GIVE ME LIBERTY!

AN AMERICAN HISTORY

Seagull Seventh Edition

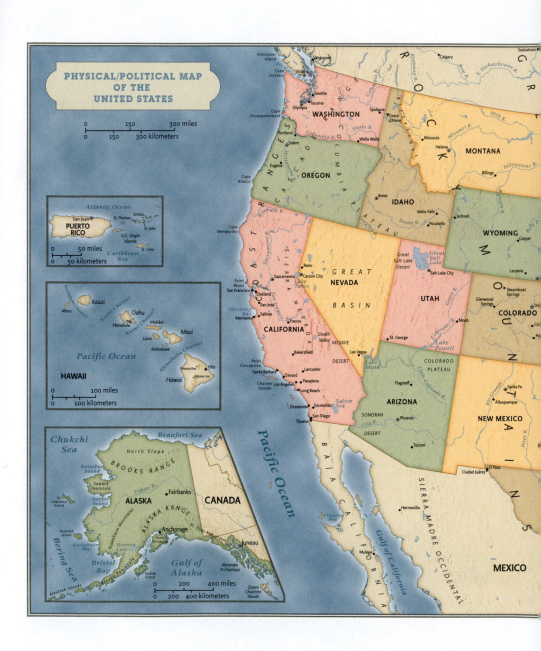

PHYSICAL/POLITICAL MAP OF THE UNITED STATES

0   150   300 miles

0   150   300 kilometers

PUERTO RICO

Atlantic Ocean

San Juan · St. Thomas · Tortola
U.S. Virgin Islands · St. John · St. Croix

Caribbean Sea

0   50 miles
0   50 kilometers

HAWAII

Niihau · Kauai
Kauai Channel
Oahu · Honolulu · Molokai · Maui
Lanai · Kahoolawe
Mauna Kea · Hilo
Mauna Loa · Hawaii

Pacific Ocean

0   100 miles
0   100 kilometers

ALASKA

Chukchi Sea
Beaufort Sea
North Slope
BROOKS RANGE
Kotzebue Sound
Seward Peninsula
Norton Sound
St. Lawrence Island
Nunivak Island
Kuskokwim Bay
Bristol Bay
Bering Sea
Aleutian Islands
Kodiak Island
Gulf of Alaska
Alexander Archipelago
Queen Charlotte Islands

ALASKA RANGE
Fairbanks
Anchorage
St. Elias Mountains
Juneau

CANADA

Yukon R.
Kuskokwim Mountains
Iliamna Lake
Alaska Peninsula

0   200   400 miles
0   200   400 kilometers

Pacific Ocean

Main map labels

Vancouver Island
Vancouver · Victoria
Cape Flattery
Cape Disappointment

WASHINGTON
Seattle · Tacoma · Olympia · Spokane · Coeur d'Alene · Walla Walla
Columbia R. · Snake R. · Missoula · Helena

MONTANA
Billings · Yellowstone R. · Milk R. · Missouri R.
Calgary · Saskatoon · S. Saskatchewan R. · Bow R.

Portland · Salem · Eugene
OREGON
Cape Blanco
Willamette R.

IDAHO
Boise · Idaho Falls · Jackson · Pocatello · Snake R.

WYOMING
Casper · Laramie · Belle Fourche R.

Cape Mendocino
Klamath R.
Sacramento R.

Reno · Carson City · Lake Tahoe
GREAT NEVADA BASIN
Great Salt Lake Desert · Great Salt Lake · Salt Lake City

UTAH
Moab · Green R. · Lake Powell · Colorado R.

COLORADO
Steamboat Springs · Glenwood Springs · Santa Fe

Point Reyes · San Francisco · Oakland · San Jose
Monterey Bay · Salinas · Monterey · Fresno
CALIFORNIA
Death Valley · MOJAVE DESERT
Bakersfield
Las Vegas · St. George · Lake Mead

ARIZONA
COLORADO PLATEAU
Flagstaff · Little Colorado R.
Phoenix · Tucson
SONORAN DESERT · Gila R.

NEW MEXICO
Albuquerque · Santa Fe
El Paso · Ciudad Juárez · Pecos R. · Rio Grande

Point Conception · Santa Barbara
Channel Islands · Oxnard · Los Angeles · Pasadena · Lancaster · Long Beach
Oceanside · Escondido · San Diego · Tijuana
Salton Sea

BAJA CALIFORNIA
Vizcaino Bay · Mulege
Gulf of California
SIERRA MADRE OCCIDENTAL
Hermosillo
MEXICO

ROCKY MOUNTAINS

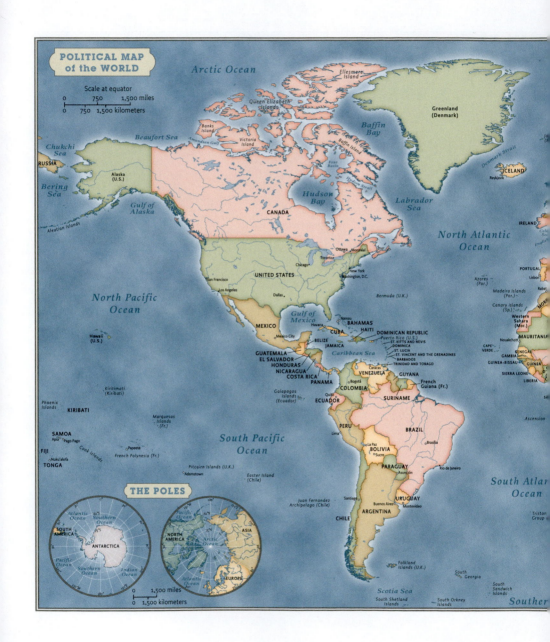

POLITICAL MAP of the WORLD

Scale at equator

0   750   1,500 miles
0   750   1,500 kilometers

Arctic Ocean

Ellesmere Island

Queen Elizabeth Islands

Greenland (Denmark)

Banks Island

Beaufort Sea

Baffin Bay

Amundsen Gulf

Victoria Island

Baffin Island

Denmark Strait

Chukchi Sea

RUSSIA

Alaska (U.S.)

Gulf of Alaska

Fox Basin

Hudson Strait

ICELAND

Reykjavik

Bering Sea

Aleutian Islands

Hudson Bay

Labrador Sea

IRELAND

CANADA

North Atlantic Ocean

North Pacific Ocean

Chicago

Ottawa   Montréal

Toronto

New York

Washington, D.C.

PORTUGAL

Lisbon

San Francisco

UNITED STATES

Azores (Por.)

MO

Los Angeles

Dallas

Bermuda (U.K.)

Madeira Islands (Por.)

Rabat

Hawaii (U.S.)

Gulf of Mexico

Canary Islands (Sp.)

Western Sahara (Mor.)

MEXICO

Nassau

BAHAMAS

Mexico City

Havana

CUBA

HAITI

DOMINICAN REPUBLIC

MAURITANIA

Puerto Rico (U.S.)

Nouakchott

CAPE VERDE

BELIZE

JAMAICA

ST. KITTS AND NEVIS

DOMINICA

GUATEMALA

ST. LUCIA

SENEGAL

GAMBIA

EL SALVADOR

Caribbean Sea

ST. VINCENT AND THE GRENADINES

BARBADOS

GUINEA-BISSAU

GUINEA

HONDURAS

TRINIDAD AND TOBAGO

NICARAGUA

SIERRA LEONE

COSTA RICA

Caracas

VENEZUELA

GUYANA

LIBERIA

PANAMA

French Guiana (Fr.)

SH

Bogotá

Kiritimati (Kiribati)

COLOMBIA

SURINAME

Galapagos Islands (Ecuador)

Quito

ECUADOR

Ascension

Phoenix Islands

KIRIBATI

PERU

Lima

BRAZIL

Marquesas Islands (Fr.)

Brasília

SAMOA

Apia

Pago Pago

La Paz

BOLIVIA

South Pacific Ocean

Sucre

Rio de Janeiro

FIJI

Cook Islands

Papeete

PARAGUAY

Nuku'alofa

French Polynesia (Fr.)

Asunción

TONGA

Pitcairn Islands (U.K.)

Adamstown

Easter Island (Chile)

URUGUAY

South Atlantic Ocean

Juan Fernandez Archipelago (Chile)

Santiago

Buenos Aires

Montevideo

CHILE

ARGENTINA

Tristan

THE POLES

Falkland Islands (U.K.)

South Georgia

Southern

South Sandwich Islands

Atlantic Ocean

Southern Ocean

Pacific Ocean

ASIA

NORTH AMERICA

Arctic Ocean

SOUTH AMERICA

ANTARCTICA

Pacific Ocean

Southern Ocean

Indian Ocean

Atlantic Ocean

EUROPE

Scotia Sea

South Shetland Islands

South Orkney Islands

0   1,500 miles
0   1,500 kilometers

GIVE ME
LIBERTY!

AN AMERICAN HISTORY

Seagull Seventh Edition

ERIC FONER
KATHLEEN DuVAL
LISA McGIRR

W. W. NORTON & COMPANY
Celebrating a Century of Independent Publishing

W. W. Norton & Company has been independent since its founding in 1923, when William Warder Norton and Mary D. Herter Norton first published lectures delivered at the People's Institute, the adult education division of New York City's Cooper Union. The firm soon expanded its program beyond the Institute, publishing books by celebrated academics from America and abroad. By midcentury, the two major pillars of Norton's publishing program—trade books and college texts—were firmly established. In the 1950s, the Norton family transferred control of the company to its employees, and today—with a staff of five hundred and hundreds of trade, college, and professional titles published each year—W. W. Norton & Company stands as the largest and oldest publishing house owned wholly by its employees.

Editor: Justin Cahill
Senior Project Editor: Jennifer Barnhardt
Associate Editor: Angie Merila
Managing Editor, College: Marian Johnson
Production Manager: Sean Mintus
Media Editor: Carson Russell
Associate Media Editor: Hillary Roegelein
Media Project Editor: Rachel Mayer
Media Assistant Editor: Jennifer Jussel
Managing Editor, College Digital Media: Kim Yi
Ebook Producer: Kate Barnes
Marketing Manager, History: Sarah England Bartley
Design Director: Rubina Yeh
Designers: Chin-yee Lai, Marisa Nakasone
Director of College Permissions: Megan Schindel
College Permissions Specialist: Joshua Garvin
Photo Editor: Stephanie Romeo
Composition: Six Red Marbles
Illustrations: Mapping Specialists, Ltd.
Manufacturing: Transcontinental

Permission to use copyrighted material is included on page A-89.

The Library of Congress has cataloged the Full Edition as follows:

Names: Foner, Eric, 1943- author. | DuVal, Kathleen, author. | McGirr,
   Lisa, 1962- author.
Title: Give me liberty! : an American history / Eric Foner, Kathleen DuVal,
   Lisa McGirr.
Description: Seventh edition. | New York, NY : W.W. Norton & Company,
   [2023] | Includes bibliographical references and index.
Identifiers: LCCN 2022036515 | **ISBN 9781324040798 (hardcover)** | ISBN
   9781324040873 (ebook other)
Subjects: LCSH: United States—History—Textbooks. | Liberty—History.
Classification: LCC E178 .F66 2023 | DDC 973—dc23/eng/20220801
LC record available at https://lccn.loc.gov/2022036515

ISBN this edition: 978-1-324-04119-1

W. W. Norton & Company, Inc., 500 Fifth Avenue, New York, NY 10110

wwnorton.com

W. W. Norton & Company Ltd., 15 Carlisle Street, London W1D 3BS

1 2 3 4 5 6 7 8 9 0

★

For my mother, Liza Foner (1909–2005), an accomplished
artist who lived through most of the twentieth century and
into the twenty-first ★ For Calvin and Quentin DuVal-Smith ★
For Noah and Pascal Beckert-McGirr

★

CONTENTS

LIST OF MAPS, TABLES, AND FIGURES

MAPS

TABLES AND FIGURES

ABOUT THE AUTHORS

ERIC FONER is DeWitt Clinton Professor Emeritus of History at Columbia University. His teaching and scholarship focus on the Civil War and Reconstruction, slavery, and nineteenth-century America. He has served as president of the Organization of American Historians, Society of American Historians, and American Historical Association. In 2006 he received the Presidential Award for Outstanding Teaching from Columbia University. His most recent books are *The Fiery Trial: Abraham Lincoln and American Slavery*, winner of the Bancroft and Lincoln Prizes and the Pulitzer Prize for History, *Gateway to Freedom: The Hidden History of the Underground Railroad*, winner of the New York Historical Society Book Prize, and *The Second Founding: How the Civil War and Reconstruction Remade the Constitution*.

KATHLEEN DuVAL is Professor of History at the University of North Carolina at Chapel Hill, where she teaches early American history. Her research focuses on how various Native American, European, and African people interacted from the sixteenth through the early nineteenth centuries. Her most recent book, *Independence Lost: Lives on the Edge of the American Revolution*, won multiple awards for its rich retelling of the history of the Revolutionary Era as experienced by enslaved people, Native Americans, and women living in the Gulf South. DuVal has also won the Guggenheim Fellowship in U.S. History, a National Humanities Center Fellowship, and a postdoctoral fellowship from the Andrew W. Mellon Foundation.

LISA McGIRR is Charles Warren Professor of American History at Harvard University. She specializes in the political and social history of the twentieth-century United States. Her most recent book, *The War on Alcohol: Prohibition and the Rise of the American State*, won acclaim for excavating the significant but neglected state-building legacies of national Prohibition. Her award-winning first book, *Suburban Warriors: The Origins of the New American Right*, investigates grassroots conservative politics in the post–World War II United States. She has received multiple fellowships, including from the American Council of Learned Societies, the Pew Program for Religion and American History, and the Fulbright Program. She has been a fellow at the Radcliffe Institute for Advanced Studies and the Freiburg Institute for Advanced Studies and is a distinguished lecturer for the Organization of American Historians.

PREFACE

Give Me Liberty! An American History is a survey of American history from the earliest interactions of Indigenous peoples, Europeans, and Africans to the first decades of the twenty-first century. It offers students a clear, concise narrative whose central theme is the changing contours of American freedom.

We are extremely gratified by the response to the first six editions of *Give Me Liberty!*, which have been used in survey courses at many hundreds of two- and four-year colleges and universities throughout the country. The comments we have received from instructors and students encourage us to think that *Give Me Liberty!* has worked well in their classrooms. Their comments have also included many valuable suggestions for revisions, which we greatly appreciate. These have ranged from corrections of typographical and factual errors to thoughts about subjects that needed more extensive treatment. In making revisions for this Seventh Edition, we have tried to take these suggestions into account. We have also incorporated the findings and insights of new scholarship that has appeared since the original edition was written.

The most significant change in this edition, immediately visible on the book's cover and title page, is the addition of two new co-authors, Professor Kathleen DuVal of the University of North Carolina at Chapel Hill and Professor Lisa McGirr of Harvard University. Both are accomplished scholars with national and international reputations. For further details about their careers, see About the Authors above.

For the initial edition of *Give Me Liberty!*, which appeared in 2005, and the five subsequent revised editions, Eric Foner was solely responsible for all the writing as well as the choice of images and document excerpts in each chapter. This required, among other tasks, keeping up with the enormous outpouring of significant books covering every aspect of American history. As time went on, this became increasingly difficult for one individual. Professors DuVal and McGirr have now joined the process of revision. For this Seventh Edition, the former is responsible for changes to Chapters 1 to 10, the latter Chapters 18 to 28. Foner took charge of Chapters 11 to 17.

The most important changes in this Seventh Edition involve heightened attention to Native American history and, in keeping with the overall theme of the book, Native Americans' ideas about freedom. This reflects both the recent burgeoning of this long-neglected field, which has produced outstanding works that change our understanding of key moments and processes in American history, and the expertise of our new co-authors.

As the original inhabitants of the lands that would become the United States, Native Americans have had a unique relationship to other Americans and with the federal government. The Constitution recognizes them as inhabitants of their own tribal sovereignties, not members of the national body politic. And sovereignty—control over ancestral lands and the ability to govern their own affairs—has been central to Native definitions of freedom. Over the centuries of American history, Indian sovereignty has eroded considerably, but it has not disappeared. Over time, it was severely challenged by European colonialism and American nationhood. Wars and forced agreements dispossessed Native Americans of much of their land but although treaties were frequently violated, they recognized Native control over the remainder. The quest to exercise authority over their own lives and to maintain traditional languages and forms of governance and social organization has been a central theme of Native American history, as has the effort of outsiders to impose their own ideas about freedom, political power, and cultural life on the Indigenous population. Throughout U.S. history, Native understanding of freedom via sovereignty has clashed with settlers' ambitions for their own freedom.

Since 1924, all Native Americans have been citizens of the United States. Even today, however, many continue to identify as citizens of Native nations as well (or instead of) as American citizens. And many tribes are recognized by U.S. courts as entities distinct from the federal and state governments, even though tribal self-government is constrained by the power of Congress and the Department of the Interior. The changing nature of Native sovereignty and its relationship to concepts of freedom within both Native American tribes and the larger society is a central theme of this Seventh Edition. Building upon past editions' inclusion of Native history and Native voices, this edition narrates the history of American Indians in three stages: a long period in which diverse Indian nations ruled most of the continent; the decline of Native power and self-government from the mid-nineteenth through early twentieth centuries, and the Native revival in the late twentieth century continuing to today.

The major revisions that illuminate the history of these themes are as follows:

Chapters 1 to 4 have been reorganized to give greater emphasis to Native American history. Chapter 1 contains more coverage of the nature of Native American societies before contact with Europeans and, in addition, an expanded discussion of West Africa on the eve of the Atlantic slave trade. Chapter 2 contains enhanced coverage of armed conflict between British settlers in Virginia and New England and the Native inhabitants, as well as new material on the early Atlantic slave trade, including the role of the Spanish, Portuguese, and Dutch, and the origins of slavery in the British colonies. Chapters 3 and 4 contain an expanded discussion of Native-colonial relations in the eighteenth century and the growth of pan-Indian coalitions that sought to halt settler intrusions.

In Chapter 5, there is greater emphasis on how the American Revolution was also a Native struggle for independence and how Native Americans fought on both sides of the conflict in pursuit of that goal. Chapter 7 contains a new section on Native nations in the West and their relations with the early American republic, which most did not wish to join. Chapters 9 and 10 deal in more detail with Indian removal in the 1830s, including how this policy was linked to the expansion of cotton production and slavery in the South, and how Native nations responded to being forced from their ancestral lands.

Chapter 14 expands the discussion of the Civil War in Indian Territory and contains a new subsection on the Dakota War, which led to the largest mass execution in American history. Chapters 15 and 16 contain new subsections on Reconstruction in Indian Territory and President Grant's attempted peace policy. In Chapter 18, there is an expanded discussion of Native American Progressivism set against the background of the continuing dispossession of Indian lands and efforts to forcibly assimilate Indian children via federally controlled boarding schools. Native American participation in World War I and debates over whether military service would lead to greater citizenship rights are discussed in Chapter 19. The subject of the Indian New Deal and its impact on Native Americans receives an expanded discussion in Chapter 21 in the context of Indigenous understandings of freedom and sovereignty, as does the role of Native Americans in World War II in Chapter 22. Chapter 23 discusses the intensified campaign, known as "termination," to abolish tribal sovereignty during the Cold War, and Chapter 24 includes a discussion of the Indian Bureau's program to move Native Americans from reservations to cities.

Chapter 25 considers "Red Power" and the American Indian Movement alongside other examples of youth-led activism in the 1960s. Chapter 26 shows how this intensified activism led to tribal revitalization, including a renaissance of Native American identity and cultural expression. In Chapter 27, readers will see how Native peoples have continued to press for self-determination in the new millennium, seeking financial restitution for past wrongs and leading grassroots movements, such as the NoDAPL movement for environmental justice.

Other revisions, not directly tied to the theme of Native American freedom but based on significant recent scholarship, include a new subsection in Chapter 12 highlighting the role of Black women in the abolitionist movement and the struggle for women's rights and in Chapter 13 an expanded discussion of John Brown's raid of 1859 with attention to the influence of Black radicals on Brown's thinking. Chapter 19 now contains material on the 1918 influenza epidemic and in Chapter 20 there is a new discussion of the Lost

Generation—the writers and artists, disillusioned with American culture of the 1920s—who found a home in Europe. Chapter 25 includes new material on Black urban uprisings in the 1960s and after, especially in relation to grievances against police behavior in minority neighborhoods. The final chapter has been substantially updated to cover the administration of Donald Trump and the election of 2020. Throughout the book there are also new selections for the Voices of Freedom and Who Is an American? document features. And this edition contains many new images—paintings, photographs, broadsides, and so on—all selected by the authors.

A NOTE ON NAMING

Readers will have noticed that in the discussion above, we have used more than one group name when discussing the people descended from the continent's original inhabitants. The proper way to identify them, as well as other groups of Americans, can be controversial. Offensive terms have recently been removed from sports arenas and geographical place names, although not without resistance. Generally speaking, we believe, people have the right to choose the words that identify them. But such preferences change over time in response to changing social and political imperatives. Often, disagreement exists within groups about their proper designation. In this edition, we have updated our terminology, recognizing that some names once widely familiar are now viewed as inappropriate or even insulting by the people to whom they are applied, while bearing in mind that changed language can seem unfamiliar and confusing to those used to an older vocabulary.

To navigate this complex question we have consulted prominent scholars who write about various groups of Americans. Most advised us to cast a wide net, using interchangeably terms that are in widespread circulation today while being wary of overusing new language that has not gained a significant foothold either among the groups themselves or in society at large. Thus, readers will find Indian, Native American, Native, and Indigenous all used to identify the people once universally called Indians. (The name Indian, as is well known, derives from Christopher Columbus's mistaken belief that his voyage to the Americas in 1492 had brought him to the East Indies rather than to a hemisphere previously unknown to Europeans.) For a time, Native peoples rejected Indian as conjuring up images of savagery. More recently it has come into wider use again, partly because of its very familiarity and partly to suggest a sense of shared identity that transcends individual tribes. Because the word Indian, despite its limitations, is so widely understood, a major organization demanding change in the 1960s intentionally chose to make the word part of its title: the American Indian Movement. This is not the only example of people turning a term considered insulting into an expression of pride.

A related question concerns the names of individual Native nations. Some groups, but by no means all, have abandoned designations that originated among white persons in favor of older Indigenous ones. While we believe, as noted above, that the group itself should decide what it wishes to be called, we realize that some changes may be confusing for many readers. In such cases we have added the previous name in parentheses, for example, Haudenosaunee (Iroquois) and Muscogee (Creek).

The heightened sensitivity to racial inequality in the aftermath of the 2020 murder of George Floyd by a Minneapolis police officer sparked a similar discussion of the proper way to designate Americans of African descent. This debate has a long history. In the revolutionary era, Black institutions often included the word African in their titles (for example, the African Methodist Episcopal Church) as a sign of a unique identity. But in response to the rise of the American Colonization Society, which claimed that Blacks, free and slave, were not truly American and should return to Africa, a wholesale reevaluation of such names took place. Meetings of Black people demanding recognition as equal members of the body politic called themselves Conventions of Colored Citizens. One of the earliest Black newspapers was titled the *Colored American*. After the end of slavery, when persons of African descent were recognized as American citizens entitled to equality of political and civil rights, Negro, from the Spanish word for the color black and for dark-skinned people, was widely used. So was Afro-American and African-American. There was debate over whether to use hyphens, and whether Negro should begin with a capital or lowercase letter. In the 1920s, when the *New York Times*, one of the nation's leading newspapers, decided to capitalize the first letter of Negro, this was hailed as an important sign of respect. More recently, the Associated Press, which informally sets journalistic standards, recommended that Black, a label that has gained wide currency since the 1960s (Black Power was one of the era's familiar slogans) should be capitalized, as an indication of the shared history and culture of persons of African descent rooted in the unique historical experience of dislocation, slavery, racial inequality, and resistance. Today, Negro and Colored are rarely used except when discussing historical situations. African American and Black are now the most common designations. The widespread elimination of the hyphen in African American has influenced how other groups are described, such as, for example, Irish Americans and Asian Americans. Again, no unanimity exists on these questions of usage. In this edition, we have used Black and African American interchangeably, while retaining Negro and Colored when quoting historical documents or using historical titles, such as the U. S. Colored Troops in the Civil War.

Then there are the Americans variously labeled Hispanic or Latino. Both designations are widely used, although neither has much historical clarity. The dictionary defines Latino as a person with roots in Latin America, a category that covers persons of every religion and race, with origins in more than a dozen countries. Hispanic refers primarily to language, meaning persons who speak Spanish (thereby excluding those Americans whose origins lie in Portuguese-speaking Brazil). It is only recently that these terms for what is now the country's largest minority group came into widespread use. The census did not include a Hispanic category until 1980. For many decades people descended from the Mexican inhabitants of lands in the Southwest acquired during the Mexican-American War viewed "Mexican" as a term of abuse and avoided it by using state-specific terms such as Tejano and Californio. The first organization of Mexican American activists purposely did not use Mexican in its title, calling itself the League of United Latin American Citizens. Later, younger radicals in California adopted Chicano, an old term of abuse, as a positive statement of identity.

There is also the problem of gendered language. In English, nouns do not have a gender as they do in Spanish. But because Latino is a masculine word, where does this leave people who do not identify as masculine? Some writers, scholars, and activists have begun using Latino/a or the gender-neutral neologism Latinx. This last term is still unfamiliar, including among most of the people it is describing. Depending on the historical context, we have decided to use Mexican American, Hispanic, Chicano, and Latino, or Chicana and Latina when specifically referencing women.

One thing is certain: language has changed over time and will continue to do so in the future. It will not be surprising if future editions of *Give Me Liberty!* employ wording that is unfamiliar or even unknown today. All this terminology is the product of our nation's ever evolving history. There is nothing unusual or pernicious in this, simply the recognition that as American society changes, the vocabulary we use to describe it changes as well.

THE FREEDOM THEME

Americans have always had a divided attitude toward history. On the one hand, they tend to be remarkably future-oriented, dismissing events of even the recent past as "ancient history" and sometimes seeing history as a burden to be overcome, a prison from which to escape. On the other hand, like many other peoples, Americans have always looked to history for a sense of personal or group identity and of national cohesiveness. This is why so many Americans devote time and energy to tracing their family trees and why they visit historical museums and National Park Service historical sites in ever-increasing numbers. Our hope is that this book will convince readers with all degrees of interest that history does matter to them.

The novelist and essayist James Baldwin once observed that history "does not refer merely, or even principally, to the past. On the contrary, the great force of history comes from the fact that we carry it within us, . . . [that] history is literally present in all that we do." As Baldwin recognized, the force of history is evident in our own world. Especially in a political democracy like the United States, whose government is designed to rest on the consent of informed citizens, knowledge of the past is essential—not only for those of us whose profession is the teaching and writing of history, but for everyone. History, to be sure, does not offer simple lessons or immediate answers to current questions. Knowing the history of immigration to the United States, and all of the tensions, turmoil, and aspirations associated with it, for example, does not tell us what current immigration policy ought to be. But without that knowledge, we have no way of understanding which approaches have worked and which have not—essential information for the formulation of future public policy.

History, it has been said, is what the present chooses to remember about the past. Rather than a fixed collection of facts, or a group of interpretations that cannot be challenged, our understanding of history is constantly changing. There is nothing unusual in the fact that each generation rewrites history to meet its own needs, or that scholars disagree among themselves on basic questions like the causes of the Civil War or the reasons for the Great Depression. Precisely because each generation asks different questions of the past, each generation formulates different answers. The past thirty years have witnessed a remarkable expansion of the scope of historical study. The experiences of groups neglected by earlier scholars, including women, African Americans, working people, and others, have received unprecedented attention from historians. New subfields—social history, cultural history, and family history among them—have taken their place alongside traditional political and diplomatic history.

Give Me Liberty! draws on this voluminous historical literature to present an up-to-date and inclusive account of the American past, paying due attention to the experience of diverse groups of Americans while in no way neglecting the events and processes Americans have experienced in common. It devotes serious attention to political, social, cultural, and economic history, and to their interconnections. The narrative brings together major events and prominent leaders with the many groups of ordinary people who make up American society. *Give Me Liberty!* has a rich cast of characters, from Thomas Jefferson to campaigners for woman suffrage, from Franklin D. Roosevelt to former slaves seeking to breathe meaning into emancipation during and after the Civil War.

Aimed at an audience of undergraduate students with little or no detailed knowledge of American history, *Give Me Liberty!* guides readers through the complexities of the subject without overwhelming them with excessive detail.

The unifying theme of freedom that runs through the text gives shape to the narrative and integrates the numerous strands that make up the American experience. This approach builds on that of Foner's earlier book, *The Story of American Freedom* (1998), although *Give Me Liberty!* places events and personalities in the foreground and is more geared to the structure of the introductory survey course.

No idea is more fundamental to Americans' sense of themselves as individuals and as a nation than freedom. The central term in our political language, freedom— or liberty, with which it is almost always used interchangeably—is deeply embedded in the record of our history and the language of everyday life. The Declaration of Independence lists liberty among mankind's inalienable rights; the Constitution announces its purpose as securing liberty's blessings. The United States fought the Civil War to bring about a new birth of freedom, World War II for the Four Freedoms, and the Cold War to defend the Free World. Americans' love of liberty has been represented by liberty poles, liberty caps, and statues of liberty, and acted out by burning stamps and burning draft cards, by running away from slavery, and by demonstrating for the right to vote. "Every man in the street, white, black, red, or yellow," wrote the educator and statesman Ralph Bunche in 1940, "knows that this is 'the land of the free' . . . 'the cradle of liberty.' "

The very universality of the idea of freedom, however, can be misleading. Freedom is not a fixed, timeless category with a single unchanging definition. Indeed, the history of the United States is, in part, a story of debates, disagreements, and struggles over freedom. Crises like the American Revolution, the Civil War, and the Cold War have permanently transformed the idea of freedom. So too have demands by various groups of Americans to enjoy greater freedom. The meaning of freedom has been constructed not only in congressional debates and political treatises but also on plantations and picket lines, in parlors and even bedrooms.

Over the course of our history, American freedom has been both a reality and a mythic ideal—a living truth for millions of Americans, a cruel mockery for others. For some, freedom has been what some scholars call a "habit of the heart," an ideal so taken for granted that it is lived out but rarely analyzed. For others, freedom is not a birthright but a distant goal that has inspired great sacrifice.

Give Me Liberty! draws attention to three dimensions of freedom that have been critical in American history: (1) the *meanings* of freedom; (2) the *social conditions* that make freedom possible; and (3) the *boundaries* of freedom that determine who is entitled to enjoy freedom and who is not. All have changed over time.

In the era of the American Revolution, for example, freedom was primarily a set of rights enjoyed in public activity—the right of a community to be governed by laws to which its representatives had consented and of individuals to engage in religious worship without governmental interference. In the nineteenth century, freedom came to be closely identified with each person's opportunity to develop to the fullest his or her innate talents. In the twentieth, the "ability to choose," in both public and private life, became perhaps the dominant understanding of freedom. This development was encouraged by the explosive growth of the consumer marketplace (a development that receives considerable attention in *Give Me Liberty!*), which offered Americans an unprecedented array of goods to satisfy their needs and desires. During the 1960s, a crucial chapter in the history of American freedom, the idea of personal freedom was extended into virtually every realm, from attire and "lifestyle" to relations between the sexes. Thus, over time, more and more areas of life have been drawn into Americans' debates about the meaning of freedom.

A second important dimension of freedom focuses on the social conditions necessary to allow freedom to flourish. What kinds of economic institutions and relationships best encourage individual freedom? In the colonial era and for more than a century after independence, the answer centered on economic autonomy, enshrined in the glorification of the independent small producer—the farmer, skilled craftsman, or shopkeeper—who did not have to depend on another person for his livelihood. As the industrial economy matured, new conceptions of economic freedom came to the fore: "liberty of contract" in the Gilded Age, "industrial freedom" (a say in corporate decision making) in the Progressive era, economic security during the New Deal, and, more recently, the ability to enjoy mass consumption within a market economy.

The boundaries of freedom, the third dimension of this theme, have inspired some of the most intense struggles in American history. Although founded on the premise that liberty is an entitlement of all humanity, the United States for much of its history deprived many of its own people of freedom. Non-whites have rarely enjoyed the same access to freedom as white Americans. The belief in equal opportunity as the birthright of all Americans has coexisted with persistent efforts to limit freedom by race, gender, and class and in other ways.

Less obvious, perhaps, is the fact that one person's freedom has frequently been linked to another's servitude. In the colonial era and nineteenth century, expanding freedom for many Americans rested on the lack of freedom—slavery, indentured servitude, the subordinate position of women—for others. By the same token, it has been through battles at the boundaries—the efforts of racial minorities, women, and others to secure greater freedom—that the meaning and experience of freedom have been deepened and the concept extended into new realms.

Time and again in American history, freedom has been transformed by the demands of excluded groups for inclusion. The idea of freedom as a universal birthright owes much both to abolitionists who sought to extend the blessings of liberty to Blacks and to immigrant groups who insisted on full recognition as American citizens. The principle of equal protection of the law without regard to race, which became a central element of American freedom, arose from the antislavery struggle and the Civil War and was reinvigorated by the civil rights revolution of the 1960s, which called itself the "freedom movement." The battle for the right of free speech by labor radicals and birth-control advocates in the first part of the twentieth century helped to make civil liberties an essential element of freedom for all Americans.

Although concentrating on events within the United States, *Give Me Liberty!* also situates American history in the context of developments in other parts of the world. Many of the forces that shaped American history, including the international migration of peoples, the development of slavery, the spread of democracy, and the expansion of capitalism, were worldwide processes not confined to the United States. Today, American ideas, culture, and economic and military power exert unprecedented influence throughout the world. But beginning with the earliest days of settlement, when European empires competed to colonize North America and enrich themselves from its trade, American history cannot be understood in isolation from its global setting.

Freedom is the oldest of clichés and the most modern of aspirations. At various times in our history, it has served as the rallying cry of the powerless and as a justification of the status quo. Freedom helps to bind our culture together and exposes the contradictions between what America claims to be and what it sometimes has been. American history is not a narrative of continual progress toward greater and greater freedom. As the abolitionist Thomas Wentworth Higginson noted after the Civil War, "revolutions may go backward." Though freedom can be achieved, it may also be taken away. This happened, for example, when the equal rights granted to former slaves immediately after the Civil War were essentially nullified during the era of segregation. As was said in the eighteenth century, the price of freedom is eternal vigilance.

In the early twenty-first century, freedom continues to play a central role in American political and social life and thought. It is invoked by individuals and groups of all kinds, from critics of economic globalization to those who seek to secure American freedom at home and export it abroad. We hope that *Give Me Liberty!* will offer beginning students a clear account of the course of American history, and of its central theme, freedom, which today remains as varied, contentious, and ever-changing as America itself. And we hope that it also enables students to understand the connections between past and current events, the historical context and antecedents of the social, political, cultural, and economic issues that the American people confront today.

ACKNOWLEDGMENTS

All works of history are, to a considerable extent, collaborative books in that every writer builds on the research and writing of previous scholars. This is especially true of a textbook that covers the entire American experience over more than five centuries. Our greatest debt is to the innumerable historians on whose work we have drawn in preparing this volume. The Suggested Reading list at the end of the book offers only a brief introduction to the vast body of historical scholarship that has influenced and informed this book. More specifically, however, we wish to thank the following scholars, who offered valuable comments, criticisms, and suggestions after generously reading portions of this work or who are using it in their classes.

Victoria Ade, West Morris Central High School
Matthew Avitabile, SUNY Cobleskill
Sheri Bartlett Browne, Tennessee State University
Brooke M. Bauer, University of South Carolina Lancaster
Jordan Bauer, University of Alabama at Birmingham
Lee Benjamins, San Jacinto College North Campus
April Braden, Dallas College
Lauren Braun-Strumfels, Raritan Valley Community College
Kate Burlingham, California State University, Fullerton
Christopher Cameron, University of North Carolina at Charlotte
David Cameron, Lone Star College–University Park
Kara Carroll, Central New Mexico Community College
Annette Chamberlin, Virginia Western Community College
Sang Chi, Santa Monica College
Jonathan Colman, University of Central Lancashire
Amy Curry, Lone Star College
Enrico Dal Lago, National University of Ireland Galway
Jewell Debnam, Morgan State University
Christopher Deutsch, University of Missouri
Alan C. Downs, Georgia Southern University
Patrick J. Doyle, Royal Holloway, University of London
Jim Dudlo, Dallas College–Brookhaven Campus
Allison Faber, Texas A&M University
Andrew Fearnley, University of Manchester
Jim Foley, St. Andrews High School
Linda C. Frank, Cayuga Community College
Malcolm Frierson, Dallas College North Lake Campus
Andrej Gaspari, Mercy College

Erik Gellman, University of North Carolina at Chapel Hill
Hillary Gleason, Laredo Community College
Teresa Hall, Central Piedmont Community College
Michael Harkins, Harper College
David C. Hsiung, Juniata College
Beth Hunter, University of Alabama at Birmingham
Courtenay Johnson, Huntington High School
Ryan William Keating, California State University, San Bernardino
Jennifer Koslow, Florida State University
Danton Kostandarithes, Bolles School
Elizabeth LaFray, Siena Heights University
Cornelia Lambert, University of North Georgia
Katherine Sharp Landdeck, Texas Woman's University
Jairo Ledesma, Miami Dade College
Paul Lubotina, Walters State Community College
Sergio Lussana, Nottingham Trent University
Thomas Massey, Cape Fear Community College
Warren Milteer Jr., University of North Carolina at Greensboro
Jen Murray, Oklahoma State University
Laura Murphy, Dutchess Community College
Joseph Myers, Delaware County Community College
Jason Newman, Consumnes River College
Jared Pack, University of Arkansas
Sarah Potter, University of Memphis
Julie Rancilio, Kapi'olani Community College
Lindsay Regele, Miami University
David Ryan, University College Cork
Ruby Smart, San Leandro High School
Matthew Stanley, Albany State University
Laura Stott, Daniel Hand High School
Katherine Scott Sturdevant, Pikes Peak Community College
Paul S. Sutter, University of Colorado Boulder
Stephen Tootle, College of the Sequoias
Felicity Turner, Georgia Southern University
Justin Vipperman, College of Southern Idaho
Dan Ware, TASIS The American School in England
Jeannie Whayne, University of Arkansas
Bryn Willcock, University of Swansea
Michael Williams, Beaumont High School
Eric Wolters, Pasco-Hernando State College
Natasha Zaretsky, University of Alabama at Birmingham

The authors are deeply indebted to the graduate students at the Departments of History at Columbia University, Harvard University, and at the University of North Carolina who helped with this project. For the Seventh Edition, David Dry, Sarah Sadlier, and Garrett Wright provided suggestions related to our guiding theme on Native Americans and freedom, with Wright conducting invaluable research. For earlier editions, Michael "Mookie" Kideckel offered significant assistance in gathering material related to borderlands and Western history and on citizenship and identity; Theresa Ventura assisted in locating material for new sections placing American history in a global context; April Holm did the same for new coverage of the history of American religion and debates over religious freedom; James Delbourgo conducted research for the chapters on the colonial era; and Beverly Gage did the same for the twentieth century. In addition, Daniel Freund provided all-around research assistance and Victoria Cain did a superb job of locating images. The authors are also grateful to the numerous undergraduate students who, while using the textbook, pointed out errors or omissions that we have corrected.

Eric Foner is particularly grateful to his colleagues in the Columbia University Department of History: Pablo Piccato, for his advice on Latin American history; Evan Haefeli and Ellen Baker, who read and made many suggestions for improvements in their areas of expertise (colonial America and the history of the West, respectively); and Sarah Phillips, who offered advice on treating the history of the environment. Foner also wants to thank his colleagues Elizabeth Blackmar and the late Alan Brinkley for offering advice and encouragement throughout the writing and revising of this book.

Many thanks go to Joshua Brown, former director of the American Social History Project, whose website, History Matters, lists innumerable online resources for the study of American history. We thank Trinidad Gonzales (South Texas College) for his indispensable help in creating a new set of resources to help adopters of *Give Me Liberty!* create more inclusive learning environments. Thanks also to the instructors who helped build our robust digital resource and ancillary package. The Norton Illumine eBook was created with the assistance of Alan Downs (Georgia Southern University), Linda Frank (Cayuga Community College), Hillary Gleason (Laredo Community College), Julie Rancilio (University of Hawai'i–Kapi'olani Community College), and Andrew Frank (Florida State University). InQuizitive for History was revised by Beth Hunter (University of Alabama at Birmingham), Sharon Ann Musher (Stockton University), Daniel Murphee (University of Central Florida), Bettye Hutchins (Vernon College), and Jen Murray (Oklahoma State University). The Instructor's Manual was thoroughly updated by Holly Hernandez (California State University, Long Beach). And our Test Bank was revised to include new questions authored by Hillary Gleason (Laredo Community College), Jared Pack (University of Arkansas), Sascha Cohen (Brandeis University), and Meghan Martinez (Florida State University).

At W. W. Norton & Company, Justin Cahill was an ideal editor who carefully guided all three authors through the revision process with wisdom, patience, and a deep understanding of history. We would also like to thank his associate editor Angie Merila for her indispensable and insightful help on all aspects of the project; Donna Mulder and Mary Kanable for their careful copyediting and proofreading work; Stephanie Romeo and Lynn Gadson for their resourceful attention to the illustrations program; Anne-Michelle Gallero, Ted Szczepanski, and Debra Morton-Hoyt for splendid work on the covers for the Seventh Edition; Jennifer Barnhardt for keeping the many threads of the project aligned and then tying them together; Sean Mintus for his efficiency and care in book production; Carson Russell and his colleagues Hillary Roegelein and Jennifer Jussel for orchestrating the rich media package that accompanies the textbook; Sarah England Bartley, Alison Hodges, Susan Hood, Carrie Polvino, and Julie Sindel for spreading the word about our book to instructors nationwide; and Julia Reidhead, Mike Wright, Steve Dunn, and Ann Shin for maintaining Norton as an independent, employee-owned publisher dedicated to excellence in its work.

Many students may have heard stories of how publishing companies alter the language and content of textbooks in an attempt to maximize sales and avoid alienating any potential reader. In this case, we can honestly say that W. W. Norton allowed us a free hand in writing and revising the book and, apart from the usual editorial corrections, did not try to influence its content at all. For this we thank them, while we accept full responsibility for the interpretations presented and for any errors the book may contain. Since no book of this length can be entirely free of mistakes, we welcome readers to send us corrections and feedback at http://seagull.wwnorton.com/DearGiveMeLiberty.

Eric Foner's greatest debt, as always, is to his family—his wife, Lynn Garafola, for her good-natured support while he was preoccupied by a project that over the years consumed more than its fair share of his time and energy, and his daughter, Daria Rose Foner, who years ago, while a ninth and tenth grader read every chapter of the First Edition as it was written. Her modest payment of twenty-five dollars per chapter was a bargain, as she offered invaluable suggestions about improving the book's clarity, logic, and grammar. Kathleen DuVal thanks her family, including Marty Smith, Quentin DuVal-Smith, Calvin DuVal-Smith, Kay DuVal, John DuVal, and Niell DuVal. She also thanks Alexa Chambers for reading the first ten chapters and giving helpful suggestions from the perspective of an APUSH student. Both Alexa and Quentin provided many happy and fruitful hours of history discussions. Lisa McGirr thanks Sven Beckert, Noah Beckert-McGirr, and Pascal Beckert-McGirr, who have offered advice, encouragement, and support. Noah (who read *Give Me Liberty!* for his U.S. history course) and Pascal have provided valuable insights from the point of view of student readers.

Eric Foner
Kathleen DuVal
Lisa McGirr
2022

RESOURCES FOR STUDENTS AND INSTRUCTORS

W. W. Norton offers a robust digital package to support teaching and learning with *Give Me Liberty!* These resources are designed to make students more effective textbook readers, while at the same time developing critical thinking and history skills.

THE NORTON ILLUMINE EBOOK

With interactive features, low-stakes assessment, and embedded audio and video, the new Norton Illumine Ebook for *Give Me Liberty!* promotes student engagement and accountability in any teaching and learning environment.

CHECK YOUR UNDERSTANDING QUESTIONS

Low-stakes, end-of-section questions focused on the chapter's core concepts motivate students and build confidence in their learning. Rich feedback explains why answers are correct or incorrect.

(Lower left and lower right) Scenes surrounding the large structure include a schoolyard, men and women voting, and Indians and whites sitting together.

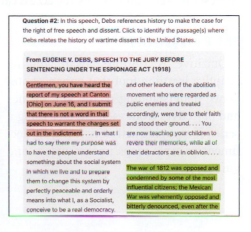

Question #2: In this speech, Debs references history to make the case for the right of free speech and dissent. Click to identify the passage(s) where Debs relates the history of wartime dissent in the United States.

From EUGENE V. DEBS, SPEECH TO THE JURY BEFORE SENTENCING UNDER THE ESPIONAGE ACT (1918)

Gentlemen, you have heard the report of my speech at Canton [Ohio] on June 16, and I submit that there is not a word in that speech to warrant the charges set out in the indictment. . . . In what I had to say there my purpose was to have the people understand something about the social system in which we live and to prepare them to change this system by perfectly peaceable and orderly means into what I, as a Socialist, conceive to be a real democracy. and other leaders of the abolition movement who were regarded as public enemies and treated accordingly, were true to their faith and stood their ground. . . . You are now teaching your children to revere their memories, while all of their detractors are in oblivion. . . . The war of 1812 was opposed and condemned by some of the most influential citizens; the Mexican War was vehemently opposed and bitterly denounced, even after the

PRIMARY SOURCE INTERACTIVES

Embedded interactives engage students with opportunities to practice critical thinking skills. Available in the ebook only, the new **"Visions of Freedom"** interactive guides students through a step-by-step visual analysis of a key image in each chapter. The popular paired document feature, **"Voices of Freedom,"** is also interactive in the Norton Illumine Ebook. Embedded audio readings invite students to listen as they read, and pop-up annotations illuminate trickier passages. After reading, students answer interactive questions that invite them to engage with each primary source.

AUTHOR VIDEOS

Over 100 videos featuring the textbook authors give students a closer look at each chapter's essential developments, difficult concepts, and "Who Is an American?" primary source documents. All videos are available with transcripts and closed captioning.

RESOURCES FOR STUDENTS

All resources are unlocked by the access card at the front of this text.

NORTON INQUIZITIVE

InQuizitive is Norton's award-winning adaptive learning tool that enhances students' understanding of the key themes and objectives from each chapter using a series of engaging activities featuring document excerpts, maps, images, videos, and guiding feedback.

HISTORY SKILLS TUTORIALS

The History Skills Tutorials are guided, interactive activities that help develop students' analytical and critical thinking skills, essential for success in the American history course. Tutorials include: analyzing primary source documents, secondary source documents, images, and maps.

RESOURCES FOR INSTRUCTORS

These and more resources are available through wwnorton.com/instructors.

RESOURCES FOR YOUR LMS

Easily add high-quality Norton digital resources to your online, hybrid, or lecture courses. Get started building your course with our easy-to-use integrated resources; all activities can be accessed right within your existing learning management system.

TEST BANK WITH NORTON TESTMAKER

Create assessments for your course from anywhere with an Internet connection, without downloading files or installing specialized software. Search and filter the more than 4,500 questions by chapter, type, difficulty, learning objectives, and other criteria, and customize test bank questions to fit your course.

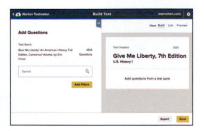

NEW EQUITY-MINDED TEACHING SUPPORT

New to the Seventh Edition are resources designed to help instructors embrace equity-minded principles in (re)designing, teaching, and reflecting on their survey course. Together with the Instructor's Manual, these resources offer sample activities and tips instructors can use to promote the success of *all* students.

GIVE ME LIBERTY!

AN AMERICAN HISTORY

Seagull Seventh Edition

CHAPTER 1

OLD WORLDS AND NEW

FOCUS QUESTIONS

- *What were the major patterns of Native American life in North America before Europeans arrived?*

- *How did Native American and European ideas of freedom differ on the eve of contact?*

- *What impelled European explorers to look west across the Atlantic?*

- *What happened when the peoples of the Americas came in contact with Europeans?*

- *What were the chief features of the Spanish empire in the Americas?*

- *What were the chief features of the French and Dutch empires in North America?*

In 1534, Mi'kmaq Indians rowed a fleet of more than forty canoes out into the Gulf of St. Lawrence to meet Frenchman Jacques Cartier's ship. Cartier was frightened until he realized that the pointed sticks the Mi'kmaqs were waving at his men had animal skins attached to them. They were signaling that they wanted to trade. Six years later and over 1,000 miles to the south, the Cacica (female leader) of Cofitachequi, a Native province in what is now South Carolina, heard that an army of foreigners had entered her country. She gathered other leaders and went out to meet them with gifts: tanned leather hides, blankets, salt, and food. She placed a necklace of pearls on the army's commander, Spaniard Hernando de Soto. Everywhere in the Americas that Europeans went, Native people met them with their own diplomatic rituals and invitations to make trading and military alliances. Although Europeans sometimes called the Americas a "new world" that Christopher Columbus "discovered," the nations and peoples of the Americas composed a world just as fully developed as those in the "old world." Fortunately for Europeans, trade with these newcomers was exactly what many of them wanted.

Human communities have always interacted. For centuries before the conquest of the Americas, Europeans had intersected with Muslim populations in North Africa and Eurasia; indeed, the very idea of Europe as a distinct community arose out of such encounters. But since the voyages of Columbus, the interconnection of cultures and peoples has taken place on a global scale. Crops new to each hemisphere crossed the Atlantic and Pacific, reshaping diets and transforming the natural environment. Building on long-standing trade with North Africa and beyond, West Africans traded with Europeans who came to their Atlantic coasts. But in Africa, Europeans built a slave trade that gave them a supply of unfree labor with which they exploited the fertile lands of the Western Hemisphere. Indeed, of approximately 10 million men, women, and children who crossed to the Americas between 1492 and 1820, the vast majority, about 7.7 million, were enslaved Africans.

Long before Columbus sailed, Europeans had dreamed of a land of abundance, riches, and ease beyond the western horizon. Once this "discovery" had taken place, they invented an America of the imagination, projecting onto it their hopes for a better life. Here, many believed, would arise unparalleled opportunities for riches, or at least liberation from poverty. Europeans envisioned America as a religious refuge, a society of equals, a source of power and glory. They searched for golden cities and fountains of eternal youth. Some sought to establish ideal communities based on the lives of the early Christian saints or other blueprints for social justice.

Some of these dreams of riches and opportunity would indeed be fulfilled. To many European settlers, America offered a far greater chance to own land and worship as they pleased than existed in Europe, with its rigid, unequal social order and official churches. Yet the conditions that enabled millions of settlers to take control of their own destinies were made possible by the debasement of millions of others. The Americas became the site of many forms of unfree labor, including indentured servitude, forced labor, and one of the most brutal and unjust systems ever devised, plantation slavery. The conquest and settlement of the Western Hemisphere opened new chapters in the long histories of both freedom and slavery.

There was a vast human diversity among the peoples thrown into contact with one another in the Americas. Exploration and settlement took place in an era of almost constant warfare among European nations, each racked by internal religious, political, and regional conflicts. Native Americans and Africans consisted of numerous nations and other polities with their own languages and cultures. They were as likely to fight one another as to unite against the European newcomers. All these peoples were changed by their integration into the new Atlantic economy. The complex interactions of these old worlds— Western Europe, North America, and West Africa—would make a new world that would change them all.

AN OLD WORLD: NORTH AMERICA

The most striking feature of Native American society at the time Europeans arrived was its sheer diversity. Each group had its own political system and set of religious beliefs, and North America was home to hundreds of mutually unintelligible languages. Indians did not define "America" as a continent or hemisphere. They did not think of themselves as a single people, and Native Americans still today identify primarily as separate nations. Identity centered on the immediate social group—a family, clan, town, nation, or confederacy. When Europeans first arrived, many Indians saw them as simply one group among many. Their first thought was how to use the newcomers to enhance their standing in relation to other Native peoples rather than to unite against them. The sharp dichotomy between "Indians" and "white" persons did not emerge until later in the colonial era.

The Settling of the Americas

During the Ice Age tens of thousands of years ago, bands of hunters and fishers crossed the Bering Strait via a land bridge. Others arrived by sea from Asia or Pacific islands earlier or later than the Bering migrants (exact dates are very

The Americas, Western Europe, and West Africa on the eve of colonization. There were countless human settlements on all four continents. People lived on farms, in villages and towns, and in cities, including the cities marked on the map.

difficult to measure). Around 14,000 years ago, when glaciers began to melt at the end of the last Ice Age, the Bering land link became submerged under water, separating the Western Hemisphere from Asia. Some Native American creation stories tell of migrations, but others describe creations within their homelands, of ancestors who fell from the sky or came into the world from a hollow log.

However people got there originally, the Americas were an ancient homeland to Native Americans by the time Europeans arrived. The hemisphere had witnessed many changes during its human history. First, the early inhabitants and their descendants spread across the two continents. Around 9,000 years ago, at the same time that agriculture was being developed in Mesopotamia, it also emerged in modern-day Mexico and the Andes and then spread to other parts of the Americas. Throughout the hemisphere, maize (corn), squash, and beans formed the basis of agriculture.

Politics and Power in Native North America

The Medieval Warm Period that began around the year 950 allowed the expansion of agriculture and the rise of cities in North America, much as it did in

Europe and West Africa. The longer growing seasons and more predictable weather of the era were ideal for farming, and large-scale farming made urban living possible. The largest city north of Mexico was Cahokia, across the Mississippi River from what is now St. Louis. In the year 1200, Cahokia's central city was home to some 12,000 people, plus a large population in outlying dependent cities, towns, and farms. Cahokia was a major manufacturing and trading center, whose prominence influenced other people throughout the Mississippi Valley to build their own cities and dependent provinces—what archaeologists call "Mississippian civilizations." Mississippian leaders ruled their realm from the large houses, halls, temples, and council chambers built on top of a central mound. Native people built scores of cities and thousands of mounds during the Mississippian era. Most of them have been destroyed, but Cahokia's central mound is still ten stories tall, even after centuries of erosion.

Ancestors of Native peoples of the arid Southwest, including the Ancestral Puebloans and the Huhugam, constructed elaborate irrigation systems in order to farm in the desert. They built great planned towns with large multi-family dwellings and conducted trade with groups as far away as central Mexico and the Mississippi Valley. Pueblo Bonito, in Chaco Canyon, New Mexico, stood five stories high and had more than 600 rooms. Like Mississippians, an elite class of leaders arose in large southwestern civilizations.

The Medieval Warm Period ended around 1250, and a colder and less predictable era called the Little Ice Age began. Large-scale agriculture became more difficult, and large centralized societies and urban populations became harder to sustain. Leaders' positions may have become more tenuous during droughts and the shorter growing seasons. It is hard to know exactly what happened, but oral histories and archaeological evidence indicate a period of growing distrust in powerful leaders and centralized political systems. People moved out of Mississippian and southwestern cities into smaller-scale, more ecologically sustainable towns and surrounding farms. When Spanish explorers came to the Southwest, they called some people the Pueblo Indians because they lived in towns, or *pueblos*. Spanish explorers in the sixteenth-century Southeast saw Mississippian cities, but the largest of them had already fallen. Mississippian descendants built smaller-scale, kin-based communities that mixed agriculture, hunting, and trade. Across North America, most Native people created a relatively egalitarian politics that emphasized consensus.

A modern visualization of Cahokia in the Mississippi River Valley, the largest Native American urban center in what is now the United States.

Towns confederated with related towns but resisted powerful leaders. In some places, larger confederacies formed to bring order to local regions or to fight together against a common enemy. In present-day New York and Pennsylvania, five nations—namely, the Mohawks, Oneidas, Cayugas, Senecas, and Onondagas—formed a **Great League of Peace**. They called their league the Haudenosaunee, "the people of the longhouse." (Their enemies called them the Iroquois, which probably meant something like "snakes.") Each year the Haudenosaunee Great Council, with male representatives chosen by the women of the five nations, met to coordinate dealings with outsiders. In the Southeast, the Choctaw, Cherokee, Chickasaw, Muscogee (Creek), and Catawba nations each eventually united dozens of towns in loose alliances.

Economics and Trade in Native North America

By the 1500s, Native leaders generally led through persuasion and reciprocity. A successful leader needed to have connections to outsiders and the ability to trade and make alliances with foreign peoples, thus bringing in valuable goods and ideas.

Exchange networks crossed North America, carrying local goods such as food, plant dyes and medicines, pottery, and quarried rock of various kinds. Trade networks also distributed goods from far away, including shell beads from the coasts, copper from the Great Lakes region, and mica from the Appalachians.

Although trading networks spanned the continent, Native Americans remained diverse. In eastern North America, hundreds of peoples inhabited towns and villages scattered from the Gulf of Mexico to present-day Canada. They lived on corn, squash, and beans, supplemented by fishing and hunting deer, turkeys, and other animals. On the densely populated Pacific coast, hundreds of distinct groups resided in independent villages and lived primarily by fishing, hunting sea mammals, and gathering wild plants and nuts. As many as 25 million salmon swam up the Columbia River each year, providing them with abundant food. On the Great Plains, with its herds of buffalo, many groups were hunters (who tracked animals on foot before the arrival of horses with the Spanish) part of the year while living in agricultural communities in the river valleys when they were not on the hunt.

Numerous land systems existed among Native Americans. Generally, however, specific families or towns had the right to farm on certain lands, and nations or confederacies claimed specific areas for hunting, fishing, and gathering. Indians saw land as a resource that particular people had the right to use but not as an economic commodity that could be bought and sold. In the nineteenth century, the Sauk leader Black Hawk explained: "The Great

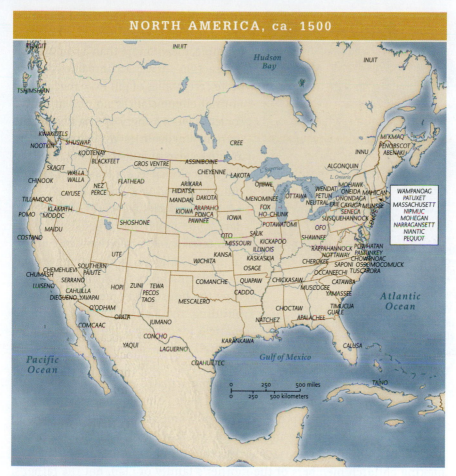

NORTH AMERICA, ca. 1500

The Native population of North America at the time of first contact with Europeans consisted of numerous peoples and nations with their own languages, religious beliefs, and economic and social structures. This map gives a sense of the large numbers of nations. By necessity, it leaves many out and includes some names that people did not call themselves in 1500.

Spirit gave it to his children to live upon, and cultivate as far as necessary for their subsistence; and so long as they occupy and cultivate it, they have a right to the soil." Few if any Native societies believed a piece of land could be fenced off and allotted forever to a single individual or family.

Nor were Native Americans devoted to the accumulation of wealth and material goods. However, status certainly mattered. Leaders tended to come from certain families or clans, and they often controlled access to resources. But their reputation and influence rested on their ability to distribute goods with their followers rather than hoarding them for themselves. Generosity was

The Village of Secoton, a drawing by John White. A central street links houses surrounded by fields of corn. In the lower part, dancers take part in a religious ceremony.

among the most valued social qualities, and gift giving was essential. Trade, for example, meant more than a commercial transaction—it was accompanied by elaborate ceremonies of gift exchange. Under normal circumstances no one in Native societies went hungry or experienced the extreme inequalities of Europe. "There are no beggars among them," reported the English colonial leader Roger Williams of Indians around New England.

Native societies were highly gendered but much more equal than the system of gender relations in Europe. In most Native communities, women had responsibility for farming and running the households, including literally building the houses. Although diplomatic leaders were usually men, women generally made the decisions about food cultivation, storage, and preparation. They participated in councils, especially when matters within the realm of women were being considered, including going to war and making peace because of women's roles in life-giving and in providing food for battle and diplomacy. Many North American societies were matrilineal—that is, tracing descent through the mother's line and making children members of the mother's family or clan, not the father's. Women generally had some power over their own sexuality and marriage, including divorce.

Religion in Native North America

For the diverse Native societies of North America, as for people all around the world in the medieval and early modern eras, religion was not simply a matter of spiritual doctrines and practices, but also systems of belief that permeated every aspect of people's lives. Their lives were steeped in religious ceremonies often directly related to farming and hunting. Spiritual power, they believed, suffused the world, and sacred spirits could be found in all kinds of living and inanimate things—animals, plants, trees, water, and wind. Through religious ceremonies, they aimed to harness the aid of powerful supernatural forces to serve human interests. Religious ceremonies sought to engage the spiritual power of nature to secure abundant crops or fend off dangerous spirits. Towns or clans also held elaborate religious rites, participation in which helped to define the boundaries of community membership. Those who seemed to possess special abilities to invoke supernatural powers—namely, shamans, medicine men, and other religious leaders—held positions of respect and authority. They did not make a sharp distinction between the natural and the supernatural, or secular and religious activities.

A major difference with Christianity, as well as with Judaism and Islam, was that Native North American religions were inclusivist. In theory at least, Christians were supposed to be exclusively Christian, rejecting all other religions' beliefs and practices as idolatry and blasphemy. Inclusivist religions, in contrast, allowed adherents to incorporate new religious beliefs and practices as part of a larger effort to make sense of the world. This fundamental difference between inclusivist and exclusivist ways of seeing religion would lead to grave misunderstandings when Christian missionaries tried to convert Native Americans.

Slavery and Freedom in Native North America

And what of liberty as the Native inhabitants of North America understood it? Many Europeans saw Indians as embodying freedom. The Haudenosaunee, wrote one colonial official, held "such absolute notions of liberty that they allow of no kind of superiority of one over another, and banish all servitude from their territories." But most colonizers quickly concluded that the notion of "freedom" was alien to Indian societies. Early English and French dictionaries of Indian languages contained no entry for "freedom" or *liberté*. Nor, wrote one early trader, did Indians have "words to express despotic power, arbitrary kings, oppressed or obedient subjects." Of course, Native Americans whose ancestors had been part of Mississippian or other hierarchical societies in previous generations did know about the dangers of excessive power. Unlike Europeans, they had rejected that way of life to develop societies with the kind of freedom that they valued.

Europeans considered Indians barbaric in part because they did not appear to live under established governments or fixed laws or have the proper respect for authority. "They are born, live, and die in a liberty without restraint," wrote one religious missionary. In a sense, they seemed *too* free, lacking the order and discipline that Europeans considered the hallmarks of civilization. When Giovanni da Verrazano described the Indians as living in "absolute freedom," he did not intend this as a compliment.

The familiar modern understanding of freedom as personal independence, often based on ownership of private property, had little meaning in Native societies. But Indians certainly had their own ideas of freedom. Although individuals were expected to think for themselves and did not always have to go along with collective decision making, men and women judged one another according to their ability to live up to widely understood ideas of appropriate behavior. Far more important than individual autonomy were kinship ties, the ability to follow one's spiritual values, and the well-being and security of one's community. Group autonomy and self-determination, and the mutual obligations that came with a sense of belonging and connectedness, took precedence over individual freedom. Indeed, the emphasis on consensus-building (rather than dictatorial decision making or majority rule) at times required someone with a dissenting point of view simply to leave a council meeting or diplomatic negotiation rather than continue to argue. The Haudenosaunee League held its leaders and representatives to a high standard: "Their hearts shall be full of peace and good will and their minds filled with a yearning for the welfare of the people. . . . Neither anger nor fury shall find lodgment in their minds and all their words and actions shall be marked by calm deliberation."

Like medieval and early modern people around the globe, many Native North American societies practiced small-scale slavery, mostly enslavement of war captives. Captives had none of the rights or privileges of members of a society. Ripped from their own societies and families, they could be forced to labor or traded away. But slavery was not inheritable, and captives could become full members of the society that adopted them.

AN OLD WORLD: WEST AFRICA

Politics and Power in West Africa

Like Native Americans and Europeans, West Africans did not consider themselves all one people. West Africans spoke dozens of different languages and hundreds of dialects. They lived under a variety of different political systems. In the late medieval and early modern eras, most West Africans lived in towns centered on kinship and run by elders. As in Native America, women in many parts of West Africa were responsible for farming and land management.

Some parts of West Africa were ruled by large empires. Gaining power in the thirteenth century, the Mali empire became the largest in West Africa, with major cities at Jenne, Gao, and Timbuktu. To the south was the smaller kingdom of Benin, in what is now Nigeria. Its capital, Edo, was an imposing city whose craftspeople produced bronze sculptures that still inspire admiration for their artistic beauty and superb casting techniques.

Economics and Trade in West Africa

The wealth of West African empires was built on trans-Saharan trade. Starting around the year 1000, Muslim traders from North Africa and the Middle East crossed the Sahara to trade with West Africa. Camel caravans carried spices, silks, and cotton south to exchange for West African products, including textiles, gold, copper, grains, nuts, and art. From North Africa, West African products reached markets in the Middle East, Asia, and Western Europe, inspiring interest among the Portuguese in establishing direct trade by sailing to West Africa.

Although connected to trading networks and regional politics, most West Africans farmed, herded, and fished locally for their living. The rice, millet, peas, okra, melons, and yams that they cultivated would spread around the world in the coming centuries, along with the products of the Americas, Europe, and Asia.

Religion in West Africa

North African traders also brought Islam to West Africa. The native religions of West Africa were well established and, like those in North America, inclusivist. Over time, many West Africans converted to Islam, in many cases blending older beliefs, practices, and rituals of planting and harvesting with Islamic doctrine. Leaders who converted to Islam built grand mosques in cities like Jenne.

Slavery and Freedom in West Africa

In addition to such products as textiles and gold, trans-Saharan trade also included enslaved people, usually war captives, criminals, or debtors. Slaves in West Africa generally worked within the households of their owners or on public works projects. They had well-defined rights, such as owning property and marrying free persons. It was not uncommon for African slaves to acquire their freedom. As in most parts of the world, slavery was one of several forms of labor, not the basis of the economy as it would become in large parts of the Americas under colonization.

Many of West Africa's rulers were converts to Islam, which forbade enslaving fellow Muslims. It allowed the enslavement of non-Muslims taken in war, as long as the owner provided religious instruction to the slave. Thus slavery was war-based and religion-based, but not race-based and not necessarily inherited.

AN OLD WORLD: WESTERN EUROPE

Politics and Power in Western Europe

Europe had been devastated by the ending of the Medieval Warm Period, famine, and the Black Death. It lost perhaps as much as half its population over the course of the fourteenth century. Whereas North Americans generally decentralized their societies and rejected authoritarian leaders in response to the crises of the thirteenth and fourteenth centuries, European monarchies grew in power and size.

Wars and strategic marriages created expansive states, including Portugal, Spain, France, England, and the Holy Roman Empire. They were ruled by dynasties that passed the crown through patrilineal lines of succession. Early modern European societies were extremely hierarchical, with marked gradations of social status ranging from the king and hereditary aristocracy down to the urban and rural poor. Inequality was built into virtually every social relationship. The king claimed to rule by the authority of God. Persons of high rank demanded deference from those below them.

Within families, men exercised authority over their wives and children. In England, the legal doctrine known as "coverture" required that when a woman married she surrendered her legal identity, which became "covered" by that of her husband. She could not own property or sign contracts in her own name, control her wages if she worked, write a separate will, or, except in the rarest of circumstances, go to court seeking a divorce. The husband conducted business and testified in court for the entire family. He had the exclusive right to his wife's "company," including domestic labor and sexual relations.

Everywhere in Europe, family life assumed male dominance and female submission. Indeed, political writers of the sixteenth century explicitly compared the king's authority over his subjects with the husband's authority over his family. Both were ordained by God. To justify this argument, they referred to a passage in the New Testament: "As the man is the head of the woman, so is Christ the head of the Church." Neither kind of authority could be challenged without threatening the fabric of social order. In Europe, women's freedoms were dramatically more restricted than in North America or West Africa.

Economics and Trade in Western Europe

As in North America and West Africa, most Western Europeans were farmers. The Medieval Warm Period had allowed them to expand agriculture into previously marginal areas, but the Little Ice Age again contracted farming. When European populations rose after the ravages of the Black Death, the fertile lands of the Americas seemed ideal for feeding the excess population.

Western Europe had only recently connected to the centuries-old trade route that stretched from the Mediterranean, Africa, and the Middle East to South Asia and China. The European conquest of the Americas would begin as an offshoot of the quest for a sea route to West Africa, India, China, and the islands of the East Indies, the sources of gold, silk, tea, sugar, spices, porcelain, and other luxury goods that Europeans had come to value.

Religion in Western Europe

States in Western Europe had converted to Christianity by the early Middle Ages and were officially Catholic until the sixteenth-century Protestant Reformation created Protestantism. As in North America and West Africa, religion was intertwined with daily life. Cathedrals were the center of towns, and calendars for schools, governments, and courts were set by the cycle of church festivals and fast days. Yet, as with Islam in West Africa, older religious traditions survived and blended with Christianity, despite its official theology of exclusivism. Many Europeans continued to believe in witches, demons, and magic.

Commercial and religious motives—namely, the desire to eliminate Islamic intermediaries and win control of the lucrative trade for Christian Western Europe—combined to inspire the quest for a direct route to West Africa and Asia. The marriage of King Ferdinand of Aragon and Queen Isabella of Castille in 1469 united their warring kingdoms. In 1492, they completed the *reconquista*—that is, the "reconquest" of Spain from the Moors, African Muslims who had occupied part of the Iberian Peninsula for centuries. To ensure Spain's religious unification, Ferdinand and Isabella ordered all Muslims and Jews to convert to Catholicism or leave the country. They hoped that ocean trade would circumvent Muslim merchants and perhaps even convert Asians to Christianity, who might help the Christian monarchs seize Jerusalem from Muslim control.

Slavery and Freedom in Western Europe

On the eve of colonization, Europeans held numerous ideas of freedom. Some were as old as the city-states of ancient Greece, while others arose during the political struggles of the early modern era. Some laid the foundations for modern conceptions of freedom, whereas others are quite unfamiliar today. Freedom was not a single idea but a collection of distinct rights and privileges, many enjoyed by only a small portion of the population.

One conception common throughout Europe was that freedom was less a political or social status than a moral or spiritual condition. Freedom meant abandoning the life of sin to embrace the teachings of Christ. "Where the Spirit of the Lord is," declares the New Testament, "there is liberty." In this definition, servitude and freedom were mutually reinforcing, not contradictory states, since those who accepted the teachings of Christ simultaneously became "free from sin" and "servants to God."

"Christian liberty" had no connection to later ideas of religious toleration, a notion that scarcely existed on the eve of colonization. Because religious systems of belief permeated every aspect of people's lives, religion was closely tied to a person's economic, political, and social position and ability to enjoy basic rights.

Every nation in Europe had an established church that decreed what forms of religious worship and belief were acceptable. Dissenters faced persecution by the state as well as condemnation by church authorities. Religious uniformity was thought to be essential to public order; the modern idea that a person's religious beliefs and practices are a matter of private choice, not legal obligation, was almost unknown. The religious wars that racked Europe in the sixteenth and seventeenth centuries centered on which religion would predominate in a kingdom or region, not the right of individuals to choose a church in which to worship.

The equating of liberty with devotion to a higher authority suggested that freedom meant obedience to law. Aristotle had described the law as liberty's "salvation," not its enemy. The identification of freedom with the rule of law did not, however, mean that all subjects of the crown enjoyed the same degree of freedom. In hierarchical European societies, liberty came from knowing one's social place and fulfilling the duties appropriate to one's rank. Most men lacked the freedom that came with economic independence. Even in places where some officials were elected, property qualifications and other restrictions limited the electorate to a minuscule part of the adult male population. The law required strict obedience of employees, and breaches of labor contracts carried criminal penalties.

European ideas of freedom still bore the imprint of the Middle Ages, when "liberties" meant formal, specific privileges such as self-government, exemption from taxation, or the right to practice a particular trade, granted to individuals or groups by contract, royal decree, or purchase. One legal dictionary defined a liberty as "a privilege ... by which men may enjoy some benefit beyond the ordinary subject." Only those who enjoyed the "freedom of the city," for example, could engage in certain economic activities. Numerous modern civil liberties did not exist. The law decreed acceptable forms of religious worship. The government regularly suppressed publications it did not like, and criticism of authority could lead to imprisonment. Personal independence was reserved for a small part of the population, and this was one reason why authorities found "masterless men"—those without regular jobs or otherwise outside the control of their social superiors—so threatening.

Nonetheless, every European country that colonized the Americas claimed to be spreading freedom—for its own population and for Native Americans.

Slavery was central to the societies of ancient Greece and Rome, and it survived for centuries in northern Europe after the collapse of the Roman empire. Germans, Vikings, and Anglo-Saxons all held slaves. In the Mediterranean world, trade in Slavic peoples survived into the fifteenth century. (The English word "slavery" derives from "Slav.") The Spanish and Portuguese took Muslim war captives during their *reconquista* and bought slaves from North African traders. As Europeans began to colonize in the Atlantic, they would look to slavery more and more for labor.

CONTACT

Chinese and Portuguese Navigation

At the beginning of the fifteenth century, one might have predicted that China would establish the world's first global empire. Between 1405 and 1433, Admiral Zheng He led seven large naval expeditions in the Indian Ocean. The first convoy consisted of 62 ships that were larger than those of any European nation, along with 225 support vessels and more than 25,000 men. On his sixth voyage, Zheng explored the coast of East Africa. China was already the world's most important trading economy, with trade routes dotting the Indian Ocean. Zheng's purpose was not discovery, but to impress other peoples with China's might. Had his ships continued westward, they could easily have reached North and South America. But as a wealthy land-based empire, China did not feel the need for overseas expansion, and after 1433 the government ended support for long-distance maritime expeditions. It fell to Portugal, situated on the western corner of the Iberian Peninsula, far removed from the overland route to Asia, to take advantage of new techniques of sailing and navigation to begin exploring the Atlantic.

The development of the **caravel**, a ship capable of long-distance travel, and of the compass and quadrant, devices that enabled sailors to determine their location and direction with greater accuracy than in the past, made it possible to sail down the coast of Africa and return to Portugal.

Portugal and West Africa

Until 1434, no European sailor had seen the coast of Africa below the Sahara. But in that year, a Portuguese ship brought a sprig of rosemary from West Africa, proof that one could sail beyond the desert and return. Little by little,

Europeans longed to trade with Asia and Africa without having to pass through the Italian city-states and Middle Eastern empires that controlled the overland route.

Portuguese ships moved farther down the coast, in 1485 reaching Benin. The Portuguese and their African trading partners established fortified trading posts on the western coast of Africa. The profits reaped by these Portuguese "factories"—so named because merchants were known as "factors"—inspired other European powers to follow in their footsteps.

Portugal also began to colonize Madeira, the Azores, and the Canary and Cape Verde Islands, which lie in the Atlantic off the African coast. Sugar plantations worked by Muslim captives and slaves from Slavic areas of Eastern Europe had flourished in the Middle Ages on Mediterranean islands like Cyprus, Malta, and Crete. Now, the Portuguese established plantations on the Atlantic islands, eventually replacing the Native populations with thousands of enslaved men and women from Africa, setting an ominous precedent. Soon, the center of sugar production would shift again, to the Western Hemisphere.

The coming of the Portuguese, soon followed by traders from other European nations, accelerated the buying and selling of captives within West Africa. At least 100,000 Africans were transported to Spain and Portugal between 1450 and 1500. In 1502, the first Africans were shipped to islands in the Caribbean. The transatlantic slave trade, and its impact on Africa, will be discussed in Chapter 4.

Having reached West Africa, Portuguese mariners pushed their explorations ever southward along the coast. Bartholomeu Dias reached the Cape of Good Hope at the continent's southern tip in 1487. In 1498, Vasco da Gama sailed around it to India, demonstrating the feasibility of a sea route to the

East. With a population of under 1 million, Portugal established a vast trading empire, with bases in India, southern China, and Indonesia. It replaced the Italian city-states as the major European commercial partner of the East. But six years before da Gama's voyage, Christopher Columbus had, he believed, discovered a new route to China and India by sailing west.

The Voyages of Columbus

On October 12, 1492, the Taíno (Arawak) people on one of the islands that today are called the Bahamas saw a strange sight. They were island people who were accustomed to vessels approaching from far away, but these ships were built in an unusual shape and had sails to catch the wind. The men wore armor made of metal and, after rowing to shore in smaller boats, raised a flag and spoke loudly in an unfamiliar language. These strangers did seem at least to know how to trade, and their needles and other pieces of metal seemed interesting and useful.

The expedition's leader, Christopher Columbus, was a seasoned mariner and fearless explorer from Genoa, a major port in northern Italy. Columbus had for years sailed the Mediterranean and North Atlantic, studying ocean currents and wind patterns. Like nearly all navigators of the time, Columbus knew the earth was round. But he drastically underestimated its size. He believed that by sailing westward he could relatively quickly cross the Atlantic and reach Asia. No one in Europe knew that two giant continents lay 3,000 miles to the west. The Vikings, to be sure, had sailed from Greenland to Newfoundland around the year 1000 and established a settlement, Vinland, at a site now known as L'Anse aux Meadows. But this outpost was abandoned after a few years and had been forgotten, except in Norse legends.

Columbus relied on a number of sources for his estimate of the size of the globe, including Marco Polo's account of his visit by land to China in the thirteenth century and, as a devout Catholic, the Bible. Most of Columbus's contemporaries, however, knew that he considerably underestimated the earth's

Columbus's Landfall, an engraving from *La lettera dell'isole* (Letter from the Islands). This 1493 pamphlet reproduced, in the form of a poem, Columbus's first letter describing his voyage of the previous year. Under the watchful eye of King Ferdinand of Spain, Columbus and his men land on a Caribbean island, while local Taínos flee.

size, which helps to explain why he had trouble gaining backers for his expedition. Eventually, King Ferdinand and Queen Isabella of Spain agreed to become sponsors, along with bankers and merchants of Spain and the Italian city-states, who desperately desired to circumvent the Muslim stranglehold on eastern trade. Columbus set sail with royal letters of introduction to Asian rulers, authorizing him to negotiate trade agreements.

After exploring the islands of the Bahamas, Hispaniola (today the site of Haiti and the Dominican Republic), and Cuba in 1492, Columbus returned the following year with seventeen ships and more than 1,000 men to establish a Spanish outpost. Before he died in 1506, Columbus made two more voyages to the Americas, in 1498 and 1502. He went to his grave believing that he had discovered a westward route to Asia. The explorations of another Italian, Amerigo Vespucci, along the coast of South America between 1499 and 1502 made plain that a continent entirely unknown to Europeans had been encountered. These lands would come to bear not Columbus's name but one based on Vespucci's—America. Vespucci also realized that the Native inhabitants were not residents of the East Indies as Columbus had believed, although the name "Indians," applied to them by Columbus, has endured to this day.

Exploration and Conquest

The technique of printing with movable type, invented in the 1450s by the German craftsman Johannes Gutenberg, made possible the rapid spread of information in Europe, at least among the educated minority. News of Columbus's achievement traveled quickly. One writer hailed him as "a hero such as the ancients made gods of." Others were inspired to follow in his wake. John Cabot, a Genoese merchant who had settled in England, reached Newfoundland in 1497. Soon, scores of fishing boats from France, Spain, and England were active in the region. Pedro Cabral claimed Brazil for Portugal in 1500.

But the Spanish took the lead in exploration and conquest. Inspired by a search for wealth, national glory, and the desire to spread Catholicism, Spanish *conquistadores*, often accompanied by religious missionaries and carrying flags emblazoned with the sign of the cross, radiated outward from Hispaniola. In 1513, Vasco Núñez de Balboa trekked across the isthmus of Panama and became the first European to gaze upon the Pacific Ocean from the Americas. Between 1519 and 1522, Ferdinand Magellan led the first expedition to sail around the world, encountering Pacific islands and peoples previously unknown to Europe. Magellan was killed in the Philippines, but his fleet completed the journey, correcting once and for all Columbus's erroneous assessment of the earth's size.

In 1519, Hernán Cortés landed on the coast of mainland Mexico and, at the urging of people he met there, decided to march on the great city of **Tenochtitlán**, the capital of the **Aztec** (Mexica) empire, whose wealth and power rested on domi-

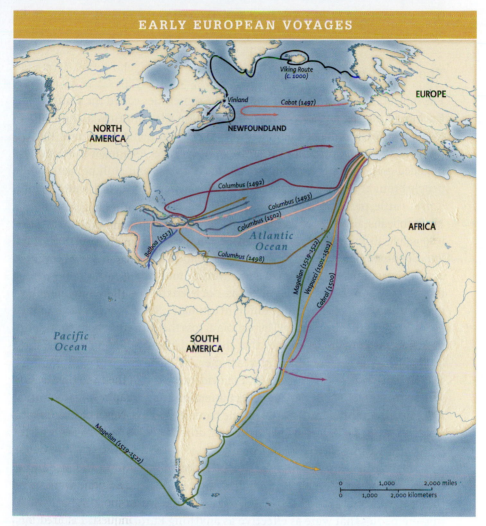

EARLY EUROPEAN VOYAGES

Viking Route (c. 1000)

EUROPE

Vinland   Cabot (1497)

NORTH AMERICA   NEWFOUNDLAND

Columbus (1492)

Columbus (1493)

Columbus (1502)

AFRICA

Balboa (1513)

Atlantic Ocean

Columbus (1498)

Magellan (1519-1522)

Vespucci (1501-1502)

Cabral (1500)

Pacific Ocean

SOUTH AMERICA

Magellan (1519-1522)

0   1,000   2,000 miles
0   1,000   2,000 kilometers

Christopher Columbus's first Atlantic crossing, in 1492, was soon followed by voyages of exploration by English, Portuguese, Spanish, and Italian explorers.

nation of numerous subordinate peoples nearby. The Aztecs were violent warriors who engaged in the ritual sacrifice of captives. This practice thoroughly alienated their neighbors who were delighted to have the Spaniards as allies.

Their thousands of warriors joined forces with the several hundred heavily armed Spaniards, plus horses, giant mastiff dogs, and smallpox, which spread from the Spaniards into the crowded city of Tenochtitlán. A few years later, Francisco Pizarro conquered the great Inca kingdom centered in modern-day Peru, similarly using brute force and taking advantage of rivalries within the kingdom. Soon, treasure fleets carrying cargoes of gold and silver from the mines of Mexico and Peru were traversing the Atlantic to enrich the Spanish crown.

The Columbian Exchange

The transatlantic flow of goods and people, sometimes called the **Columbian Exchange**, altered millions of years of evolution. Plants, animals, and cultures that had evolved independently on separate continents were now thrown together. Products introduced to Europe, Africa, and Asia from the Americas included corn, tomatoes, potatoes, peanuts, tobacco, and chili peppers, while people brought to the Americas wheat, rice, sugarcane, peaches, watermelons, horses, cattle, pigs, and sheep.

Europeans also carried germs previously unknown in the Americas. It is impossible to know how much damage European diseases did in the Americas. Smallpox helped Hernán Cortés take Tenochtitlán, and diseases certainly assisted Europeans in their conquests of North America. But trying to determine the pre-1492 population of the Americas—or even the population in the following two centuries—yields wildly different estimates. Some scholars have applied death rates in Tenochtitlán and Hispaniola across the entirety of both continents, deducing with no direct evidence that the population of the Americas declined by as much as 90 percent in the 150 years after 1492. One problem with assuming massive death rates—besides the lack of evidence—is that focusing on the indirect harm caused by disease can deflect attention from the direct violence that accompanied colonialism. Disease hit the hardest when colonizers were simultaneously cutting off access to food and water, driving people from their homes, or forcing people into slavery or missions.

Importantly, Native people actively responded to illness and attempted to curb its spread. Many instituted quarantines for sick individuals, isolated themselves from colonial settlements, and treated patients with basic nursing—remedies that were as effective as anything Europeans had at their disposal in the same era.

THE SPANISH EMPIRE

By the middle of the sixteenth century, Spain had established an immense empire that reached from Europe to the Americas and Asia. The Atlantic and Pacific oceans, once barriers separating different parts of the world, now became highways for the exchange of goods and the movement of people. Spanish galleons carried gold and silver from Mexico and Peru eastward to Spain and westward to Manila in the Philippines and on to China.

The Spanish empire included the most populous parts of the Americas and the regions richest in natural resources. Stretching from the Andes Mountains of South America through present-day Mexico and the Caribbean and into Florida and the southwestern United States, Spain's empire exceeded in size the Roman empire of the ancient world. Its center in North America was Mexico City, a magnificent capital built on the ruins of the Aztec city of Tenochtitlán that boasted churches, hospitals, monasteries, government buildings, and

Sixteenth-century Native Americans in Florida practice several healing techniques, including smoking tobacco.

the Americas' first university. Unlike the English and French empires, Spanish America was essentially an urban civilization, an "empire of towns." For centuries, its great cities, notably Mexico City, Quito, and Lima, far outshone any urban centers in other colonies and most of those in Europe.

Governing Spanish America

To rule this vast empire, the Spanish crown established a system of government headed by lawyers and bureaucrats. Authority originated with the king and flowed downward through the Council of the Indies—the main body in Spain for colonial administration—and then to viceroys in Mexico and Peru and other local officials in America. The Catholic Church also played a significant role in the administration of Spanish colonies, frequently exerting its authority on matters of faith, morals, and treatment of the Indians.

Successive kings kept elected assemblies out of Spain's empire. Royal officials were generally appointees from Spain, rather than *criollos*, or **creoles**, as persons born in the colonies of European ancestry were called. The imperial state was a real and continuous presence in Spanish America. But given the vastness of the empire, local municipal councils, universities, merchant organizations, and craft guilds enjoyed considerable independence.

Colonists in Spanish America

"The maxim of the conqueror must be to settle," said one Spanish official. The government barred non-Spaniards from emigrating to its American domains, as well as non-Christian Spaniards, including Jews and Moors. But the opportunity for social advancement drew numerous colonists from Spain—225,000

Young Woman with a Harpsichord, a colorful painting from Mexico in the early 1700s, depicts an upper-class woman. Her dress, jewelry, fan, the cross around her neck, and the musical instrument all emphasize that while she lives in the colonies, she embodies the latest in European fashion and culture.

in the sixteenth century and a total of 750,000 in the three centuries of Spain's colonial rule. Some came as laborers, craftsmen, and soldiers. Others came as government officials, priests, professionals, and minor aristocrats, all ready to direct the manual work of Indians, since living without having to labor was a sign of noble status. The most successful of these colonists enjoyed lives of luxury similar to those of the upper classes at home.

Although persons of European birth, called *peninsulares*, stood atop the social hierarchy, they never constituted more than a tiny proportion of the population of Spanish America. Unlike in the later British empire, Native inhabitants always outnumbered European colonists and their descendants in Spanish America. The Spanish forced tens of thousands of Indians to work in gold and silver mines, which supplied the empire's wealth, and on large-scale farms, or **haciendas**, controlled by Spanish landlords. Although the Spanish introduced livestock, wheat, and sugar, the main agricultural crops were the same ones grown before colonization—namely, corn, beans, and squash. Large areas remained under Native control. Like the French empire and unlike the English, Spanish authorities granted Indians certain rights within colonial society and hoped for their eventual assimilation.

In contrast, Spaniards seldom questioned the enslavement of Africans. From the early 1500s, the Spanish demand for enslaved labor fueled the Atlantic slave trade. The Spanish crown ordered wives of colonists to join them in America and demanded that single men marry. But with the population of Spanish women low at first, many single Spanish men married and had children with Native women. As early as 1514, the Spanish government formally approved of such marriages, partly as a way of bringing Christianity to the Native population. By 1600, **mestizos** (persons of mixed origin) made up a large part of the urban population of Spanish America. Over time, Spanish America evolved into a hybrid culture, part Spanish, part Native, and in some areas part

African, but with a single official faith, language, and governmental system (although Native languages survived). In 1531, a Nahua Indian, Juan Diego, reported seeing a vision of the Virgin Mary, speaking the Nahuatl language and looking like an Indian, near a Mexican village. Miracles began to be reported, and a shrine was built in her honor. The Virgin of Guadalupe would come to be revered by millions as a symbol of the mixing of Native and Spanish cultures, and later of the modern nation of Mexico.

Christianity and Conquest

What allowed one nation, the seventeenth-century Dutch legal thinker Hugo Grotius wondered, to claim possession of lands that "belonged to someone else"? This question rarely occurred to most of the Europeans who crossed the Atlantic in the wake of Columbus's voyage, or their monarchs. Following the exclusivist mandate of Christianity, they expected the people they encountered in America to abandon their own beliefs and traditions and embrace those of the newcomers. Failure to do so reinforced the conviction that these people were uncivilized "heathens" (non-Christians).

Europeans brought with them not only a long history of using violence to subdue their internal and external foes but also missionary zeal to spread the benefits of their own civilization to others, while reaping the rewards of empire. Spain was no exception. The establishment of its empire in America took place in the wake of Spain's own territorial unification, the rise of a powerful royal government, and the expulsion of Muslims and Jews in 1492. To further legitimize Spain's claim to rule the Americas, a year after Columbus's first voyage Pope Alexander VI divided the non-Christian world between Spain and Portugal, declaring that most of the Americas belonged to Spain and most of Africa belonged to Portugal. Of course, the people who lived in those places did not agree. The pope justified this pronouncement by requiring Spain and Portugal to spread Catholicism.

European Christians became religious rivals in the sixteenth century, when the Protestant Reformation divided the Catholic Church. In 1517, Martin Luther, a German priest, posted his **Ninety-Five Theses**, which accused the church of worldliness and corruption. Luther wanted to cleanse the church of abuses such as the sale of indulgences (official dispensations forgiving sins). He insisted that all believers should read the Bible for themselves, rather than relying on priests to interpret it for them. His call for reform led to the rise of new Protestant churches independent of Rome and plunged Europe into more than a century of religious and political strife.

Spain, the most powerful bastion of orthodox Catholicism, redoubled its efforts to convert Indians to the "true faith." National glory and religious mission went hand in hand. Convinced of the superiority of Catholicism to all other religions, Spain insisted that the primary goal of colonization was to save Indians from heathenism and prevent them from falling under the sway of Protestantism. The aim was neither to exterminate nor to remove Indians, but to transform them into obedient, Christian subjects of the crown. Indeed, lacking the later concept of "race" as an unchanging, inborn set of qualities and abilities, many Spanish writers insisted that Indians could in time be "brought up" to the level of European civilization. To them, this transition would require not only the destruction of Native political structures but also a transformation of their economic and spiritual lives. Religious orders established missions throughout the empire, and over time millions converted to Catholicism.

Native Rights and Freedoms in the Spanish Empire

Spaniards agreed that Indians should become Catholics, but they argued over the balance between conversion and profits. The *conquistadores* often used brutal violence to force Native men and women to submit to them, violence that many Christians found inconsistent with the mandate to convert and "civilize" Indians.

As early as 1537, Pope Paul III, who hoped to see Indians become devout subjects of Catholic monarchs, outlawed their enslavement (an edict never extended to apply to Africans). His decree declared Indians to be "truly men," who must not be "treated as dumb beasts." Starting in the 1520s, the Dominican priest **Bartolomé de Las Casas** wrote accounts of brutal Spanish atrocities toward the Native people of the Caribbean islands. Las Casas's father had sailed on Columbus's second voyage, and he himself had participated in the conquest of Cuba. But in 1514 Las Casas freed his own Indian slaves and began to preach against the injustices of Spanish rule.

Las Casas's writings denounced Spain for causing the death of millions of innocent people. He narrated in shocking detail the "strange cruelties" carried out by "the Christians," including the burning alive of men, women, and children and the imposition of forced labor. The Indians, he wrote, had been "totally deprived of their freedom and were put in the harshest, fiercest, most terrible servitude and captivity." Las Casas insisted that Spain had no grounds on which to deprive them of their lands and liberty. "The entire human race is one," he proclaimed, and while he continued to believe that Spain had a right to rule in America, largely on religious grounds, he called for Indians to enjoy "all guarantees of liberty and justice" from the moment they became subjects of Spain. "Nothing is certainly more precious in human affairs, nothing more esteemed," he wrote, "than freedom." Yet Las Casas also suggested that importing slaves from Africa would help to protect the Indians from exploitation.

Four Racial Groups, taken from a series of paintings by the eighteenth-century Mexican artist Andrés de Islas, illustrates the racial mixing that took place in the Spanish empire and some of the new vocabulary invented to describe it. *First:* The offspring of a Spaniard and Indian is a *mestizo*. *Second:* A Spaniard and a *mestiza* produce a *castizo*. *Third:* The child of an Indian and a *mestiza* is a *coyote*. *Fourth:* The child of an Indian man and African woman is a *chino*.

Largely because of Las Casas's efforts, Spain in 1542 issued a proclamation that became known as the New Laws, commanding that Indians no longer be enslaved. And the government established the **repartimiento system**, whereby Native towns were required to provide a fixed amount of labor each year on Spanish mines or farms. As tributary towns, they were ruled by Native leaders and lived according to their own laws and customs, as long as they paid their annual tribute.

Las Casas's writings, translated into several European languages, contributed to the spread of the **Black Legend**—the image of Spain as a uniquely brutal and exploitative colonizer. In reality all empires were highly exploitative. But the Black Legend would provide a potent justification for other European powers to challenge Spain's predominance in the Americas. Influenced by Las Casas, the eighteenth-century French historian Guillaume Thomas Raynal would write of Columbus's arrival in the Americas, "Tell me, reader, whether these were civilized people landing among savages, or savages among civilized people?"

Exploring North of Mexico

While the Spanish empire centered on Mexico, Peru, and the West Indies, the hope of finding a new kingdom of gold soon led Spanish explorers into new territory. In 1508, Spain established the first permanent colony in what is now the United States. That first colony was not, as many people believe, at Jamestown, Virginia, or St. Augustine, Florida, but on the island of Puerto Rico, now a U.S. "commonwealth." Unlike many other places Europeans explored north of Mexico, Puerto Rico had gold; Juan Ponce de León, who led the colony, sent

In this engraving, sixteenth-century Timucuas, Native people of northern Florida, are transporting food they have grown to the public storehouse.

a considerable amount to Spain, while keeping some for himself. In 1513, Ponce de León embarked for Florida, in search of wealth, slaves, and a fountain of eternal youth, only to be repelled by Calusa Indians. In 1528, another Spanish expedition seeking plunder landed in Florida, but the men became separated from their ships, and only four of them made it back to Mexico. For seven years, the four survivors wandered through the lands of Native peoples from Florida to the desert of the Southwest and northern Mexico. One, Álvar Núñez Cabeza de Vaca, wrote an account of his adventures, including tales told by Native inhabitants of the seven golden cities of Cibola, somewhere over the horizon.

One of the four survivors was an enslaved African named Esteban. After walking all the way to Mexico with Cabeza de Vaca in 1536, Esteban returned north, leading the expedition of Friar Marcos de Niza. Esteban went farther north than Niza, becoming the first African and first non-Indian to explore parts of northern Mexico and Arizona and the Pueblos of New Mexico.

In the late 1530s and 1540s, Juan Rodriguez Cabrillo explored the Pacific coast as far north as present-day Oregon, and expeditions led by Hernando de Soto, Francisco Vásquez de Coronado, and others marched through the Gulf region and the Southwest, fruitlessly searching for another Mexico or Peru. Coronado followed Esteban's path to the interior of the continent, reaching as far north as the Great Plains, and became the first European to encounter the immense herds of bison that roamed the West. The Coronado and de Soto expeditions, really mobile communities with hundreds of adventurers, priests, slaves, and livestock, spread devastation among Native communities. But they were unsuccessful in their quest for riches, and most of them—including de Soto—did not make it out alive.

Florida and the Spanish

The Indigenous peoples of Florida were the first to face Spanish colonization in what is now the continental United States. Spain hoped to establish a military base in present-day Florida to combat pirates who threatened the treasure fleet that each year sailed from Havana for Europe loaded with gold and silver from Mexico and Peru. Spain also wanted to forestall French incursions in the area.

EARLY SPANISH CONQUESTS AND EXPLORATIONS IN THE AMERICAS

Legend:
— Cabrillo
— Oñate
- - - Coronado
— de Soto
— Cabeza de Vaca and Esteban
····· Esteban and Niza
- - - Ponce de León
— Cortés
— Pizarro

Map labels: Cabrillo, Oñate, Cabeza de Vaca and Esteban, Coronado, Esteban and Niza, de Soto, Fort Caroline, St. Augustine, Ponce de León, Gulf of Mexico, Cortés, Mexico City, Hispaniola, Caribbean Sea, Atlantic Ocean, Pacific Ocean, Pizarro, PERU

By around 1600, New Spain had become a vast empire stretching from the modern-day American Southwest through Mexico and Central America and into the former Inca kingdom in South America. This map shows early Spanish exploration, especially in the present-day United States.

In 1565, Philip II of Spain authorized the nobleman Pedro Menéndez de Avilés to lead a colonizing expedition to Florida. Menéndez destroyed a small outpost at Fort Caroline, which a group of Huguenots (French Protestants) had established in 1562 near present-day Jacksonville. Menéndez and his men massacred the French colonists and went on to establish Spanish forts on St. Simons Island, Georgia, and at St. Augustine, Florida. The latter remains the oldest site in the continental United States continuously inhabited by European settlers and their descendants.

The Spanish did not fulfill their ambitions for Florida. After destroying the French Fort Caroline, they established forts from present-day Miami into South Carolina, as well as a Jesuit mission on Chesapeake Bay. Yet by 1574, Native people had destroyed all of these attempts besides St. Augustine and Santa Elena, near modern-day Port Royal, South Carolina. Frustrated at large expenses and no profits, in 1587 the government in Spain ordered Santa Elena abandoned and the inhabitants resettled (over their vocal protests) at St. Augustine. Having found no gold and little to attract Spanish settlers, the crown invited Franciscan missionaries to establish missions, including among the Guales north of St. Augustine in what is now Georgia, the Timucuas in central Florida, and the Apalachees in the Florida panhandle. Many Native communities were interested in the missionaries, who brought useful goods and had compelling spiritual ideas that the inclusivist nature of Indigenous religions allowed them to incorporate. Some Native leaders or communities were able to increase their power in the region by establishing permanent connections to Spanish trade. But people who lived in or near missions also found they were subjected to violence and to European diseases that wreaked havoc on the crowded mission communities.

In some places, they reached compromises that allowed the Spanish missionaries to stay. In others, the Native people threw them out. Beginning in 1597, Guale Indians planned and launched an attack on missions in their province. One Guale explained the attacks by noting that the missionaries had sought to eliminate "our dances, banquets, feasts, celebrations, and wars. . . . They persecute our old people by calling them witches." Guales and their allies ransacked missions and killed missionaries. Spanish troops and neighboring Native enemies of the Guales fought against them until the Guales agreed to peace. In general, Florida remained a Native-dominated place with an isolated post and few missions. As late as 1763, Spanish Florida had only 4,000 inhabitants of European descent.

The Southwest and the Spanish

Coronado's exploration of the Southwest was a disaster for everyone involved. Its violence repelled possible Native allies in the Southwest, and the failure to find riches decreased Spanish interest in the north. Half a century later, the

Spanish returned to the Pueblos on the Rio Grande to attempt a permanent colony called New Mexico. In 1598, Juan de Oñate led a group from Mexico of several hundred soldiers, Franciscan missionaries, and colonists, many of whom were the descendants of the early Spanish *conquistadores* and Native women from central Mexico.

Rather than establishing their own town and farms on the Rio Grande, Oñate and his followers violently moved into the Pueblos. They demanded that Native people feed and work for them, killing and raping those who did not comply. Fighting back was difficult because the Pueblos were not one people but instead inhabited over eighty independent towns and spoke six different languages.

Finally, the people of the pueblo of Acoma had enough, and they killed a Spanish patrol that included Oñate's nephew. In the ensuing battle, Oñate's forces killed an estimated 800 of Acoma's men, women, and children and captured over 500 more to keep as slaves, cutting off one foot of the adult men.

In response to protests from the missionaries and Native leaders of the Pueblos, authorities in Mexico City in 1606 deposed and punished Oñate. In 1609, they ordered the New Mexican colonists to establish a separate town and grow their own food. In the future, only married soldiers were to be stationed in New Mexico to reduce the likelihood of sexual violence. The Franciscan missionaries stayed, but most of the colonists left. Founded around 1610, the colonial town of Santa Fe would be the first permanent European settlement in the Southwest, but it remained a small settlement, surrounded by Native peoples.

The Pueblo Revolt

Some Native people left their Pueblos to build new towns farther from the Spanish. Others saw benefits in Spanish alliance, including new tools and crops and the protection of Spanish forces against their Apache and Navajo enemies. Many also found Catholicism appealing and welcomed the missionaries as a counterbalance to the depredations of soldiers and settlers. Many accepted baptism, even as they continued to practice their old religion, adding Jesus, Mary, and the Catholic saints to their already rich spiritual pantheon. But as the Inquisition—the persecution of non-Catholics—became more and more intense in Spain, so did the friars' efforts to stamp out traditional religious ceremonies in New Mexico. By burning Native sacred objects and threatening Native religious leaders, the missionaries alienated far more Indians than they converted. A prolonged drought that began around 1660 and the authorities' inability to protect the villages and missions from attacks by Navajos and Apaches added to local discontent.

The Pueblo peoples came together under the inspiring leadership of a man named Popé. A religious leader born around 1630 in San Juan Pueblo, Popé

From BARTOLOMÉ DE LAS CASAS, *HISTORY OF THE INDIES* (1528)

Las Casas was the Dominican priest who condemned the treatment of Indians in the Spanish empire. His widely disseminated writings helped to establish the Black Legend of Spanish cruelty.

The Indians [of Hispaniola] were totally deprived of their freedom and were put in the harshest, fiercest, most horrible servitude and captivity which no one who has not seen it can understand. Even beasts enjoy more freedom when they are allowed to graze in the fields. But our Spaniards gave no such opportunity to Indians and truly considered them perpetual slaves, since the Indians had not the free will to dispose of their persons but instead were disposed of according to Spanish greed and cruelty, not as men in captivity but as beasts tied to a rope to prevent free movement. When they were allowed to go home, they often found it deserted and had no other recourse than to go out into the woods to find food and to die. When they fell ill, which was very frequently because they are a delicate people unaccustomed to such work, the Spaniards did not believe them and pitilessly called them lazy dogs and kicked and beat them; and when illness was apparent they sent them home as useless. . . . They would go then, falling into the first stream and dying there in desperation; others would hold on longer but very few ever made it home. I sometimes came upon dead bodies on my way, and upon others who were gasping and moaning in their death agony, repeating "Hungry, hungry." And this was the freedom, the good treatment and the Christianity the Indians received.

About eight years passed under [Spanish rule] and this disorder had time to grow; no one gave it a thought and the multitude of people who originally lived on the island . . . was consumed at such a rate that in these eight years 90 per cent had perished. From here this sweeping plague went to San Juan, Jamaica, Cuba and the continent, spreading destruction over the whole hemisphere.

From FRIAR MARCOS DE NIZA'S ACCOUNT OF HIS VOYAGE WITH ESTEBAN (1539)

In the 1520s and 1530s, after the conquest of Mexico City, Spanish conquistadores raided Native lands to the north for captives to sell as slaves. In part due to Bartolomé de Las Casas, the Spanish monarchs outlawed Indian slavery in their empire. In 1539, Friar Marcos de Niza traveled north from Mexico City to spread the news that the slave raids would stop and priests would come instead. His guide was Esteban, an African man who had been enslaved by the Spanish. Esteban had journeyed from Florida through Texas to northern Mexico with the man who owned him under Spanish law, Andrés

Dorantes, as well as Alvar Nuñez Cabeza de Vaca. Still technically enslaved to Dorantes, Esteban now set off to lead Niza through northern Mexico to Arizona and New Mexico. Niza begins his account by explaining that two different Native groups will accompany him, Esteban, and another priest, Father Onoratto. The first are northern Indians, whom the Spanish had previously captured in the north and held in bondage near Mexico City. The Viceroy of Mexico has freed them to return home. The second group is Opatas of northwestern Mexico who came to offer to accompany Niza and Esteban as they returned the formerly enslaved people to their homes.

I took with me, as my colleague, Father Onoratto, and Dorantes' Negro Esteban and certain Indians whom the lord Viceroy freed and bought for this purpose and whom the governor of New Galicia, Francisco Vasques de Coronado turned over to me, as well as many Indians [who] came to the valley of Culiacán expressing great joy, because the freed Indians assured them that the governor sent us ahead to let them know about their freedom and that people would not be enslaving them or making war on them or mistreating them, and that this was the wish and the order of his Majesty.

With this company I made my journey . . . and on the way I found much welcome and many offerings of things to eat . . . and they made houses of straw mats and branches for me along the way where no people were living. I stayed in Petatlan for three days because my colleague Father Onoratto had fallen ill. I had to leave him there and, as I had been instructed, continue my journey, led by the Holy Spirit through no merit of my own and accompanied by the above-mentioned Esteban, Dorantes' Negro, and some of the freed Indians and many people of the region, who received me with welcome and rejoicing and triumphal arches and who gave me of their food, which wasn't much, because, they said, they had had no rain for three years and because the Indians of that region were more intent on hiding than on sowing, for fear of the Christians, who up until then had been making war on them and enslaving them. . . .

QUESTIONS

1. Why does Las Casas, after describing the ill treatment of Indians, write, "And this was the freedom, the good treatment and the Christianity the Indians received"?

2. Why did the Native peoples greet Niza and Esteban with "welcome and rejoicing"?

3. What ideas of freedom are apparent in the two documents?

was one of forty-seven Indians arrested in 1675 for "sorcery"—that is, practicing their traditional religion. Four of the prisoners were hanged, and the rest, including Popé, were brought to Santa Fe to be publicly whipped. After this humiliation, Popé returned home and began holding secret meetings in Pueblo communities.

Under Popé's leadership, Indians of the Pueblos joined in a coordinated uprising. Some 2,000 warriors destroyed isolated farms and missions, killing 400 colonists, including 21 Franciscan missionaries. They then surrounded Santa Fe. The Spanish had no choice but to abandon the town. Most of the Spanish survivors, accompanied by several hundred Christian Indians, made their way south out of New Mexico. Within a few weeks, a century of colonization in the area had been destroyed. The Pueblo Indians had reestablished the freedom lost through Spanish conquest.

The **Pueblo Revolt** was a complete victory over the Spanish. The victors turned with a vengeance on all symbols of European culture, uprooting fruit trees, destroying cattle, burning churches and images of Christ and the Virgin Mary, and wading into rivers to wash away their Catholic baptisms. They rebuilt their places of worship, called "kivas," and resumed sacred dances the friars had banned. "The God of the Spaniards," they shouted, "is dead."

The Pueblo Revolt helped to inspire revolts across northern Mexico. Other Native towns that had experienced similar troubles with the Spanish struck back in attempts to regain their independence. Apache bands took advantage of the fighting to expand their raids across the region. While the Spanish never gave up their ambitions to colonize northern Mexico, their hold on it was always tenuous.

Yet at the same time, cooperation among the Rio Grande Pueblos evaporated. By the end of the 1680s, warfare had broken out among several Pueblos, even as Apache and Navajo raids continued. Popé died around 1690. In 1692, the Spanish launched an invasion that eventually reestablished the colony of New Mexico. Some communities welcomed them back as a source of military protection. And Spain had learned a lesson. In the eighteenth century, colonial authorities adopted a more tolerant attitude toward traditional religious practices and made fewer demands on Indian labor.

THE FRENCH AND DUTCH EMPIRES

If the Black Legend inspired a sense of superiority among Spain's European rivals, the precious metals that poured from the Americas into the Spanish treasury aroused the desire to try to match Spain's success. The establishment of Spain's American empire transformed the balance of power in the world economy. The Atlantic replaced the overland route to Asia as the major axis of global trade. During the seventeenth century, the French, Dutch, and English established colonies in North America. England's mainland colonies, to be discussed in the next chapter, consisted of agricultural settlements with growing populations whose hunger for land produced incessant conflict with Native peoples. New France and New Netherland were primarily commercial ventures that, like Spanish Florida and New Mexico, never attracted large numbers of colonists. Because French and Dutch settlements were more dependent than the English on Indians as trading partners and military allies, Native Americans exercised more power and enjoyed more freedom in their relations with these settlements.

French Colonization

The first of Spain's major European rivals to embark on New World explorations was France. The French initially aimed to find gold and to locate a Northwest Passage—a sea route connecting the Atlantic to the Pacific. But early French explorers were soon disappointed, and North America came to seem little more than a barrier to be crossed, not a promising site for settlement or exploitation. For most of the sixteenth century, only explorers, fishermen, pirates preying on Spanish shipping farther south, and, as time went on, fur traders visited the eastern coast of North America. French efforts to establish settlements in Newfoundland and Nova Scotia failed, beset by Native resistance and inadequate planning and financing. Not until the seventeenth century would France, as well as England and the Netherlands, establish permanent settlements in North America.

The explorer Samuel de Champlain, sponsored by a French fur-trading company, founded Quebec in 1608. In 1673, the Jesuit priest Jacques Marquette and the fur trader Louis Joliet located the Mississippi River, and by 1681 René-Robert Cavelier, Sieur de La Salle, had descended to the Gulf of Mexico, claiming the entire Mississippi River valley for France. On European maps, New France eventually formed a giant arc along the St. Lawrence and Mississippi rivers. But the colonial population would remain small and dependent on Native alliances.

By 1700, the number of white inhabitants of New France had risen to only 19,000. With a far larger population than England, France sent many fewer emigrants to the Western Hemisphere. The government at home feared that significant emigration would undermine France's role as a European great power and might compromise its effort to establish trade and good relations with Native Americans. Unfavorable reports about America circulated widely in France. Canada was widely depicted as an icebox, a land of "savage" Indians, a dumping ground for criminals. Most French who left their homes during these years preferred to settle in the Netherlands, Spain, or the West Indies. The revocation in 1685 of the Edict of Nantes, which had extended religious toleration to French Protestants, led well over 100,000 Huguenots to flee their country. But they were not welcome in New France, which the crown desired to remain an outpost of Catholicism.

The Fur Trade

The viability of New France, with its small white population and emphasis on the fur trade rather than agricultural settlement, depended on friendly relations with Native nations. The French prided themselves on adopting a more humane policy than their imperial rivals. "Only our nation," declared one French writer, "knows the secret of winning the Indians' affection." Lacking the need for Indian labor of the Spanish and the voracious appetite for land of the English colonies, and relying on Indians to supply furs to trading posts, the French and their Native allies worked out a complex series of military, commercial, and diplomatic connections, the most enduring alliances between Indians and Europeans in colonial North America. The Jesuits, a missionary religious order, did seek, with some success, to convert Indians to Catholicism. Unlike Spanish missionaries in early New Mexico, they allowed Christian Indians to retain a high degree of independence and much of their traditional social structure, and they did not seek to suppress all traditional religious practices. Indians who converted to Catholicism were promised full membership in French colonial society. In fact, however, it was far rarer for Natives to adopt French ways than for French settlers to become attracted to the "free" life of the Indians.

Native Americans required French traders to follow their rules. The first French trading partners along the St. Lawrence River were Innus (Montagnais), Algonquins, and Wendats (Hurons), who recruited French trade and demanded good prices for furs. (Algonquins were a nation within the large linguistic grouping known as Algonquian.) When the French established Quebec, it was on Algonquin land and because Algonquin leaders invited them. As Champlain recognized, "my enterprises and discoveries . . . seem to be possible only through their means." These allies of the French also insisted that the French join their military alliance against their enemy: the Haudenosaunee (Iroquois) League, discussed previously. Thus Innus, Algonquins, and Wendats drew the French into a major war that they did not want.

It is no surprise that Native Americans wanted European trade. They incorporated European goods into their existing ways of life, using copper kettles as well as ceramic pots, adding wool blankets to animal skins and furs, and using guns for some tasks and bows and arrows (sometimes tipped with brass) for others. Some Native women married the single French men who came to New France and incorporated them and their children into Native communities.

The Dutch Empire

In 1609, Henry Hudson, an Englishman employed by the Dutch East India Company, sailed into New York Harbor searching for a Northwest Passage to Asia. Hudson and his crew became the first Europeans to sail up the river that now bears his name. Hudson did not find a route to Asia, but he did encounter Lenapes, Munsees, and Mahicans more than willing to trade furs for European goods. He claimed the area for the Netherlands, and his voyage planted the seeds for what would eventually become a great metropolis, New York City. When the powerful Mohawks of the Haudenosaunee League learned about the Dutch, they and their Mahican allies persuaded them that the most lucrative fur trade would be on the Hudson River near present-day Albany. By 1614, Dutch traders had established an outpost there at Fort Orange. Ten years later, the Dutch West India Company, which had been awarded a monopoly of Dutch trade with America, settled colonists on Manhattan Island.

These ventures formed one small part in the rise of the Dutch overseas empire. In the early seventeenth century, the Netherlands dominated international commerce, and Amsterdam was Europe's foremost shipping and banking center. The small nation had entered a golden age of rapidly accumulating wealth and stunning achievements in painting, philosophy, and the sciences. The Dutch invented the joint stock company, a way of pooling financial resources and sharing the risk of maritime voyages, which proved central to the development of modern capitalism. With a population of only 2 million, the Netherlands established a far-flung empire that reached from Indonesia to South Africa and the Caribbean and temporarily wrested control of Brazil from Portugal.

Dutch Freedom

The Dutch prided themselves on their devotion to liberty. Indeed, in the early seventeenth century they enjoyed two freedoms not recognized elsewhere in Europe—freedom of the press and of private religious practice. Even though there was an established church, the Dutch Reformed, individuals could hold whatever religious beliefs they wished. Amsterdam became a haven for persecuted Protestants from all over Europe, including French Huguenots, German Calvinists, and those, like the Pilgrims, who desired to separate from the Church of England. Jews, especially those fleeing from Spain, also found refuge there.

Other emigrants came to the Netherlands in the hope of sharing in the country's prosperity. During the seventeenth century, the nation attracted about half a million migrants from elsewhere in Europe. Many of these newcomers helped to populate the Dutch overseas empire.

Freedom in New Netherland

Despite the Dutch reputation for cherishing freedom, New Netherland was hardly governed democratically. New Amsterdam, the main population center, was essentially a fortified military outpost controlled by appointees of the Dutch West India Company. Although the governor called on prominent citizens for advice from time to time, neither an elected assembly nor a town council, the basic unit of government at home, was established. In other ways, however, the colonists enjoyed more liberty, especially in religious matters, than their counterparts elsewhere in North America.

Dutch women enjoyed far more independence than in other colonies. Unlike in England and its colonies, under Dutch law, married women retained their separate legal identity. They could go to court, borrow money, and own property. Men were used to sharing property with their wives. Their wills generally left their possessions to their widows and daughters as well as sons. Margaret Hardenbroeck, the widow of a New Amsterdam merchant, expanded her husband's business and became one of the town's richest residents after his death in 1661.

Enslaved men and women in New Netherland were able to establish some rights for themselves as well. The Dutch dominated the Atlantic slave trade in the early seventeenth century, and they introduced slaves into New Netherland as a matter of course. By 1650, the colony's 500 slaves outnumbered those in the Chesapeake. But in the 1640s a petition by a group of enslaved Africans persuaded the Dutch West India Company to institute a system of "half-freedom"— that is, they were required to pay an annual fee to the company and work for it when called upon, but they given land to support their families. Enslaved people worked on family farms or for household or craft labor, not on large plantations as in the West Indies.

The Dutch and Religious Toleration

New Netherland attracted a remarkably diverse population. As early as the 1630s, at least eighteen languages were said to be spoken in New Amsterdam, whose residents included not only Dutch settlers but also Africans, Belgians, English, French, Germans, Irish, and Scandinavians. Of course, these settlers adhered to a wide variety of religions.

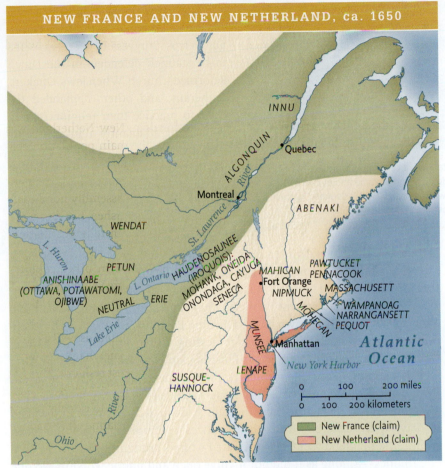

NEW FRANCE AND NEW NETHERLAND, ca. 1650

On European maps, New France and New Netherland were large land claims, but in reality they were a few trading posts and small settlements surrounded by Native nations.

The Dutch long prided themselves on being uniquely tolerant in religious matters compared to other European nations and their empires. It would be wrong, however, to attribute modern ideas of religious freedom to either the Dutch government and company at home or the rulers of New Netherland. Both Holland and New Netherland had an official religion, the Dutch Reformed Church, one of the Protestant national churches to emerge from the Reformation. The Dutch commitment to freedom of conscience extended to religious devotion exercised in private, not public worship in nonestablished churches. It did not reflect a willing acceptance of religious diversity.

THE FRENCH AND DUTCH EMPIRES ★ 37

Coastal Native Americans were adept mariners. This detail from the earliest known engraving of New Amsterdam (1627) depicts Dutch and Lenape Indian boats in the harbor.

The West India Company's officials in the colony, particularly Governor Petrus Stuyvesant, were expected to be staunch defenders of the Dutch Reformed Church. When Jews, Quakers, Lutherans, and others demanded the right to practice their religion openly, Stuyvesant adamantly refused, seeing such diversity as a threat to a godly, prosperous order. Under Stuyvesant, the colony was more restrictive in its religious policies than the Dutch government at home. Twenty-three Jews arrived in New Amsterdam in 1654 from Brazil and the Caribbean. Referring to them as "members of a deceitful race," Stuyvesant ordered the newcomers to leave. But the company overruled him, noting that Jews at home had invested "a large amount of capital" in its shares.

As a result of Stuyvesant's policies, challenges arose to the limits on religious toleration. One, known as the Flushing Remonstrance, was a 1657 petition by a group of English settlers protesting the governor's order barring Quakers from living in the town of Flushing, on Long Island. Although later seen as a landmark of religious liberty, the Remonstrance had little impact at the time. Stuyvesant ordered several signers arrested for defying his authority.

Nonetheless, it is true that the Dutch dealt with religious pluralism in ways quite different from the practices common in other European empires. Religious dissent was tolerated—often grudgingly, as in the case of Catholics—as long as it did not involve open and public worship. No one in New Netherland was forced to attend the official church, nor was anyone executed for holding the wrong religious beliefs (as would happen in Puritan New England around the time of the Flushing Remonstrance).

New Netherland and the Haudenosaunee

The Dutch came to North America to trade, and they prided themselves on getting along well with Native peoples. Mindful of the Black Legend of Spanish cruelty, the Dutch determined to treat the Native inhabitants more humanely. Having won their own independence from Spain after the longest and bloodiest war of sixteenth-century Europe, many Dutch identified with American Indians as fellow victims of Spanish oppression. From the beginning, Dutch authorities recognized Native sovereignty over the land and forbade settlement in any area unless it had been purchased.

By the 1640s, Dutch traders were exporting tens of thousands of furs each year, most of them traded from the Mohawks, one of the five nations of the Haudenosaunee League. The Mohawks dominated trade at Fort Orange (later Albany). They used their market power in furs to set prices. Colonists repeatedly complained that bakers used all of the colony's white flour to sell "sweet cake, white bread, cookies, and pretzels" to the Indians, leaving "largely bran" to sell to the colonists. The Dutch repeatedly outlawed the sale of white bread and cake, as well as liquor and guns, to Indians, but Native customers always got around the restrictions.

Some of the furs that the Mohawks sold were hunted by themselves and by other Haudenosaunee nations, but others were stolen from their enemies.

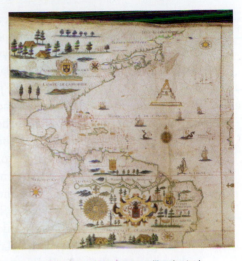

A map of the Americas from an illuminated manuscript produced in Le Havre, France, in 1613, depicting the French ambition to dominate North America. The precision of the coastline is unusual for maps of this era, although it reflects in large part the imagination of the cartographer.

Mohawks seized canoes descending the St. Lawrence River to the French posts of Montreal and Quebec. In the early decades of the 1600s, the Haudenosaunee expanded their domain far beyond their homelands, driving off or forcibly incorporating Native nations from the St. Lawrence River to the Carolinas and from the Atlantic to the Great Lakes. Although European maps labeled vast regions as New France, New Netherland, and New England, everyone knew that the Haudenosaunee were the most powerful people in the Northeast.

A Trading Colony

The Dutch were good allies to the Mohawks because they had to be, but where they attempted settlements rather than trade, they created conflict with Native neighbors. The Dutch West India Company decided that a settlement at the mouth of the Hudson River would protect Dutch trade from French and English pirates and produce grain and cattle for Fort Orange and the sugar plantations that the Dutch were establishing on Caribbean islands and the coast of South America. They gained permission to establish New Amsterdam on Manhattan Island through negotiations with Delaware (Lenape) diplomats.

In an attempt to attract settlers to North America, the Dutch West India Company promised colonists not only the right to practice their religion freely (in private) but also cheap livestock and free land after six years of labor. Eventually, it even surrendered its monopoly of the fur trade, opening this profitable commerce to all. Many settlers, Stuyvesant complained, had been lured by "an imaginary liberty" and did not display much respect for the company's authority. In 1629, the company adopted a plan of "Freedoms and Exemptions," offering large estates to *patroons*—shareholders who agreed to transport tenants for agricultural labor and purchased the land from Indians in a treaty approved by both sides. In return, the patroon was to have "freedoms" like those of a medieval lord, including the right to 10 percent of his tenants' annual income and complete authority over law enforcement within his domain. Mahicans granted land for both Fort Orange and a patroonship for Kiliaen van Rensselaer in return for benefits and payments, but no other patroonships succeeded.

The Dutch desire to attract colonists put New Amsterdam and its surrounding farms in conflict with Delawares (Lenapes and Munsees). The Dutch took more land than the Delawares had agreed to, and Dutch pigs and cattle damaged Delaware women's crops. Delawares in turn killed and ate the invasive livestock. New Netherland Governor Willem Kieft in 1639 demanded that Delawares start paying yearly tribute in corn. A group of Delawares noted that Kieft "must be a very mean fellow to come to live in this country without being invited by them, and now wish to compel them to give him their corn for nothing." A three-year conflict known as Kieft's War followed that resulted in the death of an estimated 1,000 Delawares and their allies and more than 200 colonists. Many Dutch settlers fled the colony, and the war dissuaded new settlers. Over the course of the seventeenth century, the Netherlands sent 1 million people overseas (many of them recent immigrants who were not in fact Dutch) to populate and govern their far-flung colonies. Very few, however, made North America their destination. By the mid-1660s, the European population of New Netherland numbered only 9,000. New Netherland remained a tiny backwater in the Dutch empire.

Borderlands and Empire in Early America

A **borderland**, according to one historian, is "a meeting place of peoples where geographical and cultural borders are not clearly defined." Numerous such places came into existence during the era of European conquest and settlement, including the contested region bordered by New Netherland, the Haudenosaunee League, New France, and France's Algonquian and Wendat allies. In this turbulent era, boundaries between empires and between colonists and Native peoples and between Native nations shifted constantly, overlapping claims to authority abounded, and hybrid cultures developed. In a few areas, Europeans consolidated their control and the power of nearby Native peoples weakened. But at the edges of empire, power was always unstable, and overlapping cultural interactions at the local level defied any single pattern. And beyond those edges, across most of North America, Native nations still held all of the power. European conquest was not a simple story of expanding domination over either empty space or powerless peoples but of a continual struggle to establish authority. The Spanish, French, Dutch, and English empires fought one another for dominance in various parts of the continent, and Indians wielded both economic and political power, pitting European empires against each other. Despite laws restricting commerce between empires, traders challenged boundaries, traversing lands claimed by both Europeans and Indians. People of European and Native descent married and exchanged cultural attributes.

Despite their differences, European empires shared certain features. All brought Christianity, new forms of technology and learning, new legal systems and family relations, and new forms of economic enterprise and wealth creation. They also brought savage warfare and disease. These empires were aware of one another's existence. They studied and borrowed from one another, each lauding itself as superior to the others. From the outset, dreams of freedom—for Native peoples, for settlers, for the entire world through the spread of Christianity—inspired and justified colonization. And Native peoples acted on their own dreams of freedom to fight colonialism in some times and places and, in others, to forge economic and diplomatic relationships with Europeans that they hoped would advance their own people's sovereignty and prosperity.

CHAPTER REVIEW

REVIEW QUESTIONS

1. *In the age of exploration, when different areas of the world were brought into sustained contact, how did local economies change?*

2. *One of the most striking features of Native societies at the time of the encounter with Europeans was their diversity. Support this statement with several examples.*

3. *Compare and contrast Western European, Native North American, and West African values and ways of life. Consider addressing religion, views about ownership of land, gender relations, and notions of freedom.*

4. *What were the main factors fueling European exploration and conquest?*

5. *Compare the political, economic, and religious motivations behind the French and Dutch empires with those of New Spain.*

6. *Describe how the idea of the "Black Legend" affected subsequent policies and practices of Spain as well as those of the Netherlands and France.*

7. *How would European settlers justify to Native Americans both the conquest of Native lands and terminating their freedom?*

8. *How would Native Americans explain to Europeans their own views of freedom and desires for their relationships with Europeans?*

9. *Why did Native Americans exercise more power in their relations with the Dutch and French than with the English?*

KEY TERMS

Great League of Peace (p. 6)

reconquista (p. 13)

caravel (p. 15)

conquistadores (p. 18)

Tenochtitlán (p. 18)

Aztec (p. 18)

Columbian Exchange (p. 20)

creoles (p. 21)

hacienda (p. 22)

mestizos (p. 22)

Ninety-Five Theses (p. 23)

Bartolomé de Las Casas (p. 24)

repartimiento system (p. 25)

Black Legend (p. 25)

Pueblo Revolt (p. 32)

borderland (p. 40)

Go to 🐰 **INQUIZITIVE**

To see what you know—and learn what you've missed—with personalized feedback along the way.

CHAPTER 2

EUROPEAN COLONIES AND NATIVE NATIONS

1600-1660

FOCUS QUESTIONS

- *What were the main contours of English colonization in the seventeenth century?*

- *What drew English settlers to North America, and how did Native peoples respond to incoming colonists?*

- *What was the significance of the Anglo-Powhatan Wars?*

- *How was slavery established in the western Atlantic world?*

- *What made the English settlement of New England distinctive?*

- *What were the main sources of discord in early New England?*

- *How did the English Civil War affect the colonies in America?*

In 1584, two explorers visited London. Their names were Manteo and Wanchese, and they came from what today is North Carolina's Outer Banks, a place they called Ossomocomuck. After a typically miserable two-month voyage across the Atlantic, they met with members of Parliament and Queen Elizabeth's court. As they walked around London, they could see the Tower of London and London Bridge, where the heads of traitors mounted on stakes revealed a much more hierarchical society than their own. London's population had rebounded from the Black Death, and now 150,000 people lived within its medieval city walls and the crowded suburbs right outside, starkly contrasting with the spread-out towns interspersed with farms to which Manteo and Wanchese were accustomed. They stayed in Sir Walter Raleigh's mansion on the Thames River, where they had long conversations with scholar Thomas Harriot. He asked them about profitable resources in North America while they learned about goods England could export to their people, including metal weapons. Manteo and Wanchese taught Harriot some of their Algonquian language and learned English in return. Less than a year after leaving, Manteo and Wanchese returned home on another English ship, bearing gifts from the queen and lots of news for their people.

In the era of exploration after 1492, Europeans, Native Americans, and Africans were curious about new peoples and places. Manteo and Wanchese were two of hundreds of Native Americans from the late fifteenth through nineteenth centuries who traveled to see Europe for themselves and formalize their people's alliances with Europeans.

The journey of Manteo and Wanchese and Raleigh's attempt to found an English colony at Roanoke took place at a time of heightened European involvement in North America. Interest in colonization was spurred by national and religious rivalries and the growth of a merchant class eager to invest in overseas expansion and to seize for itself a greater share of world trade. Although the Roanoke colony failed, it would be followed in the early seventeenth century by a permanent English colony at Jamestown and, as noted in Chapter 1, the founding of Quebec by France in 1608. In 1609, Henry Hudson explored the river that today bears his name, leading to the founding of the Dutch colony of New Netherland. In 1610, the Spanish established Santa Fe as the capital of New Mexico. More than a century after the voyages of Columbus, the European penetration of North America had finally begun in earnest. It occurred from many directions at once—from east to west from the Atlantic coast, north to south along the St. Lawrence and Mississippi rivers, and south to north in what is now the American Southwest. Only the English Atlantic coast efforts would draw large numbers of colonists.

English North America in the seventeenth century was a place where entrepreneurs like Walter Raleigh sought to make fortunes, religious minorities hoped to worship without governmental interference and to create societies based on biblical teachings, and aristocrats dreamed of re-creating a vanished world of feudalism. Those who drew up blueprints for settlement expected to reproduce the social structure with which they were familiar, with all its hierarchy and inequality. Women and the lower orders of men would occupy the same less-than-fully-free status as in England, subject to laws regulating their labor and depriving them of a role in politics. But for ordinary men, emigration offered an escape from lives of deprivation and inequality. "No man," wrote **John Smith**, an early leader of Jamestown, "will go from [England] to have less freedom" in America. The charter of the **Virginia Company**, granted by James I in 1606, promised that colonists would enjoy "all liberties" of those residing in "our realm of England." The male settlers of English America came to enjoy greater rights than colonists of other empires, including the power to choose members of elected assemblies, protections of the common law such as the right to trial by jury, and access to land, the key to economic independence. In some colonies, though by no means all, colonists enjoyed considerably more religious freedom than existed in Europe. Women enjoyed few of these freedoms. Women in English colonies had fewer legal rights than women in Spanish, French, or Dutch colonies. Unlike Native American societies, European women had no direct political power and unequal economic opportunities.

Many degrees of freedom coexisted in seventeenth-century North America, from enslaved men and women, stripped completely of liberty, to the independent landowner, who enjoyed a full range of rights. During a lifetime, a person might well occupy more than one place on this spectrum. The settlers' success, however, often rested on taking Native American land and, in some colonies, on importing large numbers of Africans as enslaved laborers. Freedom and lack of freedom expanded together in seventeenth-century America.

ENGLAND AND THE AMERICAS

Unifying the English Nation

Although John Cabot, sailing from England in 1497, had been the first European since the Vikings to encounter the North American continent, English exploration and colonization would wait for many years. As the case of Spain suggests, early empire building was, in large part, an extension of the consolidation of national power in Europe. But during the sixteenth century, England was a second-rate power racked by internal disunity. Henry VII, who assumed the throne in 1485, had to unify the kingdom after a long period of civil war. His son and successor, Henry VIII, launched the Reformation in England. When the pope refused to annul his marriage to Catherine of Aragon, Henry severed the nation from the Catholic Church. In its place he established the Church of England, or **Anglican Church**, with himself at the head. Decades of religious strife followed. Under Henry's son Edward VI, who became king at the age of ten in 1547, the regents who governed the country persecuted Catholics. When Edward died in 1553, his half sister Mary became queen. Mary temporarily restored Catholicism as the state religion and executed a number of Protestants. Her rule was so unpopular that reconciliation with Rome became impossible. Mary's successor, Elizabeth I (reigned 1558–1603), restored the Anglican ascendancy and executed more than 100 Catholic priests.

England and Ireland

England's long struggle to conquer and pacify Ireland, which lasted well into the seventeenth century, absorbed money and energy that might have been directed toward the Americas. In subduing Ireland, whose Catholic population was deemed a threat to the stability of Protestant rule in England, the government employed a variety of approaches, including military conquest, the slaughter of civilians, the seizure of land and introduction of English economic practices, and the dispatch of large numbers of settlers. Rather than seeking to absorb the Irish into English society, the English excluded the native population from a territory of settlement known as the Pale, where the colonists created their own social order.

Just as the "reconquest" of Spain from the Moors established patterns that would be repeated in Spanish colonization, the methods used in Ireland anticipated policies England would undertake in America. Some sixteenth-century English writers directly compared the allegedly barbaric "wild Irish" with American Indians. Like the Indians, the Irish supposedly confused liberty and license. They refused to respect English authority and resisted conversion to

English Protestantism. The early English colonies in North America and the West Indies were known as "plantations" (that is, communities "planted" from abroad among an alien population); the same term was originally used to describe Protestant settlements in Ireland.

England and North America

Not until the reign of Elizabeth I did the English turn their attention to North America, although sailors and adventurers still showed more interest in raiding Spanish towns and treasure fleets in the Caribbean than establishing settlements. The government granted charters (grants of exclusive rights and privileges) to Sir Humphrey Gilbert and Sir Walter Raleigh, authorizing them to establish colonies in North America at their own expense.

Both ventures failed. Gilbert, who had earned a reputation for brutality in the Irish wars by murdering civilians and burning their crops, established a short-lived settlement on Newfoundland in 1582. Three years later, Raleigh dispatched a fleet of five ships carrying Manteo, Wanchese, and some 100 colonists (many of them his personal servants) to set up a base on Roanoke Island, where the people of Ossomocomuck had a fishing village. To the English, it seemed a good location for raiding Spanish shipping and searching for resources, including gold. But the colonists, mostly young Englishmen, repeatedly angered local Native communities with unexpected violence. By the spring of 1586, the Native people of Ossomocomuck had trapped them on Roanoke Island, where they were dangerously short on food. When Sir Francis Drake sailed by to check on them, the English abandoned the colony. A second group of 100 settlers, composed of families that hoped to establish a permanent colony, was dispatched that year. Their fate remains a mystery. When a ship bearing supplies arrived in 1590, the sailors found the **Roanoke colony** abandoned, with the inhabitants evidently having moved to live among Manteo's people. The name of his people, "Croatoan," had been carved on a tree. Raleigh, by now nearly bankrupt, lost his enthusiasm for colonization. To establish a successful colony, it seemed clear, would require more planning and economic resources than any individual could provide.

A drawing by the artist John White shows men and women of Ossomocomuck (the North Carolina coast) dancing around a circle of posts in a religious ritual. White was a careful observer of their clothing and body markings and the objects used in the ceremony.

Spreading Protestantism

As in the case of Spain, national glory, profit, and religious mission merged in early English thinking about the Americas. The Reformation heightened the English government's sense of Catholic Spain as its mortal enemy (a belief reinforced in 1588 when a Spanish naval armada unsuccessfully attempted to invade the British Isles). Just as Spain justified its empire in part by claiming to convert Indians to Catholicism, England expressed its imperial ambitions in terms of an obligation to liberate the Americas from the tyranny of the pope. The very first justification James I offered for the English settlement of Virginia was "propagating of the Christian religion [by which he meant Protestantism] to such people as yet live in darkness and miserable ignorance of the true knowledge and worship of God." By the late sixteenth century, anti-Catholicism had become deeply ingrained in English popular culture. English translations of Bartolomé de Las Casas's writings appeared during Elizabeth's reign. One, using a common Protestant term for the Catholic Church, bore the title, "Popery Truly Displayed."

Although atrocities were hardly confined to any one nation—as England's own conduct in Ireland and Roanoke demonstrated—the idea that the empire of Catholic Spain was uniquely murderous and tyrannical enabled the English to describe their own imperial ambitions in the language of freedom. In *A Discourse Concerning Western Planting*, written in 1584 at the request of Sir Walter Raleigh, the Protestant minister and scholar Richard Hakluyt listed twenty-three reasons why Queen Elizabeth I should support the establishment of colonies. Among them was the idea that English settlements would strike a blow against Spain's empire and therefore form part of a divine mission to rescue the Americas and its inhabitants from the influence of Catholicism and tyranny. "Tied as slaves" under Spanish rule, he wrote, the Indians of the Americas were "crying out to us . . . to come and help." They would welcome English settlers and "revolt clean from the Spaniard," crying "with one voice, Liberta, Liberta, as desirous of liberty and freedom." England would repeat much of Spain's

The Armada Portrait of Queen Elizabeth I commemorates the defeat of the Spanish Armada in 1588 and appears to link it with English colonization of the Americas. England's victorious navy is visible through the window, while the queen's hand rests on a globe, with her fingers pointing to the coast of North America.

behavior in the Americas. But the English always believed that, in their case, empire and freedom would go hand in hand.

But bringing freedom to Indians was hardly the only argument Hakluyt marshaled as England prepared to step onto the world stage. National power and glory were never far from the minds of the era's propagandists of empire. Through colonization, Hakluyt and other writers argued, England, a relatively minor power in Europe at the end of the sixteenth century, could come to rival the wealth and standing of great nations like Spain and France.

The Social Crisis

Equally important, America could be a refuge for England's "surplus" population, benefiting home country and emigrants alike. The late sixteenth century was a time of social crisis in England, with economic growth unable to keep pace with the needs of a population that grew from 3 million in 1550 to about 4 million in 1600. For many years, English peasants had enjoyed a secure hold on their plots of land. But in the sixteenth and seventeenth centuries, landlords sought profits by raising sheep for the expanding trade in wool and introducing more productive farming practices such as crop rotation. They evicted small farmers and fenced off "commons" previously open to all.

While many landlords, farmers, and town merchants benefited from the **enclosure movement**, as this process was called, thousands of persons were uprooted from the land. Many flooded into England's cities, where wages fell dramatically. Others, denounced by authorities as rogues, vagabonds, and vagrants, wandered the roads in search of work. Their situation grew worse as prices throughout Europe rose, buoyed by the influx of gold and silver from the mines of Latin America into Spain. A pioneering study of English society conducted at the end of the seventeenth century estimated that half the population lived at or below the poverty line. The cost of poor relief fell mainly on local communities. "All our towns," wrote the Puritan leader John Winthrop in 1629, shortly before leaving England for Massachusetts, "complain of the burden of poor people and strive by all means to rid any such as they have." England, he added somberly, "grows weary of her inhabitants."

The government struggled to deal with this social crisis. Under Henry VIII, those without jobs could be whipped, branded, forced into the army, or hanged. During Elizabeth's reign, a law authorized justices of the peace to regulate hours and wages and put the unemployed to work. "Vagrants" were required to accept any job offered to them and could be punished if they sought to change employment. Another solution was to encourage the unruly poor to leave for the Americas. Richard Hakluyt wrote of the advantages of settling in America

NOVA BRITANNIA.

OFFERING MOST

Excellent fruites by Planting in
VIRGINIA.

Exciting all such as be well affected
to further the same.

LONDON
Printed for SAMVEL MACHAM, and are to be sold at
his Shop in Pauls Church-yard, at the
Signe of the Bul-head.
1609.

A pamphlet published in 1609 promoting emigration to Virginia.

"such needy people of our country who now trouble the commonwealth and . . . commit outrageous offenses." As colonists, they could become productive citizens, contributing to the nation's wealth.

Masterless Men

As early as 1516, when Thomas More published *Utopia*, a fictional account of an imaginary island in the Western Hemisphere, the image of America as a place where settlers could escape from the economic inequalities of Europe had been circulating in England. This ideal coincided with the goals of ordinary Englishmen. Although authorities saw wandering or unemployed "masterless men" as a danger to society and tried to force them to accept jobs, popular attitudes viewed economic dependence as lack of freedom. Only those who controlled their own labor could be regarded as truly free. Indeed, popular tales and ballads romanticized the very vagabonds, highwaymen, and even beggars denounced by the propertied and powerful, since despite their poverty they at least enjoyed freedom from wage work.

The image of the Americas as a unique place of opportunity, where the English laboring men could regain economic independence by acquiring land and where even criminals would enjoy a second chance, was deeply rooted from the earliest days of settlement. John Smith had scarcely landed in Virginia in 1607 when he wrote that in America "every man may be the master and owner of his own labor and land." In 1623, the royal letter approving the recruitment of emigrants to New England promised that any settler could easily become "lord of 200 acres of land"—an amount far beyond the reach of most Englishmen. The main lure for emigrants from England to the Americas was not so much riches in gold and silver as the promise of independence that followed from owning land. Economic freedom and the possibility of passing it on to one's children attracted the largest number of English colonists.

EARLY ENGLISH EXPLORATION AND COLONIZATION

English Emigrants

Seventeenth-century North America was an unstable and dangerous environment. Warfare, disease, and starvation killed so many colonists that, without sustained immigration, most settlements would have collapsed. With a population of between 4 million and 5 million, or about half that of Spain and a quarter of that of France, England produced a far larger number of men, women, and children willing to brave the dangers of emigration to the Americas. In large part, this was because economic conditions in England were so bad. Between 1600 and 1700, more than half a million people left England to seek opportunities in Ireland, the sugar plantations of the West Indies, and England's mainland American colonies. Many had already moved from place to place in England. Colonial settlement was in many ways an extension of the migration at home of an increasingly mobile English population.

Indentured Servants

Settlers who could pay for their own passage—government officials, clergymen, merchants, artisans, landowning farmers, members of the lesser nobility, and the families of these men—arrived in America as free persons. Most of the men quickly acquired land. In the seventeenth century, however, nearly two-thirds of English settlers came as indentured servants, who voluntarily surrendered their freedom for a specified time (usually five to seven years) in exchange for passage to America.

Like slaves, servants could be bought and sold, could not marry without the permission of their owner, were subject to physical punishment, and saw their obligation to labor enforced by the courts. To ensure uninterrupted work by female servants, the law lengthened the term of their indenture if they became pregnant. "Many Negroes are better used," complained Elizabeth Sprigs, an indentured servant in Maryland who described being forced to work "day and night . . . then tied up and whipped." But, unlike slaves, servants could look forward to a release from bondage. Assuming they survived their period of labor, servants would receive a payment known as "freedom dues" and become free members of society.

For most of the seventeenth century, however, indentured servitude was not a guaranteed route to economic autonomy. Given the high death rate, many servants did not live to the end of their terms. Freedom dues were sometimes so meager that they did not enable recipients to acquire land. Many

This 1681 painting portrays Robin Cassacinamon, an influential Pequot leader and friend of John Winthrop II, a governor of colonial Connecticut, who originally owned the painting. Cassacinamon's portrait shows how Indians incorporated European goods, such as the loincloth's fabric, into their own styles of dress. Note the wampum beads around his neck and in his headdress. The importation of European-manufactured beads and iron drills for making shell beads greatly increased the availability of wampum throughout the Northeast.

servants found the reality of life in the Americas less appealing than they had anticipated. Employers constantly complained of servants running away, not working diligently, or being unruly, all manifestations of what one commentator called their "fondness for freedom."

Land and Liberty

Land, English settlers believed, was the basis of liberty. Owning land gave men control over their own labor and, in most colonies, the right to vote. The promise of immediate access to land lured free settlers, and freedom dues that included land persuaded potential immigrants to sign contracts as indentured servants. Land in America also became a way for the king to reward relatives and allies. Each colony was launched with a huge grant of land from the crown, either to a company or to a private individual known as a proprietor. Some grants, if taken literally, stretched from the Atlantic Ocean to the Pacific.

Land was a source of wealth and power for colonial officials and their favorites, who acquired enormous estates. Without labor, however, land would have little value. Since immigrants did not come to America intending to work the land of others (except temporarily in the case of indentured servants), the very abundance of "free" land eventually led many property owners to turn to an enslaved workforce.

The Native Atlantic Coast

Land in North America, of course, was already occupied. The large number of English settlers in the Chesapeake and New England placed far greater pressure on their Native neighbors than the lightly populated colonies of New France, New Mexico, and Florida. The English were chiefly interested in displacing the Indians and settling on their land, not intermarrying with them, trading with them, or making them subjects of the crown. Yet trading with the English appealed to many Native Americans. Native men and women quickly integrated items like woolen cloth, metal kettles, iron axes, fishhooks, hoes, and guns into their daily lives. European manufacturers began to make products specifically for the Indian market, such as glass beads (called wampum in the Algonquian language of the people of Long Island) and light flintlock muskets easy to carry during hunting and raiding.

Native people who lived near English settlements sought trade and alliance with them. Some traders from English colonies also traveled out into the realm of Native nations, where, as with French and Dutch traders, Native men and women incorporated them into their family networks and economic systems.

But the combination of a growing population and promises of land for freed servants and new settlers meant that the English colonies were a dangerous neighbor. Settlers fenced in more and more land and let their pigs and cattle roam freely, trampling Native women's cornfields. Colonists' need for wood to build and heat homes and export to England depleted forests in eastern North America, as had happened in Europe in previous generations. "Since you are here strangers, and come into our country," a Native diplomat told early settlers in the Chesapeake, "you should rather conform yourselves to the customs of our country, than impose yours on us." The seventeenth century was marked by recurrent warfare between colonists and Indians. Over time the English displaced the original inhabitants more thoroughly than any other European empire.

THE CHESAPEAKE

The Jamestown Colony

On April 26, 1607, three small ships carrying colonists from England sailed out of the morning mist at what is now called Cape Henry into the mouth of Chesapeake Bay. After exploring the area for a little over two weeks, they chose a site sixty miles inland on the James River for their settlement, hoping to protect themselves from marauding Spanish warships. Here they established Jamestown (named for the king of England) as the capital of the colony of Virginia (named for his predecessor, Elizabeth I, the "virgin queen"). The voyage was sponsored by the Virginia Company, a private business organization whose shareholders included merchants, aristocrats, and members of Parliament, and to which the queen had given her blessing before her death in 1603. When the three ships returned home, 104 settlers remained in Virginia. All were men, for the Virginia Company had more interest in searching for gold and in other ways of exploiting the area's natural resources than in establishing a functioning society. Nevertheless, Jamestown became the first permanent English settlement in the area that is now the United States.

THE CHESAPEAKE, ca. 1640

0   25   50 miles
0   25   50 kilometers
MARYLAND
(1632)

MARYLAND
(1632)

NANTAUGHTACUND ONAWMANIENT
MATTAPONI   CHICACOAN
RAPPAHANNOCK
CHICKAHOMINY   WICOCOMOCO
CUTTATOWOMEN
PAMUNKEY   ACCOHANNOCK
VIRGINIA CHISKIAK
(1607)   ACCOMAC
APPOMATTOC
Jamestown
WEYANOCK

NANSEMOND

Roanoke R.

(1607) Date of settlement
English settlement, ca. 1640

Roanoke
Island

Most of the Native nations shown in this map were under Powhatan's rule. By 1640, English settlement in the Chesapeake had spread well beyond the initial colony at Jamestown, as to-bacco planters sought fertile land near navigable waterways.

The early history of Jamestown was, to say the least, not promising. The colony's leadership changed repeatedly, its inhabitants suffered an extraordinarily high death rate, and, with the company seeking a quick profit, supplies from England proved inadequate. The hopes of locating riches such as the Spanish had found in Mexico were quickly dashed. "Silver and gold they have none," one Spanish observer commented, their local resources were "not much to be regarded," and they had "no commerce with any nation." The first settlers were "a quarrelsome band of gentlemen and servants." They included few farmers and laborers and numerous sons of English gentry and high-status craftsmen (jewelers, stone-cutters, and the like), who preferred to prospect for gold rather than farm. They "would rather starve than work," declared John Smith, one of the colony's first leaders.

Jamestown lay beside a swamp containing malaria-carrying mosquitoes, and the garbage settlers dumped into the local river bred germs that caused dysentery and typhoid fever. Disease and lack of food took a heavy toll. By the end of the first year, the original population of 104 had fallen by half. New arrivals (including the first two women, who landed in 1608) brought the numbers up to 400 in 1609, but by 1610, after a winter long remembered as the "starving time," only 65 settlers remained alive. At one point, the survivors abandoned Jamestown and sailed for England, only to be intercepted and persuaded to return to Virginia by ships carrying a new governor, 250 colonists, and supplies. By 1616, about 80 percent of the immigrants who had arrived in the first decade were dead.

Only rigorous military discipline held the colony together. John Smith was a forceful man whose career before coming to America included a period fighting the Turks in Hungary, where he was captured and for a time enslaved. He imposed a regime of forced labor on company lands. "He that will not work, shall not eat," Smith declared. Smith's autocratic mode of governing alienated many of the colonists. After being injured in an accidental gunpowder explosion in 1609, he was forced to return to England. But his immediate successors continued his iron rule.

From Company to Society

The Virginia Company slowly realized that for the colony to survive it would have to abandon the search for gold, grow its own food, and find a marketable commodity. It would also have to attract more settlers. With this end in view, it announced new policies in 1618 that powerfully shaped Virginia's development as a functioning society rather than an outpost of London-based investors. Instead of retaining all the land for itself, the company introduced the **headright system**, awarding fifty acres of land to any colonist who paid for his own or another's passage. Thus, anyone who brought in a sizable number of servants would immediately acquire a large estate. In place of the governor's militaristic regime, a "charter of grants and liberties" was issued, including the establishment of a **House of Burgesses**. When it convened in 1619, this became the first elected assembly in colonial America.

The House of Burgesses was hardly a model of democracy—only freemen could vote, and the company and its appointed governor retained the right to nullify any measure the body adopted. But its creation established a political precedent that all English colonies would eventually follow. Also in 1619, the first enslaved Africans arrived in Virginia. The full significance of these two events would not be apparent until years later. But they laid the foundation for a society that would one day be dominated economically and politically by slaveowning planters.

Powhatan and Pocahontas

When the English arrived at Jamestown, they landed in an area inhabited by some 15,000 to 25,000 Algonquian-speaking people living in numerous agricultural towns. Most acknowledged the rule of Wahunsonacock, a shrewd and forceful leader from a town near present-day Richmond. Usually referred to by his title Powhatan, he had recently consolidated his authority over the region and collected tribute from over 100 subordinate towns, collectively known as the Powhatans. Like Native leaders throughout the Americas, Powhatan quickly realized the advantages of trade with the newcomers. For its part, mindful of Las Casas's condemnation of Spanish behavior and the failures at Roanoke, the Virginia Company instructed its colonists to treat the Powhatans fairly and to try to convert them to Christianity. Realizing that the colonists depended on the Native women's farming for food, John Smith tried to stop settlers from

The only portrait of Pocahontas during her lifetime was engraved by Simon van de Passe in England in 1616. This is a later copy. After converting to Christianity, she took the name Rebecca.

seizing produce from nearby villages, lest Powhatan cut off all trade.

In the first two years of Jamestown's existence, relations were mostly peaceful. At one point, Smith was captured and threatened with execution by Powhatan, only to be rescued by Pocahontas, reputedly the favorite among his many children by dozens of wives. The incident has come down in legend and film as an example of a rebellious, love-struck teenager defying her father. In fact, it was probably part of an elaborate ceremony designed by Powhatan to demonstrate his power over the colonists and incorporate them into his realm. To Powhatan, Jamestown was one of the many towns under his rule. Pocahontas subsequently became an intermediary between the two peoples.

But after Pocahontas married a fellow Powhatan and stopped coming to Jamestown and John Smith returned to England, tension grew between the two groups. The First **Anglo-Powhatan War** broke out in 1610, with Powhatans killing settlers who stole corn and the English indiscriminately killing Powhatans and destroying towns to try to scare them into feeding the colony. Pocahontas herself was captured and held as a hostage by the settlers in 1613. As part of the restoration of peace, she converted to Christianity and in 1614 married the English colonist John Rolfe. Two years later, she accompanied him to England, where she caused a sensation in the court of James I as a symbol of Anglo-Indian harmony and missionary success. In England, she became sick and died in 1617. Her father died the following year.

The Second and Third Anglo-Powhatan Wars

Once it became clear that the English were interested in establishing a constantly expanding colony, not a trading post, conflict with the Powhatans was inevitable. The peace that began in 1614 ended abruptly in 1622 when Powhatan's brother and successor, Opechancanough, led a brilliantly planned surprise attack that in a single day wiped out a quarter of Virginia's settler population of 1,200. Opechancanough hoped the English would abandon Virginia or submit to his rule, but instead the surviving 900 colonists organized themselves into military bands, which then massacred scores of Powhatans and devastated their towns. By going to war, declared Governor Francis Wyatt, the Powhatans had forfeited any claim to the land. Virginia's policy, he continued, must now be nothing less than the "expulsion of the savages to gain the free range of the country."

Native Americans remained a significant presence in Virginia and on its western border, but the English victory in the Second Anglo-Powhatan War began to shift the balance of power. Although most of the settlers whom the Virginia Company had sent had died from war, starvation, or disease, more kept coming. The Third Anglo-Powhatan War, which began in 1644, caused the deaths of some 500 colonists. But by then, colonists outnumbered Powhatans, whose population was reduced due to war, disease, and flight. After the war ended in 1646 with Opechancanough's death, Virginia forced a treaty on the peoples who had been part of Powhatan's realm. The treaty acknowledged their subordination to the government at Jamestown and required them to move to reservations and not enter areas of European settlement without permission. This policy of separation followed the precedent already established in Ireland. Settlers spreading inland continued to seize Native lands.

The destruction caused by the First and Second Anglo-Powhatan Wars had already doomed the Virginia Company. Investors had never turned a profit. In 1624, the company surrendered its charter and Virginia became the first royal colony, its governor now appointed by the crown. The government in London for years was preoccupied with affairs at home and paid little attention to Virginia. Henceforth, the local elite controlled the colony's development. And that elite was growing rapidly in wealth and power thanks to the cultivation of a crop introduced from the West Indies by John Rolfe—tobacco.

A Tobacco Colony

King James I considered tobacco "harmful to the brain and dangerous to the lungs" and issued a spirited warning against its use. But increasing numbers of Europeans enjoyed smoking and believed the tobacco plant had medicinal benefits. As a commodity with an ever-expanding mass market in Europe, tobacco became Virginia's substitute for gold. It enriched an emerging class of tobacco planters, as well as members of the colonial government who assigned good land to themselves. The crown profited from customs duties (taxes on tobacco that entered or left the kingdom). By 1624, more than 200,000 pounds were being grown, producing startling profits for landowners. Forty years later, the crop totaled 15 million pounds, and it doubled again by the 1680s. The spread of tobacco farming produced a dispersed society with few towns and little social unity. It inspired a get-rich-quick attitude and a frenzied scramble for land and labor. By the middle of the seventeenth century, a new influx of immigrants with ample financial resources—sons of merchants and English gentlemen—had taken advantage of the headright system and governmental connections to acquire large estates along navigable rivers. They established themselves as the colony's social and political elite.

The expansion of tobacco cultivation also led to an increased demand for field labor, met for most of the seventeenth century by young, male indentured servants. Despite harsh conditions of work in the tobacco fields, a persistently high death rate, and laws mandating punishments from whipping to an extension of service for those who ran away or were unruly, the abundance of land continued to attract migrants. Of the 120,000 English immigrants who entered the Chesapeake region during the seventeenth century, three-quarters came as servants.

ORIGINS OF AMERICAN SLAVERY

No European nation embarked on the colonization of the Americas with the intention of relying on enslaved Africans for the bulk of its labor force. But the incessant demand for workers spurred by the spread of tobacco cultivation eventually led Chesapeake planters to turn to the transatlantic trade in slaves. Compared with employing indentured servants, planters saw many advantages to enslaved labor. Africans could not claim the protections of English common law. Slaves' terms of service never expired, and they therefore did not become a population of unruly landless men. Their children could be enslaved, and their skin color made it more difficult for them to escape into the surrounding society. African men and women, moreover, unlike Native American men, were accustomed to agricultural labor, and they had encountered many diseases known in Europe and developed resistance to them so were less likely to succumb to epidemics.

Englishmen and Africans

The English had long viewed alien peoples with disdain, including the Irish, Native Americans, and Africans. They described these strangers in remarkably similar language as savage, pagan, and uncivilized, often comparing them to animals. "Race"—the idea that humanity is divided into well-defined groups associated with skin color—is a concept that had not fully developed in the seventeenth century. Nor had "racism"—an ideology based on the belief that some races are inherently superior to others and entitled to rule over them. The main lines of division within humanity were thought to be civilization versus barbarism or Christianity versus heathenism, not color or race.

Nonetheless, anti-Black stereotypes flourished in seventeenth-century England. Africans were seen as so alien—in color, religion, and social practices—that they were "enslavable" in a way that poor English people were not. Most English also deemed Indians to be uncivilized, and some were sold into slavery in the Caribbean. But it is difficult to enslave a people on or near their native soil. Slaves are almost always outsiders, transported from elsewhere to their place of forced labor.

Slavery in History

Slavery has existed for nearly the entire span of human history, as we have seen (see Chapter 1). In the Mediterranean world, trade in Slavic peoples survived into the fifteenth century. (The English word "slavery" derives from "Slav.") Pirates from the Barbary Coast of North Africa regularly seized Christians from ships and enslaved them. In West Africa, as noted in Chapter 1, slavery and a slave trade predated the coming of Europeans, and captive-based slavery existed among Native Americans. But slavery in nearly all these instances differed greatly from the institution that developed in American colonies.

In the Americas, slavery was based on the **plantation**, an agricultural enterprise that brought together large numbers of workers under the control of a single owner. This imbalance magnified the possibility of slave resistance, and so enslavers policed the system rigidly. It encouraged the creation of a sharp boundary between slavery and freedom. Labor on slave plantations was far more demanding than in small-scale slavery, and the death rate among slaves was much higher. In the Americas, slavery would come to be associated with race, a concept that drew a permanent line between whites and Blacks. Unlike in earlier systems of slavery, in which enslavement was often a temporary social position and not the result of long-distance forced migration, enslaved Africans in the Americas who became free always carried with them in their skin color the mark of prior bondage.

Slavery in the West Indies

Europeans' belief that Africans were alien and inferior enabled American slavery but did not alone create and expand it. For this institution to take root, planters and government authorities had to be convinced that importing enslaved Africans was the best way to solve their persistent shortage of labor. During the seventeenth century, the shipping of slaves from Africa to the Americas became a major international business. But only a relative handful was brought to England's mainland colonies. By the time plantation slavery became a major feature of life in English North America, it was already well entrenched elsewhere in the Western Hemisphere. By 1600, huge sugar plantations worked by enslaved Africans had made their appearance in Brazil, a colony of Portugal. In the seventeenth century, England, Holland, Denmark, and France joined Spain in colonizing West Indian islands. In 1650, the English population of the West Indies exceeded that in all of North America. Generally, the first settlers established mixed economies with small farms worked by white indentured servants. But as sugar planters engrossed the best land, they forced white farmers off island after island. White indentured servants proved as discontented as elsewhere. In 1629, when a Spanish expedition attacked the British island of Nevis, servants in the local militia joined them shouting, "Liberty, joyful liberty!"

For the back-breaking, monotonous work of sugar cultivation, the massive importation of enslaved Africans began. In 1645, for example, Barbados, a tiny island owned by England, was home to around 11,000 white farmers and indentured servants and 5,000 slaves. As sugar cultivation intensified, planters turned increasingly to slave labor. By 1660, the island's population had grown to 40,000, half European and half African. Ten years later, the slave population had risen to 82,000, concentrated on some 750 sugar plantations. Meanwhile, the white population stagnated. By the end of the seventeenth century, huge sugar plantations with hundreds of slaves dominated the West Indian economy, and on most of the islands the African population far outnumbered that of European origin.

Sugar was the first crop to be mass-marketed to consumers in Europe. Before its emergence, international trade consisted largely of precious metals like gold and silver and luxury goods aimed at an elite market, like the spices and silks imported from Asia. Sugar was by far the most important product of the British, French, and Portuguese empires, and sugar plantations in the Americas produced immense profits for planters, merchants, and imperial governments. Saint Domingue, modern-day Haiti, was the jewel of the French empire. In 1660, Barbados generated more trade than all the other English colonies combined.

1619

In August 1619, white Virginians bought enslaved Africans for the first time. British pirates sailing under the Dutch flag had seized these men and women from a Portuguese ship that had taken them from Angola, on the southwestern coast of Africa. They were farmers and herders who spoke a Bantu language and had been captured and forced to march over 100 miles from their homes and then packed into slave ships for a frightening and horrific journey across the Atlantic. The English at Jamestown bought between twenty and thirty men and women from the pirates and sent them to work on tobacco plantations and farms and in colonial households. It is rare to know much about enslaved women in the early seventeenth century, but we know that one of the Africans sold in Virginia in 1619 was a woman called Angela, who later worked in the household of a wealthy planter.

Compared to its rapid introduction in Brazil and the West Indies, slavery developed slowly in North America. Slaves cost more than indentured servants, and the high death rate among tobacco workers made it economically disadvantageous to pay for a lifetime of labor. As late as 1680, there were only 4,500 Blacks in the Chesapeake, a little more than 5 percent of the region's population. The most important social distinction in the seventeenth-century Chesapeake was not between Black and white but between the white plantation owners who dominated politics and society and everybody else—namely, the small farmers, indentured servants, and slaves. But the arrival of enslaved African men and women in 1619 would shape the future of Virginia and the United States for centuries to come.

Processing tobacco was as labor-intensive as caring for the plant in the fields. Here slaves and indentured servants work with the crop after it has been harvested.

Women and the Family

Virginia's white society increasingly came to resemble that of England, with a wealthy landed gentry at the top; a group of small farmers, mostly former indentured servants who had managed to acquire land, in the middle; and an army of poor laborers—servants and landless former indentured servants—at the bottom. By 1700, the region's white population had grown to nearly 90,000. Virginia, however, lacked one essential element of English society—stable family life.

The colony avidly promoted the immigration of women, including several dozen "tobacco brides" who arrived in 1620 and 1621 for arranged marriages. But given the demand for male servants to work in the tobacco fields, men in the Chesapeake outnumbered women for most of the seventeenth century by four or five to one. The vast majority of women who immigrated to the region came as indentured servants. Since they usually had to complete their terms of service before marrying, they did not begin to form families until their mid-twenties. The high death rate, unequal ratio between the sexes, and late age of marriage for those who found partners produced a society with large numbers of single men, widows, and orphans. Although patriarchal ideals remained intact in Virginia, in practice the traditional authority of husbands and fathers was weakened. Because of their own low life expectancy, fathers found it difficult to supervise the careers and marriages of their children.

In the English colonies as in England, a married woman possessed certain rights before the law, including a claim to **dower rights** of one-third of her husband's property in the event that he died before she did. Because of coverture, however, when the widow died, the property passed to the husband's male heirs. (Because Spanish, French, and Dutch law did not include coverture, in those colonies a woman could hold independently any property inherited from her parents, and a man and wife owned jointly all the wealth accumulated during a marriage.)

Social conditions in the colonies, however, opened the door even in English colonies to roles women rarely assumed in Europe. Widows and the few women who never married took advantage of their legal status as *feme sole* (a "woman alone," who enjoyed an independent legal identity denied to married women) to make contracts and conduct business. Margaret Brent, who arrived in the Chesapeake in 1638, acquired land, managed her own plantation, and acted as a lawyer in court. Some widows were chosen to administer their husbands' estates or were willed their husbands' property outright, rather than receiving only the one-third "dower rights." But because most women came to Virginia as indentured servants, they could look forward only to a life of hard labor in the tobacco fields and early death. Servants were frequently subjected to sexual abuse by their masters. Those who married often found themselves in poverty when their husbands died.

The Maryland Experiment

Although it began under very different sponsorship and remained much smaller than Virginia during the seventeenth century, the second Chesapeake colony, Maryland, followed a similar course of development. As in Virginia, tobacco came to dominate the economy and tobacco planters the society. But in other ways, Maryland's history was strikingly different.

Maryland was established in 1632 as a proprietary colony, that is, a grant of land and governmental authority to a single individual. This was Cecil Calvert, Lord Baltimore, the son of a recently deceased favorite of King Charles I. The charter made Lord Baltimore proprietor of the colony and granted him "full, free, and absolute power," including control of trade and the right to initiate all legislation, with an elected assembly confined to approving or disapproving his proposals. Lord Baltimore imagined Maryland as a feudal domain. Land would be laid out in manors with the owners paying "quitrents" to the proprietor. Lord Baltimore disliked representative institutions and believed ordinary people should not meddle in governmental affairs. On the other hand, the charter also guaranteed to colonists "all privileges, franchises, and liberties" of Englishmen. While these were not spelled out, they undoubtedly included the idea of a government limited by the law. Here was a recipe for conflict, and Maryland had more than its share during the seventeenth century.

Religion in Maryland

Further aggravating instability in the colony was the fact that Lord Baltimore, a Catholic, envisioned Maryland as a refuge for his persecuted coreligionists, especially the younger sons of Catholic gentry who had few economic or political prospects in England. In Maryland, he hoped, Protestants and Catholics could live in a harmony unknown in Europe. The first group of 130 colonists included a number of Catholic gentlemen and two priests. Most appointed officials were also Catholic, including relatives of the proprietor, as were those to whom he awarded the choicest land grants. But Protestants always formed a majority of the settlers. Most, as in Virginia, came as indentured servants, but others took advantage of Maryland's generous headright system to acquire land by transporting workers to the colony.

As in Virginia, the death rate remained very high. In one county, half the marriages during the seventeenth century lasted fewer than eight years before one partner died. Almost 70 percent of male settlers in Maryland died before reaching the age of fifty, and half the children born in the colony did not live to adulthood. But at least initially, Maryland seems to have offered servants greater opportunity for landownership than Virginia. Unlike in the older colony, freedom dues in Maryland included fifty acres of land. As tobacco planters engrossed the best land later in the century, however, the prospects for landless men diminished.

THE NEW ENGLAND WAY

The Rise of Puritanism

As Virginia and Maryland evolved toward societies dominated by a small aristocracy ruling over numerous bound laborers, a very different social order emerged in seventeenth-century New England. The early history of that region is intimately connected to the religious movement known as "Puritanism," which arose in England late in the sixteenth century. The term was initially coined by opponents to ridicule those not satisfied with the progress of the Protestant Reformation in England, who called themselves not Puritans but "godly" or "true Protestants." Puritanism came to define a set of religious principles and a view of how society should be organized. **Puritans** differed among themselves on many issues. But all shared the conviction that the Church of England retained too many elements of Catholicism in its religious rituals and doctrines. Puritans saw elaborate church ceremonies, the rule that priests could not marry, and ornate church decorations as vestiges of "popery." Many rejected the Catholic structure of religious authority descending from a pope or king to archbishops, bishops, and priests. Only independent local congregations, they believed, should choose clergymen and determine modes of worship. These Puritans were called "Congregationalists." All Puritans shared many of the beliefs of the Church of England and the society as a whole, including a hatred of Catholicism and a pride in England's greatness as a champion of liberty. But they believed that neither the church nor the nation was living up to its ideals.

Puritans considered religious belief a complex and demanding matter and urged believers to seek the truth by reading the Bible and listening to sermons by educated ministers, rather than devoting themselves to sacraments administered by priests and to what Puritans considered formulaic prayers. The sermon was the central rite of Puritan practice. In the course of a lifetime, according to one estimate, the average Puritan listened to some 7,000 sermons. In their religious beliefs, Puritans followed the ideas of the French-born Swiss theologian John Calvin. The world, Calvin taught, was divided between the elect and the damned. All persons sought salvation, but whether one was among the elect destined to be saved had already been determined by God. His will, ultimately, was unknowable, and nothing one did on earth—including prayers, good works, and offerings—would make any difference. But while there were no guarantees of salvation, worldly success—leading a good life, prospering economically—might well be indications of God's grace. Idleness and immoral behavior were sure signs of damnation.

Moral Liberty

Puritanism, however, was not simply a set of ideas but a state of mind, a zealousness in pursuing the true faith that alienated many who held differing religious views. A minority of Puritans (such as those who settled in Plymouth Colony) became separatists, abandoning the Church of England entirely to form their own independent churches. Most, however, hoped to purify the church from within. But in the 1620s and 1630s, as Charles I seemed to be moving toward a restoration of Catholic ceremonies and the Church of England dismissed Puritan ministers and censored their writings, many Puritans decided to emigrate. They departed England not so much because of persecution, but because they feared that "Popish" practices had grown to such "an intolerable height," as one minister complained, that "the consciences of God's saints . . . could no longer bear them." When Puritans emigrated to New England, they hoped to escape what they believed to be the religious and worldly corruptions of English society. They would establish a "city set upon a hill," a Bible Commonwealth whose influence would flow back across the Atlantic and rescue England from godlessness and social decay.

Like so many other immigrants to America, Puritans came in search of liberty, especially the right to worship and govern themselves in what they deemed a truly Christian manner. Freedom for Puritans was primarily a spiritual affair. It implied the opportunity and the responsibility to obey God's will through self-government and self-denial. It certainly did not mean unrestrained action, improper religious practices, or sinful behavior, of which, Puritans thought, there were far too many examples in England. In a 1645 speech to the Massachusetts legislature explaining the Puritan conception of freedom, **John Winthrop**, the colony's governor, distinguished sharply between two kinds of liberty. "Natural" liberty, or acting without restraint, suggested "a liberty to do evil." This was the false idea of freedom supposedly adopted by the Irish, Indians, and bad Christians generally. Genuine "moral" liberty—the Christian liberty described in Chapter 1—meant "a liberty to that only which is good." It was quite compatible with severe restraints on speech, religion, and personal behavior. True freedom, Winthrop insisted, depended on "subjection to authority," both religious and secular; otherwise, anarchy was sure to follow. To Puritans, liberty meant that the elect had a right to establish churches and govern society, not that others could challenge their beliefs or authority.

The Pilgrims at Plymouth

The first Puritans to arrive in America were a group of separatists known as the **Pilgrims**. They had already fled to the Netherlands in 1608, believing that Satan had begun "to sow errors, heresies and discords" in England. A decade later, fearing that their children were being corrupted by being drawn into the surrounding culture, they decided to emigrate to Virginia. The expedition was financed by a group of English investors who hoped to establish a base for profitable trade. In September 1620, the *Mayflower*, carrying 150 settlers and crew (among them many non-Puritans), embarked from England. Blown off course, they landed not in Virginia but hundreds of miles to the north, on Cape Cod. Here the 102 who survived the journey established the colony of Plymouth. Before landing, the Pilgrim leaders drew up the **Mayflower Compact**, in which the forty-one adult men going ashore agreed to obey "just and equal laws" enacted by representatives of their own choosing. This was the first written frame of government in what is now the United States. Men not normally signatories to such documents—printers, carpenters, even indentured servants—were among those who affixed their names. (This was over 200 years before most working-class men were allowed to vote in Great Britain.)

A century earlier, when Giovanni da Verrazano explored the Atlantic coast of North America, he encountered thickly settled towns. By the time the Pilgrims landed, hundreds of European fishing vessels had operated off New England, landing to trade with Indians and bringing, as elsewhere, epidemics. The Pilgrims arrived in an area whose Native population had recently been devastated by smallpox. They established Plymouth on the site of an abandoned Patuxet Indian town whose fields had been cleared before the epidemic and were ready for cultivation. Nonetheless, the settlers arrived six weeks before winter without food or farm animals. Half died during the first winter. The colonists only survived through the help of local Indians, notably Squanto, a Patuxet man who had grown up in the town where the Pilgrims settled. With twenty other Indians, Squanto had been kidnapped and brought to Spain in 1614 by English sailors, who sold them as slaves. Squanto somehow made his way to London, where he learned English. He returned

An early-seventeenth-century engraving shows Algonquian-speaking Native Americans greeting the English explorer Bartholomew Gosnold. Gosnold landed at Cape Cod in 1602 and then established a small outpost on nearby Cutty-hunk Island. The region's Native peoples had much experience with Europeans before Pilgrims settled there.

home in 1619 only to find his town abandoned. He taught the Pilgrims where to fish and how to plant corn and served as an interpreter between them and Massasoit, chief of the powerful Wampanoags. They agreed to an alliance, in which the Wampanoags would help to feed and defend Plymouth and the Pilgrims would help to fight the Wampanoags' enemies, including the Narragansetts. The celebration and renewal of this treaty one year later, in the autumn of 1621, later became known as the first Thanksgiving.

The Pilgrims hoped to establish a society based on the lives of the early Christian saints. Their government rested on the principle of consent, and voting was not restricted to church members. All land was held in common until 1627, when it was divided among the settlers. Plymouth survived as an independent colony until 1691, but it was soon overshadowed by Massachusetts Bay to its north.

The Great Migration

Chartered in 1629, the Massachusetts Bay Company was founded by a group of London merchants who hoped to further the Puritan cause and turn a profit through trade with the Indians. The first ships sailed from England in 1630, and by 1642 some 21,000 Puritans had immigrated to Massachusetts. Long remembered as the **Great Migration**, this flow of population represented less than one-third of English emigration in the 1630s. Far more English settlers arrived in Ireland, the Chesapeake, and the Caribbean. After 1640, migration to New England virtually ceased, and in some years more colonists left the region than arrived. Nonetheless, the Great Migration established the basis for a stable and thriving society.

In many ways, the settling of New England was unique. Although servants represented about one-quarter of the Great Migration, most settlers arrived in Massachusetts in families. They came for many reasons, including the desire to escape religious persecution, anxiety about the future of England, and the prospect of economic betterment. Compared with colonists in Virginia and Maryland, they were older and more prosperous, and the number of men and women more equally balanced. Because of the even sex ratio and New England's healthier climate, the population grew rapidly, doubling every twenty-seven years. Although the region received only a small fraction of the century's migration, by 1700 New England's white population of 91,000 outnumbered that of both the Chesapeake and the West Indies. Nearly all were descendants of those who crossed the Atlantic during the Great Migration.

The Puritan Family

While the imbalance between male and female migrants made it difficult for patriarchal family patterns fully to take root in the Chesapeake until the end of the seventeenth century, they emerged very quickly in New England. Whatever

The Savage Family, a 1779 painting by the New England artist Edward Savage, depicts several generations of a typically numerous Puritan family.

their differences with other Englishmen on religious matters, Puritans shared with the larger society a belief in male authority within the household as well as an adherence to coverture, the common-law tradition that severely limited married women's legal and economic rights. Puritans in America carefully emulated the family structure of England, insisting that the obedience of women, children, and servants to men's will was the foundation of social stability. They believed that the father's authority was vital in a farming society without large numbers of slaves or servants because control over the labor of one's family was essential to a man's economic success.

To be sure, Puritans deemed women to be the spiritual equals of men, and women were allowed to become full church members. Although all ministers were men, the Puritan belief in the ability of believers to interpret the Bible opened the door for some women to claim positions of religious leadership. The ideal Puritan marriage was based on reciprocal affection and companionship, and divorce was legal. Yet within the household, the husband's authority was virtually absolute. Indeed, a man's position as head of his family was thought to replicate God's authority in spiritual matters and the authority of the government in the secular realm. Magistrates sometimes intervened to protect wives from physical abuse, but they also enforced the power of fathers over their children and husbands over their wives. Moderate physical "correction" was considered appropriate for women who violated their husbands' sense of proper behavior.

Their responsibilities as wives and mothers defined women's lives. In his 1645 speech on liberty, John Winthrop noted that a woman achieved genuine freedom by fulfilling her prescribed social role and embracing "subjection to her husband's authority." The family was the foundation of strong communities, and unmarried adults seemed a danger to the social fabric. An early law of Plymouth declared that "no single person be suffered to live of himself." The typical New England woman married at twenty-two, a younger age than her English counterparts, and gave birth seven times. Because New England was a far healthier environment than the Chesapeake, more children survived infancy. Thus, much of a woman's adult life was devoted to bearing and rearing children.

Government and Society in Massachusetts

In a sermon aboard the *Arabella*, on which he sailed for Massachusetts in 1630, John Winthrop spoke of the settlers binding themselves together "in the bond of brotherly affection" in order to promote the glory of God and their own "common good." Puritans feared excessive individualism and lack of social unity. Unlike the dispersed plantation-centered society of the Chesapeake, the leaders of Massachusetts organized the colony in self-governing towns. Groups of settlers received a land grant from the colony's government and then subdivided it, with residents awarded house lots in a central area and land on the outskirts for farming. Much land remained in commons, either for collective use or to be divided among later settlers or the sons of the town's founders. Each town had its own Congregational Church. Each, according to a law of 1647, was required to establish a school, since the ability to read the Bible was central to Puritan belief. To train an educated ministry, Harvard College was established in 1636 (nearly a century after the Royal University of Mexico, founded in 1551), and two years later the first printing press in English America was established in Cambridge.

The government of Massachusetts reflected the Puritans' religious and social vision. Wishing to rule the colony without outside interference and to prevent non-Puritans from influencing decision making, the shareholders of the Massachusetts Bay Company emigrated to America, taking the charter with them and transforming a commercial document into a form of government. At first, the eight shareholders chose the men who ruled the colony. In 1634, a group of deputies elected by freemen (landowning church members) was added to form a single ruling body, the General Court. Ten years later, company officers and elected deputies were divided into two legislative houses. Unlike Virginia, whose governors were appointed first by a faraway company and after 1624 by the crown, or Maryland, where authority rested with a single proprietor, the freemen of Massachusetts elected their governor.

The principle of consent was central to Puritanism. Church government was decentralized—each congregation, as one minister put it, had "complete liberty to stand alone." Churches were formed by voluntary agreement among members, who elected the minister. No important church decision was made without the agreement of the male members. Towns governed themselves, and local officials, delegates to the General Court, and the colonial governor were all elected. Puritans, however, were hardly believers in equality. Church membership, a status that carried great prestige and power, was a restrictive category. Anyone could worship at a church, or, as the Puritans preferred to call it, meeting house, but to be a full member required demonstrating that one had experienced divine grace and could be considered a "visible saint," usually by testifying about a conversion experience. Although male property holders generally chose local officials, voting in colony-wide elections was limited to men who had been accepted as full church members. As time went on, this meant that a smaller and smaller percentage of the population controlled the government. Puritan democracy was for those within the circle of church membership; those outside the boundary occupied a secondary place in the Bible Commonwealth.

Church and State in Puritan Massachusetts

Seventeenth-century New England was a hierarchical society in which socially prominent families were assigned the best land and the most desirable seats in church. "Some must be rich and some poor, some high and eminent in power and dignity; others mean and in subjection," declared John Winthrop. This was part of God's plan, reinforced by man-made law and custom. The General Court forbade ordinary men and women from wearing "the garb of gentlemen." Ordinary settlers were addressed as "goodman" and "goodwife," while the better sort were called "gentleman" and "lady" or "master" and "mistress." When the General Court in 1641 issued a Body of Liberties outlining the rights and responsibilities of Massachusetts colonists, it adopted the traditional understanding of liberties as privileges that derived from one's place in the social order. While some liberties applied to all inhabitants, there were separate lists of rights for freemen, women, children, and servants. The Body of Liberties also allowed for slavery. The first African slave appears in the records of Massachusetts Bay in 1640.

Massachusetts forbade ministers from holding office so as not to interfere with their spiritual responsibilities. But church and state were closely interconnected. The law required each town to establish a church and to levy a tax to support the minister. There were no separate church courts, but the state enforced religious devotion. The Body of Liberties affirmed the rights of free speech and assembly and equal protection of the law for all within the colony, but the laws of Massachusetts prescribed the death penalty for, among other things, worshiping "any god, but the lord god," practicing witchcraft, or committing blasphemy.

Like many others in the seventeenth century, Puritans believed that religious uniformity was essential to social order. They did not believe in religious toleration—there was one truth, and their faith embodied it. Religious liberty meant the liberty to practice this truth. The purpose of the Puritan experiment was to complete the Reformation and, they hoped, spread it back to England. But they set their experiment up in the land of the Wampanoags, who had their own ideas about order, religion, and liberty.

Native Nations and New England

Massasoit and the Wampanoags sought alliance with the Pilgrims in order to change the balance of power in the region. The epidemic that destroyed Squanto's town had also hit the Wampanoags, but it had not reached the Narragansetts, who used the devastation to force the Wampanoags to pay them tribute. After forging an alliance and trading partnership with the English, Massasoit was able to persuade the Narragansetts to back down. The Wampanoags became intermediaries between the English and other Native groups, profiting from the trade and increasing their regional power. Massasoit consolidated diverse Native communities that had been torn apart by disease, including Squanto's Patuxets, into a strong and prosperous Wampanoag nation.

Like the Pilgrims, the English colonists who came to Massachusetts Bay established Boston and other settlements on formerly Native towns and fields and were recruited as allies and trading partners by local Indians. These included the Massachusetts Indians, on whose land they settled, and the Narragansetts, who had been shut out of Plymouth trade by the Wampanoags.

Although Puritans announced that they intended to bring Christian faith to the Indians, they made no sustained conversion efforts in the early two decades of settlement. Instead, always concerned that sinful persons might prefer a life of ease to hard work, New England's leaders feared that Native Americans might convert colonists. To Puritans, Native people enjoyed freedom, but the wrong kind—what Winthrop condemned as undisciplined "natural liberty" rather than the "moral liberty" of the Christian. In 1642, the Connecticut General Court set a penalty of three years at hard labor for any colonist who abandoned "godly society" to live with Indians. To counteract the attraction of Native life, the leaders of New England also encouraged the publication of **captivity narratives** by those captured by Indians. The most popular was *The Sovereignty and Goodness of God* by Mary Rowlandson, who had immigrated with her parents as a child in 1639 and was seized along with a group of other settlers and held for three months until ransomed in the 1670s. Rowlandson acknowledged that she had been well treated and suffered "not the least abuse or unchastity," but her book's overriding theme was her determination to return to Christian society.

The Pequot War

Like the Wampanoags, the Pequots on the north shore of Long Island Sound and the lower Connecticut River valley became a regional power through European trade and alliance, in their case with the Dutch of New Netherland. The Pequots forced their neighbors the Mohegans and the Narragansetts to pay them tribute and conduct Dutch trade through them. But in the 1630s, the Narragansetts and their Mohegan allies used their alliance with the Massachusetts Bay Colony to fight the Pequots.

An engraving from John Underhill's *News from America*, published in London in 1638, shows the destruction of the Pequot town on the Mystic River in 1637. The colonial forces are firing guns, while the Narragansetts and Mohegans shoot bows and arrows.

In May 1637, a force of 500 Narragansetts, 70 Mohegans, and 90 English colonists from Massachusetts and newer settlements in the Connecticut River valley marched on the Pequots. The fighting was fiercest at a Pequot town on the Mystic River. The English commanders set the village ablaze, killing over 500 Pequot men, women, and children.

By the end of the **Pequot War** a few months later, around one-quarter of the Pequot population of 3,000 had been killed. Survivors were enslaved in the homes of New England colonists, sold into slavery in the West Indies or Bermuda, or absorbed into other Native communities. The treaty that restored peace decreed that their name be wiped from the historical record and that surviving Pequots no longer call themselves by that name (neither decree succeeded). Although the Narragansetts and Mohegans had won the war, they also learned that the English were more dangerous enemies than they had realized.

NEW ENGLANDERS DIVIDED

Colonists in New England also clashed among themselves. The Puritans exalted individual judgment—hence their insistence on reading the Bible, yet modern ideas of individualism, privacy, and personal freedom would have struck Puritans as quite strange. They considered too much emphasis on the "self" dangerous to social harmony and community stability. In the closely knit towns of New England, residents carefully monitored one another's behavior and chastised or expelled those who violated communal norms. In the Puritan view, as one colonist put it, the main freedom possessed by dissenters was the "liberty to keep away from us." Towns banished individuals for such offenses as criticizing the church or government, complaining about the colony in letters home to England, or, in the case of one individual, Abigail Gifford, for being "a very burdensome woman." Tolerance of difference was not high on the list of Puritan values.

Rhode Island and Connecticut

Differences of opinion about how to organize a Bible Commonwealth, however, emerged almost from the founding of Massachusetts. With its emphasis on individual interpretation of the Bible, Puritanism contained the seeds of its own fragmentation. The first sustained criticism of the existing order came from the young minister Roger Williams, who arrived in Massachusetts in 1631 and soon began to insist that its congregations withdraw from the Church of England and that church and state be separated. "Soul liberty," Williams believed, required that individuals be allowed to follow their consciences wherever they led. To most Puritans, the social fabric was held together by certain religious truths, which could not be questioned. To Williams, any law-abiding citizen should be allowed to practice whatever form of religion he chose. For the government to "molest any person, Jew or Gentile, for either professing doctrine or practicing worship" violated the principle that genuine religious faith is voluntary. Williams rejected the conviction that Puritans were an elect people on a divine mission to spread the true faith. He denied that God had singled out any group as special favorites.

Banished from Massachusetts in 1636, Williams and his followers moved south, where they established the colony of Rhode Island, which eventually received a charter from London. In a world in which the right of individuals to participate in religious activities without governmental interference barely existed, Rhode Island became a beacon of religious freedom. It had no established church, no religious qualifications for voting until the eighteenth century, and no requirement that citizens attend church. It became a haven for **Dissenters** (Protestants who belonged to denominations other than the established church) and Jews persecuted in other colonies. Rhode Island's frame of government was also more democratic. The assembly was elected twice a year, the governor annually, and town meetings were held more frequently than elsewhere in New England.

Religious disagreements in Massachusetts generated other colonies as well. In 1636, the minister Thomas Hooker established a settlement at Hartford. Its system of government, embodied in the Fundamental Orders of 1639, was modeled on that of Massachusetts—with the significant exception that men did not have to be church members to vote. Quite different was the colony of New Haven, founded in 1638 by immigrants who wanted an even closer connection between church and state. In 1662, Hartford and New Haven received a royal charter that united them as the colony of Connecticut.

The Trial of Anne Hutchinson

More threatening to the Puritan establishment, both because of her gender and because she attracted a large and influential following, was Anne Hutchinson. A midwife and the daughter of a clergyman, Hutchinson, wrote John Winthrop, was "a woman of a ready wit and bold spirit." She arrived in Massachusetts with her husband in 1634 to join their minister, John Cotton, who had been expelled from his pulpit in England by church authorities. Hutchinson began holding meetings in her home, where she led discussions of religious issues among men and women, including a number of prominent merchants and public officials. In Hutchinson's view, salvation was God's direct gift to the elect and could not be earned by good works, devotional practices, or other human effort. Most Puritans shared this belief. What set Hutchinson apart was her charge

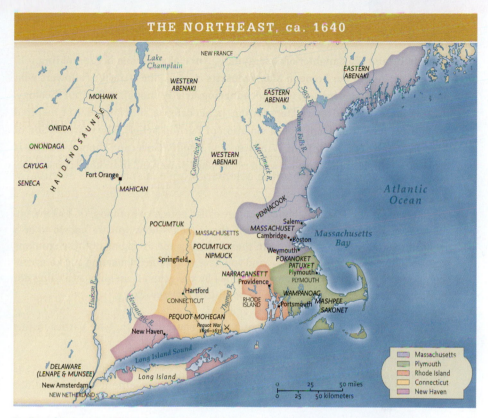

THE NORTHEAST, ca. 1640

By the mid-seventeenth century, English settlement in New England had spread inland and up and down the Atlantic coast.

that nearly all the ministers in Massachusetts were guilty of faulty preaching for distinguishing "saints" from the damned on the basis of activities such as church attendance and moral behavior rather than an inner state of grace.

In Massachusetts, where church and state reinforced each other, both ministers and magistrates were intent on suppressing any views that challenged their own leadership. Their critics denounced Cotton and Hutchinson for Antinomianism (a term for putting one's own judgment or faith above both human law and the teachings of the church). In 1637, she was placed on trial before a civil court for sedition (expressing opinions dangerous to authority). Her position as a "public woman" made her defiance seem even more outrageous. Her meetings, said Governor Winthrop, were neither "comely in the sight of God nor fitting to your sex." At her trial, Hutchinson ably debated interpretation of the Bible with her university-educated accusers. But when she spoke of divine revelations, of God speaking to her directly rather than through ministers or the Bible, she

From "THE TRIAL OF ANNE HUTCHINSON" (1637)

A midwife and the daughter of a clergyman, Anne Hutchinson began holding religious meetings in her home in Massachusetts in 1634. She attracted followers who believed that most ministers were not adhering strictly enough to Puritan theology. In 1637 she was placed on trial for sedition. In her defense, she claimed to be inspired by a direct revelation from God, a violation of Puritan beliefs. The examination of Hutchinson by Governor John Winthrop and Deputy Governor Thomas Dudley is a classic example of the clash between established power and individual conscience.

GOV. JOHN WINTHROP: Mrs. Hutchinson, you are called here as one of those that have troubled the peace of the commonwealth and the churches here; you are known to be a woman that hath had a great share in the promoting and divulging of those opinions that are the cause of this trouble, . . . and you have maintained a meeting and an assembly in your house that hath been condemned by the general assembly as a thing not tolerable nor comely in the sight of God nor fitting for your sex. . . .

MRS. ANNE HUTCHINSON: What have I said or done?

GOV. JOHN WINTHROP: [Y]ou did harbor and countenance those that are parties in this faction. . . .

MRS. ANNE HUTCHINSON: That's matter of conscience, Sir.

GOV. JOHN WINTHROP: Your conscience you must keep, or it must be kept for you.

★ ★ ★

GOV. JOHN WINTHROP: Your course is not to be suffered for. Besides we find such a course as this to be greatly prejudicial to the state. . . . And besides that it will not well stand with the commonwealth that families should be neglected for so many neighbors and dames and so much time spent. We see no rule of God for this. We see not that any should have authority to set up any other exercises besides what authority hath already set up. . . .

MRS. ANNE HUTCHINSON: I bless the Lord, he hath let me see which was the clear ministry and which the wrong. . . . Now if you do condemn me for speaking what in my conscience I know to be truth I must commit myself unto the Lord.

MR. NOWEL (ASSISTANT TO THE COURT): How do you know that was the spirit?

MRS. ANNE HUTCHINSON: How did Abraham know that it was God that bid him offer his son, being a breach of the sixth commandment?

DEP. GOV. THOMAS DUDLEY: By an immediate voice.

MRS. ANNE HUTCHINSON: So to me by an immediate revelation.

DEP. GOV. THOMAS DUDLEY: How! an immediate revelation.

★ ★ ★

GOV. JOHN WINTHROP: Mrs. Hutchinson, the sentence of the court you hear is that you are banished from out of our jurisdiction as being a woman not fit for our society, and are to be imprisoned till the court shall send you away.

From JOHN WINTHROP, SPEECH TO THE MASSACHUSETTS GENERAL COURT (JULY 3, 1645)

John Winthrop, governor of the Massachusetts Bay Colony, describes two very different definitions of liberty in this speech.

The great questions that have troubled the country, are about the authority of the magistrates and the liberty of the people. . . . Concerning liberty, I observe a great mistake in the country about that. There is a twofold liberty, natural (I mean as our nature is now corrupt) and civil or federal. The first is common to man with beasts and other creatures. By this, man, as he stands in relation to man simply, hath liberty to do what he lists; it is a liberty to do evil as well as to [do] good. This liberty is incompatible and inconsistent with authority, and cannot endure the least restraint of the most just authority. The exercise and maintaining of this liberty makes men grow more evil, and in time to be worse than brute beasts. . . . This is that great enemy of truth and peace, that wild beast, which all the ordinances of God are bent against, to restrain and subdue it.

The other kind of liberty I call civil or federal, it may also be termed moral. . . . This liberty is the proper end and object of authority, and cannot subsist without it; and it is a liberty to that only which is good, just, and honest. . . . This liberty is maintained and exercised in a way of subjection to authority; it is of the same kind of liberty wherewith Christ hath made us free. The woman's own choice makes . . . a man her husband; yet being so chosen, he is her lord, and she is to be subject to him, yet in a way of liberty, not of bondage; and a true wife accounts her subjection her honor and freedom, and would not think her condition safe and free, but in her subjection to her husband's authority. Such is the liberty of the church under the authority of Christ.

QUESTIONS

1. *To what extent does Hutchinson's being a woman play a part in the accusations against her?*

2. *Why does Winthrop consider "natural" liberty dangerous?*

3. *How do Hutchinson and Winthrop differ in their understanding of religious liberty?*

violated Puritan doctrine and sealed her own fate. Such a claim, the colony's leaders felt, posed a threat to the very existence of organized churches—and, indeed, to all authority. Hutchinson and a number of her followers were banished. Her family made its way to Rhode Island and then to the religious refuge of New Netherland, where Hutchinson and most of her relatives perished during Kieft's War (see Chapter 1) between the Dutch and Delaware Indians.

Anne Hutchinson lived in New England for only eight years, but she left her mark on the region's religious culture. As in the case of Roger Williams, her career showed how the Puritan belief in each individual's ability to interpret the Bible could easily lead to criticism of the religious and political establishment. Although religious toleration became a value in New Netherland, Maryland, and to some extent Rhode Island, Massachusetts rejected it as a violation of "moral liberty" and social harmony.

The New England Economy

The leaders of the New England colonies prided themselves on the idea that religion was the primary motivation for emigration. "We all came into these parts of America," proclaimed an official document of the 1640s, "with one and the same end and aim, namely, to advance the kingdom of our Lord Jesus Christ and to enjoy the liberties of the Gospel in purity with peace." But economic motives were hardly unimportant. One promotional pamphlet of the 1620s spoke of New England as a place "where religion and profit jump together."

Most Puritans sought in New England not only religious liberty but also economic advancement—if not riches, then at least a "competency," the economic independence that came with secure landownership or craft status. When one preacher proclaimed that the "main end" of settlement was to honor God, a man in the congregation cried out, "Sir, you are mistaken . . . our main end was to catch fish." But to Puritans no contradiction existed between piety and profit so long as one did not forget the needs of the larger community. Success in one's calling might be a sign of divine grace.

Lacking a marketable staple like sugar or tobacco, New Englanders turned to fishing and timber for exports. But the economy centered on family farms producing food for their own use and a small marketable surplus. Although the Body of Liberties of 1641, as noted above, made provision for slavery in the Bible Commonwealth, there were very few slaves in seventeenth-century New England. Nor were indentured servants as central to the economy as in the Chesapeake. Most households relied on the labor of their own members, including women in the home and children in the fields. Sons remained unmarried into their mid-twenties, when they could expect to receive land from their fathers, from local authorities, or by moving to a new town. Indeed, while religious divisions spawned new settlements, the desire for land among younger families and newcomers was the major motive for New England's expansion. In Sudbury, Massachusetts, for example, one resident proposed in 1651 that every adult man be awarded an equal parcel of land. When a town meeting rejected the idea, a group of young men received a grant from the General Court to establish their own town farther west.

The Merchant Elite

Per capita wealth in New England lagged far behind that of the Chesapeake, but it was much more equally distributed. A majority of New England families achieved the goal of owning their own land, the foundation for a comfortable independence. Nonetheless, as in the Chesapeake, economic development produced a measure of social inequality. On completing their terms, indentured servants rarely achieved full church membership or received grants of land. Most became disenfranchised wage earners.

New England assumed a growing role within the British empire based on trade. As early as the 1640s, New England merchants shipped and marketed the staples of other colonies to markets in Europe and Africa. They engaged in a particularly profitable trade with the West Indies, whose growing slave plantations they supplied with fish, timber, and agricultural produce gathered at home. Thus, New England's economy greatly profited from the Atlantic slave trade and plantation slavery. In Boston, a powerful class of merchants arose who challenged some key Puritan policies, including the subordination of economic activity to the common good. Indeed, merchants were among the most prominent backers of Anne Hutchinson's challenge to colonial authority. Some left Boston to establish a new town at Portsmouth, in the region eventually chartered as the royal colony of New Hampshire. Although the Puritans never abandoned the idea that economic activity should serve the general welfare, Boston merchants soon came to exercise a decisive influence in public affairs. Eventually, the Puritan experiment would evolve into a merchant-dominated colonial government.

The Half-Way Covenant

In the mid-seventeenth century, some Puritan leaders began to worry about their society's growing commercialization and declining piety, or "declension." By 1650, less than half the population of Boston had been admitted to full church membership. Massachusetts churches were forced to deal with a growing problem—the religious status of the third generation. Children of the elect could be baptized, but many never became full church members because they were unable to demonstrate the necessary religious commitment or testify to a conversion experience. What was the status of their children? New Englanders

Mrs. Elizabeth Freake and Baby Mary. Painted by an anonymous artist in the 1670s, this portrait depicts the wife and daughter of John Freake, a prominent Boston merchant and lawyer. To illustrate the family's wealth, Mrs. Freake wears a triple strand of pearls, a garnet bracelet, and a gold ring, and her child wears a yellow silk dress.

faced a difficult choice. They could uphold rigorous standards of church admission, which would limit the size and social influence of the Congregational Church. Or they could make admission easier, which would keep the church connected to a larger part of the population but would raise fears about a loss of religious purity.

The **Half-Way Covenant** of 1662 tried to address this problem by allowing for the baptism and a kind of subordinate, or "half-way," membership for grandchildren of those who arrived during the Great Migration. But church membership continued to stagnate.

By the 1660s and 1670s, ministers were regularly castigating the people for selfishness, manifestations of pride, violations of the Sabbath, and a "great back-sliding" from the colony's original purposes. These warnings, called "jeremiads" after the ancient Hebrew prophet Jeremiah, interpreted crop failures, disease, and war as signs of divine disapproval and warned of further punishment to come if New Englanders did not mend their ways. Yet hard work and commercial success in one's chosen calling had always been central Puritan values. In this sense, the commercialization of New England was as much a fulfillment of the Puritan mission in America as a betrayal.

RELIGION, POLITICS, AND FREEDOM

The Rights of Englishmen

Even as English emigrants began the settlement of colonies in North America, England itself became enmeshed in political and religious conflict, in which ideas of liberty played a central role. The struggle over **English liberty** in the first half of the seventeenth century expanded the definition of freedom at home and spilled over into early English North America.

By 1600, the traditional definition of "liberties" as a set of privileges confined to one or another social group still persisted, but alongside it had arisen the idea that certain "rights of Englishmen" applied to all within the kingdom. This tradition rested on the Magna Carta (or Great Charter) of 1215. An agreement between King John and a group of barons—local lords whose private armies frequently fought against each other and the crown—the Magna Carta attempted to put an end to a chronic state of civil unrest. It listed a series of "liberties" granted by the king to "all the free men of our realm." This was a restricted group at the time, since a large part of the English population still lived as serfs—peasants working land owned by feudal lords and legally bound to provide labor and other services. The liberties mentioned in the Magna Carta included protection against arbitrary imprisonment and the seizure of one's property without due process of law.

The principal beneficiaries of the Magna Carta were the barons, who obtained the right to oversee the king's conduct and even revolt if he violated their privileges. But over time, the document came to be seen as embodying the idea of "English liberty"—that the king was subject to the rule of law, and that all persons should enjoy security of person and property. These rights were embodied in the common law, whose provisions, such as habeas corpus (a protection against being imprisoned without a legal charge), the right to face one's accuser, and trial by jury came to apply to all free subjects of the English crown. And as serfdom slowly disappeared, the number of Englishmen considered "freeborn," and therefore entitled to these rights, expanded enormously, although women continued to be entirely excluded.

The English Civil War

At the beginning of the seventeenth century, when English immigrants began arriving in the Americas, "freedom" still played only a minor role in England's political debates. But the political upheavals of that century elevated the notion of "English freedom" to a central place. The struggle for political supremacy between Parliament and the Stuart monarchs James I and Charles I culminated in the English Civil War of the 1640s and early 1650s. This long-running battle arose from religious disputes about how fully the Church of England should distance its doctrines and forms of worship from Catholicism. Conflict also developed over the respective powers of the king and Parliament, a debate that produced numerous invocations of the idea of the "freeborn Englishman" and led to a great expansion of the concept of English freedom. The belief in freedom as the common heritage of all Englishmen and the conception of the British empire as the world's guardian of liberty helped to legitimize English colonization in the Western Hemisphere and to cast imperial wars against Catholic France and Spain as struggles between freedom and tyranny.

From HENRY CARE, *ENGLISH LIBERTIES, OR, THE FREE-BORN SUBJECT'S INHERITANCE* (1680)

Before the United States existed as an independent nation, settlers in England's North American colonies shared a sense of identity linked with the idea that liberty was a unique possession of Englishmen. Care was an English journalist and writer on politics. His book was an influential example of how seventeenth-century identities rested, in part, on negative images of other nations. Well into the eighteenth century, it was widely reprinted in the colonies as well as the mother country.

The Constitution of our English government (the best in the world) is no arbitrary tyranny like the Turkish Grand Seignior's, or the French Kings, whose wills (or rather lusts) dispose of the lives and fortunes of their unhappy subjects; nor an Oligarchy where the great men (like fish in the ocean) prey upon, and live by devouring the lesser at their pleasure. Nor yet a Democracy or popular State, much less an Anarchy, where all confusedly are hail fellows well met, but a most excellently mixt or qualified Monarchy, where the King is vested with large prerogatives sufficient to support majesty; and restrained only from power of doing himself and his people harm, which would be contrary to the end of all government, . . . the nobility adorned with privileges to be a screen to majesty, and a refreshing shade to their inferiors, and the commonality, too, so guarded in their persons and properties by the fence of law, [which] renders them Freemen, not Slaves.

In France and other nations the mere will of the prince is law, his word takes off any . . . head, imposes taxes, or seizes any man's estate, when, how, and as often as he wishes. . . . But in England, the law is both the measure and the bond of every subject's duty and allegiance, each man having a fixed fundamental right born with him as to the freedom of his person and property in his estate, which he cannot be deprived of, but either by his consent, or some crime for which the law has imposed . . . a penalty. . . .

This original happy frame of government is truly and properly called an Englishman's liberty, a privilege not to [be] exempt from the law, but to be freed in person and estate, from arbitrary violence and oppression.

QUESTIONS

1. *Why does Care consider the English system of "balanced" government the best in the world?*

2. *How does his view of other countries affect his pride in being English?*

The leaders of the House of Commons (the elective body that, along with the hereditary aristocrats of the House of Lords, made up the English Parliament) accused the Stuart kings of endangering liberty by imposing taxes without parliamentary consent, imprisoning political foes, and leading the nation back toward Catholicism. Civil war broke out in 1642, resulting in a victory for the forces of Parliament. In 1649, Charles I was beheaded, the monarchy abolished, and England declared "a Commonwealth and Free State"—a nation governed by the will of the people. Oliver Cromwell, the head of the victorious Parliamentary army, ruled for almost a decade after the execution of the king. In 1660, the monarchy was restored and Charles II assumed the throne. But by then, the breakdown of authority had stimulated intense discussions of liberty, authority, and what it meant to be a "freeborn Englishman."

England's Debate over Freedom

The idea of freedom suddenly took on new and expanded meanings between 1640 and 1660. The writer John Milton, who in 1649 called London "the mansion-house of liberty," called for freedom of speech and of the press. New religious sects sprang up, demanding the end of public financing and special privileges for the Anglican Church and religious toleration for all Protestants. The Levellers, history's first democratic political movement, proposed a written constitution, the Agreement of the People, which began by proclaiming "at how high a rate we value our just freedom," and went on to list inalienable rights Parliament could not infringe upon. At a time when "democracy" was still widely seen as the equivalent of anarchy and disorder, the document proposed to abolish the monarchy and House of Lords and to greatly expand the right to vote. "The poorest he that lives in England hath a life to live as the greatest he," declared the Leveller Thomas Rainsborough, and therefore "any man that is born in England . . . ought to have his voice in election." Rainsborough even condemned slavery.

The Levellers offered a glimpse of the modern definition of freedom as a universal entitlement in a society based on equal rights, not a function of social class. Another new group, the Diggers, went even further, hoping to give freedom an economic underpinning through the common ownership of land. Previous discussion of freedom, declared Gerard Winstanley, the Diggers' leader, had been misguided: "You are like men in a mist, seeking for freedom and know not what it is." True freedom applied equally "to the poor as well as the rich"; all were entitled to "a comfortable livelihood in this their own land." Even before the restoration of the monarchy, the Levellers, Diggers, and other radical movements spawned by the English Civil War had been crushed or driven underground. But some of the ideas of liberty that flourished during the 1640s and 1650s would be carried to America by English immigrants. Thomas

Rainsborough, for example, was killed in the Civil War, but his brother William and other Levellers sailed for Massachusetts.

The Civil War and English America

These struggles, accompanied by vigorous discussions of the rights of freeborn Englishmen, inevitably reverberated in England's colonies, dividing them from one another and internally. Most New Englanders sided with Parliament in the Civil War of the 1640s. Some returned to England to join the Parliamentary army or take up pulpits to help create a godly commonwealth at home. But Puritan leaders were increasingly uncomfortable as the idea of religious toleration for Protestants gained favor in England. It was the revolutionary Parliament that in 1644 granted Roger Williams his charter for the Rhode Island colony he had founded after being banished from Massachusetts.

Meanwhile, a number of followers of Anne Hutchinson became Quakers, one of the sects that sprang up in England during the Civil War. Quakers held that the spirit of God dwelled within every individual, not just the elect, and that this "inner light," rather than the Bible or teachings of the clergy, offered the surest guidance in spiritual matters. When Quakers appeared in Massachusetts, colonial officials had them whipped, fined, and banished. In 1659 and 1660, four Quakers who returned from exile were hanged, including Mary Dyer, a former disciple of Hutchinson. The treatment of Quakers gave Massachusetts a reputation in England as a hotbed of religious persecution. When Charles II, after the restoration of the monarchy in 1660, reaffirmed the Massachusetts

The execution of Charles I in 1649, a central event of the English Civil War.

charter, he ordered the colony to recognize the "liberty of conscience" of all Protestants. But while hangings ceased, efforts to suppress the Quakers continued, as did attacks on Baptists, whose disdain for a learned ministry also seemed to threaten Puritan beliefs.

The Crisis in Maryland

Unlike the New England colonies, Virginia sided with Charles I. Its leaders even proclaimed Charles II king after his father's execution in 1649, although Oliver Cromwell's government in London soon brought the rebellious colony under control. In Maryland, the combination of the religious and political battles of the Civil War, homegrown conflict between Catholic and Protestant settlers, and anti-proprietary feeling produced a violent civil war within the colony, later recalled as the "plundering time." Indeed, Maryland in the 1640s verged on total anarchy, with a pro-Parliament force assaulting those loyal to Charles I. The emerging Protestant planter class longed to seize power from the Catholic elite created by Lord Baltimore. The assembly's Protestant majority rejected laws proposed by the proprietor and claimed the same power to legislate and levy taxes enjoyed by the House of Commons in England.

To stabilize the colony and attract more settlers, Lord Baltimore appointed a Protestant governor and offered refuge to Protestant Dissenters being persecuted in Virginia, where Anglicanism was the established religion and laws restricted the religious and political rights of others. In 1649, Maryland adopted an **Act Concerning Religion (or Maryland Toleration Act)**, which institutionalized the principle of toleration that had prevailed from the colony's beginning. All Christians were guaranteed the "free exercise" of religion. The act did not establish religious liberty in a modern sense, since it punished those who denied the divinity of Jesus Christ or the doctrine of the Holy Trinity. Indeed, a Jewish physician was soon arrested under its provisions. Nonetheless, the law was a milestone in the history of religious freedom in colonial America.

Turmoil, however, continued. During the 1650s, the Commonwealth government in London placed Maryland under the control of a Protestant council, which repealed the Toleration Act and forbade Catholics from openly practicing their religion. In 1657, however, Lord Baltimore's authority was restored and with it Maryland's experiment in religious freedom.

Cromwell and the Empire

Oliver Cromwell, who ruled England from 1649 until his death in 1658, undertook an aggressive policy of colonial expansion, the promotion of Protestantism, and commercial empowerment in the British Isles and the Western Hemisphere. His army forcibly extended English control over Ireland, massacring civilians, banning the public practice of Catholicism, and seizing land owned by Catholics. In the Caribbean, England seized Jamaica, a valuable sugar island, from Spain. In 1651, as will be related in Chapter 3, Parliament passed the first Navigation Act, which sought to challenge the Dutch hold on international commerce by forcing English colonies to trade with only English ships and ports.

Thus, by the middle of the seventeenth century, several English colonies existed along the Atlantic coast of North America along with New France, New Netherland, Spanish Florida, and hundreds of Native nations. Established as part of an ad hoc process rather than arising under any coherent national plan, the English colonies differed enormously in economic, political, and social structure. The seeds had been planted, in the Chesapeake, for the development of plantation societies based on unfree labor and, in New England, for settlements centered on small towns and family farms. Throughout the colonies, many residents enjoyed freedoms they had not possessed at home, especially access to land and the right to worship as they desired. Others found themselves confined to unfree labor for many years or an entire lifetime.

The next century would be a time of crisis and consolidation as the English colonial population expanded, England moved to exert greater control over its flourishing North American colonies, and conflicts erupted both within the English colonies and between them and their Native and European neighbors.

North America in 1660

As tensions about freedom simmered in England and in its North American colonies, in 1660, the vast majority of the continent was still controlled and solely inhabited by Native Americans. Besides Spain's substantial colony in central Mexico, European settlement was confined to the small Spanish posts at Santa Fe and St. Augustine, the French trading posts of Quebec and Montreal on the St. Lawrence River, Dutch New Amsterdam and Fort Orange (Albany), and the English settlements all within 100 miles of the Atlantic Ocean: on the James River, the shore of the Chesapeake Bay, the lower Connecticut River valley, Rhode Island, and eastern Massachusetts. A whole history was happening far from European colonies.

The power of the Haudenosaunee was more greatly feared in the 1660s than the power of the Europeans. Armed with Dutch weapons, they had launched a successful series of wars against their enemies north of the St. Lawrence River and in the eastern Great Lakes. One Frenchman described the Haudenosaunee ambition to make the whole region into "one people and one land." To the west, on the northern plains, Lakotas and Dakotas (collectively known as Oceti Sakowin or Sioux) endured attacks from people to their east such as the Ottawas, who had acquired European firearms through trade with the French at Montreal.

Native North Americans developed methods of diplomacy as well as warfare. Many used the calumet (or peace pipe) ceremony to forge alliances with newcomers, neighbors, and former enemies. Probably originating among Caddoan peoples in the thirteenth century in what is now Texas, the calumet ceremony spread throughout the West as the most important diplomatic ritual between Native peoples and, eventually, in cross-cultural encounters with European travelers. Centered upon the ritual smoking of a calumet, this ceremony made strangers into fictive kin. Breaking the bonds created by the calumet ceremony was thus like betraying family.

Wampum strings and belts served a similar function in the Northeast, from eastern Canada, through present-day New York and New England, to the upper Chesapeake. Since at least the sixteenth century, the Haudenosaunee and other nations used them for opening and closing diplomatic and trade negotiations, to propose that allies join a battle, to make peace among enemies, and to console the bereaved both beyond and within their nations. Strings of beads helped an orator remember a complicated speech, and they embodied the pledges that people made to one another. Recipients who accepted the wampum were agreeing to the relationship and reciprocal responsibilities it conveyed. As Europeans began to venture deeper into the continent in the century to come, they would have to learn Native ways of peace and war.

CHAPTER REVIEW

REVIEW QUESTIONS

1. *Compare and contrast settlement patterns, religion, and relations with Native Americans of the Spanish and English in the Americas.*

2. *For English settlers, land was the basis of independence and liberty. Explain the reasoning behind that concept and how it differed from Native conceptions of land.*

3. *Describe the factors promoting and limiting religious freedom in the New England and Chesapeake colonies.*

4. *Describe who chose to emigrate to North America from England in the seventeenth century and explain their reasons.*

5. *In what ways did the economy, government, and household structure differ in New England and the Chesapeake colonies?*

6. *The English believed that, unlike the Spanish, their motives for colonization were pure, and that the growth of empire and freedom would always go hand in hand. How did the expansion of the English empire affect the freedoms of Native Americans, the Irish, and even many English citizens?*

7. *Considering politics, social tensions, and debates over the meaning of liberty, how do the events and aftermath of the English Civil War demonstrate that the English colonies in North America were part of a larger Atlantic community?*

8. *How did the tobacco economy draw the Chesapeake colonies into the greater Atlantic world?*

9. *How did the idea of freedom help legitimize English colonization?*

KEY TERMS

John Smith (p. 45)

Virginia Company (p. 45)

Anglican Church (p. 46)

Roanoke colony (p. 47)

enclosure movement (p. 49)

headright system (p. 55)

House of Burgesses (p. 55)

Anglo-Powhatan Wars (p. 56)

plantation (p. 59)

dower rights (p. 62)

Puritans (p. 64)

John Winthrop (p. 65)

Pilgrims (p. 66)

Mayflower Compact (p. 66)

Great Migration (p. 67)

captivity narratives (p. 71)

Pequot War (p. 73)

Dissenters (p. 74)

Half-Way Covenant (p. 80)

English liberty (p. 80)

Act Concerning Religion (or Maryland Toleration Act) (p. 85)

Go to 🐰 **INQUIZITIVE**

To see what you know—and learn what you've missed—with personalized feedback along the way.

★ **CHAPTER 3** ★

CREATING ANGLO-AMERICA

1660–1750

FOCUS QUESTIONS

- *How did the English empire in America expand in the mid-seventeenth century?*

- *How was slavery established in the Western Atlantic world?*

- *What major social and political crises rocked the colonies in the late seventeenth century?*

- *What were the directions of social and economic change in the eighteenth-century colonies?*

- *How did patterns of class and gender roles change in eighteenth-century America?*

- *What was the extent of Native power across the continent by the mid-eighteenth century?*

In the last quarter of the seventeenth century, a series of crises rocked the European colonies of North America. Social and political tensions boiled over in sometimes ruthless conflicts between rich and poor, free and slave, settler and Indian, and members of different religious groups. At the same time, struggles within and between European empires echoed in the colonies. Colonists and Native Americans got dragged into one another's wars. Aggrieved groups seized upon the language of freedom to advance their goals. Although each conflict had its own local causes, taken together they added up to a general crisis of colonial society in the area that would become the United States.

In 1675, a Native alliance launched attacks on New Englanders whose farms and settlements were encroaching on their lands. It was the most dramatic and violent warfare in the region in the entire seventeenth century. New Englanders called the conflict **King Philip's War**, believing that the Wampanoag leader **Metacom** (known to the colonists as King Philip) was the war's mastermind. In fact it had many leaders, including a Wampanoag woman named Weetamoo. By this time, New England's colonial population considerably outnumbered the Wampanoags. But the fate of the New England colonies hung in the balance for several months. By 1676, Wampanoags and their allies had attacked nearly half of New England's ninety towns. Twelve in Massachusetts were destroyed. As English refugees fled eastward, the line of settlement was pushed back almost to the Atlantic coast. Some 1,000 settlers, out of a population of 52,000, perished in the fighting.

In mid-1676, the tide of battle turned when the Mohawks joined the fight against the Wampanoags and their allies. Together, colonial and Native forces inflicted devastating punishment on the Wampanoags. New Englanders beheaded Metacom and Weetamoo and mounted their heads on stakes. Native towns were destroyed, and thousands of men, women, and children were killed or sold into slavery in the West Indies. Most of the survivors fled to Canada or New York. Even the "praying Indians"—that is, about 2,000 Native peoples who had converted to Christianity and lived in autonomous communities under Puritan supervision—were targeted. Removed from their towns to Deer Island in Boston Harbor, supposedly for their own protection, many perished from disease and lack of food and some were shipped to the West Indies as though they were war captives.

In the long run, King Philip's War produced a broadening of freedom for white New Englanders by expanding their access to land. But this freedom rested on the death or dispossession of most of the region's Native peoples.

GLOBAL COMPETITION AND THE EXPANSION OF ENGLAND'S EMPIRE

The Mercantilist System

As the Americas became a battleground in European nations' endless contests for wealth and power, England moved to seize control of Atlantic trade, solidify its hold on North America's eastern coast, and exert greater control over its empire. By the middle of the seventeenth century, it was apparent that the colonies could be an important source of wealth for England. According to the prevailing theory known as **mercantilism**, the government should regulate economic activity so as to promote national power. It should encourage manufacturing and commerce by special bounties, monopolies, and other measures. Above all, trade should be controlled so that more gold and silver flowed into the country than left it. That is, exports of goods, which generated revenue from abroad, should exceed imports, which required paying foreigners for their products. In the mercantilist outlook, the role of colonies was to serve the interests of the home country by producing marketable raw materials and importing manufactured goods from home. "Foreign trade," declared an influential work written in 1664 by a London merchant, formed the basis of "England's treasure." Commerce was to be the foundation of empire.

Under Oliver Cromwell, Parliament passed in 1651 the first **Navigation Act**, which aimed to wrest control of world trade from the Dutch, whose merchants profited from free trade with all parts of the world and all existing empires. Additional measures followed in 1660 and 1663. England's new economic policy, mercantilism, rested on the idea that England should monopolize the profits arising from the English empire.

According to the Navigation laws, certain "enumerated" goods—essentially, the most valuable colonial products, such as tobacco and sugar—had to be transported in English ships and sold initially in English ports, although they could then be re-exported to foreign markets. Similarly, most European goods imported into the colonies had to be shipped through England, where customs duties were paid. This enabled English merchants, manufacturers,

	CHRONOLOGY
1651	First Navigation Act issued by Parliament
1664–1674	Anglo-Dutch Wars, which result in New Netherland becoming New York
1670	First English settlers arrive in Carolina
1675–1676	King Philip's War
1676	Bacon's Rebellion
1677	Covenant Chain alliance
1682	Charter of Liberty drafted by William Penn
1683	Charter of Liberties and Privileges drafted by New York assembly
1686–1689	Dominion of New England
1688	Glorious Revolution in England
1689	Parliament enacts a Bill of Rights
	Leisler's Rebellion
	Parliament passes Toleration Act
1691	Plymouth Colony absorbed into Massachusetts
1692	Salem witch trials
1705	Virginia passes Slave Code
1715–1717	Yamasee War
1718	New Orleans founded
1718	San Antonio founded
1729–1730	Natchez War
1737	Walking Purchase

shipbuilders, and sailors to reap the benefits of colonial trade and the government to enjoy added income from taxes. As members of the empire, American colonies would profit as well, since their ships were considered English. Indeed, the Navigation Acts stimulated the rise of New England's shipbuilding industry.

The Conquest of New Netherland

The restoration of the English monarchy when Charles II assumed the throne in 1660 sparked a new period of colonial expansion. The government chartered new trading ventures, notably the Royal African Company, which was given a monopoly of the slave trade. Within a generation, the number of English colonies in North America doubled. First to come under English control was New Netherland, seized during a series of Anglo-Dutch wars between 1664 and 1674 that also saw England gain control of Dutch trading posts in Africa. Charles II awarded the colony to his younger brother James, the duke of York, with "full and absolute power" to govern as he pleased. (Hence the colony's name became New York.)

New Netherland had always remained peripheral to the far-flung Dutch empire. English rule transformed this minor military and trading base into an important imperial outpost, a seaport trading with the Caribbean and Europe, and a launching pad for military operations against the French. New York's European population, around 9,000 when the English assumed control, rose to 20,000 by 1685.

New York and the Rights of Englishmen and Englishwomen

English rule preserved the freedom of some New Yorkers, while reducing that of others. Many English observers had concluded that Dutch prosperity—what one writer called "the prodigious increase of the Netherlanders in their domestic and foreign trade"—stemmed from "their toleration of different opinions in matters of religion," which attracted "many industrious people of other countries." Thus, the terms of surrender guaranteed that the English would respect the religious beliefs and property holdings of the colony's many ethnic communities. But that guarantee did not extend to women's legal rights. The English law of coverture ended the Dutch tradition by which married women conducted business in their own name. As colonists of Dutch origin adapted to English rule, their wills directed more attention to advancing the fortunes of their sons than providing for their wives and daughters. There had been many female traders and business owners in New Amsterdam, but few remained by the end of the seventeenth century.

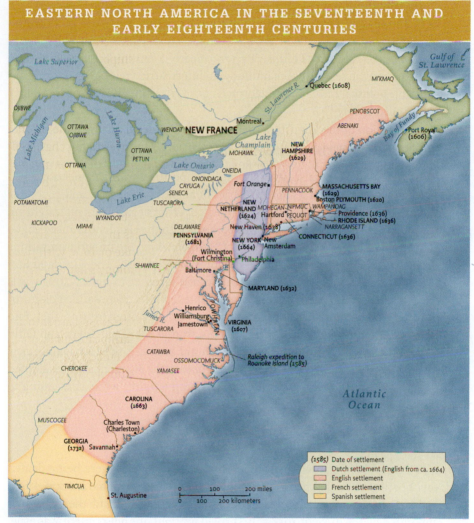

EASTERN NORTH AMERICA IN THE SEVENTEENTH AND EARLY EIGHTEENTH CENTURIES

Legend:
- (1585) Date of settlement
- Dutch settlement (English from ca. 1664)
- English settlement
- French settlement
- Spanish settlement

By the early eighteenth century, numerous English colonies populated eastern North America, while the French had established their own presence to the north and west. Native nations still ruled the vast interior.

The English increased the slave trade into New York City and issued the colony's first slave code, similar to that of Virginia and other southern colonies. In a reversal of Dutch practice, the English expelled free Blacks from many skilled jobs. As we shall see in Chapter 4, New York City would have a slave rebellion in 1712 and a conspiracy against the colony by enslaved and free Blacks united with English and Irish dockworkers.

A few families benefited enormously from English rule. The duke of York and his appointed governors continued the Dutch practice of awarding immense land grants to favorites, including 160,000 acres to Robert Livingston and 90,000 to Frederick Philipse. By 1700, nearly 2 million acres of land were owned by only five New York families who intermarried regularly, exerted considerable political influence, and formed one of colonial America's most tightly knit landed elites.

New York and the Haudenosaunee

Initially, English rule also strengthened the position of the Haudenosaunee (Iroquois) League. After a complex series of negotiations in the mid-1670s, Sir Edmund Andros, who had been appointed governor of New York after fighting the French in the Caribbean, linked New York with the Haudenosaunee League in an alliance known as the **Covenant Chain**, in which the imperial ambitions of the English and Haudenosaunee reinforced one another. The Five (later Six) Haudenosaunee Nations and New York joined together to fight Native rivals and the French. Andros, for his part, accepted the Haudenosaunee claim to authority over Native communities in the vast area stretching to the Ohio River. But beginning in the 1680s, Indians around the Great Lakes and Ohio Valley began to regroup and with French aid attacked the Haudenosaunee, pushing them back east. By the end of the century, the Haudenosaunee adopted a policy of careful neutrality with the European empires while continuing to profit from the fur trade.

The Charter of Liberties

Many colonists, meanwhile, began to complain that they were being denied the "liberties of Englishmen," especially the right to consent to taxation. There had been no representative assembly under the Dutch, and the governors appointed by the duke of York at first ruled without one. Discontent was especially strong on Long Island, which had been largely settled by New Englanders used to self-government.

In 1683, the duke agreed to call an elected assembly, whose first act was to draft a Charter of Liberties and Privileges. The charter required that elections be held every three years among male property owners and the freemen of New York City; it also reaffirmed traditional English rights such as trial by jury and security of property, as well as religious toleration for all Protestants. In part, the charter reflected an effort by newer English colonists to assert dominance over older Dutch settlers by establishing the principle that the "liberties" to which New Yorkers were entitled were those enjoyed by Englishmen at home.

The Founding of Carolina

For more than three decades after the establishment of Maryland in 1632, no new English settlement was planted in North America. Then, in 1663, Charles II awarded to eight proprietors the right to establish a colony to the north of Florida, as a barrier to Spanish expansion. Not until 1670 did the first settlers arrive to found Carolina. In its early years, Carolina was the "colony of a colony." It began as an offshoot of the tiny island of Barbados. In the mid-seventeenth century, Barbados was the Caribbean's richest plantation economy, but a shortage of available land led wealthy planters to seek opportunities in Carolina for their sons. The early settlers of Carolina sought Native allies by offering guns for deer hides and captives, a policy that unleashed widespread raiding among Indians for slaves to sell. The colonists also encouraged Native allies to attack Indians in Spanish Florida; in one series of wars between 1704 and 1706 Yamasee, Muscogee (Creek), and allied raiders captured almost 10,000 Florida Indians, most of them shipped to other mainland colonies and the West Indies as slaves. Indeed, between 1670 and 1720, the number of Indian slaves exported from Charleston was larger than the number of African slaves imported.

In 1715, the Yamasees, alarmed by the debts they had incurred in trade with the settlers, the lower prices Englishmen had begun paying for captives, and slave traders' raids into their own territory, decided to fight the English in what became known as the **Yamasee War**. The Yamasees recruited their Muscogee allies to join them, and they persuaded the Spanish to provide them with weapons. The Yamasees and Muscogees killed nearly 100 English traders, attacked plantations, and killed settlers. But the English recruited the Cherokees to join the war on their side, and the combined English and Cherokee force defeated the Yamasees and Muscogees. Most of the surviving Yamasees were enslaved or driven out of the colony into Spanish Florida, from where they occasionally launched raids against English settlements. As a result of the Yamasee War, the Carolina colonists decided that the Indian slave trade was too dangerous. From then on, they would buy almost exclusively enslaved Africans.

The Fundamental Constitutions of Carolina, issued by the proprietors in 1669, proposed to establish a feudal society with a hereditary nobility, serfs, and slaves. Needing to attract settlers quickly, however, the proprietors also provided for an elected assembly and religious toleration—by now recognized as essential to enticing migrants to North America. They also instituted a generous headright system, offering 150 acres for each member of an arriving family and 100 acres to male servants who completed their terms.

Intending to replicate the plantation economy of Barbados, the proprietors instituted a rigorous legal code that promised slaveowners "absolute power and authority" over their human property and granted each slaveholder an additional 150 acres for each enslaved person brought to the colony. Thus, any persons who settled in Carolina and brought with them slaves, including planters from Barbados, instantly acquired large new landholdings. In its early days, however, the economy centered on cattle raising and trade with local Indians, not agriculture. Carolina grew slowly until planters discovered the staple—rice—that would make them the wealthiest elite in the mainland English colonies and deeply entrench slavery in the future United States.

The Holy Experiment

The last English colony to be established in the seventeenth century was Pennsylvania. The proprietor, William Penn, envisioned it as a place where those facing religious persecution in Europe could enjoy spiritual freedom, and colonists and Native Americans would coexist in harmony. Penn's late father had been a supporter and creditor of Charles II. To cancel his debt to the Penn family and bolster the English presence in North America, the king in 1681 granted Penn a vast tract of land south and west of New York, as well as the old Swedish-Dutch colony that became Delaware.

A devout member of the **Society of Friends**, or **Quakers**, Penn was particularly concerned with establishing a refuge for his coreligionists, who faced increasing persecution in England. He had already assisted a group of English Quakers in purchasing half of what became the colony of New Jersey from Lord John Berkeley, who had received a land grant from the duke of York. Penn was largely responsible for the frame of government announced in 1677, the West Jersey Concessions, one of the most liberal of the era. Based on Quaker ideals, it created an elected assembly with a broad suffrage and established religious liberty. Penn hoped that West Jersey would become a society of small farmers, not large landowners.

Quaker Liberty

Like the Puritans, Penn considered his colony a "holy experiment," but of a different kind—"a free colony for all mankind that should go hither." He hoped that Pennsylvania could be governed according to Quaker principles, among them the equality of all persons (including women, Blacks, and Indians) before God and the primacy of the individual conscience. To Quakers, liberty was a universal entitlement, not the possession of any single people—a position that would eventually make them the first group of whites to repudiate slavery. Penn also treated Indians with a respect unique in the English colonial experience, purchasing land before reselling it to colonists and offering refuge to Native communities driven out of other colonies by warfare. Since Quakers were pacifists who came to America unarmed and did not even organize a militia until the 1740s, peace with Pennsylvania's Native neighbors was essential.

Religious freedom was Penn's most fundamental principle. He condemned attempts to enforce "religious Uniformity" for depriving thousands of "free inhabitants" of England of the right to worship as they desired. His Charter of Liberty, approved by the assembly in 1682, offered "Christian liberty" to all who affirmed a belief in God and did not use their freedom to promote "licentiousness." There was no established church in Pennsylvania, and attendance at religious services was entirely voluntary, although Jews were barred from office by a required oath affirming belief in the divinity of Jesus Christ. At the same time, the Quakers upheld a strict code of personal morality. Penn's Frame of Government prohibited swearing, drunkenness, and adultery, as well as popular entertainments of the era such as "revels, bull-baiting, and cock-fighting." Private religious belief may not have been enforced by the government, but moral public behavior certainly was. Not religious uniformity but a virtuous citizenry would be the foundation of Penn's social order.

Land in Pennsylvania

Given the power to determine the colony's form of government, Penn established an appointed council to originate legislation and an assembly elected by male taxpayers and "freemen" (owners of 100 acres of land for free immigrants and 50 acres for former indentured servants). These rules made a majority of the male population eligible to vote. Penn owned all the colony's land and sold it to settlers at low prices rather than granting it outright. Like other proprietors, he expected to turn a profit, and like most of them, he never really did. But if Penn did not prosper, Pennsylvania did. A majority of the early settlers were Quakers from the British Isles. But Pennsylvania's religious toleration, healthy climate, and inexpensive land, along with Penn's aggressive efforts to publicize the colony's advantages, soon attracted immigrants from all over Western Europe.

Ironically, the freedoms Pennsylvania offered to European immigrants contributed to the deterioration of freedom for others. The colony's successful efforts to attract settlers would eventually come into conflict with Penn's benevolent Indian policy. And the opening of Pennsylvania led to an immediate decline in the number of indentured servants choosing to sail for Virginia and

A Quaker Meeting, a painting by an unidentified British artist, dating from the late eighteenth or early nineteenth century. It illustrates the prominent place of women in Quaker gatherings.

Maryland, a development that did much to shift those colonies toward reliance on slave labor.

ENTRENCHMENT OF AMERICAN SLAVERY

In the mid-1600s, slavery in mainland North America was a small-scale form of labor that existed alongside indentured and free laborers doing similar work. By the 1800s, it would become a deeply entrenched institution that touched every part of American life. Gradually, starting in the second half of the 1600s, some colonies developed plantations worked by hundreds of enslaved men and women and legalized their permanent oppression through severe legal codes. Colonies less dependent on slave labor began to benefit from the Atlantic trade that enslavement of Africans made possible.

Slavery and the Law

Centuries before the voyages of Columbus, Spain had enacted *Las Siete Partidas*, a series of laws granting enslaved people certain rights relating to marriage, the holding of property, and access to freedom. These laws were transferred to Spain's American empire. They were often violated, but nonetheless enslaved people used them to claim rights under the law. Moreover, the Catholic Church often encouraged slaveholders to free individual slaves, and military service was at times a route to freedom for enslaved men. The law of slavery in English North America would become far more repressive than in the Spanish empire, especially on the all-important question of whether avenues existed by which slaves could obtain freedom.

For much of the seventeenth century, however, the line between slavery and freedom in the English mainland colonies was more permeable than it would later become. Although seventeenth-century Black arrivals were treated as slaves, at least some managed to become free after serving a term of years. To be sure, racial distinctions were enacted into law from the outset and generally were stricter than in French, Spanish, and Dutch colonies. As early as the 1620s, the law barred Black men from serving in the Virginia militia. The government punished sexual relations outside of marriage between Africans and Europeans more severely than the same acts involving two white persons. In 1643, a poll tax (a tax levied on individuals) was imposed on African but not white women. In both Virginia and Maryland, however, free Black men could sue and testify in court, and some even managed to acquire land and purchase white servants or African slaves. Anthony Johnson, who apparently arrived in Virginia as a slave during the 1620s, obtained his freedom and by the 1640s was

In *Free Women of Color with Their Children and Servants in a Landscape*, Agostino Brunias, an Italian artist who was sent to the West Indies by the British government in the 1760s to paint the local population, portrays an outing of fashionable free women with their children and slaves, some dressed in livery. Although the scene depicted is in the Caribbean, the work resembles numerous paintings of the leisure activities of the well-to-do in Britain. The painting reflects the three-race system that developed in the British Caribbean—the free women are light-skinned but not considered white. The woman at the center looks directly at the viewer, emphasizing her aristocratic bearing.

the owner of slaves and of several hundred acres of land on Virginia's eastern shore. Blacks and whites labored side by side in the tobacco fields, sometimes ran away together, and established intimate relationships.

The Rise of Chesapeake Slavery

Evidence of Blacks being enslaved for life appears in the historical record of the 1640s. In registers of property, for example, white servants are listed by the number of years of labor, while Blacks, with higher valuations, have no terms of service associated with their names. Not until the 1660s, however, did the laws of Virginia and Maryland refer explicitly to slavery. As tobacco planting spread and the demand for labor increased, the condition of Black and white servants diverged sharply. Authorities sought to improve the status of white servants, hoping to counteract the widespread impression in England that Virginia was a death trap. At the same time, access to freedom for Blacks receded.

A Virginia law of 1662 provided that in the case of a child of a free person and a slave, the status of the offspring followed that of the mother. This provision not only reversed the European practice of defining a child's status through the father but also made the sexual abuse of enslaved women profitable for slaveholders, since any children that resulted remained the owner's property. In 1667, the Virginia House of Burgesses decreed that religious conversion did not release a slave from bondage. Thus, Christians could own other Christians as slaves. Moreover, authorities sought to prevent the growth of the free Black population by defining all offspring of interracial relationships as illegitimate, severely punishing white women who begat children with Black men, and prohibiting the freeing of any slave unless he or she was transported out of the colony. By 1680, even though the Black population was still small, notions of racial difference were well entrenched in the law. In England's American empire, wrote one contemporary, "these two words, Negro and Slave [have] by custom grown homogenous and convertible." In British North America, unlike the Spanish empire, no distinctive mixed-race class existed; the law treated everyone with African ancestry as Black.

Bacon's Rebellion: Land and Labor in Virginia

Virginia's shift from white indentured servants to African slaves as the main plantation labor force was accelerated by one of the most dramatic confrontations of this era, **Bacon's Rebellion** of 1676. Governor William Berkeley had for thirty years run a corrupt regime in alliance with an inner circle of the colony's wealthiest tobacco planters. He rewarded his followers with land grants and lucrative offices. At first, Virginia's tobacco boom had benefited not only planters but also smaller farmers, some of them former servants who managed to acquire farms. But as tobacco farming spread inland, planters connected with the governor engrossed the best lands, leaving freed servants (a growing population, since Virginia's death rate was finally falling) with no options but to work as tenants or to move to the frontier. At the same time, heavy taxes on tobacco and falling prices because of overproduction reduced the prospects of small farmers. By the 1670s, poverty among whites had reached levels reminiscent of England. In addition, the right to vote, previously enjoyed by all adult men, was confined to landowners in 1670. Governor Berkeley maintained peaceful relations with Virginia's Native population. His refusal to encourage white settlement on Native land bordering Virginia angered many land-hungry colonists.

In 1676, long-simmering social tensions coupled with widespread resentment against the Berkeley regime erupted in Bacon's Rebellion. The spark was a confrontation between colonists and Doeg and Susquehannock Indians. Settlers demanded that the governor authorize the extermination or removal of Indians on the colony's borders to open more land for whites. Fearing all-out warfare and continuing to profit from the deerskin trade, Berkeley refused. An uprising followed, beginning with Bacon's unauthorized and shocking massacre of Occaneechi allies of Virginia. It quickly grew into a full-fledged rebellion against Berkeley and his system of rule.

To some extent, Bacon's Rebellion was a conflict within the Virginia elite. The leader, Nathaniel Bacon, a wealthy and ambitious planter who had arrived in Virginia in 1673, disdained Berkeley's coterie as men of "mean education and employments." His backers included men of wealth outside the governor's circle of cronies. But Bacon's call for the removal of all Indians from the colony, a reduction of taxes at a time of economic recession, and an end to rule by "grandees" rapidly gained support from small farmers, landless men, indentured servants, and even some Africans. The bulk of his army consisted of discontented men who had recently been servants.

The End of the Rebellion and Its Consequences

Bacon promised freedom (including access to Indian lands) to all who joined his ranks. His supporters invoked the tradition of "English liberties" and spoke of the poor being "robbed" and "cheated" by their social superiors. In 1676, Bacon gathered an armed force for an unauthorized and indiscriminate campaign against those he called the governor's "protected and darling Indians." He refused Berkeley's order to disband and marched on Jamestown, burning it to the ground. The governor fled, and Bacon became the ruler of Virginia. His forces plundered the estates of Berkeley's supporters. Only the arrival of a squadron of warships from England restored order. Bacon's Rebellion was over.

Twenty-three of his supporters were hanged (Bacon himself had taken ill and died shortly after Berkeley's departure).

The specter of a civil war among whites greatly frightened Virginia's ruling elite, who took dramatic steps to consolidate their power and improve their image. They restored property qualifications for voting, which Bacon had rescinded. At the same time, planters developed a new political style in which they cultivated the support of poorer neighbors. Meanwhile, the authorities reduced taxes and began granting fifty acres of land to servants who completed their indentures.

Sir William Berkeley, governor of colonial Virginia, 1641–1652 and 1660–1677. Berkeley's authoritarian rule helped to spark Bacon's Rebellion.

English colonists united to expand their own freedoms at the expense of others. A more aggressive Indian policy took lands from Native peoples on Virginia's borders and gave them to landless

MARYLAND ACT CONCERNING NEGROES AND OTHER SLAVES (1664)

Like Virginia, Maryland in the 1660s enacted laws to clarify questions arising from the growing importance of slavery. This law made all Black servants in the colony slaves for life, and required a white woman who married an enslaved man to serve her husband's owner.

Be it enacted by the Right Honorable the Lord Proprietary by the advice and consent of the upper and lower house of this present General Assembly, that all Negroes or other slaves already within the province, and all Negroes and other slaves to be hereafter imported into the province, shall serve durante vita [for life]. And all children born of any Negro or other slave shall be slaves as their fathers were, for the term of their lives.

And forasmuch as divers freeborn English women, forgetful of their free condition and to the disgrace of our nation, marry Negro slaves, by which also divers suits may arise touching the issue [children] of such women, and a great damage befalls the masters of such Negroes for prevention whereof, for deterring such freeborn women from such shameful matches. Be it further enacted by the authority, advice, and consent aforesaid, that whatsoever freeborn woman shall marry any slave from and after the last day of this present Assembly shall serve the master of such slave during the life of her husband. And that all the issue of such freeborn women so married shall be slaves as their fathers were. And be it further enacted, that all the issues of English or other freeborn women that have already married Negroes shall serve the masters of their parents till they be thirty years of age and no longer.

LETTER BY AN INDENTURED SERVANT
(MARCH 20, 1623)

Only a minority of emigrants from Europe to the English colonies were fully free. Indentured servants were men and women who surrendered their freedom for a specified period of time in exchange for passage to the Americas. This letter that Richard Frethorne sent from Virginia to his parents in England expresses complaints voiced by many indentured servants.

LOVING AND KIND FATHER AND MOTHER:

My most humble duty remembered to you, hoping in god of your good health, as I myself am. . . . This is to let you understand that I your child am in a most heavy case by reason of the country, [which] is such that it causeth much sickness, [such] as the scurvy and the bloody flux and divers [many] other diseases, which maketh the body very poor and weak. And when we are sick there is nothing to comfort us; for since I came out of the ship I never ate anything but peas, and loblollie (that is, water gruel). As for deer or venison I never saw any since I came into this land. . . . And I have nothing to comfort me, nor is there nothing to be gotten here but sickness and death, except [in the event] that one had money to lay out in some things for profit. But I have nothing at all—no, not a shirt to my back but two rags, nor clothes but one poor suit, nor but one pair of shoes, but one pair of stockings, but one cap, [and] but two bands [collars]. . . .

And indeed so I find it now, to my great grief and misery; and [I] saith that if you love me you will redeem me suddenly, for which I do entreat and beg. And if you cannot get the merchants to redeem me for some little money . . . Wherefore, for God's sake, pity me. I pray you to remember my love to all my friends and kindred. I hope all my brothers and sisters are in good health, and as for my part I have set down my resolution that certainly will be; that is, that the answer of this letter will be life or death to me.

ROT
Richard Frethorne

QUESTIONS

1. *What does the Maryland law tell us about how the consolidation of slavery affected ideas about racial difference?*

2. *What reasons does Richard Frethorne give for wanting his parents to "redeem" him (that is, pay off his indenture)?*

3. *What do these documents suggest about the limits of freedom in early colonial America?*

white Virginians, many of whom prospered from a rise in tobacco prices after 1680. To avert the further growth of a rebellious population of landless former indentured servants, Virginia's authorities accelerated the shift to slaves (who would never become free) on the tobacco plantations.

A Slave Society

Between 1680 and 1700, slave labor began to supplant indentured servitude on Chesapeake plantations. Bacon's Rebellion was only one among several factors that contributed to this development. As the death rate finally began to fall, it became more economical to purchase a laborer for life. Improving conditions in England reduced the number of transatlantic migrants, and the opening of Pennsylvania, where land was readily available, attracted those who still chose to leave for America. Finally, the ending of a monopoly on the English slave trade previously held by the Royal African Company opened the door to other traders and reduced the price of imported African slaves.

By 1700, Blacks constituted more than 10 percent of Virginia's population. Fifty years later, they made up nearly half. Recognizing the growing importance of slavery, the House of Burgesses in 1705 enacted a new slave code, bringing together the scattered legislation of the previous century and adding new provisions that embedded the principle of white supremacy in the law. Slaves were property, completely subject to the will of their enslavers and, more generally, of the white community. They could be bought and sold, leased, fought over in court, and passed on to descendants. Henceforth, Blacks and whites were tried in separate courts. No Black person, free or enslaved, could own arms, strike a white man, or employ a white servant. Any white person could stop any Black to demand a certificate of freedom or a pass giving permission to be off the plantation. Virginia had changed from a "society with slaves," in which slavery was one system of labor among others, to a "slave society," where slavery stood at the center of the economic process.

Notions of Freedom

Throughout history, enslaved men and women have run away and in other ways resisted bondage. They did the same in the colonial Chesapeake. Colonial newspapers were filled with advertisements for runaway slaves. These notices described the appearance and skills of the person and included such comments as "ran away without any cause" or "he has great notions of freedom." Some of the Blacks brought to the region during the seventeenth century were the offspring of sex between European traders and Africans on the western coast of Africa or the Caribbean. Familiar with European culture and fluent in English, they turned to the colonial legal system in their quest for freedom. Throughout the seventeenth century, Blacks appeared in court claiming their liberty, at first on the basis of conversion to Christianity or having a white father. This was one reason Virginia in the 1660s closed these pathways to freedom. But although legal avenues to liberty receded, the desire for freedom did not. After the suppression of a slave conspiracy in 1709, Alexander Spotswood, the governor of Virginia, warned planters to be vigilant. The desire for freedom, he reminded them, can "call together all those who long to shake off the fetters of slavery."

COLONIES IN CRISIS

King Philip's War of 1675–1676 and Bacon's Rebellion the following year coincided with disturbances in other colonies. In Maryland, where the proprietor, Lord Baltimore, in 1670 suddenly restricted the right to vote to owners of fifty acres of land or a certain amount of personal property, a Protestant uprising unsuccessfully sought to oust his government and restore the suffrage for all freemen. As the English colonies grew in population, wars broke out with their Native allies as the balance of power shifted and with Native nations on their borders, as settlers squatted on Native hunting and gathering lands. The Pueblo Revolt in 1680 (discussed in Chapter 1) indicated that the crisis of colonial authority was not confined to the British empire.

The Glorious Revolution

Turmoil in England also reverberated in the colonies. In 1688, the long struggle for domination of English government between Parliament and the crown reached its culmination in the **Glorious Revolution**, which established parliamentary supremacy once and for all and secured the Protestant succession to the throne. Under Charles II, Parliament had increased its authority, but when he died in 1685, he was succeeded by his brother James II (formerly the duke of York), a practicing Catholic and a believer that kings ruled by divine right. In 1687, James decreed religious toleration for both Protestant Dissenters and Catholics. The following year, the birth of James's son raised the prospect of a Catholic succession, alarming those who equated "popery" with tyranny. A group of English aristocrats invited the Dutch nobleman William of Orange to assume the throne with his wife, James's Protestant daughter Mary, in the name of English liberties. William arrived in England in November 1688 with an army of 21,000 men, two-thirds of them Dutch. As the landed elite and leaders of the Anglican Church rallied to William and Mary's cause, James II fled and the revolution was complete.

Unlike the broad social upheaval that marked the English Civil War of the 1640s, the Glorious Revolution was in effect a coup engineered by a small group of aristocrats in alliance. They had no intention of challenging the institution of the monarchy. But the overthrow of James II entrenched more firmly than ever the notion that liberty was the birthright of all Englishmen and that the king was subject to the rule of law. To justify the ouster of James II, Parliament in 1689 enacted an **English Bill of Rights**, which listed parliamentary powers such as control over taxation as well as rights of individuals, including trial by jury. These were the "ancient" and "undoubted . . . rights and liberties" of all Englishmen. In the following year, the Toleration Act allowed Protestant Dissenters (but not Catholics) to worship freely, although only Anglicans could hold public office.

As always, English politics were mirrored in the American colonies. After the Glorious Revolution, Protestant domination was secured in most of the colonies, with the established churches of England (Anglican) and Scotland (Presbyterian) growing the fastest, while Catholics and Dissenters suffered various forms of discrimination. Despite the new regime's language of liberty, however, religious freedom was far more advanced in some American colonies, such as Rhode Island, Pennsylvania, and Carolina, than in England. Nonetheless, throughout English America the Glorious Revolution powerfully reinforced among the colonists the sense of sharing a proud legacy of freedom and Protestantism with England.

The Glorious Revolution in America

The Glorious Revolution exposed fault lines in colonial society and offered local elites an opportunity to regain authority that had recently been challenged. Until the mid-1670s, the North American colonies had essentially governed themselves, with little interference from England. Governor Berkeley ran Virginia as he saw fit; proprietors in New York, Maryland, and Carolina governed in any fashion they could persuade colonists to accept; and New England colonies elected their own officials and openly flouted trade regulations. In 1675, England established the **Lords of Trade** to oversee colonial affairs. Three years later, the Lords questioned the Massachusetts government about its compliance with the Navigation Acts. They received the surprising reply that since the colony had no representatives in Parliament, the acts did not apply to it unless the Massachusetts General Court approved.

In the 1680s, England moved to reduce colonial autonomy. Shortly before his death, Charles II revoked the Massachusetts charter, citing wholesale violations of the Navigation Acts. Hoping to raise more money from America in order to reduce his dependence on Parliament, James II between 1686 and 1689 combined Connecticut, Plymouth, Massachusetts, New Hampshire, Rhode Island, New York, and East and West Jersey into a single super-colony, the **Dominion of New England**. It was ruled by the former New York governor Sir Edmund Andros, who did not have to answer to an elected assembly. These events reinforced the impression that James II was an enemy of freedom. In New England, Andros's actions alienated nearly everyone not dependent on his administration for favors. He appointed local officials in place of elected ones, imposed taxes without the approval of elected representatives, declared earlier land grants void unless approved by him, and enforced religious toleration for all Protestants. His rule threatened both English liberties and the church-state relationship at the heart of the Puritan order.

Colonial Uprisings

In 1689, news of the overthrow of James II triggered rebellions in several American colonies. In April, the Boston militia seized and jailed Edmund Andros and other officials, whereupon the New England colonies reestablished the governments abolished when the Dominion of New England was created. In May, a rebel militia headed by Captain Jacob Leisler established a Committee of Safety and took control of New York. Two months later, Maryland's Protestant Association overthrew the government of the colony's Catholic proprietor, Lord Baltimore.

All of these new regimes claimed to have acted in the name of English liberties and looked to London for approval. But the degrees of success of these coups varied markedly. Most triumphant were the Maryland rebels. Concluding that Lord Baltimore had mismanaged the colony, William and Mary revoked his charter (although the proprietor retained his land and rents) and established a new, Protestant-dominated government. Catholics retained the right to practice their religion but were barred from voting and holding office. In 1715, after the Baltimore family had converted to Anglicanism, proprietary power was restored. But the events of 1689 transformed the ruling group in Maryland and put an end to the colony's unique history of religious toleration.

The outcome in New York was far different. The German-born Leisler, one of the wealthiest merchants in the city, was a fervent Calvinist who feared that James II intended to reduce England and its empire to "popery and slavery." Although it was not his intention, Leisler's regime divided the colony along ethnic and economic lines. Members of the Dutch majority seized the opportunity to reclaim local power after more than two decades of English rule, while bands of rebels ransacked the homes of wealthy New Yorkers. Prominent English colonists, joined by some wealthy Dutch merchants and fur traders, protested to London that Leisler was a tyrant. William and Mary refused to recognize Leisler's authority and dispatched a new governor, backed by troops. Many of Leisler's followers were imprisoned, and he himself was condemned to be executed. The grisly manner of his death—Leisler was hanged and then had his head cut off and body cut into four parts—reflected the depths of hatred the rebellion had inspired. For generations, the rivalry between Leisler and anti-Leisler parties polarized New York politics.

Changes in New England

After deposing Governor Andros, the New England colonies lobbied hard in London for the restoration of their original charters. Most were successful, but Massachusetts was not. In 1691, the crown issued a new charter that absorbed Plymouth into Massachusetts and transformed the political structure of the Bible Commonwealth. Town government remained intact, but henceforth property ownership, not church membership, would be the requirement to vote in elections for the General Court. The governor was now appointed in London rather than elected. Thus, Massachusetts became a royal colony, the majority of whose voters were no longer Puritan "saints." Moreover, it was required to abide by the **English Toleration Act** of 1689—that is, to allow all Protestants to worship freely. The demise of the "New England way" greatly benefited non-Puritan merchants and large landowners, who came to dominate the new government.

These events produced an atmosphere of considerable tension in Massachusetts, exacerbated by raids by allied Native and French fighters on the northern border of New England. The advent of religious toleration heightened anxieties among the Puritan clergy, who considered other Protestant denominations a form of heresy. "I would not have a hand in setting up their Devil worship," one minister declared of the Quakers. Indeed, quite a few Puritans thought they saw the hand of Satan in the events of 1690 and 1691.

The Prosecution of Witches

Belief in magic, astrology, and witchcraft was widespread in seventeenth-century Europe and America, existing alongside the religion of the clergy and churches. Many Puritans believed in supernatural interventions in the affairs of the world. They interpreted as expressions of God's will such events as lightning that struck one house but spared another, and epidemics that reduced the population of their Native enemies. Evil forces could also affect daily life. Witches were individuals, usually women, who were accused of having entered into a pact with the devil to obtain supernatural powers, which they used to harm others or to interfere with natural processes. When a child was stillborn or crops failed, many believed that witchcraft was at work.

An engraving from Ralph Gardiner's *England's Grievance Discovered*, published in 1655, depicts women hanged as witches in England. The letters identify local officials: A is the hangman, B the town crier, C the sheriff, and D a magistrate.

In Europe and the colonies, witchcraft was punishable by execution. It is estimated that between the years 1400 and 1800, more than 50,000 people were executed in Europe after being convicted of witchcraft. Witches were, from time to time, hanged in seventeenth-century New England. Most were women beyond childbearing age who were outspoken, economically independent, or estranged from their husbands, or who in other ways violated traditional gender norms. The witch's alleged power challenged both God's will and the standing of men as heads of family and rulers of society.

The Salem Witch Trials

Until 1692, the prosecution of witches had been local and sporadic. But in the heightened anxiety caused by war and religious strife, a series of trials and executions took place in the town of Salem, Massachusetts, that made its name to this day a byword for fanaticism and persecution. The crisis began late in 1691 when several girls began to suffer fits and nightmares, attributed by their elders to witchcraft. Soon, three "witches" had been named, including Tituba, a Native woman from the Caribbean who was enslaved in the home of one of the girls. Since the only way to avoid prosecution was to confess and name others, accusations of witchcraft began to snowball. By the middle of 1692, hundreds of residents of Salem had come forward to accuse their neighbors. Some, it appears, used the occasion to settle old scores within the Salem community. Local authorities took legal action against nearly 150 persons, the large majority of them women. Many confessed to save their lives, but fourteen women and five men were hanged, protesting their innocence to the end. One man was pressed to death (crushed under a weight of stones) for refusing to enter a plea.

In the **Salem witch trials**, accusations of witchcraft spread far beyond the usual profile of middle-aged women to include persons of all ages (one was a child of four) and those with no previous history of assertiveness or marital discord. As accusations and executions multiplied, it became clear that something was seriously wrong with the colony's system of justice. Toward the end of 1692, the governor of Massachusetts dissolved the Salem court and ordered the remaining prisoners released. At the same time, the prominent clergyman Increase Mather published an influential treatise, *Cases of Conscience Concerning Evil Spirits*, warning that juries should not take seriously either the testimony of those who claimed to be possessed or the confessions and accusations of persons facing execution. The events in Salem discredited the tradition of prosecuting witches and accelerated a commitment among prominent colonists to finding scientific explanations for natural events like comets and illnesses, rather than attributing them to magic. In future years, only two accused witches would be brought to trial in Massachusetts, and both were found not guilty.

THE GROWTH OF COLONIAL AMERICA

The Salem witch trials took place precisely two centuries after Columbus's initial voyage. In North America, three very different empires had arisen, competing for wealth and power. The urban-based Spanish empire, with a settler elite and growing *mestizo* population directing a large Native labor force, still relied for wealth primarily on the gold and silver mines of Mexico and South America. The French empire centered on Saint Domingue, Martinique, and Guadeloupe, plantation islands of the West Indies. On the mainland, it consisted of a thinly settled string of farms and trading posts in the St. Lawrence Valley. In North America north of the Rio Grande, the English claimed less land than their rivals but outpaced them in population.

As stability returned after the crises of the late seventeenth century, English North America experienced an era of remarkable growth. Between 1700 and 1770, crude backwoods settlements became bustling provincial capitals. The hazards of starvation and disease among colonists diminished, agricultural settlement pressed westward, and hundreds of thousands of newcomers arrived from Europe. Thanks to a high birthrate and continuing immigration, the population of England's mainland colonies, 265,000 in 1700, grew nearly tenfold, to over 2.3 million seventy years later. At the same time, in places where Europeans brought war, enslavement, and destruction of natural resources, Native populations declined, directly because of Europeans or indirectly from their diseases. When Native people had time to recover from diseases, the effects were manageable, but when disease was accompanied by intensive colonization, the effects were catastrophic. In 1700, Native Americans still outnumbered Europeans in North America, but over the course of the next century, the population of English colonies would outstrip everyone else.

A Diverse Population

Probably the most striking characteristic of eighteenth-century British colonial society was its diversity. In 1700, the colonies were essentially English outposts. Relatively few Africans had yet been brought to the mainland, and the overwhelming majority of the white population—close to 90 percent—was of English origin. In the eighteenth century, African and non-English European arrivals skyrocketed, while the number emigrating from England declined.

As economic conditions in England improved, the government began to rethink the policy of encouraging emigration. No longer concerned with an excess population of vagabonds and "masterless men," authorities began to worry that large-scale emigration was draining labor from the mother country. About 40 percent of European immigrants to the colonies during the eighteenth

TABLE 3.1 Origins of Free and Unfree Newcomers to British North American Colonies, 1700–1775

	Total	Slaves	Indentured Servants	Convicts	Free
Africa	278,400	278,400	—	—	—
Ireland	108,600	—	39,000	17,500	52,100
Germany	84,500	—	30,000	—	54,500
England/ Wales	73,100	—	27,200	32,500	13,400
Scotland	35,300	—	7,400	2,200	25,700
Other	5,900	—	—	—	5,900
TOTAL	**585,800**	**278,400**	**103,600**	**52,200**	**151,600**

century continued to arrive as bound laborers who had temporarily sacrificed their freedom to make the voyage to the Americas. But as the colonial economy prospered, poor indentured migrants were increasingly joined by professionals and skilled craftsmen—teachers, ministers, weavers, carpenters—whom England could ill afford to lose. This brought to an end official efforts to promote English emigration.

Attracting Settlers

Yet while worrying about losing desirable members of its population, the government in London remained convinced that colonial development enhanced the nation's power and wealth. To bolster the Chesapeake labor force, nearly 50,000 convicts (a group not desired in Britain) were sent to work in the tobacco fields. Officials also actively encouraged Protestant immigration from the non-English (and less prosperous) parts of the British Isles and from the European continent, promising newcomers easy access to land and the right to worship freely. A law of 1740 even offered European immigrants British citizenship after seven years of residence, something that in England could be obtained only by a special act of Parliament. The widely publicized image of America as an asylum for those "whom bigots chase from foreign lands," in the words of a 1735 poem, was in many ways a by-product of Britain's efforts to attract settlers from non-English areas to its colonies.

Among eighteenth-century migrants from the British Isles, the 80,000 English newcomers (a majority of them convicted criminals) were considerably outnumbered by 145,000 from Scotland and Ulster, the northern part of Ireland, where many Scots had settled as part of England's effort to subdue the island. Scottish and Scots-Irish immigrants had a profound impact on colonial society. Mostly Presbyterians, they added significantly to religious diversity in North America. Their numbers included not only poor farmers seeking land but also numerous merchants, teachers, and professionals (indeed, a large majority of the physicians in eighteenth-century America were of Scottish origin).

The German Migration

Germans, 110,000 in all, formed the largest group of newcomers from the European continent. Most came from the valley of the Rhine River, which stretches through present-day Germany into Switzerland. In the eighteenth century, Germany was divided into numerous small states, each with a ruling prince who determined the official religion. Those who found themselves worshiping the "wrong" religion—Lutherans in Catholic areas, Catholics in Lutheran areas, and everywhere, followers of small Protestant sects such as Mennonites, Moravians, and Dunkers—faced persecution. Many decided to emigrate. Other

DIVERSITY IN THE EUROPEAN SETTLEMENTS, ATLANTIC COAST OF NORTH AMERICA, 1760

Legend:
- English
- French
- German
- Dutch
- Africans
- Scots-Irish
- Highland Scots
- J Jews
- S Swedes
- W Welsh
- F French Huguenots

Among the most striking features of eighteenth-century British colonial society was the racial and ethnic diversity of the population (except in New England). This resulted from increased immigration from the non-English parts of the British Isles and from mainland Europe, as well as the rapid expansion of the slave trade from Africa. Also note how little of the continent Europeans possessed in 1760, after nearly two centuries of colonial attempts.

migrants were motivated by persistent agricultural crises and the difficulty of acquiring land. Indeed, the emigration to America represented only a small part of a massive reshuffling of the German population within Europe. Millions of Germans left their homes during the eighteenth century, most of them migrating eastward to Austria-Hungary and the Russian empire, which made land available to newcomers.

Wherever they moved, Germans tended to travel in entire families. English and Dutch merchants created a well-organized system whereby **redemptioners** (as indentured families were called) received passage in exchange for a promise to work off their debt in America. Most settled in frontier areas—rural New York, western Pennsylvania, and the southern backcountry—where they formed tightly knit farming communities in which German for many years remained the dominant language. Their arrival greatly enhanced the ethnic and religious diversity of Britain's colonies.

Religious Diversity

Eighteenth-century British America was not a "melting pot" of cultures. Ethnic groups tended to live and worship in relatively homogeneous communities. But outside of New England, which received few immigrants and retained its overwhelmingly English ethnic character, American society had a far more diverse population than Britain. Nowhere was this more evident than in the practice of religion. In 1700, nearly all the churches in the colonies were either Congregational (in New England) or Anglican. In the eighteenth century, the Anglican presence expanded considerably. But the number of Dissenting congregations also multiplied.

Apart from New Jersey, Rhode Island, and Pennsylvania, the colonies did not adhere to a modern separation of church and state. Nearly every colony levied taxes to pay the salaries of ministers of an established church, and most barred Catholics and Jews from voting and holding public office. But increasingly, de facto toleration among Protestant denominations flourished, fueled by the establishment of new churches by immigrants, as well as new Baptist, Methodist, and other congregations created as a result of the Great Awakening, a religious revival that will be discussed in Chapter 4. By the mid-eighteenth century, Dissenting Protestants in most colonies had gained the right to worship as they pleased and own their churches, although many places still barred them from holding public office and taxed them to support the official church. Although few in number (perhaps 2,000 at their peak in eighteenth-century America), Jews also contributed to the religious diversity. German Jews, in particular, were attracted by the chance to escape the rigid religious restrictions of German-speaking parts of Europe; many immigrated to London and some,

From BENJAMIN FRANKLIN, *OBSERVATIONS CONCERNING THE INCREASE OF MANKIND* (1751)

Only a minority of immigrants from Europe to British North America in the eighteenth century came from the British Isles. Some prominent colonists found the growing diversity of the population quite disturbing. Benjamin Franklin was particularly troubled by the large influx of newcomers from Germany into Pennsylvania in the mid-eighteenth century.

Why should the Palatine [German] boors be suffered to swarm into our settlements, and by herding together establish their language and manners to the exclusion of ours? Why should Pennsylvania, founded by the English, become a Colony of *Aliens*, who will shortly be so numerous as to Germanize us instead of our Anglifying them, and will never adopt our language or customs, any more than they can acquire our complexion?

Which leads me to add one remark: That the number of purely white people in the world is proportionably very small. All Africa is black or tawny. Asia chiefly tawny. America (exclusive of the newcomers) wholly so. And in Europe, the Spaniards, Italians, French, Russians and Swedes, are generally of what we call a swarthy complexion; as are the Germans also, the Saxons only excepted, who with the English, make the principal body of white people on the face of the earth. I could wish their numbers were increased. And while we are, as I may call it, *scouring* our planet, by clearing America of woods, and so making this side of our globe reflect a brighter light to the eyes of inhabitants in Mars or Venus, why should we . . . darken its people? Why increase the sons of Africa, by planting them in America, where we have so fair an opportunity, by excluding all Blacks and Tawneys, of increasing the lovely White and Red? But perhaps I am partial to the complexion of my country, for such kind of partiality is natural to mankind.

QUESTIONS

1. *What is Franklin's objection to the growing German presence?*

2. *What does Franklin's characterization of the complexions of various groups suggest about the reliability of his perceptions of non-English peoples?*

from there, to Charleston and Philadelphia. A visitor to Pennsylvania in 1750 described the colony's religious diversity: "We find there Lutherans, Reformed, Catholics, Quakers, Menonists or Anabaptists, Herrnhuters or Moravian Brethren, Pietists, Seventh Day Baptists, Dunkers, Presbyterians, . . . Jews, Mohammedans, Pagans."

"Liberty of conscience," wrote a German newcomer in 1739, was the "chief virtue" of British North America, "and on this score I do not repent my immigration." Equally important to eighteenth-century immigrants, however, were other elements of freedom, especially the availability of land, the lack of a military draft, and the absence of restraints on economic opportunity common in Europe. Skilled workers were in great demand. "They earn what they want," one immigrant wrote to his brother in Switzerland in 1733. Letters home by immigrants spoke of low taxes, the right to enter trades and professions without paying exorbitant fees, and freedom of movement. "In this country," one wrote, "there are abundant liberties in just about all matters."

Native-Colonial Relations

The tide of newcomers, who equated liberty with possession of land, threatened to engulf Native nations on the Atlantic coast. By the eighteenth century, Native people were well integrated into global trade networks, and those who lived near colonial populations had established direct economic and diplomatic connections with Europeans. New confederacies, including the Catawbas of South Carolina and the Muscogee (Creek) Confederacy to the west of South Carolina and Georgia, united formerly independent towns and also absorbed Indigenous refugees from colonial wars. Few Indians chose to live among whites rather than in their own communities, even if preserving their independence from colonists required moving their towns farther away and becoming more interdependent with selected other Native peoples. In the 1690s, for example, Shawnees fleeing Haudenosaunee and Chickasaw raids in the Ohio Valley accepted an invitation by Delaware Indians to move onto their lands along the Delaware and Susquehanna rivers. In the 1720s and 1730s, when English, German, and Scots-Irish immigrants flooded into Pennsylvania onto those same lands, Shawnees and Delawares gradually moved upriver to preserve their independence from both the Pennsylvanians and the Haudenosaunee, who claimed them as their subordinate allies. Eventually, the Shawnees moved back to their old Ohio Valley homeland, inviting the Delawares to join them.

Like many other Native peoples in the eighteenth century, the Delawares had built strong economic and diplomatic relationships with colonies, only to be undermined by the large numbers of immigrants pushing west.

In 1734, representatives of the Muscogee (Creek) Confederacy traveled to London to conduct diplomacy with British King George II and other officials, including the trustees of the colony of Georgia, pictured in this painting. Included in the Muscogee delegation are Chief Tomochichi, his wife Senawchi, and a Muscogee boy in the center. The eagle in the bottom right corner was a gift from the Muscogees to the king.

While European traders saw potential profits in Native towns, nations, and confederacies, and British officials saw allies against France and Spain, farmers and planters viewed Indians as little more than an obstacle to their desire for land. The infamous **Walking Purchase** of 1737 brought the fraudulent dealing so common in other colonies to Pennsylvania. Colonists pressured Delawares into agreeing to an arrangement to cede a tract of land bounded by the distance a man could walk in thirty-six hours. To their amazement, Governor James Logan hired a team of swift runners, who marked out an area far in excess of what the Indians had anticipated.

By 1760, when Pennsylvania's population, a mere 20,000 in 1700, had grown to 220,000, Native-colonist relations, initially the most harmonious in British North America, had become poisoned by suspicion and hostility. One group of Susquehannas declared "that the white people had abused them and taken their lands from them, and therefore they had no reason to think that they were now concerned for their happiness." They pointedly reminded Pennsylvanians that "old William Penn" treated them with fairness and respect.

Regional Diversity

By the mid-eighteenth century, the different regions of the British colonies had developed distinct economic and social orders. Small farms tilled by family labor and geared primarily to production for local consumption predominated in New England and the new settlements of the **backcountry** (the area stretching from central Pennsylvania southward through the Shenandoah Valley of Virginia and into upland North and South Carolina). The backcountry was the most rapidly growing region in North America. In 1730, the only white residents in what was then Indian country were the occasional hunter and trader. By the eve of the American Revolution, the region contained one-quarter of Virginia's population and half of South Carolina's. Most were farm families raising grain and livestock, but slaveowning planters, seeking fertile soil for tobacco farming, also entered the area.

In the older portions of the Middle Colonies of New York, New Jersey, and Pennsylvania, farmers were more oriented to commerce than on the frontier, growing grain both for their own use and for sale abroad and supplementing the work of family members by employing wage laborers, tenants, and in some instances slaves. Because large landlords had engrossed so much desirable land, New York's growth lagged behind that of neighboring colonies. "What man will be such a fool as to become a base tenant," wondered Richard Coote, New York's governor at the beginning of the eighteenth century, "when by crossing the Hudson river that man can for a song purchase a good freehold?" With its fertile soil, favorable climate, initially peaceful Indian relations, generous governmental land distribution policy, and rivers that facilitated long-distance trading, Pennsylvania came to be known as "the best poor man's country." Ordinary colonists there enjoyed a standard of living unimaginable in Europe.

The Consumer Revolution

During the eighteenth century, Great Britain eclipsed the Dutch as the leading producer and trader of inexpensive consumer goods, including colonial products like coffee and tea, and such manufactured goods as linen, metalware, pins, ribbons, glassware, ceramics, and clothing. Trade integrated the British empire. As the American colonies were drawn more and more fully into the system of Atlantic commerce, they shared in the era's consumer revolution. In port cities and small inland towns, shops proliferated and American newspapers were filled with advertisements for British goods. British merchants supplied American traders with loans to enable them to import these products, and traveling peddlers carried them into remote frontier areas.

Consumerism in a modern sense—the mass production, advertising, and sale of consumer goods—did not exist in colonial America. Nonetheless, eighteenth-century estate inventories—records of people's possessions at the time of death—revealed the wide dispersal in American homes of European and even Asian products. In the seventeenth century, most colonists had lived in a pioneer world of homespun clothing and homemade goods. Now, even modest farmers and artisans owned books, ceramic plates, metal cutlery, and items made of imported silk and cotton. Tea, once a luxury enjoyed only by the wealthy, became virtually a necessity of life.

This 1772 broadside offers a rare view of the interior of a Philadelphia shop and lists some of the many European and West Indian goods on sale, including rum, tea, spices, and gunpowder—a sign of the ongoing consumer revolution linked to international trade.

Colonial Cities

Britain's mainland colonies were overwhelmingly agricultural. Nine-tenths of the population resided in rural areas and made their livelihood from farming. Colonial cities like Boston, New York, Philadelphia, and Charleston were quite small by the standards of Europe or Spanish America. In 1700, when the population of Mexico City stood at 100,000, Boston had 6,000 residents and New York 4,500. As late as 1750, eight cities in Spanish America exceeded in size any in English North America.

English American cities served mainly as gathering places for agricultural goods and for imported items to be distributed to the countryside. Nonetheless, the expansion of trade encouraged the rise of port cities, home to a growing population of colonial merchants and artisans (skilled craftsmen) as well as an increasing number of poor. In 1770, with some 30,000 inhabitants, Philadelphia was, after London and Liverpool, the empire's third-busiest port. The financial, commercial, and cultural center of British America, its growth rested on economic integration with the rich agricultural region nearby. Philadelphia merchants organized the collection of farm goods, supplied rural storekeepers, and extended credit to consumers. They exported flour, bread, and meat to the West Indies and Europe.

Colonial Artisans

Cities were also home to a large population of furniture makers, jewelers, and silversmiths serving wealthier citizens, and hundreds of lesser artisans like weavers, blacksmiths, coopers, and construction workers. The typical artisan owned his own tools and labored in a small workshop, often his home, assisted by family members and young journeymen and apprentices learning the trade. The artisan's skill, which set him apart from the common laborers below him in the social scale, was the key to his existence, and it gave him a far greater degree of economic freedom than those dependent on others for a livelihood. "He that hath a trade, hath an estate," wrote Benjamin Franklin, who had worked as a printer before achieving renown as a scientist and statesman.

Despite the influx of British goods, colonial craftsmen benefited from the expanding consumer market. Most journeymen enjoyed a reasonable chance of rising to the status of master and establishing a workshop of their own. Some achieved remarkable success. Born in New York City in 1723, Myer Myers, a Jewish silversmith of Dutch ancestry, became one of the city's most prominent artisans. Myers produced jewelry, candlesticks, coffeepots, tableware, and other gold and silver objects for the colony's elite, as well as religious ornaments for both synagogues and Protestant churches. He used some of his profits to acquire land in New Hampshire and Connecticut. Myers's career reflected the opportunities colonial cities offered to skilled men of diverse ethnic and religious backgrounds.

An Atlantic World

People, ideas, and goods flowed back and forth across the Atlantic, knitting together the empire and its diverse populations and creating webs of interdependence among the European empires. Sugar, tobacco, deerskin leather, and other products of the Western Hemisphere were marketed as far away as Eastern Europe. London bankers financed the slave trade between Africa and Portuguese Brazil. Spain spent its gold and silver importing goods from other countries. As trade expanded, the North American and West Indian colonies became a major market. Like colonists, Native Americans bought British manufactured goods in return for furs and deerskins. Although most colonial output was consumed at home, North Americans shipped farm products to Britain, the West Indies, and, with the exception of goods like tobacco "enumerated" under the Navigation Acts, outside the empire. Virtually the entire Chesapeake tobacco crop was marketed in Britain, with most of it then re-exported to Europe by British merchants. Most of the bread and flour exported from the colonies was destined for the West Indies. Africans enslaved there grew sugar that could be distilled into rum, a product increasingly popular in North America. The mainland colonies carried on a flourishing trade in fish and grains with southern Europe. Ships built in New England made up one-third of the British empire's trading fleet.

Membership in the empire had many advantages for the colonists. Most Americans did not complain about British regulation of their trade because commerce enriched the colonies as well as England and lax enforcement of the Navigation Acts allowed smuggling to flourish. In a dangerous world the Royal Navy protected American shipping. Eighteenth-century English America drew closer and closer to, and in some ways became more and more similar to, England itself.

SOCIAL CLASSES IN THE BRITISH COLONIES

The Colonial Elite

Most free Americans benefited from economic growth, but as colonial society matured an elite emerged that, while neither as powerful nor as wealthy as the aristocracy of England, increasingly dominated politics and society. Indeed, the gap between rich and poor probably grew more rapidly in the eighteenth century than in any other period of American history. In New England and the Middle Colonies, expanding trade made possible the emergence of a powerful upper class of merchants, often linked by family or commercial ties to great trading firms in London. There were no banks in colonial America. Credit and money were in short supply, and mercantile success depended on personal connections as much as business talent. By 1750, the Chesapeake and Lower South were dominated by slave plantations producing **staple crops**, especially tobacco and rice, for the world market. Here great planters accumulated enormous wealth from the forced labor of enslaved women and men. The colonial elite also included the rulers of proprietary colonies like Pennsylvania and Maryland.

America had no titled aristocracy as in Britain. It had no system of legally established social ranks or family pedigrees stretching back to medieval times. Apart from the De Lanceys, Livingstons, and van Rensselaers of New York, the Penn family in Pennsylvania, and a few southern planters, it had no one whose landholdings, in monetary value, rivaled those of the British aristocracy. But throughout British America, men of prominence controlled colonial

This portrait of Jane Beekman—daughter of James Beekman, one of the wealthiest colonists—was painted by the artist John Durand in 1767. It is unusual in depicting a young girl with a book (a collection, in Latin, of the works of the Renaissance scholar Erasmus), rather than simply emphasizing fashionable attire. The Beekman family was of Dutch and French Huguenot heritage, and both cultures emphasized the importance of education, including education for women.

government. In Virginia, the upper class was so tight-knit and intermarried so often that the colony was said to be governed by a "cousinocracy." Members of the gentry controlled the vestries, or local governing bodies, of the established Anglican Church, dominated the county courts (political as well as judicial institutions that levied taxes and enacted local ordinances), and were prominent in Virginia's legislature. In the 1750s, seven members of the same generation of the Lee family sat in the House of Burgesses.

Eighteenth-century Virginia was a far healthier environment than in the early days of settlement. Planters could expect to pass their wealth down to the next generation, providing estates for their sons and establishing family dynasties. Nearly every Virginian of note achieved prominence through family connections. The days when self-made men could rise into the Virginia gentry were long gone; by 1770, nearly all upper-class Virginians had inherited their wealth. Thomas Jefferson's grandfather was a justice of the peace (an important local official), militia captain, and sheriff, and his father a member of the House of Burgesses. George Washington's father, grandfather, and great-grandfather had been justices of the peace. The Virginia gentry used its control of provincial government to gain possession of large tracts of land as the colony pushed west onto Native land. Grants of 20,000 to 40,000 acres were not uncommon. Robert "King" Carter, a speaker of the House of Burgesses, acquired 300,000 acres of land and 1,000 slaves by the time of his death in 1732.

Cultures of the Americas

Before the American Revolution, there was no real "American" identity. In the seventeenth century, the term "Americans" tended to be used to describe Indians rather than colonists. Europeans often depicted the colonies pictorially with an image of a Native American. Many European immigrants maintained traditions, including the use of languages other than English, from their home countries. Some cultures mixed more than others: intermarriage with other groups was more common among Huguenots (French Protestants) than among Jews, for example. Those from the British Isles sought to create a dominant "English" identity in the Americas. This involved convincing Britons that the colonists were like themselves.

Many in Great Britain, however, saw the colonists as a collection of convicts, religious dissidents, and impoverished servants. This, in turn, inspired many colonists to assert a claim to Britishness more strongly. They insisted that British identity meant allegiance to certain values, among them free commerce and "English liberty." Yet many colonists saw some people, including American Indians, Africans, and all women, as unable to wield the responsibilities of liberty due to their place of birth, culture, or inborn traits. They must be ruled over, not take part in governance.

British identity in the colonies was defined, in part, in opposition to others, including Spanish and French Catholics, Africans, and Native Americans. As early as the late sixteenth century, in his writings on colonization, Richard Hakluyt wrote that there was "no greater glory" than "to conquer the barbarian, to recall the savage and the pagan to civility, to draw the ignorant within the orbit of reason, and to fill with reverence for divinity the godless and the ungodly." But the colonists did not include Indians or Africans in a collective colonial identity. As noted in Chapter 1, intermarriage and culture exchange between settlers and Indians was far more common in the Spanish and French empires. But in all colonies, men of primarily or exclusively European descent held most of the wealth and power.

Anglicization

For much of the eighteenth century, the British colonies had more regular trade and communications with Britain than among themselves. Elites in different regions slowly developed a common lifestyle and sense of common interests. But rather than thinking of themselves as distinctively American, they became more and more English—a process historians call "Anglicization."

Wealthy colonists tried to model their lives on British etiquette and behavior. Somewhat resentful at living in provincial isolation—"at the end of the world," as one Virginia aristocrat put it—they sought to demonstrate their status and legitimacy by importing the latest London fashions and literature, sending their sons to Britain for education, and building homes equipped with fashionable furnishings modeled on the country estates and town houses of the English gentry. Their residences included large rooms for entertainment, display cases for imported luxury goods, and elaborate formal gardens. Some members of the colonial elite, like George Washington, even had coats of arms designed for their families, in imitation of English upper-class practice.

Desperate to follow an aristocratic lifestyle, many planters fell into debt. William Byrd III of Virginia lived so extravagantly that by 1770 he had accumulated a debt of £100,000, an amount almost unheard of in England or America. But so long as the world market for tobacco thrived, so did Virginia's gentry.

The South Carolina Aristocracy

The richest group of mainland colonists were South Carolina planters (although planters in Jamaica far outstripped them in wealth). Elite South Carolinians often traveled north to enjoy summer vacations in the cooler climate of Newport, Rhode Island, and they spent much of the remainder of their time in Charleston, the only real urban center south of Philadelphia and the richest city in British North America. Here aristocratic social life flourished, centered on theaters, literary societies, and social events. Like their Virginia counterparts, South Carolina grandees lived a lavish lifestyle amid imported furniture, fine wines, silk clothing, and other items from England. They surrounded themselves with house slaves dressed in specially designed uniforms. In 1774, the per capita wealth in the Charleston District was £2,300, more than four times that of tobacco areas in Virginia and eight times the figure for Philadelphia or Boston. But wealth in South Carolina was highly concentrated. The richest 10 percent of the colony owned half the wealth in 1770, the poorest quarter less than 2 percent.

Throughout the colonies, elite men emulated what they saw as England's balanced, stable social order. Liberty, in their eyes, meant, in part, the power to rule—the right of those blessed with wealth and prominence to dominate over others. They viewed society as a hierarchical structure in which some men were endowed with greater talents than others and destined to rule. The social order, they believed, was held together by webs of influence that linked patrons and those dependent on them. Each place in the hierarchy carried with it different responsibilities, and one's status was revealed in dress, manners, and the splendor of one's home. "Superiority" and "dependence," as one colonial newspaper put it, were natural elements of any society. An image of refinement served to legitimize wealth and political power. Colonial elites prided themselves on developing aristocratic manners and cultivating the arts. On both sides of the Atlantic, elites viewed work as something reserved for common folk and slaves. Freedom from labor was the mark of gentlemen and ladies.

Poverty in the Colonies

At the other end of the social scale, poverty emerged as a visible feature of eighteenth-century colonial life. Although not considered by most colonists part of their society, the growing number of slaves lived in impoverished conditions. Among free Americans, poverty was hardly as widespread as in Britain, where in the early part of the century between one-quarter and one-half of the people regularly required public assistance. But as the colonial population expanded, access to land diminished rapidly, especially in long-settled areas. In New England, which received few immigrants, the high birthrate fueled population growth. With the supply of land limited, sons who could not hope to inherit farms were forced to move to other colonies or to try their hand at a trade in the region's towns. By mid-century, tenants and wage laborers were a growing presence on farms in the Middle Colonies. In colonial cities, the number of propertyless wage earners subsisting at the poverty line steadily increased. Taking the colonies as a whole, half of the wealth at mid-century was concentrated in the hands of the richest 10 percent of the population.

Attitudes and policies toward poverty in colonial America mirrored British precedents. The better-off colonists generally viewed the poor as lazy, shiftless, and responsible for their own plight. Both rural communities and cities did accept responsibility for assisting their own. But to minimize the burden on taxpayers, poor persons were frequently set to labor in workhouses, where they produced goods that reimbursed authorities for part of their upkeep. Their children were sent to work as apprentices in local homes or workshops. And most communities adopted stringent measures to "warn out" unemployed and propertyless newcomers who might become dependent on local poor relief. This involved town authorities either expelling the unwanted poor from an area or formally declaring certain persons ineligible for assistance. In Essex County, Massachusetts, the number of poor persons warned out each year rose from 200 in the 1730s to 1,700 in the 1760s. Many were members of families headed by widowed or abandoned women.

The Middle Ranks

The large majority of free Americans lived between the extremes of wealth and poverty. Along with racial and ethnic diversity, what distinguished the mainland colonies from Europe was the wide distribution of land and the economic autonomy of most ordinary free families. The anonymous author of the book *American Husbandry*, published in 1775, reported that "little freeholders who live upon their own property" made up "the most considerable part" of the people, especially in the northern colonies and the nonplantation parts of the South. Altogether, perhaps two-thirds of the free male population were farmers who owned their own land. England, to be sure, had no class of laborers as exploited as American slaves, but three-fifths of its people owned no property at all.

By the eighteenth century, colonial farm families viewed landownership almost as a right, the social precondition of freedom. They strongly resented

The Residence of David Twining, a painting of a Pennsylvania farm as it appeared in the eighteenth century. Edward Hicks, who lived there as a youth, painted the scene from memory in the 1840s. Hicks depicts a prosperous farm, largely self-sufficient but also producing for the market, typical of colonial eastern Pennsylvania. One of the farm workers is a slave. Five-year-old Edward himself is pictured in the lower right-hand corner, listening to Mrs. Twining read the Bible.

efforts, whether by Native Americans, great landlords, or colonial governments, to limit their access to land. A dislike of personal dependence and an understanding of freedom as not relying on others for a livelihood sank deep roots in British North America. These beliefs, after all, accorded with social reality—a wide distribution of property that made economic independence part of the lived experience of large numbers of white colonists.

Women and the Household Economy

In the eighteenth-century British mainland colonies, the family was the center of economic life. Most work revolved around the home, and all members—men, women, and children—contributed to the family's livelihood. The independence of the small farmer depended in considerable measure on the labor of dependent women and children. "He that hath an industrious family shall soon be rich," declared one colonial saying, and the high birthrate in part reflected the need for as many hands as possible on colonial farms. Most farmers concentrated first on growing food for their own consumption and acquiring enough land to pass it along to their sons. But the consumer revolution and expanding networks of Atlantic trade drew increasing numbers of farmers into production for the market as well.

As the population grew and the death rate declined, family life stabilized and more marriages became lifetime commitments. Free women were expected to devote their lives to being good wives and mothers. Already enshrined in law and property relations, male domination took on greater and greater social reality. In several colonies, the law mandated primogeniture—meaning that estates must be passed intact to the oldest son. As colonial society became more structured, coverture was more strictly enforced. In Connecticut, for example, the courts were informal and unorganized in the seventeenth century, and women often represented themselves. In the eighteenth century, it became necessary to hire a lawyer as one's spokesman in court. Women, barred from practicing as attorneys, disappeared from judicial proceedings. Because of the desperate need for labor, men and women in the seventeenth century both did various kinds of work. In the eighteenth century, the division of labor along gender lines solidified. Women's work was clearly defined, including cooking, cleaning, sewing, making butter, and assisting with agricultural chores. Still, women's work remained vital to the economy. The work of farmers' wives and daughters often spelled the difference between a family's self-sufficiency and poverty.

"Women's work is never done." This popular adage was literally true. Even as the consumer revolution reduced the demands on many women by making available store-bought goods previously produced at home, women's work seemed to increase. Lower infant mortality meant more time spent on child care and domestic chores. The demand for new goods increased the need for all family members to contribute to family income. For most women, work was incessant and exhausting. "I am dirty and distressed, almost wearied to death," wrote Mary Cooper, a Long Island woman, in her diary in 1769. "This day," she continued, "is forty years since I left my father's house and come here, and here have I seen little else but hard labor and sorrow."

NORTH AMERICA AT MID-CENTURY

By the mid-eighteenth century, the area that would become the United States was home to a remarkable diversity of peoples and different kinds of social organization, from Pueblos of the Southwest to tobacco plantations of the Chesapeake, towns and small farms of New England, landholdings in the Hudson Valley that resembled feudal estates, and fur-trading outposts on Indian land. Despite European claims, Native Americans still held most of the power in North America.

French and Spanish Colonies

In the late 1600s and early 1700s, French traders established trading posts among the Anishinaabe and Illinois peoples in the Great Lakes region. From there, they pushed south into the Mississippi River valley, as well as north from the coast of the Gulf of Mexico, where they established Biloxi in 1699, Mobile in 1702, and New Orleans in 1718. The French claimed both sides of the Mississippi River from the Gulf to the Great Lakes as the vast colony of Louisiana. French officials hoped that Louisiana, having a warmer climate than Canada, would become a thriving plantation colony. The French bought and enslaved Native captives, and the first enslaved Africans arrived in Louisiana in 1719.

But Native Americans far outnumbered French colonists, who were not able to make Louisiana the colony they planned. In 1729, the Natchez Indians expelled the French from the plantations they were building on the Mississippi River. Although the French and their Native allies eventually won the **Natchez War**, to prevent further conflict the French scaled back their plans and halted the slave trade into Louisiana.

In the meantime, French expansion in the Mississippi Valley worried Spanish officials, who considered the region to belong to them. The Spanish, unable to attract settlers, allowed Franciscan friars to expand their missions from northern Mexico into Texas. After several attempts in eastern Texas failed to attract Native converts, Spanish friars and soldiers established a mission, presidio (military outpost), and trading post at San Antonio in 1718, followed by Los Adaes on the border with French Louisiana.

The Great Plains

In the Great Plains, Native people began riding and breeding horses, first brought by Spaniards in the sixteenth century. Rather than hunting and farming seasonally as their ancestors had, some peoples, including Apaches, Comanches, and Kiowas, developed an equestrian life with large herds of horses, living all year on the continent's vast central flatland. A bustling Plains economy developed, as Comanches and other Plains Indians traded at major trading centers, including the Pueblos and Spanish New Mexico in the west and French Louisiana in the east. They also traded with Native peoples who continued to farm in the river valleys of the Plains, including the Mandans, Pawnees, Wichitas, and Caddos. Trading products included horses, bison products, war captives, food, and firearms.

Demand for European guns grew in the west during the eighteenth century. The Wichitas positioned themselves as intermediaries between the Comanches and their trading partners in the west (who were unable to buy guns from

Spaniards in New Mexico because Spain had outlawed the gun trade) and the French, who were more liberal when it came to trading firearms, in Louisiana.

Freedom in the British Colonies

Within all European empires, elites tied to imperial centers of power dominated political and economic life. But large numbers of male colonists in the British empire enjoyed far greater opportunities for freedom—namely, access to the vote, prospects of acquiring land, the right to worship as they pleased, and an escape from oppressive government—than existed in Europe. Free colonists enjoyed a relatively high standard of living for their era. The colonies' economic growth contributed to a high birthrate, long life expectancy, and expanding demand for consumer goods.

Yet many others found themselves confined to the partial freedom of indentured servitude or coverture or to the complete absence of freedom in slavery. Both timeless longings for freedom and new and unprecedented forms of unfreedom had been essential to the British North American colonies' remarkable development. To many colonists, American Indians represented freedom from the constraints of European hierarchies and social divisions. To American Indians who lost their lands to the expanding colonies or people of African descent held in bondage, Europeans represented the greatest threat to their freedom and independence.

CHAPTER REVIEW

REVIEW QUESTIONS

1. *Both the Puritans and William Penn viewed their colonies as "holy experiments." How did they differ?*

2. *Examine the economic forces, events, and laws that shaped the experiences of enslaved people.*

3. *How did English leaders understand the place and role of the American colonies in England's empire?*

4. *How did King Philip's War, Bacon's Rebellion, and the Salem witch trials illustrate a widespread crisis in British North America in the late seventeenth century?*

5. *The social structure of the eighteenth-century colonies was growing more open for some but not for others. Consider the statement with respect to men and women, whites and Blacks, and rich and poor.*

6. *By the end of the seventeenth century, commerce was the foundation of empire and the leading cause of competition between European empires. Explain how the North American colonies were directly linked to Atlantic commerce by laws and trade.*

7. *If you traveled from New England to the South, how would you describe the diversity you saw between the different colonies?*

8. *What impact did the family's being the center of economic life have on gender relations and the roles of women?*

9. *What experiences caused people in the colonies to be like people in England, and what experiences served to make them different?*

10. *How did the adoption of horses change life on the Great Plains?*

KEY TERMS

King Philip's War (p. 90)

Metacom (p. 90)

mercantilism (p. 91)

Navigation Acts (p. 91)

Covenant Chain (p. 94)

Yamasee War (p. 95)

Society of Friends (Quakers) (p. 96)

Bacon's Rebellion (p. 100)

Glorious Revolution (p. 105)

English Bill of Rights (p. 106)

Lords of Trade (p. 106)

Dominion of New England (p. 107)

English Toleration Act (p. 108)

Salem witch trials (p. 110)

redemptioners (p. 114)

Walking Purchase (p. 117)

backcountry (p. 118)

staple crops (p. 121)

Natchez War (p. 128)

Go to 🐰 INQUIZITIVE

To see what you know—and learn what you've missed—with personalized feedback along the way.

CHAPTER 4

SLAVERY, FREEDOM, AND THE STRUGGLE FOR EMPIRE

TO 1763

FOCUS QUESTIONS

- *How did African slavery differ regionally in eighteenth-century North America?*

- *What factors led to distinct African American cultures in the eighteenth century?*

- *What were the meanings of British liberty in the eighteenth century?*

- *What concepts and institutions dominated colonial politics in the eighteenth century?*

- *How did the Great Awakening challenge the religious and social structure of British North America?*

- *How did the Spanish and French empires in America develop in the eighteenth century?*

- *What was the impact of the Seven Years' War on imperial and Indian–European relations?*

Sometime in the mid-1750s, Olaudah Equiano, the eleven-year-old son of a West African village chief, was kidnapped by slave traders. He soon found himself on a ship headed for Barbados. After a short stay on that Caribbean island, Equiano was sold to a plantation owner in Virginia and then purchased by a British sea captain, who renamed him Gustavus Vassa. He accompanied his owner on numerous voyages on Atlantic trading vessels. While still a slave, he enrolled in a school in England where he learned to read and write, and then enlisted in the Royal Navy. He fought in Canada under General James Wolfe in 1758 during the Seven Years' War. In 1763, however, Equiano was sold once again and returned to the Caribbean. Three years later, he was able to purchase his freedom. Equiano went on to live through shipwrecks, took part in an English colonizing venture in Central America, and even participated in an expedition to the Arctic Circle.

Equiano eventually settled in London, and in 1789 he published *The Interesting Narrative of the Life of Olaudah Equiano, or Gustavus Vassa, the African*, which he described as a "history of neither a saint, a hero, nor a tyrant," but of a victim of slavery who through luck or fate ended up more fortunate than most of his people. He condemned the idea that Africans were inferior to Europeans and therefore deserved to be slaves. He urged the European reader to recall that "his ancestors were once, like the Africans, uncivilized" and asked, "Did nature make them inferior . . . and should they too have been made slaves?" Persons of all races, he insisted, were capable of intellectual improvement. The book became the era's most widely read account by a slave of his own experiences. Equiano died in 1797.

While Equiano may have included in his book some experiences that happened to other enslaved people as well as to himself, his narrative illuminates broad patterns of eighteenth-century American history. As noted in the previous chapter, this was a period of sustained development for British North America. Compared to England and Scotland—united to create Great Britain by the Act of Union of 1707—the colonies were growing much more rapidly. Some contemporaries spoke of British America as a "rising empire" that would one day eclipse the home country in population and wealth.

It would be wrong, however, to see the first three-quarters of the eighteenth century simply as a prelude to American independence. As Equiano's life illustrates, the Atlantic was more a bridge than a barrier. Ideas, people, and goods flowed back and forth across the ocean. Even as the colonies' populations became more diverse, they were increasingly integrated into the British empire. Their laws and political institutions were extensions of those of Britain, their ideas about society and culture reflected British values, and their economies were geared to serving the empire's needs. As European powers jockeyed for advantage in North America, British colonists were drawn into an almost continuous series of wars with France and its Native allies, which reinforced their sense of identification with and dependence on Great Britain.

Equiano's life also underscores the greatest irony or contradiction in the history of the eighteenth century—the simultaneous expansion of freedom and slavery. This was the era when the idea of the "freeborn Englishman" became powerfully entrenched in the outlook of both colonists and Britons. More than any other principle, liberty was seen as what made the British empire distinct. Yet the eighteenth century was also the height of the Atlantic slave trade, a commerce increasingly dominated by British merchants and ships. One of the most popular songs of the period included the refrain, "Britons never, never, never will be slaves." But during the eighteenth century, more than half the Africans shipped to the Americas as slaves were carried on British vessels. Most were destined for the plantations of the West Indies and Brazil, but slaves also made up around 280,000 of the 585,000 persons who arrived in Britain's mainland colonies between 1700 and 1775. Although concentrated in the Chesapeake and areas farther south, slavery existed in every colony of British North America. And unlike Equiano, very few slaves were fortunate enough to gain their freedom.

SLAVERY AND EMPIRE

Of the estimated 10 million Africans transported to the Americas between 1492 and 1820, more than half arrived between 1700 and 1800. The **Atlantic slave trade** would later be condemned as a crime against humanity. But in the eighteenth century, it was a regularized business in which European merchants,

A detail from a 1775 map of Virginia and Maryland depicts a tobacco wharf. A planter negotiates with a merchant or sea captain, while enslaved men go about their work.

African traders, and American planters engaged in complex bargaining over human lives, all with the expectation of securing a profit. The slave trade was a vital part of world commerce. Every European empire in the Americas utilized slave labor and battled for control of this lucrative trade. The *asiento*—an agreement whereby Spain subcontracted to a foreign power the right to provide slaves to Spanish America—was an important diplomatic prize. Britain's acquisition of the *asiento* from the Dutch in the Treaty of Utrecht of 1713 was a major step in its rise to commercial supremacy.

In the British empire of the eighteenth century, free laborers working for wages were atypical and slavery was the norm. Slave plantations contributed mightily to English economic development. The first mass consumer goods in international trade were produced by enslaved men and women—sugar, rice, coffee, and tobacco. The rising demand for these products fueled the rapid growth of the Atlantic slave trade.

Atlantic Trade

In the eighteenth century, the Caribbean remained the commercial focus of the British empire and the major producer of revenue for the crown. But plantation grown products from the mainland occupied a larger and larger part of Atlantic commerce. A series of triangular trading routes crisscrossed the Atlantic,

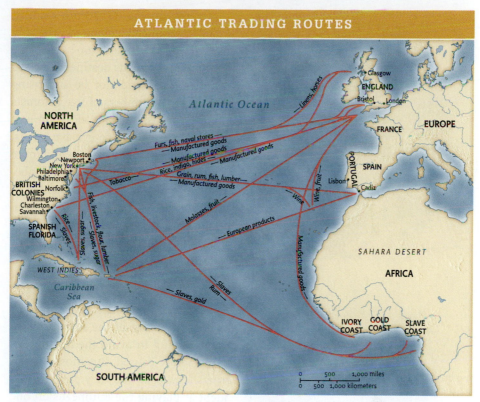

ATLANTIC TRADING ROUTES

A series of trading routes crisscrossed the Atlantic, bringing manufactured goods to Africa and Britain's American colonies, enslaved Africans to the Americas, and colonial products to Europe.

carrying British manufactured goods to Africa and the colonies, colonial products to Europe, and captured Africans to the Americas. Most colonial vessels, however, went back and forth between cities like New York, Charleston, and Savannah, and to ports in the Caribbean. Areas that had few enslaved people also profited from slavery. Merchants in New York, Massachusetts, and Rhode Island participated actively in the slave trade, shipping enslaved Africans to the Caribbean or the mainland colonies. The slave economies of the West Indies were the largest market for fish, grain, livestock, and lumber exported from New England and the Middle Colonies. Indeed, one historian writes, "The growth and prosperity of the emerging society of free colonial British America ... were achieved as a result of slave labor." In Britain itself, the profits from slavery and the slave trade stimulated the rise of ports such as Liverpool and Bristol and the growth of banking, shipbuilding, and insurance. They also helped to finance the early industrial revolution.

The frontispiece of Olaudah Equiano's account of his life, the best-known narrative by an eighteenth-century slave. The portrait of Equiano in European dress and holding a Bible challenged stereotypes of Blacks as "savages" incapable of becoming civilized.

Overall, in the eighteenth century, Atlantic commerce consisted primarily of enslaved Africans, crops that they produced, and goods destined for slave societies. It should not be surprising that for large numbers of free colonists and Europeans, freedom meant in part the power and right to enslave others. And as slavery became more and more entrenched, so too, as the Quaker abolitionist John Woolman commented in 1762, did "the idea of slavery being connected with the black color, and liberty with the white."

Africa and the Slave Trade

A few African societies, like Benin for a time, opted out of the Atlantic slave trade, hoping to avoid the disruptions it inevitably caused. But most African rulers took part, and they proved quite adept at playing the Europeans off one another, collecting taxes from foreign merchants, and keeping the capture and sale of slaves under their own control. Few Europeans ventured inland from the coast. Traders remained in their "factories" and purchased captives brought to them by African rulers and dealers.

The transatlantic slave trade made Africa a major market for European goods, especially textiles and guns. Both disrupted relationships within and among African societies. Cheap imported textiles undermined traditional craft production, while guns encouraged the further growth of slavery, since the only way to obtain European weapons was to supply slaves. By the eighteenth century, militarized states like Ashanti and Dahomey would arise in West Africa, with large armies using European firearms to prey on their neighbors in order to capture slaves. From a minor institution, slavery grew to become more and more central to West African society, a source of wealth for African merchants and of power for newly emerging African kingdoms. But the loss every year of tens of thousands of men and women in the prime of their lives to the slave trade was a horrifying loss to West Africa.

THE SLAVE TRADE IN THE ATLANTIC WORLD, 1460–1770

The Atlantic slave trade expanded rapidly in the eighteenth century. The mainland colonies received only a tiny proportion of the Africans brought to the Americas, most of whom were transported to Brazil and the West Indies.

The Middle Passage

The voyage across the Atlantic—known as the **Middle Passage** because it was the second, or middle, leg in the triangular trading routes linking Europe, Africa, and America—was a harrowing experience. Men, women, and children were crammed aboard vessels as tightly as possible to maximize profits. "The height, sometimes, between decks," wrote one slave trader, "was only eighteen inches, so that the unfortunate human beings could not turn around, or even on their sides . . . and here they are usually chained to the decks by their necks and legs." Equiano, who later described "the shrieks of the women and the groans of the dying," survived the Middle Passage, but many Africans did not. Diseases like measles and smallpox spread rapidly, and about one in five perished before reaching the Americas. Ship captains were known to throw the sick overboard in order to prevent the spread of epidemics.

Only a small proportion (less than 5 percent) of slaves carried across the Middle Passage were destined for mainland North America. The vast majority landed in Brazil or the West Indies, where the high death rate on the sugar plantations led to a constant demand for new slave imports. As late as 1700, only about 20,000 Africans had landed in Britain's colonies in North America. In the eighteenth century, however, their numbers increased steadily. Overall,

This image, made by a sailor in 1769 for the ship's owner, a merchant in Nantes, France, depicts a slave-trading vessel, the *Marie-Séraphique*, anchored off the African coast, and the ship's interior. The cargo carried in barrels, generally guns, cloth, and metal goods, was to be traded for slaves. The third image from the left depicts the conditions under which slaves endured the Middle Passage across the Atlantic. The ship carried over 300 people. The broadside also included a calculation of the profit of the voyage.

the area that was to become the United States imported between 400,000 and 600,000 slaves. By 1770, due to the natural reproduction of the slave population, around one-fifth of the estimated 2.3 million persons living in the English colonies of North America were Africans and their descendants.

Chesapeake Slavery

By the mid-eighteenth century, three distinct slave systems were well entrenched in Britain's mainland colonies: tobacco-based plantation slavery in the Chesapeake, rice-based plantation slavery in South Carolina and Georgia, and nonplantation slavery in New England and the Middle Colonies. The largest and oldest of these was the tobacco plantation system of the Chesapeake, where more than 270,000 slaves resided in 1770, nearly half of the region's population. On the eve of the Revolution, Virginia and Maryland were as closely tied to Britain as any other colonies and their economies were models of mercantilist policy (described in Chapter 3). They supplied the home country with a valuable agricultural product, imported large amounts of British goods, and were closely linked in culture and political values to London. As we have seen, the period after 1680 witnessed a rapid shift from indentured servitude to slavery on the region's tobacco plantations. In the eighteenth century, the growing world demand for tobacco encouraged continued slave imports.

As Virginia expanded westward, so did slavery. By the eve of the American Revolution, the center of gravity of slavery in the colony had shifted from the Tidewater (the region along the coast) to the Piedmont farther inland. Most enslaved women and men in the Chesapeake worked in the fields, but thousands labored as teamsters, as boatmen, and in skilled crafts. Numerous enslaved women became cooks, seamstresses, dairy maids, and personal servants. The son of George Mason, one of Virginia's leading planters and statesmen, recorded that his father's slaves included "coopers, sawyers, blacksmiths, tanners, shoemakers, spinners, weavers, knitters, and even a distiller." Slavery was common on small farms as well as plantations; nearly half of Virginia's white families owned at least one slave in 1770.

Slavery laid the foundation for the consolidation of the Chesapeake elite, a landed gentry that, in conjunction with merchants who handled the tobacco trade and lawyers who defended the interests of slaveholders, dominated the region's society and politics. As slavery expanded, planters engrossed the best lands, and wealth among the white population became more and more concentrated. Slavery transformed Chesapeake society into an elaborate hierarchy of degrees of freedom. At the top stood large planters, below them numerous lesser planters and landowning yeomen, and at the bottom a large population of convicts, indentured servants, tenant farmers, and slaves.

Freedom and Slavery in the Chesapeake

With the consolidation of a slave society in the Chesapeake, planters filled the law books with measures enhancing the master's power over his human property and restricting Blacks' access to freedom. Violence lay at the heart of the slave system. Even a planter like Landon Carter, who prided himself on his concern for the well-being of his slaves, noted casually in his diary, "They have been severely whipped day by day."

Race took on more and more importance as a line of social division. Whites increasingly considered free Blacks dangerous and undesirable. Free Blacks lost the right to employ white servants and to bear arms, were subjected to special taxes, and could be punished for striking a white person, regardless of the cause. In 1723, Virginia revoked the voting privileges of property-owning free Blacks. When the Lords of Trade in London asked Virginia's governor to justify discriminating among "freemen, merely upon account of their complexion," he responded that "a distinction ought to be made between their offspring and the descendants of an Englishman, with whom they never were to be accounted equal." Because Virginia law required that freed slaves be sent out of the colony, free Blacks remained only a tiny part of the population—less than 4 percent in 1750. "Free" and "white" had become virtually identical.

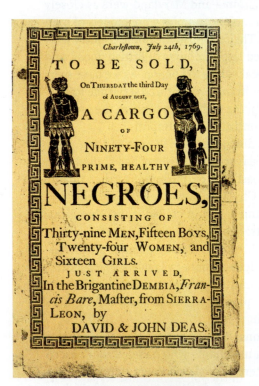

Slave Sale Broadside. This 1769 broadside advertises the sale of ninety-four slaves who had just arrived in Charleston from West Africa. Broadsides like this one were displayed prominently by slave traders to drum up business.

The Rice Kingdom in South Carolina

Farther south, a different slave system based on rice production emerged in South Carolina and Georgia. The Barbadians who initially settled South Carolina in the 1670s were quite familiar with African slavery, but their first victims were Native Americans. As noted in Chapter 3, Indians initially welcomed the settlers and began selling them war captives, most of whom were sold to the West Indies. But after the Yamasee War, the Indian slave trade largely ended, and African labor became dominant in South Carolina.

As in early Virginia, frontier conditions allowed leeway to South Carolina's small population of African-born slaves, who farmed, tended livestock, and were initially allowed to serve in the militia to fight the Spanish and Indians. And as in Virginia, the introduction of a marketable staple crop, in this case rice, led directly to economic development, the large-scale importation of slaves, and a growing divide between white and Black. South Carolina was the first mainland colony to have a Black majority. By the 1730s (by which time North Carolina had become a separate colony), two-thirds of its population was Black. In the 1740s, another staple, indigo (a crop used in producing blue dye), was developed. Like rice, indigo required large-scale cultivation and was grown by slaves.

Ironically, it was Africans, familiar with the crop at home, who taught English settlers how to cultivate rice, which then became the foundation of South Carolina slavery and of the wealthiest slaveowning class on the North American mainland. Since rice production requires considerable capital investment to drain swamps and create irrigation systems, it is economically advantageous for rice plantations to be as large as possible. Thus, South Carolina planters owned far more land and slaves than their counterparts in Virginia. Moreover, since mosquitoes bearing malaria (a disease to which Africans had developed partial immunity) flourished in the watery rice fields, planters tended to leave plantations under the control of overseers and the slaves themselves.

In the Chesapeake, field slaves worked in groups under constant supervision. Under the "task" system that developed in eighteenth-century South Carolina, individual slaves were assigned daily jobs, the completion of which allowed them time for leisure or to cultivate crops of their own. In 1762, one rice district had a population of only 76 white men among 1,000 slaves. Fearful of the ever-increasing Black population majority, South Carolina's legislature took steps to encourage the immigration of "poor Protestants," offering each newcomer a cash bounty and occasionally levying taxes on slave imports, only to see such restrictions overturned in London. By 1770, the number of South Carolina slaves had reached 75,000, well over half the colony's population.

The Georgia Experiment

Rice cultivation also spread into Georgia in the mid-eighteenth century. The colony was founded in 1732 by a group of philanthropists led by James Oglethorpe, a wealthy reformer whose causes included improved conditions for imprisoned debtors and the abolition of slavery. Oglethorpe hoped to establish a haven where the "worthy poor" of England could enjoy economic opportunity. The government in London supported the creation of Georgia to protect South

TABLE 4.1 Slave Population as Percentage of Total Population of Original Thirteen Colonies, 1770

Colony	Slave Population	Percentage
Virginia	187,600	42%
South Carolina	75,168	61
North Carolina	69,600	35
Maryland	63,818	32
New York	19,062	12
Georgia	15,000	45
New Jersey	8,220	7
Connecticut	5,698	3
Pennsylvania	5,561	2
Massachusetts	4,754	2
Rhode Island	3,761	6
Delaware	1,836	5
New Hampshire	654	1

Carolina against the Spanish and their Native allies in Florida.

Initially, the proprietors banned the introduction of both liquor and slaves, leading to continual battles with settlers, who desired both. By the 1740s, Georgia offered the spectacle of colonists pleading for the "English liberty" of self-government so that they could enact laws introducing slavery. In 1751, the proprietors surrendered the colony to the crown. The colonists quickly won the right to an elected assembly, which met in Savannah, Georgia's main settlement. It repealed the ban on slavery (and liquor), as well as an early measure that had limited land holdings to 500 acres. Georgia became a miniature version of South Carolina. By 1770, as many as 15,000 slaves labored on its coastal rice plantations.

Slavery in the North

Compared with the plantation regions, slavery was less central to the economies of New England and the Middle Colonies, where small farms predominated. Enslaved people made up only a small percentage of these colonies' populations, and it was unusual for even rich families to own more than one or two slaves. Nonetheless, slavery was not marginal to northern colonial life. African slavery existed in New England from the outset, and many of the region's leaders owned slaves, including the prominent theologian Cotton Mather. Trade with the West Indies was central to the New England economy. Slaves worked as farm hands, in artisan shops, as stevedores loading and unloading ships, and as personal servants. With slaves so small a part of the population that they seemed to pose no threat to the white majority, laws were less harsh than in the South. In New England, where in 1770 the 15,000 slaves represented less than 3 percent of the region's population, marriages between enslaved women and men were recognized in law, severe physical punishment was prohibited, and enslaved men could bring suits in court, testify against whites, and own property and pass it on to their children—rights unknown in the South.

Slavery had been present in New York from the earliest days of Dutch settlement. With white immigration lagging behind that of Pennsylvania, the colony's Hudson Valley landlords, small farmers, and craftsmen continued to use considerable amounts of slave labor in the eighteenth century. As New York City's role in the slave trade expanded, so did slavery in the city. In 1746, its 2,440 slaves amounted to one-fifth of the city's total population. Some 30 percent of its laborers were enslaved, a proportion second only to Charleston among American cities. Most were domestic workers, but slaves worked in all sectors of the economy. In 1770, about 27,000 slaves lived in New York and New Jersey, 10 percent of their total population. Slavery was also a significant presence in Philadelphia, although the institution stagnated after 1750 as artisans

A portrait of Ayuba Diallo, a Muslim merchant in Senegal who became a victim of the slave trade in 1731 and was transported to Maryland. He escaped in 1733 and with the help of wealthy patrons regained his freedom. Because of Diallo's unusual talents—he knew both English and Arabic and could recite the Koran from memory—he became a celebrity in England, which he visited in 1733. He returned to his homeland in 1734.

and merchants relied increasingly on wage laborers, whose numbers were augmented by population growth and the completion of the terms of indentured servants. In an urban economy that expanded and contracted according to the ups and downs of international trade, many employers concluded that relying on wage labor, which could be hired and fired at will, made more economic sense than a long-term investment in slaves.

SLAVE CULTURES AND SLAVE RESISTANCE

Becoming African American

The nearly 300,000 Africans brought to the mainland colonies during the eighteenth century were not a single people. They came from different cultures, spoke different languages, and practiced many religions. Eventually, an African

Music and Dance in Beaufort County, a late-eighteenth-century watercolor, depicts slaves dancing in a plantation's slave quarters, perhaps at a wedding. The musical instruments and pottery are African in origin while much of the clothing is of European manufacture, indicating the mixing of African and white cultures among the era's slaves. The artist has recently been identified as John Rose, owner of a rice plantation near Beaufort, South Carolina.

American people would emerge from the diverse groups transported to the British colonies in the Middle Passage. Slavery threw together individuals who would never otherwise have encountered one another and who had never considered their color or residence on a single continent a source of identity or unity. Their bond was not kinship, language, or even "race," but slavery itself. The process of creating a cohesive culture and community took many years, and it proceeded at different rates in different regions. But by the nineteenth century, slaves no longer identified themselves as Ibo, Ashanti, Yoruba, and so on, but as African Americans. In music, art, folklore, language, and religion, their cultural expressions emerged as a synthesis of African traditions, European elements, and new conditions in America.

For most of the eighteenth century, the majority of American slaves were African by birth. Advertisements seeking information about runaways often described them by African origin ("young Gambia Negro," "new Banbara Negro fellow"). Indeed, during the eighteenth century, Black life in the colonies was "re-Africanized" as the earlier creoles (slaves born in the Americas) came to be outnumbered by large-scale importations from Africa. Compared with the earliest generation of slaves, the newcomers died earlier and had less access to freedom. Charles Hansford, a white Virginia blacksmith, noted in a 1753 poem that he had frequently heard slaves speak of their desire to "reenjoy" life in Africa:

> I oft with pleasure have observ'd how they
> Their sultry country's worth strive to display
> In broken language, how they praise their case
> And happiness when in their native place ...
> How would they dangers court and pains endure
> If to their country they could get secure!

Although some Africans came to the colonies familiar with Christianity or Islam, the majority of North American slaves practiced traditional African religions well into the eighteenth century. When they did adopt Protestant religious beliefs and practices, many slaves did so within the inclusivism of their African religions (discussed in Chapter 1). They added the Christian God and figures from the Bible to their own pantheon of spirits, whom they continued to worship. A similar process occurred in slave societies like Brazil and Cuba, where African spirits merged with Catholic saints.

African American Cultures

By the mid-eighteenth century, the three slave systems in British North America had produced distinct African American cultures. In the Chesapeake, the enslaved population began to reproduce itself by 1740, creating a more balanced sex ratio than in the seventeenth century and making possible the creation of family-centered slave communities. Because of the small size of most plantations and the large number of white **yeoman farmers**, slaves here soon learned English, and many were swept up in the religious revivals known as the Great Awakening, discussed later in this chapter.

In South Carolina and Georgia, two very different Black societies emerged. On the rice plantations, slaves lived in extremely harsh conditions and had a low birthrate throughout the eighteenth century, making rice production dependent on continued slave imports from Africa. The slaves seldom came into contact with whites and enjoyed far more autonomy than elsewhere in the colonies. The larger structures of their lives were established by slavery, but they were able to create an African-based culture. They constructed African-style houses, chose African names for their children, and spoke Gullah, a language that mixed various African roots and was unintelligible to most whites. Despite a continuing slave trade in which young, single males predominated, slaves slowly created families and communities that bridged generations. The experience of slaves who labored in Charleston and Savannah as servants and skilled workers was quite different. Like enslaved people in the Chesapeake, they learned English. Some gained their freedom and founded communities of free people of color in both Charleston and Savannah.

In the northern colonies, slaves represented a smaller part of the population, dispersed in small holdings among the white population. They lived in close proximity to whites and had less independence in their daily lives than slaves on large plantations, although their physical conditions tended to be less harsh. They had fewer opportunities to marry and have children or to create a cohesive Black community.

RUN AWAY

THE 18th Inſtant at Night from the Subſcriber, in the City of New-York, four Negro Men, Viz. LESTER, about 40 Years of Age, had on a white Flannel Jacket and Drawers, Duck Trowſers and Home-ſpun Shirt. CÆSAR, about 18 Years of Age, cloth-ed in the ſame Manner. ISAAC, aged 17 Years cloathed in the ſame Manner, except that his Breeches were Leather; and MINGO, 15 Years of Age, with the the ſame Clothing as the 2 firſt, all of them of a middling Size, Whoever delivers either of the ſaid Negroes to the Subſcriber, ſhall receive TWENTY SHILLINGS Reward for each beſide all reaſon-able Charges. If any perſon can give Intelligence of their being harbour'd, a reward of TEN POUNDS will be paid upon conviction of the Offender. All Maſters of Veſſels and others are forewarn'd not to Tranſport them from the City, as I am reſolved to proſecute as far as the Law will allow.   WILLIAM BULL.

N. B. If the Negroes return, they ſhall be pardon'd.   - 88

An advertisement seeking the return of four men who escaped slavery in New York City. Note the careful description of their clothing and the diversity of their names, presumably given by their enslavers—two common English names, one of African origin and one alluding to ancient Rome. The reward offered is a substantial amount of money in the colonial era. "The 18th Instant" means the 18th of this month.

Resistance to Slavery

The common threads that linked these regional African American cultures were the experience of slavery and the desire for freedom. Throughout the eighteenth century, Blacks risked their lives in efforts to resist enslavement. Colonial newspapers, especially in the southern colonies, were filled with advertisements for escaped slaves. Most were young African men who had arrived recently. In South Carolina and Georgia, they fled to Spanish Florida, to uninhabited coastal and river swamps, or to Charleston and Savannah, where they could pass for free. In the Chesapeake and Middle Colonies, freedom seek-ers tended to be familiar with English language and culture and therefore, as one advertisement put it, could "pretend to be free."

What Edward Trelawny, the colonial governor of Jamaica, called "a danger-ous spirit of liberty" was widespread among people enslaved in the Americas.

The eighteenth century's first slave uprising occurred in New York City in 1712, when a group of slaves set fire to houses on the outskirts of the city and killed the first nine whites who arrived on the scene. Subsequently, eighteen conspirators were executed; some were tortured and burned alive in a public spectacle meant to intimidate the enslaved population. During the 1730s and 1740s, continuous warfare involving European empires and Indians opened the door to slave resistance. In 1731, slaves in Louisiana took advantage of the Natchez War to start a rebellion. There were uprisings throughout the West Indies, including in the Virgin Islands, owned by Denmark, and on the French island of Guadeloupe. On Jamaica, a major British center of sugar production, communities of fugitive slaves known as "maroons" waged outright warfare against British authorities until a treaty of 1739 recognized their freedom, in exchange for which they agreed to return future escapees. Tacky's Revolt, which broke out in Jamaica in 1760, was the largest slave uprising in the eighteenth-century British colonies.

The Crisis of 1739–1741

On the mainland, slaves seized the opportunity for rebellion offered by the War of Jenkins' Ear, which pitted England against Spain. In September 1739, a group of South Carolina slaves, most of them recently arrived from Kongo where some, it appears, had been soldiers, gathered near the Stono River and together seized a store containing numerous weapons. Beating drums to attract followers, the armed band marched southward toward Florida, burning houses and barns, killing whites they encountered, and shouting "Liberty." (They knew that Florida's Spanish rulers offered "Liberty and Protection" to fugitives from the British colonies.) The group eventually swelled to some 100 slaves. After a pitched battle with the colony's militia, the rebels were dispersed. The rebellion took the lives of more than two dozen whites and as many as 200 slaves, including many who had no connection to the rebellion. Some rebels managed to reach Florida, where in 1740 they were armed by the Spanish to help repel an attack on St. Augustine by a force from Georgia. The **Stono Rebellion** led to a severe tightening of the South Carolina slave code and the temporary imposition of a prohibitive tax on imported slaves.

In 1741, a panic (which some observers compared to the fear of witches in Salem in the 1690s) swept New York City. After a series of fires broke out, rumors spread that slaves, with some white allies, planned to burn part of the city, seize weapons, and either turn New York over to Spain or murder the white population. More than 150 Blacks and 20 whites were arrested, and 34 alleged conspirators were executed. Historians still disagree as to how extensive the plot was or whether it existed at all. But dramatic events like revolts, along with the constant stream of runaways, disproved the idea, voiced by the governor of South Carolina, that slaves had "no notion of liberty." In eighteenth-century America, dreams of freedom knew no racial boundary.

AN EMPIRE OF FREEDOM

British Patriotism

Despite the centrality of slavery to its empire, eighteenth-century Britons believed that Great Britain was the world's most advanced and freest nation. It was not only the era's greatest naval and commercial power but also the home of a complex governmental system with a powerful Parliament representing the interests of a self-confident landed aristocracy and merchant class. In London, the largest city in Europe with a population approaching 1 million by the end of the eighteenth century, Britain possessed a single political-cultural-economic capital. It enjoyed a common law, common language, and, with the exception of a small number of Jews, Catholics, and Africans, common devotion to Protestantism. For much of the eighteenth century, Britain found itself at war with France, which had replaced Spain as its major continental rival. This situation led to the development of a large military establishment, high taxes, and the creation of the Bank of England to help finance European and imperial conflicts. For Britons in Britain and in the colonies, war helped to sharpen a sense of national identity against foreign foes.

British patriotic sentiment became more and more assertive as the eighteenth century progressed. Symbols of British identity proliferated: the songs "God Save the King" and "Rule, Britannia," and even the modern rules of cricket, the national sport. The rapidly expanding British economy formed another point of pride uniting Britons at home and abroad. Continental peoples, according to a popular saying, wore "wooden shoes"—that is, their standard of living was far below that of Britons. Especially in contrast to France, Britain saw itself as a realm of widespread prosperity, individual liberty, the rule of law, and the Protestant faith. Wealth, religion, and freedom went together.

The British Constitution

Central to this sense of British identity was the concept of liberty. The fierce political struggles of the English Civil War and the Glorious Revolution bequeathed to eighteenth-century British men an abiding conviction that liberty was their unique possession. They believed power and liberty to be natural antagonists. To mediate between them, advocates of British freedom celebrated the rule of law, the right to live under legislation to which one's representatives had consented, restraints on the arbitrary exercise of political authority, and rights like trial by jury enshrined in the common law. On both sides of the Atlantic, every political cause, it seemed, wrapped itself in the language of liberty and claimed to be defending the "rights of Englishmen." European writers dissatisfied with the lack of liberty in their own countries looked to Britain as a model. The House of Commons, House of Lords, and king each checked the power of the others. This structure, wrote the French political philosopher Baron Montesquieu, made Britain "the one nation in the world whose constitution has political liberty for its purpose." Until the 1770s, most colonists believed themselves to be part of the freest political system humankind had ever known.

As the coexistence of slavery and liberty within the empire demonstrated, British freedom was anything but universal. It was closely identified with the Protestant religion and was invoked to contrast Britons with the "servile" subjects of Catholic countries. It viewed nearly every other nation on earth

The Polling, by the renowned eighteenth-century British artist William Hogarth, satirizes the idea that British elections are decided by the reasoned deliberations of upstanding property owners. Inspired by a corrupt election of 1754, Hogarth depicts a scene in which the maimed and dying are brought to the polls to cast ballots. At the center, lawyers argue over whether a man who has a hook for a hand can swear on the Bible.

as "enslaved"—to popery, tyranny, or barbarism. One German military officer commented in 1743 on the British "contempt" of foreigners: "They [pride] themselves not only upon their being free themselves, but being the bulwarks of liberty all over Europe; and they vilify most of the Nations on the continent ... for being slaves, as they call us." British liberty was fully compatible with wide gradations in personal rights most obviously those of women and enslaved people. Yet in the minds of the free men of Great Britain and its North American colonies, liberty was the bond of empire.

These ideas sank deep roots not only within the "political nation"—those who voted, held office, and engaged in structured political debate—but also far more broadly in British and colonial society. Laborers, sailors, and artisans spoke the language of British freedom as insistently as pamphleteers and parliamentarians. Although most white men in Britain and many in the colonies lacked the right to vote, they influenced public life in other ways, including serving on juries. Men and women of all kinds took to the streets to protest what they considered oppressive authority. Ordinary persons challenged efforts by merchants to raise the cost of bread above the traditional "just price," and the Royal Navy's practice of "impressment"—kidnapping poor men on the streets for maritime service.

Republican Liberty and Liberal Freedom

Liberty was central to two sets of political ideas that flourished in the Anglo-American world. One is termed by scholars **republicanism** (although few in eighteenth-century England used the word, which literally meant a government without a king and conjured up memories of the beheading of Charles I). Republicanism celebrated active participation in public life by economically independent citizens as the essence of liberty. Republicans assumed that only property-owning citizens possessed "virtue"—defined in the eighteenth century not simply as a personal moral quality but as the willingness and ability to subordinate self-interest to the pursuit of the public good. "Only a virtuous people are capable of freedom," wrote Benjamin Franklin.

The second set of eighteenth-century political ideas celebrating freedom came to be known as **liberalism** (although its meaning was quite different from what the word suggests today). Whereas republican liberty had a public and social quality, liberalism was essentially individual and private. The leading philosopher of liberty was John Locke. In his *Two Treatises of Government,* written around 1680, he wrote that government was formed by a mutual agreement among equals (the parties being male heads of households, not all persons). In this "social contract," men surrendered a part of their right to govern themselves in order to enjoy the benefits of the rule of law. They retained, however, their natural rights, whose existence predated the establishment of political authority. Protecting the security of life, liberty, and property required shielding a realm of private life and personal concerns—including family relations, religious preferences, and economic activity—from interference by the state. During the eighteenth century, Lockean ideas—individual rights, the consent of the governed, the right of rebellion against unjust or oppressive government—would become familiar on both sides of the Atlantic.

Like other Britons, Locke spoke of liberty as a universal right yet seemed to exclude many persons from its full benefits. While Locke was one of the first theorists to defend the property rights of women and even their access to divorce, and condemned slavery as a "vile and miserable estate of man," the free individual in liberal thought was essentially the propertied white man. Nonetheless, by proclaiming that all individuals possess natural rights that no government may violate, Lockean liberalism opened the door to the poor, women, and even slaves to challenge limitations on their own freedom.

In the eighteenth century, republicanism and liberalism overlapped and often reinforced each other. Both political outlooks could inspire a commitment to constitutional government and restraints on despotic power. Both emphasized the security of property as a foundation of freedom. Both traditions were transported to eighteenth-century America. Ideas about liberty imported from Britain to the colonies would eventually help to divide the empire.

THE PUBLIC SPHERE

Colonial politics for most of the eighteenth century was considerably less tempestuous than in the seventeenth, with its bitter struggles for power and frequent armed conflicts. Political stability in Britain coupled with the maturation of local elites in America made for more tranquil government. New York stood apart from this development. With its diverse population and bitter memories of Leisler's rebellion (see Chapter 3), New York continued to experience intense political strife among its many economic interests and ethnic groups. By the 1750s, semipermanent political parties competed vigorously for popular support in New York elections. But in most other colonies, although differences over policies of one kind or another were hardly absent, they rarely produced the civil disorder or political passions of the previous century.

The Right to Vote

In many respects, politics in eighteenth-century America had a more republican quality than in Great Britain. Suffrage requirements varied from colony to colony, but as in Britain the linchpin of voting laws was the property qualification. Its purpose was to ensure that men who possessed an economic stake in society and the independence of judgment that supposedly went with it determined the policies of the government. The "foundation of liberty," the parliamentary leader Henry Ireton had declared during the English Civil War of the 1640s, "is that those who shall choose the lawmakers shall be men freed from dependence upon others." Slaves, servants, tenants, adult sons living in the homes of their parents, the poor, and all women lacked a "will of their own" and were therefore ineligible to vote. The wide distribution of property in the colonies, however, meant that a far higher percentage of the population enjoyed voting rights than in Britain. It is estimated that between 50 and 80 percent of adult white men could vote in eighteenth-century colonial America, as opposed to fewer than 5 percent in Britain.

Colonial politics, however, was hardly democratic in a modern sense. In a few instances—some towns in Massachusetts and on Long Island—propertied women, generally widows, cast ballots. But voting was almost everywhere considered a male prerogative. In some colonies, Jews, Catholics, and Protestant Dissenters like Baptists and Quakers could not vote. Propertied free Blacks, who enjoyed the franchise in the early days of settlement, lost that right in many places. Native Americans generally participated in politics within their own towns and nations and did not vote in colonial elections.

Political Cultures

Despite the relatively broad electorate among white men, "the people" existed only on election day. Between elections, members of colonial assemblies remained out of touch with their constituents. Strongly competitive elections were the norm only in the Middle Colonies. Elsewhere, many elections went uncontested, either because only one candidate presented himself or because the local culture stressed community harmony, as in many New England towns. Considerable power in colonial politics rested with those who held appointive, not elective, office. Governors and councils were appointed by the crown in the nine royal colonies and by the proprietors of Pennsylvania and Maryland. Only in Rhode Island and Connecticut were these offices elective. Moreover, laws passed by colonial assemblies could be vetoed by governors or in London. In New England, most town officers were elected, but local officials in other colonies were appointed by the governor or by powerful officials in London. The duke of Newcastle alone could appoint eighty-three colonial officials.

Property qualifications for officeholding were far higher than for voting. In South Carolina, for example, nearly every free adult male could meet the voting qualification of fifty acres of land or payment of twenty shillings in taxes, but to sit in the assembly one had to own 500 acres of land and ten slaves or town property worth £1,000. As a result, throughout the eighteenth century nearly all of South Carolina's legislators were planters or wealthy merchants. Despite

This 1765 engraving depicting an election in Pennsylvania suggests the intensity of political debate in the Middle Colonies, as well as the social composition of the electorate. Those shown arguing outside the Old Court House in Philadelphia include physicians (with wigs and gold-topped canes), ministers, and lawyers. A line of men wait on the steps to vote.

its boisterous and competitive politics, New York's diminutive assembly, with fewer than thirty members, was dominated by relatives and allies of the great landed families, especially the Livingstons and De Lanceys. Of seventy-two men who sat in the New York Assembly between 1750 and 1776, fifty-two were related to the families who owned the great Hudson River estates.

In some colonies, a majority of free men possessed the right to vote, but an ingrained tradition of "deference"—the assumption among ordinary people that wealth, education, and social prominence carried a right to public office—sharply limited effective choice in elections. Virginia politics, for example, combined political democracy for white men with the tradition that voters should choose among candidates from the gentry. Aspirants for public office actively sought to ingratiate themselves with ordinary voters, distributing food and liquor freely at the courthouse where balloting took place. In Thomas Jefferson's first campaign for the House of Burgesses in 1768, his expenses included hiring two men "for bringing up rum" to the polling place. Even in New England, with its larger number of elective positions, town leaders were generally the largest property holders and offices frequently passed from generation to generation in the same family.

Colonial Government

Preoccupied with events in Europe and imperial rivalries, successive British governments during the first half of the eighteenth century adopted a policy of **salutary neglect**, leaving the colonies largely to govern themselves. With imperial authority so weak, the large landowners, merchants, and lawyers who dominated colonial assemblies increasingly claimed the right to control local politics.

Convinced that they represented the will of the people, elected colonial assemblies used their control of finance to exert influence over appointed governors and councils. Although governors desired secure incomes for themselves and permanent revenue for their administrations (Robert Hunter of New York demanded a life salary), assemblies often authorized salaries only one year at a time and refused to levy taxes except in exchange for concessions on appointments, land policy, and other issues. Typically members of the British gentry who had suffered financial reversals and hoped to recoup their fortunes in America, governors learned that to rule effectively they would have to cooperate with the colonial elite.

The Rise of the Assemblies

In the seventeenth century, the governor was the focal point of political authority, and colonial assemblies were weak bodies that met infrequently. But in the eighteenth, as economic development enhanced the power of American elites, the assemblies they dominated became more and more assertive. Their leaders insisted that assemblies possessed the same rights and powers in local affairs as the House of Commons enjoyed in Britain.

The most powerful assembly was Pennsylvania's, where a new charter, adopted in 1701, eliminated the governor's council, establishing the only unicameral (one-house) legislature in the colonies. Controlled until mid-century by an elite of Quaker merchants, the assembly wrested control of finance, appointments, and the militia from a series of governors representing the Penn family. Close behind in terms of power and legislative independence were the assemblies of New York, Virginia, South Carolina, and Massachusetts, which successfully resisted governors' demands for permanent salaries for appointed officials. Many of the conflicts between governors and elected assemblies stemmed from the colonies' economic growth. To deal with the scarcity of gold and silver coins, the only legal form of currency, some colonies printed paper money, although this was strongly opposed by the governors, authorities in London, and British merchants who did not wish to be paid in what they considered worthless paper. Numerous battles also took place over land policy (sometimes involving divergent attitudes toward relations with Native Americans) and the level of rents charged to farmers on land owned by the crown or proprietors.

In their negotiations and conflicts with royal governors, leaders of the assemblies drew on British political philosophers who emphasized the constant tension between liberty and political power and the dangers of executive influence over the legislature. As the colonial embodiment of the rights of Englishmen and the principle of popular consent to government, the assemblies saw themselves as defenders of "the people's liberty," in the words of one New York legislator.

Politics in Public

This language reverberated outside the relatively narrow world of elective and legislative politics. The "political nation" was dominated by the American gentry, whose members addressed each other in letters, speeches, newspaper articles, and pamphlets filled with Latin expressions and references to classical learning. But especially in colonial towns and cities, the eighteenth century witnessed a considerable expansion of the "public sphere"—the world of political organization and debate independent of the government, where an informed citizenry openly discussed questions that had previously been the preserve of officials.

In Boston, New York, and Philadelphia, clubs proliferated where literary, philosophical, scientific, and political issues were debated. Among the best known was the Junto, a "club for mutual improvement" founded by Benjamin Franklin in Philadelphia in 1727 for weekly discussion of political and economic questions. Beginning with only a dozen members, it eventually evolved into the much larger American Philosophical Society. Such groups were generally composed of men of property and commerce, but some drew ordinary citizens into discussions of public affairs. Colonial taverns and coffeehouses also became important sites not only for social conviviality but also for political debates. Philadelphia had a larger number of drinking establishments per capita than Paris. In Philadelphia, one clergyman commented, "the poorest laborer thinks himself entitled to deliver his sentiments in matters of religion or politics with as much freedom as the gentleman or scholar."

The Colonial Press

Neither the Spanish possessions of Florida and New Mexico nor New France and French Louisiana possessed a printing press, although missionaries had established one in Mexico City in the 1530s. In British North America, however, the press expanded rapidly during the eighteenth century. So did the number of political broadsides and pamphlets published, especially at election time. Widespread literacy created an expanding market for printed materials. By the eve of the American Revolution, some three-quarters of the free adult male population in the colonies and more than one-third of free adult women could read and write, and a majority of American families owned at least one book. Philadelphia boasted no fewer than seventy-seven bookshops in the 1770s.

Circulating libraries appeared in many colonial cities and towns, making possible a wider dissemination of knowledge at a time when books were still expensive. The first, the Library Company of Philadelphia, was established by Benjamin Franklin in 1731. "So few were the readers at that time, and the majority of us so poor," Franklin recalled in his *Autobiography* (1791), that he could find only fifty persons, mostly "young tradesmen," anxious for self-improvement and willing to pay for the privilege of borrowing books. But reading, he added, soon "became fashionable." Libraries sprang up in other towns, and ordinary Americans came to be "better instructed and more intelligent than people of the same rank" abroad.

The first continuously published colonial newspaper, the *Boston News-Letter*, appeared in 1704 (a predecessor, *Publick Occurrences, Both Foreign and Domestick*, established in Boston in 1690, had been suppressed by authorities after a single issue for criticizing military cooperation with the Haudeno-saunee). There were twenty-five colonial newspapers by 1765, mostly weeklies with small circulations—an average of 600 sales per issue. Probably the best-edited was the *Pennsylvania Gazette*, established in 1728 in Philadelphia and purchased the following year by Benjamin Franklin, who had earlier worked as an apprentice printer on his brother's Boston periodical, the *New England Courant*. At its peak, the *Gazette* attracted 2,000 subscribers. Newspapers initially devoted most of their space to advertisements, religious affairs, and reports on British society and government. But by the 1730s, political commentary was widespread in the American press.

Freedom of Expression and Its Limits

The public sphere thrived on the free exchange of ideas. But free expression was not generally considered one of the ancient rights of Englishmen. The phrase "freedom of speech" originated in Britain during the sixteenth century in Parliament's struggle to achieve the privilege of unrestrained debate. A right of legislators, not ordinary citizens, it referred to the ability of members of Parliament to express their views without fear of reprisal, on the grounds that only in this way could they effectively represent the people. Outside of Parliament, free speech had no legal protection. A subject could be beheaded for accusing the king of failing to hold "true" religious beliefs, and language from swearing to criticism of the government exposed a person to criminal penalties.

As for freedom of the press, governments on both sides of the Atlantic viewed this as extremely dangerous, partly because they considered ordinary citizens prone to be misled by inflammatory printed materials. During the English Civil War of the 1640s, the Levellers had called for guarantees of religious liberty and freedom of the press. But until 1695, when a British law requiring the licensing of printed works before publication lapsed, no newspaper, book, or pamphlet could legally be printed without a government license. The instructions of colonial governors included a warning about the "great inconveniences that may arise by the liberty of printing." After 1695, the government could not censor newspapers, books, and pamphlets before they appeared in print, although it continued to try to manage the press by direct payments to publishers and individual journalists. Authors and publishers could still be prosecuted for "seditious libel"—a crime that included defaming government officials—or punished for contempt.

Elected assemblies, not governors, most frequently discouraged freedom of the press in colonial America. Dozens of publishers were hauled before assemblies and forced to apologize for comments regarding one or another member. If they refused, they were jailed. James Franklin, Benjamin's older brother, spent a month in prison in 1722 after publishing a piece satirizing public authorities in Massachusetts. Colonial newspapers vigorously defended freedom of the press as a central component of liberty, insisting that the citizenry had a right to monitor the workings of government and subject public officials to criticism. Many newspapers reprinted passages from an influential series of essays published in the British press entitled *Cato's Letters* strongly opposing prosecutions for libel. "Without freedom of thought," they declared, "there can be no such thing as wisdom, and no such thing as public liberty, without freedom of speech." But since government printing contracts were crucial for economic success, few newspapers attacked colonial governments unless financially supported by an opposition faction.

The Trial of Zenger

The most famous colonial court case involving freedom of the press demonstrated that popular sentiment opposed prosecutions for criticism of public officials. This was the 1735 trial of John Peter Zenger, a German-born printer who had immigrated to New York as a youth. Financed by wealthy opponents of Governor William Cosby, Zenger's newspaper, the *Weekly Journal*, lambasted the governor for corruption, influence peddling, and "tyranny." New York's council ordered four issues burned and had Zenger himself arrested and tried for seditious libel. The judge instructed the jurors to consider only whether Zenger had actually published the offending words, not whether they were accurate. But Zenger's attorney, Andrew Hamilton, urged the jury to judge not the publisher but the governor. If they decided that Zenger's charges were correct, they must acquit him, and, Hamilton proclaimed, "every man who prefers freedom to a life of slavery will bless you."

Zenger was found not guilty. The case sent a warning to prosecutors that libel cases might be very difficult to win, especially in the superheated atmosphere of New York partisan politics. To be sure, had Zenger lambasted the assembly rather than the governor, he would in all likelihood have been lodged in jail. But the outcome helped to promote the idea that the publication of truth should always be permitted, and it demonstrated that the idea of free expression was becoming ingrained in the popular imagination.

The American Enlightenment

During the eighteenth century, many educated Americans began to be influenced by the outlook of the European **Enlightenment**. This philosophical movement, which originated among French thinkers and soon spread to Britain, sought to apply the scientific method of careful investigation based on research and experiment to political and social life. Enlightenment ideas crisscrossed the Atlantic along with goods and people. Enlightenment thinkers insisted that every human institution, authority, and tradition be judged before the bar of reason. The self-educated Benjamin Franklin's wide range of activities—establishing a newspaper, debating club, and library; publishing the widely circulated *Poor Richard's Almanack;* and conducting experiments to demonstrate that lightning is a form of electricity—exemplified the Enlightenment spirit and made him probably the best-known American in the eighteenth-century world.

One inspiration for the American Enlightenment was a reaction against the bloody religious wars that racked Europe in the seventeenth century. Enlightenment thinkers hoped that "reason," not religious enthusiasm, could govern human life. The criticism of social and political institutions based on tradition and hereditary privilege rather than the dictates of reason could also be applied to established churches. John Locke himself had published *The Reasonableness of Christianity* in 1695, which insisted that religious belief should rest on scientific evidence. During the eighteenth century, many prominent Americans moved toward the position called Arminianism, which taught that reason alone was capable of establishing the essentials of religion. Others adopted **Deism**, a belief that God essentially withdrew after creating the world, leaving it to function according to scientific laws without divine intervention. Belief in miracles, in the revealed truth of the Bible, and in the innate sinfulness of mankind were viewed by Arminians, Deists, and others as outdated superstitions that should be abandoned in the modern age.

In the seventeenth century, the English scientist Isaac Newton had revealed the natural laws that governed the physical universe. Here, Deists believed, was the purest evidence of God's handiwork. Many Protestants of all denominations could accept Newton's findings while remaining devout churchgoers (as Newton himself had). But Deists concluded that the best form of religious devotion was to study the workings of nature, rather than to worship in organized churches or appeal to divine grace for salvation. By the late colonial era, a small but influential group of leading Americans, including Benjamin Franklin and Thomas Jefferson, could be classified as Deists.

THE GREAT AWAKENING

Like freedom of the press, religion was another realm where the actual experience of liberty outstripped its legal recognition. Religion remained central to eighteenth-century American life. Sermons, theological treatises, and copies of the Bible were by far the largest category of material produced by colonial printers. Religious disputes often generated more public attention than political issues. Yet many church leaders worried about lax religious observance as colonial economic growth led people to be more and more preoccupied with worldly affairs.

Religious Revivals

Many ministers were concerned that westward expansion, commercial development, the growth of Enlightenment rationalism, and lack of individual engagement in church services were undermining religious devotion. These fears helped to inspire the revivals that swept through the colonies beginning in the 1730s. Known as the **Great Awakening**, the revivals were less a coordinated movement than a series of local events united by a commitment to a "religion of the heart," a more emotional and personal Christianity than that offered by existing churches. The revivals redrew the religious landscape of the colonies.

The eighteenth century witnessed a resurgence of religious fundamentalism in many parts of the world, in part a response to the rationalism of the Enlightenment and a desire for greater religious purity. In the Middle East and Central Asia, where Islam was widespread, followers of a form of the religion known as Wahhabism called for a return to the practices of the religion's early days. In Eastern Europe, Hasidic Jews emphasized the importance of faith and religious joy as opposed to what they considered the overly academic study of Jewish learning and history in conventional Judaism. Methodism and other forms of enthusiastic religion were flourishing in Europe. Like other intellectual currents of the time, the Great Awakening was a transatlantic movement.

During the 1720s and 1730s, the New Jersey Dutch Reformed clergyman Theodore Frelinghuysen, his Presbyterian neighbors William and Gilbert Tennent, and the Massachusetts Congregationalist minister Jonathan Edwards pioneered an intensely emotional style of preaching. Edwards's famous sermon *Sinners in the Hands of an Angry God* portrayed sinful man as a "loathsome insect" suspended over a bottomless pit of eternal fire by a slender thread that might break at any moment. Edwards's preaching, declared a member of his congregation, inspired worshipers to cry out, "What shall I do to be saved— oh, I am going to hell!" Only a "new birth"—immediately acknowledging one's sins and pleading for divine grace—could save men from eternal damnation. "It is the new birth that makes [sinners] free," declared the Reverend Joshua Tufts.

The Preaching of Whitefield

More than any other individual, the English minister George Whitefield, who declared "the whole world his parish," sparked the Great Awakening. For two years after his arrival in America in 1739, Whitefield brought his highly emotional brand of preaching to colonies from Georgia to New England. God, Whitefield proclaimed, was merciful. Rather than being predestined for damnation, men and women could save themselves by repenting of their sins. Whitefield appealed to the passions of his listeners, powerfully sketching the boundless joy of salvation and the horrors of damnation. In every sermon, he asked his listeners to look into their own hearts and answer the question, "Are you saved?" If not, they must change their sinful ways and surrender their lives to Christ.

Tens of thousands of colonists flocked to Whitefield's sermons, which were widely reported in the American press, making him a celebrity and helping to establish the revivals as the first major intercolonial event in North American history. In Whitefield's footsteps, a host of traveling preachers, or "evangelists" (meaning, literally, bearers of good news), held revivalist meetings, often to the alarm of established ministers.

Critics of the Great Awakening produced sermons, pamphlets, and newspaper articles condemning the revivalist preachers for lacking theological training, encouraging disrespect for "the established church and her ministers," and filling churches with "general disorder." Connecticut sought to stem the revivalist tide through laws punishing disruptive traveling preachers. By the time they subsided in the 1760s, the revivals had changed the religious configuration of the colonies and enlarged the boundaries of liberty. Whitefield inspired the emergence of numerous Dissenting churches. Congregations split into factions headed by Old Lights (traditionalists) and New Lights (revivalists), and new churches proliferated—Baptist, Methodist, Presbyterian, and others. Many of these new churches began to criticize the colonial practice of levying taxes to support an established church; they defended religious freedom as one of the natural rights government must not restrict.

The Awakening's Impact

Although the revivals were primarily a spiritual matter, the Great Awakening reflected existing social tensions, threw into question many forms of authority, and inspired criticism of aspects of colonial society. They attracted primarily men and women of modest means—"rude, ignorant, void of manners, education or good breeding," one Anglican minister complained. Revivalist preachers frequently criticized commercial society, insisting that believers should make salvation, not profit, "the one business of their lives." In New England, they condemned merchants who ensnared the unwary in debt as greedy and unchristian. Preaching to the small farmers of the southern backcountry, Baptist and Methodist revivalists criticized the worldliness of wealthy planters and attacked as sinful activities such as gambling, horse racing, and lavish entertainments on the Sabbath.

A few preachers explicitly condemned slavery. And a few converts, such as Robert Carter III, the grandson of the wealthy planter Robert "King" Carter, emancipated their slaves after concluding that Black and white were brothers and sisters in Christ. Carter ultimately freed some 500 men, women, and children, against the opposition of many white Virginians. Most owners managed to reconcile Christianity and slaveholding. But especially in the Chesapeake, the revivals brought numerous Black women and men into the Christian fold, an important step in creating an African American culture. Some Blacks, touched by the word of God, became Christian preachers. The revivals also spawned a group of female exhorters, who for a time shattered the male monopoly on preaching.

The revivals broadened the range of religious alternatives available to Americans, thereby leaving them more divided than before and at the same time more fully integrated into transatlantic religious developments. But the impact of the Great Awakening spread beyond purely spiritual matters. The newspaper and pamphlet wars it inspired greatly expanded the circulation of printed material in the colonies. The revivals encouraged many colonists to trust their own views rather than those of established elites. In listening to the sermons of self-educated preachers, forming Bible study groups, and engaging in intense religious discussions, ordinary colonists asserted the right to independent judgment. "The common people," proclaimed Baptist minister Isaac Backus, "claim as good a right to judge and act for themselves in matters of religion as civil rulers or the learned clergy." The revivalists' aim was spiritual salvation, not social or political revolution. But the independent frame of mind they encouraged would have significant political consequences.

IMPERIAL RIVALRIES

The rapid growth of Britain's North American colonies took place at a time of increased jockeying for power among European empires, involving much of the area today included in the United States. Spain, France, and Britain all wanted to expand their coastal colonies and establish a presence in the vast Native interior. But the colonies of England's rivals remained thinly populated and economically and militarily weak. The northern claims of the Spanish empire encompassed an area that stretched from the Pacific coast and New Mexico into the Great Plains and eastward through Texas, plus Florida on the Atlantic coast. On paper a vast territorial empire, Spanish North America (north of central Mexico) actually consisted of a few small and isolated urban clusters, most prominently St. Augustine in Florida, San Antonio in Texas, and Santa Fe and Albuquerque in New Mexico.

This illustration of friars preaching, from an eighteenth-century work by the missionary Pablo de Beaumont, depicts demons dispatched by the devil as an ever-present threat to the missionaries' efforts to convert Native Americans.

The Spanish in the Southwest

In the second half of the century, the Spanish government made a concerted effort to reinvigorate its empire north of the Rio Grande. It sought to stabilize relations with Indians, especially the nomadic Comanches and Apaches, who controlled much of the land claimed by Spain and whose raids on mines and ranches and settled Native communities wreaked havoc. Spain was also alarmed by the growing number of French merchants who made their way into the region from Louisiana.

During the reigns of Carlos II and Carlos III, Spanish reformers, like other Enlightenment figures, hoped that applying scientific methods to society would bring about progress, but at the same time they hoped to preserve the absolutist monarchy and Spain's American empire. They collected data about the area's Native population and debated whether Indians were capable of being integrated into Spanish society or should remain subject peoples. Reformers condemned Spain's past treatment of Indians and called for more humane policies. They pointed out that despite the Black Legend of unique Spanish cruelty, Indians comprised well over half of the inhabitants of New Spain but now amounted to less than 6 percent of the population of the mainland English colonies. In the northern reaches of their empire, Spanish officials used a combination of coercion, gifts, and trade to woo Native allies. These tactics to some extent strengthened Spain's hold on the northern part of its American empire against its European rivals while strengthening its Native allies.

Spain's weakness in the northern part of its American empire in large part stemmed from the small size of its settler population there. New Mexico in 1750 had fewer than 10,000 colonists, living in communities with larger numbers of Native Puebloans. Some of the Spanish were "crypto-Jews"—Jews who continued to practice their religion after converting to Catholicism, as required by Spanish law. Many had moved from Mexico City to escape the Inquisition there. Although ranching had expanded, the economy of New Mexico essentially rested on trading with Native allies. The manpower demands of wars in Europe made it impossible for the Spanish government to meet local military commanders' requests for more troops. The powerful Comanches and Apaches continued to dominate large parts of northern New Spain.

Similar problems existed in Texas. Spain had begun the colonization of Texas at the beginning of the eighteenth century, partly as a buffer to prevent French commercial influence, then spreading in the Mississippi Valley, from intruding into New Mexico. After founding San Antonio and Los Adaes earlier in the century, the Spanish established more missions and *presidios* including La Bahía on the Gulf Coast. But the region attracted few settlers. Texas had only 1,200 Spanish colonists in 1760.

Spanish Florida

Like New Mexico and Texas, Florida remained a mostly Native place with few European colonists. As we have seen, it also became a refuge for people of African descent who fled slavery in British South Carolina. In 1693, Spanish King Carlos II decreed that slaves who fled Carolina would be free in Florida if they became Catholic. The king knew that attracting former slaves to Florida—which had few Spanish settlers—would increase its population

EUROPEAN EMPIRES IN NORTH AMERICA, MID-EIGHTEENTH CENTURY

Three great empires—the British, French, and Spanish—competed for influence in North America for much of the eighteenth century. This map shows European land claims on the eve of the Seven Years' War, plus missions that Spain founded in the 1760s and 1770s.

while weakening the English colonies. Many enslaved people took up the offer over the course of the eighteenth century.

After some Spanish Floridians violated the king's decree and re-enslaved people seeking freedom in Florida, Francisco Menéndez, a captain of Florida's free Black militia who could write in Spanish, wrote petitions for their freedom. If it was not granted, he warned, his fellow Afro-Floridians might join the English against the Spanish. The petitions succeeded. The former slaves wrote the king to thank him for "ordering us to be given freedom for having come to this country and for being Christian and following the true religion [Catholicism] that saves us." These former slaves built their own settlement in 1738 outside St. Augustine and named it Gracia Reál (Royal Grace) de Santa Teresa de Mose. Francisco Menéndez led this community, which lasted until 1763.

The Spanish in California

The clash of empires also took place on the Pacific coast. In the mid-eighteenth century, empire builders in Moscow dreamed of challenging the Spanish for control of the region's fur trade, minerals, and ports. Russian traders established a series of forts in Alaska and then moved southward toward modern-day California. As late as 1812, Russians founded Fort Ross, only 100 miles north of San Francisco.

Even though only a small number of Russians actually appeared in California, the alarmed Spanish in 1769 launched the "Sacred Experiment" to take control of the coast north of San Diego to prevent its occupation by foreigners. In 1774, Juan Bautista de Anza, an explorer and military officer, led an expedition that discovered a usable overland route to California from northern Mexico. In 1776, he founded a new *presidio* and mission at San Francisco. But in 1781 Quechan (Yuma) Indians wrested control of the overland route from the Spanish. Given the distance and difficulties of communication, authorities in Mexico City decided to establish missions in California, run by the Franciscan religious order, rather than sending colonists. The friars intended to set up ranching and farming activities and convert Indians into loyal Spaniards.

A string of Spanish missions and *presidios* soon dotted the California coastline, from San Diego to Los Angeles, Santa Barbara, Monterey, San Francisco, and Sonoma. Born on the Spanish Mediterranean island of Mallorca, **Father Junípero Serra** became one of the most controversial figures in California's early history. He founded the first California mission, in San Diego, in 1769 and administered the mission network until his death in 1784. Serra was widely praised in Spain for converting thousands of Native Californians to Christianity, teaching them Spanish, and working to transform their hunting-and-gathering economies by introducing settled agriculture. In 2015, he was elevated to sainthood by the Catholic Church. But forced labor and disease took a heavy toll among Indians who lived at the missions Serra directed. Many ran away, and the friars responded with whippings and imprisonment. "Naturally we want our liberty," one fugitive from the missions remarked.

Present-day California was a densely populated area, with a Native population of perhaps 250,000 when Spanish settlement began. But the coming of soldiers and missionaries proved a disaster for the Indians. More than any other Spanish colony, California was a mission frontier. These outposts served simultaneously as religious institutions and centers of government and labor. Their aim was to transform the culture of the local population and eventually assimilate it into Spanish civilization. Father Serra and other missionaries hoped to convert the Natives to Christianity and settled farming, although Serra accommodated Native traditions such as dancing and traditional healing.

Although painted in the twentieth century, this portrait of Father Junípero Serra is based on one that dates from the eighteenth century, when Serra conducted missionary work in present-day California.

The missions also relied on forced Indian labor to grow grain, work in orchards and vineyards, and tend cattle. The combination of new diseases, environmental changes caused by the introduction of Spanish crops and animals, and the resettlement of thousands of Indians in villages around the missions devastated Native society. California did not attract Spanish settlers. In 1800, Los Angeles, with a population of 300, was the largest town. When Spanish rule came to an end in 1821, twenty missions were operating, with an average population of over 1,000 Indians, but *Californios* (California residents of Spanish descent) numbered only 3,200.

The French Empire

Spain's North American colonies remained peripheral parts of its empire when compared with its possessions in Central and South America and the Caribbean. Native peoples retained far more power in the parts of North America claimed by Spain than in areas of English settlement. The same was true when it came to a greater rival to British power in North America—as well as in Europe and the Caribbean—France. During the eighteenth century, the population and economy of Canada expanded. In the St. Lawrence River valley of French Canada, prosperous farming communities developed. By 1750, the area had a population of about 55,000 colonists. Another 10,000 (about half Europeans, half African American slaves) resided in Louisiana, mostly concentrated on the lower Mississippi River and along the Gulf Coast. By mid-century, sugar plantations had sprung up in the area between New Orleans and Baton Rouge. New Orleans already had a vibrant social life as well as an established community with churches, schools, and governmental buildings.

Nonetheless, the population of French North America continued to be dwarfed by the British colonies. Around 1750, the 1.5 million British colonists (including slaves) greatly outnumbered the 65,000 French in North America. The giant Louisiana colony consisted of a core area around New Orleans, controlled by Europeans, and a vast interior dominated by multiple Native nations.

Prejudice against emigration to North America remained widespread in France. A French novel written in 1731, known today as the basis for the nineteenth-century opera *Manon,* told the story of a prostitute punished by being transported to Louisiana and of her noble lover who followed her there. It expressed the popular view of the colony as a place of cruel exile for criminals and social outcasts. Nonetheless, by claiming control of a large arc of territory and by establishing close trading and military relations with many Native nations, the French empire posed a real challenge to the British. French forts and trading posts ringed the British colonies. In present-day Mississippi and Alabama and in the western regions of Georgia and the Carolinas, French and British traders competed to form Native alliances and control the trade in deerskins. The French were a presence on the New England and New York frontiers and in western Pennsylvania.

BATTLE FOR THE CONTINENT

The Ohio Valley

The Ohio Valley would be the flashpoint of both the French-British rivalry and struggles over Native sovereignty as those two empires pushed farther into Native lands. Earlier in the century, Shawnees had returned to their Ohio Valley homeland, accompanied by Delawares (Lenapes) pushed out of Pennsylvania. They allied with Anishinaabe, Wendat, and Illinois communities in the vast area between the Ohio River, the Great Lakes, and the Mississippi River. Among other interests, these varied peoples shared justified suspicions that the Haudenosaunee, the British, and the French all were dangers to their independence. As one Delaware spokesman remarked, it was impossible to know "where the Indians' land lay, for the French claimed all the land on one side of the Ohio River and the English on the other side."

Native nations in the Ohio Valley and Great Lakes regions hoped that allying together would protect their independence from Europeans pressing in on their territories. They shared the hunting lands south of the Ohio River with one another and with Cherokees and Chickasaws, and they traded deerskins, furs, and food with French and British traders.

This area would soon become hotly contested, but in 1750, few white settlers inhabited the Ohio Valley. The area was known to European settlers more by rumor than by observation, and contemporary maps bore little resemblance to the actual geography. Nonetheless, many prominent colonists dreamed of establishing a new empire west of the British colonies. Many others saw the West as a place where they could easily acquire land, and the freedom that went

NORTH AMERICA IN 1750

In 1750, most of North America still was populated and controlled by Native nations, although Britain, France, and Spain claimed the continent.

with it. Already, Scots-Irish and German immigrants, Virginia planters, and land speculators were eyeing the region's fertile soil. In 1749, the government of Virginia awarded an immense land grant—half a million acres—to the Ohio Company, an example of the huge domains being parceled out to those with political connections. The company's members included the colony's royal governor, Robert Dinwiddie, and the elite of Virginia society—Lees, Carters, and Washingtons. The land grant threatened the region's Native nations as well as Pennsylvania land speculators, who also had claims in the area. It sparked the French to bolster their presence in the region. It was the Ohio Company's demand for French recognition of its land claims that inaugurated the **Seven Years' War** (known in the British colonies as the **French and Indian War**), the first of the century's imperial wars to begin in the colonies and the first to result in a decisive victory for one combatant. It permanently altered the global balance of power.

The Seven Years' War

Before 1688, England was a marginal power. Spain's empire was far more extensive, France had greater influence in Europe, and the Dutch dominated overseas trade and finance. Only in the eighteenth century, after numerous wars against its rivals, did Britain emerge as the world's leading empire and its center of trade and banking. The War of the Spanish Succession (known in the colonies as Queen Anne's War) lasted from 1702 to 1713; the War of Jenkins' Ear (named after a British seaman mistreated by the Spanish) from 1739 to 1742; and King George's War from 1740 to 1748. To finance these wars, Britain's public expenditures, taxes, and national debt rose enormously. The high rate of taxation inspired discontent at home and would later help to spark the American Revolution.

By the 1750s, British possessions and trade reached around the globe. "Every part of the world affects us, in some way or another," remarked the duke of Newcastle. The existence of global empires implied that warfare among them would also be global. What became a worldwide struggle for imperial domination, which eventually spread to Europe, West Africa, and Asia, began in 1754 with British efforts to dislodge the French from forts they had constructed in western Pennsylvania. In the previous year, George Washington, then only twenty-one years old, had been dispatched by the colony's governor on an unsuccessful mission to persuade French soldiers to abandon a fort they were building on lands claimed by the Ohio Company (as well as the Shawnees, Delawares, and Haudenosaunee). In 1754, Washington returned to the area with two companies of soldiers. He hastily constructed Fort Necessity. After an ill-considered attempt to defend it against a larger French and Indian force, resulting in the loss of one-third of his men, Washington was forced to surrender.

Soon afterward, an expedition led by British General Edward Braddock marched against Fort Duquesne (today's Pittsburgh). Braddock's superiors hoped that the Ohio Valley's Native nations would join their side against the French, but Braddock alienated them. In a meeting with representatives of several Native nations, Delaware Chief Shingas asked Braddock "what he intended to do with the land if he could drive the French and their Indians away." Braddock unwisely replied, "The English should inhabit and inherit the land." Unsurprisingly, the assembled Native leaders answered that "if they might not have liberty to live on the land they would not fight for it." Some of them immediately went to join forces with the French. A Native and French force ambushed Braddock, killing him and leaving two-thirds of his 3,000 soldiers dead or wounded.

For two years, the war went against the British. French and Indian forces captured British forts in northern New York. The western borders of Pennsylvania, Virginia, the Carolinas, and Georgia were ablaze with brutal fighting among British forces, colonists, and Indians. Native American fighters killed hundreds of colonists in western Pennsylvania and pushed the line of settlement all the way back to Carlisle, only 100 miles west of Philadelphia. In Nova Scotia, the

THE
AMERICAN MAGAZINE,

PRÆVALEBIT ÆQUIOR.

AND

MONTHLY CHRONICLE for the BRITISH Colonies.
Vol. I. Nº. VI. FOR MARCH 1758.

This image from the cover of a magazine published in Pennsylvania in 1758 depicts an Englishman and a Frenchman attempting to trade with an Indian. The Frenchman offers a tomahawk and musket, the Englishman a Bible and cloth. Of course, the depictions reflect pro-British stereotypes.

British rounded up around 5,000 local French residents, called Acadians, confiscated their land, and expelled them from the region, selling their farms to settlers from New England. Some of those expelled eventually returned to France; others ended up as far away as Louisiana, where their descendants came to be known as Cajuns.

As the British government raised huge sums of money and poured men and naval forces into the war, the tide of battle turned. Secretary of State William Pitt, who took office in 1757, devised a strategy of providing funds to Prussia to enable it to hold the line against France and its ally Spain in Europe, while the British struck at the French weak point, its colonies. By 1759, Britain—with colonial and Haudenosaunee fighters playing a major role—had captured the pivotal French outposts of Forts Duquesne, Ticonderoga (north of Albany), and Louisbourg on Cape Breton Island, which guarded the mouth of the St. Lawrence River. In September of that year, a French army was defeated on the Plains of Abraham near Quebec. British forces also seized nearly all of France's islands in the Caribbean and posts in India. In Europe, meanwhile, Prussia managed to fend off the coalition of France, Russia, and Spain.

A World Transformed

"As long as the world has stood there has not been such a war," declared a British emissary to the Delaware Indians. Britain's victory fundamentally reshaped the world balance of power. In the Peace of Paris in 1763, France ceded Canada to Britain, receiving back in return the sugar islands of Guadeloupe and Martinique (far more lucrative colonies from the point of view of French authorities). As part of the reshuffling of imperial possessions, Spain ceded Florida to Britain in exchange for the return of the Philippines and Cuba (seized by the British during the war). Spain acquired from France the part of the vast Louisiana colony that lay west of the Mississippi River, plus the busy port of New Orleans at its mouth. The British received the part of Louisiana that lay east of the Mississippi (including Mobile) and renamed it, along with Florida's panhandle, West Florida, with its capital at the small post of Pensacola. France's 200-year-old North American empire had come to an end. With the exception of two tiny islands retained by France off the coast of Newfoundland, the entire continent east of the Mississippi River was now claimed by Britain, while Spain's claims stretched from the southern tip of South America to New Orleans and St. Louis.

"Peace," remarked Prime Minister Pitt, "will be as hard to make as war." Eighteenth-century warfare, conducted on land and sea across the globe, was enormously expensive. The Seven Years' War put strains on all the participants. The war's cost produced a financial crisis in France that almost three decades later would help to spark the French Revolution. The British would try to recoup part of the cost of war by increasing taxes on their American colonies. "We no sooner leave fighting our neighbors, the French," commented the British writer Dr. Samuel Johnson, "but we must fall to quarreling among ourselves." In fact, the Peace of Paris was soon followed by open warfare in North America between the British and Native Americans in lands recently ceded by France.

Pontiac's War and Native Freedom

Among other consequences, the Seven Years' War helped lay the foundation for the emergence of a distinct Native American identity. American Indians had traditionally identified most strongly along lines of kinship, shared language, and common geographical residence, including towns, nations, and confederacies rather than as one people or race. The violence directed against Indians by soldiers and settlers during the war led many Native leaders to envision more centralized Native nations and stronger alliances with one another. Others, including the Delaware Prophet **Neolin** and his Ottawa follower Pontiac, advocated something more radical: a pan-Indian identity. In the religious movement that emerged during the Seven Years' War, prophets like Neolin urged their peoples to think of themselves as one Native American race rather than separate nations. Some even developed racial theories, arguing that the Creator had made Europeans, Africans, and Native Americans as separate creations and meant for the three races to stay in the continents where he had originally put them. As Pontiac put it, according to the Creator, Native Americans should send Europeans "back to the lands I made for them, and let them stay there."

The idea of a single Native American identity was controversial even among the Delawares, Ottawas, Shawnees, and others in the Ohio Valley and Great Lakes who had seen the worst of the fighting against British colonial expansion. They had serious debates about the best way to secure their individual and

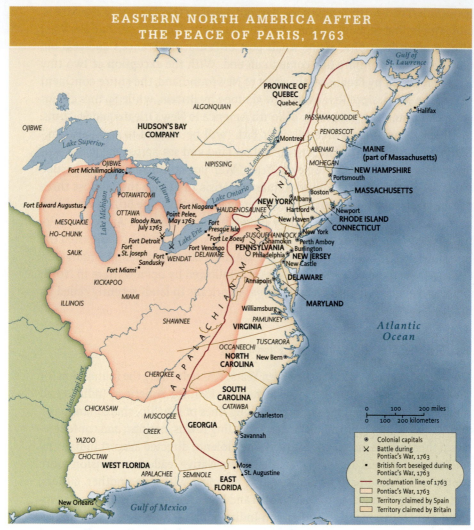

EASTERN NORTH AMERICA AFTER THE PEACE OF PARIS, 1763

Gulf of St. Lawrence

OJIBWE

Lake Superior

HUDSON'S BAY COMPANY

ALGONQUIAN

PROVINCE OF QUEBEC
Quebec

PASSAMAQUODDIE

Halifax

Montreal

PENOBSCOT

OJIBWE
Fort Michilimackinac

NIPISSING

ABENAKI

MAINE
(part of Massachusetts)

MOHEGAN

NEW HAMPSHIRE

Portsmouth

Lake Huron

Lake Michigan

POTAWATOMI

Albany

Boston

MASSACHUSETTS

Fort Edward Augustus

OTTAWA
Bloody Run,
July 1763

Fort Niagara
Point Pelee,
May 1763

Lake Ontario

NEW YORK

HAUDENOSAUNEE

Hartford

Newport

MESQUAKIE

Fort
Presque Isle

New Haven

RHODE ISLAND
CONNECTICUT

HO-CHUNK

Fort Detroit

Fort Le Boeuf

New York

SAUK

Fort
St. Joseph

Fort Venango
DELAWARE

Fort
Sandusky

WENDAT

SUSQUEHANNOCK
Shamokin

Perth Amboy

PENNSYLVANIA

Burlington

Fort Miami

Philadelphia

NEW JERSEY

New Castle

KICKAPOO

MIAMI

Annapolis

DELAWARE

ILLINOIS

MARYLAND

Williamsburg

SHAWNEE

PAMUNKEY

VIRGINIA

Atlantic
Ocean

OCCANEECHI

TUSCARORA

CHEROKEE

NORTH
CAROLINA

New Bern

Mississippi River

APPALACHIAN

SOUTH
CAROLINA

CHICKASAW

MUSCOGEE

CATAWBA

Charleston

YAZOO

CREEK

GEORGIA

Savannah

CHOCTAW

WEST FLORIDA

APALACHEE

SEMINOLE

Mose
St. Augustine

EAST
FLORIDA

New Orleans

Gulf of Mexico

| 0 | 100 | 200 miles |
| 0 | 100 | 200 kilometers |

⊛ Colonial capitals
✕ Battle during Pontiac's War, 1763
▪ British fort beseiged during Pontiac's War, 1763
— Proclamation line of 1763
▢ Pontiac's War, 1763
▢ Territory claimed by Spain
▢ Territory claimed by Britain

In the Peace of Paris, which ended the Seven Years' War, France ceded all of North America east of the Mississippi to Britain, ending the French presence on the continent. Pontiac's War challenged the British assumption that the treaty with France gave them control over Native land west of the Appalachians.

collective independence. It was one thing for two Native nations to build strong alliances to support one another and resist the British. It was quite another to ask them to give up their separate languages and identities. Indeed, although a Native American identity eventually developed, separate national identities such as Shawnee, Delaware, and Ottawa remained strong, and still continue today. Native nations maintained their separate independence despite pressures from many sides to give it up.

Native nations such as the Muscogees and Chickasaws that bordered on the area that was now the Spanish colony of Louisiana established trade and diplomacy with Spain, but for those in the Northeast, the abrupt departure of the French in the aftermath of the Seven Years' War eliminated the balance-of-power diplomacy that the Haudenosaunee and others had practiced for a century. Indians had fought on both sides in the war. But their primary aim was to maintain their independence from both empires. As one British observer put it in 1764, the Six Nations and other Indians "having never been conquered, either by the English or French, nor subject to the laws, consider themselves as a free people." Without consulting them, the French had ceded Indians' land to the British. To Indians on the British colonies' borders, it was clear that continued colonial expansion posed a dire threat.

In 1763, in the wake of the French defeat, Indians of the Ohio Valley and Great Lakes launched a major military assault on the British. Known among the colonists as **Pontiac's War**, it was led by several war leaders inspired by the teachings of the Delaware prophet Neolin. During a religious vision, the Master of Life instructed Neolin that his people must reject European technology, free themselves from commercial ties with whites and dependence on alcohol, clothe themselves in the garb of their ancestors, and drive the British from their territory (although friendly French inhabitants could remain). Neolin combined this message with the relatively new idea of pan-Indian identity. All Indians, he preached, were a single people, and only through cooperation could they regain their lost independence. In the spring and summer of 1763, Ottawa, Wendat (Huron), Delaware, Shawnee, and other Native fighters besieged British forts and settlements on the Great Lakes and Ohio River, seizing or destroying most of them. They killed hundreds of white settlers who had intruded onto their lands.

The Proclamation Line

Pontiac's War inspired the government in London to issue the **Proclamation of 1763**, prohibiting further colonial settlement west of the Appalachian Mountains. These lands were acknowledged as belonging to Indians. Moreover, the proclamation banned the sale of Indian lands to private individuals. Henceforth, only colonial governments could arrange such purchases.

The British aim was less to protect the Indians than to stabilize the situation on the colonial frontier and to avoid being dragged into an endless series of costly border conflicts. But the proclamation enraged both settlers and speculators hoping to take advantage of the expulsion of the French to consolidate

From SCAROUYADY, SPEECH TO PENNSYLVANIA PROVINCIAL COUNCIL (1756)

The Seven Years' War inflamed relations between Native Americans and white settlers in the Ohio Valley. Scarouyady, an Oneida diplomat told Pennsylvania's leaders that he hoped that a fort could be built at the Native town of Shamokin in the Susquehanna River valley, to protect friendly Indians and keep armed whites in check.

You told us that you must now build a Fort at Shamokin; we are glad to hear it; it is a good thing.... The Fort at Shamokin is not a thing of little consequence; it is of the greatest importance to us as well as you. Your people are foolish; for want of this Fort, the Indians, who are your friends, can be of no service to you, having no place to go to where they can promise themselves protection. They cannot be called together; they can do nothing for you; they are not secure any where. At present your people cannot distinguish foes from friends; they think every Indian is against them; they blame us all without distinction, because they see nobody appear for them; the common people to a man entertain this notion, and insult us wherever we go. We bear their ill usage, though very irksome; but all this will be set right when you have built the Fort, and you will see that we in particular are sincere, and many others will come to your assistance. We desire when the fort is built, you will put into the command of so important a place some of your people; grave, solid, and sensible men, who are in repute amongst you, and in whom we can place a Confidence.... Your people are foolish; they are extremely heavy, move slow, and are liable to surprizes, if you go by yourselves. We are a light Body; we can trip nimbly thro' the Woods, look over a large Extent of Country and see that all is clear, and no Enemy lying concealed to cut you off when you think nothing of it. We must likewise tell you not to make a trifling Peace. You have no doubt heard we are a People who never lay down our Arms; it is true our young People now tell you that they will fight whilst they can find one of the Enemy to fight with, so do not make a trifling Peace. Do yourselves and us Justice, and bring your Enemies to a due Sense of themselves, and to offer just Terms, and then, and not till then, think of a Peace. This is our Advice.

From PONTIAC, SPEECHES (1762 AND 1763)

Pontiac was a leader of the pan-Indian resistance to English rule known as Pontiac's War, which followed the end of the Seven Years' War. Neolin was a Delaware religious prophet who helped to inspire the war.

Englishmen, although you have conquered the French, you have not yet conquered us! We are not your slaves. These lakes, these woods, and mountains were left to us by our ancestors. They are our inheritance; and we will part with them to none. Your nation supposes that we, like the white people, cannot live without bread and pork and beef! But you ought to know that He, the Great Spirit and Master of Life, has provided food for us in these spacious lakes, and on these woody mountains.

[The Master of Life has said to Neolin:]

I am the Maker of heaven and earth, the trees, lakes, rivers, and all else. I am the Maker of all mankind; and because I love you, you must do my will. The land on which you live I have made for you and not for others. Why do you suffer the white man to dwell among you? My children, you have forgotten the customs and traditions of your forefathers. Why do you not clothe yourselves in skins, as they did, use bows and arrows and the stone-pointed lances, which they used? You have bought guns, knives, kettles and blankets from the white man until you can no longer do without them; and what is worse, you have drunk the poison firewater, which turns you into fools. Fling all these things away; live as your wise forefathers did before you. And as for these English—these dogs dressed in red, who have come to rob you of your hunting grounds, and drive away the game—you must lift the hatchet against them. Wipe them from the face of the earth, and then you will win my favor back again, and once more be happy and prosperous.

QUESTIONS

1. *What aspects of white behavior does Scarouyady object to?*

2. *What elements of Indian life does Neolin criticize most strongly?*

3. *How do Scarouyady and Pontiac differ in the ways they address white audiences?*

their claims to western lands. Many of them ignored the new policy. George Washington himself ordered his agents to buy up as much Indian land as possible, while keeping the transactions "a profound secret" because of their illegality.

War on Pennsylvania's Border

The Seven Years' War not only redrew the map of the world but produced dramatic changes within the American colonies as well. Nowhere was this more evident than in Pennsylvania, where the conflict shattered the decades-old rule of the Quaker elite and dealt the final blow to the colony's policy of accommodation with the Indians. During the war, with the frontier ablaze with battles between settlers and French and Indian warriors, western Pennsylvanians demanded that colonial authorities adopt a more aggressive stance. When the governor declared war on the Delawares, raised a militia, and offered a bounty for Indian scalps, many of the assembly's pacifist Quakers resigned their seats, effectively ending their control of Pennsylvania politics. The war deepened the antagonism of western farmers toward Indians and witnessed numerous indiscriminate assaults on Native communities, both allies and enemies.

In December 1763, while Pontiac's War still raged, a party of fifty armed men, mostly Scots-Irish farmers from the vicinity of the Pennsylvania town of Paxton, destroyed the Susquehannock town of Conestoga, massacring half a dozen men, women, and children who lived there under the protection of Pennsylvania's governor. They then marched on Lancaster, where they killed fourteen additional Native Americans. Like participants in Bacon's Rebellion nearly a century earlier, they accused colonial authorities of siding with Indians rather than colonists. They petitioned the legislature to remove all Native people from the colony. The Indians' "claim to freedom and independency," they insisted, threatened Pennsylvania's stability. When the Paxton Boys marched on Philadelphia in February 1764, intending to attack Moravian Indians who resided near the city, the governor ordered the expulsion of much of the Indian population. By the 1760s, Pennsylvania's Holy Experiment was at an end and with it William Penn's promise of "true friendship and amity" between colonists and Native Americans. No other large colony had a smaller Native population or a more remorseless determination on the part of settlers to eliminate those who remained.

Colonial Identities

Like some Native Americans, British colonists emerged from the Seven Years' War with a heightened sense of collective identity. Before the war, the colonies had been largely isolated from one another. Outside of New England, more Americans probably traveled to England than from one colony to another. In 1751, Governor George Clinton of New York had called for a general conference on Indian relations, but only three colonies bothered to send delegates. The **Albany Plan of Union** of 1754, drafted by Benjamin Franklin at the outbreak of the Seven Years' War, envisioned the creation of a Grand Council composed of delegates from each colony, with the power to levy taxes and deal with Indian relations and the common defense. Rejected by the colonial assemblies, whose powers Franklin's proposal would curtail, the plan was never sent to London for approval.

Participation in the Seven Years' War created greater bonds among the colonies. But the war also strengthened colonists' pride in being members of the British empire. It has been said that Americans were never more British than in 1763. Colonial militiamen and British regulars fought alongside each other against the French. Tensions developed between the professional British military and the often undisciplined American citizen-soldiers, but the common experience of battle and victory also forged bonds between them. For much of the century, New Englanders had called for the conquest of Canada as a blow for "Protestant freedom" against "popish slavery." The defeat of the Catholic French and their Native allies reinforced the equation of British nationality, Protestantism, and freedom.

In fact, however, after 1763 Britain's global empire was not predominantly Protestant or British or free. Slavery remained central to its economy. It now included tens of thousands of French Catholics and millions of persons in India governed as subjects rather than as citizens. The English statesman Edmund Burke wondered whether British liberty could be reconciled with rule over this "vast, heterogeneous, intricate mass of interests." Burke was almost alone in seeing the newly expanded empire as a challenge to the principles of British freedom. But soon, the American colonists would come to believe that membership in the empire jeopardized their liberty. When they did, they set out on a road that led to independence.

CHAPTER REVIEW

REVIEW QUESTIONS

1. *How did Great Britain's position in North America change relative to the other European powers during the first three-quarters of the eighteenth century?*

2. *How did the ideas of republicanism and liberalism differ in eighteenth-century British North America?*

3. *Three distinct slave systems were well entrenched in Britain's mainland colonies. Describe the main characteristics of each system.*

4. *How and why did the colonists' sense of a collective British identity change during the years before 1764?*

5. *What ideas generated by the American Enlightenment and the Great Awakening prompted challenges to religious, social, and political authorities in the British colonies?*

6. *How were colonial merchants in British America involved in the Atlantic economy, and what was the role of the slave trade in that economy?*

7. *We often consider the impact of the slave trade only on the United States, but its impact extended much further. How did it affect West African nations and society, other regions of the Americas, and the nations of Europe?*

8. *How was an African American collective identity created in these years, and what role did slave rebellions play in that process?*

9. *How did a distinct Native American identity start to emerge after the Seven Years' War?*

KEY TERMS

Atlantic slave trade (p. 133)

Middle Passage (p. 137)

yeoman farmers (p. 145)

Stono Rebellion (p. 147)

republicanism (p. 150)

liberalism (p. 150)

salutary neglect (p. 154)

Enlightenment (p. 158)

Deism (p. 158)

Great Awakening (p. 159)

Father Junípero Serra (p. 165)

Seven Years' War (p. 168)

French and Indian War (p. 168)

Neolin (p. 171)

Pontiac's War (p. 173)

Proclamation of 1763 (p. 173)

Albany Plan of Union (p. 177)

Go to ⚏ INQUIZITIVE

To see what you know—and learn what you've missed—with personalized feedback along the way.

CHAPTER 5

THE AMERICAN REVOLUTION

1763–1783

FOCUS QUESTIONS

- *What were the roots and significance of the Stamp Act controversy?*

- *What key events sharpened the divisions between Britain and the colonists in the late 1760s and early 1770s?*

- *What key events marked the move toward American independence?*

- *How did Native nations and European empires side in the Revolutionary War, and how were American forces able to prevail?*

O n the night of August 26, 1765, a violent crowd of Bostonians assaulted the elegant home of Thomas Hutchinson, chief justice and lieutenant governor of Massachusetts. Hutchinson and his family were eating dinner when the rioters arrived. They barely had time to escape before the crowd broke down the front door and proceeded to destroy or carry off most of their possessions, including paintings, furniture, silverware, and notes for a history of Massachusetts Hutchinson was writing. By the time they departed, only the outer walls of the home remained standing.

The immediate cause of the riot was the **Stamp Act**, a recently enacted British tax that many colonists felt violated their liberty. Critics of the measure had spread a rumor that Hutchinson had written to London encouraging its passage (in fact, he privately opposed it). Only a few days earlier, Hutchinson had helped to disperse a crowd attacking a building owned by his relative Andrew Oliver, a merchant who had been appointed to help administer the new law. Both crowds were led by Ebenezer Mackintosh, a shoemaker who had fought against the French during the Seven Years' War and enjoyed a wide following among Boston's working people. Arrested after the destruction of Hutchinson's home, Mackintosh was released after the intervention of the Loyal Nine, a group of merchants and craftsmen who had taken the lead in opposing the Stamp Act. The violence had gone far beyond what the Loyal Nine intended, and they promised authorities that resistance to the Stamp Act would henceforth be peaceful. The riot, nonetheless, convinced Hutchinson that for Britain to rule America effectively, "there must be an abridgement of what are called English liberties." Whether colonists would accept such an abridgement, however, was very much in doubt.

The riot of August 26 was one small episode in a series of events that launched a half-century of popular protest and political upheaval throughout the Atlantic world. The momentous era that came to be called the Age of Revolution began in British North America, spread to Europe and the Caribbean, and culminated in the Latin American wars for independence. In all these struggles, "Liberty" emerged as the foremost rallying cry for popular discontent. Rarely has the idea played so central a role in political debate and social upheaval.

If the attack on Hutchinson's home demonstrated the depths of feeling aroused by Britain's efforts to impose greater control over its empire, it also revealed that revolution is a dynamic process whose consequences no one can anticipate. The crowd's fury expressed resentments against the rich and powerful quite different from colonial leaders' objections to Parliament's attempt to tax the colonies. The Stamp Act crisis inaugurated not only a struggle for colonial liberty in relation to Great Britain but also a multisided battle to define and extend liberty within the new nation.

THE CRISIS BEGINS

When George III assumed the throne of Great Britain in 1760, no one on either side of the Atlantic imagined that within two decades Britain's American colonies would separate from the empire. But the Seven Years' War, which left Britain with an enormous debt and vastly enlarged overseas possessions to defend, led successive governments in London to seek ways to make the colonies share the cost of empire. Having studied the writings of British opposition thinkers who insisted that power inevitably seeks to encroach upon liberty, colonial leaders came to see these measures as part of a British design to undermine their freedom. Only recently they had gloried in their enjoyment of "British liberty," but they came to conclude that membership in the empire was a threat to freedom, rather than its foundation. This conviction set the colonies on the road to independence.

Consolidating the Empire

The Seven Years' War, to which the colonists contributed soldiers and economic resources, underscored for rulers in London how important the empire was to Britain's well-being and its status as a great power. Now, they believed, new regulations were needed to help guarantee the empire's continued strength and prosperity. Before 1763, Parliament had occasionally acted to forbid the issuance of paper money in America and to restrict colonial economic activities that competed with businesses at home. The Wool Act of 1699, Hat Act of 1732, and Iron Act of 1750 forbade colonial manufacture of these items. The Molasses Act of 1733 sought to curtail trade between New England and the French Caribbean by imposing a prohibitive tax on French-produced molasses used to make rum in American distilleries. And the Navigation Acts, discussed in Chapter 3, sought to channel key American exports like tobacco through British ports. The colonists frequently ignored all these measures.

As to internal affairs within the colonies, the British government frequently seemed uninterested. There was no point, one official said, in worrying about the behavior of colonists who "plant tobacco and Puritanism only, like fools." Beginning in the late 1740s, the Board of Trade, which was responsible for overseeing colonial affairs, attempted to strengthen imperial authority. It demanded that colonial

· CHRONOLOGY ·

1760	George III assumes the British throne
1764	Sugar Act
1765	Stamp Act
	Sons of Liberty organized
	Stamp Act Congress
1767	Townshend Acts
	Daughters of Liberty organized
1768	British troops stationed in Boston
1770	Boston Massacre
1773	Tea Act
	Boston Tea Party
1774	Intolerable Acts
	First Continental Congress
1775	Battles at Lexington and Concord
	Lord Dunmore's proclamation
1776	Thomas Paine's *Common Sense*
	Declaration of Independence
	Battle of Trenton
1777	Battle of Saratoga
1778	Treaty with France
1779	Sullivan expedition
1781	Cornwallis surrenders at Yorktown
1783	Treaty of Paris

The Massachusetts. CALENDAR;
OR AN
ALMANACK
FOR THE
Year of our Lord Christ 1774;
Being the second after Bissextile or Leap Year
By EZRA GLEASON.

The Wicked Statesman, or the Traitor to his Country, at the Hour of DEATH.

An engraving from a Massachusetts almanac published in 1774 depicts Lieutenant Governor Thomas Hutchinson, whose house had been destroyed by a mob nine years earlier. The devil carries a list of Hutchinson's "crimes." It was common in this period to use religious symbols to demonize political opponents.

laws conform to royal instructions and encouraged colonial assemblies to grant permanent salaries to royal governors. But the outbreak of the Seven Years' War suspended this initiative.

Having treated the colonists as allies during the war, Britain reverted in the mid-1760s to seeing them as subordinates whose main role was to enrich the mother country. Americans, Britons felt, should be grateful to the empire. To fight the Seven Years' War, Britain had borrowed from banks and individual investors more than £150 million (the equivalent of tens of trillions of dollars in today's money). Interest on the debt absorbed half the government's annual revenue. The tax burden in Britain had reached unprecedented heights. It seemed only reasonable that the colonies should help pay this national debt, foot part of the bill for continued British protection, and stop cheating the treasury by violating the Navigation Acts.

Nearly all Britons, moreover, believed that Parliament represented the entire empire and had a right to legislate for it. Millions of Britons, including the residents of major cities like Manchester and Birmingham, had no representatives in Parliament. But according to the widely accepted theory of **virtual representation**—which held that each member represented the entire empire, not just his own district—the interests of all who lived under the British crown were supposedly taken into account. When Americans began to insist that because they were unrepresented in Parliament, the British government could not tax the colonies, they won little support in England. To their surprise, however, successive British governments found that the effective working of the empire required the cooperation of local populations. Time and again, British officials backed down in the face of colonial resistance, only to return with new measures to centralize control of the empire that only stiffened colonial resolve.

The British government had already alarmed many colonists by issuing "writs of assistance" to combat smuggling. These were general search warrants that allowed customs officials to search anywhere they chose for smuggled goods. In a celebrated court case in Boston in 1761, the lawyer James Otis insisted that the writs were "an instrument of arbitrary power, destructive to English liberty, and the fundamental principles of the [British] Constitution," and that Parliament therefore had no right to authorize them. Many colonists were also outraged by the Proclamation of 1763 (mentioned in the previous chapter) barring further settlement on Native lands west of the Appalachian Mountains.

Taxing the Colonies

In 1764, the **Sugar Act**, introduced by Prime Minister George Grenville, reduced the existing tax on molasses imported into North America from the French West Indies from six pence to three pence per gallon. But the act also established a new machinery to end widespread smuggling by colonial merchants. And to counteract the tendency of colonial juries to acquit merchants charged with violating trade regulations, it strengthened the admiralty courts, where accused smugglers could be judged without benefit of a jury trial. Thus, colonists saw the measure not as a welcome reduction in taxation but as an attempt to get them to pay a levy they would otherwise have evaded.

At the same time, a Revenue Act placed goods such as wool and hides, which had previously been traded freely with Holland, France, and southern Europe, on the enumerated list, meaning they had to be shipped through England. Together, these measures threatened the profits of colonial merchants and seemed certain to aggravate an already serious economic recession resulting from the end of the Seven Years' War. They were accompanied by the Currency Act, which reaffirmed the earlier ban on colonial assemblies issuing paper as "legal tender"—that is, money that individuals are required to accept in payment of debts.

The Stamp Act Crisis

The Sugar Act was an effort to strengthen the long-established (and long-evaded) Navigation Acts. The Stamp Act of 1765 represented a new departure in imperial policy. For the first time, Parliament attempted to raise money from direct taxes in the colonies rather than through the regulation of trade. The act required that all sorts of printed material produced in the colonies—such as newspapers, books, court documents, commercial papers, land deeds, and almanacs—carry a stamp purchased from authorities. Its purpose was to help finance the operations of the empire, including the cost of stationing British troops in North America, without seeking revenue from colonial assemblies.

Whereas the Sugar Act had mainly affected residents of colonial ports, the Stamp Act managed to offend virtually every free colonist—rich and poor, farmers, artisans, and merchants. It was especially resented by members of the public sphere who wrote, published, and read books and newspapers and followed political affairs. The prospect of a British army permanently stationed on American soil also alarmed many colonists. And by imposing the stamp tax without colonial consent, Parliament directly challenged the authority of local elites who, through the assemblies they controlled, had established their power over the raising and spending of money. They viewed the empire as an association of equals in which free inhabitants overseas enjoyed the same rights as Britons at home. Colonists in other outposts of the empire, such as India, the West Indies, and Canada, echoed this outlook. All, in the name of liberty, claimed the right to govern their own affairs. British residents of Calcutta, India, demanded the "rights inherent in Englishmen." The British government and its appointed representatives in America, by contrast, saw the empire as a system of unequal parts in which different principles governed different areas, and all were subject to the authority of Parliament.

Opposition to the Stamp Act was the first great drama of the revolutionary era and the first major split between colonists and Great Britain over the meaning of freedom. Nearly all colonial political leaders opposed the act. In voicing their grievances, they invoked the rights of the freeborn Englishman, which, they insisted, colonists should also enjoy. Opponents of the act drew on time-honored British principles such as a community's right not to be taxed except by its elected representatives. Liberty, they insisted, could not be secure where property was "taken away without consent."

"No taxation without representation" became the rallying cry of opponents of the Stamp Act. Virginia's House of Burgesses approved four resolutions offered by the fiery orator Patrick Henry. They insisted that the colonists enjoyed the same "liberties, privileges, franchises, and immunities" as residents in England and that the right to consent to taxation was a cornerstone of "British freedom." (The House of Burgesses rejected as too radical three other resolutions, including Henry's call for outright resistance to unlawful taxation, but these were also reprinted in colonial newspapers.)

In October 1765, the Stamp Act Congress, with twenty-seven delegates from nine colonies, including some of the most prominent men in America, met in New York and endorsed Virginia's position. Its resolutions began by affirming the "allegiance" of all colonists to the "Crown of Great Britain" and their "due subordination" to Parliament. But they went on to insist that the right to consent to taxation was "essential to the freedom of a people." Soon, merchants throughout the colonies agreed to boycott British goods until Parliament repealed the Stamp Act. In a sense, by seeking to impose uniformity on the colonies rather than dealing with them individually as in the past, Parliament had inadvertently sparked the first major cooperative action among Britain's mainland colonies.

The Stamp Act crisis, however, did not lead inevitably to revolution. There were twenty-six British colonies in the Western Hemisphere and nearly all of them protested the tax, including Jamaica and others in the West Indies, Canadian colonies, and East and West Florida. But only nine sent delegates to the Stamp Act Congress. At this point, most colonists continued to believe that their liberties and material interests were safer inside the British empire than outside of it.

Liberty and Resistance

No word was more frequently invoked by critics of the Stamp Act than "liberty." Throughout the colonies, opponents of the new tax staged mock funerals in which liberty's coffin was carried to a burial ground only to have the occupant miraculously revived at the last moment, whereupon the assembled crowd repaired to a tavern to celebrate. As the crisis continued, symbols of liberty proliferated. The large elm tree in Boston on which protesters had hanged an effigy of the stamp distributor Andrew Oliver to persuade him to resign his post came to be known as the Liberty Tree. Its image soon began to appear in prints and pamphlets throughout the colonies. Open-air meetings were held beneath the tree, and as a result the space came to be called Liberty Hall. In New York City, a pine mast erected in 1766 as a meeting place for opponents of the Stamp Act was called the Liberty Pole.

Colonial leaders resolved to prevent the new law's implementation, and by and large they succeeded. Even before the passage of the Stamp Act, a **Committee of Correspondence** in Boston communicated with other colonies to encourage opposition to the Sugar and Currency Acts. Now, such committees sprang up in other colonies, exchanging ideas and information about resistance. Initiated by colonial elites, the movement against the Stamp Act quickly drew in a far broader range of Americans. The act, wrote John Adams, a Boston lawyer who drafted a set of widely reprinted resolutions against the measure, had inspired "the people, even to the lowest ranks," to become "more attentive to their liberties, more inquisitive about them, and more determined to defend them, than they were ever before known." Political debate, Adams added, pervaded the colonies—"our presses have groaned, our pulpits have thundered, our legislatures have resolved, our towns have voted."

Politics in the Streets

Opponents of the Stamp Act, however, did not rely solely on debate. Even before the law went into effect, crowds forced those chosen to administer it to resign and destroyed shipments of stamps. In New York City, processions involving hundreds of residents shouting "Liberty" paraded through the streets nearly every night in late 1765. They were organized by the newly created **Sons of Liberty**. While they enjoyed no standing among the colony's wealthy elite and carried little weight in municipal affairs, the Sons' leaders enjoyed a broad following among the city's craftsmen, laborers, and sailors.

The Sons posted notices reading "Liberty, Property, and No Stamps" and took the lead in enforcing the boycott of British imports. Their actions were viewed with increasing alarm by the aristocratic Livingston and De Lancey families, who dominated New York politics. As the assault on Thomas Hutchinson's house in Boston demonstrated, crowds could easily get out of hand. In Novem-

A British engraving from 1766 marking the repeal of the Stamp Act. A funeral procession on the banks of the River Thames in London includes Prime Minister George Grenville carrying a coffin noting that the act was born in 1765 and died a year later. Two large containers are labeled "Stamps from America"—stamps returned because no longer needed—and "black cloth from America," for use at the funeral. In the background, a warehouse contains goods to be "ship'd for America," now that the boycott of British imports has ended.

ber 1765, a New York crowd reportedly composed of white and Black sailors, laborers, and youths hurled stones at Fort George at the tip of Manhattan Island. They then proceeded to destroy the home of Major Thomas James, a British officer who was said to have boasted that he would force the stamps down New Yorkers' throats.

Stunned by the ferocity of American resistance and pressured by London merchants and manufacturers who did not wish to lose their American markets, the British government retreated. In 1766, Parliament repealed the Stamp Act. But this concession was accompanied by the Declaratory Act, which rejected Americans' claims that only their elected representatives could levy taxes. Parliament, proclaimed this measure, possessed the power to pass laws for "the colonies and people of America . . . in all cases whatsoever." Since the debt-ridden British government continued to need money raised in the colonies, passage of the Declaratory Act promised further conflict.

The Regulators

The Stamp Act crisis was not the only example of violent social turmoil. Beginning in the mid-1760s, a group of wealthy residents of the South Carolina backcountry calling themselves **Regulators** protested the underrepresentation of western settlements in the colony's assembly and the legislators' failure to establish local governments that could regularize land titles and suppress bands of outlaws. The lack of courts in the area, they claimed, had led to a breakdown of law and order, allowing "an infernal gang of villains" to commit "shocking outrages" on persons and property. They added: "We are *Free-men*— British subjects—Not Born Slaves."

A parallel movement in North Carolina mobilized small farmers, who complained not about a lack of government but about corrupt county authorities. Demanding the democratization of local government, the Regulators, who at their peak numbered around 8,000, condemned the "rich and powerful" (the colony's elite). The region remained in turmoil until 1771 when, in the "battle of Alamance," the farmers were suppressed by the colony's militia.

Also in the mid-1760s, tenants on the Livingston, Philipse, and Cortland manors along the Hudson River north of New York City stopped paying rent and began seizing land. Like opponents of the Stamp Act, they called themselves the Sons of Liberty. The original Sons, however, opposed their uprising, and it was soon suppressed by British and colonial troops. The emerging rift between Britain and America eventually superimposed itself on conflicts within the colonies. But the social divisions revealed in the Stamp Act riots and backcountry uprisings made some members of the colonial elite fear that opposition to British measures might unleash turmoil at home. As a result, they were more reluctant to challenge British authority when the next imperial crisis arose.

THE ROAD TO REVOLUTION

The Townshend Crisis and Colonial Boycotts

In 1767, the government in London decided to impose a new set of taxes on Americans, known as the **Townshend Acts**. They were devised by the chancellor of the Exchequer (the cabinet's chief financial minister), Charles Townshend. In opposing the Stamp Act, some colonists had seemed to suggest that they would not object if Britain raised revenue by regulating trade. Taking them at their word, Townshend persuaded Parliament to impose new taxes on goods imported into the colonies and to create a new board of customs commissioners to collect them and suppress smuggling. In response, leaders in several colonies decided in 1768 to reimpose the ban on importing British goods.

The boycott began in Boston and soon spread to the southern colonies. Reliance on American rather than British goods, on homespun clothing rather than imported finery, became a symbol of American resistance. It also reflected, as the colonists saw it, a virtuous spirit of self-sacrifice as compared with the self-indulgence and luxury many Americans were coming to associate with Britain. Because women made many of the buying decisions in colonial households, their support was essential to the boycott's success. Women formed **Daughters of Liberty** chapters, in which they signed agreements not to buy British products or shop at stores that sold them. They held public spinning and weaving bees, inviting reporters to see them demonstrate that it was patriotic to make homespun rather than purchase British cloth. The *Boston Evening Post* noted that "the industry and frugality of American ladies . . . show how greatly they are contributing to bring about the political salvation of a whole Continent."

The idea of using homemade rather than imported goods appealed to Chesapeake planters, who found themselves owing increasing amounts of money to British merchants. Nonimportation, wrote George Washington, reflecting Virginia planters' concern about their growing burden of debt, gave "the extravagant man" an opportunity to "retrench his expenses" by reducing the purchase of British luxuries, without having to advertise to his neighbors that he might be in financial distress. Virginia's leaders also announced a temporary ban on the importation of slaves, but smaller planters in the Piedmont region away from the coast, where the institution was expanding, ignored this restriction.

Urban artisans, who welcomed an end to competition from imported British manufactured goods, strongly supported the boycott. Philadelphia and New York merchants at first were reluctant to take part, although they eventually agreed to go along. Nonimportation threatened their livelihoods and raised the prospect of unleashing further lower-class turmoil. As had happened during the Stamp Act crisis, the streets of American cities filled with popular protests against the new duties.

The Boston Massacre

Boston once again became the focal point of conflict. Royal troops had been stationed in the city in 1768 after rioting that followed the British seizure of the ship *Liberty* for violating trade regulations. The soldiers, who competed for jobs on Boston's waterfront with the city's laborers, became more and more unpopular. On March 5, 1770, a fight between a snowball-throwing crowd and British troops escalated into an armed confrontation that left five Bostonians dead. One of those who fell in what came to be called the **Boston Massacre** was **Crispus Attucks**, a sailor of mixed African-Native-white

The Boston Massacre. Less than a month after the Boston Massacre of 1770, in which five colonists died, Paul Revere produced this engraving of the event. Although it inaccurately depicts what was actually a disorganized brawl between residents of Boston and British soldiers, this image became one of the most influential pieces of political propaganda of the revolutionary era.

ancestry. Attucks would later be remembered as the "first martyr of the American Revolution." The commanding officer and eight soldiers were put on trial in Massachusetts. Ably defended by John Adams, who viewed lower-class crowd actions as a dangerous method of opposing British policies, seven were found not guilty, while two were convicted of manslaughter. But Paul Revere, a member of the Boston Sons of Liberty and a silversmith and engraver, helped to stir up indignation against the British army by producing a widely circulated (and quite inaccurate) print of the Boston Massacre depicting a line of British soldiers firing into an unarmed crowd.

By 1770, as merchants' profits shriveled and many members of the colonial elite found they could not do without British goods, the nonimportation movement was collapsing. The value of British imports to the colonies declined by about one-third during 1769, but then rebounded to its former level. British merchants, who wished to remove a possible source of future interruption of trade, pressed for repeal of the Townshend duties. When the British ministry agreed, leaving in place only a tax on tea, and agreed to remove troops from Boston, American merchants quickly abandoned the boycott.

Once again, an immediate crisis had been resolved. Nonetheless, many Americans concluded that Britain was succumbing to the same pattern of political corruption and decline of liberty that afflicted other countries. In addition, rumors circulated in the colonies that the Anglican Church in England planned to send bishops to America to establish religious courts like those that had once persecuted Dissenters.

The Tea Act

The next crisis underscored how powerfully events in other parts of Britain's global empire affected the American colonies. The East India Company, a giant trading monopoly, effectively governed recently acquired British possessions in India. Numerous British merchants, bankers, and other individuals had invested heavily in its stock. A classic speculative bubble ensued, with the price of stock in the company rising sharply and then collapsing. To rescue the company and its investors, the British government decided to help it market its enormous holdings of Chinese tea in North America.

Tea, once a preserve of the wealthy, had become a drink consumed by all social classes in England and the colonies. To further stimulate its sales and bail out the East India Company, the British government, now headed by Frederick Lord North, offered the company a series of rebates and tax exemptions. These enabled it to dump low-priced tea on the American market, undercutting both established merchants and smugglers. Money raised through the taxation of imported tea would be used to help defray the costs of colonial government, thus threatening, once again, the assemblies' control over finance.

The tax on tea was not new. But many colonists insisted that to pay it on this large new body of imports would acknowledge Britain's right to tax the colonies. As tea shipments arrived, resistance developed in the major ports. On December 16, 1773, a group of colonists disguised as Indians boarded three ships at anchor in Boston Harbor and threw more than 300 chests of tea into the water. The event became known as the **Boston Tea Party**. The loss to the East India Company was around £10,000 (the equivalent of more than $4 million today).

The Intolerable Acts

The British government, declared Lord North, must now demonstrate "whether we have, or have not, any authority in that country." Its response to the Boston Tea Party was swift and decisive. Parliament closed the port of Boston to all trade until the tea was paid for. It radically altered the Massachusetts Charter of 1691 by curtailing town meetings and authorizing the governor to appoint members to the council—positions previously filled by election. Parliament also empowered military commanders to lodge soldiers in private homes. These measures, called the Coercive or **Intolerable Acts** by

Americans, united the colonies in opposition to what was widely seen as a direct threat to their political freedom.

At almost the same time, Parliament passed the Quebec Act. This extended the southern boundary of that Canadian province to the Ohio River and granted legal toleration to the Roman Catholic Church in Canada. With an eye to the growing tensions in colonies to the south, the act sought to secure the allegiance of Quebec's Catholics by offering rights denied to their coreligionists in Britain, including practicing their faith freely and holding positions in the civil service. The act not only threw into question land claims in the Ohio country but persuaded many colonists that the government in London was conspiring to strengthen Catholicism—dreaded by most Protestants—in its American empire. Fears of religious and political tyranny mingled in the minds of many colonists. Especially in New England, the cause of liberty became the cause of God. A gathering of 1,000 residents of Farmington, Connecticut, in May 1774 adopted resolutions proclaiming that, as "the sons of freedom," they would resist every attempt "to take away our liberties and properties and to enslave us forever." They accused the British ministry of being "instigated by the devil."

THE COMING OF INDEPENDENCE

The Continental Congress

Opposition to the Intolerable Acts now spread to small towns and rural areas that had not participated actively in previous resistance. In September 1774, in the town of Worcester, Massachusetts, 4,600 militiamen from thirty-seven towns (half the adult male population of the entire county) lined both sides of Main Street as the British-appointed officials walked between them. That month, a convention of delegates from Massachusetts towns approved a series of resolutions (called the Suffolk Resolves for the county in which Boston is located) that urged Americans to refuse obedience to the new laws, withhold taxes, and prepare for war.

To coordinate resistance to the Intolerable Acts, a **Continental Congress** convened in Philadelphia, bringing together the most prominent political leaders of twelve mainland colonies (Georgia and East and West Florida did not send representatives). From Massachusetts came John Adams and his more radical cousin Samuel. Virginia's seven delegates included George Washington, Richard Henry Lee, and the renowned orator Patrick Henry. "The distinctions between Virginians, Pennsylvanians, New Yorkers, and New Englanders," Henry declared, "are no more. I am not a Virginian, but an American." In March 1775, Henry concluded a speech urging a Virginia convention to begin military preparations with a legendary credo: "Give me liberty, or give me death!"

The Continental Association

Before it adjourned at the end of October 1774 with an agreement to reconvene the following May if colonial demands had not been met, the Congress endorsed the Suffolk Resolves and adopted the Continental Association, which called for an almost complete halt to trade with Great Britain and the West Indies (at South Carolina's insistence, exports of rice to Europe were exempted). The association also encouraged domestic manufacturing and denounced "every species of extravagance and dissipation." Congress authorized local Committees of Safety to implement its mandates and to take action against "enemies of American liberty," including businessmen who tried to profit from the sudden scarcity of goods.

The Committees of Safety began the process of transferring effective political power from established governments whose authority derived from Great Britain to extralegal grassroots bodies reflecting the will of the people. By early 1775, some 7,000 men were serving on local committees throughout the colonies, a vast expansion of the "political nation." The committees became training grounds where small farmers, city artisans, propertyless laborers, and other men who had heretofore had little role in government discussed political issues and exercised political power. In Philadelphia, the extralegal committees of the 1760s that oversaw the boycott of British goods had been composed almost entirely of prominent lawyers and merchants. But younger merchants, shopkeepers, and artisans dominated the committee elected in November 1774 to enforce the Continental Association. They were determined that resistance to British measures not be dropped as it had been in 1770. When the New York assembly refused to endorse the association, local committees continued to enforce it anyway.

The Sweets of Liberty

By 1775, talk of liberty pervaded the colonies. The past few years had witnessed an endless parade of pamphlets with titles like *A Chariot of Liberty* and *Oration on the Beauties of Liberty* (the latter, a sermon delivered in Boston by Joseph Allen in 1772, became the most popular public address of the years before independence). Sober men spoke longingly of the "sweets of liberty." While sleeping, Americans dreamed of liberty. One anonymous essayist reported a "night vision" of the word written in the sun's rays. Commented a British immigrant who arrived in Maryland early in 1775: "They are all liberty mad."

The right to resist oppressive authority and the identification of liberty with the cause of God, so deeply ingrained by the imperial struggles of the eighteenth century, were now invoked against Britain itself, by colonists of all backgrounds. The first mass meeting in the history of Northampton County, Pennsylvania, whose population was overwhelmingly of German ancestry, gathered in 1774. By the following year, a majority of the county's adult population had joined militia associations. Many German settlers, whose close-knit communities had earlier viewed with some suspicion "the famous English liberty" as a byword for selfish individualism, now claimed all the "rights and privileges of natural-born subjects of his majesty."

As the crisis deepened, Americans increasingly based their claims not simply on the historical rights of Englishmen but on the more abstract language of natural rights and universal freedom. The First Continental Congress defended its actions by appealing to the "principles of the English constitution," the "liberties of free and natural-born subjects within the realm of England," and the "immutable law of nature." John Locke's theory of natural rights offered a powerful justification for colonial resistance. Americans, declared Thomas Jefferson in *A Summary View of the Rights of British America* (written in 1774 to instruct Virginia's delegates to the Continental Congress), were "a free people claiming their rights, as derived from the laws of nature, and not as the gift of their chief magistrate." Americans, Jefferson insisted, still revered the king. But he demanded that empire henceforth be seen as a collection of equal parts held together by loyalty to a constitutional monarch, not a system in which one part ruled over the others.

The Outbreak of War

By the time the Second Continental Congress convened in May 1775, war had broken out between British soldiers and armed citizens of Massachusetts. On April 19, a force of British soldiers marched from Boston toward the nearby town of Concord to seize arms being stockpiled there. Riders from Boston, among them Paul Revere, warned local leaders of the troops' approach. Militiamen took up arms and tried to resist the British advance. Skirmishes between Americans and British soldiers took place, known as the **Battles of Lexington and Concord**. By the time the British retreated to the safety of Boston, some forty-nine Americans and seventy-three members of the Royal Army lay dead.

What the philosopher Ralph Waldo Emerson would later call "the shot heard 'round the world" began the American War of Independence. It reverberated throughout the colonies. When news of the skirmish reached Lemuel Roberts, a poor New York farmer, he felt his "bosom glow" with the "call of liberty." Roberts set off for Massachusetts to enlist in the army. In May 1775, Ethan Allen and the Green Mountain Boys, together with militiamen from Connecticut led by Benedict Arnold, surrounded Fort Ticonderoga in New York and forced it to surrender. The following winter, Henry Knox, George Washington's commander of artillery, arranged for some of the Ticonderoga cannon to be dragged hundreds of miles to the east to reinforce the siege of Boston, where British forces were ensconced. On June 17, 1775, two months after Lexington and Concord, the British had dislodged colonial militiamen from Breed's Hill, although only at a heavy cost in casualties. (The battle came to be named the **Battle of Bunker Hill**, after the nearby Bunker Hill.) But the arrival of American cannon in March 1776 and their entrenchment above the city made the British position in Boston untenable. The British army under the command of Sir William Howe was forced to abandon the city. Before leaving, Howe's forces cut down the original Liberty Tree.

Meanwhile, the Second Continental Congress authorized the raising of a **Continental army**, printed money to pay for it, and appointed George Washington its commander. Washington, who had gained considerable fighting experience during the Seven Years' War, was not only the colonies' best-known military officer but also a prominent Virginian. John Adams, who proposed his name, recognized that having a southerner lead American forces would reinforce colonial unity. In response, Britain declared the colonies in a state of rebellion, dispatched thousands of troops, and ordered the closing of all colonial ports.

Independence?

By the end of 1775, the breach with Britain seemed irreparable. But many colonists shied away from the idea of independence. Pride in membership in the British empire was still strong, and many political leaders, especially in colonies that had experienced internal turmoil, feared that a complete break with the mother country might unleash further conflict. Anarchy from below, in their view, was as much a danger as tyranny from above. Many advocates of independence, one opponent warned, would find it "very agreeable" to divide the property of the rich among the poor.

Such fears affected how colonial leaders responded to the idea of independence. The elites of Massachusetts and Virginia, who felt supremely confident of their ability to retain authority at home, tended to support a break with Britain. Massachusetts had borne the brunt of the Intolerable Acts. Southern leaders not only were highly protective of their political liberty but also were outraged by a proclamation issued in November 1775 by the earl of Dunmore, the British governor and military commander in Virginia. **Lord Dunmore's proclamation** offered freedom to any slave who escaped to British lines and bore arms for the king.

In New York and Pennsylvania, however, the diversity of the population made it difficult to work out a consensus on how far to go in resisting British measures. Here opposition to previous British laws had unleashed demands by small farmers and urban artisans for a greater voice in political affairs. As a result, many established leaders drew back from further resistance. Joseph

Galloway, a Pennsylvania leader and delegate to the Second Continental Congress who worked to devise a compromise between British and colonial positions, warned that independence would be accompanied by constant disputes within America. He even predicted a war between the northern and southern colonies. Americans, Galloway declared, could only enjoy "true liberty"—self-government and security for their persons and property—by remaining within the empire.

Common Sense

As 1776 dawned, America presented the unusual spectacle of colonists at war against the British empire but still pleading for their rights within it. Even as fighting raged, Congress in July 1775 had addressed the Olive Branch Petition to George III, reaffirming Americans' loyalty to the crown and hoping for a "permanent reconciliation." Ironically, it was a recent emigrant from England, not a colonist from a family long established on American soil, who grasped the inner logic of the situation and offered a vision of the broad significance of American independence. An English craftsman and minor government official, Thomas Paine had emigrated to Philadelphia late in 1774. He quickly became associated with a group of advocates of the American cause, including John Adams and Dr. Benjamin Rush, a leading Philadelphia physician. It was Rush who suggested to Paine that he write a pamphlet supporting American independence.

Its author listed only as "an Englishman," **Common Sense** appeared in January 1776. The pamphlet began not with a recital of colonial grievances but with an attack on the "so much boasted Constitution of England" and the principles of hereditary rule and monarchical government. Rather than being the most perfect system of government in the world, Paine wrote, the English monarchy was headed by "the royal brute of England," and the English constitution was composed in large part of "the base remains of two ancient tyrannies . . . monarchical tyranny in the person of the king [and] aristocratical tyranny in the persons of the peers." "Of more worth is one honest man to society, and in the sight of God," he continued, "than all the crowned ruffians that ever lived." Far preferable than monarchy would be a democratic system based on frequent elections, with citizens' rights protected by a written constitution.

Turning to independence, Paine drew on the colonists' experiences to make his case. "There is something absurd," he wrote, "in supposing a Continent to be perpetually governed by an island." Within the British empire, America's prospects were limited; liberated from the Navigation Acts and trading freely with the entire world, its "material eminence" was certain. With independence, moreover, the colonies could for the first time insulate themselves from involvement in the endless imperial wars of Europe. Britain had "dragged" its

From SAMUEL SEABURY, *AN ALARM TO THE LEGISLATURE OF THE PROVINCE IN NEW-YORK* (1775)

An Anglican minister and graduate of Yale College, Samuel Seabury was a devoted Loyalist, who in 1774 and 1775 published several pamphlets opposing the revolutionary movement. He remained in the United States after the War of Independence and became the new nation's first Episcopal bishop.

The unhappy contention we have entered into with our parent state, would inevitably be attended with many disagreeable circumstances, with many and great inconveniences to us, even were it conducted on our part, with propriety and moderation. What then must be the case, when all proper and moderate measures are rejected? . . . When every scheme that tends to peace, is branded with ignominy; as being the machination of slavery! When nothing is called FREEDOM but SEDITION! Nothing LIBERTY but REBELLION!

I will not presume to encroach so far upon your time, as to attempt to point out the causes of our unnatural contention with Great Britain. . . . Nor will I attempt to trace out the progress of that infatuation, which hath so deeply, so miserably, infected the Colonies. . . . Most, if not all the measures that have been adopted, have been illegal in their beginning, tyrannical in their operation. . . . A Committee, chosen in a tumultuous, illegal manner, usurped the most despotic authority over the province. They entered into contracts, compacts, combinations, treaties of alliance, with the other colonies, without any power from the legislature of the province. They agreed with the other Colonies to send Delegates to meet in convention at Philadelphia, to determine upon the rights and liberties of the good people of this province, unsupported by any Law. . . .

The state to which the Grand Congress, and the subordinate Committees, have reduced the colonies, is really deplorable. They have introduced a system of the most oppressive tyranny that can possibly be imagined;—a tyranny, not only over the actions, but over the words, thoughts, and minds, of the good people of this province. People have been threatened with the vengeance of a mob, for speaking in support of order and good government. . . .

Behold, Gentlemen, behold the wretched state to which we are reduced! A foreign power is brought in to govern this province. Laws made at Philadelphia, by factious men from New-England, New-Jersey, Pennsylvania, Maryland, Virginia, and the Carolinas, are imposed upon us by the most imperious menaces. Money is levied upon us without the consent of our representatives. . . . Mobs and riots are encouraged, in order to force submission to the tyranny of the Congress.

From THOMAS PAINE, COMMON SENSE (1776)

A recent emigrant from England, Thomas Paine in January 1776 published *Common Sense*, a highly influential pamphlet that in stirring language made the case for American independence.

In the following pages I offer nothing more than simple facts, plain arguments, and common sense....

Male and female are the distinctions of nature, good and bad the distinctions of heaven; but how a race of men came into the world so exalted above the rest, and distinguished like some new species, is worth enquiring into, and whether they are the means of happiness or of misery to mankind.... One of the strongest *natural* proofs of the folly of hereditary right in kings, is, that nature disapproves it, otherwise she would not so frequently turn it into ridicule, by giving mankind an *ass for a lion*....

The sun never shined on a cause of greater worth. 'Tis not the affair of a city, a country, a province, or a kingdom, but of a continent—of at least one eighth part of the habitable globe. 'Tis not the concern of a day, a year, or an age; posterity are virtually involved in the context, and will be more or less affected, even to the end of time, by the proceedings now. Now is the seed time of continental union, faith and honor....

I challenge the warmest advocate for reconciliation to show a single advantage that this continent can reap by being connected with Great Britain.... But the injuries and disadvantages which we sustain by that connection, are without number.... Any submission to, or dependence on, Great Britain, tends directly to involve this Continent in European wars and quarrels, and set us at variance with nations who would otherwise seek our friendship, and against whom we have neither anger nor complaint.

O ye that love mankind! Ye that dare oppose, not only the tyranny, but the tyrant, stand forth! Every spot of the old world is overrun with oppression. Freedom hath been hunted round the globe. Asia, and Africa, have long expelled her. Europe regards her like a stranger, and England hath given her warning to depart. O! Receive the fugitive, and prepare in time an asylum for mankind.

QUESTIONS

1. *Why does Seabury believe the Continental Congress and local committees are undermining Americans' liberties?*

2. *What does Paine see as the global significance of the American struggle for independence?*

3. *How do the two writers differ in their view of the main threats to American freedom?*

American colonies into conflicts with countries like Spain and France, which "never were . . . our enemies as *Americans*, but as our being the subjects of Great Britain." Membership in the British empire, Paine insisted, was a burden to the colonies, not a benefit.

Toward the close of the pamphlet, Paine moved beyond practical considerations to outline a breathtaking vision of the historical importance of the American Revolution. "The cause of America," he proclaimed in stirring language, "is in great measure, the cause of all mankind." The new nation would become the home of freedom, "an asylum for mankind."

Paine's Impact

Few of Paine's ideas were original. What made *Common Sense* unique was his mode of expressing them and the audience he addressed. Previous political writings had generally been directed toward the educated elite. "When I mention the public," declared John Randolph of Virginia in 1774, "I mean to include the rational part of it. The ignorant vulgar are unfit . . . to manage the reins of government." Just as evangelical ministers had shattered the trained clergy's monopoly on religious preaching, Paine pioneered a new style of political writing, one designed to expand dramatically the public sphere where political discussion took place. He wrote clearly and directly, and he avoided the complex language and Latin phrases common in pamphlets aimed at educated readers. *Common Sense* quickly became one of the most successful and influential pamphlets in the history of political writing, selling, by Paine's estimate, some 150,000 copies. Paine directed that his share of the profits be used to buy supplies for the Continental army.

The intensification of fighting in the winter of 1775–1776, when Americans unsuccessfully invaded Canada while the British burned Falmouth (now Portland), Maine, and bombarded Norfolk, Virginia, gave added weight to the movement for independence. In the spring of 1776, scores of American communities adopted resolutions calling for a separation from Britain. Only six months elapsed between the appearance of *Common Sense* and the decision by the Second Continental Congress to sever the colonies' ties with Great Britain.

The Declaration of Independence

On July 2, 1776, the Congress formally declared the United States an independent nation. Two days later, it approved the Declaration of Independence, written by Thomas Jefferson and revised by the Congress before approval. (See the Appendix for the full text.) Most of the Declaration consists of a lengthy list of grievances directed against King George III, ranging from quartering troops in colonial homes to imposing taxes without the colonists' consent. Britain's aim, it declared, was to establish "absolute tyranny" over the colonies. One clause in Jefferson's draft, which condemned the inhumanity of the slave trade and criticized the king for overturning colonial laws that sought to restrict the importation of slaves, was deleted by the Congress at the insistence of Georgia and South Carolina.

The Declaration's enduring impact came not from the complaints against George III but from Jefferson's preamble, especially the second paragraph, which begins, "We hold these truths to be self-evident, that all men are created equal, that they are endowed by their Creator with certain unalienable Rights, that among these are Life, Liberty, and the pursuit of Happiness." By

America as a Symbol of Liberty, a 1775 engraving from the cover of the *Pennsylvania Magazine*, edited by Thomas Paine soon after his arrival in America. The shield displays the colony's coat of arms. The female figure holding a liberty cap is surrounded by weaponry of the patriotic struggle, including a cartridge box marked "liberty," hanging from a tree (*right*).

"unalienable rights," Jefferson meant rights so basic, so rooted in human nature itself (or in what John Locke had called the state of nature), that no government could take them away.

Jefferson then went on to justify the breach with Britain. Government, he wrote, derives its powers from "the consent of the governed." When a government threatens its subjects' natural rights, the people have the authority "to alter or to abolish it." The Declaration of Independence is ultimately an assertion of the right of revolution.

The Declaration and American Freedom

The **Declaration of Independence** changed forever the meaning of American freedom. It completed the shift from the rights of Englishmen to the rights of mankind as the object of American independence. In Jefferson's language, "the Laws of Nature and of Nature's God," not the British constitution or the heritage of the freeborn Englishman, justified independence. No longer a set of specific rights, no longer a privilege to be enjoyed by a corporate body or people in certain social circumstances, liberty had become a universal entitlement.

Jefferson's argument (natural rights, the right to resist arbitrary authority, etc.) drew on the writings of John Locke, who, as explained in the previous chapter, saw government as resting on a "social contract," violation of which destroyed the legitimacy of authority. But when Jefferson substituted the "pursuit of happiness" for property in the familiar Lockean triad that opens the Declaration, he tied the new nation's star to an open-ended, democratic process whereby individuals develop their own potential and seek to realize their own life goals. Individual self-fulfillment, unimpeded by government, would become a central element of American freedom. Tradition would no longer rule the present, and Americans could shape their society as they saw fit.

An Asylum for Mankind

A distinctive definition of nationality resting on American freedom was born in the Revolution. From the beginning, the idea of "American exceptionalism"—the belief that the United States has a special mission to serve as a refuge from tyranny, a symbol of freedom, and a model for the rest of the world—has occupied a central place in American nationalism. The new nation declared itself, in the words of Virginia leader James Madison, the "workshop of liberty to the Civilized World." Paine's remark in *Common Sense*, "we have it in our power to begin the world over again," and his description of the new nation as an "asylum for mankind" expressed a sense that the Revolution was an event of global historical importance. Countless sermons, political tracts, and newspaper articles of the time repeated this idea. Unburdened by the institutions—monarchy, aristocracy, hereditary privilege—that oppressed the peoples of the Old World, America and America alone was the place where the principle of universal freedom could take root. This was why Jefferson addressed the Declaration to "the opinions of mankind," not just the colonists themselves or Great Britain.

First to add his name to the Declaration of Independence was the Massachusetts merchant John Hancock, president of the Second Continental Congress, with a signature so large, he declared, according to legend, that King George III could read it without his spectacles.

The Global Declaration of Independence

Even apart from the Declaration of Independence, 1776 was a momentous year in North America. Spain established Mission Dolores, the first European settlement at San Francisco, in an effort to block Russian advances on the Pacific coast. In San Diego, local Indians rebelled, unsuccessfully, against Spanish rule. The Lakota Sioux, migrating westward from Minnesota, settled in the Black Hills of North Dakota, their homeland for the next century. All these places and peoples would eventually become part of the United States, but, of course, no one knew this in 1776.

Meanwhile, the struggle for independence reverberated around the globe. The American colonists were less concerned with securing human rights for all mankind than with winning international recognition in their struggle for independence from Britain. But Jefferson hoped that this rebellion would become "the signal of arousing men to burst the chains . . . and to assume the blessings and security of self-government." And for more than two centuries, the Declaration has remained an inspiration not only to generations of Americans denied the enjoyment of their natural rights, but to colonial peoples around the world seeking independence. The Declaration quickly appeared in French and German translations, although not, at first, in Spanish, since the government feared it would inspire dangerous ideas among the peoples of Spain's American empire.

In the years since 1776, numerous anticolonial movements have modeled their own declarations of independence on America's. Today, more than half the countries in the world, in places as far-flung as China (issued after the revolution of 1911) and Vietnam (1945), have such declarations. Many of these documents, like Jefferson's, listed grievances against an imperial power to justify revolution. Few of these documents, however, have affirmed the natural rights—life, liberty, and the pursuit of happiness—Jefferson invoked. Over time, the Declaration in a global context has become an assertion of the right of various groups to form independent states, rather than a list of the rights of citizens that their governments could not abridge.

But even more than the specific language of the Declaration, the principle that legitimate political authority rests on the will of "the people" has been adopted around the world. In 1780, even as the American War of Independence raged, a Jesuit-educated Indian of Peru took the name of the last Inca ruler, Túpac Amaru, and led an uprising against Spanish rule. By the time it was suppressed in 1783, some 10,000 Spanish and 100,000 Indians had perished. In the Dutch, French, and Spanish empires, where European governments had been trying to tighten their control much as the British had done in North America, local elites demanded greater autonomy, often drawing on the constitutional arguments of American patriots. The idea that "the people" possess rights was quickly internationalized. Slaves in the Caribbean, colonial subjects in India, and indigenous inhabitants of Latin America could all speak this language, to the dismay of those who exercised power over them.

SECURING INDEPENDENCE

The Balance of Power

Declaring Americans independent was one thing; winning independence another. The newly created American army confronted the greatest military power on earth. Viewing the Americans as traitors, Britain resolved to crush

American Foot Soldiers, Yorktown Campaign, a 1781 watercolor by a French officer, includes a Black soldier from the First Rhode Island Regiment, an all-Black unit of 250 men.

the rebellion. On the surface, the balance of power seemed heavily weighted in Britain's favor. It had a well-trained army (supplemented by hired soldiers from German states such as Hesse), the world's most powerful navy, and experienced military commanders. The Americans had to rely on local militias and an inadequately equipped Continental army. Washington himself felt that militiamen were too "accustomed to unbounded freedom" to accept the "proper degree of subordination" necessary in soldiers. Moreover, many Americans were not enthusiastic about independence, and some actively supported the British.

On the other hand, many American soldiers did not lack military experience, having fought in the Seven Years' War or undergone intensive militia training in the early 1770s. They were fighting on their own soil for a cause that inspired devotion and sacrifice. During the eight years of war from 1775 to 1783, some 200,000 men bore arms in the American army and militias. As the war progressed, enlistment waned among propertied Americans, and the Continental army increasingly drew on young men with limited economic prospects—landless sons of farmers, indentured servants, laborers, and African Americans. The patriots suffered dearly for the cause. Of the colonies' free white male population aged sixteen to forty-five, one in twenty died in the War of Independence, the equivalent of nearly 3 million deaths in today's population. But so long as the Americans maintained an army in the field, the idea of independence remained alive no matter how much territory the British occupied.

Despite British power, to conquer the thirteen colonies would be an enormous and expensive task, and it was not at all certain that the public at home wished to pay the additional taxes that a lengthy war would require. The British, moreover, made a string of serious mistakes. From the outset they misjudged the degree of support for independence among the American population, as well as the capacity of American citizen-soldiers. "These people," admitted the British general Thomas Gage, "show a spirit and conduct against us that they never showed against the French [in the Seven Years' War], and everybody has judged them from their former appearance and behavior, which has led many into great mistakes." Moreover, European rivals, notably France and Spain, welcomed the prospect of a British defeat. If the Americans could forge an alliance with Britain's imperial rivals, it would go a long way toward equalizing the balance of forces.

Blacks in the Revolution

In 1776, Harry Washington escaped from Mount Vernon. Born in West Africa and enslaved in Virginia by the commander-in-chief of the Continental army, he volunteered his services to the other side. To men and women enslaved in the rebelling British colonies, the War of Independence offered an unprecedented opportunity to seize their own freedom. Many pursued this goal by fighting in one of the opposing armies.

At the war's outset, George Washington refused to accept Black recruits. But he changed his mind after Lord Dunmore's 1775 proclamation, which offered freedom to slaves who joined the British cause. Some 5,000 Black men enlisted in state militias and the Continental army and navy. Since individuals were able to avoid the draft by providing a substitute, enslaved men suddenly gained considerable bargaining power. Not a few acquired their freedom by agreeing to serve in place of an owner or his son. In 1778, Rhode Island, with a higher

Prince Simbo, a former Connecticut slave who served in the Continental army, engraved this powder horn with an all-seeing eye, a symbol of protection. Simbo was one of several thousand Black soldiers who fought for American independence.

British ships landing sailors on the New Jersey side of the Hudson River in November 1776. They quickly scaled the palisades and began pursuing George Washington's retreating army.

proportion of slaves in its population than any other New England state, formed a Black regiment and promised freedom to slaves who enlisted, while compensating their former enslavers. Blacks who fought under George Washington and in state militias did so in racially integrated companies (although invariably under white officers). They were the last Black American soldiers to do so officially until the Korean War (except for the few Black and white soldiers who fought alongside each other in irregular units at the end of World War II).

Except for South Carolina and Georgia, the southern colonies also enrolled free Blacks and slaves to fight. They were not explicitly promised freedom, but many received it individually after the war ended. And in 1783, the Virginia legislature emancipated slaves who had "contributed towards the establishment of American liberty and independence" by serving in the army.

The side of the British offered more opportunities for freedom. Harry Washington was among tens of thousands of enslaved men, women, and children who fled to British lines to claim their freedom. He joined Lord Dunmore's Ethiopian Regiment, whose members reportedly wore uniforms that bore the motto "Liberty to Slaves." During the war, Black soldiers fought with the British in campaigns in New York, New Jersey, and South Carolina. Other escaped slaves served the Royal Army as spies, guided their troops through swamps, and worked as military cooks, laundresses, and construction workers. Besides Harry Washington, sixteen other people enslaved by George Washington fled to the British. "There is not a man of them, but would leave us, if they believed they could make their escape," his cousin Lund Washington reported. "Liberty is sweet."

The First Years of the War

Had the British commander, Sir William Howe, prosecuted the war more vigorously at the outset, he might have nipped the rebellion in the bud by destroying Washington's army. But while Washington suffered numerous defeats in the first years of the war, he generally avoided direct confrontations with the British and managed to keep his army intact. Having abandoned Boston, Howe attacked New York City in the summer of 1776. Washington's army had likewise moved from Massachusetts to Brooklyn to defend the city. Howe pushed American forces back and almost cut off Washington's retreat across the East River. Washington managed to escape to Manhattan and then north to Peekskill, where he crossed the Hudson River to New Jersey. But the 3,000 men he had left behind at Fort Washington on Manhattan Island were captured by Howe.

Howe pursued the American army but never managed to inflict a decisive defeat. Demoralized by successive failures, however, many American soldiers simply went home. Once 28,000 men, Washington's army dwindled to fewer than 3,000. Indeed, Washington feared that without a decisive victory, it would melt away entirely. To restore morale and regain the initiative, he launched successful surprise attacks on Hessian soldiers at Trenton, New Jersey, on December 26, 1776, and on a British force at Princeton on January 3, 1777. Shortly before crossing the Delaware River to attack the Hessians, Washington had Thomas Paine's inspiring essay *The American Crisis* read to his troops. "These are the times that try men's souls," Paine wrote. "The summer soldier and the sunshine patriot will, in this crisis, shrink from the service of their country; but he that stands it *now*, deserves the love and thanks of man and woman."

The Battle of Saratoga

In the summer of 1777, a second British army, led by General John Burgoyne, advanced south from Canada hoping to link up with Howe and isolate New England. But in July, Howe instead moved his forces from New York City to attack Philadelphia. In September, the Continental Congress fled to Lancaster, in central Pennsylvania, and Howe occupied the City of Brotherly Love. Not having been informed of Burgoyne's plans, Howe had unintentionally abandoned him. American forces blocked Burgoyne's way, surrounded his army, and on October 17, 1777, forced him to surrender at the **Battle of Saratoga**. The victory provided a significant boost to American morale.

During the winter of 1777–1778, the British army, now commanded by Sir Henry Clinton, was quartered in Philadelphia. (In the Revolution, as in most eighteenth-century wars, fighting came to a halt during the winter.) British officers took part in an elegant social life complete with balls and parties. Meanwhile, Washington's army remained encamped at Valley Forge,

Benjamin Franklin designed this three-dollar bill for the new nation. It depicts an eagle fighting a crane with a Latin motto meaning "the outcome is in doubt."

where they suffered terribly from the frigid weather. Men who had other options simply went home. By the end of that difficult winter, recent immigrants and African Americans made up half the soldiers at Valley Forge and most of the rest were landless or unskilled laborers.

A Global War

Saratoga helped to persuade the French that American victory was possible. In 1778, American diplomats led by Benjamin Franklin concluded a Treaty of Amity and Commerce in which France recognized the United States and agreed to supply military assistance. Still smarting from their defeat in the Seven Years' War, the French hoped to weaken Britain, their main European rival, and perhaps regain some of their lost influence and territory in the Western Hemisphere. The Spanish and Dutch soon also joined the war against Britain.

European financial and military assistance would play a decisive role in Britain's defeat. Yet France, Spain, and the Netherlands all focused on their own war objectives despite pleas by the Continental Congress that they send troops to aid George Washington. The French and Dutch, concerned about British expansion around the globe, fought British ships in the Caribbean, the Atlantic, and the Indian Ocean. At the same time, Spain sought to expand its North American empire. Spanish forces seized the British colony of West Florida (including Natchez, Mobile, and Pensacola) as well as the Bahamas. The entry of Britain's European rivals transformed the War of Independence into a global conflict. By putting the British on the defensive in places ranging from Gibraltar to the West Indies to England itself and by helping to finance the American rebellion, it greatly complicated their military prospects.

Native America and the Revolution

The American Revolution and its aftermath would also be a Native American struggle for independence. Despite the Proclamation of 1763, discussed in Chapter 4, colonists had continued to move westward during the 1760s and early 1770s onto Native land. Lord Dunmore, Virginia's royal governor, observed in 1772 that he had found it impossible "to restrain the Americans. . . . They do not conceive that government has any right to forbid their taking possession of a vast tract of country" or to force them to honor treaties with Indians. Many patriot leaders, including George Washington, Patrick Henry, and Thomas Jefferson, were deeply involved in western land speculation. Washington himself had acquired more than 60,000 acres of land in western Pennsylvania after the Seven Years' War by purchasing land vouchers (a form of soldiers' wages) from his men at discount rates.

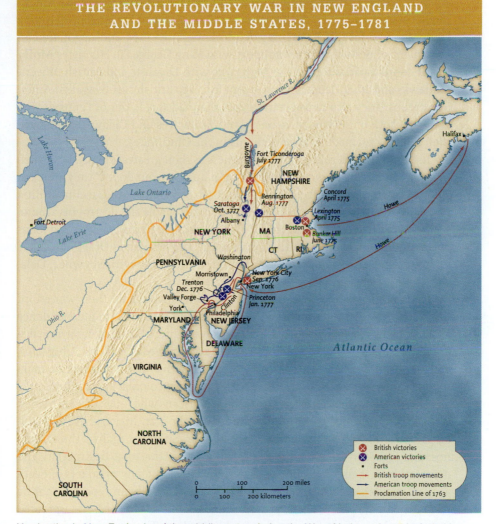

THE REVOLUTIONARY WAR IN NEW ENGLAND AND THE MIDDLE STATES, 1775–1781

Key battles in New England and the middle states during the War of Independence included Lexington and Concord, which began the armed conflict; the campaign in New York and New Jersey; and Saratoga, sometimes called the turning point of the war.

About 200,000 Native Americans lived east of the Mississippi River in 1790. During the War of Independence, they chose the side they felt would advance their own ideas of liberty. Some sided with the rebelling Americans. The Catawbas joined their Carolina neighbors in fighting the British at the Battle of Guilford Courthouse and other battles throughout the war. The Oneidas joined the Americans despite the fact that most of the rest of the Haudenosaunee (Iroquois) League allied with the British.

Most Native nations, communities, and individuals who joined the American Revolution fought on the British side in hopes of pushing settlers off Native land. Mohawk **Joseph Brant** traveled to London in 1775 and negotiated an agreement of mutual military support with King George III. His sister **Molly Brant** coordinated the efforts of Mohawks with Loyalists and British officers. Mohawks and other Haudenosaunee sent forces to British battles against American troops. They also raided settlements that had spread out of Pennsylvania and New York onto Haudenosaunee land. Shawnees and Delawares renewed their fighting against illegal settlements in the Ohio Valley.

In the South, Cherokees also saw settlers as their greatest enemy. Disgusted that they could "see the smoke of the Virginians from our doors," they attacked colonists who were squatting on their lands. North and South Carolina militia struck back in the fall of 1776, burning Cherokee towns and destroying Cherokee women's harvest. Most of the Cherokees decided to make peace and focus on rebuilding their towns, although a young fighter named Dragging Canoe led some Cherokees in continuing raids, in conjunction with Shawnee, Delaware, and Mohawk forces.

British officials hoped that large Native forces would aid their war effort. But Britain's Native allies put their highest priority on their own independence and safety. British officials called Chickasaw fighters "absolutely at our disposal," but in fact Chickasaw Chief **Paya Mataha** urged Cherokees, Choctaws, and other southeastern Native peoples not to join the war but to work on making firm alliances with one another to stand against colonial encroachment.

The war brought destruction to Native Americans who fought on both sides. British troops burned Catawba towns during the war. In 1779, Washington dispatched an expedition, led by General John Sullivan, against the Haudenosaunee (except the Oneidas) with the aim of "the total destruction and devastation of their settlements and the capture of as many prisoners of every age and sex as possible." After his campaign ended, Sullivan reported that he had burned forty towns, destroyed thousands of bushels of corn, and uprooted a vast number of fruit trees and vegetable gardens. The American victory in the Revolution would bring independence to the United States but would have grave consequences for Native independence.

The War in the South

In 1778, the focus of the war shifted to the South. Here the British hoped to exploit the social tensions between backcountry farmers and wealthy planters that had surfaced in the Regulator movements, to enlist the support of the numerous colonists in the region who remained loyal to the crown, and to disrupt the economy by encouraging slaves to escape. In December 1778, British

THE REVOLUTIONARY WAR IN THE SOUTH, 1775–1781

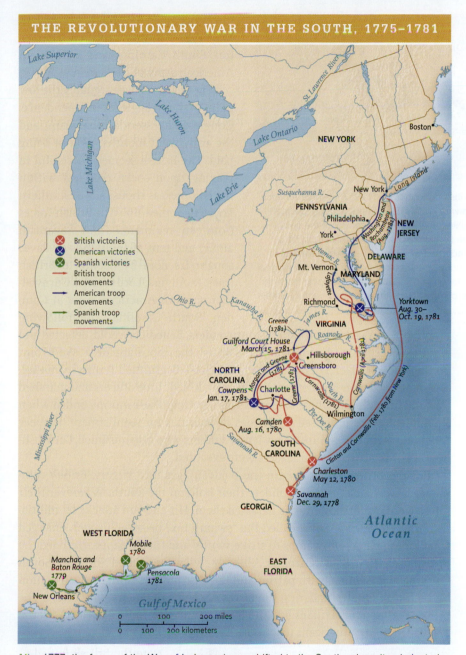

After 1777, the focus of the War of Independence shifted to the South, where it culminated in 1781 with the British defeat at Yorktown.

A British cartoon from 1779, *The Horse America Throwing His Master*, lampoons King George III for being unable to keep control of the colonies. In the background, a French officer carries a flag adorned with the fleur-de-lys, a symbol of that country, the colonists' ally. Powerful satirical attacks on public authorities, including the king, were commonplace in eighteenth-century Britain.

forces occupied Savannah, Georgia. In May 1780, Clinton captured Charleston, South Carolina, and with it an American army of 5,000 men.

The year 1780 was arguably the low point of the struggle for independence. Congress was essentially bankrupt, and the army went months without being paid. The British seemed successful in playing upon social conflicts within the colonies, as thousands of southern Loyalists joined up with British forces (fourteen regiments from Savannah alone) and tens of thousands of slaves sought freedom by fleeing to British lines. In August, Lord Charles Cornwallis routed an American army at Camden, South Carolina. The following month one of Washington's ablest commanders, Benedict Arnold, defected and almost succeeded in turning over to the British the important fort at West Point on the Hudson River. On January 1, 1781, 1,500 disgruntled Pennsylvania soldiers stationed near Morristown, New Jersey, killed three officers and marched toward Philadelphia, where Congress was meeting. Their mutiny ended when the soldiers were promised discharges or bounties for reenlistment. Harsher treatment awaited a group of New Jersey soldiers who also mutinied. On Washington's orders, two of their leaders were executed.

But the British failed to turn these advantages into victory. British commanders were unable to consolidate their hold on the South. Wherever their forces went, American militias harassed them. Hit-and-run attacks by militiamen under Francis Marion, called the "swamp fox" because his men emerged from hiding places in swamps to strike swiftly and then disappear, eroded the British position in South Carolina. A bloody civil war engulfed North and South Carolina and Georgia, with patriot and Loyalist militias inflicting retribution on each other and plundering the farms of their opponents' supporters. The brutal treatment of civilians by British forces under Colonel Banastre Tarleton persuaded many Americans to join the patriot cause.

Victory at Last

In January 1781, American forces under Daniel Morgan dealt a crushing defeat to Tarleton at Cowpens, South Carolina. Two months later, at Guilford Courthouse, North Carolina, General Nathanael Greene, while conducting a campaign of

EUROPEAN AND U.S. CLAIMS IN NORTH AMERICA, 1783

The newly independent United States occupied only a small part of the North American continent in 1783. Other European empires claimed much larger swaths of land, almost all of which were actually governed by hundreds of Native nations and inhabited by hundreds of thousands of American Indians.

strategic retreats, inflicted heavy losses on Cornwallis, the British commander in the South. Cornwallis moved into Virginia and encamped at Yorktown, located on a peninsula that juts into Chesapeake Bay. Brilliantly recognizing the opportunity to surround Cornwallis, Washington rushed his forces, augmented by French troops under the Marquis de Lafayette, to block a British escape by land. Meanwhile, a French fleet controlled the mouth of the Chesapeake, preventing supplies and reinforcements from reaching Cornwallis's army.

Imperial rivalries had helped to create the American colonies. Now, the rivalry of European empires helped to secure American independence. Taking land and sea forces together, more Frenchmen than Americans participated in the decisive **Battle of Yorktown**. On October 19, 1781, Cornwallis surrendered his army of 8,000 men. When the news reached London, public support for the war evaporated and peace negotiations soon began. Given its immense military prowess, Britain abandoned the struggle rather quickly. Many in Britain felt the West Indies were more valuable economically than the mainland colonies and knew Spain was planning an invasion of Jamaica. In any event, British merchants expected to continue to dominate trade with the United States and did so for many years.

Two years later, in September 1783, American and British negotiators concluded the **Treaty of Paris**. The American delegation—John Adams, Benjamin Franklin, and John Jay—achieved one of the greatest diplomatic triumphs in the country's history. They not only won recognition of American independence but also persuaded the British to cede the entire region between Canada and Florida east of the Mississippi River as well as giving Americans the right to fish in Atlantic waters off of Canada, which was a matter of considerable importance to New Englanders. (Spain and many Native nations would dispute the extensive borders that the United States agreed to with Britain.) At British insistence, the Americans agreed that colonists who had remained loyal to Britain would not suffer persecution and that Loyalists' property that had been seized by local and state governments would be restored.

Until independence, the thirteen colonies had formed part of Britain's American empire, along with East and West Florida and the colonies in Canada and the West Indies. But Canada and the Floridas rebuffed repeated calls to join the War of Independence, and leaders of the West Indies, fearful of slave uprisings, also remained loyal to the crown. With the Treaty of Paris, the United States of America became the Western Hemisphere's first independent nation. Its boundaries reflected not so much the long-standing unity of a geographical region, but the circumstances of its birth.

CHAPTER REVIEW

REVIEW QUESTIONS

1. *How important was the Stamp Act crisis in bringing about the American Revolution?*

2. *How did colonial women exercise economic and political power in the protests against British taxation?*

3. *Patrick Henry proclaimed that he was not a Virginian, but rather an American. What unified the colonists and what divided them at the time of the Revolution?*

4. How did enslaved people react to the American Revolution? What were the policies of the British and Continental armies regarding the enlistment of slaves?

5. Why did the colonists reach the conclusion that membership in the empire threatened their freedoms rather than guaranteed them?

6. How did new ideas of liberty contribute to tensions between the social classes in the American colonies?

7. Why did people in other countries believe that the American Revolution (or the Declaration of Independence) was important to them or their own countries?

8. Summarize the difference of opinion between British officials and colonial leaders over the issues of taxation and representation.

9. How did the actions of the British authorities help to unite the American colonists during the 1760s and 1770s?

10. Why were Native American nations more likely to side with Britain in the war?

KEY TERMS

Stamp Act (p. 179)

virtual representation (p. 182)

Sugar Act (p. 183)

"No taxation without representation" (p. 184)

Committee of Correspondence (p. 185)

Sons of Liberty (p. 186)

Regulators (p. 187)

Townshend Acts (p. 188)

Daughters of Liberty (p. 188)

Boston Massacre (p. 189)

Crispus Attucks (p. 189)

Boston Tea Party (p. 190)

Intolerable Acts (p. 190)

Continental Congress (p. 191)

Battles of Lexington and Concord (p. 193)

Battle of Bunker Hill (p. 194)

Continental army (p. 194)

Lord Dunmore's proclamation (p. 194)

Common Sense (p. 195)

Declaration of Independence (p. 199)

Battle of Saratoga (p. 205)

Joseph and Molly Brant (p. 208)

Paya Mataha (p. 208)

Battle of Yorktown (p. 212)

Treaty of Paris (p. 212)

Go to 🐰 INQUIZITIVE

To see what you know—and learn what you've missed—with personalized feedback along the way.

CHAPTER 6

THE REVOLUTION WITHIN

FOCUS QUESTIONS

- *How did equality become a stronger component of American freedom after the Revolution?*

- *How did the expansion of religious liberty after the Revolution reflect the new American ideal of freedom?*

- *How did the definition of economic freedom change after the Revolution, and who benefited from the changes?*

- *How did the Revolution diminish the freedoms of both Loyalists and Native Americans?*

- *What was the impact of the Revolution on slavery?*

- *How did the Revolution affect the status of women?*

B orn in Massachusetts in 1744, at a time when educational opportunities for girls were extremely limited, Abigail Adams nonetheless became one of the revolutionary era's great thinkers and writers. She taught herself by reading books in the library of her father, a Congregational minister. In 1764, she married John Adams, a young lawyer about to emerge as a leading advocate of resistance to British taxation and, eventually, of American independence. During the War of Independence, with her husband away in Philadelphia and Europe serving the American cause, she stayed behind at their Massachusetts home, raising their four children and managing the family's farm. The letters they exchanged form one of the most remarkable correspondences in American history. She addressed John as "Dear friend" and signed her letters "Portia"—after Brutus's devoted wife in Shakespeare's play *Julius Caesar*. Though denied an official role in politics, Abigail Adams was a keen observer of public affairs. She kept her husband informed of events in Massachusetts and offered opinions on political matters. Later, when Adams served as president, he relied on her advice more than on members of his cabinet.

In March 1776, a few months before the Second Continental Congress declared American independence, Abigail Adams wrote her best-known letter to her husband. She began by commenting indirectly on the evils of slavery. How strong, she wondered, could the "passion for Liberty" be among those "accustomed to deprive their fellow citizens of theirs?" She went on to urge Congress, when it drew up a "Code of Laws" for the new republic, to "remember the ladies." All men, she warned, "would be tyrants if they could." Women, she playfully suggested, "will not hold ourselves bound by any laws in which we have no voice or representation."

1700	Samuel Sewall's *The Selling of Joseph*, first antislavery tract in America
1765	Phillis Wheatley publishes her first poem
1770s	Slaves begin presenting freedom petitions to courts and legislatures
1776	Adam Smith's *The Wealth of Nations*
1777	Vermont state constitution bans slavery
1779	Thomas Jefferson writes Bill for Establishing Religious Freedom
	Philipsburg Proclamation
1780	Ladies' Association of Philadelphia founded
1782	Deborah Sampson enlists in Continental army
1783	Elizabeth Freeman's and Quock Walker's freedom suits result in the abolition of slavery in Massachusetts

It was the leaders of colonial society who initiated resistance to British taxation. But, as Abigail Adams's letter illustrates, the struggle for American liberty emboldened other colonists to demand more liberty for themselves. All revolutions enlarge the public sphere, inspiring previously marginalized groups to express their own dreams of freedom. At a time when so many Americans—slaves, indentured servants, women, Indians living within the colonies, apprentices, propertyless men—were denied full freedom, the struggle against Britain threw into question many forms of authority and inequality.

Yet the American Revolution left some of the old relationships of dependency in place. Despite the efforts of Abigail Adams, coverture and women's subordinate economic and political status to men would continue. Slavery would end in some places while becoming more deeply entrenched in others. The farm ownership that was the basis of independence for white families would be built by taking Native land. As political participation was extended to more and more white men, the boundaries of full citizenship became more rigidly based on gender and race.

Abigail Adams's letter is widely remembered today. Less familiar is John Adams's response, which illuminated how the Revolution had unleashed challenges to all sorts of inherited ideas of deference and authority: "We have been told that our struggle has loosened the bands of government everywhere; that children and apprentices were disobedient; that schools and colleges were grown turbulent; that Indians slighted their guardians, and negroes grew insolent to their masters." To John Adams, this upheaval, including his wife's claim to greater freedom, was an affront to the natural order of things. To others, it formed the essence of the American Revolution.

DEMOCRATIZING FREEDOM

The Dream of Equality

The American Revolution took place at three levels simultaneously. It was a struggle for national independence, a phase in a century-long continental and global battle among multiple European empires and many Native nations, and a conflict over what kind of nation an independent America should be.

With its wide distribution of property, lack of a legally established hereditary aristocracy, and established churches far less powerful than in Britain, colonial America was a society with deep democratic potential. But it took the struggle for independence to transform it into a nation that celebrated equality and opportunity. The Revolution unleashed public debates and political and social struggles that enlarged the scope of freedom and challenged inherited structures of power within America. In rejecting the crown and the principle of hereditary aristocracy, many Americans also rejected the society of privilege, patronage, and fixed status that these institutions embodied. To be sure, the men who led the Revolution from start to finish were by and large members of the American elite. The lower classes did not rise to power as a result of independence, nor did patriarchy and slavery end. Nonetheless, the idea of liberty became a revolutionary rallying cry, a standard by which to judge and challenge homegrown institutions as well as imperial ones.

Jefferson's seemingly straightforward assertion in the Declaration of Independence that "all men are created equal" announced a radical principle whose full implications no one could anticipate. In both Britain and its colonies, a well-ordered society was widely thought to depend on obedience to authority—the power of rulers over their subjects, husbands over wives, parents over children, employers over servants and apprentices, slaveholders over slaves. Inequality had been fundamental to the colonial social order; the Revolution challenged it in many ways. Henceforth, American freedom would be forever linked with the idea of equality—equality before the law, equality in political rights, equality of economic opportunity, and, for some, equality of condition. "Whenever I use the words *freedom* or *rights*," wrote Thomas Paine, "I desire to be understood to mean a perfect equality of them. . . . The floor of Freedom is as level as water."

Expanding the Political Nation

With liberty and equality as their rallying cries, previously marginalized groups advanced their demands. Long-accepted relations of dependency and restrictions on freedom suddenly appeared illegitimate—a process not intended by most of the leading patriots. In political, social, and religious life, Americans challenged the previous domination by a privileged few. In the end, the Revolution did not undo the obedience to which male heads of household were entitled from their wives and children and, at least in the southern states, their slaves. For free men, however, the democratization of freedom was dramatic. Nowhere was this more evident than in challenges to the traditional limitation of political participation to those who owned property.

In the political thought of the eighteenth century, "democracy" had several meanings. One, derived from the writings of Aristotle, defined democracy as a system in which the entire people governed directly. However, this was thought to mean mob rule. Another definition viewed democracy as the condition of primitive societies, which was not appropriate for the complex modern world. Yet another understanding revolved less around the structure of government than the principle that government should serve the interests of the people rather than an elite. In the wake of the American Revolution, the term came into wider use to express the popular aspirations for greater equality inspired by the struggle for independence.

"We are all, from the cobbler up to the senator, become politicians," declared a Boston letter writer in 1774. Throughout the colonies, election campaigns became freewheeling debates on the fundamentals of government. Universal male suffrage, religious toleration, and even the abolition of slavery were discussed not only by the educated elite but by artisans, small farmers, and laborers, now emerging as a self-conscious element in politics. In many colonies-turned-states, the militia, composed largely of members of the "lower orders," became a "school of political democracy." Its members demanded the right to elect all their officers and to vote for public officials whether or not they met age and property qualifications. They helped to thereby establish the tradition that service in the army enabled excluded men to stake a claim to full citizenship.

The Revolution in Pennsylvania

The Revolution's radical potential was more evident in Pennsylvania than in any other state. Elsewhere, the established leadership either embraced independence by the spring of 1776 or split into pro-British and pro-independence factions (in New York, for example, the Livingstons and their supporters ended up as patriots, the De Lanceys as Loyalists). But in Pennsylvania nearly the entire prewar elite opposed independence, fearing that severing the tie with Britain would lead to rule by the "rabble" and to attacks on property.

The vacuum of political leadership opened the door for the rise of a new pro-independence grouping, based on the artisan and lower-class communities of Philadelphia and organized in extralegal committees and the local militia. Their leaders included Thomas Paine (the author of *Common Sense*), Benjamin Rush (a local physician), Timothy Matlack (the son of a local brewer), and Thomas Young (who had already been involved in the Sons of Liberty in Albany and Boston). As a group, these were men of modest wealth who stood outside the merchant elite, had little political influence before 1776, and believed strongly in democratic reform. They formed a temporary alliance with supporters of independence in the Second Continental Congress (then meeting in Philadelphia), who disapproved of their strong belief in equality but hoped to move Pennsylvania toward a break with Britain.

Americans have frequently defined the idea of freedom in relation to its opposite, which in the eighteenth century meant the highly unequal societies of Europe. This engraving, *The Coronation of Louis XVI of France*, reveals the splendor of the royal court but also illustrates the world of fixed, unequal classes and social privilege repudiated by American revolutionaries.

As the public sphere expanded far beyond its previous boundaries, equality became the rallying cry of Pennsylvania's radicals. They particularly attacked property qualifications for voting. "God gave mankind freedom by nature," declared the anonymous author of the pamphlet *The People the Best Governors*, "and made every man equal to his neighbors." The people, therefore, were "the best guardians of their own liberties," and every free man should be eligible to vote and hold office. In June 1776, a broadside (a printed sheet posted in public places) warned citizens to distrust "great and over-grown rich men" who were inclined "to be framing distinctions in society." Three months after independence, Pennsylvania adopted a new state constitution that sought to institutionalize democracy by concentrating power in a one-house legislature elected annually by all men over age twenty-one who paid taxes. It abolished the office of governor, dispensed with property qualifications for officeholding, and provided that schools with low fees be established in every county. It also included clauses guaranteeing "freedom of speech, and of writing," and religious liberty.

The New Constitutions

Like Pennsylvania, every state adopted a new constitution in the aftermath of independence. Nearly all Americans now agreed that their governments must be republics, meaning that their authority rested on the consent of the governed, and that there would be no king or hereditary aristocracy. The essence of a **republic**, Paine wrote, was not the "particular form" of government, but its object: the "public good." But as to how a republican government should be structured so as to promote the public good, there was much disagreement.

Pennsylvania's new constitution reflected the belief that since the people had a single set of interests, a single legislative house was sufficient to represent it. In part to counteract what he saw as Pennsylvania's excessive radicalism, John Adams in 1776 published *Thoughts on Government*, which insisted that the new constitutions should create balanced governments whose structure would reflect the division of society between the wealthy (represented in the upper house) and ordinary men (who would control the lower). A powerful governor and judiciary would ensure that neither class infringed on the liberty of the other. Adams's call for two-house legislatures was followed by every state except Pennsylvania, Georgia, and Vermont. But only his own state, Massachusetts, gave the governor an effective veto over laws passed by the legislature. Americans had long resented efforts by appointed governors to challenge the power of colonial assemblies. They preferred power to rest with the legislature.

The Right to Vote

The issue of requirements for voting and officeholding proved far more contentious. Conservative patriots struggled valiantly to reassert the rationale for the old voting restrictions. It was ridiculous, wrote one pamphleteer, to think that "every silly clown and illiterate mechanic [artisan]" deserved a voice in government. To John Adams, as conservative on the internal affairs of America as he had been radical on independence, freedom and equality were opposites. Men without property, he believed, had no "judgment of their own," and the removal of property qualifications, therefore, would "confound and destroy all distinctions, and prostrate all ranks to one common level."

The provisions of the new state constitutions reflected the balance of power between advocates of internal change and those who feared excessive democracy. The least democratization occurred in some of the southern states, whose highly deferential political traditions enabled the landed gentry to retain their control of political affairs. In Virginia and South Carolina, the new constitutions retained property qualifications for voting and authorized the gentry-dominated legislature to choose the governor. Maryland combined a low property qualification for voting with high requirements for officeholding, including £5,000—a fortune—for the governor.

The most democratic new constitutions moved much of the way toward the idea of voting as an entitlement rather than a privilege, but they generally stopped short of universal **suffrage**, even for free men. Vermont's constitution of 1777 was the only one to sever voting completely from financial considerations, eliminating not only property qualifications but also the requirement that voters pay taxes. Pennsylvania's constitution no longer required ownership of property, but it retained the taxpaying qualification. As a result, it enfranchised nearly all of the state's free male population but left a small number, mainly paupers and domestic servants, still barred from voting. Nonetheless, even with the taxpaying requirement, it represented a dramatic departure from the colonial practice of restricting the suffrage to those who could claim to be economically independent. It elevated "personal liberty," in the words of one essayist, to a position more important than property ownership in defining the boundaries of the political nation.

Democratizing Government

Overall, the Revolution led to a great expansion of the right to vote. By the 1780s, with the exceptions of Virginia, Maryland, and New York, a large majority of the adult white male population could meet voting requirements. New Jersey's new state constitution of 1776 granted the suffrage to all "inhabitants" who met a property qualification. Until the state added the word "male" (along with "white") in 1807, property-owning women, mostly widows, did cast ballots. The new constitutions also expanded the number of legislative seats, with the result that numerous men of lesser property assumed political office. The debate over the suffrage would, of course, continue for many decades. For white men, the process of democratization did not run its course until the Age of Jackson; for women and non-whites, it would take much longer. Who should vote remains controversial to this day.

Even during the Revolution, however, in the popular language of politics, if not in law, freedom and an individual man's right to vote had become interchangeable. "The suffrage," declared a 1776 petition of disenfranchised North Carolinians, was "a right essential to and inseparable from freedom." A proposed new constitution for Massachusetts was rejected by a majority of the towns in 1778, partly because it contained a property qualification for voting. "All men were born equally free and independent," declared the town of Lenox. How could they defend their "life and liberty and property" without a voice in electing public officials? A new draft, which retained a substantial requirement for voting in state elections but allowed virtually all men to vote for town officers, was approved in 1780. And every state except South Carolina provided for annual legislative elections, to ensure that representatives remained closely accountable to the people. Henceforth, political freedom would mean not only, as in the past, a people's right to be ruled by their chosen representatives but also an individual's right to political participation.

John Dickinson's copy of the Pennsylvania constitution of 1776, with handwritten proposals for changes. Dickinson, one of the more conservative advocates of independence, felt the new state constitution was far too democratic. He crossed out a provision that all "free men" should be eligible to hold office and another declaring the people not bound by laws that did not promote "the common good."

TOWARD RELIGIOUS TOLERATION

As remarkable as the expansion of political freedom was the Revolution's impact on American religion. Religious toleration, declared one Virginia patriot, was part of "the common cause of Freedom." In Britain, Dissenters—Protestants who belonged to other denominations than the Anglican Church—had long invoked the language of liberty in seeking repeal of the laws that imposed various disabilities on non-Anglicans. (Few, however, included Catholics in their ringing calls for religious freedom.) We have already seen that Rhode Island and Pennsylvania had long made a practice of toleration. But freedom of worship before the Revolution arose more from the reality of religious pluralism than from a well-developed theory of religious liberty. Apart from Rhode Island, New England had little homegrown experience of religious pluralism. Indeed, authorities in England had occasionally pressed the region's rulers to become more tolerant. Before the Revolution, most colonies supported religious institutions with public funds and discriminated in voting and officeholding against Catholics, Jews, and even Dissenting Protestants. On the very eve of independence, Baptists who refused to pay taxes to support local Congregational ministers were still being jailed in Massachusetts. "While our country are pleading so high for liberty," the victims complained, "yet they are denying of it to their neighbors."

Catholic Americans

The War of Independence weakened the deep tradition of American anti-Catholicism. The First Continental Congress denounced the Quebec Act of 1774, which, as noted in the previous chapter, allowed Canadian Catholics to worship freely, as part of a plot to establish "popery" in North America. But a year later, when the Second Continental Congress decided on an ill-fated invasion of Canada, it invited the inhabitants of Quebec to join in the struggle against Britain, assuring them that Protestants and Catholics could readily cooperate. In 1778, the United States formed an alliance with France, a Catholic nation. Benedict Arnold justified his treason, in part, by saying that an alliance with "the enemy of the protestant faith" was too much for him to bear. But the indispensable assistance provided by France and Spain to American victory strengthened the idea that Catholics had a role to play in the newly independent nation. This represented a marked departure from the traditional notion that the full rights of Englishmen only applied to Protestants.

The Founders and Religion

The end of British rule immediately threw into question the privileged position enjoyed by the Anglican Church in many colonies. In Virginia, for example, backcountry Scots-Irish Presbyterian farmers demanded relief from taxes supporting the official Anglican Church. "The free exercise of our rights of conscience," one patriotic meeting resolved, formed an essential part of "our liberties."

Many of the leaders of the Revolution considered it essential for the new nation to shield itself from the unruly passions and violent conflicts that religious differences had inspired during the past three centuries. Men like Thomas Jefferson, John Adams, James Madison, and Alexander Hamilton believed religion necessary as a foundation of public morality. But they viewed religious doctrines through the Enlightenment lens of rationalism and skepticism. They believed in a benevolent Creator but not in supernatural interventions into the affairs of men. Jefferson wrote a version of the Bible and a life of Jesus that insisted that while Jesus had lived a deeply moral life, he was not divine and performed no miracles. In discussing the natural history of the Blue Ridge Mountains in his book *Notes on the State of Virginia*, he rejected the biblical account of creation in favor of a prolonged process of geological change.

Separating Church and State

The drive to separate church and state brought together Deists like Jefferson, who hoped to erect a "wall of separation" that would free politics and the exercise of the intellect from religious control, with members of evangelical sects, who sought to protect religion from the corrupting embrace of government. Religious leaders continued to adhere to the traditional definition of Christian liberty—submitting to God's will and leading a moral life—but increasingly felt this could be achieved without the support of government. Christ's kingdom, as Isaac Backus, the Baptist leader, put it, was "not of this world."

The movement toward religious freedom received a major impetus during the revolutionary era. Throughout the new nation, states disestablished their established churches—that is, deprived them of public funding and special legal privileges—although in some cases they appropriated money for the general support of Protestant denominations. The seven state constitutions that began with declarations of rights all declared a commitment to "the free exercise of religion."

To be sure, every state but New York—whose constitution of 1777 established complete religious liberty—kept intact colonial provisions barring Jews from voting and holding public office. Seven states limited officeholding to Protestants. Massachusetts retained its Congregationalist establishment well into the nineteenth century. Its new constitution declared church attendance compulsory while guaranteeing freedom of individual worship. It would not end public financial support for religious institutions until 1833. Throughout the country, however, Catholics gained the right to worship without persecution. Maryland's constitution of 1776 restored to the large Catholic population the civil and political rights that had been denied them for nearly a century.

Religious Liberty

In Virginia, Thomas Jefferson drew up a **Bill for Establishing Religious Freedom**, which was introduced in the House of Burgesses in 1779 and adopted, after considerable controversy, in 1786. "I have sworn upon the altar of God," he would write in 1800, "eternal hostility against every form of tyranny over the mind of man." Jefferson viewed established churches as a major example of such despotism and, as his statement reveals, believed that religious liberty served God's will. Jefferson's bill, whose preamble declared that God "hath created the mind free," eliminated religious requirements for voting and officeholding and

In Side of the Old Lutheran Church in 1800, York, Pa. A watercolor by a local artist depicts the interior of one of the numerous churches that flourished after independence. While the choir sings, a man chases a dog out of the building and another man stokes the stove. The institutionalization of religious liberty was one of the most important results of the American Revolution.

government financial support for churches, and barred the state from "forcing" individuals to adopt one or another religious outlook. Late in life, Jefferson would list this measure, along with the Declaration of Independence and the founding of the University of Virginia, as the three accomplishments (leaving out his two terms as president) for which he wished to be remembered.

Religious liberty became the model for the revolutionary generation's definition of "rights" as private matters that must be protected from governmental interference. In an overwhelmingly Christian (though not necessarily church-going) nation, the separation of church and state drew a sharp line between public authority and a realm defined as "private." It also offered a new justification for the idea of the United States as a beacon of liberty. In successfully opposing a Virginia tax for the general support of Christian churches, James Madison insisted that one reason for the complete separation of church and state was to reinforce the principle that the new nation offered "asylum to the persecuted and oppressed of every nation and religion."

The Revolution and the Churches

Thus, the Revolution enhanced the diversity of American Christianity and expanded the idea of religious liberty. But even as the separation of church and state created the social and political space that allowed all kinds of religious institutions to flourish, the culture of individual rights of which that separation was a part threatened to undermine church authority.

One example was the experience of the Moravian Brethren, who had emigrated from Germany to North Carolina on the eve of independence. To the dismay of the Moravian elders, younger members of the community, like so many other Americans of the revolutionary generation, insisted on asserting "their alleged freedom and human rights." Many rejected the community's tradition of arranged marriages, insisting on choosing their own husbands and wives. To the elders, the idea of individual liberty—which they called, disparagingly, "the American freedom"—was little more than "an opportunity for temptation," a threat to the spirit of self-sacrifice and communal loyalty essential to Christian liberty.

But despite such fears, the Revolution did not end the influence of religion on American society—quite the reverse. American churches, in the words of one Presbyterian leader, learned to adapt to living at a time when "a spirit of liberty prevails." Thanks to religious freedom, the early republic witnessed an amazing proliferation of religious denominations. The most well-established churches—Anglican, Presbyterian, and Congregationalist—found themselves constantly challenged by upstarts like Free-Will Baptists and Universalists. Today, even as debate continues over the proper relationship between spiritual and political authority, more than 1,300 religions are practiced in the United States.

Christian Republicanism

Despite the separation of church and state, colonial leaders were not hostile to religion. Indeed, religious and secular language merged in the struggle for independence, producing an outlook scholars have called Christian Republicanism. Proponents of evangelical religion and of republican government both believed that in the absence of some kind of moral restraint (provided by religion and government), human nature was likely to succumb to corruption and vice. Both believed that personal virtue was the foundation of a free society and that, by the same token, freedom—religious and political—was necessary for the development of virtue. Samuel Adams, for example, believed the new nation would become a "Christian Sparta," in which Christianity and personal self-discipline underpinned both personal and national progress. American religious leaders interpreted the American Revolution as a divinely sanctioned event, part of God's plan to promote the development of a good society. Rather than being so sinful that it would have to be destroyed before Christ returned, as many ministers had previously preached, the world, the Revolution demonstrated, could be perfected.

Most leaders of the Revolution were devout Christians, and even Deists who attended no organized church believed religious values reinforced the moral qualities necessary for a republic to prosper. Public authority continued to support religious values, in laws barring non-Christians from office and in the continued prosecution of blasphemy and breaches of the Sabbath. Pennsylvania's new democratic constitution required citizens to acknowledge the existence of God, and it directed the legislature to enact "laws for the prevention of vice and immorality." In the nineteenth century, Pennsylvania's lawmakers took this mandate so seriously that the state became as famous for its laws against swearing and desecrating the Sabbath as it had been in colonial times for religious freedom.

Patriot leaders worried about the character of future citizens, especially how to encourage the quality of "virtue," the ability to sacrifice self-interest for the public good. Some, like Jefferson, John Adams, and Benjamin Rush, put forward plans for the establishment of free, state-supported public schools. These would instruct future citizens in what Adams called "the principles of freedom," equipping them for participation in the now-expanded public sphere and for the wise election of representatives. A broad diffusion of knowledge was essential for a government based on the will of the people to survive. No nation, Jefferson wrote, could "expect to be ignorant and free."

DEFINING ECONOMIC FREEDOM

Toward Free Labor

In economic as well as political and religious affairs, the Revolution rewrote the definition of freedom. In colonial America, slavery was one part of a broad spectrum of kinds of unfree labor. In the generation after independence, with the rapid decline of indentured servitude and apprenticeship and the transformation of paid domestic service into an occupation for Blacks and white women, the halfway houses between slavery and freedom disappeared, at least for white men. The decline of these forms of labor had many causes. Wage workers became more available as indentured servants completed their terms of required labor, and considerable numbers of servants and apprentices took advantage of the turmoil of the Revolution to escape from their masters.

The lack of freedom inherent in apprenticeship and servitude increasingly came to be seen as incompatible with republican citizenship. Ebenezer Fox, a young apprentice on a Massachusetts farm, later recalled how he and other youths "made a direct application of the doctrines we heard daily, in relation to the oppression of the mother country, to our own circumstance. . . . I thought that I was doing myself a great injustice by remaining in bondage, when I ought to go free." Fox became one of many apprentices during the Revolution

View from Bushongo Tavern, an engraving from *The Columbian Magazine*, 1788, depicts the landscape of York County, Pennsylvania, exemplifying the kind of rural independence many Americans thought essential to freedom.

who decided to run away—or, as he put it, to "liberate myself." On the eve of the battles of Lexington and Concord in 1775, Fox and a friend set off for Rhode Island. After briefly working as a sailor, Fox, still a teenager, joined the Continental army.

In 1784, a group of "respectable" New Yorkers released a newly arrived ship-load of indentured servants on the grounds that their status was "contrary to . . . the idea of liberty this country has so happily established." By 1800, indentured servitude had all but disappeared from the United States. This development sharpened the distinction between freedom and slavery, and between a northern economy relying on what would come to be called "free labor" (that is, working for wages or owning a farm or shop) and a southern economy ever more heavily dependent on the labor of enslaved men and women.

The Soul of a Republic

Americans of the revolutionary generation were preoccupied with the social conditions of freedom. Could a republic survive with a sizable dependent class of citizens? "A general and tolerably equal distribution of landed property," proclaimed the educator and newspaper editor Noah Webster, "is the whole basis of national freedom." "Equality," he added, was "the very soul of a republic." Even a conservative like John Adams, who distrusted the era's democratic upsurge, hoped that every member of society could acquire land, "so that the multitude may be possessed of small estates" and the new nation could avoid the emergence of fixed and unequal social classes. At the Revolution's radical edge, some patriots believed that government had a responsibility to limit accumulations of property in the name of equality. To most free Americans, however, "equality" meant equal opportunity, rather than equality of condition. Many leaders of the Revolution nevertheless assumed that in the exceptional circumstances of America with its vast land and large population of independent farmers and artisans, the natural workings of society would produce justice, liberty, and equality.

Like many other Americans of his generation, Thomas Jefferson believed that to lack economic resources was to lack freedom. His proudest achievements included laws passed by Virginia abolishing entail (the limitation of inheritance to a specified line of heirs to keep an estate within a family) and primogeniture (the practice of passing a family's land entirely to the eldest son). These measures, he believed, would help to prevent the rise of a "future aristocracy." To the same end, Jefferson proposed to award fifty acres of land to every adult man who did not already possess it, another way government could enhance the liberty of its subjects. Of course, the land that men like Noah Webster and Thomas Jefferson hoped would secure American liberty was not empty. It belonged to Native Americans.

The Politics of Inflation

The Revolution thrust to the forefront of politics debates over whether local and national authorities should take steps to bolster household independence and protect Americans' livelihoods by limiting price increases. Economic dislocations sharpened the controversy. To finance the war, Congress issued hundreds of millions of dollars in paper money. Coupled with wartime disruption of agriculture and trade and the hoarding of goods by some Americans hoping to profit from shortages, this produced an enormous **inflation** as prices rapidly rose. The country, charged a letter to a Philadelphia newspaper in 1778, had been "reduced to the brink of ruin by the infamous practices of monopolizers."

Between 1776 and 1779, more than thirty incidents took place in which crowds confronted merchants accused of holding scarce goods off the market. Often, they seized stocks of food and sold them at the traditional "just price," a form of protest common in eighteenth-century England. In one such incident, a crowd of 100 Massachusetts women accused an "eminent, wealthy, stingy merchant" of hoarding coffee, opened his warehouse, and carted off the goods. "A large concourse of men," wrote Abigail Adams, "stood amazed, silent spectators of the whole transaction."

The Debate over Free Trade

In 1779, with inflation totally out of control (in one month, prices in Philadelphia jumped 45 percent), Congress urged states to adopt measures to fix wages and prices. The policy embodied the belief that the task of republican government was to promote the public good, not individuals' self-interest. Bitter comments appeared in the Philadelphia press about the city's elite expending huge sums on "public dinners and other extravaganzas" while many in the city were "destitute of the necessities of life." But when a Committee of Safety tried to enforce price controls, it met spirited opposition from merchants and other advocates of a free market.

Against the traditional view that men should sacrifice for the public good, believers in **free trade** argued that economic development arose from economic self-interest. Just as Newton had revealed the inner workings of the natural universe, so the social world also followed unchanging natural laws, among them that supply and demand regulated the prices of goods. Adam Smith's great treatise on economics, *The Wealth of Nations*, published in England in 1776, was beginning to become known in the United States. Smith's argument that the "invisible hand" of the free market directed economic life more effectively and fairly than governmental intervention offered intellectual justification for those who believed that the economy should be left to regulate itself.

Advocates of independence had envisioned America, released from the British Navigation Acts, trading freely with all the world. Opponents of price controls advocated free trade at home as well. "Let trade be as free as air," wrote one merchant. "Natural liberty" would regulate prices. Here were two competing conceptions of economic freedom—one based on the traditional view that the interests of the community took precedence over the property rights of individuals, the other insisting that unregulated economic freedom would produce social harmony and public gain. After 1779, the latter view gained ascendancy. State and federal efforts to regulate prices ceased. But the clash between these two visions of economic freedom would continue long after independence had been achieved.

"Yield to the mighty current of American freedom." So a member of the South Carolina legislature implored his colleagues in 1777. The current of freedom swept away not only British authority but also the principle of hereditary rule, the privileges of established churches, long-standing habits of deference and hierarchy, and old limits on the political nation. Yet in other areas, the tide of freedom encountered obstacles that did not yield as easily to its powerful flow.

THE LIMITS OF LIBERTY

Colonial Loyalists

Not all Americans shared in the democratization of freedom brought on by the American Revolution. **Loyalists**—those who retained their allegiance to the crown—experienced the conflict and its aftermath as a loss of liberty. Many leading Loyalists had supported American resistance in the 1760s but drew back at the prospect of independence and war. Loyalists included some of the most prominent Americans and some of the most humble. Altogether, an estimated 20 to 25 percent of free Americans remained loyal to the British, and nearly 20,000 fought on their side. At some points in the war, Loyalists serving with the British outnumbered Washington's army.

There were Loyalists in every colony, but they were most numerous in New York, Pennsylvania, and the backcountry of the Carolinas and Georgia. Some were wealthy men whose livelihoods depended on close working relationships with Britain—lawyers, merchants, Anglican ministers, and imperial officials. Many feared anarchy in the event of an American victory. "Liberty," one wrote, "can have no existence without obedience to the laws."

The struggle for independence heightened existing tensions between ethnic groups and social classes within the colonies. Some Loyalist ethnic minorities, like Highland Scots in North Carolina, feared that local majorities would

LOYALISM IN THE AMERICAN REVOLUTION

Legend:
- Strongly Loyalist colonists
- Native Nations or Loyalist colonists
- Neutral colonists
- Strong patriot support
- Spanish Colony

The Revolutionary War was, in some ways, a civil war within the colonies. There were Loyalists in every colony; they were most numerous in New York, North and South Carolina, and of course the nonrebelling Floridas, Canadian colonies, and West Indies.

infringe on their freedom to enjoy cultural autonomy. In the South, many backcountry farmers who had long resented the domination of public affairs by wealthy planters sided with the British. So did tenants on the New York estates of patriot landlords like the Livingston family. Robert Livingston had signed the Declaration of Independence. When the army of General Burgoyne approached Livingston's manor in 1777, tenants rose in revolt, hoping the British would confiscate his land and distribute it among themselves. Their hopes were dashed by Burgoyne's defeat at Saratoga. In the South, numerous slaves sided with the British, hoping an American defeat would bring them freedom.

The Loyalists' Plight

The War of Independence was in some respects a civil war among Americans. "This country," wrote a German colonel fighting with the British, "is the scene of the most cruel events. Neighbors are on opposite sides, children are against their fathers." Freedom of expression is often a casualty of war, and many Americans were deprived of basic rights in the name of liberty. After Dr. Abner Beebe, of East Haddam, Connecticut, spoke "very freely" in favor of the British, a mob attacked his house and destroyed his gristmill. Beebe himself was "assaulted, stripped naked, and hot pitch [tar] was poured upon him." The new state governments, or crowds of patriots, suppressed newspapers thought to be loyal to Britain.

Pennsylvania arrested and seized the property of Quakers, Mennonites, and Moravians—pacifist denominations who refused to bear arms because of their religious beliefs. With the approval of Congress, many states required residents to take oaths of allegiance to the new nation. Those who refused were denied the right to vote and in many cases forced into exile. "The flames of discord," wrote one British observer, "are sprouting from the seeds of liberty." Some wealthy Loyalists saw their land confiscated and sold at auction. Twenty-eight estates belonging to New Hampshire governor John Wentworth and his family were seized, as were the holdings of great New York Loyalist landlords like the De Lancey and Philipse families. Most of the buyers of this land were merchants, lawyers, and established landowners. Unable to afford the purchase price, tenants had no choice but to continue to labor for the new owners.

The Revolution as a Borderlands Conflict

When the war ended, as many as 60,000 Loyalists were banished from the United States or emigrated voluntarily—mostly to Britain, Canada, or the West Indies—rather than live in an independent United States. So many Loyalists went to Nova Scotia in Canada that a new province, New Brunswick, was created to accommodate them. For those Loyalists who remained in the United States, hostility proved to be short-lived. In the Treaty of Paris of 1783, as noted in Chapter 5, Americans pledged to end the persecution of Loyalists by state and local governments and to restore property seized during the war. American leaders believed the new nation needed to establish an international reputation for fairness and civility. States soon repealed their test oaths for voting and officeholding. Loyalists who did not leave the country were quickly reintegrated into American society, although despite the promise of the Treaty of Paris, confiscated Loyalist property was not returned.

The Loyalists' exile had a profound impact on the future development of North America. The War of Independence severed the British colonies of Nova Scotia and Quebec from the thirteen that formed the United States. Despite rejecting American independence, many Loyalists who settled in Canada brought with them not only a loyalty to the British crown but also a commitment to self-rule. They went on to agitate for responsible government in their new homeland. Their ideas would help to inspire rebellions in Canada in 1837 that helped close out the Age of Revolution the American revolt had launched. Although crushed by the British, the rebellions led eventually to the creation in 1867 of a single government for the Canadian provinces.

Thus, the American Revolution transformed the old boundary separating New England and New York from Quebec as provinces of the British empire into an international border. The consequences were profound. Without this development, Canada would not have been a refuge for slaves who escaped across the border later in the nineteenth century. Nor would Irish nationalists have been shielded from British law during and after the Civil War when they congregated in upstate New York and launched raids across the northern border as a way of striking a blow against British rule of their homeland. In Canada, the Loyalist exiles would long be viewed as national founding fathers, and Canadians would often define their identity in opposition to their powerful neighbor to the south, even though goods and ideas always flowed easily across the border (today, each country is the other's largest trading partner).

White Freedom, Indian Freedom

American independence created governments democratically accountable to voters who coveted Native American land. Indeed, to many patriots, Native land was one of the fruits of American victory. Driving the Indians from the Ohio Valley, wrote Jefferson, would "add to the Empire of Liberty an extensive and fertile country." Most Americans did not consider Native Americans' desires for liberty or rights to independence. "The whites were no sooner free themselves," Pequot William Apess would later write, than they turned on "the poor Indians." Independence offered the opportunity to complete the process of dispossessing Native nations of their rich lands in upstate New York, the Ohio Valley, and the southern backcountry without the impediment of Britain's

Proclamation of 1763. Even as the war raged, Americans forced the Cherokee Nation to cede 100,000 square miles of land that would become parts of South Carolina and Tennessee. Native nations between the Mississippi River and the western border of the United States would struggle in the coming decades to hold onto their land and their independence.

In 1784, a delegation of 260 Cherokee, Shawnee, Chickasaw, Choctaw, Delaware, and Haudenosaunee (Iroquois) representatives told Spanish officials in St. Louis that the creation of the United States was "the greatest blow that could have been dealt us." Now that the colonists were no longer part of the British empire, the delegates at St. Louis explained, the Americans were "extending themselves like a plague of locusts."

Those who had fought on the British side felt particularly betrayed. In the Treaty of Paris, the British agreed that the United States could have all of the land east of the Mississippi River, land that was not Britain's to give away. As Muscogee (Creek) leader Alexander McGillivray explained, "It is well known that His British Majesty has never possessed these lands neither by right of cession, by sale, nor by conquest. On the contrary it is well known that, from the beginning of the settlement of the English colonies of Carolina and Georgia until the date of said treaty, never have they had title to, or pretended to own, these our lands."

Like other Americans, Indians appropriated the language of the Revolution and interpreted it according to their own experiences. They used it to express long-standing territorial sovereignty and the right to set their own policies regarding land use and trade. The Haudenosaunee, declared one spokesman, were "a free people subject to no power on earth." Muscogees and Choctaws denied having done anything to forfeit their "independence and natural rights." When Massachusetts established a system of state "guardianship" over previously self-governing tribes, a group of Mashpees petitioned the legislature, claiming for themselves "the rights of man" and complaining of this "infringement of freedom." "Freedom" had not played a major part in Indians' vocabulary before the Revolution. By the early nineteenth century, dictionaries of Native languages for the first time began to include the word. But Native independence and sovereignty would clash with the new nation bent on creating an empire in the West.

SLAVERY AND THE REVOLUTION

While Native nations experienced American independence as a real threat to their own liberty, African Americans saw in the ideals of the Revolution and the reality of war an opportunity to claim freedom. When the United States declared its independence in 1776, the enslaved population had grown to 500,000, about one-fifth of the new nation's inhabitants. Slaveowning and slave trading were accepted routines of colonial life. Advertisements announcing the sale of slaves and seeking the return of runaways filled colonial newspapers. Sometimes, the same issues of patriotic newspapers that published accounts of the activities of the Sons of Liberty or arguments against the Stamp Act also contained slave sale notices.

The Language of Slavery and Freedom

Slavery played a central part in the language of revolution. Apart from "liberty," it was the word most frequently invoked in the era's legal and political litera-ture. Eighteenth-century writers frequently juxtaposed freedom and slavery as "the two extremes of happiness and misery in society." Yet in debates over Brit-ish rule, slavery was primarily a political category, shorthand for the denial of one's personal and political rights by arbitrary government. Those who lacked a voice in public affairs, declared a 1769 petition demanding an expansion of the right to vote in Britain, were "enslaved." By the eve of independence, the contrast between Britain, "a kingdom of slaves," and America, a "country of free men," had become a standard part of the language of resistance. Such language was employed without irony even in areas where more than half the popula-tion in fact was enslaved. South Carolina, one writer declared in 1774, was a "sacred land" of freedom, where it was impossible to believe that "slavery shall soon be permitted to erect her throne."

Advertisement for newly arrived slaves, in a Savannah newspaper, 1774. Even as colo-nists defended their own liberty against the British, the buying and selling of human beings continued.

Excelsior (Latin for "ever upward"), a large oil painting by an unknown artist, is probably an early representation of the coat of arms of New York, adopted in 1778 as one part of the transition from colony to state. It contains numerous symbols of liberty, independence, and optimism for the future—including a cap of liberty, the sunrise, an eagle atop a world globe, Justice with her scales, and an olive branch of peace.

Colonial writers of the 1760s occasionally made a direct connection between slavery as a reality and slavery as a metaphor. Few were as forthright as James Otis of Massachusetts, whose pamphlets did much to popularize the idea that Parliament lacked the authority to tax the colonies and regulate their commerce. Freedom, Otis insisted, must be universal: "What man is or ever was born free if every man is not?" Otis wrote of Blacks not as examples of the loss of rights awaiting free Americans, but as flesh and blood British subjects "entitled to all the civil rights of such."

Otis was hardly typical of patriot leaders. But the presence of hundreds of thousands of literally enslaved people powerfully affected the meaning of freedom for the leaders of the American Revolution. In a famous speech to Parliament warning against attempts to intimidate the colonies, the British statesman Edmund Burke suggested that familiarity with slavery made colonial leaders unusually sensitive to threats to their own liberties. Where freedom was a privilege, not a common right, he observed, "those who are free are by far the most proud and jealous of their freedom." On the other hand, many British observers could not resist pointing out the colonists' apparent hypocrisy. "How is it," asked Dr. Samuel Johnson, "that we hear the loudest yelps for liberty from the drivers of negroes?"

Obstacles to Abolition

The contradiction between freedom and slavery seems so self-evident that it is difficult today to appreciate the power of the obstacles to **abolition**. At the time of the Revolution, slavery was already an old institution in America. It existed in every colony and formed the basis of the economy and social structure from Maryland southward. At least 40 percent of Virginia's population and even higher proportions in Georgia and South Carolina were slaves.

Virtually every founding father owned slaves at one point in his life, including not only southern planters but also northern merchants, lawyers, and farmers. (John Adams and Thomas Paine were notable exceptions.) Thomas

Jefferson owned more than 100 slaves when he wrote of mankind's unalienable right to liberty, and everything he cherished in his own manner of life, from lavish entertainments to the leisure that made possible the pursuit of arts and sciences, ultimately rested on slave labor.

Some patriots, in fact, argued that slavery for Blacks made freedom possible for whites. Owning slaves offered a route to the economic autonomy widely deemed necessary for genuine freedom, a point driven home by a 1780 Virginia law that rewarded veterans of the War of Independence with 300 acres of land—and a slave. South Carolina and Georgia promised every white military volunteer a slave at the war's end.

So, too, the Lockean vision of the political community as a group of individuals contracting together to secure their natural rights could readily be invoked to defend bondage. Nothing was more essential to freedom, in this view, than the right of self-government and the protection of property against outside interference. These principles suggested that for the government to seize property—including slave property—against the owner's will would be an infringement on liberty. According to this logic, to require owners to give up their slave property would reduce *them* to slavery.

The Cause of General Liberty

Nonetheless, by imparting so absolute a value to liberty and defining freedom as a universal entitlement rather than a set of rights specific to a particular place or people, the Revolution inevitably raised questions about the status of slavery in the new nation. Before independence, there had been little public discussion of the institution, even though enlightened opinion in the Atlantic world had come to view slavery as morally wrong and economically inefficient, a relic of a barbarous past.

As early as 1688, a group of German Quakers issued a "protest" regarding the rights of Blacks, declaring it as unjust "to have them slaves, as it is to have other white ones." Samuel Sewall, a Boston merchant, published *The Selling of Joseph* in 1700, the first antislavery tract printed in America. All "the sons of Adam," Sewall insisted, were entitled to "have equal right unto liberty." During the course of the eighteenth century, antislavery sentiments had spread among Pennsylvania's Quakers, whose belief that all persons possessed the divine "inner light" made them particularly receptive. But it was during the revolutionary era that slavery for the first time became a focus of public debate.

Petitions for Freedom

The Revolution inspired widespread hopes that slavery could be removed from American life. Most dramatically, enslaved people themselves appreciated that by defining freedom as a universal right, the leaders of the Revolution had devised a weapon that the enslaved could use against their own bondage. The language of liberty echoed in slave communities, North and South. Living amid freedom but denied its benefits, enslaved and free Blacks appropriated the patriotic ideology for their own purposes. The most insistent advocates of freedom as a universal entitlement were African Americans, who demanded that the leaders of the struggle for independence live up to their self-proclaimed creed. As early as 1766, white Charlestonians had been shocked when their opposition to the Stamp Act inspired a group of Blacks to parade about the city crying "Liberty."

The first concrete steps toward emancipation in revolutionary America were **freedom petitions**—arguments for liberty presented to New England's courts and legislatures beginning in the early 1770s by enslaved African Americans. How, one such petition asked, could America "seek release from English tyranny and not seek the same for disadvantaged Africans in her midst?"

Some slaves sued in court for being "illegally detained in slavery." In 1783, Elizabeth Freeman (also known as Mum Bett) sued her owner for her freedom and won, arguing that her enslavement was inconsistent with the statement in the Massachusetts state constitution that "all men are born free and equal." Later that year, an enslaved man named Quock Walker sued for his freedom in the Superior Court of Massachusetts in which he cited Freeman's case. Walker's case ultimately culminated in the abolition of slavery in Massachusetts, with the judge ruling that "the idea of slavery is inconsistent with our own conduct and constitution; and there can be no such thing as a perpetual servitude of a rational creature, unless his liberty is forfeited by some criminal conduct or given up by personal consent or contract." When asked why she brought suit, Elizabeth Freeman explained, "Anytime, anytime while I was a slave, if one minute's freedom had been offered to me, and I had been told I must die at the end of that minute, I would have taken it—just to stand one minute on God's earth a free woman—I would." Enslaved people in the South drew upon Freeman's and Walker's cases and sued for their freedom as well, sometimes winning their freedom.

The turmoil of war offered other avenues to freedom. Many slaves ran away from their masters and tried to pass as freeborn. The number of fugitive-slave advertisements in colonial newspapers rose dramatically in the 1770s and 1780s. As one slaveholder put it in accounting for the escape of a man named Jim, "I believe he has nothing in view but freedom."

In 1776, the year of American independence, **Lemuel Haynes**, a Black member of the Massachusetts militia and later a celebrated minister, urged that Americans "extend" their conception of freedom. If liberty were truly "an innate principle" for all mankind, Haynes insisted, "even an African [had] as equally good a right to his liberty in common with Englishmen." Blacks sought to make white Americans understand slavery as a concrete reality—the denial of all the essential elements of freedom—not merely as a metaphor for the loss of political self-determination. Petitioning for their freedom in 1773, a group of New England slaves exclaimed, "We have no property! We have no wives! No children! We have no city! No country!"

Most slaves of the revolutionary era were only one or two generations removed from Africa. They did not need the ideology of the Revolution to persuade them that freedom was a birthright—their experience and that of their parents and grandparents suggested as much. "My love of freedom," wrote the Black poet Phillis Wheatley in 1783, arose from the "cruel fate" of being "snatch'd from Afric's" shore. Brought as a slave to Boston in 1761, Wheatley learned to read and published her first poem in a New England newspaper in 1765, when she was around twelve years old. The fact that a volume of her poems had to be printed with a testimonial from prominent citizens, including patriot leader John

Miss Breme Jones, a late-eighteenth-century watercolor depicting an enslaved woman in South Carolina. The inscription on the left, based on a passage from John Milton's *Paradise Lost*, reads: "Grave in her steps / Heaven in her eyes / And all her movement / Dignity and Love." The work was commissioned by Jones's owner John Rose, possibly as recognition of how she helped him raise his two small children after the death of his wife.

Hancock, affirming that she was in fact the author, illustrates that many whites found it difficult to accept the idea of Blacks' intellectual ability. Yet by invoking the Revolution's ideology of liberty to demand their own rights and by defining freedom as a universal entitlement, Blacks demonstrated how American they had become, even as they sought to redefine what American freedom in fact meant.

British Emancipators

As noted in the previous chapter, some 5,000 slaves fought for American independence and many thereby gained their freedom. Yet far more slaves obtained liberty from the British. Lord Dunmore's proclamation of 1775 and the Philipsburg Proclamation of General Henry Clinton issued four years later offered sanctuary to slaves, except those owned by Loyalists, who escaped to

British lines. Numerous signers of the Declaration of Independence lost slaves as a result. Thirty of Thomas Jefferson's slaves ran away to the British, as did slaves owned by Patrick Henry and James Madison. All told, tens of thousands of slaves, including one-quarter of all the slaves in South Carolina and one-third of those in Georgia, deserted their owners and fled to British lines. This was by far the largest exodus from the plantations until the outbreak of the Civil War.

Some of these escaped slaves were recaptured as the tide of battle turned in the patriots' favor. But at the war's end, some 20,000 were living in three enclaves of British control—New York, Charleston, and Savannah. George Washington insisted they must be returned. Sir Guy Carleton, the British commander in New York, replied that to do so would be "a dishonorable violation of the public faith," since they had been promised their freedom. In the end, more than 15,000 Black men, women, and children accompanied the British out of the country. They ended up in Nova Scotia, England, and Sierra Leone, a settlement for former slaves established by the British on the coast of West Africa. Some were captured and illegally re-enslaved in the West Indies. Harry Washington, mentioned in Chapter 5, eventually ended up in Sierra Leone, where in 1800 he took part in an unsuccessful uprising by Black settlers against the British-appointed government.

The issue of compensating slaveholders for the slaves who departed with the British poisoned relations between Britain and the new United States for decades to come. Finally, in 1827, Britain agreed to make payments to 1,100 Americans who claimed they had been improperly deprived of their slave property.

Voluntary Emancipations

For a brief moment, the revolutionary upheaval appeared to threaten the continued existence of slavery. During the War of Independence, nearly every state prohibited or discouraged the further importation of slaves from Africa. The war left much of the plantation South in ruins. During the 1780s, a considerable number of slaveholders, especially in Virginia and Maryland, voluntarily emancipated their slaves. In 1796, Robert Carter III, a member of one of Virginia's wealthiest families, provided for the emancipation of the more than 400 slaves he owned. In the same year, Richard Randolph, a member of another prominent Virginia family, drafted a will that condemned slavery as an "infamous practice," provided for the freedom of about ninety slaves, and set aside part of his land for them to own.

In South Carolina, however, the abolition process never got under way. When the British invaded South Carolina during the war, John Laurens, whose father Henry was Charleston's leading merchant and revolutionary-era statesman, proposed to "lead a corps of emancipated blacks in the defense of liberty." South Carolina's leaders rejected the idea. They would rather lose the war than lose their slaves.

Abolition in the North

Between 1777 (when Vermont drew up a constitution that banned slavery) and 1804 (when New Jersey acted), every state north of Maryland took steps toward emancipation, the first time in recorded history that legislative power had been invoked to eradicate slavery. But even here, where slavery was not central to the economy, the method of abolition reflected how property rights impeded emancipation. Generally, abolition laws did not free living slaves. Instead, they provided for the liberty of any child born in the future to an enslaved mother, but only after the child had served the mother's master until adulthood as compensation for the owner's future economic loss. Children born to enslaved mothers in Pennsylvania after passage of the state's emancipation act of 1780 had to serve the owner for twenty-eight years, far longer than had been customary for white indentured servants. These laws gave indentured servitude, rapidly declining among whites, a new lease on life in the case of northern Blacks.

Abolition in the North was a slow, drawn-out process. For slaves alive when the northern laws were passed, hopes for freedom rested on their own ability to escape and the voluntary actions of their owners. And many northern slaveholders proved reluctant indeed when it came to liberating their slaves. New York City, where one-fifth of the white families owned at least one slave in 1790, recorded only seventy-six such voluntary acts between 1783 and 1800. The first national census, in 1790, recorded 21,000 slaves still living in New York and 11,000 in New Jersey. New Yorker John Jay, chief justice of the United States, owned five slaves in 1800. As late as 1830, the census revealed that there were still 3,500 slaves in the North. The last slaves in Connecticut did not become free until 1848. In 1860, eighteen elderly slaves still resided in New Jersey.

Free Black Communities

All in all, the Revolution had a contradictory impact on American slavery and, therefore, on American freedom. Gradual as it was, the abolition of slavery in the North drew a line across the new nation, creating the dangerous division between free and slave states. Abolition in the North, voluntary manumissions in the Upper South, and the escape of thousands from bondage created, for the first time in American history, a sizable **free Black** population (many of whose members took new family names like Freeman or Freeland).

On the eve of independence, virtually every Black person in the British colonies had been enslaved. Now, free communities, with their own churches,

This engraving depicts a parade welcoming George Washington and the Continental army into New York City on November 25, 1783, shortly after British forces evacuated the city, which they had occupied for almost the entire War of Independence. Women take part in the celebration alongside men. But the crowd is shown as entirely white—even though many Blacks and some Native Americans resided in the city.

schools, and leaders, came into existence. They formed a standing challenge to the logic of slavery, a haven for fugitives, and a springboard for further efforts at abolition. In 1776, fewer than 10,000 free Blacks resided in the United States. By 1810, their numbers had grown to nearly 200,000, most of them living in Maryland and Virginia. In all the states except Virginia, South Carolina, and Georgia, free men of color (whether of African or Native American ancestry) who met taxpaying or property qualifications enjoyed the right to vote under new state constitutions. As the widespread use of the term "citizens of color" suggests, the first generation of free Blacks, at least in the North, formed part of the political nation.

For many Americans, white as well as Black, the existence of slavery would henceforth be recognized as a standing affront to the ideal of American freedom, a "disgrace to a free government," as a group of New Yorkers put it. In 1792, when Samuel Jennings of Philadelphia painted *Liberty Displaying the Arts and Sciences*, he included among the symbols of freedom a slave's broken chain, graphically illustrating how freedom had become identified not simply with political independence, but with emancipation. Nonetheless, the stark fact is that slavery survived the War of Independence and, thanks to the natural increase of the enslaved population, continued to grow. The national census of 1790 revealed that despite all those who had become free through state laws, voluntary emancipation, and escape, the number of slaves in the United States had grown to 700,000, numbering 200,000 more than in 1776.

DAUGHTERS OF LIBERTY

Revolutionary Women

The revolutionary generation included numerous women who contributed to the struggle for independence. Deborah Sampson, the daughter of a poor Massachusetts farmer, disguised herself as a man and in 1782, at age twenty-one, enlisted in the Continental army. Sampson displayed remarkable courage, participating in several battles and extracting a bullet from her own leg so as not to have a doctor discover her identity. A woodcut widely reprinted during the War of Independence shows Hannah Snell, who allegedly joined the British army in 1745 disguised as a man and fought in Scotland and India. Ultimately, her commanding officer learned her secret but kept it to himself, and she was honorably discharged at the end of the war. Years later, the British army awarded her a soldier's pension, and her story inspired women who wanted to serve in the military. Other patriotic women participated in crowd actions against merchants accused of seeking profits by holding goods off the market until their prices rose, contributed homespun goods to the army, and passed along information about British army movements.

A woodcut widely reprinted during the War of Independence shows Hannah Snell, who allegedly joined the British army in 1745 disguised as a man. It suggests that women could take up arms in their country's cause.

In Philadelphia, Esther Reed, the wife of patriot leader Joseph Reed, and Sarah Franklin Bache, the daughter of Benjamin Franklin, organized a Ladies' Association to raise funds to assist American soldiers. They issued public broadsides calling for the "women of America" to collect funds and forward them to the governor's wife or, if he were unmarried, to "Mistress Washington." Referring to themselves as "brave Americans" who had been "born for liberty," the Ladies' Association raised large amounts of money and illustrated how the Revolution was propelling women into new forms of public activism.

Within American households, women participated in the political discussions unleashed by independence. "Was not every fireside," John Adams later recalled, "a theater of politics?" Adams's own wife, Abigail Adams, as has been mentioned, was a shrewd analyst of public affairs. Mercy Otis Warren—the sister of James Otis and wife of James Warren, a founder of the Boston Committee of Correspondence—was another commentator on politics. She promoted the revolutionary cause in poems and dramas and later published a history of the struggle for independence.

Gender and Politics

Gender formed a boundary limiting those entitled to the full blessings of American freedom. Lucy Knox, the wife of General Henry Knox, wrote her husband during the war that when he returned home he should not consider himself "commander in chief of your own house, but be convinced that there is such a thing as equal command." But the winning of independence did not alter the family law inherited from Britain. The principle of **coverture** (first discussed in Chapter 1) remained intact in the new nation. The husband still held legal authority over the person, property, and choices of his wife. The words "to have and to hold" appeared both in deeds conveying land from one owner to another and in common marriage vows. The expansion of democracy to more white men made politics even more starkly a male realm.

For men, political freedom meant the right to self-government, the power to consent to the individuals and political arrangements that ruled over them. For women, however, the marriage contract superseded the social contract. A woman's relationship to the larger society was mediated through her relationship with her husband. In both law and economic reality, women lacked the essential qualification of political participation—autonomy based on ownership of property or control of one's own person. Since the common law included women within the legal status of their husbands, women could not be said to have property in themselves in the same sense as men.

Men claimed that qualities like independence and masculinity distinguished them from women, and they still considered control over their families an element of freedom. Among the deprivations of slavery cited by a group of Black male petitioners in 1774 was that it prevented their wives from "submitting themselves to husbands in all things," as the natural order of the universe required. Many women who entered public debate felt the need to apologize for their forthrightness. A group of Quaker women who petitioned Congress during the War of Independence protesting the mistreatment of men who would not take an oath of loyalty hoped the lawmakers would "take no offense at the freedom of women."

Most men considered women to be naturally submissive and dependent, and therefore unfit for citizenship. While public debate in the revolutionary era viewed men's rights as natural entitlements, discussions of women's roles emphasized duty and obligations, not individual liberty. Their rights were nonpolitical, deriving from their roles as wives and mothers.

The republican citizen was, by definition, male. In a notable case, a Massachusetts court returned to James Martin confiscated property previously owned by his mother, who had fled the state during the Revolution with her Loyalist husband. Like other states, Massachusetts seized the land of those who had supported the British. But, the court ruled, it was unreasonable to expect a wife to exercise independent political judgment. To rebel against the king was one thing, but one could hardly ask Mrs. Martin to rebel against her husband. Therefore, the court reasoned, she should not have been punished for taking the British side.

Republican Motherhood

According to the ideology of **republican motherhood** that emerged as a result of independence, women played an indispensable role by training future citizens. The "foundation of national morality," wrote John Adams, "must be laid in private families." Republican motherhood both ruled out direct female involvement in politics and encouraged the expansion of educational opportunities for women so that they could impart political wisdom to their sons. Women, wrote Benjamin Rush, needed to have a "suitable education," to enable them to "instruct their sons in the principles of liberty and government."

The idea of republican motherhood reinforced the trend, already evident in the eighteenth century, toward the idea of "companionate" marriage, a voluntary union held together by affection and mutual dependency rather than male authority. In her letter to John Adams quoted earlier, Abigail Adams recommended that men should willingly give up "the harsh title of Master for the more tender and endearing one of Friend."

The structure of family life itself was altered by the Revolution. In colonial America, those living within the household often included indentured servants, apprentices, and slaves. After independence, southern slaves remained, rhetorically at least, members of the owner's "family." In the North, however, with the rapid decline of various forms of indentured servitude and apprenticeship, a more modern definition of the household as consisting of parents and their children took hold. Hired workers, whether domestic servants or farm laborers, were not considered part of the family.

Keep Within the Compass, a late-eighteenth-century engraving, illustrates the happiness of a "virtuous woman" if she remains within the world of home and family and some of the "troubles" awaiting her if she ventures outside. The woman appears in a space marked off by a compass, an instrument for drawing a circle.

From ABIGAIL ADAMS TO JOHN ADAMS, BRAINTREE, MASS. (MARCH 31, 1776)

From their home in Massachusetts, Abigail Adams maintained a lively correspondence with her husband while he was in Philadelphia serving in the Continental Congress. In this letter, she suggests some of the limits of the patriots' commitment to liberty.

I wish you would ever write me a letter half as long as I write you; and tell me if you may where your fleet are gone? What sort of defence Virginia can make against our common enemy? Whether it is so situated as to make an able defence? . . . I have sometimes been ready to think that the passion for Liberty cannot be equally strong in the breasts of those who have been accustomed to deprive their fellow creatures of theirs. Of this I am certain that it is not founded upon that generous and Christian principal of doing to others as we would that others should do unto us . . .

I long to hear that you have declared an independency—and by the way in the new Code of Laws which I suppose it will be necessary for you to make I desire you would remember the ladies and be more generous & favorable to them than your ancestors. Do not put such unlimited power into the hands of the husbands. Remember all men would be tyrants if they could. If particular care and attention is not paid to the ladies, we are determined to foment a rebellion, and will not hold ourselves bound by any laws in which we have no voice or representation—that your sex are naturally tyrannical is a truth so thoroughly established as to admit of no dispute, but such of you as wish to be happy willingly give up the harsh title of master for the more tender and endearing one of friend why then, not put it out of the power of the vicious and the lawless to use us with cruelty and indignity with impunity. Men of sense in all ages abhor those customs which treat us only as the vassals of your sex. Regard us then as beings placed by providence under your protection & in imitation of the Supreme Being make use of that power only for our happiness.

From PETITIONS OF SLAVES TO THE MASSACHUSETTS LEGISLATURE (1773 AND 1777)

Many slaves saw the struggle for independence as an opportunity to assert their own claims to freedom. Among the first efforts toward abolition were petitions by Massachusetts slaves to their legislature.

The efforts made by the legislative of this province in their last sessions to free themselves from slavery, gave us, who are in that deplorable state, a high degree of satisfaction. We expect great things from men who have made such a noble stand against the designs of their *fellow-men* to enslave them. We cannot but wish and hope Sir, that you will have the same grand object, we mean civil and religious liberty, in view in your next session. The divine spirit of *freedom*, seems to fire every breast on this continent. . . .

★ ★ ★

Your petitioners apprehend that they have in common with all other men a natural and unalienable right to that freedom which the great parent of the universe hath bestowed equally on all mankind and which they have never forfeited by any compact or agreement whatever but [they] were unjustly dragged by the hand of cruel power from their dearest friends and . . . from a populous, pleasant, and plentiful country and in violation of laws of nature and of nations and in defiance of all the tender feelings of humanity brought here . . . to be sold like beast[s] of burden . . . among a people professing the mild religion of Jesus. . . .

In imitation of the laudable example of the good people of these states your petitioners have long and patiently waited the event of petition after petition by them presented to the legislative body. . . . They cannot but express their astonishment that it has never been considered that every principle from which America has acted in the course of their unhappy difficulties with Great Britain pleads stronger than a thousand arguments in favor of your petitioners [and their desire] to be restored to the enjoyment of that which is the natural right of all men.

QUESTIONS

1. *What does Abigail Adams have in mind when she refers to the "unlimited power" husbands exercise over their wives?*

2. *How do the slaves employ the principles of the Revolution for their own aims?*

3. *What do these documents suggest about the boundaries of freedom in the era of the American Revolution?*

Like slaves, some free women adapted the rhetoric of the Revolution to their own situation. Ann Baker Carson later recalled how she became estranged from the tyrannical husband she had married at age sixteen. "I was an American," she wrote. "A land of liberty had given me birth. I felt myself his equal." She left the marriage rather than continue as a "female slave." Although individual women would argue for gender equality, the subordination of women did not become a major source of public debate until long after American independence.

The Arduous Struggle for Liberty

As a result of the long struggle against British rule, the public sphere, and with it the right to vote, expanded markedly among white men. Bound labor among whites declined dramatically, religious groups enjoyed greater liberty, and Blacks mounted a challenge to slavery in which many won their freedom. On the other hand, for many Loyalists and the majority of slaves, American independence meant a deprivation of freedom. White women would see no expansion of political or legal rights. And Native nations would lose independence in the coming years as the U.S. population spread westward.

A new nation, which defined itself as an embodiment of freedom, had taken its place on the world stage. "Not only Britain, but all Europe are spectators of the conflict, the arduous struggle for liberty," wrote Ezra Stiles, the future president of Yale College, in 1775. "We consider ourselves as laying the foundation of a glorious future empire, and acting a part for the contemplation of the ages."

Like Stiles, many other Americans were convinced that their struggle for independence had worldwide significance. American independence, indeed, formed part of a larger set of movements that transformed the Atlantic world. The year 1776 saw not only Paine's *Common Sense* and Jefferson's Declaration but also the publication in England of Adam Smith's *The Wealth of Nations*, which attacked the British policy of closely regulating trade, and Jeremy Bentham's *Fragment on Government*, which criticized the nature of British government.

The winds of change were sweeping across the Atlantic world. The ideals of the American Revolution helped to inspire countless subsequent struggles for social equality and national independence, from the French Revolution, which exploded in 1789, to the uprising that overthrew the slave system in Haiti in the 1790s, the Latin American wars for independence in the early nineteenth century, and numerous struggles of colonial peoples for nationhood in the twentieth. But within the new republic, the debate over who should enjoy the blessings of liberty would continue long after independence had been achieved.

CHAPTER REVIEW

REVIEW QUESTIONS

1. For the lower classes, colonial society had been based on inequality, deference, and obedience. How did the American Revolution challenge that social order?

2. Why did the Revolution cause more radical changes in Pennsylvania than elsewhere, and how was this radicalism demonstrated in the new state constitution?

3. How did ideas of political freedom affect people's ideas about economic rights and relationships?

4. What role did the founders foresee for religion in American government and society?

5. What was the impact of the American Revolution on Native Americans?

6. What were the most important features of the new state constitutions?

7. How did popular views of property rights prevent slaves from enjoying all the freedoms of the social contract?

8. How did revolutionary America affect women's roles and rights?

KEY TERMS

republic (p. 219)

suffrage (p. 220)

Bill for Establishing Religious Freedom (p. 224)

inflation (p. 229)

free trade (p. 229)

The Wealth of Nations (p. 229)

Loyalists (p. 230)

abolition (p. 236)

freedom petitions (p. 238)

Lemuel Haynes (p. 238)

free Blacks (p. 241)

coverture (p. 244)

republican motherhood (p. 245)

Go to INQUIZITIVE

To see what you know—and learn what you've missed—with personalized feedback along the way.

CHAPTER 7

FOUNDING A NATION

1783–1791

FOCUS QUESTIONS

- *What were the achievements and problems of the Confederation government?*

- *What major disagreements and compromises molded the final content of the Constitution?*

- *How did Anti-Federalist concerns raised during the ratification process lead to the creation of the Bill of Rights?*

- *How did the definition of citizenship in the new republic apply differently to different people?*

During June and July of 1788, civic leaders in cities up and down the Atlantic coast organized colorful pageants to celebrate the ratification of the United States Constitution. For one day, Benjamin Rush commented of Philadelphia's parade, social class "forgot its claims," as thousands of marchers—rich and poor, businessman and apprentice—joined in a common public ceremony. New York's Grand Federal Procession was led by farmers, followed by the members of every craft in the city from butchers and coopers (makers of wooden barrels) to bricklayers, blacksmiths, and printers. Lawyers, merchants, and clergymen brought up the rear. The parades testified to the strong popular support for the Constitution in the nation's cities. And the prominent role of skilled artisans reflected how the Revolution had secured their place in the American public sphere. Elaborate banners and floats gave voice to the hopes inspired by the new structure of government. "May commerce flourish and industry be rewarded," declared Philadelphia's mariners and shipbuilders.

Throughout the era of the Revolution, Americans spoke of their nation as a "rising empire," destined to populate and control North America—though most only thought as far west as the Mississippi River. While Europe's empires were governed by force, America's would be different. In Jefferson's phrase, it would be "an empire of liberty," bound together by a common devotion to the principles of the Declaration of Independence. Already, the United States exceeded in size Great Britain, Spain, and France combined. As a new nation, it possessed many advantages, including physical isolation from the Old World (a significant asset between 1789 and 1815, when European powers were almost constantly at war), a youthful population certain to grow much larger, and a broad distribution of property ownership and literacy among white citizens.

But the United States was only one of many powers on the continent. Nearly all of the 3.9 million Americans recorded in the first national census of 1790 lived near the Atlantic coast. Large areas between the Appalachian Mountains and the Mississippi River remained in Native hands. The British retained military posts on American territory near the Great Lakes. The Spanish had won West and East Florida from the British during the Revolutionary War and controlled the important port of New Orleans at the mouth of the Mississippi. The United States had no claims west of the Mississippi River. There lay the Spanish colonies of Louisiana, Texas, New Mexico, and California as well as hundreds of Native nations that had never been under the power of any Europeans.

Away from navigable waterways, communication and transportation in the fledgling United States were primitive. The country was overwhelmingly rural—fewer than one American in thirty lived in a place with 8,000 inhabitants or more. The population consisted of numerous ethnic and religious groups and some 700,000 slaves, making unity difficult to achieve. No republican government had ever been established over so vast a territory or with so diverse a population. Local loyalties outweighed national patriotism. "We have no Americans in America," commented John Adams. It would take time for consciousness of a common nationality to sink deep roots.

Today, it is difficult to recall that in 1783 the future seemed precarious indeed for the fragile nation seeking to make its way in a world of hostile powers. Profound questions needed to be answered. What course of development should the United States follow? How could the competing claims of local self-government, sectional interests, and national authority be balanced? Who should be considered full-fledged members of the American people, entitled to the blessings of liberty? These issues became the focus of heated debate as the first generation of Americans sought to consolidate their new republic.

AMERICA UNDER THE CONFEDERATION

The Articles of Confederation

The first written constitution of the United States was the **Articles of Confederation**, drafted by Congress in 1777 and ratified by the states four years later. The Articles sought to balance the need for national coordination of the War of Independence with widespread fear that centralized political power posed a danger to liberty. It explicitly declared the new national government to be a "perpetual union." But it resembled less a blueprint for a common government than a treaty for mutual defense—in its own words, a "firm league of friendship" among the states. Under the Articles, the thirteen states retained their individual "sovereignty, freedom, and independence." The national government consisted of a one-house Congress, in which each state, no matter how large or populous, cast a single vote. There was no president to enforce the laws and no judiciary to interpret them. Major decisions required the approval of nine states rather than a simple majority.

The only powers specifically granted to the national government by the Articles of Confederation were those essential to the struggle for independence—declaring war, conducting foreign affairs, and making treaties with other governments. Congress had no real financial resources. It could coin money but lacked the power to levy taxes or regulate commerce. Its revenue came mainly from contributions by the individual states. To amend the Articles required the unanimous consent of the states, a formidable obstacle to change. Various amendments to strengthen the national government were proposed during the seven years (1781–1788) when the Articles of Confederation were in effect, but none received the approval of all the states.

The Articles made energetic national government impossible. But Congress in the 1780s did not lack for accomplishments. The most important was establishing national rules for distributing and settling western lands. Disputes over access to western land almost prevented ratification of the Articles in the first place. Citing their original royal charters, which granted territory running all the way to the "South Sea" (the Pacific Ocean), states such as Virginia, the Carolinas, and Connecticut claimed immense tracts of western land. Land speculators, politicians, and prospective settlers from states with clearly defined boundaries insisted that such land must belong to the nation at large. Only after the land-rich states, in the interest of national unity, ceded their western claims to the central government did the Articles win ratification.

Congress and the West

Establishing rules for the settlement of this national domain—namely, the area controlled by the federal government, stretching from the western boundaries of existing states to the Mississippi River—was by no means easy. Although some Americans spoke of it as if it were empty, more than 100,000 Indians inhabited the region. In the immediate aftermath of independence, Congress took the position that by aiding the British, Indians had forfeited the right to their lands. Little distinction was made among those who had sided with the enemy, those who had aided the patriots, and those in the interior who had played no part in the war at all. At peace conferences at Fort Stanwix, New York, in 1784 and Fort McIntosh near Pittsburgh the following year, American representatives persuaded diplomats from some Native nations to cede land north of the Ohio River. But others would dispute the legality of those treaties and would continue their fight against U.S. encroachment after the Revolutionary War ended.

When it came to disposing of western land and regulating its settlement, the Confederation government faced conflicting pressures. Many leaders believed that the economic health of the new republic required that farmers have access to land in the West. But they also saw land sales as a potential source of revenue and worried that unregulated settlement would produce endless conflicts with Indians. Land companies, which lobbied Congress vigorously, hoped to profit by purchasing real estate and reselling it to settlers.

Settlers and the West

The arrival of peace triggered a large population movement from settled parts of the original states into areas like upstate New York and across the Appalachian Mountains into Kentucky and Tennessee. To settlers, the right to take possession of western lands was an essential element of American freedom. When a group of Ohioans petitioned Congress in 1785, assailing landlords and speculators who monopolized available acreage and asking that preference in land ownership be given to "actual settlements," their motto was "Grant us Liberty." Settlers paid no heed to Indian land titles and urged the government to set a low price on public land or give it away. They frequently occupied land to which they had no legal title. By the 1790s, Kentucky courts were filled with lawsuits over land claims, and many settlers lost land they thought they owned. Eventually, disputes over land titles forced many early settlers (including the parents of Abraham Lincoln) to leave Kentucky for opportunities in other states.

At the same time, however, like British colonial officials before them, many leaders of the new nation feared that an unregulated flow of population across the Appalachian Mountains would provoke constant warfare with Indians. Moreover, they viewed frontier settlers as disorderly and lacking in proper respect for authority—"our debtors, loose English people, our German servants, and slaves," Benjamin Franklin had once called them. Establishing law and order in the West and strict rules for the occupation of land there seemed essential to attracting a better class of settlers to the West and avoiding discord between the settled and frontier parts of the new nation.

The Land Ordinances

A series of measures approved by Congress during the 1780s defined the terms by which western land would be marketed and settled. Drafted by Thomas Jefferson, the **Ordinance of 1784** established stages of self-government for the West. The region would be divided into districts initially governed by Congress and eventually admitted to the Union as member states. By a single vote, Congress rejected a clause that would have prohibited slavery throughout the West. A second resolution, the **Ordinance of 1785**, regulated land sales in the region north of the Ohio River, which came to be known as the Old Northwest. Land would be surveyed by the government and then sold in "sections" of a square mile (640 acres) at one dollar per acre. In each township, one section would be set aside to provide funds for public education. The system promised to control and concentrate settlement and raise money for Congress. But settlers violated the rules by pressing westward before the surveys had been completed.

Like the British before them, American officials found it difficult to regulate the thirst for new land. The minimum purchase price of $640, however, put public land out of the financial reach of most settlers. They generally ended up buying smaller parcels from speculators and land companies. In 1787, Congress decided to sell off large tracts to private groups, including 1.5 million

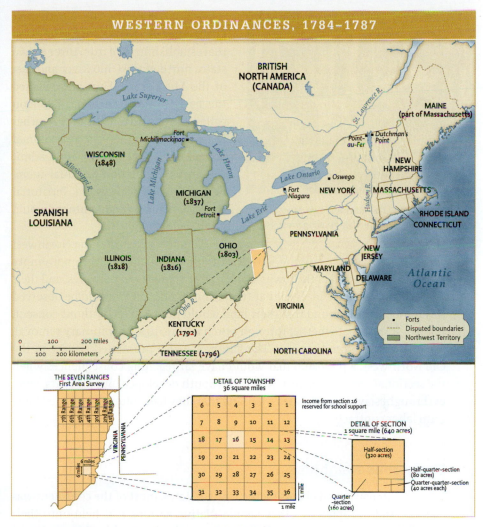

WESTERN ORDINANCES, 1784–1787

A series of ordinances in the 1780s provided for both the surveying and sale of lands in the public domain north of the Ohio River and the eventual admission of states carved from the area as equal members of the Union. (To see competing territorial claims by Native nations, see map on p. 257.)

acres to the Ohio Company, organized by New England land speculators and army officers. (This was a different organization from the Ohio Company of the 1750s, mentioned in Chapter 4.) For many years, national land policy benefited private land companies and large buyers more than individual settlers. And for decades, actual and prospective settlers pressed for a reduction in the price of government-owned land, a movement that did not end until the Homestead Act of 1862 offered free land in the public domain.

An engraving from *The Farmers' and Mechanics' Almanac* shows farm families moving west.

A final measure, the **Northwest Ordinance of 1787**, called for the eventual establishment of from three to five states north of the Ohio River and east of the Mississippi. Thus was enacted the basic principle of what Jefferson called the **empire of liberty**—rather than ruling over the West as a colonial power, the United States would admit the area's population as equal members of the political system. Territorial expansion and self-government would grow together.

The new states that the Northwest Ordinance imagined were not empty lands. They were full of the towns and farms of Shawnees, Delawares, and their allies. The Ordinance pledged that "the utmost good faith" would be observed toward local Indians and that their land would not be taken without consent, but it assumed that whether through purchase, treaties, or voluntary removal, Indians would soon disappear. The Ordinance also prohibited slavery in the Old Northwest, a provision that would have far-reaching consequences when the sectional conflict between North and South developed. But for years, owners brought slaves into the area, claiming that they had voluntarily signed long-term labor contracts.

Dangerous Neighbors

Despite extensive land claims by the United States, most of the continent was claimed and occupied by other people. Native nations still held onto their homelands throughout most of the area west of the Appalachian Mountains. In the South, the still powerful Muscogees (Creeks), Choctaws, Chickasaws, Cherokees, and smaller nations formed alliances with one another and with Spain to protect their lands and independence. The Spanish claimed what today is Florida and most of Alabama and Mississippi, in addition to the two-thirds of the continent that lay between the Mississippi River and the Pacific Ocean. With few colonists for this vast area, the Spanish were eager for Native allies against the American threat. In 1784, the Spanish, Muscogees, Chickasaws, and Choctaws agreed to a mutual alliance. Knowing that the United States threatened Native sovereignty, the alliance agreements pointedly stated that each of the Native parties was a "free nation." The Spanish pledged that "the generous mind of his Most Catholic Majesty is far from exacting lands from the Indians."

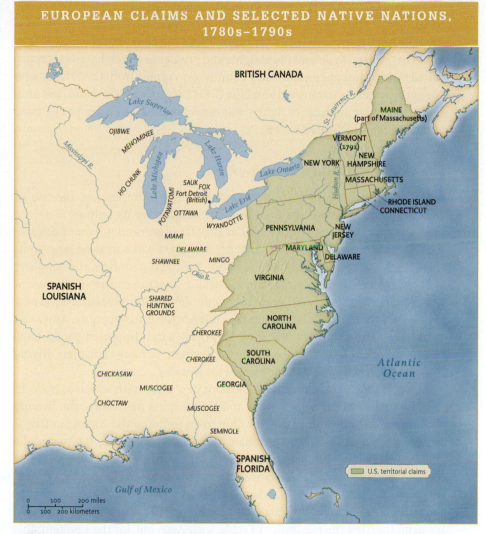

EUROPEAN CLAIMS AND SELECTED NATIVE NATIONS, 1780s–1790s

BRITISH CANADA

Lake Superior

OJIBWE

MENOMINEE

Mississippi R.

HO CHUNK

Lake Michigan

Lake Huron

POTAWATOMI

SAUK FOX
Fort Detroit
(British)

OTTAWA

WYANDOTTE

MIAMI

DELAWARE

SHAWNEE   MINGO

Ohio R.

SPANISH
LOUISIANA

SHARED
HUNTING
GROUNDS

CHEROKEE

CHEROKEE

CHICKASAW

MUSCOGEE

CHOCTAW

MUSCOGEE

SEMINOLE

Lake Erie

Lake Ontario

St. Lawrence R.

MAINE
(part of Massachusetts)

VERMONT
(1791)

NEW YORK

NEW
HAMPSHIRE

Hudson R.

MASSACHUSETTS

RHODE ISLAND
CONNECTICUT

PENNSYLVANIA

NEW
JERSEY

MARYLAND

DELAWARE

VIRGINIA

NORTH
CAROLINA

SOUTH
CAROLINA

GEORGIA

*Atlantic
Ocean*

SPANISH
FLORIDA

Gulf of Mexico

0   100   200 miles
0   100   200 kilometers

U.S. territorial claims

In the decades following the American Revolution, the United States claimed most of the region between the Atlantic Ocean and the Mississippi River. The Spanish empire contested those claims based on its victories in the war, and Native nations fought to retain their hold over the trans-Appalachian west.

This alliance allowed the Muscogees to continue defending against settlers pushing west from Georgia and the Carolinas.

At the same time, Native nations in the Ohio Valley and Great Lakes regions—those places that Congress would designate for the Western Ordinances—continued their warfare against settlers moving into and beyond their Kentucky hunting lands. In December 1786, Shawnee, Delaware, Wendat,

Ojibwe, Potawatomi, Ottawa, and Miami diplomats wrote together to Congress declaring the Ohio River the border between their nations and the United States. If Americans insisted on invading north of the river, they wrote, they would be "obliged to defend those rights and privileges which have been transmitted to us by our ancestors." They counted on support from the British, who had not evacuated their forts around the Great Lakes. Congress could pass ordinances, but it would have to fight a war it could not afford to make the Ohio country part of the United States.

The Confederation's Weaknesses

Whatever the achievements of the Confederation government, in the eyes of many influential Americans they were outweighed by its failings. Both the national government and the country at large faced worsening economic problems. To finance the War of Independence, Congress had borrowed large sums of money by selling interest-bearing bonds and paying soldiers and suppliers in notes to be redeemed in the future. Lacking a secure source of revenue, it found itself unable to pay either interest or the debts themselves or to fund new Indian wars. With the United States now outside the British empire, American ships were barred from trading with the West Indies. Imported goods, however, flooded the market, undercutting the business of many craftsmen, driving down wages, and draining money out of the country.

Some American businessmen looked for new areas with which to trade. In 1784, financed by leading New York and Philadelphia merchants, the *Empress of China* set sail for Canton, the first ship to do so flying the American flag. It carried furs, wine, Spanish silver dollars, and American ginseng. It returned the following year with silk, tea, and Chinese porcelain, a glazed ceramic widely admired for its beauty and resistance to heat and water (and commonly known simply as "China"). One set had been ordered by George Washington for his home in Mount Vernon, Virginia. The investors turned a large profit. The voyage demonstrated the feasibility of trade with Asia, but for the moment, this could not compensate for the loss of nearby markets in the British West Indies.

With Congress unable to act, the states adopted their own economic policies. Several imposed tariff duties on goods imported from abroad. Indebted farmers, threatened with the loss of land because of failure to meet tax or mortgage payments, pressed state governments for relief, as did urban craftsmen who owed money to local merchants. In order to increase the amount of currency in circulation and make it easier for individuals to pay their debts, several states printed large sums of paper money. Others enacted laws postponing debt collection. Creditors considered such measures attacks on their property rights. In a number of states, legislative elections produced boisterous campaigns in which candidates for office denounced creditors for oppressing the poor and importers of luxury goods for undermining republican virtue.

Shays's Rebellion

In late 1786 and early 1787, crowds of debt-ridden farmers closed the courts in western Massachusetts to prevent the seizure of their land for failure to pay taxes. The uprising came to be known as **Shays's Rebellion**, a name affixed to it by its opponents, after Daniel Shays, one of the leaders and a veteran of the War for Independence. Massachusetts had resisted pressure to assist needy debtors. The participants in Shays's Rebellion believed they were acting in the spirit of the Revolution. They modeled their tactics on the crowd activities of the 1760s and 1770s and employed liberty trees and liberty poles as symbols of their cause. They received no sympathy from Governor James Bowdoin, who dispatched an army headed by former Revolutionary War general Benjamin Lincoln. The rebels were dispersed in January 1787, and more than 1,000 were arrested. Without adherence to the rule of law, Bowdoin declared, Americans would descend into "a state of anarchy, confusion and slavery."

Observing Shays's Rebellion from Paris where he was serving as ambassador, Thomas Jefferson refused to be alarmed. "A little rebellion now and then is a good thing," he wrote to a friend. "The tree of liberty must be refreshed from time to time with the blood of patriots and tyrants." But the uprising was the culmination of a series of events in the 1780s that persuaded an influential group of Americans that the national government must be strengthened so that it could develop uniform economic policies and protect property owners from infringements on their rights by local majorities.

Among proponents of stronger national authority, liberty had lost some of its luster. The danger to individual rights, they came to believe, now arose not from a tyrannical central government, but from the people themselves. "Liberty," declared James Madison, "may be endangered by the abuses of liberty as well as the abuses of power." To put it another way, private liberty, especially the secure enjoyment of property rights, could be endangered by public liberty—unchecked power in the hands of the people.

Nationalists of the 1780s

Madison, a disciple and ally of Thomas Jefferson, thought deeply and creatively about the nature of political freedom. He was among the group of talented and well-organized men who spearheaded the movement for a stronger national government. Another was Alexander Hamilton, who had come to North America as a youth from the West Indies, served at the precocious age of twenty

as an army officer during the War of Independence, and married into a prominent New York family. Hamilton was perhaps the most vigorous proponent of
an "energetic" government that would enable the new nation to become a powerful commercial and diplomatic presence in world affairs. Genuine liberty,
he insisted, required "a proper degree of authority, to make and exercise the
laws." Men like Madison and Hamilton came to believe during the 1780s that
Americans were squandering the fruits of independence and that the country's
future greatness depended on enhancing national authority.

The concerns voiced by critics of the Articles found a sympathetic hearing
among men who had developed a national consciousness during the Revolution. Nationalists included army officers, members of Congress accustomed to
working with individuals from different states, and diplomats who represented
the country abroad. In the army, John Marshall (later a chief justice of the
Supreme Court) developed "the habit of considering America as my country,
and Congress as my government." Influential economic interests also desired a
stronger national government. Among these were bondholders who despaired
of being paid so long as Congress lacked a source of revenue, urban artisans
seeking tariff protection from foreign imports, merchants desiring access to
British markets, and all those who feared that the states were seriously interfering with property rights. While these groups did not agree on many issues,
they all believed in the need for a stronger national government.

In September 1786, delegates from six states met at Annapolis, Maryland, to
consider ways for better regulating interstate and international commerce. The
delegates proposed another gathering, in Philadelphia, to amend the Articles of
Confederation. Shays's Rebellion greatly strengthened the nationalists' cause. "The
late turbulent scenes in Massachusetts," wrote Madison, underscored the need for
a new constitution. "No respect," he complained, "is paid to the federal authority."
Without a change in the structure of government, either anarchy or monarchy was
the likely outcome, bringing to an end the experiment in republican government.
Every state except Rhode Island, which had gone the furthest in developing its
own debtor relief and trade policies, sent delegates to the Philadelphia convention.
When they assembled in May 1787, they decided to scrap the Articles of Confederation entirely and draft a new constitution for the United States.

A NEW CONSTITUTION

The fifty-five men who gathered for the **Constitutional Convention** included
some of the most prominent Americans. Thomas Jefferson and John Adams,
serving as diplomats in Europe, did not take part. But among the delegates were
George Washington (whose willingness to lend his prestige to the gathering

and to serve as presiding officer was an enormous asset), George Mason (author of Virginia's Declaration of Rights of 1776), and Benjamin Franklin (who had returned to Philadelphia after helping to negotiate the Treaty of Paris of 1783 and was now eighty-one years old). John Adams described the convention as a gathering of men of "ability, weight, and experience." He might have added, "and wealth." Although a few, like Alexander Hamilton, had risen from humble origins, most had been born into propertied families. They earned their livings as lawyers, merchants, planters, and large farmers. Nearly half, including a number of Northerners, owned slaves. George Washington owned over 200, three of whom he brought to Philadelphia.

At a time when fewer than one-tenth of 1 percent of Americans attended college, more than half the delegates had college educations. A majority had participated in interstate meetings of the 1760s and 1770s, and twenty-two had served in the army during the Revolution. Their shared social status and political experiences bolstered their common belief in the need to strengthen national authority and curb what one called "the excesses of democracy."

The Structure of Government

It quickly became apparent that the delegates agreed on many points. The new Constitution would create a legislature, an executive, and a national judiciary. Congress would have the power to raise money without relying on the states. States would be prohibited from infringing on the rights of property. And the government would represent the people. Hamilton's proposal for a president and Senate serving life terms, like the king and House of Lords of England, received virtually no support. Most delegates hoped to find a middle ground between the despotism of monarchy and aristocracy and what they considered the excesses of popular self-government. "We had been too democratic," observed George Mason, but he warned against the danger of going to "the opposite extreme." The key to stable, effective republican government was finding a way to balance the competing claims of liberty and power.

Differences quickly emerged over the proper balance between the federal and state governments and between the interests of large and small states. Early in the proceedings, Madison presented what came to be called the **Virginia Plan**. It proposed the creation of a two-house legislature with a state's population determining its representation in each. Smaller states, fearing that populous Virginia, Massachusetts, and Pennsylvania would dominate the new government, rallied behind the **New Jersey Plan**. This called for a single-house Congress in which each state cast one vote, as under the Articles of Confederation. In the end, a compromise was reached—a two-house Congress consisting of a Senate in which each state had two members, and a House of Representatives apportioned according to population. Senators would be chosen by state legislatures for six-year terms. They were thus insulated from sudden shifts in public opinion. Representatives were to be elected every two years directly by the people.

The Limits of Democracy

Under the Articles of Confederation, no national official had been chosen by popular vote. Thus, the mode of choosing the House of Representatives represented an expansion of democracy. Popular election of at least one part of the political regime, Madison declared, was "essential to every plan of free government." The Constitution, moreover, imposed neither property nor religious qualifications for voting, leaving it to the states to set voting rules.

Overall, however, the new structure of government was less than democratic. The delegates sought to shield the national government from the popular enthusiasms that had alarmed them during the 1780s and to ensure that the right kind of men held office. The people would remain sovereign, but they would choose among the elite to serve in the new government. The delegates assumed that the Senate would be composed of each state's most distinguished citizens. They made the House of Representatives quite small (initially 65 members, at a time when the Massachusetts assembly had 200), on the assumption that only prominent individuals could win election in large districts.

This portrait of George Washington, painted in the early 1790s by Charles Peale Polk, is based on one executed in 1787 by Polk's uncle, Charles Willson Peale. It depicts Washington as he looked when he presided over the Constitutional Convention in Philadelphia.

Nor did the delegates provide for direct election of either federal judges or the president. Members of the Supreme Court would be appointed by the president for life terms. The president would be chosen either by members of an electoral college or by the House of Representatives. The number of electors for each state was determined by adding together its allocation of senators and representatives. Electors would be prominent, well-educated individuals better qualified than ordinary voters to choose the head of state.

The actual system of election seemed a recipe for confusion. Each elector was to cast votes for two candidates for president, with the second-place finisher becoming vice president. If no candidate received a majority of the electoral ballots—as the delegates seem to have assumed would normally be the case—the president would be chosen from among the top three finishers by the House of Representatives, with each state casting one vote. The Senate would then elect the vice president. The delegates devised this extremely cumbersome system of indirect election because they did not trust ordinary voters to choose the president and vice president directly.

The Division and Separation of Powers

Hammered out in four months of discussion and compromise, the Constitution is a spare document of only 4,000 words that provides only the briefest outline of the new structure of government. (See the Appendix for the full text.) It embodies two basic political principles—**federalism**, sometimes called the **division of powers**, and the system of **checks and balances** between the different branches of the national government, also known as the **separation of powers**.

Federalism refers to the relationship between the national government and the states. Compared to the Articles of Confederation, the Constitution significantly strengthened national authority. It charged the president with enforcing the law and commanding the military. It empowered Congress to levy taxes, borrow money, regulate commerce, declare war, deal with foreign nations (including Native American nations), and promote the "general welfare." Madison proposed to allow Congress to veto state laws, but this proved too far-reaching for most delegates. The Constitution did, however, declare national legislation the "supreme Law of the Land." And it included strong provisions to prevent the states from infringing on property rights. They were barred from issuing paper money, impairing contracts, interfering with interstate commerce, and levying their own import or export duties. On the other hand, most day-to-day affairs of government, from education to law enforcement, remained in the hands of the states. This principle of divided sovereignty was a recipe for debate, which continues to this day, over the balance of power between the national government and the states.

The "separation of powers," or the system of "checks and balances," refers to the way the Constitution seeks to prevent any branch of the national government from dominating the other two. To prevent an accumulation of power dangerous to liberty, authority within the government is diffused and balanced against itself. Congress enacts laws, but the president can veto them, and a two-thirds majority is required to pass legislation over his objection. Federal judges are nominated by the president and approved by the Senate, but to ensure their independence, the judges then serve for life. The president can be impeached by the House and removed from office by the Senate for "high crimes and misdemeanors."

The Debate over Slavery

The structure of government was not the only source of debate at the Constitutional Convention. As Madison recorded, "the institution of slavery and its implications" divided the delegates at many sessions. Madison, like Jefferson a Virginia slaveholder who detested slavery, told the convention that the "distinction of color" had become the basis for "the most oppressive dominion ever exercised by man over man." Yet he later assured the Virginia ratifying convention that the Constitution offered slavery "better security than any that now exists."

The words "slave" and "slavery" do not appear in the original Constitution—a concession to the sensibilities of delegates who feared they would "contaminate the glorious fabric of American liberty." As Luther Martin of Maryland wrote, his fellow delegates "anxiously sought to avoid the admission of expressions which might be odious to the ears of Americans." But, he continued, they were "willing to admit into their system those *things* which the *expressions signified*." The document prohibited Congress from abolishing the importation of slaves from abroad for twenty years. It required states to return to their owners fugitives from bondage. And the **three-fifths clause** provided that three-fifths of the enslaved population would be counted in determining each state's representation in the House of Representatives and its electoral votes for president.

This advertisement by a slave-trading company appeared in a Richmond, Virginia, newspaper only a few months after the signing of the Constitution. The company seeks to buy 100 slaves to sell to purchasers in states farther south. Slavery was a major subject of debate at the Constitutional Convention.

South Carolina's delegates had come to Philadelphia determined to defend slavery, and they had a powerful impact on the final document. They originated the fugitive slave clause and the electoral college. They insisted on strict limits on the power of Congress to levy taxes within the states, fearing future efforts to raise revenue by taxing slave property. They threatened disunion if the Atlantic slave trade were prohibited immediately, as the New England states and Virginia, with its abundance of native-born slaves, demanded. Their threats swayed many delegates. Gouverneur Morris, one of Pennsylvania's delegates, declared that he was being forced to decide between offending the southern states and doing injustice to "human nature." For the sake of national unity, he said, he would choose the latter.

Nonetheless, the Constitution did provide a basis for later antislavery political movements. Many of the framers, including slaveholders from the Upper South, hoped that the institution would eventually die out, and they successfully resisted efforts to place an explicit national recognition of property in human beings in the document. Slavery remained an institution created by state, not national, law. This opened the door to efforts to bar slavery in places of national jurisdiction, especially the western territories.

Slavery in the Constitution

The Constitution's slavery clauses were compromises, efforts to find a middle ground between the institution's critics and defenders. Taken together, however, they embedded slavery more deeply than ever in American life and politics. The slave trade clause allowed a commerce condemned by civilized society—one that had been suspended during the War of Independence—to continue until 1808. On January 1, 1808, the first day that Congress was allowed under the Constitution, it prohibited the further importation of slaves. But in the interim, partly to replace slaves who had escaped to the British and partly to provide labor for the expansion of slavery to fertile land away from the coast, some 170,000 Africans were brought to the new nation as slaves. South Carolina and Georgia imported 100,000. This number represented more than one-quarter of all the slaves brought to mainland North America after 1700.

The fugitive slave clause accorded slave laws "extraterritoriality"—that is, the condition of bondage remained attached to a person even if he or she escaped to a state where slavery had been abolished. In the famous Somerset case of 1772, the lawyer for a West Indian slave brought to Britain had obtained his client's freedom by invoking the memorable words, "the air of England is too pure for a slave to breathe" (that is, the moment any person sets foot on British soil, he or she becomes free). Yet the new federal Constitution required all the states, North and South, to help police the institution of slavery. Nonetheless, the clause was strikingly ambiguous. It did not say who was responsible for apprehending a fugitive slave or what judicial procedures would be employed to return him or her to bondage. As time went on, these questions would become a major source of conflict between the North and the South.

The Constitution gave the national government no power to interfere with slavery in the states. And the three-fifths clause allowed the white South to exercise far greater power in national affairs than the size of its free population warranted. The clause greatly enhanced the number of southern votes in the

House of Representatives and in the electoral college. Of the first sixteen presidential elections, between 1788 and 1848, all but four placed a southern slaveholder in the White House.

Even the initial failure to include a Bill of Rights resulted, in part, from the presence of slavery. As South Carolina delegate Charles C. Pinckney explained, "such bills generally begin with declaring that all men are by nature born free," a declaration that would come "with a very bad grace, when a large part of our property consists in men who are actually born slaves."

But some slaveholders detected a potential threat buried in the Constitution. Patrick Henry, who condemned slavery but feared abolition, warned that, in time of war, the new government might take steps to arm and liberate the slaves. "May Congress not say," he asked, "that every black man must fight? Did we not see a little of this [in the] last war?" What Henry could not anticipate was that the war that eventually destroyed slavery would be launched by the South itself to protect the institution.

The Final Document

Gouverneur Morris put the finishing touches on the final draft of the new Constitution, trying to make it, he explained, "as clear as our language would permit." For the original preamble, which began, "We the people of the States of New Hampshire, Massachusetts," etc., he substituted the far more powerful "We the people of the United States." He added a statement of the Constitution's purposes, including to "establish justice," promote "the general welfare," and "secure the blessings of liberty"—things the Articles of Confederation, in the eyes of most of the delegates, had failed to accomplish.

The last session of the Constitutional Convention took place on September 17, 1787. Benjamin Franklin urged the delegates to put aside individual objections and approve the document, whatever its imperfections. "The older I grow," he remarked, "the more apt I am to . . . pay more respect to the judgment of others." Of the forty-five delegates who remained in Philadelphia, thirty-nine signed the Constitution. It was then sent to the states for ratification.

The Constitution created a new framework for American development. By assigning to Congress power over tariffs, interstate commerce, the coining of money, patents, rules for bankruptcy, and weights and measures, and by prohibiting states from interfering with property rights, it made possible a national economic market. It created national political institutions, reduced the powers of the states, and sought to place limits on popular democracy. "The same enthusiasm, now pervades all classes in favor of government," observed Benjamin Rush, "that actuated us in favor of liberty in the years 1774 and 1775." Whether "all classes" truly agreed may be doubted, for the ratification process unleashed a nationwide debate over the best means of preserving American freedom.

THE RATIFICATION DEBATE AND THE ORIGIN OF THE BILL OF RIGHTS

The Federalist

Even though the Constitution provided that it would go into effect when nine states, not all thirteen as required by the Articles of Confederation, had given their approval, ratification was by no means certain. Each state held an election for delegates to a state ratifying convention. A fierce public battle ensued, producing hundreds of pamphlets and newspaper articles and spirited campaigns to elect delegates. To generate support, Hamilton, Madison, and John Jay composed a series of eighty-five essays that appeared in newspapers under the pen name Publius and were gathered as a book, ***The Federalist***, in 1788.

This satirical engraving by Amos Doolittle (who created the image of the Battle of Concord; see Chapter 5) depicts some of the issues in the debate over the ratification of the Constitution. The wagon in the center is carrying Connecticut and sinking into the mud under the weight of debts and paper money as "Federals" and "Antifederals" try to pull it out. Federals call for the state to "comply with Congress" (that is, to pay money requisitioned by the national government); the Antifederals reply, "Tax luxury" and "Success to Shays," a reference to Shays's Rebellion. Underneath the three merchant ships is a phrase criticizing the tariffs that states were imposing on imports from one another (which the Constitution prohibited).

Hamilton wrote fifty, Madison thirty, and Jay the remainder. Today, the essays are regarded as among the most important American contributions to political thought. At the time, however, they represented only one part of a much larger national debate over ratification, reflected in innumerable pamphlets, newspaper articles, and public meetings.

Again and again, Hamilton and Madison repeated that rather than posing a danger to Americans' liberties, the Constitution in fact protected them. Hamilton's essays sought to disabuse Americans of their fear of political power. Government, he insisted, was an expression of freedom, not its enemy. Any government could become oppressive, but with its checks and balances and division of power, the Constitution made political tyranny almost impossible. At the New York ratifying convention, Hamilton assured the delegates that the Constitution had created "the perfect balance between liberty and power."

Madison, too, emphasized how the Constitution was structured to prevent abuses of authority. But in several essays, especially *Federalist* nos. 10 and 51, he moved beyond such assurances to develop a strikingly new vision of the relationship between government and society in the United States. Madison identified the essential dilemma, as he saw it, of the new republic—government must be based on the will of the people, yet the people had shown themselves susceptible to dangerous enthusiasms. Most worrisome, they had threatened property rights, whose protection was the "first object of government." The problem of balancing democracy and respect for property would only grow in the years ahead because, he warned, economic development would inevitably increase the numbers of poor. What was to prevent them from using their political power to secure "a more equal distribution" of wealth by seizing the property of the rich?

The answer, Madison explained, lay not simply in the way power balanced power in the structure of government, but in the nation's size and diversity. Previous republics had existed only in small territories—the Dutch republic, or Italian city-states of the Renaissance. But, argued Madison, the very size of the United States was a source of stability, not, as many feared, weakness. "Extend the sphere," he wrote. In a nation as large as the United States, so many distinct interests—economic, regional, and political—would arise, that no single one would ever be able to take over the government and oppress the rest. Every majority would be a coalition of minorities, and thus "the rights of individuals" would be secure.

In arguing that the size of the republic helped to secure Americans' rights, Madison's writings reinforced the tradition that saw continuous westward expansion as essential to freedom. And in basing the preservation of freedom on the structure of government and size of the republic, not the character of the people, his essays represented a major shift away from the "republican" emphasis on a virtuous citizenry devoted to the common good as the foundation of proper government. Madison helped to popularize the "liberal" idea that people are generally motivated by self-interest, and that the good of society arises from the clash of these private interests.

The Anti-Federalists

Opponents of ratification, called **Anti-Federalists**, insisted that the Constitution shifted the balance between liberty and power too far in the direction of the latter. Anti-Federalists lacked the coherent leadership of the Constitution's defenders. They included state politicians fearful of seeing their influence diminish, among them such revolutionary heroes as Samuel Adams, John Hancock, and Patrick Henry. Small farmers, many of whom supported the state debtor-relief measures of the 1780s that the Constitution's supporters deplored, also saw no need for a stronger central government. Some opponents of the Constitution denounced the document's protections for slavery; others warned that the powers of Congress were so broad that it might enact a law for abolition.

Anti-Federalists repeatedly predicted that the new government would fall under the sway of merchants, creditors, and others hostile to the interests of ordinary Americans. Popular self-government, they claimed, flourished best in small communities, where rulers and ruled interacted daily. Only men of wealth, "ignorant of the sentiments of the middling and lower class of citizens," would have the resources to win election to a national government. The result of the Constitution, warned Melancton Smith of New York, a member of Congress under the Articles of Confederation, would be domination of the "common people" by the "well-born."

"Liberty" was the Anti-Federalists' watchword. America's happiness, they insisted, "arises from the freedom of our institutions and the limited nature of our government," both threatened by the new Constitution. Maryland Anti-Federalists had caps manufactured bearing the word "Liberty," to wear to the polls when members of the state's ratification convention were elected. To the vision of the United States as an energetic great power, Anti-Federalists counterposed a way of life grounded in local, democratic institutions. "What is Liberty?" asked James Lincoln of South Carolina. "The power of governing yourselves. If you adopt this constitution, have you this power? No."

Anti-Federalists also pointed to the Constitution's lack of a **Bill of Rights**, which left unprotected rights such as trial by jury and freedom of speech and the press. The absence of a Bill of Rights, declared Patrick Henry, was "the most absurd thing to mankind that ever the world saw." State constitutions had bills of rights, yet the states, Henry claimed, were now being asked to surrender most of their powers to the federal government, with no requirement that it respect Americans' basic liberties.

Banner of the Society of Pewterers. A banner carried by one of the many artisan groups that took part in New York City's Grand Federal Procession of 1788 celebrating the ratification of the Constitution. The banner depicts artisans at work in their shop and some of their products. The words "Solid and Pure," and the inscription at the upper right, link the quality of their pewter to their opinion of the new frame of government and hopes for the future. The inscription reads:

"The Federal Plan Most Solid and Secure Americans Their Freedom Will Endure All Arts Shall Flourish in Columbia's Land And All Her Sons Join as One Social Band."

In general, pro-Constitution sentiment flourished in the nation's cities and in rural areas closely tied to the commercial marketplace. The Constitution's most energetic supporters were men of substantial property. But what George Bryan of Pennsylvania, a supporter of ratification, called the "golden phantom" of prosperity also swung urban artisans, laborers, and sailors behind the movement for a government that would use its "energy and power" to revive the depressed economy. Anti-Federalism drew its support from small farmers in more isolated rural areas such as the Hudson Valley of New York, western Massachusetts, and the southern backcountry.

In the end, the supporters' energy and organization, coupled with their domination of the colonial press, carried the day. Ninety-two newspapers and magazines existed in the United States in 1787. Of these, only twelve published a significant number of Anti-Federalist pieces. Madison also won support for the new Constitution by promising that the first Congress would enact a Bill of Rights. By mid-1788, the required nine states had ratified. Although there was strong dissent in Massachusetts, New York, and Virginia, only Rhode Island and North Carolina voted against ratification, and they subsequently had little choice but to join the new government. Anti-Federalism died. But as with other movements in American history that did not immediately achieve their goals—for example, the Populists of the late nineteenth century—some of the Anti-Federalists' ideas eventually entered the political mainstream. To this day, their belief that a too-powerful central government is a threat to liberty continues to influence American political culture.

The Bill of Rights

Ironically, the parts of the Constitution Americans most value today—the freedoms of speech, the press, and religion; protection against unjust criminal procedures; equality before the law—were not in the original document. All of these but the last (which was enshrined in the Fourteenth Amendment after the Civil War) were contained in the first ten amendments, known as the Bill of Rights. Madison was so convinced that the balances of the Constitution would protect liberty that he believed a Bill of Rights "redundant or pointless." Amendments restraining federal power, he believed, would have no effect on the danger to liberty posed by unchecked majorities in the states, and no list of rights could ever anticipate the numerous ways that Congress might operate in the future. "Parchment barriers" to the abuse of authority, he observed, would prove least effective when most needed. Madison's prediction would be amply borne out at future times of popular hysteria, such as during the Red Scare following World War I and the McCarthy era of the 1950s, when all branches of government joined in trampling on freedom of expression, and during World War II, when hatred of a foreign enemy led to the internment of more than 100,000 Japanese Americans, most of them citizens of the United States.

Nevertheless, every new state constitution contained some kind of declaration of citizens' rights, and large numbers of Americans—Federalist and Anti-Federalist alike—believed the new national Constitution should also have one. In order to "conciliate the minds of the people," as Madison put it, he presented to Congress a series of amendments that became the basis of the Bill of Rights, which was ratified by the states in 1791. The First Amendment prohibited Congress from legislating with regard to religion or infringing on freedom of speech, freedom of the press, or the right of assembly. The Second Amendment upheld the people's right to "keep and bear arms" in conjunction with "a well-regulated militia." Others prohibited abuses such as arrests without warrants and forcing a person accused of a crime to testify against himself and reaffirmed the right to trial by jury.

From DAVID RAMSAY, *THE HISTORY OF THE AMERICAN REVOLUTION* (1789)

A member of the Continental Congress from South Carolina, David Ramsay published his history of the Revolution the year after the Constitution was ratified. In this excerpt, he lauds the principles of representative government and the right of future amendment, embodied in the state constitutions and adopted in the national one, as unique American political principles and the best ways of securing liberty.

The world has not hitherto exhibited so fair an opportunity for promoting social happiness. It is hoped for the honor of human nature, that the result will prove the fallacy of those theories that mankind are incapable of self government. The ancients, not knowing the doctrine of representation, were apt in their public meetings to run into confusion, but in America this mode of taking the sense of the people, is so well understood, and so completely reduced to system, that its most populous states are often peaceably convened in an assembly of deputies, not too large for orderly deliberation, and yet representing the whole in equal proportion. These popular branches of legislature are miniature pictures of the community, and from their mode of election are likely to be influenced by the same interests and feelings with the people whom they represent. . . .

In no age before, and in no other country, did man ever possess an election of the kind of government, under which he would choose to live. The constituent parts of the ancient free governments were thrown together by accident. The freedom of modern European governments was, for the most part, obtained by concessions, or liberality of monarchs, or military leaders. In America alone, reason and liberty concurred in the formation of constitutions. . . . In one thing they were all perfect. They left the people in the power of altering and amending them, whenever they pleased. In this happy peculiarity they placed the science of politics on a footing with the other sciences, by opening it to improvements from experience, and the discoveries of future ages. By means of this power of amending American constitutions, the friends of mankind have fondly hoped that oppression will one day be no more.

From JAMES WINTHROP, ANTI-FEDERALIST ESSAY SIGNED "AGRIPPA" (1787)

A local official in Middlesex, Massachusetts, James Winthrop published sixteen public letters between November 1787 and February 1788 opposing ratification of the Constitution.

It is the opinion of the ablest writers on the subject, that no extensive empire can be governed upon republican principles, and that such a government will degenerate into a despotism, unless it be made up of a confederacy of smaller states, each having the full powers of internal regulation. This is precisely the principle which has hitherto preserved our freedom. No instance can be found of any free government of considerable extent which has been supported upon any other plan. Large and consolidated empires may indeed dazzle the eyes of a distant spectator with their splendor, but if examined more nearly are always found to be full of misery. . . . It is under such tyranny that the Spanish provinces languish, and such would be our misfortune and degradation, if we should submit to have the concerns of the whole empire managed by one empire. To promote the happiness of the people it is necessary that there should be local laws; and it is necessary that those laws should be made by the representatives of those who are immediately subject to [them]. . . .

It is impossible for one code of laws to suit Georgia and Massachusetts. They must, therefore, legislate for themselves. Yet there is, I believe, not one point of legislation that is not surrendered in the proposed plan. Questions of every kind respecting property are determinable in a continental court, and so are all kinds of criminal causes. The continental legislature has, therefore, a right to make rules in all cases. . . . No rights are reserved to the citizens. . . . This new system is, therefore, a consolidation of all the states into one large mass, however diverse the parts may be of which it is composed. . . .

A bill of rights . . . serves to secure the minority against the usurpation and tyranny of the majority. . . . The experience of all mankind has proved the prevalence of a disposition to use power wantonly. It is therefore as necessary to defend an individual against the majority in a republic as against the king in a monarchy.

QUESTIONS

1. *Why does Ramsay feel that the power to amend the Constitution is so important a political innovation?*

2. *Why does Winthrop believe that a Bill of Rights is essential in the Constitution?*

3. *How do Ramsay and Winthrop differ concerning how the principle of representation operates in the United States?*

In a sense, the Bill of Rights offered a definition of the "unalienable rights" Jefferson had mentioned in the Declaration of Independence—rights inherent in the human condition. Not having been granted by government in the first place, they could not be rescinded by government. In case any had been accidentally omitted, the Ninth Amendment declared that rights not specifically mentioned in the Constitution were "retained by the people." Its suggestion that the Constitution was not meant to be complete opened the door to future legal recognition of rights not grounded in the actual text (such as the right to privacy). The Tenth Amendment, meant to answer fears that the federal government would ride roughshod over the states, affirmed that powers not delegated to the national government or prohibited to the states continued to reside with the states.

The roots and even the specific language of some parts of the Bill of Rights lay far back in English history. Other provisions reflected the changes in American life brought about by the Revolution. The most remarkable of these was constitutional recognition of religious freedom. Unlike the Declaration of Independence, which invokes the blessing of divine providence, the Constitution is a purely secular document that contains no reference to God and bars religious tests for federal officeholders. The First Amendment prohibits the federal government from legislating on the subject of religion—a complete departure from British and colonial precedent. Under the Constitution it was and remains possible, as one critic complained, for "a papist, a Mohomatan, a deist, yea an atheist" to become president of the United States. Madison was so adamant about separating church and state that he even opposed the appointment of chaplains to serve Congress and the military.

Today, when Americans are asked to define freedom, many instinctively turn to the Bill of Rights and especially the First Amendment, with its guarantees of freedom of speech, the press, and religion. Yet the Bill of Rights aroused little enthusiasm on ratification and for decades was all but ignored. Not until the twentieth century would it come to be revered as an indispensable expression of American freedom. Nonetheless, the Bill of Rights subtly affected the language of liberty. Applying only to the federal government, not the states, it reinforced the idea that concentrated national power posed the greatest threat to freedom. And it contributed to the long process whereby freedom came to be discussed in the vocabulary of rights.

Among the most important rights were freedom of speech and the press, vital building blocks of a democratic public sphere. Once an entitlement of members of Parliament and colonial assemblies, free speech came to be seen as a basic right of citizenship. Although the legal implementation remained to be worked out, and serious infringements would occur at many points in American history, the Bill of Rights did much to establish freedom of expression as a cornerstone of the popular understanding of American freedom.

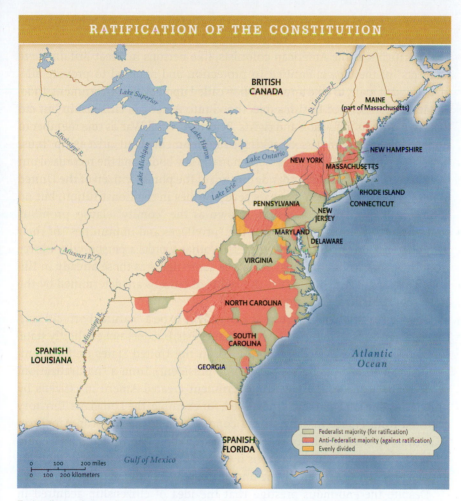

RATIFICATION OF THE CONSTITUTION

Legend:
- Federalist majority (for ratification)
- Anti-Federalist majority (against ratification)
- Evenly divided

Federalists—those who supported the new Constitution—tended to be concentrated in cities and nearby rural areas, while backcountry farmers were more likely to oppose the new frame of government.

"WE THE PEOPLE"

Who Belongs? The Constitution and American Citizenship

A nation, in one scholar's famous phrase, is more than a political entity or a specific piece of territory—it is also "an imagined political community," whose borders are as much intellectual as geographic. The creation of the United States required creating "Americans," that is, people who considered themselves members of the new nation, not simply of individual states. But who qualified as an American citizen? The Constitution did not say.

In British law, the American colonists, like persons in Great Britain, were "subjects" of the crown, entitled to protection and required to provide allegiance and, if male, to take up arms when called upon by the government. Independence transformed British subjecthood into American citizenship but did little to clarify its definition and rights. Before the Civil War, as one member of Congress later noted, a person seeking enlightenment about citizenship "must have been pained by the fruitless search in the law books and the records of our courts for a clear and satisfactory definition of the phrase 'citizen of the United States.'" The word "citizen" appears several times in the Constitution, but no definition is given. One provision, known as the "comity" clause, prohibits states from discriminating between the "privileges and immunities" of their own citizens and those of other states. In other words, a person who moves from New York to Illinois must enjoy the same rights as those already in Illinois. This language assumes that the rights of citizens are determined by the states, not the federal government.

The Constitution does require the president to be a "natural born citizen," that is, a person born in the country. This suggests, but does not explicitly state, that citizenship derives either from birth in the United States or, for immigrants from abroad (ineligible to become president), from a "naturalization" process. On occasion, the federal government created American citizens by purchasing the land on which they lived, for example, the Louisiana Territory acquired from France in 1803, or via conquest, as in the Mexican-American War. In both cases, residents of territory acquired by the United States could choose to become American citizens if they so desired (although whether this applied to Native Americans living under tribal sovereignty remained unclear).

Despite the enormous prestige that the idea of citizenship acquired in the first half of the nineteenth century, there was no commonly agreed-upon understanding of the rights that went with it or the role of the federal government in defining and guaranteeing those rights. Whites, male and female, born in the United States were commonly assumed to be citizens, but white women lacked basic rights enjoyed by men, and if a woman married a foreigner, she generally lost her U.S. citizenship. Slaves were not American citizens, nor were Indians who lived in their own sovereign nations. But the status of free people of color, whether of African or of Native American descent, born in the United States remained highly controversial. Free men of color voted in elections that chose delegates to the state conventions that ratified the Constitution. In the 1790s, the federal government issued certificates affirming the citizenship of Black and Native sailors to prevent them from being seized by the British and "impressed" into the Royal Navy. Yet as time went on, the slave states placed increasingly severe restrictions on the lives of free people of color and refused to recognize them as citizens. Some northern states and some local communities in southern states did, however, and all of the northern states accorded Black men basic rights such as property ownership, trial by jury, and the ability to hold public meetings, publish newspapers, and establish their own churches. But nowhere did they enjoy full equality before the law. One judge referred to free Blacks as "quasi citizens." Not until the Reconstruction era that followed the Civil War was a clear statement added to the Constitution affirming the principle of "birthright citizenship"—that is, anyone born in the United States, no matter one's race, language, religion, national origin, or the legal situation of one's parents, is an American citizen and entitled to the equal protection of the laws.

National Identity

The colonial population had been divided by ethnicity, religion, class, and status and united largely by virtue of its allegiance to Britain. The Revolution created not only a new nation but also a new collective body, the American people, whose members were to enjoy freedom as citizens in a new political community. Since government in the United States rested on the will of the people, it was all the more important to identify who the people were.

The Constitution opens with the words "We the People," describing those who, among other things, are to possess "the Blessings of Liberty" as a birthright and pass them on to "Posterity." (Abraham Lincoln would later cite these words to argue that because the nation had been created by the people, not the states, the states could not dissolve it.) Although one might assume that the "people" of the United States included all those living within the nation's borders, the text made clear that this was not the case. The Constitution identifies three populations inhabiting the United States: Indians who were members of independent nations and not part of the American body politic; "other persons"—that is, slaves; and the "people." Only the third were entitled to American freedom.

Every nation confronts the task of defining its identity. Historians have traditionally distinguished between "civic nationalism," which envisions the nation as a community open to all those devoted to its political institutions and social values, and "ethnic nationalism," which defines the nation as a community of descent based on a shared ethnic heritage, language, and culture. At first glance, the United States appears to conform to the civic model. It lacked a clear ethnic identity or long-established national boundaries—the political principles of the Revolution held Americans together. To be an American, all one had to do was commit oneself to an ideology of liberty, equality, and democracy. From the outset, however, American nationality combined both civic and ethnic definitions. For most of our history, American citizenship has been defined by blood as well as by political allegiance.

Native Nations on the U.S. Border

The early republic's policies toward Indians and African Americans illustrate the conflicting principles that shaped American nationality. American leaders agreed that the West belonged to the United States. Therefore, Indians must either move to lands even farther west, die off, or assimilate into white "civilization" with the expectation that they might one day become part of American society. During Washington's administration, Secretary of War Henry Knox hoped to deal with Indians with a minimum of warfare and without undermining the new nation's honor. His conciliatory policy had mixed results. Congress forbade the transfer of Indian land without federal approval. But as with Britain's Proclamation of 1763, this directive was very unpopular, and individuals and even some states continued to negotiate their own agreements or just take Native land.

Native Americans continued to fight back. In 1791, Miami leader Little Turtle led the Ohio Valley Indian Confederacy to victory over American forces

The Plan of Civilization. Painted circa 1800 by an unidentified artist, this work depicts U.S. Indian agent Benjamin Hawkins explaining the advantages of settled agriculture as part of a plan to promote "civilization" among Native Americans.

WHO IS AN AMERICAN?

FROM J. HECTOR ST. JOHN DE CRÈVECOEUR, *LETTERS FROM AN AMERICAN FARMER* (1782)

In the era of the Revolution, many foreigners celebrated the United States as not only an independent nation but also a new society, in which individuals could enjoy opportunities unknown in the Old World and where a new nationality was being forged from the diverse populations of Europe. No one promoted this image of America more enthusiastically than J. Hector St. John de Crèvecoeur, a Frenchman who had settled in New York, married the daughter of a prominent landowner, and later returned to Europe and wrote about his experiences in America.

[The European who comes to the United States] beholds fair cities, substantial villages, extensive fields, an immense country filled with decent houses, good roads, orchards, meadows, and bridges, where an hundred years ago all was wild, woody and uncultivated. . . . A modern society offers itself to his contemplation, different from what he had hitherto seen. It is not composed, as in Europe, of great lords who possess every thing and of a herd of people who have nothing. Here are no aristocratical families, no courts, no kings, no bishops, no ecclesiastical dominion. . . . We have no princes, for whom we toil, starve, and bleed: we are the most perfect society now existing in the world. Here man is free; as he ought to be. . . .

The next wish of this traveler will be to know whence came all these people? They are a mixture of English, Scotch, Irish, French, Dutch, Germans, and Swedes. From this promiscuous breed, that race now called Americans have arisen. . . . In this great American asylum, the poor of Europe have by some means met together. . . . Urged by a variety of motives, here they came. . . .

What then is the American, this new man? He is either an European, or the descendant of an European, hence that strange mixture of blood, which you will find in no other country . . . . He is an American, who leaving behind him all his ancient prejudices and manners, receives new ones from the new mode of life he has embraced, the new government he obeys, and the new rank he holds. . . . Here individuals of all nations are melted into a new race of men.

QUESTIONS

1. *What characteristics of American life does Crèvecoeur believe unite people of different origins in the United States into one people?*

2. *What aspects of society, and what parts of the American people, are left out of his description?*

led by Arthur St. Clair, the American governor of the Northwest Territory. With 630 dead, this was the costliest loss ever suffered by the United States Army at the hands of Indians. In 1794, 3,000 American troops under Anthony Wayne defeated Little Turtle's forces at the Battle of Fallen Timbers. This battle, combined with the British refusal to assist the Native forces, led directly to the **Treaty of Greenville** of 1795, in which twelve Native nations ceded most of what became Ohio and Indiana to the federal government. The treaty also established the **annuity system**—that is, a system of yearly payments of federal money in return for land cessions. Annuities provided goods and funds for Native nations to use but also gave the government leverage over nations that had signed treaties because federal Indian agents could at times withhold these payments.

American leaders urged Native Americans to give up their independent nations as well as their languages, religions, and cultures to assimilate to white America. Thomas Jefferson believed that Indians could become full-fledged members of the republic by abandoning communal landholding and hunting in favor of family-owned farms. Once they "possessed property," Jefferson told one Indian group, they could "join us in our government" and, indeed, "mix your blood with ours." To pursue the goal of assimilation, Congress in the 1790s authorized President Washington to distribute agricultural tools and livestock to Native men and spinning wheels and looms to Native women. To whites, the adoption of American gender norms, with men working the land and women tending to their homes, would be a crucial sign that the Indians were becoming "civilized." But the vast majority of Native Americans had no desire to give up their independent nations to become Americans. To them, freedom meant retaining their own nations' autonomy and identity, including their own languages, governing structures, and gendered divisions of labor. "Since our acquaintance with our brother white people," declared a Mohawk speaker at a 1796 treaty council, "that which we call freedom and liberty, becomes an entire stranger to us." The American empire of liberty depended on seizing liberty and property from Native nations.

Native Nations in the West

In the meantime, the vast region west of the Mississippi River was controlled by Native nations with little interest in the United States. Those close to European posts had forged alliances and trading relationships that sometimes gave them military and economic advantages over those without access to Europeans. The Osages along the Missouri River had increased their hunting, selling hides and furs to French traders in exchange for weapons, which they used to expand their territory at the expense of the Caddos and Wichitas. The smaller

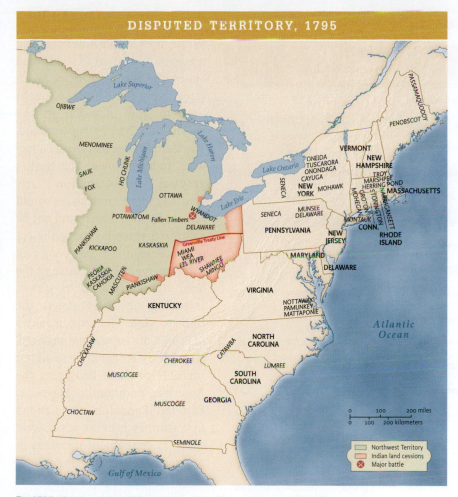

DISPUTED TERRITORY, 1795

By 1795, the area west of the Appalachian Mountains was still Indian country.

Quapaw nation had similarly used French trade and alliance to defend their lands at the confluence of the Arkansas and Mississippi rivers against their rivals. When France gave Louisiana to Spain at the end of the Seven Years' War, the Osages and Quapaws built strong alliances with Spain.

Farther west, on the Great Plains, the Comanches had become a powerful horse-riding people who forged alliances with some Native peoples while violently displacing others. They pushed Apaches, for example, into Texas and New Mexico, where they raided Pueblo and Spanish communities. The Comanches and other Plains peoples amassed huge horse herds and terrified their enemies.

Blacks and the Republic

While most Native Americans had no desire to be part of the United States, the 700,000 African Americans living there by 1790 sought freedom and inclusion in the nation they had helped to build. The status of free Blacks was somewhat indeterminate. The North's **gradual emancipation** acts assumed that former slaves would remain in the country and not be colonized abroad. During the era of the Revolution, free people of color enjoyed at least some of the legal rights accorded to whites, including, in most states, the right to vote. The large majority of Blacks, of course, were enslaved, and slavery rendered them all but invisible to those imagining the American community. Slaves, as Edmund Randolph, the nation's first attorney general, put it, were "not . . . constituent members of our society," and the language of liberty did not apply to them.

Like Randolph, many white Americans excluded Blacks from their conception of the American people. The Constitution empowered Congress to create a uniform system by which immigrants became citizens, and the Naturalization Act of 1790 offered the first legislative definition of American nationality. With no debate, Congress restricted the process of becoming a citizen from abroad to "free white persons."

The law initiated a policy that some historians, with only partial accuracy, call **open immigration**. For Europeans, the process was indeed open.

TABLE 7.1 Population of the United States, 1790

State	Total Population	Slaves	Free People of Color
New England:			
New Hampshire	141,899	158	630
Vermont*	85,341	0	271
Massachusetts	378,556	0	5,369
Connecticut	237,655	2,764	2,771
Rhode Island	69,112	948	3,484
Maine**	96,643	0	536
Middle States:			
New York	340,241	21,324	4,682
New Jersey	184,139	11,423	2,762
Pennsylvania	433,611	3,737	6,531
South:			
Delaware	59,096	8,887	3,899
Maryland	319,728	103,036	8,043
Virginia	747,610	292,627	12,866
North Carolina	395,005	100,572	5,041
South Carolina	249,073	107,094	1,801
Georgia	82,548	29,264	398
Kentucky*	73,677	12,430	114
Tennessee*	35,691	3,417	361
Total	3,929,625	697,681	59,559

*Vermont, Kentucky, and Tennessee were territories that had not yet been admitted as states.
**Maine was part of Massachusetts in 1790.

Only in the last quarter of the nineteenth century were groups of whites, beginning with prostitutes, convicted felons, "lunatics," and persons likely to become a "public charge," barred from entering the country. For the first century of the republic, virtually the only white persons in the entire world ineligible to claim American citizenship were those unwilling to renounce hereditary titles of nobility, as required in an act of 1795. And yet, the word "white" in the Naturalization Act excluded a large majority of the world's population from emigrating to the "asylum for mankind" and partaking in the blessings of American freedom. For eighty years, no non-white immigrant could become a naturalized citizen. Africans were allowed to do so in 1870, but not until the 1940s did persons of Asian origin become eligible. Some individual Native men gained U.S. citizenship, but Native Americans as a group were not granted American citizenship until 1924. Full citizenship rights were only gradually extended to women of any race.

This portrait from around 1825 depicts Euphemia Toussaint, the New York–born niece of Pierre Toussaint, a slave who had been brought to the city by his owner from the French colony Saint Domingue (modern-day Haiti) around 1787. Toussaint gained his freedom in 1807 and renamed himself in honor of the leader of the Haitian Revolution of the 1790s. He became a successful hairdresser and contributor to various charities in the city. Born in 1815, Euphemia died at the age of fourteen.

Jefferson, Slavery, and Race

Man's liberty, John Locke had written, flowed from "his having reason." To deny liberty to those who were not considered rational beings did not seem to be a contradiction. White Americans increasingly viewed Blacks as permanently deficient in the qualities that made freedom possible—namely, the capacity for self-control, reason, and devotion to the larger community. These were the characteristics that Jefferson, in a famous pseudoscientific comparison of the races in his book **Notes on the State of Virginia**, published in 1785, claimed Blacks lacked. Jefferson hypothesized that the Blacks "are inferior to the whites in the endowments both of body and mind." As much as Jefferson claimed to want to believe in the possibility of equality, he nonetheless saw African Americans as permanently inferior and incapable of republican citizenship.

Benjamin Banneker, a free African American from Maryland who had taught himself the principles of mathematics, sent Jefferson a copy of an astronomical almanac he had published, along with a plea for the abolition of slavery. Jefferson replied, "Nobody wishes more than I do to see such proofs as you exhibit, that nature has given to our black brethren, talents equal to the other colors of men." To his friend Joel Barlow, however, Jefferson suggested that a white person must have helped Banneker with his calculations. Jefferson believed he had reached his conclusions about race through neutral observations, yet in fact his prejudices blinded him to Banneker's evidence and arguments.

"Nothing is more certainly written in the book of fate," wrote Jefferson, "than that these people are to be free." Yet he felt that America should have a homogeneous citizenry with common experiences, values, and inborn abilities. Black Americans, Jefferson affirmed, should eventually enjoy the natural rights enumerated in the Declaration of Independence, but in Africa or the Caribbean, not in the United States—an idea that came to be known as "colonization." He foresaw Indians merging with whites and ceasing to be Indians, but he expressed horror at the idea of sex or marriage between Blacks and whites. Unlike Indians, Blacks, he believed, were unfit for economic independence and political self-government. Freeing the slaves without removing them from the country would endanger the nation's freedom.

Yet Jefferson himself had children with a woman he enslaved, Sally Hemings, the half-sister of his wife. Although in his will Jefferson freed her and their children, he continued to believe that people of African descent were inferior to himself and he freed no other slaves. When he died in 1826, Jefferson owed so much money that most of his more than 200 slaves were sold at auction. Some slaveholding men of Jefferson's generation did hope that Blacks could become part of the American nation. Edward Coles, an early governor of Illinois, brought his slaves from Virginia, freed them, and settled them on farms. Washington, who died in 1799, provided in his will that his 277 slaves would become free after the death of his wife, Martha. (Feeling uncomfortable living among men and women who looked forward to her death, she emancipated them the following year.) But too few slaveholders acted, and slavery continued to grow.

Principles of Freedom

Even as the decline of apprenticeship and indentured servitude narrowed the gradations of freedom among the white population, the Revolution widened the divide between free Americans and those who remained in slavery. Race, one among many kinds of legal and social inequality in colonial America, now emerged as a convenient justification for the existence of slavery in a land that claimed to be committed to freedom. Blacks' "natural faculties," Alexander

Hamilton noted in 1779, were "probably as good as ours." But the existence of slavery, he added, "makes us fancy many things that are founded neither in reason nor experience."

"We the people" increasingly meant only white Americans. "Principles of freedom, which embrace only half mankind, are only half systems," declared the anonymous author of a Fourth of July speech in Hartford, Connecticut, in 1800. "Declaration of Independence," he wondered, "where art thou now?" The answer came from a Richmond newspaper: "Tell us not of principles. Those principles have been annihilated by the existence of slavery among us."

CHAPTER REVIEW

REVIEW QUESTIONS

1. *How did the limited central government created by the Articles of Confederation reflect the issues behind the Revolution and fears for individual liberties?*

2. *What were the ideas and motivations that pushed Americans to expand west?*

3. *How did the United States pursue a policy of assimilation, and how did Native peoples respond?*

4. *What events and ideas led to the belief in 1786 and 1787 that the Articles of Confederation were not working well?*

5. *The Constitution has been described as a "bundle of compromises." Which compromises were the most significant in shaping the direction of the new nation and why?*

6. *What were the major arguments in support of the Constitution given by the Federalists?*

7. *What were the major arguments against the Constitution put forth by the Anti-Federalists?*

8. *How did the Constitution address the status of American slavery?*

9. *How did the Constitution address the question of who is an American citizen?*

10. *How did the idea of citizenship change in the first half of the nineteenth century?*

KEY TERMS

Articles of Confederation (p. 252)

Ordinance of 1784 (p. 254)

Ordinance of 1785 (p. 254)

Northwest Ordinance of 1787 (p. 256)

empire of liberty (p. 256)

Shays's Rebellion (p. 259)

Go to 🐰 INQUIZITIVE

To see what you know—and learn what you've missed—with personalized feedback along the way.

CHAPTER 8

SECURING THE REPUBLIC

1791–1815

FOCUS QUESTIONS

- *What issues made the politics of the 1790s so divisive?*
- *How did competing views of freedom and global events promote the political divisions of the 1790s?*
- *What were the achievements and failures of Jefferson's presidency?*
- *What were the causes and significant results of the War of 1812?*

O n April 30, 1789, in New York City, the nation's temporary capital, George Washington became the first president under the new Constitution. All sixty-nine electors had awarded him their votes. Dressed in a plain suit of "superfine American broad cloth" rather than European finery, Washington took the oath of office on the balcony of Federal Hall before a large crowd that reacted with "loud and repeated shouts" of approval. He then retreated inside to deliver his inaugural address before members of Congress and other dignitaries.

Washington's speech expressed the revolutionary generation's conviction that it had embarked on an experiment of enormous historical importance, whose outcome was by no means certain. "The preservation of the sacred fire of liberty and the destiny of the republican model of government," Washington proclaimed, depended on the success of the American experiment in self-government. Most Americans seemed to agree that freedom was the special genius of American institutions. In a resolution congratulating Washington on his inauguration, the House of Representatives observed that he had been chosen by "the freest people on the face of the earth." When the time came to issue the nation's first coins, Congress directed that they bear the image not of the head of state (as would be the case in a monarchy) but "an impression emblematic of liberty," with the word itself prominently displayed.

American leaders believed that the success of the new government depended, above all, on maintaining political harmony. They were especially anxious to avoid the emergence of organized political parties, which had already appeared in several states. Parties were considered divisive and disloyal. "They serve to organize faction," Washington would later declare, and to substitute the aims of "a small but artful" minority for the "will of the nation." The Constitution makes no mention of political parties, and the original method of electing the president assumes that candidates will run as individuals, not on a party ticket (otherwise, the second-place finisher would not have become vice president). Nonetheless, national political parties quickly arose. Originating in Congress, they soon spread to the general populace. Instead of harmony, the 1790s became, in the words of one historian, an "age of passion," with each party questioning the loyalty of the other and lambasting its opponent in the most extreme terms. Political rhetoric became inflamed because the stakes seemed so high—nothing less than the legacy of the Revolution, the new nation's future, and the survival of American freedom.

POLITICS IN AN AGE OF PASSION

President Washington provided a much-needed symbol of national unity. Having retired to private life after the War of Independence (despite some army officers' suggestion that he set himself up as a dictator), he was a model of self-sacrificing republican virtue. His vice president, John Adams, was widely respected as one of the main leaders in the drive for independence. Washington brought into his cabinet some of the new nation's most prominent political leaders, including Thomas Jefferson as secretary of state and Alexander Hamilton to head the Treasury Department. He also appointed a Supreme Court of six members, headed by John Jay of New York. But harmonious government proved short-lived.

Hamilton's Program

Political divisions first surfaced over the financial plan developed by Hamilton in 1790 and 1791. His immediate aims were to establish the nation's financial stability, bring to the government's support the country's most powerful financial interests, and encourage economic development. His long-term goal was to make the United States a major commercial and military power. Hamilton's model was Great Britain. The goal of national greatness, he believed, could never be realized if the government suffered from the same weaknesses as under the Articles of Confederation.

Hamilton's program had five parts. The first step was to establish the new nation's creditworthiness—that is, to create conditions under which persons would loan money to the government by purchasing its bonds, confident that they would be repaid. Hamilton proposed that the federal government assume responsibility for paying off at its full face value the national debt inherited from the War of Independence, as well as outstanding debts of the states. Second, he called for the creation of a new national debt. The old debts would be replaced by new interest-bearing bonds issued to the government's creditors. This would give men of economic substance a stake in promoting the new nation's stability, since the stronger and more economically secure the federal government, the more likely it would be to pay its debts.

The third part of Hamilton's program called for the creation of a **Bank of the United States**, modeled on the Bank of England, to serve as the nation's main financial agent. A private corporation rather than a branch of the government, it would hold public funds, issue banknotes that would serve as currency, and make loans to the government when necessary, all the while returning a tidy profit to its stockholders. Fourth, to raise revenue, Hamilton proposed a tax on producers of whiskey. Finally, in a Report on Manufactures delivered to Congress in December 1791, Hamilton called for the imposition of a tariff (a tax on imported foreign goods) and government subsidies to encourage the development of factories that could manufacture products currently purchased from abroad. Privately, Hamilton promoted an unsuccessful effort to build an industrial city at present-day Paterson, New Jersey. He also proposed the creation of a national army to deal with uprisings like Shays's Rebellion.

The Emergence of Opposition

Hamilton's vision of a powerful commercial republic won strong support from American financiers, manufacturers, and merchants. But it alarmed those who believed the new nation's destiny lay in charting a different path of development. Hamilton's plans hinged on close ties with Britain, America's main trading partner. To James Madison and Thomas Jefferson, the future lay in westward expansion, not connections with Europe. They had little desire to promote manufacturing or urban growth or to see economic policy shaped in the interests of bankers and business leaders. Their goal was a republic of independent farmers marketing grain, tobacco, and other products freely to the entire world. Free trade, they believed, not a system of government favoritism through tariffs and subsidies, would promote American prosperity while fostering greater social equality. Jefferson and Madison quickly concluded that the greatest threat to American freedom lay in the alliance of a powerful central government with an emerging class of commercial capitalists, such as Hamilton appeared to envision.

To Jefferson, Hamilton's system "flowed from principles adverse to liberty, and was calculated to undermine and demolish the republic." Hamilton's plans for a standing army seemed to his critics a bold threat to freedom. The national bank and assumption of state debts, they feared, would introduce into American politics the same corruption that had undermined British liberty, and enrich those already wealthy at the expense of ordinary Americans. During the 1780s, speculators had bought up at great discounts (often only a few cents on the dollar) government bonds and paper notes that had been used to pay those who fought in the Revolution or supplied the army. Under Hamilton's plan, speculators would reap a windfall by being paid at face value while the original holders received nothing. Because transportation was so poor, moreover, many backcountry farmers were used to distilling their grain harvest into whiskey, which could then be carried more easily to market. Hamilton's whiskey tax seemed to single them out unfairly in order to enrich bondholders.

The Jefferson–Hamilton Bargain

At first, opposition to Hamilton's program arose almost entirely from the South, the region that had the least interest in manufacturing development and the least diversified economy. It also had fewer holders of federal bonds than the Middle States and New England. (Virginia had pretty much paid off its war debt; it did not see why it should be taxed to benefit states like Massachusetts that had failed to do so.) Hamilton insisted that all his plans were authorized by the Constitution's ambiguous clause empowering Congress to enact laws for the "general welfare." As a result, many southerners who had supported the new Constitution now became "strict constructionists," who insisted that the federal government could only exercise powers specifically listed in the document. Jefferson, for example, believed the new national bank unconstitutional, since the right of Congress to create a bank was not mentioned in the Constitution.

Opposition in Congress threatened the enactment of Hamilton's plans. Behind-the-scenes negotiations followed. They culminated at a famous dinner in 1790 at which Jefferson brokered an agreement whereby southerners accepted Hamilton's fiscal program (with the exception of subsidies to manufacturers) in exchange for the establishment of the permanent national capital on the Potomac River between Maryland and Virginia.

Liberty and Washington, painted by an unknown artist around 1800, depicts a female figure of liberty placing a wreath on a bust of the first president. She carries an American flag and stands on a royal crown, which has been thrown to the ground. In the background is a liberty cap. Washington had died in 1799 and was now immortalized as a symbol of freedom, independence, and national pride.

Southerners hoped that the location would enhance their own power in the government while removing it from the influence of the northern financiers and merchants with whom Hamilton seemed to be allied. Major Pierre Charles L'Enfant, a French-born veteran of the War of Independence, designed a grandiose plan for the "federal city" modeled on the great urban centers of Europe, with wide boulevards, parks, and fountains. The job of surveying was done, in part, by Benjamin Banneker, the free African American scientist mentioned in the previous chapter. When it came to constructing public buildings in the nation's new capital, most of the labor was done by slaves.

The Impact of the French Revolution

In the 1790s, the French Revolution set Great Britain and France on the path to war. Yet British merchants, aware of the enthusiasm for revolutionary France in the United States, produced items for sale to Americans that celebrated the bonds between "the two great republics." This pitcher is adorned with the flags of the two countries and a liberty cap.

Political divisions began over Hamilton's fiscal program, but they deepened in response to events in Europe. When the French Revolution began in 1789, nearly all Americans welcomed it, inspired in part by the example of their own rebellion. John Marshall later recalled, "I sincerely believed human liberty to depend in a great measure on the success of the French Revolution." But in 1793, the Revolution took a more radical turn with the execution of King Louis XVI along with numerous aristocrats and other foes of the new government, and war broke out between France and Great Britain.

Events in France became a source of bitter conflict in America. Jefferson and his followers believed that despite its excesses the Revolution marked a historic victory for the idea of popular self-government, which must be defended at all costs. Enthusiasm for France inspired a rebirth of symbols of liberty. Liberty poles and caps reappeared on the streets of American towns and cities. To Washington, Hamilton, and their supporters, however, the Revolution raised the specter of anarchy. America, they believed, had no choice but to draw closer to Britain.

American leaders feared being divided into parties "swayed by rival European powers," in the words of John Quincy Adams. But the rivalry between Britain and France did much to shape early American politics. The "permanent" alliance between France and the United States, which dated to 1778, complicated the situation. No one advocated that the United States should become involved in the European war, and Washington in April 1793 issued a proclamation of American neutrality. But that spring the French Revolution's American admirers organized tumultuous welcomes for Edmond Genet, a French envoy seeking to arouse support for his beleaguered government. When Genet began commissioning American ships to attack British vessels under the French flag, the Washington administration asked for his recall. (Deeming the situation in France too dangerous, he decided to remain in America and married the daughter of George Clinton, the governor of New York.)

Meanwhile, the British seized hundreds of American ships trading with the French West Indies and resumed the hated practice of **impressment**—kidnapping sailors, including American citizens of British origin, to serve in their navy. Sent to London to present objections, while still serving as chief justice, John Jay negotiated an agreement in 1794 that produced the greatest public controversy of Washington's presidency. **Jay's Treaty** contained no British concessions on impressment or the rights of American shipping. Britain did agree to abandon outposts on the western frontier, which it was supposed to have done in 1783. In return, the United States guaranteed favored treatment to British imported goods. Critics of the administration charged that the treaty aligned the United States with monarchical Britain in its conflict with republican France. Ultimately, Jay's Treaty sharpened political divisions in the United States and led directly to the formation of an organized opposition party.

Political Parties

By the mid-1790s, two increasingly coherent parties had appeared in Congress, calling themselves **Federalists** and **Republicans**. (The latter had no connection with today's Republican Party, which was founded in the 1850s.) Both parties laid claim to the language of liberty, and each accused its opponent of engaging in a conspiracy to destroy it.

The Federalists, supporters of the Washington administration, favored Hamilton's economic program and close ties with Britain. Prosperous merchants, farmers, lawyers, and established political leaders (especially outside the South) tended to support the Federalists. Their outlook was generally elitist, reflecting the traditional eighteenth-century view of society as a fixed hierarchy and of public office as reserved for men of economic substance—the "rich, the able, and the well-born," as Hamilton put it. Freedom, Federalists insisted, did not mean the right to stand up in opposition to the government. Federalists feared that the "spirit of liberty" unleashed by the American Revolution was degenerating into anarchy and "licentiousness." When the New York Federalist leader Rufus King wrote an essay on the "words . . . with wrong meaning" that had "done great harm" to American society, his first example was "Liberty."

The Whiskey Rebellion

Hamilton's tax on whiskey became a clash over liberty. The **Whiskey Rebellion** of 1794 broke out when backcountry Pennsylvania farmers sought to block collection of the new tax on distilled spirits. The "rebels" invoked the symbols of 1776, displaying liberty poles and banners reading "Liberty or Death." "The citizens of the western country," one group wrote to the president, "consider [the tax] as repugnant to liberty, [and] an invasion of those privileges which the revolution bestowed upon them."

But Washington dispatched 13,000 militiamen to western Pennsylvania (a larger force than he had commanded during the Revolution). He accompanied them part of the way to the scene of the disturbances, the only time in American history that the president has actually commanded an army in the field. The "rebels" dispersed. His vigorous response, Washington wrote, was motivated in part by concern for "the impression" the restoration of public order "will make on others"—the "others" being Europeans who did not believe the American experiment in self-government could survive.

The Republican Party

Republicans, led by Madison and Jefferson, were more sympathetic to France than the Federalists and had more faith in democratic self-government. They drew their support from an unusual alliance of wealthy southern planters and ordinary farmers throughout the country. Enthusiasm for the French Revolution increasingly drew urban artisans into Republican ranks as well. Republicans preferred what a New Hampshire editor called the "boisterous sea of liberty" to the "calm of despotism." They were far more critical than the Federalists of social and economic inequality and more accepting of broad democratic participation as essential to freedom.

Each emerging party considered itself the representative of the nation and the other an illegitimate "faction." Federalists denounced Republicans as French agents, anarchists, and traitors. Republicans called their opponents monarchists intent on transforming the new national government into a corrupt, British-style aristocracy. Each charged the other with betraying the principles of the War of Independence and of American freedom. Washington himself received mounting abuse. When he left office, a Republican newspaper declared that his name had become synonymous with "political iniquity" and "legalized corruption."

An Expanding Public Sphere

The debates of the 1790s produced not only one of the most intense periods of partisan warfare in American history but also an enduring expansion of the public sphere, and with it the democratic content of American freedom. More and more citizens attended political meetings and became avid readers of pamphlets and newspapers. The establishment of nearly 1,000 post offices made possible the wider circulation of personal letters and printed materials. The era witnessed the rapid growth of the American press—the number of newspapers rose from around 100 to 260 during the 1790s and reached nearly 400 by 1810.

Hundreds of "obscure men" wrote pamphlets and newspaper essays and formed political organizations. The decade's democratic ferment was reflected in *The Key of Liberty* by William Manning, a self-educated Massachusetts farmer who had fought at the battle of Concord that began the War of Independence. Although not published until many years later, Manning's work, addressed to "friends to liberty and free government," reflected the era's popular political thought. The most important division in society, Manning declared, was between the "few" and the "many." He called for the latter to form a national political association to prevent the "few" from destroying "free government" and "tyrannizing over" the people.

The Democratic-Republican Societies

Inspired by the Jacobin clubs of Paris, supporters of the French Revolution and critics of the Washington administration in 1793 and 1794 formed nearly fifty **Democratic-Republican societies**. The Republican press publicized their meetings, replete with toasts to French and American liberty. The declaration of the Democratic Society of Addison County, Vermont, was typical: "That all men are naturally free, and possess equal rights. That all legitimate government originates in the voluntary social compact of the people."

Federalists saw the societies as another example of how liberty was getting out of hand. The government, not "self-created societies," declared the president, was the authentic voice of the American people. But the societies, "free inquiry" and "free communication" formed the first line of defense of "the unalienable rights of free men." Political liberty meant not simply voting at elections but constant involvement in public affairs. "We make no apology for thus associating ourselves," declared the Addison County society. "Political freedom" included the right to "exercise watchfulness and inspection, upon the conduct of public officers." Blamed by Federalists for helping to inspire the Whiskey Rebellion, the societies disappeared by the end of 1795. But much of their organization and outlook was absorbed into the emerging Republican Party. They helped to legitimize the right of "any portion of the people," regardless of station in life, to express political opinions and take an active role in public life.

The Republicans also gained support from immigrants from the British Isles, where war with France inspired a severe crackdown on dissent. Thomas Paine had returned to Britain in 1787. Five years later, after publishing *The Rights of Man*, a defense of the French Revolution and a stirring call for democratic change at home, he was forced to flee to France one step ahead of the law. But his writings inspired the emergence of a mass movement for political and social change, which British authorities brutally suppressed.

The Rights of Women

The democratic ferment of the 1790s inspired renewed discussion about women's rights. In 1792, Mary Wollstonecraft published in England her extraordinary pamphlet, *A Vindication of the Rights of Woman*. Inspired by Paine's *Rights of Man*, she asserted that the "rights of humanity" should not be "confined to the male line." Wollstonecraft did not directly challenge traditional gender roles. Her call for greater access to education and to paid employment for women rested on the idea that this would enable single women to support themselves and married women to perform more capably as wives and mothers. But she did "drop a hint," as she put it, that women "ought to have representation" in government. Within two years, American editions of Wollstonecraft's work had appeared, along with pamphlets defending and attacking her arguments. A short-lived women's rights magazine was published in 1795 in New York City. For generations, Wollstonecraft's writings would remain an inspiration to women seeking greater rights. "She is alive and active," the British novelist Virginia Woolf wrote in the 1920s, "she argues and experiments, we hear her voice and trace her influence even now among the living."

The expansion of the public sphere offered new opportunities to women. Increasing numbers began expressing their thoughts in print. Hannah Adams of Massachusetts became the first American woman to support herself as an author, publishing works on religious history and the history of New England. Other women took part in political discussions, read newspapers, and listened to orations, even though outside of New Jersey none could vote.

Judith Sargent Murray, one of the era's most accomplished American women, wrote essays for the *Massachusetts Magazine* under the pen name "The Gleaner." Murray's father, a prosperous Massachusetts merchant, had taken an enlightened view of his daughter's education. Although she could not attend college because of her sex, she studied alongside her brother with a tutor preparing the young man for admission to Harvard. In her essay "On the Equality of the Sexes," written in 1779 and published in 1790, Murray insisted that women had as much right as men to exercise all their talents and should be allowed equal educational opportunities to enable them to do so. Women's apparent mental inferiority to men, she insisted, simply reflected the fact that they had been denied "the opportunity of acquiring knowledge." "The idea of the incapability of women," she maintained, was "totally inadmissable in this enlightened age."

Women and the Republic

Were women part of the new body politic? Until after the Civil War, the word "male" did not appear in the Constitution. Women were counted fully in determining representation in Congress, and there was nothing explicitly limiting the rights outlined in the Constitution to men. A few contributors to the pamphlet debate on women's rights admitted that, according to the logic of democracy, women ought to have a voice in government. The Constitution's use of the word "he" to describe officeholders, however, reflected an assumption so widespread that it scarcely required explicit defense: politics was a realm for men. The women's rights debates of the 1790s did not include a broad assault on gender inequality. But like the activities of the Democratic-Republican societies, the discussion of women's status helped to popularize the language of rights in the new republic.

The men who wrote the Constitution did not envision the active and continuing involvement of ordinary citizens in affairs of state. But the rise of political parties seeking to mobilize voters in hotly contested elections, the emergence of the "self-created societies," the stirrings of women's political consciousness, and even armed uprisings like the Whiskey Rebellion broadened and deepened the democratization of public life set in motion by the American Revolution.

An engraving from *The Lady's Magazine and Repository of Entertaining Knowledge*, published in Philadelphia in 1792. A woman identified as the "Genius of the Ladies Magazine" kneels before Liberty, presenting a petition for the "Rights of Women." In the foreground are symbols of the arts, science, and literature—knowledge that should be available to women as well as men.

THE ADAMS PRESIDENCY

In 1792, Washington won unanimous reelection. Four years later, he decided to retire from public life, in part to establish the precedent that the presidency is not a life office. In his Farewell Address (mostly drafted by Hamilton and published in the newspapers rather than delivered orally), Washington defended his administration against criticism, warned against the party spirit, and advised his countrymen to steer clear of international power politics by avoiding "permanent alliances with any portion of the foreign world."

From JUDITH SARGENT MURRAY, "ON THE EQUALITY OF THE SEXES" (1790)

A prominent writer of plays, novels, and poetry, Judith Sargent Murray of Massachusetts was one of the first women to demand equal educational opportunities for women.

Is it upon mature consideration we adopt the idea, that nature is thus partial in her distributions? Is it indeed a fact, that she hath yielded to one half of the human species so unquestionable a mental superiority? I know that to both sexes elevated understandings, and the reverse, are common. But, suffer me to ask, in what the minds of females are so notoriously deficient, or unequal. . . .

Are we deficient in reason? We can only reason from what we know, and if an opportunity of acquiring knowledge hath been denied us, the inferiority of our sex cannot fairly be deduced from thence. . . . Will it be said that the judgment of a male of two years old, is more sage than that of a female's of the same age? I believe the reverse is generally observed to be true. But from that period what partiality! How is the one exalted, and the other depressed, by the contrary modes of education which are adopted! The one is taught to aspire, and the other is early confined and limited. As their years increase, the sister must be wholly domesticated, while the brother is led by the hand through all the flowery paths of science. Grant that their minds are by nature equal, yet who shall wonder at the *apparent* superiority. . . . At length arrived at womanhood, the uncultivated fair one feels a void, which the employments allotted her are by no means capable of filling. . . . She herself is most unhappy; she feels the want of a cultivated mind. . . . Should it . . . be vociferated, "Your domestic employments are sufficient"—I would calmly ask, is it reasonable, that a candidate for immortality, for the joys of heaven, an intelligent being, who is to spend an eternity in contemplating the works of Deity, should at present be so degraded, as to be allowed no other ideas, than those which are suggested by the mechanism of a pudding, or the sewing the seams of a garment? . . .

Yes, ye lordly, ye haughty sex, our souls are by nature *equal* to yours.

From ADDRESS OF THE DEMOCRATIC-REPUBLICAN SOCIETY OF PENNSYLVANIA (DECEMBER 18, 1794)

The creation of around fifty Democratic-Republican societies in 1793 and 1794 reflected the expansion of the public sphere. The Pennsylvania society issued an address defending itself against critics who questioned its right to criticize the administration of George Washington.

The principles and proceedings of our Association have lately been calumniated [tarred by malicious falsehoods]. We should think ourselves unworthy to be ranked as Freemen, if awed by the name of any man, however he may command the public gratitude for past services, we could suffer in silence so sacred a right, so important a principle, as the freedom of opinion to be infringed, by attack on Societies which stand on that constitutional basis.

Freedom of thought, and a free communication of opinions by speech through the medium of the press, are the safeguards of our Liberties. . . . By the freedom of opinion, cannot be meant the right of thinking merely; for of this right the greatest Tyrant cannot deprive his meanest slave; but, it is freedom in the communication of sentiments [by] speech or through the press. This liberty is an imprescriptable [unlimitable] right, independent of any Constitution or social compact; it is as complete a right as that which any man has to the enjoyment of his life. These principles are eternal—they are recognized by our Constitution; and that nation is already enslaved that does not acknowledge their truth. . . .

If freedom of opinion, in the sense we understand it, is the right of every Citizen, by what mode of reasoning can that right be denied to an assemblage of Citizens? . . . The Society are free to declare that they never were more strongly impressed with . . . the importance of associations . . . than at the present time. The germ of an odious Aristocracy is planted among us—it has taken root. . . . Let us remain firm in attachment to principles. . . . Let us be particularly watchful to preserve inviolate the freedom of opinion, assured that it is the most effectual weapon for the protection of our liberty.

QUESTIONS

1. *How does Murray answer the argument that offering education to women will lead them to neglect their "domestic employments"?*

2. *Why does the Democratic-Republican Society insist on the centrality of "free communication of opinions" in preserving American liberty?*

3. *How do these documents reflect expanding ideas about who should enjoy the freedom to express one's ideas in the early republic?*

The Election of 1796

George Washington's departure unleashed fierce party competition over the choice of his successor. In this, the first contested presidential election, two tickets presented themselves: John Adams, with Thomas Pinckney of South Carolina for vice president, representing the Federalists, and Thomas Jefferson, with Aaron Burr of New York, for the Republicans. In a majority of the sixteen states (Vermont, Kentucky, and Tennessee had been added to the original thirteen during Washington's presidency), the legislature chose presidential electors. But in the six states where the people voted for electors directly, intense campaigning took place. Adams received seventy-one electoral votes to Jefferson's sixty-eight. Because of factionalism among the Federalists, Pinckney received only fifty-nine votes, so Jefferson, the leader of the opposition party, became vice president. Voting fell almost entirely along sectional lines: Adams carried New England, New York, and New Jersey, while Jefferson swept the South, along with Pennsylvania.

In 1797, John Adams assumed leadership of a divided nation. Brilliant but austere, stubborn, and self-important, he was disliked even by those who honored his long career of service to the cause of independence. His presidency was beset by crises.

On the international front, the country was nearly dragged into the ongoing European war. As a neutral nation, the United States claimed the right to trade nonmilitary goods with both Britain and France, but both countries seized American ships with impunity. In 1797, American diplomats were sent to Paris to negotiate a treaty to replace the old alliance of 1778. French officials presented them with a demand for bribes before negotiations could proceed. When Adams made public the envoys' dispatches, the French officials were designated by the last three letters of the alphabet. This **XYZ affair** poisoned America's relations with its former ally. By 1798, the United States and France were engaged in a "quasi-war" at sea, with French ships seizing American vessels in the Caribbean and a newly enlarged American navy harassing the French. In effect, the United States had become a military ally of Great Britain. But despite pressure from Hamilton, who desired a declaration of war, Adams in 1800 negotiated peace with France.

Adams was less cautious in domestic affairs. Unrest continued in many rural areas. In 1799, farmers in southeastern Pennsylvania obstructed the assessment of a tax on land and houses that Congress had imposed to help fund an expanded army and navy. A crowd led by John Fries, a local militia leader and auctioneer, released arrested men from prison. No shots were fired in what came to be called Fries's Rebellion, but Adams dispatched units of the federal army to the area. The army arrested Fries for treason and proceeded to terrorize his supporters, tear down liberty poles, and whip Republican newspaper editors. Adams pardoned Fries in 1800, but the area, which had supported his election in 1796, never again voted Federalist.

The "Reign of Witches"

But the greatest crisis of the Adams administration arose over the **Alien and Sedition Acts** of 1798. Confronted with mounting opposition, some of it voiced by immigrant pamphleteers and editors, Federalists moved to silence their critics. A new Naturalization Act extended from five to fourteen years the residency requirement for immigrants seeking American citizenship. The Alien Act allowed the deportation of persons from abroad deemed "dangerous" by federal authorities. The Sedition Act (which was set to expire in 1801, by which time Adams hoped to have been reelected) authorized the prosecution of virtually any public assembly or publication critical of the government. While more lenient than many such measures in Europe (it did not authorize legal action before publication and allowed for trials by jury), the new law meant that opposition editors could be prosecuted for almost any political comment they printed. The main target was the Republican press, seen by Federalists as a group of upstart workingmen (most editors had started out as printers) whose persistent criticism of the administration fomented popular rebelliousness and endangered "genuine liberty."

The passage of these measures launched what Jefferson—recalling events in Salem, Massachusetts, a century earlier—termed a "reign of witches." Eighteen individuals, including several Republican newspaper editors, were charged under the Sedition Act. Ten were convicted for spreading "false, scandalous, and malicious" information about the government. Matthew Lyon, a member of Congress from Vermont and editor of a Republican newspaper, *The Scourge of Aristocracy*, received a sentence of four months in prison and a fine of $1,000. (Lyon had been the first former printer and most likely the first former indentured servant elected to Congress.) In Massachusetts, authorities indicted several men for erecting a liberty pole bearing the inscription "No Stamp Act, no Sedition, no Alien Bill, no Land Tax; Downfall to the Tyrants of America."

The Virginia and Kentucky Resolutions

The Alien and Sedition Acts failed to silence the Republican press. Some newspapers ceased publication, but new ones, with names like *Sun of Liberty* and *Tree of Liberty*, entered the field. The Sedition Act thrust freedom of expression to the center of discussions of American liberty. Madison and Jefferson mobilized opposition, drafting resolutions adopted by the Virginia and Kentucky legislatures. The **Virginia and Kentucky resolutions** attacked the Sedition Act as an unconstitutional violation of the First Amendment. Virginia's, written by Madison, called on the federal courts to protect free speech. The original version of Jefferson's Kentucky resolution went further, asserting that states could nullify laws of Congress that violated the Constitution—that is, states could unilaterally prevent the enforcement of such laws within their borders. The legislature prudently deleted this passage. The resolutions were directed against assaults on freedom of expression by the federal government, not the states. Jefferson took care to insist that the states "fully possessed" the authority to punish "seditious" speech, even if the national government did not. Indeed, state-level prosecutions of newspapers for seditious libel did not end when the Sedition Act expired in 1801.

No other state endorsed the Virginia and Kentucky resolutions. Many Americans, including many Republicans, were horrified by the idea of state action that might endanger the Union. But the "crisis of freedom" of the late 1790s strongly reinforced the idea that "freedom of discussion" was an indispensable attribute of American liberty and of democratic government. Free speech, as Massachusetts Federalist Harrison Gray Otis noted, had become the people's "darling privilege." The broad revulsion against the Alien and Sedition Acts contributed greatly to Jefferson's election as president in 1800.

The "Revolution of 1800"

"Jefferson and Liberty" became the watchword of the Republican campaign. By this time, Republicans had developed effective techniques for mobilizing voters, such as printing pamphlets, handbills, and newspapers and holding mass meetings to promote their cause. The Federalists, who viewed politics as an activity for a small group of elite men, found it difficult to match their opponents' mobilization. Nonetheless, they still dominated New England and enjoyed considerable support in the Middle Atlantic states. Jefferson triumphed, with seventy-three electoral votes to Adams's sixty-five.

Before assuming office, Jefferson was forced to weather an unusual constitutional crisis. Each party arranged to have an elector throw away one of his two votes for president, so that its presidential candidate would come out a vote ahead of the vice presidential. But the designated Republican elector failed to do so. As a result, both Jefferson and his running mate, Aaron Burr, received seventy-three electoral votes. With no candidate having a majority, the election was thrown into the House of Representatives that had been elected in 1798, where the Federalists enjoyed a slight majority. For thirty-five ballots, neither man received a majority of the votes. Finally, Hamilton intervened. He disliked Jefferson but believed him enough of a statesman to recognize that the Federalist financial system could not be dismantled. Burr, he warned, was obsessed with power, "an embryo Caesar."

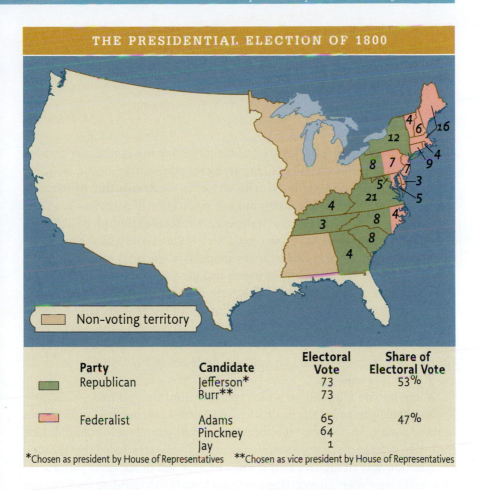

THE PRESIDENTIAL ELECTION OF 1800

Non-voting territory

Party	Candidate	Electoral Vote	Share of Electoral Vote
Republican	Jefferson*	73	53%
	Burr**	73	
Federalist	Adams	65	47%
	Pinckney	64	
	Jay	1	

*Chosen as president by House of Representatives   **Chosen as vice president by House of Representatives

Hamilton's support for Jefferson tipped the balance. To avoid a repetition of the crisis, Congress and the states soon adopted the Twelfth Amendment to the Constitution, requiring electors to cast separate votes for president and vice president. The election of 1800 also set in motion a chain of events that culminated four years later when Burr killed Hamilton in a duel. Burr appears to have subsequently engaged in a plot to form a new nation in the West from land detached from the United States and the Spanish empire. Acquitted of treason in 1807, he went into exile in Europe, eventually returning to New York, where he practiced law until his death in 1836.

The events of the 1790s demonstrated that a majority of Americans believed ordinary people had a right to play an active role in politics, express their opinions freely, and contest the policies of their government. His party, wrote Samuel Goodrich, a prominent Connecticut Federalist, was overthrown because democracy had become "the watchword of popular liberty." To their credit, Federalists never considered resistance to the election result. Adams's acceptance of defeat established the vital precedent of a peaceful transfer of power from a defeated party to its successor.

Slavery and Politics

Lurking behind the political battles of the 1790s lay the potentially divisive issue of slavery. Jefferson, after all, received every one of the South's forty-one electoral votes. He always referred to his victory as the **Revolution of 1800** and saw it not simply as a party success but as a vindication of American freedom, securing for posterity the fruits of independence. Yet the triumph of "Jefferson and Liberty" would not have been possible without slavery. Had three-fifths of the slaves not been counted in apportionment of electoral votes among the states, John Adams would have been reelected in 1800.

The issue of slavery would not disappear. The very first Congress under the new Constitution received petitions calling for emancipation. One bore the weighty signature of Benjamin Franklin, who in 1787 had agreed to serve as president of the Pennsylvania Abolition Society. The blessings of liberty, Franklin's petition insisted, should be available "without distinction of color to all descriptions of people."

A long debate followed, in which speakers from Georgia and South Carolina vigorously defended the institution and warned that behind northern criticism of slavery they heard "the trumpets of civil war." Madison found their forthright defense of slavery an embarrassment. But he concluded that the slavery question was so divisive that it must be kept out of national politics. He opposed Congress's even receiving a petition from North Carolina slaves on the grounds that they were not part of the American people and had "no claim" on the lawmakers' "attention." In 1793, to implement the Constitution's fugitive slave clause, Congress enacted a law providing for local officials to facilitate the return of escaped slaves.

The Haitian Revolution

Events during the 1790s underscored how powerfully slavery defined and distorted American freedom. The same Jeffersonians who hailed the French Revolution as a step in the universal progress of liberty reacted in horror against the slave revolution that began in 1791 in Saint Domingue, the jewel of the French overseas empire situated not far from the southern coast of the United States. Toussaint L'Ouverture, who had been enslaved on a sugar plantation, forged the rebellious slaves into an army able to defeat British forces seeking to seize the island and then an expedition hoping to reestablish French authority. The slave uprising led to the establishment of Haiti as an independent nation in 1804.

Although much of the country was left in ruins by years of warfare, the **Haitian Revolution** affirmed the universality of the revolutionary era's creed of liberty. It inspired hopes for freedom among slaves in the United States. Throughout the nineteenth century, Black Americans would look to L'Ouverture as a hero and celebrate the winning of Haitian independence. During the 1820s, several thousand free African Americans emigrated to Haiti, whose government promised newcomers political rights and economic opportunity they did not enjoy in the United States.

Among white Americans, the response to the Haitian Revolution was different. Thousands of white refugees from Haiti poured into the United

Toussaint L'Ouverture, leader of the slave revolution in Saint Domingue (modern-day Haiti). Painted in 1800 as part of a series of portraits of French military leaders, it depicts him as a courageous general.

States, fleeing the upheaval. Many spread tales of the massacres of slaveowners and the burning of their plantations, which reinforced white Americans' fears of slave insurrection at home. To most whites, the rebellious slaves seemed not men and women seeking liberty in the tradition of 1776 but a danger to American institutions. The Adams administration, which hoped that American merchants could replace their French counterparts in the island's lucrative sugar trade, encouraged the independence of Black Haiti. When Jefferson became president, on the other hand, he sought to quarantine and destroy the hemisphere's second independent republic.

Gabriel's Rebellion

The momentous year of 1800 witnessed not only the "revolution" of Jefferson's election but also an attempted real one, a plot by slaves in Virginia itself to gain their freedom. It was organized by a Richmond blacksmith, Gabriel, and his brothers Solomon, also a blacksmith, and Martin, a preacher. The conspirators planned to march on the city, which had recently become the state capital, from surrounding plantations. They would kill some white inhabitants and hold the rest, including Governor James Monroe, hostage until their demand for the abolition of slavery was met. Gabriel hoped that "poor white people" would join the insurrection, and he ordered that Quakers and Methodists (many of whom were critics of slavery) and "French people" (whose country was engaged in the "quasi-war" with the United States described earlier) be spared. On the night when the slaves were to gather, a storm washed out the roads to Richmond. The plot was soon discovered and the leaders arrested. Twenty-six slaves, including Gabriel, were hanged and dozens more transported out of the state.

Blacks in 1800 made up half of Richmond's population. One-fifth were free. A Black community had emerged in the 1780s and 1790s, and the conspiracy was rooted in its institutions. Gabriel gathered recruits at Black Baptist churches, funerals, barbecues, and other gatherings. In cities like Richmond, many enslaved skilled craftsmen, including Gabriel himself, could read and write and hired themselves out to employers—that is, negotiated their own labor arrangements, with their owner receiving their "wages." Their relative autonomy helps account for enslaved artisans' prominent role in the conspiracy.

Gabriel's Rebellion was a product of its age. Gabriel himself had been born in 1776. Like other Virginians, the participants in the conspiracy spoke the language of liberty forged in the American Revolution and reinvigorated during the 1790s. The rebels even planned to carry a banner emblazoned with the slogan, reminiscent of Patrick Henry, "Death or Liberty." "We have as much right," one conspirator declared, "to fight for our liberty as any men." Another likened himself to George Washington, who had rebelled against established authority to "obtain the liberty of [his] countrymen."

If Gabriel's conspiracy demonstrated anything, commented the prominent Virginian St. George Tucker, it was that slaves possessed "the love of freedom" as fully as other men. Gabriel's words, he added, reflected "the advance of knowledge" among Virginia's slaves, including knowledge of the American language of liberty. When slaves escaped to join Lord Dunmore during the War of Independence, he wrote, "they sought freedom merely as a good; now they also claim it as a right." Tucker believed Virginians should emancipate their slaves and settle them outside of the state. The legislature, however, moved in the opposite direction. It tightened controls over the Black population—making it illegal for them to congregate on Sundays without white supervision—and severely restricted the possibility of masters voluntarily freeing their slaves. Any slave freed after 1806 was required to leave Virginia or be sold back into slavery. The door to manumission, thrown open during the American Revolution, had been slammed shut.

JEFFERSON IN POWER

The first president to begin his term in Washington, D.C., Jefferson assumed office on March 4, 1801. The city, with its unpaved streets, impoverished residents, and unfinished public buildings, scarcely resembled L'Enfant's grand plan. At one point, part of the roof of the Capitol collapsed, narrowly missing the vice president. The city's condition seemed to symbolize Jefferson's intention to reduce the importance of the national government in American life.

Jefferson's inaugural address was conciliatory toward his opponents. "Every difference of opinion," he declared, "is not a difference of principle. . . . We are all Republicans, we are all Federalists." He went on to expound the policies his administration would follow—economy in government, unrestricted trade, freedom of religion and the press, friendship to all nations but "entangling alliances" with none. America, "the world's best hope," would flourish if a limited government allowed its citizens to be "free to regulate their own pursuits."

Jefferson hoped to dismantle as much of the Federalist system as possible. Among his first acts as president was to pardon all those imprisoned under the Sedition Act. During his eight years as president, he reduced the number of government employees and slashed the army and navy. He abolished all taxes except the tariff, including the hated tax on whiskey, and paid off part of the national debt. He aimed to minimize federal power and eliminate government oversight of the economy. His policies ensured that the United States would not become a centralized state on a European model, as Hamilton had envisioned.

Judicial Review

Nonetheless, as Hamilton predicted, it proved impossible to uproot national authority entirely. Jefferson distrusted the unelected judiciary and always believed in the primacy of local self-government. But during his presidency, and for many years thereafter, Federalist John Marshall headed the Supreme Court. Marshall had served John Adams as secretary of state and was appointed by the president to the Court shortly before Jefferson took office. A strong believer in national supremacy, Marshall established the Court's power to review laws of Congress and the states.

The first landmark decision of the Marshall Court came in 1803, in the case of *Marbury v. Madison*. On the eve of leaving office, Adams had appointed a number of justices of the peace for the District of Columbia. Madison, Jefferson's secretary of state, refused to issue commissions (the official documents entitling them to assume their posts) to these "midnight judges." Four, including William Marbury, sued for their offices. Marshall's decision declared unconstitutional the section of the Judiciary Act of 1789 that allowed the courts to order executive officials to deliver judges' commissions. It exceeded the power of Congress as outlined in the Constitution and was therefore void. Marbury, in other words, may have been entitled to his commission, but the Court had no power under the Constitution to order Madison to deliver it. On the immediate issue, therefore, the administration got its way. But the cost, as Jefferson saw it, was high. The Supreme Court had assumed the right to determine whether an act of Congress violates the Constitution—a power known as "judicial review."

Seven years later, in *Fletcher v. Peck*, the Court extended judicial review to state laws. In 1794, four land companies had paid nearly every member of the state legislature, Georgia's two U.S. senators, and a number of federal judges to secure their right to purchase land in present-day Alabama and Mississippi claimed by Georgia. They then sold the land to individual buyers at a large profit. Two years later, many of the corrupt lawmakers were defeated for reelection and the new legislature rescinded the land grant and subsequent sales. Whatever the circumstances of the legislature's initial action, Marshall declared, the Constitution forbade Georgia from taking any action that impaired a contract. Therefore, the individual purchasers could keep their land and the legislature could not repeal the original grant.

The Louisiana Purchase

But the greatest irony of Jefferson's presidency involved his greatest achievement, the **Louisiana Purchase**. This resulted not from astute American diplomacy but because the rebelling slaves of Saint Domingue (Haiti) defeated forces sent by the ruler of France, Napoleon Bonaparte, to reconquer the island. Moreover, to take advantage of the sudden opportunity to purchase Louisiana, Jefferson had to abandon his conviction that the federal government was limited to powers specifically mentioned in the Constitution, since the document said nothing about buying territory from a foreign power.

This vast Louisiana Territory, which stretched from the Gulf of Mexico to Canada and from the Mississippi River to the Rocky Mountains, had been ceded by France to Spain in 1762 as part of the reshuffling of colonial possessions at the end of the Seven Years' War. France secretly reacquired it in 1800. Soon after taking office, Jefferson learned of the arrangement. He had long been concerned about American access to the port of New Orleans, which lay within Louisiana at the mouth of the Mississippi River. He dispatched envoys to France offering to purchase the city.

Needing money for military campaigns in Europe and with his dreams of American empire in ruins because of his inability to reestablish control over Saint Domingue, Napoleon offered to sell the entire Louisiana Territory. The cost, $15 million (the equivalent of perhaps $250 million in today's money), made the Louisiana Purchase one of history's greatest real-estate bargains.

The Louisiana Purchase of 1803 doubled the land area of the United States.

In a stroke, Jefferson had doubled the size of the United States and ended the French presence in North America. Federalists were appalled. "We are to give money, of which we have too little," one declared, "for land, of which we already have too much." Jefferson admitted that he had "done an act beyond the Constitution." But he believed the benefits justified his transgression. Farmers, Jefferson had written, were "the chosen people of God," and the country would remain "virtuous" as long as it was "chiefly agricultural." Madison, in *Federalist* no. 10, had explained that the large size of the republic made self-government possible. Now, Jefferson believed, he had ensured the agrarian character of the United States and its political stability for centuries to come.

In reality, neither the French nor Spanish had settled the vast majority of the land exchanged in the Louisiana Purchase. It remained the homelands of tens of thousands of Native Americans and dozens of Native nations. Powerful peoples like the Mandans, Pawnees, Wichitas, Comanches, Osages, and others had curbed European expansion into the heart of the continent for nearly three centuries. Jefferson's goals for Louisiana assumed these Native peoples would surrender their lands and sovereignty.

Lewis and Clark

Within a year of the purchase, Jefferson dispatched an expedition led by Meriwether Lewis and William Clark, two Virginia-born veterans of Indian wars in the Ohio Valley, to explore the new territory. Their objectives were scientific, commercial, and diplomatic. They were to study the area's plants, animal life, and geography, to discover how the region could be exploited economically, and to open relations between the United States and the Native nations of the West. As Jefferson told Lewis, "It will now be proper you should inform those through whose country you will pass . . . that henceforth we become their fathers and friends." Jefferson hoped the **Lewis and Clark expedition** would establish trading relations with western Indians and locate a water route to the Pacific Ocean—an updated version of the old dream of a Northwest Passage that could facilitate commerce with Asia.

In the spring of 1804, Lewis and Clark's fifty-member "corps of discovery" set out from St. Louis on the most famous exploring party in American history. They spent the winter in the area of present-day North Dakota and then resumed their journey in April 1805. They were now accompanied by a fifteen-year-old Shoshone woman, Sacajawea, the wife of a French fur trader, who served as their guide and interpreter. After crossing the Rocky Mountains, the expedition reached the Pacific Ocean in the area of present-day Oregon (which lay beyond the nation's new boundaries) in November 1805. They returned in 1806, bringing with them an immense amount of information about the region as well as numerous plant and animal specimens. Reports about geography, plant and animal life, and Native peoples filled their daily journals. Although Lewis and Clark failed to find a commercial route to Asia, they demonstrated the possibility of overland travel to the Pacific coast.

Indians in the trans-Mississippi West were accustomed to dealing with European traders and were already connected to global markets. People all along the journey, including Otoes, Shohones, Mandans, Blackfeet, Chinooks, Lakotas, Hidatsas, and Arikaras, gladly agreed to American trade and alliance. But they rejected Americans' claim that their nations were now part of the United States. As a delegation of Osage and other diplomats who traveled to Washington to meet with President Jefferson in 1806 put it, "We are powerful and strong, and we know how to fight," although "we do not wish to fight" and prefer "peace and amity."

Incorporating Louisiana

The only part of the Louisiana Purchase with a significant non-Indian population in 1803 was the region around New Orleans. When the United States took control, the city had around 8,000 inhabitants, including nearly 3,000 slaves and 1,300 free persons of color. Incorporating this diverse population into the United States was by no means easy. French and Spanish law accorded free Blacks, many of whom were the offspring of unions between white military officers and enslaved women, nearly all the rights of white citizens. Slaves in Louisiana, as in Florida and Texas under Spanish rule, had legal rights unknown in the United States. Enslaved men and women had the right to purchase their freedom, if they could raise the money, and slaveholders had the right to manumit their slaves. Enslaved women had the right to go to court for protection against cruelty or rape by their owners.

The treaty that transferred Louisiana to the United States promised that all free inhabitants would enjoy "the rights, advantages, and immunities of citizens." Spanish and French civil codes, unlike British and American law, recognized women as co-owners of family property. Under American rule, Louisiana retained this principle of "community property" within marriage. But free Blacks suffered a steady decline in status. And the local legislature soon adopted one of the most sweeping slave codes in the South, forbidding Blacks to "ever consider themselves the equal of whites" and limiting the practice of manumission and access to the courts. Louisiana's enslaved and free Blacks had enjoyed more freedom under the rule of supposedly tyrannical Spain than as part of the liberty-hailing United States.

The Barbary Wars

Among other things, the Louisiana Purchase demonstrated that despite its vaunted isolation from the Old World, the United States continued to be deeply affected by events throughout the Atlantic world. At a time when Americans still relied on British markets to purchase their farm produce and British suppliers for imported manufactured goods, European wars directly influenced the livelihood of American farmers, merchants, and artisans. Jefferson hoped to avoid foreign entanglements, but he found it impossible as president to avoid being drawn into the continuing wars of Europe. Even as he sought to limit the power of the national government, foreign relations compelled him to expand it. The first war fought by the United States was to protect American commerce in a dangerous world.

Only a few months after taking office, Jefferson employed the very navy whose expansion by John Adams he had strongly criticized. The Barbary states on the northern coast of Africa had long preyed on shipping in the Mediterranean and Atlantic, receiving tribute from several countries, including the United States, to protect their vessels. Between 1785 and 1796, pirates captured thirteen American ships and held more than 100 sailors as "slaves," paralyzing American trade with the Mediterranean. The federal government paid hundreds of thousands of dollars in ransom and agreed to annual sums to purchase peace. In 1801, Jefferson refused demands for increased payments, and the pasha of Tripoli, in modern-day Libya, declared war on the United States. The naval conflict lasted until 1804, when an American squadron won a victory at Tripoli Harbor (a victory commemorated in the official hymn of the Marine Corps, which mentions fighting on "the shores of Tripoli"). The treaty ending the war guaranteed the freedom of American commerce, but Tripoli soon resumed harassing American ships. Only after the War of 1812 and one final American show of force did Barbary interference with American shipping end.

The **Barbary Wars** were the new nation's first encounter with the Islamic world. In the 1790s, as part of an attempt to establish peaceful relations, the federal government declared that the United States was "not, in any sense, founded on the Christian religion." But the conflicts helped to establish a long-lasting pattern in which many Americans viewed Muslims as an exotic people whose way of life did not adhere to Western standards.

The Embargo

Far more serious in its impact on the United States was warfare between Britain and France, which resumed in 1803 after a brief lull. According to international law, neutral nations had a right to trade nonmilitary goods with countries at

O-Grab-Me, or, the American Snapping-Turtle, a cartoon criticizing Jefferson's Embargo (spelled backward as o-grab-me), which banned all American shipping to foreign ports.

war. By 1806, however, each combatant had declared the other under blockade, seeking to deny trade with America to its rival. Engaged in a life-and-death struggle with Napoleon, Britain needed thousands of new sailors each year. The Royal Navy resumed the practice of impressment. By the end of 1807, it had seized more than 6,000 American sailors (claiming they were British citizens and deserters), including men from the U.S. warship *Chesapeake*, which the British frigate *Leopard* bombarded in American waters off the coast of Maryland.

To Jefferson, the economic health of the United States required freedom of trade with which no foreign government had a right to interfere. American farmers needed access to markets in Europe and the Caribbean. As colonial patriots had done in the 1760s and 1770s, he decided to use trade as a weapon. In December 1807, he persuaded Congress to enact the **Embargo Act**, a ban on all American vessels sailing for foreign ports. For a believer in limited government, this was an amazing exercise of federal power.

Enforcement of the Embargo brought back memories of Britain's Intolerable Acts of 1774, with the navy sealing off ports and seizing goods without warrants and the army arresting accused smugglers. Jefferson hoped it would lead Europeans to stop their interference with American shipping and also reduce the occasion for impressment. In 1808, American exports plummeted by 80 percent. Unfortunately, neither Britain nor France took much notice. But the Embargo devastated the economies of American port cities. Just before his term ended, in March 1809, Jefferson signed the Non-Intercourse Act, banning trade only with Britain and France but providing that if either side rescinded its edicts against American shipping, commerce with that country would resume.

Madison and Pressure for War

Jefferson left office at the lowest point of his career. He had won a sweeping reelection in 1804, receiving 162 electoral votes to only 14 for the Federalist candidate, Charles C. Pinckney. With the exception of Connecticut, he even carried the Federalist stronghold of New England. Four years later, his handpicked successor, James Madison, also won an easy victory. The Embargo, however, failed to achieve its diplomatic aims and was increasingly violated by American shippers and resented by persons whose livelihoods depended on trade. In 1810, Madison adopted a new policy. Congress allowed trade to resume but provided that if either France or Britain ceased interfering with American rights, the president could reimpose an embargo on the other. With little to lose, since Britain controlled the seas, the French emperor Napoleon announced that he had repealed his decrees against neutral shipping. But the British continued to attack American vessels and, with their navy hard-pressed for manpower, stepped up the impressment of American sailors. In the spring of 1812, Madison reimposed the embargo on trade with Britain.

Meanwhile, a group of younger congressmen, mostly from the West, were calling for war with Britain. Known as the War Hawks, this new generation of political leaders had come of age after the winning of independence and were ardent nationalists. Their leaders included Henry Clay of Kentucky, elected Speaker of the House of Representatives in 1810, and John C. Calhoun of South Carolina. The War Hawks spoke passionately of defending the national honor against British insults, but they also had more practical goals in mind, notably the annexation of Canada. Many southern War Hawks also pressed for the conquest of Florida, a haven for fugitive slaves owned by Britain's ally Spain. Members of Congress also spoke of the necessity of upholding the principle of free trade and liberating the United States once and for all from European infringements on its independence. Unimpeded access to overseas markets was essential if the agrarian republic were to prosper.

THE "SECOND WAR OF INDEPENDENCE"

The growing crisis between the United States and Britain took place against the background of deteriorating Indian relations in the West, which also helped propel the United States down the road to war. Jefferson had long favored the removal of Native Americans beyond the Mississippi River. The Louisiana Purchase made this policy more feasible. "The acquisition of Louisiana," he wrote, "will, it is hoped, put in our power the means of inducing all the Indians on this side [of the Mississippi River] to transplant themselves to the other side." Jefferson enthusiastically pursued efforts to purchase Indian lands between the Appalachian Mountains and the Mississippi. He encouraged traders to lend money to Indians, in the hope that accumulating debt would force them to sell some of their holdings, thus freeing up more land for "our increasing numbers." At the same time, the government continued President Washington's assimilationist "civilization policy," which advised Native Americans to give up most of their land and their independence. Jefferson told Native Americans that they had to choose between retaining individual small farms in the east, surrounded by white American farms, or surrendering their homelands to leave for an unknown future west of the Mississippi.

Native Nations and Continued Freedom

By 1800, nearly 400,000 American settlers lived west of the Appalachian Mountains. They now outnumbered Indians east of the Mississippi River. Under pressure, Native leaders envisioned different ways of sharing the continent with the United States. Many worked on new economic strategies to replace the declining deerskin trade as well as political changes to centralize nations that previously had been more loosely affiliated towns and bands. Shawnee Chief Black Hoof, a veteran of earlier wars against the United States who reluctantly signed the Treaty of Greenville, led economic changes designed to allow the Shawnees to remain independent on their reduced lands. Shawnees started raising cattle and selling meat, butter, and cheese and growing cash crops. They built a blacksmith forge, a gristmill, and a sawmill. They leased out tribal land, thereby embedding their land title—their legal claim to its ownership—in the kind of paper-

War Party at Fort Douglas, a watercolor by the Swiss-born Canadian artist Peter Rindisbacher. Painted in 1823, it depicts an incident during the War of 1812 when Indian allies of Great Britain fired rifles into the air to greet their commander, Captain Andrew Bulger, pictured on the far right.

work that they hoped would hold up in U.S. courts. Black Hoof used the annuity that the United States paid every year for land ceded in the 1795 Treaty of Greenville to finance these developments.

Like Black Hoof, Cherokee leaders also encouraged economic development to preserve and promote their nation. With the decline of hunting, Cherokee men raised livestock, operated ferries and taverns, and built mills and cotton gins. A few, such as Major Ridge and John Ross, established plantations like those of their wealthy white neighbors, buying enslaved Black men and women to grow cotton and exporting it to textile factories in the northern United States and in England. Cherokees began to centralize power in a national legislature and, eventually, a national court system.

Other Native Americans looked for spiritual answers to explain and respond to the U.S. threat. Prophets including Handsome Lake of the Senecas, who had overcome an addiction to alcohol, preached that Indians must refrain from fighting, gambling, drinking, and sexual promiscuity. Handsome Lake advised the Senecas and other Haudenosaunee to focus on rebuilding their Great League and preserve their sovereignty and land through diplomacy rather than military conflict.

Tenskwatawa and Tecumseh

A more militant message was expounded by two Shawnee brothers, **Tecumseh and Tenskwatawa**. In 1805, Tenskwatawa had a vision in which the Master of Life promised, "If you Indians will do everything I tell you I will turn over

From TECUMSEH, SPEECH TO THE OSAGE (1810)

While some Native Americans claimed rights as Americans and others worked for the independence of their specific Native nation, the Shawnee brothers Tenskwatawa and Tecumseh asserted a pan-Indian identity, insisting that all Native Americans shared a common set of values and a common future of freedom and autonomy rather than assimilation or removal. Tecumseh traveled widely to rally Indians to unite as one people. This speech, to Osage Indians, was recorded by John P. Hunter, who had been held captive by the Osage since childhood.

Brothers—We all belong to one family; we are all children of the Great Spirit; we walk in the same path; slake our thirst at the same spring; and now affairs of the greatest concern lead us to smoke the pipe around the same council fire!

Brothers—we are friends; we must assist each other to bear our burdens. The blood of many of our fathers and brothers has run like water on the ground, to satisfy the avarice of the white men. We, ourselves, are threatened with a great evil; nothing will pacify them but the destruction of all the red men.

Brothers—The white men are not friends to the Indians: at first, they only asked for land sufficient for a wigwam; now, nothing will satisfy them but the whole of our hunting grounds, from the rising to the setting sun. . . .

Brothers—My people are brave and numerous; but the white people are too strong for them alone. I wish you to take up the tomahawk with them. If we all unite, we will cause the rivers to stain the great waters with their blood.

Brothers—if you do not unite with us, they will first destroy us, and then you will fall an easy prey to them. They have destroyed many nations of red men because they were not united. . . . They wish to make us enemies, that they may sweep over and desolate our hunting grounds, like devastating winds, or rushing waters.

Brothers—Our Great Father over the great waters [the king of England] is angry with the white people, our enemies. He will send his brave warriors against them; he will send us rifles, and whatever else we want—he is our friend, and we are his children.

Brothers—We must be united; we must smoke the same pipe; we must fight each other's battles; and more than all, we must love the Great Spirit; he is for us; he will destroy our enemies, and make his red children happy.

QUESTIONS

1. *How does Tecumseh's understanding of national identity compare with that of most white Americans of his era? How does it compare with Pontiac's vision in the mid-eighteenth century?*

2. *Why does he claim that the king of England is the Indians' ally, and what does this suggest about his attitudes toward white people?*

the land so that the white people are covered and you alone shall possess the land." Like previous prophets, Tenskwatawa told Indians to give up alcohol and goods manufactured in Europe, to practice monogamy, and not to fight one another. But Tenskwatawa's prophesy went further. Indians should get rid of not only European influences but also their separate political identities and religious practices and renounce their national leaders. They should stop being Shawnees or Delawares and become united Indians. Persuaded by his older brother's prophesies, Tecumseh traveled to Native towns all across the middle of the continent to recruit converts to the movement, a revival of Neolin's and Pontiac's pan-Indian alliance of the 1760s (discussed in Chapter 4). The alternative to unified resistance was extermination, he argued. "Where today are the Pequot?" he asked. "Where are the Narragansett, the Mohican, the Pocanet, and other powerful tribes of our people? They have vanished before the avarice [greed] and oppression of the white man, as snow before the summer sun." Indians, he proclaimed, must recognize that they were a single people and unite in claiming "a common and equal right in the land." He repudiated chiefs like Black Hoof who had once fought the United States but now had sold land to the federal government: "Sell a country! Why not sell the air, the great sea, as well as the earth? Did not the Great Spirit make them all for the use of his children?" In 1810, Tecumseh called for attacks on American frontier settlements. In November 1811, while he was recruiting among the Muscogees and other southern Native nations, American forces under William Henry Harrison destroyed Prophetstown in the Battle of Tippecanoe. But Tenskwatawa, Tecumseh, and their followers regrouped and prepared for a war that they hoped would expel the United States once and for all.

The War of 1812

In 1795, James Madison had written that war is the greatest enemy of "true liberty." "War," he explained, "is the parent of armies; from these proceed debts and taxes, and armies, and debts, and taxes are the known instruments for bringing the many under the domination of the few." Nonetheless, Madison became a war president. Reports that the British were encouraging Tecumseh's efforts contributed to the coming of the **War of 1812**. In June 1812, with assaults on American shipping continuing, Madison asked Congress for a declaration of war. American nationality, the president declared, was at stake—would Americans remain "an independent people" or become "colonists and vassals" of Great Britain? The vote revealed a deeply divided country. Both Federalists and Republicans representing the states from New Jersey northward, where most of the mercantile and financial resources of the country were concentrated, voted against war. The South and West were strongly in favor. The bill passed the House by a vote of 79–49 and the Senate by 19–13. It was the first time the United States declared war on another country, and was approved by the smallest margin of any declaration of war in American history.

In retrospect, it seems remarkably foolhardy for a disunited and militarily unprepared nation to go to war with one of the world's two major powers. And with the expiration in 1811 of the charter of the Bank of the United States and the refusal of northern merchants and bankers to loan money, the federal government found it increasingly difficult to finance the war. Before the conflict ended, it was essentially bankrupt. Fortunately for the United States, Great Britain at the outset was preoccupied with the struggle in Europe. But it easily repelled two feeble American invasions of Canada and imposed a blockade that all but destroyed American commerce. In 1814, having finally defeated Napoleon, Britain invaded the United States. Its forces seized Washington, D.C., and burned the Capitol and the White House, while the government fled for safety.

Americans did enjoy a few military successes. In August 1812, the American frigate *Constitution* defeated the British warship *Guerriere*. Commodore Oliver H. Perry defeated a British naval force in September 1813 on Lake Erie (a startling result considering that Britain prided itself on having the world's most powerful navy—although the Americans outgunned them on the Great Lakes). In the following year, a British assault on Baltimore was repulsed when **Fort McHenry** at the entrance to the harbor withstood a British bombardment. This was the occasion when Francis Scott Key composed "The Star-Spangled Banner," an ode to the "land of the free and home of the brave" that became the national anthem during the 1930s.

The bombardment of Fort McHenry in Baltimore harbor in September 1814 was of minor military importance, but it is remembered as the inspiration for Francis Scott Key's poem, "The Star-Spangled Banner."

Like the War of Independence, the War of 1812 was a two-front struggle—against the British and against Native forces allied with Britain. In 1813, pan-Indian forces led by Tecumseh (who had been commissioned a general in the British army) were defeated, and he himself was killed, at the Battle of the Thames, near Detroit, by an American force led by William Henry Harrison. In the South, the Muscogees descended into civil war. On one side were the Red Sticks, a militant religious movement that supported Tenskwatawa and Tecumseh and fought against the United States. On the other side were Muscogees who thought the Red Sticks were an even greater threat. In March 1814, anti–Red Stick Muscogees joined Cherokees and an army of Americans under the command of Andrew Jackson to defeat the Red Sticks at the Battle of Horseshoe Bend in Alabama, killing more than 800 of them. Despite the alliance between Jackson's forces and the anti-Red Stick Muscogees, he forced all of them to cede more than half their land, more than 23 million acres in all, to the federal government.

Jackson then proceeded to New Orleans, where he engineered the war's greatest American victory, fighting off a British invasion in January 1815. Although a slaveholder, Jackson recruited the city's free men of color into his forces, appealing to them as "sons of freedom" and promising them the same pay and land bounties as white recruits. Jackson and Harrison would ride their reputations as military heroes all the way to the White House. Colonel Richard M. Johnson, who claimed to have actually killed Tecumseh, would later be elected vice president.

With neither side wishing to continue the conflict, the United States and Britain signed the Treaty of Ghent, ending the war. Although the treaty was signed in December 1814, ships carrying news of the agreement did not reach America until after the **Battle of New Orleans** had been fought. The treaty restored the previous status quo. No territory exchanged hands, nor did any provisions relate to impressment or neutral shipping rights. The United States agreed to return to Indians "all the possessions, rights, and privileges which they may have enjoyed or been entitled to" before the war began. Considering that the war had not been a military success for the United States, the Treaty of Ghent was about as good an outcome as the United States could expect.

As in the War of Independence, thousands of slaves found freedom by escaping to British forces during the War of 1812. The peace treaty specified that they must be returned, but the British refused to hand them over to their former owners. After five years of inconclusive negotiations, both countries agreed to international arbitration of the dispute—by one of the world's leading despots, Czar Nicholas I of Russia. He ruled in favor of the United States, and Britain paid a few million dollars in compensation. The freed slaves themselves mostly settled in Nova Scotia, Canada.

The War's Aftermath

A number of contemporaries called the War of 1812 the Second War of Independence. Despite widespread opposition to the conflict, it confirmed the ability of a republican government to conduct a war without surrendering its institutions. Jackson's victory at New Orleans not only made him a national hero but also became a celebrated example of the ability of a republic to defeat the forces of despotic Europe.

Moreover, despite the Treaty of Ghent, in the postwar years the United States would establish control over the vast region between the Appalachians and the Mississippi River. White settlers poured into Indiana, Michigan, Alabama, and Mississippi, bringing with them their distinctive forms of social organization. "I have no doubt," Jackson wrote to his wife, "but in a few years the banks of the Alabama [River] will present a beautiful view of elegant mansions and extensive rich and productive farms." He did not mention that those mansions would be built and the farms worked by slaves.

The War of 1812 and the Canadian Borderland

Like the American Revolution, the War of 1812 had a profound impact along the border between the United States and Canada, further solidifying it as a dividing line. Much of the fighting took place on this porous border in the long-contested region near Detroit and on the Great Lakes. A great deal of trade had developed between Vermont and Quebec, and across the lakes, which became a flourishing smuggling business during Jefferson's Embargo. When war broke out, Canadians began to see American traders as spies. The unsuccessful American attacks on Canada during the war (some led by Irish immigrants resentful at British rule over their country of birth) strengthened anti-Americanism even among Canadians not connected to revolutionary-era Loyalists. To be sure, as in so many borderland regions, many people had family ties on both sides and the exchange of goods and ideas continued after the war ended. But far more Americans now turned their sights toward the western frontier rather than Canada. For both Canadians and Americans, the war reaffirmed a sense of national identity, and both came to see the conflict as a struggle for freedom—for the United States, freedom from dependence on Great Britain; for Canada, freedom from domination by the United States.

Britain's defeat of Napoleon inaugurated a long period of peace in Europe. With diplomatic affairs playing less and less of a role in American public life, Americans' sense of separateness from the Old World grew ever stronger. The war also strengthened a growing sense of nationalism in Canada, based in part on separateness from the United States. As in 1775, Canadians did not rise up to welcome an army from the south, but instead repelled the invading American

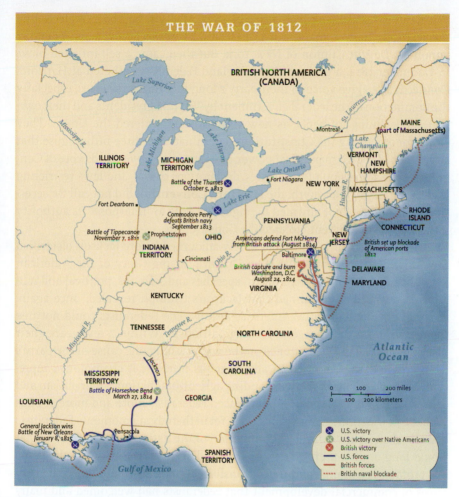

THE WAR OF 1812

BRITISH NORTH AMERICA (CANADA)

Lake Superior

MAINE
(part of Massachusetts)

Montreal

St. Lawrence R.

Lake Champlain

VERMONT

ILLINOIS TERRITORY

MICHIGAN TERRITORY

Lake Michigan

Lake Huron

NEW HAMPSHIRE

Battle of the Thames
October 5, 1813

Fort Niagara

NEW YORK

MASSACHUSETTS

Hudson R.

Fort Dearborn

Commodore Perry defeats British navy
September 1813

Lake Erie

RHODE ISLAND

CONNECTICUT

Battle of Tippecanoe
November 7, 1811

Prophetstown

OHIO

PENNSYLVANIA

Americans defend Fort McHenry from British attack (August 1814)

NEW JERSEY

British set up blockade of American ports 1812

INDIANA TERRITORY

Cincinnati

Ohio R.

Baltimore

British capture and burn Washington, D.C.
August 24, 1814

DELAWARE

MARYLAND

VIRGINIA

KENTUCKY

TENNESSEE

Tennessee R.

NORTH CAROLINA

Atlantic Ocean

Mississippi R.

Jackson

SOUTH CAROLINA

MISSISSIPPI TERRITORY

Battle of Horseshoe Bend
March 27, 1814

GEORGIA

LOUISIANA

General Jackson wins Battle of New Orleans
January 8, 1815

Pensacola

SPANISH TERRITORY

Gulf of Mexico

0   100   200 miles
0   100   200 kilometers

Legend:
- ⊗ U.S. victory
- ⊗ U.S. victory over Native Americans
- ⊗ British victory
- — U.S. forces
- — British forces
- ····· British naval blockade

Although the British burned the nation's capital, the War of 1812 essentially was a military draw.

forces, to the puzzlement of Americans who could not understand why they did not wish to become part of the empire of liberty. Each side developed stereotypes of the other that resonate to this day: Americans saw Canadians as monarchical, European, and lacking in an understanding of liberty; Canadians viewed Americans as a people unusually prone to violence.

The End of the Federalist Party

Jefferson and Madison succeeded in one major political aim—the elimination of the Federalist Party. At first, the war led to a revival of Federalist fortunes.

With antiwar sentiment at its peak in 1812, Madison had been reelected by the relatively narrow margin of 128 electoral votes to 89 over his Federalist opponent, DeWitt Clinton of New York. But then came a self-inflicted blow. In December 1814, a group of New England Federalists gathered at Hartford, Connecticut, to give voice to their party's long-standing grievances, especially the domination of the federal government by Virginia presidents and their own region's declining influence as new western states entered the Union. They called for amending the Constitution to eliminate the three-fifths clause that strengthened southern political power, and to require a two-thirds vote of Congress for the admission of new states, declarations of war, and laws restricting trade. Contrary to later myth, the **Hartford Convention** did not call for secession or disunion. But it affirmed the right of a state to "interpose" its authority if the federal government violated the Constitution.

The Hartford Convention had barely adjourned before Jackson electrified the nation with his victory at New Orleans. "Rising Glory of the American Republic," one newspaper exulted. In speeches and sermons, political and religious leaders alike proclaimed that Jackson's triumph revealed, once again, that a divine hand oversaw America's destiny. The Federalists could not free themselves from the charge of lacking patriotism. Within a few years, their party no longer existed. Its stance on the war was only one cause of the party's demise. The urban commercial and financial interests it championed represented a small minority in an expanding agricultural nation. Their elitism and distrust of popular self-government placed Federalists more and more at odds with the new nation's democratic ethos. Yet in their dying moments Federalists had raised an issue—southern domination of the national government—that would long outlive their political party. And the country stood on the verge of a profound economic and social transformation that strengthened the very forces of commercial development that Federalists had welcomed and many Republicans feared.

CHAPTER REVIEW

REVIEW QUESTIONS

1. *Identify the major parts of Hamilton's financial plan, who supported these proposals, and why they created such passionate opposition.*

2. *How did the French Revolution and ensuing global struggle between Great Britain and France shape early American politics?*

3. *How did the United States become involved in foreign affairs in this period?*

4. *How did the expansion of the public sphere and a new language of rights offer opportunities to women?*

5. *What caused the demise of the Federalists?*

6. *What impact did the Haitian Revolution have on the United States?*

7. *How did the Louisiana Purchase affect the situation of Native Americans in that region?*

8. *Whose status was changed the most by the War of 1812—that of Great Britain, the United States, or Native Americans?*

KEY TERMS

Bank of the United States (p. 289)

impressment (p. 293)

Jay's Treaty (p. 293)

Federalists and Republicans (p. 293)

Whiskey Rebellion (p. 293)

Democratic-Republican societies (p. 295)

Judith Sargent Murray (p. 296)

XYZ affair (p. 300)

Alien and Sedition Acts (p. 301)

Virginia and Kentucky resolutions (p. 301)

Revolution of 1800 (p. 304)

Haitian Revolution (p. 305)

Gabriel's Rebellion (p. 306)

Marbury v. Madison (p. 307)

Louisiana Purchase (p. 308)

Lewis and Clark expedition (p. 310)

Barbary Wars (p. 312)

Embargo Act (p. 313)

Tecumseh and Tenskwatawa (p. 315)

War of 1812 (p. 317)

Fort McHenry (p. 318)

Battle of New Orleans (p. 319)

Hartford Convention (p. 322)

Go to 🐰 INQUIZITIVE

To see what you know—and learn what you've missed—with personalized feedback along the way.

CHAPTER 9

THE MARKET REVOLUTION

1800–1840

FOCUS QUESTIONS

- *What were the main elements of the market revolution?*
- *What were the opportunities and costs of westward expansion?*
- *How did the market revolution spark social change?*
- *How did the meanings of American freedom change in this period?*
- *How did the market revolution affect the lives of workers, women, and African Americans?*

In 1824, the Marquis de Lafayette visited the United States. Nearly fifty years had passed since, as a youth of twenty, the French nobleman fought at Washington's side in the War of Independence. Now, his thirteen-month tour became a triumphant Jubilee of Liberty. Since 1784, when he last journeyed to the United States, the nation's population had tripled to nearly 12 million, its land area had more than doubled, and its political institutions had thrived. Lafayette's tour demonstrated how profoundly the nation had changed. The thirteen states of 1784 had grown to twenty-four, and he visited every one—a journey that would have been almost impossible forty years earlier. Lafayette traveled up the Mississippi and Ohio rivers by steamboat, a recent invention

This engraving celebrates General Lafayette's landing at Battery Park, New York City, for his 1824 visit to the United States. In the foreground is a steamboat, invented since the American Revolution. This and other images of Lafayette's visit were mounted on walls and printed on china plates, teapots, silverware, and playing cards to commemorate the French-American alliance and display American patriotism.

that was helping to bring economic development to the trans-Appalachian West, and crossed upstate New York via the Erie Canal, the world's longest man-made waterway, which linked the region around the Great Lakes with the Atlantic coast via the Hudson River.

Americans in the first half of the nineteenth century were fond of describing liberty as the defining quality of their new nation, the unique genius of its institutions. The poet Walt Whitman wrote of his countrymen's "deathless attachment to freedom." Likenesses of the goddess of liberty, a familiar figure in eighteenth-century British visual imagery, became even more common in the United States, appearing in paintings and sculpture and on folk art from weather vanes to quilts and tavern signs. Never, declared President Andrew Jackson in his farewell address in 1837, had any population "enjoyed so much freedom and happiness as the people of these United States." The celebration of freedom could be found in sermons, newspaper editorials, and political pronouncements in every region of the country. In *Democracy in America,* the French historian and politician Alexis de Tocqueville wrote of the "holy cult of freedom" he encountered on his own visit to the United States during the early 1830s.

Even as Lafayette, Tocqueville, and numerous other visitors from abroad toured the United States, however, Americans' understandings of freedom were changing. Three historical processes unleashed by the Revolution accelerated after the War of 1812: the spread of market relations, the westward movement of the population, and the rise of a vigorous political democracy. (The first two will be discussed in this chapter, the third in Chapter 10.) All powerfully affected the development of American society. They also helped to reshape the idea of freedom, identifying it ever more closely with economic opportunity, physical mobility, and participation in a vibrantly democratic political system.

But American freedom also continued to be shaped by the presence of slavery. Lafayette, who had purchased a plantation in the West Indies and freed its slaves, once wrote, "I would never have drawn my sword in the cause of America if I could have conceived that thereby I was founding a land of slavery." Yet slavery was moving westward with the young republic. The same steamboats and canals that enabled millions of farm families to send their goods to market also facilitated the growth of slave-based cotton plantations in the South. And slavery drew a strict racial boundary around American democracy, making voting, officeholding, and participation in the public sphere privileges for white men alone. In several southern cities, public notices warned "persons of color" to stay away from the ceremonies honoring Lafayette. Half a century after the winning of independence, the coexistence of liberty and slavery, and their simultaneous expansion, remained the central contradiction of American life.

A NEW ECONOMY

In the first half of the nineteenth century, an economic transformation known to historians as the market revolution swept over the United States. Its catalyst was a series of innovations in transportation and communication. American technology had hardly changed during the colonial era. No important alterations were made in sailing ships, no major canals were built, and manufacturing continued to be done by hand, with skills passed on from artisan to journeyman and apprentice. At the dawn of the nineteenth century, most roads were little more than rutted paths through the woods. Transporting goods thirty miles inland by road cost as much as shipping the same cargo from England. In 1800, it took fifty days to move goods from Cincinnati to New York City, via a flatboat ride down the Mississippi River to New Orleans and then a journey by sail along the Gulf and Atlantic coasts.

To be sure, the market revolution represented an acceleration of developments already under way in the colonial era. As noted in previous chapters, southern planters were selling the products of slave labor in the international market as early as the seventeenth century. By the eighteenth, many colonists had been drawn into Britain's commercial empire. Consumer goods like sugar and tea, and market-oriented tactics like the boycott of British goods, had been central to the political battles leading up to independence.

Nonetheless, as Americans moved across the Appalachian Mountains, and into interior regions of the states along the Atlantic coast, they found themselves more and more isolated from markets. In 1800, American farm families produced at home most of what they needed, from clothing to farm implements. What they could not make themselves, they obtained by bartering with their neighbors or purchasing from local stores and from rural craftsmen like blacksmiths and shoemakers. Those farmers not located near cities or navigable waterways found it almost impossible to market their produce.

The early life of Abraham Lincoln was typical of those who grew up in the pre-market world. Lincoln was born in Kentucky in 1809 and seven years later moved with his family to Indiana, where he lived until 1831. His father occasionally took pork down the Ohio and Mississippi rivers to market in New Orleans, and Lincoln himself at age nineteen traveled by flatboat to that city to sell the goods of a local merchant. But essentially, the Lincoln family was self-sufficient. They hunted game for much of their food and sewed most of their clothing at home. They relied little on cash; Lincoln's father sometimes sent young Abraham to work for neighbors as a way of settling debts. As an adult, however, Lincoln embraced the market revolution. In the Illinois legislature in the 1830s, he eagerly promoted the improvement of rivers to facilitate access to markets. As a lawyer, he eventually came to represent the Illinois Central Railroad, which opened large areas of Illinois to commercial farming.

Roads and Steamboats

In the first half of the nineteenth century, in rapid succession, the **steamboat**, canal, railroad, and telegraph wrenched America out of its economic past. These innovations opened new land to settlement, lowered transportation costs, and made it far easier for economic enterprises to sell their products. They linked farmers to national and world markets and made them major consumers of manufactured goods. Americans, wrote Tocqueville, had "annihilated space and time."

The first advance in overland transportation came through the construction of toll roads, or "turnpikes," by localities, states, and private companies. Between 1800 and 1830, the New England and Middle Atlantic states alone chartered more than 900 companies to build new roads. In 1806, Congress authorized the construction of the paved National Road from Cumberland, Maryland, to the Old Northwest. It reached Wheeling, on the Ohio River, in 1818 and by 1838 extended to Illinois, where it ended.

Because maintenance costs were higher than expected and many towns built "shunpikes"—short detours that enabled residents to avoid tollgates—most private toll roads never turned a profit. Even on the new roads, horse-drawn wagons remained an inefficient mode of getting goods to market, except over short distances. It was improved water transportation that most dramatically increased the speed and lowered the expense of commerce.

Robert Fulton, a Pennsylvania-born artist and engineer, had experimented with steamboat designs while living in France during the 1790s. He even launched a steamboat on the Seine River in Paris in 1803. But not until 1807, when Fulton's ship the *Clermont* navigated the Hudson River from New York City to Albany, was the steamboat's technological and commercial feasibility demonstrated. The invention made possible upstream commerce (that is, travel against the current) on the country's major rivers as well as rapid transport across the Great Lakes and, eventually, the Atlantic Ocean. By 1811, the first steamboat had been introduced on the Mississippi River; twenty years later some 200 plied its waters.

The Erie Canal

The completion in 1825 of the 363-mile **Erie Canal** across upstate New York (a remarkable feat of engineering at a time when America's next-largest canal was only twenty-eight miles long) allowed goods to flow between the Great Lakes and New York City. Almost instantaneously, the canal attracted an influx of farmers migrating from New England, giving birth to cities like Buffalo, Rochester, and Syracuse along its path. Its water, wrote the novelist Nathaniel Hawthorne after a trip on the canal, served as a miraculous "fertilizer," for "it causes towns with their masses of brick and stone, their churches and theaters, their business . . . to spring up."

New York governor DeWitt Clinton, who oversaw the construction of the state-financed canal, predicted that it would make New York City "the granary

THE MARKET REVOLUTION: ROADS AND CANALS, 1840

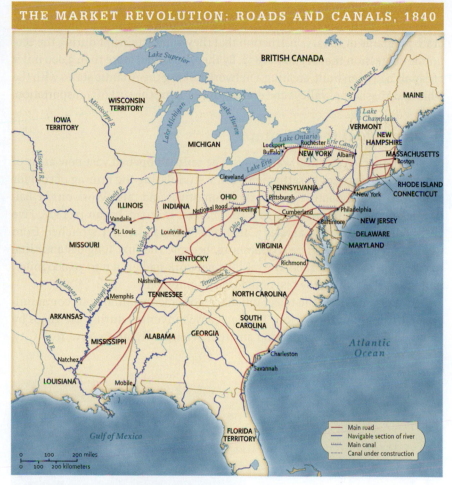

The improvement of existing roads and building of new roads and canals sharply reduced transportation times and costs and stimulated the growth of the market economy.

of the world, the emporium of commerce, the seat of manufactures, the focus of great moneyed operations." And, indeed, the canal gave New York City primacy over competing ports in access to trade with the Old Northwest. In its financing by the state government, the Erie Canal typified the developing transportation infrastructure. With the federal government generally under the control of political leaders hostile to federal funding for internal improvements, the burden fell on the states. Between 1787 and 1860, the federal government spent about $60 million building roads and canals and improving harbors; the states spent nearly ten times that sum.

A NEW ECONOMY ★ 329

The completion of the Erie Canal set off a scramble among other states to match New York's success. Several borrowed so much money to finance elaborate programs of canal construction that they went bankrupt during the economic depression that began in 1837. By then, however, more than 3,000 miles of canals had been built, creating a network linking the Atlantic states with the Ohio and Mississippi valleys and drastically reducing the cost of transportation.

Railroads and the Telegraph

Canals connected existing waterways. The railroad opened vast new areas of the American interior to settlement, while stimulating the mining of coal for fuel and the manufacture of iron for locomotives and rails. Work on the Baltimore and Ohio, the nation's first commercial railroad, began in 1828. Five years later, the South Carolina Canal and Railroad, which stretched from Charleston across the state to Hamburg, became the first long-distance line to begin operation. By 1860, the railroad network had grown to 30,000 miles, more than the total in the rest of the world combined.

At the same time, the telegraph made possible instantaneous communication throughout the nation. The device was invented during the 1830s by Samuel F. B. Morse, an artist and amateur scientist living in New York City,

An 1884 watercolor, *Locomotive DeWitt Clinton*, recalls the early days of rail travel. The train is driven by a steam-powered locomotive and the cars strongly resemble horse-drawn stagecoaches.

and was put into commercial operation in 1844. Using Morse code, messages could be sent over electric wires, with each letter and number represented by its own pattern of electrical pulses. Within sixteen years, some 50,000 miles of telegraph wire had been strung. Initially, the telegraph was a service for businesses, and especially newspapers, rather than individuals. It helped speed the flow of information and brought uniformity to prices throughout the country.

THE RISE OF THE WEST

Improvements in transportation and communication made possible the rise of the West as a powerful, self-conscious region of the new nation. Between 1790 and 1840, some 4.5 million people crossed the Appalachian Mountains—more than the entire U.S. population at the time of Washington's first inauguration. Most of this migration took place after the War of 1812, which unleashed a flood of land-hungry settlers moving from eastern states. In the six years following the end of the war in 1815, six new states entered the Union (Indiana, Illinois, Missouri, Alabama, Mississippi, and Maine—the last an eastern frontier for New England).

Few Americans moved west as lone pioneers. More frequently, people traveled in groups and, once they arrived in the West, cooperated with each other to clear land, build houses and barns, and establish communities. One stream of migration, including both small farmers and planters with their slaves, flowed out of the South to create the new Cotton Kingdom of Alabama, Mississippi, Louisiana, and Arkansas. Many farm families from the Upper South crossed into southern Ohio, Indiana, and Illinois. A third population stream moved from New England across New York to the Upper Northwest—northern Ohio, Indiana, and Illinois, and Michigan and Wisconsin.

Some western migrants became "squatters," setting up farms on land without a clear legal title. Those who purchased land acquired it either from the federal government, at the price, after 1820, of $1.25 per acre payable in cash, or from land speculators on long-term credit. By 1840, settlement had reached the Mississippi River and two large new regions—the Old Northwest and Old Southwest—had entered the Union. The West became the home of regional cultures very much like those the migrants had left behind. Upstate New York and the Upper Northwest resembled New England, with its small towns, churches, and schools, while the Lower South replicated the plantation-based society of the southern Atlantic states.

As population moved west, the nation's borders expanded. National boundaries made little difference to territorial expansion—in Florida, and later in Texas

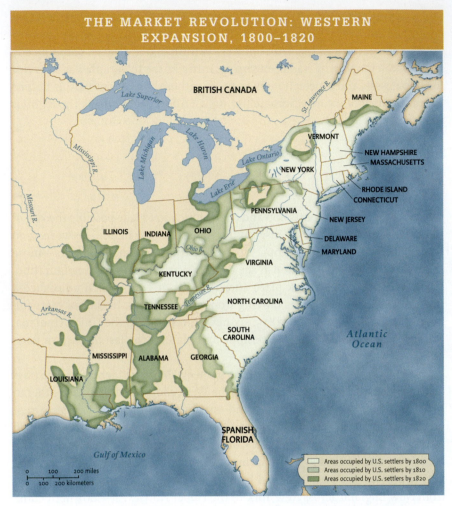

THE MARKET REVOLUTION: WESTERN EXPANSION, 1800–1820

BRITISH CANADA

MAINE

Lake Superior

Lake Michigan

Lake Huron

Lake Ontario

Lake Erie

VERMONT

NEW HAMPSHIRE
MASSACHUSETTS

NEW YORK

RHODE ISLAND
CONNECTICUT

PENNSYLVANIA

NEW JERSEY

DELAWARE

MARYLAND

Mississippi R.

Missouri R.

ILLINOIS

INDIANA

OHIO

Ohio R.

VIRGINIA

KENTUCKY

Arkansas R.

TENNESSEE

Tennessee R.

NORTH CAROLINA

SOUTH CAROLINA

Atlantic Ocean

MISSISSIPPI

ALABAMA

GEORGIA

LOUISIANA

SPANISH FLORIDA

Gulf of Mexico

0   100   200 miles
0 100 200 kilometers

☐ Areas occupied by U.S. settlers by 1800
☐ Areas occupied by U.S. settlers by 1810
■ Areas occupied by U.S. settlers by 1820

In the first two decades of the nineteenth century, the westward movement of the U.S. population brought settlers to and across the Mississippi River. Before canals—and later railroads—opened previously landlocked areas to commercial farming, settlement was concentrated near rivers.

and Oregon, American settlers rushed in to claim land under the jurisdiction of foreign countries (Spain, Mexico, and Britain) or Native nations, confident that American sovereignty would soon follow in their wake. Nor did the desire of local inhabitants to remain outside the American republic deter the nation's expansion. Florida, for example, fell into American hands despite the resistance of local Indians and Spain's rejection of American offers to buy the area. In 1810, American residents of West Florida rebelled and seized Baton Rouge, and the

United States soon annexed the area. The drive for the acquisition of East Florida was spurred by Georgia and Alabama planters who wished to eliminate a refuge for fugitive slaves and hostile Seminole Indians. Andrew Jackson led troops into the area in 1818. While on foreign soil, he created an international crisis by executing two British traders and a number of Indian chiefs. Although Jackson withdrew, Spain, aware that it could not defend the territory, sold it to the United States in the Adams-Onís Treaty of 1819 negotiated by John Quincy Adams.

Successive censuses told the remarkable story of western growth. In 1840, by which time the government had sold to settlers and land companies nearly 43 million acres of land, 7 million Americans—two-fifths of the total population—lived beyond the Appalachian Mountains. Between 1810 and 1830, Ohio's population grew from 231,000 to more than 900,000. It reached nearly 2 million in 1850, when it ranked third among all the states. The careers of the era's leading public figures reflected the westward movement. Andrew Jackson, Henry Clay, and many other statesmen had been born in states along the Atlantic coast but made their mark in politics after moving west.

An Internal Borderland

Because the Northwest Ordinance of 1787 prohibited slavery in the Old Northwest, the Ohio River came to mark a boundary between free and slave societies. But for many years it was easier for people and goods to travel between the slave state Kentucky and the southern counties of Ohio, Indiana, and Illinois than to the northern parts of those states. The region stretching northward from the Ohio River retained much of the cultural flavor of the Upper South. Its food, speech, settlement patterns, family ties, and economic relations had more in common with Kentucky and Tennessee than with the northern counties of their own states, soon to be settled by New Englanders. Until the 1850s, farmers in the southern counties of Ohio, Indiana, and Illinois were far more likely to ship their produce southward via the Ohio and Mississippi rivers than northward or to the East. The large concentration of people of southern ancestry would make Indiana and Illinois key political battlegrounds as the slavery controversy developed.

The Cotton Kingdom

Although the market revolution and westward expansion occurred simultaneously in the North and the South, their combined effects heightened the nation's sectional divisions. In some ways, the most dynamic feature of the American economy in the first thirty years of the nineteenth century was the rise of the **Cotton Kingdom**. The early industrial revolution, which began in England and soon

TABLE 9.1	Population Growth of Selected Western States, 1810–1850 (Excluding Indians)		
State	1810	1830	1850
Alabama	9,000	310,000	772,000
Illinois	12,000	157,000	851,000
Indiana	25,000	343,000	988,000
Louisiana	77,000	216,000	518,000
Mississippi	31,000	137,000	607,000
Missouri	20,000	140,000	682,000
Ohio	231,000	938,000	1,980,000

spread to parts of the North, centered on factories producing cotton textiles with water-powered spinning and weaving machinery. These factories generated an immense demand for cotton, a crop the Lower South was particularly suited to growing because of its climate and soil fertility. Until 1793, the marketing of cotton had been slowed by the laborious task of removing seeds from the plant itself. But in that year, Eli Whitney, a Yale graduate working in Georgia as a private tutor, invented the **cotton gin**. A fairly simple device consisting of rollers and brushes, the gin quickly separated the seed from the cotton fibers. It made possible the growing and selling of cotton on a large scale.

Coupled with rising demand for cotton and the opening of new lands in the West to settlement, Whitney's invention revolutionized American slavery. An institution that many Americans had expected to die out because its major crop, tobacco, exhausted the soil, now embarked on a period of unprecedented expansion. In the first decade of the nineteenth century, cotton plantations spread into the South Carolina upcountry (the region inland from the Atlantic coast previously dominated by small farms), a major reason why the state reopened the African slave trade between 1803 and 1808. After the War of 1812, the federal government moved to consolidate American control over the Lower South, forcing defeated Indians to cede land, encouraging white settlement, and acquiring Florida. With American sovereignty came the expansion of slavery. Settlers from the older southern states flooded into the region. Planters monopolized the most fertile land, while poorer farmers were generally confined to less productive and less accessible areas in the "hill country" and piney woods. After Congress prohibited the Atlantic slave trade in 1808, a massive trade in slaves developed within the United States, supplying the labor force required by the new Cotton Kingdom.

Unfree Westward Movement

Historians estimate that around 1 million enslaved men, women, and children were forced to move from the older states to the Lower South between 1800 and 1860. Some traveled with their owners to newly established plantations, but the

THE MARKET REVOLUTION: THE SPREAD OF COTTON CULTIVATION, 1820–1840

Maps of cotton production graphically illustrate the rise of the Cotton Kingdom stretching from Virginia to Louisiana.

majority were transported by slave traders to be sold at auction for work in the cotton fields. Slave trading became a well-organized business, with firms gathering slaves in Maryland, Virginia, and South Carolina and shipping them to markets in Mobile, Natchez, and New Orleans. Slave coffles—groups chained to one another on forced marches to the Lower South—became a common sight. A British visitor to the United States in the 1840s encountered what he called a "disgusting and hideous spectacle," a file of "about two hundred slaves, manacled and chained together," being marched from Virginia to Louisiana. A source of greater freedom for many whites, the westward movement meant to African Americans the destruction of family ties, the breakup of long-standing communities, and receding opportunities for liberty.

In 1793, when Whitney designed his invention, the United States produced 5 million pounds of cotton. By 1820, the crop had grown to nearly 170 million pounds. As the southern economy expanded westward, it was cotton produced on slave plantations that became the linchpin of southern development and by far the most important export of the empire of liberty.

MARKET SOCIETY

Since cotton was produced solely for sale in national and international markets, the South was in some ways the most commercially oriented region of the United States. Yet rather than spurring economic change, the South's expansion westward simply reproduced the agrarian, slave-based social order of the older states. The region remained overwhelmingly rural. In 1860, roughly 80 percent of southerners worked the land—the same proportion as in 1800. The South's transportation and banking systems remained adjuncts of the plantation economy, geared largely to transporting cotton and other staple crops to market and financing the purchase of land and slaves.

Commercial Farmers

In the North, however, the market revolution and westward expansion set in motion changes that transformed the region into an integrated economy of commercial farms and manufacturing cities. As in the case of Lincoln's family, the initial pioneer stage of settlement reinforced the farmer's self-sufficiency, for the tasks of felling trees, building cabins, breaking the soil, and feeding the family left little time for agriculture geared to the market. But as the Old Northwest became a more settled society, bound by a web of transportation and credit to eastern centers of commerce and banking, farmers found themselves drawn into the new market economy. They increasingly concentrated on growing crops and raising livestock for sale, while purchasing at stores goods previously produced at home.

Western farmers found in the growing cities of the East a market for their produce and a source of credit. Loans originating with eastern banks and insurance companies financed the acquisition of land and supplies and, in the 1840s and 1850s, the purchase of fertilizer and new agricultural machinery to expand production. The steel plow, invented by John Deere in 1837 and mass-produced by the 1850s, made possible the rapid subduing of the western prairies. The reaper, a horse-drawn machine that greatly increased the amount of wheat a farmer could harvest, was invented by Cyrus McCormick in 1831 and produced in large quantities soon afterward. Tens of thousands were in use on the eve of the Civil War. Between 1840 and 1860, America's output of wheat nearly tripled. Unlike cotton, however, the bulk of the crop was consumed within the country. Eastern farmers, unable to grow wheat and corn as cheaply as their western counterparts, increasingly concentrated on producing dairy products, fruits, and vegetables for nearby urban centers.

The Growth of Cities

From the beginning, cities formed part of the western frontier. Western cities like Cincinnati and St. Louis that stood at the crossroads of interregional trade experienced extraordinary growth. Cincinnati was known as **Porkopolis**, after its slaughterhouses, where hundreds of thousands of pigs were butchered each year and the meat then shipped to eastern consumers. The greatest of all the western cities was Chicago. In the early 1830s, it was a tiny settlement on the shore of Lake Michigan. By 1860, thanks to the railroad, Chicago had become the nation's fourth-largest city, where farm products from throughout the Northwest were gathered to be sent east.

Like rural areas, urban centers witnessed dramatic changes due to the market revolution. The number of cities with populations exceeding 5,000 rose from 12 in 1820 to nearly 150 three decades later, by which time the urban population numbered more than 6 million. Urban merchants, bankers, and master craftsmen took advantage of the economic opportunities created by the expanding market among commercial farmers. The drive among these businessmen to increase production and reduce labor costs fundamentally altered the nature of work. Traditionally, skilled artisans had manufactured goods at home, where they controlled the pace and intensity of their own labor. Now, entrepreneurs gathered artisans into large workshops in order to oversee their work and subdivide their tasks. Craftsmen who traditionally produced an entire pair of shoes or piece of furniture saw the labor process broken down into numerous steps requiring far less skill and training. They found themselves subjected to constant supervision by their employers and relentless pressure for greater output and lower wages.

The Factory System

In some industries, most notably textiles, the factory superseded traditional craft production altogether. Factories gathered large groups of workers under central supervision and replaced hand tools with power-driven machinery. Samuel Slater, an immigrant from England, established America's first factory

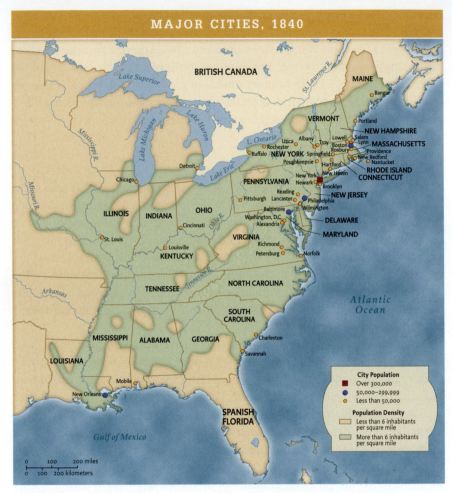

MAJOR CITIES, 1840

Although the United States was still predominantly agricultural, by 1840 major cities had arisen in the northern and northwestern states. The South lagged far behind in urban growth. Most cities were located on navigable waterways—either the Atlantic coast or inland rivers—or on rivers that provided water power for early factories.

in 1790 at Pawtucket, Rhode Island. Since British law made it illegal to export the plans for industrial machinery, Slater, a skilled mechanic, built from memory a power-driven spinning jenny, one of the key inventions of the early industrial revolution.

Spinning factories such as Slater's produced yarn, which was then sent to traditional hand-loom weavers and farm families to be woven into cloth. This "outwork" system, in which rural men and women earned money by taking in jobs from factories, typified early industrialization. Before shoe production was fully mechanized, for example, various parts of the shoe were produced in factories, then stitched together in nearby homes, and then returned to the factories for finishing. Eventually, however, the entire manufacturing process in textiles, shoes, and many other products was brought under a single factory roof.

The cutoff of British imports because of the Embargo of 1807 and the War of 1812 stimulated the establishment of the first large-scale American factory utilizing power looms for weaving cotton cloth. This was constructed in 1814 at Waltham, Massachusetts, by a group of merchants who came to be called the Boston Associates. In the 1820s, they expanded their enterprise by creating an entirely new factory town (incorporated as the city of Lowell in 1836) on the Merrimack River, twenty-seven miles from Boston. Here they built a group of modern textile factories that brought together all phases of production from the spinning of thread to the weaving and finishing of cloth. By 1850, Lowell's fifty-two mills employed more than 10,000 workers. Across New England, small industrial cities sprang up patterned on Waltham and Lowell. Massachusetts soon became the second most industrialized region of the world, after Great Britain.

The earliest factories, including those at Pawtucket, Waltham, and Lowell, were located along the "fall line," where waterfalls and river rapids could be harnessed to provide power for spinning and weaving machinery. By the 1840s, steam power made it possible for factory owners to locate in towns like New Bedford nearer to the coast and in large cities like Philadelphia and Chicago with their immense local markets. In 1850, manufacturers produced in factories not only textiles but also a wide variety of other goods, including tools, firearms, shoes, clocks, ironware, and agricultural machinery. What came to be called the **American system of manufactures** relied on the mass production of interchangeable parts that could be rapidly assembled into standardized finished products. This technique was first perfected in the manufacture of clocks by Eli Terry, a Connecticut craftsman, and in small-arms production by Eli Whitney, who had previously invented the cotton gin. More impressive, in a way, than factory production was the wide dispersion of mechanical skills throughout northern society. Every town, it seemed, had its sawmill, paper mill, ironworks, shoemaker, hatmaker, tailor, and a host of other such small enterprises.

The early industrial revolution was largely confined to New England and a few cities outside it. Lacking a strong internal market, and with its slaveholding class generally opposed to industrial development, the South lagged in factory production. And outside New England, most northern manufacturing was still done in small-scale establishments employing a handful of workers, not in factories. In Cincinnati, for example, most workers in 1850 still labored in small unmechanized workshops.

COTTON MILLS, 1820s

Lake Champlain

MAINE

NEW YORK

VERMONT

NEW HAMPSHIRE

Lake Ontario

Connecticut R.

Merrimack R.

Somersworth
Dover

Mohawk R.

Hudson R.

Lowell

MASSACHUSETTS

Waltham

Cumberland

Smithfield

Atlantic Ocean

Fall River

CONNECTICUT

Warwick

Susquehanna R.

Delaware R.

Paterson

RHODE ISLAND

PENNSYLVANIA

0   50   100 miles
0   50   100 kilometers

Delaware County

NEW JERSEY

• Towns with 50–499 cotton-mill employees
• Towns with 500–999 cotton-mill employees
• Towns with 1,000 or more cotton-mill employees

MARYLAND

DELAWARE

The early industrial revolution was concentrated in New England, where factories producing textiles from raw cotton sprang up along the region's many rivers, taking advantage of water power to drive their machinery.

The Industrial Worker

The market revolution helped to change Americans' conception of time itself. Farm life continued to be regulated by the rhythms of the seasons. But in cities, clocks became part of daily life, and work time and leisure time came to be clearly marked off from one another. In artisan workshops of the colonial and early national eras, bouts of intense work alternated with periods of leisure. Artisans would set down their tools to enjoy a drink at a tavern or attend a political discussion. As the market revolution accelerated, work in factories and workshops and even for servants in Americans' homes took place for a specified number of hours per day. In colonial America, an artisan's pay was known as his "price," since it was linked to the goods he produced. In the nineteenth century, pay increasingly became a "wage," paid according to an hourly or daily rate. The increasing reliance on railroads, which operated according to fixed schedules, also made Americans more conscious of arranging their lives according to "clock time."

Closely supervised work tending a machine for a period determined by a clock seemed to violate the independence Americans considered an essential element of freedom. Consequently, few native-born men could be attracted to work in the early factories. Employers turned instead to those who lacked other ways of earning a living.

The "Mill Girls"

Although some factories employed entire families, the early New England textile mills relied largely on female labor. At Lowell, the most famous center of early textile manufacturing, young unmarried women from Yankee farm families dominated the workforce that tended the spinning machines. To persuade parents to allow their daughters to leave home to work in the mills, Lowell owners set up boardinghouses with strict rules regulating personal behavior. They also established lecture halls and churches to occupy the women's free time.

The constant supervision of the workers' private lives seems impossibly restrictive from a modern point of view. But this was the first time in history that large numbers of women left their homes to participate in the public world. Many complained about low wages and long hours. Others valued the opportunity to earn money independently at a time when few other jobs were open to women. Home life, Lucy Larcom later recalled, was narrow and confining, while living and working at Lowell gave the **mill girls** a "larger, firmer idea of womanhood," teaching them "to go out of themselves and enter into the lives of others. . . . It was like a young man's pleasure in entering upon business for himself." But women like Larcom did not become a permanent class of factory workers. They typically remained in the factories for only a few years, after which they left to return home, marry, or move west. Larcom herself migrated to Illinois, where she became a teacher and writer. The shortage of industrial labor continued, easing only when large-scale immigration began in the 1840s and 1850s.

The Growth of Immigration

Economic expansion fueled a demand for labor, which was met, in part, by increased immigration from abroad. Between 1790 and 1830, immigrants contributed only marginally to American population growth. But between 1840 and 1860, over 4 million people (more than the entire population of 1790) entered the United States, the majority from Ireland and Germany. About 90 percent headed for the northern states, where job opportunities were most abundant and the new arrivals would not have to compete with slave labor. Immigrants were virtually unknown in the slave states, except in cities on the periphery of the South, such as New Orleans, St. Louis, and Baltimore. In the North, however, they became a visible presence in both urban and rural areas. In 1860, the 814,000 residents of New York City, the major port of entry, included more than 384,000 immigrants, and one-third of the population of Wisconsin was foreign-born.

Numerous factors inspired this massive flow of population across the Atlantic. In Europe, the modernization of agriculture and the industrial revolution disrupted centuries-old patterns of life, pushing peasants off the land and eliminating the jobs of traditional craft workers. The introduction of the oceangoing steamship and the railroad made long-distance travel more practical. The Cunard Line began regular sailings with inexpensive fares from Britain to Boston and New York City in the 1840s. Beginning around 1840, emigration from Europe accelerated, not only to the United States but to Canada and Australia as well. Frequently, a male family member emigrated first; he would later send back money for the rest of the family to follow.

Irish and German Newcomers

To everyone discontented in Europe, commented the *New York Times*, "thoughts come of the New Free World." America's political and religious freedoms attracted Europeans who chafed under the continent's repressive governments and rigid social hierarchies, including political refugees from the failed revolutions of 1848. "In America," wrote a German newcomer, "there aren't any masters, here everyone is a free agent."

The largest number of immigrants, however, were refugees from disaster—Irish men and women fleeing the Great Famine of 1845–1851, when a blight destroyed the potato crop on which the island's diet rested. An estimated 1 million persons starved to death and another million emigrated in those years, most of them to the United States. Lacking industrial skills and capital, these impoverished agricultural laborers and small farmers ended up filling the low-wage unskilled jobs native-born Americans sought to avoid. Male Irish immigrants built America's railroads, dug canals, and worked as common laborers, servants, longshoremen, and factory operatives. Irish women frequently went to work as servants in the homes of native-born Americans, although some preferred factory work

TABLE 9.2 Total Number of Immigrants by Five-Year Period

Years	Number of Immigrants
1841–1845	430,000
1846–1850	1,283,000
1851–1855	1,748,000
1856–1860	850,000

to domestic service. "It's the freedom that we want when the day's work is done," one Irish woman explained. "Our day is ten hours long, but when it's done it's done"; however, servants were on call at any time. By the end of the 1850s, the Lowell textile mills had largely replaced Yankee farm women with immigrant Irish families. Four-fifths of Irish immigrants remained in the Northeast. In Boston, New York, and smaller industrial cities, they con-gregated in overcrowded urban ghet-tos notorious for poverty, crime, and disease.

The second-largest group of immi-grants, Germans, included a consider-ably larger number of skilled craftsmen than the Irish. Germans also settled in

Although our image of the West emphasizes the lone pioneer, many migrants settled in tightly knit communities and worked cooperatively. This painting by Olof Krans, who came to the United States from Sweden with his family in 1850 at the age of twelve, shows a group of women pre-paring to plant corn at the immigrant settlement of Bishop Hill, Illinois.

tightly knit neighborhoods in eastern cities, but many were able to move to the West, where they established themselves as craftsmen, shopkeepers, and farmers. The "German triangle," as the cities of Cincinnati, St. Louis, and Mil-waukee were sometimes called, attracted large German populations. A vibrant German-language culture, with its own schools, newspapers, associations, and churches, developed wherever large numbers of Germans settled. "As one passes along the Bowery," one observer noted of a part of New York City known as Kleindeutschland (Little Germany), "almost everything is German."

Some 40,000 Scandinavians also emigrated to the United States in these years, most of whom settled on farms in the Old Northwest. The continuing expansion of industry and the failure of the Chartist movement of the 1840s, which sought to democratize the system of government in Britain, also inspired many English workers to emigrate to the United States.

The Rise of Nativism

Immigrants from England (whose ranks included the actor Junius Brutus Booth, father of John Wilkes Booth) were easily absorbed, but those from Ire-land encountered intense hostility. As Roman Catholics, they faced discrimi-nation in a largely Protestant society in which the tradition of "anti-popery" still ran deep. The Irish influx greatly enhanced the visibility and power of the Catholic Church, previously a minor presence in most parts of the country.

From SARAH BAGLEY, UNTITLED ESSAY IN *VOICE OF INDUSTRY* (1845)

Born to a New Hampshire farm family in 1806, Sarah Bagley came to Lowell in 1837 after her father suffered financial reverses. She soon became one of the most outspoken leaders of the labor movement. In 1845 she became the editor of the *Voice of Industry*, which spoke for the male and female labor movement of New England.

Whenever I raise the point that it is immoral to shut us up in a close room twelve hours a day in the most monotonous and tedious of employment, I am told that we have come to the mills voluntarily and we can leave when we will. Voluntary! Let us look a little at this remarkable form of human freedom. Do we from mere choice leave our fathers' dwellings, the firesides where all of our friends, where too our earliest and fondest recollections cluster, for the factory and the corporation's boarding house? . . . A slave too goes voluntarily to his task, but his will is in some manner quickened by the whip of the overseer.

The whip which brings us to Lowell is NECESSITY. We must have money; a father's debts are to be paid, an aged mother to be supported, a brother's ambition to be aided, and so the factories are supplied. Is this to act from free will? . . . Is any one such a fool as to suppose that out of six thousand factory girls of Lowell, sixty would be there if they could help it? Everybody knows that it is necessity alone, in some form or other, that takes us to Lowell and keeps us there. Is this freedom? To my mind it is slavery quite as really as any in Turkey or Carolina. It matters little as to the fact of slavery, whether the slave be compelled to his task by the whip of the over-seer or the wages of the Lowell Corporation. In either case it is not free will, leading the laborer to work, but an outward necessity that puts free will out of the question.

LETTER OF MARGARET McCARTHY TO HER FAMILY (1850)

Between 1840 and 1860, over 4 million people (more than the entire population of 1790) entered the United States, the majority from Ireland and Germany. Many sent money home to help family members join them, a process today sometimes called chain migration. In this letter, Margaret McCarthy, a young immigrant writing from New York City, offers advice to her family in Ireland.

My dear father I must only say that this is a good place and a good country for if one place does not suit a man he can go to another and can very easy please himself. . . . [But] I would advise no one to come to America that would not have some money after landing here that [will] enable them to go west in case they would get no work to do here. But any man or woman without a family are fools that would not venture and come to this plentiful country where no man or woman ever hungered or ever will. . . .

Come you all together courageously and bid adieu to that lovely place the land of our birth. . . . But alas I am now told it's the gulf of misery, oppression, degradation and ruin. . . . This, my dear father induces me to remit to you in this letter 20 dollars. . . . Dan Keliher tells me that you knew more of house carpentry than he did himself and he can earn from twelve to fourteen shilling a day and he also tells me that Florence will do very well and that Michael can get a place right off. . . . It is not for slavery I want you to come here no its for affording my brothers and sisters and I an opportunity of showing our kindness and gratitude and coming on your senior days . . . [so] that you my dear father and mother could walk about leisurely and independently. . . .

Oh how happy I feel [that] the Lord had not it destined for me to get married . . . at home [and] after a few months he and I may be an encumbrance on you or perhaps in the poor house.

QUESTIONS

1. *Why does Sarah Bagley compare the situation of female factory workers with slavery?*

2. *What aspirations seem to be uppermost in Margaret McCarthy's mind?*

3. *What do these documents suggest about how Americans of different backgrounds experienced and responded to economic conditions during the first half of the nineteenth century?*

During the 1840s and 1850s, Archbishop John Hughes of New York City made the church a more assertive institution. Hughes condemned the use of the Protestant King James Bible in New York City's public schools, pressed Catholic parents to send their children to an expanding network of parochial schools, and sought government funding to pay for them. He aggressively sought to win converts from Protestantism.

In the eyes of many Protestants, the newly assertive activities of the Catholic Church raised anew the question of national identity—the question "Who is an American?" and its close relative, "What kinds of immigrants should the country welcome?" Catholicism, they feared, threatened American institutions and American freedom. In 1834, Lyman Beecher, a prominent Presbyterian minister (and father of the religious leader Henry Ward Beecher and the writers Harriet Beecher Stowe and Catharine Beecher), delivered a sermon in Boston, soon published as "A Plea for the West." Beecher warned that Catholics were seeking to dominate the American West, where the future of Christianity in the world would be worked out. His sermon inspired a mob to burn a Catholic convent in the city.

The idea of the United States as a refuge for those seeking economic opportunity or an escape from oppression has always coexisted with suspicion of and hostility to foreign newcomers. American history has witnessed periods of intense anxiety over immigration. The Alien Act of 1798 reflected fear of immigrants with radical political views. During the early twentieth century, there was widespread hostility to the "new immigration" from southern and eastern Europe. The question of how many persons should be allowed to enter the United States, and under what circumstances, remains a volatile political issue.

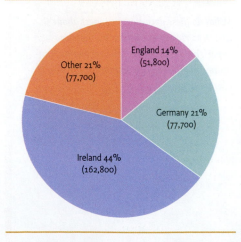

FIGURE 9.1 SOURCES OF IMMIGRATION, 1850

England 14% (51,800)

Other 21% (77,700)

Germany 21% (77,700)

Ireland 44% (162,800)

The Irish influx of the 1840s and 1850s thoroughly alarmed many native-born Americans. Those who feared the impact of immigration on American political and social life were called "nativists." They blamed immigrants for urban crime, political corruption, and a fondness for intoxicating liquor, and they accused them of undercutting native-born skilled laborers by working for starvation wages. The Irish were quickly brought into the urban political machines of the Democratic Party, whose local bosses provided jobs and poor relief to struggling newcomers. Nativists contended that the Irish, supposedly unfamiliar with American conceptions of liberty and subservient to the Catholic Church, posed a threat to democratic institutions, social reform, and public education. Stereotypes similar to those directed at Blacks flourished regarding the Irish as well—seen as childlike, lazy, and slaves of their passions, they were said to be unsuited for republican freedom.

Nativism would not become a national political movement until the 1850s, as we will see in Chapter 13. But in the 1840s, nativism found expression both in the streets and at the ballot box. New York City and Philadelphia witnessed violent anti-immigrant, anti-Catholic riots. Appealing mainly to skilled native-born workers who feared that immigrants were taking their jobs and undercutting their wages, a nativist candidate was elected New York City's mayor in 1844.

The Transformation of Law

American law increasingly supported the efforts of entrepreneurs to participate in the market revolution, while shielding them from interference by local governments and liability for some of the less desirable results of economic growth. The corporate form of business organization became central to the new market economy. A corporate firm enjoys special privileges and powers granted in a charter from the government, among them that investors and directors are not personally liable for the company's debts. Unlike companies owned by an individual, family, or limited partnership, in other words, a corporation can fail without ruining its directors and stockholders. Corporations were therefore able to raise far more capital than the traditional forms of enterprise. By the 1830s, many states had replaced the granting of charters through specific acts of legislation with "general incorporation laws," allowing any company to obtain a corporate charter if it paid a specified fee.

Many Americans distrusted corporate charters as a form of government-granted special privilege. But the courts upheld their validity, while opposing efforts by established firms to limit competition from newcomers. In ***Dartmouth College v. Woodward*** (1819), John Marshall's Supreme Court defined corporate charters issued by state legislatures as contracts, which future lawmakers could not alter or rescind. Five years later, in ***Gibbons v. Ogden***, the Court struck down a monopoly the New York legislature had granted for steamboat navigation. And in 1837, with Roger B. Taney now the chief justice, the Court ruled that the Massachusetts legislature did not infringe the charter of an existing company that had constructed a bridge over the Charles River when it empowered a second company to build a competing bridge. The community, Taney declared, had a legitimate interest in promoting transportation and prosperity.

Local judges, meanwhile, held businessmen blameless for property damage done by factory construction (such as the flooding of upstream farmlands and the disruption of fishing when dams were built to harness water power). Numerous court decisions also affirmed employers' full authority over the workplace and invoked the old common law of conspiracy to punish workers who sought to strike for higher wages. Not until 1842, in **Commonwealth v. Hunt**, did Massachusetts chief justice Lemuel Shaw decree that there was nothing inherently illegal in workers organizing a union or a strike.

THE FREE INDIVIDUAL

By the 1830s, the market revolution and westward expansion had produced a society that amazed European visitors: energetic, materialistic, and seemingly in constant motion. Arriving in Chicago in 1835, the British writer Harriet Martineau found the streets "crowded with land speculators, hurrying from one sale to another. . . . As the gentlemen of our party walked the streets, store-keepers hailed them from their doors, with offers of farms, and all manner of land-lots, advising them to speculate before the price of land rose higher." Alexis de Tocqueville was struck by Americans' restless energy and apparent lack of attachment to place. "No sooner do you set foot on American soil," he observed, "than you find yourself in a sort of tumult. All around you, everything is on the move." Westward migration and urban development created a large mobile population no longer tied to local communities who sought to seize the opportunities offered by economic change. "In the United States," wrote Tocqueville, "a man builds a house in which to spend his old age, and sells it before the roof is on; he plants a garden and [rents] it just as the trees are coming into bearing; he brings a field into tillage and leaves other men to gather the crops."

The West and Freedom

Westward expansion and the market revolution profoundly affected the lives of all Americans. They reinforced some older ideas of freedom and helped to create new ones. American freedom, for example, had long been linked with the availability of land in the West. A New York journalist, John L. O'Sullivan, first employed the phrase "**manifest destiny**," meaning that the United States had a divinely appointed mission, so obvious as to be beyond dispute, to occupy all of North America. Americans, he proclaimed, had a far better title to western lands than could be provided by any international treaty, right of discovery, or long-term settlement. Their right to the continent was provided by the nation's divinely inspired mission to extend the area of freedom. Other peoples' claims,

O'Sullivan wrote, must give way to "our manifest destiny to overspread and to possess the whole of the continent which Providence has given us for the development of the great experiment in liberty." Those who stood in the way of expansion—European powers like Great Britain and Spain, Native Americans, Mexicans—were by definition obstacles to the progress of freedom.

O'Sullivan wrote these words in 1845, but the essential idea was familiar much earlier. As the population moved across the Appalachian Mountains, so did the linkage between westward expansion and freedom. "The Goddess of Liberty," declared Senator John Breckinridge of Kentucky, was not "governed by geographical limits." A sense of spatial openness, of the constant opportunity to pick up and move when the pursuit of happiness seemed to demand it, became more and more a central component of American freedom. Freedom in the United States, wrote the French historian Michel Chevalier, one of the many Europeans who visited the country in the 1830s, was a "practical idea" as much as a "mystical one"—it meant "a liberty of action and motion which the American uses to expand over the vast territory that Providence has given him and to subdue it to his uses."

In national myth and ideology, the West would long remain, as the writer Wallace Stegner later put it, "the last home of the freeborn American." The settlement and economic exploitation of the West promised to prevent the United States from following down the path of Europe and becoming a society with fixed social classes and a large group of wage-earning poor. With population and the price of land rising dramatically in the older states and young men's prospects for acquiring a farm or setting up an independent artisan shop declining, the West still held out the chance for white American men to achieve economic independence, the social condition of freedom.

The Transcendentalists

The restless, competitive world of the market revolution strongly encouraged the identification of American freedom with the absence of restraints on self-directed individuals seeking economic advancement and personal development. The "one important revolution" of the day, the philosopher Ralph Waldo Emerson wrote in the 1830s, was "the new value of the private man." The opportunity for personal growth offered a new definition of Jefferson's pursuit of happiness, one well suited to a world in which territorial expansion and the market revolution had shattered traditional spatial and social boundaries and made moving from place to place and status to status common features of American life.

In a widely reprinted 1837 address, "The American Scholar," Emerson called on the person engaged in writing and thinking to "feel all confidence in

The daguerreotype, an early form of photography, required the sitter to remain perfectly still for twenty seconds or longer, meaning that the subject usually looked rather stiff. Nonetheless, Henry David Thoreau, pictured here in 1856, wrote, "My friends think it is pretty good though better looking than I."

himself, . . . to never defer to the popular cry," and to find and trust his own "definition of freedom." In Emerson's definition, rather than a preexisting set of rights or privileges, freedom was an open-ended process of self-realization by which individuals could remake themselves and their own lives. The keynote of the times, he declared, was "the new importance given to the single person" and the "emancipation" of the individual, the "American idea."

Emerson was perhaps the most prominent member of a group of New England intellectuals known as the **transcendentalists**, who insisted on the primacy of individual judgment over existing social traditions and institutions. Emerson's Concord, Massachusetts, neighbor, the writer Henry David Thoreau, echoed his call for individual self-reliance. "Any man more right than his neighbors," Thoreau wrote, "is a majority of one."

Individualism

Ironies abounded in the era's "individualism" (a term that first entered the language in the 1820s). For even as the market revolution promoted commercial connections between far-flung people, the idea of the "sovereign individual" proclaimed that Americans should depend on no one but themselves. Of course, personal independence had long been associated with American freedom. But eighteenth-century thinkers generally saw no contradiction between private happiness and self-sacrificing public virtue, defined as devotion to the common good. Now, Tocqueville observed, individualism led "each member of the community to sever himself from the mass of his fellows and to draw apart with his family and his friends . . . [leaving] society at large to itself." Americans increasingly understood the realm of the self—which came to be called "privacy"—as one with which neither other individuals nor government had a right to interfere. As will be discussed in the next chapter, individualism also helped to inspire the expansion of democracy. Ownership of one's self rather than ownership of property now made a person capable of exercising the right to vote.

Looking back from the 1880s, Emerson would recall the era before the Civil War as a time when "social existence" gave way to "the enlargement and independency of the individual, ... driven to find all his resources, hopes, rewards, society, and deity within himself." In his own life, Thoreau illustrated Emerson's point about the primacy of individual conscience in matters political, social, and personal, and the need to find one's own way rather than following the crowd. Thoreau became persuaded that modern society stifled individual judgment by making men "tools of their tools," trapped in stultifying jobs by their obsession with acquiring wealth. Even in "this comparatively free country," he wrote, most persons were so preoccupied with material things that they had no time to contemplate the beauties of nature.

To escape this fate, Thoreau retreated for two years to a cabin on Walden Pond near Concord, where he could enjoy the freedom of isolation from the "economical and moral tyranny" he believed ruled American society. He subsequently published *Walden* (1854), an account of his experiences and a critique of how the market revolution was, in his opinion, degrading both Americans' values and the natural environment. An area that had been covered with dense forest in his youth, he observed, had been so transformed by woodcutters and farmers that it was almost completely devoid of trees and wild animals. In one famous passage, Thoreau noted how his enjoyment of nature was disturbed by the distant sound of a locomotive whistle—a symbol of how it seemed impossible to escape the market revolution. Thoreau appealed to Americans to "simplify" their lives rather than become obsessed with the accumulation of wealth. Genuine freedom, he insisted, lay within.

The Second Great Awakening

The popular religious revivals that swept over the country during the **Second Great Awakening** added a religious underpinning to the celebration of personal self-improvement, self-reliance, and self-determination. These revivals, which began at the turn of the century, were originally organized by established religious leaders alarmed by low levels of church attendance in the young republic (perhaps as few as 10 percent of white Americans regularly attended church during the 1790s). But they quickly expanded far beyond existing churches. They peaked in the 1820s and early 1830s, when the Reverend Charles Grandison Finney held months-long revival meetings in upstate New York and New York City.

The son of Connecticut farmers, Finney had been inspired to preach after attending a religious revival in 1821. Like the evangelists (traveling preachers) of the first Great Awakening of the mid-eighteenth century, discussed in Chapter 4, Finney warned of hell in vivid language while offering the promise of salvation to converts who abandoned their sinful ways. He became a national celebrity after his success in Oneida County in upstate New York. After Finney's preaching, according to one report, the area had been "completely overthrown by the Holy Ghost" so that "the theater has been deserted, the tavern sanctified . . . and far higher and purer enjoyment has been found in exercises of devotion."

The Second Great Awakening spread to all regions of the country and democratized American Christianity, making it a truly mass enterprise. At the time of independence, fewer than 2,000 Christian ministers preached in the United States. In 1845, they numbered 40,000. Evangelical denominations like the Methodists and Baptists enjoyed explosive growth in membership, and smaller sects proliferated. By the 1840s, Methodism, with more than 1 million members, had become the country's largest denomination. Deism, a form of religious belief hostile to organized churches, had been prominent among the generation of the founding fathers. It now waned, and Christianity became even more central to American culture. Americans, wrote Tocqueville, "combine the notions of Christianity and of liberty so intimately in their minds that it is impossible to make them conceive the one without the other."

New religious prophets seemed to appear regularly in early-nineteenth-century America, determined, in novelist Herman Melville's phrase, to "gospelize the world anew." At large camp meetings, especially prominent on the frontier, fiery revivalist preachers rejected the idea that man is a sinful creature with a preordained fate, promoting instead the doctrine of human free will. At these gatherings, rich and poor, male and female, and in some instances whites and Blacks worshiped alongside one another and pledged to abandon worldly sins in favor of the godly life.

The Awakening's Impact

Even more than its predecessor of several decades earlier, the Second Great Awakening stressed the right of private judgment in spiritual matters and the possibility of universal salvation through faith and good works. Every person, Finney insisted, was a "moral free agent"—that is, a person free to choose between a Christian life and sin. Sinners could experience a "change of heart" and embrace spiritual freedom.

Revivalist ministers seized the opportunities offered by the market revolution to spread their message. They raised funds, embarked on lengthy preaching tours by canal, steamboat, and railroad, and flooded the country with mass-produced, inexpensive religious tracts. The revivals' opening of religion to mass participation and their message that ordinary Americans could shape their own spiritual destinies resonated with the spread of market values.

To be sure, evangelical preachers can hardly be described as cheerleaders for a market society. They regularly railed against greed and indifference to the welfare of others as sins. Finney called selfishness—an extreme form of individualism encouraged by the scramble for wealth—"the law of Satan's empire," not God's. Yet the revivals thrived in areas caught up in the rapid expansion of the market economy, such as the region of upstate New York along the path of the Erie Canal. Most of Finney's converts here came from the commercial and professional classes. Evangelical ministers promoted what might be called a controlled **individualism** as the essence of freedom. In stressing the importance of industry, sobriety, and self-discipline as examples of freely chosen moral behavior, evangelical preachers promoted the very qualities necessary for success in a market culture.

The Emergence of Mormonism

The Second Great Awakening illustrated how the end of governmental support for established churches promoted religious pluralism. Competition among religious groups kept religion vibrant and promoted the emergence of new denominations. Among the most successful of the religions that sprang up, hoping to create a Kingdom of God on earth, was the **Church of Jesus Christ of Latter-Day Saints**, or Mormons. The Mormons were founded in the 1820s by Joseph Smith, a farmer in upstate New York who as a youth began to experience religious visions. He claimed to have been led by an angel to a set of golden plates covered with strange writing. Smith translated and published them as *The Book of Mormon*, after a fourth-century prophet.

Depending on one's point of view, *The Book of Mormon* is either a divinely inspired holy book or an impressive work of American literature. It tells the story of three families who traveled from the ancient Middle East to the Americas, where they eventually evolved into Native American tribes. Jesus Christ plays a prominent role in the book, appearing to one of the family groups in the Western Hemisphere after his death and resurrection. The second coming of Christ would take place in the New World, where Smith was God's prophet. Smith mortgaged his farm to help pay for an edition of 5,000 copies, which appeared in 1830.

Mormonism emerged in a center of the Second Great Awakening, upstate New York. The church founded by Smith responded to the disruptions caused by the market revolution. It was self-consciously democratic, admitting anyone, regardless of wealth or occupation, who accepted Smith's message. (African Americans could join, but could not enter the priesthood—a policy not overturned until 1978.) Like Jesus, Smith condemned the selfishness of the rich—in the ideal ancient society described in *The Book of Mormon* "there was no poor among them." At a time when paper money seemed to have little intrinsic worth, gold remained an unchallenged standard of value, which may help to explain the appeal of a religious text written on golden plates.

Gradually, however, Smith began to receive visions that led to more controversial doctrines, notably polygamy, which allows one man to have more than one wife. By the end of his life, Smith had married no fewer than thirty women. Along with the absolute authority Smith exercised over his followers, this doctrine outraged the Mormons' neighbors. Mobs drove Smith and his followers out of New York, Ohio, and Missouri before they settled in 1839 in Nauvoo, Illinois, where they hoped to await the Second Coming. There, five years later, Smith was arrested on the charge of inciting a riot that destroyed an anti-Mormon newspaper. While in jail awaiting trial, Smith was murdered by a group of intruders. In 1847, his successor as Mormon leader, Brigham Young, led more than 2,000 followers across the Great Plains and Rocky Mountains to the shores of the Great Salt Lake in present-day Utah, seeking a refuge where they could practice their faith undisturbed. (The area was then part of Mexico; the United States annexed it in 1848.) By 1852, the number of Mormons in various settlements in Utah had reached 16,000. The experience of expulsion helped to shape Mormon theology. Their distinctive practice of posthumous baptism, in which modern members of the church retrospectively baptize long-dead ancestors, seeks to unite across generations families separated not only by death but also by migration. The practice has also led the church to gather and make publicly available an enormous library of genealogical records from around the world—a gold mine for scholars of every religion.

The Mormons' experience revealed the limits of religious toleration in nineteenth-century America but also the opportunities offered by religious pluralism. Today, Mormons constitute the fourth-largest church in the United States and *The Book of Mormon* has been translated into over 100 languages.

THE LIMITS OF PROSPERITY

Liberty and Prosperity

As the market revolution progressed, the right to compete for economic advancement became a touchstone of American freedom. Official imagery linked the goddess of liberty ever more closely to emblems of material wealth. New Jersey, whose official seal, adopted in 1776, had paired liberty with Ceres, the Roman goddess of agriculture, in 1821 added the motto "Liberty and Prosperity." The state seal of Arkansas, admitted to the Union in 1836, pictured liberty atop an image of a steamboat and two overflowing horns of plenty.

Many enterprising Americans seized the opportunities offered by the market revolution to enrich themselves. John Jacob Astor, the son of a poor German butcher who emigrated to the United States at the end of the War of Independence, earned large profits in the early nineteenth century by shipping furs to China and importing teas and silk. Astor invested his wealth in Manhattan real estate, which was rapidly rising in value, and built Astor House, which quickly became the nation's most famous hotel. He died in 1848 the richest man in the United States, leaving a fortune of perhaps $10 million, the equivalent of hundreds of millions of dollars today.

Astor's story seemed to exemplify the opportunities open to the "self-made man," a term that came into use during his lifetime. According to this idea, those who achieved success in America did so not as a result of hereditary privilege or government favoritism as in Europe, but through their own intelligence and hard work. In the extent of his wealth, of course, Astor was hardly typical. But the market revolution and the quickening of commercial life enriched numerous bankers, merchants, industrialists, and planters. It produced a new middle class—an army of clerks, accountants, and other office employees who staffed businesses in Boston, New York, and elsewhere. It created new opportunities for farmers who profited from the growing demand at home and abroad for American agricultural products, and for skilled craftsmen like Thomas Rodgers, a machine builder who established a successful locomotive factory in Paterson, New Jersey. New opportunities for talented men opened in professions like law, medicine, and teaching. By the early 1820s, there were an estimated 10,000 physicians in the United States.

Pat Lyon at the Forge, an 1826–1827 painting of a prosperous blacksmith. Proud of his accomplishments as a self-made man who had achieved success through hard work and skill rather than inheritance, Lyon asked the artist to paint him in his shop wearing his work clothes.

Race and Opportunity

The market revolution affected the lives of all Americans. But not all were positioned to take advantage of its benefits. Most Blacks were enslaved, but even free Blacks found themselves excluded from the new economic opportunities.

The 220,000 Blacks living in the free states on the eve of the Civil War (less than 2 percent of the North's population) suffered discrimination in every phase of their lives. Although virtually every northern county east of the Mississippi River reported some Black residents, the majority of Blacks lived in the poorest, unhealthiest sections of cities like New York, Philadelphia, and Cincinnati. And even these neighborhoods were subjected to occasional violent assault by white mobs, like the armed bands that attacked Blacks and destroyed their homes and businesses in Cincinnati in 1829.

Barred from schools and other public facilities, free Blacks laboriously constructed their own institutional life, centered on mutual aid and educational societies, as well as independent churches, most notably the African Methodist Episcopal Church. Richard Allen of Philadelphia, a Methodist preacher, had been spurred to found it after being forcibly removed from his former church for praying at the altar rail, a place reserved for whites.

While many white Americans could look forward to a life of economic accumulation and individual advancement, large numbers of free Blacks experienced downward mobility. At the time of abolition, because of widespread slave ownership among eighteenth-century artisans, a considerable number of northern Blacks possessed craft skills. But it became more and more difficult for Blacks to utilize these skills once they became free. Although many white artisans criticized slavery, most viewed the freed slaves as low-wage competitors and sought to bar them from skilled employment. "They are leaders in the cause of equal rights for themselves," a Black editor commented of New York City's artisans in the 1830s.

Hostility from white craftsmen, however, was only one of many obstacles that kept Blacks confined to the lowest ranks of the labor market. White employers refused to hire them in anything but menial positions, and white customers did not wish to be served by them. The result was a rapid decline in economic status, until by mid-century, the vast majority of northern Blacks labored for wages in unskilled jobs and as domestic servants. The state census of 1855 revealed 122 Black barbers and 808 Black servants in New York City, but only 1 lawyer and 6 doctors. Nor could free Blacks take advantage of the opening of the West to improve their economic status, a central component of American freedom. Federal law barred them from access to public land, and by 1860 four states—Indiana, Illinois, Iowa, and Oregon—prohibited them from entering their territory altogether.

The Cult of Domesticity

White women, too, found many of the opportunities opened by the market revolution closed to them. As the household declined as a center of economic production, many saw their traditional roles undermined by the availability of mass-produced goods previously made at home. Some women, as noted above, followed work as it moved from household to factory. Others, whose husbands had jobs that paid well enough that their wives did not have to work outside the home, embraced a new definition of femininity, which glorified not a woman's contribution to the family's economic well-being but her ability to create a private environment shielded from the competitive tensions of the market economy. In this way of thinking, a woman's "place" was in the home, a site increasingly emptied of economically productive functions as work moved from the household to workshops and factories. Her role was to sustain nonmarket values like love, friendship, and mutual obligation, providing men with a shelter from the competitive marketplace.

The earlier ideology of "republican motherhood," which allowed women a kind of public role as mothers of future citizens, subtly evolved into the mid-nineteenth-century **cult of domesticity**. "Virtue," which in the eighteenth century was a political characteristic of men essential to the success of republican government, came to be redefined as a personal moral quality associated more and more closely with women. "Virtue" for a woman meant not only sexual innocence but also beauty, frailty, and dependence on men. "In whatever situation of life a woman is placed from her cradle to her grave," declared *The Young Lady's Book*, one of numerous popular magazines addressed to female audiences of the 1820s and 1830s, "a spirit of obedience and submission, pliability of temper, and humility of mind, are required from her." These magazines carried articles such as "Woman, a Source of Comfort," "Woman, a Being to Come Home To," and "Woman—Man's Best Friend."

With more and more men leaving the home for work, women did exercise considerable power over personal affairs within the family. The rapid decline in the American birthrate during the nineteenth century (from an average of seven children per woman in 1800 to four in 1900) cannot be explained except by the conscious decision of millions of women to limit the number of children they bore. But the idea of domesticity minimized women's even indirect participation in the outside world. For both sexes, freedom meant fulfilling their respective "inborn" qualities. Men were supposedly rational, aggressive, and domineering, while women were nurturing, selfless, ruled by the emotions, and thus less fitted for public life. If submission to the will of another increasingly seemed inadmissible for free men, it remained a condition expected of women. Men moved freely between the public and private "spheres"; women were supposed to remain cloistered in the private realm of the family.

Women and Work

Prevailing ideas concerning gender bore little relation to the experience of those women who worked for wages at least some time in their lives. They did so despite severe disadvantages. Women could not compete freely for employment, since only low-paying jobs were available to them. Coverture was still in force, so married women could not sign independent contracts or sue in their own name, and not until after the Civil War did they, not their husbands, control the wages they earned. Nonetheless, for poor city dwellers and farm families, the labor of all family members was essential to economic survival. Thousands of poor women found jobs as domestic servants, factory workers, and seamstresses. Early industrialization enhanced the availability of paid work for northern women, as the spread of the putting-out system in such industries as shoemaking, hatmaking, and clothing manufacture allowed women laboring at home to contribute to family income even as they retained responsibility for domestic chores.

For the expanding middle class, however, it became a badge of respectability for wives to remain at home, outside the disorderly new market economy, while husbands conducted business in their offices, shops, and factories. In larger cities, where families of different social classes had previously lived alongside one another, fashionable middle-class neighborhoods populated by merchants, factory owners, and professionals like lawyers and doctors began to develop. Much of the work in middle-class homes was done by domestic servants, the largest employment category for women in nineteenth-century America. The freedom of the middle-class woman—defined in part as freedom from labor—rested on the employment of other women within her household.

Even though most women were anything but idle, in a market economy where labor increasingly meant work that created monetary value, it became more and more difficult to think of labor as encompassing anyone but men. Lydia Maria Child wrote a popular book, *The Frugal Housewife*, published in 1829, that sought to prepare women for the ups and downs of the market revolution (one chapter was entitled "How to Endure Poverty"). Child supported her family by her writing and became a prominent advocate of antislavery and of greater rights for women. Her diary reveals that in a single year she also sewed thirty-six pieces of clothing, prepared more than 700 meals, and spent much time supervising household help.

By any reasonable definition, Child worked—at home and as a writer. But discussions of labor rarely mentioned housewives, domestic servants, and female outworkers, except as an indication of how the spread of capitalism was degrading men. The idea that the male head of household should command a **family wage** that enabled him to support his wife and children became a popular definition of social justice. It sank deep roots not only among middle-class Americans but among working-class men as well. Capitalism, said the newspaper *Workingman's Advocate*, tore women from their role as "happy and independent mistresses" of the domestic sphere and forced them into the labor market, thereby undermining the natural order of the household and the authority of its male head.

The Early Labor Movement

As this complaint suggests, many Americans experienced the market revolution not as an enhancement of the power to shape their own lives, but as a loss of freedom. The period between the War of 1812 and 1840 witnessed a sharp economic downturn in 1819, a full-fledged depression starting in 1837, and numerous ups and downs in between, during which employment was irregular and numerous businesses failed. For every aspiring American who rode the tide of economic progress, another seemed to sink beneath the waves. The economic transformation produced an explosive growth in the nation's output and trade and a rise in the general standard of living. But especially in the growing cities of the Northeast, it significantly wid-

The Intelligence Office, an 1849 painting by the artist William Henry Burr, depicts a female employment office. The two women at the left are responding to an ad for a domestic worker printed in a New York City newspaper, which lies crumpled on the ground. The seated woman is the prospective employer, and in the middle is the agent who runs the office. Domestic work was the largest category of female employment throughout the nineteenth century.

ened the gap between wealthy merchants and industrialists on the one hand and impoverished factory workers, unskilled dockworkers, and seamstresses laboring at home on the other. In Massachusetts, the most industrialized state in the country, the richest 5 percent of the population owned more than half the wealth. Inequality was even more pronounced in Philadelphia, where the top 1 percent possessed more wealth than the rest of the population combined. Bankruptcy was a common fact of life, and men unable to pay their debts filled the prisons of major cities.

Alarmed at the erosion of traditional skills and the threat of being reduced to the status of dependent wage earners, skilled craftsmen in the late 1820s created the world's first Workingmen's Parties, short-lived political organizations that sought to mobilize lower-class support for candidates who would press for free public education, an end to imprisonment for debt, and legislation limiting work to ten hours per day. In the 1830s, a time of rapidly rising prices, union organization spread and strikes became commonplace. Along with demands for higher wages and shorter hours, the early labor movement called for free homesteads for settlers on public land and an end to the imprisonment of union leaders for conspiracy.

No More Grinding the Poor—But Liberty and the Rights of Man, a labor movement cartoon of the 1830s. The devil and a millionaire conspire to buy an election with money (in the box at the lower left), while an honest workingman hands his ballot to a female figure of liberty. The worker's motto is "Liberty, Equity, Justice, and the Rights of Man."

The "Liberty of Living"

But over and above these specific issues, workers' language of protest drew on older ideas of freedom linked to economic autonomy, public-spirited virtue, and social equality. The conviction of twenty New York tailors in 1835 under the common law of conspiracy for combining to seek higher wages inspired a public procession marking the "burial of liberty." Such actions and language were not confined to male workers. The mill women of Lowell walked off their jobs in 1834 to protest a reduction in wages and again two years later when employers raised rents at their boardinghouses. They carried banners affirming their rights as "daughters of free men," and, addressing the factory owners, charged that "the oppressive hand of avarice [greed] would enslave us." Freedom, Noah Webster's *American Dictionary* declared in 1828, was "a state of exemption from the power or control of another." The labor movement asked how many wage earners truly enjoyed such "exemption." Some labor spokesmen, like Langdon Byllesby of Philadelphia, went so far as to describe wage labor itself as the "very essence of slavery," since dependence on another person for one's economic livelihood was incompatible with freedom.

Rooted in the traditions of the small producer and the identification of freedom with economic independence, labor's critique of the market economy directly challenged the idea that individual improvement—Emerson's "self-trust, self-reliance, self-control, self-culture"—offered an adequate response to social inequality. "Wealth and labor," wrote Orestes Brownson in his influential essay "The Laboring Classes" (1840), were at war. Workers' problems, he went on, must be understood as institutional, not individual. They had their root in "the constitution of society," and their solution required not a more complete individualism, but a "radical change [in] existing social arrangements" so as to produce "equality between man and man."

"We are free," wrote Peter Rödel, an immigrant German shoemaker, "but not free enough. . . . We want the liberty of living." Here lay the origins of the idea, which would become far more prominent in the late nineteenth and twentieth centuries, that economic security—a standard of life below which no person would fall—formed an essential part of American freedom.

Thus, the market revolution transformed and divided American society and its conceptions of freedom. It encouraged a new emphasis on individualism and physical mobility among white men, while severely limiting the options available to everyone else. It opened new opportunities for economic freedom for many Americans, while leading others to fear that their traditional economic independence was being eroded. In a democratic society, it was inevitable that the debate over the market revolution and its consequences for freedom would be reflected in American politics.

CHAPTER REVIEW

REVIEW QUESTIONS

1. *Identify the major transportation improvements in this period and explain how they influenced the market economy.*

2. *How did state and local governments promote the national economy in this period?*

3. *What motivated U.S. settlers to move westward—and how did they respond to competing territorial claims by European or Native nations?*

4. *How did the market economy and westward expansion intensify the institution of slavery?*

5. *How did westward expansion and the market revolution drive each other?*

6. *What role did immigrants play in the new market society?*

7. *How did changes in the law promote development in the economic system?*

8. As it democratized American Christianity, the Second Great Awakening both took advantage of the market revolution and criticized its excesses. Explain.

9. How did the market revolution change women's work and family roles?

10. Give some examples of the rise of individualism in these years.

11. How did immigration and nativism address the question of who is an American?

KEY TERMS

steamboat (p. 327)

Erie Canal (p. 328)

Cotton Kingdom (p. 333)

cotton gin (p. 334)

Porkopolis (p. 337)

American system of manufactures (p. 339)

mill girls (p. 341)

nativism (p. 347)

Dartmouth College v. Woodward (p. 347)

Gibbons v. Ogden (p. 347)

Commonwealth v. Hunt (p. 348)

manifest destiny (p. 348)

transcendentalists (p. 350)

Second Great Awakening (p. 351)

individualism (p. 353)

Church of Jesus Christ of Latter-Day Saints (p. 353)

cult of domesticity (p. 357)

family wage (p. 358)

Go to 🐰 INQUIZITIVE

To see what you know—and learn what you've missed—with personalized feedback along the way.

CHAPTER 10

DEMOCRACY IN AMERICA

1815–1840

FOCUS QUESTIONS

- *Whom did the flourishing democracy of the early mid-nineteenth century include, and whom did it leave out?*

- *What efforts were made in this period to strengthen the economic integration of the nation, and what major crises hindered these efforts?*

- *What were the major areas of conflict between nationalism and sectionalism?*

- *In what ways did Andrew Jackson embody the contradictions of democratic nationalism?*

- *Why did Indian Removal happen, and how did Native nations respond?*

- *How did the Bank War influence the economy and party competition?*

The inauguration of Andrew Jackson on March 4, 1829, made it clear that something had changed in American politics. The swearing-in of the president had previously been a small, dignified event. Jackson's inauguration attracted a crowd of some 20,000 people who poured into the White House after the ceremony, ruining furniture and breaking china and glassware in the crush. It was "the reign of King Mob," lamented Justice Joseph Story of the Supreme Court.

Jackson aroused powerful feelings, pro and con. His supporters viewed his election as the advent of genuine democracy, the coming to power of the "common man." Philip Hone, a New York political leader who kept a detailed diary for more than thirty years, recorded that Jackson was "the most popular man we have ever known." Hone had voted for President John Quincy Adams in 1828, but he recognized that Jackson's democratic bearing and beliefs "suit [the people] exactly." Jackson's critics, on the other hand, considered him a tyrant. They called him King Andrew I, and when they organized politically they borrowed their name, the Whig Party, from the opponents of royal power in eighteenth-century England.

The 1830s and 1840s have been called the Age of Jackson, or the period of Jacksonian Democracy. No one individual can capture the full complexity of any period of history, but Andrew Jackson's career did embody the major developments of his era—the market revolution, the westward movement, the violent expulsion of Indians, the expansion of slavery, and the growth of democracy. He was a symbol of the self-made man. Unlike previous presidents, Jackson rose to prominence from a humble background, reflecting his era's democratic opportunities. Born in 1767 on the South Carolina frontier, he had been orphaned during the American Revolution. Early on, Jackson displayed the courage and impetuousness for which he would later become famous. While still a youth, he served as a courier for patriotic forces during the War of Independence. Captured and imprisoned, he was almost killed when a British officer struck him with a sword after Jackson refused an order to polish the officer's boots.

As a young man, Jackson moved to Tennessee, where he studied law, became involved in local politics, won election to the House of Representatives and the Senate, and became a judge on the state supreme court. His military campaigns against the British, Spanish, and Indians helped to consolidate American control over the Lower South, making possible the rise of the Cotton Kingdom. He himself acquired a large plantation in Tennessee. But more than anything else, to this generation of Americans Andrew Jackson symbolized one of the most crucial features of national life—the triumph of political democracy.

Americans pride themselves on being the world's oldest democracy. Like most firsts, there are competing definitions of the first democracy. For example, New Zealand's constitution of 1893 gave women and Maoris (the Native population) the right to vote. Even in the nineteenth century, when democracy meant male suffrage, some Latin American nations extended the right to vote to free Blacks and the descendants of the Indigenous population well before the United States did. Europe lagged far behind. Britain did not achieve universal male suffrage until the 1880s. France instituted it in 1793, abandoned it in 1799, reintroduced it in 1848, and abandoned it again a few years later. More to the point, perhaps, democracy became a central part of the definition of American nationality and the American idea of freedom.

THE TRIUMPH OF DEMOCRACY

Property and Democracy

The market revolution and territorial expansion were intimately connected with a third central element of American freedom—political democracy. The challenge to property qualifications for voting, begun during the American Revolution, reached its culmination in the early nineteenth century. Not a single state that entered the Union after the original thirteen required ownership of property to vote. In the older states, constitutional conventions during the 1820s and 1830s reconsidered democracy's economic basis. Even as the expansion of industry and commercial agriculture increased the number of wage earners in cities and older rural areas, men who could not meet property requirements insisted that they were as fit as others to exercise the rights of citizens. Their insistent pressure did much to democratize American politics.

Owning property, declared a petition by "non-freeholders" (landless men) of Richmond to the Virginia constitutional convention of 1829, did not necessarily mean the possession of "moral or intellectual endowments" superior to those of the poor. "They alone deserve to be called free," they continued, "who participate in the formation of their political institutions." By this time, only North Carolina, Rhode Island, and Virginia still retained property requirements. The large slaveholders who dominated Virginia politics successfully resisted demands for changes in voting qualifications until a constitutional convention in 1850 eliminated the property requirement.

Rhode Island's legislature resisted lifting the property requirements for voting out of fear of letting factory workers and immigrants vote. A center of factory production, Rhode Island had a

· CHRONOLOGY ·

1811	Bank of the United States charter expires
1816	Second Bank of the United States established
1817	Inauguration of James Monroe
1819	Panic of 1819
	McCulloch v. Maryland
1820	Missouri Compromise
1823	Monroe Doctrine
1825	Inauguration of John Quincy Adams
1827	Cherokee Constitution
1828	"Tariff of abominations"
1829	Inauguration of Andrew Jackson
1830	Indian Removal Act
1830–1860	Forced Indian Removals
1832	Nullification crisis
	Worcester v. Georgia
1833	Force Act
1835	Tocqueville's *Democracy in America*
1835–1842	Second Seminole War
1837	Inauguration of Martin Van Buren
1837–1843	Panic of 1837 and ensuing depression
1838–1839	Trail of Tears
1841	Inauguration of William Henry Harrison
	Dorr War

steadily growing population of propertyless wage earners unable to vote. Leaders of the state's labor movement complained repeatedly about the absence of "free suffrage." In October 1841, proponents of democratic reform organized a People's Convention, which drafted a new state constitution. It enfranchised all adult white men while eliminating Blacks entirely (although in a subsequent referendum, Blacks' right to vote was restored). When the reformers ratified their constitution in an extralegal referendum and proceeded to inaugurate Thomas Dorr, a prominent Rhode Island lawyer, as governor, President John Tyler dispatched federal troops to the state. The movement collapsed, and Dorr subsequently served nearly two years in prison for treason. The Dorr War demonstrated the passions aroused by the continuing exclusion of any group of white men from voting. And the legislature soon eliminated the property qualification for native-born men, Black as well as white, although it retained it for immigrants until 1888. With the exception of Rhode Island, by 1860 all states had ended property requirements for voting (though several continued to bar persons accepting poor relief on the grounds that they lacked genuine independence). The personal independence necessary in the citizen now rested not on ownership of property but on ownership of one's self—a reflection of the era's individualism.

Tocqueville on Democracy

By 1840, more than 90 percent of adult white men were eligible to vote. A flourishing democratic system had been consolidated. American politics was boisterous, highly partisan, and sometimes violent, and it engaged the energies of massive numbers of citizens. In a country that lacked more traditional bases of nationality—a powerful and menacing neighbor, historic ethnic, religious, and cultural unity—democratic political institutions came to define the nation's sense of its own identity.

Alexis de Tocqueville, the French writer who visited the United States in the early 1830s, returned home to produce *Democracy in America* in 1835, a classic account of a society in the midst of a political transformation. Tocqueville had come to the United States to study prisons. But he soon realized that to understand America, one must understand democracy (which as a person of aristocratic background he rather disliked). His key insight was that democracy by this time meant far more than either the right to vote or a particular set of political institutions. It was a "habit of the heart," a culture that encouraged individual initiative, belief in equality, and an active public sphere populated by numerous voluntary organizations that sought to improve society. Democracy, Tocqueville saw, had become an essential attribute of American freedom.

As Tocqueville recognized, the rise of democracy represented a profound political transformation. The idea that sovereignty belongs to the mass of ordinary citizens was a new departure in Western thought. As long ago as Aristotle, political philosophers had warned that democracy inevitably degenerated into anarchy and tyranny. For centuries, doctrines of divine right and hierarchical authority had dominated political thought. The founders of the republic, who believed that government must rest on the consent of the governed, also sought to shield political authority from excessive influence by ordinary people (hence the electoral college, Supreme Court, and other undemocratic features of the Constitution). Nonetheless, thanks to persistent pressure from those originally excluded from political participation, democracy—for white males—triumphed by the Age of Jackson.

Justice's Court in the Back Woods, an 1852 painting by Tompkins Harrison Matteson, depicts the expansion of the public sphere to include ordinary Americans. A court is in session in a local tavern. The justice of the peace, who presides, is a shoemaker who has set aside his tools but still wears his leather work apron. A lawyer appeals to the jury, composed of average (male) citizens. The case has to do with an assault. The plaintiff, his head bandaged, leans on the table at the right, while a woman consoles the defendant on the far left.

Democracy reinforced a sense of equality among those who belonged to the political nation, and it deepened the divide separating them from those who did not. Participation in elections and the pageantry surrounding them—parades, bonfires, mass meetings, party conventions—helped to define the "people" of the United States. The right to vote increasingly became the emblem of American citizenship. In law, voting was still, strictly speaking, a privilege rather than a right, subject to regulation by the individual states. But Noah Webster's *American Dictionary* noted that according to common usage and understanding in America (but not in Europe), the term "citizen" had become synonymous with the right to vote. Suffrage, said one advocate of democratic reform, was "the first mark of liberty, the only true badge of the freeman."

The Information Revolution

The market revolution and political democracy produced a large expansion of the public sphere and an explosion in printing sometimes called the "information revolution." The application of steam power to newspaper printing led to

From THE SECOND CONSTITUTION OF NEW YORK STATE (1821)

As political democracy expanded, older states, including New York, rewrote their constitutions and changed the qualifications for voting. By the late 1820s, only North Carolina, Rhode Island, and Virginia still required property qualifications for voting for white men. But as political rights expanded for white men, they became more out of reach for women and people of color.

We, the people of the state of New York, acknowledging with gratitude the grace and beneficence of God, in permitting us to make choice of our form of government, do establish this constitution.

    ARTICLE I. Section 1. The legislative power of this state shall be vested in a senate and an assembly.

    Section 2. The senate shall consist of thirty-two members. The senators shall be chosen for four years, and shall be freeholders. The assembly shall consist of one hundred and twenty-eight members, who shall be annually elected....

    ARTICLE II. Section 1. Every male citizen of the age of twenty-one years, who shall have been an inhabitant of this state one year preceding any election ... and shall have ... paid a tax to the state or county, assessed upon his real or personal property; or shall by law be exempted from taxation; or ... shall have performed ... military duty in the militia of this state; or who shall be exempted from performing militia duty in consequence of being a fireman ... [or] shall have been, within the last year, assessed to labor upon the public highways ... shall be entitled to vote ... but no man of colour, unless he shall have been for three years a citizen of this state, and ... shall be ... possessed of a freehold estate of the value of two hundred and fifty dollars, over and above all debts and incumbrances charged thereon; and shall have been actually rated, and paid a tax thereon, shall be entitled to vote at any such election.

From THE CONSTITUTION OF THE CHEROKEE NATION (1827)

Native Americans participated in nineteenth-century political changes, but the vast majority identified with their own Native nations rather than as citizens of the United States. Several Native nations drafted and ratified constitutions. The 1827 Constitution of the Cherokee Nation shows how Cherokee priorities both differed from and paralleled those of white Americans. Today, over 400 Native nations within the United States operate under written constitutions, most of which, like the U.S. and state constitutions, have over time been amended or even rewritten entirely.

We, the Representatives of the people of the Cherokee Nation, in Convention assembled, in order to establish justice, ensure tranquility, promote our common welfare, and secure to ourselves and our posterity the blessings of liberty; acknowledging with humility and gratitude the goodness of the sovereign Ruler of the Universe, ... do ordain and establish this Constitution for the Government of the Cherokee Nation.

ARTICLE I. Section 1—The boundaries of this Nation, embracing the lands solemnly guarantied and reserved forever to the Cherokee Nation by the Treaties concluded with the United States, are as follows, and shall forever hereafter remain unalterably the same: [describes the boundaries of the nation].

Section 2. The sovereignty and Jurisdiction of this Government shall extend over the country within the boundaries above described, and the lands therein are, and shall remain, the common property of the Nation; but the improvements made thereon, and in the possession of the citizens of the Nation, are the exclusive and indefensible property of the citizens respectively who made; or may rightfully be in possession of them; Provided, that the citizens of the Nation ... shall possess no right nor power to dispose of their improvements in any manner whatever to the United States, individual states, nor individual citizens thereof. ...

ARTICLE II. Section 1. The power of this Government shall be divided into three distinct departments; the Legislative, the Executive, and Judicial. ...

Section 4. No person shall be eligible to a seat in the General Council [the Legislature], but a free Cherokee male citizen, who shall have attained to the age of twenty-five years. The descendants of Cherokee men by all free women, except the African race, whose parents may have been living together as man and wife, according to the customs and laws of this Nation, shall be entitled to all the rights and privileges of this Nation, as well as the posterity of Cherokee women by all free men. No person who is of negro or mulatto parentage, either by the father or mother side, shall be eligible to hold any office of profit, honor or trust under this Government.

QUESTIONS

1. *What similarities do you see between the New York State Constitution and the Cherokee Nation Constitution?*

2. *Why do you think Article I of the Cherokee Constitution exists?*

3. *Neither colonists nor Cherokees in 1700 would have considered writing constitutions. How did their beliefs about governance and freedom change in the century that followed?*

Militia Training, an 1841 painting by the British-born artist James G. Clonney, depicts the Fourth of July celebration of an all-white militia company. Black dancers perform in the foreground while militia members socialize and, on the left, recuperate from too much drinking. A handful of women are also present.

a great increase in output and the rise of the mass-circulation "penny press," priced at one cent per issue instead of the traditional six. Newspapers like the *New York Sun and New York Herald* introduced a new style of journalism, appealing to a mass audience by emphasizing sensationalism, crime stories, and exposés of official misconduct. By 1840, according to one estimate, the total weekly circulation of newspapers in the United States, with a population of 17 million, exceeded that of Europe, with 233 million people.

Thanks to low postal rates, many newspapers circulated far beyond their places of publication. Indeed, by the 1830s, newspapers accounted for most postal traffic, outstripping private letters. The emergence of organized political parties also spurred newspaper publication. Each major party needed to have newspapers supporting its views in every part of the country, and government printing contracts were essential to most newspapers' survival. The publication of all sorts of magazines, travel guides, advice manuals, religious titles, and other reading materials also rose dramatically.

The reduction in the cost of printing made possible the appearance of many new newspapers in the late 1820s and early 1830s, including *Freedom's Journal* (the first Black newspaper), *Philadelphia Mechanic's Advocate* and other labor publications, the abolitionist weekly *The Liberator*, and the *Cherokee Phoenix*, the first Native American newspaper.

The growth of the reading public, yet another facet of the democratization of American life, opened the door for the rise of a new generation of women writers. Lydia Maria Child, Catharine Maria Sedgwick, Catharine Beecher, and others published stories, poetry, essays, and guides to domestic life. By the 1830s, moreover, through participation in religious and reform movements, thousands of women would establish a public presence, as will be described in Chapter 12. Nonetheless, once New Jersey added the word "male" to its voting requirements in 1807, no woman anywhere in the United States, whether married or single, proprietor or dependent, enjoyed the right to vote.

The Limits of Democracy

By the 1830s, the time of Andrew Jackson's presidency, the axiom that "the people" ruled had become a universally accepted part of American politics. Those who opposed this principle, wrote Tocqueville, "hide their heads." But the very centrality of democracy to the definition of both freedom and nationality made it all the more necessary to define the boundaries of the political nation. As older economic exclusions fell away, others survived and new ones were added. The vigorous public life of antebellum America was simultaneously expansive and exclusive, and its limits were as essential to its nature as its broad scope. Democracy in America could absorb native-born poor white men as well as waves of immigrant men, yet it erected impenetrable barriers to the participation of women and non-white men—groups also excluded, as noted in the previous chapter, from full participation in the market revolution.

The "principle of universal suffrage," declared the *United States Magazine and Democratic Review* in 1851, meant that "white males of age constituted the political nation." How could the word "universal" be reconciled with barring people of color and women from political participation? As democracy triumphed, the intellectual grounds for exclusion shifted from economic dependency to natural incapacity. Gender and racial differences were widely understood as part of a single, natural hierarchy of innate endowments. A boundary drawn by nature itself was not really exclusion at all. "How did woman first become subject to man, as she now is all over the world?" asked the *New York Herald* in 1852. "By her nature, her sex, just as the negro is and always will be, to the end of time, inferior to the white race, and, therefore, doomed to subjection." In the colonial era, women had been seen as a threat to the political order because they were prone to be swayed by passion (unlike men, supposedly governed by reason). In the nineteenth century, women came to be seen as too pure to risk contamination in the rough-and-tumble world of politics. Paradoxically, therefore, while freedom for white men involved an open-ended process of personal transformation, developing to the fullest the potential inherent within each human being, the limits of American democracy rested on the belief that the character and abilities of non-whites and women were forever fixed by nature.

The debate over which people are and are not qualified to take part in American democracy has lasted into the twenty-first century. Not until 1920 was the Constitution amended to require states to allow women to vote. The Voting Rights Act of 1965 swept away restrictions on Black voting imposed by many southern states. Even today, controversy persists over the voting rights of immigrants, persons who have served prison terms, and the poor.

The political world of the nineteenth century, so crucial an arena for the exercise of American freedom, was in part defined in contrast to the feminine sphere of the home. The "most rabid Radical," Ralph Waldo Emerson remarked in his journal in 1841, was likely to be conservative "in relation to the theory of Marriage." Beyond the right to "decent treatment" by her husband and to whatever property the law allowed her to control, declared the *New York Herald*, a woman had "no rights . . . with which the public have any concern."

A Racial Democracy

If the exclusion of women from political freedom continued a long-standing practice, the increasing identification of democracy and whiteness marked something of a departure. Tocqueville noted that by the 1830s, "equality" had become an American obsession. In contrast to the highly stratified societies of Europe, white Americans of all social classes dressed the same, traveled in the same stagecoaches and railroad cars, and stayed in the same hotels. Yet at the same time, Blacks were increasingly considered a group apart.

Racist imagery became the stock-in-trade of popular theatrical presentations like minstrel shows, in which white actors in blackface entertained the audience by portraying African Americans as stupid, dishonest, and altogether ridiculous. With the exception of Herman Melville, who portrayed complex, sometimes heroic Black characters in works like *Moby-Dick* and *Benito Cereno* (the latter a fictionalized account of a shipboard slave rebellion), American authors either ignored Blacks entirely or presented them as stereotypes—happy slaves prone to superstition or long-suffering but devout Christians. Meanwhile, the somewhat tentative thinking of the revolutionary era about the status of non-whites flowered into an elaborate ideology of racial superiority and inferiority, complete with "scientific" underpinnings. These developments affected the boundaries of the political nation.

In the revolutionary era, only Virginia, South Carolina, and Georgia explicitly confined the vote to whites, although elsewhere, custom often made it difficult for free Blacks to exercise the **franchise**. As late as 1800, no northern state barred Blacks from voting. But every state that entered the Union after that year, with the single exception of Maine, limited the right to vote to white males. And, beginning with Kentucky in 1799 and Maryland two years later, several states that had allowed Blacks to vote rescinded the privilege.

Race and Class

In 1821, the same New York constitutional convention that removed property qualifications for white voters raised the requirement for Blacks to $250, a sum beyond the reach of nearly all of the state's Black residents. North Carolina disenfranchised free Blacks in 1835, and Pennsylvania, home of an economically successful Black community in Philadelphia, did the same three years later. One delegate to the Pennsylvania constitutional convention refused to sign the completed document because of its provision limiting suffrage to whites. This was Thaddeus Stevens, who would later become a leader in the drive for equal rights for African Americans after the Civil War. By 1860, Blacks could vote on the same basis as whites in only five New England states, which contained only 4 percent of the nation's free Black population. A delegate to the Pennsylvania convention of 1837 described the United States as "a political community of white persons."

JIM CROW.
NEW YORK.
Published by Firth & Hall, No / Franklin Sq

Jim Crow, a piece of sheet music from 1829. Minstrel shows were a form of nineteenth-century entertainment in which white actors impersonated Blacks. One of the most popular characters was Jim Crow, the happy, child-like plantation slave created by the performer Thomas D. Rice. Years later, "Jim Crow" would come to mean the laws and customs of southern segregation.

Despite racial inequalities, many whites of the revolutionary generation had thought of African American men as "citizens of color," potential members of the body politic. But in the nineteenth century, the definition of the political nation became more and more associated with race. The federal government barred Black men from service in state militias and the army (although the navy did enroll some Black sailors). No state accorded free Blacks what today would be considered full equality before the law. In Illinois, for example, Blacks could not vote, testify or sue in court, serve in the militia, or attend public schools. Blacks were aliens, not Americans, "intruders among us," declared a political leader in Minnesota.

In effect, race had replaced class as the boundary between those American men who were entitled to enjoy political freedom and those who were not. Even as this focus on race limited America's political community as a whole, it helped to solidify a sense of national identity among the diverse groups of

European origin. In a country where the right to vote had become central to the meaning of freedom, it is difficult to overstate the importance of the fact that white male immigrants could vote in some states almost from the moment they landed in America, while nearly all free Blacks (and, of course, enslaved men and women), whose ancestors had lived in the country for centuries, could not vote at all.

NATIONALISM AND ITS DISCONTENTS

The American System

The War of 1812, which the United States and Great Britain—the world's foremost military power—fought to a draw, inspired an outburst of nationalist pride. But the war also revealed how far the United States still was from being a truly integrated nation. With the Bank of the United States having gone out of existence when its charter expired in 1811, the country lacked a uniform currency and found it almost impossible to raise funds for the war effort. Given the primitive state of transportation, it proved very difficult to move men and goods around the country. One shipment of supplies from New England had taken seventy-five days to reach New Orleans. With the coming of peace, the manufacturing enterprises that sprang up while trade with Britain had been suspended faced intense competition from low-cost imported goods. A younger generation of Republicans, including Henry Clay and John C. Calhoun, who had led the call for war in 1812, believed these "infant industries" deserved national protection. While retaining their Jeffersonian belief in an agrarian republic, they insisted that agriculture must be complemented by a manufacturing sector if the country were to become economically independent of Britain.

In 1806, Congress, as noted in the previous chapter, had approved using public funds to build a paved National Road from Cumberland, Maryland, to the Ohio Valley. Two years later, Albert Gallatin, Jefferson's secretary of the treasury, outlined a plan for the federal government to tie the vast nation together by constructing roads and canals up and down the eastern seaboard, and by connecting the Atlantic coast with the Great Lakes and Ohio and Mississippi rivers. Gallatin's proposal fell victim to regional rivalries and fears of excessive national power. But the idea revived after the War of 1812.

In his annual message (now known as the State of the Union address) to Congress in December 1815, President James Madison put forward a blueprint for government-promoted economic development that came to be known as the **American System**, a label coined by Henry Clay. (It should not be confused with the "American system of manufactures" mentioned in the previous chapter, which referred to a way of mass-producing goods with interchange-able parts, not a political program for economic growth.) The plan rested on three pillars: a new national bank, a tariff on imported manufactured goods to protect American industry, and federal financing of improved roads and canals. The last was particularly important to those worried about the dangers of disunity. "Let us bind the nation together, with a perfect system of roads and canals," John C. Calhoun implored Congress in 1815. "Let us conquer space." When believers in strict construction of the Constitution objected, Calhoun replied: "If we are restricted in the use of money to the enumerated powers, on what principle can the purchase of Louisiana be justified?"

Government-sponsored internal improvements, as the construction of roads and canals was called, proved to be the most controversial part of the plan. Congress enacted an internal improvements program drafted by Calhoun only to be astonished when the president, on the eve of his retirement from office in March 1817, vetoed the bill. Since calling for its enactment, Madison had become convinced that allowing the national government to exercise powers not mentioned in the Constitution would prove dangerous to individual lib-erty and southern interests. A constitutional amendment would be necessary, he declared, before the federal government could build roads and canals. The other two parts of his plan, however, became law. The **tariff of 1816** offered pro-tection to goods that could be produced in the United States, especially cheap cotton textiles, while admitting tax-free those that could not be manufactured at home. Many southerners supported the tariff, believing that it would enable their region to develop a manufacturing base to rival New England's. And in 1816, a new Bank of the United States was created, with a twenty-year charter from Congress.

Banks and Money

The Second Bank of the United States soon became the focus of public resent-ment. Like its predecessor, it was a private, profit-making corporation that served as the government's financial agent, issuing paper money, collecting taxes, and paying the government's debts. It was also charged with ensuring that paper money issued by local banks had real value. The number of local banks had risen to more than 200—a sign of the accelerating market revolu-tion. They promoted economic growth by helping to finance manufacturing and commerce and extending loans to farmers for the purchase of land, tools, consumer goods, and, in the South, slaves. They also printed paper money.

Today, only the federal government issues paper money, and the total is determined by the Federal Reserve Bank, not the amount of gold held at the repository at Fort Knox. But in the nineteenth century, paper money consisted of notes promising to pay the bearer on demand a specified amount of "specie" (gold or silver). The value of the currency issued by individual banks depended on their reputation for stability. Since banks often printed far more money than the specie in their vaults, the value of paper currency fluctuated wildly. No one knew if the notes issued by many banks had any value. Public confidence was essential to a bank's success. The Bank of the United States was supposed to prevent the overissuance of money. Because it held all the funds of the federal government, it accumulated a large amount of paper money issued by local banks, which had been used to purchase public land. The Bank of the United States could demand payment in gold and silver from a local bank in exchange for that bank's paper money. This prospect was supposed to prevent local banks from acting improperly, for if it could not provide the specie when asked, it would have to suspend operations.

The Panic of 1819

But instead of effectively regulating the currency and loans issued by local banks, the Bank of the United States participated in a speculative fever that swept the country after the end of the War of 1812. The resumption of trade with Europe created a huge overseas market for American cotton and grain. Coupled with the rapid expansion of settlement into the West, this stimulated demand for loans to purchase land, which local banks and branches of the Bank of the United States were only too happy to meet by printing more money. The land boom was especially acute in the South, where the Cotton Kingdom was expanding.

Early in 1819, as European demand for American farm products returned to normal levels, the economic bubble burst. During the resulting **Panic of 1819**, the demand for land plummeted, and speculators lost millions as the price of western land fell. At this time, loans tended to be of short duration and banks could demand repayment at any time. The Bank of the United States, followed by state banks, began asking for payments from those to whom it had loaned money. Farmers and businessmen who could not repay declared bankruptcy, and unemployment rose in eastern cities.

The Panic of 1819 lasted little more than a year, but it severely disrupted the political harmony of the previous years. Those suffering from the economic downturn pressed the state and national governments for assistance. To the consternation of creditors, many states, especially in the West, responded by suspending the collection of debts. Kentucky went even further, establishing a state bank that flooded the state with paper money that creditors were required to accept in repayment of loans. This eased the burden on indebted farmers but injured those who had loaned them the money. Overall, the Panic deepened many Americans' traditional distrust of banks. The Second Bank of the United States was widely blamed for causing the Panic. Several states retaliated against the national bank by taxing its local branches.

These tax laws produced another of John Marshall's landmark Supreme Court decisions, in the case of **McCulloch v. Maryland** (1819). Reasserting his broad interpretation of governmental powers, Marshall declared the Bank a legitimate exercise of congressional authority under the Constitution's clause that allowed Congress to pass "necessary and proper" laws. Marshall's interpretation of the Constitution directly contradicted the "strict construction" view that limited Congress to powers specifically granted in the Constitution.

The Missouri Controversy

In 1816, James Monroe handily defeated Federalist candidate Rufus King, becoming the last of the Virginia presidents. By 1820, the Federalists fielded electoral tickets in only two states, and Monroe carried the entire country. (One elector, William Plumer of New Hampshire, however, cast his vote for John Quincy Adams, whom he deemed more qualified than Monroe to be president. The legend later arose that Plumer voted as he did because he wished George Washington to remain the only president elected unanimously.) Monroe's two terms in office were years of one-party government, sometimes called the **Era of Good Feelings**. Plenty of bad feelings, however, surfaced during his presidency. In the absence of two-party competition, politics was organized along lines of competing sectional interests.

Even as political party divisions faded and John Marshall aligned the Supreme Court with the aggressive nationalism of Clay and Calhoun, the issue of slavery again threatened to disrupt the nation's unity. In 1819, Congress considered a request from Missouri, an area carved out of the Louisiana Purchase, to form a constitution in preparation for admission to the Union as a state. Missouri's enslaved population already exceeded 10,000. James Tallmadge, a Republican congressman from New York, moved that the introduction of more slaves be prohibited and that children of those already in Missouri be freed at age twenty-five.

Tallmadge's proposal sparked two years of controversy, during which Republican unity shattered along sectional lines. His restriction passed the House, where most northern congressmen supported it over the objections of southern representatives. It died in the Senate, however. When Congress reconvened in 1820, Senator Jesse Thomas of Illinois proposed a compromise with three parts. Missouri would be authorized to draft a constitution without Tallmadge's restriction. Maine, which prohibited slavery, would be admitted to the Union to maintain the sectional balance between free and slave states. And slavery would be

THE MISSOURI COMPROMISE, 1820

OREGON TERRITORY
(Joint U.S.-British occupation of disputed territory)

BRITISH NORTH AMERICA

ME (Admitted as a free state, 1820)

REMAINING LOUISIANA PURCHASE

MICHIGAN TERRITORY

NEW SPAIN (Independent Mexico, 1821)

MO (Admitted as a slave state, 1821)

Missouri Compromise line 36°30′

ARKANSAS TERRITORY

Pacific Ocean

Atlantic Ocean

Territory closed to slavery by the Missouri Compromise
Free states and territories
Territory opened to slavery by the Missouri Compromise
Slave states and territories

Gulf of Mexico

FLORIDA TERRITORY

0   250   500 miles
0   250   500 kilometers

The Missouri Compromise temporarily settled the question of the expansion of slavery by dividing the Louisiana Purchase into free and slave areas.

prohibited in all remaining territory within the Louisiana Purchase north of latitude 36°30′ (Missouri's southern boundary). Congress adopted Thomas's plan as the **Missouri Compromise**.

A year later, Missouri presented to Congress its new constitution, which not only protected slavery but also prohibited free Blacks from entering the state. Since some northern states considered Blacks citizens, this seemed to violate the federal Constitution's "comity" clause, which requires each state to recognize the rights of citizens of other states. Henry Clay engineered a second Missouri Compromise, according to which Congress accepted the state's constitution as written, but instructed Missouri that it could not deprive the citizens of any states of their rights under the U.S. Constitution. Missouri, however, largely ignored this provision.

The Slavery Question

Thomas Jefferson, who had drafted the clause of the Northwest Ordinance of 1787 prohibiting slavery north of the Ohio River, strenuously opposed efforts to keep the institution out of Missouri. He saw the entire controversy as an attempt by Federalists to revive their party by setting northern and southern Republicans against each other. Jefferson was correct that political power, not moral scruples, motivated most northern congressmen. But Republicans, not the few remaining Federalists, provided the bulk of the votes against slavery in Missouri. Twenty-eight years of Virginia presidents, interrupted only by the single term of John Adams of Massachusetts, had persuaded many northerners that the South exercised undue influence in Washington. More slave states meant more southern congressmen and electoral votes.

The Missouri controversy raised for the first time what would prove to be a fatal issue—the westward expansion of slavery. The sectional division it revealed aroused widespread feelings of dismay. "This momentous question," wrote Jefferson, "like a fire bell in the night, awakened and filled me with terror. I considered it at once as the knell of the union." John Quincy Adams wrote of the debate in his diary:

> [It] disclosed a secret: it revealed the basis for a new organization of parties. . . . Here was a new party really formed . . . terrible to the whole Union, but portentously terrible to the South—threatening in its progress the emancipation of all their slaves, threatening in its immediate effect that southern domination which has swayed the Union for the last twenty years.

The "dissolution of the Union" over the issue of slavery, Adams mused, disastrous as that might be, would result in civil war and the "extirpation of slavery from this whole continent." It would take more than forty years for Adams's prediction to be fulfilled. For the moment, the slavery issue faded once again from national debate.

NATION, SECTION, AND PARTY

The United States and the Latin American Wars of Independence

Between 1810 and 1822, Spain's Latin American colonies rose in rebellion and established a series of independent nations, including Mexico, Venezuela, Ecuador, and Peru. By 1825, Spain's once vast American empire had been reduced to the islands of Cuba and Puerto Rico. The uprisings inspired a wave of sympathy in the United States. In 1822, the Monroe administration became the first government to extend diplomatic recognition to the new Latin American republics.

Parallels existed between the Spanish-American revolutions and the one that had given birth to the United States. In both cases, the crisis of empire was precipitated by programs launched by the imperial country aimed in large measure at making the colonies contribute more to its finances. The government in Spain had been trying to strengthen its hold on the empire since the late eighteenth century. A French army under Napoleon occupied Spain in 1808 and overthrew the monarchy, inspiring assertions of local control throughout Spanish America. A new constitution adopted by Spain in 1812 granted greater local rights in Spain and the colonies. When the king was restored in 1814, he repudiated the constitution and moved to reassert control over the colonies. As had happened in British North America, local elites demanded status and treatment equal to residents of the imperial power. The Spanish-American declarations of independence borrowed directly from that of the United States. The first, issued in 1811, even before the restoration of the monarchy in Spain, declared that the "United Provinces" of Venezuela now enjoyed "among the sovereign nations of the earth the rank which the Supreme Being and nature has assigned us"—language strikingly similar to Jefferson's.

Unlike the British empire, Spain's dissolved into seventeen different nations. The Spanish empire was too vast and disconnected for a common sense of nationhood to emerge. The Spanish government had imposed severe restrictions on printing, thereby making communication between the various parts of the empire more difficult than in the British colonies. The first printing press in Bogotá, a major city in South America, was not established until the 1770s. Nonetheless, imported books had circulated widely, spreading the era's revolutionary ideas.

Most of the new Latin American constitutions were more democratic than that of the United States. Most sought to implement the transatlantic ideals of rights and freedom by creating a single national "people" out of the diverse populations that made up the Spanish empire. To do so, they extended the right to vote to Indians and free Blacks. The Latin American wars of independence, in which Black soldiers participated on both sides, also set in motion the gradual abolition of slavery. But the Latin American wars of independence lasted longer—sometimes more than a decade—and were more destructive than the one in the United States had been. In some countries, independence was followed by civil war. As a result, it proved far more difficult for the new Latin American republics to achieve economic development than for the United States.

The Monroe Doctrine

John Quincy Adams, who was serving as James Monroe's secretary of state, was devoted to consolidating the power of the national government at home and abroad. Adams feared that Spain would try to regain its Latin American colonies. In 1823, he drafted a section of the president's annual message to Congress that

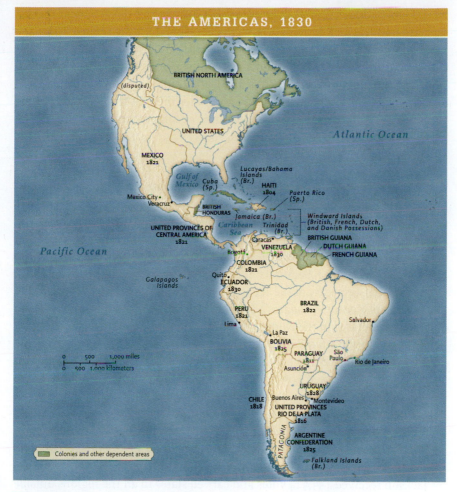

THE AMERICAS, 1830

BRITISH NORTH AMERICA

(disputed)

UNITED STATES

Atlantic Ocean

MEXICO
1821

Gulf of Mexico

Lucayas/Bahama Islands (Br.)

Cuba (Sp.)

HAITI 1804

Puerto Rico (Sp.)

Mexico City •
Veracruz•

BRITISH HONDURAS

Jamaica (Br.)

Caribbean Sea

Trinidad (Br.)

Windward Islands (British, French, Dutch, and Danish Possessions)

UNITED PROVINCES OF CENTRAL AMERICA 1821

Caracas•

VENEZUELA 1830

BRITISH GUIANA
DUTCH GUIANA
FRENCH GUIANA

Bogotá •

COLOMBIA 1821

Pacific Ocean

Galapagos Islands

Quito •

ECUADOR 1830

PERU 1821

BRAZIL 1822

Lima •

Salvador•

La Paz •

BOLIVIA 1825

PARAGUAY 1811

São Paulo•

Rio de Janeiro

0   500   1,000 miles
0   500 1,000 kilometers

Asunción•

URUGUAY 1828

CHILE 1818

Buenos Aires•

•Montevideo

UNITED PROVINCES RIO DE LA PLATA 1816

ARGENTINE CONFEDERATION 1825

PATAGONIA

Falkland Islands (Br.)

Colonies and other dependent areas

This map depicts the Western Hemisphere after most of Spain's colonies achieved their independence.

became known as the **Monroe Doctrine**. It expressed three principles. First, the United States would oppose any further efforts at colonization by European powers in the Americas (a statement aimed not only against Spain but also at France, which had designs on Cuba, and at Russia, which was seeking to expand its holdings on the Pacific coast). Second, the United States would abstain from involvement in the wars of Europe. Finally, Monroe warned European powers not to interfere with the newly independent states of Latin America.

The Monroe Doctrine is sometimes called America's diplomatic declaration of independence. For many decades, it remained a cornerstone of American foreign policy. Based on the assumption that Europe and the Americas formed separate political and diplomatic systems, it claimed for the United States the role of dominant power in the Western Hemisphere. For Adams, the commercial implications were as important as the political ones. In 1823, Latin America was a major market for British goods, and British citizens were heavily involved in mining, banking, and commercial enterprises there. Adams hoped that the United States could eventually assume Britain's economic role.

The Election of 1824

The Monroe Doctrine reflected a rising sense of American nationalism. But sectionalism seemed to rule domestic politics. As the election of 1824 approached, only Andrew Jackson could claim truly national support. Jackson's popularity rested not on any specific public policy—few voters knew his views—but on military victories over the British at the Battle of New Orleans and over the Muscogee (Creek) and Seminole Indians. Other candidates included John Quincy Adams, Secretary of the Treasury William H. Crawford of Georgia, and Henry Clay of Kentucky. Adams's support was concentrated in New England and, more generally, in the North, where Republican leaders insisted the time had come for the South to relinquish the presidency. Crawford represented the South's Old Republicans, who wanted the party to reaffirm the principles of states' rights and limited government. Clay was one of the era's most popular politicians, but his support in 1824 lay primarily in the West. A caucus of Republican congressmen traditionally chose the party's nominee for president. The caucus selected Crawford, but this did not deter the other candidates, a sign that at a time of expanding democracy a small group of officials could no longer determine who ran for office.

Jackson received 153,544 votes and carried states in all the regions outside of New England. But with four candidates in the field, none received a majority of the electoral votes. As required by the Constitution, Clay, who finished fourth, was eliminated, and the choice among the other three fell to the House of Representatives. Sincerely believing Adams to be the most qualified candidate and the one most likely to promote the American System, and probably calculating that the election of Jackson, a westerner, would impede his own presidential ambitions, Clay gave his support to Adams, helping to elect him. He soon became secretary of state in Adams's cabinet. The charge that he had made a "corrupt bargain"—bartering critical votes in the presidential contest for a public office—clung to Clay for the rest of his career, making it all but impossible for him to reach the White House. The election of 1824 laid the groundwork for a new system of political parties. Supporters of Jackson and Crawford would soon unite in a new organization, the Democratic Party, determined to place Jackson in the White House in 1828. The alliance of Clay and Adams became the basis for the Whig Party of the 1830s.

The Nationalism of John Quincy Adams

John Quincy Adams enjoyed one of the most distinguished pre-presidential careers of any American president. The son of John Adams, he had witnessed the Battle of Bunker Hill at age eight and at fourteen had worked as private secretary and French interpreter for an American envoy in Europe. He had gone on to serve as ambassador to Prussia, the Netherlands, Britain, and Russia, and as senator from Massachusetts. Although elected as a Federalist, Adams cast one of New England's few votes in favor of Jefferson's embargo policy, arguing that his region must rise above sectional self-interest to defend the national good. Given the intense political passions of the time, he had been forced to resign his seat as a result of his vote, and he soon abandoned the Federalist Party.

Adams was not an engaging figure. He described himself as "a man of cold, austere, and foreboding manners." But he had a clear vision of national greatness. At home, he strongly supported the American System of government-sponsored economic development. Abroad, he hoped to encourage American commerce throughout the world and, as illustrated by his authorship of the Monroe Doctrine, enhance American influence in the Western Hemisphere. As Monroe's secretary of state, he had been the only cabinet member to oppose reprimanding Andrew Jackson for his violent incursion into Florida. In 1819, as noted in the previous chapter, Adams negotiated a treaty by which the United States acquired Florida from Spain. He also concluded an agreement with Great Britain fixing the Canadian-American border at the forty-ninth parallel, the northern boundary of the Louisiana Purchase. An ardent expansionist, Adams was certain that the United States would eventually, and peacefully, absorb Canada, Cuba, and at least part of Mexico. Indeed, he once said, the "proper domain" of the United States was "the entire continent of North America."

"Liberty Is Power"

Adams held a view of federal power far more expansive than most of his contemporaries. In his first message to Congress, in December 1825, he set forth a comprehensive program for an activist national state. "The spirit of improvement is abroad in the land," Adams announced, and the federal government should be its patron. He called for legislation promoting agriculture, commerce, manufacturing, and "the mechanical and elegant arts." His plans included the establishment of a national university, an astronomical observatory, and a naval academy. At a time when many Americans felt that governmental authority posed the greatest threat to freedom, Adams astonished many listeners with the bold statement "Liberty is power."

Adams's proposals alarmed all believers in strict construction of the Constitution. His administration spent more on internal improvements than his five predecessors combined, and it enacted a steep increase in tariff rates in 1828. But the rest of Adams's ambitious ideas received little support in Congress. Not until the twentieth century would the kind of national economic and educational planning envisioned by Adams be realized. Some of his proposals, like the adoption by the United States of the metric system of weights and measures used by nearly every other nation in the world, and the building of a national university, have yet to be implemented.

Martin Van Buren and the Democratic Party

Adams's program handed his political rivals a powerful weapon. With individual liberty, states' rights, and limited government as their rallying cries, Jackson's supporters began to organize for the election of 1828 almost as soon as Adams assumed office. Martin Van Buren, a senator from New York, oversaw the task. The clash between Adams and Van Buren demonstrated how democracy was changing the nature of American politics. Adams typified the old politics—he was the son of a president and, like Jefferson and Madison, a man of sterling intellectual accomplishments. Van Buren represented the new political era. The son of a tavern keeper, he was a talented party manager, not a person of great vision or intellect.

But Van Buren did have a compelling idea. Rather than being dangerous and divisive, as the founding generation had believed, political parties, he insisted, were a necessary and indeed desirable element of political life. Party competition provided a check on those in power and offered voters a real choice in elections. And by bringing together political leaders from different regions in support of common candidates and principles, national parties could counteract the sectionalism that had reared its head during the 1820s. Like many of his contemporaries, Van Buren had been alarmed when politics divided along sectional lines in the Missouri debates and again in the election of 1824. He attributed this in part to a loss of discipline within the ruling Republican Party. "Party attachment," Van Buren wrote to Virginia editor Thomas Ritchie, "in former times furnished a complete antidote for sectional prejudices by producing counteracting feelings. It was not until that defense had been broken down that the clamor against southern influence and African slavery could be made effectual in the North." National political parties, Van Buren realized, formed a bond of unity in a divided nation. He set out to reconstruct the Jeffersonian political alliance between "the planters of the South and the plain republicans [the farmers and urban workers] of the North."

The Election of 1828

By 1828, Van Buren had established the political apparatus of the Democratic Party, complete with local and state party units overseen by a national committee and a network of local newspapers devoted to the party. Adams, for his part, disdained political organization. Despite Clay's urging, he refused to dismiss federal officeholders who campaigned for Jackson and did little to promote his own reelection.

Apart from a general commitment to limited government, Jackson's supporters made few campaign promises, relying on their candidate's popularity and the workings of party machinery to get out the vote. The 1828 election campaign was scurrilous. Jackson's supporters accused Adams of having had a series of mistresses while serving as a diplomat in Europe. They praised their candidate's frontier manliness and ridiculed Adams's intellectual attainments. ("Vote for Andrew Jackson who can fight, not John Quincy Adams who can write," declared one campaign slogan.) Jackson's opponents condemned him as a murderer for having executed army deserters and killing men in duels. They

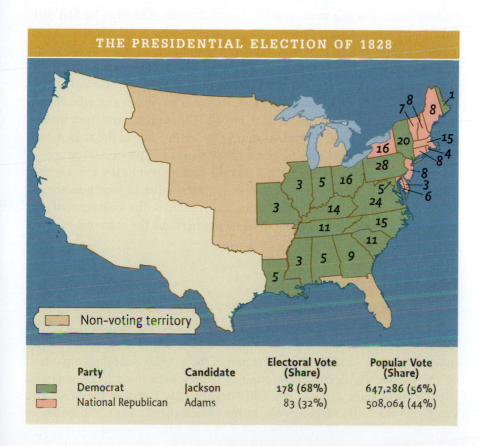

THE PRESIDENTIAL ELECTION OF 1828

☐ Non-voting territory

Party	Candidate	Electoral Vote (Share)	Popular Vote (Share)
Democrat	Jackson	178 (68%)	647,286 (56%)
National Republican	Adams	83 (32%)	508,064 (44%)

questioned the morality of his wife, Rachel, because she had married Jackson before her divorce from her first husband had become final. Jackson always believed his opponents' slanders had contributed to his wife's death shortly after the election.

By 1828, voters, not the legislature, chose presidential electors in every state except South Carolina, a fact that helped to encourage vigorous campaigning and high turnout. Nearly 57 percent of the eligible electorate cast ballots, more than double the percentage four years earlier. Jackson won a resounding victory, with around 650,000 votes to 500,000 for Adams. He carried the entire South and West, along with Pennsylvania. Jackson's election was the first to demonstrate how the advent of universal white male voting, organized by national political parties, had transformed American politics. For better or worse, the United States had entered the Age of Jackson.

THE AGE OF JACKSON

Andrew Jackson was a man of many contradictions. Although he had little formal education (Adams called him "a barbarian who could not write a sentence of grammar"), Jackson was capable of genuine eloquence in his public statements. He was a self-proclaimed champion of the common man, but his vision of democracy excluded any role for Indians, who he believed should be pushed west of the Mississippi River, and African Americans, who should remain enslaved or be freed and sent abroad. Although he rose from modest beginnings on the South Carolina frontier to become one of the richest men in Tennessee, he had an abiding suspicion of banks and paper money, and he shared the fears of many Americans that the market revolution was a source of moral decay rather than progress. A strong nationalist, Jackson nonetheless believed that the states, not Washington, D.C., should be the focal point of governmental activity. He opposed federal efforts to shape the economy or interfere in individuals' private lives.

The Party System

By the time of Jackson's presidency, politics had become more than a series of political contests—it was a spectacle, a form of mass entertainment, a part of Americans' daily lives. Every year witnessed elections to some office—local, state, or national—and millions took part in the parades and rallies organized by the parties. Politicians were popular heroes with mass followings and popular nicknames. Jackson was Old Hickory, Clay Harry of the West, and Van Buren the Little Magician (or, to his critics, the Sly Fox). Thousands of

Americans willingly attended lengthy political orations and debates. An audience of 100,000 was said to have gathered on a Massachusetts hillside to hear a speech by the Whig political leader Daniel Webster.

"Politics," one newspaper editor remarked, "seems to enter into everything." Indeed, party machines, headed by professional politicians, reached into every neighborhood, especially in cities. They provided benefits like jobs to constituents and ensured that voters went to the polls on election day. Party functionaries were rewarded with political offices. Government posts, Jackson declared, should be open to the people, not reserved for a privileged class of permanent bureaucrats. He introduced the principle of rotation in office (called the **spoils system** by opponents) into national government, making loyalty to the party the main qualification for jobs like postmaster and customs official.

Large national conventions where state leaders gathered to hammer out a platform now chose national candidates. Newspapers played a greater and greater role in politics. Nearly 400 were published in 1830, compared to 90 in 1790. Every significant town, it seemed, had its Democratic and Whig papers whose job was not so much to report the news as to present the party's position on issues of the day. Jackson's Kitchen Cabinet—an informal group of advisers who helped to write his speeches and supervise communication between the White House and local party officials—mostly consisted of newspaper editors.

Democrats and Whigs

There was more to party politics, however, than spectacle and organization. Jacksonian politics revolved around issues spawned by the market revolution and the continuing tension between national and sectional loyalties. The central elements of political debate were the government's stance toward banks, tariffs, currency, and internal improvements, and the balance of power between national and local authority. Although both parties were coalitions of groups with varied, sometimes contradictory approaches to the issues of the day, the market revolution did much to determine their views and makeup. Democrats tended to be alarmed by the widening gap between social classes. They warned that "nonproducers"—bankers, merchants, and speculators— were seeking to use connections with government to enhance their wealth to the disadvantage of the "producing classes" of farmers, artisans, and laborers. They believed the government should adopt a hands-off attitude toward the economy and not award special favors to entrenched economic interests.

"All bank charters, all acts of incorporation," declared a Democratic newspaper, "are calculated to enhance the power of wealth, produce inequalities among the people and to subvert liberty." If the national government removed itself from the economy, ordinary Americans could test their abilities in the fair competition of the self-regulating market. The Democratic Party attracted aspiring entrepreneurs who resented government aid to established businessmen, as well as large numbers of farmers and city workingmen suspicious of new corporate enterprises. Poorer farming regions isolated from markets, like the lower Northwest and the southern backcountry, tended to vote Democratic.

Whigs united behind the American System, believing that via a protective tariff, a national bank, and aid to internal improvements, the federal government could guide economic development. They were strongest in the Northeast, the most rapidly modernizing region of the country. Most established businessmen and bankers supported their program of government-promoted economic growth, as did farmers in regions near rivers, canals, and the Great Lakes, who benefited from economic changes or hoped to do so. The counties of upstate New York along the Erie Canal, for example, became a Whig stronghold, while more isolated rural communities tended to vote Democratic. Many slaveholders supported the Democrats, believing states' rights to be slavery's first line of defense. But like well-to-do merchants and industrialists in the North, the largest southern planters generally voted Whig.

Public and Private Freedom

The party battles of the Jacksonian era reflected the clash between "public" and "private" definitions of American freedom and their relationship to governmental power, a persistent tension in the nation's history. For Democrats, liberty was a private entitlement best secured by local governments and endangered by powerful national authority. "The limitation of power, in every branch of our government," wrote a Democratic newspaper in 1842, "is the only safeguard of liberty." A "splendid" government was always "built upon the ruins of popular rights."

Under Jackson, even as democracy expanded, the power of the national government waned. Weak national authority, in the Democratic view, was essential to both private freedom and states' rights—"the freedom of the individual in the social union, [and] the freedom of the State in the Federative Union." Ralph Waldo Emerson called antebellum Americans "fanatics in freedom," whose obsession expressed itself in hatred of "tolls, taxes, turnpikes, banks, hierarchies, governors, yea, almost laws." Democrats regularly condemned the faraway federal government as the greatest "danger to liberty" in America and identified government-granted privilege as the root cause of social inequality. During Jackson's presidency, Democrats reduced expenditures, lowered the tariff, killed the national bank, and refused pleas for federal aid to internal improvements. By 1835, Jackson even managed to pay off the national debt.

As a result, states replaced the federal government as the country's main economic actors, planning systems of canals and roads and chartering banks and other corporations.

Politics and Morality

Democrats, moreover, considered individual morality a private matter, not a public concern. They opposed attempts to impose a unified moral vision on society, such as "temperance" legislation, which restricted or outlawed the production and sale of liquor, and laws prohibiting various kinds of entertainment on Sundays. As noted in Chapter 9, Catholic Irish and German immigrants who began arriving in significant numbers in the 1830s flocked to the Democratic Party. One reason was that they did not wish to have Protestant moral standards enforced by the government. "In this country," declared the New York *Journal of Commerce* in 1848, "liberty is understood to be the *absence* of government from private affairs." The test of public policies was not whether they enhanced the common good but the extent to which they allowed scope for "free agency"—that is, for individuals to make decisions, pursue their interests, and cultivate their unique talents without outside interference.

Whigs, for their part, insisted that liberty and power reinforced each other. An activist national government could enhance the realm of freedom. Liberty, Whigs believed, required a prosperous and moral America. The government should create the conditions for balanced and regulated economic development, thereby promoting a prosperity in which all classes and regions would share. Like the Federalists before them, wealthy Whigs tended to view society as a hierarchy of social classes, in contrast to the disorderly world of unrestrained individual competition embraced by many Democrats. But unlike most Federalists, they insisted that in the United States class status was not fixed, since any individual could achieve upward mobility.

Whigs, moreover, rejected the premise that the government must not interfere in private life. To function as free—that is, self-directed and self-disciplined—moral agents, individuals required certain character traits, which government could help to instill. The role of government, declared one New York Whig, was not simply to stand aside but actively to "promote the welfare of the people." Many evangelical Protestants supported the Whigs, convinced that via public education, the building of schools and asylums, temperance legislation, and the like, democratic governments could inculcate the "principles of morality." And during the Jacksonian era, popularly elected local authorities enacted numerous laws, ordinances, and regulations that tried to shape public morals by banning prostitution and the consumption of alcohol, and regulating other kinds of personal behavior.

South Carolina and Nullification

Andrew Jackson, it has been said, left office with many more principles than he came in with. Elected as a military hero backed by an efficient party machinery, he was soon forced to define his stance on public issues. Despite his commitment to states' rights, Jackson's first term was dominated by a battle to uphold the supremacy of federal over state law. The tariff of 1828, which raised taxes on imported manufactured goods made of wool as well as on raw materials like iron, had aroused considerable opposition in the South, nowhere more than in South Carolina, where it was called the **tariff of abominations**. Insisting that the tariff on imported manufactured goods raised the prices paid by southern consumers to benefit the North, the legislature threatened to "nullify" it—that is, declare it null and void within their state.

The state with the largest proportion of enslaved people in its population (55 percent in 1830), South Carolina was controlled by a tightly knit group of large planters. They maintained their grip on power by a state constitution that gave plantation counties far greater representation in the legislature than their population warranted, as well as through high property qualifications for officeholders. They had been thoroughly alarmed by the Missouri crisis and by the steady strengthening of national authority by John Marshall's Supreme Court. Behind their economic complaints against the tariff lay the conviction that the federal government must be weakened lest it one day take action against slavery.

John C. Calhoun soon emerged as the leading theorist of nullification. As the South began to fall behind the rest of the country in population, Calhoun had evolved from the nationalist of 1812 into a powerful defender of southern sectionalism. Having been elected vice president in 1828, Calhoun at first remained behind the scenes, secretly drafting the *Exposition and Protest* in which the South Carolina legislature justified nullification, drawing on the arguments in the Virginia and Kentucky resolutions of 1798 (discussed in Chapter 8). The national government, Calhoun insisted, had been created by an agreement among sovereign states, each of which retained the right to prevent the enforcement within its borders of acts of Congress that exceeded the powers specifically spelled out in the Constitution.

Almost from the beginning of Jackson's first term, Calhoun's influence in the administration waned, while Secretary of State Martin Van Buren emerged as the president's closest adviser. One incident that helped set Jackson against Calhoun occurred a few weeks after the inauguration. Led by Calhoun's wife, Floride, Washington society women ostracized Peggy Eaton, the wife of Jackson's secretary of war, because she was the daughter of a Washington tavern keeper and, allegedly, a woman of "easy virtue." Van Buren stood by her, as did

Jackson, who identified criticism of Peggy Eaton with the abuse his own wife had suffered during the campaign of 1828.

Debate over nullification further divided Jackson and Calhoun. In January 1830, Daniel Webster gave a speech in the Senate declaring that the people, not the states, created the Constitution, making the federal government sovereign. He called nullification illegal, unconstitutional, and treasonous. Webster's ending was widely hailed throughout the country—"Liberty *and* Union, now and forever, one and inseparable." A few weeks later, at a White House dinner, Jackson delivered a toast while fixing his gaze on Calhoun: "Our Federal Union—it must be preserved." Calhoun's reply came immediately: "The Union—next to our liberty most dear." By 1831, Calhoun had publicly emerged as the leading theorist of states' rights.

The Nullification Crisis

Nullification was not a purely sectional issue. South Carolina stood alone during the **nullification crisis**, and several southern states passed resolutions condemning its action. Nonetheless, the elaboration of the compact theory of the Constitution gave the South a political philosophy to which it would turn when sectional conflict became more intense. Calhoun denied that nullification was a step toward disunion. On the contrary, the only way to ensure the stability of a large, diverse nation was for each state to be assured that national actions would never trample on its rights or vital interests. According to Calhoun's theory of the "concurrent majority," each major interest, including slaveholders, should have a veto over all measures that affected it.

To Jackson, however, nullification amounted to nothing less than disunion. He dismissed Calhoun's constitutional arguments out of hand: "Can anyone of common sense believe the absurdity, that a faction of any state, or a state, has a right to secede and destroy this union, and the liberty of the country with it?" The issue came to a head in 1832, when a new tariff was enacted. Despite a reduction in rates, South Carolina declared the tax on imported goods null and void in the state after the following February. In response, Jackson persuaded Congress to pass the **Force Act** authorizing him to use the army and navy to collect customs duties.

To avert a confrontation, Henry Clay, with Calhoun's assistance, engineered the passage of a new tariff, in 1833, further reducing duties. South Carolina then rescinded the ordinance of nullification, although it proceeded to "nullify" the Force Act. Calhoun abandoned the Democratic Party for the Whigs, where, with Clay and Webster, he became part of a formidable trio of political leaders (even though the three agreed on virtually nothing except hostility toward Jackson). It is perhaps ironic that Andrew Jackson, a firm believer in states' rights and limited government, did more than any other individual to give an emotional aura to the idea of Union and to offer an example of willingness to go to war, if necessary, to preserve what he considered the national government's legitimate powers.

INDIAN REMOVAL

For all of their differences, Jackson and Calhoun agreed that Native Americans should have no place in the United States. As the market revolution demanded roads and canals to connect regions, and cotton cultivation spread into new southern states, white Americans took Native Americans' land and excluded them from the nation's prosperity. "Extending the area of slavery," proclaimed Missouri senator Thomas Hart Benton, required "converting Indian soil into slave soil." During the 1820s, Missouri forced its Native population to leave the state. Soon, such expulsion would become federal policy. Congress passed the **Indian Removal Act** of 1830 to provide funds to states and territories for uprooting Native nations from the East.

The law marked a repudiation of the Jeffersonian idea that "civilized" Indians could be assimilated into the American population. In his messages to Congress, Jackson repeatedly referred to them as "savages" and supported states' efforts to seize Native Americans' land and violate their sovereignty.

The sheer scale of Indian Removal is breathtaking. Between 1830 and 1860, the United States deported around 88,000 men, women, and children from over thirty different nations east, west, north, and south of Indian Territory. Well over 10,000 people died as a result.

From just west of the Appalachian Mountains to the Mississippi Valley, poor white farmers, many of them veterans who had been promised land for their service, squatted on Native land. At the same time, speculators secured government approval to sell the land in small plots and build roads and canals. In a typical instance, one day in the spring of 1789, Shawnees discovered men on Shawnee land surveying and laying out streets for what would become Cincinnati.

Native Responses

Native Americans in 1830 were diverse. They were Catholics, Methodists, Presbyterians, and followers of Native religions. East of the Mississippi, many lived in houses like their white neighbors. The Cherokee Nation had a written constitution and a printing press. Some Indians were antislavery, and others were slaveholders. Some were tightly woven into the local economy of their white neighbors, while others hunted and farmed far from the U.S. population. Some had fought against the United States in the War of 1812, while others had fought on the U.S. side. But proponents of Indian Removal painted them as one group: primitive, violent, rapidly declining, and doomed to extinction unless rescued and removed by the government.

The engraving by J. R. Chapin depicts a meeting between U.S. General Andrew Jackson and Muscogee Chief William Weatherford in Jackson's military tent. The two leaders fought each other in the Red Stick War, part of the War of 1812. Both were war leaders, as the engraving shows, as well as political officeholders and owners of plantations. Two decades later, Jackson's Indian Removal policy would forcibly deport Weatherford's Muscogees from their homeland.

Native nations responded in various ways. The Sauk and Fox nations reluctantly moved west of the Mississippi River in 1828, but four years later Sauk war leader Black Hawk, who had fought against the United States in the War of 1812, led over 1,000 followers back to their homelands in Illinois. In the 1832 Black Hawk War, they fought several battles against militia from Illinois and Michigan before surrendering. In 1829 and 1831, Shawnees and Delawares moved across the Mississippi River, following kinspeople who had already given up on the East. Senecas, Ottawas, and Wyandots who had lived with them in the multiethnic region of the Ohio Valley joined them in the West. Between 1830 and 1860, Ho-Chunks in the western Great Lakes were repeatedly forced to move, each time promised a "permanent home." The United States used violence and starvation tactics against Kickapoos and Potawatomis to force them to move west of the Mississippi.

Most of the deportations resulting from the Indian Removal Act were in the South. White southerners wanted the rich lands of the Cherokee, Chickasaw, Choctaw, Muscogee, and Seminole nations for cotton plantations, worked by enslaved people of African descent.

Cherokee leaders went to court to protect their rights, guaranteed by the U.S. Constitution and treaties with the federal government. In 1831, the state of Georgia was attempting to extend its jurisdiction over the Cherokee Nation on its border. Georgians arrested and convicted eleven U.S. citizens, including missionary and postmaster Samuel Worcester, who had refused to swear an oath of allegiance to Georgia. Worcester and the others contended that, as U.S. citizens living in the Cherokee Nation with its permission, they were not subject to Georgia's laws.

A lithograph from 1836 depicts Sequoyah, with the syllabary of the Cherokee language that he developed. Cherokees used his writing system to publish a newspaper, transact government business, and write personal letters. It is still the writing system for Cherokee today.

The Cherokee Nation appealed on their behalf in the case called ***Worcester v. Georgia***. In its 1832 decision, the U.S. Supreme Court ruled for Worcester and the Cherokees. Although the Court did not rule that the Cherokee Nation was a foreign nation, as the Cherokees' lawyers had argued, it did accept the argument that Indian nations were distinct peoples with the right to maintain separate political identities. They must be dealt with by the federal government, not the states, and Georgia's actions violated the Cherokees' treaties with Washington. But despite his strong assertion of national supremacy in the nullification crisis, Jackson refused to recognize the validity of the *Worcester* ruling. "John Marshall has made his decision," he supposedly declared, "now let him enforce it." In effect, Georgia nullified the U.S. Supreme Court decision.

With legal appeals exhausted, one faction of the Cherokee Nation agreed to cede their lands, but the majority, led by John Ross, who had been elected principal chief under the Cherokee Constitution, adopted a policy of passive resistance. Federal soldiers forcibly removed them during the presidency of Jackson's successor, Martin Van Buren. The army herded 18,000 men, women, and children into stockades and then forced them to move west. At least one-quarter perished during the winter of 1838–1839 on the **Trail of Tears**, as the removal route from Georgia to present-day Oklahoma came to be called. (In the Cherokee language, it was called "the trail on which we cried.") Among the Cherokees removed were people of African descent who were enslaved by Cherokee plantation owners. By then, the Choctaws, Chickasaws, and Muscogees had also been deported. Under threats of invasion by the U.S. Army, Choctaw leaders signed a removal treaty in 1830, against the protests of women who attended the council. At least 2,000 Choctaws died on their disastrous journey west. Chickasaw leaders agreed in 1830 to send a delegation to see the offered lands in the West but stipulating that if the delegation could not find "a country suitable to their wants and conditions" then the treaty would be "null and void." When the delegation returned, it reported that western lands were indeed unsuitable. Those negotiations delayed removal,

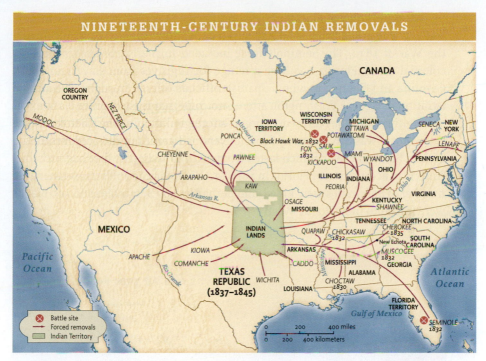

NINETEENTH-CENTURY INDIAN REMOVALS

The United States forcibly removed Native people from many locations east and west of the Mississippi River. Many suffered multiple moves (consolidated in this map).

but in 1838 Chickasaws had to move west. Although many Chickasaws were vaccinated against smallpox, several hundred died from the disease and the conditions of removal.

The Muscogees also resisted removal for years. In 1832, Muscogee leaders sent a memorial to Congress, which dwelled on the meaning of freedom and what they considered to be oppression by Alabama's lawmakers. "We never have been slaves," they proclaimed, "we have been born free. As freemen we have assisted in fighting the battles of our white brethren." Yet now their people were being "subjected to the penalties of forfeiture" of their land. The Muscogees were claiming a place in the nation's life, but identification with their own nation came before identity as Americans. And freedom meant maintaining their cultural, political, and economic independence, which, in turn, required keeping possession of ancestral lands. Some Muscogees went west starting in 1834, but the majority resisted removal, some taking refuge in the Cherokee Nation and others fighting militarily. In response, federal troops captured Muscogee warriors and deported 12,000 more Muscogees, several thousand of whom died on the journey or soon after reaching Oklahoma.

INDIAN REMOVAL ★ 395

The Seminoles of Florida resisted militarily. Osceola, one of the Seminole leaders, was a Red Stick who had survived Andrew Jackson's assault during the War of 1812. The Seminole force included formerly enslaved people. In colonial times, Florida had been a refuge for fugitives from slavery in South Carolina and Georgia to whom Spanish officials offered freedom. The administration of George Washington attempted to persuade the Seminoles to expel the fugitives, but they refused. Georgia sent the militia into Florida to recapture them, but it was driven out by Seminole and African American fighters. In the Second Seminole War, which lasted from 1835 to 1842 (the first had preceded American acquisition of Florida in 1819), 1,500 American soldiers and the same number of Seminoles were killed, and perhaps 3,000 Seminoles and 500 Blacks were forced to move to the West.

First published in 1829, *A Son of the Forest* was the autobiography of Pequot activist, preacher, and writer William Apess (sometimes spelled Apes). In it, he argued against Indian Removal and for Native Americans' place in the United States. This 1831 edition included his portrait.

Remaining in the East

Indian Removal was a systematic expulsion designed to eliminate every Native person east of the Mississippi, yet tens of thousands of Native Americans managed to remain in their homelands. Some retreated onto parts of their lands less desired by white Americans, including over 1,000 Cherokees (now the Eastern

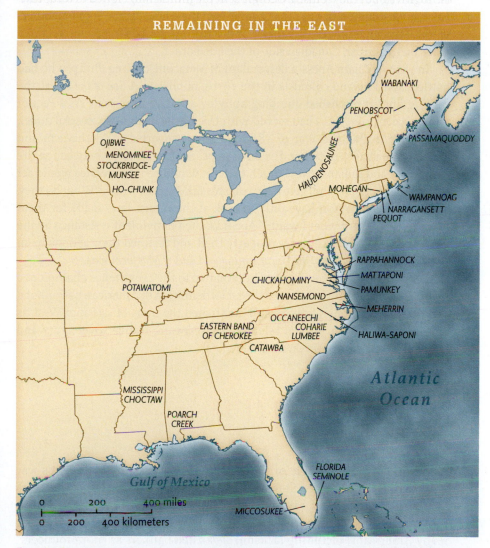

REMAINING IN THE EAST

Some Native nations and communities managed to avoid removal and stay in their homelands east of the Mississippi River. Several of these peoples, but by no means all, are represented here.

Band of the Cherokee Nation) who remained in the most mountainous part of the Cherokee Nation. Some Native communities used the support of white neighbors with whom they did business or went to church. Some held onto land by gaining individual title to it. The Catawbas employed that strategy, putting land in the name of one of their prominent women, Sally New River, but continuing to live and farm on it communally. The Haudenosaunee (Iroquois) held onto some land by using the moral leverage of having signed a treaty with George Washington in 1794 that guaranteed their land rights. Some members of the Haudenosaunee, Wabanaki, and Anishinaabe confederacies retained lands on the British Canadian side of the U.S. border.

In 1829, William Apess, a descendant of Metacom, or King Philip, who had battled New England colonists in the 1670s, published *A Son of the Forest*, the first significant published autobiography by a Native American. As a Pequot and an American, Apess had served with U.S. forces in an unsuccessful attack on Canada during the War of 1812. He later converted to Methodism and became a revivalist preacher. His book appealed for harmony between white Americans and Indians. "How much better it would be if the whites would act like civilized people [and] give every one his due," Apess wrote. "What do they, the Indians, want? You have only to look at the unjust laws made for them and say, 'They want what I want.'" Apess assisted nonviolent resistance by the Mashpees of Cape Cod against property theft and justified their actions in an 1825 book, *Nullification of the Unconstitutional Laws of Massachusetts*.

Removal was white Americans' alternative to the coexistence championed by Apess. It powerfully reinforced the racial definition of American nationhood and freedom. Although Indians still dominated the trans-Mississippi West, as American settlement pushed relentlessly westward, Native sovereignty and freedom would also be threatened there.

THE BANK WAR AND AFTER

Biddle's Bank

A central political struggle of the Age of Jackson was the president's war on the Bank of the United States. The Bank symbolized the hopes and fears inspired by the market revolution. The expansion of banking helped to finance the nation's economic development, including Indian Removal. But many Americans, including Jackson, distrusted bankers as "nonproducers" who contributed nothing to the nation's wealth but profited from the labor of others. The tendency of banks to overissue paper money, whose deterioration in value reduced the real income of wage earners, reinforced this conviction. Jackson himself had long believed that "hard money"—gold and silver—was the only honest currency. Nonetheless, when he assumed office there was little reason to predict a **Bank War**.

Heading the Bank was Nicholas Biddle of Pennsylvania, who during the 1820s had effectively used the institution's power, discussed earlier in this chapter, to curb the overissuing of money by local banks and to create a stable currency throughout the nation. Biddle was as strong-willed as Jackson and as unwilling to back down in a fight. In 1832, he told a congressional committee that his Bank had the ability to "destroy" any state bank. He hastened to add that he had never "injured" any of them. But Democrats wondered whether any institution, public or private, ought to possess such power. Many called it the Monster Bank, an illegitimate union of political authority and entrenched economic privilege. The issue of the Bank's future came to a head in 1832. Although the institution's charter would not expire until 1836, Biddle's allies persuaded Congress to approve a bill extending it for another twenty years. Jackson saw the tactic as a form of blackmail—if he did not sign the bill, the Bank would use its considerable resources to oppose his reelection.

Jackson's veto message is perhaps the central document of his presidency. In a democratic government, Jackson insisted, it was unacceptable for Congress to create a source of concentrated power and economic privilege unaccountable to the people. "It is to be regretted," he declared, "that the rich and powerful too often bend the acts of government to their selfish purposes." Exclusive privileges like the Bank's charter widened the gap between the wealthy and "the humble members of society—the farmers, mechanics, and laborers." Jackson presented himself as the defender of these "humble" Americans.

The Bank War reflected how Jackson enhanced the power of the presidency during his eight years in office, proclaiming himself the symbolic representative of all the people. He was the first president to use the veto power as a major weapon and to appeal directly to the public for political support, over the head of Congress. Whigs denounced him for usurping the power of the legislature. They insisted that Congress, not the president, represented the will of the people and that the veto power, while created by the Constitution, should be used only in extraordinary circumstances. But Jackson's effective appeal to democratic popular sentiments helped him win a sweeping reelection victory in 1832 over the Whig candidate, Henry Clay. His victory ensured the death of the Bank of the United States. (Ironically, Jackson's image today adorns the twenty-dollar bill issued by the Federal Reserve Bank, in some respects a successor of the Bank of the United States.)

The Pet Banks and the Economy

What, however, would take the Bank's place? Two very different groups applauded Jackson's veto—state bankers who wished to free themselves from

Biddle's regulations and issue more paper currency (called **soft money**), and **hard money** advocates who opposed all banks, whether chartered by the states or the federal government, and believed that gold and silver formed the only reliable currency.

During Jackson's second term, state bankers were in the ascendancy. Not content to wait for the charter of the Bank of the United States to expire in 1836, Jackson authorized the removal of federal funds from its vaults and their deposit in local banks. Not surprisingly, political and personal connections often determined the choice of these **pet banks**. The director of the Maine Bank of Portland, for example, was the brother-in-law of Levi Woodbury, a member of Jackson's cabinet. Two secretaries of the treasury refused to transfer federal money to the pet banks, since the law creating the Bank had specified that government funds could not be removed except for a good cause as communicated to Congress. Jackson finally appointed Attorney General Roger B. Taney, a loyal Maryland Democrat, to the treasury post, and he carried out the order. When John Marshall died in 1835, Jackson rewarded Taney by appointing him chief justice.

Without government deposits, the Bank of the United States lost its ability to regulate the activities of state banks. They issued more and more paper money, partly to help finance the rapid expansion of industrial development in New England, agriculture in the South and West, and canal and railroad systems planned by the states. The value of bank notes in circulation rose from $10 million in 1833 to $149 million in 1837.

Prices rose dramatically, and even though wages also increased, they failed to keep pace. As a result, workers' "real wages"—the actual value of their pay—declined. Numerous labor unions emerged, which attempted to protect the earnings of urban workers. Speculators hastened to cash in on rising land prices. Using paper money, they bought up huge blocks of public land, which they resold to farmers or to eastern purchasers of lots in entirely nonexistent western towns.

The Panic of 1837

Inevitably, the speculative boom collapsed. The government sold 20 million acres of federal land in 1836, ten times the amount sold in 1830, nearly all of it paid for in paper money, often of questionable value. In July 1836, the Jackson administration issued the Specie Circular, declaring that henceforth it would accept only gold and silver as payment for public land. At the same time, the Bank of England, increasingly suspicious about the value of American banknotes, demanded that American merchants pay their creditors in London in gold or silver. Then, an economic downturn in Britain dampened demand for American cotton, the country's major export.

The Times, an 1837 engraving that blames Andrew Jackson's policies for the economic depression. The Custom House is idle, while next door a bank is mobbed by worried depositors. Beneath Jackson's hat, spectacles, and clay pipe (with the ironic word "glory"), images of hardship abound.

Taken together, these events triggered an economic collapse in the United States, the **Panic of 1837**, followed by a depression that lasted to 1843. Prices fell by 25 percent in the first year of the downturn. Businesses throughout the country failed, and many farmers, unable to meet mortgage payments because of declining income, lost their land. Tens of thousands of urban workers saw their jobs disappear. The fledgling labor movement collapsed as strikes became impossible given the surplus of unemployed labor. By 1842, nine states had defaulted on their debts, mostly incurred to finance ambitious internal improvement projects. During the 1840s, states amended their constitutions to prohibit legislatures from borrowing money, issuing corporate charters, and buying stock in private enterprises. For the time being, the Jacksonians had succeeded in separating government—both federal and state—from the economy.

The president forced to deal with the depression was Martin Van Buren, who had been elected in 1836 over three regional candidates put forward by the Whigs in an attempt to maximize the party's electoral vote and throw the election into the House of Representatives. Under Van Buren, the hard-money, anti-bank wing of the Democratic Party came to power. In 1837, the administration announced its intention to remove federal funds from the pet banks and hold them in the Treasury Department in Washington under the control of government officials. In 1840, Congress approved the new policy, known as the Independent Treasury, which completely separated the federal government from the nation's banking system. Making federal funds unavailable for banks to use for investment would have dampened future economic growth had not the discovery of gold in California in 1848 poured new money into the economy. The Independent Treasury split the Democratic Party. Business-oriented Democrats, often connected with the state banks, strongly opposed Van Buren's policy and shifted wholesale to the Whigs. Meanwhile, the party's "agrarian" wing—small farmers and urban laborers opposed to all banking and paper money and uncomfortable with the market revolution in general—rallied to Van Buren. Many advocates of state sovereignty who had joined the Whigs after the nullification crisis now returned to the Democratic fold, including Van Buren's old nemesis, John C. Calhoun.

The Election of 1840

Despite his reputation as a political magician, Van Buren found that without Jackson's personal popularity he could not hold the Democratic coalition together. In 1840, he also discovered that his Whig opponents had mastered the political techniques he had helped to pioneer. Confronting an unprecedented opportunity for victory because of the continuing economic depression, the Whigs abandoned their most prominent leader, Henry Clay, and nominated William Henry Harrison. Like Jackson when he first sought the presidency, Harrison's main claim to fame was military success against the British and Indians during the War of 1812.

The party nominated Harrison without a platform. In a flood of publications, banners, parades, and mass meetings, they promoted him as the "log cabin" candidate, the champion of the common man. This tactic proved enormously effective, even though it bore little relationship to the actual life of the wealthy Harrison. The Whigs also denounced Van Buren as an aristocrat who had squandered the people's hard-earned money on "expensive furniture, china, glassware, and gold spoons" for the White House. Harrison's running mate was John Tyler, a states'-rights Democrat from Virginia who had joined the Whigs after the nullification crisis and did not follow Calhoun back to the Democrats. On almost every issue of political significance, Tyler held views totally opposed to those of other Whigs. But party leaders hoped he could expand their base in the South.

By 1840, the mass democratic politics of the Age of Jackson had absorbed the logic of the marketplace. Selling candidates and their images was as important as the positions for which they stood. With two highly organized parties competing throughout the country, voter turnout soared to 80 percent of those eligible, a level at which it remained for the rest of the nineteenth century. Harrison won a sweeping victory. "We have taught them how to conquer us," lamented a Democratic newspaper.

His Accidency

Whig success proved short-lived. Immediately upon assuming office, Harrison contracted pneumonia. He died a month later, and John Tyler succeeded him. When the Whig majority in Congress tried to enact the American System into law, Tyler vetoed nearly every measure, including a new national bank and higher tariff. Most of the cabinet resigned, and his party repudiated him. Whig newspapers were soon calling the president "His Accidency" and "The Executive Ass."

Tyler's four years in office were nearly devoid of accomplishment. If the campaign that resulted in the election of Harrison demonstrated how a flourishing system of democratic politics had come into existence, Tyler's lack of success showed that political parties had become central to American government. Without a party behind him, a president could not govern. But a storm was now gathering that would test the stability of American democracy and the statesmanship of its political leaders and of the party system itself.

CHAPTER REVIEW

REVIEW QUESTIONS

1. *What global changes prompted the Monroe Doctrine? What were its key provisions? How does it show America's growing international presence?*

2. *How did Andrew Jackson represent the major developments of the era: westward movement, the market revolution, and the expansion of democracy for some alongside the limits on it for others?*

3. *How did the expansion of white male democracy run counter to the ideals of the founders, who believed government should be sheltered from excessive influence by ordinary people?*

4. *What were the components of the American System, and how were they designed to promote the national economy under the guidance of the federal government?*

5. *How did the Missouri Compromise and the nullification crisis demonstrate increasing sectional competition and disagreements over slavery?*

6. *According to Martin Van Buren, why were political parties a desirable element of public life? What did he do to build the party system?*

7. How was *Indian Removal connected to the market revolution and other developments of the Jacksonian era?*

8. What rights did the *Muscogee nation seek to confirm in its 1832 memorial to Congress? On what bases did Native peoples make claims?*

9. What were the *key issues that divided the Democratic and Whig parties? Where did each party stand on those issues?*

10. Explain the *causes and effects of the Panic of 1837.*

KEY TERMS

Democracy in America (p. 366)

franchise (p. 372)

American System (p. 374)

tariff of 1816 (p. 375)

Panic of 1819 (p. 376)

McCulloch v. Maryland (p. 377)

Era of Good Feelings (p. 377)

Missouri Compromise (p. 378)

Monroe Doctrine (p. 381)

spoils system (p. 387)

tariff of abominations (p. 390)

Exposition and Protest (p. 390)

nullification crisis (p. 391)

Force Act (p. 391)

Indian Removal Act (p. 392)

Worcester v. Georgia (p. 394)

Trail of Tears (p. 394)

Bank War (p. 399)

soft money and hard money (p. 400)

pet banks (p. 400)

Panic of 1837 (p. 401)

Go to ⚄ INQUIZITIVE

To see what you know—and learn what you've missed—with personalized feedback along the way.

CHAPTER 11

THE
PECULIAR INSTITUTION

FOCUS QUESTIONS

- *How did slavery shape social and economic relations in the Old South?*

- *What were the legal and material constraints on slaves' lives and work?*

- *How did family, gender, religion, and values combine to create a distinct slave culture in the Old South?*

- *What were the major forms of resistance to slavery?*

I n an age of "self-made" men, no American rose more dramatically from humble origins to national and international distinction than Frederick Douglass. Born into slavery in 1818, he became a major figure in the crusade for abolition, the drama of emancipation, and the effort during Reconstruction to give meaning to Black freedom.

Douglass was the son of a slave mother and an unidentified white man, possibly his owner. As a youth in Maryland, he gazed out at the ships in Chesapeake Bay, seeing them as "freedom's swift-winged angels." In violation of Maryland law, Douglass learned to read and write, initially with the assistance of his owner's wife and then, after her husband forbade her to continue, with the help of local white children. "From that moment," he later wrote, he understood that knowledge was "the pathway from slavery to freedom." Douglass experienced slavery in all its variety, from work as a house servant and as a skilled craftsman in a Baltimore shipyard to labor as a plantation field hand. When he was fifteen, Douglass's owner sent him to a "slave breaker" to curb his independent spirit.

After numerous whippings, Douglass defiantly refused to allow himself to be disciplined again. This confrontation, he recalled, was "the turning-point in my career as a slave." It rekindled his desire for freedom. In 1838, having borrowed the free papers of a Black sailor, he escaped to the North.

Frederick Douglass went on to become the most influential African American of the nineteenth century and the nation's preeminent advocate of racial equality. "He who has endured the cruel pangs of slavery," he wrote, "is the man to advocate liberty." Douglass lectured against slavery throughout the North and the British Isles, and he edited a succession of antislavery publications. He published a widely read autobiography that offered an eloquent condemnation of slavery and racism. Indeed, his own accomplishments testified to the incorrectness of prevailing ideas about Blacks' inborn inferiority. Douglass was also active in other reform movements, including the campaign for women's rights. During the Civil War, he advised Abraham Lincoln on the employment of Black soldiers and became an early advocate of giving the right to vote to the emancipated slaves. Douglass died in 1895 as a new system of white supremacy based on segregation and disenfranchisement was being fastened upon the South.

Throughout his career, Douglass insisted that slavery could only be overthrown by continuous resistance. "Those who profess to favor freedom, and yet deprecate agitation," he declared, "are men who want crops without plowing up the ground, they want rain without thunder and lightning, they want the ocean without the awful roar of its many waters." In effect, Douglass argued that in their desire for freedom, the slaves were truer to the nation's underlying principles than the white Americans who annually celebrated the Fourth of July while allowing the continued existence of slavery.

THE OLD SOUTH

When Frederick Douglass was born, slavery was already an old institution in America. Two centuries had passed since the first twenty Africans were landed in Virginia from a Dutch ship. After abolition in the North, slavery had become **the "peculiar institution"** of the South—that is, an institution unique to southern society. The Mason-Dixon Line, drawn by two surveyors in the eighteenth century to settle a boundary dispute between Maryland and Pennsylvania, eventually became the dividing line between slavery and freedom.

Despite the hope of some of the founders that slavery might die out, in fact the institution survived the crisis of the American Revolution and rapidly expanded westward. During the first forty years of Douglass's life, the number of slaves and the economic and political importance of slavery continued to grow. On the eve of the Civil War, the enslaved population had risen to nearly 4 million, its high rate of natural increase more than making up for the prohibition in 1808 of further slave imports from Africa. In the South as a whole, slaves made up one-third of the total population, and in the cotton-producing states of the Lower South, around half. By the 1850s, slavery had crossed the Mississippi River and was expanding rapidly in Arkansas, Louisiana, and eastern Texas. In 1860, one-third of the nation's cotton crop was grown west of the Mississippi.

Cotton Is King

In the nineteenth century, cotton replaced sugar as the world's major crop produced by slave labor. And although slavery survived in Brazil and the Spanish and French Caribbean, its abolition in the British empire in 1833 made the United States indisputably the center of slavery in the Americas.

When measured by slavery's geographic extent, the numbers held in bondage, and the institution's economic importance both regionally and nationally, the Old South was the largest and most powerful slave society the modern world has known. Its strength rested on a virtual monopoly of cotton, the South's "white gold." Cotton had been grown for thousands of years in many parts of the globe. The *conquistador* Hernán Cortés was impressed by the high quality of woven cotton clothing worn by the Aztecs. But in the nineteenth century, cotton assumed an unprecedented role in the world economy.

Because the early industrial revolution centered on factories using cotton as the raw material to manufacture cloth, cotton became by far the most important commodity in international trade. And three-fourths of the world's cotton supply came from the southern United States. Throughout the world, hundreds of thousands of workers loaded, unloaded, spun, and wove cotton, and thousands of manufacturers and merchants owed their wealth to the cotton trade. Textile manufacturers in places as far-flung as Massachusetts, Lancashire

· C H R O N O L O G Y ·	
1791–1804	Haitian Revolution
1800	Gabriel's Rebellion
1811	Slave revolt in Louisiana
1822	Denmark Vesey's slave conspiracy
1830s	States legislate against teaching slaves to read or write
1831	William Lloyd Garrison's *The Liberator* debuts
	Nat Turner's Rebellion
1831–1832	Slave revolt in Jamaica
1832	Virginia laws tighten the slave system
1833	British Parliament mandates emancipation
1838	Great Britain abolishes slavery within its empire
	Frederick Douglass escapes slavery
1839	Slaves take control of the *Amistad*
1841	Slave uprising on the *Creole*
1849	Harriet Tubman escapes slavery
1855	Trial of Celia

in Great Britain, Normandy in France, and the suburbs of Moscow depended on a regular supply of American cotton.

Cotton sales earned the money from abroad that allowed the United States to pay for imported manufactured goods. On the eve of the Civil War, cotton represented well over half of the total value of American exports. In 1860, the economic investment represented by the slave population exceeded the value of the nation's factories, railroads, and banks combined.

The Second Middle Passage

As noted in Chapter 9, to replace the slave trade from Africa, which had been prohibited by Congress in 1808, a massive trade in slaves developed within the United States. More than 2 million slaves were sold between 1820 and 1860, a majority to local buyers but hundreds of thousands from older states to "importing" states of the Lower South, resulting in what came to be known as the **Second Middle Passage**. Slave trading was a visible, established business. The main commercial districts of southern cities contained the offices of slave traders, complete with signs reading "Negro Sales" or "Negroes Bought Here." Auctions of slaves took place at public slave markets, as in New Orleans, or at courthouses. Southern newspapers carried advertisements for slave sales, southern banks financed slave trading, southern ships and railroads carried enslaved men, women, and children from buyers to sellers, and southern states and municipalities earned revenue by taxing the sale of slaves. The Cotton Kingdom could not have arisen without the internal slave trade, and the economies of older states like Virginia came increasingly to rely on the sale of slaves.

Slavery and the Nation

Slavery, Henry Clay proclaimed in 1816, "forms an exception . . . to the general liberty prevailing in the United States." But Clay, like many of his contemporaries, underestimated slavery's impact on the entire nation. The "free states" had ended slavery, but they were hardly unaffected by it. The Constitution, as we have seen, enhanced the power of the South in the House of Representatives and electoral college and required all states to return fugitives from bondage. Slavery shaped the lives of all Americans, white as well as Black. It helped to determine where they lived, how they worked, and under what conditions they could exercise their freedoms of speech, assembly, and the press.

Northern merchants and manufacturers participated in the slave economy and shared in its profits. Money earned in the cotton trade helped to finance industrial development and internal improvements in the North. Northern ships carried cotton to New York and Europe, northern bankers financed cotton plantations, northern companies insured slave property, and northern

HAULING THE WHOLE WEEK8 PICKING

In this painting from 1842, slaves—men, women, and children—accompany an oxcart carrying the week's cotton crop to New Orleans.

factories turned cotton into cloth. New York City's rise to commercial prominence depended as much on the establishment of shipping lines that gathered the South's cotton and transported it to Europe as on the Erie Canal. The Lords of the Loom (New England's early factory owners) relied on cotton supplied by the Lords of the Lash (southern slaveowners). Northern manufacturers like Brooks Brothers supplied cheap fabrics (called "Negro cloth") to clothe the South's slaves.

The Southern Economy

There was no single South before the Civil War. In the eight slave states of the Upper South, slaves and slaveowners made up a smaller percentage of the total population than in the seven Lower South states that stretched from South Carolina west to Texas. The Upper South had major centers of industry in Baltimore, Richmond, and St. Louis, and its economy was more diversified than that of the Lower South, which was heavily dependent on cotton. Not surprisingly, during the secession crisis of 1860–1861, the Lower South states were the first to leave the Union.

Nonetheless, slavery led the South down a very different path of economic development than the North's, limiting the growth of industry, discouraging immigrants from entering the region, and inhibiting technological progress. The South did not share in the urban growth experienced by the rest of the country. Most southern cities were located on the region's periphery and served mainly as centers for gathering and shipping cotton. Southern banks existed primarily to help finance the plantations. They loaned money for the purchase of land and slaves, not manufacturing development. Southern railroads mostly consisted of short lines that brought cotton from the interior to coastal ports.

Slave distribution
(one dot represents 200 slaves)

Rather than being evenly distributed throughout the South, the slave population was concentrated in areas with the most fertile soil and easiest access to national and international markets. By 1860, a significant percentage of the slave population had been transported from the Atlantic coast to the Lower South via the internal slave trade.

In the Cotton Kingdom, the only city of significant size was New Orleans. With a population of 168,000 in 1860, New Orleans ranked as the nation's sixth-largest city. As the gathering point for cotton grown along the Mississippi River and sugar from the plantations of southeastern Louisiana, it was the world's leading exporter of slave-grown crops. Unlike other cities with slavery (apart from St. Louis and Baltimore, on the periphery of the South), New Orleans also attracted large numbers of European immigrants. In 1860, 40 percent of its population was foreign-born. And New Orleans's rich French heritage and close connections with the Caribbean produced a local culture quite different from that of the rest of the United States, reflected in the city's distinctive music, dance, religion, and cuisine.

In 1860, the South produced less than 10 percent of the nation's manufactured goods. Many northerners viewed slavery as an obstacle to American economic progress. But as New Orleans showed, slavery and economic growth could go hand in hand. In general, the southern economy was hardly stagnant, and slavery proved

The Slave Auction, by the British artist Lefevre Cranstone, who visited Virginia in 1859 and 1860. A slave sale is in progress, while on the right, slaves wait apprehensively for their turn to be sold. A child clings to her mother, perhaps for the last time, while potential buyers examine the seated women.

very profitable for most owners. The profits produced by slavery for the South and the nation as a whole formed a powerful obstacle to abolition. Senator James Henry Hammond of South Carolina declared, "No power on earth dares to make war upon it. **Cotton is king.**"

Plain Folk of the Old South

The foundation of the Old South's economy, slavery powerfully shaped race relations, politics, religion, and the law. Its influence was pervasive: "Nothing escaped," writes one historian, "nothing and no one." This was true despite the fact that the majority of white southerners—three out of four white families—owned no slaves. Since planters monopolized the best land, most small white farmers lived outside the plantation belt in hilly areas unsuitable for cotton production. They worked the land using family labor rather than slaves or hired workers.

Many southern farmers lived lives of economic self-sufficiency remote from the market revolution. They raised livestock and grew food for their families, purchasing relatively few goods at local stores. Those residing on marginal land in isolated hill areas and the Appalachian Mountains were often desperately poor and, since nearly all the southern states lacked systems of free

TABLE 11.1 Growth of the Enslaved Population

Years	Slave Population
1790	697,624
1800	893,602
1810	1,191,362
1820	1,538,022
1830	2,009,043
1840	2,487,355
1850	3,204,313
1860	3,953,760

public education, were more often illiterate than their northern counterparts. Not until the arrival of railroads and coal mining later in the nineteenth century would such areas become integrated into the market economy. Most yeoman farmers enjoyed a comfortable standard of living, and many owned a slave or two. But even successful small farmers relied heavily on home production to supply their basic needs. Unlike northern farmers, therefore, they did not provide a market for manufactured goods. This was one of the main reasons why the South did not develop an industrial base.

Some poorer whites resented the power and privileges of the great planters. Politicians like Andrew Johnson of Tennessee and Joseph Brown of Georgia rose to power as self-proclaimed spokesmen of the common man against the "slavocracy." But most poor whites made their peace with the planters in whose hands economic and social power was concentrated. Racism, kinship ties, common participation in a democratic political culture, and regional loyalty in the face of outside criticism all served to cement bonds between planters and the South's "plain folk." In the plantation regions, moreover, small farmers manned the slave patrols that kept a lookout for runaway slaves and those on the roads without permission. Non-slaveholders regularly elected slaveowners to public offices in the South. Like other white southerners, most small farmers believed their economic and personal freedom rested on slavery.

TABLE 11.2 Slaveholding, 1850 (in Round Numbers)

Number of Slaves Owned	Slaveholders
1	68,000
2–4	105,000
5–9	80,000
10–19	55,000
20–49	30,000
50–99	6,000
100–199	1,500
200 +	250

The Planter Class

Even among slaveholders, the planter was far from typical. In 1850, a majority of slaveholding families owned five or fewer slaves. Fewer than 40,000 families possessed the twenty or more slaves that qualified them as planters. Fewer than 2,000 families owned 100 slaves or more. Nonetheless, the planter's values and aspirations dominated southern life. The plantation, wrote Frederick Douglass, was "a little nation by itself, with its own language, its own rules, regulations, and customs." These rules and customs set the tone for southern society.

Ownership of slaves provided the route to wealth, status, and influence. Planters not only held the majority of slaves, but they controlled the most fertile land, enjoyed the highest incomes, and dominated state and local offices and the leadership of both political parties. Small slaveholders aspired to move up into the ranks of the planter class. Those who acquired wealth almost always invested it in land and slaves. But as the price of a "prime field hand" rose from $1,000 in 1840 to $1,800 in 1860 (the latter figure equivalent to around $60,000 today), it became more and more difficult for poorer white southerners to become slave-holders.

Slavery, of course, was a profit-making system, and slaveowners kept close watch on world prices for their products and invested in enterprises such as railroads and canals. They paid careful attention to every detail of their operations, adopted the most modern business and accounting practices, and carefully monitored market conditions and their own profits. Their wives—the "plantation mistresses" idealized in southern lore for femininity, beauty, and dependence on men—were hardly idle. They cared for sick slaves, directed the domestic servants, and supervised the entire plantation when their husbands were away. Of course, owners' sexual exploitation of slave women produced deep resentment among their wives, who sometimes took it out on the slaves themselves.

Many of the richest planters squandered their wealth in a lifestyle complete with lavish entertainments and summer vacations in Newport and Saratoga. House slaves were so numerous in Charleston, wrote one visitor to the city, that "the Charlestonians are obliged to exercise their wits to devise sufficient variety to keep them employed." On the cotton frontier, many planters lived in crude log homes. But in the older slave states, and as settled society developed in the Lower South, they constructed elegant mansions adorned with white columns in the Greek Revival style of architecture.

The Paternalist Ethos

The slave plantation was deeply embedded in the world market, and planters sought to accumulate land, slaves, and profits. But planters' values glorified not the competitive capitalist marketplace, but a hierarchical, agrarian society in which slaveholding gentlemen took personal responsibility for the physical and moral well-being of their dependents—women, children, and slaves. "The master," wrote one planter, "as the head of the system, has a right to the obedience and labor of the slave, but the slave has also his mutual rights in the master; the right of protection, the right of counsel and guidance, the right of subsistence, the right of care and attention in sickness and old age."

Louisa, an enslaved woman, with her charge in an 1858 photograph. The slave had been purchased at age twenty-two at a slave auction in New Orleans to serve as a nursemaid. Because of a death in the white family, the child was her legal owner.

This outlook, known as **paternalism** (from the Latin word for "father"), had been a feature of American slavery even in the eighteenth century. But it became more ingrained after the closing of the African slave trade in 1808, which narrowed the cultural gap between master and slave. Unlike the absentee planters of the West Indies, many of whom resided in Great Britain, southern slaveholders lived on their plantations and thus had year-round contact with their slaves.

The paternalist outlook both masked and justified the brutal reality of slavery. It enabled slaveowners to think of themselves as kind, responsible masters even as they bought and sold their human property—a practice at odds with the claim that slaves formed part of the master's "family." Some slaveowners tried to reform the system to eliminate its most oppressive features. The Reverend Charles C. Jones, a wealthy planter in Georgia, organized his neighbors to promote the religious instruction of slaves, improve slave housing, diet, and medical care, and discourage severe punishments. But even Jones believed African Americans so "degraded" and lacking in moral self-discipline that he could not contemplate an end to slavery.

The Code of Honor

As time went on, the dominant southern conception of the good society diverged more and more sharply from that of the egalitarian, competitive, individualistic North. In the South, for example, both upper- and lower-class whites adhered to a code of personal honor, in which men were expected to defend, with violence if necessary, their own reputation and that of their families. Although dueling was illegal, many prominent southerners took part in duels to avenge supposed insults. In 1826, Henry Clay and John Randolph, two of the most important southern political leaders, fought a duel with pistols after Clay took exception to criticisms by Randolph on the floor of Congress. Fortunately, each missed the other. Twenty years later, however, John H. Pleasants, editor of the *Richmond Whig*, died in a duel with the son of a rival newspaperman.

Just as southern men had a heightened sense of their own honor and masculinity, white southern women, even more than in the North, were confined within the "domestic circle." "A man loves his children," wrote George Fitzhugh, a Virginia lawyer and author of numerous books and articles on social issues, "because they are weak, helpless, and dependent. He loves his wife for similar reasons." As will be discussed in the next chapter, many northern women before the Civil War became part of a thriving female culture centered on voluntary religious and reform organizations. Few parallels existed in the South, and plantation mistresses often complained of loneliness and isolation.

The Proslavery Argument

Some southerners worried about their standing in the eyes of the world, especially how others viewed the intellectual life of their region. "We of the South," one wrote, "must, to Europe, continue to appear inferior to the North in intellectual cultivation." The free states outstripped the slave states in public education, in the number of colleges, and in newspapers, literary journals, and other publications. Nonetheless, the life of the mind flourished in the Old South, and the region did not lack for novelists, political philosophers, scientists, and the like.

In the thirty years before the outbreak of the Civil War, however, even as northern criticism of the "peculiar institution" began to deepen, proslavery thought came to dominate southern public life. "Many in the South," John C. Calhoun proclaimed in 1837, "once believed that [slavery] was a moral and political evil. . . . That folly and delusion are gone; we see it now in its true light, and regard it as the most safe and stable basis for free institutions in the world."

Even those who had no direct stake in slavery shared with planters a deep commitment to white supremacy. Indeed, racism—the belief that Blacks were innately inferior to whites and unsuited for life in any condition other than slavery—formed one pillar of the **proslavery argument**. Most slaveholders also found legitimation for slavery in biblical passages such as the injunction that servants should obey their masters. Others argued that slavery was essential to human progress. Had not the ancient republics of Greece and Rome and the great European empires of the seventeenth and eighteenth centuries rested on slave labor? Without slavery, planters would be unable to cultivate the arts, sciences, and other civilized pursuits.

White southerners thought slavery was "modern," in tune with the times. Despite British emancipation, other forms of unfree labor were spreading in the world. The products of slave labor, especially cotton, were essential to the nineteenth-century economy. Southern planters were hardly parochial. They took a deep interest in international affairs. They felt a community of interest with owners in Cuba and Brazil and used their power in the federal government

SIZE OF SLAVEHOLDINGS, 1860

Average number of slaves
per slaveholding, 1860
- 20+
- 15–20
- 10–15
- 5–10
- 0–5

Most southern slaveholders owned fewer than five slaves. The largest plantations were concentrated in coastal South Carolina and along the Mississippi River.

to insist that American foreign policy promote the interests of slavery throughout the hemisphere.

Still other defenders of slavery insisted that the institution guaranteed equality for whites by preventing the growth of a class doomed to a life of unskilled labor. Like northerners, they claimed to be committed to the ideal of freedom. Slavery for Blacks, they declared, was the surest guarantee of "perfect equality" among whites, liberating them from the "low, menial" jobs like factory labor and domestic service performed by wage laborers in the North. Slavery made possible the considerable degree of economic autonomy (the social condition of freedom) enjoyed not only by planters but also by non-slaveholding whites. Because of slavery, claimed one congressman, white southerners were as "independent as the bird which cleaves the air." And because independence was necessary for citizenship, slavery was the "cornerstone of our republican edifice."

Abolition in the Americas

American slaveowners were well aware of developments in slave systems elsewhere in the Western Hemisphere. As noted in Chapter 8, the slave revolution in Haiti sent shock waves of fear throughout the American South. White southerners observed carefully the results of the wave of emancipations that swept the hemisphere in the first four decades of the century. In these years, slavery was abolished in most of Spanish America and in the British empire.

In most Latin American nations, the end of slavery followed the pattern established earlier in the northern United States—gradual emancipation accompanied by some kind of recognition of the owners' legal right to property in slaves. Abolition was far swifter in the British empire, where Parliament in 1833 mandated almost immediate emancipation, with a transitional period of "apprenticeship." The law appropriated 20 million pounds to compensate the owners.

The experience of emancipation in other parts of the hemisphere strongly affected debates over slavery in the United States. Southern slaveowners judged the vitality of the Caribbean economy by how much sugar and other crops it produced for the world market. Since many former slaves preferred to grow food for their own families, defenders of slavery in the United States charged that British emancipation had been a failure, as sugar production declined. Abolitionists disagreed, pointing to the rising standard of living of freed slaves, the spread of education among them, and other improvements in their lives. In a hemispheric perspective, slavery was a declining institution. By 1840, slavery had been outlawed in Mexico, Central America, and Chile, and only small numbers of aging slaves remained in Venezuela, Colombia, and Peru. During the European revolutions of 1848, France and Denmark emancipated their colonial slaves. At midcentury, significant New World slave systems remained only in Cuba, Puerto Rico, Brazil—and the United States. Nonetheless, because of the rapid growth of the slave population in the Old South, there were more slaves in the hemisphere in 1860 than at any earlier point.

Slavery and Liberty

Many white southerners declared themselves the true heirs of the American Revolution. They claimed to be inspired by "the same spirit of freedom and independence" that motivated the founding generation. Like their ancestors of the 1760s and 1770s, their political language was filled with contrasts between liberty and slavery and complaints that outsiders proposed to reduce them to "slaves" by interfering with their local institutions. Southern state constitutions enshrined the idea of equal rights for free men, and the South participated fully in the movement toward political democracy for whites.

Beginning in the 1830s, however, proslavery writers began to question the ideals of liberty, equality, and democracy so widely shared elsewhere in the nation. South Carolina, where a majority of white families owned slaves, became the home of an aggressive defense of slavery that repudiated the idea that freedom and equality were universal entitlements. The insistence of the

RAFFLE

Mr. Joseph Jennings respectfully informs his friends and the public that, at the request of many acquaintances, he has been induced to purchase from Mr. Osborne, of Missouri, the celebrated

DARK BAY HORSE, "STAR,"

Aged five years, square trotter and warranted sound; with a new light Trotting Buggy and Harness; also, the dark, stout

MULATTO GIRL, "SARAH,"

Aged about twenty years, general house servant, valued at *nine hundred dollars*, and guaranteed, and

Will be Raffled for

At 4 o'clock P. M., February first, at the selection hotel of the subscribers. The above is as represented, and those persons who may wish to engage in the usual practice of raffling, will, I assure them, be perfectly satisfied with their destiny in this affair.
The whole is valued at its just worth, fifteen hundred dollars; fifteen hundred

CHANCES AT ONE DOLLAR EACH.

The Raffle will be conducted by gentlemen selected by the interested subscribers present. Five nights will be allowed to complete the Raffle. BOTH OF THE ABOVE DESCRIBED CAN BE SEEN AT MY STORE, No. 78 Common St., second door from Camp, at from 9 o'clock A. M. to 2 P. M. Highest throw to take the first choice; the lowest throw the remaining prize, and the fortunate winners will pay twenty dollars each for the refreshments furnished on the occasion.
N. B. No chances recognized unless paid for previous to the commencement.

JOSEPH JENNINGS.

A poster advertising the raffle of a horse and a slave, treated as equivalents, at a Missouri store.

Declaration of Independence that all men were created equal and entitled to liberty was "the most false and dangerous of all political errors," insisted John C. Calhoun.

As the sectional controversy intensified after 1830, a number of southern writers and politicians came to defend slavery less as the basis of equality for whites than as the foundation of an organic, hierarchical society. Inequality and hence the submission of inferior to superior—Black to white, female to male, lower classes to upper classes—was a "fundamental law" of human existence. A hierarchy of "ranks and orders in human society," insisted John B. Alger, a Presbyterian minister in South Carolina, formed part of the "divine arrangement" of the world.

Slavery and Civilization

The Virginia writer George Fitzhugh took the argument to its most radical conclusion. Far from being the natural condition of mankind, Fitzhugh wrote, "universal liberty" was the exception, an experiment carried on "for a little while" in "a corner of Europe" and the northern United States. Taking the world and its history as a whole, slavery, "without regard to race and color," was "the general, . . . normal, natural" basis of "civilized society." Indeed, wrote Fitzhugh, slaveowners and slaves shared a "community of interest" unknown in "free society." Since they lacked economic cares, he contended, "the Negro slaves of the South are the happiest, and, in some degree, the freest people in the world." White workers in both the North and South, according to Fitzhugh, would fare better having individual owners, rather than living as "slaves" of the economic marketplace.

Abraham Lincoln would later observe that the essential function of the proslavery argument was to serve the interests of those who benefited from a system of extreme inequality. He imagined Dr. Frederick A. Ross, a leading proslavery clergyman, considering whether he should free his slave Sambo. God's view of the subject, Lincoln noted, was not entirely clear, and "no one thinks of asking Sambo's opinion." Therefore, it fell to Dr. Ross to decide the question. "If he decides that God wills Sambo to continue a slave," Lincoln wrote, "he thereby retains his own comfortable position; but if he decides that

God wills Sambo to be free, he thereby has to walk out of the shade, take off his gloves, and [work] for his own bread." Under these circumstances, it was hardly surprising that Dr. Ross found the argument that Sambo should remain a slave very persuasive.

After 1830, southern writers, newspaper editors, politicians, and clergymen increasingly devoted themselves to spreading the defense of slavery. The majority of white southerners came to believe that freedom for whites rested on the power to command the labor of Blacks. In the words of the Richmond *Enquirer*, "freedom is not possible without slavery."

LIFE UNDER SLAVERY

Slaves and the Law

For slaves, the "peculiar institution" meant a life of incessant toil, brutal punishment, and the constant fear that their families would be destroyed by sale. Under the law, slaves were property. Although they had a few legal rights (all states made it illegal to kill a slave except in self-defense, and slaves accused of serious crimes were entitled to their day in court, before all-white judges and juries), these were haphazardly enforced. Slaves could be sold or leased by their owners at will and lacked any voice in the governments that ruled over them. They could not testify in court against a white person, sign contracts or acquire property, own firearms, hold meetings unless a white person was present, or leave the farm or plantation without the permission of their owner. By the 1830s, it was against the law to teach a slave to read or write.

Not all of these laws were rigorously enforced. Some members of slaveholding families taught slave children to read (although rather few, since well over 90 percent of the slave population was illiterate in 1860). In the South Carolina rice fields, owners allowed some slaves to carry shotguns, in defiance of the law, to scare off birds feasting on rice seeds. It was quite common throughout the South for slaves to gather without white supervision at crossroads villages and country stores on Sunday, their day of rest.

The slave, declared a Louisiana law, "owes to his master . . . a respect without bounds, and an absolute obedience." Not only did the owner have the legal right to what Alabama's legal code called the "time, labor, and services" of his slaves, but no aspect of their lives, from the choice of marriage partners to how they spent their free time, was immune from his interference. The entire system of southern justice, from the state militia and courts down to armed patrols in each locality, was designed to enforce the master's control over the person and labor of his slaves.

In one famous case, a Missouri court considered the case of Celia, a slave who had killed her owner in 1855 while resisting a sexual assault. State law deemed "any woman" in such circumstances to be acting in self-defense. But Celia, the court ruled, was not a "woman" in the eyes of the law. She was a slave, whose owner had complete power over her person. The court sentenced her to death. However, since Celia was pregnant, her execution was postponed until the child was born, so as not to deprive her owner's heirs of their property rights.

Conditions of Slave Life

As the nineteenth century progressed, some southern states enacted laws to prevent the mistreatment of slaves, and their material living conditions improved. Food supplies and wild game were abundant in the South, and many slaves supplemented the food provided by their owners (primarily cornmeal and pork or bacon) with chickens and vegetables they raised themselves, animals they hunted in the forests, and, not infrequently, items they stole from the plantation smokehouse. Compared with their counterparts in the West Indies and Brazil, American slaves enjoyed better diets, lower rates of infant mortality, and longer life expectancies. Many factors contributed to improving material conditions. One was the growing strength of the planters' paternalist outlook. Douglass himself noted that "not to give a slave enough to eat, is regarded as the most aggravated development of meanness, even among slaveholders." Most of the South, moreover, lies outside the geographical area where tropical diseases like malaria, yellow fever, and typhoid fever flourish, so health among all southerners was better than in the Caribbean. And with the price of slaves rising dramatically after the closing of the African slave trade, it made economic sense for owners to become concerned with the health and living conditions of their human property.

These improvements were meant to strengthen slavery, not undermine it. Even as the material lives of the majority of slaves improved, the South drew tighter and tighter the chains of bondage. In Brazil, it was not uncommon for an owner to free slaves as a form of celebration—on the occasion of a wedding in the owner's family, for example—or to allow slaves to purchase their freedom. Although slavery in Brazil lasted until 1888, more than half the population of African descent was already free in 1850. (The comparable figure in the American South was well below 10 percent.) In the nineteenth-century South, more and more states set limits on voluntary manumission, requiring that such acts be approved by the legislature. "All the powers of earth," declared Abraham Lincoln in 1857, seemed to be "rapidly combining" to fasten bondage ever more securely upon American slaves. Few slave societies in history have so systematically closed off all avenues to freedom as the Old South.

Free Blacks in the Old South

The existence of slavery helped to define the status of those Blacks who did enjoy freedom. On the eve of the Civil War, nearly half a million free

Blacks lived in the United States, a majority in the South. Most were the descendants of slaves freed by southern owners in the aftermath of the Revolution or by the gradual emancipation laws of the northern states. Their numbers were supplemented by slaves who had been voluntarily liberated by their owners, who had been allowed to purchase their freedom, or who succeeded in running away.

When followed by "Black" or "Negro," the word "free" took on an entirely new meaning. Whites defined their freedom, in part, by their distance from slavery. But among Blacks, wrote Douglass, "the distinction between the slave and the free is not great." Northern free Blacks, as noted in Chapter 10, generally could not vote and enjoyed few economic opportunities. Free Blacks in the South could legally own property and marry and, of course, could not be bought and sold. But many regulations restricting the lives of slaves also applied to them. Free Blacks had no voice in selecting public officials. Like slaves, they

TABLE 11.3 Free Black Population, 1860

Region	Free Black Population	Percentage of Total Black Population
North	226,152	100%
South	261,918	6.2
Upper South	224,963	12.8
Lower South	36,955	1.5
Delaware	19,829	91.7
Washington, D.C.	11,131	77.8
Kentucky	10,684	4.5
Maryland	83,942	49.1
Missouri	3,572	3.0
North Carolina	30,463	8.4
Tennessee	7,300	2.6
Virginia	58,042	10.6
Alabama	2,690	0.6
Arkansas	144	0.1
Florida	932	1.5
Georgia	3,500	0.8
Louisiana	18,647	5.3
Mississippi	773	0.2
South Carolina	9,914	2.4
Texas	355	0.2

were prohibited from owning dogs, firearms, or liquor, and they could not strike a white person, even in self-defense. They were not allowed to testify in court against whites or serve on juries, and they had to carry at all times a certificate of freedom. Poor free Blacks who required public assistance could be bound out to labor alongside slaves. "Free negroes," declared a South Carolina judge in 1848, "belong to a degraded caste of society" and should learn to conduct themselves "as inferiors."

As noted above, nineteenth-century Brazil had a large free Black population. In the West Indies, many children of white owners and female slaves gained their freedom, becoming part of a "free colored" population sharply

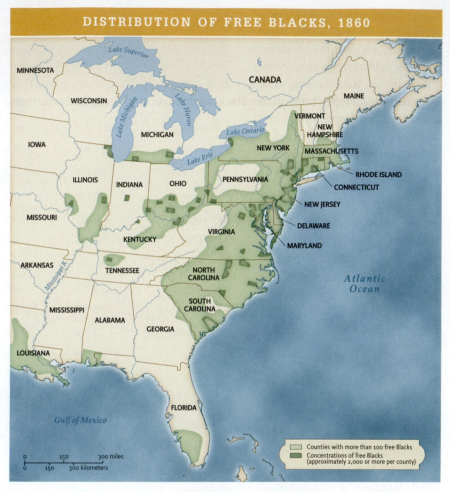

DISTRIBUTION OF FREE BLACKS, 1860

Legend:
- Counties with more than 100 free Blacks
- Concentrations of free Blacks (approximately 2,000 or more per county)

The nation's population in 1860 included nearly 500,000 free Blacks. The majority lived in the slave states, especially Maryland and Virginia.

distinguished from both whites above them and slaves below. In the absence of a white lower middle class, free Blacks in Jamaica and other Caribbean islands operated shops and worked as clerks in government offices.

In the United States, a society that equated "Black" and "slave" and left little room for a mixed-race group between them, free Blacks were increasingly considered undesirable, a potential danger to the slave system. By the 1850s, most southern states prohibited free Blacks from entering their territory and a few states even moved to expel them altogether, offering the choice of enslavement or departure. Nonetheless, a few free Blacks managed to prosper within slave society. William Johnson, a Natchez barber, acquired enough money to purchase a plantation with fifteen slaves; he hunted with upper-class whites and loaned them money. But he suffered from the legal disadvantages common to his race. He could not, for example, testify against his debtors in court when they failed to pay. In Virginia, the slaves freed and given land by the will of Richard Randolph (noted in Chapter 6) established a vibrant community they called Israel Hill. Despite the legal restrictions on free Blacks in the state, they prospered as farmers and skilled craftsmen.

The Upper and Lower South

Very few free Blacks (around 37,000 persons, or less than 2 percent of the area's Black population) lived in the Lower South in 1860. Like William Johnson, a majority of them resided in cities. Mississippi, an overwhelmingly rural state with no real urban centers, had fewer than 800 free Blacks on the eve of the Civil War. In New Orleans and Charleston, on the other hand, relatively prosperous free Black communities developed, mostly composed of mixed-race descendants of unions between white men and slave women. Some became truly wealthy— Antoine Dubuclet of Louisiana, for example, owned 100 slaves. Many free Blacks in these cities acquired an education and worked as skilled craftsmen such as tailors, carpenters, and mechanics. They established churches for their communities and schools for their children. Some New Orleans free Blacks sent their children to France for an education. These elite free Blacks did everything they could to maintain a separation from the slave population. The Brown Fellowship Society of Charleston, for example, would not even allow dark-skinned free men to join. Even in these cities, however, most free Blacks were poor unskilled laborers.

In the Upper South, where the large majority of southern free Blacks lived, they generally worked for wages as farm laborers. Here, where tobacco had exhausted the soil, many planters shifted to grain production, which required less year-round labor. They sold off many slaves to the Lower South and freed others. By 1860, half the African American population of Maryland was free. Planters hired local free Blacks to work alongside their slaves at harvest time. Free Blacks in Virginia and Maryland were closely tied to the slave community and often had relatives in bondage. Some owned slaves, but usually these were free men who had purchased their slave wives and children but could not liberate them because the law required any slave who became free to leave the state. Overall, in the words of Willis A. Hodges, a member of a free Virginia family that helped runaways to reach the North, free Blacks and slaves were "one man of sorrow."

Slave Labor

First and foremost, slavery was a system of labor; "from sunup to first dark," with only brief interruptions for meals, work occupied most of the slaves' time.

From LETTER BY JOSEPH TAPER TO JOSEPH LONG (1840)

No one knows how many slaves succeeded in escaping from bondage before the Civil War. Some settled in northern cities like Boston, Cincinnati, and New York. But because the Constitution required that fugitives be returned to slavery, many continued northward until they reached Canada.

One successful fugitive was Joseph Taper, a slave in Frederick County, Virginia, who in 1837 ran away to Pennsylvania with his wife and children. Two years later, learning that a "slave catcher" was in the neighborhood, the Tapers fled to Canada. In 1840, Taper wrote to a white acquaintance in Virginia recounting some of his experiences.

The biblical passage to which Taper refers reads: "And I will come near to you to judgment; and I will be a swift witness against the sorcerers, and against the adulterers, and against false swearers, and against those that oppress the hireling in his wages, the widow, and the fatherless, and that turn aside the stranger from his right, and fear not me, saith the Lord of hosts."

Dear sir,

I now take the opportunity to inform you that I am in a land of liberty, in good health. . . . Since I have been in the Queen's dominions I have been well contented, Yes well contented for Sure, man is as God intended he should be. That is, all are born free and equal. This is a wholesome law, not like the Southern laws which puts man made in the image of God, on level with brutes. O, what will become of the people, and where will they stand in the day of Judgment. Would that the 5th verse of the 3d chapter of Malachi were written as with the bar of iron, and the point of a diamond upon every oppressor's heart that they might repent of this evil, and let the oppressed go free. . . .

We have good schools, and all the colored population supplied with schools. My boy Edward who will be six years next January, is now reading, and I intend keeping him at school until he becomes a good scholar.

I have enjoyed more pleasure within one month here than in all my life in the land of bondage. . . . My wife and self are sitting by a good comfortable fire happy, knowing that there are none to molest [us] or make [us] afraid. God save Queen Victoria. The Lord bless her in this life, and crown her with glory in the world to come is my prayer,

Yours With much respect

most obt, Joseph Taper

From "SLAVERY AND THE BIBLE" (1850)

White southerners developed an elaborate set of arguments defending slavery in the period before the Civil War. One pillar of proslavery thought was the idea that the institution was sanctioned by the Bible, as in this essay from the influential southern magazine *De Bow's Review*.

A very large party in the United States believe that holding slaves is morally wrong; this part founds its belief upon precepts taught in the Bible, and takes that book as the standard of morality and religion.

. . . We think we can show; that the Bible teaches clearly and conclusively that the holding of slaves is right; and if so, no deduction from general principles can make it wrong, if that book is true.

From the earliest period of time down to the present moment, slavery has existed in some form or under some name, in almost every country of the globe. It existed in every country known, even by name, to any one of the sacred writers, at the time of his writing; yet no one of them condemns it in the slightest degree. Would this have been the case had it been wrong in itself? Would not some of the host of sacred writers have spoken of this alleged crime, in such terms as to show, in a manner not to be misunderstood, that God wished all men to be equal?

. . . Abraham, the chosen servant of God, had his bond servants, whose condition was similar to, or worse than, that of our slaves. He considered them as his property, to be bought and sold as any other property which he owned.

. . . We find, that both the Old and New Testaments speak of slavery—that they do not condemn the relation, but, on the contrary, expressly allow it or create it; and they give commands and exhortations, which are based upon its legality and propriety. It can not, then, be wrong.

QUESTIONS

1. *How does Taper's letter reverse the rhetoric, common among white Americans, that saw the United States as a land of freedom and the British empire as lacking in liberty?*

2. *Why does De Bow feel that it is important to show that the Bible sanctions slavery?*

3. *How do Taper and De Bow differ in their understanding of the relationship of slavery and Christianity?*

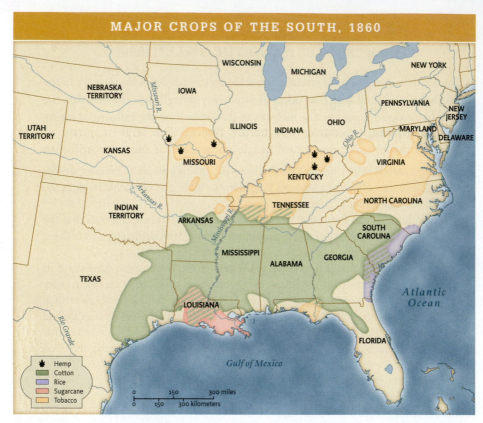

MAJOR CROPS OF THE SOUTH, 1860

Cotton was the major agricultural crop of the South—and, indeed, the nation—but slaves also grew rice, sugarcane, tobacco, and hemp.

Large plantations were diversified communities, where slaves performed all kinds of work. The 125 slaves on one plantation, for instance, included a butler, two waitresses, a nurse, a dairymaid, a gardener, ten carpenters, and two shoemakers. Other plantations counted among their slaves engineers, blacksmiths, and weavers, as well as domestic workers from cooks to coachmen.

Slaves cut wood to provide fuel for steamboats, worked in iron and coal mines, manned the docks in southern seaports, and laid railroad track. They were set to work by local authorities to construct and repair bridges, roads, and other facilities and by the federal government to build forts and other public buildings in the South. Businessmen, merchants, lawyers, and civil servants owned slaves, and by 1860 some 200,000 worked in industry, especially in the ironworks and tobacco factories of the Upper South. Reliance on unfree labor, moreover, extended well beyond the ranks of slaveholders, for, as noted earlier, many small farmers and manufacturers rented slaves from plantation owners. A few owners gave trusted slaves extensive responsibilities. Simon Gray's owner made him the head of a riverboat crew on the Mississippi. Gray supervised both white and enslaved workers, sold his owner's lumber at urban markets, and handled large sums of money.

Gang Labor and Task Labor

Gray's experience, of course, was hardly typical. The large majority of slaves—75 percent of women and nearly 90 percent of men, according to one study—worked in the fields. The precise organization of their labor varied according to the crop and the size of the holding. On small farms, the owner often toiled side by side with his slaves. The largest concentration of slaves, however, lived and worked on plantations in the Cotton Belt, where men, women, and children labored in gangs, often under the direction of an overseer and perhaps a slave "driver" who assisted him. Among slaves, overseers had a reputation for meting out brutal treatment. "The requisite qualifications for an overseer," wrote Solomon Northup, a free Black who spent twelve years in slavery after being kidnapped from the North, "are utter heartlessness, brutality, and cruelty. It is his business to produce large crops, no matter [what the] cost."

The 150,000 slaves who worked in the sugar fields of southern Louisiana also labored in large gangs. Conditions here were among the harshest in the South, for the late fall harvest season required round-the-clock labor to cut and process the sugarcane before it spoiled. On the rice plantations of South Carolina and Georgia, the system of task labor, which had originated in the colonial era, prevailed. With few whites willing to venture into the malaria-infested swamps, slaves were assigned daily tasks and allowed to set their own pace of work. Once a slave's task had been completed, he or she could spend the rest of the day hunting, fishing, or cultivating garden crops.

Slavery in the Cities

Skilled urban craftsmen also enjoyed considerable autonomy. Most city slaves were servants, cooks, and other domestic laborers. But owners sometimes allowed those with craft skills to "hire their own time." This meant that they could make work arrangements individually with employers, with most of the wages going to the slave's owner. Many urban slaves even lived on their own. But slaveholders increasingly became convinced that, as one wrote, the growing independence of skilled urban slaves "exerts a most injurious influence upon the relation of master and servant." For this reason, many owners in the 1850s sold city slaves to the countryside and sought replacements among skilled white labor.

During his time in Baltimore, Frederick Douglass "sought my own employment, made my own contracts, and collected my own earnings." Compared to conditions on the plantation, he concluded, "I was really well off." Douglass hastened to add, however, that his favored treatment in no way lessened his desire for freedom—"it was *slavery*, not its mere incidents, that I hated."

Maintaining Order

Slaveowners employed a variety of means in their attempts to maintain order and discipline among their human property and persuade them to labor productively. At base, the system rested on force. Masters had almost complete discretion in inflicting punishment, and rare was the slave who went through his or her life without experiencing a whipping. Josiah Henson, who escaped to the North and published an autobiography, wrote that he could never erase from his memory the traumatic experience of seeing his father brutally whipped for striking a white man. Any infraction of plantation rules, no matter how minor, could be punished by the lash. One Georgia planter recorded in his journal that he had whipped a slave "for not bringing over milk for my coffee, being compelled to take it without."

Subtler means of control supplemented violence. Owners encouraged and exploited divisions among the slaves, especially between field hands and house servants. They created systems of incentives that rewarded good work with time off or even money payments. Probably the most powerful weapon wielded by slaveowners was the threat of sale, which separated slaves from their immediate families and from the communities that, despite overwhelming odds, African Americans created on plantations throughout the South.

SLAVE CULTURE

Slaves never abandoned their desire for freedom or their determination to resist total white control over their lives. In the face of grim realities, they succeeded in forging a semi-independent culture, centered on the family and church. This enabled them to survive the experience of bondage without surrendering their self-esteem and to pass from generation to generation a set of ideas and values fundamentally at odds with those of their owners.

Slave culture drew on the African heritage. African influences were evident in the slaves' music and dances, style of religious worship, and the use of herbs by slave healers to combat disease. (Given the primitive nature of professional medical treatment, some whites sought out slave healers instead of trained physicians.) Unlike the plantation regions of the Caribbean and Brazil, where the African slave trade continued into the nineteenth century and the

Black population far outnumbered the white, most slaves in the United States were American-born and lived amid a white majority. Slave culture was a new creation, shaped by African traditions and American values and experiences.

The Slave Family

At the center of the slave community stood the family. On the sugar plantations of the West Indies, the number of males far exceeded that of females, the workers lived in barracks-type buildings, and settled family life was nearly impossible. The United States, where the slave population grew from natural increase rather than continued importation from Africa, had an even male-female ratio, making the creation of families far more possible. To be sure, the law did not recognize the legality of slave marriages. The owner had to consent before a man and woman could "jump over the broomstick" (the slaves' marriage ceremony), and families stood in constant danger of being broken up by sale.

Nonetheless, most adult slaves married, and their unions, when not disrupted by sale, typically lasted for a lifetime. To solidify a sense of family continuity, slaves frequently named children after cousins, uncles, grandparents, and other relatives. Nor did the slave family simply mirror kinship patterns among whites. Slaves, for example, did not marry first cousins, a practice common among white southerners. Because of constant sales, the slave community had a significantly higher number of female-headed households than among whites, as well as families in which grandparents, other relatives, or even non-kin assumed responsibility for raising children.

The Threat of Sale

As noted above, the threat of sale, which disrupted family ties, was perhaps the most powerful disciplinary weapon slaveholders possessed. As the domestic slave trade expanded with the rise of the Cotton Kingdom, about one slave marriage in three in slave-selling states like Virginia was broken by sale. Many children were separated from their parents by sale. According to one estimate, at least 10 percent of the teenage slaves in the Upper South were sold in the interstate slave trade. Fear of sale permeated slave life, especially in the Upper South. "Mother, is Massa going to sell us tomorrow?" ran a line in a slave song. As a reflection of their paternalist responsibilities, some owners encouraged slaves to marry. Others, however, remained unaware of their slaves' family connections, and their interest in slave children was generally limited to the children's ability to work in the fields. The federal census broke down the white population by five-year age categories, but it divided slaves only once, at age

This 1842 engraving depicts an estate sale in New Orleans. At the center, a family of slaves is being sold. On the extreme right and left, auctioneers sell other property, including paintings.

ten, the point at which they became old enough to enter the plantation labor force.

Slave traders gave little attention to preserving family ties. A public notice, "Sale of Slaves and Stock," announced the 1852 auction of property belonging to a recently deceased Georgia planter. It listed thirty-six individuals ranging from an infant to a sixty-nine-year-old woman and ended with the proviso "Slaves will be sold separate, or in lots, as best suits the purchaser." Sales like this were a human tragedy. "My dear wife," a Georgia slave wrote in 1858, "I take the pleasure of writing you these few [lines] with much regret to inform you that I am sold. . . . Give my love to my father and mother and tell them good bye for me, and if we shall not meet in this world I hope to meet in heaven. My dear wife for you and my children my pen cannot express the grief I feel to be parted from you all."

Gender Roles among Slaves

In some ways, gender roles under slavery differed markedly from those in the larger society. Slave men and women experienced, in a sense, the equality of powerlessness. The nineteenth century's "cult of domesticity," which defined the home as a woman's proper sphere, did not apply to slave women, who regularly worked in the fields. Enslaved men could not act as the economic providers for their families. Nor could they protect their wives from physical or sexual abuse by owners and overseers (a frequent occurrence on many plantations) or determine when and under what conditions their children worked.

When slaves worked "on their own time," however, more conventional gender roles prevailed. Slave men chopped wood, hunted, and fished, while women washed, sewed, and assumed primary responsibility for the care of children. Some planters allowed their slaves small plots of land on which to grow food to supplement the rations provided by the owner; women usually took charge of these "garden plots." But whatever its internal arrangements, the family was central to the slave community, allowing for the transmission of values, traditions, and survival strategies—in a word, of slave culture—from one generation to the next.

Slave Religion

A distinctive version of Christianity also offered solace to slaves in the face of hardship and hope for liberation from bondage. Some Blacks, free and slave, had taken part in the Great Awakening of the colonial era, and even more were swept into the South's Baptist and Methodist churches during the religious revivals of the late eighteenth and early nineteenth centuries. As one preacher recalled of the great camp meeting that drew thousands of worshipers to Cane Ridge, Kentucky, in 1801, no distinctions were made "as to age, sex, color, or anything of a temporary nature; old and young, male and female, Black and white, had equal privilege to minister the light which they received, in whatever way the Spirit directed."

Even though the law prohibited slaves from gathering without a white person present, every plantation, it seemed, had its own Black preacher. Usually the preacher was a "self-called" slave who possessed little or no formal education but whose rhetorical abilities and familiarity with the Bible made him one of the most respected members of the slave community. Especially in southern cities, slaves also worshiped in biracial congregations with white ministers, where they generally were required to sit in the back pews or in the balcony. Urban free Blacks established their own churches, sometimes attended by slaves.

To owners, Christianity offered another means of social control. Many required slaves to attend services conducted by white ministers, who preached that theft was immoral and that the Bible required servants to obey their masters. One slave later recalled being told in a white minister's sermon "how good God was in bringing us over to this country from dark and benighted Africa, and permitting us to listen to the sound of the gospel." Several slaves walked out of the service during a sermon by Charles C. Jones stressing that God had commanded servants to obey their masters and that they should not try to run away. One man came up to Jones at the end and said, "The doctrine is *one-sided.*"

The Gospel of Freedom

The slaves transformed the Christianity they had embraced, turning it to their own purposes. A blend of African traditions and Christian belief, slave religion was practiced in secret nighttime gatherings on plantations and in "praise meetings" replete with shouts, dances, and frequent emotional interchanges between the preacher and the congregation. One former slave later recalled typical secret religious gatherings: "We used to slip off into the woods in the old slave days on Sunday evening way down in the swamps to sing and pray to our own liking. We prayed for this day of freedom."

The biblical story of Exodus, in which God chose Moses to lead the enslaved Jews of Egypt into a promised land of freedom, played a central role in Black

The "Negro church" on Rockville Plantation near Charleston, South Carolina, in an 1863 photograph. Few plantations had such a building; most slaves worshiped secretly or in biracial churches with white ministers.

Christianity. Slaves identified themselves as a chosen people, whom God in the fullness of time would deliver from bondage. At the same time, the figure of Jesus Christ represented to slaves a personal redeemer, one who truly cared for the oppressed. Slaves found other heroes and symbols in the Bible as well: Jonah, who overcame hard luck and escaped from the belly of a whale; David, who vanquished the more powerful Goliath; and Daniel, who escaped from the lion's den. And the Christian message of brotherhood and the equality of all souls before the Creator, in the slaves' eyes, offered an irrefutable indictment of the institution of slavery.

The Desire for Liberty

If their masters developed an elaborate ideology defending the South's "peculiar institution," slave culture rested on a conviction of the unjustness of bondage and the desire for freedom. "Nobody," the British political philosopher Edmund Burke had written during the American Revolution, "will be argued into slavery." Whatever proslavery writers asserted and ministers preached, Blacks thought of themselves as a working people unjustly deprived of the fruits of their labor by idle planters who lived in luxury. "We bake the bread / they give us the crust," said a line from one slave song.

Most slaves fully understood the impossibility of directly confronting the system. Their folktales had no figures equivalent to Paul Bunyan, the powerful, larger-than-life backwoodsman popular in white folklore. Slaves' folklore, such as the Brer Rabbit stories, glorified the weak hare who outwitted stronger foes like the bear and fox, rather than challenging them directly. Their religious songs, or spirituals, spoke of lives of sorrow ("I've been 'buked and I've been scorned"), while holding out hope for ultimate liberation ("Didn't my Lord deliver Daniel?"). When they sang, "I'm bound for the land of Canaan," slaves meant not only relief from worldly woes in an afterlife but also escaping to the North or, in God's good time, witnessing the breaking of slavery's chains.

"Freedom," declared a Black minister after emancipation, "burned in the Black heart long before freedom was born." Even the most ignorant slave, observed Solomon Northup, could not "fail to observe the difference between their own condition and the meanest white man's, and to realize the injustice of laws which place it within [the owner's] power not only to appropriate the profits of their industry, but to subject them to unmediated and unprovoked punishment without remedy."

Owners attempted to prevent slaves from learning about the larger world. But slaves created neighborhood networks that transmitted information between plantations. Skilled craftsmen, preachers, pilots on ships, and other privileged slaves spread news of local and national events. Owners found that slaves knew more about political events than they expected. James Henry Hammond of South Carolina was "astonished and shocked" to find that his slaves understood the political views of the presidential candidates of 1844, Henry Clay and James K. Polk, and knew "most of what the abolitionists are doing."

The world of most rural slaves was bounded by their local communities and kin. They became extremely familiar with the local landscape, crops, and population but had little knowledge of the larger world. Nonetheless, slaves could not remain indifferent to the currents of thought unleashed by the American Revolution or to the language of freedom in the society around them. The social and political agenda African Americans would put forward in the Reconstruction era that followed emancipation—stressing civil and political equality, the strengthening of the Black community, and autonomy in their working lives—flowed directly out of their experience in slavery.

RESISTANCE TO SLAVERY

Confronted with federal, state, and local authorities committed to preserving slavery, and outnumbered within the South as a whole by the white population, slaves could only rarely express their desire for freedom by outright rebellion. Compared to Brazil and the West Indies, which experienced numerous uprisings, involving hundreds or even thousands of slaves, revolts in the United States were smaller and less frequent. There was no parallel, of course, to the successful slave revolution in Haiti discussed in Chapter 8 or to the unsuccessful 1831 rebellion in Jamaica that appears to have involved as many as 20,000 slaves. This does not, however, mean that slaves in the United States placidly accepted the system under which they were compelled to live. Resistance to slavery took many forms in the Old South, from individual acts of defiance to occasional uprisings. These actions posed a constant challenge to the slaveholders' self-image as benign paternalists and their belief that slaves were obedient subjects grateful for their owners' care.

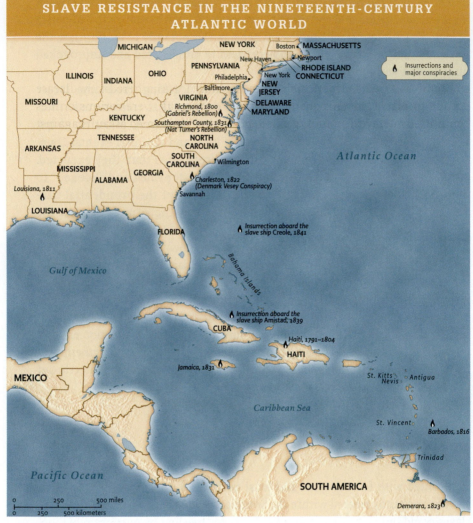

SLAVE RESISTANCE IN THE NINETEENTH-CENTURY ATLANTIC WORLD

Instances of slave resistance occurred throughout the Western Hemisphere on land and at sea. This map shows the location of major events in the nineteenth century.

Forms of Resistance

The most widespread expression of hostility to slavery was "day-to-day resistance" or "silent sabotage"—doing poor work, breaking tools, abusing animals, and in other ways disrupting the plantation routine. Frederick Law Olmsted, a northerner who toured the South in the 1850s, took note of "gates left open, rails removed from fences by the negroes, mules lamed and implements broken, a flat boat set adrift in the river, men ordered to cart rails for a new fence, depositing them so that a double expense of labor would be required to lay them." Many slaves made believe that they were ill to avoid work (although almost no slaves reported themselves sick on Sunday, their only day of rest). Then there was the theft of food, a form of resistance so common that one southern physician diagnosed it as a hereditary disease unique to Blacks. Less frequent, but more dangerous, were serious crimes committed by slaves, including arson, poisoning, and armed assaults against individual whites.

Fugitive Slaves

Even more threatening to the stability of the slave system were slaves who ran away. As we have seen, war provided the opportunity for mass escapes. Thousands of slaves gained their freedom by running away to British lines during the War of Independence and War of 1812. Generally, however, formidable obstacles confronted the prospective **fugitive slave**. As Solomon Northup recalled, "Every white man's hand is raised against him, the patrollers are watching for him, the hounds are ready to follow in his track." Slaves had little or no knowledge of geography, apart from understanding that following the North Star led to freedom. Not surprisingly, most of those who succeeded lived, like Frederick Douglass, in the Upper South, especially Maryland, Virginia, and Kentucky, which bordered on the free states. Douglass, who escaped at age twenty, was also typical in that the large majority of fugitives were young men. Most slave women were not willing to leave children behind, and to take them along on the arduous escape journey was nearly impossible.

In the Lower South, fugitives tended to head for cities like New Orleans or Charleston, where they hoped to hide "in plain sight" among the growing communities of free Blacks. A study of Tennessee newspaper advertisements for runaways finds that around 40 percent were thought to have remained in the local neighborhood and 30 percent to have headed to other locations in the South, while only 25 percent tried to reach the North. Other escapees fled to remote areas like the Great Dismal Swamp of Virginia or the Florida Everglades, where the Seminole Indians offered refuge before being forced to move west. Indeed, many Native American peoples assisted fugitive slaves. In the Old Northwest, Ottawas and Shawnees helped runaways reach freedom in Canada. After Mexico abolished slavery in 1829, that country also became a refuge for thousands of slaves escaping from Lower South slave states, including Texas after it became part of the United States.

The Underground Railroad

The **Underground Railroad**, a loose organization of sympathetic abolitionists who hid fugitives in their homes and sent them on to the next "station," assisted some runaway slaves. A few courageous individuals made forays into the South to liberate slaves. The best known was **Harriet Tubman**. Born in Maryland in 1820, Tubman escaped to Philadelphia in 1849 and during the next decade risked her life by making numerous trips back to her state of birth to lead relatives and other slaves to freedom. Recent scholarship suggests that she rescued about seventy-five men, women, and children from slavery. But most who managed to reach the North did so on their own initiative, sometimes showing remarkable ingenuity. William and Ellen Craft impersonated a sickly owner traveling with his slave. Henry "Box" Brown had himself packed by a friend inside a crate and literally shipped from Richmond, Virginia, to freedom in the North. When his crate was opened, Brown emerged "with a face radiant with joy" and launched into a "hymn of praise." But because fugitives were always vulnerable to recapture, Brown soon departed for England, where he became a fixture on the antislavery lecture circuit.

Rather than a single, centralized system with tunnels, codes, and clearly defined routes and stations, the Underground Railroad was a series of interlocking local networks involving Black and white abolitionists. These networks communicated with each other and together helped a substantial number of fugitives reach safety in the free states and Canada. One estimate is that around 30,000 fugitives managed to escape from the South in the three decades before the Civil War. The number was hardly sufficient to undermine the slave system, which counted nearly 4 million slaves in 1860, but enough to become a major source of consternation in the slave states.

By the 1850s, slaves were using numerous means of escape, not simply running away on foot but hiding on boats with the help of sympathetic captains and sailors, taking an owner's horse and carriage, and boarding trains, as Frederick Douglass had done. They had many motives—brutality by the owners, fear of sale, or simply, as one said, because "I was tired of being a slave." Their actions had a profound impact on national politics. Running away undermined proslavery propaganda about contented slaves. The status of fugitives became a major irritant in diplomatic relations as successive administrations demanded, without success, that Canada and Mexico return escaped slaves. Efforts to recapture fugitives on northern soil showed that the power of slavery reached into the free states and forced many northerners who were not abolitionists to confront the question of the relationship between individual conscience and obedience to law.

The *Amistad*

In a few instances, large groups of slaves collectively seized their freedom. The most celebrated instance involved fifty-three slaves who in 1839 took control of **the *Amistad***, a ship transporting them from one port in Cuba to another, and tried to force the navigator to steer it to Africa. The *Amistad* wended its way up the Atlantic coast, until an American vessel seized it off the coast of Long Island. President Martin Van Buren favored returning the slaves to Cuba. But abolitionists brought their case to the Supreme Court, where former president John Quincy Adams argued that since they had been recently brought from Africa in violation of international treaties banning the slave trade, the captives should be freed. The Court accepted Adams's reasoning, and most of the captives made their way back to Africa.

The *Amistad* case had no legal bearing on slaves within the United States. But it may well have inspired a similar uprising in 1841, when 135 slaves being transported by sea from Norfolk, Virginia, to New Orleans seized control of the ship *Creole* and sailed for Nassau in the British Bahamas. Their leader had the evocative name Madison Washington. To the dismay of the Tyler administration, the British gave refuge to the *Creole* slaves.

Slave Revolts

Resistance to slavery occasionally moved beyond such individual and group acts of defiance to outright rebellion. The four largest conspiracies in American history occurred within the space of thirty-one years in the early nineteenth century. The first, organized by the Virginia slave Gabriel in 1800, was discussed in Chapter 8. It was followed eleven years later by an uprising on sugar plantations upriver from New Orleans. Some 500 men and women, armed with sugarcane knives, axes, clubs, and a few guns, marched toward the city, destroying property as they proceeded and shouting, "Freedom or death." The white population along the route fled in panic to New Orleans. Within two days, the militia

Cinqué, a leader of the slave revolt on the *Amistad*, in an 1839 painting by Nathaniel Jocelyn, a prominent Connecticut artist.

and regular army troops met the rebels and dispersed them in a pitched battle, killing sixty-six. Soon afterward, the principal leaders were executed. They seem to have been inspired by the recent success of the slave revolution in Haiti.

The next major conspiracy was organized in 1822 by Denmark Vesey, a slave carpenter in Charleston, South Carolina, who had purchased his freedom after winning a local lottery. An outspoken, charismatic leader, he rebuked Blacks who stepped off the city's sidewalks to allow whites to pass and took a leading role in the local African Methodist Church. **Denmark Vesey's conspiracy** reflected the combination of American and African influences then circulating in the Atlantic world and coming together in Black culture. "He studied the Bible a great deal," recalled one of his followers, "and tried to prove from it that slavery and bondage is against the Bible." Vesey also quoted the Declaration of Independence, pored over newspaper reports of the debates in Congress regarding the Missouri Compromise, and made pronouncements like "all men had equal rights, Blacks as well as whites." And he read to his co-conspirators accounts of the slave revolution in Haiti. The African heritage was present in the person of Vesey's lieutenant Gullah Jack, a religious "conjurer" from Angola who claimed to be able to protect the rebels against injury or death. The plot was discovered before it could reach fruition.

As in the case of many slave conspiracies, evidence about the Vesey plot is contradictory and disputed. Much of it comes from a series of trials in which the court operated in secret and failed to allow the accused to confront those who testified against them. The state's attorney general noted that to try a "free white man" under such circumstances would clearly violate his fundamental rights. But, he added, "slaves are not entitled to these rights," since "all the provisions of our constitution in favor of liberty are intended for freemen only." In the end, thirty-five slaves and free Blacks, among them Vesey and three slaves belonging to the governor, were executed and an equal number banished from the state.

Nat Turner's Rebellion

The best known of all slave rebels was Nat Turner, a slave preacher and religious mystic in Southampton County, Virginia, who came to believe that God had chosen him to lead a Black uprising. Turner traveled widely in the county conducting religious services. He told of seeing Black and white angels fighting in the sky and the heavens running red with blood. Perhaps from a sense of irony, Turner initially chose July 4, 1831, for his rebellion only to fall ill on the appointed day. On August 22, he and a handful of followers marched from farm to farm assaulting the white inhabitants. Most of their victims were women and children, for many of the area's men were attending a religious revival across the border in North Carolina. By the time the militia put down the uprising, about eighty slaves had joined Turner's band, and some sixty whites had been killed. Turner was subsequently captured and, with seventeen other rebels, condemned to die. Asked before his execution whether he regretted what he had done, Turner responded, "Was not Christ crucified?"

Nat Turner's Rebellion was the last large-scale rebellion before the Civil War. Like Gabriel's and Vesey's conspiracies, Turner's took place outside the heart of the plantation South, where slavery was most rigidly policed. Because Turner began with only a handful of followers, he faced less chance of discovery or betrayal than Gabriel or Vesey. Nonetheless, his revolt demonstrated conclusively that in a region where whites outnumbered Blacks and the white community was armed and united, slaves stood at a fatal disadvantage in any violent encounter. Only an outside force could alter the balance of power within the South.

Turner's rebellion sent shock waves through the entire South. "A Nat Turner," one white Virginian warned, "might be in any family." In the panic that followed the revolt, hundreds of innocent slaves were whipped and scores executed. For one last time, Virginia's leaders openly debated whether steps ought to be taken to do away with the "peculiar institution." "The blood of Turner and his innocent victims," declared a Richmond newspaper, "has opened the doors which have been shut for fifty years." But a proposal for gradual emancipation and the removal of the Black population from the state failed to win legislative approval.

Instead of moving toward emancipation, the Virginia legislature of 1832 decided to fasten even more tightly the chains of bondage. New laws prohibited Blacks, free or slave, from acting as preachers (a measure that proved impossible to enforce), strengthened the militia and patrol systems, banned free Blacks from owning firearms, and prohibited teaching slaves to read. Other southern states followed suit. In the debate's aftermath, Thomas R. Dew, a professor at the College of William and Mary in Virginia, published an influential pamphlet pointing to the absurdity of deporting the bulk of the state's labor force. The state, he insisted, faced a stark choice—retain slavery, or free the slaves and absorb them into Virginia society. Few critics of slavery were willing to accept the latter alternative.

In some ways, 1831 marked a turning point for the Old South. In that year, Parliament debated a program for abolishing slavery throughout the British empire, underscoring the South's growing isolation. Turner's rebellion, following only a few months after the appearance in Boston of William Lloyd

Garrison's abolitionist journal, *The Liberator*, suggested that American slavery faced enemies both within and outside the South. The proslavery argument increasingly permeated southern intellectual and political life, while dissenting opinions were suppressed. Some states made membership in an abolitionist society a criminal offense, while mobs drove critics of slavery from their homes. The South's "great reaction" produced one of the most thoroughgoing suppressions of freedom of speech in American history. Even as reform movements arose in the North that condemned slavery as contrary to Christianity and to basic American values, and national debate over the peculiar institution intensified, southern society closed in defense of slavery.

CHAPTER REVIEW

REVIEW QUESTIONS

1. *Given that most northern states had abolished slavery by the 1830s, how is it useful to think of slavery as a national—rather than regional—economic and political system?*

2. *While some poor southern whites resented the dominance of the "slavocracy," most supported the institution and accepted the power of the planter class. Why did the "plain folk" continue to support slavery?*

3. *How did the planters' paternalism serve to justify the system of slavery? How did it hide the reality of life for slaves?*

4. *Identify the basic elements of the proslavery defense and those points aimed especially at non-southern audiences.*

5. *In what sense did southern slaveholders consider themselves forward-looking?*

6. *Compare slaves in the Old South with those elsewhere in the world, focusing on health, diet, and opportunities for freedom.*

7. *Describe the difference between gang labor and task labor for slaves, and explain how slaves' tasks varied by region across the Old South.*

8. *How did enslaved people create community and a culture that allowed them to survive in an oppressive society?*

9. *Identify the different types of resistance to slavery. Which ones were the most common, the most effective, and the most demonstrative?*

KEY TERMS

the "peculiar institution" (p. 406)

Second Middle Passage (p. 408)

"Cotton is king" (p. 411)

paternalism (p. 414)

proslavery argument (p. 415)

fugitive slaves (p. 435)

Underground Railroad (p. 436)

Harriet Tubman (p. 436)

the *Amistad* (p. 437)

Denmark Vesey's conspiracy (p. 438)

Nat Turner's Rebellion (p. 439)

Go to 🐰 INQUIZITIVE

To see what you know—and learn what you've missed—with personalized feedback along the way.

CHAPTER 12

AN AGE OF REFORM

1820–1840

FOCUS QUESTIONS

- *What were the major movements and goals of antebellum reform?*
- *What were the different varieties of abolitionism?*
- *How did abolitionism challenge barriers to racial equality and free speech?*
- *What were the diverse sources of the antebellum women's rights movement and its significance?*

Among the many Americans who devoted their lives to the crusade against slavery, few were as selfless or courageous as Abby Kelley. Born in Massachusetts in 1811, she was educated at a Quaker boarding school in Rhode Island. As a teacher in Lynn, Massachusetts, she joined the Female Anti-Slavery Society and, like thousands of other northern women, threw herself into the abolitionist movement. In 1838, Kelley began to give public speeches about slavery. Her first lecture outside of Lynn was literally a baptism of fire. Enraged by reports that abolitionists favored "amalgamation" of the races—that is, sexual relations between whites and Blacks—residents of Philadelphia stormed the meeting hall and burned it to the ground.

For two decades, Kelley traveled throughout the North, speaking almost daily in churches, public halls, and antislavery homes on "the holy cause of human rights." Her career illustrated the interconnections of the era's reform movements. In addition to abolitionism, she was active in pacifist organizations—which opposed the use of force, including war, to settle disputes—and was a pioneer in the early struggle for women's rights. "In striving to strike [the slave's] irons off," she wrote, women "found most surely that we were manacled ourselves." Kelley was not the first American woman to speak in public. But she covered more miles and gave more speeches than any other female orator. She forthrightly challenged her era's assumption that a woman's "place" was in the home. More than any other individual, remarked Lucy Stone, another women's rights advocate, Kelley "earned for us all the right of free speech."

Abby Kelley's private life was as unconventional as her public career. She enjoyed a long and happy marriage to Stephen S. Foster, a strong-willed abolitionist given to interrupting Sunday sermons to denounce ministers who failed to condemn slavery. She gave birth to a daughter in 1847 but soon returned to lecturing. When criticized for not devoting herself to the care of her infant, Kelley replied: "I have done it for the sake of the mothers whose babies are sold away from them. The most precious legacy I can leave my child is a free country."

THE REFORM IMPULSE

"In the history of the world," wrote Ralph Waldo Emerson in 1841, "the doctrine of reform has never had such hope as at the present hour." Abolitionism was only one of the era's numerous efforts to improve American society. During his visit in the early 1830s, Alexis de Tocqueville noted how in the absence of a powerful national government, Americans' political and social activities were organized through voluntary associations—churches, fraternal orders, political clubs, and the like. The reform impulse was part of this proliferation of voluntary groups. Americans established organizations that worked to prevent the manufacture and sale of liquor, end public entertainments and the delivery of the mail on Sunday, improve conditions in prisons, expand public education, uplift the condition of wage laborers, and reorganize society on the basis of cooperation rather than competitive individualism.

Nearly all these groups worked to convert public opinion to their cause. They sent out speakers, gathered signatures on petitions, and published pamphlets. Like Abby Kelley, many reformers were active in more than one crusade. Some reform movements, like restraining the consumption of liquor and alleviating the plight of the blind and insane, flourished throughout the nation. Others, including women's rights, labor unionism, and educational reform, were weak or nonexistent in the South, where they were widely associated with antislavery sentiment. Reform was an international crusade. Peace, temperance, women's rights, and antislavery advocates regularly crisscrossed the Atlantic to promote their ideas.

Reformers adopted a wide variety of tactics to bring about social change. Some relied on "moral suasion" to convert people to their cause. Others, like opponents of the "demon rum," sought to use the power of the government to force sinners to change their ways. Some reformers decided to withdraw altogether from the larger society and establish their own cooperative settlements. They hoped to change American life by creating "heavens on earth," where they could demonstrate by example the superiority of a collective way of life. Reformers never amounted to anything like a majority of the population, even in the North, but they had a profound impact on both politics and society.

Utopian Communities

About 100 reform communities were established in the decades before the Civil War. Historians call them "utopian" after Thomas More's sixteenth-century novel *Utopia*, an outline of a perfect society. (The word has also come to imply that such plans are impractical and impossible to realize.) These communities differed greatly in structure and motivation. Some were subject to the iron discipline of a single leader, while others operated in a democratic fashion. Most arose from religious conviction, but others were inspired by the secular desire to counteract the social and economic changes set in motion by the market revolution.

Nearly all the communities set out to reorganize society on a cooperative basis, hoping to restore social harmony to a world of excessive individualism and to narrow the widening gap between rich and poor. Through their efforts, the words "socialism" and "communism," meaning a social organization in which productive property is owned by the community rather than private individuals, entered the language of politics. Most **utopian communities** also tried to find substitutes for conventional gender relations and marriage patterns. Some prohibited sexual relations between men and women altogether; others allowed them to change partners at will. But nearly all insisted that the abolition of private property must be accompanied by an end to men's "property" in women.

The Shakers

Religious communities attracted those who sought to find a retreat from a society permeated by sin, "a refuge from the evils of this Sodom," as the founders of Zoar, in Ohio, put it. But the **Shakers**, the most successful of the religious communities, also had a significant impact on the outside world. At their peak during the 1840s, cooperative Shaker settlements, which stretched from Maine to Kentucky, included more than 5,000 members. The Shakers were founded in the late eighteenth century by Mother Ann Lee, the daughter of an English blacksmith, who became a religious exhorter and claimed that Christ had directed her to emigrate with her followers to America. The first Shaker community was established in upstate New York in 1787.

God, the Shakers believed, had a "dual" personality, both male and female, and thus the two sexes were spiritually equal. Their work was deemed equally important (although each man was assigned a "sister" to take care of his washing and sewing). "Virgin purity" formed a pillar of the Shakers' faith. They completely abandoned traditional family life. Men and women lived separately in large dormitory-like structures and ate in communal dining rooms. Their numbers grew by attracting converts and adopting children from orphanages rather than through natural increase. Numerous outsiders visited Shaker communities to observe the religious services that gave the group its name, in which men and women, separated by sex, engaged in frenzied dancing. Although they rejected the individual accumulation of private property, the Shakers proved remarkably successful economically. They were among the first to market vegetable and flower seeds and herbal medicines commercially and to breed cattle for profit. Their beautifully crafted furniture is still widely admired today.

Oneida

Another influential and controversial community was **Oneida**, founded in 1848 in upstate New York by John Humphrey Noyes, the Vermont-born son of a U.S. congressman. Noyes took the revivalists' message that man could achieve moral perfection to an atypical extreme. He preached that he and his followers had become so perfect that they had achieved a state of complete "purity of heart," or sinlessness.

In 1836, Noyes and his disciples formed a small community in Putney, Vermont. Like the Shakers, Noyes did away with private property and abandoned traditional marriage. But in contrast to Shaker celibacy, he taught that all members of his community formed a single "holy family" of equals. The community became notorious for what Noyes called "complex marriage," whereby any man could propose sexual relations to any woman, who had the right to reject or accept his invitation, which would then be registered in a public record book. The great danger was "exclusive affections," which, Noyes felt, destroyed social harmony.

After being indicted for adultery by local officials, Noyes in 1848 moved his community to Oneida, where it survived until 1881. Oneida was an extremely

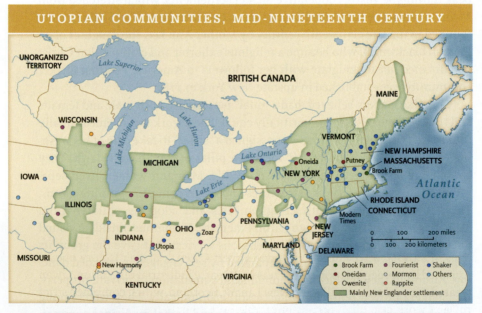

UTOPIAN COMMUNITIES, MID-NINETEENTH CENTURY

In the first half of the nineteenth century, dozens of utopian communities were established in the United States, where small groups of men and women attempted to establish a more perfect social order within the larger society.

dictatorial environment. To become a member of the community, one had to demonstrate command of Noyes's religious teachings and live according to his rules. Members carefully observed each other's conduct and publicly criticized those who violated Noyes's regulations. By the 1860s, a committee was even determining which couples would be permitted to have children—an early example of "eugenics," as the effort to improve the human race by regulating reproduction came to be known.

Worldly Communities

To outside observers, utopian communities like Oneida seemed a case of "voluntary slavery." But because of their members' selfless devotion to the teachings and rules laid down by their leader, spiritually oriented communities often achieved remarkable longevity. The Shakers survived well into the twentieth century. Communities with a more worldly orientation tended to be beset by internal divisions and therefore lasted for much shorter periods.

In 1841, New England transcendentalists established **Brook Farm** not far from Boston, where they hoped to demonstrate that manual and intellectual labor could coexist harmoniously. They modeled the community in part on the ideas of the French social reformer Charles Fourier, who envisioned communal living and working arrangements, while retaining private property. Fourier's blueprint for "phalanxes," as he called his settlements, planned everything to the last detail, from the number of residents (2,000) to how much income would be generated by charging admission to sightseers. With leisure time devoted to music, dancing, dramatic readings, and intellectual discussion, Brook Farm was like an exciting miniature university. But it attracted mostly writers, teachers, and ministers, some of whom disliked farm labor. The novelist Nathaniel Hawthorne, a resident for a time, complained about having to shovel manure. Brook Farm disbanded after a few years, and Hawthorne offered a skeptical view of life there in his 1852 novel *The Blithedale Romance*.

The Owenites

The most important secular communitarian (meaning a person who plans or lives in a cooperative community) was Robert Owen, a British factory owner. Appalled by the degradation of workers in the early industrial revolution, Owen created a model factory village at New Lanark, Scotland, which combined strict rules of work discipline with comfortable housing and free public education. Around 1815, its 1,500 employees made New Lanark the largest center of cotton manufacturing in the world. Convinced that the "rich and the poor, the governors and the governed, have really but one interest," Owen promoted

The Drunkard's Progress, an 1826 anti-liquor broadside illustrating how drinking leads a respectable man and his family to ruin.

communitarianism as a peaceful means of ensuring that workers received the full value of their labor. In 1824, he purchased the Harmony community in Indiana—originally founded by the German Protestant religious leader George Rapp, who had emigrated to America with his followers at the beginning of the nineteenth century. Here, Owen established **New Harmony**, where he hoped to create a "new moral world."

"The character of man is, without a single exception, always formed for him," Owen declared. Individuals could be transformed by changing the circumstances in which they lived. In Owen's scheme, children would be removed at an early age from the care of their parents to be educated in schools where they would be trained to subordinate individual ambition to the common good. Owen also defended women's rights, especially access to education and the right to divorce. At New Harmony, he promised, women would no longer be "enslaved" to their husbands, and "false notions" about innate differences between the sexes would be abandoned.

Harmony eluded the residents of New Harmony. They squabbled about everything from the community's constitution to the distribution of property. Owen's settlement survived for only a few years, but it strongly influenced the labor movement, educational reformers, and women's rights advocates. Owen's vision resonated with the widely held American belief that a community of equals could be created in the New World.

Religion and Reform

Most Americans saw the ownership of property as the key to economic independence—and, therefore, to freedom—and marriage as the foundation of the social order. Few were likely to join communities that required them to surrender both. Far more typical of the reform impulse were movements that aimed at liberating men and women either from restraints external to themselves, such as slavery and war, or from forms of internal "servitude" like drinking, illiteracy, and a tendency toward criminality. Drinkers, proclaimed one reformer, could not be considered free: they were "chained to alcohol, bound to the demon rum." Many of these reform movements drew their inspiration from the religious revivalism of the Second Great Awakening, discussed in Chapter 9, and many of the leaders of reform movements had had transformative religious experiences. If, as the revivalist preachers maintained, God had created man as a "free moral agent," sinners could not only reform themselves but could also remake the world.

The revivals popularized the outlook known as **perfectionism**, which saw both individuals and society at large as capable of indefinite improvement. Regions like upstate New York and northern Ohio became known as "burned-over districts" because of the intense revivals they experienced in the 1820s and 1830s. Such areas became fertile soil for the era's reform movements and their vision of a society freed from sin. Under the impact of the revivals, older reform efforts moved in a new, radical direction. Temperance (which literally means moderation in the consumption of liquor) was transformed into a crusade to eliminate drinking entirely. Criticism of war became outright pacifism. And, as will be related below, critics of slavery now demanded not gradual emancipation but immediate and total abolition.

The Temperance Movement

To members of the North's emerging middle-class culture, reform became a badge of respectability, an indication that individuals had taken control of their own lives and had become morally accountable. The American Temperance Society, founded in 1826, sought to redeem not only habitual drunkards but also the occasional drinker. It claimed by the 1830s to have persuaded hundreds of thousands of Americans to renounce liquor. By 1840, the consumption of alcohol per person had fallen to less than half the level of a decade earlier. (It had peaked in 1830 at seven gallons per person per year, compared with around two gallons today.) During the 1840s, the Washingtonian Society gathered reformed drinkers in "experience meetings," where they offered public testimony about their previous sins.

The **temperance movement** aroused considerable hostility. One person's sin is another's pleasure or cherished custom. Those Americans who enjoyed

Sunday recreation or a stiff drink from time to time did not think they were any less moral than those who had been reborn at a religious camp meeting, had abandoned drinking, and devoted the Sabbath to religious observances.

Critics of Reform

Many Americans saw the reform impulse as an attack on their own freedom. Drinking was a prominent feature of festive celebrations and events like militia gatherings. As in the colonial era, taverns were popular meeting places for workingmen, sites not only of drinking but also of political discussions, organizational meetings, and popular recreations. A "Liberty Loving Citizen" of Worcester, Massachusetts, wondered what gave one group of citizens the right to dictate to others how to conduct their personal lives.

American Catholics, their numbers growing because of Irish and German immigration, proved hostile to the reform impulse. Catholics understood freedom in ways quite different from Protestant reformers. They viewed sin as an inescapable burden of individuals and society. The perfectionist idea that evil could be banished from the world struck them as an affront to genuine religion, and they bitterly opposed what they saw as reformers' efforts to impose their own version of Protestant morality on their neighbors. While reformers spoke of man as a free moral agent, Catholics tended to place less emphasis on individual independence and more on the importance of communities centered on family and church. "Man," declared Archbishop John Hughes of New York, the nation's most prominent Catholic leader, was not an autonomous creature but "by his nature, a being of society."

Reformers and Freedom

Reformers had to reconcile their desire to create moral order with their quest to enhance personal freedom. They did this through a vision of freedom that was liberating and controlling at the same time. On the one hand, reformers insisted that their goal was to enable Americans to enjoy genuine liberty. In a world in which personal freedom increasingly meant the opportunity to compete for economic gain and individual self-improvement, they spoke of liberating Americans from various forms of "slavery" that made it impossible to succeed—slavery to drink, to poverty, to sin.

On the other hand, reformers insisted that self-fulfillment came through self-discipline. Their definition of the free individual was the person who internalized the practice of self-control. Philip Schaff, a German minister who emigrated to Pennsylvania in 1843, wrote that "true national freedom, in the American view . . . rests upon a moral groundwork, upon the virtue of self-possession and self-control in individual citizens." In some ways, reformers believed, American society suffered from an excess of liberty—the anarchic "natural liberty" John Winthrop had warned against in the early days of Puritan Massachusetts, as opposed to the "Christian liberty" of the morally upright citizen.

Many religious groups in the East worried that settlers in the West and immigrants from abroad lacked self-control and led lives of vice, exhibited by drinking, violations of the Sabbath, and lack of Protestant devotion. They formed the American Tract Society, the American Bible Society, and other groups that flooded eastern cities and the western frontier with copies of the gospel and pamphlets promoting religious virtue. Between 1825 and 1835, the pamphlets distributed by the Tract Society amounted to more than 500 million pages. Both their understanding of freedom and their ability to take advantage of new printing technologies influenced the era's reform movements.

The Invention of the Asylum

The tension between liberation and control in the era's reform movements was vividly evident in the proliferation of new institutions that reformers hoped could remake human beings into free, morally upright citizens. In colonial America, crime had mostly been punished by whipping, fines, or banishment. The poor received relief in their own homes, orphans lived with neighbors, and families took care of mentally ill members.

During the 1830s and 1840s, Americans embarked on a program of institution building—jails for criminals, poorhouses for the destitute, asylums for the insane, and orphanages for children without families. These institutions differed in many respects, but they shared with believers in "perfectionism" the idea that social ills once considered incurable could in fact be eliminated. The way to "cure" undesirable elements of society was to place them in an environment where their character could be transformed. Today, prisons and asylums have become overcrowded places where rehabilitating the inmates seems less important than simply holding them at bay, away from society. At the outset, however, these institutions were inspired by the conviction that those who passed through their doors could eventually be released to become productive, self-disciplined citizens.

The Common School

The largest effort at institution building before the Civil War came in the movement to establish **common schools**—that is, tax-supported state school systems open to all children. In the early nineteenth century, most children were educated in locally supported schools, private academies, charity schools, or at home, and many had no access to learning at all. School reform reflected the numerous purposes that came together in the era's reform impulse. Horace

This daguerreotype from around 1850 captures the students at the Emerson School, the most prominent educational institution for girls in Boston. A male teacher stands at the far right.

Mann, a Massachusetts lawyer and Whig politician who served as director of the state's board of education, was the era's leading educational reformer. His annual reports, widely read throughout the country, combined conservatism and radicalism, liberation and social control.

Mann hoped that universal public education could restore equality to a fractured society by bringing the children of all classes together in a common learning experience and equipping the less fortunate to advance in the social scale. Education would "equalize the conditions of men"—in effect, it would serve as industrial society's alternative to moving west to acquire a farm. At the same time, Mann argued that the schools would reinforce social stability by rescuing students from the influence of parents who failed to instill the proper discipline. To some extent, the schools' "silent curriculum"—obedience to authority, promptness in attendance, organizing one's day according to predetermined time periods that changed at the ringing of a bell—helped to prepare students for work in the new industrial economy.

The schools, Mann believed, were training free individuals—meaning persons who internalized self-discipline. But he encountered persistent opposition from parents who did not wish to surrender the moral education of their children to teachers and bureaucrats. Nonetheless, with labor organizations, factory owners, and middle-class reformers all supporting the idea, every northern state by 1860 had established tax-supported school systems for its children. The common school movement created the first real career opportunity for women, who quickly came to dominate the ranks of teachers. The South, where literate Blacks were viewed as a danger to social order and planters had no desire to tax themselves to pay for education for poor white children, lagged far behind. This was one of many ways in which North and South seemed to be growing apart.

THE CRUSADE AGAINST SLAVERY

Compared with drinking, Sabbath-breaking, and illiteracy, the greatest evil in American society at first appeared to attract the least attention from reformers. For many years, it seemed that the only Americans willing to challenge the existence of slavery were Quakers, slaves, and free Blacks. After the antislavery impulse spawned by the Revolution died out, the slavery question faded from national life, with occasional eruptions like the Missouri controversy of 1819–1821.

Colonization

Before the 1830s, those white Americans willing to contemplate an end to bondage almost always coupled calls for abolition with the "colonization" of freed slaves—their deportation to Africa, the Caribbean, or Central America. In 1816, proponents of this idea founded the **American Colonization Society**, which promoted the gradual abolition of slavery and the settlement of Black Americans in Africa. It soon established Liberia on the coast of West Africa, an outpost of American influence whose capital, Monrovia, was named for President James Monroe.

Colonization struck many observers as totally impractical. When the English writer Harriet Martineau visited the United States in the 1830s, she was amazed that former president James Madison endorsed the idea. "How such a mind as his" could be convinced that slavery would not end unless Blacks were deported from the country she could not understand.

Nonetheless, numerous prominent political leaders of the Jacksonian era—including Henry Clay, John Marshall, and Jackson himself—supported the Colonization Society. Many northerners saw colonization as the only way to rid the nation of slavery. Southern supporters devoted most of their energy to persuading those African Americans who were already free to leave the United States. Free Blacks, they insisted, were a "degraded" group whose presence posed a danger to white society. Other colonizationists believed that slavery and racism were so deeply embedded in American life that Blacks could never achieve equality if freed and allowed to remain in the country. Like Indian removal, colonization rested on the premise that America is fundamentally a white society.

Blacks and Colonization

In the decades before the Civil War, several thousand Black Americans did emigrate to Liberia with the aid of the Colonization Society. Some were slaves emancipated by their owners on the condition that they depart, while others left voluntarily, motivated by a desire to spread Christianity in Africa or to enjoy rights denied them in the United States. Having experienced "the legal slavery of the South and the social slavery of the North," wrote one emigrant on leaving for Liberia, he knew he could "never be a free man in this country."

But most African Americans adamantly opposed the idea of colonization. In fact, the formation of the American Colonization Society galvanized free

PROTEST AGAINST COLONIZATION MOVEMENT, PHILADELPHIA (1817)

The establishment of the American Colonization Society, which advocated removing the Black population from the United States, posed a direct threat to the goal of equal citizenship for African Americans. In early 1817, a mass meeting in Philadelphia insisted on Blacks' status as part of American society. The reference to the city's "hour of danger" refers to the Black population's work to care for victims of the yellow fever epidemic of 1793, when thousands of white residents fled the city.

At a numerous meeting of the people of color, convened at Bethel church, to take into consideration the propriety of remonstrating [protesting] against the contemplated measure, that is to exile us from the land of our nativity, . . . the following resolutions were adopted, without one dissenting voice.

Whereas our ancestors (not of choice) were the first successful cultivators of the wilds of America, we their descendants feel ourselves entitled to participate in the blessings of her luxuriant soil, which their blood and sweat manured; and that any measure or system of measures, having a tendency to banish us from her bosom, would not only be cruel, but in direct violation of those principles, which have been the boast of this republic.

Resolved, That we view with deep abhorrence the unmerited stigma attempted to be cast upon the reputation of the free people of color, by the promoters of this measure, 'that they are a dangerous and useless part of the community,' when in the state of disfranchisement in which they live, in the hour of danger they ceased to remember their wrongs, and rallied around the standard of their country.

Resolved, That we never will separate ourselves voluntarily from the slave population in this country; they are our brethren by the ties of consanguinity, of suffering, and of wrong; and we feel that there is more virtue in suffering privations with them, than fancied advantages for a season.

Resolved, That without arts, without science, without a proper knowledge of government, to cast into the savage wilds of Africa the free people of color, seems to us the circuitous route through which they must return to perpetual bondage.

QUESTIONS

1. *What arguments do the resolutions advance in claiming the status of Americans*

2. *In what way do the resolutions reflect prevailing American beliefs about Africa?*

Blacks to claim their rights as Americans. Early in 1817, some 3,000 free Blacks assembled in Philadelphia for the first national Black convention. Their resolutions insisted that Blacks were Americans, entitled to the same freedom and rights enjoyed by whites. In the years that followed, a number of Black organizations removed the word "African" from their names to eliminate a possible reason for being deported from the land of their birth.

Militant Abolitionism

The abolitionist movement that arose in the 1830s differed profoundly from its genteel, conservative predecessor. Drawing on the religious conviction that slavery was an unparalleled sin and the secular one that it contradicted the values enshrined in the Declaration of Independence, a new generation of reformers rejected the traditional approach of gradual emancipation and demanded immediate abolition. Also unlike their predecessors, they directed explosive language against slavery and slaveholders and insisted that Blacks, once free, should be incorporated as equal members of the republic rather than being deported. White abolitionists themselves were hardly free of the racism that pervaded American society. Nonetheless, nearly all abolitionists insisted that economic, civil, and political rights in the United States should be equally enjoyed without regard to race. Perfecting American society, they insisted, meant rooting out not just slavery, but racism in all its forms.

An abolitionist banner. Antislavery organizations adopted the Liberty Bell as a symbol of their campaign to extend freedom to Black Americans. Previously, the bell, forged in Philadelphia in the eighteenth century, had simply been known as the Old State House Bell.

The first indication of the new spirit of abolitionism came in 1829 with the appearance of *An Appeal to the Coloured Citizens of the World* by David Walker, a free African American who had been born in North Carolina and now operated a used-clothing store in Boston. A passionate indictment of slavery and racial prejudice, the *Appeal* warned whites that the nation faced divine punishment if it did not mend its sinful ways. Walker invoked the Bible and the Declaration of Independence, but he went beyond these familiar arguments to call on Blacks to take pride in the achievements of ancient African civilizations and to claim all their rights as Americans.

The Emergence of Garrison

Walker's language alarmed both slaveholders and many white critics of slavery. When free Black sailors secretly distributed the pamphlet in the South, some southern states put a price on Walker's head. Walker, however, did not create an abolitionist organization, and he died in mysterious circumstances in 1830. Not until the appearance in 1831 of the *Liberator*, William Lloyd Garrison's weekly journal published in Boston, did the new breed of abolitionism find a permanent voice. "I will be as harsh as truth," Garrison announced, "and as uncompromising as justice. On this subject, I do not wish to think, or speak, or write, with moderation. . . . I will not equivocate—I will not excuse—I will not retreat a single inch—and I will be heard."

And heard he was, partly because southerners, outraged by his inflammatory rhetoric (one editorial called slaveowners "an adulterous and perverse generation, a brood of vipers"), reprinted Garrison's editorials in their own newspapers in order to condemn them, thus providing him with instant notoriety. Some of Garrison's ideas, such as his suggestion that the North abrogate the Constitution and dissolve the Union to end its complicity in the evil of slavery, were rejected by most abolitionists. But his call for the immediate abolition of slavery echoed throughout antislavery circles. Garrison's pamphlet *Thoughts on African Colonization* persuaded many foes of slavery that Blacks must be recognized as part of American society, not viewed as aliens to be shipped overseas.

Spreading the Abolitionist Message

Beginning with a handful of activists, the abolitionist movement expanded swiftly throughout the North. Antislavery leaders took advantage of the rapid development of print technology and the expansion of literacy due to common school education to spread their message. Like radical pamphleteers of the American Revolution and evangelical ministers of the Second Great Awakening, they recognized the democratic potential in the production of printed material. Abolitionists seized upon the recently invented steam printing press to produce millions of copies of pamphlets, newspapers, petitions, novels, and broadsides. Between the formation of the **American Anti-Slavery Society** in 1833 and the end of the decade, some 100,000 northerners joined local groups devoted to abolition. Most were ordinary citizens—farmers, shopkeepers, craftsmen, and laborers, along with a few prominent businessmen like the merchants Arthur and Lewis Tappan of New York.

A is an Abolitionist—
 A man who wants to free
The wretched slave—and give to all
 An equal liberty.

C is the Cotton-field, to which
 This injured brother's driven,
When, as the white man's *slave*, he toils
 From early morn till even.

B is a Brother with a skin
 Of somewhat darker hue,
But in our Heavenly Father's sight,
 He is as dear as you.

D is the Driver, cold and stern,
 Who follows, whip in hand,
To punish those who dare to rest,
 Or disobey command.

Pages from an abolitionist book for children. Abolitionists sought to convince young and old of the evils of slavery.

If Garrison was the movement's most notable propagandist, Theodore Weld, a young minister who had been converted by the evangelical preacher Charles G. Finney, helped to create its mass constituency. A brilliant orator, Weld trained a band of speakers who brought the abolitionist message into the heart of the rural and small-town North. Their methods were those of the revivals—fervent preaching, calls for individuals to renounce their immoral ways—and their message was a simple one: slavery is a sin.

There was far more to Weld's moralistic approach than a concern for religious righteousness. Identifying slavery as a sin was essential to discrediting the traditional strategies of gradual emancipation and colonization. The only proper response to the sin of slavery, abolitionist speakers proclaimed, was the institution's immediate elimination. Weld also supervised the publication of abolitionist pamphlets, including his own *Slavery As It Is* (1839), a compilation of accounts of the maltreatment of slaves. Since Weld took all his examples from the southern press, they could not be dismissed as figments of the northern imagination.

Abolitionists also pioneered modern ways of raising funds, especially charity fairs or "bazaars," where women sold clothing and embroidery made by local sewing circles and luxury items such as silks, porcelain, jewelry, and works of art dispatched by antislavery groups in the British Isles. Generally, fairs were held just before Christmas and included a large assortment of dolls, toys, and other gifts for children. Indeed, abolitionists helped to establish the idea of a Christmas shopping season when people exchanged presents bought at commercial venues. With their slogan, "Buy for the Sake of the Slave," the fairs offered a foretaste of later consumer activism. The grandest of these fairs was the National Anti-Slavery Bazaar in Boston, organized by the wealthy and stylish reformer Maria Weston Chapman, which by the 1850s was raising several thousand dollars per year for the cause, but smaller versions proliferated throughout the North.

Slavery and Moral Suasion

Many southerners feared that the abolitionists intended to spark a slave insurrection, a belief strengthened by the outbreak of Nat Turner's Rebellion a few months after *The Liberator* made its appearance. Yet not only was Garrison completely unknown to Turner, but nearly all abolitionists, despite their militant language, rejected violence as a means of ending slavery. Many were pacifists or "non-resistants," who believed that coercion should be eliminated from all human relationships and institutions. Their strategy was **moral suasion**— the belief that peacefully converting people to Christian values, rather than violence, was the best way to achieve social change. Their arena was the public sphere. Slaveholders must be convinced of the sinfulness of their ways, and the North of its complicity in the peculiar institution.

Standing outside established institutions, abolitionists adopted the role of radical social critics. Among the first to appreciate the key role of public opinion in a mass democracy, they focused their efforts not on infiltrating the existing political parties, but on awakening the nation to the moral evil of slavery. Their language was deliberately provocative, calculated to seize public attention. "Slavery," said Garrison, "will not be overthrown without excitement, without a most tremendous excitement."

Abolitionists and the Idea of Freedom

The abolitionist crusade both reinforced and challenged common understandings of freedom in Jacksonian America. Abolitionists helped to popularize the concept, fortified by the market revolution, that personal freedom derived not from the ownership of productive property such as land but from ownership of one's self and the ability to enjoy the fruits of one's labor. Abolitionists repudiated the idea of "wage slavery," which had been popularized by the era's labor movement and by southern defenders of slavery. Compared with the slave, the person working for wages, they insisted, was an embodiment of freedom: the free laborer could change jobs if he wished, accumulate property, and enjoy a stable family life. Only slavery, wrote the abolitionist William Goodell, deprived human beings of their "grand central right—the inherent right of self-ownership." On the other hand, abolitionists argued that the inherent, natural, and absolute right to personal liberty, regardless of race, took precedence over other forms of freedom, such as the right of citizens to accumulate and hold property or self-government by local political communities.

A rare photograph of an abolitionist meeting in New York State around 1850. Frederick Douglass is at the left of the woman at the center.

Birthright Citizenship

The crusade against slavery gave birth to a new understanding of citizenship and the rights it entailed—a new answer to the question, "Who is an American?" Long before the Civil War, abolitionists Black and white developed a definition of national citizenship severed from the concept of race, with citizens' rights enforced by the federal government. The first legal treatise on the rights of free Black Americans came from the pen of a white abolitionist, William Yates, in 1838. Abolitionists campaigned for northern free Blacks' right to vote, access to education, and equal treatment by transportation companies and public accommodations such as hotels and theaters. They put forward ideas that would be incorporated into the laws and Constitution after the Civil War: that any person born in the United States was entitled to American citizenship and that citizens should enjoy full equality, regardless of race.

The antislavery conventions organized by free Blacks promoted the principle of "birthright citizenship," commonly describing themselves as gatherings of "colored citizens." "Nothing could be plainer," declared the National Convention of Colored Citizens in 1843, "than that native free born men must be citizens." They seized upon the Constitution's language requiring the president to be a "natural born citizen" to argue that American citizenship derived from place of birth, not ancestry or race. Black leaders insistently claimed the same civil and political rights as enjoyed by white citizens, as well as what they called "public rights," which encompassed equal access to businesses serving the public such as hotels, theaters, streetcars, steamships, and railroads, which regularly excluded Blacks. Free Blacks and their white allies used a variety of tactics to press for citizenship rights. They launched campaigns for the right to vote, sued streetcar companies that excluded Black passengers, and challenged discriminatory laws in local, state, and federal courts. Their efforts were usually unsuccessful, but they did win a few victories, such as the repeal of Ohio's discriminatory Black Laws in 1849 and the racial integration of Boston's public schools in 1855. These campaigns helped to establish a new discourse of citizens' rights.

A New Vision of America

In a society in which the rights of citizenship had become more and more closely associated with whiteness, the antislavery movement sought to reinvigorate the idea of freedom as a truly universal entitlement. The origin of the idea of an American people unbounded by race lies not with the founders, who by and large made their peace with slavery, but with the abolitionists. The antislavery crusade viewed slaves and free Blacks as members of the national community, a position summarized in the title of Lydia Maria Child's popular treatise of 1833, *An Appeal in Favor of That Class of Americans Called Africans*. Child's text insisted that Blacks should no more be considered Africans than whites were Englishmen. Abolitionists also pioneered the modern idea that human rights took precedence over national sovereignty. They urged the United States to participate in the courts that brought together judges from Britain and other countries to punish those who violated the ban on the Atlantic slave trade. These courts were perhaps the first example of transnational human rights enforcement. But with southerners exerting powerful influence in Washington, the United States did not join the court system until 1862, in the midst of the Civil War.

The crusade against slavery, wrote Angelina Grimké, who became a leading abolitionist speaker, was the nation's preeminent "school in which human rights are ... investigated." Abolitionists debated the Constitution's relationship to slavery. William Lloyd Garrison burned the document, calling it a covenant with the devil; Frederick Douglass came to believe that it offered no national protection to slavery. But despite this difference of opinion, abolitionists developed an alternative, rights-oriented view of constitutional law, grounded in their universalistic understanding of liberty. Seeking to define the core rights to which all Americans were entitled—the meaning of freedom in concrete legal terms—abolitionists invented the concept of equality before the law regardless of race, one all but unknown in American life before the Civil War. Abolitionist literature also helped to expand the definition of cruelty. The graphic descriptions of the beatings, brandings, and other physical sufferings of the slaves helped to popularize the idea of bodily integrity as a basic right that slavery violated.

Despite being denounced by their opponents as enemies of American principles, abolitionists consciously identified their movement with the revolutionary heritage. The Declaration of Independence was not as fundamental to public oratory in the early republic as it would later become. Abolitionists seized upon it, interpreting the document's preamble as a condemnation of slavery. The Liberty Bell, later one of the nation's most venerated emblems of freedom, did not achieve that status until abolitionists adopted it as a symbol and gave it its name, as part of an effort to identify their principles with those of the founders. (Prior to the 1830s, it was simply the Old State House Bell, used at various times to mark the death of prominent citizens, summon students at the University of Pennsylvania to their classes, and celebrate patriotic holidays.) Of course, Americans of all regions and political beliefs claimed the Revolution's legacy. Mobs that disrupted abolitionist meetings invoked the "spirit of '76," as did southern defenders of slavery. Abolitionists never represented more than a small part of the North's population. But as the slavery controversy intensified, the belief spread far beyond abolitionist circles that slavery contradicted the nation's heritage of freedom.

BLACK AND WHITE ABOLITIONISM

Black Abolitionists

Blacks played a leading role in the antislavery movement. Even before the appearance of *The Liberator*, as we have seen, northern free Blacks had organized in opposition to the Colonization Society. James Forten, a successful Black sailmaker in Philadelphia, helped to finance *The Liberator* in its early years. As late as 1834, northern Blacks, attracted by Garrison's rejection of colonization and his demand for equal rights for Black Americans, made up a majority of the journal's subscribers. Several Blacks served on the board of directors of the American Anti-Slavery Society, and northern-born Blacks and fugitive slaves quickly emerged as major organizers and speakers.

Frederick Douglass was only one among many former slaves who published accounts of their lives in bondage; these works convinced thousands of northerners of the evils of slavery. Indeed, the most effective piece of antislavery literature of the entire period, Harriet Beecher Stowe's novel

Uncle Tom's Cabin, was to some extent modeled on the autobiography of fugitive slave Josiah Henson. Serialized in 1851 in a Washington antislavery newspaper and published as a book the following year, *Uncle Tom's Cabin* sold more than 1 million copies by 1854, and it also inspired numerous stage versions. By portraying slaves as sympathetic men and women, and as Christians at the mercy of slaveholders who split up families and set bloodhounds on innocent mothers and children, Stowe's melodrama gave the abolitionist message a powerful human appeal.

Abolitionism and Race

The first racially integrated social movement in American history and the first to give equal rights for Blacks a central place in its political agenda, abolitionism was nonetheless a product of its time and place. Racism, as we have seen, was pervasive in nineteenth-century America, North as well as South. White abolitionists could not free themselves entirely from this prejudice. They monopolized the key decision-making posts, charged Black spokesman Martin R. Delany, relegating Blacks to "a mere secondary, underling position." By the 1840s, Black abolitionists sought an independent role within the movement, regularly holding their own conventions. The Black abolitionist Henry Highland Garnet, who as a child had escaped from slavery in Maryland with his father, proclaimed at one such gathering in 1843 that slaves should rise in rebellion to throw off their shackles. His position was so at odds with the prevailing belief in moral suasion that the published proceedings entirely omitted the speech. Not until 1848 did Garnet's speech appear in print, along with Walker's *Appeal*, in a pamphlet partially financed by an obscure abolitionist named John Brown.

What is remarkable, however, is not that white abolitionists reflected the prejudices of their society, but the extent to which they managed to rise above them. The abolitionist emblem—a portrait of a slave in chains coupled with the motto "Am I Not a Man and a Brother?"—challenged white Americans to face up to the reality that men and women no different from themselves were being held in bondage.

Most adamant in contending that the struggle against slavery required a redefinition of both freedom and Americanness were Black members of the abolitionist crusade. Black abolitionists developed an understanding of freedom that went well beyond the usage of most of their white contemporaries.

Slavery and American Freedom

At every opportunity, Black abolitionists rejected the nation's pretensions as a land of liberty. Many free Blacks dramatically reversed the common association of the United States with the progress of freedom. Black communities in the North devised an alternative calendar of "freedom celebrations" centered on January 1, the date in 1808 on which the slave trade became illegal, and August 1, the anniversary of West Indian emancipation, rather than July 4. Thanks to its embrace of emancipation in the 1830s, declared a group of Black abolitionists in Philadelphia, Britain had become a model of liberty and justice, while the United States remained a land of tyranny.

Black abolitionists also identified the widespread poverty of the free Black population as a consequence of slavery and insisted that freedom possessed an economic dimension. It must be part of the "great work" of the antislavery crusade, insisted Charles L. Reason, "to abolish not only chattel slavery, but that other kind of slavery, which, for generation after generation, dooms an oppressed people to a condition of dependence and pauperism."

The greatest oration on American slavery and American freedom was delivered in Rochester in 1852 by Frederick Douglass. Speaking just after the annual Independence Day celebration, Douglass posed the question, "What, to the Slave, is the Fourth of July?". He answered that Fourth of July festivities revealed the hypocrisy of a nation that proclaimed its belief in liberty yet daily committed "practices more shocking and bloody" than any other country on earth. Like other abolitionists, however, Douglass also laid claim to the founders' legacy. The Revolution had left a "rich inheritance of justice, liberty, prosperity, and independence," from which subsequent generations had tragically strayed. Only by abolishing slavery and freeing the "great doctrines" of the Declaration of Independence from the "narrow bounds" of race could the United States recapture its original mission.

Gentlemen of Property and Standing

At first, abolitionism aroused violent hostility from northerners who feared that the movement threatened to disrupt the Union, interfere with profits wrested from slave labor, and overturn white supremacy. Led by "**gentlemen of property and standing**" (often merchants with close commercial ties to the South), mobs disrupted abolitionist meetings in northern cities. In 1835, a Boston crowd led William Lloyd Garrison through the streets with a rope around his neck. The editor barely escaped with his life. In the following year, a Cincinnati mob destroyed the printing press of James G. Birney, a former slaveholder who had been converted to abolitionism by Theodore Weld and had been forced to flee Kentucky for the North. Antislavery editor Elijah P. Lovejoy became the movement's first martyr in 1837 when he was killed by a mob in Alton, Illinois, while defending his press. In 1838, a mob in Philadelphia burned to the ground Pennsylvania Hall, which abolitionists had built to hold their meetings. Before starting the fire, however, the mob patriotically carried a portrait of George Washington to safety.

Elsewhere, crowds of southerners, with the unspoken approval of Andrew Jackson's postmaster general, Amos Kendall, burned abolitionist literature that they had removed from the mail. In 1836, when abolitionists began to flood Washington with petitions calling for emancipation in the nation's capital, the House of Representatives adopted the notorious **gag rule**, which prohibited their consideration. The rule was repealed in 1844, thanks largely to the tireless opposition of former president John Quincy Adams, who from 1831 represented Massachusetts in the House.

Slavery and Civil Liberties

Far from stemming the movement's growth, however, mob attacks and attempts to limit abolitionists' freedom of speech convinced many northerners that slavery was incompatible with the democratic liberties of white Americans. In a speech after Lovejoy's murder, Theodore Weld commented on the contrast between Americans' self-confident claims to freedom and the reality of anti-abolitionist violence: "The empty name is everywhere—*free* government, *free* men, *free* speech, *free* schools, and *free* churches. Hollow counterfeits all!" "We commenced the present struggle," announced abolitionist William Jay, "to obtain the freedom of the slave; we are compelled to continue it to preserve our own. We are now contending . . . for the liberty of speech, of the press, and of conscience."

The abolitionist movement now broadened its appeal so as to win the support of northerners who cared little about the rights of Blacks but could be convinced that slavery endangered their own cherished freedoms. The gag rule aroused considerable resentment in the North. "If the government once begins to discriminate as to what is orthodox and what is heterodox in opinion," wrote the *New York Evening Post*, hardly a supporter of abolitionism, "farewell, a long farewell to our freedom."

Am I Not a Man and a Brother? The most common abolitionist depiction of a slave, this image both presents African Americans as unthreatening individuals seeking white assistance and calls upon white Americans to recognize Blacks as fellow men unjustly held in bondage.

For many years, the American public sphere excluded discussion of slavery. Tocqueville had noted that in a democracy, individual dissenters found it difficult to stand up against the overwhelming power of majority opinion. Americans valued free speech, he wrote, but he did "not know any country where, in general, less independence of mind and genuine freedom of discussion reign than in America." The fight for the right to debate slavery openly and without reprisal led abolitionists to elevate "free opinion"—freedom of speech and of the press and the right of petition—to a central place in what Garrison called the "gospel of freedom." In defending free speech, abolitionists claimed to have become custodians of the "rights of every freeman."

THE ORIGINS OF FEMINISM

The Rise of the Public Woman

"When the true history of the antislavery cause shall be written," Frederick Douglass later recalled, "women will occupy a large space in its pages." Much of the movement's grassroots strength derived from northern women, who joined by the thousands. Most were evangelical Protestants, New England Congregationalists, or Quakers convinced, as Martha Higginson of Vermont wrote, that slavery was "a disgrace in this land of Christian light and liberty." A few became famous, but most antislavery women remain virtually unknown to history. One such activist was Lucy Colman, whose mother sang her antislavery songs when she was a child. She became an abolitionist lecturer, a teacher at a school for Blacks in upstate New York, an advocate of women's rights, and an opponent of capital punishment.

The public sphere was open to women in ways government and party politics were not. Women's letters and diaries reveal a keen interest in political issues, from slavery to presidential campaigns. Long before they could vote, women circulated petitions, attended mass meetings, marched in political parades, delivered public lectures, and raised money for political causes. Women organized a petition campaign against the policy of Indian removal. Although unsuccessful, the experience helped to produce a generation of women who then turned their attention to abolitionism, temperance, and other reforms. Harriet Beecher (later the author of *Uncle Tom's Cabin*) participated in the movement against Indian removal—of which her sister, Catharine, was a major organizer. **Dorothea Dix**, a Massachusetts schoolteacher, was the leading advocate of more humane treatment of the insane, who at the time generally were placed in jails alongside debtors and hardened criminals. Thanks to her efforts, twenty-eight states constructed mental hospitals before the Civil War. In 1834, middle-class women in New York City organized the Female Moral Reform Society, which sought to redeem prostitutes from lives of sin and to protect the morality of single women. They attacked the era's sexual double standard by publishing lists of men who frequented prostitutes or abused women. By 1840, the society had been replicated in hundreds of American communities.

Women and Free Speech

All these activities enabled women to carve out a place in the public sphere. But it was participation in abolitionism that inspired the early movement for women's rights. In working for the rights of the slave, not a few women developed a new understanding of their own subordinate status. The daughters of a prominent South Carolina slaveholder, Angelina and Sarah Grimké had been converted first to Quakerism and then to abolitionism while visiting Philadelphia. During the 1830s, they began to deliver popular lectures that offered a scathing condemnation of slavery from the perspective of those who had witnessed its evils firsthand.

The Grimké sisters were neither the first women to lecture in public nor the first to be feverishly condemned by self-proclaimed guardians of female modesty. Frances Wright, a Scottish-born follower of reformer Robert Owen, spoke at New York's Hall of Science in the late 1820s and early 1830s, on subjects ranging from communitarianism to slavery, women's rights, and the plight of northern laborers. One New York newspaper called Wright a "female monster" for "shamefully obtruding herself upon the public." Maria Stewart, a Black Bostonian, in 1832 became the first American woman to lecture to mixed male and female audiences. She, too, received intense criticism. "I have made myself contemptible in the eyes of many," Stewart wrote. "This is the land of freedom," she added, "and we claim our rights," including the right to speak in public.

Stewart left Boston in 1833 and rarely lectured again. The Grimké sisters, however, used the controversy over their speeches as a springboard for a vigorous argument against the idea that taking part in assemblies, demonstrations, and lectures was unfeminine. Outraged by the sight of females sacrificing all "modesty and delicacy" by appearing on the public lecture platform, a group of Massachusetts clergymen denounced the sisters. In reply, they forthrightly defended not only the right of women to take part in political debate but also their right to share the social and educational privileges enjoyed by men. "Since I engaged in the investigation of the rights of the slave," declared Angelina Grimké, "I have necessarily been led to a better understanding of my own." Her sister Sarah proceeded to publish *Letters on the Equality of the Sexes* (1838), a powerful call for equal rights for women. The book raised numerous issues familiar even today, including what later generations would call "equal pay for equal work." Why, Sarah Grimké wondered, did male teachers invariably receive higher wages than women, and a male tailor earn "two or three times as much" as a female counterpart "although the work done by each may be equally good?"

Women's Rights

The Grimkés were the first to apply the abolitionist doctrine of universal freedom and equality to the status of women. When the prominent writer Catharine Beecher reprimanded the sisters for stepping outside "the domestic and social sphere," urging them to accept the fact that "heaven" had designated man "the superior" and woman "the subordinate," Angelina Grimké issued a stinging answer. "I know nothing," she wrote, "of men's rights and women's rights. My doctrine, then is, that whatever it is morally right for man to do, it is morally right for woman to do." Like their predecessors Frances Wright and Maria Stewart, the Grimké sisters soon retired from the fray, unwilling to endure the intense criticism to which they were subjected. But their writings helped to spark the movement for women's rights, which arose in the 1840s.

The May Session of the Woman's Rights Convention, a cartoon published in *Harper's Weekly*, June 11, 1859. A female orator addresses the audience of men and women, while hecklers in the balcony disrupt the proceedings.

Elizabeth Cady Stanton and Lucretia Mott, the key organizers of the Seneca Falls Convention of 1848, were veterans of the antislavery crusade. In 1840, they had traveled to London for the World Anti-Slavery Convention, only to be barred from participating because of their sex. The Seneca Falls Convention, a gathering on behalf of women's rights held in the upstate New York town where Stanton lived, raised the issue of woman's suffrage for the first time. Stanton, the principal author, modeled the Seneca Falls Declaration of Sentiments on the Declaration of Independence. But the document added "women" to Jefferson's axiom "all men are created equal," and in place of a list of injustices committed by George III, it condemned the "injuries and usurpations on the part of man toward woman." The first was denying her the right to vote. As Stanton told the convention, only the vote would make woman "free as man is free," since in a democratic society, freedom was impossible without access to the ballot. The argument was simple and irrefutable: in the words of Lydia Maria Child, "either the theory of our government is *false*, or women have a right to vote."

Seneca Falls marked the beginning of the seventy-year struggle for **woman suffrage**. The vote, however, was hardly the only issue raised at the convention. The Declaration of Sentiments condemned the entire structure of inequality that denied women access to education and employment, gave husbands control over the property and wages of their wives and custody of children in the event of divorce, deprived women of independent legal status after they married, and restricted them to the home as their "sphere of action." Equal rights became the rallying cry of the early movement for women's rights, and equal rights meant claiming access to all the prevailing definitions of freedom.

Organizing among Black Women

Although ignored until recently by historians, Black women played a leading role in the abolitionist movement and the struggle for other forms of equality. Black women built their own organizations, often connected to Black churches, and worked alongside white abolitionists and feminists, claiming a role in public debate. Among the first women to address what critics called "promiscuous" audiences (those that consisted of both men and women) were the traveling minister and teacher Jarena Lee, Maria Stewart, mentioned previously, and Sarah Mapps Douglass, who lectured in Philadelphia against slavery before the Grimké sisters. Mary Ann Shadd Carey, born free in Delaware in 1823, emigrated to Canada, where she founded the *Provincial Freeman*, the first newspaper edited by a Black woman. She published articles demanding the abolition of slavery and equal rights for women and gave assistance to fugitive slaves who succeeded in reaching Canada. She returned to the United States during the Civil War to help recruit Black soldiers for the Union army.

Feminism and Freedom

Like abolitionism, temperance, and other reforms, **feminism** was an international movement. Lacking broad backing at home, early feminists found allies abroad. "Women alone will say what freedom they want," declared an article in the *Free Woman*, a journal established in Paris in 1832. With their household chores diminished because of the availability of manufactured goods and domestic servants, many middle-class women chafed at the restrictions that made it impossible for them to gain an education, enter the professions, and in other ways exercise their talents. Whether married or not, early feminists insisted, women deserved the range of individual choices—the possibility of self-realization—that constituted the essence of freedom.

The artist Thomas Hicks painted this portrait of the feminist writer and editor Margaret Fuller in 1848, two years before she died in a shipwreck as she was returning from a sojourn in Europe.

Women, wrote Margaret Fuller, had the same right as men to develop their talents, to "grow . . . to live freely and unimpeded." The daughter of a Jeffersonian congressman, Fuller was educated at home. (She learned Latin before the age of six.) She became part of New England's transcendentalist circle (discussed in Chapter 9) and from 1840 to 1842 edited *The Dial*, a magazine that reflected the group's views. In 1844, Fuller became literary editor of the *New York Tribune*, the first woman to achieve so important a position in American journalism.

In *Woman in the Nineteenth Century*, published in 1845, Fuller sought to apply to women the transcendentalist idea that freedom meant a quest for personal development. "Every path" to self-fulfillment, she insisted, should be "open to woman as freely as to man." Fuller singled out Abby Kelley as a "gentle hero" for continuing to speak in public despite being denounced by men for venturing "out of her sphere." Fearing that marriage to an American would inevitably mean subordination to male dictation, Fuller traveled to Europe as a correspondent for the *Tribune*. There she married an Italian patriot. Along with her husband and baby, she died in a shipwreck in 1850 while returning to the United States.

Women and Work

Women also demanded the right to participate in the market revolution. At an 1851 women's rights convention, the Black abolitionist Sojourner Truth insisted that the movement devote attention to the plight of poor and working-class women and repudiate the idea that women were too delicate to engage in work outside the home. Born a slave in New York State around 1799, Truth did not obtain her freedom until slavery finally ended in the state in 1827. A listener at her 1851 speech (which was not recorded at the time) later recalled that Truth had spoken of her years of hard physical labor, flexed her arm to show her strength, and exclaimed, "And aren't I a woman?"

Although those who convened at Seneca Falls were predominantly from the middle class—no representatives of the growing number of "factory girls" and domestic servants took part—the participants rejected the identification of the home as a woman's "sphere." Women, wrote Pauline Davis in 1853, "must go *to work*" to emancipate themselves from "bondage." During the 1850s, some feminists tried to popularize a new style of dress, devised by Amelia Bloomer, consisting of a loose-fitting tunic and trousers. In her autobiography, published in 1898, Elizabeth Cady Stanton recalled that women who adopted Bloomer's attire were ridiculed by the press and insulted by "crowds of boys in the streets." They found that "the physical freedom enjoyed did not compensate for the persistent persecution and petty annoyances suffered at every turn." The target of innumerable male jokes, the "bloomer" costume attempted to make a serious point—that the long dresses, tight corsets, and numerous petticoats considered to be appropriate female attire were so confining that they made it almost impossible for women to claim a place in the public sphere or to work outside the home.

In one sense, feminism demanded an expansion of the boundaries of freedom rather than a redefinition of the idea. Women, in the words of one reformer, should enjoy "the rights and liberties that every 'free white male citizen' takes to himself as God-given." But even as it sought to apply prevailing notions of freedom to women, the movement posed a fundamental challenge to some of society's central beliefs—that the capacity for independence and rationality were male traits, that the world was properly divided into public and private realms, and that issues of justice and freedom did not apply to relations within the family. In every realm of life, including the inner workings of the family, declared Elizabeth Cady Stanton, there could be "no happiness without freedom."

The Slavery of Sex

The dichotomy between freedom and slavery powerfully shaped early feminists' political language. Just as the idea of "wage slavery" enabled northern workers to challenge the inequalities of the market revolution, the concept of the "slavery of sex" empowered the women's movement to develop an all-encompassing critique of male authority and their own subordination. Feminists of the 1840s and 1850s pointed out that the law of marriage made nonsense of the description of the family as a "private" institution independent of public authority. When the abolitionists and women's rights activists Lucy Stone and Henry Blackwell married, they felt obliged to repudiate New York's laws that clothed the husband "with legal powers which ... no man should possess."

Feminist abolitionists did not invent the analogy between marriage and slavery. The English writer Mary Wollstonecraft had invoked it as early as the 1790s in *A Vindication of the Rights of Woman* (discussed in Chapter 8). But the analogy between free women and slaves gained prominence as it was swept up in the accelerating debate over slavery. "Woman is a slave, from the cradle to the grave," asserted Ernestine Rose. "Father, guardian, husband—master still. One conveys her, like a piece of property, over to the other." For their part, southern defenders of slavery frequently linked slavery and marriage as natural and just forms of inequality. Eliminating the former institution, they charged, would threaten the latter.

Am I Not a Woman and a Sister?, an illustration from *The Liberator*, 1849. Identifying with the plight of the female slave enabled free women to see more clearly the inequalities they themselves faced.

Marriage was not, literally speaking, equivalent to slavery. The married woman, however, did not enjoy the fruits of her own labor—a central element of freedom. Beginning with Mississippi in 1839, numerous states enacted married women's property laws, shielding from a husband's creditors property brought into a marriage by his wife. Such laws initially aimed not to expand women's rights as much as to prevent families from losing their property during the depression that began in 1837. But in 1860, New York enacted a more far-reaching measure, allowing married women to sign contracts, buy and sell property, and keep their own wages. In most states, however, property accumulated after marriage, as well as wages earned by the wife, still belonged to the husband.

"Social Freedom"

Influenced by abolitionism, women's rights advocates turned another popular understanding of freedom—self-ownership, or control over one's own person—in

From ANGELINA GRIMKÉ, LETTER IN THE LIBERATOR (AUGUST 2, 1837)

The daughters of a prominent South Carolina slaveholder, Angelina and Sarah Grimké became abolitionists after being sent to Philadelphia for education. In this article, Angelina Grimké explains how participation in the movement against slavery led her to a greater recognition of women's lack of basic freedoms.

Since I engaged in the investigation of the rights of the slave, I have necessarily been led to a better understanding of my own; for I have found the Anti-Slavery cause to be . . . the school in which human rights are more fully investigated, and better understood and taught, than in any other [reform] enterprise. . . . Here we are led to examine why human beings have any rights. It is because they are moral beings. . . . Now it naturally occurred to me, that if rights were founded in moral being, then the circumstance of sex could not give to man higher rights and responsibilities, than to woman. . . .

When I look at human beings as moral beings, all distinction in sex sinks to insignificance and nothingness; for I believe it regulates rights and responsibilities no more than the color of the skin or the eyes. My doctrine, then is, that whatever it is morally right for man to do, it is morally right for woman to do. . . . This regulation of duty by the mere circumstance of sex . . . has led to all that [numerous] train of evils flowing out of the anti-christian doctrine of masculine and feminine virtues. By this doctrine, man has been converted into the warrior, and clothed in sternness . . . whilst woman has been taught to lean upon an arm of flesh, to . . . be admired for her personal charms, and caressed and humored like a spoiled child, or converted into a mere drudge to suit the convenience of her lord and master. . . . It has robbed woman of . . . the right to think and speak and act on all great moral questions, just as men think and speak and act. . . .

The discussion of the wrongs of slavery has opened the way for the discussion of other rights, and the ultimate result will most certainly be . . . the letting of the oppressed of every grade and description go free.

From CATHARINE BEECHER, *AN ESSAY ON SLAVERY AND ABOLITIONISM* (1837)

Most men, and many women, did not approve of women taking part in public debate. The writer Catharine Beecher responded to the activities of the Grimké sisters by urging them to accept that "heaven" had designated man "the superior" and woman "the subordinate."

I have . . . been informed, that you contemplate a tour, during the ensuing year, for the purpose of exerting your influence to form Abolition Societies among ladies of the non-slave-holding States. . . . The object I have in view, is to present some reasons why it seems unwise and inexpedient for ladies of the non-slave-holding States to unite themselves in Abolition Societies; and thus, at the same time, to exhibit the inexpediency of the course you propose to adopt. . . .

Heaven has appointed to one sex the superior, and to the other the subordinate station, and this without any reference to the character or conduct of either. It is therefore as much for the dignity as it is for the interest of females, in all respects to conform to the duties of this relation. . . . But while woman holds a subordinate relation in society to the other sex, it is not because it was designed that her duties or her influence should be any the less important, or all-pervading. But it was designed that the mode of gaining influence and of exercising power should be altogether different and peculiar. . . . Woman is to win every thing by peace and love; by making herself so much respected, esteemed and loved, that to yield to her opinions and to gratify her wishes, will be the free-will offering of the heart. But this is to be all accomplished in the domestic and social circle. . . . The moment woman begins to feel the promptings of ambition, or the thirst for power, her ægis of defence is gone. All the sacred protection of religion, all the generous promptings of chivalry, all the poetry of romantic gallantry, depend upon woman's retaining her place as dependent and defenceless, and making no claims, and maintaining no right but what are the gifts of honour, rectitude and love.

A woman may seek the aid of cooperation and combination among her own sex, to assist her in her appropriate offices of piety, charity, maternal and domestic duty; but whatever, in any measure, throws a woman into the attitude of a combatant, either for herself or others—whatever binds her in a party conflict—whatever obliges her in any way to exert coercive influences, throws her out of her appropriate sphere. . . . In this country, petitions to congress, in reference to the official duties of legislators, seem, IN ALL CASES, to fall entirely without the sphere of female duty. Men are the proper persons to make appeals to the rulers whom they appoint, and if their female friends, by arguments and persuasions, can induce them to petition, all the good that can be done by such measures will be secured.

QUESTIONS

1. *What consequences does Grimké believe follow from the idea of rights being founded in the individual's "moral being"?*

2. *How does Beecher believe women should exert power within American society?*

3. *How do the two definitions of women's freedom differ from one another?*

an entirely new direction. The emphasis in abolitionist literature on the violation of the slave woman's body by her master helped to give the idea of self-ownership a concrete reality that encouraged application to free women as well. The law of domestic relations presupposed the husband's right of sexual access to his wife and to inflict corporal punishment on her. Courts proved reluctant to intervene in cases of physical abuse so long as it was not "extreme" or "intolerable." "Women's Rights," declared a Boston meeting in 1859, included "freedom and equal rights in the family." The demand that women should enjoy the rights to regulate their own sexual activity and procreation and to be protected by the state against violence at the hands of their husbands challenged the notion that claims for justice, freedom, and individual rights should stop at the household's door.

The issue of women's private freedom revealed underlying differences within the movement for women's rights. Belief in equality between the sexes and in the sexes' natural differences coexisted in antebellum feminist thought. Even as they entered the public sphere and thereby challenged some aspects of the era's "cult of domesticity" (discussed in Chapter 9), many early feminists accepted other elements. Allowing women a greater role in the public sphere, many female reformers argued, would bring their "inborn" maternal instincts to bear on public life, to the benefit of the entire society.

Even feminists critical of the existing institution of marriage generally refrained from raising in public the explosive issue of women's "private" freedom. The question frequently arose, however, in the correspondence of feminist leaders. "Social Freedom," Susan B. Anthony observed to Lucy Stone, "lies at the bottom of all—and until woman gets that, she must continue the slave of men in all other things." Women like Anthony, who never married, and Stone, who with her husband created their own definition of marriage, reflected the same dissatisfactions with traditional family life as the women who joined communitarian experiments. Not until the twentieth century would the demand that freedom be extended to intimate aspects of life inspire a mass movement. But the dramatic fall in the birthrate over the course of the nineteenth century suggests that many women were quietly exercising "personal freedom" within their families.

The Abolitionist Schism

Even in reform circles, the demand for a greater public role for women remained extremely controversial. Massachusetts physician Samuel Gridley Howe pioneered humane treatment of the blind and educational reform, and he was an ardent abolitionist. But Howe did not support his wife's participation in the movement for female suffrage, which, he complained, caused her to "neglect domestic relations." When abolitionism split into two wings in 1840, the immediate cause was a dispute over the proper role of women in antislavery work. Abby Kelley's election to the business committee of the American Anti-Slavery Society sparked the formation of a rival abolitionist organization, the American and Foreign Anti-Slavery Society, which believed it wrong for a woman to occupy so prominent a position. The antislavery poet John Greenleaf Whittier compared Kelley to Eve, Delilah, and Helen of Troy, women who had sown the seeds of male destruction.

Behind the split lay the fear among some abolitionists that Garrison's radicalism on issues like women's rights, as well as his refusal to support the idea of abolitionists voting or running for public office, impeded the movement's growth. Determined to make abolitionism a political movement, the seceders formed the **Liberty Party**, which nominated James G. Birney as its candidate for president. He received only 7,000 votes (about one-third of 1 percent of the total). In 1840, antislavery northerners saw little wisdom in "throwing away" their ballots.

While the achievement of most of their demands lay far in the future, the women's rights movement succeeded in making "the woman question" a permanent part of the transatlantic discussion of social reform. As for abolitionism, although it remained a significant presence in northern public life until emancipation was achieved, by 1840 the movement had accomplished its most important work. More than 1,000 local antislavery societies were now scattered throughout the North, representing a broad constituency awakened to the moral issue of slavery. The "great duty of freedom," Ralph Waldo Emerson had declared in 1837, was "to open our halls to discussion of this question." The abolitionists' greatest achievement lay in shattering the conspiracy of silence that had sought to preserve national unity by suppressing public debate over slavery.

CHAPTER REVIEW

REVIEW QUESTIONS

1. *How did the utopian communities challenge existing ideas about property and marriage?*

2. *How did the supporters and opponents of temperance understand the meaning of freedom differently?*

3. *What were the similarities and differences between the common school and institutions like asylums, orphanages, and prisons that were created by reformers?*

4. *Why did so many prominent white Americans, from both the North and South, support the colonization of freed slaves?*

5. *How was the abolition movement affected by other social and economic changes such as the rise in literacy, new print technology, and ideas associated with the market revolution?*

6. *How was racism evident even in the abolitionist movement, and what steps did some abolitionists take to fight racism in American society?*

7. *How could antebellum women participate in the public sphere even though they were excluded from government and politics?*

8. *How did white women's participation in the abolitionist movement push them to a new understanding of their own rights and oppression?*

9. *How did advocates for women's rights in these years both accept and challenge existing gender beliefs and social roles?*

10. *To what degree was antebellum reform international in scope?*

11. *How did the antislavery movement give rise to a new understanding of citizenship and the rights it afforded?*

KEY TERMS

utopian communities (p. 445)

Shakers (p. 445)

Oneida (p. 446)

Brook Farm (p. 447)

communitarianism (p. 448)

New Harmony (p. 448)

perfectionism (p. 449)

temperance movement (p. 449)

common school (p. 451)

American Colonization Society (p. 453)

American Anti-Slavery Society (p. 456)

moral suasion (p. 458)

Uncle Tom's Cabin (p. 462)

"gentlemen of property and standing" (p. 463)

gag rule (p. 464)

Dorothea Dix (p. 465)

woman suffrage (p. 468)

feminism (p. 469)

Liberty Party (p. 475)

Go to 🐰 INQUIZITIVE

To see what you know—and learn what you've missed—with personalized feedback along the way.

CHAPTER 13

A HOUSE DIVIDED

1840–1861

- What were the major factors contributing to U.S. territorial expansion in the 1840s?

- Why did the expansion of slavery become the most divisive political issue in the 1840s and 1850s?

- What combination of issues and events fueled the creation of the Republican Party in the 1850s?

- What enabled Lincoln to emerge as president from the divisive party politics of the 1850s?

- What were the final steps on the road to secession?

In 1855, Thomas Crawford, one of the era's most prominent American sculptors, was asked to design a statue to adorn the Capitol's dome, still under construction in Washington, D.C. He proposed a statue of Freedom, a female figure wearing a liberty cap. Secretary of War Jefferson Davis of Mississippi, one of the country's largest slaveholders, objected to Crawford's plan. A familiar symbol in the colonial era, the liberty cap had fallen into disfavor among some Americans after becoming closely identified with the French Revolution. Davis's disapproval, however, rested on other grounds. Ancient Romans, he noted, regarded the cap as "the badge of the freed slave."

Its use, he feared, might suggest that there was a connection between the slaves' longing for freedom and the liberty of freeborn Americans. Davis ordered the liberty cap replaced with a less controversial military symbol, a feathered helmet.

Crawford died in Italy, where he had spent most of his career, in 1857. Two years later, the colossal Statue of Freedom, which weighed 15,000 pounds, was transported to the United States in several pieces and assembled at a Maryland foundry under the direction of Philip Reed, a slave craftsman. In 1863, it was installed atop the Capitol, where it can still be seen today. By the time it was put in place, the country was immersed in the Civil War and Jefferson Davis had become president of the Confederate States of America. The dispute over the Statue of Freedom offers a small illustration of how, by the mid-1850s, nearly every public question was being swept up into the gathering storm over slavery.

FRUITS OF MANIFEST DESTINY

Continental Expansion

In the 1840s, slavery moved to the center stage of American politics. It did so not in the moral language or with the immediatist program of abolitionism, but as a result of the nation's territorial expansion. By 1840, with the completion of Indian removal, virtually all the land east of the Mississippi River was in white hands. The depression that began in 1837 sparked a large migration of settlers farther west. Some headed to Oregon, whose Willamette Valley was reputed to be one of the continent's most beautiful and fertile regions. Until the 1840s, the American presence in the area had been limited to a few fur traders and explorers. But between 1840 and 1845, some 5,000 emigrants made the difficult 2,000-mile journey by wagon train to Oregon from jumping-off places on the banks of the Missouri River. By 1860, nearly 300,000 men, women, and children braved disease, starvation, the natural barrier of the Rocky Mountains, and occasional Indian attacks to travel overland to Oregon and California.

During most of the 1840s, the United States and Great Britain jointly administered Oregon, and Utah was part of Mexico. This did not stop Americans from settling in either region. National boundaries meant little to those who moved west. The 1840s witnessed an intensification of the old belief that God intended the American nation to reach all the way to the Pacific Ocean. As noted in Chapter 9, the term that became a shorthand for this expansionist spirit was "manifest destiny."

The Mexican Frontier: New Mexico and California

Settlement of Oregon did not directly raise the issue of slavery, although the prospect of new states in a region that did not seem hospitable to slavery alarmed some southerners. But the nation's acquisition of part of Mexico did. When Mexico achieved its independence from Spain in 1821, it was nearly as large as the United States and its population of 6.5 million was about two-thirds that of its northern neighbor. Mexico's northern provinces—California, New Mexico, and Texas—however, were isolated and sparsely settled outposts surrounded by Indian country. New Mexico's population at the time of Mexican independence consisted of around 30,000 persons of Spanish origin, 10,000 Pueblo Indians, and an indeterminate number of nomadic Indians—bands of Apaches, Comanches, Navajos, and Utes. With the opening in 1821 of the Santa Fe Trail linking that city with Independence, Missouri, the northern periphery of the new Mexican nation was quickly incorporated into the sphere of influence of the rapidly expanding western United States. New Mexico's commerce with the United States eclipsed trade with the rest of Mexico.

California's non-Indian population in 1821, some 3,200 missionaries, soldiers, and settlers, was vastly outnumbered by about 20,000 Native Americans living and working on land owned by religious missions and by 150,000 members of unsubdued tribes in the interior. In 1834, in the hope of reducing the power of the Catholic Church and attracting Mexican and foreign settlers to California, the Mexican government dissolved the great mission landholdings and emancipated Indians working for the friars. Most of the land ended up in the hands of a new class of Mexican cattle ranchers, the *Californios*, who defined their own identity in large measure

• CHRONOLOGY •

1820	Moses Austin receives Mexican land grant
1836	Texas independence from Mexico
1845	Inauguration of James Polk
	United States annexes Texas
1846	Wilmot Proviso
1846–1848	Mexican War
1848	Treaty of Guadalupe Hidalgo
	Gold discovered in California
	Free Soil Party organized
1849	Inauguration of Zachary Taylor
1850	Compromise of 1850
	Fugitive Slave Act
1853	Inauguration of Franklin Pierce
1854	Kansas-Nebraska Act
	Know-Nothing Party established
	Ostend Manifesto
	Republican Party organized
1856	Bleeding Kansas
1857	Inauguration of James Buchanan
	Dred Scott decision
1858	Lincoln-Douglas debates
1859	John Brown's raid on Harpers Ferry
1860	South Carolina secedes
1861	Inauguration of Abraham Lincoln
	Fort Sumter fired upon

American Progress. This 1872 painting by John Gast, commissioned by the author of a travel guide to the Pacific coast, reflects the ebullient spirit of manifest destiny. A female figure descended from earlier representations of the goddess of liberty wears the star of empire and leads the movement westward while Indians retreat before her. Symbols of civilization abound: the eastern city in the upper right corner, railroads, fenced animals, stagecoaches, and telegraph wires and a "school book" held by the central figure.

against the surrounding Indian population. *Californios* referred to themselves as *gente de razón* (people capable of reason) as opposed to the *indios*, whom they called *gente sin razón* (people without reason). For the "common good," Indians were required to continue to work for the new landholders.

By 1840, California was already linked commercially with the United States. New England ships were trading with the region. In 1846, Alfred Robinson, who had moved from Boston, published *Life in California*. "In this age of annexation," he wondered, "why not extend the 'area of freedom' by the annexation of California?"

The Texas Revolt

The first part of Mexico to be settled by significant numbers of Americans was Texas, whose non-Indian population of Spanish origin (called **Tejanos**) numbered only about 2,000 when Mexico became independent. In order to develop the region, the Spanish government had accepted an offer by Moses Austin, a Connecticut-born farmer, to colonize it with Americans. In 1820, Austin received a large land grant. He died soon afterward and his son Stephen continued the plan, now in independent Mexico, reselling land in smaller plots to American set-tlers at twelve cents per acre. Settlers were required to become Mexican citizens. By 1830, the population of American origin had reached around 7,000, consider-ably exceeding the number of *Tejanos*.

Alarmed that its grip on the area was weakening, the Mexican government in 1830 annulled existing land contracts and barred future emigration from the United States. Led by Stephen Austin, American settlers demanded greater autonomy within Mexico. Part of the area's tiny *Tejano* elite joined them. Mostly ranchers and large farmers, they had welcomed the economic boom that accompanied the settlers and had formed economic alliances with American traders. The issue of slavery further exacerbated matters. Mexico had abolished slavery, but local authorities allowed American settlers to bring slaves with them. When Mexico's ruler, General **Antonio López de Santa Anna**, sent an army in 1835 to impose central authority, a local committee charged that his purpose was "to give liberty to our slaves and make slaves of ourselves."

Westward migration in the early and mid-1840s took American settlers across Indian country into the Oregon Territory, ownership of which was disputed with Great Britain. The Mormons migrated west to Salt Lake City, then part of Mexico.

The appearance of Santa Anna's army sparked the chaotic **Texas revolt**. The rebels formed a provisional government that soon called for Texan independence. On March 6, 1836, Santa Anna's army stormed the Alamo, a mission compound in San Antonio, killing its 187 American and *Tejano* defenders. "Remember the Alamo" became the Texans' rallying cry. In April, forces under Sam Houston, a former governor of Tennessee, routed Santa Anna's army at the Battle of San Jacinto and forced him to recognize Texan independence. Houston was soon elected the first president of the Republic of Texas. In 1837, the Texas Congress called for union with the United States. But fearing the political disputes certain to result from an attempt to add another slave state to the Union, President Martin Van Buren shelved the question. Settlers from the United States nonetheless poured into the region, many of them slaveowners taking up fertile cotton land. By 1845, the population of Texas reached nearly 150,000.

The Election of 1844

Texas annexation remained on the political back burner until President John Tyler revived it in the hope of rescuing his failed administration and securing southern support for renomination in 1844. In April 1844, a letter by John C. Calhoun, whom Tyler had appointed secretary of state, was leaked to the press. It linked the idea of absorbing Texas directly to the goal of strengthening slavery in the United States. Some southern leaders, indeed, hoped that Texas could be divided into several states, thus further enhancing the South's power in Congress. Late that month, Henry Clay and former president Van Buren, the prospective Whig and Democratic candidates for president and two of the party system's most venerable leaders, met at Clay's Kentucky plantation. They agreed to issue letters rejecting immediate annexation on the grounds that it might provoke war with Mexico. Clay and Van Buren were reacting to the slavery issue in the traditional manner—by trying to keep it out of national politics.

A campaign handkerchief from 1844 depicts the Whig candidate for president, Henry Clay, surrounded by images of national unity and the economic progress that, Whigs argued, would follow from the enactment of a protective tariff. Clay and his running mate, Theodore Frelinghuysen, were narrowly defeated by the Democrat James K. Polk.

Clay went on to receive the Whig nomination, but for Van Buren the letters proved to be a disaster. At the Democratic convention, southerners bent on annexation deserted Van Buren's cause, and he failed to receive the two-thirds majority necessary for nomination. The delegates then turned to the little-known James K. Polk, a former governor of Tennessee whose main assets were his support for annexation and his close association with Andrew Jackson, still the party's most popular figure. Like nearly all the presidents before him, Polk was a slaveholder. He owned substantial cotton plantations in Tennessee and Mississippi, where conditions were so brutal that only half of the slave children lived to the age of fifteen and adults frequently ran away. To soothe injured feelings among northern Democrats over the rejection of Van Buren, the party platform called for not only the "reannexation" of Texas (implying that Texas had been part of the Louisiana Purchase and therefore already belonged to the United States) but also the "reoccupation" of all of Oregon. "Fifty-four forty or fight"—American control of Oregon all the way to its northern boundary at north latitude 54°40′—became a popular campaign slogan. But the bitterness of the northern Van Burenites over what they considered to be a betrayal on the part of the South would affect American politics for years to come.

Polk was the first "dark horse" candidate for president—that is, one whose nomination was completely unexpected. In the fall, he defeated Clay in an extremely close election. Polk's margin in the popular vote was less than 2 percent. Had not James G. Birney, running again as the Liberty Party candidate, received 16,000 votes in New York, mostly from antislavery Whigs, Clay would have been elected. In March 1845, only days before Polk's inauguration, Congress declared Texas part of the United States.

The Road to War

James K. Polk may have been virtually unknown, but he assumed the presidency with a clearly defined set of goals: to reduce the tariff, reestablish the Independent Treasury system, settle the dispute over ownership of Oregon, and bring California into the Union. Congress soon enacted the first two goals, and the third was accomplished in an agreement with Great Britain dividing Oregon at the forty-ninth parallel. Many northerners were bitterly disappointed by this compromise, considering it a betrayal of Polk's campaign promise not to give up any part of Oregon without a fight. But the president secured his main objectives, the Willamette Valley and the magnificent harbor of Puget Sound.

Acquiring California proved more difficult. Polk dispatched an emissary to Mexico offering to purchase the region, but the Mexican government refused to negotiate. By the spring of 1846, Polk was planning for military action. In April,

American soldiers under Zachary Taylor moved into the region between the Nueces River and the Rio Grande, land claimed by both countries on the disputed border between Texas and Mexico. This action made conflict with Mexican forces inevitable. When fighting broke out, Polk claimed that the Mexicans had "shed blood upon American soil" and called for a declaration of war.

The War and Its Critics

The **Mexican War** was the first American conflict to be fought primarily on foreign soil and the first in which American troops occupied a foreign capital. Inspired by the expansionist fervor of manifest destiny, a majority of Americans supported the war. But a significant minority in the North dissented, fearing that far from expanding the "great empire of liberty," the administration's real aim was to acquire new land for the expansion of slavery. Ulysses S. Grant, who served with distinction in Mexico, later called the war "one of the most unjust ever waged by a stronger nation against a weaker nation." Henry David Thoreau was jailed in Massachusetts in 1846 for refusing to pay taxes as a protest against the war. Defending his action, Thoreau wrote an important essay, "On Civil Disobedience," which inspired such later advocates of nonviolent resistance to unjust laws as Martin Luther King Jr.

Among the war's critics was Abraham Lincoln, who had been elected to Congress in 1846 from Illinois. Like many Whigs, Lincoln questioned whether the Mexicans had actually inflicted casualties on American soil, as Polk claimed, and in 1847 he introduced a resolution asking the president to specify the precise "spot" where blood had first been shed. Lincoln's stance proved unpopular in Illinois. He had already agreed to serve only one term in Congress, but when Democrats captured his seat in 1848, many blamed the result on Lincoln's criticism of the war. But the concerns he raised regarding the president's power to "make war at pleasure" would continue to echo in the twentieth and twenty-first centuries.

Combat in Mexico

More than 60,000 American volunteers enlisted and did most of the fighting. Combat took place on three fronts. In June 1846, a band of American insurrectionists proclaimed California freed from Mexican control and named Captain John C. Frémont, head of a small scientific expedition in the West, its ruler. Their aim was California's incorporation into the United States, but for the moment they adopted a flag depicting a large bear as the symbol of the area's independence. A month later, the U.S. Navy sailed into Monterey and San Francisco harbors, raised the American flag, and put an end to the "bear flag republic." At almost the same time, 1,600 American troops under General Stephen W. Kearny occupied Sante Fe without resistance and then set out for southern California, where they helped to put down a Mexican uprising against American rule.

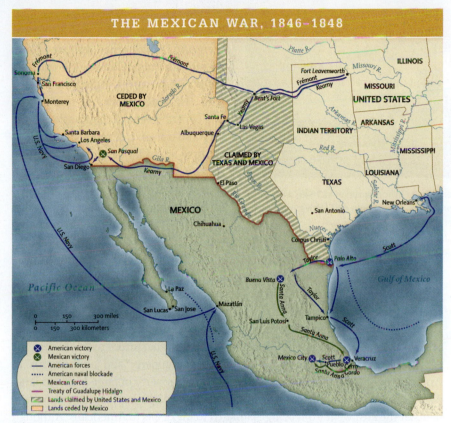

The Mexican War was the first in which an American army invaded another country and occupied its capital. As a result of the war, the United States acquired a vast new area in the modern-day Southwest.

The bulk of the fighting occurred in central Mexico. In February 1847, Taylor defeated Santa Anna's army at the Battle of Buena Vista. When the Mexican government still refused to negotiate, Polk ordered American forces under Winfield Scott to march inland from the port of Veracruz toward Mexico City. Scott's forces routed Mexican defenders and in September occupied the country's capital. In February 1848, the two governments agreed to the Treaty of Guadalupe Hidalgo, which confirmed the annexation of Texas and ceded California and present-day New Mexico, Arizona, Nevada, and Utah to the United States. In exchange, the United States paid Mexico $15 million. The Mexican Cession, as the land annexed from Mexico was called, established the present territorial boundaries on the North American continent except for the **Gadsden Purchase**, a parcel of additional land bought from Mexico in 1853, and Alaska, acquired from Russia in 1867.

A scene on a California ranch in 1849, with *Californios* (on horseback) and Native Americans at work.

The Mexican War is only a footnote in most Americans' historical memory. Unlike other wars, few public monuments celebrate the conflict. Mexicans, however, regard the war (or "the dismemberment," as it is called) as a central event of their national history and a source of resentment over a century and a half after it was fought. As the Mexican negotiators of 1848 complained, it was unprecedented to launch a war because a country refused to sell part of its territory to a neighbor.

With the end of the Mexican War, the United States absorbed half a million square miles of Mexico's territory, one-third of that nation's total area. A region that for centuries had been united was suddenly split in two, dividing families and severing trade routes. An estimated 75,000 to 100,000 Spanish-speaking Mexicans and more than 150,000 Indians inhabited the Mexican Cession. The Treaty of Guadalupe Hidalgo guaranteed to "male citizens" of the area "the free enjoyment of their liberty and property" and "all the rights" of Americans—a provision designed to protect the property of large Mexican landowners in California. Thus, in the first half of the nineteenth century, some residents of the area went from being Spaniards to Mexicans to Americans. Although not newcomers, they had to adjust to a new identity as if they were immigrants. As to Indians whose homelands and hunting grounds suddenly became part of the United States, the treaty referred to them only as "savage tribes" whom the United States must prevent from launching incursions into Mexico across the new border. Decades of Indian raids and warfare in northern Mexico in which Comanches, Kiowas, Apaches, and others attacked Mexican towns and ranches, and to which Mexico responded in kind, had led to the death of thousands of people and had undermined Mexico's economy. American leaders claimed that because of Mexico's inability to control its northern territories, annexation to the United States was an act of salvation for the region's population.

The Texas Borderland

After achieving independence in 1836, Texas became a prime example of a western borderland. *Anglos* (white settlers from the East) and *Tejanos* had fought together to achieve independence, but soon relations between them soured. *Anglos* in search of land and resources expelled some Mexicans, including former allies, now suspected of loyalty to Mexico. Juan Seguín, a *Tejano*, had played an active role in the revolt and served for a time as mayor of San Antonio. In 1842, still mayor, he was driven from the town by vigilantes. He had become, he lamented, "a foreigner in my native land."

Facing pressures to Americanize, some *Tejano* families sent their children to English-language schools established by Protestant missionaries from the East. But most refused to convert from Catholicism, despite the declining power of the church after Texas became part of the United States. Increasingly, *Tejanos* were confined to unskilled agricultural or urban labor. Some *Tejanos* used their ambiguous identities to their own advantage. During the Civil War, some *Tejano* men avoided the Confederate draft by claiming to be citizens of Mexico.

Meanwhile, in southern Texas, the disputed territory between the Nueces River and the Rio Grande, claimed by both Texas and Mexico but actually controlled by Comanche Indians, became a site of continual conflict. Authority in the area remained contested until Texas became part of the much more powerful United States and even then, Comanche power would not be broken until the 1860s and 1870s.

Race and Manifest Destiny

The spirit of manifest destiny gave a new stridency to ideas about racial superiority. During the 1840s, territorial expansion came to be seen as proof of the innate superiority of the "Anglo-Saxon race" (a mythical construct defined largely by its opposites: Blacks, Indians, Hispanics, and Catholics). "*Race*," declared John L. O'Sullivan's *Democratic Review*, was the "key" to the "history of nations."

"Race" in the mid-nineteenth century was an amorphous notion involving color, culture, national origin, class, and religion. Newspapers, magazines, and scholarly works popularized the link between American freedom and the supposedly innate liberty-loving qualities of Anglo-Saxon Protestants. The annexation of Texas and conquest of much of Mexico became triumphs of civilization, progress, and liberty over the tyranny of the Catholic Church and the incapacity of "mongrel races." Indeed, calls by some expansionists for the United States to annex all of Mexico failed in part because of fear that the nation could not assimilate its large non-white Catholic population, supposedly unfit for citizenship in a republic.

The imposition of the American system of race relations proved detrimental to many inhabitants of the newly acquired territories. Texas had already demonstrated as much. Mexico had abolished slavery and declared persons of Spanish, Indian, and African origin equal before the law. The Texas Constitution adopted after independence not only included protections for slavery but also denied civil rights to Indians and persons of African origin. Only whites were permitted to purchase land, and the entrance of free Blacks into

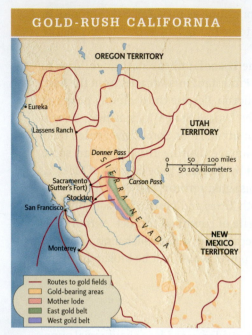

GOLD-RUSH CALIFORNIA

OREGON TERRITORY

Eureka

Lassens Ranch

UTAH
TERRITORY

Donner Pass

0   50   100 miles
0 50 100 kilometers

Sacramento
(Sutter's Fort)   Carson Pass

Stockton

San Francisco

NEW
MEXICO
TERRITORY

Monterey

— Routes to gold fields
  Gold-bearing areas
  Mother lode
  East gold belt
  West gold belt

The gold rush brought thousands of fortune seekers, from nearly every corner of the globe, to California.

the state was prohibited altogether. "Every privilege dear to a free man is taken away," one free Black resident of Texas complained.

Local circumstances affected racial definitions in the former Mexican territories. Texas defined "Spanish" Mexicans, especially those who occupied important social positions, as white. But the residents of New Mexico of both Mexican and Indian origin were long deemed "too Mexican" for democratic self-government. With white migration lagging, Congress did not allow New Mexico to become a state until 1912.

Gold-Rush California

California had a non-Indian population of fewer than 15,000 when the Mexican War ended. For most of the 1840s, five times as many Americans emigrated to Oregon as to California. But this changed dramatically after January 1848, when gold was discovered in the foothills of the Sierra Nevada Mountains at a sawmill owned by the Swiss immigrant Johann A. Sutter. A mania for gold spread throughout the world, fanned by newspaper accounts of instant wealth acquired by early migrants. By ship and land, newcomers poured into California, in what came to be called the **gold rush**. The non-Indian population rose to 200,000 by 1852 and more than 360,000 eight years later.

California's gold-rush population was incredibly diverse. Experienced miners flooded in from Mexico and South America. Tens of thousands of Americans who had never seen a mine arrived from the East, and from overseas came Irish, Germans, Italians, and Australians. Nearly 25,000 Chinese landed between 1849 and 1852, almost all of them young men who had signed long-term labor contracts with Chinese merchants, who in turn leased them to mining and railroad companies and other employers. San Francisco, a town of 1,000 in 1848, became the gateway to the El Dorado of northern California. By 1850, it had 30,000 residents and had become perhaps the world's most racially and ethnically diverse city. Unlike the families who settled farming frontiers, most of the gold-rush migrants were young men. Women played many roles in western mining communities, running restaurants and boardinghouses and working as laundresses, cooks, and prostitutes. But as late as 1860, California's male population outnumbered females by nearly three to one.

California and the Boundaries of Freedom

As early surface mines quickly became exhausted, they gave way to underground mining that required a large investment of capital. This economic development worsened conflicts among California's many racial and ethnic groups engaged in fierce competition for gold. The law was very fragile in gold-rush California. In 1851 and 1856, "committees of vigilance" took control of San Francisco, sweeping aside established courts to try and execute those accused of crimes. White miners organized extralegal groups that expelled "foreign

A hand-colored engraving from the 1850s advertises the sale of a sixteen-year-old Southern California Native American woman. The price, listed in French, is a pound of gunpowder and a bottle of brandy. Slavery had been abolished in California law but persisted in some parts of the state.

miners"—Mexicans, Chileans, Chinese, French, and American Indians—from areas with gold. The state legislature imposed a tax of twenty dollars per month on foreign miners, driving many of them from the state.

California would long remain in the American imagination a place of infinite opportunity, where newcomers could start their lives anew. But the boundaries of freedom there were tightly drawn. The state constitution of 1850 limited voting and the right to testify in court to whites, excluding Indians, Asians, and the state's few Blacks (who numbered only 962). California landowners who claimed Spanish descent or had intermarried with American settlers were deemed to be white. But with land titles derived from Mexican days challenged in court, many sold out to newcomers from the East.

The Chinese encountered considerable prejudice, with white miners organizing to drive them from the gold fields. Even though Chinese immigrants included teachers, merchants, and other professionals, Governor John Bigler denounced all Chinese as "coolies," an ethnic slur that suggested they worked for wages so low that they undercut the conditions of free white labor. Chinese women were widely described as prostitutes. These prejudicial images would survive for many decades and would fuel later efforts to exclude people from China from the United States.

For California's Indians, the gold rush and absorption into the United States proved to be disastrous. Gold seekers overran Indian communities. Miners, ranchers, and vigilantes murdered thousands of Indians. Determined to reduce the native population, state officials paid millions in bounties to private militias that launched attacks on the state's Indians. Although California was a free state, thousands of Indian children, declared orphans or vagrants by local courts, were bought and sold as slaves. By 1860, California's Indigenous population, nearly 150,000 when the Mexican War ended, had been reduced to around 30,000.

Opening Japan

The Mexican War ended with the United States in possession of the magnificent harbors of San Diego and San Francisco, long seen as jumping-off points for trade with the Far East. Between 1848 and 1860 American trade with China tripled.

In the 1850s, the United States took the lead in opening Japan, a country that had closed itself to nearly all foreign contact for more than two centuries. In 1853 and 1854, American warships under the command of **Commodore Matthew Perry** (the younger brother of Oliver Perry, a hero of the War of 1812) sailed into Tokyo Harbor. Perry, who had been sent by President Millard Fillmore to negotiate a trade treaty, demanded that the Japanese deal with him. Alarmed by European intrusions into China and impressed by Perry's armaments as well as a musical pageant he presented that included a blackface minstrel show, Japanese leaders agreed to do so. In 1854, they opened two ports to American shipping. Two years later, Townsend Harris, a merchant from New York City, arrived as the first American consul (and, according to some accounts, the inspiration for Puccini's great opera, *Madama Butterfly*, about an American who marries and then abandons a Japanese woman). Harris persuaded the Japanese to allow American ships into additional ports and to establish full diplomatic relations between the two countries. Japan soon launched a process of modernization that transformed it into the region's major military power.

A DOSE OF ARSENIC

Victory over Mexico added more than 1 million square miles to the United States—an area larger than the Louisiana Purchase. But the acquisition of this vast territory raised the fatal issue that would disrupt the political system and plunge the nation into civil war—whether slavery should be allowed to expand into the West. Events soon confirmed Ralph Waldo Emerson's prediction that if the United States gobbled up part of Mexico, "it will be as the man who swallows arsenic. . . . Mexico will poison us."

Already, the bonds of union were fraying. In 1844 and 1845, the Methodists and Baptists, the two largest evangelical churches, divided into northern and southern branches. But it was the entrance of the slavery issue into the heart of American politics as the result of the Mexican War that eventually dissolved perhaps the strongest force for national unity—the two-party system.

The Wilmot Proviso

Before 1846, the status of slavery in all parts of the United States had been settled, either by state law or by the Missouri Compromise, which determined slavery's status in the Louisiana Purchase. The acquisition of new land reopened the question of slavery's expansion. The divisive potential of this issue became clear in 1846, when Congressman David Wilmot of Pennsylvania proposed a resolution prohibiting slavery from all territory acquired from Mexico. Party lines crumbled as every northerner, Democrat and Whig alike, supported what came to be known as the **Wilmot Proviso**, while nearly all southerners opposed it. The measure passed the House, where the more populous North possessed a majority, but failed in the Senate, with its even balance of free and slave states. The proviso, said one newspaper, "as if by magic, brought to a head the great question that is about to divide the American people."

In 1848, opponents of slavery's expansion organized the **Free Soil Party** and nominated Martin Van Buren for president and Charles Francis Adams, the son of John Quincy Adams, as his running mate. Democrats nominated Lewis Cass of Michigan, who proposed that the decision on whether to allow slavery should be left to settlers in the new territories (an idea later given the name "popular sovereignty"). Van Buren was motivated in part by revenge against the South for jettisoning him in 1844. But his campaign struck a chord among northerners opposed to the expansion of slavery, and he polled some 300,000 votes, 14 percent of the northern total. Victory in 1848 went to the Whig candidate, Zachary Taylor, a hero of the Mexican War and a Louisiana sugar planter. But the fact that one former president and the son of another abandoned their parties to run on a Free Soil platform showed that antislavery sentiment had spread far beyond abolitionist ranks. "Antislavery," commented Senator William H. Seward of New York, "is at length a respectable element in politics."

The Free Soil Appeal

The Free Soil position had a popular appeal in the North that far exceeded the abolitionists' demand for immediate emancipation and equal rights for Blacks. While Congress possessed no constitutional power to abolish slavery within a state, well-known precedents existed for keeping territories (areas that had not yet entered the Union as states) free from slavery. Congress had done this in 1787 in the Northwest Ordinance and again in the Missouri Compromise of 1820–1821. Many northerners had long resented what they considered southern domination of the federal government. The idea of preventing the creation of new slave states appealed to those who favored policies, such as the protective tariff and government aid to internal improvements, that the majority of southern political leaders opposed.

For thousands of northerners, moreover, the ability to move to the new western territories held out the promise of economic betterment. The depression of the early 1840s had reinforced the traditional equation of landownership with economic freedom. The labor movement promoted

CONTINENTAL EXPANSION THROUGH 1853

Original 13 states 1783
Great Britain Cession 1783
Louisiana Purchase 1803
Acquired from Great Britain 1818
Florida Purchase 1819
1912 Date of organization as territory

Acquired from Great Britain 1842
Texas Annexation 1845
Oregon Country 1846
Mexican Cession 1848
Gadsden Purchase 1853
(1912) Date of statehood

Borders represent present-day state borders

By 1853, with the Gadsden Purchase, the present boundaries of the United States in North America, with the exception of Alaska, had been created.

access to western land as a way of combating unemployment and low wages in the East. "Freedom of the soil," declared George Henry Evans, the editor of a pro-labor newspaper, offered the only alternative to permanent economic dependence for American workers.

Such views merged easily with opposition to the expansion of slavery. If slave plantations were to occupy the fertile lands of the West, northern migration would be effectively blocked. The term "free soil" had a double meaning. The Free Soil platform of 1848 called both for barring slavery from western territories and for the federal government to provide free homesteads to settlers in the new territories. Unlike abolitionism, the "free soil" idea also appealed to the racism so widespread in northern society. Wilmot himself insisted that his controversial proviso aimed to advance "the cause and rights of the free white man," in part by preventing him from having to compete with "Black labor."

To white southerners, the idea of barring slavery from territory acquired from Mexico seemed a violation of their equal rights as members of the Union. Southerners had fought and died to win these territories; surely they had a right to share in the fruits of victory. A majority of slaves in 1848 lived in states that had not even existed when the Constitution was adopted. Just as northerners believed westward expansion essential to their economic well-being, southern leaders became convinced that slavery must expand or die. Southern interests would not be secure in a Union dominated by non-slaveholding states.

Crisis and Compromise

In world history, the year 1848 is remembered as the "springtime of nations," a time of democratic uprisings against the monarchies of Europe and demands by ethnic minorities for national independence. American principles of liberty and self-government appeared to be triumphing in the Old World. The Chartist movement in Great Britain organized massive demonstrations in support of democratic reforms. The French replaced their monarchy with a republic. Hungarians proclaimed their independence from Austrian rule. Patriots in Italy and Germany, both divided into numerous states, demanded national unification. But the revolutionary tide receded. Chartism faded away. In France, the Second Republic was soon succeeded by the reign of Emperor Napoleon III. Revolts in Budapest, Rome, and other cities were crushed. Would their own experiment in self-government, some Americans wondered, suffer the same fate as the failed revolutions of Europe?

With the slavery issue appearing more and more ominous, established party leaders moved to resolve differences between the sections. Some disputes were of long standing, but the immediate source of controversy arose from the acquisition of new lands after the Mexican War. In 1850, California asked to be admitted to the Union as a free state. Many southerners opposed the measure, fearing that it would upset the sectional balance in Congress. Senator Henry Clay offered a plan with four main provisions that came to be known as the Compromise of 1850. California would enter the Union as a free state. The slave trade, but not slavery itself, would be abolished in the nation's capital. A stringent new law would help southerners reclaim runaway slaves. And the status of slavery in the remaining territories acquired from Mexico would be left to the decision of the local white inhabitants. The United States would also agree to pay off the massive debt Texas had accumulated while independent.

The Great Debate

In the Senate debate on the Compromise, powerful leaders spoke for and against compromise. Daniel Webster of Massachusetts announced his willingness to abandon the Wilmot Proviso and accept a new fugitive slave law if this were the price of sectional peace. John C. Calhoun, again representing South Carolina, was too ill to speak. A colleague read his remarks rejecting the very idea of compromise. Slavery, Calhoun insisted, must be protected by the national government and extended into all the new territories. The North must yield or the Union could not survive. William H. Seward of New York also opposed compromise. To southerners' talk of their constitutional rights, Seward responded that a "higher law" than the Constitution condemned slavery—the law of morality. Here was the voice of abolitionism, now represented in the U.S. Senate.

President Zachary Taylor, like Andrew Jackson a southerner but a strong nationalist, was alarmed by talk of disunion. He accused southern leaders in Congress of holding California hostage to their own legislative aims and insisted that all Congress needed to do was admit California to the Union. But Taylor died suddenly of an intestinal infection on July 9, 1850. His successor, Millard Fillmore of New York, threw his support to Clay's proposals. Fillmore helped to break the impasse in Congress and secure adoption of the **Compromise of 1850**.

The Fugitive Slave Issue

For one last time, political leaders had removed the dangerous slavery question from congressional debate. The new **Fugitive Slave Act**, however, made further controversy inevitable. The law allowed special federal commissioners to determine the fate of alleged fugitives without benefit of a jury trial or even testimony by the accused individual. It prohibited local authorities from interfering with the capture of fugitives and required individual citizens to

THE COMPROMISE OF 1850

Legend:
- Unorganized territory
- Free states and territories
- Slave states
- Open to slavery by popular sovereignty (Compromise of 1850)

The Compromise of 1850 attempted to settle issues arising from the acquisition of territory from Mexico by admitting California as a free state and providing that the status of slavery in Utah and New Mexico would be determined by the settlers. The area labeled "unorganized territory" was home to many Native American nations but no U.S. territorial governments had been established there.

assist in such capture when called upon by federal agents. Thus, southern leaders, usually strong defenders of states' rights and local autonomy, supported a measure that brought federal agents into communities throughout the North, armed with the power to override local law enforcement and judicial procedures to secure the return of runaway slaves. The security of slavery was more important to them than states'-rights consistency.

The law further widened sectional divisions and reinvigorated the Underground Railroad. In a series of dramatic confrontations, fugitives, aided by abolitionist allies, violently resisted recapture. A large crowd in 1851 rescued the escaped slave Jerry from jail in Syracuse, New York, and spirited him off to Canada. In the same year, an owner who attempted to recapture a fugitive was killed in Christiana, Pennsylvania. Later in the decade, Margaret Garner, a Kentucky slave who had escaped with her family to Ohio, killed her own young daughter rather than see her returned to slavery by federal marshals. (At the end of the twentieth century, this incident would become the basis for Toni Morrison's celebrated novel *Beloved*.)

THE FUGITIVE SLAVE LAW....HAMLET IN CHAINS.

An engraving from the *National Anti-Slavery Standard*, October 17, 1850, depicts James Hamlet, the first person returned to slavery under the Fugitive Slave Act of 1850, in front of City Hall in New York. Flags fly from the building, emblazoned with popular American maxims violated by Hamlet's rendition. By the time this appeared in print, New Yorkers had raised the money to purchase Hamlet's freedom and he was back in the city.

Less dramatically, the men and women involved in the Underground Railroad redoubled their efforts to assist fugitives. Thanks to the consolidation of the railroad network in the North, it was now possible for escaping slaves who reached the free states to be placed on trains that would take them to safety in Canada in a day or two. In 1855 and 1856, Sydney Howard Gay, an abolitionist editor in New York City and a key Underground Railroad operative, recorded in a notebook the arrival of over 200 fugitives—men, women, and children—a majority of whom had been sent by train from Philadelphia. Gay dispatched them to upstate New York and Canada.

Overall, several thousand fugitives and freeborn Blacks, worried that they might be swept up in the stringent provisions of the Fugitive Slave Act, fled to safety in Canada. The sight of so many refugees seeking liberty in a foreign land challenged the familiar image of the United States as an asylum for freedom. "Families are separating," reported a Toronto newspaper in October 1850, "leaving their homes, and flying in all directions to seek in Canada, under the British flag, the protection denied to them in the free republic."

Douglas and Popular Sovereignty

At least temporarily, the Compromise of 1850 seemed to restore sectional peace and party unity. In the 1852 presidential election, Democrat Franklin Pierce won a sweeping victory over the Whig Winfield Scott on a platform that recognized the Compromise as a final settlement of the slavery controversy. Pierce received a broad popular mandate, winning 254 electoral votes to Scott's 42. Yet his administration turned out to be one of the most disastrous in American history.

In 1854, the party system finally succumbed to the disruptive pressures of sectionalism. Early in that year, Illinois senator Stephen A. Douglas introduced a bill to provide territorial governments for Kansas and Nebraska, located within the Louisiana Purchase. With Calhoun, Clay, and Webster (the "great triumvirate") all having died between 1850 and 1852, Douglas, although only forty-one, saw himself as the new leader of the Senate. A strong believer in western development, he hoped that a transcontinental railroad could be constructed through Kansas or Nebraska. But he feared that this could not be accomplished unless formal governments had been established in these territories. Southerners in Congress, however, seemed adamant against allowing the organization of new free territories that might further upset the sectional balance. Douglas hoped to satisfy them by applying the principle of **popular sovereignty**, whereby the status of slavery would be determined by the votes of local settlers, not Congress. To Douglas, popular sovereignty embodied the idea of local self-government and offered a middle ground between the extremes of North and South. It was a principle on which all parts of the Democratic Party could unite, and which might enable him to capture the presidential nomination in 1856 to succeed the ineffectual Pierce.

The Kansas-Nebraska Act

Unlike the lands taken from Mexico, Kansas and Nebraska lay in the nation's heartland, directly in the path of westward migration. Slavery, moreover, was prohibited there under the terms of the Missouri Compromise, which Douglas's bill would repeal. In response, a group of antislavery congressmen issued the *Appeal of the Independent Democrats*. Written by two abolitionists from Ohio—Congressman Joshua Giddings and Senator Salmon P. Chase— the *Appeal* proved to be one of the most effective pieces of political persuasion in American history. It arraigned Douglas's bill as a "gross violation of a sacred pledge," part and parcel of "an atrocious plot" to convert free territory into a "dreary region of despotism, inhabited by masters and slaves." It helped to convince millions of northerners that southern leaders aimed at nothing less than extending their peculiar institution throughout the West.

Thanks to Douglas's energetic leadership, the **Kansas-Nebraska Act** became law. But it shattered the Democratic Party's unity. Even as Congress debated, protest meetings sprang up throughout the North. Fearing that the bill's unpopularity among their constituents would harm their chances for reelection, half the northern Democrats in the House cast negative votes. It is difficult to think of a piece of legislation in American history that had a more profound impact on national life. During the next two years, the Whig Party, unable to develop a unified response to the political crisis, collapsed. The South became solidly Democratic. Most northern Whigs, augmented by thousands of disgruntled Democrats, joined a new organization, the Republican Party, dedicated to preventing the further expansion of slavery.

THE KANSAS-NEBRASKA ACT, 1854

BRITISH CANADA

WASHINGTON TERRITORY

OREGON TERRITORY

MINNESOTA TERRITORY

NEBRASKA TERRITORY

WI

ME

VT
NH

MI

NY

MA

IA

PA

RI
CT

UTAH TERRITORY

IL IN OH

Mason-Dixon Line

NJ
DE

CA

KANSAS TERRITORY

see inset

MO

KY

VA

MD

Missouri Compromise Line 36°30'N

TN

NC

NEW MEXICO TERRITORY

INDIAN TERRITORY

AR

SC

MS AL GA

TX

LA

FL

BLEEDING KANSAS
Atchison
Leavenworth
Lecompton
Missouri R.
KANSAS
TERRITORY
Lawrence   **MISSOURI**
Pottawatomie ✗   ✗ Osawatomie
Massacre

☐ Free states and territories
☐ Slave states
☐ Indian territory
☐ Open to slavery by popular sovereignty under the Compromise of 1850
☐ Open to slavery by popular sovereignty under the Kansas-Nebraska Act, 1854

0   250   500 miles
0   250   500 kilometers

The Kansas-Nebraska Act opened a vast area in the nation's heartland to the possible spread of slavery by repealing the Missouri Compromise and providing that settlers would determine the status of slavery in these territories.

THE RISE OF THE REPUBLICAN PARTY

The Northern Economy

The disruptive impact of slavery on the traditional parties was the immediate cause of political transformation in the mid-1850s. But the rise of the Republican Party also reflected underlying economic and social changes, notably the completion of the market revolution and the beginning of mass immigration from Europe. The period from 1843, when prosperity returned, to 1857, when another economic downturn hit, witnessed explosive economic growth, especially in the North. The catalyst was the completion of the railroad network. From 5,000 miles in 1848, railroad track mileage grew to 30,000 by 1860, with most of the construction occurring in Ohio, Illinois, and other states of the Old Northwest. Four great trunk railroads now linked eastern cities with western farming and commercial centers. The railroads completed the reorientation of the Northwest's trade from the South to the East. As late as 1850, most western farmers still shipped their produce down the Mississippi River. Ten years later, however, railroads transported nearly all their crops to the East, at a fraction of the previous cost. The economic integration of the Northwest and Northeast created the groundwork for their political unification in the Republican Party.

By 1860, the North had become a complex, integrated economy, with eastern industrialists marketing manufactured goods to the commercial farmers of the West, while residents of the region's growing cities consumed the food westerners produced. Northern society stood poised between old and new ways. The majority of the population still lived not in large cities but in small towns and rural areas, where the ideal of economic independence—owning one's own farm or shop—still lay within reach. Yet the majority of the northern workforce no longer labored in agriculture, and the industrial revolution was spreading rapidly.

Two great areas of industrial production had arisen. One, along the Atlantic coast, stretched from Boston to Philadelphia and Baltimore. A second was centered on or near the Great Lakes, in inland cities like Buffalo, Cleveland, Pittsburgh, and Chicago. Driven by railroad expansion, coal mining and iron manufacturing were growing rapidly. Chicago, the Old Northwest's major rail center and the jumping-off place for settlers heading for the Great Plains, had become a complex manufacturing center, producing 5,000 reapers each year, along with barbed wire, windmills, and prefabricated "balloon frame" houses, all of which facilitated further western settlement. New York City by 1860 had become the nation's preeminent financial, commercial, and manufacturing center. Although the southern economy was also growing and the continuing expansion of cotton production brought wealth to slaveholders, the South did not share in these broad economic changes.

The Rise and Fall of the Know-Nothings

As noted in Chapter 9, nativism—hostility to immigrants, especially Catholics—emerged as a local political movement in the 1840s. But in 1854, with the party system in crisis, it burst on the national political scene with the sudden appearance of the American, or Know-Nothing, Party (so called because it began as a secret organization whose members, when asked about its existence, were supposed to respond, "I know nothing"). The **Know-Nothing Party** trumpeted its dedication to reserving political office for native-born Americans and to resisting the "aggressions" of the Catholic Church, such as its supposed efforts to undermine public school systems. The Know-Nothings swept the 1854 state elections in Massachusetts, electing the governor, all of the state's congressmen, and nearly every member of

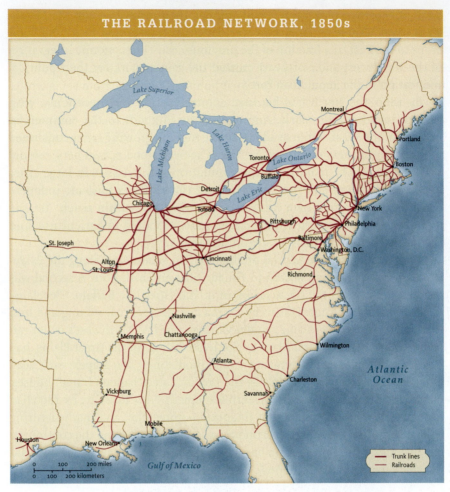

Trunk lines
Railroads

The rapid expansion of the railroad network in the 1850s linked the Northeast and Old Northwest in a web of commerce. The South's rail network was considerably less developed, accounting for only 30 percent of the nation's track mileage.

the state legislature. They captured the mayor's office in cities like Philadelphia, Chicago, and San Francisco as well. In many states, nativists emerged as a major component of victorious "anti-Nebraska" coalitions of voters opposed to the Kansas-Nebraska Act. In the North, the Know-Nothings' appeal combined anti-Catholic and antislavery sentiment, with opposition to the sale of liquor often added to the equation. After all, most Catholics, as noted in the previous chapter, vigorously opposed the reform movements inspired by evangelical Protestantism, especially antislavery and temperance. The 1854 elections, said one observer, revealed "a deep seated feeling in favor of human freedom and also a fine determination that hereafter none but Americans shall rule America."

Despite severe anti-Irish discrimination in jobs, housing, and education, however, it is remarkable how little came of demands that immigrants be barred from the political nation. All European immigrants benefited from being white. During the 1850s, free Blacks found immigrants pushing them out of the jobs as servants and common laborers previously available to them. The newcomers had the good fortune to arrive after white male suffrage had become the norm and automatically received the right to vote. Even as New England states sought to reduce immigrant political power (Massachusetts and Connecticut made literacy a voting requirement, and Massachusetts mandated a two-year waiting period between becoming a naturalized citizen and voting), western states desperate for labor allowed immigrants to vote well before they became citizens. In a country where the suffrage had become essential to understandings of freedom, it is significant that white male immigrants could vote almost from the moment they landed in America, while Blacks and Native Americans, whose ancestors had lived in the country for centuries, could not.

The Free Labor Ideology

By 1856, it was clear that the Republican Party —a coalition of antislavery Democrats, northern Whigs, Free Soilers, and Know-Nothings opposed to the further expansion of slavery—would become the major alternative to the Democratic Party in the North. Republicans managed to convince most northerners that **the Slave Power**, as they called the South's proslavery political leadership, posed a more immediate threat to their liberties and aspirations than "popery" and immigration. The party's appeal rested on the idea of "free labor." In Republican hands, the antithesis between "free society" and "slave society" coalesced into a comprehensive worldview that glorified the North as the home of progress, opportunity, and freedom.

The defining quality of northern society, Republicans declared, was the opportunity it offered each laborer to move up to the status of landowning farmer or independent craftsman, thus achieving the economic independence essential to freedom. Slavery, by contrast, spawned a social order consisting of degraded slaves, poor whites with no hope of advancement, and idle aristocrats. The struggle over the territories was a contest about which of two antagonistic labor systems would dominate the West and, by implication, the nation's future. If slavery were to spread into the West, northern free laborers would be barred and their chances for social advancement severely diminished. Slavery, Republicans insisted, must be kept out of the territories so that free labor could flourish.

To southern claims that slavery was the foundation of liberty, Republicans responded with the rallying cry "freedom national"—meaning not abolition, but ending the federal government's support of slavery. Under the banner of free labor, northerners of diverse backgrounds and interests rallied in defense of the superiority of their own society.

Republicans were not abolitionists—they focused on preventing the spread of slavery, not attacking it where it existed. Nonetheless, many party leaders viewed the nation's division into free and slave societies as an "irrepressible conflict," as Senator William H. Seward of New York put it in 1858, that eventually would have to be resolved. These "two systems" of society, Seward insisted, were "incompatible" within a single nation. The market revolution, Seward argued, by drawing the entire nation closer together in a web of transportation and commerce, heightened the tension between freedom and slavery. The United States, he predicted, "must and will, sooner or later, become either entirely a slaveholding nation, or entirely a free-labor nation."

Bleeding Kansas and the Election of 1856

Their free labor outlook, which resonated so effectively with deeply held northern values, helps to explain the Republicans' rapid rise to prominence. But dramatic events also fueled the party's growth. When Kansas held elections in 1854 and 1855, hundreds of proslavery Missourians crossed the border to cast fraudulent ballots. President Franklin Pierce recognized the legitimacy of the resulting proslavery legislature. Settlers from free states soon established a rival government, and a sporadic civil war broke out in Kansas in which some 200 persons eventually lost their lives. In one incident, in May 1856, a proslavery mob attacked the free-soil stronghold of Lawrence, burning public buildings and pillaging private homes.

"**Bleeding Kansas**" seemed to discredit Douglas's policy of leaving the decision on slavery up to the local population, thus aiding the Republicans. The party also drew strength from an unprecedented incident in the halls of Congress. South Carolina representative Preston Brooks, wielding a gold-tipped cane, beat the antislavery senator Charles Sumner of Massachusetts unconscious after Sumner delivered a denunciation of "The Crime

THE PRESIDENTIAL ELECTION OF 1856

Non-voting territory

Party	Candidate	Electoral Vote (Share)	Popular Vote (Share)
Democrat	Buchanan	174 (59%)	1,838,169 (45%)
Republican	Frémont	114 (39%)	1,341,264 (33%)
American	Fillmore	8 (3%)	874,534 (22%)

against Kansas." Many southerners applauded Brooks, sending him canes emblazoned with the words "Hit him again!"

In the election of 1856, the Republican Party chose as its candidate John C. Frémont and drafted a platform that strongly opposed the further expansion of slavery. Stung by the northern reaction to the Kansas-Nebraska Act, the Democrats nominated James Buchanan, who had been minister to Great Britain in 1854 and thus had no direct connection with that divisive measure. The Democratic platform endorsed the principle of popular sovereignty as the only viable solution to the slavery controversy. Meanwhile, the Know-Nothings presented ex-president Millard Fillmore as their candidate. Frémont outpolled Buchanan in the North, carrying eleven of sixteen free states—a remarkable achievement for an organization that had existed for only two years. But Buchanan won the entire South and the key northern states of Illinois, Indiana, and Pennsylvania, enough to ensure his victory. Fillmore carried only Maryland.

The 1856 election returns made starkly clear that parties had reoriented themselves along sectional lines. One major party had been destroyed, another had been seriously weakened, and a new one had arisen, devoted entirely to the interests of the North.

THE EMERGENCE OF LINCOLN

The final collapse of the party system took place during the administration of a president who epitomized the old political order. Born during George Washington's presidency, James Buchanan had served in Pennsylvania's legislature, in both houses of Congress, and as secretary of state under James K. Polk. A staunch believer in the Union, he committed himself to pacifying inflamed sectional emotions. Few presidents have failed more disastrously in what they set out to accomplish.

The Dred Scott Decision

Even before his inauguration, Buchanan became aware of an impending Supreme Court decision that held out the hope of settling the slavery controversy once and for all. This was the case of ***Dred Scott v. Sandford***. During the 1830s, Scott had accompanied his owner, Dr. John Emerson of Missouri, to Illinois, where slavery had been prohibited by the Northwest Ordinance of 1787 and by state law, and to Wisconsin Territory, where it was barred by the Missouri Compromise. After returning to Missouri, Scott sued for his freedom, claiming that residence on free soil had made him free.

Dred Scott as painted in 1857, the year the Supreme Court ruled that he and his family must remain in slavery.

The Dred Scott decision, one of the most famous—or infamous—rulings in the long history of the Supreme Court, was announced in March 1857, two days after Buchanan's inauguration. The justices addressed three questions. Could a Black person be a citizen and therefore sue in federal court? Did residence in a free state make Scott free? Did Congress possess the power to prohibit slavery in a territory? All nine justices issued individual opinions. But essentially, the Court divided 6–3 (with Justice Robert C. Grier of Pennsylvania, at Buchanan's behind-the-scenes urging, joining a southern majority). Seventeen years earlier, in the little-known case *United States v. Dow*, which involved a person from the Philippines, Chief Justice Roger B. Taney had made clear his conviction that only white persons were eligible to be part of the American body politic. Whites, he wrote, were the "master race," protected by the Constitution, while the rights of non-whites could be limited by state legislatures, even to the extent of being enslaved. Now, Taney declared that only white persons could be citizens of the United States. The nation's founders, Taney insisted, believed that Blacks "had no rights which the white man was bound to respect." Ironically, one reason for Taney's ruling was his robust understanding of what citizenship entailed. Being a citizen, he declared, meant freedom from legal discrimination and full enjoyment of the rights specified in the Constitution, among them the ability to travel anywhere in the country and the right "to keep and carry arms wherever they went." These were not rights he thought Black people, free or slave, should enjoy.

The case could have ended there, since Scott had no right to sue, but inspired by the idea of resolving the slavery issue, Taney pressed on. Scott, he declared, remained a slave. Illinois law had no effect on him after his return to Missouri. As for his residence in Wisconsin, Congress possessed no power under the Constitution to bar slavery from a territory. The Missouri Compromise, recently repealed by the Kansas-Nebraska Act, had been unconstitutional, and so was any measure interfering with southerners' right to bring slaves into the western territories. The decision in effect declared unconstitutional

From OPINION OF THE COURT, CHIEF JUSTICE ROGER B. TANEY, THE DRED SCOTT DECISION (1857)

In the Dred Scott decision, the Supreme Court attempted to resolve a divisive question: Were free African Americans citizens of the United States? The Court answered no. For the majority, Chief Justice Roger B. Taney insisted that American citizenship was for white persons alone.

The words "people of the United States" and "citizens" are synonymous terms, and mean the same thing. They both describe the political body who, according to our republican institutions, form the sovereignty, and who hold the power and conduct the government through their representatives. They are what we familiarly call the "sovereign people," and every citizen is one of this people and a constituent member of this sovereignty. The question before us is, whether the class of persons described in the plea . . . compose a portion of this people, and are constituent members of this sovereignty? We think they are not, and that they are not included, and were not intended to be included, under the word "citizens" in the Constitution, and can therefore claim none of the rights and privileges which that instrument provides for and secures to citizens of the United States. On the contrary, they were at that time considered as a subordinate and inferior class of beings, who had been subjugated by the dominant race, and, whether emancipated or not, yet remained subject to their authority, and had no rights or privileges but such as those who held the power and the government might choose to grant them. . . .

They had for more than a century before been regarded as beings of an inferior order, and altogether unfit to associate with the white race, either in social or political relations; and so far inferior, that they had no rights which the white man was bound to respect. . . .

The general words [of the Declaration of Independence] would seem to embrace the whole human family, . . . but it is too clear for dispute, that the enslaved African race were not intended to be included. [The authors] perfectly understood the meaning of the language they used, and they knew that it would not in any part of the civilized world be supposed to embrace the Negro race.

QUESTIONS

1. *What evidence does Taney present that Blacks were not considered citizens by the authors of the Declaration of Independence and the Constitution?*

2. *Why do you think he bases his argument on what he says were the intentions of the founders rather than the situation of free Blacks in the 1850s?*

the Republican platform of restricting slavery's expansion. It also seemed to undermine Douglas's doctrine of popular sovereignty. For if Congress lacked the power to prohibit slavery in a territory, how could a territorial legislature created by Congress do so? The Court, a Georgia newspaper exulted, "covers every question regarding slavery and settles it in favor of the South."

The Decision's Aftermath

Perhaps the person least directly affected by the Dred Scott decision was the plaintiff himself, for a new owner immediately emancipated Scott and his family. Scott died in 1858, having enjoyed his freedom for less than two years. Harriet Scott lived until 1876, long enough to see Taney's ruling invalidated by the laws and constitutional amendments of Reconstruction. Their youngest daughter, Lizzie, survived to the age of 99. She died in 1954, having experienced the long era of segregation and the birth of the modern civil rights movement. Among the decision's casualties was the reputation of the Court itself, which, in the North, sank to the lowest level in all of American history.

The Dred Scott decision caused a furor in the North and put the question of Black citizenship on the national political agenda. James McCune Smith, a Black physician, author, and antislavery activist, carefully dissected Taney's reasoning, citing legal precedents going back to "the annals of lofty Rome" to demonstrate that all free persons born in the United States, Black as well as white, "must be citizens." Many Republicans also rejected Taney's reasoning. In a stinging dissent, Justice John McLean of Ohio insisted that regardless of race, "birth on the soil of a country both creates the duties and confers the rights of citizenship."

Slavery, announced President Buchanan, henceforth existed in all the territories, "by virtue of the Constitution." In 1858, his administration attempted to admit Kansas as a slave state under the Lecompton Constitution, which had been drafted by a pro-southern convention and never submitted to a popular vote. Outraged by this violation of popular sovereignty, Douglas formed an unlikely alliance with congressional Republicans to block the attempt. Kansas remained a territory; it would join the Union as a free state on the eve of the Civil War. The Lecompton battle convinced southern Democrats that they could not trust their party's most popular northern leader.

Lincoln and Slavery

The depth of Americans' divisions over slavery was brought into sharp focus in 1858 in one of the most storied election campaigns in the nation's history. Seeking reelection to the Senate as both a champion of popular sovereignty and the man who had prevented the administration from forcing slavery on the people of Kansas, Douglas faced an unexpectedly strong challenge from Abraham Lincoln, then little known outside of Illinois. Born into a modest farm family in Kentucky in 1809, Lincoln had moved as a youth to frontier Indiana and then Illinois. Although he began running for public office at the age of twenty-one, until the mid-1850s his career hardly seemed destined for greatness. He had served four terms as a Whig in the state legislature and one in Congress from 1847 to 1849.

Lincoln reentered politics in 1854 as a result of the Kansas-Nebraska Act. He once said that he "hated slavery as much as any abolitionist." Unlike abolitionists, however, Lincoln was willing to compromise with the South to preserve the Union. "I hate to see the poor creatures hunted down," he once wrote of fugitive slaves, "but I bite my lip and keep silent." But on one question he was inflexible—stopping the expansion of slavery.

Lincoln developed a critique of slavery and its expansion that gave voice to the central values of the emerging Republican Party and the millions of northerners whose loyalty it commanded. His speeches combined the moral fervor of the abolitionists with the respect for order and the Constitution of more conservative northerners. "I hate it," he said in 1854 of the prospect of slavery's expansion, "because of the monstrous injustice of slavery itself. I hate it because it deprives our republican example of its just influence in the world—enables the enemies of free institutions, with plausibility, to taunt us as hypocrites—causes the real friends of freedom to doubt our sincerity."

In a sense, Lincoln's own life personified the free labor ideology and the opportunities northern society offered to laboring men. "I want every man to have the chance," said Lincoln, "and I believe a black man is entitled to it, in which he *can* better his condition." Blacks might not be the equal of whites in all respects, but in their "natural right" to the fruits of their labor, they were "my equal and the equal of all others."

The Lincoln-Douglas Campaign

The campaign against Douglas, the North's preeminent political leader, created Lincoln's national reputation. Accepting his party's nomination for the Senate in June 1858, Lincoln etched sharply the differences between them. "A house divided against itself," he announced, "cannot stand. I believe this government cannot endure, permanently half *slave* and half *free*." Lincoln's point was not that civil war was imminent, but that Americans must choose between favoring and opposing slavery. There could be no middle ground. Douglas's policy of popular sovereignty, he insisted, reflected a moral indifference that could only result in the institution's spread throughout the entire country.

The **Lincoln-Douglas debates**, held in seven Illinois towns and attended by tens of thousands of listeners, remain classics of American political oratory. Clashing definitions of freedom lay at their heart. To Lincoln, freedom meant opposition to slavery. The nation needed to rekindle the spirit of the founding fathers, who, he claimed, had tried to place slavery on the path to "ultimate extinction." Douglas argued that the essence of freedom lay in local self-government and individual self-determination. A large and diverse nation could only survive by respecting the right of each locality to determine its own institutions. In response to a question posed by Lincoln during the Freeport debate, Douglas insisted that popular sovereignty was not incompatible with the Dred Scott decision. Although territorial legislatures could no longer exclude slavery directly, he argued, if the people wished to keep slaveholders out, all they needed to do was refrain from giving the institution legal protection.

Douglas insisted that politicians had no right to impose their own moral standards on society as a whole. "I deny the right of Congress," he declared, "to force a good thing upon a people who are unwilling to receive it." If a community wished to own slaves, it had a right to do so. Of course, when Douglas spoke of the "people," he meant whites alone. He spent much of his time in the debates attempting to portray Lincoln as a dangerous radical whose positions threatened to degrade white Americans by reducing them to equality with Blacks. The United States government, Douglas proclaimed, had been created "by white men for the benefit of white men and their posterity for ever."

Lincoln shared many of the racial prejudices of his day. He opposed giving Illinois Blacks the right to vote or serve on juries and spoke frequently of colonizing Blacks overseas as the best solution to the problems of slavery and race. Yet, unlike Douglas, Lincoln did not use appeals to racism to garner votes. And he refused to exclude Blacks from the human family. No less than whites, they were entitled to the inalienable rights of the Declaration of Independence, which applied to "all men, in all lands, everywhere," not merely to Europeans and their descendants.

The Illinois election returns revealed a state sharply divided, like the nation itself. Southern Illinois, settled from the South, voted strongly Democratic, while the rapidly growing northern part of the state was firmly in the Republican column. Douglas was reelected. His victory was all the more remarkable because elsewhere in the North Republicans swept to victory in 1858.

John Brown at Harpers Ferry

On October 16, 1859, an armed assault by twenty-two abolitionists, five of them Black, on the federal arsenal at **Harpers Ferry, Virginia**, further heightened sectional tensions. Militarily, the plan made little sense. The band was soon surrounded and its men killed or captured by a detachment of federal soldiers headed by Colonel Robert E. Lee. The leader of the raid, the white abolitionist John Brown, was inspired, in part, by the tradition of violent resistance to slavery, including the Haitian Revolution and Nat Turner's Rebellion. Throughout the 1830s and 1840s, despite constantly being in debt, he financed antislavery publications and befriended fugitive slaves and radical Black activists including David Walker, Martin Delany, and Henry Highland Garnet, who believed that abolitionists who advocated moral suasion alone were naïve. No oppressed people, Garnet declared in 1843, had ever secured their liberty without violence.

Two years after the end of the Civil War in 1867, the artist Thomas Satterwhite Noble, a veteran of the Confederate army, painted *John Brown's Blessing*, commemorating an apocryphal incident in which a slave woman presented her child to Brown as he was being led to the gallows. Two white children, accompanied by their Black nurse, look on.

Like other abolitionists, Brown was a deeply religious man. His God, however, was not the forgiving Jesus of the revivals, who encouraged men and women to save themselves through conversion, but the vengeful Father of the Old Testament. During the civil war in Kansas, Brown traveled to the territory. In May 1856, after the attack on Lawrence, he and a few followers murdered five proslavery settlers at Pottawatomie Creek. For the next two years, he traveled through the North and Canada, raising funds and enlisting followers for a war against slavery. He sought military and financial support from radical abolitionists including Frederick Douglass and Harriet Tubman. A group of white abolitionists known as the Secret Six and a Black activist, Mary Ellen Pleasant, became key financiers of the raid at Harpers Ferry.

When Virginia's governor, Henry A. Wise, spurned pleas for clemency and ordered Brown executed, he turned Brown into a martyr in much of the North. Henry David Thoreau pronounced him "a crucified hero." To the South, the failure of the assault on Harpers Ferry seemed less significant than the adulation it aroused from much of the northern public. The raid and Brown's execution further widened the breach between the sections.

Since Brown's death, radicals of both the left and right have revered him as a man willing to take direct action against an institution he considered immoral. Black leaders have long hailed him as a rare white person willing to sacrifice himself for the cause of racial justice. Brown's last letter was a brief, prophetic statement: "I, John Brown, am quite certain that the crimes of this guilty land will never be purged away but with blood."

The Rise of Southern Nationalism

With the Republicans continuing to gain strength in the North, Democrats might have been expected to put a premium on party unity as the election of 1860 approached. By this time, however, a sizable group of southerners viewed their region's prospects as more favorable outside the Union than within it. Throughout the 1850s, influential writers and political leaders kept up a drumbeat of complaints about the South's problems. The sky-high price of slaves made it impossible for many planters' sons and upwardly mobile small farmers to become planters in their own right. Many white southerners felt that the opportunity was eroding for economic independence through ownership of land and slaves—liberty as they understood it. The North, secessionists charged, reaped the benefits of the cotton trade, while southerners fell deeper and deeper into debt. To remain in the Union meant to accept "bondage" to the North. But an independent South could become the foundation of a slave empire ringing the Caribbean and embracing Cuba, other West Indian islands, Mexico, and parts of Central America.

More and more southerners were speaking openly of southward expansion. In 1854, Pierre Soulé of Louisiana, the American ambassador to Spain, persuaded the ministers to Britain and France to join him in signing the Ostend Manifesto, which called on the United States to purchase or seize Cuba, where slavery was still legal, from Spain. Meanwhile, the military adventurer William Walker led a series of "filibustering" expeditions (the term derived from the Spanish word for pirate, *filibustero*) in Central America.

Born in Tennessee, Walker had headed to California to join the gold rush. Failing to strike it rich, he somehow decided to try to become the leader of a Latin American country. Walker moved to establish himself as ruler of Nicaragua in Central America and to open that country to slavery. Nicaragua at the time was engaged in a civil war, and one faction invited Walker to assist it by bringing 300 armed men. In 1855, Walker captured the city of Granada and in the following year proclaimed himself president. The administration of Franklin Pierce recognized Walker's government, but neighboring countries sent in troops, who forced Walker to flee. His activities represented clear violations of American neutrality laws. But Walker won acclaim in the South, and when federal authorities placed him on trial in New Orleans in 1858, the jury acquitted him.

By the late 1850s, southern leaders were bending every effort to strengthen the bonds of slavery. "Slavery is our king," declared a South Carolina politician in 1860. "Slavery is our truth, slavery is our divine right." New state laws further restricted access to freedom. One in Louisiana stated simply: "After the passage of this act, no slave shall be emancipated in this state." Some southerners called for the reopening of the African slave trade, hoping that an influx of new slaves would lower the price, thereby increasing the number of whites with a vested interest in the peculiar institution. By early 1860, seven states of the Lower South had gone on record demanding that the Democratic platform pledge to protect slavery in all the territories that had not yet been admitted to the Union as states. Virtually no northern politician could accept this position. For southern leaders to insist on it would guarantee the destruction of the Democratic Party as a national institution. But southern nationalists, known as "fire-eaters," hoped to split the party and the country and form an independent southern Confederacy.

The Democratic Split

When the Democratic convention met in April 1860, Douglas's supporters commanded a majority but not the two-thirds required for a presidential nomination. Because of his fight against Kansas's Lecompton Constitution and his refusal to support congressional laws imposing slavery on all the territories, Douglas had become unacceptable to political leaders of the Lower South. When the convention adopted a platform reaffirming the doctrine of popular sovereignty, delegates from seven slave states walked out and the gathering recessed in confusion. Six weeks later, it reconvened, replaced the bolters with Douglas supporters, and nominated him for president. In response, southern Democrats placed their own ticket in the field, headed by John C. Breckinridge of Kentucky. Breckinridge insisted that slavery must be protected in the western territories.

The Democratic Party, the last great bond of national unity, had been shattered. National conventions had traditionally been places where party managers, mindful of the need for unity in the fall campaign, reconciled their differences. But in 1860, neither northern nor southern Democrats were interested in conciliation. Southern Democrats no longer trusted their northern counterparts. Douglas's backers, for their part, would not accept a platform that doomed their party to certain defeat in the North.

The Nomination of Lincoln

Meanwhile, Republicans gathered in Chicago and chose Lincoln as their standard-bearer. Although he entered the convention with fewer delegates than William H. Seward, Lincoln did not suffer from Seward's political liabilities. Former Know-Nothings, a majority of whom had by now joined Republican ranks, bitterly resented Seward's efforts as governor of New York to channel state funds to Catholic schools. Seward had a not entirely deserved reputation for radicalism as a result of his "higher law" and "irrepressible conflict" speeches, discussed earlier.

Lincoln's devotion to the Union appealed to moderate Republicans, and his emphasis on the moral dimension of the sectional controversy made him acceptable to Republicans from abolitionist backgrounds. Having never associated with the Know-Nothings, he could appeal to immigrant voters, and nativists preferred him to the hated Seward. Most important, coming from Illinois, Lincoln was better positioned to carry the pivotal "doubtful states" essential for Republican victory. On the third ballot, he was nominated. The party platform denied the validity of the Dred Scott decision, reaffirmed Republicans' opposition to slavery's expansion, and added economic planks designed to appeal to a broad array of northern voters—free homesteads in the West, a protective tariff, and government aid in building a transcontinental railroad.

The Election of 1860

A colorful Republican campaign banner from the 1860 campaign emphasizes the party's opposition to the expansion of slavery and promise of free homesteads for settlers in the West.

In effect, two presidential campaigns took place in 1860. In the North, Lincoln and Douglas were the combatants. In the South, the Republicans had no presence and three candidates contested the election—Douglas, Breckinridge, and John Bell of Tennessee, the candidate of the hastily organized Constitutional Union Party. A haven for Unionist former Whigs, this new party adopted a platform consisting of a single pledge—to preserve "the Constitution as it is [that is, with slavery] and the Union as it was [without sectional discord]."

The most striking thing about the election returns was their sectional character. Lincoln carried all of the North except New Jersey, receiving 1.8 million popular votes (54 percent of the regional total and 40 percent of the national) and 180 electoral votes (a clear majority). Breckinridge captured most of the slave states, although Bell carried three Upper South states and about 40 percent of the southern vote as a whole. Douglas placed first only in Missouri, but his 1.3 million popular votes were second in number only to Lincoln's. Douglas was the only candidate with significant support in all parts of the country, a vindication, in a sense, of his long effort to transcend sectional divisions. But his failure to carry either section suggested that a traditional political career based on devotion to the Union was no lon-

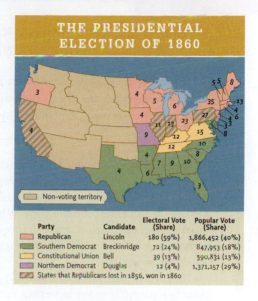

THE PRESIDENTIAL ELECTION OF 1860

Non-voting territory

Party	Candidate	Electoral Vote (Share)	Popular Vote (Share)
Republican	Lincoln	180 (59%)	1,866,452 (40%)
Southern Democrat	Breckinridge	72 (24%)	847,953 (18%)
Constitutional Union	Bell	39 (13%)	590,831 (13%)
Northern Democrat	Douglas	12 (4%)	1,371,157 (29%)
States that Republicans lost in 1856, won in 1860			

ger possible. Without a single vote in ten southern states, Lincoln was elected the nation's sixteenth president. He failed to secure a majority of the national popular vote. But because of the North's superiority in population, Lincoln would still have carried the electoral college and thus been elected president even if the votes of his three opponents had all been cast for a single candidate.

THE IMPENDING CRISIS

The Secession Movement

In the eyes of many white southerners, Lincoln's victory placed their future at the mercy of a party avowedly hostile to their region's values and interests. Those advocating secession did not believe Lincoln's administration would take immediate steps against slavery in the states. But if, as seemed quite possible, the election of 1860 marked a fundamental shift in power, the beginning of a long period of Republican rule, who could say what the North's antislavery sentiment would demand in five years, or ten? Slaveowners, moreover, feared Republican efforts to extend their party into the South by appealing to non-slaveholders. Rather than accept permanent minority status in a nation governed by their opponents, Lower South political leaders boldly struck for their region's independence. At stake, they believed, was not a single election but an entire way of life.

From WILLIAM LYMAN AND OTHERS, LETTER TO THE *MIDDLETOWN SENTINEL AND WITNESS* (1850)

The passage of the Fugitive Slave Act in 1850 raised in the most direct way the relationship between law and liberty. Six residents of Middletown, Connecticut, in a letter to the local newspaper, explained why they would not obey the new law.

The undersigned are friends of law. We reverence law. We are of the party of law and order.... Even an imperfect law we will respect and bear with, till we can obtain its modification or repeal. But all is not law which calls itself law. When iniquity frames itself into law, the sacredness of law is gone. When an enactment, falsely calling itself law, is imposed upon us, which disgraces our country, which invades our conscience, which dishonors our religion, which is an outrage upon our sense of justice, we take our stand against the imposition.

The Fugitive Slave Law commands all good citizens to be slave catchers. Good citizens *cannot* be slave catchers, any more than light can be darkness. You tell us, the Union will be endangered if we oppose this law. We reply, that greater things than the Union will be endangered, if we submit to it: Conscience, Humanity, Self-respect are greater than the Union.... When our sense of decency is clean gone forever, we will turn slave catchers; till then, never. You tell us that great men made this law. If great men choose to disgrace themselves, choose to put off all manliness, and plunge all over into meanness and dishonor, it does not follow that small men should do so too. If Beacon Street [a chief commercial street in Boston] and Marshfield [Daniel Webster's estate] choose to turn slave catchers, let them. We farmers and working men choose to stay by our plows and mills.... We are not yet ready to give ourselves over to all manner of villainy. Be the consequence what it may, come fines, come imprisonment, come what will, this thing you call law *we will not obey*.

From THE DECLARATION OF THE IMMEDIATE CAUSES OF SECESSION (1860)

In December 1860, South Carolina declared its secession from the Union. Like the American Revolutionaries of 1776, the legislature issued a document explaining to the world why the state had taken this step.

The non-slaveholding States . . . have assumed the right of deciding upon the propriety of our domestic institutions; and have denied the rights of property established in fifteen of the States and recognized by the Constitution; they have denounced as sinful the institution of slavery; they have permitted open establishment among them of societies, whose avowed object is to disturb the peace and to eloign [take away] the property of the citizens of other States. They have encouraged and assisted thousands of our slaves to leave their homes; and those who remain, have been incited by emissaries, books and pictures to servile insurrection.

For twenty-five years this agitation has been steadily increasing, until it has now secured to its aid the power of the common Government. . . . A geographical line has been drawn across the Union, and all the States north of that line have united in the election of a man to the high office of President of the United States, whose opinions and purposes are hostile to slavery. He is to be entrusted with the administration of the common Government, because he has declared that that "government cannot endure permanently half slave, half free," and that the public mind must rest in the belief that slavery is in the course of ultimate extinction. . . .

On the 4th of March next this party will take possession of the Government. It has announced that the South shall be excluded from the common territory, that the Judicial tribunal shall be made sectional, and that a war must be waged against slavery until it shall cease throughout the United States.

The guarantees of the Constitution will then no longer exist; the equal rights of the states will be lost. The slaveholding states will no longer have the power of self-government, or self-protection, and the federal government will have become their enemy.

QUESTIONS

1. *Whom do the Connecticut writers seem to blame for the Fugitive Slave Act?*

2. *What is the main motivation for South Carolina's secession?*

3. *What do these documents indicate about the rule of law in the nineteenth-century United States?*

In the months that followed Lincoln's election, seven states stretching from South Carolina to Texas seceded from the Union. These were the states of the Cotton Kingdom, where slaves represented a larger part of the total population than in the Upper South. First to secede was South Carolina, the state with the highest percentage of slaves in its population and a long history of political radicalism. On December 20, 1860, the legislature unanimously voted to leave the Union. Its *Declaration of the Immediate Causes of Secession* placed the issue of slavery squarely at the center of the crisis. Secessionists equated their movement with the struggle for American independence. Proslavery ideologue George Fitzhugh, however, later claimed that southern secession was even more significant than the "commonplace affair" of 1776, since the South rebelled not merely against a particular government but against the erroneous modern idea of freedom based on "human equality" and "natural liberty."

The Secession Crisis

As the Union unraveled, President Buchanan seemed paralyzed. He denied that a state could secede, but he also insisted that the federal government had no right to use force against it. Other political leaders struggled to find a formula to resolve the crisis. Senator John J. Crittenden of Kentucky, a slave state on the border between North and South, offered the most widely supported compromise plan of the secession winter. Embodied in a series of unamendable constitutional amendments, Crittenden's proposal would have guaranteed the future of slavery in the states where it existed, and extended the Missouri Compromise line to the Pacific Ocean, dividing between slavery and free soil all territories "now held, or hereafter acquired." The seceding states rejected the compromise as too little, too late. But many in the Upper South and North saw it as a way to settle sectional differences and prevent civil war.

Crittenden's plan, however, foundered on the opposition of Abraham Lincoln. Willing to conciliate the South on issues like the return of fugitive slaves, Lincoln took an unyielding stand against the expansion of slavery. Here, he informed one Republican leader, he intended to "hold firm, as with a chain of steel." A fundamental principle of democracy, Lincoln believed, was at stake. "We have just carried an election," he wrote, "on principles fairly stated to the people. Now we are told in advance that the government shall be broken up unless we surrender to those we have beaten, before we take the offices. . . . If we surrender, it is the end of us and the end of the government." Lincoln, moreover, feared that Crittenden's reference to land "hereafter acquired" offered the South a thinly veiled invitation to demand the acquisition of Cuba, Mexico, and other territory suited to slavery.

Before Lincoln assumed office on March 4, 1861, the seven seceding states formed the Confederate States of America, adopted a constitution, and chose as their president Jefferson Davis of Mississippi. With a few alterations—the president served a single six-year term; cabinet members, as in Britain, could sit in Congress—the Confederate constitution was modeled closely on that of the United States. It departed from the federal Constitution, however, in explicitly guaranteeing slave property both in the states and in any territories the new nation acquired. Confederates were confident their new nation would thrive on the global stage. They looked forward to aggressively pursuing a proslavery foreign policy in the Caribbean and annexing new areas.

And the War Came

When Lincoln became president, eight slave states of the Upper South remained in the Union. Here, large parts of the white population did not believe Lincoln's election justified dissolving the Union. Even within the Confederacy, whites had divided over secession, with considerable numbers of non-slaveholding farmers in opposition. In time, Lincoln believed, secession might collapse from within.

In his inaugural address, Lincoln tried to be conciliatory. He rejected the right of secession but denied any intention of interfering with slavery in the states. He said nothing of retaking the forts, arsenals, and customs houses the Confederacy had seized, although he did promise to "hold" remaining federal property in the seceding states. But Lincoln also issued a veiled warning: "In your hands, my dissatisfied fellow countrymen, and not in mine, is the momentous issue of civil war."

In his first month as president, Lincoln walked a tightrope. He avoided any action that might drive more states from the Union, encouraged southern Unionists to assert themselves within the Confederacy, and sought to quiet a growing clamor in the North for forceful action against secession. Knowing that the risk of war existed, Lincoln strove to ensure that if hostilities did break out, the South, not the Union, would fire the first shot. And that is precisely what happened on April 12, 1861, at **Fort Sumter**, an enclave of Union control in the harbor of Charleston, South Carolina.

A few days earlier, Lincoln had notified South Carolina's governor that he intended to replenish the garrison's dwindling food supplies. Viewing Fort Sumter's presence as an affront to southern nationhood, and perhaps hoping to force the wavering Upper South to join the Confederacy, Jefferson Davis ordered batteries to fire on the fort. On April 14, its commander surrendered. The following day, Lincoln proclaimed that an insurrection existed in the South and called for 75,000 troops to suppress it. Civil war had begun. Within weeks, Virginia, North Carolina, Tennessee, and Arkansas joined the Confederacy. "Both sides deprecated war," Lincoln later said, "but one of them would *make* war rather than let the nation survive; and the other would *accept* war rather than let it perish. And the war came."

In 1842, Henry Wadsworth Longfellow published *Poems on Slavery*, a collection that included a work entitled simply "The Warning." In it, Longfellow compared the American slave to the mighty biblical figure of Samson, who after being blinded and chained, managed to destroy the temple of his tormentors:

> There is a poor, blind Samson in this land,
> Shorn of his strength, and bound in bonds of steel,
> Who may, in some grim revel, raise his hand,
> And shake the pillars of this Commonweal,
> Till the vast Temple of our liberties
> A shapeless mass of wreck and rubbish lies.

In 1861, Longfellow's warning came to pass. The Union created by the founders lay in ruins. The struggle to rebuild it would bring about a new birth of American freedom.

CHAPTER REVIEW

REVIEW QUESTIONS

1. *Explain the justifications for the doctrine of manifest destiny, including material and idealistic motivations.*

2. *Why did many Americans criticize the Mexican War? How did they see expansion as a threat to American liberties?*

3. *How did the concept of "race" develop by the mid-nineteenth century, and how did it enter into the manifest destiny debate?*

4. *How did western expansion affect the sectional tensions between the North and South?*

5. *How did the market revolution contribute to the rise of the Republican Party? How did those economic and political factors serve to unite groups in the Northeast and in the Northwest, and why was that unity significant?*

6. *What was the "Slave Power," and why did many northerners feel threatened by it?*

7. *How did the Dred Scott decision spark new debates over citizenship for African Americans?*

8. Based on the Lincoln-Douglas debates, how did the two differ on the expansion of slavery, equal rights, and the role of the national government? Use examples of their words to illustrate your points.

9. Why did Stephen Douglas, among others, believe that "popular sovereignty" could resolve sectional divisions of the 1850s? Why did the idea not work out?

10. Explain how sectional voting patterns in the 1860 presidential election allowed southern "fire-eaters" to justify secession.

11. What do the California gold rush and the opening of Japan reveal about the United States' involvement in a global economic system?

KEY TERMS

Tejanos (p. 480)

Antonio López de Santa Anna (p. 481)

Texas revolt (p. 482)

Mexican War (p. 484)

Gadsden Purchase (p. 485)

gold rush (p. 488)

Commodore Matthew Perry (p. 490)

Wilmot Proviso (p. 491)

Free Soil Party (p. 491)

Compromise of 1850 (p. 494)

Fugitive Slave Act (p. 494)

popular sovereignty (p. 497)

Kansas-Nebraska Act (p. 497)

Know-Nothing Party (p. 499)

the Slave Power (p. 501)

"Bleeding Kansas" (p. 502)

Dred Scott v. Sandford (p. 503)

Lincoln-Douglas debates (p. 508)

Harpers Ferry, Virginia (p. 508)

Fort Sumter (p. 517)

Go to INQUIZITIVE

To see what you know—and learn what you've missed—with personalized feedback along the way.

CHAPTER 14

A NEW BIRTH OF FREEDOM: THE CIVIL WAR

1861–1865

FOCUS QUESTIONS

- *Why is the Civil War considered the first modern war?*

- *How did a war to preserve the Union become a war to end slavery?*

- *How did the Civil War transform the national economy and create a stronger nation-state?*

- *How was the society and economy of the Confederacy affected by the war effort?*

- *What were the military and political turning points of the war?*

- *What were the most important wartime "rehearsals for Reconstruction"?*

Like hundreds of thousands of other Americans, Marcus M. Spiegel volunteered in 1861 to fight in the Civil War. Born into a Jewish family in Germany in 1829, Spiegel took part in the failed German revolution of 1848. In the following year he emigrated to Ohio, where he married the daughter of a local farmer. When the Civil War broke out, the nation's 150,000 Jews represented less than 1 percent of the total population. But Spiegel shared wholeheartedly in American patriotism. He went to war, he wrote to his brother-in-law, to defend "the flag that was ever ready to protect you and me and every one who sought its protection from oppression."

Spiegel rose to the rank of colonel in the 120th Ohio Infantry and saw action in Virginia, Mississippi, and Louisiana. He corresponded frequently with his wife, Caroline. "I have seen and learned much," he wrote in 1863. "I have seen men dying of disease and mangled by the weapons of death; I have witnessed hostile armies arrayed against each other, the charge of infantry, [and] cavalry hunting men down like beasts." But he never wavered in his commitment to the "glorious cause" of preserving the Union and its heritage of freedom.

What one Pennsylvania recruit called "the magic word *Freedom*" shaped how many Union soldiers understood the conflict. The war's purpose, wrote Samuel McIlvaine, a sergeant from Indiana, was to preserve the American nation as "the beacon light of liberty and freedom to the human race." But as the war progressed, prewar understandings of liberty gave way to something new. Millions of northerners who had not been abolitionists became convinced that preserving the Union as an embodiment of liberty required the destruction of slavery.

Marcus Spiegel's changing views mirrored the transformation of a struggle to save the Union into a war to end slavery. Spiegel was an ardent Democrat. He shared the era's racist attitudes and thought Lincoln's Emancipation Proclamation a serious mistake. Yet as the Union army penetrated the heart of the Lower South, Spiegel became increasingly opposed to slavery. "Since I am here," he wrote to his wife from Louisiana in January 1864, "I have learned and seen . . . the horrors of slavery. You know it takes me long to say anything that sounds antidemocratic [opposed to Democratic Party policies], but . . . never hereafter will I either speak or vote in favor of slavery."

Marcus Spiegel was killed in a minor engagement in Louisiana in May 1864, one of hundreds of thousands of Americans to perish in the Civil War.

THE FIRST MODERN WAR

The American Civil War is often called the first modern war. Never before had mass armies confronted each other on the battlefield with the deadly weapons created by the industrial revolution. The resulting casualties dwarfed anything in the American experience. Beginning as a battle of army versus army, the war became a conflict of society against society, in which the distinction between military and civilian targets often disappeared. In a war of this kind, the effectiveness of political leadership, the ability to mobilize economic resources, and a society's willingness to keep up the fight despite setbacks are as crucial to the outcome as success or failure on individual battlefields.

The Two Combatants

Almost any comparison between Union and Confederacy seemed to favor the Union. The population of the North and the loyal border slave states numbered 22 million in 1860, while only 9 million persons lived in the Confederacy, 3.5 million of them enslaved. In manufacturing, railroad mileage, and financial resources, the Union far outstripped its opponent. On the other hand, the Union confronted by far the greater task. To restore the shattered nation, it had to invade and conquer an area larger than Western Europe. Like Washington's forces during the American Revolution, southern armies could lose most of the battles and still win the war if their opponent tired of the struggle. "No people," Confederate general P. G. T. Beauregard later claimed, "ever warred for independence with more relative advantages than the Confederacy."

On both sides, the outbreak of war stirred powerful feelings of patriotism. Recruits rushed to enlist, expecting a short, glorious war. Later, as enthusiasm waned the Confederacy in the spring of 1862 passed the first draft law in American history, and the North soon followed. By 1865, more than 2 million men had served in the Union army and 900,000 in the Confederate army. Each was a cross section of its society: the North's was composed largely of farm boys, shopkeepers, artisans, and urban workers, while the South's consisted mostly of non-slaveholding small farmers, with slaveowners dominating the officer corps.

Few recruits had any military experience. Ideas about war were highly romantic, based on novels, magazine articles, and lithographs of soldiers covering themselves with glory. One private wrote home in 1862 that his notion of combat had come from the pictures of battles he had seen: "They would all be in a line, all standing in a nice level field fighting, a number of ladies taking care of the wounded, etc. But it isn't so." Nor were the recruits ready for military regimentation. "It comes rather hard at first to be deprived of liberty," wrote an Illinois soldier. Initially, the constant round of drilling, ditch digging, and other chores was only occasionally interrupted by fierce bursts of fighting on the battlefield.

The Technology of War

Neither the soldiers nor their officers were prepared for the way technology had transformed warfare. The Civil War was the first major conflict in which the railroad transported troops and supplies and the first to see railroad junctions such as Atlanta and Petersburg become major military objectives. The famous sea battle between the Union vessel *Monitor* and the Confederate *Merrimac* in 1862 was the first demonstration of the superiority of ironclads over wooden ships, revolutionizing naval warfare. The war saw the use of the telegraph for military communication, the introduction of observation balloons to view enemy lines, and even primitive hand grenades and submarines.

Perhaps most important, a revolution in arms manufacturing had replaced the traditional musket, accurate at only a short range, with the more modern rifle, deadly at 600 yards or more because of its grooved (or "rifled") barrel. This development changed the nature of combat, emphasizing the importance of heavy fortifications and elaborate trenches and giving those on the defensive—usually southern armies—a significant advantage over attacking forces. "My men," said Confederate general Thomas "Stonewall" Jackson, "sometimes fail to drive the enemy from his position, but to hold one, never." The war of rifle and trench produced the appalling casualty statistics of Civil War battles. The most recent estimate of those who perished in the war—around 750,000 men—represents the equivalent, in terms of today's population, of more than 7 million. These figures do not include the thousands of civilians who became victims of battles or who perished in disease-ridden camps for runaway slaves or in conflicts between Unionist and Confederate families that raged in parts of the South. The death toll in the Civil War exceeds the total number of Americans who died in all the nation's other wars, from the Revolution to the wars in Iraq and Afghanistan.

Nor was either side ready for other aspects of modern warfare. Medical care remained primitive. "I believe the doctors kill more than they cure," wrote an Alabama private in 1862. Diseases like measles, dysentery, malaria, and typhus swept through army camps, killing more men than did combat. The Civil War was the first war in which large numbers of Americans were captured by the

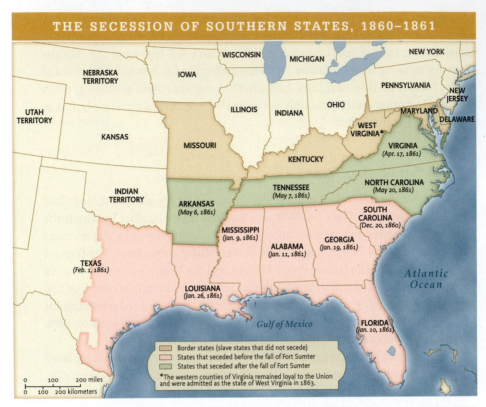

THE SECESSION OF SOUTHERN STATES, 1860–1861

Border states (slave states that did not secede)
States that seceded before the fall of Fort Sumter
States that seceded after the fall of Fort Sumter

*The western counties of Virginia remained loyal to the Union and were admitted as the state of West Virginia in 1863.

By the time secession ran its course, eleven slave states had left the Union.

enemy and held in dire conditions in military prisons. Some 50,000 men died in these prisons, victims of starvation and disease, including 13,000 Union soldiers at Andersonville, Georgia.

The Public and the War

Another modern feature of the Civil War was that both sides employed a vast propaganda effort to mobilize public opinion. In the Union, an outpouring of lithographs, souvenirs, sheet music, and pamphlets issued by patriotic organizations and the War Department reaffirmed northern values, tarred the Democratic Party with the brush of treason, and accused the South of numerous crimes against Union soldiers and loyal civilians. Comparable items appeared in the Confederacy.

At the same time, the war's brutal realities were brought home with unprecedented immediacy to the public at large. War correspondents accompanied the armies, and newspapers reported the results of battles on the following day and

quickly published long lists of casualties. The infant art of photography
carried images of war into millions
of American living rooms. The camera, in the words of one journalist,
"brought the bodies and laid them in
our door-yards." Mathew Brady, who
organized a corps of photographers
to cover the war, found the conflict a
passport to fame and wealth. For photography itself, it was a turning point
in its growth as an art and a business
enterprise.

Mobilizing Resources

The outbreak of the war found both
sides unprepared. In 1861, there was no
national railroad gauge (the distance
separating the two rails), so trains built
for one line could not run on another.
There were no national banking system, no tax system capable of raising
the enormous funds needed to finance
the war, and not even accurate maps of
the southern states. Soon after the firing on Fort Sumter, Lincoln proclaimed
a naval blockade of the South. But
the navy, charged with patrolling the
3,500-mile coastline, consisted of only
ninety vessels, fewer than half of them
steam powered. Not until late in the
war did the blockade become effective.

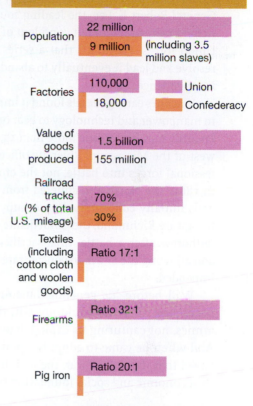

FIGURE 14.1 RESOURCES FOR WAR: UNION VERSUS CONFEDERACY

	Union	Confederacy
Population	22 million	9 million (including 3.5 million slaves)
Factories	110,000	18,000
Value of goods produced	1.5 billion	155 million
Railroad tracks (% of total U.S. mileage)	70%	30%
Textiles (including cotton cloth and woolen goods)	Ratio 17:1	
Firearms	Ratio 32:1	
Pig iron	Ratio 20:1	

In nearly every resource for warfare, the Union enjoyed a distinct advantage. But this did not make Union victory inevitable; as during the War of Independence, the stronger side sometimes loses.

Then there was the problem of purchasing and distributing the food,
weapons, and other supplies required by the soldiers. The Union army eventually became the best-fed and best-supplied military force in history. By the
war's third year, on the other hand, southern armies were suffering from acute
shortages of food, uniforms, and shoes. Yet the chief of the Confederacy's Ord-
nance Bureau, Josiah Gorgas (a transplanted northerner), proved brilliantly
resourceful in arming southern troops. Under his direction, the Confederate
government imported weapons from abroad and established arsenals of its
own to turn out rifles, artillery, and ammunition.

Military Strategies

Each side tried to find ways to maximize its advantages. Essentially, the Confederacy adopted a defensive strategy, with occasional thrusts into the North. General Robert E. Lee, the leading southern commander, was a brilliant battlefield tactician who felt confident of his ability to fend off attacks by larger Union forces. He hoped that a series of defeats would weaken the North's resolve and lead it eventually to abandon the conflict and recognize southern independence.

Lincoln's early generals found it impossible to bring the Union's advantages in manpower and technology to bear on the battlefield. In April 1861, the regular army numbered little more than 15,000 men, most of whom were stationed west of the Mississippi River. Its officers had been trained to lead small, professional forces into battle, not the crowds of untrained men who assembled in 1861. The North also suffered from narrowness of military vision. Its generals initially concentrated on occupying southern territory and attempting to capture Richmond, the Confederate capital. They attacked sporadically and withdrew after a battle, thus sacrificing the North's manpower superiority and allowing the South to concentrate its smaller forces when an engagement impended.

Well before his generals, Lincoln realized that simply capturing and occupying territory would not win the war and that defeating the South's armies, not capturing its capital, had to be the North's battlefield objective. And when he came to adopt the policy of emancipation, Lincoln acknowledged that to win the war, the Union must make the institution that lay at the economic and social foundation of southern life a military target.

The War Begins

In the East, most of the war's fighting took place in a narrow corridor between Washington and Richmond—a distance of only 100 miles—as a succession of Union generals led the Army of the Potomac (as the main northern force in the East was called) toward the Confederate capital, only to be turned back by southern forces. The first significant engagement, the **first Battle of Bull Run**, took place in northern Virginia on July 21, 1861. It ended with the chaotic retreat of the Union soldiers, along with the sightseers and politicians who had come to watch the battle. Almost 800 men died at Bull Run, a toll eclipsed many times in the years to come, but more Americans than had been killed in any previous battle in the nation's history.

In the wake of Bull Run, George B. McClellan, an army engineer who had recently won a minor engagement with Confederate troops in western Virginia, assumed command of the Union's Army of the Potomac. A brilliant organizer,

McClellan succeeded in welding his men into a superb fighting force. He seemed reluctant, however, to commit them to battle, since he tended to overestimate the size of enemy forces. And as a Democrat, he hoped that compromise might end the war without large-scale loss of life or a weakening of slavery. Months of military inactivity followed.

The War in the East, 1862

Not until the spring of 1862, after a growing clamor for action by Republican newspapers, members of Congress, and an increasingly impatient Lincoln, did McClellan lead his army of more than 100,000 men into Virginia. Here they confronted the smaller Army of Northern Virginia under the command of the Confederate general Joseph E. Johnston, and after he was wounded, Robert E. Lee. Lee had been offered a command in the Union army but chose to fight for the Confederacy because of his devotion to Virginia. In the Seven Days' Campaign, a series of engagements in June 1862 on the peninsula south of

THE CIVIL WAR IN THE EAST, 1861–1862

During the first two years of the war, most of the fighting took place in Virginia and Maryland.

Richmond, Lee blunted McClellan's attacks and forced him to withdraw to the vicinity of Washington, D.C. In August 1862, Lee again emerged victorious at the **second Battle of Bull Run** against Union forces under the command of General John Pope.

Successful on the defensive, Lee now launched an invasion of the North. He hoped to bring the border slave states into the Confederacy, persuade Britain and France to recognize southern independence, influence the North's fall elections, and perhaps capture Washington, D.C. At the **Battle of Antietam**, in Maryland, McClellan and the Army of the Potomac repelled Lee's advance. In a single day of fighting, nearly 4,000 men were killed and 18,000 wounded (2,000 of whom later died of their injuries). The dead, one survivor recalled, lay three deep in the field, mowed down "like grass before the scythe." More Americans died on September 17, 1862, when the Battle of Antietam was fought, than on any other day in the nation's history, including Pearl Harbor and D-Day in World War II and the terrorist attacks of September 11, 2001.

Since Lee was forced to retreat, the North could claim Antietam as a victory. It was to be the Union's last success in the East for some time. In December 1862, the Union suffered one of its most disastrous defeats of the war when General Ambrose E. Burnside, who had replaced McClellan as the head of the Army of the Potomac, assaulted Lee's army, which was entrenched on heights near Fredericksburg, Virginia. "It was not a fight," wrote one Union soldier to his mother, "it was a massacre."

The War in the West

While the Union accomplished little in the East in the first two years of the war, events in the West followed a different course. Here, the architect of early success was Ulysses S. Grant. A West Point graduate who had resigned from the army in 1854 in part because of allegations of excessive drinking, Grant had been notably unsuccessful in civilian life. When the war broke out, he was working as a clerk in his brother's leather store in Galena, Illinois. But after being commissioned as a colonel in an Illinois regiment, Grant quickly displayed the daring, the logical mind, and the grasp of strategy he would demonstrate throughout the war.

In February 1862, Grant won the Union's first significant victory when he captured Forts Henry and Donelson in Tennessee. In April, naval forces under Admiral David G. Farragut steamed into New Orleans, giving the Union control of the South's largest city and the rich sugar plantation parishes to its south and west. At the same time, Grant withstood a surprise Confederate attack at Shiloh, Tennessee. But Union momentum in the West then stalled.

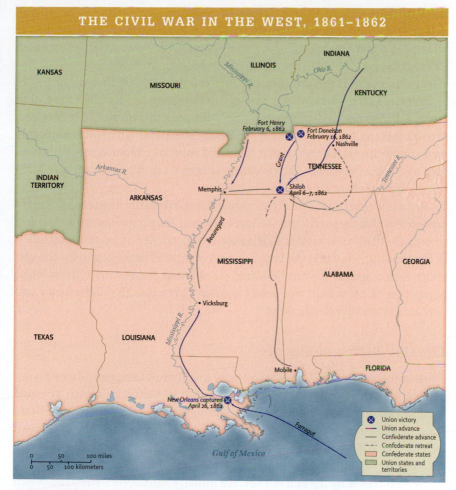

THE CIVIL WAR IN THE WEST, 1861–1862

Most of the Union's victories in the first two years of the war occurred in the West, especially at Shiloh and New Orleans.

THE COMING OF EMANCIPATION

Slavery and the War

War, it has been said, is the midwife of revolution. And the Civil War produced far-reaching changes in American life. The most dramatic of these was the destruction of slavery, the central institution of southern society. Between 1831, when the British abolished slavery in their empire, and 1888, when emancipation came to Brazil, some 6 million slaves gained their freedom in the Western Hemisphere. Of these, nearly 4 million, two-thirds of the total, lived in the southern United States. In numbers, scale, and the economic power of the institution of slavery, American emancipation dwarfed that of any other country (although far more people were liberated in 1861 when Czar Alexander II abolished serfdom in the Russian empire).

At the outset of the war, Lincoln invoked time-honored northern values to mobilize public support. In a message to Congress, he identified the Union cause with the fate of democracy for the "whole family of man." He declared, "This is essentially a people's struggle. On the side of the Union, it is a struggle for maintaining in the world, that form and substance of government, whose leading object is to elevate the condition of men . . . to afford all, an unfettered start, and a fair chance, in the race of life."

But while appealing to free labor values, Lincoln initially insisted that slavery was irrelevant to the conflict. In the war's first year, his paramount concerns were to keep the border slave states—Delaware, Maryland, Kentucky, and Missouri—in the Union and to build the broadest base of support in the North for the war effort. Action against slavery, he feared, would drive the border, with its white population of 2.6 million and nearly 500,000 slaves, into the Confederacy and alienate conservative northerners.

The Unraveling of Slavery

Thus, in the early days of the war, a nearly unanimous Congress adopted a resolution proposed by Senator John J. Crittenden of Kentucky, which affirmed that the Union had no intention of interfering with slavery. Northern military commanders even returned fugitive slaves to their owners, a policy that raised an outcry in antislavery circles. Yet as the Confederacy set slaves to work as military laborers and Blacks began to escape to Union lines, the policy of ignoring slavery unraveled. By the end of 1861, the military had adopted the plan, begun in Virginia by General Benjamin F. Butler, of treating escaped Blacks as contraband of war—that is, property of military value subject to confiscation. Butler's order added a word to the war's vocabulary. Escaping slaves became known as **"the contrabands."** They were housed by the army in "contraband camps" and educated in new "contraband schools."

Meanwhile, slaves took actions that helped propel a reluctant white America down the road to emancipation. Well before Lincoln made emancipation a war aim, Blacks, in the North and the South, were calling the conflict the "freedom war." In 1861 and 1862, as the federal army occupied Confederate territory, slaves by the thousands headed for Union lines. Unlike fugitives before the war, these runaways included large numbers of women and children, as entire families abandoned the plantations. Not a few passed along military intelligence and detailed knowledge of the South's terrain. In southern Louisiana, the arrival of the Union army in 1862 led slaves to sack plantation houses

Thoughts of Liberia: Emancipation, an enigmatic painting by the artist Edwin White from 1861, depicts a Black man sitting before the hearth of a modest cabin, holding a cane and newspaper. On the wall on the left is a poster, "Hayti." The man is evidently thinking of emigrating to Liberia, the outpost in Africa established years earlier by the American Colonization Society, or perhaps to Haiti. The painting has been interpreted as a reassuring message to whites who feared that abolition would produce a large class of free Blacks, suggesting instead that emancipated slaves wanted to leave the United States. But the reference to Haiti also reminds us of the revolution that overthrew slavery there.

and refuse to work unless wages were paid. Slavery there, wrote a northern reporter, "is forever destroyed and worthless, no matter what Mr. Lincoln or anyone else may say on the subject."

Steps toward Emancipation

At first, Blacks' determination to seize the opportunity presented by the war proved a burden to the army and an embarrassment to the administration. But the failure of traditional strategies to produce victory strengthened the hand of antislavery northerners. Since slavery stood at the foundation of the southern economy, they insisted, emancipation was necessary to weaken the South's ability to sustain the war.

The most uncompromising opponents of slavery before the war, abolitionists and **Radical Republicans**, quickly concluded that the institution must become a target of the Union war effort. Outside of Congress, few pressed the case for emancipation more eloquently than Frederick Douglass. From the outset, he insisted that it was futile to "separate the freedom of the slave from the victory of the government." "Fire must be met with water," Douglass declared, "darkness with light, and war for the destruction of liberty must be met with war for the destruction of slavery."

These appeals won increasing support in a Congress frustrated by lack of military success. In March 1862, Congress prohibited the army from returning fugitive slaves. Then came abolition in the District of Columbia (with monetary compensation for slaveholders) and the territories, followed in July by the Second Confiscation Act, which liberated slaves of disloyal owners in Union-occupied territory, as well as slaves who escaped to Union lines.

Throughout these months, Lincoln struggled to retain control of the emancipation issue. In August 1861, John C. Frémont, commanding Union forces in Missouri, a state racked by a bitter guerrilla war between pro-northern and pro-southern bands, decreed the freedom of its slaves. Fearful of the order's impact on the border states, Lincoln swiftly rescinded it. In November, the president proposed that the border states embark on a program of gradual emancipation with the federal government paying owners for their loss of property. He also revived the idea of colonization. In August 1862, Lincoln met at the White House with a delegation of Black leaders and urged them to promote emigration from the United States. "You and we are different races," he declared. "It is better for us both to be separated." As late as December 1862, the president signed an agreement with a shady entrepreneur to settle former slaves on an island off the coast of Haiti.

Lincoln's Decision

During the summer of 1862, Lincoln concluded that emancipation had become a political and military necessity. Many factors contributed to his decision— lack of military success, hope that emancipated slaves might help meet the army's growing manpower needs, changing northern public opinion, and the calculation that making slavery a target of the war effort would counteract sentiment in Britain for recognition of the Confederacy. But on the advice of Secretary of State William H. Seward, Lincoln delayed his announcement until after a Union victory, lest it seem an act of desperation. On September 22, 1862, five days after McClellan's army forced Lee to retreat at Antietam, Lincoln issued the Preliminary Emancipation Proclamation. It warned that unless the South laid down its arms by the end of 1862, he would decree abolition.

The initial northern reaction was not encouraging. In the fall elections of 1862, Democrats made opposition to emancipation the centerpiece of their campaign, warning that the North would be "Africanized"—inundated by freed slaves who would compete for jobs and seek to marry white women. The Republicans suffered sharp reverses. In his annual message to Congress, early in December, Lincoln tried to calm northerners' racial fears, reviving the ideas of gradual emancipation and colonization. He concluded, however, on a higher note: "Fellow citizens, we cannot escape history. . . . The fiery trial through which we pass, will light us down, in honor or dishonor, to the latest generation. . . . In giving freedom to the slave, we assure freedom to the free— honorable alike in what we give, and what we preserve."

The Emancipation Proclamation

On January 1, 1863, after greeting visitors at the annual White House New Year's reception, Lincoln retired to his study to sign the **Emancipation Proclamation**. The document did not liberate all the slaves—indeed, on the day it was issued, it applied to very few. Because its legality derived from the president's authority as military commander-in-chief to combat the South's rebellion, the Proclamation exempted areas firmly under Union control (where the war, in effect, had already ended). Thus, it did not apply to the loyal border slave states that had never seceded or to areas of the Confederacy occupied by Union soldiers, such as Tennessee and parts of Virginia and Louisiana. But the vast majority of the South's slaves—more than 3 million men, women, and children—it declared "henceforward shall be free." Since most of these slaves were still behind Confederate lines, however, their liberation would have to await Union victories.

Despite its limitations, the Proclamation set off scenes of jubilation among free Blacks and abolitionists in the North and "contrabands" and slaves in the South. "Sound the loud timbrel o'er Egypt's dark sea," intoned a Black preacher at a celebration in Boston. "Jehovah hath triumphed, his people are free." By making the Union army an agent of emancipation and wedding the goals of Union and abolition, the Proclamation sounded the eventual death knell of slavery.

Not only did the Emancipation Proclamation alter the nature of the Civil War and the course of American history, but it also represented a turning point in Lincoln's own thinking. It contained no reference to compensation to slaveholders or to colonization of the freed people. For the first time, it committed the government to enlisting Black soldiers in the Union army. Lincoln now became in his own mind the Great Emancipator—that is, he assumed the role that history had thrust upon him, and he tried to live up to it. He would later

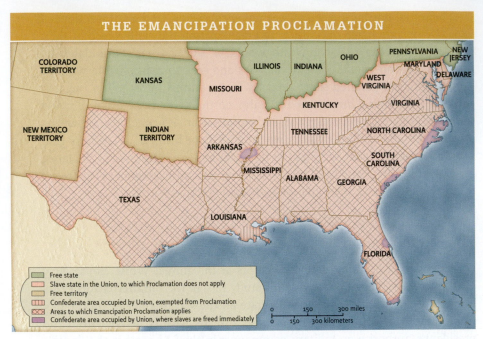

THE EMANCIPATION PROCLAMATION

Legend:
- Free state
- Slave state in the Union, to which Proclamation does not apply
- Free territory
- Confederate area occupied by Union, exempted from Proclamation
- Areas to which Emancipation Proclamation applies
- Confederate area occupied by Union, where slaves are freed immediately

0   150   300 miles
0   150   300 kilometers

With the exception of a few areas, the Emancipation Proclamation applied only to slaves in parts of the Confederacy not under Union control on January 1, 1863. Lincoln did not "free the slaves" with a stroke of his pen, but the Proclamation did change the nature of the Civil War.

refuse suggestions that he rescind or modify the Proclamation in the interest of peace. Were he to do so, he told one visitor, "I should be damned in time and eternity."

The Civil War, begun to preserve the prewar Union, now portended a far-reaching transformation in southern life and a redefinition of American freedom and citizenship. Decoupling emancipation from colonization meant that the freed slaves would become part of American life. A new system of labor, politics, and race relations would have to replace the shattered institution of slavery. "Up to now," wrote the socialist thinker Karl Marx, observing events from London, "we have witnessed only the first act of the Civil War— the constitutional waging of war. The second act, the revolutionary waging of war, is at hand."

Enlisting Black Troops

Of the Proclamation's provisions, few were more radical in their implications than the enrollment of Blacks into military service. Since sailor had been one of the few occupations open to free Blacks before the war, Secretary of the Navy Gideon

Welles had already allowed African Americans to serve on Union warships. Early in the war, Harry Jarvis, a Virginia slave, escaped to Fortress Monroe and offered to enlist in the Union army. General Benjamin F. Butler, Jarvis later recalled, "said *it wasn't a Black man's war. I told him it would be a Black man's war* before they got through."

At the outset, the administration feared that whites would not be willing to fight alongside Blacks, and that enlisting Black soldiers would alienate the border slave states that remained in the Union. Preliminary steps to enlist combat troops were taken in a few parts of the South in 1862. White abolitionist Thomas Wentworth Higginson was sent to the South Carolina Sea Islands, which the Union navy had seized early in the war, to enroll slaves in the First South Carolina Volunteers. But only after the Emancipation Proclamation did the recruitment of Black soldiers begin in earnest.

The regimental banner and motto of a unit of African American soldiers embodies the hope that service in the Union army will lead to citizenship in the postwar world.

By the end of the war, more than 180,000 Black men had served in the Union army and 24,000 in the navy. Some Black units won considerable notoriety, among them the Fifty-fourth Massachusetts Volunteers, a company of free Blacks from throughout the North commanded by Robert Gould Shaw, a young reformer from a prominent Boston family. The bravery of the Fifty-fourth in the July 1863 attack on Fort Wagner, South Carolina, where nearly half the unit, including Shaw, perished, helped to dispel widespread doubts about Blacks' ability to withstand the pressures of the Civil War battlefield. (The exploits of Shaw and the Fifty-fourth Massachusetts were popularized in the 1989 film *Glory*.)

Most Black soldiers were emancipated slaves who joined the army in the South. After Union forces in 1863 seized control of the rich plantation lands of the Mississippi Valley, General Lorenzo Thomas raised fifty regiments of Black soldiers—some 76,000 men in all. Another large group hailed from the border states exempted from the Emancipation Proclamation, where enlistment was, for most of the war, the only route to freedom. Here Black military service undermined slavery, for Congress expanded the Emancipation Proclamation to liberate the families of Black soldiers.

THE COMING OF EMANCIPATION ★ 535

The Black Soldier

A photograph of a Black washerwoman for the Union army wearing a small American flag reflects how the war and emancipation led African Americans to identify strongly with the nation.

For Black soldiers themselves, military service proved to be a liberating experience. "No negro who has ever been a soldier," wrote a northern official in 1865, "can again be imposed upon; they have learned what it is to be free and they will infuse their feelings into others." Service in the army established men as community leaders and opened a door to political advancement. Out of the army came many of the leaders of the Reconstruction era. At least 130 former soldiers served in political office after the Civil War. In time, the memory of Black military service would fade from white America's collective memory. Of the hundreds of Civil War monuments that still dot the northern landscape, fewer than a dozen contain an image of a Black soldier. But well into the twentieth century, it remained a point of pride in Black families throughout the United States that their fathers and grandfathers had fought for freedom.

The Union navy treated Black sailors pretty much the same as white sailors. Conditions on ships made racial segregation impossible. Black and white sailors received equal pay and had the same promotion opportunities. Within the army, however, Black soldiers received treatment that was anything but equal. Organized into segregated units under sometimes abusive white officers, they initially received lower pay (ten dollars per month, compared to sixteen dollars for white soldiers). They were disproportionately assigned to labor rather than combat, and they could not rise to the rank of commissioned officer until the very end of the war. If captured by Confederate forces, they faced the prospect of sale into slavery or immediate execution. In a notorious incident in 1864, 200 of 262 Black soldiers died when southern troops under the command of Nathan B. Forrest overran Fort Pillow in Tennessee. Some of those who perished had been killed after surrendering.

Nonetheless, Black soldiers played a crucial role not only in winning the Civil War but also in defining the war's consequences. "Once let a Black man get upon his person the brass letters U.S.," wrote Frederick Douglass in urging Blacks to enlist, "and there is no power on earth which can deny that he has earned the right to citizenship in the United States." As Douglass predicted, thanks in part to Black military service many Republicans in the last two years of the war came to believe that emancipation must bring with it equal protection of the laws regardless of race. One of the first acts of the federal government to recognize this principle was the granting of retroactive equal pay to Black soldiers early in 1865.

The service of Black soldiers affected Lincoln's own outlook. He insisted that they must be treated the same as whites when captured and suspended prisoner-of-war exchanges when the Confederacy refused to include Black troops. In 1864, Lincoln, who before the war had never supported suffrage for African Americans, urged the governor of Union-occupied Louisiana to work for the partial enfranchisement of Blacks, singling out soldiers as especially deserving. At some future time, he observed, they might again be called upon to "keep the *jewel of Liberty* in the family of freedom."

THE SECOND AMERICAN REVOLUTION

"Old things are passing away," wrote a Black resident of California in 1862, "and eventually old prejudices must follow. The revolution has begun, and time alone must decide where it is to end." The changing status of Black Americans was only one dramatic example of what some historians call the **Second American Revolution**—the transformation of American government and society brought about by the Civil War.

Liberty and Union

Never was freedom's contested nature more evident than during the Civil War. "We all declare for liberty," Lincoln observed in 1864, "but in using the same *word* we do not all mean the same *thing*." To the North, he continued, freedom meant for "each man" to enjoy "the product of his labor." To southern whites, it conveyed mastership—the power to do "as they please with other men, and the product of other men's labor." The Union's triumph consolidated the northern understanding of freedom as the national norm.

The attack on Fort Sumter crystallized in northern minds the direct conflict between freedom and slavery that abolitionists had insisted upon for decades. The war, as Frederick Douglass recognized as early as 1862, merged "the cause of the slaves and the cause of the country." "Liberty and Union," he continued, "have become identical." As during the American Revolution, religious and secular understandings of freedom joined in a celebration of national destiny. "As He died to make men holy, let us die to make men free," proclaimed the popular song "Battle Hymn of the Republic," written by Julia Ward Howe and published in 1862.

Lincoln's Vision

But it was Lincoln himself who linked the conflict with the deepest beliefs of northern society. It is sometimes said that the American Civil War was part of a broader nineteenth-century process of nation building. Throughout the world, powerful, centralized nation-states developed in old countries, and new nations emerged where none had previously existed. The Civil War took place as modern states were consolidating their power and reducing local autonomy.

Lincoln has been called the American equivalent of Giuseppe Mazzini or Otto von Bismarck, who during this same era created nation-states in Italy and Germany from disunited collections of principalities. But Lincoln's nation was different from those being constructed in Europe. They were based on the idea of unifying a particular people with a common ethnic, cultural, and linguistic heritage. To Lincoln, the American nation embodied, instead, a set of universal ideas, centered on political democracy and human liberty.

Lincoln summarized his conception of the war's meaning in November 1863 in brief remarks at the dedication of a military cemetery at the site of the war's greatest battle. The Gettysburg Address is considered his finest speech. In less than three minutes, he identified the nation's mission with the principle that "all men are created equal," spoke of the war as bringing about a "new birth of freedom," and defined the essence of democratic government. The sacrifices of Union soldiers, he declared, would ensure that "government of the people, by the people, for the people, shall not perish from the earth."

The mobilization of the Union's resources for modern war brought into being a new American nation-state with greatly expanded powers and responsibilities. The United States remained a federal republic with sovereignty divided between the state and national governments. But the war forged a new national self-consciousness, reflected in the increasing use of the word "nation"—a unified political entity—in place of the older "Union" of separate states. In his inaugural address in 1861, Lincoln used the word "Union" twenty times, while making no mention of the "nation." By 1863, "Union" does not appear at all in the 269-word Gettysburg Address, while Lincoln referred five times to the "nation."

The War and American Religion

The upsurge of patriotism, and of national power, was reflected in many aspects of American life. Even as the war produced unprecedented casualties, the northern Protestant clergy strove to provide it with a religious justification and to reassure their congregations that the dead had not died in vain. The religious press now devoted more space to military and political developments than to spiritual matters. In numerous wartime sermons, Christianity and patriotism were joined in a civic religion that saw the war as God's mechanism for ridding the United States of slavery and enabling it to become what it had never really been—a land of freedom. Lincoln, one of the few American presidents who never joined a church, shrewdly marshaled religious symbolism to generate public support, declaring days of Thanksgiving after northern victories and encouraging northern clergymen

The Sisters of Charity, an order of nuns, photographed with doctors and soldiers at a hospital in Philadelphia in 1863. Many of the wounded from the Battle of Gettysburg were sent here for treatment. The Catholic contribution to the Union war effort mitigated the nativist bias so prominent in the 1850s.

to support Republican candidates for office. Of course, the southern clergy was equally convinced that the Confederate cause represented God's will.

Religious beliefs enabled Americans to cope with mass death. Of course, equating death with eternal life is a central tenet of Christianity. But the war led to what one historian calls a "transformation of heaven," as Americans imagined future celestial family reunions. Some Americans could not wait until their own deaths to see the departed. Spiritualism—belief in the ability to communicate with the dead—grew in popularity. Mary Todd Lincoln held seances in the White House to experience again the presence of her young son Willie, who succumbed to disease in 1862.

Coping with death also required unprecedented governmental action, from notifying next of kin to accounting for the dead and missing. Both the Union and Confederacy established elaborate systems for gathering statistics and maintaining records of dead and wounded soldiers, an effort supplemented by private philanthropic organizations. After the war ended, the federal government embarked on a program to locate and re-bury hundreds of thousands of Union soldiers in national military cemeteries. Between 1865 and 1871, the government reinterred more than 300,000 Union (but not Confederate) soldiers—including Black soldiers, who were buried in segregated sections of military cemeteries.

Liberty in Wartime

This intense new nationalism made criticism of the war effort—or of the policies of the Lincoln administration—seem to Republicans equivalent to treason. Although there had been sporadic persecution of opponents of the Mexican-American War, the Civil War presented, for the first time since the Revolution, the issue of the limits of wartime dissent. During the conflict, declared the Republican *New York Times*, "the safety of the nation is the supreme law." Arbitrary arrests numbered in the thousands. They included opposition newspaper editors, Democratic politicians, individuals who discouraged enlistment in the army, and ordinary civilians like the Chicago man briefly imprisoned for calling the president a "damned fool." With the Constitution unclear as to who possessed the power to suspend the writ of habeas corpus (thus allowing prisoners to be held without charge), Lincoln claimed the right under the presidential war powers and twice suspended the writ throughout the entire Union for those accused of "disloyal activities."

The courts generally gave the administration a free hand. They refused to intervene when a military court convicted Clement L. Vallandigham, a leading Ohio Democrat known for his blistering antiwar speeches, of treason. On Lincoln's order, Vallandigham was banished to the Confederacy. In 1861, Chief Justice Roger B. Taney ordered the president to release John Merryman, a civilian who had been arrested by military authorities in Maryland, but the president ignored him. Not until 1866, after the fighting had ended, did the Supreme Court, in the case *Ex parte Milligan*, declare it unconstitutional to bring accused persons before military tribunals where civil courts were operating. The Constitution, declared Justice David Davis, is not suspended in wartime.

Lincoln was not a despot. Most of those arrested were quickly released, the Democratic press continued to flourish, and contested elections were held throughout the war. But the policies of the Lincoln administration offered proof—to be repeated during later wars—of the fragility of civil liberties in the face of assertive patriotism and wartime demands for national unity.

The North's Transformation

Even as he invoked traditional values, Lincoln presided over far-reaching changes in northern life. The effort to mobilize the resources of the Union greatly enhanced the power not only of the federal government but also of a rising class of capitalist entrepreneurs. Unlike the South, which suffered economic devastation, the North experienced the war as a time of prosperity.

Nourished by wartime inflation and government contracts, the profits of industry boomed. New England mills worked day and night to supply the army with blankets and uniforms, and Pennsylvania coal mines and ironworks rapidly expanded their production. Mechanization proceeded apace in many industries, especially those like boot and shoe production and meatpacking that supplied the army's ever-increasing needs. Agriculture also flourished, for even as farm boys by the hundreds of thousands joined the army, the frontier of cultivation pushed westward, with machinery and immigrants replacing lost labor. Wisconsin furnished 90,000 men to the Union army, yet its population, grain production, and farm income continued to grow.

Government and the Economy

Congress adopted policies that promoted economic growth and permanently altered the nation's financial system. With the South now unrepresented, the lawmakers adopted policies long advocated by many northerners. To spur agricultural development, the **Homestead Act** offered 160 acres of free public land to settlers in the West. It took effect on January 1, 1863, the same day as the Emancipation Proclamation, and like the Proclamation, tried to implement a vision of freedom. By the 1930s, more than 400,000 families had acquired farms under its provisions. In addition, the Morrill Land Grant College Act, named for Justin S. Morrill of Vermont, who introduced the measure, assisted the states in establishing "agricultural and mechanic colleges."

Congress also made huge grants of money and land for internal improvements, including up to 100 million acres to the Union Pacific and Central Pacific, two companies chartered in 1862 and charged with building a railroad from the Missouri River to the Pacific coast. (These were the first corporate charters issued by the federal government since the Second Bank of the United States in 1816.)

When first proposed in 1846, the idea of a **transcontinental railroad** had been considered by Congress "too gigantic" and "entirely impracticable." And, indeed, the project was monumental. The Central Pacific progressed only twenty miles a year for the first three years of construction because the Sierra Nevada range was almost impassable. It required some 20,000 men to lay the tracks across prairies and mountains, a substantial number of them immigrant Chinese contract laborers. Hundreds of Chinese workers died blasting tunnels and building bridges through this treacherous terrain. When it was completed in 1869, the transcontinental railroad, which ran from Omaha, Nebraska, to San Francisco, reduced the time of a cross-country journey from four or five months to six days. It expanded the national market, facilitated the spread of settlement and investment in the West, and heralded the doom of the Plains Indians.

The West and the War

Most accounts of the Civil War say little or nothing about the West. Yet the conflict engulfed Missouri, Kansas, and Indian Territory and spread into the South-

This photograph from 1861 depicts Native American volunteer soldiers being enrolled in the Union army. Indian soldiers were recruited well before the army admitted Blacks.

west borderlands. The war divided western communities as residents flocked to both armies.

Since the beginning of the republic, the question of slavery had been tied up with the status of new western lands. Jefferson Davis had long been interested in the expansion of slavery into the Southwest. In pursuit of this goal, in October 1861, Confederate units from Texas launched an invasion of New Mexico (which Texans had long claimed as part of their state). They hoped to conquer the region as a gateway to acquisition of southern California and northern Mexico, a continuation of a southern version of manifest destiny. But the Confederates were defeated at Glorieta Pass in March 1862 by a small Union army contingent reinforced by volunteers from Colorado and California. With their retreat to Texas died the dream of a slave empire in the Far West.

Indian Territory and the War

The war had a profound impact on western Indians. One of Lincoln's first orders as president was to withdraw federal troops from the West so that they could protect Washington, D.C. Recognizing that this would make it impossible for the army to keep white interlopers from intruding on Indian land, as treaties required it to do, Indian leaders begged Lincoln to reverse this decision, but to no avail.

When the war began, around 70,000 persons lived in Indian Territory, mostly members of the Five Tribes, who had been removed from the Southeast under Jackson and Van Buren, but also numerous other groups that claimed part of the region as their own homelands. Indian nations were divided and Native soldiers participated on both sides of the conflict. Some Native soldiers, such as 3,000 Cherokee, fought for the Confederacy to help preserve slavery. Most Indians made decisions based on what they considered the best way to maintain their nations' sovereignty. Early in the war, a flood of pro-Union refugees fled to Kansas from areas controlled by pro-Confederate tribes. A year before issuing the Emancipation Proclamation, Lincoln authorized the recruitment of Native American soldiers into the Union army. By the summer of 1863, Union forces, including Indigenous soldiers, had established control of Indian Territory.

Although Lincoln did not share the visceral hatred of Indians of many westerners, he pursued policies that had disastrous effects on Native peoples. Key legislation discussed previously—for example, the Homestead Act that offered free public land to settlers in the West, the Morrill Act that set aside vast acreages for states to use to finance higher education, and the acts that granted land to companies to build the transcontinental railroad—made subjugating western Indians all the more pressing for Union leaders.

The Dakota War

One of Lincoln's most dramatic and controversial wartime decisions arose from the outbreak of conflict in Minnesota between Dakota Indians and the U.S. Army. In 1851, the Dakotas had signed treaties with the federal government confining them to a small reservation in exchange for annual supplies of needed goods and monetary payments. Because of corruption within the federal government's Indian Office, these supplies and payments failed to materialize. Meanwhile white settlers continued to encroach on Dakota land.

After suffering multiple treaty violations, in the summer of 1862 Dakota soldiers launched a series of attacks on settlers and army posts. An army regiment defeated the Dakota Indians, took 1,500 prisoners, established a military tribunal, and sentenced more than 300 to death. Lincoln stayed the executions until he could personally review the trial proceedings. When warned by Minnesota's governor that commuting the sentences would be politically harmful, Lincoln replied that he would not execute men to gain votes. In the end, he commuted over 260 sentences, the largest such action in American history. But he also approved 38 death sentences, leading to the nation's largest official execution. And hundreds of Indigenous persons, including the bulk of the Dakota population as well as Ho-Chunks who had nothing to do with the uprising, were removed to Dakota Territory.

As the war continued, sporadic fighting took place between Union forces and Indian nations. The administration pressed forward with forcing Indians to sign treaties giving up much of their land and with efforts to remove Native peoples to reservations. In his annual messages to Congress, Lincoln announced how much Indian land had been ceded to the government—3 million acres in 1862 and 1863 alone.

The Sand Creek Massacre

Inevitably, conflict flared in the West between Native Americans and white settlers with disastrous results. In November 1864, Colorado militiamen attacked

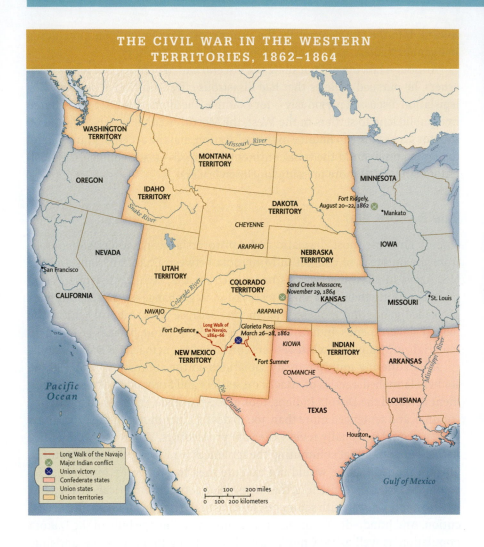

THE CIVIL WAR IN THE WESTERN TERRITORIES, 1862–1864

WASHINGTON TERRITORY

MONTANA TERRITORY

Missouri River

OREGON

IDAHO TERRITORY

MINNESOTA

DAKOTA TERRITORY

Fort Ridgely, August 20–22, 1862

*Mankato

Snake River

CHEYENNE

NEVADA

ARAPAHO

NEBRASKA TERRITORY

IOWA

*San Francisco

UTAH TERRITORY

Colorado River

COLORADO TERRITORY

Sand Creek Massacre, November 29, 1864

St. Louis

CALIFORNIA

NAVAJO

ARAPAHO

KANSAS

MISSOURI

Fort Defiance

Long Walk of the Navajo, 1864–66

Glorieta Pass, March 26–28, 1862

KIOWA

INDIAN TERRITORY

ARKANSAS

NEW MEXICO TERRITORY

*Fort Sumner

COMANCHE

Mississippi River

Pacific Ocean

Rio Grande

LOUISIANA

TEXAS

Houston

Gulf of Mexico

— Long Walk of the Navajo
● Major Indian conflict
✖ Union victory
▢ Confederate states
▢ Union states
▢ Union territories

0   100   200 miles
0   100 200 kilometers

a group of around 700 Cheyennes and Arapahos camped along Sand Creek in Colorado. Led by Colonel John Chivington, an abolitionist and a former Methodist minister, the soldiers were bent on punishing Indians responsible for raids on nearby settlements. They failed to locate the "hostile Indians" but chose to assault the peaceful encampment with rifles and artillery, killing more than 150 men, women, and children. The incident sparked intensified warfare on the southern plains, as Cheyennes and Arapahos retaliated with attacks of their own. It also helped to inspire a movement for the reform of Indian policies to emphasize peaceful assimilation over military conquest. Congress investigated the massacre and condemned Chivington's actions. It even promised reparations to the survivors.

The Union army also launched a series of campaigns in the Southwest against tribes like the Kiowas and Comanches, whose violent raids on ranches and settlements had been an essential, although disruptive, part of the borderlands economy, organized around trading and exchanging captives (usually women), livestock, and horses. They had taken tens of thousands of horses and cattle each year, to use as a kind of currency in trade with other Indians and white persons.

The army also made war on the Navajo, who were more victims than perpetrators of these raids. Indian raiding parties had stolen more than 50,000 sheep from their settlements in 1860 alone. Union forces destroyed their orchards and sheep and forced 8,000 people to move to a reservation set aside by the government. The **Navajo's Long Walk** became as central to their historical experience as the Trail of Tears to the Cherokee (see Chapter 10). Unlike the eastern Indians, however, the Navajo were eventually allowed to return to a portion of their lands. The wars against Native Americans, a small part of the violence that engulfed the nation during the Civil War, would continue for more than two decades after the sectional conflict ended.

Ironically, the Confederacy, although defending slavery, treated Native Americans more fairly than the Union. The Confederate Constitution provided for Indian tribes to elect representatives to Congress, and the Davis administration removed state jurisdiction over Indian reservations, allowing them complete self-government.

A New Financial System

The need to pay for the war produced dramatic changes in financial policy. To raise money, the Union government increased the tariff to unprecedented heights (thus promoting the further growth of northern industry), imposed new taxes on the production and consumption of goods, and enacted the nation's first income tax. It also borrowed more than $2 billion by selling interest-bearing bonds, thus creating an immense national debt. And it printed more than $400 million worth of paper money, called "greenbacks," declared to be legal tender—that is, money that must be accepted for nearly all public and private payments and debts. To rationalize banking, Congress established a system of nationally chartered banks, which were required to purchase government bonds and were given the right to issue banknotes as currency. A heavy tax drove money issued by state banks out of existence. Thus, the United States, whose money supply before the war was a chaotic mixture of paper notes issued by state and local banks, now had essentially two kinds of national paper currency—greenbacks printed directly by the federal government, and notes issued by the new national banks.

Along with profitable contracts to supply goods for the military effort, wartime economic policies greatly benefited northern manufacturers, railroad men, and financiers. Numerous Americans who would take the lead in reshaping the nation's postwar economy created or consolidated their fortunes during the Civil War, among them iron and steel entrepreneur Andrew Carnegie, oil magnate John D. Rockefeller, financiers Jay Gould and J. P. Morgan, and Philip D. Armour, who earned millions supplying beef to the Union army. These and other "captains of industry" managed to escape military service, sometimes by purchasing exemptions or hiring substitutes, as allowed by the draft law.

Taken together, the Union's economic policies vastly increased the power and size of the federal government. The federal budget for 1865 exceeded $1 billion—nearly twenty times that of 1860. With its new army of clerks, tax collectors, and other officials, the government became the nation's largest employer. And while much of this expansion proved temporary, the government would never return to its weak and fragmented condition of the prewar period.

Women and the War

For many northern women, the conflict opened new doors of opportunity. Women took advantage of the wartime labor shortage to move into jobs in factories and into certain largely male professions, particularly nursing. The expansion of the activities of the national government opened new jobs for women as clerks in government offices. Many of these wartime gains were short-lived, but in white-collar government jobs, retail sales, and nursing, women found a permanent place in the workforce.

Some northern women took a direct part in military campaigns. Clara Barton, a clerk in the Patent Office in Washington, D.C., when the war began, traveled with the Army of Virginia, helping to organize supply lines and nursing wounded soldiers. Barton worked alone rather than as a part of the Department of Female Nurses, and she never received compensation from the government.

Hundreds of thousands of northern women took part in organizations that gathered money and medical supplies for soldiers and sent books, clothing, and food to freedmen. The United States Sanitary Commission emerged as a centralized national relief agency to coordinate donations on the northern home front. Although control at the national level remained in male hands, patriotic women did most of the grassroots work. Women played the leading role in organizing **Sanitary Fairs**—grand bazaars that displayed military banners, uniforms, and other relics of the war and sold goods to raise money for soldiers' aid. New York City's three-week fair of 1864 attracted a crowd of 30,000 and raised more than $1 million.

Many men understood women's war work as an extension of their "natural" capacity for self-sacrifice. But the very act of volunteering to work in local soldiers' aid societies brought many northern women into the public sphere and offered them a taste of independence. The suffrage movement suspended operations during the war to devote itself to the Union and emancipation. But women's continuing lack of the vote seemed all the more humiliating as their involvement in war work increased.

From the ranks of this wartime mobilization came many of the leaders of the postwar movement for women's rights. Mary Livermore, the wife of a Chicago minister, toured military hospitals to assess their needs, cared for injured and dying soldiers, and organized two Sanitary Fairs. She emerged from the war with a deep resentment of women's legal and political subordination and organized her state's first woman suffrage convention. After the war, Clara Barton not only became an advocate of woman suffrage but also, as president of the American National Red Cross, lobbied for the United States to endorse the First Geneva Convention of 1864, which mandated the humane treatment of battlefield casualties. Largely as a result of Barton's efforts, the Senate ratified the convention in 1882. (Subsequent Geneva Conventions in the twentieth century would deal with the treatment of prisoners of war and civilians during wartime.)

The Divided North

Despite Lincoln's political skills, the war and his administration's policies divided northern society. Republicans labeled those opposed to the war Copperheads, after a poisonous snake that strikes without warning. Mounting casualties and rapid societal changes divided the North. Disaffection was strongest among the large southern-born population of states like Ohio, Indiana, and Illinois and working-class Catholic immigrants in eastern cities.

As the war progressed, it heightened existing social tensions and created new ones. The growing power of the federal government challenged traditional notions of local autonomy. The Union's draft law, which allowed individuals to provide a substitute or buy their way out of the army, caused widespread indignation. Workers resented manufacturers and financiers who reaped large profits while their own real incomes dwindled because of inflation. The war witnessed the rebirth of the northern labor movement, which organized numerous strikes for higher wages. The prospect of a sweeping change in the status of Blacks called forth a racist reaction in many parts of the North. Throughout the war, the Democratic Party subjected Lincoln's policies to withering criticism, although it remained divided between "War Democrats," who supported the military effort while criticizing emancipation and the draft, and those who favored immediate peace.

On occasion, dissent degenerated into outright violence. In July 1863, the introduction of the draft provoked four days of rioting in New York City. The mob, composed largely of Irish immigrants, assaulted symbols of the new order being created by the war—draft offices, the mansions of wealthy Republicans, industrial establishments, and the city's Black population, many of whom fled to New Jersey or took refuge in Central Park. Only the arrival of Union troops quelled the uprising, but not before more than 100 persons had died.

THE CONFEDERATE NATION

Leadership and Government

The man charged with the task of rallying public support for the Confederacy proved unequal to the task. Born in 1808 in Kentucky, within eight months and 100 miles of Lincoln's birth, Jefferson Davis moved to Mississippi as a youth, attended West Point, and acquired a large plantation. Aloof, stubborn, and humorless, he lacked Lincoln's common touch and political flexibility. Although known before the war as the "Cicero of the Senate" for his eloquent speeches, Davis, unlike Lincoln, proved unable to communicate the war's meaning effectively to ordinary men and women. Moreover, the Confederacy's lack of a party system proved to be a liability. Like the founders of the American republic, southern leaders saw parties as threats to national unity. As a result, Davis lacked a counterpart to the well-organized Republican Party, which helped to mobilize support for the Lincoln administration.

Under Davis, the Confederate nation became far more centralized than the Old South had been. The government raised armies from scratch, took control of southern railroads, and built manufacturing plants. But it failed to find an effective way of utilizing the South's major economic resource, cotton. In the early part of the war, the administration tried to suppress cotton production, urging planters to grow food instead and banning cotton exports. This, it was hoped, would promote economic self-sufficiency and force Great Britain, whose textile mills could not operate without southern cotton, to intervene on the side of the Confederacy.

"**King Cotton diplomacy**" turned out to be ineffective. Large crops in 1859 and 1860 had created a huge stockpile in English warehouses. By the time distress hit the manufacturing districts in 1862, the government of Prime Minister Palmerston had decided not to intervene, partly because Britain needed northern wheat almost as much as southern cotton. But the Confederate policy had far-reaching global consequences. Recognizing their overdependence on

The centrality of slavery to the Confederacy is illustrated by the paper money issued by state governments and private banks, which frequently juxtaposed scenes of slaves at work with other revered images. The ten-dollar note of the Eastern Bank of Alabama depicts slaves working in the field and at a port, along with an idealized portrait of southern white womanhood. Alabama's five-dollar bill includes an overseer directing slaves in the field and a symbol of liberty.

southern cotton, other nations moved to expand production. Britain promoted cultivation of the crop in Egypt and India, and Russia did the same in parts of Central Asia. As a result, the resumption of American cotton production after the war led directly to a worldwide crisis of overproduction that drove down the price of cotton, impoverishing farmers around the world.

Nor did Davis deal effectively with obstructionist governors like Joseph E. Brown of Georgia, who denounced the Confederate draft as "a dangerous usurpation" of states' rights and individual liberty. All in all, Davis was so inferior to Lincoln as a wartime leader that one historian has suggested that had the North and South exchanged presidents, the South would have won the war.

From ALEXANDER H. STEPHENS, THE CORNERSTONE SPEECH, SAVANNAH (1861)

Alexander H. Stephens, one of Georgia's most prominent political leaders, opposed secession in the winter of 1860–1861, but once his state acted he agreed to serve as vice president of the Confederacy. In March 1861, he delivered a speech that offered an explanation for the dissolution of the Union.

We are passing through one of the greatest revolutions in the annals of the world. . . . The new constitution has put at rest, forever, all the agitating questions relating to our peculiar institution African slavery as it exists amongst us and the proper status of the negro in our form of civilization. This was the immediate cause of the late rupture and present revolution. Jefferson . . . had anticipated this, as the "rock upon which the old Union would split." He was right. What was conjecture with him, is now a realized fact. But whether he fully comprehended the great truth upon which that rock stood and stands, may be doubted. The prevailing ideas entertained by him and most of the leading statesmen at the time of the formation of the old constitution, were that the enslavement of the African was in violation of the laws of nature; that it was wrong in principle, socially, morally, and politically. . . . Those ideas, however, were fundamentally wrong. They rested upon the assumption of the equality of races. This was an error. . . .

Our new government is founded upon exactly the opposite idea; its foundations are laid, its corner-stone rests, upon the great truth that the negro is not equal to the white man; that slavery, subordination to the superior race, is his natural and normal condition. This, our new government, is the first, in the history of the world, based upon this great physical, philosophical, and moral truth . . . . Many who hear me, perhaps, can recollect well, that this truth was not generally admitted, even within their day. The errors of the past generation still clung to many as late as twenty years ago. Those at the North, who still cling to these errors, with a zeal above knowledge, we justly denominate fanatics. . . . They assume that the negro is equal, and hence conclude that he is entitled to equal privileges and rights with the white man. . . . They were attempting to make things equal which the creator had made unequal. . . . With us, all of the white race, however high or low, rich or poor, are equal in the eye of the law. Not so with the negro. Subordination is his place. [This is] the real corner-stone in our new edifice.

From ABRAHAM LINCOLN, ADDRESS AT SANITARY FAIR, BALTIMORE (1864)

Abraham Lincoln's speech at a Sanitary Fair (a grand bazaar that raised money for the care of Union soldiers) offers a dramatic illustration of the contested meaning of freedom during the Civil War.

The world has never had a good definition of the word liberty, and the American people, just now, are much in want of one. We all declare for liberty; but in using the same *word* we do not all mean the same *thing*. With some the word liberty may mean for each man to do as he pleases with himself, and the product of his labor; while with others the same word may mean for some men to do as they please with other men, and the product of other men's labor. Here are two, not only different, but incompatible things, called by the same name—liberty. And it follows that each of the things is, by the respective parties, called by two different and incompatible names—liberty and tyranny.

The shepherd drives the wolf from the sheep's throat, for which the sheep thanks the shepherd as a *liberator*, while the wolf denounces him for the same act as the destroyer of liberty, especially as the sheep was a black one. Plainly the sheep and the wolf are not agreed upon a definition of the word liberty; and precisely the same difference prevails today among us human creatures, even in the North, and all professing to love liberty. Hence we behold the process by which thousands are daily passing from under the yoke of bondage, hailed by some as the advance of liberty, and bewailed by others as the destruction of all liberty. Recently, as it seems, the people of Maryland have been doing something to define liberty [abolishing slavery in the state]; and thanks to them that, in what they have done, the wolf's dictionary, has been repudiated.

QUESTIONS

1. *How does Stephens describe changes in southern ideas about slavery since the nation's founding?*

2. *What does Lincoln identify as the essential difference between northern and southern definitions of freedom?*

3. *How do Stephens and Lincoln differ in their definitions of liberty and whether it applies to African Americans?*

The Inner Civil War

As the war progressed, social change and internal turmoil engulfed much of the Confederacy. At the outset, most white southerners rallied to the Confederate cause. No less fervently than northern troops, southern soldiers spoke of their cause in the language of freedom. "We are fighting for our liberty," wrote one volunteer, without any sense of contradiction, "against tyrants of the North . . . who are determined to destroy slavery." But public disaffection eventually became an even more serious problem for the Confederacy than for the Union.

One grievance was the draft. Like the Union, the Confederacy allowed individuals to provide a substitute. Because of the accelerating disintegration of slavery, it also exempted one white male for every twenty slaves on a plantation (thus releasing many overseers and planters' sons from service). The "twenty-negro" provision convinced many yeomen that the struggle for southern independence had become "a rich man's war and a poor man's fight."

Economic Problems

Economic deprivation also sparked disaffection. As the blockade tightened, areas of the Confederacy came under Union occupation, and production by slaves declined, shortages arose of essential commodities such as salt, corn, and meat. The war left countless farms, plantations, businesses, and railroads in ruins. The economic crisis, which stood in glaring contrast to the North's boom, was an unavoidable result of the war. But Confederate policies exaggerated its effects. War requires sacrifice, and civilian support for war depends, in part, on the belief that sacrifice is being fairly shared. Many non-slaveholders, however, became convinced that they were bearing an unfair share of the war's burdens.

Like the Union, the Confederacy borrowed heavily to finance the war. Unlike federal lawmakers, however, the planter-dominated Confederate Congress proved unwilling to levy heavy taxes that planters would have to pay. It relied on paper money, of which it issued $1.5 billion, far more than the North's greenbacks. The Confederate Congress also authorized military officers to seize farm goods to supply the army, paying with increasingly worthless Confederate money. Small farmers deeply resented this practice, known as "impressment." Numerous yeoman families, many of whom had gone to war to preserve their economic independence, sank into poverty and debt. Food riots broke out in many places, including Richmond, Virginia, and Mobile, Alabama, where in 1863 large crowds of women plundered army food supplies.

In 1862, Joshua B. Moore, a slaveholder in northern Alabama, commented on how slavery threatened the Confederate war effort: "Men who have no interest in it," he wrote, "are not going to fight through a long war to save it— never. They will tire of it and quit." As the war progressed, desertion became what one officer called a "crying evil" for the southern armies. By the war's end, more than 100,000 men had deserted, almost entirely from among "the poorest class of nonslaveholders whose labor is indispensable to the daily support of their families." Men, another official noted, "cannot be expected to fight for the government that permits their wives and children to starve."

Southern Unionists

Continued loyalty to the Union was a dangerous stance in the Confederate South. Georgia in 1861 passed a law making it punishable by death (hardly the action of a government committed to individual liberty and the rights of minorities). Nonetheless, by 1864, organized peace movements had appeared in several southern states, and secret societies such as the Heroes of America were actively promoting disaffection. Confederate military tribunals imprisoned hundreds of Unionists. Others were violently driven from their homes, and a few were executed by the army or civilian authorities. But southerners loyal to the Union made a significant contribution to northern victory. By the end of the war, an estimated 50,000 white southerners had fought in the Union armies.

One of the most celebrated Union heroes of the war was Elizabeth Van Lew of Richmond, who had persuaded her mother to free the family's slaves when her father died in 1843. During the war she frequently visited Libby Prison in the Confederate capital, bringing supplies to Union prisoners of war and helping some of them to escape. With the aid of Mary Elizabeth Bowser, a former slave of the Van Lew family who worked as a servant in the southern White House, Van Lew passed information about Confederate plans to Union forces.

Women and the Confederacy

Even more than in the North, the war placed unprecedented burdens on southern white women. Left alone on farms and plantations, they were often forced to manage business affairs and discipline slaves, previously the responsibility of men. As in the North, women mobilized to support soldiers in the field and stepped out of their traditional "sphere" to run commercial establishments and work in arms factories. In Richmond, "government girls" staffed many of the clerkships in the new Confederate bureaucracy. Rose Greenhow, the widow of a former American diplomat, headed an espionage ring in Washington, D.C., that passed valuable information about Union troop movements to the Confederacy early in the war. Even after her arrest and jailing, she managed to smuggle out intelligence until she was exiled to Richmond in 1862. Jefferson Davis rewarded Greenhow with $2,500 for her services.

The war led to the political mobilization, for the first time, of non-slaveholding white women. Lacking the aid of slave labor, they found that the absence of their husbands from their previously self-sufficient farms made it impossible to feed their families. They flooded Confederate authorities with petitions seeking assistance, not as charity but as a right. Politicians could not ignore the pleas of soldiers' wives, and state governments began to distribute supplies to needy families.

Southern women's self-sacrificing devotion to the cause became legendary. But as the war went on and the death toll mounted, increasing numbers of women came to believe that the goal of independence was not worth the cost. The growing disaffection of southern white women, conveyed in letters to loved ones at the front, contributed to the decline in civilian morale and encouraged desertion from the army.

Black Soldiers for the Confederacy

The growing shortage of white manpower eventually led Confederate authorities to a decision no one could have foreseen when the war began: they authorized the arming of slaves to fight for the South. As early as September 1863, a Mississippi newspaper had argued for freeing and enlisting able-bodied Black men. "Let them," it wrote, "be declared free, placed in the ranks, and told to fight for their homes and country." But many slaveholders fiercely resisted this idea, and initially, the Confederate Senate rejected it. Not until March 1865, after Robert E. Lee had endorsed the plan, did the Confederate Congress authorize the arming of slaves. To be sure, enlisting Blacks in the Confederate army did not necessarily mean the end of slavery. Both the British and Americans had used slave soldiers in the War of Independence, but slavery survived, as it undoubtedly would have had the Confederacy managed to win the Civil War.

The war ended before substantial recruitment of Black Confederate soldiers—the only ones who reached the front were two companies impressed into service in Richmond a few days before the city's surrender. But the Confederate army did employ numerous Blacks, nearly all of them slaves, as laborers. This later led to some confusion over whether Blacks actually fought for the Confederacy—apart from a handful who "passed" for white, none in fact did. But the South's decision to raise Black troops illustrates how the war undermined not only slavery but also the proslavery ideology. "The day you make soldiers of them is the beginning of the end of the revolution," declared Howell Cobb, a Georgia planter and politician. "If slaves make good soldiers, our whole theory of slavery is wrong."

TURNING POINTS

Gettysburg and Vicksburg

Despite the accelerating demise of slavery and the decline of morale in the South, the war's outcome remained very much in doubt for much of its third and fourth years. In April 1863, "Fighting Joe" Hooker, who had succeeded Ambrose E. Burnside as the Union commander in the East, brought the Army of the Potomac into central Virginia to confront Lee. Outnumbered two to one, Lee repelled Hooker's attack at Chancellorsville, although he lost his ablest lieutenant, "Stonewall" Jackson, who died after being mistakenly shot by his own soldiers.

Lee now gambled on another invasion of the North, although his strategic objective remains unclear. Perhaps he believed a defeat on its own territory would destroy the morale of the northern army and public. In any event, the two armies, with Union soldiers now under the command of General George

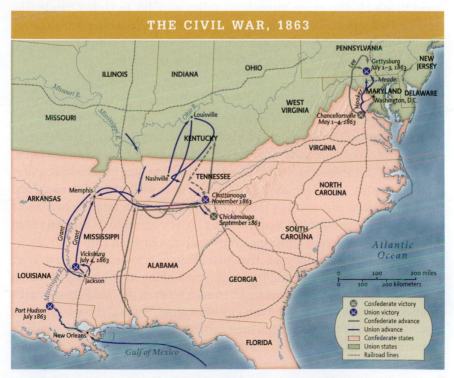

THE CIVIL WAR, 1863

In July 1863, the Union won major victories at Gettysburg and Vicksburg.

G. Meade, met at Gettysburg, Pennsylvania, on the first three days of July 1863. With 165,000 troops involved, the **Battle of Gettysburg** remains the largest battle ever fought on the North American continent. Lee found himself in the unusual position of confronting entrenched Union forces. After two days of failing to dislodge them, he decided to attack the center of the Union line. On July 3, Confederate forces, led by Major General George E. Pickett's crack division, marched across an open field toward Union forces. Withering artillery and rifle fire met the charge, and most of Pickett's soldiers never reached Union lines. Later remembered as "the high tide of the Confederacy," Pickett's Charge was also Lee's greatest blunder. His army retreated to Virginia, never again to set foot on northern soil.

On the same day that Lee began his retreat from Gettysburg, the Union achieved a significant victory in the West. Late in 1862, Grant had moved into Mississippi toward the city of Vicksburg. From its heights, defended by miles of trenches and earthworks, the Confederacy commanded the central Mississippi River. When direct attacks failed, as did an attempt to divert the river by digging a canal, Grant launched a siege. On July 4, 1863, Vicksburg surrendered, and with it John C. Pemberton's army of 30,000 men, a loss the Confederacy could ill afford. The entire Mississippi Valley now lay in Union hands. The simultaneous defeats at Gettysburg and the **Battle of Vicksburg** dealt a heavy blow to southern morale. "Today absolute ruin seems our portion," one official wrote in his diary. "The Confederacy totters to its destruction."

1864

Nearly two years, however, would pass before the war ended. Brought east to take command of Union forces, Grant in 1864 began a war of attrition against Lee's army in Virginia. That is, he was willing to accept high numbers of casualties, knowing that the North could replace its manpower losses while the South could not. Grant understood that to bring the North's manpower advantage into play, he must attack continuously "all along the line," thereby preventing the enemy from concentrating its forces or retreating to safety after an engagement.

In May 1864, the 115,000-man Army of the Potomac crossed the Rapidan River to do battle with Lee's forces in Virginia. A month of the war's bloodiest fighting followed. Grant and Lee first encountered each other in the Wilderness, a wild, shrub-covered region where, one participant recalled, "it was as though Christian men had turned to fiends, and hell itself had usurped the place of earth." Grant's army suffered 18,000 casualties, while Lee's far smaller forces incurred 7,500. Previous Union generals had broken off engagements after losses of this magnitude. But Grant continued to press forward, attacking again at Spotsylvania and then at Cold Harbor. At the end of six weeks of fighting, Grant's casualties stood at

60,000—almost the size of Lee's entire army—while Lee had lost 30,000 men. The sustained fighting in Virginia was a turning point in modern warfare. With daily combat and a fearsome casualty toll, it had far more in common with the trench warfare of World War I (discussed in Chapter 19) than the almost gentlemanly fighting with which the Civil War began.

Grant had become the only Union general to maintain the initiative against Lee, but at a cost that led critics to label him a "butcher of men." Victory still eluded him. Grant attempted to capture Petersburg, which controlled the railway link to Richmond, but Lee got to Petersburg first, and Grant settled in for a prolonged siege. Meanwhile, General William T. Sherman, who had moved his forces into Georgia from Tennessee, encountered dogged resistance from Confederate troops. Not until September 1864 did he finally enter Atlanta, seizing Georgia's main railroad center.

As casualty rolls mounted in the spring and summer of 1864, northern morale sank to its lowest point of the war. Lincoln for a time believed he would be unable to win reelection. In May, hoping to force Lincoln to step aside, Radical Republicans nominated John C. Frémont on a platform calling for a constitutional amendment to abolish slavery, federal protection of the freedmen's rights, and confiscation of the land of leading Confederates. The Democratic candidate for president, General George B. McClellan, was hampered from the outset of the campaign by a platform calling for an immediate cease-fire and peace conference—a plan that even war-weary northerners viewed as equivalent to surrender. In the end, Frémont withdrew, and buoyed by Sherman's capture of Atlanta, Lincoln won a sweeping victory. He captured every state but Kentucky, Delaware, and New Jersey. The result ensured that the war would continue until the Confederacy's defeat.

REHEARSALS FOR RECONSTRUCTION AND THE END OF THE WAR

As the war drew toward a close and more and more parts of the Confederacy came under Union control, federal authorities found themselves presiding over the transition from slavery to freedom. In South Carolina, Louisiana, and other parts of the South, debates took place over issues—access to land, control of labor, and the new structure of political power—that would reverberate in the postwar world.

The Sea Islands Experiment

The most famous "rehearsal for Reconstruction" took place on the Sea Islands just off the coast of South Carolina. The war was only a few months old when, in November 1861, the Union navy occupied the islands. Nearly the entire white population fled, leaving behind some 10,000 slaves. The navy was soon followed by other northerners—army officers, Treasury agents, prospective investors in cotton land, and a group known as Gideon's Band, which included Black and white reformers and teachers committed to uplifting the freed slaves. Each of these groups, in addition to the islands' Black population, had its own view of how the transition to freedom should be organized. And journalists reported every development on the islands to an eager reading public in the North.

Convinced that education was the key to making self-reliant, productive citizens of the former slaves, northern-born teachers like Charlotte Forten, a member of one of Philadelphia's most prominent Black families, and Laura M. Towne, a white native of Pittsburgh, devoted themselves to teaching the freed Blacks. Towne, who in 1862 helped to establish Penn School on St. Helena Island, remained there as a teacher until her death in 1901. Like many of the Gideonites, Towne and Forten assumed that Blacks needed outside guidance to appreciate freedom. But they sympathized with the former slaves' aspirations, central to which was the desire for land.

Other northerners, however, believed that the transition from slave to free labor meant not giving Blacks land but enabling them to work for wages in more humane conditions than under slavery. When the federal government put land on the islands up for sale, most was acquired not by former slaves but by northern investors bent upon demonstrating the superiority of free wage labor and turning a tidy profit at the same time. By 1865, the **Sea Islands experiment** was widely held to be a success. Black families were working for wages, acquiring education, and enjoying better shelter and clothing and a more varied diet than under slavery. But the experiment also bequeathed to postwar Reconstruction the contentious issue of whether landownership should accompany Black freedom.

Wartime Reconstruction in the West

A very different rehearsal for Reconstruction, involving a far larger area and population than the Sea Islands, took place in Louisiana and the Mississippi Valley. After the capture of Vicksburg, the Union army established regulations for plantation labor. Military authorities insisted that the emancipated slaves must sign labor contracts with plantation owners who took an oath of loyalty. But, unlike before the war, the laborers would be paid wages and provided with education, physical punishment was prohibited, and their families were safe from disruption by sale.

Neither side was satisfied with the new labor system. Blacks resented having to resume working for whites and being forced to sign labor contracts. Planters complained that without the whip, discipline could not be enforced. But only occasionally did army officers seek to implement a different vision of freedom. At Davis Bend, Mississippi, site of the cotton plantations of Jefferson Davis and his brother Joseph, General Grant decided to establish a "negro paradise." Here, rather than being forced to labor for white owners, the emancipated slaves saw the land divided among themselves. In addition, a system of government was established that allowed the former slaves to elect their own judges and sheriffs.

The Politics of Wartime Reconstruction

As the Civil War progressed, the future political status of African Americans emerged as a key dividing line in public debates. Events in Union-occupied Louisiana brought the issue to national attention. Hoping to establish a functioning civilian government in the state, Lincoln in 1863 announced his **Ten-Percent Plan of Reconstruction**. He essentially offered an amnesty and full restoration of rights, including property except for slaves, to nearly all white southerners who took an oath affirming loyalty to the Union and support for emancipation. When 10 percent of the voters of 1860 had taken the oath, they could elect a new state government, which would be required to abolish slavery. Lincoln's plan offered no role to Blacks in shaping the post-slavery order. His leniency toward southern whites seems to have been based on the assumption that many former slaveholders would come forward to accept his terms, thus weakening the Confederacy, shortening the war, and gaining white support for the ending of slavery.

Another group now stepped onto the stage of politics—the free Blacks of New Orleans, who saw the Union occupation as a golden opportunity to press for equality before the law and a role in government for themselves. Their complaints at being excluded under Lincoln's Reconstruction plan won a sympathetic hearing from Radical Republicans in Congress. By the summer of 1864, dissatisfaction with events in Louisiana helped to inspire the **Wade-Davis Bill**, named for two leading Republican members of Congress. This bill required a majority (not one-tenth) of white male southerners to pledge support for the Union before Reconstruction could begin in any state, and it guaranteed Blacks equality before the law, although not the right to vote. The bill passed Congress only to die when Lincoln refused to sign it and Congress adjourned. As the war drew to a close, it was clear that while slavery was dead, no agreement existed as to what social and political system should take its place.

Victory at Last

After Lincoln's reelection, the war hastened to its conclusion. In November 1864, Sherman and his army of 60,000 set out from Atlanta on their March to the Sea. Cutting a sixty-mile-wide swath through the heart of Georgia, they destroyed railroads, buildings, and all the food and supplies they could not use. His aim, Sherman wrote, was "to whip the rebels, to humble their pride, to follow them to their innermost recesses, and make them fear and dread us." Here was modern war in all its destructiveness, even though few civilians were physically harmed. In January 1865, after capturing Savannah, Sherman moved into South Carolina, bringing even greater destruction. Anarchy reigned on the plantations as slaves drove off remaining overseers, destroyed planters' homes, plundered smokehouses and storerooms, and claimed the land for themselves.

On January 31, 1865, Congress approved the **Thirteenth Amendment**, which abolished slavery throughout the entire Union—and in so doing, introduced the word "slavery" into the Constitution for the first time. In March, in his second inaugural address, Lincoln called for reconciliation: "With malice toward none, with charity for all, . . . let us . . . bind up the nation's wounds." Yet he also leveled a harsh judgment on the nation's past. Unlike the northern and southern clergy, who were sure of what God intended, Lincoln suggested that man does not know God's will—a remarkably modest statement on the eve of Union victory. Perhaps, Lincoln suggested, God had brought on the war to punish the entire nation, not just the South, for the sin of slavery. And if God willed that the war continue until all the wealth created by 250 years of slave labor had been destroyed, and "every drop of blood drawn with the lash shall be paid by another drawn with the sword," this too would be an act of justice.

April 1865 brought some of the most momentous events in American history. On April 2, Grant finally broke through Lee's lines at Petersburg, forcing the Army of Northern Virginia to abandon the city and leaving Richmond defenseless. The following day, Union soldiers occupied the southern capital. At the head of one Black army unit marched its chaplain, Garland H. White, a former fugitive from slavery. Called upon by a large crowd to make a speech, White, as he later recalled, proclaimed "for the first time in that city freedom to all mankind." Then the "doors of all the slave pens were thrown open and thousands came out shouting and praising God, and Father, or Master Abe."

On April 4, heedless of his own safety, Lincoln walked the streets of Richmond accompanied only by a dozen sailors. At every step he was besieged by former slaves, some of whom fell on their knees before the embarrassed president, who urged them to remain standing. Meanwhile, Lee and his army headed west, only to be encircled by Grant's forces. Realizing that further resistance was useless, Lee surrendered at **Appomattox Courthouse,**

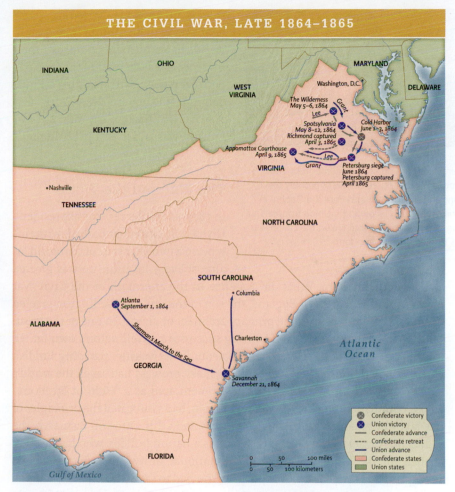

THE CIVIL WAR, LATE 1864–1865

The military defeat of the Confederacy came in the East, with Sherman's March to the Sea, Grant's occupation of Richmond, and the surrender of Robert E. Lee's army.

Virginia, on April 9. Although some Confederate units remained in the field, the Civil War was over.

Lincoln did not live to savor victory. On April 11, in what proved to be his last speech, he called publicly for the first time for limited Black suffrage in the South. Three days later, while attending a performance at Ford's Theatre in Washington, D.C., the president was mortally wounded by John Wilkes Booth, one of the nation's most celebrated actors. Lincoln died the next morning. A train carried the president's body to its final resting place in Illinois on a winding 1,600-mile journey that illustrated how tightly the railroad now bound the northern states. Grieving crowds lined the train route, and

A painting by the artist A. A. Lamb from 1864 depicts a militant figure of liberty proudly displaying the American flag before the Capitol in Washington, D.C., followed by Union troops. This is one of many images that linked the Union war effort to the cause of freedom.

solemn processions carried the president's body to lie in state in major cities so that mourners could pay their respects. It was estimated that 300,000 persons passed by the coffin in Philadelphia, 500,000 in New York, and 200,000 in Chicago. On May 4, 1865, Lincoln was laid to rest in Springfield.

The War and the World

In 1877, soon after retiring as president, Ulysses S. Grant embarked with his wife on a two-year tour of the world. At almost every location, he was greeted as a modern-day hero. What did America in the aftermath of the Civil War represent to the world? In England, the son of the duke of Wellington greeted Grant as a military genius, the primary architect of victory in one of the greatest wars in human history, and a fitting successor to Wellington's own father, the general who had vanquished Napoleon. In Newcastle, parading English workers hailed him as the man whose military prowess had saved the world's leading experiment in democratic government, and as a "Hero of Freedom," whose commander-in-chief, Abraham Lincoln, had vindicated the principles of free labor by emancipating America's slaves. In Berlin, Otto von Bismarck, the chancellor of Germany, welcomed Grant as a nation-builder, who had accomplished on the battlefield something—national unity—that Bismarck was attempting to create for his own people. "You had to save the Union," Bismarck commented, "just as we had to save Germany." Grant corrected him—"Not only to save the Union, but to destroy slavery."

The War in American History

The Civil War laid the foundation for modern America, guaranteeing the Union's permanence, destroying slavery, and shifting power in the nation from the South to the North (and, more specifically, from slaveowning planters to northern capitalists). It dramatically increased the power of the federal government and accelerated the modernization of the northern economy. And it placed on the postwar agenda the challenge of defining and protecting African American freedom.

Paradoxically, both sides lost something they had gone to war to defend. Slavery was the cornerstone of the Confederacy, but the war led inexorably to slavery's destruction. In the North, the war hastened the transformation of Lincoln's America—the world of free labor, of the small shop and independent farmer—into an industrial giant. Americans, in the words of the abolitionist Wendell Phillips, would "never again . . . see the republic in which we were born."

Late in May 1865, some 200,000 veterans paraded through Washington, D.C., for the Grand Review of the Union armies, a final celebration of the nation's triumph. The scene inspired the poet Bret Harte to imagine a very different parade—a "phantom army" of the Union dead:

> The martyred heroes of Malvern Hill,
> Of Gettysburg and Chancellorsville,
> The men whose wasted figures fill
> The patriot graves of the nation . . .
> And marching beside the others,
> Came the dusky martyrs of Pillow's fight.

To Harte, the war's meaning ultimately lay in the sacrifices of individual soldiers. He included in his reverie the Black troops, including those massacred at Fort Pillow. Blacks, Harte seemed to be saying, had achieved equality in death. Could the nation give it to them in life?

Here was the problem that confronted the United States as the postwar era known as Reconstruction began. "Verily," as Frederick Douglass declared, "the work does not *end* with the abolition of slavery, but only *begins*."

CHAPTER REVIEW

REVIEW QUESTIONS

1. *What made the American Civil War the first modern war?*

2. *How was the North's victory over the South tied to the different ways the market revolution had developed in the two regions?*

3. *Describe how President Lincoln's war aims evolved between 1861 and 1863, changing from simply preserving the Union to also ending slavery.*

4. *How did the actions of slaves themselves, northern military strategy, and the Emancipation Proclamation combine to end slavery?*

5. *What role did Blacks play in winning the Civil War and in defining the war's consequences?*

6. *How did federal policies undertaken during the Civil War transform the United States into a stronger nation-state—economically, politically, and ideologically?*

7. *What was the impact of the Civil War on civil liberties?*

8. *Compare and contrast women's efforts in the North and South to support the war effort and their families.*

9. *In what ways did the outcome of the Civil War change the United States' status in the world?*

10. *Why did some Native nations join forces with the Union and some with the Confederacy?*

KEY TERMS

first Battle of Bull Run (p. 526)

second Battle of Bull Run (p. 528)

Battle of Antietam (p. 528)

"the contrabands" (p. 530)

Radical Republicans (p. 532)

Emancipation Proclamation (p. 533)

Second American Revolution (p. 537)

Ex parte Milligan (p. 540)

Homestead Act (p. 541)

transcontinental railroad (p. 541)

Navajo's Long Walk (p. 545)

Sanitary Fairs (p. 546)

"King Cotton diplomacy" (p. 548)

Battle of Gettysburg (p. 556)

Battle of Vicksburg (p. 556)

Sea Islands experiment (p. 558)

Ten-Percent Plan of Reconstruction (p. 559)

Wade-Davis Bill (p. 559)

Thirteenth Amendment (p. 560)

Appomattox Courthouse, Virginia (p. 560)

Go to 🐰 INQUIZITIVE

To see what you know—and learn what you've missed—with personalized feedback along the way.

"WHAT IS FREEDOM?": RECONSTRUCTION

1865–1877

FOCUS QUESTIONS

- *What visions of freedom did the former slaves and slaveholders pursue in the postwar South?*

- *What were the sources, goals, and competing visions for Reconstruction?*

- *What were the social and political effects of Radical Reconstruction in the South?*

- *What were the main factors, in both the North and South, for the overthrow of Reconstruction?*

O n the evening of January 12, 1865, less than a month after Union forces captured Savannah, Georgia, twenty leaders of the city's Black community gathered for a discussion with General William T. Sherman and Secretary of War Edwin M. Stanton. Mostly Baptist and Methodist ministers, the group included several men who within a few years would assume prominent positions during the era of Reconstruction that followed the Civil War. Ulysses S. Houston, pastor of the city's Third African Baptist Church, and James Porter, an Episcopal religious leader who had operated a secret school for Black children before the war, in a few years would win election to the Georgia legislature. James D. Lynch, who had been born free in Baltimore and educated in New Hampshire, went on to serve as secretary of state of Mississippi.

The conversation revealed that the Black leaders brought out of slavery a clear definition of freedom. Asked what he understood by slavery, Garrison Frazier, a Baptist minister chosen as the group's spokesman, responded that it meant one person's "receiving by irresistible power the work of another man, and not by his consent." Freedom he defined as "placing us where we could reap the fruit of our own labor, and take care of ourselves." The way to accomplish this was "to have land, and turn it and till it by our own labor." Frazier insisted that Blacks possessed "sufficient intelligence" to maintain themselves in freedom and enjoy the equal protection of the laws.

Sherman's meeting with the Black leaders foreshadowed some of the radical changes that would take place during the era known as Reconstruction (meaning, literally, the rebuilding of the shattered nation). In the years following the Civil War, former slaves and their white allies, North and South, would seek to redefine the meaning and boundaries of American freedom and citizenship. Previously an entitlement of whites, these would be expanded to include Black Americans. The laws and Constitution would be rewritten to guarantee African Americans, for the first time in the nation's history, recognition as citizens and equality before the law. Black men would be granted the right to vote, ushering in a period of interracial democracy throughout the South. Black schools, churches, and other institutions would flourish, laying the foundation for the modern African American community. Many of the advances of Reconstruction would prove temporary, swept away during a campaign of violence in the South and the North's retreat from the ideal of equality. But Reconstruction laid the foundation for future struggles to extend freedom to all Americans.

All this, however, lay in the future in January 1865. Four days after the meeting, Sherman responded to the Black delegation by issuing Special Field Order 15. This set aside the Sea Islands and a large area along the South Carolina and Georgia coasts for the settlement of Black families on forty-acre plots of land. He also offered them broken-down mules that the army could no longer use. In Sherman's order lay the origins of the phrase "forty acres and a mule," which would reverberate across the South in the next few years. By June, some 40,000 freed slaves had been settled on "Sherman land." Among the emancipated slaves, Sherman's order raised hopes that the end of slavery would be accompanied by the economic independence that they, like other Americans, believed essential to genuine freedom.

THE MEANING OF FREEDOM

With the end of the Civil War, declared an Illinois congressman in 1865, the United States was a "new nation," for the first time "wholly free." The destruction of slavery, however, made the definition of freedom the central question on the nation's agenda. "What is freedom?" asked Congressman James A. Garfield in 1865. "Is it the bare privilege of not being chained? If this is all, then freedom is a bitter mockery, a cruel delusion." Did freedom mean simply the absence of slavery, or did it imply other rights for the former slaves, and if so, which ones: equal civil rights, the vote, ownership of property? During Reconstruction, freedom became a terrain of conflict, its substance open to different, often contradictory interpretations. Out of the conflict over the meaning of freedom arose new kinds of relations between Black and white southerners, and a new definition of the rights of all Americans.

Blacks and the Meaning of Freedom

African Americans' understanding of freedom was shaped by their experiences as slaves and their observation of the free society around them. To begin with, freedom meant escaping the numerous injustices of slavery—punishment by the lash, the separation of families, denial of access to education, the sexual exploitation of Black women by their owners—and sharing in the rights and opportunities of American citizens. "If I cannot do like a white man," Henry Adams, an emancipated slave in Louisiana, told his former owner in 1865, "I am not free."

Blacks relished the opportunity to demonstrate their liberation from the regulations, significant and trivial, associated with slavery. They openly held mass meetings and religious services free of white supervision, and they acquired dogs, guns, and liquor, all barred to them under slavery. No longer required to obtain a pass from their owners to travel, former slaves throughout the South left the plantations in search of better jobs, family members, or simply a taste of personal liberty. Many moved to southern towns and cities, where, it seemed, "freedom was free-er."

Families in Freedom

With slavery dead, institutions that had existed before the war, like the Black family, free Blacks' churches and schools, and the secret slave church, were strengthened, expanded, and freed from white supervision. The family was central to the postemancipation Black community. Former slaves made remarkable efforts to locate loved ones from whom they had been separated under slavery. One northern reporter in 1865 encountered a freedman who had walked more than 600 miles from Georgia to North Carolina, searching for the wife and children from whom he had been sold away before the war. Meanwhile, widows of Black soldiers successfully claimed survivors' pensions, forcing the federal government to acknowledge the validity of prewar relationships that slavery had attempted to deny.

But while Reconstruction witnessed the stabilization of family life, freedom subtly altered relationships within the family. Emancipation increased the power of Black men and brought to many Black families the nineteenth-century notion that men and women should inhabit separate "spheres." Immediately after the Civil War, planters complained that freedwomen had "withdrawn" from field labor and work as house servants. Many Black women preferred to devote more time to their families than had been possible under slavery, and men considered it a badge of honor to see their wives remain at home. Eventually, the dire poverty of the Black community would compel a far higher proportion of Black women than white women to go to work for wages.

Church and School

At the same time, Blacks abandoned white-controlled religious institutions to create churches of their own. On the eve of the Civil War, 42,000 Black Methodists worshiped in biracial South Carolina churches; by the end of Reconstruction, only 600 remained. The rise of the independent Black church, with Methodists and Baptists commanding the largest followings, redrew the religious map of the South. As the major institution independent of white control, the church played a central role in the Black community. A place of worship, it also housed schools, social events, and political gatherings. Black ministers came to play a major role in politics. Some 250 held public office during Reconstruction.

Another striking example of the freedpeople's quest for individual and community improvement was their desire for education. Education, declared a Mississippi freedman, was "the next best thing to liberty." The thirst for learning sprang from many sources—a desire to read the Bible, the need to prepare for the economic marketplace, and the opportunity, which arose in 1867, to take part in politics. Blacks of all ages flocked to the schools established by northern missionary societies, the Freedmen's Bureau, and groups of ex-slaves. Northern journalist Sidney Andrews, who toured the South in 1865, was impressed by how much education also took place outside of the classroom: "I had occasion very frequently to notice that porters in stores and laboring men in warehouses, and cart drivers on the streets, had spelling books with them, and were studying them during the time they were not occupied with their work." Before the Civil War, few colleges admitted Black students (an exception was Wilberforce University in Ohio, an institution for Blacks founded by the African Methodist Episcopal Church in 1856). During Reconstruction, Black colleges proliferated, including Fisk in Tennessee, Hampton Institute in Virginia, and Howard in the nation's capital.

Family Record, a lithograph marketed to former slaves after the Civil War, is an idealized portrait of a middle-class Black family with scenes of slavery and freedom.

Political Freedom

In a society that had made political participation a core element of freedom, the right to vote inevitably became central to the former slaves' desire for empowerment and equality. As Frederick Douglass put it soon after the South's surrender in 1865, "Slavery is not abolished until the Black man has the ballot." In a "monarchial government," Douglass explained, no "special" disgrace applied to those denied the right to vote. But in a democracy, "where universal suffrage is the rule," excluding any group meant branding them with "the stigma of inferiority." As soon as the Civil War ended, and in some parts of the South even earlier, free Blacks and emancipated slaves claimed a place in the public sphere. They came together in conventions, parades, and petition drives to demand the right to vote and, on occasion, to organize their own "freedom ballots." Anything less than full citizenship, Black spokesmen insisted, would betray the nation's democratic promise and the war's meaning.

Land, Labor, and Freedom

Former slaves' ideas of freedom, like those of rural people throughout the world, were directly related to landownership. Only land, wrote Merrimon Howard, a freedman from Mississippi, would enable "the poor class to enjoy the sweet boon of freedom." On the land they would develop independent communities free of white control. Many former slaves insisted that through their unpaid labor, they had acquired a right to the land. "The property which they hold," declared an Alabama Black convention, "was nearly all earned by the sweat of *our* brows." In some parts of the South, Blacks in 1865 seized property, insisting that it belonged to them. On one Tennessee plantation, former slaves claimed to be "joint heirs" to the estate and, the owner complained, took up residence "in the rooms of my house."

In its individual elements and much of its language, former slaves' definition of freedom resembled that of white Americans—self-ownership, family stability, religious liberty, political participation, and economic autonomy. But these elements combined to form a vision very much their own. For whites, freedom, no matter how defined, was a given, a birthright to be defended. For African Americans, it was an open-ended process, a transformation of every aspect of their lives and of the society and culture that had sustained slavery in the first place. Although the freedpeople failed to achieve full freedom as they understood it, their definition did much to shape national debate during the turbulent era of Reconstruction.

Masters without Slaves

Most white southerners reacted to military defeat and emancipation with dismay, not only because of the widespread devastation but also because they must now submit to northern demands. The appalling loss of life, a disaster without parallel in the American experience, affected all classes of southerners. Nearly 260,000 men died for the Confederacy—more than one-fifth of the South's adult male white population. The wholesale destruction of work animals, farm buildings, and machinery ensured that economic revival would be slow and painful. In 1870, the value of property in the South, not counting that represented by slaves, was 30 percent lower than before the war.

Planter families faced profound changes in the war's aftermath. Many lost not only their slaves but also their life savings, which they had patriotically invested in now-worthless Confederate bonds. Some, whose slaves departed the plantation, for the first time found themselves compelled to do physical labor. General Braxton Bragg and his wife, a woman "raised in affluence," lived for a time in a slave cabin.

Southern planters sought to implement an understanding of freedom quite different from that of the former slaves. As they struggled to accept the reality of emancipation, most planters defined Black freedom in the narrowest manner. As journalist Sidney Andrews discovered late in 1865, "The whites seem wholly unable to comprehend that freedom for the negro means the same thing as freedom for them. They readily enough admit that the government has made him free, but appear to believe that they have the right to exercise the same old control." To southern leaders, freedom still meant hierarchy and mastery; it

THE BARROW PLANTATION

1860

1881

Two maps of the Barrow plantation illustrate the effects of emancipation on rural life in the South. In 1860, slaves lived in communal quarters near the owner's house. Twenty-one years later, former slaves working as sharecroppers lived scattered across the plantation and had their own church and school.

was a privilege not a right, a carefully defined legal status rather than an open-ended entitlement. Certainly, it implied neither economic autonomy nor civil and political equality. A Kentucky newspaper summed up the stance of much of the white South: the former slave was "*free*, but free only to labor."

The Free Labor Vision

Along with former slaves and former masters, the victorious Republican North tried to implement its own vision of freedom. Central to its definition was the antebellum principle of free labor, now further strengthened as a definition of the good society by the Union's triumph. In the free labor vision of a reconstructed South, emancipated Blacks, enjoying the same opportunities for advancement as northern workers, would labor more productively than they had as slaves. At the same time, northern capital and migrants would energize the economy. The South would eventually come to resemble the "free society" of the North, complete with public schools, small towns, and independent farmers. Unified on the basis of free labor, proclaimed Carl Schurz, a refugee from the failed German revolution of 1848 who rose to become a leader of the Republican Party, America would become "a republic, greater, more populous, freer, more prosperous, and more powerful" than any in history.

With planters seeking to establish a labor system as close to slavery as possible, and former slaves demanding economic autonomy and access to land, a long period of conflict over the organization and control of labor followed on plantations throughout the South. It fell to the **Freedmen's Bureau**, an agency established by Congress in March 1865, to attempt to establish a working free labor system.

The Freedmen's Bureau

Under the direction of General O. O. Howard, a graduate of Bowdoin College in Maine and a veteran of the Civil War, the Bureau took on responsibilities that can only be described as daunting. The Bureau was an experiment in government social policy that seems to belong more comfortably to the New Deal of the 1930s or the Great Society of the 1960s (see Chapters 21 and 25, respectively) than to nineteenth-century America. Bureau agents were supposed to establish schools, provide aid to the poor and aged, settle disputes between whites and Blacks and among the freedpeople, and secure for former slaves and white Unionists equal treatment before the courts. "It is not . . . in your power to fulfill one-tenth of the expectations of those who framed the Bureau," General William T. Sherman wrote to Howard. "I fear you have Hercules' task."

Winslow Homer's 1876 painting *The Cotton Pickers*, one of a series of studies of rural life in Virginia, portrays two Black women as dignified figures, without a trace of the stereotyping so common in the era's representations of former slaves. The expressions on their faces are ambiguous, perhaps conveying disappointment that eleven years after the end of slavery they are still at work in the fields.

The Bureau lasted from 1865 to 1870. Even at its peak, there were fewer than 1,000 agents in the entire South. Nonetheless, the Bureau's achievements in some areas, notably education and health care, were striking. While the Bureau did not establish schools itself, it coordinated and helped to finance the activities of northern societies committed to Black education. By 1869, nearly 3,000 schools, serving more than 150,000 pupils in the South, reported to the Bureau. Bureau agents also assumed control of hospitals established by the army during the war, and expanded the system into new communities. They provided medical care to both Black and white southerners. In economic relations, however, the Bureau's activities proved far more problematic.

The Failure of Land Reform

The idea of free labor, wrote one Bureau agent, was "the noblest principle on earth." All that was required to harmonize race relations in the South was fair wages, good working conditions, and the opportunity to improve the laborer's situation in life. But Blacks wanted land of their own, not jobs on plantations. One provision of the law establishing the Bureau gave it the authority to divide abandoned and confiscated land into forty-acre plots for rental and eventual sale to the former slaves.

In the summer of 1865, however, President Andrew Johnson, who had succeeded Lincoln, ordered nearly all land in federal hands returned to its former owners. A series of confrontations followed, notably in South Carolina and Georgia, where the army forcibly evicted Blacks who had settled on "Sherman land." When O. O. Howard, head of the Freedmen's Bureau, traveled to the Sea Islands to inform Blacks of the new policy, he was greeted with disbelief and protest. A committee of former slaves drew up petitions to Howard and President Johnson. "We want Homesteads," they declared, "we were promised Homesteads by the government." Land, the freedmen insisted, was essential to the meaning of freedom. Without it, they declared, "we have not bettered our condition" from the days of slavery—"you will see, this is not the condition of really free men."

Because no land distribution took place, the vast majority of rural freedpeople remained poor and without property during Reconstruction. They had no alternative but to work on white-owned plantations, often for their former owners. Far from being able to rise in the social scale through hard work, Black men were largely confined to farm work, unskilled labor, and service jobs, and Black women to positions in private homes as cooks and maids. Their wages remained too low to allow for any accumulation. By the turn of the century, a significant number of southern African Americans had managed to acquire small parcels of land. But the failure of land reform produced a deep sense of betrayal that survived among the former slaves and their descendants long after the end of Reconstruction. "No sir," Mary Gaffney, an elderly ex-slave, recalled in the 1930s, "we were not given a thing but freedom."

Toward a New South

Out of the conflict on the plantations, new systems of labor emerged in the different regions of the South. The task system, under which workers were assigned daily tasks, completion of which ended their responsibilities for that day, survived in the rice kingdom of South Carolina and Georgia. Closely supervised wage labor predominated on the sugar plantations of southern Louisiana. Sharecropping came to dominate the Cotton Belt and much of the Tobacco Belt of Virginia and North Carolina.

Sharecropping initially arose as a compromise between Blacks' desire for land and planters' demand for labor discipline. The system allowed each Black family to rent a part of a plantation, with the crop divided between worker and owner at the end of the year. Sharecropping guaranteed the planters a stable resident labor force. Former slaves preferred it to gang labor because it offered

SHARECROPPING IN THE SOUTH, 1880

Percentage of farms
sharecropped (by county)

- 35–80%
- 26–34%
- 20–25%
- 13–19%
- 0–12%

VIRGINIA

TENNESSEE

NORTH CAROLINA

ARKANSAS

SOUTH
CAROLINA

TEXAS

MISSISSIPPI

GEORGIA

ALABAMA

LOUISIANA

*Atlantic
Ocean*

Gulf of Mexico

FLORIDA

0   150   200 miles

0   150   200 kilometers

By 1880, sharecropping had become the dominant form of agricultural labor in large parts of the South. The system involved both white and Black farmers.

them the prospect of working without day-to-day white supervision. But as the years went on, sharecropping became more and more oppressive. Share-croppers' economic opportunities were severely limited by a world market in which the price of farm products suffered a prolonged decline.

The White Farmer

The plight of the small farmer was not confined to Blacks in the postwar South. Wartime devastation set in motion a train of events that permanently altered the independent way of life of white yeomen, leading to what they considered a loss of freedom. Before the war, most small farmers had concentrated on raising food for their families and grew little cotton. With much of their property destroyed, many yeomen saw their economic condition worsened by successive crop failures after the war. To obtain supplies from merchants, farmers were forced to take up the growing of cotton and pledge a part of the crop as collateral (property the creditor can seize if a debt is not paid). This system became known as the **crop lien**. Since interest rates were extremely high and the price

From PETITION OF COMMITTEE IN BEHALF OF THE FREEDMEN TO ANDREW JOHNSON (1865)

In the summer of 1865, President Andrew Johnson ordered land that had been distributed to freed slaves in South Carolina and Georgia returned to its former owners. A committee of freedmen drafted a petition asking for the right to obtain land. Johnson did not, however, change his policy.

We the freedmen of Edisto Island, South Carolina, have learned from you through Major General O. O. Howard . . . with deep sorrow and painful hearts of the possibility of [the] government restoring these lands to the former owners. We are well aware of the many perplexing and trying questions that burden your mind, and therefore pray to god (the preserver of all, and who has through our late and beloved President [Lincoln's] proclamation and the war made us a free people) that he may guide you in making your decisions and give you that wisdom that cometh from above to settle these great and important questions for the best interests of the country and the colored race.

Here is where secession was born and nurtured. Here is where we have toiled nearly all our lives as slaves and treated like dumb driven cattle. This is our home, we have made these lands what they were, we are the only true and loyal people that were found in possession of these lands. We have been always ready to strike for liberty and humanity, yea to fight if need be to preserve this glorious Union. Shall not we who are freedmen and have always been true to this Union have the same rights as are enjoyed by others? . . . Are not our rights as a free people and good citizens of these United States to be considered before those who were found in rebellion against this good and just government? . . .

[Are] we who have been abused and oppressed for many long years not to be allowed the privilege of purchasing land but be subject to the will of these large land owners? God forbid. Land monopoly is injurious to the advancement of the course of freedom, and if government does not make some provision by which we as freedmen can obtain a homestead, we have not bettered our condition. . . .

We look to you . . . for protection and equal rights with the privilege of purchasing a homestead—a homestead right here in the heart of South Carolina.

From A SHARECROPPING CONTRACT (1866)

Few former slaves were able to acquire land in the post–Civil War South. Most ended up as sharecroppers, working on white-owned land for a share of the crop at the end of the growing season. This contract, typical of thousands of others, originated in Tennessee. The laborers signed with an X, as they were illiterate.

Thomas J. Ross agrees to employ the Freedmen to plant and raise a crop on his Rosstown Plantation. . . . On the following Rules, Regulations and Remunerations.

The said Ross agrees to furnish the land to cultivate, and a sufficient number of mules & horses and feed them to make and house said crop and all necessary farming utensils to carry on the same and to give unto said Freedmen whose names appear below one half of all the cotton, corn and wheat that is raised on said place for the year 1866 after all the necessary expenses are deducted out that accrues on said crop. Outside of the Freedmen's labor in harvesting, carrying to market and selling the same the said Freedmen . . . covenant and agrees to and with said Thomas J. Ross that for and in consideration of one half of the crop before mentioned that they will plant, cultivate, and raise under the management control and Superintendence of said Ross, in good faith, a cotton, corn and oat crop under his management for the year 1866. And we the said Freedmen agrees to furnish ourselves & families in provisions, clothing, medicine and medical bills and all, and every kind of other expenses that we may incur on said plantation for the year 1866 free of charge to said Ross. Should the said Ross furnish us any of the above supplies or any other kind of expenses, during said year, [we] are to settle and pay him out of the net proceeds of our part of the crop the retail price of the county at time of sale or any price we may agree upon—The said Ross shall keep a regular book account, against each and every one or the head of every family to be adjusted and settled at the end of the year.

We furthermore bind ourselves to and with said Ross that we will do good work and labor ten hours a day on an average, winter and summer. . . . We further agree that we will lose all lost time, or pay at the rate of one dollar per day, rainy days excepted. In sickness and women lying in childbed are to lose the time and account for it to the other hands out of his or her part of the crop. . . .

We furthermore bind ourselves that we will obey the orders of said Ross in all things in carrying out and managing said crop for said year and be docked for disobedience. All is responsible for all farming utensils that is on hand or may be placed in care of said Freedmen for the year 1866 to said Ross and are also responsible to said Ross if we carelessly, maliciously maltreat any of his stock for said year to said Ross for damages to be assessed out of our wages.

Samuel (X) Johnson, Thomas (X) Richard, Tinny (X) Fitch, Jessie (X) Simmons, Sophe (X) Pruden, Henry (X) Pruden, Frances (X) Pruden, Elijah (X) Smith

QUESTIONS

1. *Why do the Black petitioners believe that owning land is essential to the enjoyment of freedom?*

2. *In what ways does the contract limit the freedom of the laborers?*

3. *What do these documents suggest about competing definitions of Black freedom in the aftermath of slavery?*

of cotton fell steadily, many farmers found themselves still in debt after marketing their portion of the crop at year's end. They had no choice but to continue to plant cotton to obtain new loans. By the mid-1870s, white farmers, who cultivated only 10 percent of the South's cotton crop in 1860, were growing 40 percent, and many who had owned their land had fallen into dependency as sharecroppers, who now rented land owned by others.

Both Black and white farmers found themselves caught in the sharecropping and crop-lien systems. A far higher percentage of Black than white farmers in the South rented land rather than owned it. But every census from 1880 to 1940 counted more white than Black sharecroppers. The workings of sharecropping and the crop-lien system are illustrated by the case of Matt Brown, a Mississippi farmer who borrowed money each year from a local merchant. He began 1892 with a debt of $226 held over from the previous year. By 1893, although he produced cotton worth $171, Brown's debt had increased to $402, because he had borrowed $33 for food, $29 for clothing, $173 for supplies, and $112 for other items. Brown never succeeded in getting out of debt. He died in 1905; the last entry under his name in the merchant's account book is a coffin.

The Urban South

Even as the rural South stagnated economically, southern cities experienced remarkable growth after the Civil War. As railroads penetrated the interior, they enabled merchants in market centers like Atlanta to trade directly with the North, bypassing coastal cities that had traditionally monopolized southern commerce. A new urban middle class of merchants, railroad promoters, and bankers reaped the benefits of the spread of cotton production in the postwar South.

Thus, Reconstruction brought about profound changes in the lives of southerners, Black and white, rich and poor. In place of the prewar world of master, slave, and self-sufficient yeoman, the postwar South was peopled by new social classes—landowning employers, Black and white sharecroppers, cotton-producing white farmers, wage-earning Black laborers, and urban entrepreneurs. Each of these groups turned to Reconstruction politics in an attempt to shape to its own advantage the aftermath of emancipation.

Aftermath of Slavery

The United States, of course, was not the only society to confront the transition from slavery to freedom. In similar struggles across the Western Hemisphere, former planters (or, in Haiti, where the planter class had been destroyed, the government itself) tried to encourage or require former slaves to go back to work on plantations to grow the same crops as under slavery. Planters elsewhere held the same stereotypical views of Black laborers as were voiced by their counterparts in the United States—former slaves were supposedly lazy, were lacking in ambition, and thought that freedom meant an absence of labor.

For their part, former slaves throughout the hemisphere tried to carve out as much independence as possible, both in their daily lives and in their labor. They attempted to reconstruct family life by withdrawing women and children from field labor (in the West Indies, women turned to

Chinese laborers at work on a Louisiana plantation during Reconstruction.

marketing their families' crops to earn income). Wherever possible, former slaves acquired land of their own and devoted more time to growing food for their families than to growing crops for the international market. In many places, the plantations either fell to pieces, as in Haiti, or continued operating with a new labor force composed of indentured servants from India and China, as in Jamaica, Trinidad, and British Guiana. Southern planters in the United States brought in a few Chinese laborers in an attempt to replace freedmen, but since the federal government opposed such efforts, the Chinese remained only a tiny proportion of the southern workforce.

But if struggles over land and labor united its postemancipation experience with that of other societies, in one respect the United States was unique. Only in the United States were former slaves, within two years of the end of slavery, granted the right to vote and, thus, given a major share of political power. Few anticipated this development when the Civil War ended. It came about as the result of one of the greatest political crises of American history—the battle between President Andrew Johnson and Congress over Reconstruction. The struggle resulted in profound changes in the nature of citizenship, the structure of constitutional authority, and the meaning of American freedom.

THE MAKING OF RADICAL RECONSTRUCTION

Andrew Johnson

To Lincoln's successor, Andrew Johnson, fell the task of overseeing the restoration of the Union. Born in poverty in North Carolina, as a youth Johnson worked as a tailor's apprentice. After moving to Tennessee, he achieved success through politics. Beginning as an alderman (a town official), he rose to serve in the state legislature, Congress, and for two terms as governor of Tennessee. Johnson identified himself as the champion of his state's "honest yeomen" and a foe of large planters, whom he described as a "bloated, corrupted aristocracy." A strong defender of the Union, he became the only senator from a seceding state to remain at his post in Washington, D.C., when the Civil War began. When northern forces occupied Tennessee, Abraham Lincoln named him military governor. In 1864, Republicans nominated him to run for vice president as a symbol of the party's hope of extending its organization into the South.

In personality and outlook, Johnson proved unsuited for the responsibilities he shouldered after Lincoln's death. A lonely, stubborn man, he was intolerant of criticism and unable to compromise. He lacked Lincoln's political skills and keen sense of public opinion. A fervent believer in states' rights, Johnson insisted that since secession was illegal, the southern states had never actually left the Union or surrendered the right to govern their own affairs. Moreover, while Johnson had supported emancipation once Lincoln made it a goal of the war effort, he held deeply racist views. African Americans, Johnson believed, had no role to play in Reconstruction.

The Failure of Presidential Reconstruction

A little over a month after Lee's surrender at Appomattox, and with Congress out of session until December, Johnson in May 1865 outlined his plan for reuniting the nation. He issued a series of proclamations that began the period of Presidential Reconstruction (1865–1867). Johnson offered a pardon (which restored political and property rights, except for slaves) to nearly all white southerners who took an oath of allegiance to the Union. He excluded Confederate leaders and wealthy planters whose prewar property had been valued at more than $20,000. This exemption suggested at first that Johnson planned a more punitive Reconstruction than Lincoln had intended. Most of those exempted, however, soon received individual pardons from the president. Johnson also appointed provisional governors and ordered them to call state conventions, elected by whites alone, that would establish loyal governments in the South. Apart from the requirement that they abolish slavery, repudiate secession, and refuse to pay the Confederate debt—all unavoidable consequences of southern defeat—he granted the new governments a free hand in managing local affairs.

At first, most northerners believed Johnson's policy deserved a chance to succeed. The conduct of the southern governments elected under his program, however, turned most of the Republican North against the president. By and large, white southern voters returned prominent Confederates and members of the old elite to power. Reports of violence directed against former slaves and northern visitors in the South further alarmed Republicans.

The Black Codes

But what aroused the most opposition to Johnson's Reconstruction policy were the **Black Codes**, laws passed by the new southern governments that attempted to regulate the lives of the former slaves. These laws granted Blacks certain rights, such as legalized marriage, ownership of property, and limited access to the courts. But they denied them the rights to testify against whites, to serve on juries or in state militias, or to vote. And in response to planters' demands that the freedpeople be required to work on the plantations, the Black Codes declared that those who failed to sign yearly labor contracts could be arrested and hired out to white landowners. Some states limited the occupations open to Blacks and barred them from acquiring land, and others provided that judges could assign Black children to work for their former owners without the consent of the parents. "We are not permitted to own the land whereon to build a schoolhouse or a church," complained a Black convention in Mississippi. "Where is justice? Where is freedom?"

Clearly, the death of slavery did not automatically mean the birth of freedom. But the Black Codes so completely violated free labor principles that they called forth a vigorous response from the Republican North. Wars—especially civil wars—often generate hostility and bitterness. But few groups of rebels in history have been treated more leniently than the defeated Confederates. A handful of southern leaders were arrested but most were quickly released. Only one was executed—Henry Wirz, the commander of Andersonville prison, where thousands of Union prisoners of war had died. Most of the Union army was swiftly demobilized. What motivated the North's turn against Johnson's policies was not a desire to "punish" the white South, but the inability of the South's political leaders to accept the reality of emancipation. "We must see to it," announced Republican senator William Stewart of Nevada, "that the man made free by the Constitution of the United States is a freeman indeed."

The Radical Republicans

When Congress assembled in December 1865, Johnson announced that with loyal governments functioning in all the southern states, the nation had been reunited. In response, Radical Republicans, who had grown increasingly disenchanted with Johnson during the summer and fall, called for the dissolution

Thaddeus Stevens, leader of the Radical Republicans in the House of Representatives during Reconstruction.

of these governments and the establishment of new ones with "rebels" excluded from power and Black men guaranteed the right to vote. Radicals tended to represent constituencies in New England and the "burned-over" districts of the rural North that had been home to religious revivalism, abolitionism, and other reform movements. Although they differed on many issues, Radicals shared the conviction that Union victory created a golden opportunity to institutionalize the principle of equal rights for all, regardless of race.

The Radicals fully embraced the expanded powers of the federal government born during the Civil War. Traditions of federalism and states' rights, they insisted, must not obstruct a sweeping national effort to protect the rights of all Americans. The most prominent Radicals in Congress were Charles Sumner, a senator from Massachusetts, and Thaddeus Stevens, a lawyer and iron manufacturer who represented Pennsylvania in the House of Representatives. Before the Civil War, both had been outspoken foes of slavery and defenders of Black rights. "The same national authority," declared Sumner, "that destroyed slavery must see that this other pretension [racial inequality] is not permitted to survive."

Thaddeus Stevens's most cherished aim was to confiscate the land of disloyal planters and divide it among former slaves and northern migrants to the South. "The whole fabric of southern society," he declared, "*must* be changed. Without this, this Government can never be, as it has never been, a true republic." But his plan to make "small independent landholders" of the former slaves proved too radical even for many of his Radical colleagues. Congress, to be sure, had already offered free land to settlers in the West in the Homestead Act of 1862. But this land had been in the possession of the federal government, not private individuals (although originally, of course, it had belonged to Indians). Most congressmen believed too deeply in the sanctity of property rights to be willing to take land from one group of owners and distribute it to others. Stevens's proposal failed to pass.

The Origins of Civil Rights

With the South unrepresented, Republicans enjoyed an overwhelming majority in Congress. But the party was internally divided. Most Republicans were moderates, not Radicals. Moderates believed that Johnson's plan was flawed, but they desired to work with the president to modify it. They feared that neither northern nor southern whites would accept Black suffrage. Moderates and Radicals joined in refusing to seat the southerners recently elected to Congress, but moderates broke with the Radicals by leaving the Johnson governments in place.

Early in 1866, Senator Lyman Trumbull of Illinois proposed two bills, reflecting the moderates' belief that Johnson's policy required modification. The first extended the life of the Freedmen's Bureau, which had originally been established for only one year. The second, the **Civil Rights Bill of 1866**, was described by one congressman as "one of the most important bills ever presented to the House for its action." It defined all persons born in the United States as citizens and spelled out rights they were to enjoy without regard to race. Equality before the law was central to the measure—no longer could states enact laws like the Black Codes discriminating between white and Black citizens. So were free labor values. According to the law, no state could deprive any citizen of the right to make contracts, bring lawsuits, or enjoy equal protection of one's person and property. These, said Trumbull, were the "fundamental rights belonging to every man as a free man." The bill made no mention of the right to vote for Blacks. In constitutional terms, the Civil Rights Bill represented the first attempt to give concrete meaning to the Thirteenth Amendment, which had abolished slavery, to define in law the essence of freedom.

To the surprise of Congress, Johnson vetoed both bills. Both, he said, would centralize power in the national government and deprive the states of the authority to regulate their own affairs. Moreover, he argued, Blacks did not deserve the rights of citizenship. By acting to secure their rights, Congress was discriminating "against the white race." The vetoes made a breach between the president and nearly the entire Republican Party inevitable. Congress failed by a single vote to muster the two-thirds majority necessary to override the veto of the Freedmen's Bureau Bill (although later in 1866, it did extend the Bureau's life to 1870). But in April 1866, the Civil Rights Bill became the first major law in American history to be passed over a presidential veto.

The Fourteenth Amendment

Congress now proceeded to adopt its own plan of Reconstruction. In June, it approved and sent to the states for ratification the **Fourteenth Amendment**, which placed in the Constitution the principle of birthright citizenship, except for Native Americans subject to tribal authority, and empowered the federal government to protect the rights of all Americans. The amendment prohibited the states from abridging the "privileges or immunities" of citizens or denying to any person the "equal protection of the laws." This broad language opened the door for future Congresses and the federal courts to breathe meaning into the guarantee of legal equality.

In a compromise between the radical and moderate positions on Black suffrage, the amendment did not grant Blacks the right to vote. But it did provide that if a state denied the vote to any group of men, that state's representation in Congress would be reduced. (This penalty did not apply when states barred women from voting.) The abolition of slavery threatened to increase southern political power, since now all Blacks, not merely three-fifths as in the case of slaves, would be counted in determining a state's representation in Congress. The Fourteenth Amendment offered the leaders of the white South a choice—allow Black men to vote and keep their state's full representation in the House of Representatives, or limit the vote to whites and sacrifice part of their political power.

The Fourteenth Amendment produced an intense division between the parties. Not a single Democrat in Congress voted in its favor, and only 4 of 175 Republicans were opposed. Radicals, to be sure, expressed their disappointment that the amendment did not guarantee Black suffrage. (It was far from perfect, Stevens told the House, but he intended to vote for it, "because I live among men and not among angels.") Nonetheless, by writing into the Constitution the principle that equality before the law regardless of race is a fundamental right of all Americans, the amendment made the most important change in that document since the adoption of the Bill of Rights.

The Reconstruction Act

The Fourteenth Amendment became the central issue of the political campaign of 1866. Johnson embarked on a speaking tour of the North, called by journalists the "swing around the circle," to urge voters to elect members of Congress committed to his own Reconstruction program. Denouncing his critics, the president made wild accusations that the Radicals were plotting to assassinate him. His behavior further undermined public support for his policies, as did riots that broke out in Memphis and New Orleans, in which white policemen and citizens killed dozens of Blacks.

In the northern congressional elections that fall, Republicans opposed to Johnson's policies won a sweeping victory. Nonetheless, at the president's urging, every southern state but Tennessee refused to ratify the Fourteenth Amendment. The intransigence of Johnson and the bulk of the white South

Reconstruction, an elaborate allegory of national reconciliation, equality, and progress, designed by Horatio Bateman and printed in 1867. The overall message is that Reconstruction, grounded in liberty and equality, will restore goodwill between the sections and races. The structure at the center symbolizes the federal government; it is being rebuilt as Black and white men carry new pillars, representing the states, to support it. The old bases of some of the columns, called "Foundations of Slavery," are being replaced by new ones representing Liberty, Justice, and Education. Under the dome, former rivals shake hands, including Generals Grant and Lee, and Republican editor Horace Greeley and Jefferson Davis. Scenes surrounding it include a schoolyard, men and women voting, and Indians and whites sitting together. At the top are the heads of great figures of American history, as well as other historical characters including Joan of Arc, John Milton, and Jesus Christ. The eagle at the center carries a streamer reading: "All men are born free and equal."

pushed moderate Republicans toward the Radicals. In March 1867, over Johnson's veto, Congress adopted the **Reconstruction Act**, which temporarily divided the South into five military districts and called for the creation of new state governments, with Black men given the right to vote. Thus began the period of Radical Reconstruction, which lasted until 1877. But the conflict between President Johnson and Congress did not end with the passage of the Reconstruction Act.

Impeachment and the Election of Grant

In March 1867, Congress adopted the **Tenure of Office Act**, barring the president from removing certain officeholders, including cabinet members, without the consent of the Senate. Johnson considered this an unconstitutional restriction on his authority. In February 1868, he dismissed Secretary of War Edwin M. Stanton, an ally of the Radicals. The House of Representatives responded by approving articles of **impeachment**—that is, it presented charges against Johnson to the Senate, which had to decide whether to remove him from office.

That spring, for the first time in American history, a president was placed on trial before the Senate for "high crimes and misdemeanors." By this point, virtually all Republicans considered Johnson a failure as president. But some moderates disliked Benjamin F. Wade, a Radical who, as temporary president of the Senate, would become president if Johnson were removed. Others feared that conviction would damage the constitutional separation of powers between Congress and the executive. Johnson's lawyers assured moderate Republicans that, if acquitted, he would stop interfering with Reconstruction policy. The final tally was 35–19 to convict Johnson, one vote short of the two-thirds necessary to remove him. Seven Republicans joined the Democrats in voting to acquit the president.

A few days after the vote, Republicans nominated Ulysses S. Grant, the Union's most prominent military hero, as their candidate for president. Grant's Democratic opponent was Horatio Seymour, the former governor of New York. Reconstruction became the central issue of the bitterly fought 1868 campaign. Republicans identified their opponents with secession and treason, a tactic known as "waving the bloody shirt." Democrats denounced Reconstruction as unconstitutional and condemned Black suffrage as a violation of America's political traditions. They appealed openly to racism. Seymour's running mate, Francis P. Blair Jr., charged Republicans with placing the South under the rule of "a semi-barbarous race" who longed to "subject the white women to their unbridled lust."

The Fifteenth Amendment

Grant won the election of 1868, although by a margin—300,000 of 6 million votes cast—that many Republicans found uncomfortably slim. The result led Congress to adopt the era's third and final amendment to the Constitution. In February 1869, it approved the **Fifteenth Amendment**, which prohibited the federal and state governments from denying any citizen the right to vote because of race. Bitterly opposed by the Democratic Party, it was ratified in 1870.

Although the Fifteenth Amendment left the door open to suffrage restrictions not explicitly based on race—literacy tests, property qualifications, and poll taxes—and did not extend the right to vote to women, it marked the culmination of four decades of abolitionist agitation. As late as 1868, even after Congress had enfranchised Black men in the South, only eight northern states allowed African American men to vote. With the Fifteenth Amendment, the American Anti-Slavery Society disbanded, its work, its members believed, now complete. "Nothing in all history," exclaimed veteran abolitionist William Lloyd Garrison, equaled "this wonderful, quiet, sudden transformation of four millions of human beings from . . . the auction-block to the ballot-box."

The Second Founding

The laws and amendments of Reconstruction reflected the intersection of two products of the Civil War era—a newly empowered national state and the idea of a national citizenry enjoying equality before the law. What Republican leader Carl Schurz called the "great Constitutional revolution" of Reconstruction transformed the federal system and with it, the language of freedom so central to American political culture.

The principle of equality before the law, moreover, did not apply only to the South. The Reconstruction amendments voided many northern laws discriminating on the basis of race. As one congressman noted, the amendments expanded the liberty of whites as well as Blacks, including "the millions of people of foreign birth who will flock to our shores."

The new amendments also transformed the relationship between the federal government and the states. The Bill of Rights had linked civil liberties to the autonomy of the states. Its language—"Congress shall make no law"—reflected the belief that concentrated national power posed the greatest threat to freedom. The authors of the Reconstruction amendments assumed that rights required national power to enforce them. Rather than a threat to liberty, the federal government, in Charles Sumner's words, had become "the custodian of freedom."

The Reconstruction amendments transformed the Constitution from a document primarily concerned with federal-state relations and the rights of property into a vehicle through which members of vulnerable minorities could stake a claim to freedom and seek protection against misconduct by all levels of government. In the twentieth century, many of the Supreme Court's most important decisions expanding the rights of American citizens were based on the Fourteenth Amendment, including the 1954 *Brown* ruling that outlawed school segregation and the decision in 2015 preventing states from discriminating against gay Americans in the right to marry.

Together with far-reaching congressional legislation meant to secure to former slaves access to the courts, ballot box, and public accommodations, and to protect them against violence, the Reconstruction amendments transferred much of the authority to define citizens' rights from the states to the nation. They were crucial in creating the world's first biracial democracy, in which people only a few years removed from slavery exercised significant political power. Introducing into the Constitution for the first time the words "equal protection of the law" and "the right to vote" (along with "male," to the outrage of the era's advocates of women's rights), the amendments both reflected and reinforced a new era of individual rights consciousness among Americans of all races and backgrounds.

Today, the legal doctrine of birthright citizenship sets the United States apart. Most countries, including every one in Europe, limit automatic access to citizenship via ethnicity, culture, or religion. Birthright citizenship remains an eloquent statement about the nature of American society and a repudiation of a long history of equating citizenship with whiteness.

So profound were these changes that the amendments are frequently seen not simply as an alteration of an existing structure but as a second founding, which created a fundamentally new document with a new definition of both the status of Blacks and the rights of all Americans.

Boundaries of Freedom

Reconstruction redrew the boundaries of American freedom. Lines of exclusion that limited the privileges of citizenship to white men had long been central to the practice of American democracy. Only in an unparalleled crisis could they have been replaced, even temporarily, by the vision of a republic of equals embracing Black Americans as well as white. That the United States was a "white man's government" had been a widespread belief before the Civil War. It is not difficult to understand why Andrew Johnson, in one of his veto messages, claimed that federal protection of Blacks' civil rights violated "all our experience as a people."

Another illustration of the new spirit of racial inclusiveness was the Burlingame Treaty, negotiated by Anson Burlingame, an antislavery congressman from Massachusetts before being named American envoy to China. Other treaties with China had been one-sided, securing trading and political advantages for European powers. The Burlingame Treaty reaffirmed China's national sovereignty, and provided reciprocal protection for religious freedom and against discrimination for citizens of each country emigrating or visiting the other. When Burlingame died, Mark Twain wrote a eulogy that

From FREDERICK DOUGLASS, "THE COMPOSITE NATION" (1869)

In a remarkable speech delivered in Boston, Frederick Douglass condemned anti-Asian discrimination and called for giving Chinese immigrants all the rights of other Americans, including the right to vote. Douglass's vision of a country made up of people of all races and national origins—and enjoying equal rights—was too radical for the time and remains controversial today.

We are a country of all extremes, ends and opposites; the most conspicuous example of composite nationality in the world. Our people defy all the ethnological and logical classifications. In races we range all the way from Black to white, with intermediate shades which . . . no man can name a number. . . . Our land is capable of supporting one fifth of all the globe. Here, labor is abundant and here labor is better remunerated than anywhere else. All moral, social and geographical causes conspire to bring to us the peoples of all other over-populated countries.

Europe and Africa are already here, and the Indian was here before either. . . . Heretofore the policy of our government has been governed by race pride, rather than by wisdom. . . . Before the relations of [Blacks and Indians] are satisfactorily settled, and in spite of all opposition, a new race is making its appearance within our borders, and claiming attention [the Chinese]. . . . Do you ask, if I favor such immigration. I answer *I would.* Would you have them naturalized, and have them invested with all the rights of American citizenship? *I would.* Would you allow them to hold office? *I would.* . . .

There are such things in the world as human rights. They rest upon no conventional foundation, but are external, universal, and indestructible. Among these, is the right of locomotion; the right of migration; the right which belongs to no particular race, but belongs alike to all. . . . We shall mold them all . . . into Americans; Indian and Celt, Negro and Saxon, Latin and Teuton, Mongolian and Caucasian, Jew and Gentile, all shall here bow to the same law, speak the same language, support the same government, enjoy the same liberty.

QUESTIONS

1. *What is Douglass's answer to the question, "Who is an American?"*

2. *Why does he believe that being able to move freely from one country to another should be considered a universal human right?*

praised him for "outgrow[ing] the narrow citizenship of a state [to] become a citizen of the world."

Reconstruction Republicans' belief in universal rights had its limits. In his remarkable "Composite Nation" speech of 1869, Frederick Douglass condemned prejudice against immigrants from China. America's destiny, he declared, was to transcend race by serving as an asylum for people from all corners of the globe. A year later, Charles Sumner moved to strike the word "white" from naturalization requirements. Senators from the western states objected. At their insistence, the naturalization law was amended to make Africans eligible to obtain citizenship when immigrating from abroad. But Asians remained ineligible. The racial boundaries of nationality had been redrawn but not eliminated. The juxtaposition of the amended naturalization law and the Fourteenth Amendment created a significant division in the Asian American community. Well into the twentieth century, Asian immigrants could not become citizens, but their U.S.-born children automatically did.

Reconstruction in Indian Territory

Even though they had not been part of the Union, enjoying their own sovereignty, Indian nations that had sided with the Confederacy were treated after the Civil War as secessionists. During Reconstruction, federal agents negotiated new treaties with pro-Confederate Native American nations in Indian Territory. They included provisions for the abolition of slavery and, in some cases, citizenship and equal rights for former slaves of Native Americans. They required tribes to cede much of their land to the federal government and provided for the construction of railroads through Indian Territory. In some cases, Native nations were forced to provide land to their former slaves—the only slaveholders anywhere in the United States who were required to do so. Like many southern whites, former Indian slaveholders for generations rejected the equality of their emancipated slaves. Indeed, the status of the descendants of Native Americans' slaves remains a source of controversy to this day. The Cherokee Constitution was recently amended to exclude them from citizenship, leading to lawsuits that have yet to be resolved.

The Rights of Women

"The contest with the South that destroyed slavery," wrote the Philadelphia lawyer Sidney George Fisher in his diary, "has caused an immense increase in the popular passion for liberty and equality." But advocates of women's rights encountered the limits of the Reconstruction commitment to equality. Women activists saw Reconstruction as the moment to claim their own emancipation.

The rewriting of the Constitution, declared suffrage leader Olympia Brown, offered the opportunity to sever the blessings of freedom from sex as well as race and to "bury the Black man and the woman in the citizen."

The destruction of slavery led feminists to search for ways to make the promise of free labor real for women. Every issue of the new women's rights journal, *The Agitator*, edited by Mary Livermore, who had led fund-raising efforts for aid to Union soldiers during the war, carried stories complaining of limited job opportunities and unequal pay for females who entered the labor market. Other feminists debated how to achieve "liberty for married women." Demands for liberalizing divorce laws (which generally required evidence of adultery, desertion, or extreme abuse to terminate a marriage) and for recognizing "woman's control over her own body" (including protection against domestic violence and access to what later generations would call birth control) moved to the center of many feminists' concerns. "Our rotten marriage institution," one Ohio woman wrote, "is the main obstacle in the way of woman's freedom."

Feminists and Radicals

In one place, women's political rights did expand during Reconstruction—not, however, in a bastion of radicalism such as Massachusetts, but in the Wyoming territory. This had less to do with the era's egalitarian impulse than with the desire to attract female immigrants to an area where men outnumbered women five to one. In 1869, Wyoming's diminutive legislature (it consisted of fewer than twenty men) extended the right to vote to women, and the bill was then signed by the governor, a federal appointee. Wyoming entered the Union in 1890, becoming the first state since New Jersey in the late eighteenth century to allow women to vote.

In general, however, talk of woman suffrage and redesigning marriage found few sympathetic male listeners. Even Radical Republicans insisted that Reconstruction was the "Negro's hour" (the hour, that is, of the Black male). The Fourteenth Amendment for the first time introduced the word "male" into the Constitution, in its clause penalizing a state for denying any group of men the right to vote. The Fifteenth Amendment outlawed discrimination in voting based on race but not gender. These measures produced a bitter split both between feminists and Radical Republicans, and within feminist circles.

Some leaders, like Stanton and Susan B. Anthony, opposed the Fifteenth Amendment because it did nothing to enfranchise women. They denounced their former abolitionist allies and moved to sever the women's rights movement from its earlier moorings in the antislavery tradition. On occasion, they appealed to racial and ethnic prejudices, arguing that native-born white

A Delegation of Advocates of Woman Suffrage Addressing the House Judiciary Committee, an engraving from *Frank Leslie's Illustrated Newspaper*, February 4, 1871. The group includes Elizabeth Cady Stanton, seated just to the right of the speaker, and Susan B. Anthony, at the table on the extreme right.

women deserved the vote more than non-whites and immigrants. "Patrick and Sambo and Hans and Yung Tung, who do not know the difference between a monarchy and a republic," declared Stanton, had no right to be "making laws for [feminist leader] Lucretia Mott."

Other abolitionist-feminists, like Abby Kelley and Lucy Stone, insisted that despite their limitations, the Reconstruction amendments represented steps in the direction of truly universal suffrage and should be supported. Even though the Fifteenth Amendment did nothing to secure their right to vote, most Black women activists felt that the enfranchisement of Black men was necessary for the advancement of the entire race.

The result was a split in the movement and the creation in 1869 of two hostile women's rights organizations—the National Woman Suffrage Association, led by Stanton, and the American Woman Suffrage Association, with Lucy Stone as president. They would not reunite until 1890. Few Black women joined either organization. Instead, they created their own local clubs and associations, often based in Black churches, to press not only for the right to vote but also for the ability to travel freely without encountering harassment as well as action against lynching.

Thus, even as it rejected the racial definition of freedom that had emerged in the first half of the nineteenth century, Reconstruction left the gender boundary largely intact. When women tried to use the rewritten legal code and Constitution to claim equal rights, they found the courts unreceptive. Myra Bradwell invoked the idea of free labor in challenging an Illinois rule limiting the practice of law to men, but the Supreme Court in 1873 rebuffed her claim. Free labor principles, the justices declared, did not apply to women, since "the law of the Creator" had assigned them to "the domestic sphere."

Despite their limitations, the Fourteenth and Fifteenth Amendments and the Reconstruction Act of 1867 marked a radical departure in American history. "We have cut loose from the whole dead past," wrote Timothy Howe, a Republican senator from Wisconsin, "and have cast our anchor out a hundred years" into the future. The Reconstruction Act of 1867 inaugurated America's first real experiment in interracial democracy.

RADICAL RECONSTRUCTION IN THE SOUTH

"The Tocsin of Freedom"

Among the former slaves, the passage of the Reconstruction Act inspired an outburst of political organization. At mass political meetings—community gatherings attended by men, women, and children—African Americans staked their claim to equal citizenship. Blacks, declared an Alabama meeting, deserved "exactly the same rights, privileges and immunities as are enjoyed by white men. We ask for nothing more and will be content with nothing less."

These gatherings inspired direct action to remedy long-standing grievances. Hundreds took part in sit-ins that integrated horse-drawn public streetcars in cities across the South. Plantation workers organized strikes for higher wages. Speakers, male and female, fanned out across the South. Frances Ellen Watkins Harper, a black veteran of the abolitionist movement, embarked on a two-year tour, lecturing on "Literacy, Land, and Liberation." She addressed her remarks to white southerners as well as emancipated slaves: "We are all bound up together in one great bundle of humanity, and society cannot trample on the weakest and feeblest of its members without receiving the curse in its own soul."

Determined to exercise their new rights as citizens, thousands joined the Union League, an organization closely linked to the Republican Party, and the vast majority of eligible African Americans registered to vote. James K. Green, a former slave in Hale County, Alabama, and a League organizer, went on to serve eight years in the Alabama legislature. In the 1880s, Green looked back on his political career. Before the war, he declared, "I was entirely ignorant; I knew nothing more than to obey my master; and there were thousands of us in the same attitude. . . . But the tocsin [warning bell] of freedom sounded and knocked at the door and we walked out like free men and shouldered the responsibilities."

By 1870, all the former Confederate states had been readmitted to the Union, and in a region where the Republican Party had not existed before the war, nearly all were under Republican control. Their new state constitutions, drafted in 1868 and 1869 by the first public bodies in American history with substantial Black representation, marked a considerable improvement over those they replaced. The constitutions established the region's first state-funded systems of free public education and created new penitentiaries, orphan asylums, and homes for the insane. They guaranteed equality of civil and political rights and abolished practices of the antebellum era such as whipping as a punishment for crime, property qualifications for officeholding, and imprisonment for debt. A few states initially barred former Confederates from voting, but this policy was quickly abandoned by the new state governments.

The Black Officeholder

From the Plantation to the Senate, an 1883 lithograph celebrating African American progress during Reconstruction. Among the Black leaders pictured at the top are Reconstruction congressmen Benjamin S. Turner, Josiah T. Walls, and Joseph H. Rainey; Hiram Revels of Mississippi, the first African American senator; religious leader Richard Allen; and abolitionists Frederick Douglass and William Wells Brown. At the center emancipated slaves work in the cotton fields, and below children attend school and a Black family stands outside its home.

Throughout Reconstruction, Black voters provided the bulk of the Republican Party's support. But African Americans did not control Reconstruction politics, as their opponents frequently charged. The highest offices remained almost entirely in white hands, and only in South Carolina, where Blacks made up 60 percent of the population, did they form a majority of the legislature. Nonetheless, the fact that some 2,000 African Americans occupied public offices during Reconstruction represented a fundamental shift of power in the South and a radical departure in American government.

African Americans were represented at every level of government. Fourteen were elected to the national House of Representatives. Two Blacks served in the U.S. Senate during Reconstruction, both representing Mississippi. Hiram Revels, who had been born free in North Carolina, was educated in Illinois, and served as a chaplain in the wartime Union army, in 1870 became the first Black senator in American history. The second, Blanche K. Bruce, a former slave, was elected in 1875. The next African American elected to the Senate was Edward W. Brooke of Massachusetts, who served 1967–1978.

Pinckney B. S. Pinchback of Louisiana, the Georgia-born son of a white planter and a free Black woman, served briefly during the winter of 1872–1873 as America's first Black governor. More than a century would pass before L. Douglas Wilder of Virginia, elected in 1989, became the second. Some 700 Blacks sat in state legislatures during Reconstruction, and scores held local offices ranging from justice of the peace to sheriff, tax assessor, and policeman. The presence of Black officeholders and their white allies made a real difference in southern life, ensuring that Blacks accused of crimes would be tried before juries of their peers and enforcing fairness in such aspects of local government as road repair, tax assessment, and poor relief.

In South Carolina and Louisiana, homes of the South's wealthiest and best-educated free Black communities, most prominent Reconstruction office-holders had never experienced slavery. In addition, a number of Black Reconstruction officials, like Pennsylvania-born Jonathan J. Wright, who served on the South Carolina Supreme Court, had come from the North after the Civil War. The majority, however, were former slaves who had established their leadership in the Black community by serving in the Union army, working as ministers, teachers, or skilled craftsmen, or engaging in Union League organizing. Among the most celebrated Black officeholders was Robert Smalls, who had worked as a slave on the Charleston docks before the Civil War and who won national fame in 1862 by secretly guiding the *Planter*, a Confederate vessel, out of the harbor and delivering it to Union forces. Smalls became a powerful political leader on the South Carolina Sea Islands and was elected to five terms in Congress.

Carpetbaggers and Scalawags

The new southern governments also brought to power new groups of whites. Many Reconstruction officials were northerners who for one reason or another made their homes in the South after the war. Their opponents dubbed them **carpetbaggers**, implying that they had packed all their belongings in a suitcase and left their homes in order to reap the spoils of office in the South. Some carpetbaggers were undoubtedly corrupt adventurers. The large majority, however, were former Union soldiers who decided to remain in the South when the war ended, before there was any prospect of going into politics. Others were investors in land and railroads who saw in the postwar South an opportunity to combine personal economic advancement with a role in helping to substitute, as one wrote, "the civilization of freedom for that of slavery." Teachers, Freedmen's Bureau officers, and others who came to the region genuinely hoping to assist the former slaves represented another large group of carpetbaggers.

Most white southern Republicans had been born in the South. Former Confederates reserved their greatest scorn for these **scalawags**, whom they considered traitors to their race and region. Some southern-born Republicans were men of stature and wealth, like James L. Alcorn, the owner of one of Mississippi's largest plantations and the state's first Republican governor.

Most scalawags, however, were non-slaveholding white farmers from the southern upcountry. Many had been wartime Unionists, and they now cooperated with the Republicans in order to prevent "rebels" from returning to power. Others hoped Reconstruction governments would help them recover from wartime economic losses by suspending the collection of debts and enacting laws protecting small property holders from losing their homes to creditors. In states like North Carolina, Tennessee, and Arkansas, Republicans initially commanded a significant minority of the white vote. Even in the Lower South, the small white Republican vote was important, because the population remained almost evenly divided between Blacks (almost all of whom voted for the party of Lincoln) and whites (overwhelmingly Democratic).

Southern Republicans in Power

In view of the daunting challenges they faced, the remarkable thing is not that Reconstruction governments in some respects failed, but how much they did accomplish. Perhaps their greatest achievement lay in establishing the South's first state-supported public schools. The new educational systems served both Black and white children, although generally in schools segregated by race. Only in New Orleans were the public schools integrated during Reconstruction, and only in South Carolina did the state university admit Black students (elsewhere, separate colleges were established). By the 1870s, in a region whose prewar leaders had made it illegal for slaves to learn and had done little to provide education for poorer whites, more than half the children, Black and white, were attending public schools. The new governments also pioneered civil rights legislation. Their laws made it illegal for railroads, hotels, and other institutions to discriminate on the basis of race. Enforcement varied considerably from locality to locality, but Reconstruction established for the first time at the state level a standard of equal citizenship and a recognition of Blacks' right to a share of public services.

Republican governments also took steps to strengthen the position of rural laborers and promote the South's economic recovery. They passed laws to ensure that agricultural laborers and sharecroppers had the first claim on harvested crops, rather than merchants to whom the landowner owed money. South Carolina created a state Land Commission, which by 1876 had settled 14,000 Black families and a few poor whites on their own farms.

The Quest for Prosperity

Rather than land distribution, however, the Reconstruction governments pinned their hopes for southern economic growth and opportunity for African Americans and poor whites alike on regional economic development. Railroad construction, they believed, was the key to transforming the South into a society of booming factories, bustling towns, and diversified agriculture. "A free and living republic," declared a Tennessee Republican, would "spring up in the track of the railroad." Every state during Reconstruction helped to finance railroad construction, and through tax reductions and other incentives tried to attract northern manufacturers to invest in the region. The program had mixed results. Economic development in general remained weak. With abundant opportunities existing in the West, few northern investors ventured to the Reconstruction South.

To their supporters, the governments of Radical Reconstruction presented a complex pattern of disappointment and accomplishment. A revitalized southern economy failed to materialize, and most African Americans remained locked in poverty. On the other hand, biracial democratic government, a thing unknown in American history, for the first time functioned effectively in many parts of the South. Public facilities were rebuilt and expanded, school systems established, and legal codes purged of racism. The conservative elite that had dominated southern government from colonial times to 1867 found itself excluded from political power, while poor whites, newcomers from the North, and former slaves cast ballots, sat on juries, and enacted and administered laws. "We have gone through one of the most remarkable changes in our relations to each other," declared a white South Carolina lawyer in 1871, "that has been known, perhaps, in the history of the world." It is a measure of how far change had progressed that the reaction against Reconstruction proved so extreme.

THE OVERTHROW OF RECONSTRUCTION

Reconstruction's Opponents

The South's traditional leaders—planters, merchants, and Democratic politicians—bitterly opposed the new governments. They denounced them as corrupt, inefficient, and examples of "Black supremacy." "Intelligence, virtue, and patriotism" in public life, declared a protest by prominent southern Democrats, had given way to "ignorance, stupidity, and vice." Corruption did exist during Reconstruction, but it was confined to no race, region, or party. The rapid growth of state budgets and the benefits to be gained from public aid led in some states to a scramble for influence that produced bribery, insider dealing, and a get-rich-quick atmosphere. Southern frauds, however, were dwarfed by those practiced in these years by the Whiskey Ring, which involved high officials of the Grant administration, and by New York's Tweed Ring, controlled by the Democrats, whose thefts ran into the tens of millions of dollars. (These are discussed in the next chapter.) The rising taxes needed to pay for schools and other new public facilities and to assist railroad development were another cause of opposition to Reconstruction. Many poor whites who had initially supported the Republican Party turned against it when it became clear that their economic situation was not improving.

The most basic reason for opposition to Reconstruction, however, was that most white southerners could not accept the idea of former slaves voting, holding office, and enjoying equality before the law. In order to restore white supremacy in southern public life and to ensure planters a disciplined, reliable labor force, they believed, Reconstruction must be overthrown. Opponents launched a campaign of violence in an effort to end Republican rule. Their actions posed a fundamental challenge both for Reconstruction governments in the South and for policymakers in Washington, D.C.

"A Reign of Terror"

The Civil War ended in 1865, but violence remained widespread in large parts of the postwar South. In the early years of Reconstruction, violence was mostly local and unorganized. Blacks were assaulted and murdered for refusing to give way to whites on city sidewalks, using "insolent" language, challenging end-of-year contract settlements, and attempting to buy land. The violence that greeted the advent of Republican governments after 1867, however, was far more pervasive and more directly motivated by politics. In wide areas of the South, secret societies sprang up with the aim of preventing Blacks from voting and destroying the organization of the Republican Party by assassinating local leaders and public officials.

The most notorious such organization was the **Ku Klux Klan**, which in effect served as a military arm of the Democratic Party in the South. The Klan was a terrorist organization. Led by planters, merchants, and Democratic politicians, men who liked to style themselves the South's "respectable citizens," the Klan committed some of the most brutal criminal acts in American history. In many counties, it launched what one victim called a "reign of terror" against Republican leaders, Black and white.

The Klan's victims included white Republicans, among them wartime Unionists and local officeholders, teachers, and party organizers. William Luke, an Irish-born teacher in a Black school, was lynched in 1870. But African Americans—local political leaders, those who managed to acquire land, and others who in one way or another defied the norms of white supremacy—bore the brunt of the violence. In York County, South Carolina, where nearly the entire white male population joined the Klan (and women participated by sewing the robes and hoods Klansmen wore as disguises), the organization committed eleven murders and hundreds of whippings. Black schoolhouses, tangible evidence of African American freedom, were frequent targets of anti-Reconstruction violence. One historian has identified over 600 schools destroyed.

On occasion, violence escalated from assaults on individuals to mass terrorism and even local insurrections. In Meridian, Mississippi, in 1871, some thirty Blacks were murdered in cold blood, along with a white Republican judge. The bloodiest act of violence during Reconstruction took place in Colfax, Louisiana, in 1873, where armed whites assaulted the town with a small cannon. Scores of former slaves were murdered, including fifty members of a Black militia unit after they had surrendered.

Unable to suppress the Klan, the new southern governments appealed to Washington for help. In 1870 and 1871, Congress adopted three **Enforcement Acts**, outlawing terrorist societies and allowing the president to use the army against them. These laws continued the expansion of national authority during Reconstruction. They defined crimes that aimed to deprive citizens of their civil and political rights as federal offenses rather than violations of state law. In 1871, President Grant dispatched federal marshals, backed up by troops in some areas, to arrest hundreds of accused Klansmen. Many Klan leaders fled the South. After a series of well-publicized trials, the Klan went out of existence. In 1872, for the first time since before the Civil War, peace reigned in most of the former Confederacy.

The Liberal Republicans

Despite the Grant administration's effective response to Klan terrorism, the North's commitment to Reconstruction waned during the 1870s. Many Radicals, including Thaddeus Stevens, who died in 1868, had passed from the scene. Within the Republican Party, their place was taken by politicians less committed to the ideal of equal rights for Blacks. Northerners increasingly felt that the South should be able to solve its own problems without constant interference from Washington. The federal government had freed the slaves, made them citizens, and given them the right to vote. Now, Blacks should rely on their own resources, not demand further assistance.

In 1872, an influential group of Republicans, alienated by corruption within the Grant administration and believing that the growth of federal power during and after the war needed to be curtailed, formed their own party. They included Republican founders like Lyman Trumbull and prominent editors and journalists such as E. L. Godkin of *The Nation*. Calling themselves Liberal Republicans, they nominated Horace Greeley, editor of the *New York Tribune*, for president.

The Liberals' alienation from the Grant administration initially had little to do with Reconstruction. They claimed that corrupt politicians had come to power in the North by manipulating the votes of immigrants and workingmen, while men of talent and education like themselves had been pushed aside. Democratic criticisms of Reconstruction, however, found a receptive audience among the Liberals. As in the North, they became convinced, the "best men" of the South had been excluded from power while "ignorant" voters controlled politics, producing corruption and misgovernment. Power in the South should be returned to the region's "natural leaders." During the campaign of

1872, Greeley repeatedly called on Americans to "clasp hands across the bloody chasm" by putting the Civil War and Reconstruction behind them.

Greeley had spent most of his career, first as a Whig and then as a Republican, denouncing the Democratic Party. But with the Republican split presenting an opportunity to repair their political fortunes, Democratic leaders endorsed Greeley as their candidate. Many rank-and-file Democrats, unable to bring themselves to vote for Greeley, stayed at home on election day. As a result, Greeley suffered a devastating defeat by Grant, whose margin of more than 700,000 popular votes was the largest in a nineteenth-century presidential contest. But Greeley's campaign placed on the northern agenda the one issue on which the Liberal reformers and the Democrats could agree—a new policy toward the South.

The North's Retreat

The Liberal attack on Reconstruction, which continued after 1872, contributed to a resurgence of racism in the North. Journalist James S. Pike, a leading Greeley supporter, in 1874 published *The Prostrate State*, an influential account of a visit to South Carolina. The book depicted a state engulfed by political corruption and under the control of "a mass of black barbarism." The South's problems, Pike insisted, arose from "Negro government." The solution was to restore leading whites to political power. Newspapers that had long supported Reconstruction now began to condemn Black participation in southern government. Engravings depicting the former slaves as heroic Civil War veterans, upstanding citizens, or victims of violence were increasingly replaced by caricatures presenting them as little more than unbridled animals. Resurgent racism offered Blacks' alleged incapacity as a convenient explanation for the "failure" of Reconstruction.

Other factors also weakened northern support for Reconstruction. In 1873, the country plunged into a severe economic depression. Distracted by economic problems, Republicans were in no mood to devote further attention to the South. The depression dealt the South a severe blow and further weakened the prospect that Republicans could revitalize the region's economy. Democrats made substantial gains throughout the nation in the elections of 1874. For the first time since the Civil War, their party took control of the House of Representatives. Before the new Congress met, the old one enacted a final piece of Reconstruction legislation, the **Civil Rights Act of 1875**. This outlawed racial discrimination in places of public accommodation like hotels and theaters. But it was clear that the northern public was retreating from Reconstruction.

The Supreme Court whittled away at the guarantees of Black rights Congress had adopted. In the *Slaughterhouse Cases* (1873), white butchers excluded from a state-sponsored monopoly in Louisiana went to court, claiming that their right to pursue a livelihood, a privilege of American citizenship guaranteed by the Fourteenth Amendment, had been violated. The justices rejected their claim,

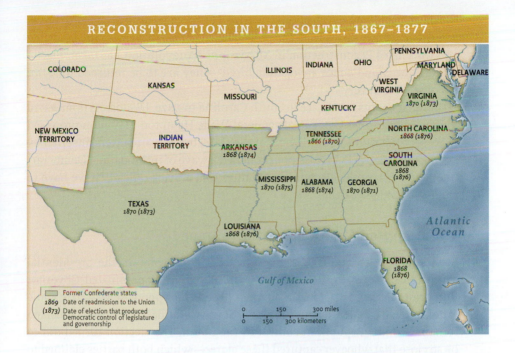

RECONSTRUCTION IN THE SOUTH, 1867–1877

ruling that the amendment had not altered traditional federalism. Most of the rights of citizens, it declared, remained under state control. Three years later, in *United States v. Cruikshank*, the Court gutted the Enforcement Acts by throwing out the convictions of some of those responsible for the Colfax Massacre of 1873.

The Triumph of the Redeemers

By the mid-1870s, Reconstruction was clearly on the defensive. Democrats had already regained control of states with substantial white voting majorities such as Tennessee, North Carolina, and Texas. The victorious Democrats called themselves **Redeemers**, since they claimed to have "redeemed" the white South from corruption, misgovernment, and northern and Black control.

In those states where Reconstruction governments survived, violence again erupted. This time, the Grant administration showed no desire to intervene. In contrast to the Klan's activities—conducted at night by disguised men—the violence of 1875 and 1876 took place in broad daylight, as if to underscore Democrats' conviction that they had nothing to fear from Washington. In Mississippi, in 1875, white rifle clubs drilled in public and openly assaulted and murdered Republicans. When Governor Adelbert Ames, a Maine-born Union general, frantically appealed to the federal government for assistance, President Grant responded that the northern public was "tired out" by southern problems. On election day, armed Democrats destroyed ballot boxes and drove former slaves from the polls. The result was a Democratic landslide and the end of Reconstruction in Mississippi. "A revolution has taken place," wrote Ames, "and a race are disfranchised—they are to be returned to . . . an era of second slavery."

Similar events took place in South Carolina in 1876. Democrats nominated for governor former Confederate general Wade Hampton. Hampton promised to respect the rights of all citizens of the state, but his supporters, inspired by Democratic tactics in Mississippi, launched a wave of intimidation. Democrats intended to carry the election, one planter told a Black official, "if we have to wade in blood knee-deep."

The Disputed Election and Bargain of 1877

Events in South Carolina directly affected the outcome of the presidential campaign of 1876. To succeed Grant, the Republicans nominated Governor Rutherford B. Hayes of Ohio. Democrats chose as his opponent New York's governor, Samuel J. Tilden. By this time, only South Carolina, Florida, and Louisiana remained under Republican control in the South. The election turned out to be so close that whoever captured these states—which both parties claimed to have carried—would become the next president.

Unable to resolve the impasse on its own, Congress in January 1877 appointed a fifteen-member Electoral Commission, composed of senators, representatives, and Supreme Court justices. Republicans enjoyed an 8–7 majority on the commission, and to no one's surprise, the members decided by that margin that Hayes had carried the disputed southern states and had been elected president. Even as the commission deliberated, however, behind-the-scenes negotiations took place between leaders of the two parties. Hayes's representatives agreed to recognize Democratic control of the entire South and to avoid further intervention in local affairs. They also pledged that Hayes would place a southerner in the cabinet position of postmaster general and that he would work for federal aid to the Texas and Pacific railroad, a transcontinental line projected to follow a southern route. For their part, Democrats promised not to dispute Hayes's right to office and to respect the civil and political rights of Blacks.

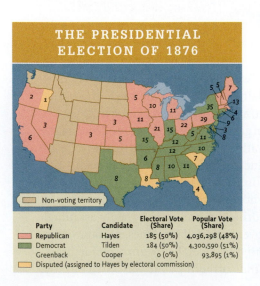

THE PRESIDENTIAL ELECTION OF 1876

Non-voting territory

Party	Candidate	Electoral Vote (Share)	Popular Vote (Share)
Republican	Hayes	185 (50%)	4,036,298 (48%)
Democrat	Tilden	184 (50%)	4,300,590 (51%)
Greenback	Cooper	0 (0%)	93,895 (1%)
Disputed (assigned to Hayes by electoral commission)			

Thus was concluded the **Bargain of 1877**. Not all of its parts were fulfilled. But Hayes became president, and he did appoint David M. Key of Tennessee as postmaster general. Hayes quickly ordered federal troops to stop guarding the state houses in Louisiana and South Carolina, allowing Democratic claimants to become governor. (Contrary to legend, Hayes did not remove the last soldiers from the South—he simply ordered them to return to their barracks.) But the Texas and Pacific never did get its land grant. Of far more significance, the triumphant southern Democrats failed to live up to their pledge to recognize Blacks as equal citizens.

The End of Reconstruction

As a historical process—the nation's adjustment to the destruction of slavery—Reconstruction continued well after 1877. Blacks continued to vote and, in some states, hold office into the 1890s. But as a distinct era of national history—when Republicans controlled much of the South, Blacks exercised significant political power, and the federal government accepted the responsibility for protecting the fundamental rights of all American citizens—Reconstruction had come to an end. Despite its limitations, Reconstruction was a remarkable chapter in the story of American freedom. Nearly a century would pass before the nation again tried to bring equal rights to the descendants of slaves. The civil rights era of the 1950s and 1960s would sometimes be called the Second Reconstruction.

Even while it lasted, however, Reconstruction revealed some of the tensions inherent in nineteenth-century discussions of freedom. The policy of granting Black men the vote while denying them the benefits of land ownership strengthened the idea that the free citizen could be a poor, dependent laborer. Reconstruction placed on the national agenda a problem that would dominate political discussion for the next half-century—how, in a modern society, to define the economic essence of freedom.

CHAPTER REVIEW

REVIEW QUESTIONS

1. *In 1865, former Confederate general Robert Richardson remarked that "the emancipated slaves own nothing, because nothing but freedom has been given to them." Explain whether this would be an accurate assessment of Reconstruction twelve years later.*

2. *The women's movement split into two separate national organizations in part because the Fifteenth Amendment did not give women the vote. Explain why the two groups split.*

3. *In what sense did the Reconstruction amendments mark a second founding of the United States?*

4. *What is birthright citizenship and why is it important?*

5. *How did Black families, churches, schools, and other institutions contribute to the development of African American culture and political activism in this period?*

6. *Why did ownership of land and control of labor become major points of contention between former slaves and whites in the South?*

7. *By what methods did southern whites seek to limit African American civil rights and liberties? How did the federal government respond?*

8. *How did the failure of land reform and continued poverty lead to new forms of servitude for both Blacks and whites?*

9. *What caused the confrontation between President Johnson and Congress over Reconstruction policies?*

10. *What national issues and attitudes combined to bring an end to Reconstruction by 1877?*

11. *By 1877, how did the condition of former slaves in the United States compare with that of freedpeople around the globe?*

KEY TERMS

Freedmen's Bureau (p. 572)

sharecropping (p. 574)

crop lien (p. 575)

Black Codes (p. 581)

Civil Rights Bill of 1866 (p. 583)

Fourteenth Amendment (p. 583)

Reconstruction Act (p. 585)

Tenure of Office Act (p. 586)

impeachment (p. 586)

Fifteenth Amendment (p. 586)

carpetbaggers (p. 595)

scalawags (p. 595)

Ku Klux Klan (p. 598)

Enforcement Acts (p. 599)

Civil Rights Act of 1875 (p. 600)

Redeemers (p. 601)

Bargain of 1877 (p. 603)

Go to 🐰 INQUIZITIVE

To see what you know—and learn what you've missed—with personalized feedback along the way.

CHAPTER 16

AMERICA'S GILDED AGE

1870–1890

FOCUS QUESTIONS

- *What factors combined to make the United States a mature industrial society after the Civil War?*

- *How did the economic development of the Gilded Age affect American freedom?*

- *How did reformers of the period approach the problems of an industrial society?*

- *How was the West transformed economically and socially in this period?*

- *Was the Gilded Age political system effective in meeting its goals?*

An immense crowd gathered in New York harbor on October 28, 1886, for the dedication of *Liberty Enlightening the World*, a fitting symbol for a nation now wholly free. The idea for the statue originated in 1865 with Édouard de Laboulaye, a French educator and the author of several books on the United States, as a response to the assassination of Abraham Lincoln. The statue, de Laboulaye hoped, would celebrate both the historic friendship between France and the United States and the triumph, through the Union's victory in the Civil War, of American freedom. Measuring more than 150 feet from torch to toe and standing atop a huge pedestal, the edifice was the tallest man-made structure in the Western Hemisphere. It exceeded in height, newspapers noted with pride, the Colossus of Rhodes, a wonder of the ancient world.

In time, the Statue of Liberty, as it came to be called, would become Americans' most revered national icon. For over a century it has stood as a symbol of freedom. The statue has offered welcome to millions of immigrants—the "huddled masses yearning to breathe free" celebrated in a poem by Emma Lazarus inscribed on its base in 1903. In the years since its dedication, the statue's familiar image has been reproduced by folk artists in every conceivable medium and has been used by advertisers to promote everything from cigarettes and lawn mowers to war bonds. As its use by Chinese students demanding democracy in the Tiananmen Square protests of 1989 showed, it has become a powerful international symbol as well.

Although the Civil War was over, the country in the late nineteenth century was racked by violence, by not only white supremacists in the South but also widespread labor conflict, warfare against Native Americans in the West, and political assassinations. Indeed, the year of the statue's dedication, 1886, also witnessed the "great upheaval," a wave of strikes and labor protests that touched every part of the nation. The 600 dignitaries (598 of them men) who gathered on what is now called Liberty Island for the dedication hoped the Statue of Liberty would inspire renewed devotion to the nation's political and economic system. But for all its grandeur, the statue could not conceal the deep social divisions and fears about the future of American freedom that accompanied the country's emergence as the world's leading industrial power. Nor did the celebrations address the crucial questions that moved to the center stage of American public life during the 1870s and 1880s and remained there for decades to come: What are the social conditions that make freedom possible, and what role should the national government play in defining and protecting the liberty of its citizens?

THE SECOND INDUSTRIAL REVOLUTION

1896	Utah gains statehood
1899	Thorstein Veblen's *The Theory of the Leisure Class*
1905	*Lochner v. New York*

Between the end of the Civil War and the early twentieth century, the United States underwent one of the most rapid and profound economic revolutions any country has ever experienced. There were numerous causes for this explosive economic growth. The country enjoyed abundant natural resources, a growing supply of labor, an expanding market for manufactured goods, and the availability of capital for investment. In addition, the federal government actively promoted industrial and agricultural development. It enacted high tariffs that protected American industry from foreign competition, granted land to railroad companies to encourage construction, and used the army to remove Indians from western lands desired by farmers and mining companies.

The Industrial Economy

The rapid expansion of factory production, mining, and railroad construction in all parts of the country except the South signaled the transition from Lincoln's America—a world centered on the small farm and artisan workshop—to a mature industrial society. Americans of the late nineteenth century marveled at the triumph of the new economy. "One can hardly believe," wrote the philosopher John Dewey, "there has been a revolution in history so rapid, so extensive, so complete."

By 1913, the United States produced one-third of the world's industrial output—more than the total of Great Britain, France, and Germany combined. Half of all industrial workers now labored in plants with more than 250 employees. On the eve of the Civil War, the first industrial revolution, centered on the textile industry, had transformed New England into a center of manufacturing. But otherwise, the United States was still primarily an agricultural nation. By 1880, for the first time, the Census Bureau found a majority of the workforce engaged in non-farming jobs. By 1890, two-thirds of Americans worked for wages, rather than owning a farm, business, or craft shop. Drawn to factories by the promise of employment, a new working class emerged in these years. Between 1870 and 1920, almost 11 million Americans moved from farm to city, and another 25 million immigrants arrived from overseas.

Most manufacturing now took place in industrial cities. New York, with its new skyscrapers and hundreds of thousands of workers in all sorts of manufacturing establishments, symbolized dynamic urban growth. After merging with Brooklyn in 1898, its population exceeded 3.4 million. The city, along with Boston, financed industrialization and westward expansion, its banks and stock exchange funneling capital to railroads, mines, and factories. But the heartland of the second industrial revolution was the region around the Great Lakes, with its factories producing iron and steel, machinery, chemicals, and packaged foods. Pittsburgh had become the world's center of iron and steel manufacturing. Chicago, by 1900 the nation's second-largest city, with 1.7 million inhabitants, was home to factories producing steel and farm machinery and giant stockyards where cattle were processed into meat products for shipment east in refrigerated railcars. Smaller industrial cities also proliferated, often concentrating on a single industry—cast-iron stoves in Troy, New York, furniture in Grand Rapids, Michigan.

Railroads and the National Market

The railroad made possible what is sometimes called the "second industrial revolution." Spurred by private investment and massive grants of land and money by federal, state, and local governments, the number of miles of railroad track in the United States tripled between 1860 and 1880 and tripled again by 1920, opening vast new areas to commercial farming and creating a

TABLE 16.1 Indicators of Economic Change, 1870–1920

	1870	1900	1920
Farms (millions)	2.7	5.7	6.4
Land in farms (million acres)	408	841	956
Wheat grown (million bushels)	254	599	843
Employment (millions)	14	28.5	44.5
In manufacturing (millions)	2.5	5.9	11.2
Percentage of workforce[a]			
Agricultural	52	38	27
Industry[b]	29	31	44
Trade, service, administration[c]	20	31	27
Railroad track (thousands of miles)	53	258	407
Steel produced (thousands of tons)	0.8	11.2	46
Gross national product (billions of dollars)	7.4	18.7	91.5
Per capita (in 1920 dollars)	371	707	920
Life expectancy at birth (years)	42	47	54

[a] Percentages are rounded and do not total 100.
[b] Includes manufacturing, transportation, mining, and construction.
[c] Includes trade, finance, and public administration.

THE RAILROAD NETWORK, 1880

By 1880, the transnational rail network made possible the creation of a truly national market for goods.

truly national market for manufactured goods. In 1886, the railroads adopted a standard national gauge (the distance separating the two rails), making it possible for the first time for trains of one company to travel on any other company's track. By the 1890s, five transcontinental lines transported the products of western mines, farms, ranches, and forests to eastern markets and carried manufactured goods to the West. The railroads reorganized time itself. In 1883, the major companies divided the nation into the four time zones still in use today.

The growing population formed an ever-expanding market for the mass production, mass distribution, and mass marketing of goods, essential elements of a modern industrial economy. The spread of national brands like Ivory soap and Quaker Oats symbolized the continuing integration of the economy. So did the growth of national chains, most prominently the Atlantic and Pacific Tea Company, better known as A & P grocery stores. Based in Chicago, the national mail-order firms Montgomery Ward and Sears, Roebuck & Co. sold clothing, jewelry, farm equipment, and numerous other goods to rural families throughout the country.

The Greatest Department Store on Earth, a cartoon from *Puck*, November 29, 1899, depicts Uncle Sam selling goods, mostly manufactured products, to the nations of the world. The search for markets overseas would be a recurring theme of twentieth-century American foreign policy.

The Spirit of Innovation

A remarkable series of technological innovations spurred rapid communication and economic growth. The opening of the Atlantic cable in 1866 made it possible to send electronic telegraph messages instantaneously between the United States and Europe. During the 1870s and 1880s, the telephone, typewriter, and handheld camera came into use.

Scientific breakthroughs poured forth from research laboratories in Menlo Park and West Orange, New Jersey, created by the era's greatest inventor, Thomas A. Edison. During the course of his life, Edison helped to establish entirely new industries that transformed private life, public entertainment, and economic activity, including the phonograph, lightbulb, motion picture, and a system for generating and distributing electric power. He opened the first electric generating station in Manhattan in 1882 to provide power to streetcars, factories, and private homes, and he established, among other companies, the forerunner of General Electric to market electrical equipment. The spread of electricity was essential to industrial and urban growth, providing a more reliable and flexible source of power than water or steam.

Competition and Consolidation

Economic growth was dramatic but highly volatile. The combination of a market flooded with goods and the federal monetary policies (discussed later in this chapter) that removed money from the national economy led to a relentless fall in prices. The world economy suffered prolonged downturns in the 1870s and 1890s.

Businesses engaged in ruthless competition. Railroads and other companies tried various means of bringing order to the chaotic marketplace. They formed "pools" that divided up markets between supposedly competing firms and fixed prices. They established **trusts**—legal devices whereby the affairs of several rival companies were managed by a single director. Such efforts to coordinate the economic activities of independent companies generally proved short-lived, disintegrating as individual firms continued their intense pursuit of profits.

To avoid cutthroat competition, more and more corporations battled to control entire industries. The process of economic concentration culminated between 1897 and 1904, when some 4,000 firms vanished into larger corporations that served national markets and exercised an unprecedented degree of control over the economy. By the time the wave of mergers had been completed, giant corporations like U.S. Steel (created by financier J. P. Morgan in 1901 by combining ten large steel companies into the first billion-dollar economic enterprise), Standard Oil, and International Harvester (a manufacturer of agricultural machinery) dominated major industries.

The Rise of Andrew Carnegie

In an era without personal or corporate income taxes, some business leaders accumulated enormous fortunes and economic power. Under the aggressive leadership of Thomas A. Scott, the Pennsylvania Railroad—for a time the nation's largest corporation—forged an economic empire that stretched across the continent and included coal mines and oceangoing steamships. With an army of professional managers to oversee its far-flung activities, the railroad pioneered modern techniques of business organization.

Another industrial giant was Andrew Carnegie, who emigrated with his family from his native Scotland at the age of thirteen and as a teenager worked in a Pennsylvania textile factory. During the depression that began in 1873, Carnegie set out to establish a steel company that incorporated **vertical integration**—that is, one that controlled every phase of the business from raw materials to transportation, manufacturing, and distribution. By the 1890s, he dominated the steel industry and had accumulated a fortune worth hundreds of millions of dollars. Carnegie's complex of steel factories at Homestead, Pennsylvania, was the most technologically advanced in the world.

Carnegie's father, an immigrant Scottish weaver who had taken part in popular efforts to open the British political system to working-class participation, had instilled in his son a commitment to democracy and social equality. From his mother, Carnegie learned that life was a ceaseless struggle in which one must strive to get ahead or sink beneath the waves. His life reflected the tension between these elements of his upbringing. Believing that the rich had a moral obligation to promote the advancement of society, Carnegie denounced the "worship of money" and distributed much of his wealth to various philanthropies, especially the creation of public libraries in towns throughout the country. But he ran his companies with a dictatorial hand. His factories operated nonstop, with two twelve-hour shifts every day of the year except the Fourth of July. Carnegie's rise from humble beginnings to great wealth reinforced the "rags to riches" ideal that flourished during the Gilded Age. But such success was hardly available to his own poorly paid employees.

The Triumph of John D. Rockefeller

If any single name became a byword for enormous wealth, it was John D. Rockefeller, who began his working career as a clerk for a Cleveland merchant and rose to dominate the oil industry. He drove out rival firms through cutthroat competition, arranging secret deals with railroad companies, and fixing prices and production quotas. Rockefeller began with **horizontal expansion**—buying out competing oil refineries. But like Carnegie, he soon established a vertically integrated monopoly, which dominated the drilling, refining, storage, and distribution of oil. By the 1880s, his Standard Oil Company controlled 90 percent of the nation's oil industry. Like Carnegie, Rockefeller gave much of his fortune away, establishing foundations to promote education and medical research. And like Carnegie, he bitterly fought his employees' efforts to organize unions.

These and other industrial leaders inspired among ordinary Americans a combination of awe, admiration, and hostility. Depending on one's point of view, they were "captains of industry," whose energy and vision pushed the economy forward, or **"robber barons,"** who wielded power without any accountability in an unregulated marketplace. Most rose from modest backgrounds and seemed examples of how inventive genius and business sense enabled Americans to seize opportunities for success. But their dictatorial attitudes, unscrupulous methods, repressive labor policies, and exercise of power without any democratic control led to fears that they were undermining political and economic freedom. Concentrated wealth degraded the political process, declared Henry Demarest Lloyd in *Wealth against Commonwealth* (1894), an exposé of how

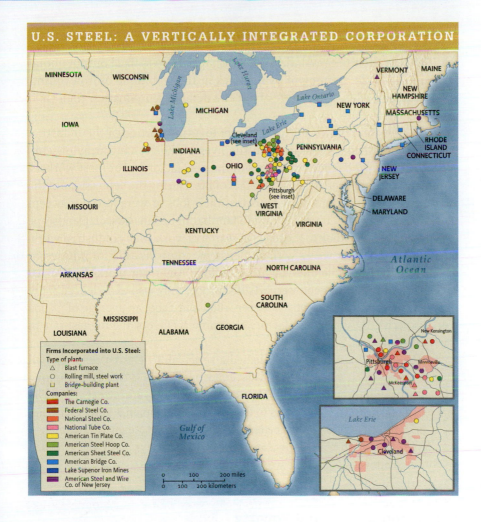

U.S. STEEL: A VERTICALLY INTEGRATED CORPORATION

Rockefeller's Standard Oil Company made a mockery of economic competition and political democracy by manipulating the market and bribing legislators. "Liberty and monopoly," Lloyd concluded, "cannot live together."

Workers' Freedom in an Industrial Age

Remarkable as it was, the country's economic growth distributed its benefits very unevenly. For a minority of workers, the rapidly expanding industrial system created new forms of freedom. In some industries, skilled workers commanded high wages and exercised considerable control over the production process. A worker's economic independence now rested on technical skill rather than ownership of one's own shop and tools as in earlier times.

What was known as "the miner's freedom" consisted of elaborate work rules that left skilled underground workers free of managerial supervision on the job. Through their union, skilled iron- and steelworkers fixed output quotas and controlled the training of apprentices in the technique of iron rolling. These workers often knew more about the details of production than their employers did.

Such "freedom," however, applied only to a tiny portion of the industrial labor force and had little bearing on the lives of the growing army of semi-skilled workers who tended machines in the new factories. For most workers, economic insecurity remained a basic fact of life. During the depressions of the 1870s and 1890s, millions of workers lost their jobs or were forced to accept reductions of pay. The "tramp" became a familiar figure on the social landscape as thousands of men took to the roads in search of work. Many industrial workers labored sixty-hour weeks with no pensions, compensation for injuries, or protections against unemployment. Although American workers received higher wages than their counterparts in Europe, they also experienced more dangerous working conditions. Between 1880 and 1900, an average of 35,000 workers perished each year in factory and mine accidents, the highest rate in the industrial world.

In 1888, the *Chicago Times* published a series of articles by reporter Nell Cusack under the title "City Slave Girls," exposing wretched conditions among women working for wages in the city's homes, factories, and sweatshops. The articles unleashed a flood of letters to the editor from women workers. One singled out domestic service—still the largest employment category for women—as "a slave's life," with "long hours, late and early, seven days in the week, bossed and ordered about as before the war."

Increasing Wealth and Poverty

At the other end of the economic spectrum, the era witnessed an unprece-dented accumulation of wealth. Class divisions became more and more visible. In frontier days, all classes in San Francisco, for example, lived near the waterfront. In the late nineteenth century, upper-class families built mansions on Nob Hill and Van Ness Avenue (known as "millionaire's row"). In eastern cities as well, the rich increasingly resided in their own exclusive neighbor-hoods and vacationed among members of their own class at exclusive resorts like Newport, Rhode Island. The growing urban middle class of professionals, office workers, and small businessmen moved to new urban and suburban neighborhoods linked to central business districts by streetcars and commuter railways. "Passion for money," wrote the novelist Edith Wharton in *The House of Mirth* (1905), dominated society. Wharton's book traced the difficulties of Lily Bart, a young woman of modest means pressured by her mother and New York high society to "barter" her beauty for marriage to a rich husband.

By 1890, the richest 1 percent of Americans received the same total income as the bottom half of the population and owned more property than the remaining 99 percent. Many of the wealthiest Americans consciously pursued an aristocratic lifestyle, building palatial homes, attending exclusive social clubs, schools, and colleges, holding fancy-dress balls, and marrying into each other's families. In 1899, the economist and social historian Thorstein Veblen published *The Theory of the Leisure Class*, a devastating critique of an upper-class culture focused on "conspicuous consumption"—that is, spending money not on needed or even desired goods, but simply to demonstrate the possession of wealth. One of the era's most widely publicized spectacles was an elaborate costume ball organized in 1897 by Mrs. Bradley Martin, the daughter of a New York railroad financier. The theme was the royal court of prerevolutionary France. The Waldorf-Astoria Hotel was decorated to look like the palace of Versailles, the guests wore the dress of the French nobility, and the hostess bedecked herself with the actual jewels of Queen Marie Antoinette.

Not that far from the Waldorf, much of the working class lived in desperate conditions. Jacob Riis, in *How the Other Half Lives* (1890), offered a shocking account of living conditions among the urban poor, complete with photographs of apartments in dark, airless, overcrowded tenement houses.

FREEDOM IN THE GILDED AGE

The era from 1870 to 1890 is the only period of American history commonly known by a derogatory name—**the Gilded Age**, after the title of an 1873 novel by Mark Twain and Charles Dudley Warner. "Gilded" means covered with a layer of gold, but it also suggests that the glittering surface masks a core of little real value and is therefore deceptive. Twain and Warner were referring not only to the remarkable expansion of the economy in this period but also to the corruption caused by corporate dominance of politics and to the oppressive treatment of those left behind in the scramble for wealth. "Get rich, dishonestly if we can, honestly if we must," was the era's slogan, according to *The Gilded Age*.

The Social Problem

As the United States matured into an industrial economy, Americans struggled to make sense of the new social order. Debates over political economy engaged the attention of millions, reaching far beyond the tiny academic world into the public sphere inhabited by self-educated workingmen and farmers, reformers of all kinds, newspaper editors, and politicians. This broad public discussion produced thousands of books, pamphlets, and articles on such technical issues as land taxation and currency reform, as well as widespread debate over the social and ethical implications of economic change.

Many Americans sensed that something had gone wrong in the nation's social development. Talk of "better classes," "respectable classes," and "dangerous classes" dominated public discussion, and bitter labor strife seemed to have become the rule. During the Gilded Age, Congress and a number of states established investigating committees to inquire into the relations between labor and capital. In 1881, the Massachusetts Bureau of Labor Statistics reported that virtually every worker it interviewed in Fall River, the nation's largest center of textile production, complained of overwork, poor housing, and tyrannical employers.

Freedom, Inequality, and Democracy

The appearance of what Massachusetts cotton manufacturer Edward Atkinson called "a permanent factory population" living on the edge of poverty alongside a growing class of millionaires posed a sharp challenge to traditional definitions of freedom. "The great curse of the Old World—the division of society into classes," declared *The Nation*, had come to America. It became increasingly difficult to view wage labor as a temporary resting place on the road to economic independence.

Given the vast expansion of the nation's productive capacity, many Americans viewed the concentration of wealth as inevitable, natural, and justified by progress. By the turn of the century, advanced economics taught that wages were determined by the iron law of supply and demand and that wealth rightly flowed not to those who worked the hardest but to men with business skills and access to money. The close link between freedom and equality, forged in the Revolution and reinforced during the Civil War, appeared increasingly out of date. The task of social science, wrote iron manufacturer Abram Hewitt, was to devise ways of making "men who are equal in liberty" content with the "inequality in . . . distribution" inevitable in modern society.

Among the first to take up this challenge were the self-styled "liberal" reformers. (Their beliefs were quite different from those called liberals in modern America, who advocate that an activist government try to address social needs.) This group of editors and professionals broke with the Republican Party in 1872 and helped to bring about a change in northern opinion regarding Reconstruction. But their program was not confined to the South.

Gilded Age liberals feared that with lower-class groups seeking to use government to advance their own interests, democracy was becoming a threat to individual liberty and the rights of property. Some urged a return to the long-abandoned principle that voting should be limited to property owners. During the 1830s, Alexis de Tocqueville had reported that opponents of democracy "hide their heads." By the 1870s, wrote one observer, "expressions of doubt and distrust in regard to universal suffrage are heard constantly . . . [at] the top of our society."

Prayer Time in the Nursery, Five Points House of Industry, taken by Jacob Riis around 1889, offers a striking contrast to the bleak homes of New York City's poor families, depicted in many of his photographs.

One of the most influential statements of this outlook came from the pen of the historian Francis Parkman in an 1879 essay, "The Failure of Universal Suffrage." Democracy, Parkman complained, transferred power "from superior to inferior types of men," resulting in the reign of "organized ignorance." The solution was to limit those entitled to vote.

Social Darwinism in America

The idea of the natural superiority of some groups to others, which before the Civil War had been invoked to justify slavery in an otherwise free society, now reemerged in the vocabulary of modern science to explain the success and failure of individuals and social classes. In 1859, the British scientist Charles Darwin published *On the Origin of Species*. One of the most influential works of science ever to appear, it expounded the theory of evolution whereby plant and animal species best suited to their environment took the place of those less able to adapt.

In a highly oversimplified form, language borrowed from Darwin or developed by his followers, such as "natural selection," "the struggle for existence," and "the survival of the fittest," entered public discussion of social problems. According to what came to be called **Social Darwinism**, evolution was as natural a process in human society as in nature, and government must not interfere. Especially misguided, in this view, were efforts to uplift those at the bottom of the social order, such as laws regulating conditions of work or public assistance to the poor. The giant industrial corporation, Social Darwinists believed, had emerged because it was better adapted to its environment than earlier forms of enterprise. To restrict its operations by legislation would reduce society to a more primitive level.

Even the depressions of the 1870s and 1890s did not shake the widespread view that the poor were essentially responsible for their own fate. Charity workers and local governments spent much time and energy distinguishing the "deserving" poor (those, like widows and orphans, destitute through no fault of their own) from the "undeserving," a far larger number. Failure to advance in society was widely thought to indicate a lack of character, an absence of self-reliance and determination in the face of adversity.

The era's most influential Social Darwinist was Yale professor William Graham Sumner. For Sumner, freedom meant "the security given to each man" that he can acquire, enjoy, and dispose of property "exclusively as he chooses," without interference from other persons or from government. Freedom thus defined required frank acceptance of inequality. Society faced two and only two alternatives: "liberty, inequality, survival of the fittest; not-liberty, equality, survival of the unfittest." In 1883, Sumner published *What Social Classes Owe to Each Other*. His answer, essentially, was nothing: "In a free state," no one was entitled to claim "help from, and cannot be charged to [offer] help to, another." Government, Sumner believed, existed only to protect "the property of men and the honor of women," not to upset social arrangements decreed by nature.

Liberty of Contract

The growing influence of Social Darwinism helped to popularize an idea that would be embraced by the business and professional classes in the last quarter of the nineteenth century—a "negative" definition of freedom as limited government and an unrestrained free market. Central to this social vision was the idea of contract. "The laws of contract," wrote one reformer, "are the foundation of civilization." So long as labor relations were governed by contracts freely arrived at by independent individuals, neither the government nor unions had a right to interfere with working conditions, and Americans had no grounds to complain of a loss of freedom.

Demands by workers that the government enforce an eight-hour day, provide relief to the unemployed, or in other ways intervene in the economy struck liberals as an example of how the misuse of political power posed a threat to liberty. The principle of free labor, which originated as a celebration of the independent small producer in a society of broad equality and social harmony, was transformed into a defense of the unrestrained operations of the capitalist marketplace.

The Courts and Freedom

In elevating liberty of contract from one element of freedom to its very essence, the courts played a significant role. The Fourteenth Amendment had empowered the federal government to overturn state laws that violated citizens' rights. By the 1880s, **liberty of contract**, not equality before the law for former slaves, came to be defined as the amendment's true meaning. State and federal courts regularly struck down state laws regulating economic enterprise as an interference with the right of the free laborer to choose his employment and working conditions, and of the entrepreneur to utilize his property as he saw fit. For decades, the courts viewed state regulation of business—especially laws establishing maximum hours of work and safe working conditions—as an insult to free labor.

At first, the Supreme Court was willing to accept laws regulating enterprises that represented a significant "public interest." In *Munn v. Illinois*, an 1877 decision, it upheld the constitutionality of an Illinois law that established a state board empowered to regulate fees charged by grain storage facilities. Nine years later, however, in *Wabash v. Illinois*, the Court essentially reversed itself, ruling that only the federal government, not the states, could regulate railroads engaged in interstate commerce, as all important lines were. The decision led directly to the passage of the Interstate Commerce Act of 1887, discussed below.

The courts generally sided with business enterprises that complained of a loss of economic freedom. In 1885, the New York Court of Appeals invalidated a state law that prohibited the manufacture of cigars in tenement dwellings on the grounds that such legislation deprived the worker of the "liberty" to work "where he will." Although women still lacked political rights, they were increasingly understood to possess the same economic "liberty," defined in this way, as men. On the grounds that it violated women's freedom, the Illinois Supreme Court in 1895 declared unconstitutional a state law that outlawed the production of garments in sweatshops and established a maximum forty-eight-hour workweek for women and children. In the same year, in *United States v. E. C. Knight Co.*, the U.S. Supreme Court ruled that the Sherman Antitrust Act of 1890, which barred combinations in restraint of trade, could not be used to break up a sugar refining monopoly, since the Constitution empowered Congress to regulate commerce but not manufacturing. Their unwillingness to allow regulation of the economy, however, did not prevent the courts from acting to impede labor organization. The Sherman Act, intended to prevent business mergers that stifled competition, was used by judges primarily to issue injunctions prohibiting strikes on the grounds that they illegally interfered with the freedom of trade.

In a 1905 case that became almost as notorious as *Dred Scott* and gave the name "Lochnerism" to the entire body of liberty of contract decisions, the Supreme Court in *Lochner v. New York* voided a state law establishing ten hours per day or sixty per week as the maximum hours of work for bakers. The law, wrote Associate Justice Rufus Peckham for the 5-4 majority, "interfered with the right of contract between employer and employee" and therefore infringed upon individual freedom. By this time, the Court was invoking "liberty" in ways that could easily seem absurd. In one case, it overturned as a violation of "personal liberty" a Kansas law prohibiting "yellow-dog" contracts, which made nonmembership in a union a condition of employment. In another, it struck down state laws requiring payment of coal miners in money rather than paper usable only at company-owned stores. Workers, observed mine union leader John P. Mitchell, "are being guaranteed the liberties they do not want and denied the liberty that is of real value to them."

LABOR AND THE REPUBLIC

"The Overwhelming Labor Question"

As Mitchell's remark suggests, public debate in the late nineteenth century more than at almost any other moment in American history divided along class lines. The shift from the slavery controversy to what one politician called "the overwhelming labor question" was dramatically illustrated in 1877, the year of both the end of Reconstruction and the first national labor walkout—the **Great Railroad Strike**. When workers protesting a pay cut paralyzed rail traffic in much of the country, militia units tried to force them back to work. After troops fired on strikers in Pittsburgh, killing twenty people, workers responded by burning the city's railroad yards, destroying millions of dollars in property. General strikes paralyzed Chicago and St. Louis. The strike revealed both a strong sense of solidarity among workers and the close ties between the Republican Party and the new class of industrialists. President Rutherford B. Hayes, who a few months earlier had ordered federal troops in the South to end their involvement in local politics, ordered the army into the North. The workers, the president wrote in his diary, were "put down by force."

In the aftermath of 1877, the federal government constructed armories in major cities to ensure that troops would be on hand in the event of further labor difficulties. Henceforth, national power would be used not to protect beleaguered former slaves but to guarantee the rights of property.

The Strike, an 1886 painting by the German-born artist Robert Koehler, who had grown up in a working-class family in Milwaukee. Koehler depicts a confrontation between a factory owner, dressed in a silk top hat, and angry workers. A woman and her children, presumably members of a striker's family, watch from the side while another woman, at the center, appears to plead for restraint. The threat of violence hangs in the air, and a striker in the lower right-hand corner reaches for a stone. The painting was inspired by events in Pittsburgh during the Great Railroad Strike of 1877.

The Knights of Labor and the "Conditions Essential to Liberty"

The 1880s witnessed a new wave of labor organizing. At its center stood the **Knights of Labor**. The Knights were the first group to try to organize unskilled workers as well as skilled ones, women alongside men, and Blacks as well as whites (although even the Knights excluded the despised Asian immigrants on the West Coast). The group reached a peak membership of nearly 800,000 in 1886 (making it the largest labor organization of the nineteenth century) and involved millions of workers in strikes, boycotts, political action, and educational and social activities.

Labor reformers of the Gilded Age put forward a wide array of programs, from the eight-hour day to public employment in hard times, currency reform, anarchism, socialism, and the creation of a vaguely defined "cooperative commonwealth." All these ideas arose from the conviction that the social conditions of the 1880s needed drastic change. Americans, declared

Terence V. Powderly, head of the Knights of Labor, were not "the free people that we imagine we are."

The labor movement launched a sustained assault on the understanding of freedom grounded in Social Darwinism and liberty of contract. Because of unrestrained economic growth and political corruption, the Knights charged, ordinary Americans had lost control of their economic livelihoods and their own government. Reaching back across the divide of the Civil War, labor defined employers as a new "slave power." Concentrated capital, warned George E. McNeill, a shoemaker and factory worker who became one of the movement's most eloquent writers, was now "a greater power than that of the state." The remedy was to "engraft republican principles into our industrial system" by guaranteeing a basic set of economic rights for all Americans.

Middle-Class Reformers

Dissatisfaction with social conditions in the Gilded Age extended well beyond aggrieved workers. Alarmed by fear of class warfare and the growing power of concentrated capital, social thinkers offered numerous plans for change. In the last quarter of the century, more than 150 utopian or cataclysmic novels appeared, predicting that social conflict would end either in a new, harmonious social order or in total catastrophe. One popular novel of the era, *Caesar's Column* (1891) by Ignatius Donnelly, ended with civilized society destroyed in a savage civil war between labor and capital.

Of the many books proposing more optimistic remedies for the unequal distribution of wealth, the most popular were *Progress and Poverty* (1879) by Henry George, *The Cooperative Commonwealth* (1884) by Laurence Gronlund, and Edward Bellamy's *Looking Backward* (1888). All three were among the century's greatest best-sellers, their extraordinary success testifying to what George called "a wide-spread consciousness . . . that there is something *radically* wrong in the present social organization." All three writers, though in very different ways, sought to reclaim an imagined golden age of social harmony and American freedom.

Progress and Poverty

Although it had no direct impact on government policy, *Progress and Poverty* probably commanded more public attention than any book on economics in American history. An antislavery newspaper editor in California in the 1850s and 1860s, Henry George had witnessed firsthand the rapid monopolization of land in the state. His book began with a famous statement of "the problem" suggested by its title—the growth of "squalor and misery" alongside material progress. His solution was the **single tax**, which would replace other taxes with a levy on increases in the value of real estate. The single tax would be so high that it would prevent speculation in both urban and rural land. No one knows how many of Henry George's readers actually believed in this way of solving the nation's ills. But millions responded to his clear explanation of economic relationships and his stirring account of how the "social distress" long thought to be confined to the Old World had made its appearance in the New.

Freedom lay at the heart of George's analysis. The "proper name" for the political movement spawned by his book, he once wrote, was "freedom men," who would "do for the question of industrial slavery" what the Republican Party had done for the slavery of Blacks. George rejected the traditional equation of liberty with ownership of land (since the single tax in effect made land the "common property" of the entire society). In other ways, however, his definition of freedom was thoroughly in keeping with mainstream thought. Despite calling for a single massive public intervention in the economy, George saw government as a "repressive power," whose functions in the "co-operative society" of the future would be limited to enhancing the quality of life—building "public baths, museums, libraries, gardens," and the like.

The Cooperative Commonwealth

Quite different in outlook was *The Cooperative Commonwealth*, the first book to popularize socialist ideas for an American audience. Its author, Laurence Gronlund, was a lawyer who had emigrated from Denmark in 1867. Socialism—the belief that private control of economic enterprises should be replaced by public ownership in order to ensure a fairer distribution of the benefits of the wealth produced—became a major political force in Western Europe in the late nineteenth century. In the United States, however, where access to private property was widely considered essential to individual freedom, socialist beliefs at this point were largely confined to immigrants, whose writings, frequently in foreign languages, attracted little attention.

Gronlund began the process of socialism's Americanization. While Karl Marx, the nineteenth century's most influential socialist theorist, had predicted that socialism would come into being via a working-class revolution, Gronlund portrayed it as the end result of a process of peaceful evolution, not violent upheaval. He thus made socialism seem more acceptable to middle-class Americans who desired an end to class conflict and the restoration of social harmony.

Bellamy's Utopia

Not until the early twentieth century would socialism become a significant presence in American public life. As Gronlund himself noted, the most important result of *The Cooperative Commonwealth* was to prepare an audience for Edward Bellamy's *Looking Backward*, which promoted socialist ideas while "ignoring that name" (Bellamy wrote of nationalism, not socialism). Bellamy lived virtually his entire life in the small industrial city of Chicopee Falls, Massachusetts. In *Looking Backward*, his main character falls asleep in the late nineteenth century only to awaken in the year 2000, in a world where cooperation has replaced class strife, "excessive individualism," and cutthroat competition. Inequality has been banished and with it the idea of liberty as a condition to be achieved through individual striving free of governmental restraint. Freedom, Bellamy insisted, was a social condition, resting on interdependence, not autonomy.

From today's vantage point, Bellamy's utopia—with citizens obligated to labor for years in an Industrial Army controlled by a single Great Trust—seems a chilling social blueprint. Yet the book inspired the creation of hundreds of nationalist clubs devoted to bringing into existence the world of 2000 and left a profound mark on a generation of reformers and intellectuals. Bellamy held out the hope of retaining the material abundance made possible by industrial capitalism while eliminating inequality. In proposing that the state guarantee economic security to all, Bellamy offered a far-reaching expansion of the idea of freedom.

Protestants and Moral Reform

Mainstream Protestants played a major role in seeking to stamp out sin in the late nineteenth century. What one historian calls a "Christian lobby" promoted political solutions to what it saw as the moral problems raised by labor conflict and the growth of cities, and threats to religious faith by Darwinism and other scientific advances.

Unlike the pre–Civil War period, when "moral suasion" was the preferred approach of many reformers, powerful national organizations like the Women's Christian Temperance Union, National Reform Association, and Reform Bureau now campaigned for federal legislation that would "Christianize the government" by outlawing sinful behavior. Among the proposed targets were the consumption of alcohol, gambling, prostitution, polygamy, and birth control. Most of these groups spoke less about improving society than stamping out the sins of individuals. In a striking departure from the prewar situation, southerners joined in the campaign for federal regulation of individual behavior, something whites in the region had previously strongly opposed, fearing it could lead to action against slavery. The key role played by the white South in the campaign for moral legislation helped earn the region a reputation as the Bible Belt—a place where political action revolved around religious principles. Although efforts to enact a national law requiring businesses to close on Sunday failed, the Christian lobby's efforts in the 1880s and 1890s set the stage for later legislation such as the Mann Act of 1910, banning the transportation of women across state lines for immoral purposes (an effort to suppress prostitution), and Prohibition.

A Social Gospel

Most of the era's Protestant preachers concentrated on attacking individual sins like drinking and Sabbath-breaking and saw nothing immoral about the pursuit of riches. But the outlines of what came to be called the **Social Gospel** were taking shape in the writings of Walter Rauschenbusch, a Baptist minister in New York City, Washington Gladden, a Congregational clergyman in Columbus, Ohio, and others. They insisted that freedom and spiritual self-development required an equalization of wealth and power and that unbridled competition mocked the Christian ideal of brotherhood.

The Social Gospel movement originated as an effort to reform Protestant churches by expanding their appeal in poor urban neighborhoods and making them more attentive to the era's social ills. The movement's adherents established missions and relief programs in urban areas that attempted to alleviate poverty, combat child labor, and encourage the construction of better working-class housing. They worked with the Knights of Labor and other groups demanding health and safety laws. Some suggested that a more cooperative organization of the economy should replace competitive capitalism. Within American Catholicism, as well, a group of priests and bishops emerged who attempted to alter the church's traditional hostility to movements for social reform and its isolation from contemporary currents of social thought. With most of its parishioners working men and women, they argued, the church should lend its support to the labor movement. These developments suggested the existence of widespread dissatisfaction with the "liberty of contract" understanding of freedom.

The Haymarket Affair

The year of the dedication of the Statue of Liberty, 1886, also witnessed an unprecedented upsurge in labor activity. Inspired by a successful strike by western railroad unions against lines controlled by the powerful financier Jay Gould, workers flooded into the Knights of Labor. On May 1, 1886, some 350,000 workers in cities across the country demonstrated for an eight-hour day. Having originated in the United States, May 1, or May Day as it came to be called, soon became an annual date of parades, picnics, and protests, celebrated around the world by organized labor.

The most dramatic events of 1886 took place in Chicago, a city with a large and vibrant labor movement that brought together native-born and

In a political cartoon from *Frank Leslie's Weekly*, November 13, 1886, Uncle Sam congratulates a workingman for the defeat of Henry George's candidacy for mayor of New York City on the United Labor Party ticket. A disappointed anarchist fulminates in the background. Local labor parties did win many local victories in 1886.

immigrant workers, whose outlooks ranged from immigrant socialism and anarchism to American traditions of equality and anti-monopoly. In 1885, the iron moulders union—one of the most powerful organizations of skilled industrial workers in the country—had organized a strike against a wage reduction at the great McCormick plant that produced agricultural machinery. The company brought in strikebreakers and private police, who battled in the streets with the strikers. Fearing chaos, the mayor and prominent business leaders persuaded the company to settle on the union's terms. But in February 1886, after the company installed new machinery that reduced its dependence on the iron moulders' traditional skills, it announced that henceforth the factory would operate on a nonunion basis. The result was a bitter, prolonged strike.

This time, Chicago's city government sided with the company. On May 3, 1886, four strikers were killed by police when they attempted to prevent strikebreakers from entering the factory. The next day, a rally was held in Haymarket Square to protest the killings. Near the end of the speeches, someone—whose identity has never been determined—threw a bomb into the crowd, killing a policeman. The panicked police opened fire, shooting several bystanders and a number of their own force. Employers took the opportunity presented by the **Haymarket affair** to paint the labor movement as a dangerous and un-American force, prone to violence and controlled by foreign-born radicals. Eight anarchists were charged with plotting and carrying out the bombing. Even though the evidence against them was extremely weak, a jury convicted the "Haymarket martyrs." Four were hanged, one committed suicide in prison, and the remaining three were imprisoned until John Peter Altgeld, a pro-labor governor of Illinois, commuted their sentences in 1893.

Most of the eight men accused of plotting the Haymarket bombing were foreign-born—five Germans and an English immigrant. One was of German descent. The last was Albert Parsons, a native of Alabama who had served in the Confederate army in the Civil War and edited a Republican newspaper in Texas during Reconstruction. Fearing violence because of his political views and the fact that his wife, Lucy Parsons, a former slave, was Black, Albert Parsons moved to Chicago during the 1870s. Having survived the Ku Klux Klan in Reconstruction Texas, Parsons perished on the Illinois gallows for a crime that he, like the other "Haymarket martyrs," did not commit. Lucy Parsons went on to become one of the era's most celebrated radical orators. She probably addressed more Americans than any other Black speaker in the nineteenth century except Frederick Douglass.

Labor and Politics

The Haymarket affair took place amid an outburst of independent labor political activity. One study has identified more than 100 local political tickets associated with the Knights of Labor between 1886 and 1888, from Anniston, Alabama, to Whitewater, Wisconsin. Their major aim was to end the use of public and private police forces and court injunctions against strikes and labor organizations. At least sixty achieved some kind of electoral success. In Kansas City, a coalition of Black and Irish American workers and middle-class voters elected Tom Hanna as mayor. He proceeded to side with unions rather than employers in industrial disputes.

The most celebrated labor campaign took place in New York City, where in 1886, somewhat to his own surprise, Henry George found himself thrust into the role of labor's candidate for mayor. A few days after the dedication of the Statue of Liberty, New Yorkers flocked to the polls. Nearly 70,000 voted for George, who finished second, eclipsing the total of the Republican candidate, Theodore Roosevelt, and coming close to defeating Democrat Abram Hewitt.

In a political system that within living memory had witnessed the disappearance of the Whig Party, the rise and fall of the Know-Nothings, and the emergence of the Republicans, the events of 1886 suggested that labor might be on the verge of establishing itself as a permanent political force. In fact, that year marked the high point of the Knights of Labor. Facing increasing employer hostility and linked by the press to the violence and radicalism associated with the Haymarket events, the Knights soon declined. The major parties, moreover, proved remarkably resourceful in appealing to labor voters.

THE TRANSFORMATION OF THE WEST

Nowhere did capitalism penetrate more rapidly or dramatically than in the trans-Mississippi West, whose "vast, trackless spaces," as the poet Walt Whitman called them, were now absorbed into the expanding economy. At the close of the Civil War, the frontier of continuous white settlement did not extend very far beyond the Mississippi River. To the west lay millions of acres of fertile and mineral-rich land roamed by giant herds of buffalo whose meat and hides provided food, clothing, and shelter for a population of more than 250,000 Indians.

In 1893, the historian Frederick Jackson Turner gave a celebrated lecture, "The Significance of the Frontier in American History," in which he argued that on the western frontier the distinctive qualities of American culture were forged: individual freedom, political democracy, and economic mobility. The West, he added, acted as a "safety valve," drawing off those dissatisfied with their situation in the East and therefore counteracting the threat of social unrest. Turner's was one of the most influential interpretations of American history ever developed. But his lecture summarized attitudes toward the West that had been widely shared among Americans long before 1893. Ever since the beginning of colonial settlement in British North America, the West—a region whose definition shifted as the population expanded—had been seen as a place of opportunity.

Many Americans did indeed experience the westward movement in the way Turner described it. From farmers moving into Ohio, Indiana, and Illinois in the decades after the American Revolution to prospectors who struck it rich in the California gold rush of the mid-nineteenth century, millions of Americans and immigrants from abroad found in the westward movement a path to economic opportunity. But Turner seemed to portray the West as an empty space before the coming of white settlers. In fact, of course, it was already inhabited by Native Americans, who bore the brunt of westward expansion as people from the East invaded their homelands. Moreover, the West was hardly a uniform paradise of small, independent farmers. Landlords, railroads, and mining companies in the West also utilized Mexican migrant and indentured labor, Chinese working on long-term contracts, and, until the end of the Civil War, African American slaves.

A Diverse Region

The West, of course, was hardly a single area. West of the Mississippi River lay a variety of regions, all marked by remarkable physical beauty—the Great Plains, the Rocky Mountains, the desert of the Southwest, the Sierra Nevada, and the valleys and coastline of California and the Pacific Northwest. It would take many decades before individual settlers and corporate business enterprises penetrated all these areas. But the process was far advanced by the end of the nineteenth century.

The political and economic incorporation of the American West was part of a global process. In many parts of the world, indigenous inhabitants—the Mapuche in Chile, the Zulu in South Africa, Aboriginal peoples in Australia, American Indians— were pushed aside (often after fierce resistance) as centralizing governments brought large interior regions under their control. In the United States, the incorporation of the West required the active intervention of the federal government, which acquired Indian land by war and treaty, administered land sales, regulated territorial politics, and distributed land and money to farmers, railroads, and mining companies. Western states used land donated by the federal government, in accordance with the Morrill Land-Grant Act passed during the Civil War, to establish public universities. And, of course, the abolition of slavery by the Thirteenth Amendment decided the long contest over whether the West would be a society based on free or slave labor.

Newly created western territories such as Arizona, Idaho, Montana, and the Dakotas remained under federal control far longer than had been the pattern in the East. Eastern territories had taken an average of thirteen years to achieve statehood; it took New Mexico sixty-two years to do so, Arizona forty-nine, and Utah forty-six. Many easterners were wary of granting statehood to the territories until white and non-Mormon settlers counterbalanced the large Latino and Mormon populations.

Having been granted millions of acres of land by the federal and state governments, railroads sought to encourage emigration to the West by both Americans and immigrants so that they could sell real estate to settlers. This brochure by the Chicago, Burlington & Quincy Railroad Company, circulated in Europe, advertises land in Nebraska in Danish.

In the twentieth century, the construction of federally financed irrigation systems and dams would open large areas to commercial farming. Ironically, the West would become known (not least to its own inhabitants) as a place of rugged individualism and sturdy independence. But without active governmental assistance, the region could never have been settled and developed.

Farming on the Middle Border

Even as sporadic Indian wars raged, settlers poured into the West. Territorial and state governments eager for population, and railroad companies anxious to sell land they had acquired from the government, flooded European countries and eastern cities with promotional literature promising easy access to land. More land came into cultivation in the thirty years after the Civil War than in the previous two and a half centuries of American history. Hundreds of thousands of families acquired farms under the Homestead Act, and even more purchased land from speculators and from railroad companies that had been granted immense tracts of public land by the federal government. A new agricultural empire producing wheat and corn for national and international markets arose on the Middle Border (Minnesota, the Dakotas, Nebraska, and Kansas), whose population rose from 300,000 in 1860 to 5 million in 1900. The farmers were a diverse group, including native-born easterners, Blacks escaping the post-Reconstruction South, and immigrants from Canada, Germany, Scandinavia, and Great Britain. Although ethnic diversity is generally associated with eastern cities, in the late nineteenth century the most multicultural state in the Union was North Dakota.

Despite the promises of promotional pamphlets, farming on the Great Plains was not an easy task. Difficulties came in many forms—from the poisonous rattlesnakes that lived in the tall prairie grass to the blizzards and droughts that periodically afflicted the region. Much of the burden fell on women. Farm families generally invested in the kinds of labor-saving machinery that would bring in cash, not machines that would ease women's burdens in the household (like the backbreaking task of doing laundry). While husbands and sons tended to devote their labor to cash crops, farm wives cared for animals, grew crops for food, and cooked and cleaned. A farm woman in Arizona described her morning chores in her diary: "Get up, turn out my chickens, draw a pail of water . . . make a fire, put potatoes to cook, brush and sweep half inch of dust off floor, feed three litters of chickens, then mix biscuits, get breakfast, milk, besides work in the house, and this morning had to go half mile after calves." On far-flung homesteads, many miles from schools, medical care, and sources of entertainment, farm families suffered from loneliness and isolation—a problem especially severe for women when their husbands left, sometimes for weeks at a time, to market their crops.

Bonanza Farms

John Wesley Powell, the explorer and geologist who surveyed the Middle Border in the 1870s, warned that because of the region's arid land and limited rainfall, development there required large-scale irrigation projects. The model of family farming envisioned by the Homestead Act of 1862 could not apply: no single family could do all the work required on irrigated farms—only cooperative, communal farming could succeed, Powell maintained.

Despite the emergence of a few **bonanza farms** that covered thousands of acres and employed large numbers of agricultural wage workers, family farms still dominated the trans-Mississippi West. Even small farmers, however, became increasingly oriented to national and international markets, specializing in the production of single crops for sale in faraway places. At the same time, railroads brought factory-made goods to rural people, replacing items previously produced in farmers' homes. Farm families became more and more dependent on loans to purchase land, machinery, and industrial products, and more and more vulnerable to the ups and downs of prices for agricultural goods in the world market. Agriculture reflected how the international economy was becoming more integrated. The combination of economic depressions and expanding agricultural production in places like Argentina, Australia, and the American West pushed prices of farm products steadily downward. From Italy and Ireland to China, India, and the American South, small farmers throughout the world suffered severe difficulties in the last quarter of the nineteenth century. Many joined the migration to cities within their countries or the increasing international migration of labor.

The future of western farming ultimately lay with giant agricultural enterprises relying heavily on irrigation, chemicals, and machinery—investments far beyond the means of family farmers. A preview of the agricultural future was already evident in California, where, as far back as Spanish and Mexican days, landownership had been concentrated in large units. In the late nineteenth century, California's giant fruit and vegetable farms, owned by corporations like the Southern Pacific Railroad, were tilled not by agricultural laborers who could expect to acquire land of their own, but by migrant workers from China, the Philippines, Japan, and Mexico, who tramped from place to place following the ripening crops.

In the 1870s, California's "wheat barons," who owned ranches of 30,000 or more acres, shipped their grain from San Francisco all the way to Great Britain, while large-scale growers in the new "Orange Empire" of the southern part of the state sent fruit east by rail, packaged in crates bedecked with images of an Edenic landscape filled with lush orchards.

The Cowboy and the Corporate West

The two decades following the Civil War also witnessed the golden age of the cattle kingdom. The Kansas Pacific Railroad's stations at Abilene, Dodge City, and Wichita, Kansas, became destinations for the fabled drives of millions of cattle from Texas. A collection of white, Mexican, and Black men who

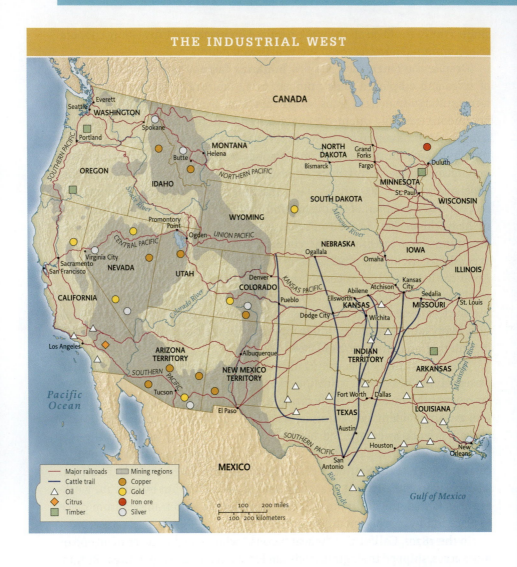

conducted the cattle drives, the cowboys became symbols of a life of freedom on the open range. Their exploits would later serve as the theme of many a Hollywood movie, and their clothing inspired fashions that remain popular today. But there was nothing romantic about the life of the cowboys, most of whom were low-paid wage workers. (Texas cowboys even went on strike for higher pay in 1883.) The days of the long-distance cattle drive ended in the mid-1880s, as farmers enclosed more and more of the open range with barbed-wire fences, making it difficult to graze cattle on the grasslands of the Great Plains, and two terrible winters destroyed millions of cattle. When the industry recuperated, it was reorganized in large, enclosed ranches close to rail connections.

The West was more than a farming empire. By 1890, a higher percentage of its population lived in cities than was the case in other regions. The economic focus of California's economy remained San Francisco, a major manufacturing center and one of the world's great trading ports. The explosive growth of southern California began in the 1880s, first with tourism, heavily promoted by railroad companies, followed by the discovery of oil in Los Angeles in 1892. Large corporate enterprises appeared throughout the West. The lumber industry, dominated by small-scale producers in 1860, came under the control of corporations that acquired large tracts of forest and employed armies of loggers. Lumbermen had cut trees in the Far West's vast forests since the days of Spanish and Mexican rule. Now, with rising demand for wood for buildings in urban centers and with new railroads making it possible to send timber quickly to the East, production expanded rapidly. Sawmills sprang up near rail lines, and lumber companies acquired thousands of acres of timber land. Loggers who had migrated from the East and Midwest and were used to cutting pine trees had to develop new techniques for felling the far larger giant redwoods of northern California. Once they did, coastal forests were decimated, with the high-quality wood being used to construct many of the buildings in San Francisco and other communities. In the early twentieth century, the desire to save the remaining redwoods would become one inspiration for the conservation movement.

Western mining, from Michigan iron ore and copper to gold and silver in California, Nevada, and Colorado, fell under the sway of companies that mobilized eastern and European investment to introduce advanced technology. Gold and silver rushes took place in the Dakotas in 1876, Idaho in 1883, Colorado in the 1890s, and Alaska at the end of the century. Railroad hubs like Albuquerque, Denver, El Paso, and Tucson flourished as gateways to the new mineral regions. But as in California after 1848, the independent prospector working a surface mine with his pick and shovel quickly gave way to deep-shaft corporate mining employing wage workers. As with other western industries, the coming of the railroad greatly expanded the possibilities for mining, making it possible to ship minerals from previously inaccessible places. Moreover, professionally trained engineers from the East and Europe introduced new scientific techniques of mining and smelting ore. For example, the town of Leadville, Colorado, which did not exist before the mid-1870s, became one of the world's great centers of lead production after August R. Meyer, a European mining engineer, analyzed the precise content of silver and lead in the area's minerals. The economic crosscurrents at work in post–Civil War mining were illustrated at Butte, Montana. In the 1880s, absentee owners from San Francisco poured millions of dollars into what they thought was a silver mine, only to learn that they had acquired one of the world's richest deposits of copper. A new town, Anaconda, quickly arose, with a population of 2,000 miners, smelters, engineers, and others, from a wide variety of ethnic backgrounds. In the early twentieth century, the company would be acquired by bankers and other investors from the East.

A similar process occurred in New Mexico, where traditional life based on sheep farming on land owned in common by Mexican villagers had continued more or less unchanged after the United States acquired the area in the Mexican War. The existence of these Spanish and Mexican communal landholdings may have influenced John Wesley Powell's recommendations concerning communal farming. Railroads reached the area in the 1870s, bringing with them eastern mining companies and commercial ranchers and farmers. Because courts only recognized Mexican-era land titles to individual plots of land, communal landholdings were increasingly made available for sale to newcomers. By 1880, three-quarters of New Mexico's sheep belonged to just twenty families. Unable to continue as sheep raisers, more and more Hispanic residents went to work for the new mines and railroads.

The Chinese Presence

Chinese immigration, which had begun at the time of the California gold rush, continued in the postwar years. Before the Civil War, nearly all Chinese newcomers had been unattached men, brought in by labor contractors to work in western gold fields, railroad construction, and factories. In the early 1870s, entire Chinese families began to immigrate. By 1880, 105,000 persons of Chinese descent lived in the United States. Three-quarters lived in California, where Chinese made up over half of the state's farm workers. But Chinese immigrants were present throughout the West and in all sorts of jobs. After the completion of the transcontinental railroad in 1869, many worked in construction on other railroad lines that sprang up throughout the region. Chinese could be found in mines in Idaho, Colorado, and Nevada, as domestic workers in urban households, and in factories producing cigars, clothing, and shoes in western cities. They built levees, drained agricultural fields, and worked on fishing boats. Many men had wives and children in China, and like members of other immigrant groups, they kept in touch by sending letters and money to their families at home and reading magazines aimed at emigrants that reported on local events in China. As will be related in the next chapter, their growing presence sparked an outpouring of anti-Chinese sentiment, leading to laws excluding virtually all Chinese from entering the country.

Conflict on the Mormon Frontier

The Mormons had moved to the Great Salt Lake Valley in the 1840s, hoping to practice their religion free of the persecution that they had encountered in the East. They envisioned their community in Utah as the foundation of a great empire they called Deseret. Given the widespread unpopularity of Mormon polygamy and the close connection of church and state in Mormon theology, conflict with both the federal government and the growing numbers of non-Mormons moving west became inevitable. In 1857, after receiving reports that the work of federal judges in Utah was being obstructed by the territorial governor, the Mormon leader Brigham Young, President James Buchanan removed Young and appointed a non-Mormon to replace him. Young refused to comply, and federal troops entered the Salt Lake Valley, where they remained until the beginning of the Civil War. During this time of tension, a group of Mormons attacked a wagon train of non-Mormon settlers traveling through Utah and intending to settle in California. What came to be called the Mountain Meadows Massacre resulted in the death of all the adults and older children in the wagon train—over 100 persons. Only a handful of young children survived. Nearly twenty years later, one leader of the assault was convicted of murder and executed.

After the Civil War, Mormon leaders sought to avoid further antagonizing the federal government. In the 1880s, Utah banned the practice of polygamy, a prohibition written into the state constitution as a requirement before Utah gained admission as a state in 1896.

The Plains Indians in a Changing West

The transcontinental railroad, a symbol of the reunited nation, brought tens of thousands of newcomers to the West and stimulated the expansion of farming, mining, and other enterprises. The incorporation of the West into the national economy spelled the doom of the world of the Plains Indians. Their lives had already undergone profound transformations. In the eighteenth century, the spread of horses, originally introduced by the Spanish, led to a wholesale shift from farming and hunting on foot to mounted hunting of buffalo. New Indian groups migrated to the Great Plains to take advantage of the horse, coalescing into the great tribes of the nineteenth century—the Cheyenne, Comanche, Crow, Kiowa, and Lakota. As newcomers sought to stake a claim on the hunting grounds of the Great Plains and existing groups fought to defend their homelands, cycles of warfare spread across the region.

Until the Civil War, Native nations ruled the Great Plains and the American presence was mostly limited to army forts and trading posts. Most migrants on the Oregon and California trails before the Civil War encountered little hostility from Indians, often trading with them for food and supplies. But as settlers encroached on Indian lands, bloody conflict between the army and Plains tribes began in the 1850s and continued for decades.

Grant's Peace Policy and Reconstruction in Indian Territory

In 1869, President Grant announced a "Peace Policy" in the West. It was designed by Ely Parker, a Seneca man who had served on Grant's staff during the war and who had written out Robert E. Lee's terms of surrender in 1865. Appointed by Grant, Commissioner of Indian Affairs Ely Parker was the first Native American to hold that office. (The first Indian Cabinet member, Secretary of the Interior Deb Haaland, was appointed by President Joe Biden in 2021.) Initially, the Peace Policy curtailed military violence in the West. Its announcement was soon followed by an act of Congress ending the practice of making treaties with Indigenous peoples—a severe blow to Native American sovereignty. Now Indian policy would be determined unilaterally by Congress and the president. The underlying assumption remained what it long had been: that Indians must accept removal to reservations and eventual assimilation into American life. In some ways, these policies offered a parallel to Reconstruction in the South. In both cases the federal government sought to consolidate its control over the entire country and to fit large numbers of conquered people—white southerners and western Indians—into a single national mold.

Despite the Peace Policy, warfare soon resumed. Drawing on methods used to defeat the Confederacy, Civil War generals like Philip H. Sheridan set out to destroy the foundations of the Indian economy—villages, horses, and especially the buffalo. Hunting by mounted Indians had already reduced the buffalo population—estimated at 30 million in 1800—but it was army campaigns and the depredations of hunters seeking buffalo hides that rendered the vast herds all but extinct. By 1886, an expedition from the Smithsonian Institution in

This pencil-and-crayon drawing by a Cheyenne Indian from the 1880s depicts a Native American fighting two Black members of the U.S. military. After the Civil War, Black soldiers, whose presence was resented by many whites, in the North as well as the South, were reassigned to the West.

Washington had difficulty finding twenty-five "good specimens." "A cold wind blew across the prairie when the last buffalo fell," said the Sioux leader Sitting Bull, "a death-wind for my people."

"Let Me Be a Free Man"

The army's relentless attacks broke the power of one tribe after another. In 1877, troops commanded by former Freedmen's Bureau commissioner O. O. Howard pursued the Nez Percé Indians and their leader, Chief Joseph, on a 1,700-mile chase across the Far West. The Nez Percé (whose name was given them by Lewis and Clark in 1805 and means "pierced nose" in French) were seeking to escape to Canada after fights with settlers who had encroached on tribal lands in Oregon and Idaho. After four months, Howard forced the Indians to surrender, and they were removed to Oklahoma and later to a reservation in Washington Territory. Until his death in 1904, Joseph would unsuccessfully petition successive presidents for his people's right to return to their beloved Oregon homeland.

Indians occasionally managed to inflict costly delay and even defeat on army units. The most famous Indian victory took place in June 1876 at the **Battle of the Little Bighorn**, when General George A. Custer and his entire command of 250 men perished. The Lakota, Arapaho, and Cheyenne warriors, led by Sitting Bull and Crazy Horse, were defending tribal land in the Black Hills of the Dakota Territory. Reserved for them in an 1868 treaty "for as long as the grass shall grow," their lands had been invaded by whites after the discovery of gold. Eventually the Indians were worn down, partly because of the decimation of the buffalo, and relinquished their claim to the Black Hills. In the Southwest, Cochise, Geronimo, and other leaders of the Apache, who had been relocated by the government a number of times, led bands that crossed and recrossed the border with Mexico, evading the army and occasionally killing civilians. They would not surrender until the mid-1880s.

Another casualty was the Comanche empire, centered in modern-day New Mexico and Colorado. Beginning in the mid-eighteenth century, the Comanche dominated much of the Great Plains and Southwest. The Comanche subordinated local Indian groups to their power, imposed a toll on trade routes like the Santa Fe Trail, and dealt for a time as an equal with the Spanish, French, and American governments. Their power was not finally broken until the 1870s.

Remaking Indian Life

"The life my people want is a life of freedom," Sitting Bull declared. The Indian idea of freedom, however, which centered on preserving their cultural and political autonomy and control of ancestral lands, conflicted with the interests and values of most white Americans. Nearly all officials believed that the

From SPEECH OF CHIEF JOSEPH OF THE NEZ PERCÉ INDIANS, IN WASHINGTON, D.C. (1879)

Chief Joseph, leader of the Nez Percé Indians, led his people on a 1,700-mile trek through the Far West in 1877 in an unsuccessful effort to escape to Canada. Two years later, he addressed an audience in Washington, D.C., that included President Rutherford B. Hayes, appealing for the freedom and equal rights enshrined in the law after the Civil War.

———————————————

I have heard talk and talk, but nothing is done. Good words do not last long unless they amount to something. Words do not pay for my dead people. They do not pay for my country, now overrun by white men. . . . Good words will not get my people a home where they can live in peace and take care of themselves. I am tired of talk that comes to nothing. It makes my heart sick when I remember all the . . . broken promises. . . .

If the white man wants to live in peace with the Indian he can live in peace. There need be no trouble. Treat all men alike. Give them the same law. Give them all an even chance to live and grow. All men were made by the same Great Spirit Chief. They are all brothers. The earth is the mother of all people, and all people should have equal rights upon it. You might as well expect the rivers to run backward as that any man who was born a free man should be contented when penned up and denied liberty to go where he pleases. . . .

When I think of our condition my heart is heavy. I see men of my race treated as outlaws and driven from country to country, or shot down like animals. I know that my race must change. We cannot hold our own with the white men as we are. We only ask an even chance to live as other men live. . . .

Let me be a free man—free to travel, free to stop, free to work, free to trade where I choose, free to choose my own teachers, free to follow the religion of my fathers, free to think and talk and act for myself—and I will obey every law, or submit to the penalty.

From LETTER BY SAUM SONG BO, AMERICAN MISSIONARY (OCTOBER 1885)

During the 1880s, Chinese Americans were subjected to discrimination in every phase of their lives. In 1882, Congress temporarily barred further immigration from China. In 1885, when funds were being raised to build a pedestal for the Statue of Liberty, Saum Song Bo, a Chinese American writer, contrasted the celebration of liberty with the treatment of the Chinese.

A paper was presented to me yesterday for inspection, and I found it to be specially drawn up for subscription among my countrymen toward the Pedestal Fund of the . . . Statue of Liberty. . . . But the word liberty makes me think of the fact that this country is the land of liberty for men of all nations except the Chinese. I consider it as an insult to us Chinese to call on us to contribute toward building in this land a pedestal for a statue of Liberty. That statue represents Liberty holding a torch which lights the passage of those of all nations who come into this country. But are the Chinese allowed to come? As for the Chinese who are here, are they allowed to enjoy liberty as men of all other nationalities enjoy it? Are they allowed to go about everywhere free from the insults, abuses, assaults, wrongs, and injuries from which men of other nationalities are free? . . .

And this statue of Liberty is a gift from another people who do not love liberty for the Chinese. [To] the Annamese and Tonquinese Chinese [colonial subjects of the French empire in Indochina], . . . liberty is as dear as to the French. What right have the French to deprive them of their liberty?

Whether this statute against the Chinese or the statue to Liberty will be the most lasting monument to tell future ages of the liberty and greatness of this country, will be known only to future generations.

QUESTIONS

1. *What are Chief Joseph's complaints about the treatment of his people?*

2. *Why does Saum Song Bo believe that the Chinese do not enjoy liberty in the United States?*

3. *What are the similarities and differences in the definition of freedom in the two documents?*

This photograph depicts Lakota, Cheyenne, and Arapaho leaders who visited the White House in 1877.

federal government should persuade or force the Plains Indians to surrender most of their land and to exchange their religion, communal property, nomadic way of life, and gender relations for Christian worship, private ownership, and small farming on reservations with men tilling the fields and women working in the home.

In 1871, Congress eliminated the treaty system that dated back to the revolutionary era, by which the federal government negotiated agreements with Indians as if they were independent nations. This step was supported by railroad companies that found tribal sovereignty an obstacle to construction and by Republicans who believed that it contradicted the national unity born of the Civil War. The federal government pressed forward with its assault on Indian culture. The Bureau of Indian Affairs established boarding schools where Indian children, removed from the "negative" influences of their parents and tribes, were dressed in non-Indian clothes, given new names, and educated in white ways.

The boarding schools established by the federal government lasted for a century and a half and during their existence housed hundreds of thousands of Indigenous children. The aim was forced assimilation: "kill the Indian and save the man," as the founder of one such school put it. The administrators imposed a regimented schedule and harsh discipline on Indian students, who were not allowed to return home, even when family members fell ill or died. Being removed from their families and communities had a long-term negative impact on many students. The boarding schools were rife with disease. Many students succumbed to tuberculosis and other illnesses and some died by suicide. The curriculum downplayed Indians' role in American history, prohibited the use of Native languages, and emphasized patriotic identification with the national government, not with individual tribes, all as part of the effort to assimilate the students into white society and to facilitate the seizure of Indian land.

The Dawes Act

The crucial step in attacking "tribalism" came in 1887 with the passage of the **Dawes Act**, named for Senator Henry L. Dawes of Massachusetts, chair of the Senate's Indian Affairs Committee. The act broke up the land of nearly all tribes into small parcels to be distributed to Indian families, with the remainder auctioned off to white purchasers. Indians who accepted the farms and "adopted the habits of civilized life" would become full-fledged American citizens. The policy proved to be a disaster, leading to the loss of much tribal land and the erosion of Indian cultural traditions. Whites, however, benefited enormously. When the government made 2 million acres of Indian land available in Oklahoma, 50,000 white settlers poured into the territory to claim farms on the single day of April 22, 1889. Further land rushes followed in the 1890s. In the half century after the passage of the Dawes Act, Indians lost 86 million of the 138 million acres of land in their possession in 1887. Overall, according to one estimate, between 1776 and today, via the "right of discovery," treaties, executive orders, court decisions, and outright theft, the United States has acquired over 1.5 billion acres of land from Native Americans, an area twenty-five times as large as Great Britain.

Are Native Americans American?

Many laws and treaties in the nineteenth century offered Indians the right to become American citizens if they left the tribal setting and assimilated into American society. But tribal identity was the one thing nearly every Indian wished to maintain, and very few took advantage of these offers. Thus, few Native Americans were recognized as American citizens. Western courts ruled that the rights guaranteed in the Civil Rights Act of 1866 and the Fourteenth and Fifteenth Amendments did not apply to them. In one of its most controversial rulings, *Elk v. Wilkins* (1884), the Supreme Court agreed.

John Elk was born in Indian Territory (in present-day Oklahoma), but gave up his tribal affiliation and moved to Omaha, where he worked and paid taxes. He tried, unsuccessfully, to claim American citizenship and register to vote. The Civil Rights Act had excluded only Indians "not taxed" from birthright citizenship, and the Fourteenth Amendment, as noted in Chapter 15, recognized as citizens all persons born in the United States and subject to its "jurisdiction." John Elk certainly seemed to meet all these criteria. Yet the Supreme Court rejected his appeal. It questioned whether any Indian had achieved the degree of "civilization" required of citizens.

By 1900, roughly 53,000 Indians had become American citizens by accepting land allotments under the Dawes Act. The following year, Congress granted citizenship to 100,000 residents of Indian Territory. The remainder would have to wait until 1919 (for those who fought in World War I). In that year there were around 300,000 Indians in the United States, of whom 125,000 were not citizens. Finally, in 1924, Congress extended citizenship to all Native Americans. But their right to cast ballots remained contested. As late as 1948, Arizona and New Mexico did not allow Indians to vote.

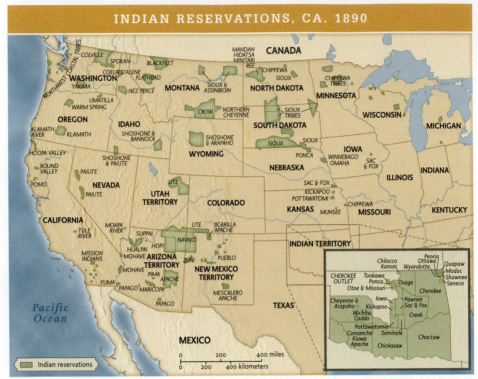

INDIAN RESERVATIONS, CA. 1890

By 1890, the vast majority of the remaining Indian population had been removed to reservations scattered across the western states.

The Ghost Dance and Wounded Knee

Some Indians sought solace in the **Ghost Dance,** a religious revitalization campaign. Its leaders foretold a day when whites would disappear, the buffalo would return, and Indians could once again practice their ancestral customs "free from misery, death, and disease." Large numbers of Native Americans gathered for days of singing, dancing, and religious observances. Fearing a general uprising, the government sent troops to the reservations. On December 29, 1890, soldiers opened fire on Ghost Dancers encamped near Wounded Knee Creek in South Dakota, killing between 150 and 200 Indians, mostly women and children.

The **Wounded Knee massacre** was widely applauded in the press. An Army Court of Inquiry essentially exonerated the troops and their commander, and twenty soldiers were later awarded the Medal of Honor, a recognition of exceptional heroism in battle, for their actions at Wounded Knee. Like federal efforts to exert control over the Mormons in Utah, the suppression of the Ghost Dance revealed the limits on Americans' efforts to seek in the West the freedom to practice nonmainstream religions.

Although violent skirmishes from Oklahoma to Minnesota in the early twentieth century showed that small-scale Indian resistance continued, the Wounded Knee massacre marked the end of four centuries of armed conflict between the continent's native population and European settlers and their descendants. By 1900, the Indian population had fallen to 250,000, the lowest point in American history. A children's book about Indians published around this time stated flatly, "The Indian pictured in these pages no longer exists." Yet despite everything, Indians survived, and in the twentieth century their numbers once again would begin to grow.

Settler Societies and Global Wests

The conquest of the American West was part of a global process whereby settlers moved boldly into the interior of regions in temperate climates around the world, bringing their familiar crops and livestock and establishing mining and other industries. Countries such as Argentina, Australia, Canada, and New Zealand, as well as the United States, are often called "settler societies," because immigrants from overseas quickly outnumbered and displaced the original inhabitants— unlike in India and most parts of colonial Africa, where fewer Europeans ventured and those who did relied on the labor of the indigenous inhabitants.

In many settler societies, native peoples were subjected to cultural reconstruction similar to policies in the United States. In Australia, the government gathered the Aboriginal populations—their numbers devastated by disease— in "reserves" reminiscent of American Indian reservations. Australia went further than the United States in the forced assimilation of surviving Aboriginal peoples. The government removed large numbers of children from their families to be adopted by whites—a policy only abandoned in the 1970s and for which the prime minister formally apologized in 2008 in a national moment of reconciliation called Sorry Day.

Myth, Reality, and the Wild West

The West has long played many roles in Americans' national self-consciousness. It has been imagined as a place of individual freedom and unbridled opportunity for those dissatisfied with their lives in the East and as a future empire that would dominate the continent and the world. Even as farms, mines, and cities spread over the landscape in the post–Civil War years, a new image of the West began to circulate—the Wild West, a lawless place ruled by cowboys and Indians (two groups by this time vastly outnumbered by other westerners), and marked by gunfights, cattle drives, and stagecoach robberies.

This image of a violent yet romantic frontier world would later become a staple of Hollywood movies. In the late nineteenth century, it was disseminated in vaudeville shows that achieved immense popularity. Although not the first, William "Buffalo Bill" Cody was the most important popularizer of this idea of the West. A former hunter and scout for the U.S. Army, Cody developed an elaborate theatrical presentation that toured for decades across the United States and Europe. Buffalo Bill's Wild West Show included reenactments of battles with Indians (including Custer's Last Stand), buffalo hunts, Indian rituals, and feats by the sharpshooter Annie Oakley. Along with Cody, other persons who had actually participated in these events appeared in the show, including the warrior Sitting Bull and a group of Indian fighters. The image of the Wild West also circulated in cheap popular books known as dime novels and sensational journalistic accounts.

Theater audiences and readers found fantasies of adventure in observing western violence from a safe distance and marveled at the skills of horseback riding, roping, and shooting on display. They imagined the West as a timeless place immune to the corruptions of civilization, which offered a striking contrast to the increasingly sedentary lives of men in eastern cities. Indeed, despite the inclusion of Oakley, this West of the imagination was emphatically a male preserve. The real West—for example, the struggles of farm families—played no role in this depiction. Nor did pervasive labor conflict in mining centers, or the role of the federal government and eastern capital in the region's development. The West's multiracial, multiethnic population also disappeared, although different groups added their own elements to the mythical west. Mexican Americans, for example, made a folk hero of Gregorio Cortez, a Texas outlaw renowned for his ability to outwit pursuers. The West Coast also had no place in the picture—the imagined West seemed to stop at the Rocky Mountains.

POLITICS IN A GILDED AGE

The Corruption of Politics

As they had earlier in the nineteenth century, Americans during the Gilded Age saw their nation as an island of political democracy in a world still dominated by undemocratic governments. In Europe, only France and Switzerland enjoyed universal male suffrage. Even in Britain, which prided itself on its tradition of political liberty, most of the working class could not vote until the passage of the Reform Act of 1884.

Nonetheless, the power of the new corporations, seemingly immune to democratic control, raised disturbing questions for the American understanding of political freedom as popular self-government. In 1873, the chief justice of the Wisconsin Supreme Court warned that a "new and dark power" threatened American democracy. "Which shall rule," he asked, "wealth or man; which shall lead, money or intellect; who shall fill public stations, educated and patriotic freemen, or the feudal slaves of corporate capital?" Political corruption was rife. "The galleries and lobbies of every legislature," observed an Illinois Republican leader, "are thronged with men seeking to procure an advantage" for one corporation or another. In Pennsylvania's legislature, the "third house" of railroad lobbyists was said to enjoy as much influence as the elected chambers. In the West, many lawmakers held stock or directorships in lumber companies and railroads that received public aid.

Urban politics fell under the sway of corrupt political machines like New York's Tweed Ring, which plundered the city of tens of millions of dollars. "Boss" William M. Tweed's organization reached into every neighborhood. He forged close ties with railroad men and labor unions, and he won support from the city's immigrant poor by fashioning a kind of private welfare system that provided food, fuel, and jobs in hard times. A combination of political reformers and businessmen tired of paying tribute to the ring ousted Tweed in the early 1870s, although he remained popular among the city's poor, who considered him an urban Robin Hood.

At the national level, many lawmakers supported bills aiding companies in which they had invested money or from which they received stock or salaries. The most notorious example of corruption came to light during Grant's presidency. This was Crédit Mobilier, a corporation formed by an inner ring of Union Pacific Railroad stockholders to oversee the line's government-assisted construction. Essentially, it enabled the participants to sign contracts with themselves, at an exorbitant profit, to build the new line. The arrangement was protected by the distribution of stock to influential politicians, including Speaker of the House Schuyler Colfax, who was elected vice president in 1868. In another example of corruption, the Whiskey Ring of the Grant administration united Republican officials, tax collectors, and whiskey manufacturers in a massive scheme that defrauded the federal government of millions of tax dollars.

The Politics of Dead Center

In national elections, party politics bore the powerful imprint of the Civil War. Republicans controlled the industrial North and Midwest and the agrarian

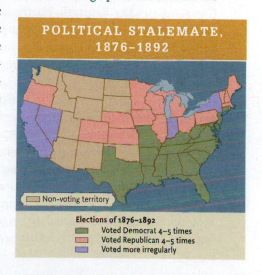

POLITICAL STALEMATE, 1876–1892

Non-voting territory

Elections of 1876–1892
- Voted Democrat 4–5 times
- Voted Republican 4–5 times
- Voted more irregularly

West and were particularly strong among members of revivalist churches, Protestant immigrants, and Blacks. Organizations of Union veterans formed a bulwark of Republican support. Every Republican candidate for president from 1868 to 1900 except James G. Blaine had fought in the Union army. (In the 1880 campaign, all four candidates—Republican James A. Garfield, Democrat Winfield Scott Hancock, Prohibitionist Neal Dow, and James B. Weaver of the Greenback-Labor Party—had been Union generals during the war.) By 1893, a lavish system of pensions for Union soldiers and their widows and children consumed more than 40 percent of the federal budget. Democrats, after 1877, dominated the South and did well among Catholic voters, especially Irish Americans, in the nation's cities.

Americans were heavily invested in national politics. Election campaigns brought forth nightly parades of torch-bearing partisans, incessant political rallies, and spellbinding oratory laced with scurrilous attacks on opponents. In saloons and on urban streetcars, Americans engaged in fistfights over politics. On election day, armed men employed by local political machines tried to prevent supporters of the opposing party from casting a ballot. One magazine described national politics as "the theater, the opera, the baseball game, the intellectual gymnasium [school], almost the church" all rolled into one.

The parties were closely divided. In three of the five presidential elections between 1876 and 1892, the margin separating the major candidates was less than 1 percent of the popular vote. Twice, in 1876 and 1888, the candidate with an electoral-college majority trailed in the popular ballot. The congressional elections of 1874, when Democrats won control of the House of Representatives, ushered in two decades of political stalemate. A succession of one-term presidencies followed: Rutherford B. Hayes (elected in 1876), James A. Garfield (succeeded, after his assassination in 1881, by Chester A. Arthur), Grover Cleveland in 1884, Benjamin Harrison in 1888, and Cleveland, elected for the second time, in 1892. Only for brief periods did the same party control the White House and both houses of Congress. More than once, Congress found itself paralyzed as important bills shuttled back and forth between the House and Senate, and special sessions to complete legislation became necessary. Gilded Age presidents made little effort to mobilize public opinion or exert executive leadership. Their staffs were quite small. Grover Cleveland himself answered the White House doorbell.

In some ways, American democracy in the Gilded Age seemed remarkably healthy. Party loyalty was intense, and 80 percent or more of eligible voters turned out to cast ballots. It was an era of spellbinding political oratory. James G. Blaine was among the members of Congress tainted by the Crédit Mobilier scandal, but Robert G. Ingersoll's speech before the Republican national convention of 1876 nearly secured Blaine's nomination for president by depicting him as a "plumed knight" who had raised his "shining lance" against the country's enemies.

Government and the Economy

The nation's political structure, however, proved ill equipped to deal with the problems created by the economy's rapid growth. Despite its expanded scope and powers arising from the Civil War, the federal government remained remarkably small by modern standards. Activities from education to medical care, business regulation, civil and criminal prosecutions, and many others were almost entirely under the control of local and state governments or private institutions. The federal workforce in 1880 numbered 100,000 (today, it exceeds 2 million).

Nationally, both parties came under the control of powerful political managers with close ties to business interests. Republicans strongly supported a high tariff to protect American industry, and throughout the 1870s they pursued a fiscal policy based on reducing federal spending, repaying much of the national debt, and withdrawing greenbacks—the paper money issued by the Union during the Civil War—from circulation. Democrats opposed the high tariff, but the party's national leadership remained closely linked to New York bankers and financiers and resisted demands from debt-ridden agricultural areas for an increase in the money supply. In 1879, for the first time since the war, the United States returned to the **gold standard**—that is, paper currency became exchangeable for gold at a fixed rate.

By reducing competition from foreign manufactured goods and leaving the banks, not the government, in control of issuing money, Republican economic policies strongly favored the interests of eastern industrialists and bankers. These policies worked to the disadvantage of southern and western farmers, who had to pay a premium for manufactured goods while the prices they received for their produce steadily declined.

Reform Legislation

Gilded Age national politics did not entirely lack accomplishments. Inspired in part by President Garfield's assassination by a disappointed office seeker, the **Civil Service Act of 1883** created a merit system for federal employees, with appointment via competitive examinations rather than political influence. Although it applied at first to only 10 percent of government workers, the act marked the first step in establishing a professional civil service and removing officeholding from the hands of political machines. (However, since funds raised from political appointees had helped to finance the political parties, civil service reform had the unintended result of increasing politicians' dependence on donations from business interests.)

In 1887, in response to public outcries against railroad practices, Congress established the **Interstate Commerce Commission** (ICC) to ensure that the rates railroads charged farmers and merchants to transport their goods were "reasonable" and did not offer more favorable treatment to some shippers. The ICC was the first federal agency intended to regulate economic activity, but since it lacked the power to establish rates on its own—it could only sue companies in court—it had little impact on railroad practices. Three years later, Congress passed the **Sherman Antitrust Act**, which banned all combinations and practices that restrained free trade. The measure posed a significant threat to corporate efforts to dominate sectors of the economy. But the courts primarily used it as a way to suppress labor unions. Nonetheless, these laws helped to establish the precedent that the national government could regulate the economy to promote the public good.

Political Conflict in the States

The nation had to weather the effects of drastic economic change and periodic economic crises without leadership from Washington. At the state and local levels, however, the Gilded Age was an era of political ferment and conflict over the proper uses of governmental authority. In the immediate aftermath of the Civil War, state governments in the North, like those in the Reconstruction South, greatly expanded their responsibility for public health, welfare, and education, and cities invested heavily in public works such as park construction and improved water and gas services. Those who suffered from economic change called on the activist state created by the war to redress their own grievances.

Third parties enjoyed significant if short-lived success in local elections. The Greenback-Labor Party proposed that the federal government stop taking "greenback" money out of circulation. This, it argued, would make more funds available for investment and give the government, not private bankers, control of the money supply. It also condemned the use of militias and private police against strikes. In the late 1870s, the party controlled local government in a number of industrial and mining communities and contributed to the election of twenty-one members of Congress independent of the two major parties.

The policies of railroad companies produced a growing chorus of protest, especially in the West. Farmers and local merchants complained of excessively high freight rates, discrimination in favor of large producers and shippers, and high fees charged by railroad-controlled grain warehouses. Critics of the railroads came together in the Patrons of Husbandry, or Grange, which moved to establish cooperatives for storing and marketing farm output in the hope of forcing the carriers "to take our produce at a fair price." Founded in 1867, the Grange claimed more than 700,000 members by the mid-1870s. It called on state governments to establish fair freight rates and warehouse charges. In several states, the Grange succeeded in having commissions established to investigate—and, in some cases, regulate—railroad practices.

Thus, America's Gilded Age witnessed deep and sometimes violent divisions over the definition of freedom in a rapidly industrializing society. The battle between upholders of Social Darwinism and laissez-faire, who saw freedom as the right of individuals to pursue their economic interests without outside restraint, and those who believed in collective efforts to create "industrial freedom" for ordinary Americans, would continue for many decades. In the early twentieth century, reformers would turn to new ways of addressing the social conditions of freedom and new means of increasing ordinary Americans' political and economic liberty. But before this, in the 1890s, the nation would face its gravest crisis since the Civil War, and the boundaries of freedom would once again be redrawn.

CHAPTER REVIEW

REVIEW QUESTIONS

1. *The American economy thrived because of federal involvement, not the lack of it. How did the federal government actively promote industrial and agricultural development in this period?*

2. *Why were railroads so important to America's second industrial revolution? What events demonstrate their influence on society and politics as well as the economy?*

3. *Why did organized efforts of farmers, workers, and local reformers largely fail to achieve substantive change in the Gilded Age?*

4. *Explain how social thinkers misapplied Charles Darwin's ideas to justify massive disparities in wealth and power and to deny government a role in equalizing opportunity.*

5. *How did social reformers such as Edward Bellamy, Henry George, and advocates of the Social Gospel conceive of liberty and freedom differently than the proponents of the liberty of contract ideal and laissez-faire?*

6. *In what ways did the West provide a "safety valve" for the problems in the industrial East? In what ways did it reveal some of the same problems?*

7. *Describe the involvement of American family farmers in the global economy after 1870 and its effects on their independence.*

8. *How did American political leaders seek to remake Native Americans and change the ways they lived?*

9. *What were some of the obstacles that made it difficult for Native Americans to claim American citizenship in the nineteenth century?*

10. *According to* The Gilded Age *by Mark Twain and Charles Dudley Warner, the era's slogan was "Get rich, dishonestly if we can, honestly if we must." Explain how this was true of the politics of the era.*

KEY TERMS

trusts (p. 611)

vertical integration (p. 611)

horizontal expansion (p. 612)

robber barons (p. 612)

the Gilded Age (p. 615)

Social Darwinism (p. 617)

liberty of contract (p. 619)

Great Railroad Strike (p. 620)

Knights of Labor (p. 621)

single tax (p. 622)

Social Gospel (p. 625)

Haymarket affair (p. 626)

bonanza farms (p. 631)

Battle of the Little Bighorn (p. 637)

Dawes Act (p. 640)

Ghost Dance (p. 642)

Wounded Knee massacre (p. 642)

gold standard (p. 647)

Civil Service Act of 1883 (p. 647)

Interstate Commerce Commission (p. 648)

Sherman Antitrust Act (p. 648)

Go to 🐰 INQUIZITIVE

To see what you know—and learn what you've missed—with personalized feedback along the way.

CHAPTER 17

FREEDOM'S BOUNDARIES, AT HOME AND ABROAD

1890–1900

FOCUS QUESTIONS

- *What were the origins and the significance of Populism?*

- *How did the liberties of Blacks after 1877 give way to legal segregation across the South?*

- *In what ways did the boundaries of American freedom grow narrower in this period?*

- *How did the United States emerge as an imperial power in the 1890s?*

One of the most popular songs of 1892 bore the title "Father Was Killed by a Pinkerton Man." It was inspired by an incident during a bitter strike at Andrew Carnegie's steelworks at Homestead, Pennsylvania, the nineteenth century's most widely publicized confrontation between labor and capital. The strike pitted one of the nation's leading industrial corporations against a powerful union, the Amalgamated Association, which represented the skilled iron- and steelworkers among the complex's 3,800 employees.

Homestead's twelve steel mills were the most profitable and technologically advanced in the world. The union contract gave the Amalgamated Association a considerable say in their operation, including the right to approve the hiring of new workers and to regulate the pace of work. To Carnegie and Henry Clay Frick, his partner and chairman of the Carnegie Steel Company, the union's power increasingly seemed an intolerable infringement on management's rights. In 1892, they decided to operate the plant on a nonunion basis. Frick surrounded the factory with a fence topped by barbed wire, constructed barracks to house strikebreakers, and fired the entire workforce. Henceforth, only workers who agreed not to join the union could work at Homestead. In response, the workers, including the unskilled laborers not included in the Amalgamated Association, blockaded the steelworks and mobilized support from the local community. The battle memorialized in song took place on July 6, 1892, when armed strikers confronted 300 private policemen from the Pinkerton Detective Agency. Seven workers and three Pinkerton agents were killed, and the Pinkertons were forced to retreat. Four days later, the governor of Pennsylvania dispatched 8,000 militiamen to open the complex on management's terms. The strikers held out until November, but the union's defeat was now inevitable. In the end, the Amalgamated Association was destroyed.

The Carnegie corporation's tactics and the workers' solidarity won the strikers widespread national sympathy. "Ten thousand Carnegie libraries," declared the *St. Louis Post-Dispatch*, "would not compensate the country for the evils resulting from Homestead." The strike became an international cause célèbre as well. British newspapers pointed out that their country restricted the use of private police forces far more severely than the United States. Britons, they claimed, understood economic liberty better than Americans.

Homestead demonstrated that neither a powerful union nor public opinion could influence the conduct of the largest corporations. The writer Hamlin Garland, who visited Homestead two years after the strike, found the workforce sullen and bitter. He described a town "as squalid and unlovely as could be imagined," with dingy houses over which hung dense clouds of black smoke. It was "American," he wrote, "only in the sense in which [it] represents the American idea of business."

In fact, two American ideas of freedom collided at Homestead—the employers' definition, based on the idea that property rights, unrestrained by union rules or public regulation, sustained the public good, and the workers' conception, which stressed economic security and independence from what they considered the "tyranny" of employers. The strife at Homestead also reflected broader battles over American freedom during the 1890s. Like the Homestead workers, many Americans came to believe that they were being denied economic independence and democratic self-government, long central to the popular understanding of freedom.

During the 1890s, millions of farmers joined the Populist movement in an attempt to reverse their declining economic prospects and to rescue the government from what they saw as control by powerful corporate interests. The 1890s witnessed the imposition of a new racial system in the South that locked African Americans into the status of second-class citizenship, denying them many of the freedoms white Americans took for granted. Increasing immigration produced heated debates over whether the country should reconsider its traditional self-definition as a refuge for foreigners seeking greater freedom on American shores. At the end of the 1890s, in the Spanish-American War, the United States for the first time acquired overseas territory and found itself ruling over subject peoples from Puerto Rico to the Philippines. Was the democratic republic, many Americans wondered, becoming an empire like those of Europe? Rarely has the country experienced at one time so many debates over both the meaning and boundaries of freedom.

THE POPULIST CHALLENGE

The Farmers' Revolt

Even as labor unrest crested, a different kind of uprising was ripening in the South and the trans-Mississippi West, a response to falling agricultural prices and growing economic dependency in rural areas. Like industrial workers, small farmers faced increasing economic insecurity. In the South, the sharecropping system, discussed in Chapter 15, locked millions of tenant farmers, white and Black, into perpetual poverty. The interruption of cotton exports during the Civil War had led to the rapid expansion of production in India, Egypt, and Brazil. The glut of cotton on the world market when southern production resumed led to declining prices (from 11 cents a pound in 1881 to 4.6 cents in 1894), throwing millions of small farmers deep into debt and threatening them with the loss of their land. In the West, farmers who had mortgaged their property to purchase seed, fertilizer, and equipment faced the prospect of losing their farms when unable to repay their bank loans. Farmers increasingly believed that their plight derived from the high freight rates charged by railroad companies, excessive interest rates for loans from merchants and bankers, and the fiscal policies of the federal government (discussed in the previous chapter) that reduced the supply of money and helped to push down farm prices.

Through the Farmers' Alliance, the largest citizens' movement of the nineteenth century, farmers sought to remedy their condition. Founded in Texas in the late 1870s, the Alliance spread to forty-three states by 1890. At first, the Alliance remained aloof from politics, attempting to improve rural conditions by the cooperative financing and marketing of crops. Alliance "exchanges" would loan money to farmers and sell their produce. But it soon became clear that farmers on their own could not finance this plan, and banks refused to extend loans to the exchanges. The Alliance therefore proposed that the federal government establish warehouses where farmers could store their crops until they were sold. Using the crops as collateral, the government would then issue loans to farmers at low interest rates, thereby ending their dependence on bankers and merchants. Since it would have to be enacted by Congress, the "subtreasury plan," as this proposal was called, led the Alliance into politics.

The People's Party

In the early 1890s, the Alliance evolved into the People's Party (or **Populists**), the era's greatest political insurgency. The party did not just appeal to farmers. It sought to speak for all the "producing classes" and achieved some of its greatest successes in states like Colorado and Idaho, where it won the support of miners and industrial workers. But its major base lay in the cotton and wheat belts of the South and West.

The Populists embarked on a remarkable effort of community organization and education. To spread their message they published numerous pamphlets on political and economic questions, established more than 1,000 local newspapers, and sent traveling speakers throughout rural America. Wearing "a huge Black sombrero and a Black Prince Albert coat," Texas Populist orator "Cyclone" Davis traveled the Great Plains accompanied by the writings of Thomas Jefferson, which he quoted to demonstrate the evils of banks and large corporations. At great gatherings on the western plains, similar in some ways to religious revival meetings, and in small-town southern country stores, one observer wrote, "people talked who had seldom spoken. . . . Little by little they commenced to theorize upon their condition."

Here was the last great political expression of the nineteenth-century vision of America as a commonwealth of small producers whose freedom rested on the ownership of productive property and respect for the dignity of labor. "Day by day," declared the *People's Party Paper* of Georgia in 1893, "the power of the individual sinks. Day by day the power of the classes, or the corporations, rises. . . . In all essential respects, the republic of our fathers is dead."

But although the Populists used the familiar language of nineteenth-century radicalism, they were hardly a backward-looking movement. They embraced the modern technologies that made large-scale cooperative enterprise possible—the railroad, the telegraph, and the national market—while looking to the federal government to regulate them in the public interest. They promoted agricultural education and believed farmers should adopt modern scientific methods of cultivation. They believed the federal government could move beyond partisan conflict to operate in a businesslike manner to promote the public good—a vision soon to be associated with the Progressive movement and, many years later, presidents Jimmy Carter and Barack Obama.

The Populist Platform

The Populist platform of 1892, adopted at the party's Omaha convention, remains a classic document of American reform. Written by Ignatius Donnelly, a Minnesota editor and former Radical Republican congressman during Reconstruction, it spoke of a nation "brought to the verge of moral, political, and material ruin" by political corruption and economic inequality. "The fruits of the toil of millions," the platform declared, "are boldly stolen to build up colossal fortunes . . . while their possessors despise the republic and endanger liberty." The platform put forth a long list of proposals to restore democracy and economic opportunity, many of which would be adopted during the next half-century: the direct election of U.S. senators, government control of the currency, a graduated income tax, a system of low-cost public financing to enable farmers to market their crops, and recognition of the right of workers to form labor unions. In addition, Populists called for public ownership of the railroads to guarantee farmers inexpensive access to markets for their crops. A generation would pass before a major party offered so sweeping a plan for political action to create the social conditions of freedom.

The Populist Coalition

THE BLUE AND THE GRAY.

"LET US CLASP HANDS ACROSS THE BLOODY CHASM."—Horace Greeley anticipated the inevitable. The Farmers' Alliance taken up his burden twenty years after he laid it down.

In an 1891 cartoon from a Texas Populist newspaper, northern and southern Civil War veterans clasp hands across the "bloody chasm" (a phrase first used by the New York editor Horace Greeley during his campaign for president in 1872). Beneath each figure is an explanation of why voting alignments have previously been based on sectionalism—the North fears "rebel" rule, the white South "Negro supremacy."

In some southern states, the Populists made remarkable efforts to unite Black and white small farmers on a common political and economic program. The obstacles to such an alliance were immense—not merely the heritage of racism and the political legacy of the Civil War, but the fact that many white Populists were landowning farmers while most Blacks were tenants and agricultural laborers. Unwelcome in the southern branches of the Farmers' Alliance, Black farmers formed their own organization, the Colored Farmers' Alliance.

In general, southern white Populists' racial attitudes did not differ significantly from those of their non-Populist neighbors. Nonetheless, recognizing the need for allies to break the Democratic Party's stranglehold on power in the South, some white Populists insisted that Black and white farmers shared common grievances and could unite for common goals. Tom Watson, Georgia's leading Populist, worked the hardest to forge a Black-white alliance. "You are kept apart," he told interracial audiences, "that you may be separately fleeced of your earnings. . . . This race antagonism perpetuates a monetary system which beggars both." While many Blacks refused to abandon the party of Lincoln, others were attracted by the Populist appeal. In 1894, a coalition of white Populists and Black Republicans won control of North Carolina, bringing to the state a "second Reconstruction" complete with increased spending on public education and a revival of Black officeholding. In most of the South, however, Democrats fended off the Populist challenge by resorting to the tactics they had used to retain power since the 1870s—mobilizing whites with warnings about "Negro supremacy," intimidating Black voters, and stuffing ballot boxes on election day.

The Populist movement also engaged the energies of thousands of reform-minded women from farm and labor backgrounds. Some, like Mary Elizabeth Lease, a former homesteader and one of the first female lawyers in Kansas, became prominent organizers, campaigners, and strategists. Lease was famous for her speeches urging farmers to "raise less corn and more hell" (although she

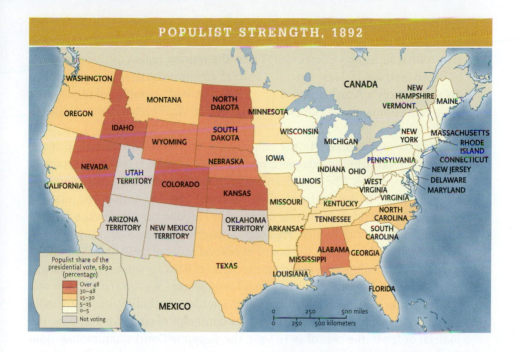

POPULIST STRENGTH, 1892

Populist share of the presidential vote, 1892 (percentage)
- Over 48
- 30–48
- 15–30
- 5–15
- 0–5
- Not voting

apparently never uttered those exact words, which would have been considered inappropriate for a woman in public). "We fought England for our liberty," Lease declared, "and put chains on four million Blacks. We wiped out slavery and . . . began a system of white wage slavery worse than the first." During the 1890s, referendums in Colorado and Idaho approved extending the vote to women, while in Kansas and California the proposal went down in defeat. Populists in all these states endorsed women's suffrage.

Populist presidential candidate James Weaver received more than 1 million votes in 1892. The party carried five western states, with twenty-two electoral votes, and elected three governors and fifteen members of Congress. In his inaugural address in 1893, Lorenzo Lewelling, the new Populist governor of Kansas, anticipated a phrase made famous seventy years later by Martin Luther King Jr.: "I have a dream. . . . In the beautiful vision of a coming time I behold the abolition of poverty. A time is foreshadowed when . . . liberty, equality, and justice shall have permanent abiding places in the republic."

The Government and Labor

Were the Populists on the verge of replacing one of the two major parties? The severe depression that began in 1893 led to increased conflict between capital and labor and seemed to create an opportunity for expanding the Populist vote. Time and again, employers brought state or federal authority to bear to protect their own economic power or put down threats to public order. Even before the economic downturn, in 1892, the governor of Idaho declared martial law and sent militia units and federal troops into the mining region of Coeur d'Alene to break a strike. In May 1894, the federal government deployed soldiers to disperse **Coxey's Army**—a band of several hundred unemployed men led by Ohio businessman Jacob Coxey, who marched to Washington demanding economic relief.

Also in 1894, workers in the company-owned town of Pullman, Illinois, where railroad sleeping cars were manufactured, called a strike to protest a reduction in wages. The American Railway Union, whose 150,000 members included both skilled and unskilled railroad laborers, announced that its members would refuse to handle trains with Pullman cars. When the boycott crippled national rail service, President Grover Cleveland's attorney general, Richard Olney (himself on the board of several railroad companies), obtained a federal court injunction ordering the strikers back to work. Federal troops and U.S. marshals soon occupied railroad centers like Chicago and Sacramento.

The strike collapsed when the union's leaders, including its charismatic president, Eugene V. Debs, were jailed for contempt of court for violating the judicial order. In the case of *In re Debs*, the Supreme Court unanimously confirmed the sentences and approved the use of injunctions against striking labor unions. On his release from prison in November 1895, more than 100,000 persons greeted Debs at a Chicago railroad depot.

The Rise of the AFL

Within the labor movement, the demise of the Knights of Labor and the ascendancy of the **American Federation of Labor** (AFL) during the 1890s reflected the shift away from a broadly reformist past to more limited goals. As the Homestead and Pullman strikes demonstrated, direct confrontations with large corporations were likely to prove suicidal. AFL founder and longtime president Samuel Gompers declared that unions should not seek economic independence, pursue the Knights' utopian dream of creating a "cooperative commonwealth," or form independent parties with the aim of achieving power in government. Rather, the labor movement should devote itself to negotiating with employers for higher wages and better working conditions for its members. Like Booker T. Washington, Gompers spoke the language of the era's business culture. Indeed, the AFL policies he pioneered were known as "business unionism." Gompers embraced the idea of "freedom of contract," shrewdly turning it into an argument against interference by judges with workers' right to organize unions.

During the 1890s, union membership rebounded from its decline in the late 1880s. But at the same time, the labor movement became less and less inclusive. Abandoning the Knights' ideal of labor solidarity, the AFL restricted membership to skilled workers—a small minority of the labor force—effectively excluding the vast majority of unskilled workers and, therefore, nearly all Blacks, women, and new European immigrants. AFL membership centered on sectors of the economy like printing and building construction that were dominated by small competitive businesses. AFL unions had little presence in basic industries like steel and rubber or in the large-scale factories that now dominated the economy.

Populism and Labor

In 1894, Populists made determined efforts to appeal to industrial workers. Populist senators supported the demand of Coxey's Army for federal unemployment relief, and Governor Davis Waite of Colorado, who had edited a labor newspaper before his election, sent the militia to protect striking miners against company police. In the state and congressional elections of that year, as the economic depression deepened, voters by the millions abandoned the Democratic Party of President Cleveland.

In rural areas, the Populist vote increased in 1894. But urban workers did not rally to the Populists, whose demand for higher prices for farm goods would raise the cost of food and reduce the value of workers' wages. Moreover, the revivalist atmosphere of many Populist gatherings and the biblical cadences of Populist speeches were alien to the largely immigrant and Catholic industrial working class. Urban working-class voters in 1894 instead shifted en masse to the Republicans, who claimed that raising tariff rates (which Democrats had recently reduced) would restore prosperity by protecting manufacturers and industrial workers from the competition of imported goods and cheap foreign labor. In one of the most decisive shifts in congressional power in American history, the Republicans gained 117 seats in the House of Representatives.

Bryan and Free Silver

In 1896, Democrats and Populists joined to support William Jennings Bryan for the presidency. A thirty-six-year-old congressman from Nebraska, Bryan won the Democratic nomination after delivering to the national convention an electrifying speech that crystallized the farmers' pride and grievances. "Burn down your cities and leave our farms," Bryan proclaimed, "and your cities will spring up again as if by magic; but destroy our farms and grass will grow in the streets of every city in the country." Bryan called for the "free coinage" of silver—the unrestricted minting of silver money. In language ringing with biblical imagery, Bryan condemned the gold standard: "You shall not press down upon the brow of labor this crown of thorns. You shall not crucify mankind upon a cross of gold."

At various points in the nineteenth century, from debates over "hard" versus "soft" money in the Jacksonian era to the greenback movement after the Civil War, the "money question" played a central role in American politics. Bryan's demand for "free silver" was the latest expression of the view that increasing the amount of currency in circulation would raise the prices farmers received for their crops and make it easier to pay off their debts.

There was more to Bryan's appeal, however, than simply free silver. A devoutly religious man, he was strongly influenced by the Social Gospel movement (discussed in the previous chapter) and tried to apply the teachings of Jesus Christ to uplifting the "little people" of the United States.

Many Populists were initially cool to Bryan's campaign. Their party had been defrauded time and again by Democrats in the South. But realizing that they could not secure victory alone, the party's leaders endorsed Bryan's candidacy. Bryan broke with tradition and embarked on a nationwide speaking tour, seeking to rally farmers and workers to his cause.

The Campaign of 1896

Republicans met the silverite challenge head on, insisting that gold was the only "honest" currency. Abandoning the gold standard, they insisted, would destroy business confidence and prevent recovery from the depression by making creditors unwilling to extend loans, since they could not be certain of the value of the money in which they would be repaid. The party nominated for president Ohio governor William McKinley, who as a congressman in 1890 had shepherded to passage the strongly protectionist McKinley Tariff.

The election of 1896 is sometimes called the first modern presidential campaign because of the amount of money spent by the Republicans and the efficiency of their national organization. Eastern bankers and industrialists, thoroughly alarmed by Bryan's call for monetary inflation and his fiery speeches denouncing corporate arrogance, poured millions of dollars into Republican coffers. (McKinley's campaign raised some $10 million; Bryan's around $300,000.) While McKinley remained at his Ohio home, where he addressed crowds of

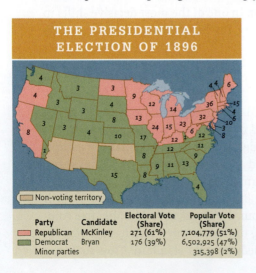

THE PRESIDENTIAL ELECTION OF 1896

Non-voting territory

Party	Candidate	Electoral Vote (Share)	Popular Vote (Share)
Republican	McKinley	271 (61%)	7,104,779 (51%)
Democrat	Bryan	176 (39%)	6,502,925 (47%)
Minor parties			315,398 (2%)

supporters from his front porch, his political manager Mark Hanna created a powerful national machine that flooded the country with pamphlets, posters, and campaign buttons.

The results revealed a nation as divided along regional lines as in 1860. Bryan carried the South and West and received 6.5 million votes. McKinley swept the more populous industrial states of the Northeast and Midwest, attracting 7.1 million. The era's bitter labor strife did not carry over into the electoral arena; indeed, party politics seemed to mute class conflict rather than to reinforce it. Industrial America, from financiers and managers to workers, now voted solidly Republican, a loyalty reinforced when prosperity returned after 1897.

McKinley's victory shattered the political stalemate that had persisted since 1876 and created one of the most enduring political majorities in American history. During McKinley's presidency, Republicans placed their stamp on economic policy by passing the Dingley Tariff of 1897, raising rates to the highest level in history, and passing the Gold Standard Act of 1900. Not until 1932, in the midst of another economic depression, would the Democrats become the nation's majority party. The election of 1896 also proved to be the last presidential election with extremely high voter turnout (in some states, over 90 percent of those eligible). From then on, voter participation began a downhill trend, although it rose again from the mid-1930s through the 1960s. Today, only around half the electorate casts ballots.

THE SEGREGATED SOUTH

The Redeemers in Power

The failure of Populism in the South opened the door for the full imposition of a new racial order. The coalition of merchants, planters, and business entrepreneurs who dominated the region's politics after 1877, who called themselves Redeemers, had moved to undo as much as possible of Reconstruction. State budgets were slashed, taxes, especially on landed property, reduced, and public facilities like hospitals and asylums closed. Hardest hit were the new public school systems. Louisiana spent so little on education that it became the only state in the Union in which the percentage of whites unable to read and write actually increased between 1880 and 1900. Black schools, however, suffered the most, as the gap between expenditures for Black and white pupils widened steadily. "What I want here is Negroes who can make cotton," declared one planter, "and they don't need education to help them make cotton."

New laws authorized the arrest of virtually any person without employment and greatly increased the penalties for petty crimes. "They send [a man] to the penitentiary if he steals a chicken," complained a former slave in North Carolina. The Thirteenth Amendment, which abolished slavery, allowed "involuntary servitude" to continue for those convicted of crime. And as the South's prison population rose, the renting out of convicts became a profitable business. Every southern state placed at least a portion of its convicted criminals, the majority of them Blacks imprisoned for minor offenses, in the hands of private businessmen. Railroads, mines, and lumber companies competed for this new form of cheap, involuntary labor. Conditions in labor camps were often barbaric, with disease rife and the death rates high. "One dies, get another" was the motto of the system's architects.

The Failure of the New South Dream

During the 1880s, Atlanta editor Henry Grady tirelessly promoted the promise of a **New South**, an era of prosperity based on industrial expansion and agricultural diversification. In fact, while planters, merchants, and industrialists prospered, the region as a whole sank deeper and deeper into poverty. Some industry did develop, including mining in the Appalachians, textile production in the Carolinas and Georgia, and furniture and cigarette manufacturing in certain southern cities. The new upcountry cotton factories offered jobs to entire families of poor whites from the surrounding countryside. But since the main attractions for investors were the South's low wages and taxes and the availability of convict labor, these enterprises made little contribution to regional economic development. With the exception of Birmingham, Alabama, which by 1900 had developed into an important center for the manufacture of iron and steel, southern cities were mainly export centers for cotton, tobacco, and rice, with little industry or skilled labor. Overall, the region remained dependent on the North for capital and manufactured goods. In 1900, southern per capita income amounted to only 60 percent of the national average. As late as the 1930s, President Franklin D. Roosevelt would declare the South the nation's "number one" economic problem.

Black Life in the South

As the most disadvantaged rural southerners, Black farmers suffered the most from the region's condition. In the Upper South, economic development offered some opportunities—mines, iron furnaces, and tobacco factories employed Black laborers, and a good number of Black farmers managed to acquire land. In the rice kingdom of coastal South Carolina and Georgia, planters found themselves unable to acquire the capital necessary to repair irrigation systems and machinery destroyed by the war. By the turn of the century, most of the great plantations had fallen to pieces, and many Blacks acquired land and took up self-sufficient farming. In most of the Lower South, however, African Americans owned a smaller percentage of the land in 1900 than they had at the end of Reconstruction.

The Black educator Mary McLeod Bethune with girls from the school she established in Florida in a photograph from around 1905.

In southern cities, the network of institutions created after the Civil War—schools and colleges, churches, businesses, women's clubs, and the like—served as the foundation for increasingly diverse Black urban communities. They supported the growth of a Black middle class, mostly professionals like teachers and physicians, or businessmen like undertakers and shopkeepers serving the needs of Black customers. But the labor market was rigidly divided along racial lines. Black men were excluded from supervisory positions in factories and workshops and white-collar jobs such as clerks in offices. A higher percentage of Black women than white worked for wages, but mainly as domestic servants. They could not find employment among the growing numbers of secretaries, typists, and department store clerks.

The Kansas Exodus

Overall, one historian has written, the New South was "a miserable landscape dotted only by a few rich enclaves that cast little or no light upon the poverty surrounding them." Trapped at the bottom of a stagnant economy, some Blacks sought a way out through emigration from the South. In 1879 and 1880, an estimated 40,000 to 60,000 African Americans migrated to Kansas, seeking political equality, freedom from violence, access to education, and economic opportunity. The name participants gave to this migration—the Exodus, derived from the biblical account of the Jews escaping slavery in Egypt—indicated that its roots lay in deep longings for the substance of freedom. Those promoting the **Kansas Exodus**, including former fugitive slave Benjamin "Pap" Singleton, the organizer of a real estate company, distributed flyers and lithographs picturing Kansas as an idyllic land of rural plenty. Lacking the capital to take up farming, however, most Black migrants ended up as unskilled laborers in towns and cities. But few chose to return to the South. In the words of one minister active in the movement, "We had rather suffer and be free."

Despite deteriorating prospects in the South, most African Americans had little alternative but to stay in the region. The real expansion of job opportunities

A photograph of townspeople in Nicodemus, a community established by members of the 1879–1880 "Exodus" of southern African Americans to Kansas.

was taking place in northern cities. But most northern employers refused to offer jobs to Blacks in the expanding industrial economy, preferring to hire white migrants from rural areas and immigrants from Europe. Not until the outbreak of World War I in Europe in 1914 cut off immigration did northern employers open industrial jobs to Blacks, setting in motion the Great Migration discussed in Chapter 19. Until then, the vast majority of African Americans remained in the South.

The Transformation of Black Politics

Neither Black voting nor Black officeholding came to an abrupt end in 1877, although Democrats solidified their control of state and local affairs by redrawing district lines and substituting appointive for elective officials in counties with Black majorities. A few Blacks even served in Congress in the 1880s and 1890s. Nonetheless, political opportunities became more and more restricted. Not until the 1990s would the number of Black legislators in the South approach the level seen during Reconstruction.

For Black men of talent and ambition, other avenues—business, the law, the church—increasingly seemed to offer greater opportunities for personal advancement and community service than politics. The banner of political leadership passed to Black women activists. The National Association of Colored Women, founded in 1896, brought together local and regional women's clubs to press for both women's rights and racial uplift. Most female activists emerged from the small urban Black middle class and preached the necessity of "respectable" behavior as part and parcel of the struggle for equal rights. They aided poor families, offered lessons in home life and childrearing, and battled gambling and drinking in Black communities. Some poor Blacks resented middle-class efforts to instruct them in proper behavior. But by insisting on the right of Black women to be considered as "respectable" as their white counterparts, the women reformers challenged the racial ideology that consigned all Blacks to the status of degraded second-class citizens.

The Emergence of Booker T. Washington

The social movements that had helped to expand the nineteenth-century boundaries of freedom now redefined their objectives so that they might be realized within the new economic and intellectual framework. Prominent Black leaders, for example, took to emphasizing economic self-help and individual advancement into the middle class as an alternative to political agitation.

Symbolizing the change was the juxtaposition, in 1895, of the death of Frederick Douglass with Booker T. Washington's widely praised speech, known as the "**Atlanta Compromise**," at the Atlanta Cotton Exposition. He urged Blacks to adjust to segregation and abandon agitation for civil and political rights. Born a slave in 1856, Washington had studied as a young man at Hampton Institute, Virginia. He adopted the outlook of Hampton's founder, General Samuel Armstrong, who emphasized that obtaining farms or skilled jobs was far

Booker T. Washington, advocate of industrial education and economic self-help.

more important to African Americans emerging from slavery than the rights of citizenship. Washington put this view into practice when he became head of Tuskegee Institute in Alabama, a center for vocational education (education focused on training for a job rather than broad learning).

In his Atlanta speech, Washington repudiated the abolitionist tradition that stressed ceaseless agitation for full equality. He urged Blacks not to try to combat segregation: "In all the things that are purely social we can be as separate as the fingers, yet one as the hand in all things essential to mutual progress." Washington advised his people to seek the assistance of white employers who, in a land racked by labor turmoil, would prefer a docile, dependable Black labor force to unionized whites. Washington's ascendancy rested in large part on his success in channeling aid from wealthy northern whites to Tuskegee and to Black politicians and newspapers who backed his program. But his support in the Black community also arose from a widespread sense that in the world of the late nineteenth century, frontal assaults on white power were impossible and that Blacks should concentrate on building up their segregated communities.

The Elimination of Black Voting

For nearly a generation after the end of Reconstruction, despite fraud and violence, Black southerners continued to cast ballots. In some states, the Republican

Party remained competitive. Despite the limits of the Populists' interracial alliance, the threat of a biracial political insurgency frightened the ruling Democrats and contributed greatly to the disenfranchisement movement.

Between 1890 and 1908, every southern state enacted laws or constitutional provisions meant to eliminate the Black vote. Since the Fifteenth Amendment prohibited the use of race as a qualification for the suffrage, how were such measures even possible? Southern legislatures drafted laws that on paper appeared color-blind but that were actually designed to end Black voting. The most popular devices were the poll tax (a fee that each citizen had to pay in order to retain the right to vote), literacy tests, and the requirement that a prospective voter demonstrate to election officials an "understanding" of the state constitution. Six southern states also adopted a **grandfather clause**, exempting from the new requirements descendants of persons eligible to vote before the Civil War (when only whites, of course, could cast ballots in the South). The racial intent of the grandfather clause was so clear that the Supreme Court in 1915 invalidated such laws for violating the Fifteenth Amendment. The other methods of limiting Black voting, however, remained on the books.

Some white leaders presented **disenfranchisement** as a "good government" measure—a means of purifying politics by ending the fraud, violence, and manipulation of voting returns regularly used against Republicans and Populists. But ultimately, as a Charleston newspaper declared, the aim was to make clear that the white South "does not desire or intend ever to include Black men among its citizens." Although election officials often allowed whites who did not meet the new qualifications to register, numerous poor and illiterate whites also lost the right to vote, a result welcomed by many planters and urban reformers. Louisiana, for example, reduced the number of Blacks registered to vote from 130,000 in 1894 to 1,342 a decade later. But 80,000 white voters also lost the right. Disenfranchisement led directly to the rise of a generation of southern "demagogues," who mobilized white voters by extreme appeals to racism. Tom Watson, who as noted above had tried to forge an interracial Populist coalition in the 1890s, reemerged early in the twentieth century as a power in Georgia public life through vicious speeches whipping up prejudice against Blacks, Jews, and Catholics.

As late as 1940, only 3 percent of adult Black southerners were registered to vote. The elimination of Black and many white voters, which reversed the nineteenth-century trend toward more inclusive suffrage, could not have been accomplished without the acquiescence of the North. In 1891, the Senate failed to pass a proposal for federal protection of Black voting rights in the South. Apart from the grandfather clause, the Supreme Court gave its approval to disenfranchisement laws. According to the Fourteenth Amendment, any state that deprived male citizens of the franchise was supposed to lose part of its representation in Congress. But like much of the Constitution, this provision was consistently violated so far as African Americans were concerned. As a result, southern congressmen wielded far greater power on the national scene than their tiny electorates warranted. As for Blacks, for decades thereafter, they would regard "the loss of suffrage as being the loss of freedom."

The Law of Segregation

Along with disenfranchisement, the 1890s saw the widespread imposition of segregation in the South. Laws and local customs requiring the separation of the races had numerous precedents. They had existed in many parts of the pre–Civil War North. Southern schools and many other institutions had been segregated during Reconstruction. In the 1880s, however, southern race relations remained unsettled. Some railroads, theaters, and hotels admitted Blacks and whites on an equal basis while others separated them by race or excluded Blacks altogether.

In 1883, in the *Civil Rights Cases*, the Supreme Court invalidated the Civil Rights Act of 1875, which had outlawed racial discrimination by hotels, theaters, railroads, and other public facilities. The Fourteenth Amendment, the Court insisted, prohibited unequal treatment by state authorities, not private businesses. In 1896, in the landmark decision in ***Plessy v. Ferguson***, the Court gave its approval to state laws requiring separate facilities for Blacks and whites. The case arose in Louisiana, where the legislature had required railroad companies to maintain a separate car for Black passengers. A Citizens Committee of Black residents of New Orleans came together to challenge the law. To create a test case, Homer Plessy, a light-skinned African American, refused a conductor's order to move to the "colored only" railroad car and was arrested.

To argue the case before the Supreme Court, the Citizens Committee hired Albion W. Tourgée, who as a judge in North Carolina during Reconstruction had waged a courageous battle against the Ku Klux Klan. "Citizenship is national and knows no color," he insisted, and racial segregation violated the Fourteenth Amendment's guarantee of equal protection before the law. But in a 7-1 decision, the Court upheld the Louisiana law, arguing that segregated facilities did not discriminate so long as they were "**separate but equal**." The lone dissenter, John Marshall Harlan, reprimanded the majority with an oft-quoted comment: "Our constitution is color-blind." Segregation, he insisted, sprang from whites' conviction that they were the "dominant race" (a phrase used by the Court's majority), and it violated the principle of equal liberty. To Harlan, freedom for the former slaves meant the right to participate fully and equally in American society.

Segregation and White Domination

As Harlan predicted, states reacted to the *Plessy* decision by passing laws mandating racial segregation in every aspect of southern life, from schools to hospitals, waiting rooms, toilets, and cemeteries. Some states forbade taxi drivers to carry members of different races at the same time. Despite the "thin disguise" (Harlan's phrase) of equality required by the Court's "separate but equal" doctrine, facilities for Blacks were either nonexistent or markedly inferior. In 1900, no public high school for Blacks existed in the entire South. Black elementary schools, one observer reported, occupied buildings "as bad as stables."

More than a form of racial separation, segregation was one part of an all-encompassing system of white domination, in which each component—disenfranchisement, unequal economic status, inferior education—reinforced the others. The point was not so much to keep the races apart as to ensure that when they came into contact with each other, whether in politics, labor relations, or social life, whites held the upper hand. For example, many Blacks could be found in "whites-only" railroad cars. But they entered as servants and nurses accompanying white passengers, not as paying customers entitled to equal treatment.

An elaborate social etiquette developed, with proper behavior differentiated by race. One sociologist who studied the turn-of-the-century South reported that in places of business, Blacks had to stand back and wait until whites had been served. They could not raise their voices or in other ways act assertively in the presence of whites, and they had to "give way" on the streets. In shops, whites but not Blacks were allowed to try on clothing.

Segregation affected other groups as well as Blacks. In some parts of Mississippi where Chinese laborers had been brought in to work the fields after the Civil War, three separate school systems—white, Black, and Chinese—were established. In California, Black, Hispanic, and American Indian children were frequently educated alongside whites, but state law required separate schools for those of "mongolian or Chinese descent." In Texas and California, although Mexicans were legally considered "white," they found themselves barred from many restaurants, places of entertainment, and other public facilities.

The Rise of Lynching

Those Blacks who sought to challenge the system, or who refused to accept the demeaning behavior that was a daily feature of southern life, faced not only overwhelming political and legal power but also the threat of violent reprisal. In every year between 1883 and 1905, more than fifty persons, the vast majority of them Black men, were lynched in the South—that is, murdered by a mob. **Lynching** continued well into the twentieth century. By 1950, the total number of victims since 1880 had reached over 4,000. Some lynchings occurred secretly at night; others were advertised in advance and attracted large crowds of onlookers. Mobs engaged in activities that shocked the civilized world. In 1899, Sam Hose, a plantation laborer who killed his employer in self-defense, was brutally murdered near Newman, Georgia, before 2,000 onlookers, some of whom arrived on a special excursion train from Atlanta. A crowd including young children watched as his executioners cut off Hose's ears, fingers, and genitals, burned him alive, and then fought over pieces of his bones as souvenirs. Law enforcement authorities made no effort to prevent the lynching or to bring those who committed the crime to justice.

Like many victims of lynchings, Hose was accused after his death of having raped a white woman. Many white southerners considered preserving the purity of white womanhood a justification for extralegal vengeance. Yet in nearly all cases, as activist Ida B. Wells argued in a newspaper editorial after a Memphis lynching in 1892, the charge of rape was a "bare lie." Born a slave in Mississippi in 1862, Wells had become a schoolteacher and editor. Her essay condemning the lynching of three Black men in Memphis led a mob to destroy her newspaper, the *Memphis Free Press*, while she was out of the city. Wells moved to the North, where she became the nation's leading antilynching crusader. She bluntly insisted that given the conditions of southern Blacks, the United States had no right to call itself the "land of the free."

A crowd at the aftermath of the lynching of Laura Nelson and her teenage son L. D. Nelson, African American residents of Okemah, Oklahoma, in 1911. They were accused of shooting to death a deputy sheriff who had come to the Nelson home to investigate the theft of livestock. A week after being lodged in jail, they were removed by a mob and taken to the bridge. Members of the mob raped Mrs. Nelson before the lynching. The photograph was reproduced as a postcard, sold at local stores. As in most lynchings, no one was prosecuted for the crime.

From IDA B. WELLS, *LYNCH LAW IN ALL ITS PHASES* (1893)

After being driven from Memphis because of her outspoken opposition to lynching, Ida B. Wells campaigned to awaken the public to racial terrorism. This is an excerpt from a speech she delivered in Boston in 1893.

I am before the American people today through no inclination of my own, but because of a deep-seated conviction that the country at large does not know the extent to which lynch law prevails in parts of the republic. . . .

Although the impression has gone abroad that most of the lynchings take place because of assaults on white women only one-third of the number lynched in the past ten years have been charged with that offense, to say nothing of those who were not guilty of the charge. . . . But the unsupported word of any white person for any cause is sufficient to cause a lynching. . . . Governors of states and officers of the law stand by and see the work well done.

And yet this Christian nation, the flower of the nineteenth century civilization, says it can do nothing to stop this inhuman slaughter. The general government is willingly powerless to send troops to protect the lives of its Black citizens. . . . The lawlessness which has been here described is like unto that which prevailed under slavery. The very same forces are at work now as then. [They] can be traced to the very first year Lee's conquered veterans marched from Appomattox to their homes in the southland. They were conquered in war, but not in spirit. They believed as firmly as ever that it was their right to rule Black men and dictate to the national government. . . . All their laws are shaped to this end—school laws, railroad car regulations . . . every device is adopted to make slaves of free men. . . . The rule of the mob is absolute. . . .

Do you ask the remedy? A public sentiment strong against lawlessness must be aroused [to demand] that equal and exact justice be accorded to every citizen of what-ever race, who finds a home within the borders of the land of the free and the home of the brave.

From W. E. B. DU BOIS, *THE SOULS OF BLACK FOLK* (1903)

Like Wells, the Black educator and activist W. E. B. Du Bois demanded equal treatment for Black Americans. In *The Souls of Black Folk*, he sought to revive the tradition of agitation for basic civil, political, and educational rights, and for recognition of Blacks as full members of American society.

The silently growing assumption of this age is that . . . the backward races of to-day are of proven inefficiency and not worth the saving. Such an assumption is the arrogance of peoples irreverent toward time and ignorant of the deeds of men. A thousand years ago such an assumption, easily possible, would have made it difficult for the Teuton to prove his right to life. Two thousand years ago such dogmatism, readily welcome, would have [refuted] the idea of blond races ever leading civilization. . . .

Your country? How came it yours? Before the Pilgrims landed we were here. Here we have brought our three gifts and mingled them with yours: a gift of story and song—soft, stirring melody in an ill-harmonized and unmelodious land; the gift of sweat and brawn to beat back the wilderness, conquer the soil, and lay the foundations of this vast economic empire two hundred years earlier than your weak hands could have done it; the third, a gift of the Spirit. Around us the history of the land has centered for thrice a hundred years. . . . Actively we have woven ourselves with the very warp and woof of this nation,—we fought their battles, shared their sorrow, mingled our blood with theirs, and generation after generation have pleaded with a headstrong, careless people to despise not Justice, Mercy, and Truth, lest the nation be smitten with a curse. Our song, our toil, our cheer, and warning have been given to this nation in blood-brotherhood. Are not these gifts worth the giving? Is not this work and striving? Would America have been America without her Negro people?

QUESTIONS

1. *Whom does Wells blame for lynching?*

2. *In what ways does Du Bois criticize and in what ways does he seem to embrace the idea of inborn racial characteristics and abilities?*

3. *How do Wells and Du Bois appeal to history to bolster their claims?*

Although many countries have witnessed outbreaks of violence against minority racial, ethnic, or religious groups, widespread lynching of individuals over so long a period was a phenomenon unknown elsewhere. Canada, for example, has experienced only one lynching in its history—in 1884, when a mob from the United States crossed the border into British Columbia to lynch an Indian teenager who had fled after being accused of murder.

Years later, Black writer Blyden Jackson recalled growing up in early-twentieth-century Louisville, Kentucky, a city in many ways typical of the New South. It was a divided society. There was the world "where white folks lived . . . the Louisville of the downtown hotels, the lower floors of the big movie houses . . . the inner sanctums of offices where I could go only as a humble client or a menial custodian." Then there was the Black world, "the homes, the people, the churches, and the schools," where "everything was Black." "I knew," Jackson later recalled, "that there were two Louisvilles and . . . two Americas."

Politics, Religion, and Memory

As the white North and South moved toward reconciliation in the 1880s and 1890s, one cost was the abandonment of the dream of racial equality written into the laws and Constitution during Reconstruction. In popular literature and memoirs by participants, at veterans' reunions and in public memorials, the Civil War came to be remembered as a tragic family quarrel among white Americans in which Blacks had played no significant part. It was a war of "brother against brother" in which both sides fought gallantly for noble causes—local rights on the part of the South, preservation of the Union for the North. Slavery increasingly came to be viewed as a minor issue, not the war's fundamental cause, and Reconstruction as a regrettable period of "Negro rule" when former slaves had power thrust upon them by a vindictive North. This outlook gave legitimacy to southern efforts to eliminate Black voting, lest the region once again suffer the alleged "horrors" of Reconstruction.

At the same time as they reduced Blacks to second-class citizenship, southern governments erected monuments to the **Lost Cause**, a romanticized version of slavery, the Old South, and the Confederate experience.

Even as white northern Protestants abandoned concern for racial justice and embraced the idea of sectional reconciliation, southern churches played a key role in keeping the values of the Old South alive by refusing to reunite with northern counterparts. In the 1840s, the Methodist and Baptist churches had divided into northern and southern branches. Methodists would not reunite until well into the twentieth century; Baptists have yet to do so. In both North and South, school history textbooks emphasized happy slaves and the evils of Reconstruction, and the role of Black soldiers in winning the war was all but forgotten. When a group of Black veterans attempted to participate in a Florida ceremony commemorating the fiftieth anniversary of the outbreak of the Civil War in 1911, a white mob tore the military insignias off their jackets and drove them away.

REDRAWING THE BOUNDARIES

The effective nullification of the laws and amendments of Reconstruction reflected nationwide patterns of thought and policy. As the nineteenth century drew to a close, American society seemed to be fracturing along lines of both class and race. The result, commented economist Simon Patten, was a widespread obsession with redrawing the boundary of freedom by identifying and excluding those unworthy of the blessings of liberty. "The South," he wrote, "has its negro, the city has its slums. . . . The friends of American institutions fear the ignorant immigrant, and the workingman dislikes the Chinese." As Patten suggested, many Americans embraced a more and more restricted definition of nationhood.

The New Immigration and the New Nativism

The 1890s witnessed a major shift in the sources of immigration to the United States. Despite the prolonged depression, 3.5 million newcomers entered the United States during the decade, seeking jobs in the industrial centers of the North and Midwest. Over half arrived not from Ireland, England, Germany, and Scandinavia, the traditional sources of immigration, but from southern and eastern Europe, especially Italy and the Russian and Austro-Hungarian empires. The **new immigrants** were widely described by native-born Americans as members of distinct "races," whose lower level of civilization explained everything from their willingness to work for substandard wages to their supposed inborn tendency toward criminal behavior. They were "beaten men from beaten races," wrote economist Francis Amasa Walker, representing "the worst failures in the struggle for existence." American cities, said an Ohio newspaper, were being overrun by foreigners who "have no true appreciation of the meaning of liberty" and therefore posed a danger to democratic government.

Immigration Restriction

The new immigration helped to trigger a resurgence of racial nationalism in the United States and elsewhere in the world. Talk of "race suicide" abounded as critics of immigration warned about the declining birthrate among native-born "Anglo-Saxon" women. Many Americans who felt aggrieved because of economic changes sought to re-create a sense of belonging, juxtaposing "our" identity against people deemed "other" because of color, religion, political views, or some other characteristic. Restricting immigration was widely seen as a way to determine who was fit to be an American and thus to upgrade the "quality" of the population.

Founded in 1894 by a group of Boston professionals, the **Immigration Restriction League** spread rapidly across the country. It made a sharp distinction between "old" and "new" immigrants and, echoing the Know-Nothings of the 1850s, blamed the latter for problems ranging from urban crime and poverty to mass unemployment. The League called for reducing immigration by barring the illiterate from entering the United States. Such a measure was adopted by Congress early in 1897 but vetoed by Grover Cleveland shortly before he left office. A law of 1903 did bar a long list of persons from entering the United States, among them "idiots, insane persons, epileptics, . . . [and] paupers," as well as anarchists, the first time those holding a specific political viewpoint were denied the right to immigrate. And with the enactment of measures to exclude the Chinese, the United States pioneered the development of a racialized immigration policy.

Northern and western states, like those in the South, experimented with ways to eliminate "undesirable" voters. Nearly all the states during the 1890s adopted the secret, or "Australian," ballot, meant both to protect voters' privacy and to limit the participation of illiterates (who could no longer receive help from party officials at polling places). Several states ended the practice of allowing immigrants to vote before becoming citizens and adopted stringent new residency and literacy requirements. None of these measures approached the scope of Black disfranchisement in the South, or the continued denial of voting rights to women in nearly all the states. But throughout the country, suffrage was increasingly becoming a privilege, not a right.

Chinese Exclusion and Chinese Rights

The boundaries of nationhood, expanded so dramatically in the aftermath of the Civil War, slowly contracted. Leaders of both parties expressed vicious opinions regarding immigrants from China—they were "odious, abominable, dangerous, revolting," declared Republican leader James G. Blaine. In 1875, Congress excluded Chinese women from entering the country. California congressman Horace Page, the bill's author, insisted that it was intended to preserve the health of white citizens by barring Chinese prostitutes. But immigration authorities enforced the Page law so as to keep out as well the wives and daughters of arriving men and of those already in the country.

Beginning in 1882 with the **Chinese Exclusion Act**, Congress abrogated the Burlingame Treaty ratified during Reconstruction and temporarily excluded all immigrants from China from entering the country. Although non-whites had long been barred from becoming naturalized citizens, this was the first time that race had been used to exclude from the country an entire group of people. Congress renewed the restriction ten years later and made it permanent in 1902. Chinese in the United States were required to register with the government and carry identification papers or face deportation. Indeed, the use of photographs for personal identification first came into widespread use as a means of enforcing Chinese exclusion. One Chinese activist complained that the photos, which bore a striking resemblance to "mug shots" of persons under arrest, criminalized people "innocent of any crime" and created a "national rogues' gallery" of Chinese residents. In 2012, Congress passed a Resolution of Regret apologizing for the exclusion laws and acknowledging their role in exacerbating racial discrimination. It was sponsored by Judy Chu, a Chinese American member of the House of Representatives from California.

By 1930, because of exclusion, the number of Chinese had declined to 75,000. On the West Coast, the Chinese suffered intense discrimination and periodic mob violence. In the late-nineteenth-century West, thousands of Chinese immigrants were expelled from towns and mining camps, and mobs assaulted Chinese residences and businesses. In 1885, twenty-eight Chinese coal miners were killed by white miners, themselves mostly European immigrants, in Rock Springs, Wyoming.

Chinese fought restrictive measures with methods both illegal and legal. Many refused to carry identification as a protest against what they called the

Beginning in 1909, as part of the enforcement of Chinese exclusion, all Chinese in the United States were required to carry a government-issued certificate, the first widespread use of photographs as proof of identity. This certificate, issued in 1924, belonged to Anna May Wong, an American-born movie star.

"dog tag" law. Some obtained fraudulent documents that created "paper identities" showing them to be a family member of a U.S. resident, or a member of a group exempted from exclusion, and thus eligible to enter the country. After the San Francisco earthquake of 1906, some claimed their citizenship papers had been destroyed in the fire that devastated much of the city.

Drawing on the legislation of the Reconstruction era, Chinese victims sued local governments for redress when their rights were violated and petitioned Congress for indemnity. Their demands for equal rights forced the state and federal courts to define the reach of the Fourteenth Amendment. For example, between 1871 and 1885, San Francisco provided no public education for Chinese children. In 1885, the California Supreme Court, in *Tape v. Hurley*, ordered the city to admit Chinese students to public schools. The state legislature responded by passing a law authorizing segregated education, and the city established a school for Chinese. But Joseph and Mary Tape, who had lived in the United States since the 1860s, insisted that their daughter be allowed to attend her neighborhood school like other children. "Is it a disgrace to be born a Chinese?" Mary Tape wrote. "Didn't God make us all!" But her protest failed. Not until 1947 did California repeal the law authorizing separate schools for the Chinese.

The U.S. Supreme Court also considered the legal status of Chinese Americans. In *Yick Wo v. Hopkins* (1886), the Court unanimously ordered San Francisco to grant licenses to Chinese-operated laundries, which the city government had refused to do. To deny a person the opportunity to earn a living, the Court declared, was "intolerable in any country where freedom prevails." Twelve years later, in *United States v. Wong Kim Ark*, the Court ruled that the Fourteenth Amendment awarded citizenship to children of Chinese immigrants born on American soil.

Thus, at the same time that it was severely limiting constitutional protections for Black Americans, the Court pushed back against efforts by the states to deny Chinese persons the rights guaranteed in the Reconstruction amendments. Ironically, John Marshall Harlan, the Court's most vigorous defender of the rights of Blacks, favored Chinese exclusion and the denial of birthright citizenship to the children of Chinese immigrants. The majority disagreed with him in *Wong Kim Ark* in part because limiting birthright citizenship might call into question the status of millions of American-born children of immigrants from Europe.

Yet the justices also affirmed the right of Congress to set racial restrictions on immigration. And in its decision in *Fong Yue Ting v. United States* (1893), the Court authorized the federal government to expel Chinese aliens without due process of law. In his dissent, Justice David J. Brewer acknowledged that the power was now directed against a people many

Americans found "obnoxious." But "who shall say," he continued, "it will not be exercised tomorrow against other classes and other people?" Brewer proved to be an accurate prophet. In 1904, the Court cited *Fong Yue Ting* in upholding the law barring anarchists from entering the United States, demonstrating how restrictions on the rights of one group can become a precedent for infringing on the rights of others.

Exclusion profoundly shaped the experience of Chinese Americans, long stigmatizing them as incapable of assimilation and justifying their isolation from mainstream society. Congress for the first time also barred groups of whites from entering the country, beginning in 1875 with prostitutes and convicted felons, "Are we still a [place of refuge] for the oppressed of all nations?" wondered James B. Weaver, the Populist candidate for president in 1892.

The Women's Era

Changes in the women's movement reflected the same combination of expanding activities and narrowing boundaries. The 1890s launched what would later be called the "women's era"—three decades during which women, although still denied the vote, enjoyed larger opportunities than in the past for economic independence and played a greater and greater role in public life. By now, nearly every state had adopted laws giving married women control over their own wages and property and the right to sign separate contracts and make separate wills. Nearly 5 million women worked for wages in 1900. Although most were young, unmarried, and concentrated in traditional jobs such as domestic service and the garment industry, a generation of college-educated women was beginning to take its place in better-paying clerical and professional positions.

Through a network of women's clubs, temperance associations, and social reform organizations, women exerted a growing influence on public affairs. Founded in 1874, the Woman's Christian Temperance Union (WCTU) grew to become the era's largest female organization, with a membership by 1890 of 150,000. Under the banner of Home Protection, it moved from demanding the prohibition of alcoholic beverages (blamed for leading men to squander their wages on drink and treat their wives abusively) to a comprehensive program of economic and political reform, including the right to vote. Women, insisted Frances Willard, the group's president, must abandon the idea that "weakness" and dependence were their nature and join assertively in movements to change society. "A wider freedom is coming to the women of America," she declared in an 1895 speech to male and female strikers in a Massachusetts shoe factory. "Too long has it been held that woman has no right to enter these movements. So much for the movements. Politics is the place for woman."

At the same time, the center of gravity of feminism shifted toward an outlook more in keeping with prevailing racial and ethnic norms. The earlier "feminism of equal rights," which claimed the ballot as part of a larger transformation of women's status, was never fully repudiated. The movement continued to argue for women's equality in employment, education, and politics. But with increasing frequency, the native-born, middle-class women who dominated the suffrage movement claimed the vote as educated members of a "superior race."

A new generation of suffrage leaders suggested that educational and other voting qualifications did not conflict with the movement's aims, so long as they applied equally to men and women. Immigrants and former slaves had been enfranchised with "ill-advised haste," declared Carrie Chapman Catt, president of the National American Woman Suffrage Association (created in 1890 to reunite the rival suffrage organizations formed after the Civil War). Indeed, Catt suggested, extending the vote to native-born white women would help to counteract the growing power of the "ignorant foreign vote" in the North and the dangerous potential for a second Reconstruction in the South. Elitism within the movement was reinforced when many advocates of suffrage blamed the "slum vote" for the defeat of a women's suffrage referendum in California. In 1895, the same year that Booker T. Washington delivered his Atlanta address, the National American Woman Suffrage Association held its annual convention in that segregated city. Eight years later, the association met in New Orleans, where the delegates sang "Dixie" and listened to speeches by former Confederate officers that denounced Blacks as barbarians. Like other American institutions, the organized movement for women's suffrage had made its peace with nativism and racism.

BECOMING A WORLD POWER

The New Imperialism

In the last years of the 1890s, the narrowed definition of nationhood was projected abroad, as the United States took its place as an imperial power on the international stage. In world history, the last quarter of the nineteenth century is known as the age of imperialism, when rival European empires carved up large parts of the world among themselves. For most of this period, the United States remained a second-rate power. In 1880, the head of the Ottoman empire decided to close three foreign embassies to reduce expenses. He chose those in Sweden, Belgium, and the United States. In that year, the American navy was smaller than Denmark's or Chile's. When European powers met at the Berlin Congress of 1884–1885 to divide most of Africa among themselves, the

United States attended because of its relationship with Liberia but did not sign the final agreement.

Throughout the nineteenth century, large empires controlled much of the globe. After 1870, a "new imperialism" arose, controlled by European powers and Japan. Belgium, Great Britain, and France consolidated their hold on colonies in Africa, and newly unified Germany acquired colonies there as well. The British and Russians sought to increase their influence in Central Asia, and all the European powers struggled to dominate parts of China. By the early twentieth century, most of Asia, Africa, the Middle East, and the Pacific had been divided among these empires. The justification for this expansion of imperial power was that it would bring modern "civilization" to the supposedly backward peoples of the non-European world. The natives, according to their colonial occupiers, would be instructed in Western values, labor practices, and the Christian religion. Eventually, they would be accorded the right of self-government, although no one could be sure how long this would take. In the meantime, "empire" was another word for "exploitation."

American Expansionism

Territorial expansion, of course, had been a feature of American life from well before independence. But the 1890s marked a major turning point in America's relationship with the rest of the world. Americans were increasingly aware of themselves as an emerging world power. "We are a great imperial Republic destined to exercise a controlling influence upon the actions of mankind and to affect the future of the world," proclaimed Henry Watterson, an influential newspaper editor.

Until the 1890s, American expansion had taken place on the North American continent. Ever since the Monroe Doctrine of 1823, to be sure, many Americans had considered the Western Hemisphere an American sphere of influence. There was persistent talk of acquiring Cuba, and President Grant had sought to annex the Dominican Republic, only to see the Senate reject the idea. The last territorial acquisition before the 1890s had been Alaska, purchased from Russia by Secretary of State William H. Seward in 1867, to much derision from those who could not see the purpose of American ownership of "Seward's icebox." Seward, however, was mostly interested in the Aleutian Islands, a part of Alaska that stretched much of the way to Asia (see the map on p. 685) and that, he believed, could be the site of coaling stations for merchant ships plying the Pacific.

Most Americans who looked overseas were interested in expanded trade, not territorial possessions. The country's agricultural and industrial production could no longer be entirely absorbed at home. By 1890, companies like Singer Sewing Machines and John D. Rockefeller's Standard Oil Company aggressively marketed their products abroad. Especially during economic downturns, business leaders insisted on the necessity of greater access to foreign customers. Middle-class American women, moreover, were becoming more and more desirous of clothing and food from abroad, and their demand for consumer goods such as "Oriental" fashions and exotic spices for cooking spurred the economic penetration of the Far East.

The Lure of Empire

One group of Americans who spread the nation's influence overseas were religious missionaries, thousands of whom ventured abroad in the late nineteenth century to spread Christianity, prepare the world for the second coming of Christ, and uplift the poor. Inspired by Dwight Moody, a Methodist evangelist, the Student Volunteer Movement for Foreign Missions sent more than 8,000 missionaries to "bring light to heathen worlds" across the globe. Missionary work offered employment to those with few opportunities at home, including Blacks and women, who made up a majority of the total.

A small group of late-nineteenth-century thinkers actively promoted American expansionism, warning that the country must not allow itself to be shut out of the scramble for empire. In *Our Country* (1885), Josiah Strong, a prominent Congregationalist clergyman, sought to update the idea of manifest destiny. Having demonstrated their special aptitude for liberty and self-government on the North American continent, Strong announced, Anglo-Saxons should now spread their institutions and values to "inferior races" throughout the world. The economy would benefit, he insisted, since one means of civilizing "savages" was to turn them into consumers of American goods.

Naval officer Alfred T. Mahan, in *The Influence of Sea Power upon History* (1890), argued that no nation could prosper without a large fleet of ships engaged in international trade, protected by a powerful navy operating from overseas bases. Mahan published his book in the same year that the census bureau announced that there was no longer a clear line separating settled from unsettled land. Thus, the frontier no longer existed. "Americans," wrote Mahan, "must now begin to look outward." His arguments influenced the outlook of James G. Blaine, who served as secretary of state during Benjamin Harrison's presidency (1889–1893). Blaine urged the president to try to acquire Hawaii, Puerto Rico, and Cuba as strategic naval bases.

Although independent, Hawaii was already closely tied to the United States through treaties that exempted imports of its sugar from tariff duties and provided for the establishment of an American naval base at Pearl Harbor. Hawaii's economy was dominated by American-owned sugar plantations that employed a workforce of native islanders and Chinese, Japanese, and Filipino laborers under long-term contracts. Early in 1893, a group of American planters organized a rebellion that overthrew the Hawaii government of Queen Liliuokalani. On the eve of leaving office, Harrison submitted a treaty of annexation to the Senate. After determining that a majority of Hawaiians did not favor the treaty, Harrison's successor, Grover Cleveland, withdrew it. In July 1898, in the midst of the Spanish-American War, the United States finally annexed the Hawaiian Islands. In 1993, the U.S. Congress passed, and President Bill Clinton signed, a resolution expressing regret to native Hawaiians for "the overthrow of the Kingdom of Hawaii . . . with the participation of agents and citizens of the United States."

Queen Liliuokalani, the last ruler of Hawaii before it was annexed by the United States.

The depression that began in 1893 heightened the belief that a more aggressive foreign policy was necessary to stimulate American exports. In the face of social conflict and the new immigration, government and private organizations promoted a unifying patriotism. These were the years when rituals like the Pledge of Allegiance and the practice of standing for the playing of "The Star-Spangled Banner" came into existence. Americans had long honored the Stars and Stripes, but the "cult of the flag," including an official Flag Day, dates to the 1890s. New, mass-circulation newspapers also promoted nationalistic sentiments. By the late 1890s, papers like William Randolph Hearst's *New York Journal* and Joseph Pulitzer's *New York World*—dubbed the "**yellow press**" by their critics after the color in which Hearst printed a popular comic strip—were selling a million copies each day by mixing sensational accounts of crime and political corruption with aggressive appeals to patriotic sentiments.

The "Splendid Little War"

All these factors contributed to America's emergence as a world power in the Spanish-American War of 1898. But the immediate origins of the war lay not at home but in the long Cuban struggle for independence from Spain. Ten years of guerrilla war had followed a Cuban revolt in 1868. The movement for independence resumed in 1895. As reports circulated of widespread suffering caused by the Spanish policy of rounding up civilians and moving them into detention camps, the Cuban struggle won growing support in the United States.

Demands for intervention escalated after February 15, 1898, when an explosion—probably accidental, a later investigation concluded—destroyed

THE SPANISH-AMERICAN WAR: THE PACIFIC

CHINA

FORMOSA (Taiwan) (Japanese)

Hong Kong (British)

Pacific Ocean

Hainan

Dewey

Luzon

PHILIPPINE ISLANDS

Manila

FRENCH INDOCHINA

South China Sea

Sulu Sea

Mindanao

BRITISH NORTH BORNEO

SARAWAK (British)

NETHERLANDS EAST INDIES

Pacific Ocean

Manila surrenders August 13, 1898

Manila

Bataan

Corregidor

Dewey

Spanish fleet destroyed May 1, 1898

0   200   400 miles
0   200   400 kilometers

THE SPANISH-AMERICAN WAR: THE CARIBBEAN

UNITED STATES

Santiago

San Juan Hill July 1, 1898

Spanish fleet destroyed July 3, 1898

Tampa

U.S.S. Maine sunk February 1898

Havana

BAHAMAS

Atlantic Ocean

CUBA

Santiago

HAITI

PUERTO RICO

JAMAICA (British)

DOMINICAN REPUBLIC

Caribbean Sea

Pacific Ocean

0   200   400 miles
0   200   400 kilometers

American victories
American forces
American naval blockade
Spanish forces
Spanish possessions

In both the Pacific and the Caribbean, the United States achieved swift victories over Spain in the Spanish-American War.

the American battleship **U.S.S. *Maine*** in Havana Harbor, with the loss of nearly 270 lives. The yellow press blamed Spain and insisted on retribution. After Spain rejected an American demand for a cease-fire on the island and eventual Cuban independence, President McKinley in April asked Congress for a declaration of war. The purpose, declared Senator Henry Teller of Colorado, was to aid Cuban patriots in their struggle for "liberty and freedom." To underscore the government's humanitarian intentions, Congress adopted the Teller Amendment, stating that the United States had no intention of annexing or dominating the island.

Secretary of State John Hay called the Spanish-American conflict a "splendid little war." It lasted only four months and resulted in fewer than 400 American combat deaths. Having shown little interest in imperial expansion before 1898, McKinley now embraced the idea. The war's most decisive engagement, in fact, took place not in Cuba but at Manila Bay, a strategic harbor in the Philippine Islands in the distant Pacific Ocean. Here, on May 1, the American navy under Admiral George Dewey defeated a Spanish fleet. Soon afterward, soldiers went ashore, becoming the first American army units to engage in combat outside the Western Hemisphere. July witnessed another naval victory off Santiago, Cuba, and the landing of American troops on Cuba and Puerto Rico.

Roosevelt at San Juan Hill

The most highly publicized land battle of the war took place in Cuba. This was the charge up San Juan Hill, outside Santiago, by Theodore Roosevelt's Rough Riders. An ardent expansionist, Roosevelt had long believed that a war would reinvigorate the nation's unity and sense of manhood, which had suffered, he felt, during the 1890s. A few months shy of his fortieth birthday when war broke out, Roosevelt resigned his post as assistant secretary of the navy to raise a volunteer cavalry unit, which rushed to Cuba to participate in the fighting. Roosevelt envisioned his unit as a cross section of American society and enrolled athletes from Ivy League colleges, western cowboys, representatives of various immigrant groups, and even some American Indians. But with the army still segregated, he excluded Blacks from his regiment. Ironically, when the Rough Riders reached the top of San Juan Hill, they found that Black units had preceded them—a fact Roosevelt omitted in his reports of the battle, which were widely reproduced in the popular press. His exploits made Roosevelt a national hero. He was elected governor of New York that fall and in 1900 became McKinley's vice president.

An American Empire

With the backing of the yellow press, the war quickly escalated from a crusade to aid the suffering Cubans to an imperial venture that ended with the United States in possession of a small overseas empire. McKinley became convinced that the United States could neither return the Philippines to Spain nor grant them independence, for which he believed the inhabitants unprepared. In an interview with a group of Methodist ministers, the president spoke of receiving a divine revelation that Americans had a duty to "uplift and civilize" the Filipino people and to train them for self-government. In the treaty with Spain that ended the war, the United States acquired the Philippines, Puerto Rico, and the Pacific island of Guam. As for Cuba, before recognizing its independence, McKinley forced the island's new government to approve the **Platt Amendment** to the new Cuban constitution (drafted by Senator Orville H. Platt of Connecticut), which authorized the United States to intervene militarily whenever it saw fit. The United States also acquired a permanent lease on naval stations in Cuba, including what is now the facility at Guantánamo Bay.

The Platt Amendment passed the Cuban Congress by a single vote. Cuban patriots were terribly disappointed. José Martí had fomented revolution in Cuba from exile in the United States and then traveled to the island to take part in the uprising, only to be killed in a battle with Spanish soldiers in 1895. "To change masters is not to be free," Martí had written. And the memory of the betrayal of 1898 would help to inspire another Cuban revolution half a century later.

American interest in its new possessions had more to do with trade than gaining wealth from natural resources or large-scale American settlement. Puerto Rico and Cuba were gateways to Latin America, strategic outposts from which American naval and commercial power could be projected throughout the hemisphere. The Philippines, Guam, and Hawaii lay astride shipping routes to the markets of Japan and China. In 1899, soon after the end of the Spanish-American War, Secretary of State John Hay announced the **Open Door Policy**, demanding that European powers that had recently divided China into commercial spheres of influence grant equal access to American exports. The Open Door referred to the free movement of goods and money, not people. Even as the United States banned the immigration of Chinese into this country, it insisted on access to the markets and investment opportunities of Asia.

The Philippine War

Many Cubans, Filipinos, and Puerto Ricans had welcomed American intervention as a way of breaking Spain's long hold on these colonies. Large planters looked forward to greater access to American markets, and local elites hoped that the American presence would fend off radical changes proposed by rebellious nationalist movements. Nationalists and labor leaders admired America's democratic ideals and believed that American participation in the destruction of Spanish rule would lead to social reform and political self-government.

But the American determination to exercise continued control, direct or indirect, led to a rapid change in local opinion, nowhere more so than in the Philippines. Filipinos had been fighting a war against Spain since 1896. After Dewey's victory at Manila Bay, their leader, Emilio Aguinaldo, established a provisional government with a constitution modeled on that of the United States. But once McKinley decided to retain possession of the islands, the Filipino movement turned against the United States. The result was a second war, far longer (it lasted from 1899 to 1903) and bloodier (it cost the lives of more than 100,000 Filipinos and 4,200 Americans) than the Spanish-American conflict. Today, the **Philippine War** is perhaps the least remembered of all American wars. At the time, however, it was closely followed and widely debated in the United States. Both sides committed atrocities. Insurgents killed Filipinos who cooperated with the Americans. The U.S. Army burned villages and moved the inhabitants into camps where thousands perished of disease, and launched a widespread campaign of torture, including the infamous "water cure" or simulated drowning, later revived in the Iraq and Afghanistan wars of the 21st century and known as waterboarding. Press reports of these practices tarnished the nation's self-image

AMERICAN EMPIRE, 1898

As a result of the Spanish-American War, the United States became the ruler of a far-flung overseas empire.

as liberators. "We do not intend to free the people of the Philippines," complained Mark Twain. "We have gone there to conquer."

The McKinley administration justified its policies on the grounds that its aim was to "uplift and civilize and Christianize" the Filipinos (although most residents of the islands were already Roman Catholics). William Howard Taft, who became governor-general of the Philippines in 1901, believed it might take a century to raise Filipinos to the condition where they could appreciate "what Anglo-Saxon liberty is."

Once in control of the Philippines, the colonial administration took seriously the idea of modernizing the islands. It expanded railroads and harbors, brought in American schoolteachers and public health officials, and sought to modernize agriculture (although efforts to persuade local farmers to substitute corn for rice ran afoul of the Filipino climate and cultural traditions). The United States, said President McKinley, had an obligation to its "little brown brothers." Yet in all the new possessions, American policies tended to serve the interests of land-based local elites—native-born landowners in the Philippines, American sugar planters in Hawaii and Puerto Rico—and such policies bequeathed enduring poverty to the majority of the rural population. Under American rule, Puerto Rico, previously an island of diversified small farmers, became a low-wage plantation economy controlled by absentee corporations. By the 1920s, its residents were among the poorest in the entire Caribbean.

Citizens or Subjects?

American rule also brought with it American racial attitudes. In an 1899 poem, the British writer Rudyard Kipling urged the United States to take up the "white man's burden" of imperialism. American proponents of empire agreed that the domination of non-white peoples by whites formed part of the progress of civilization. Among the soldiers sent to the Philippines to fight Aguinaldo were a number of Black regiments. Their letters from the front suggested that American atrocities arose from white troops applying to the Filipino population the same "treatment for colored peoples" practiced at home.

America's triumphant entry into the ranks of imperial powers sparked an intense debate over the relationship among political democracy, race, and American citizenship. The American system of government had no provision for permanent colonies. The right of every people to self-government was one of the main principles of the Declaration of Independence. The idea of an "empire of liberty" assumed that new territories would eventually be admitted as equal states and their residents would be American citizens. In the aftermath of the Spanish-American War, however, nationalism, democracy, and American freedom emerged more closely identified than ever with notions of Anglo-Saxon superiority.

Leaders of both parties, while determined to retain the new overseas possessions, feared that people of what one congressman called "an alien race and foreign tongue" could not be incorporated into the Union. The Foraker Act of 1900 declared Puerto Rico an "insular territory," different from previous territories in the West. Its 1 million inhabitants were defined as citizens of Puerto Rico, not the United States, and denied a future path to statehood. Filipinos occupied a similar status. In a series of cases decided between 1901 and 1904 and known collectively as the **Insular Cases**, the Supreme Court held that the Constitution did not fully apply to the territories recently acquired by the United States—a significant limitation of the scope of American freedom. Congress, the Court declared, must recognize the "fundamental" personal rights of residents of the Philippines and Puerto Rico. But otherwise it could govern them as it saw fit for an indefinite period of time. Thus, two principles central to American freedom since the War of Independence—no taxation without representation, and government based on the consent of the governed—were abandoned when it came to the nation's new possessions.

In the twentieth century, the territories acquired in 1898 would follow different paths. Hawaii, which had a sizable population of American missionaries and planters, became a traditional territory. Its population, except for Asian immigrant laborers, became American citizens, and it was admitted as a state in 1959. After nearly a half-century of American rule, the Philippines achieved independence in 1946. Until 1950, the U.S. Navy administered Guam, which remains today an "unincorporated" territory. As for Puerto Rico, it is sometimes called "the world's oldest colony," because ever since the Spanish conquered the island in 1493 it has lacked full self-government. Congress extended American citizenship to Puerto Ricans in 1917. Puerto Rico today remains in a kind of political limbo, poised on the brink of statehood or independence. The island has the status of a commonwealth. It elects its own government but lacks a voice in Congress (and in the election of the U.S. president), and key issues such as defense and environmental policy are controlled by the United States.

Whatever the end result, the Spanish-American War established a precedent for American intervention in the affairs of other countries, especially those in the Western Hemisphere. In the twentieth century, the United States would intervene in Latin America to change local governments, either by direct military action or via support for military coups, no fewer than forty times.

Drawing the Global Color Line

Just as American ideas about liberty and self-government had circulated around the world in the Age of Revolution, American racial attitudes had a global impact in the age of empire. The turn of the twentieth century was a time of worldwide concern about immigration, race relations, and the "white man's burden," all of which inspired a global sense of fraternity among "Anglo-Saxon" nations. Chinese exclusion in the United States strongly influenced anti-Chinese laws adopted in Canada.

One "lesson" these countries learned from the United States was that the "failure" of Reconstruction demonstrated the impossibility of multiracial democracy. The extremely hostile account of Reconstruction by the British writer James Bryce in his widely read book *The American Commonwealth* (published in London in 1888) circulated around the world. Bryce called African Americans "children of nature" and insisted that giving them the right to vote had been a terrible mistake, which had produced all kinds of corruption and misgovernment. His book was frequently cited by the founders of the Australian Commonwealth (1901) to justify their "white Australia" policy, which barred the further immigration of Asians. The Union of South Africa, inaugurated in 1911, saw its own policy of racial separation—later known as apartheid—as following in the footsteps of segregation in the United States. Even American proposals that did not become law, such as the literacy test

From THE REV. CHARLES G. AMES, ADDRESS TO ANTI-IMPERIALISM MEETING, BOSTON (1898)

The emergence of the United States as an imperial power as a result of the Spanish-American War sparked an intense debate over the relationship between political democracy, race, and citizenship. Anti-imperialists like Ames warned that acquiring an overseas empire threatened to undermine democracy at home and also wondered whether inhabitants of places conquered by the United States were worthy of citizenship.

We are told that it is "our duty" to extend to the struggling people of the Philippines the same help and protection we have pledged to Cuba. . . . Is there a man in America who wishes those seven millions of Malays, Negritos and Chinamen for fellow citizens and joint rulers of this Republic? But if we govern them without their consent, it must be by military occupation by force; that is by the Spanish method. . . .

But the scheme of conquest does not end with the acquisition of the Philippines; it only begins there. The imperial program includes a chain of island possessions. The European powers are dividing the Asiatic, African and Polynesian world among themselves; we are to go in for a share of the booty. . . .

How can we undertake to rule subject provinces in distant parts of the globe without trampling on the principles of free government? Once accepting this way of dealing with other people, how long will it be before some occasion will arise for applying it at home? In committing ourselves to permanent military methods of government anywhere, we give up the republic, for we abandon its fundamental principle, even while boasting of the name. . . .

The imperial scheme requires us to go very deeply into military and naval expenditure, that we may be ever on fighting footing. We must girdle the earth with strategic possessions, every one of which must be fortified and garrisoned. . . . We are to be a great military nation! . . . If you object, you are no patriot! But where will be the republic? . . .

The policy of imperialism threatens to change the temper of our people, and to put us into a permanent attitude of arrogance, testiness and defiance toward other nations. . . . We shall be one more bully among bullies: we shall only add one more to the list of oppressors of mankind. . . . The program of imperialism reads to me like a declaration of war for the new century.

QUESTIONS

1. *Why does Ames see imperialism as undermining democracy?*

2. *How do his views of race affect his opposition to imperialism?*

for immigrants vetoed by President Cleveland, influenced measures adopted overseas. The United States, too, learned from other countries. The Gentleman's Agreement that limited Japanese immigration early in the twentieth century (see Chapter 19) followed a similar arrangement between Japan and Canada.

"Republic or Empire?"

The emergence of the United States as an imperial power sparked intense debate. Opponents formed the **Anti-Imperialist League**. It united writers and social reformers who believed American energies should be directed at home, businessmen fearful of the cost of maintaining overseas outposts, and racists who did not wish to bring non-white populations into the United States. Among its prominent members were E. L. Godkin, the editor of *The Nation*, the novelist William Dean Howells, and the labor leader George E. McNeill. The league held meetings throughout the country and published pamphlets called

The first step towards lightening

The White Man's Burden

is through teaching the virtues of cleanliness.

Pears' Soap

An advertisement employs the idea of a White Man's Burden (borrowed from a poem by Rudyard Kipling) as a way of promoting the virtues of Pears' Soap. Accompanying text claims that Pears' is "the ideal toilet soap" for "the cultured of all nations," and an agent of civilization in "the dark corners of the earth."

Liberty Tracts, warning that empire was incompatible with democracy. America's historic mission, the league declared, was to "help the world by an example of successful self-government," not to conquer other peoples. A "republic of free men," anti-imperialists proclaimed, should assist the people of Puerto Rico and the Philippines in their own "struggles for liberty," rather than subjecting them to colonial rule.

In 1900, Democrats again nominated William Jennings Bryan to run against McKinley. The Democratic platform opposed the Philippine War for placing the United States in the "un-American" position of "crushing with military force" another people's desire for "liberty and self-government." George S. Boutwell, president of the Anti-Imperialist League, declared that the most pressing question in the election was the nation's future character—"republic or empire?"

But without any sense of contradiction, proponents of an imperial foreign policy also adopted the language of freedom. Senator Albert Beveridge of

Indiana claimed that America ventured abroad not for material gain or national power, but to bring "a new day of freedom" to the peoples of the world. Beveridge did not, however, neglect more practical considerations. American trade, he insisted, "henceforth must be with Asia. The Pacific is our ocean. . . . Where shall we turn for consumers of our surplus? Geography answers the question. China is our natural customer." Riding the wave of patriotic sentiment inspired by the war, and with the economy having recovered from the depression of 1893–1897, McKinley in 1900 repeated his 1896 triumph.

At the dawn of the twentieth century, the United States seemed poised to take its place among the world's great powers. Writers at home and overseas confidently predicted that American influence would soon span the globe. In his 1902 book *The New Empire*, Brooks Adams, a grandson of John Quincy Adams, predicted that because of its economic power, the United States would soon "outweigh any single empire, if not all empires combined." Years would pass before this prediction was fulfilled. But in 1900, many features that would mark American life for much of the twentieth century were already apparent. The United States led the world in industrial production. The merger movement of 1897–1904 (discussed in the previous chapter) left broad sections of the economy under the control of giant corporations. The political system had stabilized. The white North and South had achieved reconciliation, while rigid lines of racial exclusion—the segregation of Blacks, Chinese exclusion, Indian reservations—limited the boundaries of freedom and citizenship.

Yet the questions central to nineteenth-century debates over freedom—the relationship between political and economic liberty, the role of government in creating the conditions of freedom, and the definition of those entitled to enjoy the rights of citizens—had not been permanently answered. Nor had the dilemma of how to reconcile America's role as an empire with traditional ideas of freedom been resolved. These were the challenges bequeathed by the nineteenth century to the first generation of the twentieth.

CHAPTER REVIEW

REVIEW QUESTIONS

1. *What economic and political issues gave rise to the Populist Party, and what changes did the party advocate?*

2. *How did employers use state and federal forces to protect their own economic interests, and what were the results?*

3. *Who were the Redeemers, and how did they change society and politics in the New South?*

4. *Explain how changes in politics, economics, social factors, and violence interacted to affect the situation of African Americans in the New South.*

5. *How did religion and the idea of the Lost Cause give support to a new understanding of the Civil War?*

6. *What rights did Chinese immigrants and Chinese Americans gain in these years, and what limitations did they experience? How did their experiences set the stage for other restrictions on immigration?*

7. *Compare and contrast the goals, strategies, and membership of the American Federation of Labor and the Knights of Labor (you may want to refer back to Chapter 16).*

8. *What ideas and interests motivated the United States to create an empire in the late nineteenth century?*

9. *Compare the arguments for and against U.S. imperialism. Be sure to consider the views of Josiah Strong and Emilio Aguinaldo.*

10. *What was the Immigration Restriction League and what changes to political participation did it advocate?*

KEY TERMS

Populists (p. 654)

Coxey's Army (p. 658)

American Federation of Labor (p. 658)

New South (p. 662)

Kansas Exodus (p. 663)

Atlanta Compromise (p. 665)

grandfather clause (p. 666)

disenfranchisement (p. 666)

Plessy v. Ferguson (p. 667)

"separate but equal" (p. 667)

lynching (p. 668)

Lost Cause (p. 672)

new immigrants (p. 673)

Immigration Restriction League (p. 674)

Chinese Exclusion Act (p. 674)

yellow press (p. 681)

U.S.S. *Maine* (p. 682)

Platt Amendment (p. 683)

Open Door Policy (p. 684)

Philippine War (p. 684)

Insular Cases (p. 686)

Anti-Imperialist League (p. 689)

Go to ⚓ INQUIZITIVE

To see what you know—and learn what you've missed—with personalized feedback along the way.

CHAPTER 18

THE PROGRESSIVE ERA

1900–1916

FOCUS QUESTIONS

- *Why was the city such a central element in Progressive America?*

- *How did the labor and women's movements challenge the nineteenth-century meanings of American freedom?*

- *In what ways did Progressivism include both democratic and anti-democratic impulses?*

- *How did the Progressive presidents foster the rise of the nation-state?*

It was late afternoon on March 25, 1911, when fire broke out at the Triangle Shirtwaist Company. The factory occupied the top three floors of a ten-story building in the Greenwich Village neighborhood of New York City. Here some 500 workers, mostly young Jewish and Italian immigrant women, toiled at sewing machines producing ladies' blouses, some earning as little as three dollars per week. Those who tried to escape the blaze discovered that the doors to the stairwell had been locked—the owners' way, it was later charged, of discouraging theft and unauthorized bathroom breaks. The fire department rushed to the scene with high-pressure hoses. But their ladders reached only to the sixth floor. As the fire raged, onlookers watched in horror as girls leapt from the upper stories. By the time the blaze had been put out, 46 bodies lay on the street and 100 more were found inside the building.

The Triangle Shirtwaist Company was typical of manufacturing in the nation's largest city, a beehive of industrial production in small, crowded factories. New York was home to 30,000 manufacturing establishments with more than 600,000 employees—more industrial workers than in the entire state of Massachusetts. Triangle had already played a key role in the era's labor history. When 200 of its workers tried to join the International Ladies' Garment Workers Union (ILGWU), the owners responded by firing them. This incident helped to spark a general walkout of female garment workers in 1909—the Uprising of the 20,000. Among the strikers' demands was better safety in clothing factories. The impoverished immigrants forged an alliance with middle- and upper-class female supporters, including members of the Women's Trade Union League, which had been founded in 1903 to help bring women workers into unions. Alva Belmont, the ex-wife of railroad magnate William Vanderbilt, contributed several of her cars to a parade in support of the striking workers. By the time the walkout ended early in 1911, the ILGWU had won union contracts with more than 300 firms. But the Triangle Shirtwaist Company was not among them.

The Triangle fire was not the worst fire disaster in American history (seven years earlier, over 1,000 people had died in a blaze on the *General Slocum* excursion boat in New York harbor). But it had an unrivaled impact on public consciousness. More than twenty years later, Franklin D. Roosevelt would refer to it in a press conference as an example of why the government needed to regulate industry. In its wake, efforts to organize the city's workers accelerated, and the state legislature passed new factory inspection laws and fire safety codes.

Triangle focused attention on the social divisions that plagued American society during the first two decades of the twentieth century, a period known as the Progressive era. These were years when economic expansion produced millions of new jobs and brought an unprecedented array of goods within reach of American consumers. Cities expanded rapidly—by 1920, for the first time, more Americans lived in towns and cities than in rural areas. Yet severe inequality remained the most visible feature of the urban landscape, and persistent labor strife raised anew the question of government's role in combating it. The fire and its aftermath also highlighted how traditional gender roles were changing as women took on new responsibilities in the workplace and in the making of public policy.

The word "Progressive" came into common use around 1910 as a way of describing a broad, loosely defined political movement of individuals and groups who hoped to bring about significant change in American social and political life. Progressives included forward-looking businessmen who realized that workers must be accorded a voice in economic decision making, and labor activists bent on empowering industrial workers. Other major contributors to **Progressivism** were members of female reform organizations who hoped to protect women and children from exploitation, social scientists who believed that academic research would help to solve social problems, and members of an anxious middle class who feared that their status was threatened by the rise of big business.

Everywhere in early-twentieth-century America the signs of economic and political consolidation were apparent—in the power of a small directorate of Wall Street bankers and corporate executives, the manipulation of democracy by corrupt political machines, and the rise of new systems of managerial control in workplaces. In these circumstances, wrote Benjamin P. DeWitt, in his 1915 book *The Progressive Movement*, "the individual could not hope to compete.... Slowly, Americans realized that they were not free."

As this and the following chapter will discuss, Progressive reformers responded to the perception of declining freedom in varied, contradictory ways. The era saw the expansion of political and economic freedom through the reinvigoration of the movement for woman suffrage, the use of political power to expand workers' rights, and efforts to improve democratic government by weakening the power of city bosses and giving ordinary citizens more influence on legislation. It witnessed the flowering of understandings of freedom based on individual fulfillment and personal self-determination—the ability to participate fully in the ever-expanding consumer marketplace and, especially for women, to enjoy economic and sexual freedoms long considered the province of men. At the same time, many Progressives supported efforts to limit the full enjoyment of freedom to those deemed fit to exercise it properly. The new system of white supremacy in the 1890s became fully consolidated in the South. Growing numbers of Americans born in the United States demanded that immigrants abandon their traditional cultures and become fully "Americanized." And efforts were made at the local and national levels to place political decision making in the hands of experts who did not have to answer to the electorate. The idea of freedom remained as contested as ever in Progressive America.

1914	Ludlow Massacre
	Federal Trade Commission established
	Clayton Act

AN URBAN AGE AND A CONSUMER SOCIETY

Farms and Cities

The Progressive era was a period of explosive economic growth, fueled by increasing industrial production, a rapid rise in population, and the continued expansion of the consumer marketplace. In the first decade of the twentieth century, the economy's total output rose by about 85 percent. For the last time in American history, farms and cities grew together. As farm prices recovered from their low point during the depression of the 1890s, American agriculture entered what would later be remembered as its "golden age." The expansion of urban areas stimulated demand for farm goods. Farm families poured into the western Great Plains. More than 1 million claims for free government land were filed under the Homestead Act of 1862—more than in the previous forty years. Between 1900 and 1910, the combined population of Texas and Oklahoma rose by nearly 2 million, and Kansas, Nebraska, and the Dakotas added 800,000. Irrigation transformed the Imperial Valley of California and parts of Arizona into major areas of commercial farming.

But it was the city that became the focus of Progressive politics and of a new mass-consumer society. The United States counted twenty-one cities whose population exceeded 100,000 in 1910, the largest of them New York, with 4.7 million residents. The twenty-three square miles of Manhattan Island were home to over 2 million people, more than lived in thirty-three of the states. Fully a quarter of them inhabited the Lower East Side, a densely populated immigrant neighborhood.

The stark urban inequalities of the 1890s continued into the Progressive era. Immigrant families in New York's downtown tenements often had no electricity or indoor toilets. Three miles to the north stood the mansions of Fifth

A colored photograph from around 1900 shows the teeming street life of Mulberry Street, on New York City's densely populated Lower East Side. The massive immigration of the early twentieth century transformed the life of urban centers throughout the country and helped to spark the Progressive movement.

Avenue's Millionaire's Row. According to one estimate, J. P. Morgan's financial firm directly or indirectly controlled 40 percent of all financial and industrial capital in the United States. Alongside such wealth, reported the Commission on Industrial Relations, established by Congress in 1912, more than one-third of the country's mining and manufacturing workers lived in "actual poverty."

The city captured the imagination of artists, writers, and reformers. The glories of the American landscape had been the focal point of nineteenth-century painters (exemplified by the Hudson River school, which produced canvases celebrating the wonders of nature). Now painters like George W. Bellows and John Sloan and photographers such as Alfred Stieglitz and Edward Steichen captured the electric lights, crowded bars and theaters, and soaring skyscrapers of the urban landscape. With its youthful, exuberant energies, the city seemed an expression of modernity itself.

The Muckrakers

Others saw the city as a place where corporate greed undermined traditional American values. At a time when more than 2 million children under the age of fifteen worked for wages, Lewis Hine photographed child laborers to draw attention to persistent social inequality. A new generation of journalists writing for mass-circulation national magazines exposed the ills of industrial and urban life. *The Shame of the Cities* by Lincoln Steffens (published as a series in *McClure's Magazine* in 1901–1902 and in book form in 1904) showed how party bosses and business leaders profited from political corruption. *McClure's* also hired Ida Tarbell to expose the arrogance and economic machinations of John D. Rockefeller's Standard Oil Company. Published in two volumes in 1904, her *History of the Standard Oil Company* was the most substantial product of what Theodore Roosevelt disparaged as **muckraking**—the use of journalistic skills to expose the underside of American life.

Major novelists of the era took a similar unsparing approach to social ills. Theodore Dreiser's *Sister Carrie* (1900) traced a young woman's moral corruption in Chicago's harsh urban environment. Perhaps the era's most influential novel was Upton Sinclair's *The Jungle* (1906), whose description of unsanitary slaughterhouses and the sale of rotten meat stirred public outrage and led directly to the passage of the Pure Food and Drug Act and the Meat Inspection Act of 1906.

TABLE 18.1 Rise of the City, 1880–1920

Year	Urban Population (percentage)	Number of Cities with 100,000+ Population
1880	20%	12
1890	28	15
1900	38	18
1910	50	21
1920	68	26

Immigration as a Global Process

If one thing characterized early-twentieth-century cities, it was their immigrant character. The "new immigration" from southern and eastern Europe had begun around 1890 but reached its peak during the Progressive era. Between 1901 and the outbreak of World War I in Europe in 1914, some 13 million immigrants came to the United States, the majority from Italy, Russia, and the Austro-Hungarian empire. Progressive-era immigration formed part of a larger process of worldwide migration set in motion by industrial expansion and the decline of traditional agriculture. Poles emigrated not only to Pittsburgh and Chicago but also to work in German factories and Scottish mines. Italians sought jobs in Belgium, France, and Argentina as well as the United States. As many as 750,000 Chinese migrated to other countries each year.

Between 1840 and 1914 (when immigration to the United States would be virtually cut off, first by the outbreak of World War I and then by legislation), perhaps 40 million persons emigrated to the United States and another 20 million to other parts of the Western Hemisphere, including Canada, Argentina, and the Caribbean. This population flow formed one part of a massive shifting of peoples throughout the world.

Numerous causes inspired this uprooting of population. Rural southern and eastern Europe and large parts of Asia were regions marked by widespread poverty and illiteracy, burdensome taxation, and declining economies. Political turmoil at home, like the revolution that engulfed Mexico after 1911, also inspired emigration. Not all of these immigrants could be classified as "free laborers," however. Large numbers of Chinese, Mexican, and Italian migrants, including many who came to the United States, were bound to long-term contracts with labor agents, who then provided the workers to American employers. But all the areas attracting immigrants were frontiers—agricultural,

A photograph by Lewis Hine, who used his camera to chronicle the plight of child laborers. Shown here: a young spinner in a Vermont cotton factory.

mining, or industrial—with expanding job opportunities.

Most European immigrants to the United States entered through **Ellis Island**. Located in New York Harbor, this became in 1892 the nation's main immigrant processing and detention facility. Millions of Americans today trace their ancestry to an immigrant who passed through Ellis Island. About 2 percent of total arrivals, who failed a medical examination or were deemed to be anarchists, prostitutes, or "likely to become a public charge," were sent home.

At the same time, an influx of Asian and Mexican newcomers was taking place in the West. After the exclusion of immigrants from China in the late nineteenth century, a small number of Japanese arrived, primarily to work as agricultural laborers in California's fruit and vegetable fields and on Hawaii's sugar plantations. By 1910, the population of Japanese origin had grown to 72,000. Between 1910 and 1940, Angel Island in San Francisco Bay—the "Ellis Island of the West"—served as the main entry point for immigrants from Asia.

Far larger was Mexican immigration. Between 1900 and 1930, some 1 million Mexicans entered the United States—a number exceeded by only a few European countries. Mexicans generally entered through El Paso, Texas, the main southern gateway into the United States. Many ended up in the San Gabriel Valley of California, drawn by citrus growers searching for cheap labor.

By 1910, one-seventh of the American population was foreign-born, the highest percentage in the country's history. More than 40 percent of New York City's population had been born abroad. In Chicago and smaller industrial cities like Providence, Milwaukee, and San Francisco, the figure exceeded 30 percent. Although many newcomers moved west to take part in the expansion of farming, most clustered in industrial centers. By 1910, nearly three-fifths of the workers in the twenty leading manufacturing and mining industries were foreign-born.

The Immigrant Quest for Freedom

Like their nineteenth-century predecessors, the new immigrants arrived imagining the United States as a land of freedom, where all persons enjoyed equality before the law, could worship as they pleased, enjoyed economic opportunity, and had been emancipated from the oppressive social hierarchies of their homelands. "America is a free country," one Polish immigrant wrote home. "You don't have to be a serf to anyone." Agents sent abroad by the American government to investigate the reasons for large-scale immigration reported that the main impetus was a desire to share in the "freedom and prosperity enjoyed by the people of the United States." Freedom, they added, was largely an economic ambition—a desire to escape from "hopeless poverty" and achieve a standard of living impossible at home. While some of the new immigrants, especially Jews fleeing religious persecution in the Russian empire, thought of themselves as permanent emigrants, the majority initially planned to earn enough money to return home and purchase land. Groups like Mexicans and Italians included many "birds of passage," who remained only temporarily in the United States. In 1908, a year of economic downturn in the United States, more Italians left the country than entered.

The new immigrants clustered in close-knit "ethnic" neighborhoods with their own shops, theaters, and community organizations, and often continued to speak their native tongues. As early as 1900, more than 1,000 foreign-language newspapers were published in the United States. Churches were pillars of these immigrant communities. In New York's East Harlem, even anti-clerical Italian immigrants, who resented the close alliance in Italy between the Catholic Church and the oppressive state, participated eagerly in the annual festival of the Madonna of Mt. Carmel.

An illustration in the 1912 publication *The New Immigration* depicts the various "types" entering the United States.

Although most immigrants earned more than was possible in the impoverished regions from which they came, they endured low wages, long hours, and dangerous working conditions. In the mines and factories of Pennsylvania and the Midwest, eastern European immigrants performed low-wage unskilled labor, while native-born workers dominated skilled and supervisory jobs. The vast majority of Mexican immigrants became poorly paid agricultural, mine, and railroad laborers, with little prospect of upward economic mobility. "My people are not in America," remarked one Slavic priest, "they are under it."

Consumer Freedom

Cities, however, were also the birthplace of a mass-consumption society that added new meaning to American freedom. There was, of course, nothing unusual in the idea that the promise of American life lay, in part, in the enjoyment by the masses of citizens of goods available in other countries only to the well-to-do. Not until the Progressive era, however, did the advent of large downtown department stores, chain stores in urban neighborhoods, and retail mail-order houses for farmers and small-town residents make available to consumers throughout the country the vast array of goods now pouring from the nation's factories. By 1910, Americans could purchase, among many other items, electric sewing machines, washing machines, vacuum cleaners, and record players. Low wages, the unequal distribution of income, and the South's persistent poverty limited the consumer economy, which would not fully come into its own until after World War II. But it was in Progressive America that the promise of mass consumption became the foundation for a new understanding of freedom as access to the cornucopia of goods made available by modern capitalism.

Leisure activities also took on the characteristics of mass consumption. Amusement parks, dance halls, and theaters attracted large crowds of city dwellers. The most popular form of mass entertainment at the turn of the century was vaudeville, a live theatrical entertainment consisting of numerous short acts typically including song and dance, comedy, acrobats, magicians, and trained animals. In the 1890s, brief motion pictures were already being introduced into vaudeville shows. As the movies became longer and involved more sophisticated plot narratives, separate theaters developed. By 1910, 25 million Americans per week, mostly working-class urban residents, were attending "nickelodeons"—motion-picture theaters whose five-cent admission charge was far lower than at vaudeville shows.

The Working Woman

The new visibility of women in urban public places—at work, as shoppers, and in places of entertainment like cinemas and dance halls—indicated that traditional gender roles were changing dramatically in Progressive America. As the Triangle fire revealed, more and more women were working for wages. Black women still worked primarily as domestics or in southern cotton fields. Immigrant women were largely confined to low-paying factory employment. But for native-born white women, the kinds of jobs available expanded enormously. By 1920, around 25 percent of employed women were office workers or telephone operators, and only 15 percent worked in domestic service, the largest female job category of the nineteenth century. Female work was no longer confined to young, unmarried white women and adult Black women. In 1920, of 8 million women working for wages, one-quarter were married and living with their husbands.

TABLE 18.2 Immigrants and Their Children as Percentage of Population, Ten Major Cities, 1920

City	Percentage
New York City	76%
Cleveland	72
Boston	72
Chicago	71
Detroit	65
San Francisco	64
Minneapolis	63
Pittsburgh	59
Seattle	55
Los Angeles	45

The working woman—immigrant and native, working-class and professional—became a symbol of female emancipation. Women faced special limitations on their economic freedom, including wage discrimination and exclusion from many jobs. Yet almost in spite of themselves, union leader Abraham Bisno remarked, young immigrant working women developed a sense of independence: "They acquired the *right to a personality*," something alien to the highly patriarchal family structures of the old country. "We enjoy our independence and freedom" was the assertive statement of the Bachelor Girls Social Club, a group of female mail-order clerks in New York.

The growing number of younger women who desired a lifelong career, wrote Charlotte Perkins Gilman in her influential book *Women and Economics* (1898), offered evidence of a "spirit of personal independence" that pointed to a coming transformation of both economic and family life. Gilman's writings reinforced the claim that the road to woman's freedom lay through the workplace. In the home, she argued, women experienced not fulfillment but oppression, and the housewife was an unproductive parasite, little more than a servant to her husband and children. By condemning women to a life of domestic drudgery, prevailing gender norms made them incapable of contributing to society or enjoying freedom in any meaningful sense of the word.

TABLE 18.3 Percentage of Women 14 Years and Older in the Labor Force, 1900–1930

Year	All Women	Married Women	Women as % of Labor Force
1900	20.4%	5.6%	18%
1910	25.2	10.7	24
1920	23.3	9.0	24
1930	24.3	11.7	25

The desire to participate in the consumer society produced remarkably similar battles within immigrant families of all nationalities between parents and their self-consciously "free" children, especially daughters. Contemporaries, native and immigrant, noted how "the novelties and frivolities of fashion" appealed to young working women, who spent part of their meager wages on clothing and makeup and at places of entertainment. Daughters considered parents who tried to impose curfews or to prevent them from going out alone to dances or movies as old-fashioned and not sufficiently "American." Immigrant parents found it very difficult to adapt to what one Mexican mother called "this terrible freedom in this United States." "The Mexican girls," she told a sociologist studying immigrant life in Los Angeles, "seeing American girls with freedom, they want it too."

The Rise of Fordism

If any individual exemplified the new consumer society, it was Henry Ford. The son of an immigrant Irish farmer, Ford had worked as an apprentice in Michigan machine shops and later as an engineer for the Edison Illuminating Company. Ford did not invent the automobile, but he developed the techniques of production and marketing that brought it within the reach of ordinary Americans. In 1905, he established the Ford Motor Company, one of dozens of small automobile manufacturing firms that emerged in these years. Three years later, he introduced the Model T, a simple, light vehicle sturdy enough to navigate the country's poorly maintained roads. While early European models like the Mercedes aimed at an elite market and were superior in craftsmanship, Ford concentrated on standardizing output and lowering prices.

In 1913, Ford's factory in Highland Park, Michigan, adopted the method of production known as the moving assembly line, in which car frames were brought to workers on a continuously moving conveyor belt. The process enabled Ford to expand output by greatly reducing the time it took to produce each car. In 1914, he raised wages at his factory to the unheard-of level of five dollars per day (more than double the pay of most industrial workers), enabling him to attract a steady stream of skilled laborers. Labor conditions in the Ford plant were not as appealing as the wages, however: assembly-line work was monotonous (the worker repeated the same basic motions for the entire day), and Ford used spies and armed detectives to prevent unionization. When other businessmen criticized him for endangering profits by paying high wages, Ford replied that workers must be able to afford the goods being turned out by American factories. Ford's output rose from 34,000 cars, priced at $700 each, in 1910, to 730,000 Model T's that sold at a price of $316 (well within the reach of many workers) in 1916. The economic system based on mass production and mass consumption came to be called **Fordism**.

TABLE 18.4 Sales of Passenger Cars, 1900–1925

Year	Number of Cars (in Thousands)
1900	4.1
1905	24.2
1910	181.0
1915	895.9
1920	1,905.5
1925	3,735.1

The assembly line at the Ford Motor Company factory in Highland Park, Michigan, around 1914.

The Promise of Abundance

As economic production shifted from capital goods (steel, railroad equipment, etc.) to consumer products, the new advertising industry perfected ways of increasing sales, often by linking goods with the idea of freedom. Numerous products took "liberty" as a brand name or used an image of the Statue of Liberty as a sales device. The department-store magnate Edward Filene called consumerism a "school of freedom," since shoppers made individual choices on basic questions of living. Economic abundance would eventually come to define the "American way of life," in which personal fulfillment was to be found through acquiring material goods.

The promise of abundance shifted the quest for freedom to the realm of private life, but it also inspired political activism. Exclusion from the world of mass consumption would come to seem almost as great a denial of the rights of citizenship as being barred from voting once had been. The desire for consumer goods led many workers to join unions and fight for higher wages. "Consumers' consciousness," wrote Walter Lippmann, who emerged in these years as one of the nation's most influential social commentators, was growing rapidly, with the "high cost of living" as its rallying cry.

An American Standard of Living

The maturation of the consumer economy gave rise to concepts—a "living wage" and an "**American standard of living**"—that offered a new language for criticizing the inequalities of wealth and power in Progressive America. Father John A. Ryan's influential book *A Living Wage* (1906) described a decent standard of living (one that enabled a person to participate in the consumer economy) as a "natural and absolute" right of citizenship. Ryan had grown up in Minnesota in a family sympathetic to Henry George, the Knights of Labor, and the Populists. His book sought to translate into American terms Pope Leo XIII's powerful statement of 1891, *Rerum Novarum*, which criticized the divorce of economic life from ethical considerations, endorsed the right of workers to organize unions, and repudiated competitive individualism in favor of a more cooperative vision of the good society. Ryan's insistence that economic relationships should be governed by moral standards had a powerful influence on social thought among American Catholics.

The popularity of the idea of an American standard of living reflected, in part, the emergence of a mass-consumption society during the Progressive era. For the first time in the nation's history, mass consumption came to occupy a central place in descriptions of American society and its future. The optimistic writings of Simon W. Patten, a prophet of prosperity, announced the end of the "reign of want" and the advent of a society of abundance and leisure. In the dawning "new civilization," he proclaimed, Americans would enjoy economic equality in a world in which "every one is independent and free."

VARIETIES OF PROGRESSIVISM

For most Americans, however, Patten's "new civilization" lay far in the future. The more immediate task, in the Progressives' view, was to humanize industrial capitalism and find common ground in a society still racked by labor conflict and experiencing massive immigration from abroad. Some Progressives proposed to return to a competitive marketplace populated by small producers. Others accepted the permanence of the large corporation and looked to the government to reverse the growing concentration of wealth and to ensure social justice. Still others would relocate freedom from the economic and political worlds to a private realm of personal fulfillment and unimpeded self-expression. But nearly all Progressives agreed that freedom must be infused with new meaning to deal with the economic and social conditions of the early twentieth century. The "old democracy," wrote Walter Weyl, associate editor of *The New Republic*, a weekly magazine that became the "bible" of Progressive intellectuals, provided no answer to the problems of a world in which the "chief restrictions upon liberty" were economic, not political.

Industrial Freedom

In Progressive America, complaints of a loss of freedom came not only from the most poorly paid factory workers but from better-off employees as well. Large firms in the automobile, electrical, steel, and other industries sought to implement greater control over the work process. Efficiency expert Frederick W. Taylor pioneered what he called **scientific management**—a program that sought to streamline production and boost profits by systematically controlling costs and work practices. Through scientific study, the "one best way" of producing goods could be determined and implemented. The role of workers was to obey the detailed instructions of supervisors. Not surprisingly, many skilled workers saw the erosion of their traditional influence over the work process as a loss of freedom. "Men and women," complained Samuel Gompers, whose American Federation of Labor (AFL) represented such skilled workers, "cannot live during working hours under autocratic conditions, and instantly become sons and daughters of freedom as they step outside the shop gates."

The great increase in the number of white-collar workers—the army of salespeople, bookkeepers, salaried professionals, and corporate managers that sprang up with the new system of management—also undermined the experience of personal autonomy. For although they enjoyed far higher social status and incomes than manual workers, many, wrote one commentator, were the kind of individuals who "under former conditions, would have been . . . managing their own businesses," not working for someone else.

These developments helped to place the ideas of "industrial freedom" and "industrial democracy," which had entered the political vocabulary in the Gilded Age, at the center of political discussion during the Progressive era. Lack of "industrial freedom" was widely believed to lie at the root of the much-discussed "labor problem." Since in an industrial age the prospect of managing one's own business seemed increasingly remote, many Progressives believed that the key to increasing industrial freedom lay in empowering workers to participate in economic decision making via strong unions. Louis D. Brandeis, an active ally of the labor movement whom President Woodrow Wilson appointed to the Supreme Court in 1916, maintained that unions embodied an essential principle of freedom—the right of people to govern themselves. The contradiction between "political liberty" and "industrial slavery," Brandeis insisted, was America's foremost social problem.

The Socialist Presence

Economic freedom was also a rallying cry of American socialism, which reached its greatest influence during the Progressive era. Founded in 1901, the **Socialist Party** brought together surviving late-nineteenth-century radicals, such as Populists and followers of Edward Bellamy, with a portion of the labor movement. The party called for immediate reforms such as free college education, legislation to improve the condition of laborers, and, as an ultimate goal, democratic control over the economy through public ownership of railroads and factories. It was the task of socialism, said western labor leader John O'Neill, to "gather together the shards of liberty"—the fragments of the American heritage of freedom—scattered by a government controlled by capitalist millionaires.

By 1912, the Socialist Party claimed 150,000 dues-paying members, published hundreds of newspapers, enjoyed substantial support in the American Federation of Labor, and had elected scores of local officials. Socialism flourished in diverse communities throughout the country. On the Lower East Side of New York City, it arose from the economic exploitation of immigrant workers and Judaism's tradition of social reform. Here, a vibrant socialist culture developed, complete with Yiddish-language newspapers and theaters, as well as large public meetings and street demonstrations. In 1914, the district elected socialist Meyer London to Congress. Another center of socialist strength was Milwaukee, where Victor Berger, a German-born teacher and newspaper editor, mobilized local AFL unions into a potent political force that elected Emil Seidel mayor in 1910. Seidel's

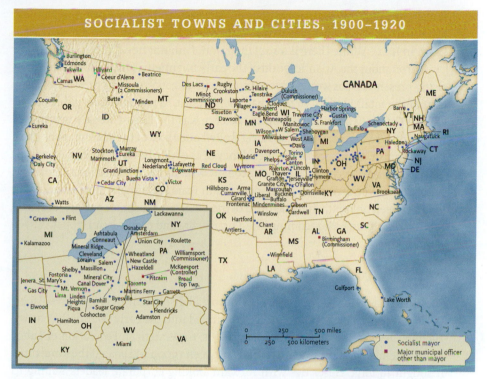

Although the Socialist Party never won more than 6 percent of the vote nationally, it gained control of numerous small and medium-sized cities between 1900 and 1920.

administration provided aid to the unemployed, forced the police to recognize the rights of strikers, and won the respect of middle-class residents for its honesty and freedom from machine domination. Socialism also made inroads among tenant farmers in old Populist areas like Oklahoma, and in the mining regions of Idaho and Montana.

The Gospel of Debs

No one was more important in spreading the socialist gospel or linking it to ideals of equality, self-government, and freedom than Eugene V. Debs, the railroad union leader who, as noted in the previous chapter, had been jailed during the Pullman Strike of 1894. For two decades, Debs crisscrossed the country preaching that control of the economy by a democratic government held out the hope of uniting "political equality and economic freedom." As a champion of the downtrodden, Debs managed to bridge the cultural divide between New York's

Jewish immigrants, prairie socialists of the West, and native-born intellectuals attracted to the socialist ideal. "While there is a lower class," proclaimed Debs, "I am in it. . . . While there is a soul in prison, I am not free."

Throughout the Atlantic world of the early twentieth century, socialism was a rising presence. Debs would receive more than 900,000 votes for president (6 percent of the total) in 1912. In that year, the socialist *Appeal to Reason*, published in Girard, Kansas, with a circulation of 700,000, was the largest weekly newspaper in the country, and socialist Max Hayes polled one-third of the vote when he challenged Samuel Gompers for the presidency of the AFL. In Western Europe, socialism experienced even more pronounced growth. In the last elections before the outbreak of World War I in 1914, socialists in France, Germany, and Scandinavia won between one-sixth and one-third of the vote. "Socialism is coming," declared the *Appeal to Reason.* "It is coming like a prairie fire and nothing can stop it."

AFL and IWW

Socialism was only one example of widespread discontent in Progressive America. The labor strife of the Gilded Age continued into the early twentieth century. Having survived the depression of the 1890s, the American Federation of Labor saw its membership triple to 1.6 million between 1900 and 1904. At the same time, it sought to forge closer ties with forward-looking corporate leaders willing to deal with unions as a way to stabilize employee relations. AFL president Gompers joined with George Perkins of the J. P. Morgan financial empire and Mark Hanna, who had engineered McKinley's election in 1896, in the National Civic Federation, which accepted the right of **collective bargaining** for "responsible" unions. It helped to settle hundreds of industrial disputes and encouraged improvements in factory safety and the establishment of pension plans for long-term workers. Most employers nonetheless continued to view unions as an intolerable interference with their authority, and resisted them stubbornly.

The AFL mainly represented the most privileged American workers—skilled industrial and craft laborers, nearly all of them white, male, and native-born. In 1905, a group of unionists who rejected the AFL's exclusionary policies formed the **Industrial Workers of the World** (IWW). Part trade union, part advocate of a workers' revolution that would seize the means of production and abolish the state, the IWW made solidarity its guiding principle, extending "a fraternal hand to every wage-worker, no matter what his religion, fatherland, or trade." The organization sought to mobilize those excluded from the AFL—the immigrant factory labor force, migrant timber and agricultural workers, women, Blacks, and even the despised Chinese on the West Coast. The IWW's most prominent leader was William "Big Bill" Haywood, who had worked in western mines as a youth. Dubbed by critics "the most dangerous man in America," Haywood became a national figure in 1906 when he was kidnapped and spirited off to Idaho, accused of instigating the murder of a former anti-union governor. Defended by labor lawyer Clarence Darrow, Haywood was found not guilty.

The New Immigrants on Strike

The Uprising of the 20,000 in New York's garment industry, mentioned earlier, was one of a series of mass strikes among immigrant workers that placed labor's demand for the right to bargain collectively at the forefront of the reform agenda. These strikes demonstrated that while ethnic divisions among workers impeded labor solidarity, ethnic cohesiveness could also be a basis of unity, so long as strikes were organized on a democratic basis. IWW organizers printed leaflets, posters, and banners in multiple languages and insisted that each nationality enjoy representation on the committee coordinating a walkout. It drew on the sense of solidarity within immigrant communities to persuade local religious leaders, shopkeepers, and officeholders to support the strikes.

The labor conflict that had the greatest impact on public consciousness took place in Lawrence, Massachusetts. The city's huge woolen mills employed 32,000 men, women, and children representing twenty-five nationalities. They worked six days per week and earned an average of sixteen cents per hour. When the state legislature in January 1912 enacted a fifty-four-hour limit to the workweek, employers reduced the weekly take-home pay of those who had been laboring longer hours. Workers spontaneously went on strike, and called on the IWW for assistance.

In February, Haywood and a group of women strikers devised the idea of sending strikers' children out of the city for the duration of the walkout. Socialist families in New York City agreed to take them in. The sight of the children, many of whom appeared pale and half-starved, marching up Fifth Avenue from the train station led to a wave of sympathy for the strikers. "I have worked in the slums of New York," wrote one observer, "but I have never found children who were so uniformly ill-nourished, ill-fed, and ill-clothed." A few days later, city officials ordered that no more youngsters could leave Lawrence. When a group of mothers and children gathered at the railroad station in defiance of the order, club-wielding police drove them away,

Children of Lawrence, Massachusetts, strikers marching in New York City during the epic labor confrontation of 1911.

producing outraged headlines around the world. The governor of Massachusetts soon intervened, and the strike was settled on the workers' terms. A banner carried by the Lawrence strikers gave a new slogan to the labor movement: "We want bread and roses, too"—a declaration that workers sought not only higher wages but the opportunity to enjoy the finer things of life.

Another highly publicized labor uprising took place in New Orleans, where a 1907 strike of 10,000 Black and white dockworkers prevented employers' efforts to eliminate their unions and reduce their wages. This was a remarkable expression of interracial solidarity at a time when segregation had become the norm throughout the South. Other strikes proved less successful. A six-month walkout of 25,000 silk workers in Paterson, New Jersey, in 1913 failed despite publicity generated by the Paterson Pageant, in which the strikers reenacted highlights of their struggle before a sympathetic audience at New York's Madison Square Garden.

A strike against the Rockefeller-owned Colorado Fuel and Iron Company was also unsuccessful. Mostly recent immigrants from Europe and Mexico, the strikers demanded recognition of the United Mine Workers of America, wage increases, an eight-hour workday, and the right to shop and live in places not owned by the company. When the walkout began, in September 1913, the mine owners evicted 11,000 strikers and their families from company housing. They moved into tent colonies, which armed militia units soon surrounded. On April 20, 1914, the militia attacked the largest tent city, at Ludlow, and burned it to the ground, killing an estimated twenty to thirty men, women, and children. Seven months after the Ludlow Massacre, the strike was called off.

Labor and Civil Liberties

The fiery organizer Mary "Mother" Jones, who at the age of eighty-three had been jailed after addressing the Colorado strikers, later told a New York audience that the union "had only the Constitution; the other side had the bayonets." Yet the struggle of workers for the right to strike and of labor radicals against restraints on open-air speaking made free speech a significant public issue in the early twentieth century. By and large, the courts rejected their claims. But these battles laid the foundation for the rise of civil liberties as a central component of freedom in twentieth-century America.

State courts in the Progressive era regularly issued injunctions prohibiting strikers from speaking, picketing, or distributing literature during labor disputes. Like the abolitionists before them, the labor movement, in the name of freedom, demanded the right to assemble, organize, and spread their views. The investigations of the Commission on Industrial Relations revealed the absence of free speech in many factory communities, with labor organizers prohibited from speaking freely under threat of either violence from private police or suppression by local authorities. "I don't think we live in a free country or enjoy civil liberties," Clarence Darrow told the commission.

The IWW's battle for civil liberties breathed new meaning into the idea of freedom of expression. Lacking union halls, its organizers relied on songs, street theater, impromptu organizing meetings, and street corner gatherings to spread their message and attract support. In response to IWW activities, officials in Los Angeles, Spokane, Denver, and more than a dozen other cities limited or prohibited outdoor meetings. To arouse popular support, the IWW filled the jails with members who defied local law by speaking in public. Sometimes, prisoners were brutally treated, as in Spokane, where three died and hundreds were hospitalized after being jailed for violating a local law requiring prior approval of the content of public speeches. In nearly all the free-speech fights, however, the IWW eventually forced local officials to give way. "Whether they agree or disagree with its methods or aims," wrote one journalist, "all lovers of liberty everywhere owe a debt to this organization for . . . [keeping] alight the fires of freedom."

The New Feminism

During the Progressive era, the word "feminism" first entered the political vocabulary. In 1914, a mass meeting at New York's Cooper Union debated the question "What is Feminism?" The meeting was sponsored by Heterodoxy, a women's club located in Greenwich Village that brought together female professionals, academics, and reformers. Feminism, said one speaker, meant woman's emancipation "both as a human being and a sex-being." Feminism's forthright attack on traditional rules of sexual behavior added a new dimension to the idea of personal freedom.

Heterodoxy was part of a new radical "bohemia" (a social circle of artists, writers, and others who reject conventional rules and practices). Its definition of feminism merged issues like the vote and greater economic opportunities with open discussion of sexuality. Its members formed discussion clubs, attended experimental theaters, and published magazines. They confidently expected to preside over the emancipation of the human spirit from the prejudices of the nineteenth century.

One symbol of the new era was Isadora Duncan, who brought from California a new, expressive dance based on the free movement of a body liberated from the constraints of traditional technique and costume. "I beheld the dance I had always dreamed of," wrote the novelist Edith Wharton on seeing a Duncan performance, "satisfying every sense as a flower does, or a phrase of Mozart's." Another sign of artistic revolution was the Armory Show of 1913, an exhibition that exposed New Yorkers to new cubist paintings from Europe by artists previously unknown in the United States, like Pablo Picasso.

From CHARLOTTE PERKINS GILMAN, *WOMEN AND ECONOMICS* (1898)

Women and Economics, by the prolific feminist social critic and novelist Charlotte Perkins Gilman, influenced the new generation of women aspiring to greater independence. It insisted that how people earned a living shaped their entire lives and that therefore women must free themselves from the home to achieve genuine freedom.

It is not motherhood that keeps the housewife on her feet from dawn till dark; it is house service, not child service. Women work longer and harder than most men. . . . A truer spirit is the increasing desire of young girls to be independent, to have a career of their own, at least for a while, and the growing objection of countless wives to the pitiful asking for money, to the beggary of their position. More and more do fathers give their daughters, and husbands their wives, a definite allowance,—a separate bank account,—something . . . all their own.

The spirit of personal independence in the women of today is sure proof that a change has come. . . . The radical change in the economic position of women is advancing upon us. . . . The growing individualization of democratic life brings inevitable change to our daughters as well as to our sons. . . . One of its most noticeable features is the demand in women not only for their own money, but for their own work for the sake of personal expression. Few girls today fail to manifest some signs of this desire for individual expression. . . .

Economic independence for women necessarily involves a change in the home and family relation. But, if that change is for the advantage of individual and race, we need not fear it. It does not involve a change in the marriage relation except in withdrawing the element of economic dependence, nor in the relation of mother to child save to improve it. But it does involve the exercise of human faculty in women, in social service and exchange rather than in domestic service solely. . . . [Today], when our still developing social needs call for an ever-increasing . . . freedom, the woman in marrying becomes the house-servant, or at least the housekeeper, of the man. . . . When women stand free as economic agents, they will [achieve a] much better fulfilment of their duties as wives and mothers and [contribute] to the vast improvement in health and happiness of the human race.

From JOHN MITCHELL, "THE WORKINGMAN'S CONCEPTION OF INDUSTRIAL LIBERTY" (1910)

During the Progressive era, the idea of "industrial liberty" moved to the center of political discussion. Progressive reformers and labor leaders like John Mitchell, head of the United Mine Workers, condemned the prevailing idea of liberty of contract in favor of a broader definition of economic freedom.

While the Declaration of Independence established civil and political liberty, it did not, as you all know, establish industrial liberty.... Liberty means more than the right to choose the field of one's employment. He is not a free man whose family must buy food today with the money that is earned tomorrow. He is not really free who is forced to work unduly long hours and for wages so low that he can not provide the necessities of life for himself and his family; who must live in a crowded tenement and see his children go to work in the mills, the mines, and the factories before their bodies are developed and their minds trained. To have freedom a man must be free from the harrowing fear of hunger and want; he must be in such a position that by the exercise of reasonable frugality he can provide his family with all of the necessities and the reasonable comforts of life. He must be able to educate his children and to provide against sickness, accident, and old age....

A number of years ago the legislatures of several coal producing States enacted laws requiring employers to pay the wages of their workmen in lawful money of the United States and to cease the practice of paying wages in merchandise. From time immemorial it had been the custom of coal companies to conduct general supply stores, and the workingmen were required, as a condition of employment, to accept products in lieu of money in return for services rendered. This system was a great hardship to the workmen.... The question of the constitutionality of this legislation was carried into the courts and by the highest tribunal it was declared to be an invasion of the workman's liberty to deny him the right to accept merchandise in lieu of money as payment of his wages.... [This is] typical of hundreds of instances in which laws that have been enacted for the protection of the workingmen have been declared by the courts to be unconstitutional, on the grounds that they invaded the liberty of the working people.... Is it not natural that the workingmen should feel that they are being guaranteed the liberties they do not want and denied the liberty that is of real value to them? May they not exclaim, with Madame Roland [of the French Revolution], "O Liberty! Liberty! How many crimes are committed in thy name!"

QUESTIONS

1. *What does Gilman see as the main obstacles to freedom for women?*

2. *What does Mitchell believe will be necessary to establish "industrial liberty"?*

3. *How do the authors differ in their view of the relationship of the family to individual freedom?*

The Rise of Personal Freedom

During the Progressive era, as journalist William M. Reedy jested, it struck "sex o'clock" in America. The founder of psychiatry, Sigmund Freud, lectured at Clark University in Worcester, Massachusetts, in 1909, and discovered that his writings on infantile sexuality, repression, and the irrational sources of human behavior were widely known "even in prudish America." Issues of intimate personal relations previously confined to private discussion blazed forth in popular magazines and public debates.

For the generation of women who adopted the word "feminism" to express their demand for greater liberty, free sexual expression and reproductive choice emerged as critical definitions of women's emancipation. Greenwich Village in New York City became a center of sexual experimentation. The aura of tolerance attracted many gay men and lesbians to the area, and although organized demands for gay rights lay far in the future, the gay community became an important element of the Village's lifestyle. But new sexual attitudes spread far beyond bohemia; they flourished among the young, unmarried, self-supporting women who made sexual freedom a hallmark of their oft-proclaimed personal independence.

The Birth-Control Movement

The growing presence of women in the labor market reinforced demands for access to birth control, an issue that gave political expression to changing sexual behavior. In the nineteenth century, the right to "control one's body" generally meant the ability to refuse sexual advances, including those of a woman's husband. Now, it suggested the ability to enjoy an active sexual life without necessarily bearing children. Emma Goldman, who had emigrated to the United States from Lithuania at the age of sixteen, toured the country lecturing on subjects from anarchism to the need for more enlightened attitudes toward homosexuality. She regularly included the right to birth control in her speeches and distributed pamphlets with detailed information about various contraceptive devices. "I demand freedom for both sexes," she proclaimed, "freedom of action, freedom in love and freedom in motherhood." Goldman constantly ran afoul of the law. By one count, she was arrested more than forty times for dangerous or "obscene" statements or simply to keep her from speaking.

By forthrightly challenging the laws banning contraceptive information and devices, Margaret Sanger, one of eleven children of an Irish American working-class family, placed the **birth-control movement** at the heart of the new feminism. In 1911, she began a column on sex education, "What Every Girl Should Know," for *The Call*, a New York socialist newspaper. By 1914, Sanger was

openly advertising birth-control devices in her own journal, *The Woman Rebel.*
"No woman can call herself free," she proclaimed, "who does not own and con-
trol her own body [and] can choose consciously whether she will or will not be
a mother." In 1916, Sanger opened a clinic in a working-class neighborhood of
Brooklyn and began distributing contraceptive devices to poor Jewish, Irish, and
Italian women, an action for which she was sentenced to a month in prison.

Among the remarkable women involved in the birth-control movement—
and radicalism more generally—was Helen Keller. Born in Alabama, she lost her
sight and hearing because of a disease at the age of nineteen months. But she
learned to read and write in braille and graduated from Radcliffe College in 1904.
Keller became known throughout the world as the author of numerous articles and books, especially an autobiography that has been translated into over
fifty languages. Keller became a leading advocate for persons with disabilities.
Less well known is that in addition to campaigning for the availability of birth
control, Keller was also an outspoken supporter of socialism, woman suffrage,
the rights of laborers, and world peace and a longtime member of the Industrial
Workers of the World.

The careers of Sanger and Keller exemplified how, for a time, the birth-
control issue became a crossroads where the paths of labor radicals, cultural
modernists, and feminists intersected. The IWW and Socialist Party distributed
Sanger's writings. Like the IWW free-speech fights and Goldman's persistent
battle for the right to lecture, Sanger's travail was part of a rich history of dissent in the Progressive era that helped to focus enlightened opinion on the ways
local authorities and national obscenity legislation set rigid limits to Americans' freedom of expression.

Slowly laws banning birth control began to change. The birth-control
movement gained increased respectability in the 1920s as doctors and professionals joined the cause, and its earlier
radicalism faded. The organization
Sanger established, the American Birth
Control League, increasingly voiced
support for improving the "quality"
of the human race by controlling the
reproduction of those deemed less fit—
namely, the poor, persons with mental illness, and those with disabilities.
However, because laws banning birth
control were determined by individual
states, even when some states liberal-
ized their laws, birth control remained
unavailable in many others.

Mothers with baby carriages wait outside
Margaret Sanger's birth-control clinic in
Brownsville, Brooklyn, 1916.

Pan-Indian Progressives and Native American Freedom

A new generation of Native American reformers participated in the Progressive impulse. The **Society of American Indians** was formed in 1911 and open to "Progressive Indians . . . and friends of Indian progress." Unlike past Indian reformers, its leaders did not believe that being a modern Indian meant eradicating Native cultures. With a professional leadership drawn from many tribal nations, the "Red Progressives," as they were sometimes known, promoted a pan-Indian identity, focusing on fostering the common cause of American Indians and on remedying injustices. In 1911, Charles Eastman, a Dakota Native American and medical doctor, published *The Soul of the Indian*, a book that promoted a vision of modern citizenship that drew upon Indian and white cultures. The organization's Indian educators such as Ella Deloria, of Lakota heritage, and Henry Roe Cloud, a Ho-Chunk Indian, pressed to include Native studies curriculum in federal boarding schools (see Chapter 17).

Frequently themselves educated at boarding schools steeped in ideals of Americanism and patriotism, the organization's leaders were supportive of the basic goals of federal Indian policy, including assimilation and the transformation of communal landholdings on reservations into individual property. But they insisted on better educational opportunities, U.S. citizenship, a special claims court, and increased independence through diminishing the power of the Bureau of Indian Affairs over Native American lives.

Society of American Indians founder Carlos Montezuma, a Yavapai Indian, was an outspoken critic of the Bureau of Indian Affairs. Raised in Chicago and trained as a doctor, he took a position with the agency and was appalled by the abject poverty and prison-like conditions on reservations. In 1916, he established a newsletter, *Wassaja*, meaning "signaling" in Yavapai, which called for the abolition of the Bureau of Indian Affairs. In his view, federal government officials' power to determine all aspects of Indian social, economic, and cultural life amounted to unfreedom. Montezuma insisted that self-determination was the only way for Indians to escape poverty and marginalization: "We must free ourselves . . . we must be independent."

While the Society of American Indians emphasized citizenship, equal rights, and individual independence, other Native groups aimed to retain or restore land as the basis for Indigenous freedom. By the late nineteenth century, the Muscogee (Creek), Cherokee, Choctaw, Seminole, and Chickasaw nations had built prosperous townships, farms, ranches, and schools in Indian Territory. When federal officials broke up their common holdings, sold "surplus" lands to settlers, and sought to dissolve their governments, their leaders vigorously protested but to little avail. By 1905, with dissolution looming, they held a convention to form the new pan-Indian state of Sequoyah in an effort to retain their political authority within the U.S. federal system. But Congress ignored their appeals, instead establishing the state of Oklahoma in 1907, which united Indian and Oklahoma Territory. After statehood, a grassroots movement among the Muscogee that had formed in 1902, known as the Crazy Snakes, continued to call for the re-establishment of their landholdings and governance. The movement remained active for over a decade. The Society of American Indians and the Crazy Snakes represented distinctive strategies for securing Indian freedom that would remain influential for years to come.

THE POLITICS OF PROGRESSIVISM

Effective Freedom

Progressivism was an international movement. In the early twentieth century, cities throughout the world experienced similar social strains arising from rapid industrialization and urban growth. In 1850, London and Paris were the only cities whose population exceeded 1 million. By 1900, there were twelve—New York, Chicago, and Philadelphia in the United States, and others in Europe, Latin America, and Asia. Facing similar social problems, reformers across the globe exchanged ideas and envisioned new social policies. Sun Yat-Sen, the Chinese leader, was influenced by the writings of Henry George and Edward Bellamy.

As governments in Britain, France, and Germany instituted old age pensions, minimum wage laws, unemployment insurance, and the regulation of workplace safety, American reformers came to believe they had much to learn from the Old World. The term "social legislation," meaning governmental action to address urban problems and the insecurities of working-class life, originated in Germany but soon entered the political vocabulary of the United States.

Progressives believed that the modern era required a fundamental rethinking of the functions of political authority, whether the aim was to combat the power of the giant corporations, protect consumers, civilize the marketplace, or guarantee industrial freedom at the workplace. Progressives sought to reinvigorate the idea of an activist, socially conscious government. Even in South Carolina, with its strong tradition of belief in local autonomy, Governor Richard I. Manning urged his constituents to modify their view of government as "a threat to individual liberty," to see it instead as "a means for solving the ills of the body politic."

Progressives could reject the traditional assumption that powerful government posed a threat to freedom, because their understanding of freedom was itself in flux. "Effective freedom," wrote the philosopher John Dewey, was a positive, not a negative, concept—the "power to do specific things." As such, it depended on "the *distribution* of powers that exists at a

A photograph from 1910 depicts needy constituents of New York political boss Timothy "Big Tim" Sullivan receiving free pairs of shoes. Each year, Sullivan distributed 2,000 pairs on his mother's birthday. Such largesse endeared political bosses to many voters, to the annoyance of municipal reformers.

given time." Thus, freedom inevitably became a political question.

Pragmatism

Dewey was one of the foremost proponents of a school of philosophy called **pragmatism** that emerged in the late nineteenth century and strongly influenced Progressive thinkers. One of the most important philosophical movements ever to emerge in the United States, pragmatism, as explained in a 1907 book of that title by the philosopher William James (brother of the famous novelist Henry James), insisted that institutions and social policies must be judged by their concrete effects, not their longevity or how well they comport with religious doctrine or traditional political beliefs.

Given the deep divisions and widespread poverty in American society, ideologies such as Social Darwinism and liberty of contract, judged by the standard of pragmatism, had manifestly failed, and new approaches to social problems were needed.

State and Local Reforms

Throughout the Western world, social legislation proliferated in the early twentieth century. In the United States, with a political structure more decentralized than in European countries, state and local governments enacted most of the era's reform measures. In cities, Progressives worked to reform the structure of government to reduce the power of political bosses, establish public control of "natural monopolies" like gas- and waterworks, and improve public transportation. They raised property taxes in order to spend more money on schools, parks, and other public facilities.

Gilded Age mayors Hazen Pingree and Samuel "Golden Rule" Jones pioneered urban Progressivism. A former factory worker who became a successful shoe manufacturer, Pingree served as mayor of Detroit from 1889 to 1897. He battled the business interests that had dominated city government, forced gas and telephone companies to lower their rates, and established a municipal power plant. Jones had instituted an eight-hour day and paid vacations at his factory that produced oil drilling equipment. As mayor of Toledo, Ohio, from 1897 to 1905, he founded night schools and free kindergartens, built new parks, and supported the right of workers to unionize. Since state legislatures defined the powers of city government, urban Progressives often carried their campaigns to the state level. Pingree became governor of Michigan in 1896, in which post he continued his battle against railroads and other corporate interests.

Progressivism in the West

Although often associated with eastern cities, Progressivism was also a major presence in the West. Former Populists and those who believed in the moral power of the frontier gravitated to Progressive programs to regulate the railroads and other large corporations, and to the idea that direct democracy could revitalize corrupt politics. Important Progressive leaders worked for reform in western states and municipalities, including Hiram Johnson of California and Robert M. La Follette of Wisconsin.

Oregon stood at the forefront of Progressive reform. The leading figure in that state was William U'Ren, a lawyer who had entered politics as a supporter of Henry George's single-tax program. U'Ren concluded that without changes to the political system, entrenched interests would always be able to block reforms such as George's. He was the founder of the Oregon System, which included such measures as the initiative, referendum, and recall. **Initiative**, also known as direct legislation, enabled citizens to propose and vote directly on laws, bypassing state legislatures. **Referendum** similarly provided for popular votes on public policies. **Recall** allowed for the removal of public officials by popular vote. Together with direct primaries, in which voters, rather than party officials, chose candidates for office, all these reforms sought to weaken the power of political bosses and transfer it to ordinary citizens. Using the initiative, Progressives won the vote for women in the state.

The Oregon System, studied and emulated in many other states, came into being via an alliance of the urban middle class with reform-minded farmers and workers. But fault lines appeared when labor-oriented Progressives tried to use the initiative and referendum to increase taxes on the well-to-do and require the state to provide jobs for the unemployed. Both measures failed. Moreover, the initiative system quickly became out of control. In the 1912 election, voters in Portland were asked to evaluate forty measures seeking to become law. Nonetheless, between 1910 and 1912, Oregon's West Coast neighbors, Washington and California, also adopted the initiative and referendum and approved woman suffrage.

In California, where a Republican machine closely tied to the Southern Pacific Railroad had dominated politics for decades, Progressives took power under Governor Hiram Johnson, who held office from 1911 to 1917. As public prosecutor, Johnson had secured the conviction for bribery of San Francisco political boss Abraham Ruef. Having promised to "kick the Southern

Pacific [Railroad] out of politics," he secured passage of the Public Utilities Act, one of the country's strongest railroad-regulation measures, as well as laws banning child labor and limiting the working hours of women.

The most influential Progressive administration at the state level was that of Robert M. La Follette, who made Wisconsin a "laboratory for democracy." After serving as a Republican member of Congress, La Follette became convinced that an alliance of railroad and lumber companies controlled state politics. Elected governor in 1900, he instituted a series of measures known as the Wisconsin Idea, including nominations of candidates for office through primary elections, the taxation of corporate wealth, and state regulation of railroads and public utilities. Other measures created a statewide system of insurance against illness, death, and accident, barred the sale to private companies of land, mineral rights, and other natural resources owned by the state, required safety devices on various forms of machinery, and prohibited child labor. To staff his administration, he drew on nonpartisan faculty members from the University of Wisconsin. Wisconsin offered the most striking merger of the social and political impulses that went under the name of Progressivism.

Progressive Democracy

"We are far from free," wrote Randolph Bourne in 1913, "but the new spirit of democracy is the angel that will free us." Progressives hoped to reinvigorate democracy by restoring political power to the citizenry and civic harmony to a divided society. Alarmed by the upsurge in violent class conflict and the unrestricted power of corporations, they believed that political reforms could help to create a unified "people" devoted to greater democracy and social reconciliation. Yet increasing the responsibilities of government made it all the more important to identify who was entitled to political participation and who was not.

The Progressive era saw a host of changes implemented in the political process, many seemingly contradictory in purpose. The electorate was simultaneously expanded and contracted, empowered and removed from direct influence on many functions of government. Democracy was enhanced by the **Seventeenth Amendment**—which provided that U.S. senators be chosen by popular vote rather than by state legislatures—by widespread adoption of the popular election of judges, and by the use of primary elections among party members to select candidates for office. The era culminated with a constitutional amendment enfranchising women—the largest expansion of democracy in American history.

But the Progressive era also witnessed numerous restrictions on democratic participation, most strikingly the disenfranchisement of Blacks in the South, a process, as noted in Chapter 17, supported by many white southern Progressives as a way of ending election fraud. To make city government more honest and efficient, many localities replaced elected mayors with appointed nonpartisan commissions or city managers—a change that insulated officials from machine domination but also from popular control. New literacy tests and residency and registration requirements, common in northern as well as southern states, limited the right to vote among the poor. Taken as a whole, the electoral changes of the Progressive era represented a significant reversal of the idea that voting was an inherent right of American citizenship. In the eyes of many Progressives, the "fitness" of voters, not their absolute numbers, defined a functioning democracy.

Government by Expert

"He didn't believe in democracy; he believed simply in government." The writer H. L. Mencken's quip about Theodore Roosevelt came uncomfortably close to the mark for many Progressive advocates of an empowered state. Most Progressive thinkers were highly uncomfortable with the real world of politics, which seemed to revolve around the pursuit of narrow class, ethnic, and regional interests. Robert M. La Follette's reliance on college professors to staff important posts in his administration reflected a larger Progressive faith in expertise. The government could best exercise intelligent control over society through a democracy run by impartial experts who were in many respects unaccountable to the citizenry.

This impulse toward order, efficiency, and centralized management—all in the name of social justice—was an important theme of Progressive reform. The title of Walter Lippmann's influential 1914 work of social commentary, *Drift and Mastery*, posed the stark alternatives facing the nation. "Drift" meant continuing to operate according to the outmoded belief in individual autonomy. "Mastery" required applying scientific inquiry to modern social problems. The new generation of educated professionals, Lippmann believed, could be trusted more fully than ordinary citizens to solve America's deep social problems. Political freedom was less a matter of direct participation in government than of qualified persons devising the best public policies.

Jane Addams and Hull House

But alongside this elitist politics, Progressivism also included a more democratic vision of the activist state. As much as any other group, organized women reformers spoke for the democratic side of Progressivism. Still barred from voting and holding office in most states, women nonetheless became central to the political history of the Progressive era. Women challenged the barriers that excluded them from formal political participation and developed a democratic, grassroots vision of Progressive government. They placed on the political agenda new understandings of female freedom. The immediate catalyst was a growing awareness among women reformers of the plight of poor immigrant communities and the emergence of the condition of women and child laborers as a major focus of public concern.

The era's most prominent female reformer was Jane Addams, who had been born in 1860, the daughter of an Illinois businessman. In 1889, she founded Hull House in Chicago, a **settlement house** devoted to improving the lives of the immigrant poor. Hull House was modeled on Toynbee Hall, which Addams had visited after its establishment in a working-class neighborhood of London in 1884. Unlike previous reformers, who had aided the poor from afar, settlement-house workers moved into poor neighborhoods. They built kindergartens and playgrounds for children, established employment bureaus and health clinics, and showed female victims of domestic abuse how to gain legal protection. By 1910, more than 400 settlement houses had been established in cities throughout the country.

"Spearheads for Reform"

Addams was typical of the Progressive era's "new woman." By 1900, there were more than 80,000 college-educated women in the United States. Many found a calling in providing social services, nursing, and education to poor families in the growing cities. The efforts of middle-class women to uplift the poor, and of laboring women to uplift themselves, helped to shift the center of gravity of politics toward activist government. Women like Addams discovered that even well-organized social work was not enough to alleviate the problems of inadequate housing, income, and health. Government action was essential. Hull House inspired an array of reforms in Chicago, soon adopted elsewhere, including stronger building and sanitation codes, shorter working hours and safer labor conditions, and the right of labor to organize.

Female activism spread throughout the country. Ironically, the exclusion of Blacks from jobs in southern textile mills strengthened the region's movement against child labor. Reformers portrayed child labor as a menace to white supremacy, depriving white children of educations they would need as adult members of the dominant race. These reformers devoted little attention to the condition of Black children. Women's groups in Alabama were instrumental in the passage of a 1903 state law restricting child labor. By 1915, every southern state had followed suit. But with textile mill owners determined to employ children and many poor families dependent on their earnings, these laws were enforced only sporadically.

The settlement houses have been called "spearheads for reform." They produced prominent Progressive figures like Julia Lathrop, the first woman to

Mayor Mary W. Howard (center) and the town council of Kanab, Utah. They served from 1912 to 1914, the first all-female municipal government in American history.

head a federal agency (the Children's Bureau, established in 1912 to investigate the conditions of mothers and children and advocate their interests). Florence Kelley, the daughter of Civil War–era Radical Republican congressman William D. Kelley and a veteran of Hull House, went on to mobilize women's power as consumers as a force for social change. In the Gilded Age, the writer Helen Campbell had brilliantly exposed the contradiction of a market economy in which fashionable women wore clothing produced by poor women in wretched sweatshops. "Emancipation on the one side," she pointedly observed, "has meant no corresponding emancipation for the other." A generation later, under Kelley's leadership, the National Consumers' League became the nation's leading advocate of laws governing the working conditions of women and children. Freedom of choice in the marketplace, Kelley insisted, enabled socially conscious consumers to "unite with wage earners" by refusing to purchase goods produced under exploitative conditions.

The Campaign for Woman Suffrage

After 1900, the campaign for woman suffrage moved beyond the mostly elite membership of the 1890s to engage a broad coalition ranging from middle-class members of women's clubs to unionists, socialists, and settlement-house workers. For the first time, it became a mass movement. Membership in the National American Woman Suffrage Association grew from 13,000 in 1893 to

Mary Pickford, one of the era's most celebrated movie stars, publicized her support for woman suffrage in this photograph from around 1910.

more than 2 million by 1917. The group campaigned throughout the country for the right to vote and began to enjoy some success. By 1900, more than half the states allowed women to vote in local elections dealing with school issues, and Wyoming, Colorado, Idaho, and Utah had adopted full woman suffrage. The West also led the way in women holding public office. The first women to become mayors of major cities, governors, and members of Congress hailed from the West—Mayor Bertha Landes in Seattle (1926–1928), Congresswoman Jeanette Rankin of Montana (elected 1916 and 1940), and, in the 1920s, governors Miriam "Ma" Ferguson of Texas and Nellie Tayloe Ross of Wyoming.

Cynics charged that Wyoming legislators used suffrage to attract more female migrants to their predominantly male state, while Utah hoped to enhance the political power of husbands in polygamous marriages banned by law but still practiced by some Mormons. In Colorado and Idaho, however, the success of referendums in the 1890s reflected the power of the Populist Party, a strong supporter of votes for women. Between 1910 and 1914, seven more western states enfranchised women. In 1913, Illinois became the first state east of the Mississippi River to allow women to vote in presidential elections.

These campaigns, which brought women aggressively into the public sphere, were conducted with a new spirit of militancy. They also made effective use of the techniques of advertising, publicity, and mass entertainment characteristic of modern consumer society. California's successful 1911 campaign utilized automobile parades, numerous billboards and electric signs, and countless suffrage buttons and badges. Nonetheless, state campaigns were difficult, expensive, and usually unsuccessful. The movement increasingly focused its attention on securing a national constitutional amendment giving women the right to vote.

Maternalist Reform

Ironically, the desire to exalt women's role within the home did much to inspire the reinvigoration of the suffrage movement. Many of the era's experiments in public policy arose from the conviction that the state had an obligation to protect women and children. Female reformers helped to launch a mass movement for direct government action to improve the living standards of poor mothers and children. Laws providing for mothers' pensions (state aid to mothers of young children who lacked male support) spread rapidly after 1910. The pensions tended to be less than generous, and local eligibility requirements opened the door to unequal treatment (white widows benefited the most, single mothers were widely discriminated against, and Black women were almost entirely excluded). **Maternalist reforms** like mothers' pensions rested on the assumption that the government should encourage women's capacity for bearing and raising children and enable them to be economically independent at the same time. Both feminists and believers in conventional domestic roles supported such measures. The former hoped that these laws would subvert women's dependence on men, the latter that they would strengthen traditional families and the mother-child bond.

Other Progressive legislation recognized that large numbers of women did in fact work outside the home, but defined them as a dependent group (like children) in need of state protection in ways male workers were not. In 1908, in the landmark case of **Muller v. Oregon**, Louis D. Brandeis filed a brief citing scientific and sociological studies to demonstrate that because women had less strength and endurance than men, long hours of labor were dangerous for women, while their unique ability to bear children gave the government a legitimate interest in their working conditions. Persuaded by Brandeis's argument, the Supreme Court unanimously upheld the constitutionality of an Oregon law setting maximum working hours for women.

Thus, three years after the notorious *Lochner* decision invalidating a New York law limiting the working hours of male bakers (discussed in Chapter 16), the Court created the first large breach in "liberty of contract" doctrine. But the cost was high: at the very time that women in unprecedented numbers were entering the labor market and earning college degrees, Brandeis's brief and the Court's opinion solidified the view of women workers as weak, dependent, and incapable of enjoying the same economic rights as men. By 1917, thirty states had enacted laws limiting the hours of labor of female workers. Many women derived great benefit from these laws; others saw them as an infringement on their freedom.

While the maternalist agenda built gender inequality into the early foundations of the welfare state, the very use of government to regulate working conditions called into question basic assumptions concerning liberty of contract. Although not all reformers were willing to take the step, it was easy to extend the idea of protecting women and children to demand that government better the living and working conditions of men as well, by insuring them against the impact of unemployment, old age, ill health, and disability.

Brandeis himself insisted that government should concern itself with the health, income, and future prospects of all its citizens.

The Idea of Economic Citizenship

Brandeis envisioned a different welfare state from that of the maternalist reformers, one rooted less in the idea of healthy motherhood than in universal economic entitlements, including the right to a decent income and protection against unemployment and work-related accidents. For him, the right to assistance derived from citizenship itself, not some special service to the nation (as in the case of mothers).

This vision, too, enjoyed considerable support in the Progressive era. By 1913, twenty-two states had enacted workmen's compensation laws to benefit workers, male or female, injured on the job. This legislation was the first wedge that opened the way for broader programs of social insurance. To avoid the stigma of depending on governmental assistance, contributions from workers' own wages funded these programs in part, thus distinguishing them from charity dispensed by local authorities to the poor. But state minimum wage laws and most laws regulating working hours applied only to women. Women and children may have needed protection, but interference with the freedom of contract of adult male workers was still widely seen as degrading. The establishment of a standard of living and working conditions beneath which no American, male or female, should be allowed to fall would await the coming of the New Deal.

THE PROGRESSIVE PRESIDENTS

Despite the ferment of Progressivism on the city and state levels, the most striking political development of the early twentieth century was the rise of the national state. The process of nationalization was occurring throughout American life. National corporations dominated the economy; national organizations like the American Medical Association came into being to raise the incomes and respect of professions. The process was even reflected in the consolidation of local baseball teams into the American and National Leagues and the advent in 1903 of the World Series. Only energetic national government, Progressives believed, could create the social conditions of freedom.

Despite creative experiments in social policy at the city and state levels, the tradition of localism seemed to most Progressives an impediment to a renewed sense of national purpose. Poverty, economic insecurity, and lack of industrial democracy were national problems that demanded national solutions. The democratic national state, wrote *New Republic* editor Herbert Croly, offered an alternative to control of Americans' lives by narrow interests that manipulated politics or by the all-powerful corporations. Croly proposed a new synthesis of American political traditions. To achieve the "Jeffersonian ends" of democratic self-determination and individual freedom, he insisted, the country needed to employ the "Hamiltonian means" of government intervention in the economy. Each in his own way, the Progressive presidents—Theodore Roosevelt, William Howard Taft, and Woodrow Wilson—tried to address this challenge.

Theodore Roosevelt

In September 1901, the anarchist Leon Czolgosz assassinated William McKinley while the president visited the Pan-American Exposition in Buffalo, New York. At the age of forty-two, Vice President Theodore Roosevelt became the youngest man ever to hold the office of president. Roosevelt was an impetuous, energetic individual with a penchant for what he called the "strenuous life" of manly adventure. In many ways, he became the model for the twentieth-century president, an official actively and continuously engaged in domestic and foreign affairs. (The foreign policies of the Progressive presidents will be discussed in the next chapter.) Roosevelt regarded the president as "the steward of the public welfare." He moved aggressively to set the political agenda.

Roosevelt's program, which he called the Square Deal, attempted to confront the problems caused by economic consolidation by distinguishing between "good" and "bad" corporations. The former, among which he included U.S. Steel, served the public interest. The latter were run by greedy financiers interested only in profit and had no right to exist.

Soon after assuming office, Roosevelt shocked the corporate world by announcing his intention to prosecute under the Sherman Antitrust Act the Northern Securities Company. Created by financier J. P. Morgan, this "holding company" owned the stock and directed the affairs of three major western railroads. It monopolized transportation between the Great Lakes and the Pacific. Morgan was outraged. "Wall Street is paralyzed," quipped one newspaper, "at the thought that a President of the United States should sink to enforce the law." In 1904, the Supreme Court ordered Northern Securities dissolved, a major victory for the antitrust movement.

Roosevelt and Economic Regulation

Roosevelt also believed that the president should be an honest broker in labor disputes, rather than automatically siding with employers as his predecessors had usually done. When a strike paralyzed the West Virginia and Pennsylvania coalfields in 1902, he summoned union and management leaders to the White

House. By threatening a federal takeover of the mines, he persuaded the owners to allow the dispute to be settled by a commission he himself would appoint.

Reelected in 1904, Roosevelt pushed for more direct federal regulation of the economy. Appealing to the public for support, he condemned the misuse of the "vast power conferred by vast wealth." He proposed to strengthen the Interstate Commerce Commission (ICC), which the Supreme Court had essentially limited to collecting economic statistics. By this time, journalistic exposés, labor unrest, and the agitation of Progressive reformers had created significant public support for Roosevelt's regulatory program. In 1906, Congress passed the Hepburn Act, giving the ICC the power to examine railroads' business records and to set reasonable rates, a significant step in the development of federal intervention in the corporate economy. That year, as has been noted, also saw the passage of the **Pure Food and Drug Act**, which established a federal agency to police the quality and labeling of food and drugs, and the Meat Inspection Act. Many businessmen supported these measures, recognizing that they would benefit from greater public confidence in the quality and safety of their products. But even they were alarmed by Roosevelt's calls for federal inheritance and income taxes and the regulation of all interstate businesses.

John Muir and the Spirituality of Nature

If the United States lagged behind Europe in many areas of social policy, it led the way in the conservation of natural resources. The first national park, Yellowstone in Wyoming, was created by Congress in 1872, partly to preserve an area of remarkable natural beauty and partly at the urging of the Northern Pacific Railroad, which was anxious to promote western tourism. In the 1890s, the Scottish-born naturalist John Muir organized the Sierra Club to help preserve forests from uncontrolled logging by timber companies.

Muir's love of nature stemmed from deep religious feelings. In nature, he believed, men could experience directly the presence of God. Muir lamented the intrusions of civilization on the natural environment and developed a broad following. As more and more Americans lived in cities, they came to see nature less as something to conquer and more as a place for recreation and personal growth.

The Conservation Movement

In the 1890s, Congress authorized the president to withdraw "forest reserves" from economic development, a restriction on economic freedom in the name of a greater social good. But it was under Theodore Roosevelt that the **conservation movement** became a concerted federal policy. A dedicated outdoorsman who built a ranch in North Dakota in the 1880s, Roosevelt moved to preserve parts of the natural environment from economic exploitation.

Relying for advice on Gifford Pinchot, the head of the U.S. Forest Service, he ordered that millions of acres be set aside as wildlife preserves and encouraged Congress to create new national parks. The creation of parks like Yellowstone, Yosemite, and Glacier required the removal of Indians who hunted and fished there as well as the reintroduction of animals that had previously disappeared. City dwellers who visited the national parks did not realize that these were to a considerable extent artificially created and managed environments, not primordial nature.

In some ways, conservation was a typical Progressive reform. Staffed by experts, the government could stand above political and economic battles, serving the public good while preventing "special interests" from causing irreparable damage to the environment. Pinchot halted timber companies' reckless assault on the nation's forests. But unlike Muir, he believed that development and conservation could go hand in hand and that logging, mining, and grazing on public lands should be controlled, not eliminated. Conservation also reflected the Progressive thrust toward efficiency and control—in this case, control of nature itself.

In the view of Progressive conservationists, the West's scarcest resource—water—cried out for regulation. Governments at all levels moved to control the power of western rivers, building dams and irrigation projects to regularize their flow, prevent waste, and provide water for large-scale agriculture and urban development. With such projects came political conflict, as cities like Los Angeles and San Francisco battled with rural areas for access to water. After secretly buying up large tracts of land in the Owens Valley east of the city, for example, the city of Los Angeles constructed a major aqueduct between 1908 and 1913, over the vigorous objections of the valley's residents. By the 1920s, so much water had been diverted to the city that the once thriving farming and ranching businesses of Owens Valley could no longer operate.

Taft in Office

Having served nearly eight years as president, Roosevelt did not run again in 1908. His chosen successor was William Howard Taft, a federal judge from Ohio who had served as governor of the Philippines after the Spanish-American War. Taft defeated William Jennings Bryan, making his third unsuccessful race for the White House. Taft's inaugural address expressed the Progressive view of the state: "The scope of a modern government ... has been widened far beyond the principles laid down by the old 'laissez-faire' school of political writers."

Although temperamentally more conservative than Roosevelt, Taft pursued antitrust policy even more aggressively. He persuaded the Supreme Court in 1911 to declare John D. Rockefeller's Standard Oil Company (one of Roosevelt's "good" trusts) in violation of the Sherman Antitrust Act and to order its breakup into separate marketing, producing, and refining companies. The government also won a case against American Tobacco, which the Court ordered to end pricing policies that were driving smaller firms out of business. In these decisions, the justices announced a new standard for judging large corporations—the "rule of reason"—which in effect implemented Roosevelt's old distinction between good and bad trusts. Big businesses were not, in and of themselves, antitrust violators, unless they engaged in policies that stifled competition.

Taft supported the **Sixteenth Amendment** to the Constitution, which authorized Congress to enact a graduated income tax (one whose rate of taxation is higher for wealthier citizens). It was ratified shortly before he left office. A 2 percent tax on incomes over $4,000 had been included in a tariff enacted in 1894 but had been quickly declared unconstitutional by the Supreme Court as a "communistic threat to property." The movement to resurrect the income tax united southern and western farmers who wished to reduce government dependence on revenue from the tariff, which they believed discriminated against nonindustrial states, and Progressives who believed that taxation should be based on the ability to pay. A key step in the modernization of the federal government, the income tax provided a reliable and flexible source of revenue for a national state whose powers, responsibilities, and expenditures were growing rapidly.

Despite these accomplishments, Taft seemed to gravitate toward the more conservative wing of the Republican Party. Only a few months after taking office, he signed the Payne-Aldrich Tariff, which reduced rates on imported goods but not nearly as much as reformers wished. Taft's rift with Progressives grew deeper when Richard A. Ballinger, the secretary of the interior, concluded that Roosevelt had exceeded his authority in placing land in forest reserves. Ballinger decided to return some of this land to the public domain, where mining and lumber companies would have access to it. Gifford Pinchot accused Ballinger of colluding with business interests and repudiating the environmental goals of the Roosevelt administration. When Taft fired Pinchot in 1910, the breach with party Progressives became irreparable. In 1912, Roosevelt challenged Taft for the Republican nomination. Defeated, Roosevelt launched an independent campaign as the head of the new **Progressive Party**.

The Election of 1912

All the crosscurrents of Progressive-era thinking about what *McClure's Magazine* called "the problem of the relation of the State and the corporation" came together in the presidential campaign of 1912. The four-way contest between Taft, Roosevelt, Democrat Woodrow Wilson, and Socialist Eugene V. Debs became a national debate on the relationship between political and economic freedom in the age of big business. At one end of the political spectrum stood Taft, who stressed that economic individualism could remain the foundation of the social order so long as government and private entrepreneurs cooperated in addressing social ills. At the other end was Debs. Relatively few Americans supported the Socialist Party's goal of abolishing the "capitalistic system" altogether, but its immediate demands—including public ownership of the railroads and banking system, government aid to the unemployed, and laws establishing shorter working hours and a minimum wage—summarized forward-looking Progressive thought.

Eugene V. Debs, the Socialist Party candidate, speaking in Chicago during the 1912 presidential campaign.

But it was the battle between Wilson and Roosevelt over the role of the federal government in securing economic freedom that galvanized public attention in 1912. The two represented competing strands of Progressivism. Both believed government action necessary to preserve individual freedom, but they differed over the dangers of increasing the government's power and the inevitability of economic concentration. Though representing a party thoroughly steeped in states' rights and laissez-faire ideology, Wilson was deeply imbued with Progressive ideas. As governor of New Jersey, Wilson had presided over the implementation of a system of workmen's compensation and state regulation of utilities and railroads.

New Freedom and New Nationalism

Strongly influenced by Louis D. Brandeis, with whom he consulted frequently during the campaign, Wilson insisted that democracy must be reinvigorated by restoring market competition and freeing government from domination by big business. Wilson feared big government as much as he feared the power of the corporations. The **New Freedom**, as he called his program, envisioned the federal government strengthening antitrust laws, protecting the right of workers to unionize, and actively encouraging small businesses—creating, in other words, the conditions for the renewal of economic competition without increasing government regulation of the economy. Wilson warned that corporations were as likely to corrupt government as to be managed by it, a forecast that proved remarkably accurate.

To Roosevelt's supporters, Wilson seemed a relic of a bygone era; his program, they argued, served the needs of small businessmen but ignored the inevitability of economic concentration and the interests of professionals, consumers, and labor. Wilson and Brandeis spoke of the "curse of bigness." What the nation actually needed, Walter Lippmann countered, was frank acceptance of the benefits of bigness, coupled with the intervention of government to counteract its abuses. Lippmann was expressing the core of the **New Nationalism**, Roosevelt's program of 1912. Only the "controlling and directing power of the government," Roosevelt insisted, could restore "the liberty of the oppressed." He called for heavy taxes on personal and corporate fortunes and federal regulation of industries, including railroads, mining, and oil.

The Progressive Party platform offered numerous proposals to promote social justice. Drafted by a group of settlement-house activists, labor reformers, and social scientists, the platform laid out a blueprint for a modern, democratic welfare state, complete with woman suffrage, federal supervision of corporate enterprise, national labor and health legislation for women and children, an eight-hour day and "living wage" for all workers, and a national system of social insurance covering unemployment, medical care, and old age. Described by Roosevelt as the "most important document" since the end of the Civil War, the platform brought together many of the streams of thought and political experiences that flowed into Progressivism. Roosevelt's campaign helped to give freedom a modern social and economic content and established an agenda that would define political liberalism for much of the twentieth century.

Roosevelt's Americanism

A redefinition of what it meant to be an American united many strands of Progressive-era thought. Theodore Roosevelt's New Nationalism was one example. Roosevelt wanted immigrants to "Americanize" rather than retain cultures and customs from their countries of origin. He also believed that fitness for citizenship—or lack thereof—was both inborn and related to past historical experience. Slaves brought from Africa and their descendants, he believed, could not assimilate properly into American culture. Only persons with the capacity for "self-control"—mainly white people—were capable of participating in democracy.

In a 1910 speech in Kansas outlining his New Nationalism, Roosevelt announced that the "prime problem of our nation is to get the right type of good citizenship." He argued that the government should provide for the well-being of its people to make them better citizens, while retaining the view that only persons with "the right kind of character" were really qualified for citizenship. Being a proper American required a certain level of material comfort. "No man can be a good citizen," he declared, "unless he has a wage more than sufficient to cover the bare cost of living. . . . We keep countless men from being good citizens by the conditions of life with which we surround them." Yet the person who lacked the qualities necessary to be "a good man in the home, a good

From MARY CHURCH TERRELL, "WHAT IT MEANS TO BE COLORED IN THE CAPITAL OF THE UNITED STATES" (1906)

The daughter of slaves, Mary Church Terrell became one of the nation's most prominent Black women. A high school teacher in Washington, D.C., she went on to serve on the city's Board of Education and became a founder of the NAACP. In 1906, Terrell delivered a speech to a women's club in Washington in which she outlined some of the forms of humiliation faced daily by African Americans in the nation's capital. They were treated, she pointed out, like aliens in their native land.

As a colored woman I might enter Washington any night, a stranger in a strange land, and walk miles without finding a place to lay my head. Unless I happened to know colored people who live here . . . I should be obliged to spend the entire night wandering about. Indians, Chinamen, Filipinos, Japanese and representatives of any other dark race can find hotel accommodations, if they can pay for them. The colored man alone is thrust out of the hotels of the national capital like a leper.

Unless I am willing to engage in a few menial occupations, in which the pay for my services would be very poor, there is no way for me to earn an honest living, if I am not a trained nurse or a dressmaker or can secure a position as teacher in the public schools. . . . If I try to enter many of the numerous vocations in which my white sisters are allowed to engage, the door is shut in my face. . . .

It is impossible for any white person in the United States, no matter how sympathetic and broad, to realize what life would mean to him if his incentive to effort were suddenly snatched away. . . . Surely nowhere in the world do oppression and persecution based solely on the color of the skin appear more hateful and hideous than in the capital of the United States, because the chasm between the principles upon which this Government was founded, in which it still professes to believe, and those which are daily practiced under the protection of the flag, yawn so wide and deep.

QUESTIONS

1. *Why does Terrell compare her situation with that of people from China, Japan, and other countries in Asia?*

2. *Why does she consider prejudice more "hateful" in the United States than in other countries?*

father, a good husband," could also never be a good citizen. Clearly, Roosevelt's idea of citizenship had a strong gender bias. Yet in 1912 he would embrace woman suffrage. And Roosevelt's concept of Americanism, although closed to Blacks and Asian Americans, was open to more people than the outlook of his contemporaries who also excluded the "new immigrants" from Europe. But its coercive potential would become starkly evident a few years later, when the United States entered World War I and the government demanded absolute loyalty of all Americans and the immediate assimilation of immigrants.

Wilson's First Term

The Republican split in 1912 ensured a sweeping victory for Wilson, who won about 42 percent of the popular vote, although Roosevelt humiliated Taft by winning about 27 percent to the president's 23 percent. In office, Wilson proved himself a strong executive leader. He established an office at the Capitol so that he could confer regularly with members of Congress about pending legislation, and he was the first president to hold regular press conferences in order to influence public opinion directly and continuously. He delivered messages personally to Congress rather than sending them in written form, as had all his predecessors since John Adams.

With Democrats in control of Congress, Wilson moved aggressively to implement his version of Progressivism. The first significant measure of his presidency was the Underwood Tariff, which substantially reduced duties on imports and, to make up for lost revenue, imposed a graduated income tax on the richest 5 percent of Americans. There followed the Clayton Act of 1914, which exempted labor unions from antitrust laws and barred courts from issuing injunctions curtailing the right to strike. In 1916 came the Keating-Owen Act outlawing child labor in the manufacture of goods sold in interstate commerce (the Supreme Court would later declare it unconstitutional), the Adamson Act establishing an eight-hour workday on the nation's railroads, and the Warehouse Act, reminiscent of the Populist subtreasury plan, which extended credit to farmers when they stored their crops in federally licensed warehouses.

The Expanding Role of Government

Some of Wilson's policies seemed more in tune with Roosevelt's New Nationalism than the New Freedom of 1912. He abandoned the idea of aggressive trust-busting in favor of greater government supervision of the economy. Wilson presided over the creation of two powerful new public agencies. In 1913, Congress created the Federal Reserve System, consisting of twelve regional banks. They were overseen by a central board appointed by the president and empowered to handle the issuance of currency, aid banks in danger of failing, and influence interest rates so as to promote economic growth. The law was a delayed response to the Panic of 1907, when the failure of several financial companies threatened a general collapse of the banking system. With the federal government lacking a modern central bank, it had been left to J. P. Morgan to assemble the funds to prop up threatened financial institutions. Morgan's actions highlighted the fact that in the absence of federal regulation of banking, power over finance rested entirely in private hands.

A second expansion of national power occurred in 1914, when Congress established the **Federal Trade Commission** (FTC) to investigate and prohibit "unfair" business activities such as price-fixing and monopolistic practices. Both the Federal Reserve and FTC were welcomed by many business leaders as a means of restoring order to the economic marketplace and warding off more radical measures for curbing corporate power. But they reflected the remarkable expansion of the federal role in the economy during the Progressive era.

By 1916, the social ferment and political mobilizations of the Progressive era had given birth to a new American state. With new laws, administrative agencies, and independent commissions, government at the local, state, and national levels had assumed the authority to protect and advance "industrial freedom." Government had established rules for labor relations, business behavior, and financial policy, protected citizens from market abuses, and acted as a broker among the groups whose conflicts threatened to destroy social harmony. But a storm was already engulfing Europe that would test the Progressive faith in empowered government as the protector of American freedom.

CHAPTER REVIEW

REVIEW QUESTIONS

1. *Identify the main groups and ideas that drove the Progressive movement.*

2. *Explain how immigration to the United States in this period was part of a global movement of peoples.*

3. *Describe how Fordism transformed American industrial and consumer society.*

4. *Socialism was a rising force across the globe in the early twentieth century. How successful was the movement in the United States?*

5. *Explain why the Industrial Workers of the World (IWW) grew so rapidly and aroused so much opposition.*

6. *How did immigrants adjust to life in America? What institutions or activities became important to their adjustment, and why?*

7. *What did Progressive-era feminists want to change in society, and how did their actions help to spearhead broader reforms?*

8. *How did ideas of women's roles, shared by maternalist reformers, lead to an expansion of activism by and rights for women?*

9. *How did Progressive-era Native Americans organize and what were their aims?*

10. *How did each Progressive-era president view the role of the federal government?*

11. *According to Theodore Roosevelt, what were the qualities that made for "the right type of good citizenship"?*

12. *Pick a Progressive-era reform (a movement, specific legislation, and organization) and describe how it shows how Progressives could work for both the expansion of democracy and restrictions on it.*

KEY TERMS

Go to 🐰 **INQUIZITIVE**

To see what you know—and learn what you've missed—with personalized feedback along the way.

CHAPTER 19

SAFE FOR DEMOCRACY: THE UNITED STATES AND WORLD WAR I

1916–1920

FOCUS QUESTIONS

- *In what ways did the Progressive presidents promote the expansion of American power overseas?*

- *How did the United States get involved in World War I?*

- *How did the United States mobilize resources and public opinion for the war effort?*

- *How did the war affect race relations in the United States?*

- *Why was 1919 such a watershed year for the United States and the world?*

At the dawn of the twentieth century, America's rising economic supremacy was the subject of frequent commentary in both Europe and the United States. The French economist Louis Bosc warned that America would soon dominate the "universe." Brooks Adams, grandson of John Quincy Adams, more admiringly commented on the "velocity and proportions" of the new "American supremacy," declaring the United States "a gigantic and growing empire." And in 1902, the English writer W. T. Stead, impressed by Americans' "exuberant energies," published a short volume with the arresting title, *The Americanisation of the World, or the Trend of the Twentieth Century*, predicting that the United States would soon emerge as "the greatest of world powers."

The United States had, indeed, emerged as a formidable empire by 1900. The conquest of Hawaii in 1893 expanded its territory halfway across the Pacific. The colonization of the Philippines and Puerto Rico after the Spanish-American War, along with the acquisition of Guam and American Samoa and in 1917 the Virgin Islands, added more than 7 million new people over whom the nation ruled. Yet the country's overseas territorial holdings remained small compared to those of Britain, France, and Germany. In 1900, Great Britain ruled over more than 300 million people in possessions scattered across the globe, and France had nearly 50 million subjects in Asia and Africa. America's empire differed significantly from those of European countries.

On the North American continent, the United States had vastly expanded since its founding. In the first half of the nineteenth century, American Indian expropriation, land purchased from European empires, and the war with Mexico more than tripled the size of its territory. By the early twentieth century, America had emerged as a continent-spanning nation with a growing population and abundant mineral and agricultural resources that helped drive its extraordinary economic growth. By 1913, the United States produced 65 percent of the world's petroleum, 56 percent of the world's copper, 39 percent of its coal, and 36 percent of its iron ore. By 1914, it produced more than one-third of the world's manufactured goods. Although Britain still dominated world banking and the

British pound remained the major currency of international trade, the United States had become the leading industrial power. Europeans complained of an "American invasion" of steel, oil, agricultural equipment, and consumer goods and many feared American products and culture would overwhelm them. "What are the chief new features of London life?" one British writer asked in 1901. "They are the telephone, the portable camera, the phonograph, the electric street car, the automobile, the typewriter. . . . In every one of these the American maker is supreme."

The fierce economic competition Europe faced from the United States intensified European countries' quest for overseas colonial control. With its own vast territory, the United States, however, was more interested in ensuring a favorable economic climate for American goods and trade abroad. America's economic supremacy, W. T. Stead remarked, was grounded in the "single-minded commitment to the pursuit of wealth." By the dawn of the twentieth century, its economic industries and corporate energies would lead the United States to promote its interests through newly energetic involvement in the affairs of other nations. As Brooks Adams wrote, the nation "must be brought into competition with rivals at the ends of the earth." America's influence was growing throughout the world.

America's burgeoning connections with the outside world led to increasing military and political involvement. In the two decades after 1900, many of the basic principles that would guide American foreign policy for the rest of the century were formulated. The "open door"—the free flow of trade, investment, information, and culture—emerged as a key principle of American foreign relations. "Since the manufacturer insists on having the world as a market," wrote Woodrow Wilson, "the flag of his nation must follow him and the doors of nations which are closed against him must be battered down."

Americans in the twentieth century often discussed foreign policy in the language of freedom. At least in rhetoric, the United States ventured abroad—including intervening militarily in the affairs of other nations—not to pursue strategic goals or to enhance American economic interests but to promote liberty and democracy. A supreme faith in America's historic destiny and in the righteousness of its ideals enabled the country's leaders to think of the United States simultaneously as an emerging great power and as the worldwide embodiment of freedom.

More than any other individual, Woodrow Wilson articulated this vision of America's relationship to the rest of the world. His foreign policy, called by historians **liberal internationalism**, rested on the conviction that economic and political progress went hand in hand. Thus, greater worldwide freedom would follow inevitably from increased American investment and trade abroad. Frequently during the twentieth century, this conviction would serve as a mask for

American power and self-interest. It would also inspire sincere efforts to bring freedom to other peoples. In either case, liberal internationalism represented a shift from the nineteenth-century tradition of promoting freedom primarily by example, to active intervention to remake the world in the American image.

American involvement in World War I provided the first great test of Wilson's belief that American power could "make the world safe for democracy." Most Progressives embraced the country's participation in the war, believing that the United States could help to spread Progressive values throughout the world. The government quickly came to view critics of American involvement not simply as citizens with a different set of opinions but as enemies of the very ideas of democracy and freedom. As a result, the war produced one of the most sweeping repressions of the right to dissent in all of American history. Rather than bringing Progressivism to other peoples, the war destroyed it at home.

AN ERA OF INTERVENTION

Just as they expanded the powers of the federal government in domestic affairs, the Progressive presidents increasingly projected American power outside the country's borders. At first, they confined their interventions to the Western Hemisphere, whose affairs the United States had claimed a special right to oversee ever since the Monroe Doctrine of 1823. Between 1901 and 1920, U.S. marines landed in Caribbean countries more than twenty times. Usually, they were dispatched to create a welcoming economic environment for American companies that wanted stable access to goods like bananas and sugar, and for bankers nervous that their loans to local governments might not be repaid.

"I Took the Canal Zone"

Just as he distinguished between good and bad trusts, Theodore Roosevelt divided the world into "civilized" and "uncivilized" nations. The former, he believed, had an obligation to establish order in an unruly world. Roosevelt became far more active in international diplomacy than most of his predecessors, helping, for example, to negotiate a settlement of the Russo-Japanese War of 1904–1905, a feat for which he was awarded the Nobel Peace Prize. Closer to home, his policies were more aggressive. "I have always been fond of the West African proverb," he wrote, "'Speak softly and carry a big stick.'" And although he declared that the United States "has not the slightest desire for territorial aggrandizement at the expense of its southern neighbors," Roosevelt pursued a policy of intervention in Central America.

In his first major action in the region, Roosevelt engineered the separation of Panama from Colombia in order to facilitate the construction of a canal linking the Atlantic and Pacific oceans. The idea of a canal across the fifty-one-mile-wide Isthmus of Panama had a long history. In 1879–1881, the French engineer Ferdinand de Lesseps attempted to construct such a waterway but failed because of inadequate funding and the toll exacted on his workers by yellow fever and malaria. Roosevelt had long been a proponent of American naval development. He was convinced that a canal would facilitate the movement of naval and commercial vessels between the two oceans. In 1903, when Colombia, of which Panama was a part, refused to cede land for the project, Roosevelt helped to set in motion an uprising by conspirators led by Philippe Bunau-Varilla, a representative of the Panama Canal Company. An American gunboat prevented the Colombian army from suppressing the rebellion.

THE PANAMA CANAL ZONE

Constructed in the first years of the twentieth century, after Theodore Roosevelt helped engineer Panama's independence from Colombia, the Panama Canal drastically reduced the time it took for commercial and naval vessels to sail between the Atlantic and the Pacific oceans.

Upon establishing Panama's independence, Bunau-Varilla signed a treaty giving the United States both the right to construct and operate a canal and sovereignty over the **Panama Canal Zone**, a ten-mile-wide strip of land through which the route would run. A remarkable feat of engineering, the canal was the largest construction project in American history to that date. Like the building of the transcontinental railroad in the 1860s and much construction work today, it involved the widespread use of immigrant labor. Most of the 60,000 workers came from the Caribbean islands of Barbados and Jamaica, but others hailed from Europe, Asia, and the United States. In keeping with American segregation policies, the best jobs were reserved for white Americans, who lived in their own communities complete with schools, churches, and libraries. The project also required a massive effort to eradicate the mosquitoes that carried the tropical diseases responsible, in part, for the failure of earlier efforts. When completed in 1914, the canal reduced the sea voyage between the East and West coasts of the United States by 8,000 miles. "I took the Canal Zone," Roosevelt exulted. But the manner in which the canal had been initiated, and the continued American rule over the Canal Zone, would long remain a source of tension. In 1977, as a symbol of a new, noninterventionist U.S. attitude toward Latin America, President Jimmy Carter negotiated treaties that led to turning over the canal's operation and control of the Canal Zone to Panama in the year 2000 (see Chapter 26).

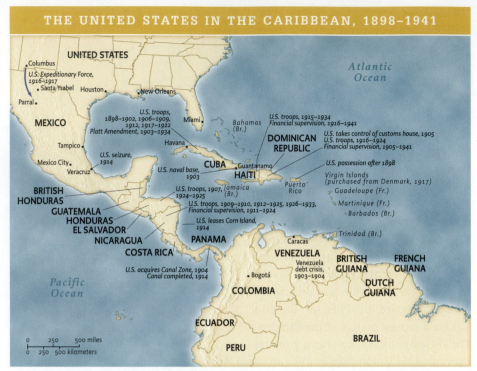

THE UNITED STATES IN THE CARIBBEAN, 1898–1941

Between 1898 and 1941, the United States intervened militarily numerous times in Caribbean countries, generally to protect the economic interests of American banks and investors.

The Roosevelt Corollary

Roosevelt's actions in Panama anticipated the full-fledged implementation of a principle that came to be called the **Roosevelt Corollary** to the Monroe Doctrine. This held that the United States had the right to exercise "an international police power" in the Western Hemisphere—a significant expansion of Monroe's pledge to defend the hemisphere against European intervention. Early in Roosevelt's administration, British, Italian, and German naval forces blockaded Venezuela to ensure the payment of debts to European bankers. Roosevelt persuaded them to withdraw, but the incident convinced him that financial instability in the New World would invite intervention from the Old. In 1904, Roosevelt ordered American forces to seize the customs houses of the Dominican Republic to ensure payment of that country's debts to European and American investors. He soon arranged an "executive agreement" giving a group of American banks control over Dominican finances. In 1906, he dispatched troops to Cuba to oversee a disputed election; they remained in the country until 1909. Roosevelt also encouraged investment by American corporations like the United Fruit Company, whose huge banana plantations soon dominated the economies of Honduras and Costa Rica.

Roosevelt's successor, William Howard Taft, landed marines in Nicaragua to protect a government friendly to American economic interests. In general, however, Taft emphasized economic investment and loans from American banks, rather than direct military intervention, as the best way to spread American influence. As a result, his foreign policy became known as **Dollar Diplomacy**. In Honduras, Nicaragua, the Dominican Republic, and even Liberia—the West African nation established in 1816 as a home for freed American slaves—Taft pressed for more efficient revenue collection, stable government, and access to land and labor by American companies.

Moral Imperialism

The son of a Presbyterian minister, Woodrow Wilson brought to the presidency a missionary zeal and a sense of his own and the nation's moral righteousness. He appointed as secretary of state William Jennings Bryan, a strong anti-imperialist. Wilson repudiated Dollar Diplomacy and promised

The *World's Constable*, a cartoon commenting on Theodore Roosevelt's "new diplomacy," in *Judge*, January 14, 1905, portrays Roosevelt as an impartial policeman, holding in one hand the threat of force and in the other the promise of the peaceful settlement of disputes. Roosevelt stands between the "undisciplined" non-white peoples of the world and the imperialist powers of Europe and Japan.

COLONIAL POSSESSIONS, 1900

American	Dutch	Ottoman
Belgian	French	Portuguese
British	German	Russian
Danish	Italian	Spanish

a new foreign policy that would respect Latin America's independence and free it from foreign economic domination. But Wilson also believed that the export of American manufactured goods and investments went hand in hand with the spread of democratic ideals. To Wilson, expanding American economic influence served a higher purpose than mere profit. Americans, he told a group of businessmen in 1916, were "meant to carry liberty and justice" throughout the world. "Go out and sell goods," he urged them, "that will make the world more comfortable and happy, and convert them to the principles of America."

Wilson's **moral imperialism** produced more military interventions in Latin America than the foreign policy of any president before or since. In 1915, he sent marines to occupy Haiti after the government refused to allow American banks to oversee its financial dealings. The United States seized control of Haitian finances, forced the dissolution of its national assembly, and rewrote the Haitian Constitution. American military rule would last until 1934. In 1916, Wilson established a military government in the Dominican Republic as well. American soldiers remained there until 1924. Wilson's foreign policy underscored a paradox of modern American history: the presidents who spoke the most about freedom were likely to intervene most frequently in the affairs of other countries.

Wilson and Mexico

Wilson's major preoccupation in Latin America was Mexico, where in 1911 a revolution led by Francisco Madero overthrew the government of dictator Porfirio Díaz. Two years later, without Wilson's knowledge but with the backing of the U.S. ambassador and of American companies that controlled Mexico's oil and mining industries, military commander Victoriano Huerta assassinated Madero and seized power.

Wilson was appalled. The United States, he announced, would not extend recognition to a "government of butchers." He would "teach" Latin Americans, he added, "to elect good men." When civil war broke out in Mexico, Wilson ordered American troops to land at Vera Cruz to prevent the arrival of weapons meant for Huerta's forces. But to Wilson's surprise, Mexicans greeted the marines as invaders rather than liberators. Vera Cruz, after all, was where the forces of the conquistador Hernán Cortés had landed in the sixteenth century and those of Winfield Scott during the Mexican-American War. More than 100 Mexicans and 19 Americans died in the fighting that followed.

Huerta resigned in 1914 and fled the country. Meanwhile, various Mexican factions contended for power. A peasant uprising in the southern part of the country, led by Emiliano Zapata, demanded land reform. The Wilson administration offered support to Venustiano Carranza, a leader devoted to economic modernization. In 1916, the war spilled over into the United States when several hundred men loyal to Francisco "Pancho" Villa, the leader of another peasant force, raided Columbus, New Mexico, a few miles north of the border, leading to the death of seventeen Americans. With Carranza's approval, Wilson ordered 10,000 troops under the command of General John J. Pershing on an expedition into Mexico that unsuccessfully sought to arrest Villa. Violence in Mexico continued—within the next few years, Zapata, Carranza, and Villa all fell victim to assassination. Mexico was a warning that it might be more difficult than Wilson assumed to use American might to reorder the internal affairs of other nations, or to apply moral certainty to foreign policy.

AMERICA AND THE GREAT WAR

In June 1914, a Serbian nationalist assassinated Archduke Franz Ferdinand, heir to the throne of the Austro-Hungarian empire, in Sarajevo. (Today, Sarajevo is the capital of Bosnia and Herzegovina.) This deed set in motion a chain of events that plunged Europe into the most devastating war the world had ever seen. In the years before 1914, European nations had engaged in a scramble to obtain colonial possessions overseas and had constructed a shifting series of alliances seeking military domination within Europe. In the aftermath of the assassination, Austria-Hungary, the major power in Eastern Europe, declared war on Serbia. Within a little more than a month, because of the European powers' interlocking military alliances, Britain, France, Russia, and Japan (the Allies) found themselves at war with the Central Powers—Germany, Austria-Hungary, and the Ottoman empire, whose holdings included modern-day Turkey and much of the Middle East.

German forces quickly overran Belgium and part of northern France. The war then settled into a prolonged stalemate, with bloody, indecisive battles succeeding one another. New military technologies—submarines, airplanes, machine guns, tanks, and poison gas—produced unprecedented slaughter. In one five-month battle at Verdun, in 1916, 600,000 French and German soldiers died—nearly as many deaths as in the entire American Civil War. By the time the war ended, an estimated 10 million soldiers, and uncounted millions of civilians, had perished.

The Great War, or World War I as it came to be called, dealt a severe blow to the optimism and self-confidence of Western civilization. For decades, philosophers, reformers, and politicians had hailed the triumph of reason and human progress. Despite increasingly bitter rivalries between European powers, especially Germany and Britain, as they competed for political and military dominance at home and carved up Asia and Africa into rival empires, mankind seemed to have moved beyond the time when disputes were settled by war. The conflict was also a shock to European socialist and labor movements. Of the two great ideologies that had arisen in the nineteenth century, nationalism and socialism, the former proved more powerful. Karl Marx had called on the "workers of the world" to unite against their oppressors. Instead, they marched off to kill each other.

Neutrality and Preparedness

As war engulfed Europe, Americans found themselves sharply divided. British Americans sided with their nation of origin, as did many other Americans who associated Great Britain with liberty and democracy and Germany with repressive government. On the other hand, German Americans identified with Germany. Irish Americans bitterly opposed any aid to the British, a sentiment reinforced in 1916 when authorities in London suppressed the Easter Rebellion, an uprising demanding Irish independence, and executed several of its leaders. Immigrants from the Russian empire, especially Jews, had no desire to see the United States aid the czar's regime. Indeed, the presence of Russia, the world's largest despotic state, as an ally of Britain and France made it difficult to see the war as a clear-cut battle between democracy and autocracy.

Many feminists, pacifists, and social reformers, moreover, had become convinced that peace was essential to further efforts to enhance social justice at home. They lobbied vigorously against American involvement. So did large numbers of religious leaders, who viewed war as a barbaric throwback to a less Christian era.

When war broke out in 1914, President Wilson proclaimed American neutrality. But as in the years preceding the War of 1812, naval warfare in Europe reverberated in the United States. Britain declared a naval blockade of Germany and began to stop American merchant vessels. Germany launched submarine warfare against ships entering and leaving British ports. In May 1915, a German submarine sank the British liner **Lusitania** (which was carrying a large cache of arms) off the coast of Ireland, causing the death of 1,198 passengers, including 124 Americans. Wilson composed a note of protest so strong that Bryan resigned as secretary of state, fearing that the president was laying the foundation for military intervention. Bryan had advocated warning Americans not to travel on the ships of belligerents, but Wilson felt this would represent a retreat from the principle of freedom of the seas.

The sinking of the *Lusitania* outraged American public opinion and strengthened the hand of those who believed that the United States must prepare for possible entry into the war. These included longtime advocates of a stronger military establishment, like Theodore Roosevelt, and businessmen with close economic ties to Britain, the country's leading trading partner and the recipient of more than $2 billion in wartime loans from American banks. Wilson himself had strong pro-British sympathies and viewed Germany as "the natural foe of liberty." By the end of 1915, he had embarked on a policy of "preparedness"—a crash program to expand the American army and navy.

The Road to War

In May 1916, Germany announced the suspension of submarine warfare against noncombatants. Wilson's preparedness program seemed to have succeeded in securing the right of Americans to travel freely on the high seas without committing American forces to the conflict. "He kept us out of war" became the slogan of his campaign for reelection. With the Republican Party reunited after its split in 1912, the election proved to be one of the closest in American history. Wilson defeated Republican candidate Charles Evans Hughes by only twenty-three electoral votes and about 600,000 popular votes out of more than 18 million cast. Partly because he seemed to promise not to send American soldiers to Europe, Wilson carried ten of the twelve states that had adopted woman suffrage. Without the votes of women, Wilson would not have been reelected.

On January 22, 1917, Wilson called for a "peace without victory" in Europe and outlined his vision for a world order including freedom of the seas, restrictions on armaments, and self-determination for nations great and small. Almost immediately, however, Germany announced its intention to resume submarine warfare against ships sailing to or from the British Isles, and several American merchant vessels were sunk. The German government realized that its actions would probably lead Wilson to intervene, but German strategists gambled that the blockade would strangle Britain economically before the arrival of American troops.

In March 1917, British spies intercepted and made public the **Zimmermann Telegram**, a message by German foreign secretary Arthur Zimmermann calling on Mexico to join in a coming war against the United States and promising to help it recover territory lost in the Mexican-American War of 1846–1848. A revolution in Russia that same month overthrew the czar and established a constitutional government, making it more plausible to believe that the United States would be fighting on the side of democracy. On April 2, Wilson went before Congress to ask for a declaration of war against Germany. "The world," he proclaimed, "must be made safe for democracy. Its peace must be planted upon the tested foundation of political liberty." The war resolution passed the Senate 82–6 and the House 373–50.

The Fourteen Points

Not until the spring of 1918 did American forces arrive in Europe in large numbers. By then, the world situation had taken a dramatic turn. In November 1917, a communist revolution headed by Vladimir Lenin overthrew the Russian government that had come to power the previous spring. Shortly thereafter, Lenin withdrew Russia from the war and published the secret treaties by which the Allies had agreed to divide up conquered territory after the war—an embarrassment for Wilson, who had promised a just peace.

Partly to assure the country that the war was being fought for a moral cause, Wilson in January 1918 issued the **Fourteen Points**, the clearest statement of American war aims and of his vision of a new international order. Among the key principles were self-determination for all peoples, freedom of the seas, free trade, open diplomacy (an end to secret treaties), the readjustment of colonial claims with colonized people given "equal weight" in deciding their futures, and the creation of a "general association of nations" to preserve the peace. Wilson envisioned this last provision, which led to the establishment after the war of the League of Nations, as a kind of global counterpart to the regulatory commissions Progressives had created at home to maintain social harmony and prevent the powerful from exploiting the weak. Although purely an American

After years of stalemate on the western front in World War I, the arrival of American troops in 1917 and 1918 shifted the balance of power and made possible the Allied victory.

program, not endorsed by the other Allies, the Fourteen Points established the agenda for the peace conference that followed the war.

The United States threw its economic resources and manpower into the war. When American troops finally arrived in Europe, they turned the tide of battle. In the spring of 1918, they helped to repulse a German advance near Paris and by July were participating in a major Allied counteroffensive. In September, in the Meuse-Argonne campaign, American soldiers under the command of General John J. Pershing, fresh from his campaigns in Mexico, helped to push back the German army. With 1.2 million American soldiers taking part and well over 100,000 dead and wounded, Meuse-Argonne, which lasted a month and a half, was the main American engagement of the war and one of the most significant and deadliest battles in American history. It formed part of a massive Allied offensive involving British, French, and Belgian soldiers and those from overseas European possessions. With his forces in full retreat, the German kaiser abdicated on

November 9. Two days later, Germany sued for peace. More than 100,000 Americans had died, a substantial number, but they were only 1 percent of the 10 million soldiers killed in the Great War.

THE WAR AT HOME

The Forgotten Pandemic

Millions died in combat during World War 1, but even more—between 20 to 40 million—were killed during the 1918–1919 flu pandemic. A mild first wave in the spring of 1918 was followed by a more virulent second wave that spread like wildfire around the globe. The pandemic reached catastrophic proportions in the United States by the fall of 1918. The disease, which hit young adults especially hard, killed 675,000 Americans within a few months.

Wartime mobilization contributed to rapid virus spread with servicemen crossing the ocean on crowded ships and living in packed military camps and trenches. In Philadelphia, a liberty loan parade escalated case numbers, and the city soon became the hardest hit municipality in the country. On the West Coast, San Francisco closed schools, churches, and public amusements and passed a mandatory mask ordinance to stem the rising tide of cases. Such mandates, as with the Covid-19 pandemic a century later, sparked opposition. An Anti-Mask League criticized the efficacy of mask wearing and decried the ordinance as a violation of personal liberty. With numbers falling by the spring of 1919, concerns turned to wartime demobilization, labor upheaval, and the Red Scare. Despite the devastating loss of life, the pandemic was largely forgotten.

The Progressives' War

Looking at American participation in the European conflict, literary critic Randolph Bourne saw the expansion of government power as a danger. Most Progressives, however, viewed it as a golden opportunity. To them, the war offered the possibility of reforming American society along scientific lines, instilling a sense of national unity and self-sacrifice, and expanding social justice. That American power could now disseminate Progressive values around the globe heightened the war's appeal.

Almost without exception, Progressive intellectuals and reformers, joined by prominent labor leaders and native-born socialists, rallied to Wilson's support. The roster included intellectuals like John Dewey, journalists such as Walter Lippmann and Herbert Croly, AFL head Samuel Gompers, socialist writers like Upton Sinclair, and prominent reformers including Florence Kelley and

Charlotte Perkins Gilman. In *The New Republic,* Dewey urged Progressives to recognize the "social possibilities of war." The crisis, he wrote, offered the prospect of attacking the "immense inequality of power" within the United States, thus laying the foundation for Americans to enjoy "effective freedom."

The Wartime State

Like the Civil War, World War I created, albeit temporarily, a national state with unprecedented powers and a sharply increased presence in Americans' everyday lives. Under the **Selective Service Act** of May 1917, 24 million men were required to register with the draft, and the army soon swelled from 120,000 to 5 million men. The war seemed to bring into being the New Nationalist state Theodore Roosevelt and so many Progressives had desired. New federal agencies moved to regulate industry, transportation, labor relations, and agriculture. Headed by Wall Street financier Bernard Baruch, the **War Industries Board** presided over all elements of war production from the distribution of raw materials to the prices of manufactured goods. To spur efficiency, it established standardized specifications for everything from automobile tires to shoe colors (three were permitted—Black, brown, and white). The Railroad Administration took control of the nation's transportation system, and the Fuel Agency rationed coal and oil. The Food Administration instructed farmers on modern methods of cultivation and promoted the more efficient preparation of meals. Its director, Herbert Hoover, mobilized the shipment of American food to the war-devastated Allies, popularizing the slogan "Food will win the war."

These agencies generally saw themselves as partners of business as much as regulators. They guaranteed government suppliers a high rate of profit and encouraged cooperation among former business rivals by suspending antitrust laws. At the same time, however, the War Labor Board, which included representatives of government, industry, and the American Federation of Labor, pressed for the establishment of a minimum wage, eight-hour workday, and the right to form unions. During the war, wages rose substantially, working conditions in many industries improved, and union membership doubled. To finance the war, corporate and individual income taxes rose enormously. By 1918, the wealthiest Americans were paying 60 percent of their income in taxes. Tens of millions of Americans answered the call to demonstrate their patriotism by purchasing Liberty bonds. Once peace arrived, the wartime state quickly withered away. But for a time, the federal government seemed well on its way to fulfilling the Progressive vision of promoting economic rationalization, industrial justice, and a sense of common national purpose.

The Propaganda War

During the Civil War, it had been left to private agencies—Union Leagues, the Loyal Publication Society, and others—to mobilize prowar public opinion. But the Wilson administration decided that patriotism was too important to leave to the private sector. Many Americans were skeptical about whether democratic America should enter a struggle between rival empires. Some vehemently opposed American participation, notably the Industrial Workers of the World (IWW) and the bulk of the Socialist Party, which in 1917 condemned the declaration of war as "a crime against the people of the United States" and called on "the workers of all countries" to refuse to fight. As the major national organization to oppose Wilson's policy, the Socialist Party became a rallying point for antiwar sentiment. In mayoral elections across the country in the fall of 1917, the Socialist vote averaged 20 percent, far above the party's previous total.

In April 1917, the Wilson administration created the Committee on Public Information (CPI) to explain to Americans and the world, as its director, George Creel, put it, "the cause that compelled America to take arms in defense of its liberties and free institutions." Enlisting academics, journalists, artists, and advertising men, the CPI flooded the country with prowar propaganda, using every available medium from pamphlets (of which it issued 75 million) to posters, newspaper advertisements, and motion pictures. It trained and dispatched across the country 75,000 Four-Minute Men, who delivered brief standardized talks (sometimes in Italian, Yiddish, and other immigrant languages) to audiences in movie theaters, schools, and other public venues.

Never before had an agency of the federal government attempted the "conscious and intelligent manipulation of the organized habits and opinions of the masses," in the words of young Edward Bernays, a member of Creel's staff who would later create the modern profession of public relations. The CPI's activities proved, one adman wrote, that it was possible to "sway the ideas of whole populations, change their habits of life, create belief, practically universal in any policy or idea." In the 1920s, advertisers would use what they had learned to sell goods. But the CPI also set a precedent for governmental efforts to shape public opinion in later international conflicts, from World War II to the Cold War and Iraq.

"The Great Cause of Freedom"

The CPI couched its appeal in the Progressive language of social cooperation and expanded democracy. Abroad, this meant a peace based on the principle of national self-determination. At home, it meant improving "industrial democracy." A Progressive journalist, Creel believed the war would accelerate the movement toward solving the "age-old problems of poverty, inequality, oppression, and unhappiness." He took to heart a warning from historian Carl Becker that a simple contrast between German tyranny and American democracy would not seem plausible to the average worker: "You talk to him of our ideals of liberty and he thinks of the shameless exploitation of labor and of the ridiculous gulf between wealth and poverty." CPI pamphlets foresaw a postwar society complete with a "universal eight-hour day" and a living wage for all.

While "democracy" served as the key term of wartime mobilization, "freedom" also took on new significance. The war, a CPI advertisement proclaimed, was being fought in "the great cause of freedom." Thousands of persons, often draftees, were enlisted to pose in giant human tableaus representing symbols of liberty. One living representation of the Liberty Bell at Fort Dix, New Jersey, included 25,000 people. The most common visual image in wartime propaganda was the Statue of Liberty, employed especially to rally support among immigrants. "You came here seeking Freedom," stated a caption on one Statue of Liberty poster. "You must now help preserve it." Buying Liberty bonds became a demonstration of patriotism. Wilson's speeches cast the United States as a land of liberty fighting alongside a "concert of free people" to secure self-determination for the oppressed peoples of the world. The idea of freedom, it seems, requires an antithesis, and the CPI found one in the German kaiser and, more generally, the German nation and people. Government propaganda whipped up hatred of the wartime foe by portraying it as a nation of barbaric Huns.

The Coming of Woman Suffrage

The enlistment of "democracy" and "freedom" as ideological war weapons inevitably inspired demands for their expansion at home. In 1916, Wilson had cautiously endorsed votes for women. America's entry into the war threatened to tear the suffrage movement apart, since many advocates had been associated with opposition to American involvement. Indeed, among those who voted against the declaration of war was the first woman member of Congress, the staunch pacifist Jeannette Rankin of Montana. "I want to stand by my country, but I cannot vote for war," she said. Although defeated in her reelection bid in 1918, Rankin would return to Congress in 1940. She became the only member to oppose the declaration of war against Japan in 1941, which ended her political career. In 1968, at the age of eighty-five, Rankin took part in a giant march on Washington to protest the war in Vietnam.

As during the Civil War, however, most leaders of woman suffrage organizations enthusiastically enlisted in the effort. Women sold war bonds, organized patriotic rallies, and went to work in war production jobs. Some 22,000 served as clerical workers and nurses with American forces in Europe. Many believed wartime service would earn them equal rights at home.

At the same time, a new generation of college-educated activists, organized in the National Woman's Party, pressed for the right to vote with militant tactics many older suffrage advocates found scandalous. The party's leader, Alice Paul, had studied in England between 1907 and 1910 when the British suffrage movement adopted a strategy that included arrests, imprisonments, and vigorous denunciations of a male-dominated political system. How could the country fight for democracy abroad, Paul asked, while denying it to women at home? She compared Wilson to the kaiser, and a group of her followers chained themselves to the White House fence, resulting in a seven-month prison sentence. When they began a hunger strike, the prisoners were force-fed.

The combination of women's patriotic service and widespread outrage over the mistreatment of Paul and her fellow prisoners pushed the administration toward full-fledged support for woman suffrage. "We have made partners of the women in this war," Wilson proclaimed. "Shall we admit them only to a partnership of suffering and sacrifice and toil and not to a partnership of privilege and right?" In 1920, the long struggle culminated in the ratification of the Nineteenth Amendment barring states from using sex as a qualification for the suffrage. The United States became the twenty-seventh country to allow women to vote.

The Nineteenth Amendment was cause for celebration, but it did not provide all women the vote. It left states free to limit voting by poll taxes and literacy clauses. Voting rights activists, such as Hallie Quinn Brown, president of the National Association of Colored Women, called upon the National Women's Party to back legislation securing the franchise for all women, but the organization rejected the proposal, declaring its work finished. In North Carolina, the Colored Women's Rights Association mobilized to ensure "all women the right of the ballot regardless of color." Concerned about such actions, state lawmakers in the South tightened voting laws further. Mississippi extended poll taxes to women that had been applied to men to prevent Black women from voting.

Prohibition

The war gave a powerful impulse to other campaigns that had engaged the energies of many women in the Progressive era. Ironically, efforts to stamp out prostitution and protect soldiers from venereal disease led the government to distribute birth-control information and devices—the very action for which Margaret Sanger had recently been jailed, as noted in the previous chapter.

Prohibition, a movement inherited from the nineteenth century that had gained new strength and militancy in Progressive America, finally achieved national success during the war. Numerous impulses flowed into the renewed campaign to ban intoxicating liquor. Employers hoped it would create a more disciplined labor force. Urban reformers believed that it would promote a more

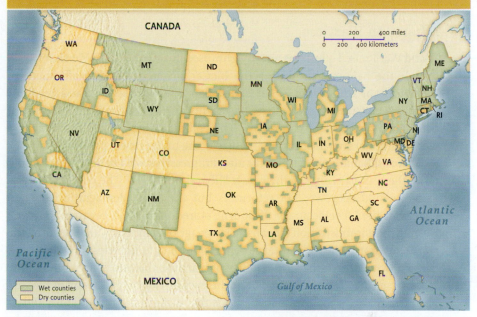

PROHIBITION, 1915: COUNTIES AND STATES THAT BANNED LIQUOR BEFORE THE EIGHTEENTH AMENDMENT (RATIFIED 1919, REPEALED 1933)

In the early years of the twentieth century, many states and localities in the South and West banned the manufacture and sale of alcoholic beverages. ("Wet" counties allowed alcoholic beverages, "dry" counties banned them.) Prohibition became national with the adoption of the Eighteenth Amendment in 1919.

orderly city environment and undermine urban political machines that used saloons as places to organize. Women reformers hoped Prohibition would protect wives and children from husbands who engaged in domestic violence when drunk or who squandered their wages at saloons. Many native-born Protestants saw Prohibition as a way of imposing "American" values on immigrants.

Like the suffrage movement, Prohibitionists first concentrated on state campaigns. By 1915, they had won victories in eighteen southern and midwestern states where the immigrant population was small and Protestant denominations like Baptists and Methodists strongly opposed drinking. But like the suffrage movement, Prohibitionists came to see national legislation as their best strategy. The war gave them added ammunition. Many prominent breweries were owned by German Americans, making beer seem unpatriotic. The Food Administration insisted that grain must be used to produce food, not distilled into beer and liquor. By December 1917, Congress had passed the **Eighteenth Amendment**, prohibiting the manufacture and sale of intoxicating liquor. It was ratified by the states in 1919 and went into effect at the beginning of 1920.

Liberty in Wartime

World War I raised questions already glimpsed during the Civil War that would trouble the nation again during the McCarthy era and in the aftermath of the terrorist attacks of 2001: What is the balance between security and freedom? Does the Constitution protect citizens' rights during wartime? Should dissent be equated with lack of patriotism? The conflict demonstrated that during a war, traditional civil liberties are likely to come under severe pressure.

In 1917, Randolph Bourne ridiculed Progressives who believed they could mold the war according to their own "liberal purposes." The conflict, he predicted, would empower not reformers but the "least democratic forces in American life." The accuracy of Bourne's prediction soon became apparent. Despite the administration's idealistic language of democracy and freedom, the war inaugurated the most intense repression of civil liberties the nation has ever known. Perhaps the very nobility of wartime rhetoric contributed to the massive suppression of dissent. For in the eyes of Wilson and many of his supporters, America's goals were so virtuous that disagreement could only reflect treason to the country's values.

The Espionage and Sedition Acts

For the first time since the Alien and Sedition Acts of 1798, the federal government enacted laws to restrict freedom of speech. The **Espionage Act** of 1917 prohibited not only spying and interfering with the draft but also "false statements" that might impede military success. The postmaster general barred from the mails numerous newspapers and magazines critical of the administration. The victims ranged from virtually the entire socialist press and many foreign-language publications to *The Jeffersonian*, a newspaper owned by ex-Populist leader Tom Watson, which criticized the draft as a violation of states' rights. In 1918, the **Sedition Act** made it a crime to make spoken or printed statements that intended to cast "contempt, scorn, or disrepute" on the "form of government," or that advocated interference with the war effort. The government charged more than 2,000 persons with violating these laws. Over half were convicted. A court sentenced Ohio farmer John White to twenty-one months in prison for saying that the murder of innocent women and children by German soldiers was no worse than what the United States had done in the Philippines in the war of 1899–1903.

The most prominent victim was Eugene V. Debs, convicted in 1918 under the Espionage Act for delivering an antiwar speech. Before his sentencing, Debs gave the court a lesson in the history of American freedom, tracing the tradition of dissent from Thomas Paine to the abolitionists and pointing out that the nation had never engaged in a war without internal opposition. Germany sent socialist leader Karl Liebknecht to prison for four years for opposing the war; in the United States, Debs's sentence was ten years. After the war's end, Wilson rejected the advice of his attorney general that he commute Debs's sentence. Debs ran for president while still in prison in 1920 and received 900,000 votes. It was left to Wilson's successor, Warren G. Harding, to release Debs from prison in 1921.

Coercive Patriotism

Even more extreme repression took place at the hands of state governments and private groups. Americans had long displayed the flag (and used it in advertisements for everything from tobacco products to variety shows). But during World War I, attitudes toward the American flag became a test of patriotism. Persons suspected of disloyalty were forced to kiss the flag in public; those who made statements critical of the flag could be imprisoned. During the war, thirty-three states outlawed the possession or display of red or black flags (symbols, respectively, of communism and anarchism), and twenty-three outlawed a newly created offense, "criminal syndicalism," the advocacy of unlawful acts to accomplish political change or "a change in industrial ownership."

"Who is the real patriot?" Emma Goldman asked while on trial for conspiring to violate the Selective Service Act. She answered, those who "love America with open eyes," who were not blind to "the wrongs committed in the name of patriotism." But from the federal government to local

A common patriotic exercise involved massive numbers of soldiers forming images of the Statue of Liberty, the Liberty Bell, or President Woodrow Wilson. Here, in 1918, some 18,000 men about to depart for the war in Europe from Camp Dodge, Iowa, create what contemporaries called a "living photograph."

OLIVER WENDELL HOLMES, MAJORITY OPINION, *SCHENCK V. UNITED STATES* (1919)

Oliver Wendell Holmes delivered the Supreme Court's majority opinion, which upheld the constitutionality of the Espionage Act and the Sedition Act and the conviction of Charles T. Schenck, a socialist who distributed anti-draft leaflets through the mails. A week later, the Court upheld Eugene Debs's conviction for a speech condemning the war. The decision in the *Schenck* case dealt a blow to civil liberties and remained the test for First Amendment cases for half a century.

We admit that in many places and in ordinary times the defendants in saying all that was said in the circular would have been within their constitutional rights. But the character of every act depends upon the circumstances in which it is done.... The most stringent protection of free speech would not protect a man in falsely shouting fire in a theatre and causing a panic. It does not even protect a man from an injunction against uttering words that may have all the effect of force.... The question in every case is whether the words used are used in such circumstances and are of such a nature as to create a clear and present danger that they will bring about the substantive evils that Congress has a right to prevent. It is a question of proximity and degree. When a nation is at war many things that might be said in times of peace are such a hindrance to its effort that their utterance will not be endured so long as men fight and that no Court could regard them as protected by any constitutional right.

From EUGENE V. DEBS, SPEECH TO THE JURY BEFORE SENTENCING UNDER THE ESPIONAGE ACT (1918)

Socialist leader Eugene V. Debs was arrested for delivering an antiwar speech and convicted of violating the Espionage Act. In his speech to the jury, he defended the right of dissent in wartime.

Gentlemen, you have heard the report of my speech at Canton [Ohio] on June 16, and I submit that there is not a word in that speech to warrant the charges set out in the indictment. . . . In what I had to say there my purpose was to have the people understand something about the social system in which we live and to prepare them to change this system by perfectly peaceable and orderly means into what I, as a Socialist, conceive to be a real democracy. . . . I have never advocated violence in any form. I have always believed in education, in intelligence, in enlightenment; and I have always made my appeal to the reason and to the conscience of the people.

In every age there have been a few heroic souls who have been in advance of their time, who have been misunderstood, maligned, persecuted, sometimes put to death. . . . Washington, Jefferson, Franklin, Paine, and their compeers were the rebels of their day. . . . But they had the moral courage to be true to their convictions. . . .

William Lloyd Garrison, Wendell Phillips, Elizabeth Cady Stanton . . . and other leaders of the abolition movement who were regarded as public enemies and treated accordingly, were true to their faith and stood their ground. . . . You are now teaching your children to revere their memories, while all of their detractors are in oblivion. . . .

The war of 1812 was opposed and condemned by some of the most influential citizens; the Mexican War was vehemently opposed and bitterly denounced, even after the war had been declared and was in progress, by Abraham Lincoln, Charles Sumner, Daniel Webster. . . . They were not indicted; they were not charged with treason. . . .

Isn't it strange that we Socialists stand almost alone today in upholding and defending the Constitution of the United States? The revolutionary fathers . . . understood that free speech, a free press and the right of free assemblage by the people were fundamental principles in democratic government. . . . I believe in the right of free speech, in war as well as in peace.

QUESTIONS

1. *What is Holmes's assessment of the proper balance between liberty and security?*

2. *How does Debs make the case for the right of free speech and dissent?*

3. *How do the documents differ in their assessment of the threats to liberty?*

authorities and private groups, patriotism came to be equated with support for the government, the war, and the American economic system, while antiwar sentiment, labor radicalism, and sympathy for the Russian Revolution became "un-American." Local authorities formally investigated residents who failed to subscribe to Liberty Loans. Throughout the country, schools revised their course offerings to ensure their patriotism and required teachers to sign loyalty oaths.

The 250,000 members of the newly formed American Protective League (APL) helped the Justice Department identify radicals and critics of the war by spying on their neighbors and carrying out "slacker raids" in which thousands of men were stopped on the streets of major cities and required to produce draft registration cards. Many private groups seized upon the atmosphere of repression as a weapon against domestic opponents. Employers cooperated with the government in crushing the Industrial Workers of the World (IWW), a move long demanded by business interests. In July 1917, vigilantes in Bisbee, Arizona, rounded up some 1,200 striking copper miners and their sympathizers, herded them into railroad boxcars, and transported them into the desert, where they were abandoned. Few ever returned to Bisbee. In August, a crowd in Butte, Montana, lynched IWW leader Frank Little. The following month, operating under one of the broadest warrants in American history, federal agents swooped down on IWW offices throughout the country, arresting hundreds of leaders and seizing files and publications.

The war experience, commented Walter Lippmann, demonstrated "that the traditional liberties of speech and opinion rest on no solid foundation." Yet while some Progressives protested individual excesses, most failed to speak out against the broad suppression of freedom of expression. Civil liberties, by and large, had never been a major concern of Progressives, who had always viewed the national state as the embodiment of democratic purpose and insisted that freedom flowed from participating in the life of society, not standing in opposition. Strong believers in the use of national power to improve social conditions, Progressives found themselves ill prepared to develop a defense of minority rights against majority or governmental tyranny. From the AFL to *New Republic* intellectuals, moreover, supporters of the war saw the elimination of socialists and alien radicals as a necessary prelude to the integration of labor and immigrants into an ordered society, an outcome they hoped would emerge from the war.

WHO IS AN AMERICAN?

In many respects, Progressivism was a precursor to major developments of the twentieth century—the New Deal, the Great Society, the socially active state. But in accepting the idea of "race" as a permanent, defining characteristic of individuals and social groups, Progressives bore more resemblance to nineteenth-century thinkers than to later twentieth-century liberals, with whom they are sometimes compared.

The "Race Problem" and the "Science" of Eugenics

Even before American participation in World War I, what contemporaries called the "race problem"—the tensions that arose from the country's increasing ethnic diversity—had become a major subject of public concern. "Race" referred to far more than Black-white relations. The *Dictionary of Races of Peoples*, published in 1911 by the U.S. Immigration Commission, listed no fewer than forty-five immigrant "races," each supposedly with its own inborn characteristics. They ranged from Anglo-Saxons at the top down to Hebrews, Northern Italians, and, lowest of all, Southern Italians—supposedly violent, undisciplined, and incapable of assimilation. Popular best-sellers like *The Passing of the Great Race*, published in 1916 by Madison Grant, president of the New York Zoological Society, warned that the influx of new immigrants and the low birthrate of native white women threatened the foundations of American civilization.

The emergence of **eugenics**, which studied the alleged mental characteristics of different groups of people, gave an air of scientific expertise to anti-immigrant sentiment. Racial "purity" became an obsession of eugenicists. The Race Betterment Foundation and the American Breeder's Association eugenics committee, both established in 1906, aimed to promote the "purity of the gene pool" and warned about the menace posed by people with "inferior blood." The Eugenic Records Office, headquartered in New York State, issued certificates to people who could demonstrate their "Nordic purity."

Eugenics taught that since many social problems, including juvenile delinquency, prostitution, and even poverty, were caused by defective genes, they could be eliminated by controlling reproduction. These ideas led to the passage of laws to "improve" the quality of the human race. Indiana in 1907 passed a law authorizing doctors to sterilize the developmentally disabled housed in state institutions so they would not pass their "defective" genes on to children. During and after World War I, numerous other states followed suit. In *Buck v. Bell* (1927), the Supreme Court upheld the constitutionality of these laws. Carrie Buck, an eighteen-year-old committed to a Virginia institution for the "feeble-minded," sued to prevent her sterilization by the state on the grounds that it violated her right to the equal protection of the laws, guaranteed by the Fourteenth Amendment. Justice Oliver Wendell Holmes's opinion rejecting her plea included the widely publicized statement, "Society can prevent those who are manifestly unfit from continuing their kind. ... Three generations of imbeciles are enough." By the time the practice ended in the 1960s, some 63,000 persons had been involuntarily sterilized. American eugenics policies for manipulating the character of the population were carefully studied in Nazi Germany.

Americanization and Pluralism

Somehow, the very nationalization of politics and economic life served to heighten awareness of ethnic and racial difference and spurred demands for "Americanization"—the creation of a more homogeneous national culture. A 1908 play by the Jewish immigrant writer Israel Zangwill, *The Melting Pot*, gave a popular name to the process by which newcomers were supposed to merge their identity into existing American nationality. Public and private groups of all kinds—including educators, employers, labor leaders, social reformers, and public officials—took up the task of Americanizing new immigrants. The Ford Motor Company's famed sociological department entered the homes of immigrant workers to evaluate their clothing, furniture, and food preferences and enrolled them in English-language courses. Ford fired those who failed to adapt to American standards after a reasonable period of time. Americanization programs often targeted women as the bearers and transmitters of culture. In Los Angeles, teachers and religious missionaries worked to teach English to Mexican American women so that they could then assimilate American values. Fearful that adult newcomers remained too stuck in their Old World ways, public schools paid great attention to Americanizing immigrants' children. The challenge facing schools, wrote one educator, was "to implant in their children, so far as can be done, the Anglo-Saxon conception of righteousness, law and order, and popular government."

With President Wilson declaring that some Americans "born under foreign flags" were guilty of "disloyalty . . . and must be absolutely crushed," the federal and state governments demanded that immigrants demonstrate their unwavering devotion to the United States. The Committee on Public Information renamed the Fourth of July, 1918, Loyalty Day and asked ethnic groups to participate in patriotic pageants. New York City's celebration included a procession of 75,000 persons with dozens of floats and presentations linking immigrants with the war effort and highlighting their contributions to American society. Leaders of ethnic groups that had suffered discrimination saw the war as an opportunity to gain greater rights. Prominent Jewish leaders promoted enlistment and expressions of loyalty.

The Anti-German Crusade

German Americans bore the brunt of forced Americanization. The first wave of German immigrants had arrived before the Civil War. By 1914, German Americans numbered nearly 9 million, including immigrants and persons of German parentage. They had created thriving ethnic institutions including clubs, sports associations, schools, and theaters. On the eve of the war, many Americans admired German traditions in literature, music, and philosophy,

From RANDOLPH S. BOURNE, "TRANS-NATIONAL AMERICA" (1916)

Probably the most penetrating rejection of the Americanization model issued from the pen of the social critic Randolph Bourne. In an article in *The Atlantic*, Bourne envisioned a democratic, cosmopolitan society in which immigrants and natives alike retained their group identities while at the same time embracing a new "trans-national" culture.

No reverberatory effect of the great war has caused American public opinion more solicitude than the failure of the "melting-pot." The discovery of diverse nationalistic feelings among our great alien population has come to most people as an intense shock. . . . We have had to listen to publicists who . . . insist that the alien shall be forcibly assimilated to that Anglo-Saxon tradition which they unquestionably label "American." . . . We act as if we wanted Americanization to take place only on our own terms, and not by the consent of the governed. . . .

The Anglo-Saxon was merely the first immigrant. . . . Colonials from the other nations have come and settled down beside him. They found no definite native culture . . . and consequently they looked back to their mother-country, as the earlier Anglo-Saxon immigrant was looking back to his. . . .

There is no distinctively American culture. It is apparently our lot rather to be a federation of cultures. This we have been for half a century, and the war has made it ever more evident that this is what we are destined to remain. . . . What we have achieved has been rather a cosmopolitan federation of national colonies, of foreign cultures, from whom the sting of devastating competition has been removed. America is already the world-federation in miniature, the continent where for the first time in history has been achieved that miracle of hope, the peaceful living side by side, with character substantially preserved, of the most heterogeneous peoples under the sun. . . . America is coming to be, not a nationality but a trans-nationality, a weaving back and forth, with the other lands, of many threads of all sizes and colors. Any movement which attempts to thwart this weaving, or to dye the fabric any one color, or disentangle the threads of the strands, is false to this cosmopolitan vision.

QUESTIONS

1. Why does Bourne believe that the "melting pot" has failed?

2. What does he mean by describing America as a "trans-nationality"?

and one-quarter of all the high school students in the country studied the German language. But after American entry into the war, the use of German and expressions of German culture became a target of prowar organizations. In Iowa, Governor William L. Harding issued a proclamation requiring that all oral communication in schools, public places, and over the telephone be conducted in English. Freedom of speech, he declared, did not include "the right to use a language other than the language of the country."

By 1919, the vast majority of the states had enacted laws restricting the teaching of foreign languages. Popular words of German origin were changed: "hamburger" became "liberty sandwich," and "sauerkraut" "liberty cabbage." Many communities banned the playing of German music. The government jailed Karl Muck, the director of the Boston Symphony and a Swiss citizen, as an enemy alien after he insisted on including the works of German composers like Beethoven in his concerts. The war dealt a crushing blow to German American culture. By 1920, the number of German-language newspapers had been reduced to 276 (one-third the number twenty years earlier), and only 1 percent of high school pupils still studied German. The census of 1920 reported a 25 percent drop in the number of Americans admitting to having been born in Germany.

Even as Americanization programs sought to assimilate immigrants into American society, the war strengthened the conviction that certain kinds of undesirable persons ought to be excluded altogether. The new immigrants, one advocate of restriction declared, appreciated the values of democracy and freedom far less than "the Anglo-Saxon," as evidenced by their attraction to "extreme political doctrines" like anarchism and socialism. Stanford University psychologist Lewis Terman introduced the term "IQ" (intelligence quotient) in 1916, claiming that this single number could measure an individual's mental capacity. Intelligence tests administered to recruits by the army seemed to confirm scientifically that Blacks and the new immigrants stood far below native white Protestants on the IQ scale, further spurring demands for immigration restriction.

Fighting for Rights and Freedom

No matter how coercive, Americanization programs assumed that European immigrants and especially their children could eventually adjust to the conditions of American life and become productive citizens enjoying the full blessings of American freedom. This assumption did not apply to non-white immigrants, non-white nationals of U.S. overseas territory, or to Blacks. Although the melting-pot idea envisioned that newcomers from Europe would leave their ethnic enclaves and join the American mainstream, non-whites confronted ever-present boundaries of exclusion.

The war led to further growth of the Southwest's Mexican population. Wartime demand for labor from the area's mine owners and large farmers led the government to exempt Mexicans temporarily from the literacy test enacted in 1917. Yet public officials in the Southwest treated them as a group apart. Segregation, by law and custom, was common in schools, hospitals, theaters, and other institutions in states with significant Mexican populations. By 1920, nearly all Mexican children in California and the Southwest were educated in their own schools or classrooms. Phoenix, Arizona, established separate public schools for Indians, Mexicans, Blacks, and whites. Although in far smaller numbers than Blacks, Mexican Americans also suffered lynchings—over 200 between 1880 and 1930. Discrimination led to the formation of La Grán Liga Mexicanista de Beneficencia y Protección, which aimed to improve the conditions of Mexicans in the United States and "to strike back at the hatred of some bad sons of Uncle Sam."

Asian Americans also experienced continued discrimination and exclusion. In 1906, the San Francisco school board ordered all Asian students confined to a single public school. When the Japanese government protested, President Theodore Roosevelt persuaded the city to rescind the order. He then negotiated the Gentlemen's Agreement of 1907 whereby Japan agreed to end migration to the United States except for the wives and children of men already in the country. In 1913, California barred all aliens incapable of becoming naturalized citizens (that is, all Asians) from owning or leasing land. And in 1917, Congress passed legislation creating an "Asiatic barred zone" banning immigration from much of Asia.

Despite such discrimination, Asian Americans and Pacific Islanders served in the military. Leaders of these groups saw such service as an opportunity to win greater freedom. The Chinese American press insisted that even those born abroad and barred from citizenship should register for the draft, to "bring honor to the people of our race." Filipino leaders, such as Manuel L. Quezon, aimed to use military service to gain greater respect under U.S. colonial rule and to strengthen the case for national independence. Despite their ambiguous status as U.S. nationals, neither citizens nor aliens, thousands of Filipinos served in the U.S. army and the navy. Many volunteered but others, such as Filipino contract workers in Hawaii, were drafted.

Puerto Ricans also occupied an ambiguous position within American society. On the eve of American entry into World War I, Congress terminated the status "citizen of Puerto Rico" and conferred American citizenship on residents of the island. The aim was to dampen support for Puerto Rican independence and to strengthen the American hold on a strategic outpost in the Caribbean. The change did not grant islanders the right to vote for president or representation in Congress. Puerto Rican men, nonetheless, were subject to the draft and fought overseas. José de Diego, the Speaker of the House of the island's legislature, wrote the president in 1917 asking that Puerto Rico be granted the democracy the United States was fighting for in Europe.

Native Americans and World War I

World War I intensified debates among Native Americans about freedom, citizenship, and the place of American Indians in U.S. society. More than 12,000 American Indians served in the military; most volunteered but many were drafted. Off-reservation boarding schools served as important sites of recruitment, with over 200 Native American soldiers recruited from the Carlisle school alone. Native Americans held conflicting views about military service. With widespread poverty and poor health conditions on reservations, the Society of American Indians (discussed in Chapter 18) saw the war as an opportunity to win freedom and citizenship. "Our American Indians are today in France on the battle line, fighting that liberty, fraternity and equality of opportunity may prevail throughout the world," wrote "Red Progressive" Arthur C. Parker. "Are they to return and find that they alone of all humankind are denied those blood-bought privileges?" Such arguments contributed to legislation in 1919 providing American Indian veterans eligibility for citizenship.

Many Native Americans, however, viewed the draft as an assault on their sovereignty. The Pueblo, Hopi, Navajo, Haudenosaunee (Iroquois), Lakota, and Ojibwe peoples opposed the draft. The Oneida and Onondaga nations insisted on fighting alongside the United States as an ally rather than for it and declared war on Germany. Native American soldiers' casualty rate was higher than other groups with white officers using Indians for dangerous tasks such as scouts.

The Color Line

George Miner (Ho-Chunk), an army corporal, stands guard in Niederahren, Germany, shortly after the end of World War I. Many Native Americans volunteered or were drafted.

By far the largest non-white group, African Americans were excluded from nearly every Progressive definition of freedom described in Chapter 18.

After their disenfranchisement in the South, few could participate in American democracy. Barred from joining most unions and from skilled employment, Black workers had little access to "industrial freedom." A majority of adult Black women worked outside the home, but for wages that offered no hope of independence. Predominantly domestic and agricultural workers, they remained unaffected by the era's laws regulating the hours and conditions of female labor. Nor could Blacks, the majority desperately poor, participate fully in the emerging consumer economy, either as employees in the new department stores (except as janitors and cleaning women) or as purchasers of the consumer goods now flooding the marketplace.

Progressive intellectuals, social scientists, labor reformers, and suffrage advocates displayed a remarkable indifference to the Black condition. Israel Zangwill did not include Blacks in the melting-pot idea popularized by his Broadway play. Walter Weyl waited until the last fifteen pages of *The New Democracy* to introduce the "race problem." His comment, quoted in the previous chapter, that the chief obstacles to freedom were economic, not political, revealed little appreciation of how the denial of voting rights underpinned the comprehensive system of inequality to which southern Blacks were subjected.

Roosevelt, Wilson, and Race

The Progressive presidents shared prevailing attitudes concerning Blacks. Theodore Roosevelt shocked white opinion by inviting Booker T. Washington to dine with him in the White House and by appointing a number of Blacks to federal offices. But in 1906, when a small group of Black soldiers shot off their guns in Brownsville, Texas, killing one resident, and none of their fellows would name them, Roosevelt ordered the dishonorable discharge of three Black companies—156 men in all, including six winners of the Congressional Medal of Honor. Roosevelt's ingrained belief in Anglo-Saxon racial destiny (he called Indians "savages" and Blacks "wholly unfit for the suffrage") did nothing to lessen Progressive intellectuals' enthusiasm for his New Nationalism. Even Jane Addams, one of the few Progressives to take a strong interest in Black rights and a founder of the National Association for the Advancement of Colored People (NAACP), went along when the Progressive Party convention of 1912 rejected a civil rights plank in its platform and barred Black delegates from the South.

Woodrow Wilson, a native of Virginia, could speak without irony of the South's "genuine representative government" and its exalted "standards of liberty." His administration imposed racial segregation in federal departments in Washington, D.C., and dismissed numerous Black federal employees. Wilson allowed D. W. Griffith's film *The Birth of a Nation*, which glorified the Ku Klux Klan as the defender of white civilization during Reconstruction, to have its premiere at the White House in 1915. "Have you a 'new freedom' for white Americans and a new slavery for your African American fellow citizens?" William Monroe Trotter, the militant Black editor of the *Boston Guardian* and founder of the all-Black National Equal Rights League, asked the president.

In one of hundreds of lynchings during the Progressive era, a white mob in Springfield, Missouri, in 1906 falsely accused three Black men of rape, hanged them from an electric light pole, and burned their bodies in a public orgy of violence. Atop the pole stood a replica of the Statue of Liberty.

W. E. B. Du Bois and the Revival of Black Protest

Black leaders struggled to find a strategy to rekindle the national commitment to equality that had flickered brightly, if briefly, during Reconstruction. No one thought more deeply, or over so long a period, about the Black condition and the challenge it posed to American democracy than the scholar and activist W. E. B. Du Bois. Born in Great Barrington, Massachusetts, in 1868, and educated at Fisk and Harvard universities, Du Bois lived to his ninety-fifth year. The unifying theme of his career was Du Bois's effort to reconcile the contradiction between what he called "American freedom for whites and the continuing subjection of Negroes." His book *The Souls of Black Folk* (1903) issued a clarion call for Blacks dissatisfied with the accommodationist policies of Booker T. Washington to press for equal rights. Du Bois believed that educated African Americans like himself—the "talented tenth" of the Black community—must use their education and training to challenge inequality.

In some ways, Du Bois was a typical Progressive who believed that investigation, exposure, and education would lead to solutions for social problems. As a professor at Atlanta University, he projected a grandiose plan for decades of scholarly study of Black life in order to make the country aware of racism and point the way toward its elimination. But he also understood the necessity of political action.

In 1905, Du Bois gathered a group of Black leaders at Niagara Falls (meeting on the Canadian side since no American hotel would provide accommodations) and organized the Niagara movement, which sought to reinvigorate the abolitionist tradition. "We claim for ourselves," Du Bois wrote in the group's manifesto, "every single right that belongs to a freeborn American, political, civil, and social; and until we get these rights we will never cease to protest and assail the ears of America." The Declaration of Principles adopted at Niagara Falls called for restoring to Blacks the right to vote, an end to racial segregation, and complete equality in economic and educational opportunity. These would remain the cornerstones of the Black struggle for racial justice for decades to come. Four years later, Du Bois joined with a group of mostly white reformers, shocked by a lynching in Springfield, Illinois (Lincoln's adult home), to create the **National Association for the Advancement of Colored People**. The NAACP, as it was known, launched a long struggle for the enforcement of the Fourteenth and Fifteenth Amendments.

The NAACP's legal strategy won a few victories. In *Bailey v. Alabama* (1911), the Supreme Court overturned southern "peonage" laws that made it a crime for sharecroppers to break their labor contracts. Six years later, it ruled unconstitutional a Louisville zoning regulation excluding Blacks from living in certain parts of the city (primarily because it interfered with whites' right to sell their property as they saw fit). Overall, however, the Progressive era witnessed virtually no progress toward racial justice.

The men who founded the Niagara movement at a 1905 meeting on the Canadian side of Niagara Falls. W. E. B. Du Bois is in the second row, second from the right, in a white hat. They pledged to renew the struggle for "every single right that belongs to a freeborn American." By the time of the second meeting, a year later, women had become part of the movement.

Military Service and the Promise of Freedom

Among Black Americans, the wartime language of freedom inspired hopes for a radical change in the country's racial system. With the notable exception of William Monroe Trotter, most Black leaders saw American participation in the war as an opportunity to make real the promise of freedom. To Trotter, much-publicized German atrocities were no worse than American lynchings; rather than making the world safe for democracy, the government should worry about "making the South safe for the Negroes." Yet the Black press rallied to the war. Du Bois himself, in widely reprinted editorials, called on African Americans to enlist in the army to help "make our own America a real land of the free."

Black participation in the Civil War had helped to secure the destruction of slavery and the achievement of citizenship. But during World War I, closing ranks did not bring significant gains. The navy barred Blacks entirely, and the segregated army confined most of the 400,000 Blacks who served in the war to supply units rather than combat. Wilson feared, as he noted in his diary, that the overseas experience would "go to their heads." And the U.S. Army campaigned strenuously to persuade the French not to treat Black soldiers as equals—not to eat or socialize with them, or even shake their hands. Contact with African colonial soldiers fighting alongside the British and French did widen the horizons of Black American soldiers. But while colonial troops marched in the victory parade in Paris, the Wilson administration did not allow Black Americans to participate.

The Great Migration and the "Promised Land"

Nonetheless, the war unleashed social changes that altered the contours of American race relations. The combination of increased wartime production and a drastic falloff in immigration from Europe opened thousands of industrial jobs to Black laborers for the first time, inspiring a large-scale migration from South to North. On the eve of World War I, 90 percent of the African American population still lived in the South. Most northern cities had tiny Black populations, and domestic and service work still predominated among both Black men and Black women in the North. But between 1910 and 1920, half a million Blacks left the South. The Black population of Chicago more than doubled, New York City's rose 66 percent, and smaller industrial cities like Akron, Buffalo, and Trenton showed similar gains.

Many motives sustained the **Great Migration**—higher wages in northern factories than were available in the South (even if Blacks remained confined to menial and unskilled positions), opportunities for educating their children, escape from the threat of lynching, and the prospect of exercising the right to vote. Migrants spoke of a Second Emancipation, of "crossing over Jordan," and of leaving the realm of pharaoh for the Promised Land. One group from Mississippi stopped to sing, "I am bound for the land of Canaan," after their train crossed the Ohio River into the North.

The Black migrants, mostly young men and women, carried with them "a new vision of opportunity, of social and economic freedom," as Alain Locke explained in the preface to his influential book *The New Negro* (1925). Yet the migrants encountered

TABLE 19.1 The Great Migration

City	Black Population, 1910	Black Population, 1920	Percent Increase
New York	91,709	152,467	66.3%
Philadelphia	84,459	134,229	58.9
Chicago	44,103	109,458	148.2
St. Louis	43,960	69,854	58.9
Detroit	5,741	40,838	611.3
Pittsburgh	25,623	37,725	47.2
Cleveland	8,448	34,451	307.8

vast disappointments—severely restricted employment opportunities, exclusion from unions, rigid housing segregation, and outbreaks of violence that made it clear that no region of the country was free from racial hostility. More white southerners than Blacks moved north during the war, often with similar economic aspirations. But the new Black presence, coupled with demands for change inspired by the war, created a racial tinderbox that needed only an incident to trigger an explosion.

Racial Violence, North and South

Dozens of Blacks were killed during a 1917 riot in East St. Louis, Illinois, where employers had recruited Black workers in an attempt to weaken unions (most of which excluded Blacks from membership). In 1919, more than 250 persons died in riots in the urban North. Most notable was the violence in Chicago, touched off by the drowning by white bathers of a Black teenager who accidentally crossed the unofficial dividing line between Black and white beaches on Lake Michigan. The riot that followed raged for five days and involved pitched battles between the races throughout the city. By the time the National Guard restored order, 38 persons had been killed and more than 500 injured.

Violence was not confined to the North. In the year after the war ended, seventy-six persons were lynched in the South, including several returning Black veterans wearing their uniforms. In Phillips County, Arkansas, attacks on striking Black sharecroppers by armed white vigilantes left as many as 200 persons dead and required the intervention of the army to restore order. The worst single incidence of racial terror in American history occurred in Tulsa, Oklahoma, in 1921, when more than 300 Blacks were killed and over 10,000 left homeless after a white mob, including police and National Guardsmen, burned an all-Black section of the city, the Greenwood District, to the ground. Its main thoroughfare was nicknamed "Negro Wall Street" by Booker T. Washington for its prosperous Black-owned businesses. The **Tulsa massacre** erupted after a group of Black veterans tried to prevent the lynching of a youth who

One of a series of paintings by the Black artist Jacob Lawrence called *The Migration Series*, inspired by the massive movement of African Americans to the North during and after World War I. For each, Lawrence composed a brief title, in this case, "In the North the Negro had better educational facilities."

had accidentally tripped and fallen on a white female elevator operator, causing rumors of rape to sweep the city.

The Rise of Garveyism

World War I kindled a new spirit of militancy. The East St. Louis riot of 1917 inspired a widely publicized Silent Protest Parade on New York's Fifth Avenue in which 10,000 Blacks silently carried placards reading, "Mr. President, Why Not Make America Safe for Democracy?" In the new densely populated Black ghettos of the North, widespread support emerged for the Universal Negro Improvement Association, a movement for African independence and Black self-reliance launched by **Marcus Garvey**, a recent immigrant from Jamaica. Freedom for Garveyites meant national self-determination. Blacks, they insisted, should enjoy the same internationally recognized identity enjoyed by other peoples in the aftermath of the war. "Everywhere we hear the cry of freedom," Garvey proclaimed in 1921. "We desire a freedom that will lift us to the common standard of all men, . . . freedom that will give us a chance and opportunity to rise to the fullest of our ambition and that we cannot get in countries where other men rule and dominate." Du Bois and other established Black leaders viewed Garvey as little more than a demagogue, but the massive movement he built testified to the popular appeal of Black nationalist ideas and the sense of betrayal that had been kindled in Black communities during and after the war. Garvey's influence spread to the Caribbean, Canada, and Africa. The government launched an investigation into Garvey in 1919 hoping to deport him as an "undesirable alien." Charged and convicted of mail fraud in 1922, Garvey was deported in 1927.

1919

A Worldwide Upsurge

The combination of militant hopes for social change and disappointment with the war's outcome was evident far beyond the Black community. In the Union of Soviet Socialist Republics (or Soviet Union), as Russia had been renamed after the revolution, Lenin's government had nationalized landholdings, banks, and factories and proclaimed the socialist dream of a workers' government. The Russian Revolution and the democratic aspirations unleashed by World War I sent tremors of hope and fear throughout the world. Like 1848 and, in the future, 1968, 1919 was a year of worldwide social and political upheaval. Inspired by Lenin's call for revolution, communist-led governments came to power in Bavaria (a part of Germany) and Hungary. General strikes demanding the fulfillment of wartime promises of "industrial democracy" took place in Belfast, Glasgow, and Winnipeg. In Spain, anarchist peasants began seizing land. Crowds in India challenged British rule, and nationalist movements in other colonies demanded independence. "We are living and shall live all our lives in a revolutionary world," wrote Walter Lippmann.

The worldwide revolutionary upsurge produced a countervailing mobilization by opponents of radical change. Even as they fought the Germans, the Allies viewed the Soviet government as a dire threat and attempted to overturn it. In the summer of 1918, Allied expeditionary forces—British, French, Japanese, and Americans—landed in Russia to aid Lenin's opponents in the civil war that had engulfed the country. The last of them did not leave until 1920.

Wilson's policies toward the Soviet Union revealed the contradictions within the liberal internationalist vision. On the one hand, in keeping with the principles of the Fourteen Points and its goal of a worldwide economic open door, Wilson hoped to foster trade with the new government. On the other, fear of communism as a source of international instability and a threat to private property inspired military intervention in Russia. The Allies did not invite the Soviet Union to the Versailles peace conference, and Wilson refused to extend diplomatic recognition to Lenin's government. The Soviet regime survived, but in the rest of the world the tide of change receded. By the fall, the mass strikes had been suppressed and conservative governments had been installed in central Europe. Anticommunism would remain a pillar of twentieth-century American foreign policy.

Upheaval in America

In the United States, 1919 also brought unprecedented turmoil. Racial violence, as noted above, was widespread. In June, bombs exploded at the homes of prominent Americans, including the attorney general, A. Mitchell Palmer, who escaped uninjured. Among aggrieved American workers, wartime language linking patriotism with democracy and freedom inspired hopes that an era of social justice and economic empowerment was at hand. In 1917, Wilson had told the AFL, "While we are fighting for freedom, we must see to it among other things that labor is free." Labor took him seriously—more seriously, it seems, than Wilson intended. The government, as one machinist put it, had "proclaimed to the World that the freedom and democracy we are fighting for shall be practiced in the industries of America."

By the war's end, many Americans believed that the country stood on the verge of what Herbert Hoover called "a new industrial order." Sidney Hillman, leader of the garment workers' union, was one of those caught up in the utopian dreams inspired by the war and reinforced by the Russian Revolution. "One can hear the footsteps of the Deliverer," he wrote. "Labor will rule and the World will be free." In 1919, more than 4 million workers engaged in strikes—the greatest wave of labor unrest in American history. There were walkouts, among many others, by textile workers, telephone operators, and Broadway actors. Throughout the country, workers appropriated the imagery and rhetoric of the war, parading in army uniforms with Liberty buttons, denouncing their employers as "kaisers," and demanding "freedom in the workplace." They were met by an unprecedented mobilization of employers, government, and private patriotic organizations.

The strike wave began in January 1919 in Seattle, where a walkout of shipyard workers mushroomed into a general strike that for once united AFL unions and the IWW. For five days, a committee of labor leaders oversaw city services, until federal troops arrived to end the strike. In September, Boston policemen struck for higher wages and shorter working hours. Declaring "there is no right to strike against the public safety," Massachusetts governor Calvin Coolidge called out the National Guard to patrol the city and fired the entire police force. In the nation's coalfields, a company manager observed, wartime propaganda had raised unrealistic expectations among workers, who took the promise of "an actual emancipation" too "literally." When the war ended, miners demanded an end to company absolutism. Their strike was ended by a court injunction obtained by Attorney General Palmer.

The Great Steel Strike

The wartime rhetoric of economic democracy and freedom helped to inspire the era's greatest labor uprising, the 1919 steel strike. It united some 365,000 mostly immigrant workers in demands for union recognition, higher wages, and an eight-hour workday. Before 1917, the steel mills were little autocracies where managers arbitrarily established wages and working conditions and suppressed all efforts at union organizing. During the war, workers flooded into the Amalgamated Association, the union that had been nearly destroyed by its defeat at Homestead a generation earlier. By the end of 1918, they had won an eight-hour day. Employers' anti-union activities resumed following the armistice that ended the fighting. "For why this war?" asked one Polish immigrant steelworker at a union meeting. "For why we buy Liberty bonds? For the mills? No, for freedom and America—for everybody. No more [work like a] horse and wagon. For eight-hour day."

In response to the strike, steel magnates launched a concerted counterattack. Employers appealed to anti-immigrant sentiment among native-born workers, many of whom returned to work, and conducted a propaganda campaign that associated the strikers with the IWW, communism, and disloyalty. "Americanism vs. Alienism" was the issue of the strike, declared the *New York Tribune*. With middle-class opinion having turned against the labor movement and the police assaulting workers on the streets, the strike collapsed in early 1920.

The Red Scare

Many Progressives hoped to see the wartime apparatus of economic planning continue after 1918. The Wilson administration, however, quickly dismantled the agencies that had established controls over industrial production and the labor market, although during the 1930s they would serve as models for some policies of Franklin D. Roosevelt's New Deal. Wartime repression of dissent, however, continued. It reached its peak with the **Red Scare of 1919–1920**, a short-lived but intense period of political intolerance inspired by the postwar

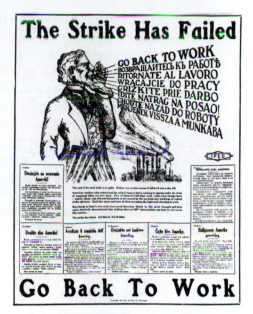

An advertisement placed by a steel company in a Pittsburgh newspaper announces, in several languages, that the steel strike of 1919 "has failed." The use of the figure of Uncle Sam illustrates how the companies clothed their anti-union stance in the language of patriotism.

strike wave and the social tensions and fears generated by the Russian Revolution.

Convinced that episodes like the steel strike were part of a worldwide communist conspiracy, Attorney General A. Mitchell Palmer in November 1919 and January 1920 dispatched federal agents to raid the offices of radical and labor organizations throughout the country. They carried search warrants so broad that they reminded those with a sense of history of the writs of assistance against which James Otis had eloquently protested as being destructive of liberty in 1761. The Palmer Raids were overseen by the twenty-four-year-old director of the Radical Division of the Justice Department, J. Edgar Hoover. More than 5,000 persons were arrested, most of them without warrants, and held for months without charge. The government deported hundreds of immigrant radicals, including Emma Goldman. Hoover also began compiling files on thousands of Americans suspected of holding radical political ideas, a practice he would later continue as head of the Federal Bureau of Investigation.

The abuse of civil liberties in early 1920 was so severe that Palmer came under heavy criticism from Congress and much of the press. Secretary of Labor Louis Post began releasing imprisoned immigrants, and the Red Scare collapsed.

Even the explosion of a bomb outside the New York Stock Exchange in September 1920, which killed forty persons, failed to rekindle it. (The perpetrators of this terrorist explosion, the worst on American soil until the Oklahoma City bombing of 1995, were never identified.) The reaction to the Palmer Raids planted the seeds for a new appreciation of the importance of civil liberties that would begin to flourish during the 1920s. But in their immediate impact, the events of 1919 and 1920 dealt a devastating setback to radical and labor organizations of all kinds and kindled an intense identification of patriotic Americanism with support for the political and economic status quo. The IWW had been effectively destroyed, and many moderate unions lay in disarray. The Socialist Party crumbled under the weight of governmental repression (the New York legislature expelled five Socialist members, and Congress denied Victor Berger the seat to which he had been elected from Wisconsin) and internal differences over the Russian Revolution.

Wilson at Versailles

The beating back of demands for fundamental social change was a severe rebuke to the hopes with which so many Progressives had enlisted in the war effort. Wilson's inability to achieve a just peace based on the Fourteen Points compounded the sense of failure. Late in 1918, the president traveled to France to attend the Versailles peace conference. Greeted by ecstatic Paris crowds, he declared that American soldiers had come to Europe "as crusaders, not merely to win a war, but to win a cause . . . to lead the world on the way of liberty." But he proved a less adept negotiator than his British and French counterparts, David Lloyd George and Georges Clemenceau.

Although the Fourteen Points had called for "open covenants openly arrived at," the negotiations were conducted in secret. The resulting **Versailles Treaty** did accomplish some of Wilson's goals. It established the **League of Nations**, the body central to his vision of a new international order. It applied the principle of self-determination to Eastern Europe and redrew the map of that region. From the ruins of the Austro-Hungarian empire and parts of Germany and czarist Russia, new European nations emerged from the war—Finland, Poland, Czechoslovakia, Austria, Hungary, Latvia, Lithuania, Estonia, and Yugoslavia. Some enjoyed ethnolinguistic unity, while others comprised unstable combinations of diverse nationalities.

Despite Wilson's pledge of a peace without territorial acquisitions or vengeance, the Versailles Treaty was a harsh document that all but guaranteed future conflict in Europe. Clemenceau won for France the right to occupy the Saar Basin and Rhineland—iron- and coal-rich parts of Germany. The treaty placed strict limits on the size of Germany's future army and navy.

Lloyd George persuaded Wilson to agree to a clause declaring Germany morally responsible for the war and setting astronomical reparations payments (they were variously estimated at between $33 billion and $56 billion), which crippled the German economy.

The Wilsonian Moment

To many people around the world, the Great War destroyed European claims that theirs was a higher civilization, which gave them the right to rule over more barbaric peoples. In this sense, it helped to heighten the international prestige of the United States, a latecomer to the war. Like the ideals of the American Revolution, the Wilsonian rhetoric of self-determination reverberated across the globe, especially among colonial peoples seeking independence. In fact, they took Wilson's rhetoric more seriously than he did. Despite his belief

EUROPE IN 1914

World War I and the Versailles Treaty redrew the map of Europe and the Middle East. The Austro-Hungarian and Ottoman empires ceased to exist, and Germany and Russia were reduced in size. A group of new states emerged in Eastern Europe, embodying the principle of self-determination, one of Woodrow Wilson's Fourteen Points.

EUROPE IN 1919

NORTHERN IRELAND (GREAT BRITAIN)

IRISH FREE STATE (after 1921)

GREAT BRITAIN

NORWAY
SWEDEN
FINLAND
ESTONIA
LATVIA
LITHUANIA

DENMARK
NETHERLANDS

EAST PRUSSIA (GERMANY)

Danzig (Free City)

RUSSIA (Union of Soviet Socialist Republics after 1922)

North Sea
Baltic Sea

LUXEMBOURG
BELGIUM
GERMANY
Rhineland
Saar
POLAND

Atlantic Ocean

FRANCE
SWITZERLAND
Lorraine
Alsace
AUSTRIA
HUNGARY
CZECHOSLOVAKIA

ROMANIA

YUGOSLAVIA

Black Sea

PORTUGAL
SPAIN
Corsica (Fr.)
ITALY
Sardinia (It.)
ALBANIA
BULGARIA
GREECE
TURKEY

Sicily

Dodecanese Is. (Italy)
Cyprus

Mediterranean Sea
Crete

New nations
Demilitarized or Allied occupied zone

in self-determination, he believed that colonial peoples required a long period of tutelage before they were ready for independence.

Nonetheless, Wilsonian ideals quickly spread around the globe—not simply the idea that government must rest on the consent of the governed but also Wilson's stress on the "equality of nations," large and small, and that international disputes should be settled by peaceful means rather than armed conflict. These stood in sharp contrast to the imperial ideas and practices of Europe. In Eastern Europe, whose people sought to carve new, independent nations from the ruins of the Austro-Hungarian and Ottoman empires, many considered Wilson a "popular saint." The leading Arabic newspaper, *Al-Ahram*, published in Egypt, then under British rule, gave extensive coverage to Wilson's speech asking Congress to declare war in the name of democracy, and to the Fourteen Points, and translated the Declaration of Independence into Arabic for its readers. In Beijing, students demanding that China free itself of foreign domination gathered at the American embassy shouting, "Long live Wilson." Japan proposed to include in the charter of the new League of Nations a clause recognizing the equality of all people, regardless of race.

Outside of Europe, however, the idea of "self-determination" was stillborn. When the peace conference opened, Secretary of State Robert Lansing warned that the phrase was "loaded with dynamite" and would "raise hopes which can never be realized." Wilson's language, he feared, had put "dangerous" ideas "into the minds of certain races" and would inspire "impossible demands, and cause trouble in many lands." As Lansing anticipated, advocates of colonial independence descended on Paris to lobby the peace negotiators. Arabs demanded that a unified independent state be carved from the old Ottoman empire in the Middle East. Nguyen That Thanh, a young Vietnamese patriot working in Paris, appealed unsuccessfully to Wilson to help bring an end to French rule in Vietnam. W. E. B. Du Bois organized a Pan-African Congress in Paris that put forward the idea of a self-governing nation to be carved out of Germany's African colonies. Koreans, Indians, Irish, and others also pressed claims for self-determination.

The British and French, however, had no intention of applying this principle to their own empires. They rebuffed the pleas of colonial peoples for self-rule. During the war, the British had encouraged Arab nationalism as a weapon against the Ottoman empire and had also pledged to create a homeland in Palestine for the persecuted Jews of Europe. In fact, the victors of World War I divided Ottoman territory into a series of new territories, including Syria, Lebanon, Iraq, and Palestine, controlled by the victorious Allies under League of Nations "mandates." South Africa, Australia, and Japan acquired former German colonies in Africa and Asia. Nor did Ireland achieve its independence at Versailles. Only at the end of 1921 did Britain finally agree to the creation of the Irish Free State, while continuing to rule the northeastern corner of the island. As for the Japanese proposal to establish the principle of racial equality, Wilson, with the support of Great Britain and Australia, engineered its defeat.

The Seeds of Wars to Come

Du Bois, as noted above, hoped that Black participation in the war effort would promote racial justice at home and self-government for colonies abroad. "We return," he wrote in *The Crisis* in May 1919. "We return from fighting, we return fighting. Make way for Democracy!" But the war's aftermath both in the United States and overseas left him bitterly disappointed. Du Bois concluded that Wilson had not meant to include Black Americans or the colonial peoples of the world in his democratic vision. "Most men today," he complained, "cannot conceive of a freedom that does not involve somebody's slavery." In 1903, in *The Souls of Black Folk*, Du Bois had made the memorable prediction that "the problem of the twentieth century is the problem of the color-line." He now forecast a "fight for freedom" that would pit "Black and brown and yellow men" throughout the world against racism and imperialism.

Disappointment at the failure to apply the Fourteen Points to the non-European world created a pervasive cynicism about Western use of the language of freedom and democracy. Wilson's apparent willingness to accede to the demands of the imperial powers helped to spark a series of popular protest movements across the Middle East and Asia, and the rise of a new anti-Western nationalism. Some leaders, like Nguyen That Thanh, who took the name Ho Chi Minh, turned to communism, in whose name he would lead Vietnam's long and bloody struggle for independence. With the collapse of the Wilsonian moment, Lenin's reputation in the colonial world began to eclipse that of the American president. But whether communist or not, these movements announced the emergence of anticolonial nationalism as a major force in world affairs, which it would remain for the rest of the twentieth century.

"Your liberalness," one Egyptian leader remarked, speaking of Britain and America, "is only for yourselves." Yet ironically, when colonial peoples demanded to be recognized as independent members of the international community, they would invoke both the heritage of the American Revolution—the first colonial struggle that produced an independent nation—and the Wilsonian language whereby the self-governing nation-state is the most legitimate political institution, and all nations deserve equal respect.

As Du Bois recognized, World War I sowed the seeds not of a lasting peace but of wars to come. German resentment over the peace terms would help to fuel the rise of Adolf Hitler and the coming of World War II. In the breakup of Czechoslovakia and Yugoslavia, violence over the status of Northern Ireland, and seemingly unending conflicts in the Middle East, the world of the late twentieth century was still haunted by the ghost of Versailles.

The Treaty Debate

One final disappointment awaited Wilson on his return from Europe. He viewed the new League of Nations as the war's finest legacy. But many Americans feared that membership in the League would commit the United States to an open-ended involvement in the affairs of other countries. Wilson asserted that the United States could not save the world without being continually involved with it. His opponents, led by Senator Henry Cabot Lodge of Massachusetts, argued that the League threatened to deprive the country of its freedom of action.

A considerable majority of senators would have accepted the treaty with "reservations" ensuring that the obligation to assist League members against attack did not supersede the power of Congress to declare war. As governor of New Jersey and as president, Wilson had proved himself to be a skilled politician capable of compromising with opponents. In this case, however, convinced that the treaty reflected "the hand of God," Wilson refused to negotiate with congressional leaders. In October 1919, in the midst of the League debate, Wilson suffered a serious stroke. Although the extent of his illness was kept secret, he remained incapacitated for the rest of his presidency. In effect, his wife, Edith, headed the government for the next seventeen months. In November 1919 and again in March 1920, the Senate rejected the Versailles Treaty.

American involvement in World War I lasted barely nineteen months, but it cast a long shadow over the following decade—and, indeed, the rest of the century. In its immediate aftermath, the country retreated from international involvements. But in the long run, Wilson's combination of idealism and power politics had an enduring impact. His appeals to democracy, open markets, and a special American mission to instruct the world in freedom, coupled with a willingness to intervene abroad militarily to promote American interests and values, would create the model for twentieth-century American international relations.

On its own terms, the war to make the world safe for democracy failed. Even great powers cannot always bend the world to their purposes. The war brought neither stability nor democracy to most of the world, and it undermined freedom in the United States. It also led to the eclipse of Progressivism. Republican candidate Warren G. Harding, who had no connection with the party's Progressive wing, swept to victory in the presidential election of 1920. Harding's campaign centered on a "return to normalcy" and a repudiation of what he called "Wilsonism." He received 60 percent of the popular vote. Begun with idealistic goals and grand hopes for social change, American involvement in the Great War laid the foundation for one of the most conservative decades in the nation's history.

CHAPTER REVIEW

REVIEW QUESTIONS

1. *Explain the role of the United States in the global economy by 1920.*

2. *What were the assumptions underlying the Roosevelt Corollary? How did the doctrine affect U.S. relations with European nations and those in the Western Hemisphere?*

3. *What did President Wilson mean by "moral imperialism," and what measures were taken to apply this to Latin America?*

4. *How did the ratification of both the Eighteenth and Nineteenth Amendments suggest both the restrictive and democratizing nature of Progressivism?*

5. Why did Progressives see in the expansion of governmental powers in wartime an opportunity to reform American society?

6. What were the goals and methods of the Committee on Public Information during World War I?

7. What are governmental and private examples of coercive patriotism during the war? What were the effects of those efforts?

8. How did the "science" of eugenics fuel anti-immigrant sentiment?

9. How did World War I and its aftermath provide African Americans with opportunities?

10. What were the major causes—both real and imaginary—of the Red Scare?

11. Identify the goals of those pressing for global change in 1919 and of those who opposed them.

KEY TERMS

liberal internationalism (p. 739)

Panama Canal Zone (p. 741)

Roosevelt Corollary (p. 742)

Dollar Diplomacy (p. 743)

moral imperialism (p. 744)

Lusitania (p. 747)

Zimmermann Telegram (p. 748)

Fourteen Points (p. 748)

Selective Service Act (p. 751)

War Industries Board (p. 751)

Eighteenth Amendment (p. 756)

Espionage Act (p. 756)

Sedition Act (p. 756)

eugenics (p. 761)

National Association for the Advancement of Colored People (p. 769)

Great Migration (p. 770)

Tulsa massacre (p. 771)

Marcus Garvey (p. 772)

Red Scare of 1919–1920 (p. 775)

Versailles Treaty (p. 776)

League of Nations (p. 776)

Go to 📖 INQUIZITIVE

To see what you know—and learn what you've missed—with personalized feedback along the way.

CHAPTER 20

FROM BUSINESS CULTURE TO GREAT DEPRESSION

THE TWENTIES, 1920–1932

FOCUS QUESTIONS

- *Who benefited and who suffered in the new consumer society of the 1920s?*

- *In what ways did the government promote business interests in the 1920s?*

- *Why did the protection of civil liberties gain importance in the 1920s?*

- *What were the major flash points between fundamentalism and pluralism in the 1920s?*

- *What were the causes of the Great Depression, and how effective were the government's responses by 1932?*

In May 1920, at the height of the postwar Red Scare, police arrested two Italian immigrants accused of participating in a robbery at a South Braintree, Massachusetts, factory in which a security guard was killed. Nicola Sacco, a shoemaker, and Bartolomeo Vanzetti, an itinerant unskilled laborer, were anarchists who dreamed of a society in which government, churches, and private property had been abolished. They saw violence as an appropriate weapon of class warfare. But very little evidence linked them to this particular crime. In the atmosphere of anti-radical and anti-immigrant fervor, however, their conviction was a certainty. "I have suffered," Vanzetti wrote from prison, "for things that I am guilty of. I am suffering because I am a radical and indeed I am a radical; I have suffered because I was an Italian, and indeed I am an Italian."

Although their 1921 trial aroused little public interest outside the Italian American community, the case of Sacco and Vanzetti attracted international attention during the lengthy appeals that followed. There were mass protests in many countries against their impending execution, including Argentina, France, and Italy. The movement to save their lives attracted the support of an impressive array of intellectuals in the United States and internationally, such as the novelist John Dos Passos, the poet Edna St. Vincent Millay, physicist Albert Einstein, and the Mexican muralist Diego Rivera. In response to the mounting clamor, the governor of Massachusetts appointed a three-member commission to review the case, headed by Abbott Lawrence Lowell, the president of Harvard University (and for many years an official of the Immigration Restriction League). The commission upheld the verdict and death sentences, and on August 23, 1927, Sacco and Vanzetti died in the electric chair. The **Sacco-Vanzetti case** laid bare some of the fault lines beneath the surface of American society during the 1920s. The case, the writer Edmund Wilson commented, "raised almost every fundamental question of our political and social system." It demonstrated how long the Red Scare extended into the 1920s and how powerfully it undermined basic American freedoms. It reflected the fierce cultural battles that raged in many communities during the decade. To many native-born Americans, the two men symbolized an alien threat to their way of life. To Italian Americans, the outcome symbolized the nativist prejudices and stereotypes that haunted immigrant communities. To Dos Passos, the executions underscored the success of the anti-radical crusade: "They are stronger. They are rich. They hire and fire the politicians, the old judges, . . . the college presidents." Dos Passos's lament was a bitter comment on the triumph of pro-business conservatism during the 1920s. For some international observers, the outcome belied America's claim of bringing freedom and democracy to the world. "America," commented one Danish newspaper, "which formerly was the country of liberty, has begun a new role: that of reaction . . . which is preparing to assume world hegemony."

In popular memory, the decade that followed World War I is recalled as the Jazz Age or the Roaring Twenties. With its flappers (young, sexually liberated women), speakeasies (nightclubs that sold liquor in violation of Prohibition), new musical and dance styles, and a soaring stock market fueled by easy credit and a get-rich-quick outlook, it seemed a time of experimentation and rebellion against moral rules inherited from the nineteenth century. Radio and movies spread mass culture throughout the nation, and Americans reveled in the new consumer goods the factories produced. Yet, in fact, the decade was one of profound tension between the growing ethnic and racial diversity of cities with their more secular and commercial culture and rural Americans, between traditional and "modern" Christianity, and between participants in the burgeoning consumer culture and those who did not share fully in the new prosperity. It was an era when U.S. cultural and economic influence continued to widen in the world as well as an era of profound political conservatism. The federal government retreated from earlier Progressive efforts to reign in the power of large corporations but, through Prohibition, became newly involved in curtailing Americans' personal freedoms.

THE BUSINESS OF AMERICA

A Decade of Prosperity

"The chief business of the American people," said Calvin Coolidge, who became president after Warren G. Harding's sudden death from a heart attack in 1923, "is business." Rarely in American history had economic growth seemed more dramatic, cooperation between business and government so close, and business values so widely shared. After a sharp postwar recession that lasted into 1922, the 1920s was a decade of prosperity. Productivity and economic output rose dramatically as new industries—chemicals, aviation, electronics—flourished and older ones like food processing and the manufacture of household appliances adopted Henry Ford's moving assembly line.

The automobile was the backbone of economic growth. The most celebrated American factories now turned out cars, not textiles and steel as in the nineteenth century. Annual automobile production tripled during the 1920s, from 1.5 to 4.8 million. General Motors, which learned the secret of marketing numerous individual models and stylish designs, surpassed Ford with its cheap, standardized Model T (replaced in 1927 by the Model A). By 1929, half of all American families owned a car (a figure not reached in England until 1980). The automobile industry stimulated the expansion of steel, rubber, and oil production, road construction, and other sectors of the economy. It promoted tourism and the growth of suburbs (already, some commuters were driving to work) and helped to reduce rural isolation.

During the 1920s, American multinational corporations extended their sway throughout the world. With Europe still recovering from the Great War, American investment overseas far exceeded that of other countries. The dollar replaced the British pound as the most important currency of international trade. American companies produced 85 percent of the world's cars and 40 percent of its manufactured goods. General Electric and International Telephone and Telegraph bought up companies in other countries. International Business Machines (IBM) was the world's leader in office supplies. American oil companies built new refineries overseas. American companies took control of raw materials abroad, from rubber in Liberia to oil in Venezuela.

One unsuccessful example of the global spread of American corporations was Fordlandia, an effort by the auto manufacturer Henry Ford to create a town in the heart of Brazil's Amazon rain forest. Ford hoped to secure a steady supply of rubber for car tires. But as in the United States, where he had compelled immigrant workers to adopt American dress and diet, he wanted to bring local inhabitants up to what he considered the proper standard of life (this meant, for example, forbidding his workers from using alcohol and tobacco and trying to get them to stop eating traditional Brazilian foods). Eventually, the climate and local insects destroyed the rubber trees that Ford's engineers, lacking experience in tropical agriculture, had planted much too close together, while the workers rebelled against the long hours of labor and regimentation of the community.

A New Society

During the 1920s, consumer goods of all kinds proliferated, marketed by salesmen and advertisers who promoted them as ways of satisfying Americans' psychological desires and everyday needs. Frequently purchased on credit through new installment buying plans, they rapidly altered daily life. Telephones made communication easier. Vacuum cleaners, washing machines, and refrigerators transformed work in the home and reduced the demand for domestic servants.

Boosted by Prohibition and an aggressive advertising campaign that, according to the company's sales director, made it "impossible for the consumer to *escape*" the product, Coca-Cola became a symbol of American life.

Americans spent more and more of their income on leisure activities like vacations, movies, and sporting events. By 1929, weekly movie attendance had reached 80 million, double the figure of 1922. Movies had been produced early in the century in several American cities, but shortly before World War I film-makers gravitated to Hollywood, a district of Los Angeles, attracted by the open space, year-round sunshine for outdoor filming, and varied scenery. In 1910, two French companies, Pathé and Gaumont, had been the world's leading film producers. By 1925, American releases outnumbered French by eight to one. In the 1920s, both companies abandoned film production for the more profitable business of distributing American films in Europe.

Radios and phonographs brought mass entertainment into Americans' living rooms. The number of radios in Americans' homes rose from 190,000 in 1923 to just under 5 million in 1929. These developments helped to create and spread a new celebrity culture, in which recording, film, and sports stars moved to the top of the list of American heroes. During the 1920s, more than 100 million records were sold each year. RCA Victor sold so many recordings of the great opera tenor Enrico Caruso that he is sometimes called the first modern celebrity. He was soon joined by the film actor Charlie Chaplin, baseball player Babe Ruth, and boxer Jack Dempsey. Ordinary Americans followed every detail of their lives. Perhaps the decade's greatest celebrity, in terms of intensive press coverage, was the aviator Charles Lindbergh, who in 1927 made the first solo nonstop flight across the Atlantic.

André Siegfried, a Frenchman who visited the United States four times, commented in 1928 that a "new society" had come into being, in which Americans considered their "standard of living" a "sacred acquisition, which they will defend at any price." In this new "mass civilization," widespread acceptance of going into debt to purchase consumer goods had replaced the values of thrift and self-denial, central to nineteenth-century notions of upstanding character.

The Limits of Prosperity

"Big business in America," remarked the journalist Lincoln Steffens, "is producing what the socialists held up as their goal—food, shelter, and clothing for all." But signs of future trouble could be seen beneath the prosperity of the 1920s. The fruits of increased production were very unequally distributed. Real wages for industrial workers (wages adjusted to take account of inflation) rose by one-quarter between 1922 and 1929, but corporate profits rose at more than twice that rate. The process of economic concentration continued unabated.

A handful of firms dominated numerous sectors of the economy. In 1929, 1 percent of the nation's banks controlled half of its financial resources. Most of the small auto companies that had existed earlier in the century had fallen by the wayside. General Motors, Ford, and Chrysler now controlled four-fifths of the industry.

At the beginning of 1929, the share of national income of the wealthiest 5 percent of American families exceeded that of the bottom 60 percent. A majority of families had no savings, and an estimated 40 percent of the population remained in poverty, unable to participate in the flourishing consumer economy. Improved productivity meant that goods could be produced with fewer workers. During the 1920s, more Americans worked in the professions, retailing, finance, and education, but the number of manufacturing workers declined by 5 percent, the first such drop in the nation's history. Parts of New England were already experiencing the chronic unemployment caused by deindustrialization. Many of the region's textile companies failed in the face of low-wage competition from southern factories or shifted production to take advantage of the South's cheap labor. Most advertisers directed their messages at businessmen and the middle class. At the end of the decade, 75 percent of American households still did not own a washing machine, and 60 percent had no radio.

The Farmers' Plight

Nor did farmers share in the decade's prosperity. The "golden age" of American farming had reached its peak during World War I, when the need to feed war-torn Europe and government efforts to maintain high farm prices had raised farmers' incomes and promoted the purchase of more land on credit. Thanks to mechanization and the increased use of fertilizer and insecticides, agricultural production continued to rise even when government subsidies ended and world demand stagnated. As a result, the price of farm products fell, farm incomes declined steadily, and banks foreclosed tens of thousands of farms whose owners were unable to meet mortgage payments.

For the first time in the nation's history, the number of farms and farmers declined during the 1920s. For example, half the farmers in Montana lost their land to foreclosure between 1921 and 1925. Extractive industries, like mining and lumber, also suffered as their products faced a glut on the world market. During the decade, some 3 million persons migrated out of rural areas. Many headed for southern California, whose rapidly growing economy needed new labor. The population of Los Angeles, the West's leading industrial center, a producer of oil, automobiles, aircraft, and, of course, Hollywood movies, rose from 575,000 to 2.2 million during the decade, largely because of an influx of displaced farmers from the Midwest. Well before the 1930s, rural America was in an economic depression.

The 1920s, however, was not simply a period of decline on the farm but of significant technological change. The mechanization of agriculture had been taking place since the mid-nineteenth century, especially in the West, but it now accelerated dramatically. New inventions came into widespread use on the Great Plains, especially the steam tractor and the disk plow, which killed weeds, chopped up the sod, and left the surface layer much easier to plant. Mechanization encouraged an increase in the scale of agriculture. From farms growing wheat to California orange groves, the western states became home to modern "factory farms," employing large numbers of migrant laborers. Massive irrigation projects completed in the previous decades made the Far West much more suitable for farming. Farm output boomed in previously arid parts of California, Arizona, New Mexico, and Texas. With immigration from Asia barred and Blacks unwanted, agribusinesses recruited workers from across the southern border, and immigrants from Mexico came to make up the vast majority of the West's low-wage farm migrants.

The Image of Business

Hollywood films spread images of "the American way of life" across the globe. America, wrote the historian Charles Beard, was "boring its way" into the world's consciousness. In high wages, efficient factories, and the mass production of consumer goods, Americans seemed to have discovered the secret of permanent prosperity. Businessmen like Henry Ford and engineers like Herbert Hoover were cultural heroes. Photographers such as Lewis Hine and Margaret Bourke-White and painters like Charles Sheeler celebrated the beauty of machines and factories. *The Man Nobody Knows*, a 1925 best-seller by advertising executive Bruce Barton, portrayed Jesus Christ as "the greatest advertiser of his day, . . . a virile go-getting he-man of business," who "picked twelve men from the bottom ranks and forged a great organization."

Kansas agricultural worker breaking new ground with a disk plow, which eased the task of readying the sod of the Great Plains for planting and encouraged the emergence of larger farms.

Persuaded by the success of World War I's Committee on Public Information, numerous firms established public relations departments to justify corporate practices to the public and counteract its long-standing distrust of big business. They succeeded in changing popular attitudes toward Wall Street. Congressional hearings of 1912–1914 headed by Louisiana congressman Arsène Pujo had laid bare the manipulation of stock prices by a Wall Street "money trust," reinforcing the widespread view of the stock market as a place where insiders fleeced small investors. But in the 1920s, as the steadily rising price of stocks made front-page news, the market attracted more investors. Many assumed that stock values would rise forever. By 1928, an estimated 1.5 million Americans owned stock—still a small minority of the country's 28 million families, but far more than in the past.

The Decline of Labor

With the defeat of the labor upsurge of 1919 and the dismantling of the wartime regulatory state, business appropriated the rhetoric of Americanism and "industrial freedom" as weapons against labor unions. Some corporations during the 1920s implemented a new style of management. They provided their employees with private pensions and medical insurance plans, job security, and greater workplace safety. They established sports programs to occupy their employees' leisure time. They spoke of "welfare capitalism," a more socially conscious kind of business leadership, and trumpeted the fact that they now paid more attention to the "human factor" in employment.

At the same time, however, employers in the 1920s embraced the American Plan, at whose core stood the open shop—a workplace free of both government regulation and unions, except, in some cases, "company unions" created and controlled by management. Collective bargaining, declared one group of employers, represented "an infringement of personal liberty and a menace to the institutions of a free people." Prosperity, they insisted, depended on giving business complete freedom of action. This message was reinforced in a propaganda campaign that linked unionism and socialism as examples of the sinister influence of foreigners on American life. Even the most forward-looking companies continued to employ strikebreakers, private detectives, and the blacklisting of union organizers to prevent or defeat strikes.

During the 1920s, organized labor lost more than 2 million members, and unions agreed to demand after demand by employers in an effort to stave off complete elimination. In cities like Minneapolis, New Orleans, and Seattle, once centers of thriving labor movements, unions all but disappeared. Uprisings by the most downtrodden workers did occur sporadically throughout the decade. Southern textile mills witnessed desperate strikes by workers who charged employers with "making slaves out of the men and women" who labored there. Facing the combined opposition of business, local politicians, and the courts, as well as the threat of violence, such strikes were doomed to defeat.

The Equal Rights Amendment

The idealistic goals of World War I, wrote the young Protestant minister Reinhold Niebuhr, seemingly had been abandoned: "We are rapidly becoming the most conservative nation on earth." Like the labor movement, feminists struggled to adapt to the new political situation. The achievement of suffrage in 1920 eliminated the bond of unity between various activists, each "struggling for her own conception of freedom," in the words of labor reformer Juliet Stuart Poyntz. Black feminists insisted that the movement must now demand the vote for all women by abolishing restrictive poll taxes and literacy clauses in the South. They won little support from white counterparts, but they continued to work through organizations like the National Association of Colored Women for women's rights and civil rights. A few prominent feminists, including Elizabeth Cady Stanton's daughter Harriot Stanton Blatch, joined the rapidly diminishing Socialist Party, convinced that women should support an independent electoral force that promoted governmental protection of vulnerable workers.

The long-standing division between two competing conceptions of woman's freedom—one based on motherhood, the other on individual autonomy and the right to work—now crystallized in the debate over an **Equal Rights Amendment** (ERA) to the Constitution promoted by Alice Paul and the National Woman's Party. This amendment proposed to eliminate all legal distinctions "on account of sex." In Paul's opinion, the ERA followed logically from winning the right to vote. Having gained political equality, she insisted, women no longer required special legal protection—they needed equal access to employment, education, and all the other opportunities of citizens. To supporters of mothers' pensions and laws limiting women's hours of labor, which the ERA would sweep away, the proposal represented a giant step backward. Apart from the National Woman's Party, every major female organization, from the League of Women Voters to the Women's Trade Union League, opposed the ERA.

In the end, none of these groups achieved success in the 1920s. The ERA campaign failed, as did a proposed constitutional amendment giving Congress the power to prohibit child labor, which farm groups and business organizations opposed. In 1929, Congress repealed the Sheppard-Towner Act of 1921, a major achievement of the maternalist reformers that had provided federal assistance to programs for infant and child health.

Women's Freedom

If political feminism faded, the prewar feminist demand for personal freedom gained new traction in the vast consumer marketplace and in the actual behavior of the decade's much publicized liberated young woman. Female liberation resurfaced as a lifestyle, the stuff of advertising and mass entertainment stripped of its earlier associations with political and economic radicalism. At a moment when the government sharply curtailed the personal liberty of Americans through the Eighteenth Amendment (ushering in Prohibition), the **flapper**, with her bobbed hair, short skirts, drinking, and public smoking, epitomized the change in standards of sexual behavior, at least in large cities, and became a popular symbol of cultural rebellion against the Prohibition law. She frequented dance halls and music clubs where dances like the Charleston and the sounds of jazz, first popular in Black communities, now found wider audiences.

What had been scandalous a generation earlier—women's self-conscious pursuit of personal pleasure—became a device to market goods from automobiles to cigarettes. In 1904, a woman had been arrested for smoking in public

(*Left*) Advertisers marketed cigarettes to women as symbols of female independence. The August 27, 1925, cover of *Life* magazine shows a young man and a young woman dressed identically at the beach in revealing bathing suits (by 1920s standards), both enjoying cigarettes. (*Right*) An ad for a washing machine promises to liberate women from the "slavery" of everyday laundering at home.

in New York City. Two decades later, Edward Bernays, the "father" of modern public relations, masterminded a campaign to persuade women to smoke, dubbing cigarettes women's "torches of freedom." The new freedom, however, was available only during one phase of a woman's life. Once she married, what Jane Addams had called the "family claim" still ruled. And marriage, according to one advertisement, remained "the one pursuit that stands foremost in the mind of every girl and woman." Having found a husband, women were expected to seek freedom within the confines of the home, finding "liberation," according to the advertisements, in the use of new labor-saving appliances.

BUSINESS AND GOVERNMENT

The Republican Era

Government policies reflected the pro-business ethos of the 1920s. Recalling the era's prosperity, one stockbroker later remarked, "God, J. P. Morgan and the Republican Party were going to keep everything going forever." Business lobbyists dominated Republican national conventions. They called on the federal government to lower taxes on personal incomes and business profits, maintain high tariffs, and support employers' continuing campaign against unions. The administrations of Warren G. Harding and Calvin Coolidge obliged. "Never before, here or anywhere else," declared the *Wall Street Journal*, "has a government been so completely fused with business." The two presidents appointed so many pro-business members of the Federal Reserve Board, the Federal Trade Commission, and other Progressive-era agencies that, complained Nebraska senator George W. Norris, they in effect repealed the regulatory system. The Harding administration did support Secretary of Commerce Herbert Hoover's successful effort to persuade the steel industry to reduce the workday from twelve to eight hours. But it resumed the practice of obtaining court injunctions to suppress strikes, as in a 1922 walkout of 250,000 railroad workers protesting a wage cut.

Under William Howard Taft, appointed chief justice in 1921, the Supreme Court remained strongly conservative. A resurgence of laissez-faire jurisprudence eclipsed the Progressive ideal of a socially active national state. The Court struck down a federal law that barred goods produced by child labor from interstate commerce. It even repudiated *Muller v. Oregon* (see Chapter 18) in a 1923 decision (*Adkins v. Children's Hospital*) overturning a minimum wage law for women in Washington, D.C. Now that women enjoyed the vote, the justices declared, they were entitled to the same workplace freedom as men. "This," lamented Florence Kelley, "is a new Dred Scott decision," which, in the name of liberty of contract, "fills those words with the bitterest and most cruel mockery."

Though the Court sided against labor regulation, it backed aggressive Prohibition enforcement. Most notably, the Court sided with the expansion of federal surveillance power in the 1928 decision **Olmstead v. United States**. The decision gave the green light to the federal government's use of wiretapping (listening in on private telephone conversations) to gain evidence to prosecute suspected criminals. In an influential dissent, Justice Louis Brandeis argued that wiretapping without a warrant constituted an unjustifiable violation by the government of citizens' reasonable expectation of privacy and the "right to be let alone—the most comprehensive of rights and the right most favored by civilized men."

Prohibition Enforcement

Prohibition, as the *Olmstead* case suggests, expanded the role of the government in crime control and the government's visibility, outside of wartime, in the lives of ordinary Americans. Declaring an entire industry illegal, the Eighteenth Amendment and the National Prohibition Act (passed by Congress to enforce the law) created a new category of crime, which the Prohibition Bureau, the Coast Guard, Customs Bureau, the newly established Border Patrol, along with state and local police, sought to rein in. Federal and state officials, however, were no match for the increasingly powerful liquor supply rings. With fabulous profits to be made, illegal manufacturers and traders paid off judges, politicians, and police. Despite rampant corruption, Prohibition was enforced, albeit selectively. Wealthy Americans enjoyed illegal liquor from protected suppliers with little risk, but small-time violators suffered arrests, fines, and jail time.

Corruption in Government

Warren G. Harding had taken office as president in 1921 promising a "return to normalcy" after an era of Progressive reform and world war. His administration, however, quickly became one of the most corrupt in American history. Although his cabinet included men of integrity and talent, like Secretary of State Charles Evans Hughes and Secretary of Commerce Herbert Hoover, Harding also surrounded himself with cronies who used their offices for private gain. For example, Attorney General Harry Daugherty accepted payments not to prosecute accused bootleggers (traders in illegal alcohol). The head of the Veterans' Bureau, Charles Forbes, received kickbacks from the sale of government supplies. The most notorious scandal involved Secretary of the Interior Albert Fall, who accepted nearly $500,000 from private businessmen to whom he leased government oil reserves at **Teapot Dome**, Wyoming. Fall became the first cabinet member in history to be convicted of a felony.

The Election of 1924

The Harding administration's corruption did not prevent the Republican Party from winning the presidency in 1924. When Harding died in 1923, he was succeeded in office by Vice President Calvin Coolidge. Coolidge was a dour man of few words, but in contrast to his predecessor he seemed to exemplify Yankee honesty. Coolidge faced off against John W. Davis, a Wall Street lawyer nominated on the 103rd ballot by a badly divided Democratic national convention. The party had split between its urban, largely Catholic and immigrant supporters, hostile to Prohibition and the revival of the Ku Klux Klan (discussed on page 805), and its more rural, Protestant southern and western wing. The Democrats suffered a crushing defeat with Coolidge reelected in a landslide.

One-sixth of the electorate in 1924 voted for Robert La Follette, running as the candidate of a new Progressive Party, which called for greater taxation of wealth, the conservation of natural resources, public ownership of the railroads, farm relief, and the end of child labor. Although such ideas had been proposed many times before World War I, Coolidge described the platform as a blueprint for a "communistic and socialistic" America. Despite endorsements from veteran Progressives like Jane Addams and John Dewey and the American Federation of Labor, La Follette could raise no more than $250,000 for his campaign. He carried only his native Wisconsin. But his candidacy demonstrated the survival of some currents of dissent in a highly conservative decade.

Economic Diplomacy

Coolidge continued his predecessor's policies. He twice vetoed the McNary-Haugen bill, the top legislative priority of congressmen from farm states. This bill sought to have the government purchase agricultural products for sale overseas in order to raise farm prices. Coolidge denounced it as an unwarranted interference with the free market. Foreign affairs also reflected the close working relationship between business and government. "Any student of modern diplomacy," declared Huntington Wilson, a State Department official, "knows that in these days of competition, capital, trade, agriculture, labor and statecraft all go hand in hand if a country is to profit." The 1920s marked a retreat from Wilson's goal of internationalism in favor of unilateral American actions mainly designed to increase exports and investment opportunities overseas. Indeed, what is sometimes called the "isolationism" of the 1920s represented a reaction against the disappointing results of Wilson's military and diplomatic pursuit of freedom and democracy abroad. The United States did play host to the Washington Naval Arms Conference

From JUSTICE LOUIS BRANDEIS, DISSENTING OPINION, *OLMSTEAD V. UNITED STATES* (1928)

In 1928 in *Olmstead v. United States*, the Supreme Court ruled that government wire-tapping without a warrant did not violate constitutional protections. In an influential dissent, Justice Brandeis argued that wiretapping of telephones, a relatively recent technology, was an even greater threat than "tampering with the mails." His dissent was notable for declaring a constitutional right to privacy and for presciently warning that new technologies might facilitate unforeseen forms of government surveillance, endangering liberty. (The Supreme Court reversed *Olmstead* in its 1967 *Katz v. United States* ruling, an important advance for civil liberties.)

When the Fourth and Fifth Amendments were adopted. . . . Force and violence were then the only means known to man by which a government could directly effect self-incrimination. . . . But 'time works changes, brings into existence new conditions and purposes'. Subtler and more far-reaching means of invading privacy have become available to the government. . . . to obtain disclosure in court of what is whispered in the closet.

. . . Whenever a telephone line is tapped, the privacy of the persons at both ends of the line is invaded, and all conversations between them upon any subject, and although proper, confidential, and privileged, may be overheard. Moreover, the tapping of one man's telephone line involves the tapping of the telephone of every other person whom he may call, or who may call him. . . .

The makers of our Constitution undertook to secure conditions favorable to the pursuit of happiness. . . . They conferred, as against the government, the right to be let alone—the most comprehensive of rights and the right most valued by civilized men. To protect that right, every unjustifiable intrusion by the government upon the privacy of the individual, whatever the means employed, must be deemed a violation of the Fourth Amendment. And the use, as evidence in a criminal proceeding, of facts ascertained by such intrusion must be deemed a violation of the Fifth. . . .

Decency, security, and liberty alike demand that government officials shall be subjected to the same rules of conduct that are commands to the citizen. In a government of laws, existence of the government will be imperiled if it fails to observe the law scrupulously. Our government is the potent, the omnipresent teacher. For good or for ill, it teaches the whole people by its example. Crime is contagious. If the government becomes a lawbreaker, it breeds contempt for law; . . . it invites anarchy. To declare that in the administration of the criminal law the end justifies the means—to declare that the government may commit crimes in order to secure the conviction of a private criminal—would bring terrible retribution. Against that pernicious doctrine this court should resolutely set its face.

From MAJORITY OPINION, JUSTICE JAMES C. MCREYNOLDS, IN *MEYER V. NEBRASKA* (1923)

A landmark in the development of civil liberties, the Supreme Court's decision in *Meyer v. Nebraska* rebuked the coercive Americanization impulse of World War I, overturning a Nebraska law that required all school instruction to take place in English.

The problem for our determination is whether the statute [prohibiting instruction in a language other than English] as construed and applied unreasonably infringes the liberty guaranteed . . . by the Fourteenth Amendment. . . .

The American people have always regarded education and acquisition of knowledge as matters of supreme importance which should be diligently promoted. . . . The calling always has been regarded as useful and honorable, essential, indeed, to the public welfare. Mere knowledge of the German language cannot reasonably be regarded as harmful. Heretofore it has been commonly looked upon as helpful and desirable. [Meyer] taught this language in school as part of his occupation. His right to teach and the right of parents to engage him so to instruct their children, we think, are within the liberty of the Amendment.

It is said the purpose of the legislation was to promote civil development by inhibiting training and education of the immature in foreign tongues and ideals before they could learn English and acquire American ideals. . . . It is also affirmed that the foreign born population is very large, that certain communities commonly use foreign words, follow foreign leaders, move in a foreign atmosphere, and that the children are therefore hindered from becoming citizens of the most useful type and the public safety is impaired.

That the State may do much, go very far, indeed, in order to improve the quality of its citizens, physically, mentally, and morally, is clear; but the individual has certain fundamental rights which must be respected. The protection of the Constitution extends to all, to those who speak other languages as well as to those born with English on the tongue. Perhaps it would be highly advantageous if all had ready understanding of our ordinary speech, but this cannot be coerced by methods which conflict with the Constitution. . . . No emergency has arisen which rendered knowledge by a child of some language other than English so clearly harmful as to justify its inhibition with the consequent infringement of rights long freely enjoyed.

QUESTIONS

1. *How does the decision in* Meyer v. Nebraska *expand the definition of liberty protected by the Fourteenth Amendment?*

2. *What does Brandeis identify as a threat to liberty?*

3. *What are the different rights these two documents emphasize and seek to protect?*

of 1922 that negotiated reductions in the navies of Britain, France, Japan, Italy, and the United States. But the country remained outside the League of Nations. Even as American diplomats continued to press for access to markets overseas, the Fordney-McCumber Tariff of 1922 raised taxes on imported goods to their highest levels in history, a repudiation of Wilson's principle of promoting free trade.

Much foreign policy was conducted through private economic relationships rather than governmental action. The United States emerged from World War I as both the world's foremost center of manufacturing and the major financial power, thanks to British and French debts for American loans that had funded their war efforts. During the 1920s, New York bankers, sometimes acting on their own and sometimes with the cooperation of the Harding and Coolidge administrations, solidified their international position by extending loans to European and Latin American governments. They advanced billions of dollars to Germany to enable the country to meet its World War I reparations payments. American industrial firms, especially in auto, agricultural machinery, and electrical equipment manufacturing, established plants overseas to supply the world market and take advantage of inexpensive labor. American investors gained control over raw materials such as copper in Chile and oil in Venezuela. In 1928, in the so-called Red Line Agreement, British, French, and American oil companies divided oil-producing regions in the Middle East and Latin America among themselves.

As before World War I, the government dispatched soldiers when a change in government in the Caribbean threatened American economic interests. Having been stationed in Nicaragua since 1912, American marines withdrew in 1925. But the troops soon returned in an effort to suppress a nationalist revolt headed by General Augusto César Sandino. Having created a National Guard headed by General Anastasio Somoza, the marines finally departed in 1933. A year later, Somoza assassinated Sandino and seized power. For the next forty-five years, he and his family ruled and plundered Nicaragua. Somoza's son was overthrown in 1979 by a popular movement calling itself the Sandinistas (see Chapter 26).

THE BIRTH OF CIVIL LIBERTIES

Among the casualties of World War I and the 1920s was Progressivism's faith that an active federal government embodied the national purpose and enhanced the enjoyment of freedom. Wartime and postwar repression, Prohibition, and the pro-business policies of the 1920s all illustrated, in the eyes of many Progressives, how public power could go grievously wrong.

This lesson opened the door to a new appreciation of civil liberties—rights an individual may assert even against democratic majorities—as essential elements of American freedom. Building on prewar struggles for freedom of expression by labor unions, socialists, and birth-control advocates, some reformers now developed a greater appreciation of the necessity of vibrant, unrestricted political debate. In the name of a "new freedom for the individual," the 1920s saw the birth of a coherent concept of civil liberties and the beginnings of significant legal protection for freedom of speech against the government.

Censorship

Wartime repression continued into the 1920s. Under the heading "Sweet Land of Liberty," *The Nation* magazine in 1923 detailed recent examples of the degradation of American freedom—lynchings in Alabama, Arkansas, and Florida; the beating by Columbia University students of an undergraduate who had written a letter defending freedom of speech and the press; the arrest of a union leader in New Jersey and 400 members of the IWW in California; a refusal to allow a socialist to speak in Pennsylvania. Throughout the 1920s, artistic works with sexual themes were subjected to rigorous censorship. The Postal Service removed from the mails books it deemed obscene. The Customs Service barred works by the sixteenth-century French satirist Rabelais, the modern novelist James Joyce, and many others from entering the country. A local crusade against indecency made the phrase "Banned in Boston" a term of ridicule among upholders of artistic freedom. Boston's Watch and Ward Committee excluded sixty-five books from the city's bookstores, including works by the novelists Upton Sinclair, Theodore Dreiser, and Ernest Hemingway.

The Woman's Christian Temperance Union, a powerful grassroots organization that had been key to winning national Prohibition, campaigned in the 1920s for the government to regulate Hollywood movie plots whose content, they believed, lowered standards of morality. Faced with such campaigns, the film industry adopted the Hays code in 1930, a sporadically enforced set of guidelines that prohibited movies from depicting nudity, long kisses, and adultery, and barred scripts that portrayed clergymen in a negative light or criminals sympathetically. Filmmakers hoped that self-censorship would prevent censorship by local governments, a not uncommon occurrence since the courts deemed movies a business subject to regulation, not a form of expression. Not until 1951, in a case involving *The Miracle*, a film many Catholics found offensive, would the Supreme Court declare movies an artistic form protected by the First Amendment.

The Lost Generation

Faced with censorship campaigns and Prohibition's curtailment of personal liberty, intellectuals ridiculed the dominant strands of American culture. H. L. Mencken, a pioneering satirical journalist, bristled with disdain for what he called the "boobus Americanus," the conformist, "moronic," "peasant," middle-class masses. Even as Europeans turned in increasing numbers to American popular culture and consumer goods, some came to view the country as a repressive cultural wasteland. British novelist D. H. Lawrence, who lived for a time in the United States, once commented that Americans prided themselves on being the "land of the free," but "the free mob" had destroyed the right to dissent. Dismayed with the conservatism of American politics, repressive moral campaigns, and the materialism of the culture, a number of influential artists and writers emigrated to Paris. This group of cultural exiles became known as the **Lost Generation** for their deep disillusionment with the ideals that had led the nation into war and the repression that followed in its wake. Novelists and poets like Ernest Hemingway, Gertrude Stein, and F. Scott Fitzgerald, among others, felt that Europe valued art and culture and appreciated unrestrained freedom of expression, including the right to drink legally.

A "Clear and Present Danger"

During World War I, the Unitarian minister John Haynes Holmes later recalled, "there suddenly came to the fore in our nation's life the new issue of civil liberties." The arrest of antiwar dissenters under the Espionage and Sedition Acts inspired the formation in 1917 of the Civil Liberties Bureau, which in 1920 became the **American Civil Liberties Union** (ACLU). For the rest of the century, the ACLU would take part in most of the landmark cases that helped to bring about a "rights revolution." Its efforts helped to give meaning to traditional civil liberties like freedom of speech and invented new ones, like the right to privacy. When it began, however, the ACLU was a small, beleaguered organization. A coalition of pacifists, Progressives shocked by wartime repression, and lawyers outraged at what they considered violations of Americans' legal rights, it saw its own pamphlets defending free speech barred from the mails by postal inspectors.

Prior to World War I, the Supreme Court had done almost nothing to protect the rights of unpopular minorities. Now, it was forced to address the question of the permissible limits on political and economic dissent. In its initial decisions, it dealt the concept of civil liberties a series of devastating blows. In 1919, the Court upheld the constitutionality of the Espionage Act and the conviction of Charles T. Schenck, a socialist who had distributed antidraft leaflets through the mails. Speaking for the Court, Justice Oliver Wendell Holmes declared that the First Amendment did not prevent Congress from prohibiting speech that presented a "clear and present danger" of inspiring illegal actions. Free speech, he observed, "would not protect a man in falsely shouting fire in a theater and causing a panic."

For the next half-century, Holmes's doctrine would remain the basic test in First Amendment cases. Since the Court usually allowed public officials to decide what speech was in fact "dangerous," it hardly provided a stable basis for the defense of free expression in times of crisis. A week after **Schenck v. United States**, the Court unanimously upheld the conviction of Eugene V. Debs for a speech condemning the war. It also affirmed the wartime jailing of the editor of a German-language newspaper whose editorials had questioned the draft's constitutionality.

The Court and Civil Liberties

Also in 1919, the Court upheld the conviction of Jacob Abrams and five other men for distributing pamphlets critical of American intervention in Russia after the Russian revolution. This time, however, Holmes and Louis Brandeis dissented, marking the emergence of a Court minority committed to a broader defense of free speech. Six years after *United States v. Abrams*, the two again dissented when the majority upheld the conviction of Benjamin Gitlow, a communist whose *Left-wing Manifesto* calling for revolution led to his conviction under a New York law prohibiting "criminal anarchy." "The only meaning of free speech," Holmes now declared, was that advocates of every set of beliefs, even "proletarian dictatorship," should have the right to convert the public to their views in the great "marketplace of ideas" (an apt metaphor for a consumer society). In approving Gitlow's conviction, the Court majority observed that the Fourteenth Amendment obligated the states to refrain from

Defendants in *United States v. Abrams*, on the day of their deportation to Russia in 1921. Jacob Abrams is on the right. They were convicted under the Espionage Act of 1918 for impeding the war effort by distributing pamphlets critical of the American intervention in Russia after the Russian revolution.

unreasonable restraints on freedom of speech and the press. The comment marked a major step in the long process by which the Bill of Rights was transformed from an ineffective statement of principle into a significant protection of Americans' freedoms.

The tide of civil-liberties decision making slowly began to turn. By the end of the 1920s, the Supreme Court had voided a Kansas law that made it a crime to advocate unlawful acts to change the political or economic system and one from Minnesota authorizing censorship of the press. The new regard for free speech went beyond political expression. In 1930, the Court threw out the conviction of Mary Ware Dennett for sending a sex-education pamphlet, *The Sex Side of Life*, through the mails. Three years later, a federal court overturned the Customs Service's ban on James Joyce's novel *Ulysses*, a turning point in the battle against the censorship of works of literature.

Meanwhile, Brandeis was crafting an intellectual defense of civil liberties on grounds somewhat different from Holmes's model of a competitive market in ideas. In 1927, the Court upheld the conviction of the prominent California socialist and women's rights activist Anita Whitney for attending a convention of the Communist Labor Party where speakers advocated violent revolution. Brandeis voted with the majority on technical grounds. But he issued a powerful defense of freedom of speech as essential to active citizenship in a democracy: "Those who won our independence believed . . . that freedom to think as you will and to speak as you think are indispensable to the discovery and spread of political truth. . . . The greatest menace to freedom is an inert people." A month after the decision, the governor of California pardoned Whitney, terming freedom of speech the "indispensable birthright of every free American." The intrepid Mrs. Whitney was soon back in court for violating a California law making it a crime to display a red flag. In 1931, the Supreme Court overturned the law as "repugnant to the guaranty of liberty contained in the Fourteenth Amendment." A judicial foundation for civil liberties was slowly being born.

THE CULTURE WARS

The Fundamentalist Revolt

Although many Americans embraced modern urban culture with its religious and ethnic pluralism, mass entertainment, and liberated sexual rules, others found it alarming. Many evangelical Protestants felt threatened by the decline of traditional values and the increased visibility of Catholicism and Judaism

A 1923 lithograph by George Bellows captures the dynamic style of the most prominent evangelical preacher of the 1920s, Billy Sunday.

because of immigration. They also resented the growing presence within mainstream Protestant denominations of "modernists" who sought to integrate science and religion and adapt Christianity to the new secular culture. "The day is past," declared Harry Emerson Fosdick, pastor of New York's First Presbyterian Church and a prominent modernist, "when you can ask thoughtful men to hold religion in one compartment of their minds and their modern world view in another."

Convinced that the literal truth of the Bible formed the basis of Christian belief, fundamentalists launched a campaign to rid Protestant denominations of modernism and to combat the new individual freedoms that seemed to contradict traditional morality. Their most flamboyant apostle was Billy Sunday, a talented professional baseball player who became a revivalist preacher. Between 1900 and 1930, Sunday drew huge crowds with a highly theatrical preaching style and a message denouncing sins ranging from Darwinism to alcohol. He was said to have preached to 100 million people during his lifetime—more than any other individual in history.

Much of the press portrayed **fundamentalism** as a movement of backwoods bigots. In fact, it was a national phenomenon. Even in New York City, the center of the new modern culture, Fosdick was removed from his ministry in 1924 (whereupon John D. Rockefeller Jr. built the interdenominational Riverside Church for him). Fundamentalism became an important strain of 1920s culture and politics.

The Scopes Trial

In 1925, a trial in Tennessee threw into sharp relief the division between traditional values and modern, secular culture. John Scopes, a teacher in a Tennessee public school, was arrested for violating a state law that prohibited the teaching of Charles Darwin's theory of evolution. His trial became a national sensation. The proceedings were even carried live on national radio.

The **Scopes trial** reflected the enduring tension between two American definitions of freedom. Fundamentalist Christians clung to the traditional idea of "moral" liberty—voluntary adherence to time-honored religious beliefs. The theory that man had evolved over millions of years from ancestors like apes contradicted the biblical account of creation. Those who upheld the Tennessee law identified evolutionists with feminists, socialists, and religious modernists, all of whom, they claimed, substituted human judgment for the word of God. To Scopes's defenders, including the American Civil Liberties Union, which had persuaded him to violate the law in order to test its constitutionality, freedom meant above all the right to independent thought and individual self-expression. To them, the Tennessee law offered a lesson in the dangers of religious intolerance and the merger of church and state.

The renowned labor lawyer Clarence Darrow defended Scopes. The trial's highlight came when Darrow called William Jennings Bryan to the stand as an "expert witness" on the Bible. Viewing the trial as a "duel to the death" between science and Christianity, he accepted Darrow's challenge. But Bryan revealed an almost complete ignorance of modern science and proved unable to respond effectively to Darrow's sarcastic questioning. Does the serpent really crawl on its belly as punishment for having tempted Eve in the Garden of Evil? When Bryan answered "yes," Darrow inquired how it got around before being cursed—on its tail? Asked whether God had actually created the world in six days, Bryan replied that these should be understood as ages, "not six days of twenty-four hours"—thus opening the door to the very nonliteral interpretation of the Bible fundamentalists rejected.

The jury found Scopes guilty, although the Tennessee Supreme Court later overturned the decision on a technicality. Shortly after the trial ended, Bryan died and the movement for anti-evolution laws disintegrated. Fundamentalists retreated for many years from battles over public education, preferring to build their own schools and colleges where teaching could be done as they saw fit and preachers were trained to spread their interpretation of Christianity. The battle would be rejoined, however, toward the end of the twentieth century, when fundamentalism reemerged as an important force in politics. To this day, the teaching of the theory of evolution in public schools arouses intense debate in parts of the United States.

The Second Klan

Few features of urban life seemed more alien to rural and small-town native-born Protestants than their immigrant populations and cultures. The wartime obsession with "100 percent Americanism" continued into the 1920s, a decade of citizenship education programs in public schools, legally sanctioned visits to immigrants' homes to investigate their household arrangements, and vigorous efforts by employers to instill appreciation for "American values." Only "an agile and determined immigrant," commented the *Chicago Tribune*, could "hope to escape Americanization by at least one of the many processes now being prepared for his special benefit." In 1922, Oregon became the only state ever to require all students to attend public schools—a measure aimed, said the state's attorney general, at abolishing parochial education and preventing "bolshevists, syndicalists and communists" from organizing their own schools.

A Ku Klux Klan parade in Red Bank, New Jersey, on Armistice Day in 1925 shows the Klan's national reach and strength during the era. Unlike the Klan of the Reconstruction era, the second Klan was more powerful in the North and West than in the South.

The most menacing expression of the idea that enjoyment of American freedom should be limited on religious, ethnic, and racial grounds was the resurgence of the Ku Klux Klan. The Klan had been reborn in 1915 in Atlanta, Georgia, to defend native-born white Protestant supremacy. Only a few thousand members joined its ranks until 1920 when membership snowballed. Post–World War I social conflict, new militancy among organized labor and Blacks, and more permissive sexual norms fueled fundamentalist Protestant anxieties over social change. Savvy promoters spread the Klan's message that it stood for "pure American values." The Klan's claim that it would "clean up" communities and put bootleggers and moonshiners out of business contributed to its growth among the American-born white Protestant religious men and women who strongly supported Prohibition.

By the mid-1920s, the Ku Klux Klan claimed between 3 and 5 million members, many of whom held respected positions in their communities. It sank deep roots not only in the South but also in the Midwest and parts of the West and North, for a time controlling the Republican Party in Indiana and Colorado. In southern California, southern Illinois, and other Klan enclaves, the Klan held large marches, cross-burnings, and auto parades making the Klan a visible (and frightening) presence. American civilization, it insisted, was endangered not only by Blacks but also by immigrants—especially Jews and Catholics—and all the forces that endangered "individual liberty": feminism, unions, immorality, and giant corporations. In some regions, the Klan supplied manpower for police anti-liquor raids, targeting heavily immigrant and Catholic communities. In places like Youngtown and Niles, Ohio, immigrants fought back against such raids. The violent social conflict that resulted eroded support for the Klan and eventually for Prohibition.

Closing the Golden Door

The Klan's influence faded after 1925, but the Klan's attacks on modern secular culture and political radicalism and its demand that control of the nation be returned to "citizens of the old stock" reflected sentiments widely shared in the 1920s. The decade witnessed a flurry of legislation that offered a new answer to the venerable question "Who is an American?" Immigration restriction had a long history. The Naturalization Act of 1790 had barred Blacks and Asians from naturalization, with the ban lifted for the former in 1870. Beginning in 1875, various classes of immigrants had been excluded, among them prostitutes, those deemed "likely to become a public charge," and those with contagious diseases. Nonetheless, prior to World War I virtually all the white persons who wished to pass through the "golden door" into the United States and become citizens were able to do so. During the 1920s, however, the pressure for wholesale immigration restriction became irresistible. One index of the changing political climate was that large employers dropped their traditional opposition. Fears of immigrant radicalism now outweighed the desire for cheap unskilled labor, especially since mechanization had halted the growth of the industrial labor force and the Great Migration of World War I had accustomed industrialists to employing African Americans.

A scene from a series of murals painted in 1933 by Thomas Hart Benton for Chicago's "Century of Progress" exposition—now displayed at Indiana University—shows scenes of Americans at work and at play. Benton's inclusion, at the center, of a Ku Klux Klan rally hints at the darker side of the politics and culture of the 1920s. The newspaperman at his typewriter symbolizes the role of the press in exposing the Klan's nefarious deeds.

In 1921, a temporary measure restricted immigration from Europe to 357,000 per year (one-third of the annual average before the war). Three years later, Congress permanently limited European immigration to 150,000 per year, distributed according to a series of national quotas that severely restricted the numbers from southern and eastern Europe. The Johnson-Reed, or Immigration, Act aimed to ensure that descendants of the old immigrants forever outnumbered the children of the new.

The 1924 law also barred the entry of all those ineligible for naturalized citizenship—that is, the entire population of Asia, even though Japan had fought on the American side in World War I. The only Asians still able to enter the United States were residents of the Philippines, who were deemed to be "American nationals" (although not citizens) because the islands had been U.S. territory since the Spanish-American War. Largely to bar further Philippine immigration, Congress in 1934 established a timetable for the islands' independence, which was finally achieved in 1946. The 1934 law established an immigration quota of fifty Filipinos a year to the mainland United States but allowed their continued entry into the Hawaiian Islands to work as plantation laborers.

The law of 1924 established, in effect, for the first time a new category— the **illegal alien**. With it came a new enforcement mechanism, the Border Patrol, charged with policing the land boundaries of the United States and empowered to arrest and deport persons who entered the country in violation of the new nationality quotas or other restrictions. Later associated almost exclusively with Latinos, "illegal aliens" at first referred mainly to southern and eastern Europeans who tried to sneak across the border from Mexico or Canada.

Native American Citizenship

Debates about the boundaries of citizenship in the 1920s provided an opportunity for Native American groups that had long campaigned for U.S. citizenship to gain a new hearing. Indian advocates for citizenship, such as Carlos Montezuma and the Society of American Indians (discussed in Chapter 18), pointed to the military service of Native American men during World War I to argue in its favor. Their campaign contributed to the passage of the 1924 **Indian Citizenship Act**, which conferred citizenship on all Indians in the United States. Many Native Americans had already obtained citizenship after accepting allotments under the Dawes Act, or through military service, but about one-third, approximately 100,000 Native Americans, lacked citizenship. The conferral of citizenship without consent, consultation, or need for an application, however, was sharply criticized by some Indian leaders who

IMMIGRATION QUOTAS UNDER THE JOHNSON-REED ACT (1924)

In 1921, Congress imposed temporary country-by-country immigration quotas, based on the number of persons counted from each nation in the 1910 census. Three years later it revised the quotas to further limit the number allowed to enter the country and changed the base date to 1890, before the arrival of most of the "new immigrants" from southern and eastern Europe. Countries in the Western Hemisphere, including Canada and Mexico, were not subject to quota limitations. The largest reductions applied to Italy (from which 283,000 immigrants had arrived in 1914) and Russia (255,000 in that year).

Country or Area of Birth	Immigration Quota
Africa (total of various countries)	1,100
Albania	100
Arabian Peninsula	100
Asia (total of various countries)	0
Bulgaria	100
Denmark	2,789
Germany	51,227
Great Britain	34,007
Greece	100
Hungary	473

Country or Area of Birth	Immigration Quota
Ireland	28,567
Italy	3,845
Latvia	142
Norway	6,453
Poland	5,982
Russia	2,248
San Marino	100
Spain	131
Sweden	9,561
Turkey	100

QUESTIONS

1. *What do the numbers tell us about which immigrants Congress considered most and least desirable?*

2. *Why do you think no quotas were established for the Western Hemisphere?*

viewed the legislation as another way for the federal government to dissolve Indian sovereignty. The Haudenosaunee (Iroquois) vocally refused U.S. citizenship, arguing that they were already citizens of their own nation that predated the United States.

Race and the Law

The new immigration law reflected the heightened emphasis on "race" as a determinant of public policy. By the early 1920s, political leaders of both North and South agreed upon the relegation of Blacks to second-class citizenship. But "race policy" meant far more than Black-white relations. "America must be kept American," declared President Coolidge in his annual message to Congress in 1923. His secretary of labor, James J. Davis, commented that immigration policy, once based on the need for labor and the notion of the United States as an asylum of liberty, must now rest on a biological definition of the ideal population.

The seemingly "scientific" calculation of the new quota system—based on the "national origins" of the American population—involved a highly speculative analysis of past census returns, with the results altered to increase allowable immigration by politically influential groups like Irish Americans. Non-whites were excluded altogether when calculating quotas—otherwise, Africa would have received a far higher quota than the tiny number allotted to it. But then, the entire concept of race as a basis for public policy lacked any rational foundation. The Supreme Court admitted as much in 1923 when it rejected the claim of Bhagat Singh Thind, an Indian-born World War I veteran, who asserted that as a "pure Aryan," he was actually white and could therefore become an American citizen. "White," the Court declared, was not a scientific concept at all, but part of "common speech, to be interpreted with the understanding of the common man" (a forthright statement of what later scholars would call the "social construction" of race).

Pluralism and Liberty

During the 1920s, some Americans challenged the idea that southern and eastern Europeans were unfit to become citizens, or could only do so by abandoning their traditions in favor of Anglo-Saxon ways. Horace Kallen, himself of German Jewish origin, in 1924 coined the phrase "cultural pluralism" to describe a society that gloried in ethnic diversity rather than attempting to suppress it. Toleration of difference was part of the "American Idea," Kallen wrote. Anthropologists like Franz Boas, Alfred Kroeber, and Ruth Benedict insisted that no scientific basis existed for theories of racial superiority or for the notion that societies and races could be ranked on a fixed scale running from "primitive" to "civilized."

These writings, however, had little immediate impact on public policy. In the 1920s, the most potent defense of a pluralist vision of American society came from the new immigrants themselves. Every major city still contained ethnic enclaves with their own civic institutions, theaters, churches, and foreign-language newspapers. Their sense of separate identity had been heightened by the emergence of independent nation-states in eastern Europe after the war. It would be wrong, to be sure, to view ethnic communities as united in opposition to Americanization. In a society increasingly knit together by mass culture and a consumer economy, few could escape the pull of assimilation. The department store, dance hall, and motion picture theater were as much agents of Americanization as the school and workplace. From the perspective of many immigrant women, moreover, assimilation often seemed not so much the loss of an inherited culture as a loosening of patriarchal bonds and an expansion of freedom. But most immigrants resented the coercive aspects of Americanization programs, so often based on the idea of the superiority of Protestant mainstream culture.

Mobilizing for Tolerance

In the face of immigration restriction, Prohibition, a revived Ku Klux Klan, and widespread anti-Semitism and anti-Catholicism, immigrant groups asserted the validity of cultural diversity and identified toleration of difference—religious, cultural, and individual—as the essence of American freedom. In effect, they reinvented themselves as "ethnic" Americans, claiming an equal share in the nation's life but, in addition, the right to remain in many respects culturally distinct. In 1924, the Catholic Holy Name Society brought 10,000 marchers to Washington to challenge the Klan and to affirm Catholics' loyalty to the nation. Throughout the country, organizations like the Anti-Defamation League of B'nai B'rith (founded in 1916 to combat anti-Semitism) and the National Catholic Welfare Council lobbied, in the name of "personal liberty," for laws prohibiting discrimination against immigrants by employers, colleges, and government agencies. The Americanization movement, declared a Polish newspaper in Chicago, had "not the smallest particle of the true American spirit, the spirit of freedom, the brightest virtue of which is the broadest possible tolerance." For many immigrants, for whom beer and wine were part of leisure and culture, Prohibition signified the coercive side of Americanization campaigns and represented a symbol of the era's intolerance. "It isn't foremost about thirst," explained one Chicago ethnic newspaper, "it was a rejection of

A Black family arriving in Chicago in 1922, as part of the Great Migration from the rural South.

morality through police handcuffs." Polish, Czech, German, and Italian ethnic leaders mobilized their communities and channeled their hostility to the law into the political process and became a potent political force in a more urban, liberal Democratic Party in 1928.

The efforts of immigrant communities to resist coerced Americanization broadened the definition of liberty for all Americans. In landmark decisions, the Supreme Court struck down Oregon's law requiring all students to attend public schools and Nebraska's prohibiting teaching in a language other than English—one of the anti-German measures of World War I. "The protection of the Constitution," the decision in *Meyer v. Nebraska* (1923) declared, "extends to all, to those who speak other languages as well as to those born with English on the tongue," a startling rebuke to enforced Americanization. The decision expanded the freedom of all immigrant groups. In its aftermath, federal courts overturned various Hawaii laws imposing special taxes and regulations on private Japanese-language schools. In these cases, the Court also interpreted the Fourteenth Amendment's guarantee of equal liberty to include the right to "marry, establish a home and bring up children" and to practice religion as one chose, "without interference from the state." The decisions gave pluralism a constitutional foundation and paved the way for the Court's elaboration, two generations later, of a constitutional right to privacy.

The Emergence of Harlem

The 1920s also witnessed an upsurge of self-consciousness among Black Americans, especially in the North's urban ghettos. With European immigration all but halted, the Great Migration of World War I continued apace. Nearly 1 million Blacks left the South during the 1920s, and the Black population of New York, Chicago, and other urban centers more than doubled. New York's Harlem gained an international reputation as the "capital" of Black America, a mecca for migrants from the South and immigrants from the West Indies, 150,000 of whom entered the United States between 1900 and 1930. Unlike the southern newcomers, most of whom had been agricultural workers, the West Indians included a large number of well-educated professional and white-collar workers. Their encounter with American racism appalled them. "I had heard of prejudice in America," wrote the poet and novelist Claude McKay, who emigrated from Jamaica in 1912, "but never dreamed of it being so intensely bitter."

The 1920s became famous for "slumming," as groups of whites visited Harlem's dance halls, jazz clubs, and speakeasies in search of exotic adventure. The illegal nightclubs, run by organized criminals, clustered in the section of the city where the police permitted the illicit traffic to flourish and neighbors lacked connections to complain. African American newspapers denounced the conditions as a "direct slap in the face" of the Black electorate but to little avail. While the Harlem of the white imagination was a place freed from the restrains of mainstream American culture, the real Harlem was a community of widespread poverty, its residents confined to low-wage jobs and, because housing discrimination barred them from other neighborhoods, forced to pay exorbitant rents. Most Harlem businesses were owned by whites; even the famed Cotton Club excluded Black customers and employed only light-skinned dancers in its renowned chorus line. Few Blacks, North or South, shared in the prosperity of the 1920s.

The Harlem Renaissance

But Harlem also contained a vibrant Black cultural community that established links with New York's artistic mainstream. Poets and novelists like Countee Cullen, Langston Hughes, and Claude McKay were befriended and sponsored by white intellectuals and published by white presses. Broadway for the first time presented Black actors in serious dramatic roles, as well as shows like *Dixie to Broadway* and *Blackbirds* that featured great entertainers including the singers Florence Mills and Ethel Waters and the tap dancer Bill Robinson. At the same time, the theater flourished in Harlem, freeing Black writers and actors from the constraints imposed by white producers.

The term "New Negro," associated in politics with pan-Africanism and the militancy of the Garvey movement, in art meant the rejection of established stereotypes and a search for Black values to put in their place. This quest led the writers of what came to be called the **Harlem Renaissance** to the roots of the Black experience—Africa, the rural South's folk traditions, and the life of the urban ghetto. Claude McKay made the major character of his novel *Home to Harlem* (1928) a free spirit who wandered from one scene of exotic life to another in search of a beautiful girl he had known. W. E. B. Du Bois feared that a novel like McKay's, with its graphic sex and violence, actually reinforced white prejudices about Black life. Harlem Renaissance writings, however, also contained a strong element of protest. This mood was exemplified by McKay's poem "If We Must Die," a response to the race riots of 1919. The poem affirmed that Blacks would no longer allow themselves to be murdered defenselessly by whites:

> If we must die, let it not be like hogs
> Hunted and penned in an inglorious spot,
> While round us bark the mad and hungry dogs,
> Making their mock at our accursed lot. . . .
> Like men we'll face the murderous, cowardly pack,
> Pressed to the wall, dying, but fighting back!

Winston Churchill would invoke McKay's words to inspire the British public during World War II.

The celebrated case of Ossian Sweet, a Black physician who moved into a previously all-white Detroit neighborhood in 1925, reflected the new spirit of assertiveness among many African Americans. When a white mob attacked his home, someone (probably Sweet's brother) fired into the crowd, killing a man. Indicted for murder along with his two brothers, Sweet was defended by Clarence Darrow, fresh from his participation in the Scopes trial. The jury proved unable to agree on a verdict. A second prosecution, of Sweet's brother, ended in acquittal.

The Election of 1928

Few men elected as president have seemed destined for a more successful term in office than Herbert Hoover. Born in Iowa in 1874, the son of a blacksmith and his schoolteacher wife, Hoover accumulated a fortune as a mining engineer working for firms in Asia, Africa, and Europe. During and immediately after World War I, he gained international fame by coordinating overseas food relief. The British economist John Maynard Keynes, a severe critic of the 1919 Versailles Treaty, called Hoover "the only man" to emerge from the peace conference "with an enhanced reputation." He "had never known failure," wrote the novelist Sherwood Anderson. Hoover seemed to exemplify what was widely called the "new era" of American capitalism. In 1922, while serving as secretary of commerce, he published *American Individualism*, which condemned government regulation as an interference with the economic opportunities of ordinary Americans, but also insisted that self-interest should be subordinated to public service. Hoover considered himself a Progressive, although he preferred what he called "associational action," in which private agencies directed regulatory and welfare policies, to government intervention in the economy. Like many other Progressives, Hoover had supported Prohibition, and he continued to stand steadfast behind the law while in office. He favored better law enforcement, which he believed would ensure the law's success. The law, after all, had shut down the boisterous public old-time ethnic saloon and reduced drinking, especially among working-class men and women who could not afford the high cost of quality bootleg liquor.

Hoover quickly emerged as the Republican Party nominee after Calvin Coolidge decided not to run. Accepting the nomination, Hoover celebrated the decade's prosperity and promised that poverty would "soon be banished from this earth." His Democratic opponent was Alfred E. Smith, the first Catholic to be nominated by a major party. Born into poverty on New York's Lower East Side, Smith had become a fixture in Tammany Hall politics. Of Irish heritage, he became a spokesman for new immigrants and championed the values of pluralism and tolerance. During his three terms as governor of New York, he helped pass Progressive laws limiting the hours of working women and children and establishing widows' pensions. He denounced the Red Scare and signed legislation repealing New York's Prohibition enforcement law. He believed Prohibition unworkable and an encroachment on personal liberty. "Rum and Romanism," a shorthand epithet for Smith's support for repeal and his religion, became the focus of the race. Protestant ministers and religious publications denounced Smith. The Methodists, at their annual conference, took the unusual step of endorsing Hoover, justifying their entry into politics due to the "moral" issue at stake.

For the first time since Reconstruction, Republicans carried several southern states, reflecting the deep hostility among religious fundamentalists toward Smith's Catholicism, his immigrant heritage, and his support for repeal. "Hoover," wrote one previously Democratic southern newspaper editor, "is sprung from

American soil and stock," while Smith represented "the aliens." But Smith, who carried the nation's twelve largest cities, drew new immigrant groups to the Democratic Party, many of whom voted in a national presidential election for the first time. He also won significant support in economically struggling farm areas. With more than 58 percent of the vote, Hoover was elected by a landslide in 1928. But Smith's campaign helped to lay the foundation for the triumphant Democratic coalition of the 1930s based on urban ethnic voters, African Americans in northern cities, farmers, and the South.

The First War on Crime

In his inaugural address, Herbert Hoover identified the first critical business of the nation as the "failure of our system of criminal justice" calling for "reform, reorganization, and strengthening of our whole judicial and enforcement system." Crime, usually understood as a local problem, had become one of national concern, driven by the Prohibition era's heightened clamor over crime. State crime commissions, "tough on crime" legislation, and the first large-scale government effort to examine the causes of crime and to propose remedies, known as the **Wickersham Commission**, were established. Hoover systematized federal crime reporting, expanded the nation's prison system to relieve overcrowding, increased the purview of the Bureau of Investigation to include kidnapping (renamed the FBI in 1935), and doubled the size of the Border Patrol established in 1924. In 1930, Hoover established the Federal Bureau of Narcotics, a precursor to the modern Drug Enforcement Administration. In 1931, he won passage of the "Alien Act" providing for the deportation of noncitizens convicted of violating narcotics laws.

THE GREAT DEPRESSION

The Coming of the Depression

On October 21, 1929, President Hoover traveled to Michigan to take part in the Golden Anniversary of the Festival of Light, organized by Henry Ford to commemorate the invention of the lightbulb by Thomas Edison fifty years earlier. Hoover's speech was a tribute to progress, and especially to the businessmen and scientists from whose efforts "we gain constantly in better standards of living, more stability of employment . . . and decreased suffering." Eight days later, on Black Tuesday, the stock market crashed. As panic selling set in, more than $10 billion in market value (equivalent to more than ten times that amount in today's money) vanished in five hours. Soon, the United States and, indeed, the entire world found themselves in the grip of the **Great Depression**, the greatest economic disaster in modern history.

The **stock market crash** did not, by itself, cause the Depression. Even before 1929, signs of economic trouble had become evident. Southern California and Florida experienced frenzied real-estate speculation and then spectacular busts, with banks failing, land remaining undeveloped, and mortgages foreclosed. The highly unequal distribution of income and the prolonged depression in farm regions reduced American purchasing power. Sales of new autos and household consumer goods stagnated after 1926. European demand for American goods also declined, partly because industry there had recovered from wartime destruction.

A fall in the bloated stock market, driven ever higher during the 1920s by speculators, was inevitable. But it came with such severity that it destroyed many of the investment companies that had been created to buy and sell stock, wiping out thousands of investors, and it greatly reduced business and consumer confidence. Around 26,000 businesses failed in 1930. Those that survived cut back on further investment and began laying off workers. The global financial system, which was based on the gold standard, was ill equipped to deal with the downturn. Germany defaulted on reparations payments to France and Britain, leading these governments to stop repaying debts to American banks. Throughout the industrial world, banks failed as depositors withdrew money, fearful that they could no longer count on the promise to redeem paper money in gold. Millions of families lost their life savings.

Although stocks recovered somewhat in 1930, they soon resumed their relentless downward slide. Between 1929 and 1932, the price of a share of U.S. Steel fell from $262 to $22, and General Motors from $73 to $8. Four-fifths of the Rockefeller family fortune disappeared. William C. Durant, one of the founders of General Motors, lost all his money and ended up running a bowling alley in Flint, Michigan. In 1932, the economy hit rock bottom. Since 1929, the gross national product (the value of all the goods and services in the country) had fallen by one-third, prices by nearly 40 percent, and more than 11 million Americans—25 percent of the labor force—could not find work. U.S. Steel, which had employed 225,000 full-time workers in 1929, had none at the end of 1932, when it was operating at only 12 percent of capacity. Those who retained their jobs confronted reduced hours and dramatically reduced wages. Every industrial economy suffered, but the United States, which had led the way in prosperity in the 1920s, was hit hardest of all.

Americans and the Depression

The Depression transformed American life. Hundreds of thousands of people took to the road in search of work. Hungry men and women lined the streets

Unemployed men lined up outside a Chicago soup kitchen in 1931. Charitable institutions like this one were overwhelmed by the advent of the Great Depression.

of major cities. In Detroit, 4,000 children stood in breadlines each day seeking food. Thousands of families, evicted from their homes, moved into ramshackle shantytowns, dubbed Hoovervilles, that sprang up in parks and on abandoned land. Cities quickly spent the little money they had available for poor relief. In Chicago, where half the working population was unemployed at the beginning of 1932, Mayor Anton Cermak telephoned people individually, begging them to pay their taxes. "We saw want and despair walking the streets," wrote a Chicago social worker, "and our friends, sensible, thrifty families, reduced to poverty." When the Soviet Union advertised its need for skilled workers, it received more than 100,000 applications from the United States.

The Depression actually reversed the long-standing movement of population from farms to cities. Many Americans left cities to try to grow food for their families. In 1935, 33 million people lived on farms—more than at any previous point in American history. But rural areas, already poor, saw families reduce the number of meals per day and children go barefoot. With the future shrouded in uncertainty, the American suicide rate rose to the highest level in the nation's history and the birthrate fell to the lowest.

"The American way of life," the confident slogan of the consumer culture, and common sayings like "safe as a bank" took on a hollow ring. The image of big business, carefully cultivated during the 1920s, collapsed as congressional investigations revealed massive irregularities committed by bankers and stockbrokers. Banks had knowingly sold worthless bonds. Prominent Wall Streeters had unloaded their own portfolios while advising small investors to maintain their holdings. Richard Whitney, the president of the New York Stock Exchange, was convicted of stealing from customers, including from a fund to aid widows and orphans. He ended up in jail.

Resignation and Protest

Many Americans reacted to the Depression with resignation or blamed themselves for economic misfortune. Others responded with protests that were at first spontaneous and uncoordinated, since unions, socialist organizations, and other groups that might have provided disciplined leadership had been decimated during the 1920s. In the spring of 1932, 20,000 unemployed World War I veterans descended on Washington to demand early payment of a bonus due in 1945, only to be driven away by federal soldiers led by the army's chief of staff, Douglas MacArthur. Throughout the country, the unemployed demonstrated for jobs and public relief. That summer, led by the charismatic Milo Reno, a former Iowa Populist, the National Farmers' Holiday Association protested low prices by temporarily blocking roads in the Midwest to prevent farm goods from getting to market.

Only the minuscule Communist Party seemed able to give a political focus to the anger and despair. "The most fully employed persons I met during the Depression," one labor leader later recalled, "were the Communists." They "brought misery out of hiding," forming unemployed councils, sponsoring marches and demonstrations for public assistance, and protesting the eviction of unemployed families from their homes. The press discussed the idea that the United States was on the verge of a revolution. The insurance firm Lloyd's of London reported an upsurge in American requests for riot insurance. The Hoover administration in 1931 opposed efforts to save money by reducing the size of the army, warning that this would "lessen our means of maintaining domestic peace and order."

"No One Has Starved"

In the eyes of many Americans, President Hoover's response to the Depression seemed inadequate and uncaring. Leading advisers, including Andrew Mellon, the wealthy secretary of the treasury, told Hoover that economic downturns were a normal part of capitalism, which weeded out unproductive firms and encouraged moral virtue among the less fortunate. Businessmen strongly opposed federal aid to the unemployed, and many publications called for individual "belt-tightening" as the road to recovery.

The federal government had never faced an economic crisis as severe as the Great Depression. Few political leaders understood how important consumer spending had become in the American economy. Most held to the conventional view that government intervention to aid those who had lost their jobs would do little to spur economic recovery and would encourage

Americans to rely on government charity to address misfortune. In 1931, Hoover quoted former president Grover Cleveland from four decades earlier: "The Government should not support the people. . . . Federal aid . . . weakens the sturdiness of our national character."

Strongly opposed on principle to direct federal intervention in the economy, Hoover remained committed to "associational action." He put his faith in voluntary steps by business to maintain investment and employment—something few found it possible to do—and efforts by local charity organizations to assist needy neighbors. He called numerous conferences of business and labor leaders and established commissions to encourage firms to cooperate in maintaining prices and wages without governmental dictation. Hoover attempted to restore public confidence, making frequent public statements that "the tide had turned." But these made him increasingly seem out of touch with reality. By 1932, even *Fortune*, a business magazine, criticized Hoover for his response. The editors published a lengthy exposé of the dire economic conditions across the nation, juxtaposing images of breadlines and bonus marchers with Hoover's declaration that "No One Has Starved" making him seem callous and out of touch.

Cameramen at the White House during the presidency of Herbert Hoover. Hoover never became comfortable dealing with the mass media.

Hoover adamantly opposed offering direct relief for the unemployed: it would do them a "disservice," he told Congress. But one action Hoover did take to open up jobs drew upon the era's heightened nativism. Secretary of Labor William Doak proposed to "make jobs for American citizens" by sharply curtailing legal immigration and deporting undocumented immigrants. The campaign hit the Mexican American community in the Southwest especially hard. With encouragement and funding from the federal government, local officials conducted raids and used coercive scare tactics to urge Mexican Americans to "voluntarily" depart, transporting them out of the country on trains, buses, and ships. A majority of those who repatriated, over 400,000 people, were recent U.S. immigrants, but among the forcibly relocated were perhaps 200,000 Mexican American children who had been born in the United States and were therefore citizens.

The Worsening Economic Outlook

Such policing did little to improve economic conditions, and some administration remedies, like the **Smoot-Hawley Tariff**, which Hoover signed with some reluctance in 1930, made the economic situation worse. Raising the already high taxes on imported goods, it inspired similar increases abroad, further reducing international trade. A tax increase Hoover pushed through Congress in 1932 in an attempt to balance the federal budget further reduced Americans' purchasing power. Other initiatives inspired ridicule. When he approved funds to provide food for livestock, one observer remarked that the president would feed "jackasses but . . . not starving babies."

By 1932, Hoover had to admit that voluntary action had failed to stem the Depression. He signed laws creating the **Reconstruction Finance Corporation**, which loaned money to failing banks, railroads, and other businesses, and the Federal Home Loan Bank System, which offered aid to home owners threatened with foreclosure. Having vetoed previous bills to create employment through public-works projects like road and bridge construction, he now approved a measure appropriating nearly $2 billion for such initiatives and helping to fund local relief efforts. These were dramatic departures from previous federal economic policy. But further than this, Hoover would not go.

Freedom in the Modern World

In 1927, the New School for Social Research in New York City organized a series of lectures on the theme of Freedom in the Modern World. Founded eight years earlier as a place where "free thought and intellectual integrity" could flourish in the wake of wartime repression, the school's distinguished faculty included the philosopher John Dewey and historian Charles Beard (who had resigned from Columbia University in 1917 to protest the dismissal of antiwar professors). The lectures painted a depressing portrait of American freedom on the eve of the Great Depression. "The idea of freedom," declared economist Walton H. Hamilton, had become "an intellectual instrument for looking backward. . . . Liberty of contract has been made the be-all and end-all of personal freedom; . . . the domain of business has been defended against control from without in the name of freedom." The free exchange of ideas, moreover, had not recovered from the crisis of World War I. The "sacred dogmas of patriotism and Big Business," said the educator Horace Kallen, dominated teaching, the press, and public debate. A definition of freedom reigned supreme that celebrated the unimpeded reign of economic enterprise yet tolerated the surveillance of private life and individual conscience.

The prosperity of the 1920s had reinforced this definition of freedom. With the economic crash, compounded by the ineffectiveness of the Hoover administration's response, it would be discredited. By 1932, the seeds had already been planted for a new conception of freedom that combined two different elements in a sometimes uneasy synthesis. One was the Progressive belief in a socially conscious state making what Dewey called "positive and constructive changes" in economic arrangements. The other, which arose in the 1920s, centered on respect for civil liberties and cultural pluralism and declared that realms of life like group identity, personal behavior, and the free expression of ideas lay outside legitimate state concern. These two principles would become the hallmarks of modern liberalism, which during the 1930s would redefine American freedom.

CHAPTER REVIEW

REVIEW QUESTIONS

1. How did consumerism and the idea of the "American way of life" affect people's understanding of American values, including the meaning of freedom, in the 1920s?

2. Which groups did not share in the prosperity of the 1920s and why?

3. How did business practices and policies lead to a decline in union membership in the 1920s?

4. President Calvin Coolidge said that "the chief business of the American people is business." How did the federal government's policies and practices in the 1920s reflect this understanding of the importance of business interests?

5. Who supported restricting immigration in the 1920s and why? Why were they more successful in gaining federal legislation to limit immigration in these years?

6. Did U.S. society in the 1920s reflect the concept of cultural pluralism as explained by Horace Kallen? Why or why not?

7. Identify the causes of the Great Depression.

8. What principles guided President Hoover's response to the Great Depression, and how did this restrict his ability to help the American people?

9. What issues were of particular concern to religious fundamentalists in these years and why?

10. In what ways did the ideas about (and the reality of) proper roles for women change in these years?

KEY TERMS

Go to 🐰 INQUIZITIVE

To see what you know—and learn what you've missed—with personalized feed-back along the way.

CHAPTER 21

THE NEW DEAL

1932 – 1940

FOCUS QUESTIONS

- *What were the major policy initiatives of the New Deal in the Hundred Days?*

- *Who were the main proponents of economic justice in the 1930s, and what measures did they advocate?*

- *What were the major initiatives of the Second New Deal, and how did they differ from the First New Deal?*

- *How did the New Deal recast the meaning of American freedom?*

- *How did New Deal benefits apply to women and minorities?*

- *How did the Popular Front influence American culture in the 1930s?*

E arly in 1941, the unemployed Woody Guthrie, soon to become one of the country's most popular songwriters and folk singers, brought his family to Portland, Oregon. He hoped to star in a film about the great public-works projects under way on the Columbia River. Given a temporary job by the Bonneville Power Authority, the public agency that controlled the Columbia dams, Guthrie produced a song every day for the next month. One, "Roll on, Columbia," became a popular statement of the benefits that resulted when government took the lead in improving the lot of ordinary citizens:

And on up the river is Grand Coulee Dam,
The mightiest thing ever built by a man,

To run the great factories and water
   the land,
It's roll on, Columbia, roll on. . . .
Your power is turning our
   darkness to dawn.
So, roll on, Columbia, roll on.©

The Columbia River winds its way on a 1,200-mile course from Canada through Washington and Oregon to the Pacific Ocean. Because of its steep descent from uplands to sea level, it produces an immense amount of energy. Residents of the Pacific Northwest had long dreamed of tapping this unused energy for electricity and irrigation to promote economic development. But not until the 1930s did the federal government launch the program of dam construction that transformed the region. The project created thousands of jobs for the unemployed, and the network of dams produced abundant cheap power.

When the Grand Coulee Dam went into operation in 1941, it was the largest manmade structure in world history. It eventually produced more than 40 percent of the nation's hydroelectric power. The dam provided the cheapest electricity in the country for towns that sprang up out of nowhere, farms on what had once been deserts in eastern Washington and Oregon, and factories that would soon be producing aluminum for World War II airplanes. The project also resulted in large environmental and human costs. The Columbia River had once been filled with salmon. But the Grand Coulee Dam made no provision for the passage of fish, and the salmon all but vanished. The dam deprived the Colville confederated tribes, who lived along the waterway, of their fishing livelihoods, and the filling of the dam reservoir led to the flooding of thousands of acres of reservation land, submerging homes and burial grounds. Promises of a portion of revenue from the dam and cheaper electricity for reservation residents were broken.

The Grand Coulee Dam was part of what one scholar has called a "public works revolution" that transformed the American economy and landscape during the 1930s. The Roosevelt administration spent far more money on building roads, dams, airports, bridges, and housing than on any other activity.

Franklin D. Roosevelt believed regional economic development like that in the Northwest would promote economic growth, ease the domestic and working lives of ordinary Americans, and keep control of key natural resources in public rather than private hands. The environmental costs and the effect on Indian interests of such projects were largely ignored at the time, becoming a source of controversy only later in the century as Americans became more attuned to environmentalism and Indigenous rights. At the time, supporters emphasized the promise of "a world replete with more freedom and happiness than mankind has ever known."

The Columbia River project reflected broader changes in American life and thought during the **New Deal** of the 1930s. Roosevelt oversaw the transformation of the Democratic Party into a coalition of farmers, industrial workers, the reform-minded urban middle class, liberal intellectuals, northern African Americans, and, somewhat incongruously, the white supremacist South, united by the belief that the federal government must provide Americans with protection against the dislocations caused by modern capitalism. "Liberalism," traditionally understood as limited government and free-market economics, took on its modern meaning. Thanks to the New Deal, it now referred to active efforts by the national government to modernize and regulate the market economy and to provide citizens a baseline of security against economic calamity.

Freedom, too, underwent a transformation during the 1930s. The Depression had discredited the ideas that social progress rests on the unrestrained pursuit of wealth and that, apart from groups like widows and orphans, most poverty is self-inflicted. The New Deal elevated a public guarantee of economic security to the forefront of American discussions of freedom. The 1930s were a decade of dramatic social upheaval. Social and political activists, most notably a revitalized labor movement, placed new issues on the political agenda. When one writer in 1941 published a survey of democratic thought beginning in the ancient world, he concluded that what distinguished his own time was its awareness of "the social conditions of freedom." Thanks to the New Deal, he wrote, "economic security" had "at last been recognized as a political condition of personal freedom." Regional economic development like that in the Northwest reflected this understanding of freedom. So did other New Deal measures, including the Social Security Act, which offered aid to the unemployed and aged, and the Fair Labor Standards Act, which established a national minimum wage.

Yet while the New Deal significantly expanded the meaning of freedom, it did not erase freedom's boundaries. Its benefits flowed to industrial workers but not tenant farmers, to men far more fully than women, and to white Americans more than Blacks, Native Americans, or other non-whites who were deprived of basic rights.

THE FIRST NEW DEAL

FDR and the Election of 1932

It is indeed paradoxical that Franklin D. Roosevelt, who had been raised in privilege on a New York country estate, came to be beloved as the symbolic representative of ordinary citizens. But like Lincoln, with whom he is often

COLUMBIA RIVER BASIN PROJECT, 1949

■ Existing dam in 1949
▲ Dam proposed or under construction in 1949
▢ Tribal lands
— Columbia River basin boundary

Completed and proposed Columbia River project dams in 1949 and their proximity to Native American lands.

compared, Roosevelt's greatness lay in his willingness to throw off the "dogmas of the quiet past" (Lincoln's words) to confront an unprecedented national crisis. FDR, as he liked to be called, was born in 1882, a fifth cousin of Theodore Roosevelt. After serving as undersecretary of the navy during World War I, he ran for vice president on the ill-fated Democratic ticket of 1920 headed by James M. Cox. In 1921, he contracted polio and lost the use of his legs, a fact he carefully concealed from the public, concerned that his disability might negatively impact his political career and his projection of vigorous presidential leadership during the 1930s and World War II. Very few Americans realized that the president needed a wheelchair for mobility.

In his speech accepting the Democratic nomination for president in 1932, Roosevelt promised a "new deal" for the American people. But his campaign offered only vague hints of what this might entail. Roosevelt spoke of the government's responsibility to guarantee "every man . . . a right to make a comfortable living." But he also advocated a balanced federal budget and criticized his opponent, President Hoover, for excessive government spending, especially to enforce the increasingly unpopular Prohibition law. The biggest difference between the parties during the campaign was the Democrats' call for the **repeal** of Prohibition. This position solidified Roosevelt's support among urban, ethnic workers who despised the law. Democrats argued that repeal would provide jobs by reopening a shuttered industry and raise government revenue. Roosevelt suggested a greater awareness of the plight of ordinary Americans and a willingness to embark on new ways to address the Great Depression. Battered by the economic crisis, Americans in 1932 were desperate for new leadership, and Roosevelt won a resounding victory. He received 57 percent of the popular vote, and Democrats swept to a commanding majority in Congress.

The Coming of the New Deal

The Depression did not produce a single pattern of international public response. For nearly the entire decade of the 1930s, conservative governments ruled Britain and France. They were more interested in preserving public order than relieving suffering or embarking on policy innovations. In Germany, Adolf Hitler, leader of the Nazi Party, established one of the most brutal dictatorships in human history beginning in 1933. Hitler banned all political opposition and launched a reign of terror against Jews and others deemed to be "un-German." In the Soviet Union, another tyrant, Joseph Stalin, embarked on successive five-year plans that at great social cost produced rapid industrialization and claimed to have eliminated unemployment.

Roosevelt conceived of the New Deal as an alternative to socialism on the left, Nazism on the right, and the inaction favored by upholders of unregulated capitalism. He hoped to reconcile democracy, individual liberty, and economic recovery and development. "You have made yourself," the British economist John Maynard Keynes wrote to FDR, "the trustee for those in every country who seek to mend the evils of our condition by reasoned experiment within the framework of the existing social system." If Roosevelt failed, Keynes added, the only remaining choice would be between "orthodoxy" (that is, doing nothing) and "revolution."

Roosevelt did not enter office with a blueprint for dealing with the Depression. At first, he relied heavily for advice on a group of intellectuals and social workers who took up key positions in his administration. They included Secretary of Labor Frances Perkins, a veteran of Hull House and the New York Consumers' League who had been among the eyewitnesses to the Triangle fire of 1911; Harry Hopkins, who had headed emergency relief efforts during Roosevelt's term as governor of New York; Secretary of the Interior Harold Ickes, a veteran of Theodore Roosevelt's Progressive campaign of 1912; and Louis Brandeis, who had advised Woodrow Wilson during the 1912 campaign and now offered political advice to FDR while serving on the Supreme Court.

The presence of these individuals reflected how Roosevelt drew on the reform traditions of the Progressive era. But Progressivism, as noted in Chapter 18, was hardly a unified movement, and Roosevelt's advisers did not speak with one voice. Brandeis believed that large corporations not only wielded excessive power but also had contributed to the Depression by keeping prices artificially high and failing to increase workers' purchasing power. They should be broken up, he insisted, not regulated. But the "brains trust"—a group of academics that included a number of Columbia University professors—saw bigness as inevitable in a modern economy. The competitive marketplace, they argued, was a thing of the past, and large firms needed to be managed and directed by the government, not dismantled. Their view prevailed during what came to be called the First New Deal.

The Banking Crisis

"This nation asks for action and action now," Roosevelt announced on taking office on March 4, 1933. The country, wrote the journalist and political commentator Walter Lippmann, "was in such a state of confused desperation that it would have followed almost any leader anywhere he chose to go." FDR spent much of 1933 trying to reassure the public. In his inaugural address, he declared that "the only thing we have to fear is fear itself."

Roosevelt confronted a banking system on the verge of collapse. As bank funds invested in the stock market and corporate bonds lost their value and panicked depositors withdrew their savings, bank after bank closed its doors.

By March 1933, banking had been suspended in a majority of the states—that is, people could not gain access to money in their bank accounts. Roosevelt declared a "bank holiday," temporarily halting all bank operations, and called Congress into special session. On March 9, it rushed to pass the **Emergency Banking Act**, which provided funds to shore up threatened institutions.

Further measures soon followed that transformed the American financial system. The Glass-Steagall Act barred commercial banks from becoming involved in the buying and selling of stocks. Until its repeal in the 1990s, the law prevented many of the irresponsible practices that had contributed to the stock market crash. The same law established the Federal Deposit Insurance Corporation (FDIC), a government system that insured the accounts of individual depositors. And Roosevelt took the United States off the gold standard—that is, he severed the link between the country's currency and its gold reserves, thus making possible the issuance of more money in the hope of stimulating business activity. Together, these measures rescued the financial system and greatly increased the government's power over it. About 5,000 banks—one-third of the nation's total—had failed between 1929 and 1933, representing a loss of tens of millions of dollars to depositors. In 1936, not a single bank failed in the United States.

The NRA

The Emergency Banking Act was the first of an unprecedented flurry of legislation during the first three months of Roosevelt's administration, a period known as the **Hundred Days**. Seizing on the sense of crisis and the momentum of his electoral victory, Roosevelt won rapid passage of laws he hoped would promote economic recovery. He persuaded Congress to create a host of new agencies, whose initials soon became part of the language of politics—NRA, AAA, CCC. Never in American history had a president exercised such power in peacetime or so rapidly expanded the role of the federal government in people's lives.

The centerpiece of Roosevelt's plan for combating the Depression, the **National Industrial Recovery Act**, was to a large extent modeled on the government–business partnership established by the War Industries Board of World War I, although in keeping with FDR's nondogmatic approach, it also owed something to Herbert Hoover's efforts to build stronger government–business cooperation. Roosevelt called it "the most important and far-reaching legislation ever enacted by the American Congress." The act established the **National Recovery Administration** (NRA), which would work with groups of business leaders to establish industry codes that set standards for output, prices, and working conditions. Thus, "cutthroat" competition (in which companies took losses to drive competitors out of business) would be ended. These industry-wide arrangements would be exempt from antitrust laws.

The NRA reflected how even in its early days, the New Deal reshaped understandings of freedom. In effect, FDR had repudiated the older idea of liberty based on the idea that the best way to encourage economic activity and ensure a fair distribution of wealth was to allow market competition to operate, unrestrained by the government. And to win support from labor, section 7a of the new law recognized the workers' right to organize unions—a departure from the "open shop" policies of the 1920s and a step toward government support for what workers called "industrial freedom."

Headed by Hugh S. Johnson, a retired general and businessman, the NRA quickly established codes that set standards for production, prices, and wages in the textile, steel, mining, and auto industries. Johnson launched a publicity campaign to promote the NRA and its symbol, the Blue Eagle, which stores and factories that abided by the codes displayed. But after initial public enthusiasm, the NRA became mired in controversy. Large companies dominated the code-writing process. An inquiry conducted by the labor lawyer Clarence Darrow in 1934 concluded that they used the NRA to drive up prices, limit production, lay off workers, and divide markets among themselves at the expense of smaller competitors. Many anti-union employers ignored section 7a. The government lacked the manpower to police the 750 codes in effect by 1935. The NRA produced neither economic recovery nor peace between employers and workers. It did, however, help to undercut the pervasive sense that the federal government was doing nothing to deal with the economic crisis.

Government Jobs

The Hundred Days also brought the government into providing relief to those in need. Roosevelt and most of his advisers shared the widespread fear that direct government payments to the unemployed would undermine individual self-reliance. Indeed, one of the first measures of the Hundred Days had been the Economy Act, which reduced federal spending in an attempt to win the confidence of the business community. But with nearly a quarter of the workforce unemployed, spending on relief was unavoidable. In May 1933, Congress created the Federal Emergency Relief Administration, to make grants to local agencies that aided those impoverished by the Depression. FDR, however, much preferred to create temporary jobs, thereby combating unemployment while improving the nation's infrastructure of roads, bridges, public buildings, and parks.

In March 1933, Congress established the **Civilian Conservation Corps** (CCC), which set unemployed young men to work on projects like forest preservation, flood control, and the improvement of national parks and wildlife preserves. By the time the program ended in 1942, more than 3 million persons had passed through CCC camps, where they received government wages of $30 per month. The CCC made a major contribution to the enhancement of the American environment.

Public-Works Projects

One section of the National Industrial Recovery Act created the **Public Works Administration** (PWA), with an appropriation of $3.3 billion. Directed by Secretary of the Interior Harold Ickes, it contracted with private construction companies to build roads, schools, hospitals, and other public facilities, including New York City's Triborough (now Robert F. Kennedy) Bridge and the Overseas Highway between Miami and Key West, Florida. In

A map published by the Public Works Administration in 1935 depicts some of the numerous infrastructure projects funded by the New Deal. Among the most famous public-works projects are the Triborough Bridge in New York City, the Overseas Highway in Florida, and the Grand Coulee Dam in Washington. Overall, the New Deal spent $250 billion (in today's money) to construct, among other things, 40,000 public buildings, 72,000 schools, 80,000 bridges, and 8,000 parks.

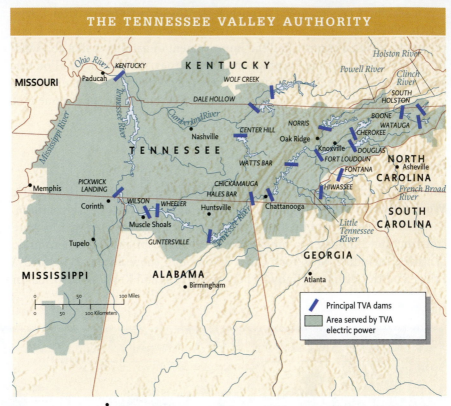

THE TENNESSEE VALLEY AUTHORITY

Principal TVA dams

Area served by TVA electric power

A map showing the reach of the Tennessee Valley Authority, covering all or parts of seven southeastern states.

November 1933, yet another agency, the Civil Works Administration (CWA), was launched. Unlike the PWA, it directly hired workers for construction projects. By January 1934, it employed more than 4 million persons in the construction of highways, tunnels, courthouses, and airports. But as the cost spiraled upward and complaints multiplied that the New Deal was creating a class of Americans permanently dependent on government jobs, Roosevelt ordered the CWA dissolved.

Some New Deal public-works initiatives looked to government-planned economic transformation as much as economic relief. The **Tennessee Valley Authority** (TVA), another product of the Hundred Days, built a series of dams to prevent floods and deforestation along the Tennessee River and to provide cheap electric power for homes and factories in a seven-state region where many families still lived in isolated log cabins. The TVA put the federal government, for the first time, in the business of selling electricity in competition with private companies. It significantly improved the lives of many southerners and offered a preview of the program of regional planning that spurred the economic development of the West.

The New Deal and Agriculture

Another policy initiative of the Hundred Days addressed the disastrous plight of American farmers. The **Agricultural Adjustment Act** (AAA) authorized the federal government to set production quotas for major crops and pay farmers to plant less in an attempt to raise farm prices. Many crops already in the field were destroyed. In 1933, the government ordered more than 6 million pigs slaughtered as part of the policy, a step critics found strange at a time of widespread hunger.

The AAA succeeded in significantly raising farm prices and incomes. But not all farmers benefited. Money flowed to property-owning farmers, ignoring the large number who worked on land owned by others. The AAA policy of paying landowning farmers not to grow crops encouraged the eviction of thousands of poor tenants and sharecroppers. Many joined the rural exodus to cities or to the farms of the West Coast.

The onset in 1930 of a period of unusually dry weather in the nation's heartland worsened the Depression's impact on rural America. By mid-decade, the region suffered from the century's most severe drought. Mechanized agriculture in this semiarid region had pulverized the topsoil and killed native grasses that prevented erosion. Winds now blew much of the soil away, creating the **Dust Bowl**, as the affected areas of Oklahoma, Texas, Kansas, and Colorado were called. A local newspaper described the situation in Cimarron County, Oklahoma: "Not a blade of wheat; cattle dying on the range, ninety percent of the poultry dead because of the sand storms, milk cows gone dry." One storm in 1934 carried dust as far as Washington, D.C. The drought and dust storms displaced more than 1 million farmers. John Steinbeck's novel *The Grapes of Wrath* (1939) and a popular film based on the book captured their plight, tracing a dispossessed family's trek from Oklahoma to California.

Another New Deal initiative, the Resettlement Administration, established in 1934, sought to relocate rural

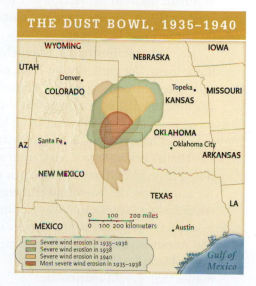

THE DUST BOWL, 1935–1940

Severe wind erosion in 1935–1936
Severe wind erosion in 1938
Severe wind erosion in 1940
Most severe wind erosion in 1935–1938

and urban families suffering from the Depression to communities planned by the federal government. Headed by Columbia University economist Rexford G. Tugwell, one of Roosevelt's advisers, it set up relief camps for migrant workers in California (many of whom had been displaced by the dust storms) and built several new communities, including Greenbelt just outside Washington, D.C.

The New Deal and Housing

Owning one's home had long been a widely shared American ambition. "A man is not a whole and complete man," Walt Whitman had written in the 1850s, "unless he owns a house and the ground it stands on." For many members of the middle class, home ownership was a mark of respectability. For workers, it offered economic security at a time of low wages, erratic employment, and limited occupational mobility. On the eve of World War I, a considerably higher percentage of immigrant workers than the native-born middle class owned their homes.

The Depression devastated the American housing industry. The construction of new residences all but ceased, and banks and savings and loan associations that had financed home ownership collapsed or, to remain afloat, foreclosed on many homes (a quarter of a million in 1932 alone). In 1931, President Hoover convened a Conference on Home Building and Home Ownership to review the housing crisis. The president called owning a home an American "birthright," the embodiment of the spirit of "enterprise, of independence, and of . . . freedom." Papers presented at the conference revealed that millions of Americans lived in overcrowded, unhealthy urban slums or in ramshackle rural dwellings. Private enterprise alone, it seemed clear, was unlikely to solve the nation's housing crisis.

Hoover's administration established a federally sponsored bank to issue home loans. Not until the New Deal, however, did the government systematically enter the housing market. Roosevelt spoke of "the security of the home" as a fundamental right akin to "the security of livelihood, and the security of social insurance." In 1933 and 1934, his administration moved energetically to protect home owners from foreclosure and to stimulate new construction. The Home Owners Loan Corporation and **Federal Housing Administration** (FHA) insured millions of long-term mortgages issued by private banks. At the same time, the federal government itself built thousands of units of low-rent housing. New Deal housing policy represented a remarkable departure from previous government practice. Thanks to the FHA and, later, the Veterans' Administration, home ownership came within the reach of tens of millions of families. It became cheaper for most Americans to buy single-family homes than to rent apartments.

Other important measures of Roosevelt's first two years in office included the establishment of the Federal Communications Commission to oversee the nation's broadcast airwaves and telephone communications; the creation of the Securities and Exchange Commission to regulate the stock and bond markets, and the ratification of the Twenty-first Amendment to the Constitution, which repealed Prohibition.

Taken together, the First New Deal was a series of experiments, some of which succeeded and some of which did not. They transformed the role of the federal government, constructed numerous public facilities, and provided relief to millions of needy persons. Public employment rescued millions of Americans from the ravages of the Depression. But while the economy improved somewhat, sustained recovery had not been achieved. Some 10 million Americans—more than 20 percent of the workforce—remained unemployed when 1934 came to an end.

The Court and the New Deal

In 1935, the Supreme Court, still controlled by conservative Republican judges who held to the nineteenth-century understanding of freedom as liberty of contract, began to invalidate key New Deal laws. First came the NRA, declared unconstitutional in May in a case brought by the Schechter Poultry Company of Brooklyn, which had been charged with violating the code adopted by the chicken industry. In a unanimous decision, the Court declared the NRA unlawful because in its codes and other regulations it delegated legislative powers to the president and attempted to regulate local businesses that did not engage in interstate commerce. In January 1936, the AAA fell in *United States v. Butler*, which declared it an unconstitutional exercise of congressional power over local economic activities. In June, by a 5-4 vote, the justices ruled that New York could not establish a minimum wage for women and children.

Having failed to end the Depression or win judicial approval, the First New Deal ground to a halt. Meanwhile, pressures were mounting outside Washington that propelled the administration toward more radical departures in policy.

THE GRASSROOTS REVOLT

Labor's Great Upheaval

The most striking development of the mid-1930s was the mobilization of millions of workers in mass-production industries that had successfully resisted unionization. "Labor's great upheaval," as this era of unprecedented militancy was called, came as a great surprise. Unlike in the past, however, the federal government now seemed to be on the side of labor, a commitment embodied in the National Industrial Recovery Act and in the Wagner Act (discussed later) of 1935, which granted workers the legal right to form unions. With the severe reduction of European immigration, ethnic differences among workers had diminished in importance. American-born children of the new immigrants now dominated the industrial labor force, and organizers no longer had to distribute materials in numerous languages as the IWW had done. And a cadre of militant labor leaders, many of them socialists and communists with long experience in organization, had survived the repression of the 1920s. They provided leadership to the labor upsurge.

American factories at the outset of the New Deal were miniature dictatorships in which unions were rare, workers could be beaten by supervisors and fired at will, and management determined the length of the workday and speed of the assembly line. In industrial communities scattered across the country, local government firmly supported the companies. "Jesus Christ couldn't speak in Duquesne for the union," declared the mayor of that Pennsylvania steel town. Workers' demands during the 1930s went beyond better wages. They included an end to employers' arbitrary power in the workplace, and basic civil liberties for workers, including the rights to picket, distribute literature, and meet to discuss their grievances. All these goals required union recognition.

Roosevelt's election as president did much to rekindle hope among those who called themselves "slaves of the depression," in the words of a worker writing to Secretary of Labor Frances Perkins, the first woman appointed to the U.S. cabinet. During the 1930s, many Americans wrote letters to the president and Perkins. These poignant letters described what a Louisiana sugar laborer called the "terrible and inhuman condition" of many workers. Labor organizers spread the message that the "political liberty for which our forefathers fought" had been "made meaningless by economic inequality" and "industrial despotism." "We are free Americans," declared the Steel Workers Organizing Committee. "We shall exercise our inalienable rights to organize into a great industrial union."

Labor's great upheaval exploded in 1934, a year that witnessed no fewer than 2,000 strikes. Many produced violent confrontations between workers and the local police. In Toledo, Ohio, 10,000 striking auto workers surrounded the Electric Auto-Lite factory, where managers had brought strikebreakers to take their jobs, leading to a seven-hour fight with police and the National Guard. In Minneapolis, a four-month strike by truck drivers led to pitched battles in the streets and the governor declaring martial law. San Francisco experienced the country's first general strike since 1919. It began with a walkout of dockworkers who demanded recognition of the International Longshoremen's Association and an end to the hated "shape up" system in which they had to gather en masse each day to wait for work assignments. The year 1934 also witnessed a strike of 400,000 textile workers in states from New England to the Deep South, demanding recognition of the United Textile Workers. Many of these walkouts, including those in Toledo, Minneapolis, and San Francisco, won at least some of the workers' demands. But the textile strike failed.

The Rise of the CIO

The labor upheaval led to the formation of a new labor organization, the **Congress of Industrial Organizations** (CIO) in 1935. In contrast to the American Federation of Labor's traditional policy of organizing workers by craft—welders or machine repairers, for example—the CIO sought to mobilize all workers in a given industry, such as steel manufacturing. Under the leadership of United Mine Workers president, John L. Lewis, the CIO aimed to create unions in the main bastions of the American economy. It aimed, said Lewis, at nothing less than to secure "economic freedom and industrial democracy" for American workers—a fair share in the wealth produced by their labor and a voice in determining the conditions under which they worked.

In December 1936, unions, most notably the United Auto Workers (UAW), a fledgling CIO union, unveiled the sit-down, a strikingly effective tactic that the IWW had pioneered three decades earlier. Rather than walking out of a plant, thus enabling management to bring in strikebreakers, workers halted production but remained inside. In the UAW's first **sit-down strike**, 7,000 General Motors workers seized control of the Fisher Auto Body plant in Cleveland. Sit-downs soon spread to GM factories in Flint, Michigan, the nerve center of automobile production. When local police tried to storm the Flint plants, workers fought them off. Democratic governor Frank Murphy, who had been elected with strong support from the CIO, declared his unwillingness to use force to dislodge the strikers. The strikers demonstrated a remarkable spirit of unity. They cleaned the plant, oiled the idle machinery, settled disputes among themselves, prepared meals, and held concerts of labor songs. Workers' wives shuttled food into the plant. "They made a palace out of what had been their prison," wrote one reporter. On February 11, General Motors agreed to negotiate with the UAW. Not until 1941 would the bitterly anti-union Henry Ford sign a labor contract. But by the end of 1937, the UAW claimed 400,000 members.

The victory in the auto industry reverberated throughout industrial America. Steelworkers had suffered memorable defeats in the struggle for unionization, notably at Homestead in 1892 and in the Great Steel Strike of 1919.

U.S. Steel, the country's single most important business firm, owner of an industrial empire that stretched across several states and employed more than 200,000 workers, had been among the strongest opponents of unionization. But in March 1937, fearing a sit-down campaign and aware that it could no longer count on the aid of state and federal authorities, the company agreed to recognize the Steel Workers Organizing Committee (forerunner of the United Steelworkers of America). Smaller steel firms, however, refused to follow suit. On Memorial Day 1937, company guards and Chicago police fired on a picnic of striking Republic Steel workers, killing ten persons. Not until 1942 would Republic sign a labor contract.

Union membership reached 9 million by 1940, more than double the number in 1930. The coming of the union, said a member of New York City's transit workers' organization, enabled workers "to go to our bosses and talk to them like men, instead of . . . like slaves." Unions demanded and won a say in workplace management, including the right to contest the amount and pace of work and the introduction of new technology. They gained new grievance procedures and seniority systems governing hiring, firing, and promotions. The CIO unions helped to stabilize a chaotic employment situation and offered members a sense of dignity and freedom.

Labor and Politics

Throughout the industrial heartland, the labor upsurge altered the balance of economic power and propelled to the forefront of politics labor's goal of a fairer, freer, more equal America. Unlike the AFL, traditionally hostile to government intervention in labor-management relations, the CIO put forward an ambitious program for federal action to shield Americans from economic and social insecurity, including public housing, universal health care, and unemployment and old age insurance.

Building on the idea, so prominent in the 1920s, that the key to prosperity lay in an American standard of living based on mass consumption, CIO leaders explained the Depression as the result of an imbalance of wealth and income. The role of unions, in cooperation with the government, they argued, was to "create a consumer's demand" by raising wages and redistributing wealth. Only in this way could society absorb the products that rolled off modern assembly lines. The pathbreaking 1937 agreement between the UAW and General Motors spoke of a "rate of pay commensurate with an American standard of living." By mid-decade, many New Dealers accepted the "underconsumptionist" explanation of the Depression, which saw lack of sufficient consumer demand as its underlying cause. They concluded that the government must act to raise dramatically wage earners' share of the national income.

Voices of Protest

Other popular movements of the mid-1930s also placed the question of economic justice on the political agenda. In California, the novelist Upton Sinclair won the Democratic nomination for governor in 1934 as the head of the End Poverty in California movement. Sinclair called for the state to use idle factories and land in cooperative ventures that would provide jobs for the unemployed. He lost the election after being subjected to one of the first modern "negative" media campaigns. Sinclair's opponents circulated false newsreels showing armies of unemployed men marching to California to support his candidacy and a fake endorsement from the Communist Party.

Huey Long, the "Kingfish" of Louisiana politics, in full rhetorical flight. The photo was probably taken in 1934, when Long was in the U.S. Senate but still running the state government.

The rise to national prominence of Huey Long offered another sign of popular dissatisfaction with the slow pace of economic recovery. Long's career embodied both Louisiana's Populist and Socialist traditions (Winn Parish, his home, had voted for both of these third parties) and the state's heritage of undemocratic politics. Driven by intense ambition and the desire to help uplift the state's "common people," Long won election as governor in 1928 and in 1930 took a seat in the U.S. Senate. From Washington, he dominated every branch of state government. He used his dictatorial power to build roads, schools, and hospitals and to increase the tax burden on Louisiana's oil companies.

One of the most colorful characters in twentieth-century American politics, Long launched the **Share Our Wealth movement** in 1934, with the slogan "Every Man a King." He called for the confiscation of most of the wealth of the richest Americans in order to finance an immediate grant of $5,000 and a guaranteed job and annual income for all citizens. In his inimitable style, Long explained his goal: "Let's pull down these huge piles of gold until there shall be a real job, not a little old sow-belly, black-eyed pea job but a real spending money, beefsteak and gravy . . . Ford in the garage . . . red, white, and blue job for every man." Long claimed a following of 5 million. He was on the verge of announcing a run for president when the son of a defeated political rival assassinated him in 1935.

Dr. Francis Townsend, a California physician, meanwhile won wide support for a plan by which the government would make a monthly payment of $200 to older Americans, with the requirement that they spend it immediately. This, he argued, would boost the economy. By the end of 1934, Townsend Clubs claimed more than 2 million members. Along with the rise of the CIO, these signs of popular discontent helped to spark the Second New Deal.

Religion on the Radio

Also in the mid-1930s, the "radio priest," Father Charles E. Coughlin, attracted millions of listeners with weekly broadcasts attacking Wall Street bankers and greedy capitalists, and calling for government ownership of key industries as a way of combating the Depression. Initially a strong supporter of FDR, Coughlin became increasingly critical of the president for what he considered the failure of the New Deal to promote social justice. His crusade would later shift to anti-Semitism and support for European fascism.

Other religious leaders of various denominations took advantage of the mass media to spread their beliefs. Many fundamentalists used the most modern techniques of communication, including the radio and popular entertainment, to promote their anti-modernist message. They found in the radio a way of bringing their views directly to ordinary Americans, bypassing established churches and their leaders. During the 1920s, Aimee Semple McPherson, a Los Angeles revivalist, had her own radio station, which broadcast sermons from the International Church of the Foursquare Gospel she had founded. McPherson also traveled the country as a revivalist preacher. Her sermons used elaborate sets, costumes, and special effects borrowed from the movie industry. In later decades, fundamentalist Christians would take advantage of television and the Internet to disseminate their religious and political views.

THE SECOND NEW DEAL

Spurred by the failure of his initial policies to pull the country out of the Depression and the growing popular clamor for greater economic equality, and buoyed by Democratic gains in the midterm elections of 1934, Roosevelt in 1935 launched the Second New Deal. The first had focused on economic recovery. The emphasis of the second was economic security—a guarantee that Americans would be protected against unemployment and poverty. "Boys," Roosevelt's relief administrator, Harry Hopkins, told his staff, "this is our hour. We've got to get everything we want—a [public] works program, social security, wages and hours, everything—now or never."

The idea that lack of consumer demand caused the Depression had been popularized by Huey Long, Francis Townsend, and the CIO. More and more New Dealers concluded that the government should no longer try to plan business recovery but should try to redistribute the national income so as to sustain mass purchasing power in the consumer economy. A series of measures in 1935 attacked head-on the problem of weak demand and economic inequality. Congress levied a highly publicized tax on large fortunes and corporate profits—a direct response to the popularity of Huey Long's Share Our Wealth campaign. It created the Rural Electrification Agency (REA) to bring electric power to homes that lacked it—80 percent of farms were still without electricity in 1934—in part to enable more Americans to purchase household appliances.

The REA proved to be one of the Second New Deal's most successful programs. By 1950, 90 percent of the nation's farms had been wired for electricity, and almost all now possessed radios, electric stoves, refrigerators, and mechanical equipment to milk cows. In addition, the federal government under the Second New Deal tried to promote soil conservation and family farming. This effort resulted from the belief that the country would never achieve prosperity so long as farmers' standard of living lagged well behind that of city dwellers, and that rural poverty resulted mainly from the poor use of natural resources. Thus, farmers received federal assistance in reducing soil loss in their fields. These measures (like those of the AAA) mainly benefited landowners, not sharecroppers, tenants, or migrant workers. In the long run, the Second New Deal failed to arrest the trend toward larger farms and fewer farmers.

The WPA and the Wagner Act

In 1934, Roosevelt had severely curtailed federal employment for those in need. Now, he approved the establishment of the **Works Progress Administration** (WPA), which hired some 3 million Americans, in virtually every walk of life, each year until it ended in 1943. Under Harry Hopkins's direction, the WPA changed the physical face of the United States. It constructed thousands of public buildings and bridges, more than 500,000 miles of roads, and 600 airports. It built stadiums, swimming pools, and sewage treatment plants. Unlike previous work relief programs, the WPA employed many out-of-work white-collar workers and professionals, even doctors and dentists.

Perhaps the most famous WPA projects were in the arts. The WPA set hundreds of artists to work decorating public buildings with murals. It hired writers to produce local histories and guidebooks to the forty-eight states and to record the recollections of ordinary Americans, including hundreds of former slaves. Its Federal Theater Project put on plays, including an all-Black production of *Macbeth* and Sinclair Lewis's drama *It Can't Happen Here*, about fascism coming to the United States. The Federal Music Project established orchestras and choral groups, and the Federal Dance Project sponsored ballet and modern dance programs. Thanks to the WPA, audiences across the country enjoyed their first glimpse of live musical and theatrical performances and their first opportunity to view exhibitions of American art. Also in 1935, Congress created the National Youth Administration to provide relief to American teenagers and young adults.

Another major initiative of the Second New Deal, the **Wagner Act**, was known at the time as "Labor's Magna Carta" (a reference to an early landmark in the history of freedom). This brought democracy into the American workplace by empowering the National Labor Relations Board to supervise elections in which employees voted on union representation. It also outlawed "unfair labor practices," including the firing and blacklisting of union organizers. The bill's main sponsor, Robert Wagner of New York, told the Senate that the ability of workers to pool their strength through collective bargaining represented the "next step" in "the evolution of American freedom." He also promised that unionization and higher wages would aid economic recovery by boosting the purchasing power of ordinary Americans.

The American Welfare State

The centerpiece of the Second New Deal was the **Social Security Act** of 1935. It embodied Roosevelt's conviction that the national government had a responsibility to ensure the material well-being of ordinary Americans. It created a system of unemployment insurance, old age pensions, and aid to people with disabilities, the elderly poor, and families with dependent children.

None of these were original ideas. The Progressive platform of 1912 had called for old age pensions. Assistance to poor families with dependent children descended from the mothers' pensions promoted by maternalist reformers. Many European countries had already adopted national unemployment insurance plans. What was new, however, was that in the name of economic security, the American government would now supervise not simply temporary relief but also a permanent system of social insurance.

The Social Security Act launched the American version of the **welfare state**—a term that originated in Britain during World War II to refer to a system of income assistance, health coverage, and social services for all citizens. The act illustrated both the extent and the limits of the changes ushered in by the Second New Deal. The American welfare state marked a radical departure from previous government policies, but compared with similar programs in Europe, it has always been far more decentralized, involved lower levels of public spending, and covered fewer citizens. The original Social Security bill, for example, envisioned a national system of health insurance. But Congress dropped this after ferocious opposition from the American Medical Association, which feared government regulation of doctors' activities and incomes.

The Social Security System

Some New Dealers desired a program funded by the federal government's general tax revenues and with a single set of eligibility standards administered by national officials. But Secretary of Labor Frances Perkins, along with powerful members of Congress, wished to keep relief in the hands of state and local authorities and believed that workers should contribute directly to the cost of their own benefits. Roosevelt himself preferred to fund Social Security by taxes on employers and workers, rather than out of general government revenues. He wanted to ensure that Social Security did not add to the federal deficit and believed that paying such taxes gave contributors "a legal, moral, and political right" to collect their old age pensions and unemployment benefits, which no future Congress could rescind.

As a result, Social Security emerged as a hybrid of national and local funding, control, and eligibility standards. Old age pensions were administered nationally but paid for by taxes on employers and employees. Such taxes also funded payments to the unemployed, but this program was highly decentralized, with the states retaining considerable control over the level of benefits. The states paid most of the cost of direct poor relief, under the program called Aid to Dependent Children, and eligibility and the level of payments varied enormously from place to place. As will be discussed later, the combination of local administration and the fact that domestic and agricultural workers were not covered by unemployment and old age benefits meant that Social Security at first excluded large numbers of Americans, especially unmarried women and non-whites.

Nonetheless, Social Security represented a dramatic departure from the traditional functions of government. The Second New Deal transformed the relationship between the federal government and American citizens. Before the 1930s, national political debate often revolved around the question of *whether* the federal government should intervene in the economy. After the New Deal, debate rested on *how* it should intervene. In addition, the government assumed a responsibility, which it has never wholly relinquished, for guaranteeing Americans a living wage and protecting them against economic and personal misfortune. "Laissez-faire is dead," wrote Walter Lippmann, "and the modern state has become responsible for the modern economy [and] the task of insuring . . . the standard of life for its people."

A RECKONING WITH LIBERTY

The Depression made inevitable, in the words of one writer, a "reckoning with liberty." For too many Americans, Roosevelt proclaimed, "life was no longer free; liberty no longer real; men could no longer follow the pursuit of happiness." The 1930s produced an outpouring of books and essays on freedom. The large majority took for granted the need for a new definition. In a volume entitled *Land of the Free* (1938), the poet Archibald MacLeish used photographs of impoverished migrants and sharecroppers to question the reality of freedom in desperate times. "We told ourselves we were free," he wrote. Now, "we wonder if the liberty is done . . . or if there's something different men can mean by Liberty."

Like the Civil War, the New Deal recast the idea of freedom by linking it to the expanding power of the national state. "Our democracy," wrote Father John A. Ryan, a prominent Catholic social critic, "finds itself . . . in a new age where not political freedom but social and industrial freedom is the most insistent cry." Influenced by Ryan, the National Catholic Welfare Conference in 1935 declared that "social justice" required a government guarantee of continuous employment and a "decent livelihood and adequate security" for all Americans.

FDR and the Idea of Freedom

Along with being a superb politician, Roosevelt was a master of political communication. At a time when his political opponents controlled most newspapers, he harnessed radio's power to bring his message directly into American homes. By the mid-1930s, more than two-thirds of American families owned radios. They listened avidly to Roosevelt's radio addresses, known as "fireside chats."

FDR delivering one of his "fireside chats." Roosevelt was the first president to make effective use of the radio to promote his policies.

Roosevelt adeptly appealed to traditional values in support of new policies. He gave the term "liberalism" its modern meaning. In the nineteenth century, liberalism had been a shorthand for limited government and free-market economics. Roosevelt consciously chose to employ it to describe a large, active, socially conscious state. He reclaimed the word "freedom" from conservatives and made it a rallying cry for the New Deal. In his second fireside chat, Roosevelt juxtaposed his own definition of liberty as "greater security for the average man" to the older notion of liberty of contract, which served the interests of "the privileged few." Henceforth, he would consistently link freedom with economic security and identify entrenched economic inequality as its greatest enemy. "The liberty of a democracy," he declared in 1938, was not safe if citizens could not "sustain an acceptable standard of living."

Even as Roosevelt invoked the word to uphold the New Deal, "liberty"—in the sense of freedom from powerful government—became the fighting slogan of his opponents. Their principal critique of the New Deal was that its "reckless spending" undermined fiscal responsibility and its new government regulations restricted American freedom. When conservative businessmen and politicians in 1934 formed an organization to mobilize opposition to Roosevelt's policies, they called it the American Liberty League. Robert Taft of Ohio, leader of the Republicans in Congress, accused Roosevelt of sacrificing "individual freedom" in a misguided effort to "improve the conditions of the poor."

As the 1930s progressed, opponents of the New Deal invoked the language of liberty with greater and greater passion. The U.S. Chamber of Commerce charged FDR with attempting to "Sovietize" America. Even though his own administration had abandoned laissez-faire in the face of economic disaster, former president Hoover launched strident attacks on his successor for endangering "fundamental American liberties." In *The Challenge to Liberty* (1934), Hoover called the New Deal "the most stupendous invasion of the whole spirit of liberty" the nation had ever seen.

The Election of 1936

By 1936, with working-class voters providing massive majorities for the Democratic Party and businesses large and small bitterly estranged from the New Deal, politics reflected class divisions more completely than at any other time in American history. Conceptions of freedom divided sharply as well. Americans, wrote George Soule, editor of *The New Republic*, confronted "two opposing systems of concepts about liberty," reflecting "the needs and purposes of two opposing [parts] of the population." One was the idea of "freedom for private enterprise," the other "socialized liberty" based on "an equitably shared abundance."

A fight for the possession of "the ideal of freedom," reported the *New York Times*, emerged as the central issue of the presidential campaign of 1936. The Democratic platform insisted that in a modern economy the government has

From FRANKLIN D. ROOSEVELT, "FIRESIDE CHAT" (1934)

President Roosevelt pioneered the use of the new mass medium of radio to speak directly to Americans in their homes. He used his "fireside chats" to mobilize support for New Deal programs, link them with American traditions, and outline his definition of freedom.

To those who say that our expenditures for public works and other means for recovery are a waste that we cannot afford, I answer that no country, however rich, can afford the waste of its human resources. Demoralization caused by vast unemployment is our greatest extravagance. Morally, it is the greatest menace to our social order. Some people try to tell me that we must make up our minds that in the future we shall permanently have millions of unemployed just as other countries have had them for over a decade. What may be necessary for those countries is not my responsibility to determine. But as for this country, I stand or fall by my refusal to accept as a necessary condition of our future a permanent army of unemployed. . . .

In our efforts for recovery we have avoided, on the one hand, the theory that business should and must be taken over into an all-embracing Government. We have avoided, on the other hand, the equally untenable theory that it is an interference with liberty to offer reasonable help when private enterprise is in need of help. The course we have followed fits the American practice of Government, a practice of taking action step by step, of regulating only to meet concrete needs, a practice of courageous recognition of change. I believe with Abraham Lincoln, that "the legitimate object of Government is to do for a community of people whatever they need to have done but cannot do at all or cannot do so well for themselves in their separate and individual capacities."

I am not for a return to that definition of liberty under which for many years a free people were being gradually regimented into the service of the privileged few. I prefer and I am sure you prefer that broader definition of liberty under which we are moving forward to greater freedom, to greater security for the average man than he has ever known before in the history of America.

From JOHN STEINBECK, *THE HARVEST GYPSIES: ON THE ROAD TO THE GRAPES OF WRATH* (1938)

John Steinbeck's popular novel *The Grapes of Wrath* (1939), and the film version that followed shortly thereafter, focused national attention on the plight of homeless migrants displaced from their farms as a result of the Great Depression. Before that book appeared, Steinbeck had published a series of newspaper articles based on eyewitness accounts of the migrants, which became the basis for his novel.

In California, we find a curious attitude toward a group that makes our agriculture successful. The migrants are needed, and they are hated. . . . The migrants are hated for the following reasons, that they are ignorant and dirty people, that they are carriers of disease, that they increase the necessity for police and the tax bill for schooling in a community, and that if they are allowed to organize they can, simply by refusing to work, wipe out the season's crops. . . .

Let us see what kind of people they are, where they come from, and the routes of their wanderings. In the past they have been of several races, encouraged to come and often imported as cheap labor. Chinese in the early period, then Filipinos, Japanese and Mexicans. These were foreigners, and as such they were ostracized and segregated and herded about. . . . But in recent years the foreign migrants have begun to organize, and at this danger they have been deported in great numbers, for there was a new reservoir from which a great quantity of cheap labor could be obtained.

The drought in the middle west has driven the agricultural populations of Oklahoma, Nebraska and parts of Kansas and Texas westward. . . . Thousands of them are crossing the borders in ancient rattling automobiles, destitute and hungry and homeless, ready to accept any pay so that they may eat and feed their children. . . .

The earlier foreign migrants have invariably been drawn from a peon class. This is not the case with the new migrants. They are small farmers who have lost their farms, or farm hands who have lived with the family in the old American way. . . . They have come from the little farm districts where democracy was not only possible but inevitable, where popular government, whether practiced in the Grange, in church organization or in local government, was the responsibility of every man. And they have come into the country where, because of the movement necessary to make a living, they are not allowed any vote whatever, but are rather considered a properly unprivileged class. . . .

As one little boy in a squatter's camp said, "When they need us they call us migrants, and when we've picked their crop, we're bums and we got to get out."

QUESTIONS

1. *What does Roosevelt mean by the difference between the definition of liberty that has existed in the past and his own "broader definition of liberty"?*

2. *According to Steinbeck, how do Depression-era migrant workers differ from those in earlier periods?*

3. *Do the migrant workers described by Steinbeck enjoy liberty as Roosevelt understands it?*

an obligation to establish a "democracy of opportunity for all the people." In his speech accepting renomination, Roosevelt launched a blistering attack against "economic royalists" who, he charged, sought to establish a new tyranny over the "average man." Economic rights, he went on, were the precondition of liberty—poor men "are not free men." Throughout the campaign, FDR would insist that the threat posed to economic freedom by the "new despotism" of large corporations was the main issue of the election.

As Roosevelt's opponent, Republicans chose Kansas governor Alfred Landon, a former Theodore Roosevelt Progressive. Landon denounced Social Security and other measures as threats to individual liberty. Opposition to the New Deal planted the seeds for the later flowering of an antigovernment conservatism bent on upholding the free market and dismantling the welfare state. But in 1936 Roosevelt won a landslide reelection, with more than 60 percent of the popular vote. He carried every state except Maine and Vermont. Roosevelt's victory was all the more remarkable in view of the heavy support most of the nation's newspapers and nearly the entire business community gave to the Republicans. His success stemmed from strong backing from organized labor and his ability to unite southern white and northern Black voters, Protestant farmers and urban Catholic and Jewish ethnics, industrial workers and middle-class home owners. These groups made up the so-called New Deal coalition, which would dominate American politics for nearly half a century.

The Court Fight

Roosevelt's second inaugural address was the first to be delivered on January 20. In order to lessen a newly elected president's wait before taking office, the recently ratified Twentieth Amendment had moved inauguration day from March 4. FDR called on the nation to redouble its efforts to aid those "who have too little." The Depression, he admitted, had not been conquered: "I see one-third of a nation ill-housed, ill-clad, and ill-nourished." Emboldened by his electoral triumph, Roosevelt now made what many considered a serious political miscalculation. On the pretense that several members of the Supreme Court were too old to perform their duties, he proposed that the president be allowed to appoint a new justice for each one who remained on the Court past age seventy (which six of the nine had already surpassed). FDR's aim, of course, was to change the balance of power on a Court that, he feared, might well invalidate Social Security, the Wagner Act, and other measures of the Second New Deal.

The plan aroused cries that the president was an aspiring dictator. Congress rejected it. But Roosevelt accomplished his underlying purpose. The Supreme Court, it is sometimes said, follows the election returns. Coming soon after Roosevelt's landslide victory of 1936, the threat of "**Court packing**" inspired an astonishing about-face on the part of key justices. Beginning in March 1937, the Court suddenly revealed a new willingness to support economic regulation by both the federal government and the states. It upheld a minimum wage law of the state of Washington similar to the New York measure it had declared unconstitutional a year earlier. It turned aside challenges to Social Security and the Wagner Act. In subsequent cases, the Court affirmed federal power to regulate wages, hours, child labor, agricultural production, and numerous other aspects of economic life.

Announcing a new judicial philosophy, Chief Justice Charles Evans Hughes pointed out that the words "freedom of contract" did not appear in the Constitution. "Liberty," however, did, and this, Hughes continued, required "the protection of law against the evils which menace the health, safety, morals, and welfare of the people." The Court's new willingness to accept the New Deal marked a permanent change in judicial policy. Having declared dozens of economic laws unconstitutional in the decades leading up to 1937, the justices have rarely done so since.

The End of the Second New Deal

Even as the Court made its peace with Roosevelt's policies, the momentum of the Second New Deal slowed. The landmark United States Housing Act did pass in 1937, initiating the first major national effort to build homes for the poorest Americans. But the Fair Labor Standards bill failed to reach the floor for over a year. When it finally passed in 1938, it banned goods produced by child labor from interstate commerce, set forty cents as the minimum hourly wage, and required overtime pay for hours of work exceeding forty per week. This last major piece of New Deal legislation established the practice of federal regulation of wages and working conditions, another radical departure from pre-Depression policies.

The year 1937 also witnessed a sharp downturn of the economy. With economic conditions improving in 1936, Roosevelt had reduced federal funding

FIGURE 21.1 UNEMPLOYMENT, 1925–1945

The New Deal did not really solve the problem of unemployment, which fell below 10 percent only in 1941, as the United States prepared to enter World War II.

for farm subsidies and WPA work relief. The result was disastrous. As government spending fell, so did business investment, industrial production, and the stock market. Unemployment, still 14 percent at the beginning of 1937, rose to nearly 20 percent by year's end.

In 1936, in *The General Theory of Employment, Interest, and Money*, John Maynard Keynes had challenged economists' traditional belief in the sanctity of balanced budgets. Large-scale government spending, he insisted, was necessary to sustain purchasing power and stimulate economic activity during downturns. Such spending should be enacted even at the cost of a budget deficit (a situation in which the government spends more money than it takes in). By 1938, Roosevelt was ready to follow this prescription, which would later be known as Keynesian economics. In April, he asked Congress for billions more for work relief and farm aid. By the end of the year, the immediate crisis had passed. But the events of 1937–1938 marked a major shift in New Deal philosophy. Rather than economic planning, as in 1933–1934, or economic redistribution, as in 1935–1936, public spending would now be the government's major tool for combating unemployment and stimulating economic growth. The Second New Deal had come to an end.

THE LIMITS OF CHANGE

Roosevelt conceived of the Second New Deal, and especially Social Security, as expanding the meaning of freedom by extending assistance to broad groups of needy Americans—the unemployed, elderly, and dependent—as a right of citizenship, not charity or special privilege. But political realities, especially the power of inherited ideas about gender and Black disenfranchisement in the South, powerfully affected the drafting of legislation. New Deal programs were justified as ways of bringing economic security to "the people" rather than to specific disadvantaged groups. But different Americans experienced the New Deal in radically different ways.

The New Deal and American Women

The New Deal brought more women into government than ever before in American history. A number of talented women, including Secretary of Labor Frances Perkins, advised the president and shaped public policy. Most prominent of all was Eleanor Roosevelt, FDR's distant cousin whom he married in 1905. She transformed the role of First Lady, turning a position with no formal responsibilities into a base for political action. She traveled widely, spoke out on public issues, wrote a regular newspaper column that sometimes disagreed openly with her husband's policies, and worked to enlarge the scope of the New Deal in areas like civil rights, labor legislation, and work relief.

But even as the New Deal increased women's visibility in national politics, organized feminism, already in disarray during the 1920s, disappeared as a political force. Indeed, the Depression inspired widespread demands for women to remove themselves from the labor market to make room for unemployed men. Because the Depression hit industrial employment harder than low-wage clerical and service jobs where women predominated, the proportion of the workforce made up of women rose. The government tried to reverse this trend. In its waning days, the Hoover administration prohibited both members of a married couple from holding federal jobs. Until the repeal of that provision in 1937, it led to the dismissal of numerous female civil service employees whose husbands worked for the government. Many states and localities prohibited the hiring of women whose husbands earned a "living wage," and employers from banks to public school systems barred married women from jobs. Although the CIO organized female workers, it, too, adhered to the idea that women should be supported by men. "The working wife whose husband is employed," said a vice president of the United Auto Workers, "should be barred from industry."

Most New Deal programs did not exclude women from benefits (although the CCC restricted its camps to men). But the ideal of the male-headed household powerfully shaped social policy. Since paying taxes on one's wages made one eligible for the most generous Social Security programs—old age pensions and unemployment insurance—they left most women uncovered, since they did not work outside the home. The program excluded the 3 million mostly female domestic workers altogether. "Those who need protection most are completely overlooked," the sister of a household worker complained to Secretary of Labor Perkins. "What about the poor domestics, both in private homes and private institutions. What have you done for them? Nothing."

The Southern Veto

Roosevelt made the federal government the symbolic representative of all the people, including racial and ethnic groups generally ignored by previous administrations. Yet the power of the Solid South helped to mold the New Deal welfare state into an entitlement of white Americans. After the South's Blacks lost the right to vote around the turn of the century, Democrats enjoyed a political monopoly in the region. Democratic members of Congress were elected again and again. With results predetermined, many whites did not bother to vote (only about 20 percent of eligible southern voters cast ballots in the election of 1920). But this tiny electorate had an enormous impact on national policy. Committee

Students from Howard University outside the National Crime Conference in Washington, D.C., in 1934. They wore nooses and the names of victims to protest the conference's failure to include the subject of lynching in its program.

chairmanships in Congress rest on seniority—how many years a member has served in office. Beginning in 1933, when Democrats took control of Congress, southerners assumed the key leadership positions. Despite his personal popularity, Roosevelt felt he could not challenge the power of southern Democrats if he wished legislation to pass. At their insistence, the Social Security law excluded agricultural and domestic workers, the largest categories of Black employment.

Roosevelt spoke of Social Security's universality, but the demand for truly comprehensive coverage came from the political left and Black organizations. Congressman Ernest Lundeen of Minnesota in 1935 introduced a bill establishing a federally controlled system of old age, unemployment, and health benefits for all wage workers, plus support for female heads of households with dependents. Black organizations like the Urban League and the NAACP supported the Lundeen bill and lobbied strenuously for a system that enabled agricultural and domestic workers to receive unemployment and old age benefits and that established national relief standards. The Social Security Act, however, not Lundeen's proposal, became law. Its limitations, complained the *Pittsburgh Courier*, a Black newspaper, reflected the power of "reactionary elements in the South who cannot bear the thought of Negroes getting pensions and compensations" and who feared that the inclusion of Black workers would disrupt the region's low-wage, racially divided labor system.

The Stigma of Welfare

Because of the "southern veto," the majority of Black workers found themselves confined to the least generous and most vulnerable wing of the new welfare state. The public assistance programs established by Social Security, notably aid to dependent children and to the poor elderly, were open to all Americans who could demonstrate financial need. But they set benefits at extremely low levels and authorized the states to determine eligibility standards, including "moral" behavior as defined by local authorities. As a result, public assistance programs allowed for widespread discrimination in the distribution of benefits. Because recipients did not pay Social Security taxes, they came to bear the humiliating stigma of dependency on government handouts, which would soon come to be known as "welfare."

In 1942, the National Resources Planning Board noted that because of their exclusion from programs "which give aid under relatively favorable conditions," Blacks were becoming disproportionately dependent on welfare, a program widely viewed with popular disfavor. The situation, the report concluded, seemed certain to stigmatize Blacks as recipients of unearned government assistance and welfare as a program for minorities, thus dooming it forever to inadequate "standards of aid." Over time, this is precisely what happened, until the federal government abolished its responsibility for welfare in 1996 entirely, during the presidency of Bill Clinton.

The Native American New Deal

The New Deal had a contradictory impact on Native Americans. Government policies that broke up collective landholdings and forced assimilation had devastated Native American economies and increased their dependence on the government. Indians suffered desperate impoverishment and poor health conditions, with tuberculosis rates twice as high as for white Americans. Commissioner of Indian Affairs John Collier launched an **Indian New Deal**. Though most Native Americans were deeply distrustful of the federal government, Christine Galler, an Okanogan Indian, summed up the sentiments of many: "Let us try a new deal. It cannot be any worse than what it has been."

Collier ended the government's ban on Native religious expressions and cultural ceremonies, replaced boarding schools intended to eradicate tribal identities with day schools, and brought more Indians into the Indian Bureau. In 1934, Collier secured passage of the Indian Reorganization Act. The act abolished the government's campaign, dating back to the Dawes Act of 1877, of forcibly dividing Indian lands into small plots for individual families and selling off "surplus" lands. It sought to rebuild the Indian land base by enabling tribes to repurchase land, and it recognized the right of Indians to govern their own affairs. For years, many Native Americans had pressed for a return of their lands and viewed self-determination as foundational to freedom. The Indian Reorganization Act acknowledged these goals, though in limited fashion. It encouraged tribes to establish governing councils and to adopt new constitutions, but it compelled them to adopt constitutions in line with government officials' expectations. Ramon Roubideaux of the Lakota tribe criticized this approach: "It is not self-government because self-government by permission is no self-government at all."

The Indian New Deal also sought to improve reservation economic conditions by providing employment and training. The Civilian Conservation Corps (CCC) Indian Division employed 80,000 Native Americans during the Depression. They built fire towers, schools, roads, and worked on forestry, soil, range, and water conservation projects. But under the CCC Indian Division,

Members of the Navajo nation at Shiprock Fair reading about the federal program for Navajos.

reservation superintendents retained control over the distribution of pay, impounding a portion of wages for distribution at their discretion.

In the case of the Navajo nation, by then the largest tribe in the United States, the Indian New Deal brought new injustices. Sheep herding was important to the Navajo political economy, but grazing had contributed to soil erosion and drought. Federal conservation officials identified an impending environmental calamity and called for drastic, immediate herd reductions. Navajos protested the policy, but federal agents seized animals, transported them to canyons or corrals, and killed them. Outraged by Collier's support of livestock reduction, the Navajos rejected the Indian Reorganization Act in June 1935. The Indian New Deal ended the devastating policy of forced assimilation and now emphasized the goal of Native sovereignty, but the Indian Reorganization Act did not significantly improve reservation living conditions, and some New Deal programs, such as livestock reduction and the Columbia River Basin project, inflicted new harms.

The New Deal and Mexican Americans

For Mexican Americans, the Depression was a wrenching experience. The deportation campaigns of the federal government and local officials discussed previously led more than 400,000 (one-fifth of the population of Mexican origin) to return to Mexico. Those who remained mostly worked in grim conditions in California's vegetable and fruit fields, whose corporate farms benefited enormously from New Deal dam construction that provided them with cheap electricity and water for irrigation. The Wagner Act and Social Security Act did not apply to agricultural laborers. When the workers tried to organize a union as part of the decade's labor upsurge, they were brutally suppressed. In his 1939 book *Factories in the Field*, the writer Carey McWilliams exposed the low wages, inadequate housing, and political repression under which the migrant laborers suffered, which the New Deal did nothing to alleviate.

Mexican American leaders struggled to develop a consistent strategy for their people. They sought greater rights by claiming to be white Americans—in order to avoid the same discrimination as African Americans—but also sought the backing of the Mexican government and promoted a mystical sense of pride and identification with Mexican heritage later given the name *la raza*.

Mexican Americans were not the only group encouraged to leave the United States. In 1935, Congress passed the Filipino Repatriation Act, offering free transportation to those born in the Philippines and willing to return there. Persons who did leave would only be able to return by applying under the Philippines' annual immigration quota of fifty. Given the lack of economic opportunity in the Philippines and fear about being permanently unable to return to the United States, of the 45,000 Filipinos in the country, only around 2,000 accepted the offer.

A New Deal for Blacks

As the "last hired and first fired," African Americans were hit hardest by the Depression. With an unemployment rate double that of whites, even those who retained their jobs now faced competition from unemployed whites who had previously considered positions like waiter and porter beneath them. Blacks benefited disproportionately from direct government relief and, especially in northern cities, jobs on New Deal public-works projects. The Depression propelled economic survival to the top of the Black agenda. Demonstrations in Harlem demanded jobs in the neighborhood's white-owned stores, with the slogan "Don't Buy Where You Can't Work." W. E. B. Du Bois abandoned his earlier goal of racial integration as unrealistic for the foreseeable future. Blacks, he wrote, must recognize themselves as "a nation within a nation," build an independent, cooperative economy within their communities, and gain control of their own separate schools (a position reminiscent of that of Booker T. Washington, whom he had earlier condemned).

Roosevelt appointed Mary McLeod Bethune, a prominent Black educator, as a special adviser on minority affairs and a number of other Blacks to important federal positions. Key members of his administration, including his wife, Eleanor, and Secretary of the Interior Harold Ickes, a former president of the Chicago chapter of the NAACP, directed national attention to the injustices of segregation, disenfranchisement, and lynching. In 1939, Eleanor Roosevelt resigned from the Daughters of the American Revolution when the organization refused to allow the Black singer Marian Anderson to present a concert at Constitution Hall in Washington. The president's wife arranged for Anderson to sing on the steps of the Lincoln Memorial and for the concert to be broadcast nationally on the radio.

Thanks to the New Deal, the decade witnessed a historic shift in Black voting patterns. In the North and West, where they enjoyed the right to vote, Blacks in 1934 and 1936 abandoned their allegiance to the party of Lincoln and emancipation in favor of Democrats and the New Deal. But their hopes for broad changes in the nation's race system were disappointed. Despite a massive lobbying campaign, southern congressmen prevented passage of a federal antilynching law. FDR offered little support. "I did not choose the tools with which I must work," he told Walter White of the NAACP; he would not jeopardize his economic programs by alienating powerful members of Congress. The CCC established segregated work camps. Because of the exclusion of agricultural and domestic workers, Social Security's old age pensions and unemployment benefits and the minimum wages established by the Fair Labor Standards Act left uncovered 60 percent of all employed Blacks and 85 percent of Black women.

Federal Discrimination

Federal housing policy, which powerfully reinforced residential segregation, revealed the racial boundaries of New Deal freedom. Nearly all municipalities, North as well as South, insisted that housing built or financially aided by the federal government be racially segregated. (In Texas, some communities financed three sets of housing projects—for whites, Blacks, and Mexicans.) The Federal Housing Administration, moreover, had no hesitation about insuring mortgages that contained clauses barring future sales to non-white buyers, and it refused to channel money into integrated neighborhoods. In some cases, the presence of a single Black family led the agency to declare an entire block off-limits for federal mortgage insurance. Along with discriminatory practices by private banks and real-estate companies, federal policy became a major factor in further entrenching housing segregation in the United States. Moreover, excluding Blacks from federally backed mortgage insurance by designating minority neighborhoods "undesirable" for credit purposes harmed Black opportunities to accumulate home equity and financial wealth.

Federal employment practices also discriminated on the basis of race. As late as 1940, of the 150,000 Blacks holding federal jobs, only 2 percent occupied positions other than clerk or custodian. In the South, many New Deal construction projects refused to hire Blacks at all. "They give all the work to white people and give us nothing," a Black resident of Mississippi wrote to FDR in 1935. The New Deal began the process of modernizing southern agriculture, but tenants, Black and white, footed much of the bill. Tens of thousands of sharecroppers, as noted earlier, were driven off the land as a result of the AAA policy of raising crop prices by paying landowners to reduce cotton acreage.

During the 1930s, the South remained rigidly segregated. This 1939 photograph by Dorthea Lange depicts a "colored" movie theater in the Mississippi Delta.

Support for civil rights would eventually become a test of liberal credentials. But in the 1930s, one could advocate Roosevelt's economic program and oppose antilynching legislation and moves to incorporate Black workers within Social Security. Theodore Bilbo, the notoriously racist senator from Mississippi, was one of the New Deal's most loyal backers. Not until the Great Society of the 1960s would those left out of Social Security and other New Deal programs—racial minorities, many women, migrants, and other less privileged workers—win inclusion in the American welfare state.

Nonetheless, in a society in which virtually all institutions, public and private, created and reinforced patterns of discrimination, the New Deal helped to create an atmosphere that made possible challenges to the racial and ethnic status quo and the rise of a new, more inclusive vision of American freedom.

A NEW CONCEPTION OF AMERICA

If the New Deal failed to dismantle the barriers that barred non-whites from full participation in American life, the 1930s witnessed the absorption of other groups into the social mainstream. With Catholics and Jews occupying prominent posts in the Roosevelt administration and new immigrant voters forming an important part of its electoral support, the New Deal made ethnic pluralism a living reality in American politics. One of Roosevelt's first acts on taking office had been to sign the Beer and Wine Revenue Act, an anticipation of the constitutional amendment repealing Prohibition. While promoted as a way to revive employment in the liquor industry and boost tax revenues, it also represented a repudiation of the linkage of politics and Protestant morality. The election of the Italian American Fiorello La Guardia as mayor of New York City in 1933 symbolized the coming to power of the new immigrants. Although a Republican, La Guardia worked closely with FDR and launched his own program of spending on housing, parks, and public works. La Guardia's program was one of numerous "little New Deals" that brought ethnic working-class voters to power in communities throughout the industrial heartland.

Thanks to the virtual cutoff of southern and Eastern European immigration in 1924, the increasing penetration of movies, chain stores, and mass advertising into ethnic communities, and the common experience of economic crisis, the 1930s witnessed an acceleration of cultural assimilation. But the process had a different content from the corporate-sponsored Americanization plans of the preceding years. For the children of the new immigrants, labor and political activism became agents of a new kind of Americanization. One could participate fully in the broader society without surrendering one's ideals and ethnic identity. "Unionism is Americanism" became a CIO rallying cry. "The Mesabi Range," a Minnesota miner wrote to Secretary of Labor Perkins, complaining of low wages and management hostility to unions in the iron-rich region, "isn't Americanized yet."

The Heyday of American Communism

In the mid-1930s, for the first time in American history, the left—an umbrella term for socialists, communists, labor radicals, and many New Deal liberals—enjoyed a shaping influence on the nation's politics and culture. The CIO and Communist Party became focal points for a broad social and intellectual impulse that helped to redraw the boundaries of American freedom. An obscure, faction-ridden organization when the Depression began, the Communist Party experienced remarkable growth during the 1930s. The party's membership never exceeded 100,000, but several times that number passed through its ranks.

The party's commitment to socialism resonated with a widespread belief that the Depression had demonstrated the bankruptcy of capitalism. But it was not so much the party's ideology as its vitality—its involvement in a mind-boggling array of activities, including demonstrations of the unemployed, struggles for industrial unionism, and a renewed movement for Black civil rights—that for a time made it the center of gravity for a broad democratic upsurge. At the height of the **Popular Front**—a period during the mid-1930s when the Communist Party sought to ally itself with socialists and New Dealers in movements for social change, urging reform of the capitalist system rather than revolution—Communists gained an unprecedented respectability.

Earl Browder, the party's leader, even appeared on the cover of *Time* magazine. It is one of the era's ironies that an organization with an undemocratic structure and closely tied to Stalin's dictatorial regime in Russia should have contributed to the expansion of freedom in the United States. But the Communist Party helped to imbue New Deal liberalism with a militant spirit and a more pluralistic understanding of Americanism.

Redefining the People

In theater, film, and dance, the Popular Front vision of American society sank deep roots and survived much longer than the political moment from which it sprang. In this broad left-wing culture, social and economic radicalism, not support for the status quo, defined true Americanism, ethnic and racial diversity was the glory of American society, and the "American way of life" meant unionism and social citizenship, not the unbridled pursuit of wealth. The American "people," viewed by many intellectuals in the 1920s as representing mean-spirited fundamentalism and crass commercialism, were suddenly rediscovered as embodiments of democratic virtue.

The "common man," Roosevelt proclaimed, embodied "the heart and soul of our country." During the 1930s, artists and writers who strove to create socially meaningful works eagerly took up the task of depicting the daily lives of ordinary farmers and city dwellers. Art about the people—such as Dorothea Lange's photographs of migrant workers and sharecroppers—and art created by the people—such as Black spirituals—came to be seen as expressions of genuine Americanism. The Federal Music Project dispatched collectors with tape recorders to help preserve American folk music. Films celebrated populist figures who challenged and defeated corrupt businessmen and politicians, as in *Mr. Smith Goes to Washington* (1939). New immigrants, especially Jews and Italians, played a prominent role in producing and directing Hollywood films of the 1930s. Their movies, however, glorified not urban ethnic communities but ordinary small-town, middle-class Americans.

Promoting Diversity

"A new conception of America is necessary," wrote the immigrant labor radical Louis Adamic in 1938. Despite bringing ethnic and northern Black voters into its political coalition, the Democratic Party said little about ethno-cultural issues, fearful of rekindling the divisive battles of the 1920s. But the Popular Front forthrightly sought to promote the idea that the country's strength lay in diversity, tolerance, and the rejection of ethnic prejudice and class privilege. The CIO avidly promoted the idea of ethnic and racial inclusiveness. It broke decisively with the AFL's tradition of exclusionary unionism. "We are the only Americans who take them into our organization as equals," wrote labor organizer Rose Pesotta, referring to the Mexican Americans who flocked to the Cannery and Agricultural Workers union.

Popular Front culture presented a heroic but not uncritical picture of the country's past. Martha Graham's modern dance masterpiece *American Document* (1938), an embodiment of Popular Front aesthetics with its emphasis on America's folk traditions and multiethnic heritage, centered its account of history on the Declaration of Independence and the Gettysburg Address. Yet Graham did not neglect what her narrator called "things we are ashamed of," including the dispossession of the Indians and the plight of the unemployed. Graham's answer to Hector St. John de Crèvecoeur's old question, "What, then, is the American, this new man?" was that Americans were not only middle-class Anglo-Saxons but also Blacks, immigrants, and the working class. Earl Robinson's song "Ballad for Americans," a typical expression of Popular Front culture that celebrated the religious, racial, and ethnic diversity of American society, became a national hit and was performed in 1940 at the Republican national convention.

Challenging the Color Line

It was fitting that "Ballad for Americans" reached the top of the charts in a version performed by the magnificent Black singer Paul Robeson. Popular Front culture moved well beyond New Deal liberalism in condemning racism as incompatible with true Americanism. In the 1930s, groups like the American Jewish Committee and the National Conference of Christians and Jews actively promoted ethnic and religious tolerance, defining pluralism as "the American way." But whether in Harlem or East Los Angeles, the Communist Party was the era's only predominantly white organization to make fighting racism a top priority. "The communists," declared Charles H. Houston, the NAACP's chief lawyer, "made it impossible for any aspirant to Negro leadership to advocate less than full economic, political and social equality."

Communist influence spread even to the South. The Communist-dominated International Labor Defense mobilized popular support for Black defendants victimized by a racist criminal justice system. It helped to make the **Scottsboro case** an international cause célèbre. The case revolved around nine young Black men arrested for the rape of two white women in Alabama in 1931. Despite the weakness of the evidence against the "Scottsboro boys" and the fact that one of the two accusers recanted, Alabama authorities three times put them on trial and three times won convictions. Landmark Supreme Court decisions overturned the first two verdicts and established legal principles that greatly expanded the definition of civil liberties—that defendants have a constitutional right to effective legal representation and that states cannot systematically exclude Blacks from juries. But the Court allowed the third set of convictions to stand, which led to prison sentences for five of the defendants. In 1937, a defense lawyer worked out a deal whereby Alabama authorities released nearly all the defendants on parole, although the last of the "Scottsboro boys" did not leave prison until thirteen years had passed.

Despite considerable resistance from white workers determined to preserve their monopoly of skilled positions and access to promotions, the CIO welcomed Black members and advocated the passage of antilynching laws and the return of voting rights to southern Blacks. The CIO brought large numbers of Black industrial workers into the labor movement for the first time and ran extensive educational campaigns to persuade white workers to recognize the interests they shared with their Black counterparts. Black workers, many of them traditionally hostile to unions because of their long experience of exclusion, responded with enthusiasm to CIO organizing efforts. The union offered the promise of higher wages, dignity in the workplace, and an end to the arbitrary power of often racist foremen. Ed McRea, a white CIO organizer in Memphis, Tennessee, reported that he had little difficulty persuading Black workers of the value of unionization: "You didn't have any trouble explaining this to Blacks, with the kinds of oppression and conditions they had. It was a question of freedom."

Labor and Civil Liberties

Another central element of Popular Front public culture was its mobilization for civil liberties, especially the right of labor to organize. The struggle to launch industrial unions encountered sweeping local restrictions on freedom of speech as well as repression by private and public police forces. Nationwide publicity about the wave of violence directed against the Southern Tenant Farmers Union in the South and the CIO in industrial communities in the North elevated the rights of labor to a central place in discussions of civil liberties. The American Civil Liberties Union, primarily concerned in the 1920s with governmental repression, by 1934 concluded that "the masters of property" posed as great a danger to freedom of speech and assembly as political authorities.

Beginning in 1936, a Senate subcommittee headed by Robert M. La Follette Jr. exposed the methods employers used to combat unionization, including spies and private police forces. Workers had "no liberties at all," an employee of General Motors wrote to the committee from Saginaw, Michigan. The extensive violence unleashed against strikers in California's cotton and lettuce fields made that state, the committee report concluded, seem more like a "European dictatorship" than part of the United States.

Labor militancy helped to produce an important shift in the understanding of civil liberties. Previously conceived of as individual rights that must be protected against infringement by the government, the concept now expanded to include violations of free speech and assembly by powerful private groups. As a result, just as the federal government emerged as a guarantor of economic security, it also became a protector of freedom of expression.

By the eve of World War II, civil liberties had assumed a central place in the New Deal understanding of freedom. In 1939, Attorney General Frank Murphy established a Civil Liberties Unit in the Department of Justice. "For the first time in our history," Murphy wrote the president, "the full weight of the Department will be thrown behind the effort to preserve in this country the blessings of liberty." Meanwhile, the same Supreme Court that in 1937 relinquished its role as a judge of economic legislation moved to expand its authority over civil liberties. The justices insisted that constitutional guarantees of free thought and expression were essential to "nearly every other form of freedom" and therefore deserved special protection by the courts. Thus, civil liberties replaced liberty of contract as the judicial foundation of freedom. In 1937, the Court overturned on free speech grounds the conviction of Angelo Herndon, a Communist organizer jailed in Georgia for "inciting insurrection." Three years later, it invalidated an Alabama law that prohibited picketing in labor disputes. Since 1937, the large majority of state and national laws overturned by the courts have been those that infringe on civil liberties, not on the property rights of business.

The new appreciation of free expression was hardly universal. In 1938, the House of Representatives established the **House Un-American Activities Committee** to investigate disloyalty. Its expansive definition of "un-American" included communists, labor radicals, and the left of the Democratic Party, and its hearings led to the dismissal of dozens of federal employees on charges of subversion. Two years later, Congress enacted the Smith Act, which made it a federal crime to "teach, advocate, or encourage" the overthrow of the government. A similar pursuit of radical views took place at the state level. The New York legislature's Rapp-Coudert Committee held sweeping hearings investigating "subversive" influences in New York City's public colleges, resulting in the firing in 1941 of some sixty faculty members charged with communist sympathies.

The End of the New Deal

By then the New Deal, as an era of far-reaching social reform, had already begun to recede. One reason was that more and more southern Democrats were finding themselves at odds with Roosevelt's policies. In 1938, the administration released a "Report on Economic Conditions in the South," along with a letter by the president referring to the region as "the nation's No. 1 economic problem." The document revealed that the South lagged far behind other parts of the country in industrialization and investment in education and public health. Its per capita income stood at half that of the rest of the nation. Also in 1938, a new generation of homegrown radicals—southern New Dealers, Black activists, labor leaders, communists, even a few elected officials—founded the Southern Conference for Human Welfare to work for unionization, unemployment relief, and racial justice.

Until the late 1930s, prominent southern Democrats had been strong supporters of the New Deal, while at the same time working to shape legislation to allow for the local administration of relief and the exclusion of most Black workers. Now, southern business and political leaders feared that continuing federal intervention in their region would encourage unionization and upset race relations. Roosevelt concluded that the enactment of future New Deal measures required a liberalization of the southern Democratic Party. In 1938, he tried to persuade the region's voters to replace conservative congressmen with ones who would support his policies. The South's small electorate dealt him a stinging rebuke. In the North, where the economic downturn, the "Court-packing" plan, and the upsurge of CIO militancy alarmed many middle-class voters, Republicans increased their congressional representation.

A period of political stalemate followed the congressional election of 1938. For many years, a conservative coalition of southern Democrats and northern Republicans dominated Congress. Further reform initiatives became almost impossible, and Congress moved to abolish existing ones, beginning with the Federal Theater Project, which had alarmed conservatives because of the presence of radicals and gay men and lesbians on its payroll. Congress repealed an earlier tax on corporate profits and rejected a proposed program of national medical insurance. The administration, moreover, increasingly focused its attention on the storm gathering in Europe. Even before December 1941, when the United States entered World War II, "Dr. Win the War," as Roosevelt put it, had replaced "Dr. New Deal."

The New Deal in American History

Given the scope of the economic calamity it tried to counter, the New Deal seems in many ways quite limited. Compared with later European welfare states' social insurance protections, Social Security remained restricted in scope and modest in cost. The New Deal failed to address the problem of racial inequality, which in some ways it actually worsened.

Yet even as the New Deal receded, its substantial accomplishments remained. It greatly expanded the federal government's role in the American economy and made it an independent force in relations between industry and labor. The government influenced what farmers could and could not plant, required employers to deal with unions, insured bank deposits, regulated the stock market, loaned money to home owners, and provided payments to a majority of the elderly and unemployed. It transformed the physical environment through hydroelectric dams, reforestation projects, rural electrification, and the construction of innumerable public facilities. It restored faith in democracy and made the government an institution directly experienced in Americans' daily lives and directly concerned with their welfare. It redrew the map of American politics. It helped to inspire, and was powerfully influenced by, a popular upsurge that recast the idea of freedom to include a public guarantee of economic security for ordinary citizens and that identified economic inequality as the greatest threat to American freedom.

The New Deal certainly improved economic conditions in the United States. But it did not generate sustained prosperity. More than 15 percent of the workforce remained unemployed in 1940. Only the mobilization of the nation's resources to fight World War II would finally end the Great Depression.

CHAPTER REVIEW

REVIEW QUESTIONS

1. *Discuss how regional planning such as the Tennessee Valley Authority and the Columbia River project reflected broader changes in American life during the New Deal.*

2. *What actions did President Roosevelt and Congress take to help the banking system recover as well as to reform how it operated in the long run?*

3. *How did the actions of the AAA benefit many farmers, injure others, and provoke attacks by conservatives?*

4. *Explain what labor did in the 1930s to rise from being "slaves of the depression" to secure "economic freedom and industrial democracy" for American workers.*

5. *How did the emphasis of the Second New Deal differ from the First New Deal?*

6. *How did the entrenched power of southern white conservatives limit African Americans' ability to enjoy the full benefits of the New Deal and eliminate racial violence and discrimination? Why did African Americans still support the Democratic Party?*

7. *Analyze the effects of the Indian Reorganization Act of 1934 on Native Americans.*

8. *Explain how New Deal programs contributed to the stigma of Blacks as welfare-dependent.*

9. *What were the political forces that informed the Filipino Repatriation Act?*

10. *How did the New Deal build on traditional ideas about the importance of home ownership to Americans, and how did it change Americans' ability to own their own homes?*

11. *What were the major characteristics of liberalism by 1939?*

KEY TERMS

New Deal (p. 825)

repeal (p. 827)

Emergency Banking Act (p. 829)

Hundred Days (p. 829)

National Industrial Recovery Act (p. 829)

National Recovery Administration (p. 829)

Civilian Conservation Corps (p. 831)

Public Works Administration (p. 831)

Tennessee Valley Authority (p. 832)

Agricultural Adjustment Act (p. 833)

Dust Bowl (p. 833)

Federal Housing Administration (p. 834)

Congress of Industrial Organizations (p. 837)

sit-down strike (p. 837)

Share Our Wealth movement (p. 839)

Works Progress Administration (p. 841)

Wagner Act (p. 842)

Social Security Act (p. 842)

welfare state (p. 842)

Court packing (p. 848)

Indian New Deal (p. 853)

Popular Front (p. 858)

Scottsboro case (p. 860)

House Un-American Activities Committee (p. 862)

Go to 📖 **INQUIZITIVE**

To see what you know—and learn what you've missed—with personalized feedback along the way.

CHAPTER 22

FIGHTING FOR THE FOUR FREEDOMS: WORLD WAR II

1941–1945

FOCUS QUESTIONS

- *What steps led to American participation in World War II?*

- *How did the United States mobilize economic resources and promote popular support for the war effort?*

- *What visions of America's postwar role began to emerge during the war?*

- *How did American minorities face threats to their freedom at home and abroad during World War II?*

- *How did the end of the war begin to shape the postwar world?*

By far the most popular works of art produced during World War II were paintings of the **Four Freedoms** by the magazine illustrator Norman Rockwell. In his State of the Union address, delivered before Congress on January 6, 1941, President Roosevelt spoke eloquently of a future world order founded on the "essential human freedoms": freedom of speech, freedom of worship, freedom from want, and freedom from fear. The Four Freedoms became Roosevelt's favorite statement of Allied aims. At various times, he compared them to the Ten Commandments, the Magna Carta, and the Emancipation Proclamation. They embodied, Roosevelt declared in a 1942 radio address, the "rights of men of every creed and every race, wherever they live," and made clear "the crucial difference between ourselves and the enemies we face today."

Rockwell's paintings succeeded in linking the Four Freedoms with the defense of traditional American values. "Words like *freedom or liberty*," declared one wartime advertisement, "draw close to us only when we break them down into the homely fragments of daily life." This insight helps to explain Rockwell's astonishing popularity. Born in New York City in 1894, Rockwell had lived in the New York area until 1939, when he and his family moved to Arlington, Vermont, where they could enjoy, as he put it, "the clean, simple country life, as opposed to the complicated world of the city." Drawing on the lives of his Vermont neighbors, Rockwell translated the Four Freedoms into images of real people situated in small-town America. Each of the paintings focuses on an instantly recognizable situation. An ordinary citizen rises to speak at a town meeting; members of different religious groups are seen at prayer; a family enjoys a Thanksgiving dinner; a mother and father stand over sleeping children.

The Four Freedoms paintings first appeared in the *Saturday Evening Post* early in 1943. Letters of praise poured in to the magazine's editors. The government produced and sold millions of reprints. The paintings toured the country as the centerpiece of the Four Freedoms Show, which included theatrical presentations, parades, and other events aimed at persuading Americans to purchase war bonds. By the end of its tour, the Four Freedoms Show had raised $133 million.

Even as Rockwell invoked images of small-town life to rally Americans to the war effort, however, the country experienced changes as deep as at any time in its history. Many of the economic trends and social movements that we associate with the last half of the twentieth century had their roots in the war years. As during World War I, but on a far larger scale, wartime mobilization expanded the size and scope of government and energized the economy. The gross national product more than doubled and unemployment disappeared as war production finally conquered the Depression. The demand for labor drew millions of women into the workforce and sent a tide of migrants from rural America to the industrial cities of the North and West, permanently altering the nation's social geography. Some 30 million Americans moved during the war, half going into military service and half taking up new jobs.

World War II gave the country a new and lasting international role and greatly strengthened the idea that American security was global in scope and could only be protected by the worldwide triumph of core American values.

Government military spending sparked the economic development of the South and West, laying the foundation for the rise of the modern Sunbelt. The war created a close link between big business and a militarized federal government—a "military-industrial complex," as President Dwight D. Eisenhower would later call it—that long survived the end of fighting.

World War II also redrew the boundaries of American nationality. In contrast to World War I, the government recognized the "new immigrants" of the early twentieth century and their children as loyal Americans. Black Americans' second-class status assumed, for the first time since Reconstruction, a prominent place on the nation's political agenda. But toleration had its limits. With the United States at war with Japan, the federal government removed more than 110,000 Japanese Americans, the majority of them American citizens, from their homes and placed them in internment camps.

As a means of generating support for the struggle, the Four Freedoms provided a crucial language of national unity. But this unity obscured divisions within American society that the war in some ways intensified, divisions reflected in debates over freedom. While some Americans looked forward to a worldwide New Deal, others envisioned "free enterprise" replacing government intervention in the economy. The war gave birth to the modern civil rights movement but strengthened the commitment of many white Americans to maintain the existing racial order. The movement of women into the labor force challenged traditional gender relations, but most men and not a few women longed for the restoration of family life with a male breadwinner and a wife responsible for the home.

Even Rockwell's popular paintings suggested some of the ambiguities within the idea of freedom. With the exception of *Freedom of Speech*, which depicts civic democracy in action, the paintings emphasized private situations. The message seemed to be that Americans were fighting to preserve freedoms enjoyed individually or within the family rather than in the larger public world. This emphasis on freedom as an element of private life would become more and more prominent in postwar America.

FIGHTING WORLD WAR II

Good Neighbors

During the 1930s, with Americans preoccupied by the economic crisis, international relations played only a minor role in public affairs. From the outset of his administration, nonetheless, FDR embarked on a number of departures in foreign policy. In 1933, hoping to stimulate American trade, he exchanged ambassadors with the Soviet Union, whose government his Republican predecessors had stubbornly refused to recognize.

Roosevelt also formalized a policy initiated by Herbert Hoover by which the United States repudiated the right to intervene militarily in the internal affairs of Latin American countries. This Good Neighbor Policy, as it was called, had mixed results. During the 1930s, the United States withdrew its troops from Haiti and Nicaragua. FDR accepted Cuba's repeal of the Platt Amendment (discussed in Chapter 17), which had authorized American military interventions on that island. These steps offered a belated recognition of the sovereignty of America's neighbors. But while Roosevelt condemned "economic royalists" (wealthy businessmen) at home, like previous presidents he felt comfortable dealing with undemocratic governments friendly to American business interests abroad. The United States lent its support to dictators like Anastasio Somoza in Nicaragua, Rafael Trujillo Molina in the Dominican Republic, and Fulgencio Batista in Cuba. "He may be a son of a bitch, but he's *our* son of a bitch," FDR said of Somoza.

However, as the international crisis deepened in the 1930s, the Roosevelt administration took steps to counter German influence in Latin America by expanding hemispheric trade and promoting respect for American culture. Nelson Rockefeller, the head of an office that hoped to expand cultural relations in the hemisphere, sent the artists of the American Ballet Caravan and the NBC Symphony Orchestra on Latin American tours. This was a far different approach to relations with Central and South America than the military interventions of the first decades of the century.

OURS...to fight for

Freedom of Speech   *Freedom of Worship*

Freedom from Want   *Freedom from Fear*

The immensely popular Office of War Information poster reproducing Norman Rockwell's paintings of the Four Freedoms, President Franklin D. Roosevelt's shorthand for American purposes in World War II. "Four Freedoms" Illustrations © SEPS licensed by Curtis Licensing Indianapolis, IN.

The Road to War

Ominous developments in Asia and Europe quickly overshadowed events in Latin America. By the mid-1930s, it seemed clear that the rule of law was disintegrating in international relations and that war was on the horizon. In 1931, seeking to expand its military and economic power in Asia, Japan invaded Manchuria, a province of northern China. Six years later, its troops moved farther into China. When the Japanese overran the city of Nanjing, they massacred an estimated 300,000 Chinese prisoners of war and civilians.

An aggressive power threatened Europe as well. After brutally consolidating his rule in Germany, Adolf Hitler embarked on a campaign to control the entire continent. In violation of the Versailles Treaty, he feverishly pursued German rearmament. In 1936, he sent troops to occupy the Rhineland, a demilitarized zone between France and Germany established after World War I. The failure of Britain, France, and the United States to oppose this action convinced Hitler that the democracies could not muster the will to halt his aggressive plans. Italian leader Benito Mussolini, the founder of fascism, a movement similar to Hitler's Nazism, invaded and conquered Ethiopia. When General Francisco Franco in 1936 led an uprising against the democratically elected government of Spain, Hitler poured in arms, seeing the conflict as a testing ground for new weaponry. In 1939, Franco emerged victorious from a bitter civil war, establishing yet another fascist government in Europe. As part of a campaign to unite all Europeans of German origin in a single empire, Hitler in 1938 annexed Austria and the Sudetenland, an ethnically German part of Czechoslovakia. Shortly thereafter, he gobbled up all of that country.

As the 1930s progressed, Roosevelt became more and more alarmed at Hitler's aggression as well as his accelerating campaign against Germany's Jews, whom the Nazis stripped of citizenship and property and began to deport to concentration camps. In a 1937 speech in Chicago, FDR called for international action to "quarantine" aggressors. But no further steps followed. Roosevelt had little choice but to follow the policy of "appeasement" adopted by Britain and France, who hoped that agreeing to Hitler's demands would prevent war. British prime minister Neville Chamberlain returned from the Munich conference of 1938, which awarded Hitler the Sudetenland, proclaiming that he had guaranteed "peace in our time."

Isolationism

To most Americans, the threat arising from Japanese and German aggression seemed very distant. Moreover, Hitler had more than a few admirers in the United States. Obsessed with the threat of communism, some Americans approved of his expansion of German power as a counterweight to the Soviet Union. Businessmen did not wish to give up profitable overseas markets. Henry Ford did business with Nazi Germany throughout the 1930s. Indeed, Ford plants there employed slave labor provided by the German government. Trade with Japan also continued, including shipments of American trucks and aircraft and considerable amounts of oil. Until 1941, 80 percent of Japan's oil supply came from the United States.

Many Americans remained convinced that involvement in World War I had been a mistake. Senate hearings in 1934–1935 headed by Gerald P. Nye of North Dakota revealed that international bankers and arms exporters had pressed the Wilson administration to enter that war and had profited handsomely from it. Pacifism spread on college campuses, where tens of thousands of students took part in a "strike for peace" in 1935. Ethnic allegiances reinforced Americans' traditional reluctance to enter foreign conflicts. Many Americans of German and Italian descent celebrated the expansion of national power in their countries of origin. Irish Americans remained strongly anti-British.

Isolationism—the 1930s version of Americans' long-standing desire to avoid foreign entanglements—dominated Congress. Beginning in 1935, lawmakers passed a series of **Neutrality Acts** that banned travel on belligerents' ships and the sale of arms to countries at war. These policies, Congress hoped, would allow the United States to avoid the conflicts over freedom of the seas that had contributed to involvement in World War I. Despite the fact that the Spanish Civil War pitted a democratic government against an aspiring fascist dictator, the Western democracies, including the United States, imposed an embargo on arms shipments to both sides. Some 3,000 Americans volunteered to fight in the Abraham Lincoln Brigade on the side of the Spanish republic. But with Germany supplying the forces of Franco, the decision by democratic countries to abide by the arms embargo contributed substantially to his victory.

War in Europe

In the Munich agreement of 1938, Britain and France had caved in to Hitler's aggression. In 1939, the Soviet Union proposed an international agreement to oppose further German demands for territory. Britain and France, who distrusted Stalin and saw Germany as a bulwark against the spread of communist influence in Europe, refused. Stalin then astonished the world by signing a nonaggression pact with Hitler, his former sworn enemy. On September 1, 1939, immediately after the signing of the Nazi–Soviet pact, Germany invaded Poland. This time, Britain and France, who had pledged to protect Poland against aggression, declared war. But Germany appeared unstoppable. Within a year, the Nazi *blitzkrieg* (lightning war) had overrun Poland and much of Scandinavia, Belgium, and the Netherlands. On June 14, 1940, German troops occupied Paris. Hitler now dominated nearly all of Europe, as well as North Africa. In September 1940, Germany, Italy, and Japan created a military alliance known as the Axis.

For one critical year, Britain stood virtually alone in fighting Germany. Winston Churchill, who became prime minister in 1940, vowed to resist a threatened Nazi invasion. In the Battle of Britain of 1940–1941, German planes launched devastating attacks on London and other cities. The Royal Air Force eventually turned back the air assault. But Churchill pointedly called on the "new world, with all its power and might," to step forward to rescue the old.

Toward Intervention

Roosevelt viewed Hitler as a mad gangster whose victories posed a direct threat to the United States. But most Americans remained desperate to remain out of the conflict. "What worries me, especially," FDR wrote to Kansas editor William Allen White, "is that public opinion over here is patting itself on the back every morning and thanking God for the Atlantic Ocean and the Pacific Ocean." After a tumultuous debate, Congress in 1940 agreed to allow the sale of arms to Britain on a "cash and carry" basis—that is, they had to be paid for in cash and transported in British ships. It also approved plans for military rearmament. But with a presidential election looming, Roosevelt was reluctant to go further.

In 1940, breaking with a tradition that dated back to George Washington, Roosevelt announced his candidacy for a third term as president. The international situation was too dangerous and domestic recovery too fragile, he insisted, for him to leave office. Republicans chose as his opponent a political amateur, Wall Street businessman and lawyer Wendell Willkie. Differences between the candidates were far more muted than in 1936. Both supported the law, enacted in September 1940, that established the nation's first peacetime draft. Willkie endorsed New Deal social legislation. He captured more votes than Roosevelt's previous opponents, but FDR still emerged with a decisive victory. Soon after his victory, in a fireside chat in December 1940, Roosevelt announced that the United States would become the "great arsenal of democracy," providing Britain and China with military supplies in their fight against Germany and Japan.

"America First" and Lend-Lease

As the United States became more closely involved in the war, a diverse group mobilized against American participation, including some liberals and socialists. But by far the largest and most influential organization was the **America First Committee**, which grew to approximately 500,000 members with over 400 chapters nationwide. Led by conservative businessmen opposed to Roosevelt's domestic and foreign policy, the organization drew upon isolationist ideas, arguing that a Nazi triumph over Great Britain was less of a threat to the United States than entry into the war. Participation in the war, they warned, would bring an end to the "American system of free enterprise" by augmenting government regulatory power. Instead, they called for building up an "impregnable" military defense.

Though the national leadership condemned Nazi support, well-known members such as Henry Ford, radio priest Father Coughlin, and aviator Charles A. Lindbergh embraced anti-Semitic and conspiratorial thinking. Both Ford and Lindbergh accepted the highest medals of honor granted to foreigners from Nazi officials in 1938. At a rally in Des Moines, Iowa, Lindbergh blamed Jews, the Roosevelt administration, and the British for pressuring the United States to enter the war. America First, along with conservative women's organizations such as the National Legion of Mothers of America and the Women's National Committee to Keep United States Out of War, energized the crusade against intervention. Well-attended speeches and rallies, especially in the Midwest, showed the grassroots resonance of such sentiments. The isolationist drumbeat proved a thorn in the side of the Roosevelt administration, though increasingly Americans began to support intervention.

By 1941, Britain was virtually bankrupt, no longer able to pay for supplies provided by the United States. At Roosevelt's urging, Congress passed the **Lend-Lease Act**, which authorized military aid so long as countries promised somehow to return it all after the war. Under the law's provisions, the United States funneled billions of dollars' worth of arms to Britain and China, as well as the Soviet Union, after Hitler renounced his nonaggression pact and invaded that country in June 1941. FDR also froze Japanese assets in the United States, halting virtually all trade between the countries, including the sale of oil vital to Japan.

Those who believed that the United States must intervene to stem the rising tide of fascism tried to awaken a reluctant country to prepare for war. Interventionists popularized slogans that would become central to wartime mobilization. In June 1941, refugees from Germany and the occupied countries of Europe joined with Americans to form the Free World Association, which sought to bring the United States into the war against Hitler. The same year saw the formation of Freedom House. With a prestigious membership that included university presidents, ministers, businessmen, and labor leaders, Freedom House described the war raging in Europe as an ideological struggle between dictatorship and the "free world." In October 1941, it sponsored a "Fight for Freedom" rally at New York's Madison Square Garden, complete with a patriotic variety show entitled "It's Fun to Be Free." The rally ended by demanding an immediate declaration of war against Germany.

Pearl Harbor

Until November 1941, the administration's attention focused on Europe. But at the end of that month, intercepted Japanese messages revealed that an assault in the Pacific was imminent. No one, however, knew where it would come. On December 7, 1941, Japanese planes, launched from aircraft carriers, bombed the naval base at Pearl Harbor in Hawaii, the first attack by a foreign power on American soil since the War of 1812. Japan launched the attack in the hope of crippling American naval power in the Pacific. With a free hand in its campaign of conquest in East Asia, Japan would gain access to supplies of oil and other resources it could no longer obtain from the United States. It hoped that destroying the American fleet would establish Japan for years to come as the dominant power in the region.

Pearl Harbor was a complete and devastating surprise. In a few hours, more than 2,000 American servicemen were killed, and 187 aircraft and 18 naval vessels, including 8 battleships, destroyed or damaged. By a stroke of fortune, no aircraft carriers—which would prove decisive in the Pacific war—happened to be docked at Pearl Harbor on December 7.

To this day, conspiracy theories abound suggesting that FDR knew of the attack and did nothing to prevent it so as to bring the United States into the war. No credible evidence supports this charge. Indeed, with the country drawing ever closer to intervention in Europe, Roosevelt hoped to keep the peace in the Pacific. But Secretary of Labor Frances Perkins, who saw the president after the attack, remarked that he seemed calm—"his terrible moral problem had been resolved." Terming December 7 "a date which will live in infamy," Roosevelt asked Congress for a declaration of war against Japan. The combined vote in Congress was 388 in favor and 1 against—pacifist Jeanette Rankin of Montana, who had also voted against American entry into World War I. The next day, Germany declared war on the United States. America had finally joined the largest war in human history.

The War in the Pacific

In retrospect, it appears inevitable that the entry of the United States, with its superior industrial might, would ensure the defeat of the **Axis powers**. But the first few months of American involvement witnessed an unbroken string of military disasters. Having earlier occupied substantial portions of French Indochina (now Vietnam, Laos, and Cambodia), Japan in early 1942 conquered Burma (Myanmar) and Siam (Thailand). Japan also took control of the Dutch East Indies (Indonesia), whose extensive oil fields could replace supplies from the United States. And it occupied Guam, the Philippines, and other Pacific islands. At Bataan, in the Philippines, the Japanese forced 78,000 American and Filipino troops to lay down their arms—the largest surrender in American

WORLD WAR II IN THE PACIFIC, 1941–1945

Although the Japanese navy never fully recovered from its defeats at the Coral Sea and Midway in 1942, it took three more years for American forces to near the Japanese homeland.

military history. Thousands perished on the ensuing "death march" to a prisoner-of-war camp, and thousands more died of disease and starvation after they arrived. At the same time, German submarines sank hundreds of Allied merchant and naval vessels during the Battle of the Atlantic.

Soon, however, the tide of battle began to turn. In May 1942, in the Battle of the Coral Sea, the American navy turned back a Japanese fleet intent on attacking Australia. The following month, it inflicted devastating losses on the Japanese navy in the Battle of Midway Island. American codebreakers had managed to decipher the Japanese communications code, so the navy was forewarned about the timing of the assault at Midway and prepared an ambush for the attacking fleet. In the battle, four Japanese aircraft carriers, along with other vessels, were destroyed. Midway was the turning point of the Pacific naval war. The victories there and in the Coral Sea allowed American forces to launch the bloody campaigns that one by one drove the Japanese from fortified islands like Guadalcanal and the Solomons in the western Pacific and brought American troops ever closer to Japan.

The War in Europe

The "Grand Alliance" of World War II in Europe brought together the United States, Great Britain, and the Soviet Union, each led by an iron-willed, larger-than-life figure: Roosevelt, Winston Churchill, and Joseph Stalin. United in their determination to defeat Nazi Germany, they differed not only in terms of the societies they represented but also in their long-range goals. Stalin was set on establishing enough control over eastern Europe that his country would never again be invaded from the west. Churchill hoped to ensure that the British Empire emerged intact from the war. Roosevelt, like Woodrow Wilson before him, hoped to establish a new international order so that world wars would never again take place.

Facing wars in two hemispheres, Roosevelt had to determine how best to deploy American manpower and resources. Bearing the brunt of the fighting after Hitler invaded the Soviet Union in 1941, Stalin demanded an early Allied attack across the English Channel to confront German forces in occupied France and relieve pressure on his beleaguered army. Churchill's strategy was to attack the "soft underbelly" of Axis power through Allied operations in the Mediterranean, starting with an invasion of North Africa. Churchill's approach prevailed, and the cross-Channel invasion did not come until 1944.

In November 1942, British and American forces invaded North Africa and by May 1943 forced the surrender of the German army. By the spring of 1943, the Allies also gained the upper hand in the Atlantic, as British and American destroyers and planes devastated the German submarine fleet. But even though

WORLD WAR II IN EUROPE, 1942–1945

Most of the land fighting in Europe during World War II took place on the eastern front between the German and Soviet armies.

Roosevelt was committed to liberating Europe from Nazi control, American troops did not immediately become involved on the European continent. As late as the end of 1944, more American military personnel were deployed in the Pacific than against Germany. In July 1943, American and British forces invaded Sicily, beginning the liberation of Italy. A popular uprising in Rome overthrew the Mussolini government, whereupon Germany occupied most of the country. Fighting there raged throughout 1944.

The major involvement of American troops in Europe did not begin until June 6, 1944. On that date, known as **D-Day**, nearly 200,000 American, British, and Canadian soldiers under the command of General Dwight D. Eisenhower landed in Normandy in northwestern France. More than a million troops followed them ashore in the next few weeks, in the most massive sea–land operation in history. After fierce fighting, German armies retreated eastward. By August, Paris had been liberated.

The crucial fighting in Europe, however, took place on the eastern front, the scene of an epic struggle between Germany and the Soviet Union. More than 3 million German soldiers took part in the 1941 invasion. After sweeping through western Russia, German armies in August 1942 launched a siege of Stalingrad, a city located deep inside Russia on the Volga River. This proved to be a catastrophic mistake. Bolstered by an influx of military supplies from the United States, the Russians surrounded the German troops and forced them to surrender. Some 800,000 Germans and 1.2 million Russians perished in the fighting. The German surrender at Stalingrad in January 1943 marked the turning point of the European war. The campaign in the east devastated Hitler's forces and sent surviving units on a long retreat back toward Germany.

Of 13.6 million German casualties in World War II, 10 million came on the Russian front. They represented only part of the war's vast toll in human lives. Millions of Poles and at least 20 million Russians, probably many more, perished—not only soldiers but also civilian victims of starvation, disease, and massacres by German soldiers. After his armies had penetrated eastern Europe in 1941, moreover, Hitler embarked on the "final solution"—the mass extermination of "undesirable" peoples—Slavs, gypsies, gay men and women, and, above all, Jews. By 1945, 6 million Jewish men, women, and children had died in Nazi death camps. What came to be called the **Holocaust** was the horrifying culmination of the Nazi belief that Germans constituted a "master race" destined to rule the world.

THE HOME FRONT

Mobilizing for War

By the end of World War II, some 50 million American men had registered for the draft and 10 million had been inducted into the military. The army exemplified how the war united American society in new ways. Military service threw together Americans from every region and walk of life, and almost every racial and ethnic background (African Americans continued to serve in segregated units). It brought into contact the children of immigrants and Americans with very different cultures and outlooks. By 1942, the federal government relied entirely on the draft for manpower. This ensured that wartime sacrifice was widely shared throughout American society. By contrast, in the decades following the Vietnam War, the armed forces have been composed entirely of volunteers, and the military today includes very few men and women from middle- and upper-class backgrounds.

World War II also transformed the role of the national government. FDR created federal agencies like the War Production Board, the War Manpower Commission, and the Office of Price Administration to regulate the allocation of labor, control the shipping industry, establish manufacturing quotas, and fix wages, prices, and rents. The number of federal workers rose from 1 million to 4 million, part of a tremendous growth in new jobs that pushed the unemployment rate down from 14 percent in 1940 to 2 percent three years later.

The government forced civilian industries to retool for war production. Michigan's auto factories now turned out trucks, tanks, and jeeps for the army. By 1944, American factories produced a ship every day and a plane every five minutes. The gross national product rose from $91 billion to $214 billion during the war, and the federal government's expenditures amounted to twice the combined total of the previous 150 years. The government marketed billions of dollars' worth of war bonds, increased taxes, and began the practice of withholding income tax directly from weekly paychecks. Before the war, only the 4 million wealthiest Americans paid income taxes; by 1945, more than 40 million did so. The government, one historian writes, moved during the war from "class taxation" to "mass taxation."

Business and the War

The relationship between the federal government and big business changed dramatically from the days of the Second New Deal. "If you are going to go to war in a capitalist country," observed Secretary of War Henry Stimson, "you had better let business make money out of the process." As corporate executives flooded into federal agencies concerned with war production, Roosevelt offered incentives to spur output—low-interest loans, tax concessions, and contracts with guaranteed profits. The great bulk of federal spending went to the largest corporations, furthering the long-term trend toward economic concentration. By the end of the war, the 200 biggest industrial companies accounted for almost half of all corporate assets in the United States.

Americans marveled at the achievements of wartime manufacturing. Thousands of aircraft, 100,000 armored vehicles, and 2.5 million trucks rolled off American assembly lines, and entirely new products like synthetic rubber replaced natural resources now controlled by Japan. Government-sponsored scientific research perfected inventions like radar, jet engines, and early computers that helped to win the war and would have a large impact on postwar life.

These accomplishments not only made it possible to win a two-front war but also helped to restore the reputation of business and businessmen, which had reached a low point during the Depression.

Federal funds reinvigorated established manufacturing areas and created entirely new industrial centers. World War II saw the West Coast emerge as a focus of military-industrial production. The government invested billions of dollars in the shipyards of Seattle, Portland, and San Francisco and in the steel plants and aircraft factories of southern California. By the war's end, California had received one-tenth of all federal spending, and Los Angeles had become the nation's second-largest manufacturing center. Nearly 2 million Americans moved to California for jobs in defense-related industries, and millions more passed through for military training and embarkation to the Pacific war.

In the South, the combination of rural out-migration and government investment in military-related factories and shipyards hastened a shift from agricultural to industrial employment. During the war, southern per capita income rose from 60 percent to 70 percent of the national average. But the South remained very poor when the war ended. Much of its rural population still lived in small wooden shacks with no indoor plumbing. The region had only two cities—Houston and New Orleans—with populations exceeding 500,000. Despite the expansion of war production, the South's economy still relied on agriculture and extractive industries—mining, lumber, oil—or manufacturing linked to farming, like the production of cotton textiles.

TABLE 22.1 Labor Union Membership

Years	Number of Members
1933	2,857,000
1934	3,728,000
1935	3,753,000
1936	4,107,000
1937	5,780,000
1938	8,265,000
1939	8,980,000
1940	8,944,000
1941	10,489,000
1942	10,762,000
1943	13,642,000
1944	14,621,000
1945	14,796,000

Labor in Wartime

Organized labor repeatedly described World War II as a crusade for freedom that would expand economic and political democracy at home and abroad and win for unions a major voice in politics and industrial management. During the war, labor entered a three-sided arrangement with government and business that allowed union membership to soar to unprecedented levels. In order to secure industrial peace and stabilize war production, the federal government forced reluctant employers to recognize unions. In 1944, when Montgomery Ward, the large mail-order company, defied a pro-union order, the army seized its headquarters and physically evicted its president. For their part, union leaders agreed not to strike and conceded employers' right to "managerial prerogatives" and a "fair profit."

WARTIME ARMY AND NAVY BASES AND AIRFIELDS

Airfields, bases, and stations
Army camps, forts, and posts
Naval bases

As this map indicates, the military and naval facilities built by the federal government during World War II were concentrated in the South and West, sparking the economic development of these regions.

Despite the gains produced by labor militancy during the 1930s, unions only became firmly established in many sectors of the economy during World War II. By 1945, union membership stood at nearly 15 million, one-third of the non-farm labor force and the highest proportion in American history. But if labor became a partner in government, it was very much a junior partner. The decline of the New Deal, already evident in the late 1930s, proceeded during the war. Congress continued to be dominated by a conservative alliance of Republicans and southern Democrats. They left intact core New Deal programs like Social Security but eliminated agencies such as the Civilian Conservation Corps, National Youth Administration, and Works Progress Administration. Congress rejected Roosevelt's call for a cap on personal incomes and set taxes on corporate profits at a level far lower than FDR requested. Despite the "no-strike" pledge, 1943 and 1944 witnessed numerous brief walkouts in which workers protested the increasing speed of assembly-line production and the disparity between wages frozen by government order and expanding corporate profits.

Fighting for the Four Freedoms

Previous conflicts, including the Mexican War and World War I, had deeply divided American society. In contrast, World War II came to be remembered as the Good War, a time of national unity in pursuit of indisputably noble goals. But all wars require the mobilization of patriotic public opinion. "To sell *goods*, we must sell *words*" had become a motto of advertisers. Foremost among the words that helped to "sell" World War II was "freedom."

Talk of freedom pervaded wartime America. To Roosevelt, the Four Freedoms expressed deeply held American values worthy of being spread worldwide. Freedom from fear meant not only a longing for peace but also a more general desire for security in a world that appeared to be out of control. Freedom of speech and religion scarcely required detailed explanation. But their prominent place among the Four Freedoms accelerated the process by which First Amendment protections of free expression moved to the center of Americans' definition of liberty. In 1941, the administration celebrated with considerable fanfare the 150th anniversary of the Bill of Rights (the first ten amendments to the Constitution). FDR described their protections against tyrannical government as defining characteristics of American life, central to the rights of "free men and free women." In 1943, the Supreme Court reversed a 1940 ruling and, on First Amendment grounds, upheld the right of Jehovah's Witnesses to refuse to salute the American flag in public schools. The decision stood in sharp contrast to the coercive patriotism of World War I, and it affirmed the sanctity of individual conscience as a bedrock of freedom, even in times of crisis. The justices contrasted the American system of constitutional protection for unpopular minorities with Nazi tyranny.

Freedom from Want

The "most ambiguous" of the Four Freedoms, *Fortune* magazine remarked, was freedom from want. Yet this "great inspiring phrase," as a Pennsylvania steelworker put it in a letter to the president, seemed to strike the deepest chord in a nation just emerging from the Depression. Roosevelt initially meant it to refer to the elimination of barriers to international trade. But he quickly came to link freedom from want to an economic goal more relevant to the average citizen— protecting the future "standard of living of the American worker and farmer" by guaranteeing that the Depression would not resume after the war. This, he declared, would bring "real freedom for the common man."

When Norman Rockwell's paintings of the Four Freedoms first appeared in the *Saturday Evening Post*, each was accompanied by a brief essay. For *Freedom from Want*, the editors chose an unknown Filipino poet, Carlos Bulosan, who had emigrated to the United States at the age of sixteen. Bulosan's essay showed how the

Four Freedoms could inspire hopes for a better future as well as nostalgia for Rockwell's imagined small-town past. Bulosan wrote of those Americans still outside the social mainstream—migrant workers, cannery laborers, Black victims of segregation—for whom freedom meant having enough to eat, sending their children to school, and being able to "share the promise and fruits of American life."

The Office of War Information

The history of the Office of War Information (OWI), created in 1942 to mobilize public opinion, illustrates how the political divisions generated by the New Deal affected efforts to promote the Four Freedoms. The liberal Democrats who dominated the OWI's writing staff sought to make the conflict "a 'people's war' for freedom." The OWI feared that Americans had only a vague understanding of the war's purposes. They utilized radio, film, the press, and other media to give the conflict an ideological meaning, while seeking to avoid the nationalist hysteria of World War I.

Wartime mobilization drew on deep-seated American traditions. The portrait of the United States holding aloft the torch of liberty in a world overrun by

Each side in World War II invoked history to rally support for its cause. "Rise of Asia" depicts Japan liberating Asia from "ABCD" imperial oppressors (Americans, British, Chinese, Dutch), while the poster issued by the Office of War Information in the United States links the words of Abraham Lincoln to the struggle against Nazi tyranny.

oppression reached back at least as far as the American Revolution. The description of a world half slave and half free recalled the Great Emancipator. But critics charged that the OWI seemed most interested in promoting the definition of freedom Roosevelt had emphasized during the 1930s. One of its first pamphlets listed as elements of freedom the right to a job at fair pay and to adequate food, clothing, shelter, and medical care. Concerned that the OWI was devoting as much time to promoting New Deal social programs as to the war effort, Congress eliminated most of its funding.

The Fifth Freedom

After Congress curtailed the OWI, the "selling of America" became overwhelmingly a private affair. Under the watchful eye of the War Advertising Council, private companies joined in the campaign to promote wartime patriotism, while positioning themselves and their brand names for the postwar world. Alongside advertisements urging Americans to purchase war bonds, guard against revealing military secrets, and grow "victory gardens" to allow food to be sent to the army, the war witnessed a burst of messages marketing advertisers' definition of freedom. Without directly criticizing Roosevelt, they repeatedly suggested that he had overlooked a fifth freedom. The National Association of Manufacturers and individual companies bombarded Americans with press releases, radio programs, and advertisements attributing the amazing feats of wartime production to "free enterprise."

Americans on the home front enjoyed a prosperity many could scarcely remember. Despite the rationing of scarce consumer items like coffee, meat, and gasoline, consumers found more goods available in 1944 than when the war began. With the memory of the Depression still very much alive, businessmen predicted a postwar world filled with consumer goods, with "freedom of choice" among abundant possibilities assured if only private enterprise were liberated from government controls. One advertisement for Royal typewriters, entitled "What This War Is All About," explained that victory would "hasten the day when you . . . can once more walk into any store in the land and buy anything you want." Certainly, ads suggested, the war did not imply any alteration in American institutions. "I'm fighting for freedom," said a soldier in an ad by the Nash-Kelvinator Corporation. "So don't anybody tell me I'll find America changed."

Women at Work

During the war, the nation engaged in an unprecedented mobilization of "womanpower" to fill industrial jobs vacated by men. OWI publications encouraged women to go to work, Hollywood films glorified the independent woman, and private advertising celebrated the achievements of Rosie the Riveter, the female industrial laborer depicted as muscular and self-reliant in Norman Rockwell's famous magazine cover. With 15 million men in the armed forces, women in 1944 made up more than one-third of the civilian labor force, and 350,000 served in auxiliary military units.

Women shipfitters on board the USS *Nereus* in 1943.

Even though most women workers still labored in clerical and service jobs, new opportunities suddenly opened in industrial, professional, and government positions previously restricted to men. On the West Coast, one-third of the workers in aircraft manufacturing and shipbuilding were women. For the first time in history, married women in their thirties outnumbered the young and single among female workers. Women forced unions like the United Auto Workers to confront issues like equal pay for equal work, maternity leave, and childcare facilities for working mothers. Having enjoyed what one wartime worker called "a taste of freedom"—doing "men's" jobs for men's wages—many women hoped to remain in the labor force once peace returned.

The Pull of Tradition

"We as a nation," proclaimed one magazine article, "must change our basic attitude toward the work of women." But change proved difficult. The government, employers, and unions depicted work as a temporary necessity, not an expansion of women's freedom. Advertisements assured women laboring in factories that they, too, were "fighting for freedom." But their language spoke of sacrifice and military victory, not rights, independence, or self-determination. One union publication even declared, "There should be a law requiring the women who have taken over men's jobs to be laid off after the war." When the war ended, most female war workers, especially those in better-paying industrial employment, did indeed lose their jobs.

Despite the upsurge in the number of working women, the advertisers' "world of tomorrow" rested on a vision of family-centered prosperity. Like Norman Rockwell's Four Freedoms paintings, these wartime discussions of freedom simultaneously looked forward to a day of material abundance and back to a time when the family stood as the bedrock of society. The "American way of life" celebrated during the war centered on the woman with "a husband to meet every night at the door," and a home stocked with household appliances and consumer goods. Men in the army seem to have assumed that they would return home to resume traditional family life. In one wartime radio program, a young man described his goal for peacetime: "Havin' a home and some kids, and breathin' fresh air out in the suburbs . . . livin' and workin' decent, like free people."

VISIONS OF POSTWAR FREEDOM

Toward an American Century

The prospect of an affluent future provided a point of unity between New Dealers and conservatives, business and labor. And the promise of prosperity to some extent united two of the most celebrated blueprints for the postwar world. One was *The American Century*, publisher Henry Luce's 1941 effort to mobilize the American people both for the coming war and for an era of postwar world leadership. Americans, Luce's book insisted, must embrace the role history had thrust upon them as the "dominant power in the world." They must seize the opportunity to share with "all peoples" their "magnificent industrial products" and the "great American ideals," foremost among which stood "love of freedom." After the war, American power and American values would underpin a previously unimaginable prosperity—"the abundant life," Luce called it—produced by "free economic enterprise."

Luce's essay anticipated important aspects of the postwar world. But its bombastic rhetoric and a title easily interpreted as a call for American global dominance aroused opposition among liberals and the left. Henry Wallace, Roosevelt's vice president after the 1940 election and one of the more liberal New Dealers, offered the liberal response in "The Price of Free World Victory," an address delivered in May 1942 to the Free World Association.

In contrast to Luce's American Century, a world of business dominance no less than of American power, Wallace predicted that the war would usher in a "century of the common man." The "march of freedom," said Wallace, would continue in the postwar world. That world, however, would be marked by international cooperation, not any single power's rule. Governments acting to "humanize" capitalism and redistribute economic resources would eliminate hunger, illiteracy, and poverty.

Luce and Wallace both spoke the language of freedom. Luce offered a confident vision of worldwide free enterprise, while Wallace anticipated a global New Deal. But they had one thing in common—a new conception of America's role in the world, tied to continued international involvement, the promise of economic abundance, and the idea that the American experience should serve as a model for all other nations. Neither took into account the ideas that other countries might have developed as to how to proceed once the war had ended.

"The Way of Life of Free Men"

Even as Congress moved to dismantle parts of the New Deal, liberal Democrats and their left-wing allies unveiled plans for a postwar economic policy that would allow all Americans to enjoy freedom from want. In 1942 and 1943, the reports of the National Resources Planning Board (NRPB) offered a blueprint for a peacetime economy based on full employment, an expanded welfare state, and a widely shared American standard of living. Economic security and full employment were the board's watchwords. It called for a "new bill of rights" that would include all Americans in an expanded Social Security system and guarantee access to education, health care, adequate housing, and jobs for able-bodied adults. The NRPB's plan for a "full-employment economy" with a "fair distribution of income," said *The Nation*, embodied "the way of life of free men."

The reports continued a shift in liberals' outlook that dated from the late 1930s. Rather than seeking to reform the institutions of capitalism, liberals would henceforth rely on government spending to secure full employment, social welfare, and mass consumption, while leaving the operation of the economy in private hands. The reports appeared to reflect the views of British economist John Maynard Keynes, who, as noted in the previous chapter, had identified government spending as the best way to promote economic growth, even if it caused budget deficits. The war had, in effect, ended the Depression by implementing a military version of Keynesianism. In calling for massive spending on job creation and public works—urban redevelopment, rural electrification, an overhaul of the transportation system, and the like—the NRPB proposed the continuation of Keynesian spending in peacetime. But this went so far beyond what Congress was willing to support that it eliminated the NRPB's funding.

An Economic Bill of Rights

Mindful that public-opinion polls showed a large majority of Americans favoring a guarantee of employment for those who could not find work, the president in 1944 called for an "Economic Bill of Rights." The original Bill of Rights restricted the power of government in the name of liberty. FDR proposed to expand its power in order to secure full employment, an adequate income, medical care, education, and a decent home for all Americans.

Already ill and preoccupied with the war, Roosevelt spoke only occasionally of the Economic Bill of Rights during the 1944 presidential campaign. The replacement of Vice President Henry Wallace by Harry S. Truman, then a little-known senator from Missouri, suggested that the president did not intend to do battle with Congress over social policy. Congress did not enact the Economic Bill of Rights. But in 1944, it extended to the millions of returning veterans an array of benefits, including unemployment pay, scholarships for further education,

low-cost mortgage loans, pensions, and job training. The Servicemen's Readjustment Act, or **GI Bill of Rights**, was one of the most far-reaching pieces of social
legislation in American history. Aimed at rewarding members of the armed
forces for their service and preventing the widespread unemployment and economic disruption that had followed World War I, it profoundly shaped postwar
society. By 1946, more than 1 million veterans were attending college under its
provisions, making up half of total college enrollment. Almost 4 million would
receive home mortgages, spurring a postwar suburban housing boom.

During 1945, unions, civil rights organizations, and religious groups urged
Congress to enact the Full Employment Bill, which tried to do for the entire
economy what the GI Bill promised veterans. The measure established a "right
to employment" for all Americans and required the federal government to
increase its level of spending to create enough jobs in case the economy failed
to do so. The target of an intense business lobbying campaign, the bill only
passed in 1946 with the word "Full" removed from its title and after its commitment to governmental job creation had been eliminated. But as the war drew to
a close, most Americans embraced the idea that the government must continue
to play a major role in maintaining employment and a high standard of living.

The Road to Serfdom

The failure of the Full Employment Bill confirmed the political stalemate
that had begun with the elections of 1938. It also revealed the renewed intellectual respectability of fears that economic planning represented a threat
to liberty. When the *New Republic* spoke of full employment as the "road to
freedom," it subtly acknowledged the impact of *The Road to Serfdom* (1944), a
surprise best-seller by Friedrich A. Hayek, a previously obscure Austrian-born
economist. Hayek claimed that even the best-intentioned government efforts
to direct the economy posed a threat to individual liberty. He offered a simple
message—"Planning leads to dictatorship."

Coming at a time when the miracles of war production had reinvigorated
belief in the virtues of capitalism, and with the confrontation with Nazism highlighting the danger of merging economic and political power, Hayek offered a
new intellectual justification for opponents of active government. In a complex
economy, he insisted, a free market mobilizes the fragmented and partial knowledge scattered throughout society far more effectively than a planned economy.

Unlike many of his disciples, Hayek was not a doctrinaire advocate of
laissez-faire. His book endorsed measures that later conservatives would
denounce as forms of socialism—minimum wage and maximum hours laws,
antitrust enforcement, and a social safety net guaranteeing all citizens a basic
minimum of food, shelter, and clothing. Hayek, moreover, criticized traditional

conservatives for fondness for social hierarchy and authoritarian government. But by equating fascism, socialism, and the New Deal and by identifying economic planning with a loss of freedom, he helped set the stage for a renewed battle over the government's proper role in society and the economy, and the social conditions of American freedom.

THE AMERICAN DILEMMA

The unprecedented attention to freedom as the defining characteristic of American life had implications that went far beyond wartime mobilization. World War II reshaped Americans' understanding of themselves as a people. The struggle against Nazi tyranny and its theory of a master race discredited ethnic and racial inequality. Originally promoted by religious and ethnic minorities in the 1920s and the Popular Front in the 1930s, a pluralist vision of American society now became part of official rhetoric. What set the United States apart from its wartime foes, the government insisted, was not only dedication to the ideals of the Four Freedoms but also the principle that Americans of all races, religions, and national origins could enjoy those freedoms equally. Racism was the enemy's philosophy; Americanism rested on toleration of diversity and equality for all. By the end of the war, the new immigrant groups had been fully accepted as loyal ethnic Americans, rather than members of distinct and inferior "races." And the contradiction between the principle of equal freedom and the actual status of Blacks had come to the forefront of national life.

Patriotic Assimilation

Among other things, World War II created a vast melting pot, especially for European immigrants and their children. Millions of Americans moved out of urban ethnic neighborhoods and isolated rural enclaves into the army and industrial plants. What one historian has called their "patriotic assimilation" differed sharply from the forced Americanization of World War I. While the Wilson administration had established Anglo-Saxon culture as a national norm, Roosevelt promoted pluralism as the only source of harmony in a diverse society. The American way of life, wrote the novelist Pearl Buck in an OWI pamphlet, rested on brotherhood—the principle that "persons of many lands can live together . . . and if they believe in freedom they can become a united people."

Government and private agencies eagerly promoted equality as the definition of Americanism and a counterpoint to Nazism. Officials rewrote history to establish racial and ethnic tolerance as the American way. To be an American,

FDR declared, had always been a "matter of mind and heart," and "never . . . a matter of race or ancestry"—a statement more effective in mobilizing support for the war than in accurately describing the nation's past. Mindful of the intolerance spawned by World War I, the OWI highlighted nearly every group's contributions to American life and celebrated the strength of a people united in respect for diversity. One OWI pamphlet described prejudice as a foreign import rather than a homegrown product and declared bigots more dangerous than spies—they were "fighting for the enemy."

Horrified by the uses to which the Nazis put the idea of inborn racial difference, biological and social scientists abandoned belief in a link among race, culture, and intelligence, an idea only recently central to their disciplines. Ruth Benedict's *Races and Racism* (1942) described racism as "a travesty of scientific knowledge." In the same year, Ashley Montagu's *Man's Most Dangerous Myth: The Fallacy of Race* became a best-seller. By the war's end, racism and nativism had been stripped of intellectual respectability, at least outside the South, and were viewed as psychological disorders.

Hollywood, too, did its part, portraying fighting units whose members, representing various regional, ethnic, and religious backgrounds, put aside group loyalties and prejudices for the common cause. *Air Force* featured a bomber crew that included an Anglo-Saxon officer, a Jewish sergeant, and a Polish American gunner. In the film *Bataan*, the ethnically balanced platoon included a Black soldier, even though the real army was racially segregated. The war's most popular motion picture, *This Is the Army*, starring, among others, future president Ronald Reagan, offered a vision of postwar society that celebrated the ethnic diversity of the American people.

Intolerance, of course, hardly disappeared from American life. One correspondent complained to Norman Rockwell that he included too many "foreign-looking" faces in his *Freedom of Worship* painting. Many business and government circles still excluded Jews. Along with the fact that early reports of the Holocaust were too terrible to be believed, anti-Semitism contributed to the government's unwillingness to allow more than a handful of European Jews (21,000 during the course of the war) to find refuge in the United States. Roosevelt himself learned during the war of the extent of Hitler's "final solution" to the Jewish presence in Europe. But he failed to authorize air strikes that might have destroyed German death camps.

Nonetheless, the war made millions of ethnic Americans, especially the children of the new immigrants, feel fully American for the first time. During the war, one New York "ethnic" recalled, "the Italo Americans stopped being Italo and started becoming Americans." But the event that inspired this comment, the Harlem race riot of 1943, suggested that patriotic assimilation stopped at the color line.

The *Bracero* Program

The war had a far more ambiguous meaning for non-white groups than for whites. On the eve of Pearl Harbor, racial barriers remained deeply entrenched in American life. Southern Blacks were still trapped in a rigid system of segregation. Asians could not immigrate to the United States or become naturalized citizens. As noted in the previous chapters, more than 400,000 Mexican Americans had been repatriated during the Depression.

The war set in motion changes that would reverberate in the postwar years. Under the ***bracero* program** agreed to by the Mexican and American governments in 1942 (the name derives from *brazo*, the Spanish word for arm), tens of thousands of contract laborers crossed into the United States to take up jobs as domestic and agricultural workers. Initially designed as a temporary response to the wartime labor shortage, the program lasted until 1964. During the period of the *bracero* program, more than 4.5 million Mexicans entered the United States under government labor contracts (while a slightly larger number were arrested for illegal entry by the Border Patrol). *Braceros* were supposed to receive decent housing and wages. But since they could not become citizens and could be deported at any time, they found it almost impossible to form unions or secure better working conditions.

Although the *bracero* program reinforced the status of immigrants from Mexico as an unskilled labor force, wartime employment opened new opportunities for second-generation Mexican Americans. Hundreds of thousands of men and women emerged from ethnic neighborhoods, or *barrios*, to work in defense industries and serve in the army (where, unlike Blacks, they fought alongside whites). For Mexican American women in particular, the war afforded new opportunities for public participation and higher incomes. "Rosita the Riveter" took her place alongside "Rosie" in the West Coast's multiethnic war production factories. Government publications and newspaper accounts celebrated their role as patriotic mothers who encouraged their sons to enlist in the army and offered moral support while they were away at war. A new "Chicano" culture—a fusion of Mexican heritage and American experience—was being born. Contact with other groups led many to learn English and sparked a rise in interethnic marriages.

Mexican American Rights

The **zoot suit riots** of 1943, in which club-wielding sailors and policemen attacked Mexican American youths wearing flamboyant clothing on the streets of Los Angeles, illustrated the limits of wartime tolerance. But the contrast between the war's rhetoric of freedom and pluralism and the reality of continued discrimination inspired a heightened consciousness of civil rights.

Mexican Americans brought complaints of discrimination before the Fair Employment Practices Commission (FEPC) to fight the practice in the Southwest of confining them to the lowest-paid work or paying them lower wages than white workers doing the same jobs.

Perhaps half a million Mexican American men and women served in the armed forces. And with discrimination against Mexicans an increasing embarrassment in view of Roosevelt's Good Neighbor Policy, Texas (the state with the largest population of Mexican descent) in 1943 unanimously passed the oddly named Caucasian Race—Equal Privileges resolution. It stated that since "all the nations of the North and South American continents" were united in the struggle against Nazism, "all persons of the Caucasian race" were entitled to equal treatment in places of public accommodation. Since Texas law had long defined Mexicans as white, the measure applied to them while not challenging the segregation of Blacks. The resolution lacked an enforcement mechanism. Indeed, because of continued discrimination in Texas, the Mexican government for a time prohibited the state from receiving laborers under the *bracero* program.

The War and Indigenous Freedom

In her 1944 book, *Speaking of Indians*, Lakota author Ella Deloria wrote that the war "wrought an overnight change in outlook, horizon, and even habits of the Indian people." As in World War I, wartime service by Native Americans intensified debates about their place in society but now brought significant changes. Among the 25,000 Native Americans who served in the war were the famous Navajo "code-talkers" who transmitted messages in their complex native language, which the Japanese could not decipher. On the home front, Native Americans worked in wartime industry in factories, on farms, and on military installations. Marge Pascale, an Ojibwe woman, joined the Women's Army Corps in 1943, explaining "One thing about the service, you get two pair of shoes and you get a bed and you get to eat."

Indeed, many Native Americans joined the military to escape impoverishment. Many others were drafted, but military service was also viewed by some as an act of tribal and American patriotism—one they hoped would foster Indigenous freedoms. One Santa Clara Pueblo man, learning that Congress was considering construction of dams that threatened tribal homes, protested, "We are fighting with Uncle Sam's army to defend the right of our people to live our own life in our own way." Most American Indian nations cooperated with the draft, but the Hopi, Ute, Seminole, Haudenosaunee (Iroquois), Yakima, and Tohono O'odham (Papago) resisted. After losing a court case seeking to exempt their nation from the draft, Haudenosaunee officials deployed the language of freedom: "After taking practically all the beautiful country that once was ours," they claimed, the United States now looked to "take from us our last possession, our freedom." For most Native Americans, self-determination, or sovereignty, was foundational to their conception of freedom.

The wartime home front brought renewed challenges to Native sovereignty. The U.S. government seized Indian land for military purposes. On the Lakota Pine Ridge reservation, the government appropriated over 350,000 acres for a gunnery range, forcing many families to leave behind their homes, crops, and livestock. Without the consent of the Pima, Mohave, and Chemehuevi Indians, and despite protests, the U.S. government built two internment camps, the Poston internment center and the Colorado River camp, on Indigenous land in Arizona. During the war, private interests and state officials eager to abolish tribal sovereignty and open Indian lands argued that Indians who moved off reservations temporarily during wartime wished to do so permanently. In response, Indian representatives from fifty tribes formed the National Congress of American Indians in 1944. The organization fought against the assault on sovereignty, called for a commission to settle land claims, and sought to gain voting rights in states like New Mexico and Arizona where Indians faced disfranchisement.

Bound by War

With China an ally in the Pacific war, Congress in 1943 ended decades of complete exclusion by establishing a nationality quota for Chinese immigrants. The annual limit of 105 hardly suggested a desire for a large-scale influx. But the image of the Chinese as gallant fighters defending their country against Japanese aggression called into question long-standing racial stereotypes. As in the case of Mexican Americans, large numbers of Chinese Americans moved out of ethnic ghettos to work alongside whites in jobs on the home front. More than 50,000 Asian Americans—the children and grandchildren of immigrants from China, Japan, Korea, and the Philippines—fought in the U.S. army, mostly in all-Asian units.

The Philippines had been granted Commonwealth status by Congress in 1934 and promised a ten-year transition from colonial rule to full independence. But many Filipinos fought under U.S. military command in the Pacific. In the battle of Bataan alone, the United States Armed Forces in the Far East included about 80,000 soldiers, the vast majority of whom were Filipino scouts and Filipino army soldiers. Among the many killed on the infamous Bataan death march and in the prison camps in the two months that followed, most were Filipino soldiers.

For Japanese Americans, the war proved a harrowing experience. Many Americans viewed the war against Germany as an ideological struggle. But

From LEAGUE OF UNITED LATIN AMERICAN CITIZENS, "WORLD WAR II AND MEXICAN AMERICANS" (1945)

Founded in 1929, the League of United Latin American Citizens (LULAC) campaigned for equal treatment for Americans of Latino descent and their full integration into American life. Soon after the war ended, an editorial in its publication *LULAC News* condemned continuing discrimination, reflecting how the war sparked a rising demand for equal rights among many minority groups.

"We do not serve Mexicans here." "You will have to get out as no Mexicans are allowed." "Your uniform and service ribbons mean nothing here. We still do not allow Mexicans."

These, and many other stronger-worded ones, are the embarrassing and humiliating retorts given our returning veterans of Latin American descent and their families. They may all be worded differently, and whereas some are toned with hate and loathness while others are toned with sympathy and remorse, still the implication remains that these so-called "Mexicans" are considered unworthy of equality, regardless of birthright or service. . . .

Why this hate, this prejudice, this tendency to discriminate against a people whose only fault seems to be that they are heirs of a culture older than any known "American Culture," to find themselves a part of a land and people they have helped to build and to defend, to find themselves a part of a minority group whose acquired passive nature keeps them from boldly demanding those rights and privileges which are rightfully theirs? Can it be the result of difference in race, nationality, language, loyalty, or ability?

There is no difference in race. Latin Americans, or so-called "Mexicans," are Caucasian or white. . . . There is no difference in nationality. These "Mexicans" were born and bred in this country and are just as American as Jones or Smith. . . . Difference in language? No, these "Mexicans" speak English. Accented, perhaps, in some cases, but English all over the United States seems to be accented. . . . Difference in loyalty? How can that be when all revere the same stars and stripes, when they don the same service uniforms for the same principles? Difference in intelligence and ability? Impossible. . . .

This condition is not a case of difference; it is a case of ignorance. . . . An ignorance of the cultural contributions of Americans of Latin American descent to the still young American Culture; . . . an ignorance of a sense of appreciation for a long, profitable, and loyal association with a group of Americans whose voice cries out in desperate supplication: "We have proved ourselves true and loyal Americans . . . now give us social, political, and economic equality."

From CARLOS BULOSAN, "FREEDOM FROM WANT" IN *THE SATURDAY EVENING POST* (1943)

When Norman Rockwell's paintings of the Four Freedoms appeared in *The Saturday Evening Post* in 1943, each was accompanied by an essay. The "Freedom from Want" essay was authored by the novelist and poet Carlos Bulosan. A Filipino who had worked as a migrant and cannery worker, Bulosan focuses on working and laboring groups on the margins of American society and emphasizes the importance of economic security as the foundation for freedom and democracy.

If you want to know what we are, look upon the farms or upon the hard pavements of the city. You usually see us working or waiting for work, and you think you know us, but our outward guise is more deceptive than our history. . . .

Our march toward security and peace is the march of freedom—the freedom that we should like to become a living part of. It is the dignity of the individual to live in a society of free men, where the spirit of understanding and belief exist; of understanding that all men are equal; that all men, whatever their color, race, religion, or estate, should be given equal opportunity to serve themselves and each other according to their needs and abilities.

To us, freedom is not an intangible thing. When we have enough to eat, then we are healthy enough to enjoy what we eat. Then we have the time and ability to read and think and discuss things. Then we are not merely living but also becoming a creative part of life. It is only then that we become a growing part of democracy. . . .

The totalitarian nations hate democracy. They hate us because we ask for a definite guaranty of freedom of religion, freedom of expression, and freedom from fear and want. Our challenge to tyranny is the depth of our faith in a democracy worth defending. . . . We are multitudes in Pennsylvania mines, in Alaskan canneries. We are millions from Puget Sound to Florida. . . .

Sometimes we walk across the land looking for something to hold on to. We cannot believe that the resources of this country are exhausted. Even when we see our children suffer humiliations, we cannot believe that America has no more place for us. We realize that what is wrong is not in our system of government, but in the ideals which were blasted away by a materialistic age. We know that we can truly find and identify our-selves with a living tradition if we walk proudly in familiar streets. It is a great honor to walk on the American earth.

Everywhere we are on the march, passing through darkness into a sphere of economic peace. When we have the freedom to think and discuss things without fear, when peace and security are assured, when the futures of our children are ensured. . . . America lives and becomes a growing part of our aspirations again.

QUESTIONS

1. *What evidence does the editorial offer that Latinos are deserving of equality?*

2. *How does Bulosan make the case that economic security is essential for freedom?*

3. *What differences and what commonalities exist between these two claims for greater rights in American society?*

both sides saw the Pacific war as a race war. Japanese propaganda depicted Americans as a self-indulgent people contaminated by ethnic and racial diversity. In the United States, long-standing prejudices and the shocking attack on Pearl Harbor combined to produce an unprecedented hatred of Japan. "In all our history," according to one historian, "no foe has been detested as were the Japanese." Government propaganda and war films portrayed the Japanese as rats, dogs, gorillas, and snakes—bestial and subhuman. They blamed Japanese aggression on a violent racial or national character, not, as in the case of Germany and Italy, on tyrannical rulers.

About 70 percent of Japanese Americans in the continental United States lived in California, where they dominated vegetable farming in the Los Angeles area. One-third were first-generation immigrants, or *issei*, but a substantial majority were *nisei*—American-born, and therefore citizens. Many of the latter spoke only English, had never been to Japan, and had tried to assimilate despite prevailing prejudice. But the Japanese American community could not remain unaffected by the rising tide of hatred. The government bent over backward to include German Americans and Italian Americans in the war effort. It ordered the arrest of only a handful of the more than 800,000 German and Italian nationals in the United States when the war began. But it viewed every person of Japanese ethnicity as a potential spy.

Japanese American Internment

California, as discussed in Chapter 19, had a long history of hostility toward the Japanese. Now, inspired by exaggerated fears of a Japanese invasion of the West Coast and pressured by whites who saw an opportunity to gain possession of Japanese American property, the military persuaded FDR to issue Executive Order 9066. Promulgated in February 1942, this ordered the relocation of all persons of Japanese descent from the West Coast. That spring and summer, authorities removed more than 110,000 men, women, and children—nearly two-thirds of them American citizens—to camps far from their homes. The order did not apply to persons of Japanese descent living in Hawaii, where they represented nearly 40 percent of the population. Despite Hawaii's vulnerability, its economy could not function without Japanese American labor. But **Japanese American internment** provided ammunition for Japan's claim that its aggressions in Asia were intended to defend the rights of non-white peoples against colonial rule and a racist United States.

The internees were subjected to a quasi-military discipline in the camps. Living in former horse stables, makeshift shacks, or barracks behind barbed-wire fences, they were awakened for roll call at 6:45 each morning and ate their meals (which rarely included the Japanese cooking to which they were accustomed) in giant mess halls. Armed guards patrolled the camps, and searchlights shone all night. Privacy was difficult to come by, and medical facilities were often non-existent. Nonetheless, the internees did their best to create an atmosphere of home, decorating their accommodations with pictures, flowers, and curtains, planting vegetable gardens, and setting up activities like sports clubs and art classes for themselves.

Internment revealed how easily war can undermine basic freedoms. There were no court hearings, no due process, and no writs of habeas corpus. One searches the wartime record in vain for public protests among non-Japanese against the gravest violation of civil liberties since the end of slavery. The press supported the policy almost unanimously. In Congress, only Senator Robert Taft of Ohio spoke out against it. Groups publicly committed to fighting discrimination, from the Communist Party to the NAACP and the American Jewish Committee, either defended the policy or remained silent.

The courts refused to intervene. In 1944, in **Korematsu v. United States**, the Supreme Court denied the appeal of Fred Korematsu, a Japanese American citizen who had been arrested for refusing to present himself for internment.

JAPANESE AMERICAN INTERNMENT, 1942–1945

More than 100,000 Japanese Americans—the majority American citizens—were forcibly moved from their homes to internment camps during World War II.

From JUSTICE ROBERT A. JACKSON, DISSENT IN *KOREMATSU V. UNITED STATES* (1944)

The decision upholding the order interning Japanese Americans during World War II is one of the most infamous in the Supreme Court's history. Justice Jackson's dissent has often been cited as a powerful warning against government-sponsored racism. In 2018, the Court repudiated the *Korematsu* decision.

Korematsu was born on our soil, of parents born in Japan. The Constitution makes him a citizen of the United States by nativity, and a citizen of California by residence. No claim is made that he is not loyal to this country. . . .

Now, if any fundamental assumption underlies our system, it is that guilt is personal and not inheritable. Even if all of one's antecedents had been convicted of treason, the Constitution forbids its penalties to be visited upon him. . . . But here is an attempt to make an otherwise innocent act a crime merely because this prisoner is the son of parents as to whom he had no choice, and belongs to a race from which there is no way to resign. . . .

In the very nature of things, military decisions are not susceptible of intelligent judicial appraisal. . . . Courts can never have any real alternative to accepting the mere declaration of the authority that issued the order that it was reasonably necessary from a military viewpoint.

Much is said of the danger to liberty from the Army program for deporting and detaining these citizens of Japanese extraction. But a judicial construction of the due process clause that will sustain this order is a far more subtle blow to liberty than the promulgation of the order itself. A military order, however unconstitutional, is not apt to last longer than the military emergency. Even during that period, a succeeding commander may revoke it all. But once a judicial opinion rationalizes such an order to show that it conforms to the Constitution, or rather rationalizes the Constitution to show that the Constitution sanctions such an order, the Court for all time has validated the principle of racial discrimination in criminal procedure and of transplanting American citizens. The principle then lies about like a loaded weapon, ready for the hand of any authority that can bring forward a plausible claim of an urgent need.

QUESTIONS

1. *Why does Justice Jackson believe that even though military authorities have the power to violate constitutional protections in time of war, the courts should not approve their actions?*

2. *What does he mean by likening the Court's decision to "a loaded weapon"?*

Speaking for a 6-3 majority, Justice Hugo Black, usually an avid defender of civil liberties, upheld the legality of the internment policy, insisting that an order applying only to persons of Japanese descent was not based on race. In 2018, in a case involving President Trump's order banning travel to the United States by citizens of several Muslim-majority countries, the Supreme Court, as an aside, declared that the *Korematsu* decision was "gravely wrong" and had no legal standing.

The government marketed war bonds to the internees. It established a loyalty oath program, expecting Japanese Americans to swear allegiance to the government that had imprisoned them and to enlist in the army. Some young men refused, and about 200 were sent to prison for resisting the draft. "Let us out and then maybe I'll think about risking my skin for 'the land of the free,'" one of the resisters remarked. But 20,000 Japanese Americans joined the armed forces from the camps, along with another 13,000 from Hawaii.

A long campaign for acknowledgment of the injustice done to Japanese Americans followed the end of the war. In 1988, Congress apologized for internment and provided $20,000 in compensation to each surviving victim. President Bill Clinton subsequently awarded Fred Korematsu the Presidential Medal of Freedom.

Blacks and the War

Although the treatment of Japanese Americans revealed the stubborn hold of racism in American life, the wartime message of freedom portended a major transformation in the status of Blacks. "There never has been, there isn't now, and there never will be," Roosevelt declared, "any race of people on the earth fit to serve as masters over their fellow men." Yet Nazi Germany cited American practices as proof of its own race policies. Washington remained a rigidly segregated city, and the Red Cross refused to mix blood from Blacks and whites in its blood banks (thereby, critics charged, in effect accepting Nazi race theories). Charles Drew, the Black scientist who pioneered the techniques of storing and shipping blood plasma—a development of immense importance to the treatment of wounded soldiers—protested bitterly against this policy, pointing out that it had no scientific basis. In 1940 and 1941, even as Roosevelt called for aid to the free peoples of Europe, thirteen lynchings took place in the United States.

The war spurred a movement of Black population from the rural South to the cities of the North and West that dwarfed the Great Migration of World War I and the 1920s. In the **second Great Migration**, about 700,000 Black migrants poured out of the South on what they called "liberty trains," seeking jobs in the industrial heartland. They encountered sometimes violent hostility. In 1943, a fight at a Detroit city park spiraled into a race riot that left thirty-four persons dead, and a "hate strike" of 20,000 workers protested the upgrading of Black employees in a plant manufacturing aircraft engines. The war failed to end lynching. Isaac Simmons, a Black minister, was murdered in 1944 for refusing to sell his land to a white man who believed it might contain oil. The criminals went unpunished. This took place in Liberty, Mississippi.

Blacks and Military Service

When World War II began, the air force and marines had no Black members. The army restricted the number of Black enlistees and contained only five Black officers, three of them chaplains. The navy accepted Blacks only as waiters and cooks.

During the war, more than 1 million Blacks served in the armed forces. They did so in segregated units, largely confined to construction, transport, and other noncombat tasks. Many northern Black draftees were sent to the South for military training, where they found themselves excluded from movie theaters and servicemen's clubs on military bases and abused when they ventured into local towns. Black soldiers sometimes had to give up their seats on railroad cars to accommodate Nazi prisoners of war. "Nothing so lowers Negro morale," wrote the NAACP's magazine, *The Crisis*, "as the frequent preferential treatment of Axis prisoners of war in contrast with Army policy toward American troops who happen to be Negro."

When southern Black veterans returned home and sought benefits through the GI Bill, they encountered even more evidence of racial discrimination. On the surface, the GI Bill contained no racial differentiation in offering benefits like health care, college tuition assistance, job training, and loans to start a business or purchase a farm. But local authorities who administered its provisions allowed southern Black veterans to use its education benefits only at segregated colleges, limited their job training to unskilled work and low-wage service jobs, and restricted loans for farm purchase to white veterans.

Birth of the Civil Rights Movement

In 1942, a public-opinion survey sponsored by the army's Bureau of Intelligence found that the vast majority of white Americans were "unaware that there is any such thing as a 'Negro problem'" and were convinced that Blacks were satisfied with their social and economic conditions. They would soon discover their mistake.

The war years witnessed the birth of the modern civil rights movement. Angered by the almost complete exclusion of African Americans from jobs in the rapidly expanding war industries (of 100,000 aircraft workers in 1940, fewer than 300 were Blacks), the Black labor leader A. Philip Randolph in July 1941 called for a March on Washington. His demands included access to defense employment, an end to segregation, and a national antilynching law. Randolph, who as founder of the Brotherhood of Sleeping Car Porters had long battled racism among both employers and unions, hurled Roosevelt's rhetoric back at the president. Randolph declared racial discrimination "undemocratic, un-American, and pro-Hitler."

The prospect of thousands of angry Blacks descending on Washington, remarked one official, "scared the government half to death." To persuade Randolph to call off the march, Roosevelt issued Executive Order 8802, which banned discrimination in defense jobs and established a Fair Employment Practices Commission (FEPC) to monitor compliance. The Black press hailed the order as a new Emancipation Proclamation.

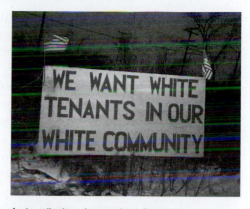

A sign displayed opposite a Detroit housing project in 1942 symbolizes one aspect of what Gunnar Myrdal called "the American Dilemma"—the persistence of racism in the midst of a worldwide struggle for freedom.

Essentially an investigative agency, the FEPC lacked enforcement powers. But its very existence marked a significant shift in public policy. Its hearings exposed patterns of racial exclusion so ingrained that firms at first freely admitted that their want ads asked for "colored" applicants for positions as porters and janitors and "white" ones for skilled jobs, and that they allowed Black women to work only as laundresses and cooks. The first federal agency since Reconstruction to campaign for equal opportunity for Black Americans, the FEPC played an important role in obtaining jobs for Black workers in industrial plants and shipyards. In southern California, the aircraft manufacturer Lockheed ran special buses into Black neighborhoods to bring workers to its plants. By 1944, more than 1 million Blacks, 300,000 of them women, held manufacturing jobs. ("My sister always said that Hitler was the one that got us out of the white folks' kitchen," recalled one Black woman.)

The Double-V

When the president "said that we should have the Four Freedoms," a Black steelworker declared, he meant to include "all races." During the war, NAACP membership grew from 50,000 to nearly 500,000. The Congress of Racial Equality (CORE), founded by an interracial group of pacifists in 1942, held sit-ins in northern cities to integrate restaurants and theaters. After a Firestone tire factory in Memphis fired a Black woman for trying to enter a city bus before white passengers had been seated, Black workers at the plant went on strike until she was reinstated.

In February 1942, the *Pittsburgh Courier* coined the phrase that came to symbolize Black attitudes during the war—the **double-V**. Victory over Germany and Japan, it insisted, must be accompanied by victory over segregation at home. While the Roosevelt administration and the white press saw the war as an expression of American ideals, Black newspapers pointed to the gap between those ideals and reality. Side by side with ads for war bonds, *The Crisis* insisted that a segregated army "cannot fight for a free world."

Surveying wartime public opinion, a political scientist concluded that "symbols of national solidarity" had very different meanings to white and Black Americans. To Blacks, freedom from fear meant, among other things, an end to lynching, and freedom from want included doing away with "discrimination in getting jobs." If, in whites' eyes, freedom was a "possession to be defended," he observed, to Blacks and other racial minorities it remained a "goal to be achieved." "*Our* fight for freedom," said a returning Black veteran of the Pacific war, "begins when we get to San Francisco."

"Imperialisms at Home"

During the war, a broad political coalition centered on the left but reaching well beyond it called for an end to racial inequality in America. The NAACP and American Jewish Congress cooperated closely in advocating laws to ban discrimination in employment and housing. Despite considerable resistance from rank-and-file white workers, CIO unions, especially those with strong left-liberal and communist influence, made significant efforts to organize Black workers and win them access to skilled positions. AFL craft unions by and large continued their long tradition of excluding Black workers. But during World War II, the CIO was probably more racially integrated than any labor organization since the Knights of Labor in the 1880s.

As Blacks demanded an end to segregation, southern politicians took up the cry of protecting white supremacy. They also spoke the language of freedom. Defenders of the racial status quo interpreted freedom to mean the right to shape their region's institutions without outside interference. The "war emergency," insisted Governor Frank Dixon of Alabama, "should not be used as a pretext to bring about the abolition of the color line." Even as the war gave birth to the modern civil rights movement, it also planted the seeds for the South's "massive resistance" to desegregation during the 1950s.

In the rest of the country, however, the status of Black Americans assumed a place at the forefront of enlightened liberalism. Far more than in the 1930s, federal officials spoke openly of the need for a dramatic change in race relations. American democracy, noted Secretary of War Stimson, had not yet addressed "the persistent legacy of the original crime of slavery." Progress came slowly. But the National War Labor Board banned racial wage differentials. In *Smith v. Allwright* (1944), the Supreme Court outlawed all-white primaries, one of the mechanisms by which southern states deprived Blacks of political rights. The government also ordered that soldiers be allowed to vote without paying a poll tax, enabling thousands of Black men to cast ballots for the first time. In 1944, the navy began assigning small numbers of Black sailors to previously all-white ships. In the final months of the war, it ended segregation altogether, and the army established a few combat units that included Black and white soldiers.

After a world tour in 1942 to rally support for the Allies, Wendell Willkie, Roosevelt's opponent of 1940, published *One World.* It sold 1 million copies, faster than any other nonfiction work in American history. Willkie's travels persuaded him that Asia, Africa, and Latin America would play a pivotal role in the postwar era. But the book's great surprise came in Willkie's attack on "our imperialisms at home." Unless the United States addressed the "mocking paradox" of racism, he insisted, its claim to world leadership would lack moral authority. "If we want to talk about freedom," Willkie wrote, "we must mean freedom for everyone inside our frontiers."

An American Dilemma

No event reflected the new concern with the status of Black Americans more than the publication in 1944 of *An American Dilemma*, a sprawling account of the country's racial past, present, and future written by the Swedish social scientist Gunnar Myrdal. The book offered an uncompromising portrait of how deeply racism was entrenched in law, politics, economics, and social behavior. But Myrdal combined this sobering analysis with admiration for what he called the American Creed—belief in equality, justice, equal opportunity, and freedom. The war, he argued, had made Americans more aware than ever of the contradiction between this creed and the reality of racial inequality. He concluded that "there is bound to be a redefinition of the Negro's status as a result of this War."

Myrdal's notion of a conflict between American values and American racial policies was hardly new—Frederick Douglass and W. E. B. Du Bois had said much the same thing. But in the context of a worldwide struggle against Nazism and rising Black demands for equality at home, his book struck a chord. It identified a serious national problem and seemed to offer an almost painless path to peaceful change, in which the federal government would take the lead in outlawing discrimination. This coupling of an appeal to American principles with federal social engineering established a liberal position on race relations that would survive for many years.

By 1945, support for racial justice had finally taken its place on the liberal-left agenda alongside full employment, civil liberties, and the expansion of the New Deal welfare state. Roosevelt himself rarely spoke out on racial issues. But many liberals insisted that racial discrimination must be confronted head-on through federal antilynching legislation, equal opportunity in the workplace, an end to segregated housing and schools, and the expansion of Social Security programs to cover agricultural and domestic workers. This wartime vision of a racially integrated full employment economy formed a bridge between the New Deal and the Great Society of the 1960s (see Chapter 25).

Black Internationalism

In the nineteenth century, Black radicals like David Walker and Martin Delany had sought to link the fate of African Americans with that of peoples of African descent in other parts of the world, especially the Caribbean and Africa. In the first decades of the twentieth century, this kind of international consciousness was reinvigorated. Garveyism (discussed in Chapter 19) was one example; another was reflected in the five Pan-African Congresses that met between 1919 and 1945. Attended by Black intellectuals from the United States, the Caribbean, Europe, and Africa, these gatherings denounced the colonial rule of Africa and sought to establish a sense of unity among all people in the African diaspora (a term used to describe the scattering of a people who share a single national, religious, or racial identity). At the home of George Padmore, a West Indian labor organizer and editor living in London, Black American leaders like W. E. B. Du Bois and Paul Robeson came into contact with future leaders of African independence movements such as Jomo Kenyatta (Kenya), Kwame Nkrumah (Ghana), and Nnamdi Azikiwe (Nigeria). "I discovered Africa in London," Robeson remarked.

Through these gatherings, Du Bois, Robeson, and others developed an outlook that linked the plight of Black Americans with that of people of color worldwide. Racism, they came to believe, originated not in irrational hatred but in the slave trade and slavery. In the modern age, it was perpetuated by colonialism. Thus, freeing Africa from colonial rule would encourage greater equality at home.

World War II stimulated among African Americans an even greater awareness of the links between racism in the United States and colonialism abroad. In 1942, the *Pittsburgh Courier*, a major Black newspaper, began publishing regular columns on events in India (where the British had imprisoned leaders of the movement for national independence) and China. In the same year, Robeson founded the Council on African Affairs, which tried to place colonial liberation at the top of the Black American agenda.

THE END OF THE WAR

As 1945 opened, Allied victory was assured. In December 1944, in a desperate gamble, Hitler launched a surprise counterattack in France that pushed Allied forces back fifty miles, creating a large bulge in their lines. The largest single battle ever fought by the U.S. Army, the Battle of the Bulge produced more than 70,000 American casualties. But by early 1945 the assault had failed.

In March, American troops crossed the Rhine River and entered the industrial heartland of Germany. Hitler took his own life, and shortly afterward Soviet forces occupied Berlin. On May 8, 1945, known as **V-E Day** (for victory in Europe), came the formal end to the war against Germany. In the Pacific, American forces moved ever closer to Japan. They reconquered Guam in August 1944 and landed in the Philippines two months later, where they destroyed most of the remainder of the enemy fleet in the naval battle of Leyte Gulf.

"The Most Terrible Weapon"

Franklin D. Roosevelt defeated Republican nominee Thomas E. Dewey, the governor of New York, to win an unprecedented fourth term in 1944. But FDR did not live to see the Allied victory. He succumbed to a stroke on April 12, 1945. To his successor, Harry S. Truman, fell one of the most momentous decisions ever confronted by an American president—whether to use the atomic bomb against Japan. Truman did not know about the bomb until after he became president. Then Secretary of War Stimson informed him that the United States had secretly developed "the most terrible weapon ever known in human history."

The bomb was a practical realization of the theory of relativity, a rethinking of the laws of physics developed early in the twentieth century by the German scientist Albert Einstein. Energy and matter, Einstein showed, represented two forms of the same phenomenon. According to his famous equation $E = mc^2$, the energy contained in matter equals its mass times the speed of light squared—an enormous amount. By using certain forms of uranium, or the man-made element plutonium, an atomic reaction could be created that transformed part of the mass into energy. This energy could be harnessed to provide a form of controlled power, or it could be unleashed in a tremendous explosion.

Having fled to the United States from Hitler's Germany, Einstein in 1939 warned Roosevelt that Nazi scientists were trying to develop an atomic weapon and urged the president to do likewise. In the following year, FDR authorized what came to be known as the **Manhattan Project**, a top-secret program in which American scientists developed an atomic bomb during

World War II. The weapon was tested successfully in the New Mexico desert in July 1945.

The Dawn of the Atomic Age

On August 6, 1945, an American plane dropped an atomic bomb that detonated over Hiroshima, Japan—a target chosen because almost alone among major Japanese cities, it had not yet suffered damage. In an instant, nearly every building in the city was destroyed. Of the city's population of 280,000 civilians and 40,000 soldiers, approximately 70,000 died immediately. Because atomic bombs release deadly radiation, the death toll kept rising in the months that followed. By the end of the year, it reached at least 140,000. Thousands more perished over the next five years. On August 9, the United States exploded a second bomb over Nagasaki, killing 70,000 persons. On the same day, the Soviet Union declared war on Japan and invaded Manchuria. Within a week, Japan surrendered.

Because of the enormous cost in civilian lives—more than twice America's military fatalities in the entire Pacific war—the use of the bomb remains controversial. The Japanese had fought ferociously while being driven from one Pacific island after another. An American invasion of Japan, some advisers warned Truman, might cost as many as 250,000 American lives. No such invasion was planned, however, until the following year, and considerable evidence had accumulated that Japan was nearing surrender. Already some of its officials had communicated a willingness to end the war if Emperor Hirohito could remain on his throne. This fell short of the Allies' demand for "unconditional surrender," but the victors would, in the end, agree to Hirohito's survival. Japan's economy had been crippled and its fleet destroyed, and it would now have to fight the Soviet Union as well as the United States. Some of the scientists who had worked on the bomb urged Truman to demonstrate its power to international observers. But Truman did not hesitate. The bomb was a weapon, he reasoned, and weapons are created to be used.

The Nature of the War

The dropping of the atomic bombs was the logical culmination of the way World War II had been fought. All wars inflict suffering on noncombatants. But never before had civilian populations been so ruthlessly targeted. Military personnel represented 90 percent of those who died in World War I. But of the estimated 50 million persons who perished during World War II (including 400,000 American soldiers), perhaps 20 million were civilians. Germany had killed millions of members of "inferior races." It had repeatedly bombed London and other cities. The Allies carried out even more deadly air assaults on civilian populations. Early in 1945, the firebombing of Dresden killed some

25,000 people, mostly women, children, and elderly men. On March 9, nearly 100,000 died in an inferno caused by the bombing of Tokyo.

Four years of war propaganda had dehumanized the Japanese in Americans' eyes, and few persons criticized Truman's decision in 1945. But public doubts began to surface, especially after John Hersey published *Hiroshima* (1946), a graphic account of the horrors suffered by the civilian population. General Dwight D. Eisenhower, who thought the use of the bomb unnecessary, later wrote, "I hated to see our country be the first to use such a weapon."

Planning the Postwar World

Even as the war raged, a series of meetings between Allied leaders formulated plans for the postwar world. Churchill, Roosevelt, and Stalin met at Tehran, Iran, in 1943, and at Yalta, in the southern Soviet Union, early in 1945, to hammer out agreements. The final "Big Three" conference took place at Potsdam, near Berlin, in July 1945. It involved Stalin, Truman, and Churchill (replaced midway in the talks by Clement Attlee, who became prime minister when his Labour Party swept the British elections). At the **Potsdam conference**, the Allied leaders established a military administration for Germany and agreed to place top Nazi leaders on trial for war crimes.

Relations among the three Allies were often uneasy, as each maneuvered to maximize its postwar power. Neither Britain nor the United States trusted Stalin. The delay in the Allied invasion of France until 1944, which left the Soviets to do the bulk of the fighting against Germany, angered the Russians. But since Stalin's troops had won the war on the eastern front, it was difficult to resist his demand that eastern Europe become a Soviet sphere of influence (a region whose governments can be counted on to do a great power's bidding).

Yalta and Bretton Woods

At the **Yalta conference**, Roosevelt and Churchill entered only a mild protest against Soviet plans to retain control of the Baltic states (Estonia, Latvia, and Lithuania) and a large part of eastern Poland, in effect restoring Russia's pre–World War I western borders. Stalin agreed to enter the war against Japan later in 1945, to include noncommunists in the pro-Soviet government of Poland, and to allow "free and unfettered elections" there. But he was intent on establishing communism in eastern Europe. He believed, as he put it to Yugoslav communist leader Josip Broz ("Tito"), that in modern war, "whoever occupies a territory also imposes his own social system." Yalta saw the high-water mark of wartime American–Soviet cooperation. But it planted seeds of conflict, since the participants soon disagreed over the fate of eastern Europe.

Tension also existed between Britain and the United States. Churchill rejected American pressure to place India and other British colonies on the road to independence. He concluded private deals with Stalin to divide southern and eastern Europe into British and Soviet spheres of influence.

Britain also resisted, unsuccessfully, American efforts to reshape and dominate the postwar economic order. A meeting of representatives of forty-five nations at Bretton Woods, New Hampshire, in July 1944 replaced the British pound with the dollar as the main currency for international transactions. During the 1930s, as noted in the previous chapter, FDR had taken the United States off the gold standard, allowing the government to issue more money in the hope of stimulating business activity. The **Bretton Woods conference** reestablished the link between the dollar and gold. It set the dollar's value at $35 per ounce of gold and gave other currencies a fixed relationship to the dollar. The conference also created two American-dominated financial institutions. The World Bank would provide money to developing countries and to help rebuild Europe. The International Monetary Fund would work to prevent governments from devaluing their currencies to gain an advantage in international trade, as many had done during the Depression.

Although the details took many years to emerge, Bretton Woods created the framework for the postwar capitalist economic system, based on a freer international flow of goods and investment and a recognition of the United States as the world's financial leader. Determined to avoid a recurrence of the Great Depression, American leaders believed that the removal of barriers to free trade would encourage the growth of the world economy, an emphasis that until the presidency of Donald Trump remained central to American foreign policy.

The United Nations

Early in the war, the Allies also agreed to establish a successor to the League of Nations. In a 1944 conference at Dumbarton Oaks, near Washington, D.C., they developed the structure of the **United Nations** (UN). There would be a General Assembly—essentially a forum for discussion where each member enjoyed an equal voice—and a Security Council responsible for maintaining world peace. Along with ten rotating members, the council would have five permanent ones—Britain, China, France, the Soviet Union, and the United States—each with the power to veto resolutions. In June 1945, representatives of fifty-one countries met in San Francisco to adopt the UN Charter, which outlawed force or the threat of force as a means of settling international disputes. In July, the U.S. Senate endorsed the charter. In contrast to the bitter dispute over membership in the League of Nations after World War I, only two senators voted against joining the UN. At the conclusion of the San Francisco conference that established the United Nations, President Truman urged Americans to recognize that "no matter how great our strength, we must deny ourselves the license to do always as we please. This is the price which each nation will have to pay for world peace. . . . And what a reasonable price that is."

A member of the U.S. Navy plays "Goin' Home" on the accordion as Franklin D. Roosevelt's body is carried from the Warm Springs Foundation where he died suddenly on April 12, 1945.

Peace, but Not Harmony

World War II produced a radical redistribution of world power. Japan and Germany, the two dominant military powers in their regions before the war, were utterly defeated. Britain and France, though victorious, were substantially weakened. Only the United States and the Soviet Union remained able to project significant influence beyond their national borders.

Overall, however, the United States was clearly the dominant world power. "What Rome was to the ancient world," wrote the journalist Walter Lippmann, "America is to be to the world of tomorrow." But peace did not usher in an era of international harmony. The Soviet occupation of eastern Europe created a division soon to be solidified in the Cold War. The dropping of the atomic bombs left a worldwide legacy of fear.

It remained to be seen how seriously the victorious Allies took their wartime rhetoric of freedom. In August 1941, four months before the United States entered the war, FDR and British prime minister Winston Churchill had met for a conference, on warships anchored off the coast of Newfoundland, and issued the **Atlantic Charter**. The charter promised that "the final destruction of Nazi tyranny" would be followed by open access to markets, the right of "all peoples" to choose their form of government, and a global extension of the New Deal so that people everywhere would enjoy "improved labor standards, economic advancement and social security." It referred specifically to two of Roosevelt's Four Freedoms—freedom from want and freedom from fear. But freedom of speech and of worship had been left out because of British reluctance to apply them to its colonial possessions, especially India.

The Four Freedoms speech and the Atlantic Charter had been primarily intended to highlight the differences between Anglo-American ideals and Nazism. Nonetheless, they had unanticipated consequences. As one of Roosevelt's speechwriters remarked, "when you state a moral principle, you are stuck with it, no matter how many fingers you have kept crossed at the moment." The language with which World War II was fought helped to lay the foundation for postwar ideals of human rights that extend to all mankind.

During the war, Mahatma Gandhi, the Indian nationalist leader, wrote to Roosevelt that the idea "that the Allies are fighting to make the world safe for freedom of the individual and for democracy seems hollow, so long as India, and for that matter, Africa, are exploited by Great Britain, and America has the Negro problem in her own home." Allied victory saved mankind from a living nightmare—a worldwide system of dictatorial rule and slave labor in which peoples deemed inferior suffered the fate of European Jews and the victims of Japanese outrages in Asia. But disputes over the freedom of colonial peoples overseas and non-whites in the United States foretold wars and social upheavals to come.

CHAPTER REVIEW

REVIEW QUESTIONS

1. *Why did most Americans support isolationism in the 1930s?*

2. *What factors after 1939 led to U.S. involvement in World War II?*

3. *How did government, business, and labor work together to promote wartime production, and how did the war affect each group?*

4. *How did different groups understand or experience the Four Freedoms differently?*

5. *Explain how conservatives in Congress and business used the war effort to attack the goals and legacy of the New Deal.*

6. *How did the war alter the lives of women on the home front, and what did different groups think would happen to the status of women after the war?*

7. *How did a war fought to bring "essential human freedoms" to the world fail to protect the home-front liberties of Blacks, Indians, Japanese Americans, and Mexican Americans?*

8. *Explain how World War II promoted an awareness of the links between racism in the United States and colonialism around the world.*

9. *What was the impact of the GI Bill of Rights on American society, including minorities?*

10. *Describe how the decisions made at the Bretton Woods conference in 1944 created the framework for postwar U.S. economic and foreign policy.*

KEY TERMS

Four Freedoms (p. 866)

isolationism (p. 871)

Neutrality Acts (p. 871)

America First Committee (p. 873)

Lend-Lease Act (p. 873)

Axis powers (p. 875)

D-Day (p. 877)

Holocaust (p. 878)

GI Bill of Rights (p. 888)

bracero program (p. 891)

zoot suit riots (p. 891)

Japanese American internment (p. 896)

Korematsu v. United States (p. 897)

second Great Migration (p. 899)

double-V (p. 902)

V-E Day (p. 905)

Manhattan Project (p. 905)

Potsdam conference (p. 907)

Yalta conference (p. 907)

Bretton Woods conference (p. 908)

United Nations (p. 908)

Atlantic Charter (p. 909)

Go to 🐇 INQUIZITIVE

To see what you know—and learn what you've missed—with personalized feedback along the way.

★ **CHAPTER 23** ★

THE UNITED STATES AND THE COLD WAR

1945–1953

FOCUS QUESTIONS

- *What series of events and ideological conflicts prompted the Cold War?*

- *How did the Cold War reshape ideas of American freedom?*

- *What major domestic policy initiatives did Truman undertake?*

- *What effects did the anticommunism of the Cold War have on American politics and culture?*

On September 16, 1947, the 160th anniversary of the signing of the Constitution, the Freedom Train opened to the public in Philadelphia. A traveling exhibition of 133 historical documents, the train, bedecked in red, white, and blue, soon embarked on a sixteen-month tour that took it to more than 300 American cities. Never before or since have so many cherished pieces of Americana—among them the Mayflower Compact, the Declaration of Independence, and the Gettysburg Address—been assembled in one place. After leaving the train, visitors were encouraged to rededicate themselves to American values by taking the Freedom Pledge and adding their names to a Freedom Scroll.

The idea for the Freedom Train, perhaps the most elaborate peacetime patriotic campaign in American history, originated in 1946 with the Department of Justice. President Harry S. Truman endorsed it as a way of contrasting American freedom with "the destruction of liberty by the Hitler tyranny." Since direct government funding raised fears of propaganda, however, the administration turned the project over to a nonprofit group, the American Heritage Foundation, headed by Winthrop W. Aldrich, chairman of Chase Manhattan Bank.

By any measure, the Freedom Train was an enormous success. It attracted more than 3.5 million visitors, and millions more took part in the civic activities that accompanied its journey, including labor-management forums, educational programs, and patriotic parades. Behind the scenes, however, the Freedom Train demonstrated that the meaning of freedom remained as controversial as ever.

The liberal staff members at the National Archives who proposed the initial list of documents had included the Wagner Act of 1935, which guaranteed workers the right to form unions, as well as President Roosevelt's Four Freedoms speech of 1941, with its promise to fight "freedom from want." The more conservative American Heritage Foundation removed these documents. They also deleted from the original list the Fourteenth and Fifteenth Amendments, which had established the principle of equal civil and political rights regardless of race after the Civil War, and FDR's 1941 order establishing the Fair Employment Practices Commission, which Congress had recently allowed to expire. In the end, nothing on the train referred to organized labor or any twentieth-century social legislation. The only documents relating to Blacks were the Emancipation Proclamation, the Thirteenth Amendment, and a 1776 letter by South Carolina patriot Henry Laurens criticizing slavery.

Many Black Americans initially voiced doubts regarding the exhibit. On the eve of the train's unveiling, the poet Langston Hughes wondered whether there would be "Jim Crow

• CHRONOLOGY •

1945	Yalta conference
1946	Philippines granted independence
1947	Truman Doctrine
	Federal Employee Loyalty program
	Jackie Robinson integrates major league baseball
	Marshall Plan
	Taft-Hartley Act
	Freedom Train exhibition
	House Un-American Activities Committee investigates Hollywood
1948	UN adopts Universal Declaration of Human Rights
	Truman desegregates military
1948– 1949	Berlin blockade and airlift
1949	North Atlantic Treaty Organization established
	Soviet Union tests atomic bomb
	People's Republic of China established
1950	McCarthy's Wheeling, W.V., speech
	NSC-68 issued
	McCarran Internal Security Act
1950– 1953	Korean War
1951	*Dennis v. United States*
1953	Julius and Ethel Rosenberg executed for spying
1954	Army-McCarthy hearings
1955	Warsaw Pact organized

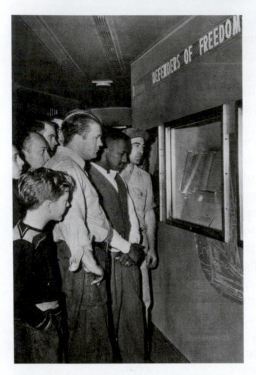
Visitors viewing historic documents aboard the Freedom Train in 1948.

on the Freedom Train." "When it stops in Mississippi," Hughes asked, "will it be made plain / Everybody's got a right to board the Freedom Train?" In fact, with the Truman administration about to make civil rights a major priority, the train's organizers announced that they would not permit segregated viewing. In an unprecedented move, the American Heritage Foundation canceled visits to Memphis, Tennessee, and Birmingham, Alabama, when local authorities insisted on separating visitors by race. The Freedom Train visited forty-seven other southern cities without incident and was hailed in the Black press for breaching, if only temporarily, the walls of segregation.

Even as the Freedom Train reflected a new sense of national unease about expressions of racial inequality, its journey also revealed the growing impact of the **Cold War**. Originally intended to contrast American freedom with Nazi tyranny, the train quickly became caught up in the emerging struggle with communism. In the spring of 1947, a few months before the train was dedicated, President Truman committed the United States to the worldwide **containment** of Soviet power and inaugurated a program to root out "disloyal" persons from government employment. Soon, Attorney General Tom C. Clark was praising the Freedom Train as a means of preventing "foreign ideologies" from infiltrating the United States and of "aiding the country in its internal war against subversive elements." The Freedom Train revealed how the Cold War helped to reshape freedom's meaning, identifying it ever more closely with anticommunism, "free enterprise," and the defense of the social and economic status quo.

ORIGINS OF THE COLD WAR

The Two Powers

The United States emerged from World War II as by far the world's greatest power. Although most of the army was quickly demobilized, the country boasted the world's most powerful navy and air force. The United States accounted for half the world's manufacturing capacity. It alone possessed the atomic bomb. As discussed in the previous chapter, the Roosevelt administration was determined to avoid a retreat to isolationism like the one that followed World War I. It believed that the United States could lead the rest of the world to a future of international cooperation, expanding democracy, and ever-increasing living standards. New institutions like the United Nations and World Bank had been created to promote these goals. American leaders also believed that the nation's security depended on the security of Europe and Asia and that American prosperity required global economic reconstruction.

The only power that in any way could rival the United States was the Soviet Union, whose armies now occupied most of eastern Europe, including the eastern part of Germany. Its crucial role in defeating Hitler and its claim that communism had wrested a vast backward nation into modernity gave the Soviet Union considerable prestige in Europe and among colonial peoples struggling for independence. Like the United States, the Soviets looked forward to a world order modeled on their own society and values. Having lost more than 20 million dead and suffered vast devastation during the war, however, Stalin's government was in no position to embark on new military adventures. "Unless they were completely out of their minds," said American undersecretary of state Dean Acheson, the Russians were hardly likely to go to war with the far more powerful United States. But having done the largest amount of fighting in the defeat of Hitler, the Soviet government remained determined to establish a sphere of influence in eastern Europe, through which Germany had twice invaded Russia in the past thirty years.

The Roots of Containment

FDR seems to have believed that the United States could maintain friendly relations with the Soviet Union once World War II ended. In retrospect, however, it seems all but inevitable that the two major powers to emerge from the war would come into conflict. Born of a common foe rather than common long-term interests, values, or history, their wartime alliance began to unravel almost from the day that peace was declared.

The first confrontation of the Cold War took place in the Middle East. At the end of World War II, Soviet troops had occupied parts of northern Iran, hoping to pressure that country to grant it access to its rich oil fields. Under British and American pressure, however, Stalin quickly withdrew Soviet forces. At the same time, the Soviets installed procommunist governments in Poland, Romania, and Bulgaria, a step they claimed was no different from American domination of Latin America or Britain's determination to maintain its own empire. But many Americans became convinced that Stalin was violating the promise of free elections in Poland that had been agreed to at the Yalta conference of 1945.

Early in 1946, in his famous **Long Telegram** from Moscow, American diplomat George Kennan advised the Truman administration that the Soviets could not be dealt with as a normal government. Communist ideology drove them to try to expand their power throughout the world, he claimed, and only the United States had the ability to stop them. While Kennan believed that the Russians could not be dislodged from control of eastern Europe, his telegram laid the foundation for what became known as the policy of "containment," according to which the United States committed itself to preventing any further expansion of Soviet power.

Shortly afterward, in a speech at Fulton, Missouri, Britain's former wartime prime minister Winston Churchill declared that an **iron curtain** had descended across Europe, partitioning the free West from the communist East. Churchill's speech helped to popularize the idea of an impending long-term struggle between the United States and the Soviets. But not until March 1947, in a speech announcing what came to be known as the **Truman Doctrine**, did the president officially embrace the Cold War as the foundation of American foreign policy and describe it as a worldwide struggle over the future of freedom.

The Truman Doctrine

Harry S. Truman never expected to become president. Until Democratic Party leaders chose him to replace Henry Wallace as Roosevelt's running mate in 1944, he was an undistinguished senator from Missouri. When he assumed the presidency after Roosevelt's death in April 1945, Truman found himself forced to decide foreign policy debates in which he had previously played virtually no role.

Convinced that Stalin could not be trusted and that the United States had a responsibility to provide leadership to a world that he tended to view in stark, black-and-white terms, Truman soon determined to put the policy of containment into effect. The immediate occasion for this epochal decision came early in 1947 when Britain informed the United States that because its economy had been shattered by the war, it could no longer afford its traditional international role. Britain had no choice but to end military and financial aid to two crucial governments—Greece, a monarchy threatened by a communist-led rebellion, and Turkey, from which the Soviets were demanding joint control of the straits linking the Black Sea and the Mediterranean. Britain asked the United States to fill the vacuum.

The Soviet Union had little to do with the internal problems of Greece and Turkey, where opposition to corrupt, undemocratic regimes was largely homegrown. Neither had held truly free elections. But they occupied strategically important sites at the gateway to southeastern Europe and the oil-rich Middle East. Truman had been told by Senate leader Arthur Vandenberg that the only way a reluctant public and Congress would support aid to these governments was for the president to "scare hell" out of the American people. To rally popular backing, Truman rolled out the heaviest weapon in his rhetorical arsenal—the defense of freedom. As the leader of the "free world," the United States must now shoulder the responsibility of supporting "freedom-loving peoples" wherever communism threatened them. Twenty-four times in the eighteen-minute speech, Truman used the words "free" and "freedom."

Building on the wartime division of the globe into free and enslaved worlds, and invoking a far older vision of an American mission to defend liberty against the forces of darkness, the Truman Doctrine created the language through which most Americans came to understand the postwar world. More than any other statement, a prominent senator would write, this speech established "the guiding spirit of American foreign policy." Truman succeeded in persuading both Republicans and Democrats in Congress to support his policy, beginning a long period of bipartisan support for the containment of communism. As Truman's speech to Congress suggested, the Cold War was, in part, an ideological conflict. Both sides claimed to be promoting freedom and social justice while defending their own security, and each offered its social system as a model the rest of the world should follow.

While his request to Congress was limited to $400 million in military aid to two governments (aid that enabled both Greece and Turkey to defeat their domestic foes), Truman's rhetoric suggested that the United States had assumed a permanent global responsibility. The speech set a precedent for American assistance to anticommunist regimes throughout the world, no matter how undemocratic, and for the creation of a set of global military alliances directed against the Soviet Union. There soon followed the creation of new national security bodies immune from democratic oversight, such as the Atomic Energy Commission, National Security Council, and Central Intelligence Agency (CIA), the last established in 1947 to gather intelligence and conduct secret military operations abroad.

The Marshall Plan

The language of the Truman Doctrine and the future it sketched of open-ended worldwide responsibilities for the United States alarmed many Americans. "Are we to shoulder the mantle of nineteenth-century British imperialism?" asked the *San Francisco Chronicle*. "Are we asking for a third world war?" But the threat of American military action overseas formed only one pillar of containment.

Secretary of State George C. Marshall spelled out the other in a speech at Harvard University in June 1947. Marshall pledged the United States to contribute billions of dollars to finance the economic recovery of Europe. Two years after the end of the war, much of the continent still lay in ruins. Food shortages were widespread and inflation rampant. The economic chaos, exacerbated by the unusually severe winter of 1946–1947, had strengthened the communist parties of France and Italy. American policymakers feared that these countries might fall into the Soviet orbit.

The **Marshall Plan** offered a positive vision to go along with containment. It aimed to combat the idea, widespread since the Great Depression, that capitalism was in decline and communism the wave of the future. It defined the threat to American security not so much as Soviet military power but as economic and political instability, which could be breeding grounds for communism. Avoiding Truman's language of a world divided between free and unfree blocs, Marshall insisted, "Our policy is directed not against any country or doctrine, but against hunger, poverty, desperation, and chaos." Freedom meant more than simply anticommunism—it required the emergence of the "political and social conditions in which free institutions can exist." In effect, the Marshall Plan envisioned a New Deal for Europe, an extension to that continent of Roosevelt's wartime Four Freedoms. As a booklet explaining the idea to Europeans put it, the aim was "a higher standard of living for the entire nation; maximum employment for workers and farmers; greater production." Or, in the words of a slogan used to popularize the Marshall Plan, "Prosperity Makes You Free."

The Marshall Plan proved to be one of the most successful foreign aid programs in history. By 1950, western European production exceeded prewar levels and the region was poised to follow the United States down the road to a mass-consumption society. Since the Soviet Union refused to participate, fearing American control over the economies of eastern Europe, the Marshall Plan further solidified the division of the

A page from a Dutch pamphlet promoting the Marshall Plan.

continent. At the same time, the United States worked out with twenty-three other Western nations the General Agreement on Tariffs and Trade (GATT), which proposed to stimulate freer trade among the participants, creating an enormous market for American goods and investment.

The Reconstruction of Japan

Under the guidance of General Douglas MacArthur, the "supreme commander" in Japan until 1948, that country adopted a new, democratic constitution and eliminated absentee landlordism so that most tenant farmers became owners of land. Thanks to American insistence, and against the wishes of most Japanese leaders, the new constitution gave women the right to vote for the first time in Japan's history. (A century after the Seneca Falls convention, woman suffrage had become an intrinsic part of American understandings of freedom.) Furthermore, Article 9 of the new constitution stated that Japan would renounce forever the policy of war and armed aggression and would maintain only a modest self-defense force.

The United States also oversaw the economic reconstruction of Japan. Initially, the United States proposed to dissolve Japan's giant industrial corporations, which had contributed so much to the nation's war effort. But this plan was abandoned in 1948 in favor of an effort to rebuild Japan's industrial base as a bastion of anticommunist strength in Asia. By the 1950s, thanks to American economic assistance, the adoption of new technologies, and low spending on the military, Japan's economic recovery was in full swing.

The Berlin Blockade and NATO

Meanwhile, the Cold War intensified and, despite the Marshall Plan, increasingly took a militaristic turn. At the end of World War II, each of the four victorious powers assumed control of a section of occupied Germany, and of Berlin, located deep in the Soviet zone. In June 1948, the United States, Britain, and France introduced a separate currency in their zones, a prelude to the creation of a new West German government that would be aligned with them in the Cold War. In response, the Soviets cut off road and rail traffic from the American, British, and French zones of occupied Germany to Berlin.

An eleven-month airlift followed, with Western planes supplying fuel and food to their zones of the city. When Stalin lifted the blockade in May 1949, the Truman administration had won a major victory. Soon, two new nations emerged, East and West Germany, each allied with a side in the Cold War. Berlin itself remained divided. Not until 1991 would Germany be reunified.

Children in Berlin celebrate the arrival of a plane bringing supplies to counter the Soviet blockade of the city in 1948.

Also in 1949, the Soviet Union tested its first atomic bomb, ending the American monopoly of the weapon. In the same year, the United States, Canada, and ten western European nations established the **North Atlantic Treaty Organization** (NATO), pledging mutual defense against any future Soviet attack. Soon, West Germany became a crucial part of NATO. Many Europeans feared German rearmament. But France and other victims of Nazi aggression saw NATO as a kind of "double containment," in which West Germany would serve as a bulwark against the Soviets while integration into the Western alliance tamed and "civilized" German power. The North Atlantic Treaty was the first long-term military alliance between the United States and Europe since the Treaty of Amity and Commerce with France during the American Revolution. The Soviets formalized their own eastern European alliance, the Warsaw Pact, in 1955.

The Growing Communist Challenge

In 1949, communists led by Mao Zedong emerged victorious in the long Chinese civil war—a serious setback for the policy of containment. Assailed by Republicans for having "lost" China (which, of course, the United States never "had" in the first place), the Truman administration refused to recognize the new government—the People's Republic of China—and blocked it from occupying China's seat at the United Nations. Until the 1970s, the United States insisted that the ousted regime, which had been forced into exile on the island of Taiwan, remained the legitimate government of China.

In the wake of Soviet-American confrontations over southern and eastern Europe and Berlin, the communist victory in China, and Soviet success in developing an atomic bomb, the National Security Council approved a call for a permanent military buildup to enable the United States to pursue a global crusade against communism. Known as **NSC-68**, this 1950 manifesto described the Cold War as an epic struggle between "the idea of freedom" and the "idea of slavery under the grim oligarchy of the Kremlin." One of the most important policy statements of the early Cold War, NSC-68 helped to spur a dramatic increase in American military spending.

The Korean War

Initially, American postwar policy focused on Europe. But it was in Asia that the Cold War suddenly turned hot. Japan's defeat in World War II ended its colonial rule over Korea. In 1945, the country was divided into Soviet and American zones. These soon evolved into two governments: communist North Korea, and anticommunist South Korea, undemocratic but aligned with the United States. In June 1950, the North Korean army invaded the south, hoping to reunify the country under communist control. North Korean soldiers soon occupied most of the peninsula. Viewing Korea as a clear test of the policy of containment, the Truman administration persuaded the United Nations Security Council to authorize the use of force to repel the invasion. (The Soviets, who could have vetoed the resolution, were boycotting Security Council meetings to protest the refusal to seat communist China.)

American troops did the bulk of the fighting on this first battlefield of the Cold War. In September 1950, General Douglas MacArthur launched a daring counterattack at Inchon, behind North Korean lines. The invading forces retreated northward, and MacArthur's army soon occupied most of North Korea. Truman now hoped to unite Korea under a pro-American government. But in October 1950, when UN forces neared the Chinese border, hundreds of thousands of Chinese troops intervened, driving them back in bloody fighting. MacArthur demanded the right to push north again and possibly even invade China and use nuclear weapons against it. But Truman, fearing an all-out war on the Asian mainland, refused. MacArthur did not fully accept the principle of civilian control of the military. When he went public with criticism of the president, Truman removed him from command. The war then settled into a stalemate around the thirty-eighth parallel, the original boundary between the two Koreas. Not until 1953 was an armistice agreed to, essentially restoring the prewar status quo. There has never been a formal peace treaty ending the **Korean War**.

More than 33,000 Americans died in Korea. The Asian death toll reached an estimated 1 million Korean soldiers and 2 million civilians (many of them victims of starvation after American bombing destroyed irrigation systems essential to rice cultivation), along with hundreds of thousands of Chinese troops. Korea made it clear that the Cold War, which began in Europe, had become a global conflict.

Taken together, the events of 1947–1953 showed that the world had moved very far from the hopes for global harmony symbolized by the founding of the United Nations in 1945. No longer did the United States speak of One World (the title of Wendell Willkie's influential wartime book). Instead, the world had been divided in two. The United States now stood as the undisputed leader of what was increasingly known as the West (although it included Japan, where

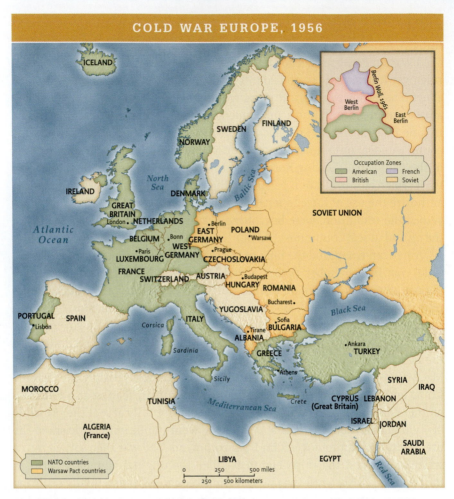

COLD WAR EUROPE, 1956

Occupation Zones
- American
- French
- British
- Soviet

- NATO countries
- Warsaw Pact countries

The division of Europe between communist and noncommunist nations, solidified by the early 1950s, would last for nearly forty years.

permanent American military bases were established), or the Free World. NATO was soon followed by SEATO in Southeast Asia and CENTO in the Middle East, forming a web of military alliances that ringed the Soviet Union and China.

Cold War Critics

In the Soviet Union, Stalin had consolidated a brutal dictatorship that jailed or murdered millions of Soviet citizens. With its one-party rule, stringent state control of the arts and intellectual life, and government-controlled

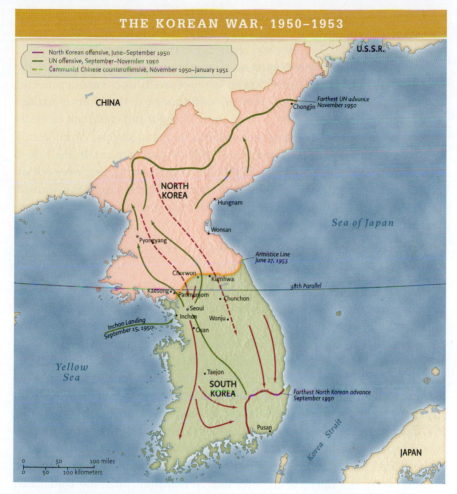

THE KOREAN WAR, 1950–1953

North Korean offensive, June–September 1950
UN offensive, September–November 1950
Communist Chinese counteroffensive, November 1950–January 1951

As this map indicates, when General Douglas MacArthur launched his surprise landing at Inchon, North Korean forces controlled nearly the entire Korean peninsula.

economy, the Soviet Union presented a stark opposite of democracy and "free enterprise." As a number of contemporary critics, few of them sympathetic to Soviet communism, pointed out, however, casting the Cold War in terms of a worldwide battle between freedom and slavery had unfortunate consequences. George Kennan, whose Long Telegram had inspired the policy of containment, observed that such language made it impossible to view international crises on a case-by-case basis, or to determine which genuinely involved either freedom or American interests.

In a penetrating critique of Truman's policies, Walter Lippmann, one of the nation's most prominent journalists, objected to turning foreign policy into an "ideological crusade." To view every challenge to the status quo as part of a contest with the Soviet Union, Lippmann correctly predicted, would require the United States to recruit and subsidize an "array of satellites, clients, dependents and puppets." It would have to intervene continuously in the affairs of nations whose political problems did not arise from Moscow and could not be easily understood in terms of the battle between freedom and slavery. World War II, he went on, had shaken the foundations of European empires. In the tide of revolutionary nationalism now sweeping the world, communists were certain to play an important role. It would be a serious mistake, Lippmann warned, for the United States to align itself against the movement for colonial independence in the name of anticommunism.

Imperialism and Decolonization

World War II had increased awareness in the United States of the problem of imperialism and had led many African Americans to identify their own struggle for equality with the strivings of non-white colonial peoples overseas. Many movements for colonial independence borrowed the language of the American Declaration of Independence in demanding the right to self-government. Liberal Democrats and Black leaders urged the Truman administration to take the lead in promoting worldwide **decolonization**, insisting that a Free World worthy of the name should not include colonies and empires. On July 4, 1946, the Philippines celebrated its independence from U.S. colonial rule, a move hailed by nationalist movements in other colonies. But as the Cold War developed, the United States backed away from pressuring its European allies to move toward granting self-government to colonies like French Indochina, the Dutch East Indies, and British possessions like the Gold Coast and Nigeria in Africa and Malaya in Asia. Even after India and Pakistan won independence in 1947, Britain was determined to retain much of its remaining empire.

In practice, geopolitical and economic interests shaped American foreign policy as powerfully as the idea of freedom. But American policymakers used the language of a crusade for freedom to justify actions around the world that had little to do with freedom by almost any definition. No matter how repressive to its own people, if a nation joined the worldwide anticommunist alliance led by the United States, it was counted as a member of the Free World. The Republic of South Africa, for example, was considered a part of the Free World even though its white minority had deprived the Black population of nearly all their rights. Was there not some way, one critic asked, that the United States could accept "the aid of tyrants" on practical grounds "without corrupting our speeches by identifying tyranny with freedom"?

THE COLD WAR AND THE IDEA OF FREEDOM

Among other things, the Cold War was a battle, in a popular phrase of the 1950s, for the "hearts and minds" of people throughout the world. Like other wars, it required popular mobilization, in which the idea of freedom played a central role. During the 1950s, freedom became an inescapable theme of academic research, popular journalism, mass culture, and official pronouncements. Henry Luce, who had popularized the idea of an American Century, explained that "freedom" was the "one word out of the whole human vocabulary" through which *Time* magazine could best explain America to the rest of the world.

The Cultural Cold War

One of the more unusual Cold War battlefields involved American culture. Under the code name "Militant Liberty," national security agencies encouraged Hollywood to produce anticommunist movies, such as *The Red Menace* (1949) and *I Married a Communist* (1950), and urged that film scripts be changed to remove references to less-than-praiseworthy aspects of American history, such as Indian removal and racial discrimination.

The Central Intelligence Agency (CIA) and Defense Department emerged as unlikely patrons of the arts. As noted in Chapter 21, the federal government had openly financed all sorts of artistic works during the 1930s. But Cold War funding for the arts remained top-secret—in part because Congress proved reluctant to spend money for this purpose, in part because Americans charged communist governments with imposing artistic conformity. In an effort to influence public opinion abroad, the Soviet Union sponsored tours of its world-famous ballet companies, folk dance troupes, and symphony orchestras. To counteract the widespread European view of the United States as a cultural backwater, the CIA secretly funded an array of overseas publications, conferences, publishing houses, concerts, and art exhibits. And to try to improve the international image of American race relations, the government sent jazz musicians and other Black performers abroad, especially to Africa and Asia.

Works produced by artists who considered themselves thoroughly nonpolitical became weapons in the cultural Cold War. The CIA promoted the so-called New York school of painters, led by Jackson Pollock. For Pollock, the essence of art lay in the process of creation, not the final product. His "action" paintings, made by spontaneously dripping and pouring paint over large canvases, produced works of vivid color and energy but without any recognizable subject matter. Many members of Congress much preferred Norman Rockwell's readily understandable illustrations of small-town life to Pollock's "abstract expressionism." Some called Pollock's works un-American and wondered aloud if they were part of a communist plot. In 1946, the State Department

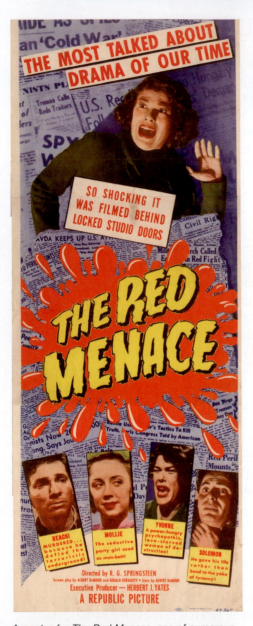

A poster for *The Red Menace*, one of numerous anticommunist films produced by Hollywood during the 1950s.

assembled a stylistically diverse exhibition of contemporary American paintings that it displayed in Europe and Latin America to demonstrate "the freedom of expression enjoyed by artists in America." But criticism emerged in Congress. Representative Fred Busbey of Illinois said the exhibit gave the impression that "the American people are despondent, broke down or of hideous shape." The State Department abandoned the project and sold the works at auction.

The CIA, however, funded the Museum of Modern Art in New York, which championed the New York School, and helped arrange for exhibitions overseas. It hoped to persuade Europeans not only that these paintings demonstrated that the United States represented artistic leadership as well as military power, but also that such art embodied the free, individual expression denied to artists in communist countries. Pollock's paintings, John Cage's musical compositions, which incorporated chance sounds rather than a fixed score, and the "graceful freedom" of George Balanchine's ballet choreography were all described as artistic reflections of the essence of American life.

Freedom and Totalitarianism

Along with freedom, the Cold War's other great mobilizing concept was **totalitarianism**. The term originated in Europe between the world wars to describe fascist Italy and Nazi Germany— aggressive, ideologically driven states that sought to subdue all of civil society, including churches, unions, and other voluntary associations, to their control. Such states, according to the theory of totalitarianism, left no room for individual rights or alternative values and therefore could never change from within. By 1950, the year the McCarran Internal Security Act barred "totalitarians" from entering the United States, the term had become a shorthand way of describing those on the other side in the Cold War. As the eventual collapse of communist governments in eastern Europe and the Soviet Union would demonstrate, the idea of totalitarianism greatly exaggerated the totality of government control of private life and thought in these countries. But its widespread use reinforced the view that the greatest danger to freedom lay in an overly powerful government.

Just as the conflict over slavery redefined American freedom in the nineteenth century and the confrontation with the Nazis shaped understandings of freedom during World War II, the Cold War reshaped them once again. Russia had already conquered America, the poet Archibald MacLeish complained in 1949, since politics was conducted "under a kind of upside-down Russian veto." Whatever Moscow stood for was by definition the opposite of freedom, including anything to which the word "socialized" could be attached. In the largest public relations campaign in American history, the American Medical Association raised the specter of "socialized medicine" to discredit and defeat Truman's proposal for national health insurance. The real-estate industry likewise mobilized against public housing, terming it "socialized housing," similar to policies undertaken by Moscow.

The Rise of Human Rights

The Cold War also affected the emerging concept of human rights. The atrocities committed during World War II, as well as the global language of the Four Freedoms and the Atlantic Charter, forcefully raised the issue of human rights in the postwar world. After the war, the victorious Allies put numerous German officials on trial before special courts at Nuremberg for crimes against humanity. For the first time, individuals were held directly accountable to the international community for violations of human rights. The trials resulted in prison terms for many Nazi officials and the execution of ten leaders.

The United Nations Charter includes strong language prohibiting discrimination on the basis of race, sex, or religion. In 1948, the UN General Assembly approved a far more sweeping document, the Universal Declaration of Human Rights, drafted by a committee chaired by Eleanor Roosevelt. It identified a broad range of rights to be enjoyed by people everywhere, including freedom of speech, religious toleration, and protection against arbitrary government, as well as social and economic entitlements like the right to an adequate standard of living and access to housing, education, and medical care. The document had no enforcement mechanism. But the core principle—that a nation's treatment of its own citizens should be subject to outside evaluation—slowly became part of the language in which freedom was discussed.

Ambiguities of Human Rights

The American and French Revolutions of the late eighteenth century had introduced into international relations the idea of basic rights belonging to all persons simply because they are human. In a sense, this was the origin of the idea of "human rights"—principles so fundamental that no government has a right to violate them. The antislavery movement had turned this idea into a powerful weapon against the legitimacy of slavery. Yet the debates over the Universal Declaration of Human Rights revealed the tensions inherent in the idea, tensions that persist to the present day. To what extent do human rights supersede national sovereignty? Who has the authority to enforce human rights that a government is violating? The United Nations? Regional bodies like the Organization of American States and the European Union? A single country (as the United States would claim to be doing in the Iraq War that began in 2003)?

One reason for the lack of an enforcement mechanism in the Universal Declaration of Human Rights was that both the United States and the Soviet Union refused to accept outside interference in their internal affairs. John Foster Dulles, an American delegate to the conference that created the UN, opposed any statement affirming human rights out of fear that it would lead to an international investigation of "the Negro question in this country." In 1947, the NAACP did file a petition with the United Nations asking it to investigate racism in the United States as a violation of human rights. Conditions in states like Mississippi should be of concern to all mankind, it argued, because if democracy failed to function in "the leading democracy in the world," the prospects for democracy were weakened everywhere. But the UN decided that it lacked jurisdiction. Nonetheless, since the end of World War II, the enjoyment of human rights has increasingly taken its place in definitions of freedom across the globe.

After the Cold War ended, the idea of human rights would play an increasingly prominent role in world affairs. But during the 1950s, Cold War imperatives shaped the concept. Neither the United States nor the Soviet Union could resist emphasizing certain provisions of the Universal Declaration while ignoring others. The Soviets claimed to provide all citizens with social and economic rights but violated democratic rights and civil liberties. Many Americans condemned the nonpolitical rights as a step toward socialism.

Eleanor Roosevelt saw the Universal Declaration of Human Rights as an integrated body of principles, a combination of traditional civil and political liberties with the social conditions of freedom outlined in her husband's Economic Bill of Rights of 1944. But to make it easier for member states to ratify the document, the UN divided it into two "covenants"—Civil and Political Rights, and Economic, Social, and Cultural Rights. It took until 1992 for the U.S. Congress to ratify the first. It has never approved the second.

THE TRUMAN PRESIDENCY

The Fair Deal

With the end of World War II, President Truman's first domestic task was to preside over the transition from a wartime to a peacetime economy. More than 12 million men remained in uniform in August 1945. Most wanted nothing more than to return home to their families. Demobilization proceeded at a rapid pace. Within a year, the armed forces had been reduced to 3 million. The majority of returning soldiers entered the labor force—one reason why more than 2 million women workers lost their jobs. Many also took advantage of the GI Bill of Rights (discussed in the previous chapter) to obtain home mortgages, set up small businesses, and embark on college educations.

In the immediate aftermath of World War II, President Truman, backed by party liberals and organized labor, moved to revive the stalled momentum of the New Deal. Truman's program, which he announced in September 1945 and would later call the **Fair Deal**, focused on improving the social safety net and raising the standard of living of ordinary Americans. He called on Congress to increase the minimum wage, enact a program of national health insurance, and expand public housing, Social Security, and aid to education. Truman, complained one Republican leader, was "out–New Dealing the New Deal."

The Postwar Strike Wave

In 1946, a new wave of labor militancy swept the country. The AFL and CIO launched **Operation Dixie**, a campaign to bring unionization to the South and, by so doing, shatter the hold of anti-labor conservatives on the region's politics. More than 200 labor organizers entered the region, seeking support especially in the southern textile industry, the steel industry in the Birmingham region, and agriculture. With war production at an end, overtime work diminished even as inflation soared following the removal of price controls. The resulting drop in workers' real income sparked the largest strike wave in American history. Nearly 5 million workers—including those in the steel, auto, coal, and other key industries—walked off their jobs, demanding wage increases. The strike of 750,000 steelworkers represented the largest single walkout in American history to that date. Even Hollywood studios shut down because of a strike of actors and other employees of the movie industry that lasted for the better part of a year. One historian calls this period "the closest thing to a national general strike in industry in the twentieth century."

President Truman feared the strikes would seriously disrupt the economy. When railroad workers stopped work and set up picket lines, the infuriated president prepared a speech in which he threatened to draft them all into the army and "hang a few traitors"—language toned down by his advisers. The walkout soon ended, as did a coal strike after the Truman administration secured a court order requiring the miners to return to work. To resolve other strikes, Truman appointed federal "fact-finding boards," which generally recommended wage increases, although not enough to restore workers' purchasing power to wartime levels.

The Republican Resurgence

In the congressional elections of 1946, large numbers of middle-class voters, alarmed by the labor turmoil, voted Republican. Many workers, disappointed by Truman's policies, stayed at home. This was a lethal combination for the Democratic Party. For the first time since the 1920s, Republicans swept to control of both houses of Congress. Meanwhile, in the face of vigorous opposition from southern employers and public officials and the reluctance of many white workers to join interracial labor unions, Operation Dixie failed to unionize the South or dent the political control of conservative Democrats in the region. The election of 1946 ensured that a conservative coalition of Republicans and southern Democrats would continue to dominate Congress.

Congress turned aside Truman's Fair Deal program. It enacted tax cuts for wealthy Americans and, over the president's veto, in 1947 passed the **Taft-Hartley Act**, which sought to reverse some of the gains made by organized labor in the past decade. The measure authorized the president to suspend strikes by ordering an eighty-day "cooling-off period," and it banned sympathy strikes and secondary boycotts (labor actions directed not at an employer but at those who did business with him). It outlawed the closed shop, which required a worker to be a union member when taking up a job, and authorized states to pass "right-to-work" laws, prohibiting other forms of compulsory union membership. It also forced union officials to swear that they were not communists. The Taft-Hartley Act made it considerably more difficult to bring unorganized workers into unions. Over time, as population and capital investment shifted to states with "right-to-work" laws like Texas, Florida, and North Carolina,

Taft-Hartley contributed to the decline of organized labor's share of the nation's workforce.

Postwar Civil Rights

During his first term, Truman reached out in unprecedented ways to the nation's Black community. The war, as noted in the previous chapter, had inspired a new Black militancy and led many whites to reject American racial practices as reminiscent of Hitler's theory of a master race. In the years immediately following World War II, the status of Black Americans enjoyed a prominence in national affairs unmatched since Reconstruction.

Between 1945 and 1951, eleven states from New York to New Mexico established fair employment practices commissions, and numerous cities passed laws against discrimination in access to jobs and public accommodations. (Some of these measures addressed other racial groups besides Blacks: for example, California in 1947 repealed its laws permitting local school districts to provide segregated education for children of Chinese descent and those barring aliens from owning land.) A broad civil rights coalition involving labor, religious groups, and Black organizations supported these measures. The NAACP, its ranks swollen during the war, launched a voter registration campaign in the South. By 1952, 20 percent of Black southerners were registered to vote, nearly a seven-fold increase since 1940. (Most of the gains took place in the Upper South—in Alabama and Mississippi, the heartland of white supremacy, the numbers barely budged.) Law enforcement agencies finally took the crime of lynching seriously. In 1952, for the first time since record keeping began seventy years earlier, no lynchings took place in the United States. In 1946, the Superman radio show devoted several episodes to the man of steel fighting the Ku Klux Klan, a sign of changing race relations in the wake of World War II.

In another indication that race relations were in flux, the Brooklyn Dodgers in 1947 challenged the long-standing exclusion of Black players from major league baseball by adding Jackie Robinson to their team. Robinson, who possessed both remarkable athletic ability and a passion for equality, had been tried and acquitted for insubordination in 1944 when he refused to move to the back of a bus at Fort Hood, Texas, while serving in the army. But he promised Dodger owner Branch Rickey that he would not retaliate when subjected to racist taunts by opposing fans and players. His dignity in the face of constant verbal abuse won Robinson nationwide respect, and his baseball prowess earned him the Rookie of the Year award. His success opened the door to the integration of baseball and led to the demise of the Negro Leagues, to which Black players had previously been confined.

To Secure These Rights

In October 1947, a Commission on Civil Rights appointed by the president issued *To Secure These Rights*, one of the most devastating indictments ever published of racial inequality in America. It called on the federal government to assume the responsibility for abolishing segregation and ensuring equal treatment in housing, employment, education, and the criminal justice system. Truman hailed the report as "an American charter of human freedom." The impact of America's race system on the nation's ability to conduct the Cold War was not far from his mind. Truman noted that if the United States were to offer the "peoples of the world" a "choice of freedom or enslavement," it must "correct the remaining imperfections in our practice of democracy."

In February 1948, Truman presented an ambitious civil rights program to Congress, calling for a permanent federal civil rights commission, national laws against lynching and the poll tax, and action to ensure equal access to jobs and education. Congress, as Truman anticipated, approved none of his proposals. But in July 1948, just as the presidential campaign was getting under way, Truman issued an executive order desegregating the armed forces. The armed services became the first large institution in American life to promote racial integration actively and to attempt to root out long-standing racist practices. The Korean War would be the first American conflict fought by an integrated army since the War of Independence.

Truman genuinely despised racial discrimination. But his focus on civil rights also formed part of a strategy to win reelection by reinvigorating and expanding the political coalition Roosevelt had created. With calls for federal health insurance, the repeal of the Taft-Hartley Act, and aid to public education, the Democratic platform of 1948 was the most progressive in the party's history. Led by Hubert Humphrey, the young mayor of Minneapolis, party liberals overcame southern resistance and added a strong civil rights plank to the platform.

Part of a series of giant murals painted between 1941 and 1948 for the lobby of the Rincon Center (formerly a post office, now a shopping mall in San Francisco), this work by the artist Anton Refregier links the Four Freedoms of World War II to a multicultural vision of American society. (In Norman Rockwell's celebrated paintings, shown in Chapter 22, all the figures depicted are white.)

The Dixiecrat and Wallace Revolts

"I say the time has come," Humphrey told the Democratic national convention, "to walk out of the shadow of states' rights and into the sunlight of human rights." Whereupon numerous southern delegates—dubbed **Dixiecrats** by the press—walked out of the gathering. They soon formed the States' Rights Democratic Party and nominated for president Governor Strom Thurmond of South Carolina. Although his platform called for the "complete segregation of the races" and his campaign drew most of its support from those alarmed by Truman's civil rights initiatives, Thurmond denied charges of racism. The real issue of the election, Thurmond insisted, was freedom—the States' Rights Democratic Party, he declared, stood for "individual liberty and freedom, the right of people to govern themselves." Truman's plans for extending federal power into the South to enforce civil rights, Thurmond charged, would "convert America into a Hitler state."

Also in 1948, a group of left-wing critics of Truman's foreign policy formed the Progressive Party and nominated former vice president Henry A. Wallace for president. Wallace advocated an expansion of social welfare programs at home and denounced racial segregation even more vigorously than Truman. When he campaigned in the South, angry white crowds attacked him. But his real difference with the president concerned the Cold War. Wallace called for international control of nuclear weapons and a renewed effort to develop a relationship with the Soviet Union based on economic cooperation rather than military confrontation. He announced his willingness to accept support from all Americans who agreed with him, including socialists and communists. The influence of the now much-reduced Communist Party in Wallace's campaign led to an exodus of New Deal liberals and severe attacks on his candidacy. A vote for Wallace, Truman declared, was in effect a vote for Stalin.

The Election of 1948

Wallace threatened to draw votes from Truman on the left and Thurmond to undermine the president's support in the South, where whites had voted solidly for the Democrats throughout the twentieth century.

Virtually every public-opinion poll and newspaper report predicted a victory for Republican Thomas E. Dewey, Truman's main opponent. Truman's success—by 303 to 189 electoral votes—represented one of the greatest upsets in American political history. For the first time since 1868, Blacks (in the North, where they enjoyed the right to vote) played a decisive role in the outcome.

Thurmond carried four Lower South states, demonstrating that the race issue, couched in terms of individual freedom, had the potential of leading traditionally Democratic white voters to desert their party. In retrospect, the States' Rights campaign offered a preview of the political transformation that by the end of the twentieth century would leave every southern state in the Republican column. As for Wallace, he suffered the humiliation of polling fewer popular votes (1.16 million) than Thurmond (1.17 million). His crushing defeat inaugurated an era in which public criticism of the foundations of American foreign policy became all but impossible.

THE ANTICOMMUNIST CRUSADE

For nearly half a century, the Cold War profoundly affected American life. It ensured that the military-industrial establishment created during World War II would be permanent, not temporary. The United States retained a large and active federal government and poured money into weapons development and overseas bases. National security became the stated reason for a host of government projects, including aid to higher education and the building of a new national highway system (justified by the need to speed the evacuation of major cities in the event of nuclear war). The Cold War encouraged a culture of secrecy and dishonesty. Not until decades later was it revealed that during the 1950s and 1960s both the Soviet and American governments conducted experiments in which unwitting soldiers were exposed to chemical, biological, and nuclear weapons. American nuclear tests, conducted on Pacific islands and in Nevada, exposed thousands of civilians to radiation that caused cancer and birth defects.

A postcard promoting tourism to Las Vegas highlights as one attraction the city's proximity to a nuclear test site. Witnessing nearby atomic explosions became a popular pastime in the city. The government failed to issue warnings of the dangers of nuclear fallout, and only years later did it admit that many onlookers had contracted diseases from radiation.

Cold War military spending helped to fuel economic growth and support scientific research that not only perfected weaponry but also led to improved aircraft, computers, medicines, and other products with a large impact on civilian life. Since much of this research took place at universities, the Cold War promoted the rapid expansion of American higher education. The Cold War reshaped immigration policy, with refugees from communism being allowed to enter the United States regardless of national-origin quotas. The international embarrassment caused by American racial policies contributed to the dismantling of segregation. And like other wars, the Cold War encouraged the drawing of a sharp line between patriotic Americans and those accused of being disloyal. Containment—not only of communism but also of unorthodox opinions of all kinds—took place at home as well as abroad. At precisely the moment when the United States celebrated freedom as the foundation of American life, the right to dissent came under attack.

Loyalty, Disloyalty, and American Identity

The fear inspired by communism became a catalyst for reconsidering American identity in the mid-twentieth century. This led to some paradoxical outcomes. In public opinion polls, many Americans expressed devotion to civil liberties while also favoring depriving communists and other nonconformists of their jobs or even citizenship. As the historian Henry Steele Commager argued in a 1947 magazine article, the anticommunist crusade promoted a new definition of American loyalty and identity: conformity. Anything other than "uncritical and unquestioning acceptance of America as it is," he wrote, could now be labeled unpatriotic. Much of the clampdown on communism fell disproportionately against people already seen as outside the American mainstream, including Jews and other immigrants, and gay persons.

The relationship between communism and citizenship was codified in the **McCarran-Walter Act** of 1952, which made it possible to revoke the citizenship and deport an American born abroad if he or she refused to testify about "subversive" activity, joined a subversive organization, or voted in a foreign election. The first major piece of immigration legislation since 1924, it passed over Truman's veto. Truman had appointed a Commission on Immigration, whose report, *Whom Shall We Welcome?*, called for replacing the quotas based on national origins with a more flexible system taking into account family reunion, labor needs, and political asylum. But the McCarran-Walter Act kept the quotas in place. They would remain the basis of immigration law until 1965.

The renewed fear of immigrants sparked by the anticommunist crusade went far beyond communists. In 1954, the government launched a program that employed military-style tactics to invade Mexican American neighborhoods and round up and deport

The anti-Communist crusade sparked renewed fear of immigrants. Migrant workers in California hold up their work permits during the federal government's massive deportation campaign in 1954.

From OSCAR HANDLIN, "THE IMMIGRATION FIGHT HAS ONLY BEGUN" (1952)

Published shortly after passage of the McCarran-Walter Act, an article by Harvard historian Oscar Handlin, himself the son of Russian Jewish immigrants, became a rallying cry for those attacking the law and demanding a new immigration policy. As was common at the time, Handlin's language had an unspoken gender dimension, using "man" to encompass both men and women.

Not since the Alien and Sedition Acts of 1798 has an act of Congress come so close to subverting the underlying assumption on which the conception of citizenship in the United States rests: the assumption that there are no degrees of citizenship, that all Americans are completely equal in rights whatever their place of birth. . . . Retaining the rigid national quotas, it [also] curtails severely the civil liberties of immigrants and resident aliens. . . .

The [immigration] laws are bad because they rest on the racist assumption that mankind is divided into fixed breeds, biologically and culturally separated from each other, and because, within that framework, they assume that Americans are Anglo-Saxons by origin and ought to remain so. To all other peoples, the laws say that the United States ranks them in terms of their racial proximity to our own "superior" stock; and upon the many, many millions of Americans not descended from the Anglo-Saxons, the laws cast a distinct imputation of inferiority.

More recent defenders of the quota system, unwilling to endorse the open racism that gave it birth, have urged that the differentiations it establishes be regarded as cultural rather than racial. The South Italian or the Syrian, it is argued, is culturally less capable of adjusting to American life than the Englishman or the German. . . . There is no evidence to support that contention. . . . Allowed to settle in peace, every variety of man has been able to make a place for himself in American life, to his own profit and to the enrichment of the society that has accepted him. The dreaded "riff-raff" of 1910—Greeks, Armenians, Magyars, Slovaks, Polish Jews—are the respected parents of respected citizens today. . . .

The Americans of the 19th century had confidence enough in their own society and in their own institutions to believe any man could become an American. More than ever do we now need to reaffirm that faith.

QUESTIONS

1. *Why does Handlin believe that basic premises of the immigration quota system have been disproven?*

2. *How does he invoke history to bolster his arguments?*

undocumented aliens. It was called "Operation Wetback," utilizing a racial slur sometimes directed at Mexican immigrants. Within a year, some 1 million Mexicans had been deported.

Dividing the world between liberty and slavery automatically made those who could be linked to communism enemies of freedom. Although the assault on civil liberties came to be known as **McCarthyism**, it began before Senator Joseph R. McCarthy of Wisconsin burst onto the national scene in 1950. In 1947, less than two weeks after announcing the Truman Doctrine, the president established a loyalty review system that required government employees to demonstrate their patriotism without being allowed to confront accusers or, in some cases, knowing the charges against them. Along with persons suspected of disloyalty, the new national security system also targeted gay men and lesbians who worked for the government. They were deemed particularly susceptible to blackmail by Soviet agents as well as supposedly lacking in the qualities needed to maintain the country's resolve in the fight against communism. Ironically, the government conducted an anti-gay campaign at the very time that gay men enjoyed a powerful presence in realms of culture and commercial life being promoted as expressions of American freedom—modern art and ballet, fashion, and advertising. The loyalty program failed to uncover any cases of espionage. But the federal government dismissed several hundred gay men and lesbians from their jobs, and thousands resigned rather than submit to investigation.

Also in 1947, the House Un-American Activities Committee (HUAC) launched a series of hearings about communist influence in Hollywood. Calling well-known screenwriters, directors, and actors to appear before the committee ensured a wave of national publicity, which its members relished. Celebrities like producer Walt Disney and actors Gary Cooper and Ronald Reagan testified that the movie industry harbored numerous communists. But ten "unfriendly witnesses" refused to answer the committee's questions about their political beliefs or to "name names" (identify individual communists) on the grounds that the hearings violated the First Amendment's guarantees of freedom of speech and political association. The committee charged the **Hollywood Ten**, who included the prominent screenwriters Ring Lardner Jr. and Dalton Trumbo, with contempt of Congress, and they served jail terms of six months to a year. Hollywood studios blacklisted them (denied them employment), along with more than 200 others who were accused of communist sympathies or who refused to name names.

The Spy Trials

A series of highly publicized legal cases followed, which fueled the growing anticommunist hysteria. Whittaker Chambers, an editor at *Time* magazine, testified before HUAC that during the 1930s, Alger Hiss, a high-ranking State

Department official, had given him secret government documents to pass to agents of the Soviet Union. Hiss vehemently denied the charge, but a jury convicted him of perjury and he served five years in prison. A young congressman from California and a member of HUAC, Richard Nixon, achieved national prominence because of his dogged pursuit of Hiss. In another celebrated case, the Truman administration put the leaders of the Communist Party on trial for advocating the overthrow of the government. In 1951, eleven of them were sentenced to five years in prison.

The most sensational trial involved Julius and Ethel Rosenberg, a working-class Jewish communist couple from New York City (quite different from Hiss, a member of the eastern Protestant "establishment"). In 1951, a jury convicted the Rosenbergs of conspiracy to pass secrets concerning the atomic bomb to Soviet agents during World War II (when the Soviets were American allies). Their chief accuser was David Greenglass, Ethel Rosenberg's brother, who had worked at the Los Alamos nuclear research center.

The case against Julius Rosenberg rested on highly secret documents that could not be revealed in court. (When they were released many years later, the scientific information they contained seemed too crude to justify the government's charge that Julius had passed along the "secret of the atomic bomb," although he may have helped the Soviets speed up their atomic program.) The government had almost no evidence against Ethel Rosenberg, and Greenglass later admitted that he had lied in some of his testimony about her. Indeed, prosecutors seem to have indicted her in the hope of pressuring Julius to confess and implicate others. But in the atmosphere of hysteria, their conviction was certain. Even though they had been convicted of conspiracy, a far weaker charge than spying or treason, Judge Irving Kaufman called their crime "worse than murder." They had helped, he declared, to "cause" the Korean War. Despite an international outcry, the death sentence was carried out in 1953. Controversy still surrounds the degree of guilt of both Hiss and the Rosenbergs, although almost no one today defends the Rosenbergs' execution. But these trials powerfully reinforced the idea that an army of Soviet spies was at work in the United States.

McCarthy and McCarthyism

In this atmosphere, a little-known senator from Wisconsin suddenly emerged as the chief national pursuer of subversives and gave a new name to the anti-communist crusade. Joseph R. McCarthy had won election to the Senate in 1946, partly on the basis of a fictional war record (he falsely claimed to have flown combat missions in the Pacific). In a speech at Wheeling, West Virginia, in February 1950, McCarthy announced that he had a list of 205 communists working for the State Department. The charge was preposterous, the numbers constantly changed, and McCarthy never identified a single person guilty of genuine disloyalty. But with a genius for self-promotion, McCarthy used the Senate subcommittee he chaired to hold hearings and level wild charges against numerous individuals as well as the Defense Department, the Voice of America, and other government agencies. Although many Republicans initially supported his rampage as a weapon against the Truman administration, McCarthy became an embarrassment to the party after the election of Republican Dwight D. Eisenhower as president in 1952. But McCarthy did not halt his campaign. He even questioned Eisenhower's anticommunism.

Few political figures had the courage to speak up against McCarthy's crusade. One who did was Margaret Chase Smith of Maine, the Senate's only woman member. On June 1, 1950, soon after McCarthy's Wheeling speech, Smith addressed the Senate with what she called a "declaration of conscience." She did not name McCarthy, but few could mistake the target of her condemnation of a "campaign of hate and character assassination." Most of her colleagues, however, remained silent.

McCarthy's downfall came in 1954, when a Senate committee investigated his charges that the army had harbored and "coddled" communists. The nationally televised **Army-McCarthy hearings** revealed McCarthy as a bully who browbeat witnesses and made sweeping accusations with no basis in fact. The dramatic high point came when McCarthy attacked the loyalty of a young attorney in the firm of Joseph Welch, the army's chief lawyer. "Let us not assassinate this lad further," Welch pleaded. "You have done enough. Have you no sense of decency, sir?" After the hearings ended, the Republican-controlled Senate voted to "condemn" McCarthy for his behavior. He died three years later. But the word "McCarthyism" had entered the political vocabulary, a shorthand for character assassination, guilt by association, and abuse of power in the name of anticommunism.

An Atmosphere of Fear

By the early 1950s, the anticommunist crusade had created a pervasive atmosphere of fear. One commentator described Washington, D.C., as a city rife with "spying, suspicion, [and] defamation by rumor," with "democratic freedoms" at risk as power slipped into the hands of those "whose values are the values of dictatorship and whose methods are the methods of the police state." But anticommunism was as much a local as a national phenomenon. States created their own committees, modeled on HUAC, that investigated suspected communists and other dissenters. States and localities required loyalty oaths of teachers, pharmacists, and members of other professions, and they banned communists from fishing, holding a driver's license, and, in Indiana, working as a professional wrestler.

Private organizations like the American Legion, National Association of Manufacturers, and Daughters of the American Revolution also persecuted individuals for their beliefs. The Better America League of southern California gathered the names of nearly 2 million alleged subversives in the region. Previous membership in organizations with communist influence or even participation in campaigns in which communists had taken part, such as the defense of the government of Spain during the Spanish Civil War of the 1930s, suddenly took on sinister implications. Throughout the country in the late 1940s and 1950s, those who failed to testify about their past and present political beliefs and to inform on possible communists frequently lost their jobs.

Local anticommunist groups forced public libraries to remove from their shelves "un-American" books like the tales of Robin Hood, who took from the rich to give to the poor. Universities refused to allow left-wing speakers to appear on campus and fired teachers who refused to sign loyalty oaths or to testify against others.

As during World War I, the courts did nothing to halt the political repression, demonstrating once again James Madison's warning that popular hysteria could override "parchment barriers" like the Bill of Rights that sought to prevent infringements on freedom. In 1951, in *Dennis v. United States*, the Supreme Court upheld the jailing of Communist Party leaders even though the charges concerned their beliefs, not any actions they had taken.

The Uses of Anticommunism

There undoubtedly were Soviet spies in the United States. Yet the tiny Communist Party hardly posed a threat to American security. And the vast majority of those jailed or deprived of their livelihoods during the McCarthy era were guilty of nothing more than holding unpopular beliefs and engaging in lawful political activities.

Anticommunism had many faces and purposes. A popular mass movement, it grew especially strong among ethnic groups like Polish Americans, with roots in eastern European countries now dominated by the Soviet Union, and among American Catholics in general, who resented and feared communists' hostility to religion. Government agencies like the Federal Bureau of Investigation (FBI) used anticommunism to expand their power. Under director J. Edgar Hoover, the FBI developed files on thousands of American citizens, including political dissenters, gay men and lesbians, and others, most of whom had no connection to communism.

Anticommunism also served as a weapon wielded by individuals and groups in battles unrelated to defending the United States against subversion. McCarthy and his Republican followers often seemed to target not so much Stalin as the legacy of Roosevelt and the New Deal. For many Democrats, aggressive anticommunism became a form of self-defense against Republican charges of disloyalty and a weapon in a struggle for the party's future. For business, anticommunism became part of a campaign to identify government intervention in the economy with socialism. For western interests, it served as a rationale to press for an end to Native Americans' "collectivist" landholdings. White supremacists employed anticommunism against Black civil rights, employers used it against unions, and upholders of sexual morality and traditional gender roles raised the cry of subversion against feminists and gay persons both supposedly responsible for eroding the country's fighting spirit.

Leaders of the National Congress of American Indians, an organization founded in1944 to protect the rights of Indigenous peoples. *Left to right:* Helen Peterson, D'Arcy McNickle, Joseph Garry, Louis Bruce, and Ruth Bronson.

Anticommunist Politics

At its height, from the late 1940s to around 1960, the anticommunist crusade powerfully structured American politics and culture. Especially after their unexpected defeat in 1948, Republicans in Congress used a drumbeat of charges of subversion to block Truman's political program. The most important actions of Congress were ones the president opposed. After launching the government's loyalty program in 1947, Truman had become increasingly alarmed at the excesses of the anticommunist crusade. He vetoed the McCarran Internal Security Act of 1950, which required "subversive" groups to register with the government, allowed the denial of passports to their members, and authorized their deportation or detention on presidential order. But Congress quickly gave the measure the two-thirds majority necessary for it to become law.

Truman did secure passage of a 1950 law that added previously excluded self-employed and domestic workers to Social Security. Otherwise, however, the idea of expanding the New Deal welfare state faded. In its place, private welfare arrangements proliferated. The labor contracts of unionized workers established health insurance plans, automatic cost of living wage increases, paid vacations, and pension plans that supplemented Social Security. Western European governments provided these benefits to all citizens. In the United States, union members in major industries enjoyed them but not the nonunionized majority of the population, a situation that created increasing inequality among laboring Americans.

From HENRY STEELE COMMAGER, "WHO IS LOYAL TO AMERICA?" *HARPER'S MAGAZINE* (1947)

In a sharply worded essay written in 1947 for *Harper's Magazine* and later published in *Freedom, Loyalty, Dissent* (1954), the prominent historian Henry Steele Commager commented on how the anticommunist crusade was stifling the expression of dissent and promoting an idea of patriotism that equated loyalty to the nation with uncritical acceptance of American society and institutions.

Increasingly Congress is concerned with the eradication of disloyalty and the defense of Americanism, and scarcely a day passes . . . that the outlines of the new loyalty and the new Americanism are not etched more sharply in public policy. . . . In the making is a revival of the red hysteria of the early 1920s, one of the shabbiest chapters in the history of American democracy, and more than a revival, for the new crusade is designed not merely to frustrate Communism but to formulate a positive definition of Americanism, and a positive concept of loyalty.

What is this new loyalty? It is, above all, conformity. It is the uncritical and unquestioning acceptance of America as it is—the political institutions, the social relationships, the economic practices. It rejects inquiry into the race question or socialized medicine, or public housing, or into the wisdom or validity of our foreign policy. It regards as particularly heinous any challenge to what is called "the system of private enterprise," identifying that system with Americanism. It abandons . . . the once popular concept of progress, and regards America as a finished product, perfect and complete.

It is, it must be added, easily satisfied. For it wants not intellectual conviction nor spiritual conquest, but mere outward conformity. In matters of loyalty, it takes the word for the deed, the gesture for the principle. It is content with the flag salute. . . . It is satisfied with membership in respectable organizations and, as it assumes that every member of a liberal organization is a Communist, concludes that every member of a conservative one is a true American. It has not yet learned that everyone who saith Lord, Lord, shall enter into the kingdom of Heaven. It is designed neither to discover real disloyalty nor to foster true loyalty.

The concept of loyalty as conformity is a false one. It is narrow and restrictive, denies freedom of thought and of conscience. . . . What do men know of loyalty who make a mockery of the Declaration of Independence and the Bill of Rights?

From DWIGHT D. EISENHOWER, FAREWELL ADDRESS (JANUARY 17, 1961)

Before departing office, Dwight D. Eisenhower issued a warning about new dangers posed to American liberty due to the convergence of military might and a powerful arms industry. With the United States' continued involvement in wars from Vietnam to Iraq, his warning has proved prescient.

My fellow Americans: . . . . This evening I come to you with a message of leave-taking and farewell, and to share a few final thoughts with you, . . . Throughout America's adventure in free government, our basic purposes have been to keep the peace; to foster progress in human achievement, and to enhance liberty, dignity and integrity among people and among nations. To strive for less would be unworthy of a free and religious people. . . . A vital element in keeping the peace is our military establishment. Our arms must be mighty, ready for instant action, so that no potential aggressor may be tempted to risk his own destruction. . . . Until the latest of our world conflicts, the United States had no armaments industry. American makers of plowshares could, with time and as required, make swords as well. But now we can no longer risk emergency improvisation of national defense; we have been compelled to create a permanent armaments industry of vast proportions. Added to this, three and a half million men and women are directly engaged in the defense establishment. We annually spend on military security more than the net income of all United States corporations.

This conjunction of an immense military establishment and a large arms industry is new in the American experience. The total influence—economic, political, even spiritual—is felt in every city, every State house, every office of the Federal government. We recognize the imperative need for this development. Yet we must not fail to comprehend its grave implications. Our toil, resources and livelihood are all involved; so is the very structure of our society.

In the councils of government, we must guard against the acquisition of unwarranted influence, whether sought or unsought, by the military-industrial complex. The potential for the disastrous rise of misplaced power exists and will persist.

We must never let the weight of this combination endanger our liberties or democratic processes. We should take nothing for granted. Only an alert and knowledgeable citizenry can compel the proper meshing of the huge industrial and military machinery of defense with our peaceful methods and goals, so that security and liberty may prosper together.

QUESTIONS

1. Why does Commager feel that the new patriotism makes a "mockery" of the Bill of Rights?

2. According to Eisenhower, what is the "military-industrial complex"?

3. What new threats to freedom during the Cold War do these documents emphasize?

The Cold War and Native Americans

Cold War anticommunist politics also brought renewed threats to Indian self-determination. Advocates of detribalization built upon earlier assimilationist efforts but now mobilized the era's heightened communist fears to argue for an end to Native American reservations. While fighting communism abroad, one prominent western senator charged, the government was promoting "natural socialist environments" at home. House resolution 108, passed in 1953, called for abolishing Indians' trust relationship with the federal government ushering in what became known as the **termination era**. Utah Senator Arthur Watkins called termination the "Indian Freedom Program," likening reservations to prisons. Such claims were contested by Native Americans whose own understandings of freedom were grounded in self-determination. Zuni World War II and Korean War veterans declared that "this is supposed to be a land of freedom" and that termination policies would "mean total destruction of all tribes." Joseph Garry, a Coeur d'Alene veteran and National Congress of American Indians (NCAI) president, argued that "reservations do not imprison us. They are ancestral homelands.... We must assert our right to maintain ownership in our own way."

The NCAI defended Indian sovereignty. D'Arcy McNickle, a prominent writer of Cree and white heritage, called on the U.S. government to provide development aid for Indian reservations, much as it did for less economically advanced nations internationally, rather than terminating tribes without their consent. Protest against termination garnered widespread support. Several smaller tribes did see their trust status abolished, but the NCAI and their non-Indian allies halted wholesale termination by the early 1960s. Their campaign, however, was not untouched by the atmosphere of Cold War conformity. The NCAI cooperated with the anticommunist crusade, carefully choosing its allies to avoid association with groups that were labeled as "subversive" by HUAC.

The Cold War and Organized Labor

Every political and social organization had to cooperate with the anticommunist crusade or face destruction, a wrenching experience for movements like labor and civil rights, in which communists had been some of the most militant organizers. After the passage of the Taft-Hartley Act of 1947, which withdrew bargaining rights and legal protection from unions whose leaders failed to swear that they were not communists, the CIO expelled numerous left-wing officials and eleven communist-led unions, representing nearly 1 million workers. Organized labor emerged as a major supporter of the foreign policy of the Cold War. Internal battles over the role of communists and their allies led to the purging of some of the most militant union leaders, often the ones most committed to advancing equal rights to women and racial minorities in the workplace.

Cold War Civil Rights

The civil rights movement also underwent a transformation. At first, mainstream Black organizations like the NAACP and Urban League protested the Truman administration's loyalty program. They wondered aloud why the program and congressional committees defined communism as "un-American," but not racism. Anticommunist investigators often cited attendance at interracial gatherings as evidence of disloyalty. But while a few prominent Black leaders, notably the singer and actor Paul Robeson and the veteran crusader for equality W. E. B. Du Bois, became outspoken critics of the Cold War, most felt they had no choice but to go along. The NAACP purged communists from local branches. When the government deprived Robeson of his passport and indicted Du Bois for failing to register as an agent of the Soviet Union, few prominent Americans, white or Black, protested. (The charge against Du Bois was so absurd that even at the height of McCarthyism, the judge dismissed it.)

The Cold War caused a shift in thinking and tactics among civil rights groups. Organizations like the Southern Conference for Human Welfare, in which communists and noncommunists had cooperated in linking racial equality with labor organizing and economic reform, had been crucial to the struggles of the 1930s and war years. Their demise left a gaping hole that the NAACP, with its narrowly legalistic strategy, could not fill. Black organizations embraced the language of the Cold War and used it for their own purposes. They insisted that by damaging the American image abroad, racial inequality played into the Russians' hands. Thus, they helped to cement Cold War ideology as the foundation of the political culture, while complicating the idea of American freedom.

President Truman, as noted above, had called for greater attention to civil rights in part to improve the American image abroad. All in all, however, the height of the Cold War was an unfavorable time to raise questions about the imperfections of American society. In 1947, two months after the Truman Doctrine speech, Undersecretary of State Dean Acheson delivered a major address defending the president's pledge to aid "free peoples" seeking to preserve their "democratic institutions." Acheson chose as his audience the Delta Council, an organization of Mississippi planters, bankers, and merchants. He seemed unaware that to make the case for the Cold War, he had ventured into what one historian has called the "American Siberia," a place of grinding poverty whose Black population (70 percent of the total) enjoyed neither genuine freedom nor democracy. Most of the Delta's citizens were denied the very liberties supposedly endangered by communism.

After 1948, little came of the Truman administration's civil rights flurry. State and local laws banning discrimination in employment and housing remained largely unenforced. In 1952, the Democrats showed how quickly the issue had faded by nominating for president Adlai Stevenson of Illinois, a candidate with little interest in civil rights, with southern segregationist John Sparkman as his running mate. The following year, Hortense Gabel, director of the eminently respectable New York State Committee Against Discrimination in Housing, reported that the shadow of fear hung over the civil rights movement. Given the persecution of dissent and the widespread sentiment that equated any criticism of American society with disloyalty, "a great many people are shying away from all activity in the civil liberties and civil rights fronts."

Time would reveal that the waning of the civil rights impulse was only temporary. But it came at a crucial moment, the late 1940s and early 1950s, when the United States experienced the greatest economic boom in its history. The rise of an "affluent society" transformed American life, opening new opportunities for tens of millions of white Americans in rapidly expanding suburbs. But it left Blacks trapped in the declining rural areas of the South and urban ghettos of the North. The contrast between new opportunities and widespread prosperity for whites and continued discrimination for Blacks would soon inspire a civil rights revolution and, with it, yet another redefinition of American freedom.

CHAPTER REVIEW

REVIEW QUESTIONS

1. *What major ideological conflicts, security interests, and events brought about the Cold War?*

2. *President Truman referred to the Truman Doctrine and the Marshall Plan as "two halves of the same walnut." Explain the similarities and differences between these two aspects of containment.*

3. *How did the tendency of both the United States and the Soviet Union to see all international events through the lens of the Cold War lessen each country's ability to understand what was happening in other countries around the world?*

4. *Why did the United States not support movements for colonial independence around the world?*

5. *How did the government attempt to shape public opinion during the Cold War?*

6. *Explain the differences between the United States' and the Soviet Union's application of the UN Universal Declaration of Human Rights.*

7. *How did the anticommunist crusade affect organized labor in the postwar period?*

8. *What accounts for the Republican resurgence in these years?*

9. *What were the major components of Truman's Fair Deal? Which ones were implemented and which ones not?*

10. *How did the Cold War affect civil liberties in the United States?*

11. *How did the McCarran-Walter Act codify the relationship between communism and citizenship? Why did the clampdown on communism fall disproportionately on those regarded as outside the American mainstream?*

KEY TERMS

Cold War (p. 914)

containment (p. 914)

Long Telegram (p. 916)

iron curtain (p. 916)

Truman Doctrine (p. 916)

Marshall Plan (p. 918)

North Atlantic Treaty Organization (p. 920)

NSC-68 (p. 920)

Korean War (p. 921)

decolonization (p. 924)

totalitarianism (p. 926)

Fair Deal (p. 929)

Operation Dixie (p. 929)

Taft-Hartley Act (p. 930)

Dixiecrats (p. 933)

McCarran-Walter Act (p. 935)

McCarthyism (p. 937)

Hollywood Ten (p. 937)

Army-McCarthy hearings (p. 939)

termination era (p. 944)

Go to 🐰 **INQUIZITIVE**

To see what you know—and learn what you've missed—with personalized feedback along the way.

★ CHAPTER 24 ★

AN AFFLUENT SOCIETY

1953–1960

FOCUS QUESTIONS

- *What were the main characteristics of the affluent society of the 1950s?*

- *How were the 1950s a period of consensus in both domestic policies and foreign affairs?*

- *What were the major thrusts of the civil rights movement in this period?*

- *What was the significance of the presidential election of 1960?*

In 1958, during a "thaw" in the Cold War, the United States and the Soviet Union agreed to exchange national exhibitions in order to allow citizens of each "superpower" to become acquainted with life in the other. The Soviet Exhibition, unveiled in New York City in June 1959, featured factory machinery, scientific advances, and other illustrations of how communism had modernized a backward country. The following month, the American National Exhibition opened in Moscow. A showcase of consumer goods and leisure equipment, complete with stereo sets, a movie theater, home appliances, and twenty-two different cars, the exhibit, *Newsweek* observed, hoped to demonstrate the superiority of "modern capitalism with its ideology of political and economic freedom." Yet the exhibit's real message was not freedom but consumption—or, to be more precise, the equating of the two.

When Vice President Richard Nixon prepared for his trip to Moscow to launch the exhibition, a former ambassador to Russia urged him to emphasize American values: "We are idealists; they are materialists." But the events of the opening day seemed to reverse these roles. Nixon devoted his address, entitled "What Freedom Means to Us," not to freedom of expression or differing forms of government, but to the "extraordinarily high standard of living" in the United States, with its 56 million cars and 50 million television sets. The United States, he declared, had achieved what Soviets could only dream of—"prosperity for all in a classless society."

The Moscow exhibition became the site of a classic Cold War confrontation over the meaning of freedom—the "kitchen debate" between Nixon and Soviet premier Nikita Khrushchev. Twice during the first day Nixon and Khrushchev engaged in unscripted debate about the merits of capitalism and communism. The first took place in the kitchen of a model suburban ranch house, the second in a futuristic "miracle kitchen" complete with a mobile robot that swept the floors. Supposedly the home of an average steelworker, the ranch house was the exhibition's centerpiece. It represented, Nixon declared, the mass enjoyment of American freedom within a suburban setting—freedom of choice among products, colors, styles, and prices. It also implied a particular role for women. Throughout his exchanges with Khrushchev, Nixon used the words "women" and "housewives" interchangeably. Pointing to the automatic floor sweeper, the vice president remarked that in the United States "you don't need a wife."

Nixon's decision to make a stand for American values in the setting of a suburban kitchen was a brilliant stroke. Nixon recognized that "soft power"—the penetration across the globe of American goods and popular culture—was an even more potent form of influence than military might. Indeed, his stance reflected the triumph during the 1950s of a conception of freedom centered on economic abundance and consumer choice within the context of traditional family life—a vision that seemed to offer far more

· CHRONOLOGY ·

1946	*Mendez v. Westminster*
1947	Levittown development starts
1950	David Riesman's *The Lonely Crowd*
1952	United States detonates first hydrogen bomb
1953	Soviet Union detonates hydrogen bomb
	CIA-led Iranian coup
1954	*Brown v. Board of Education*
	CIA-led Guatemalan coup
	Geneva Accords for Vietnam
1955	AFL and CIO merge
	Allen Ginsberg's *Howl*
1955–1956	Montgomery bus boycott
1956	Southern Manifesto
	Federal-Aid Highway Act
	Suez crisis
1957	Eisenhower Doctrine
	Southern Christian Leadership Conference organized
	Integration of Little Rock's Central High School
	Sputnik launched
	Jack Kerouac's *On the Road*
1958	National Defense Education Act
1959	Nixon-Khrushchev "kitchen debate"
1960	John F. Kennedy elected president
1962	Milton Friedman's *Capitalism and Freedom*

Vice President Richard Nixon, with hands folded, and Soviet premier Nikita Khrushchev during the "kitchen debate," a discussion, among other things, of the meaning of freedom, which took place in 1959 at the American National Exposition in Moscow. Khrushchev makes a point while a woman demonstrates a washing machine.

opportunities for the "pursuit of happiness" to men than women. In reply, Khrushchev ridiculed consumer culture and the American obsession with household gadgets. "Don't you have a machine," he quipped, "that puts food in the mouth and pushes it down?" Many of the items on display, he continued, served "no useful purpose." Yet, in a sense, the Soviet leader conceded the debate when he predicted—quite incorrectly—that within seven years his country would surpass the United States in the production of consumer goods. For if material abundance was a battleground in the Cold War, American victory was certain.

THE GOLDEN AGE

The end of World War II was followed by what one scholar has called the "golden age" of capitalism, a period of economic expansion, stable prices, low unemployment, and rising standards of living that continued until 1973. Between 1946 and 1960, the American gross national product more than doubled and much of the benefit flowed to ordinary citizens in rising wages. In every measurable way—diet, housing, income, education, recreation—most Americans lived better than their parents and grandparents had. By 1960, an estimated 60 percent of Americans enjoyed what the government defined as a middle-class standard of living. The official poverty rate, 30 percent of all families in 1950, had declined to 22 percent a decade later (still, to be sure, representing more than one in five Americans).

Numerous innovations came into widespread use in these years, transforming Americans' daily lives. They included television, home air-conditioning, automatic dishwashers, inexpensive long-distance telephone calls, and jet air travel. Services like electricity, central heating, and indoor plumbing that within living memory had been enjoyed only by the rich and solidly middle class now became features of common life.

Between 1950 and 1973, the average real wages of manufacturing workers doubled. Wages rose faster for low-income than high-income Americans, lessening economic inequality. The reduction of income inequality stemmed from many causes, among them the federal government's progressive income tax policy, according to which wealthy Americans paid a far higher rate of taxation than others. During the 1950s, 1960s, and 1970s, the tax rate for the richest Americans never fell below 70 percent. (Today, it is 43 percent, although because of numerous tax loopholes for the wealthy, few actually pay that rate.) At the time, widespread affluence, the improving economic status of working-class men and women, and the narrowing gap between rich and poor seemed to have become a permanent feature of American society. History would show that this was, in fact, an exceptional moment, made possible by government policies, a strong union movement, and the country's global economic dominance in the wake of World War II. When the long postwar boom ended in 1973 it would be succeeded by an even longer period of stagnant incomes for most Americans and increasing inequality.

A Changing Economy

Despite the economic recovery of western Europe and Japan after World War II, the United States remained the world's predominant industrial power. Major industries like steel, automobiles, and aircraft dominated the domestic and world markets for their products. Like other wars, the Cold War fueled industrial production and promoted a redistribution of the nation's population and economic resources. The West, especially the Seattle area, southern California, and the Rocky Mountain states, benefited enormously from government contracts for aircraft, guided missiles, and radar systems. The South became the home of numerous military bases and government-funded shipyards. Growth in the construction of aircraft engines and submarines counterbalanced the decline of New England's old textile and machinery industries, many of which relocated in the South to take advantage of low-cost nonunion labor.

In retrospect, the 1950s appear as the last decade of the industrial age in the United States. Since then, the American economy has shifted rapidly toward services, education, information, finance, and entertainment, while employment in manufacturing has declined. Even during the 1950s, the number of factory laborers fell slightly while clerical workers grew by nearly 25 percent and salaried employees in large corporate enterprises rose by 60 percent. Unions' very success in raising wages inspired employers to mechanize more and more elements of manufacturing in order to reduce labor costs. In 1956, for the first time in American history, white-collar workers outnumbered blue-collar factory and manual laborers.

The long-term trend toward fewer and larger farms continued. During the 1950s, the farm population fell from 23 million to 15 million, yet agricultural production rose by 50 percent, thanks to more efficient machinery, the application of chemical fertilizers and insecticides, increased use of irrigation to open land to cultivation in the West, and the development of new crop strains.

The decade witnessed an acceleration of the transformation of southern life that had begun during World War II. New tractors and harvesting machinery and a continuing shift from cotton production to less labor-intensive soybean and poultry raising reduced the need for farm workers. More than 3 million Black and white hired hands and sharecroppers migrated out of the region. The center of gravity of American farming shifted decisively to Texas, Arizona, and especially California. The large corporate farms of California, worked by Latino and Filipino migrant laborers, poured forth an endless supply of fruits and vegetables for the domestic and world markets. Items like oranges and orange juice, once luxuries, became an essential part of the American diet.

A Suburban Nation

The main engines of economic growth during the 1950s, however, were residential construction and spending on consumer goods. The postwar baby boom (discussed later) and the shift of population from cities to suburbs created an enormous demand for housing, home appliances, and cars. By 1960, suburban residents of single-family homes outnumbered urban dwellers and those living in rural areas. (Today, they outnumber both combined.)

During the 1950s, the number of houses in the United States doubled, nearly all of them built in the suburbs that sprang up across the landscape. The dream of home ownership, the physical embodiment of hopes for a better life, came within reach of the majority of Americans. Developers pioneered inexpensive mass-building techniques, and government-backed low-interest loans to returning veterans allowed working-class men and women in large numbers to purchase homes. William and Alfred Levitt, who shortly after the war built the first **Levittown** on 1,200 acres of potato fields on Long Island near New York City, became the most famous suburban developers. Levittown's more than 10,000 houses were assembled quickly from prefabricated parts and priced well within the reach of most Americans. Levittown was soon home to 40,000 people. At the same time, suburbs required a new form of shopping center—the mall—to which people drove in their cars. In contrast to traditional mixed-use city centers crowded with pedestrians, malls existed solely for shopping and had virtually no public space. Malls narrowed the grounds for controversial or political activities, with mall owners and retailers controlling the types of activities that could take place there.

The Growth of the West

The modern West emerged in the postwar years. Unlike the 1930s, when most migrants to the West came from the South and the Dust Bowl states, all parts of the country now contributed to the region's growth. Federal spending on

Ernst Haas's 1969 photograph of Albuquerque, New Mexico, could have been taken in any one of scores of American communities. As cities spread out, "strips," consisting of motels, gas stations, and nationally franchised businesses, became common. Meanwhile, older downtown business sections stagnated.

dams, highways, and military installations helped to fuel the flow of people. So did the pleasant climate of many parts of the region, and the diffusion of air-conditioning in warmer places such as Arizona and southern California. The rapid expansion of oil production (a result of the tremendous increase in automobile ownership) led to the explosive growth of urban centers connected to the oil industry such as Denver, Dallas, and Houston.

But it was California that became the most prominent symbol of the postwar suburban boom. Between World War II and 1975, more than 30 million Americans moved west of the Mississippi River. One-fifth of the population growth of the 1950s occurred in California alone. In 1963, it surpassed New York to become the nation's most populous state.

Most western growth took place in metropolitan areas, not on farms. But "centerless" western cities like Houston, Phoenix, and Los Angeles differed greatly from traditional urban centers in the East. Rather than consisting of downtown business districts linked to residential neighborhoods by public transportation, western cities were decentralized clusters of single-family homes and businesses united by a web of highways. The Los Angeles basin, the largest western suburban region, had once had an extensive system of trains, trolleys, and buses. But local governments dismantled these lines after World War II, and the state and federal governments replaced them with freeways for cars and trucks. Suburban growth spilled into farm regions like the San Fernando and San Bernardino valleys. By one estimate, one-third of southern California's land area (presumably not including mountains and deserts) was paved over with roads and parking lots. Life centered around the car; people drove to and from work and did their shopping at malls reachable only by driving. In other sections of the country as well, shopping shifted to suburban centers, and old downtown business districts stagnated. The spread of suburban homes created millions of new lawns. The water used to maintain these expansive lawns, especially in arid regions, raised few worries at the time. Only decades later, with rising awareness of environmental issues, would it cause alarm. Today, more land is cultivated in grass than any agricultural crop in the United States.

A Consumer Culture

"The consumer is the key to our economy," declared Jack Straus, chairman of the board of Macy's, New York City's leading department store. "Our ability to consume is endless. The luxuries of today are the necessities of tomorrow." The roots of the consumer culture of the 1950s date back to the 1920s and even earlier. But never before had affluence, or consumerism, been so widespread. In a consumer culture, the measure of freedom became the ability to gratify market desires. Modern society, wrote Clark Kerr, president of the University of California, may well have reduced freedom "in the workplace" by subjecting workers to stringent discipline on the job, but it offered a far greater range of "goods and services," and therefore "a greater scope of freedom" in Americans' "personal lives."

In a sense, the 1950s represented the culmination of the long-term trend in which consumerism replaced economic independence and democratic participation as central definitions of American freedom. Attitudes toward debt changed as well. Low interest rates and the spread of credit cards encouraged Americans to borrow money to purchase consumer goods. Americans became comfortable living in never-ending debt, once seen as a loss of economic freedom.

Participation in consumer capitalism became more than a way to acquire goods; mass consumption was promoted as a patriotic act, a defining feature of American identity, and one that would help the country win the Cold War. From Coca-Cola to Levi's jeans, American consumer goods, once a status symbol for the rich in other countries, were now marketed to customers around the globe. The country's most powerful weapon in the Cold War, insisted a reporter for *House Beautiful* magazine, was "the freedom offered by washing machines and dishwashers, vacuum cleaners, automobiles, and refrigerators."

The TV World

Thanks to television, images of middle-class life and advertisements for consumer goods blanketed the country. By the end of the 1950s, nearly nine of ten American families owned a TV set. Television replaced newspapers as the most common source of information about public events, and TV watching became the nation's leading leisure activity. Television changed Americans' eating habits (the frozen TV dinner, heated and eaten while watching a program, went on sale in 1954).

With a few exceptions, like the Army-McCarthy hearings mentioned in the previous chapter, TV avoided controversy and projected a bland image of middle-class life. Popular shows of the early 1950s, such as *The Goldbergs* (with Jewish immigrants as the central characters) and *The Honeymooners* (in which Jackie Gleason played a bus driver), featured working-class families living in urban apartments. By the end of the decade, they had been replaced as the dominant programs by quiz shows, westerns, and comedies set in suburban homes like *Leave It to Beaver* and *The Adventures of Ozzie and Harriet*. TV ads, aimed primarily at middle-class suburban viewers, conveyed images of the good life based on endless consumption.

A New Ford

"The concept of freedom," wrote one commentator in 1959, "has become as familiar to us as an old hat or a new Ford." And a new Ford—or Chrysler or Chevrolet—now seemed essential to the enjoyment of freedom's benefits. Along with a home and television set, the car became part of what sociologists called "the standard consumer package" of the 1950s. By 1960, 80 percent of American families owned at least one car, and 14 percent had two or more, nearly all manufactured in the United States. Most were designed to go out of style within a year or two, promoting further purchases.

Auto manufacturers and oil companies vaulted to the top ranks of corporate America. Detroit and its environs were home to immense auto factories. The River Rouge complex had 62,000 employees, Willow Run 42,000. Since the military increasingly needed high-technology goods rather than the trucks and tanks that had rolled off assembly lines in World War II, the region around the Great Lakes lagged in defense contracts. In the long term, the continued funneling of federal dollars from the North and Midwest to the Sunbelt would prove devastating to the old industrial heartland. But during the 1950s, the booming automobile industry, with its demand for steel, rubber, and other products, assured the region's continued prosperity.

The automobile transformed the nation's daily life, becoming the pivot around which a new suburban lifestyle emerged. Beginning with Congress's

THE INTERSTATE HIGHWAY SYSTEM

Begun in 1956 and completed in 1993, the interstate highway system dramatically altered the American landscape and Americans' daily lives. It made possible more rapid travel by car and stimulated the growth of suburbs along its many routes.

passage of the Federal Aid Highway Act in 1956, the **interstate highway system** changed Americans' living and travel habits. It made possible long-distance vacationing by car, commuting to work from ever-increasing distances, and decentralized suburban living. Cold War arguments—especially the need to provide rapid exit routes from cities in the event of nuclear war—justified this multibillion-dollar project creating 41,000 miles of roadway. But automobile manufacturers, oil companies, suburban builders, and construction unions had a financial stake in supporting highway construction regardless of any Soviet threat. While Americans drove 330 million miles per year on the eve of World War II and 600 million miles in 1955, that number increased to 1 billion miles by 1968. The car symbolized freedom as individual mobility and private choice. Advertising, television shows, and popular songs constantly reminded Americans that on the road, they truly enjoyed freedom.

Highways, automobiles, and suburban growth altered the American landscape, leading to the construction of motels, drive-in movie theaters, office complexes outside city centers, and roadside eating establishments (the first McDonald's fast-food restaurant opened in 1954). Although the climate costs of the carbon-rich, car-based suburban lifestyle would generate increased concern with greater environmental consciousness later in the century, at the time, the rapid growth of suburbs was celebrated by many as "a firm foundation for future national prosperity." But suburbanization was not without its critics. Urban policy planners, conservationists, and social theorists lamented the decline of open space, the emphasis on private life, and the relentless uniformity of suburban tract housing, which they claimed reinforced conformist habits among inhabitants.

Women at Work and at Home

The emergence of suburbia as a chief site of what was increasingly called the "American way of life" placed pressure on the family—and especially women—to live up to freedom's promise. After 1945, as former soldiers returned to the workforce, women lost most of the industrial jobs they had performed during the war. As during most of American history, women who worked outside the home remained concentrated in low-salary, nonunion jobs, such as clerical, sales, and service labor, rather than better-paying manufacturing positions. After a sharp postwar drop in female employment, the number of women at work soon began to rise. By 1955, it exceeded the level of World War II. But the nature and aims of women's work had changed. The modern woman, said *Look* magazine, worked part-time, to help support the family's middle-class lifestyle, not to help pull it out of poverty or to pursue personal fulfillment or an independent career. Working women in 1960 earned, on average, only 60 percent of the income of men.

Despite the increasing numbers of wage-earning women, the suburban family's breadwinner was assumed to be male, while the wife remained at home. Films, TV shows, and advertisements portrayed marriage as the most important goal of American women. And during the 1950s, men and women reaffirmed the virtues of family life, assumed to be always heterosexual. They married younger (at an average age of twenty-two for men and twenty for women), divorced less frequently than in the past, and had more children (3.2 per family). A **baby boom** that lasted into the mid-1960s followed the end of the war. At a time of low immigration, the American population rose by nearly 30 million (almost 20 percent) during the 1950s. The increase arose mostly from the large number of births, but it also reflected the fact that Americans now lived longer than in the past, thanks to the wide availability of "miracle drugs" like penicillin that had been developed during World War II to combat bacterial infections.

The family also became a weapon in the Cold War. The ability of women to remain at home, declared a government official, "separates us from the Communist world," where a high percentage of women worked. To be sure, the family life exalted during the 1950s differed from the patriarchal household of old. It was a modernized relationship, in which both partners reconciled family obligations with personal fulfillment through shared consumption, leisure

Yale Joel's 1958 photograph of a hospital maternity ward captures the postwar baby boom.

activities, and sexual pleasure. Thanks to modern conveniences, the personal freedom once associated with work could now be found at home. Frozen and prepared meals, exulted one writer in 1953, offered housewives "freedom from tedium, space, work, and their own inexperience"—quite a change from the Four Freedoms of World War II.

Like other forms of dissent, feminism seemed to have disappeared from American life or was widely dismissed as evidence of mental disorder. Prominent psychologists insisted that the unhappiness of individual women or even the desire to work for wages stemmed from a failure to accept the "maternal instinct." "The independent woman," declared the book *Modern Woman: The Lost Sex* (1947), "is a contradiction in terms." The idea of domestic life as a refuge and of full-time motherhood as a woman's "sphere" had a long history in the United States. But in the postwar suburbs, where family life was physically separated from work, relatives, and the web of social organizations typical of cities, it came close to realization.

A Segmented and Segregated Landscape

For millions of city dwellers, the suburban utopia fulfilled the dream, postponed by depression and war, of home ownership and middle-class incomes. For beneficiaries of postwar prosperity, in the words of a Boston worker who made heroic sacrifices to move his family to the suburbs, the home became "the center of freedom." The move to the suburbs also promoted Americanization, cutting residents off from urban ethnic communities and bringing them fully into the world of mass consumption. But if the suburbs offered a new site for the enjoyment of American freedom, they were never as uniform as either its celebrants or its critics claimed. There are upper-class suburbs, working-class suburbs, industrial suburbs, and "suburban" neighborhoods within city limits. With school funding, services, and amenities heavily dependent on property taxes in most American suburbs, the quality of public education one's children received and the services towns provided depended heavily on the community where one could afford to purchase a home.

If the class uniformity of suburbia has been exaggerated, its racial uniformity was all too real. As late as the 1990s, nearly 90 percent of suburban whites lived in communities with non-white populations of less than 1 percent—the legacy of decisions by government, real-estate developers, banks, and residents.

During the postwar suburban boom, federal agencies continued to insure mortgages that barred resale of houses to non-whites, thereby financing housing segregation. Even after the Supreme Court in 1948 declared such provisions legally unenforceable, banks and private developers barred non-whites from the suburbs and the government refused to subsidize their mortgages except in segregated enclaves. In 1960, Blacks represented less than 3 percent of the population of Chicago's suburbs. The vast new communities built by William Levitt refused to allow Blacks, including army veterans, to rent or purchase homes. "If we sell one house to a Negro family," Levitt explained, "then 90 or 95 percent of our white customers will not buy into the community." After a lawsuit, Levitt finally agreed during the 1960s to sell homes to non-whites, but at a pace that can only be described as glacial. In 1990, his Long Island community, with a population of 53,000, included 127 Black residents.

Public Housing and Urban Renewal

A Housing Act passed by Congress in 1949 authorized the construction of more than 800,000 units of public housing in order to provide a "decent home for every American family." But the law set an extremely low ceiling on the income of residents—a rule demanded by private contractors seeking to avoid competition from the government in building homes for the middle class. This regulation limited housing projects to the very poor. Since white urban and suburban neighborhoods successfully opposed the construction of public housing, it was increasingly confined to segregated neighborhoods in inner cities, reinforcing the concentration of poverty in urban non-white neighborhoods. At the same time, under programs of **urban renewal**, cities demolished poor neighborhoods in city centers that occupied potentially valuable real estate. In their place, developers constructed retail centers and all-white middle-income housing complexes, and states built urban public universities like Wayne State in Detroit and the University of Illinois at Chicago. Los Angeles displaced a neighborhood of mixed ethnic groups in Chavez Ravine in order to build a stadium for the Dodgers, whose move in 1958 after sixty-eight years in Brooklyn seemed to symbolize the growing importance of California on the national scene. White residents displaced by urban renewal often moved to the suburbs. Non-whites, unable to do so, found housing in run-down city neighborhoods.

Native American Relocation

Native Americans were one of the groups that increasingly found housing in dilapidated urban neighborhoods. Beginning in the 1950s, Indians increasingly moved to cities in the Midwest and West just as growing numbers of middle-class whites (along with jobs) departed for the suburbs. In 1952, the

This Bureau of Indian Affairs promotional photograph shows an Indian couple relocated to Elgin, Illinois, enjoying a seemingly middle-class life. Reality rarely matched such expectations.

federal government initiated the **Indian Urban Relocation Program** to move Indians off reservations to cities such as Chicago, Denver, and Los Angeles. Relocation was in line with earlier government campaigns to diminish Native Americans' tribal identities. The Bureau of Indian Affairs promised Indians good jobs, good housing, and good schools, holding out the hope of a better life than that available on reservations. Those who joined the program, sometimes pressured by Indian Bureau officials with recruitment quotas to meet, had their expectations quickly dashed. Housed in some of the poorest city neighborhoods, they found well-paying jobs were hard to come by, and relocation offices provided very limited support. Between 1952 and 1972, approximately 100,000 Native Americans moved to cities under the program, effectively moving from rural to urban poverty. Though many returned home; others stayed, leaving behind reservation life. Many overcame the obstacles they faced, but others experienced unemployment, alcoholism, and eventually homelessness. Indians criticized the program as the latest in a long line of injustices to their communities. But the trend of Indian urbanization has continued. Urbanization did not, as many government officials hoped, end tribal ties. In line with the paradoxical outcome of the earlier boarding school experience (discussed in Chapter 18), relocation and urbanization helped foster a new generation of pan-Indian nationalists. A group of urban Indian youth in places like St. Paul, Minneapolis, and Chicago would soon revitalize the importance of land and sovereignty as the basis of Indian freedom, forging the American Indian Movement, as we will see in the next chapter.

The Divided Society

Suburbanization hardened the racial lines of division in American life. Between 1950 and 1970, about 7 million white Americans left cities for the suburbs. Meanwhile, nearly 3 million Blacks moved from the South to the North, greatly increasing the size of existing poor, minority residential neighborhoods and creating entirely new ones. And far outpacing Native American urbanization, half a million Puerto Ricans moved to the mainland. Mostly small coffee and tobacco farmers and agricultural laborers, they were forced to relocate when

American sugar companies expanded landholdings on the island. Most ended up in New York City's East Harlem, until then an Italian American community. Although set in a different part of New York, the popular Broadway musical *West Side Story* dramatized the tensions between Puerto Rican newcomers and longtime urban residents. By the late 1960s, more Puerto Ricans lived in New York City than San Juan, the island's capital.

The process of racial exclusion became self-reinforcing. Non-whites remained concentrated in manual and unskilled jobs, the result of employment discrimination and their virtual exclusion from educational opportunities at public and private universities, including those outside the South. In 1950, only 12 percent of employed Blacks held white-collar positions, compared with 45 percent of whites. As the white population and industrial jobs fled the old city centers for the suburbs, poorer Blacks and Latinos remained trapped in poor inner-city neighborhoods, seen by many whites as places of crime, poverty, and welfare.

Suburbanites, for whom the home represented not only an emblem of freedom but the family's major investment, became increasingly fearful that any non-white presence would lower the quality of life and destroy property values. *Life* magazine quoted a white suburbanite discussing a prospective Black neighbor: "He's probably a nice guy, but every time I see him, I see $2,000 drop off the value of my house." Residential segregation was reinforced by "blockbusting"—a tactic of real estate brokers who circulated exaggerated warnings of an impending influx of non-whites, to persuade alarmed white residents to sell their homes hastily. Because of this practice, some all-white neighborhoods quickly became all-minority enclaves rather than places where members of different races lived side by side.

"Freedom is equal housing too" became a slogan in the campaign for residential integration. But suburban home ownership long remained a

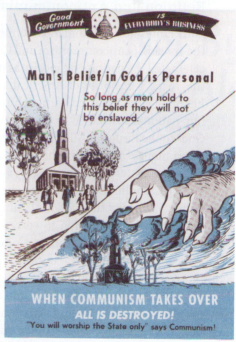

An image from a booklet issued by the American Economic Foundation illustrates the linkage of anticommunism and religious faith during the Cold War. The hairy hand in the bottom half of the drawing represents the communist threat, which endangers religious freedom in the United States.

white entitlement, with the freedom of non-whites to rent or purchase a home where they desired overridden by the claims of private property and "freedom of association." Even as the old divisions between white ethnic Americans faded in the suburban melting pot, racial barriers in housing, and therefore in public education and jobs, were reinforced.

Cold War affluence coexisted with urban decay and racism, the seeds from which protest would soon flower. Yet to many observers in the 1950s it seemed that the ills of American society had been solved. Scholars celebrated the "end of ideology" and the triumph of a democratic, capitalist "consensus" in which all Americans except the maladjusted and fanatics shared the same liberal values of individualism, respect for private property, and belief in equal opportunity. If problems remained, their solutions required technical adjustments, not structural change or aggressive political intervention.

Religion and Anticommunism

Both Protestant and Roman Catholic religious leaders played crucial roles in the spread of anticommunism and Cold War culture. Official American values celebrated the nation's religiosity as opposed to "godless" communism. During the 1950s, a majority of Americans—the highest percentage in the nation's history—were affiliated with a church or synagogue. In 1954, to "strengthen our national resistance to communism," Congress added the words "under God" to the Pledge of Allegiance. In 1957, "**In God We Trust**" was included on paper money. As noted in the previous chapter, Soviet domination of strongly Catholic eastern Europe inspired powerful currents of anticommunism among Catholic ethnic groups in the United States. Leading clerics like Bishop Fulton J. Sheen of the Catholic Church and Protestant evangelist Billy Graham used radio and television to spread to millions a religious message heavily imbued with anticommunism. Communism, Graham declared, was not only an economic and political outlook but a religion—one "inspired, directed and motivated by the Devil himself."

As for religious differences, the source of persistent tension in American history, these were absorbed within a common "Judeo-Christian" heritage, a notion that became central to the cultural and political dialogue of the 1950s. This newly invented tradition sought to demonstrate that Catholics, Protestants, and Jews shared the same history and values and had all contributed to the evolution of American society. The idea of a unified Judeo-Christian tradition overlooked the long history of hostility among religious denominations. But it reflected the decline of anti-Semitism and anti-Catholicism in the wake of World War II, as well as the ongoing secularization of American life. As Will Herberg argued in his influential book *Protestant-Catholic-Jew* (1955), religion now had less to do with spiritual activities or sacred values than with personal identity, group assimilation, and the promotion of traditional morality. In an affluent suburban society, Herberg argued, the "common religion" was the American way of life, a marriage of democratic values and economic prosperity—in a phrase, "free enterprise."

Selling Free Enterprise

The economic content of Cold War freedom increasingly came to focus on consumer capitalism, or, as it was now universally known, "free enterprise." More than political democracy or freedom of speech, which many allies of the United States outside western Europe lacked, an economic system resting on private ownership united the nations of the Free World. A week before his Truman Doctrine speech, in a major address on economic policy, the president reduced Roosevelt's Four Freedoms to three. Freedom of speech and worship remained, but freedom from want and fear had been replaced by freedom of enterprise, "part and parcel," said Truman, of the American way of life.

Even more than during World War II, what one historian calls the "selling of free enterprise" became a major industry, involving corporate advertising, school programs, newspaper editorials, and civic activities. Convinced that ads represented "a new weapon in the world-wide fight for freedom," the Advertising Council invoked cherished symbols like the Statue of Liberty and the Liberty Bell in the service of "competitive free enterprise." To be sure, the free enterprise campaigners did not agree on every issue. Some businessmen believed that defending free enterprise required rolling back much of the power that labor unions had gained in the past decade, dismantling New Deal regulations, and restricting the economic role of government. Representing what might be called business's more liberal wing, the Advertising Council, in its "American Economic System" ad campaign of 1949, reaffirmed labor's

A portrait of affluence: In this photograph by Alex Henderson, Steve Czekalinski, an employee of the DuPont Corporation, poses with his family and the food they consumed in a single year, 1951. The family spent $1,300 (around $12,000 in today's money) on food, including 699 bottles of milk, 578 pounds of meat, and 131 dozen eggs. Nowhere else in the world was food so available and inexpensive.

right to collective bargaining and the importance of government–business cooperation. Indeed, despite talk of the glories of the free market, government policies played a crucial role in the postwar boom. The rapid expansion of the suburban middle class owed much to federal tax subsidies, mortgage guarantees for home purchases, dam and highway construction, military contracts, and benefits under the GI Bill.

People's Capitalism

Free enterprise seemed an odd way of describing an economy in which a few large corporations dominated key sectors. Until well into the twentieth century, most ordinary Americans had been deeply suspicious of big business, associating it with images of robber barons who manipulated politics, suppressed economic competition, and treated their workers unfairly. Americans, wrote David Lilienthal, chairman of the Atomic Energy Commission, must abandon their traditional fear that concentrated economic power endangered "our very liberties." Large-scale production was not only necessary to fighting the Cold War, but it enhanced freedom by multiplying consumer goods. "By freedom," wrote Lilienthal, "I mean essentially *freedom to choose.* . . . It means a maximum range of choice for the consumer when he spends his dollar." By the end of the 1950s, public-opinion surveys revealed that more than 80 percent of Americans believed that "our freedom depends on the free enterprise system."

A sharp jump in the number of individuals investing in Wall Street inspired talk of a new "people's capitalism." In 1953, 4.5 million Americans—only slightly more than in 1928—owned shares of stock. By the mid-1960s, the number had grown to 25 million. In the face of widespread abundance, who could deny that the capitalist marketplace embodied individual freedom or that poverty would soon be a thing of the past? "It was American Freedom," proclaimed *Life* magazine, "by which and through which this amazing achievement of wealth and power was fashioned."

The Libertarian Conservatives

During the 1950s, a group of thinkers began the task of reviving conservatism and reclaiming the idea of freedom from liberals. Although largely ignored outside their own immediate circle, they developed ideas that would define conservative thought for the next half-century. One was opposition to a strong national government, an outlook that had been given new political life in conservatives' bitter reaction against the New Deal. To these "libertarian" conservatives, freedom meant individual autonomy and unregulated capitalism.

These ideas had great appeal to conservative entrepreneurs, especially in the rapidly growing South and West. Many businessmen who desired to pursue their economic fortunes free of government regulation, high taxes, and labor unions found intellectual reinforcement in the writings of the young economist Milton Friedman. In 1962, Friedman published *Capitalism and Freedom*, which identified the free market as the necessary foundation for individual liberty. This was not an uncommon idea during the Cold War, but Friedman pushed it to extreme conclusions. He called for turning over to the private sector virtually all government functions and the repeal of minimum wage laws, the graduated income tax, and the Social Security system. Friedman extended the idea of unrestricted free choice into virtually every realm of life. Government, he insisted, should seek to regulate neither the economy nor individual conduct.

The New Conservatism

Friedman was indirectly criticizing not only liberalism but also the "new conservatism," a second strand of thought that became increasingly prominent in the 1950s. Convinced that the Free World needed to arm itself morally and intellectually, not just militarily, for the battle against communism, "new conservatives" like writers Russell Kirk and Richard Weaver insisted that toleration of difference—a central belief of modern liberalism—offered no substitute for the search for absolute truth. Weaver's book, *Ideas Have Consequences* (1948), a rambling philosophical treatise that surprisingly became the most influential statement of this new traditionalism, warned that the West was suffering from moral decay and called for a return to a civilization based on values grounded in the Christian tradition and in timeless notions of good and evil.

Although they wanted government expelled from the economy, new conservatives expected it to regulate personal behavior, to restore a Christian morality they saw as growing weaker and weaker in American society.

Here lay the origins of a division in conservative ranks that would persist into the twenty-first century. Unrestrained individual choice and moral virtue are radically different starting points from which to discuss freedom. Was the purpose of conservatism, one writer wondered, to create the "free man" or the "good man"? Libertarian conservatives spoke the language of progress and personal autonomy; the "new conservatives" emphasized tradition, community, and moral commitment. The former believed that too many barriers existed to the pursuit of individual liberty. The latter condemned an excess of individualism and a breakdown of common values.

Fortunately for conservatives, political unity often depends less on intellectual coherence than on the existence of a common foe. And two powerful enemies became focal points for the conservative revival—the Soviet Union abroad and the federal government at home. Anticommunism, however, did not clearly distinguish conservatives from liberals, who also supported the

Cold War. What made conservatism distinct was its antagonism to "big government" in America, at least so long as it was controlled by liberals who, conservatives believed, tolerated or encouraged immorality. Republican control of the presidency did not lessen conservatives' hostility to the federal government, partly because they did not consider President Eisenhower one of their own.

THE EISENHOWER ERA

Ike and Nixon

Dwight D. Eisenhower, or "Ike," as he was affectionately called, emerged from World War II a popular war hero, having led the Allied invasion of Europe in 1944. Eisenhower's party affiliation was unknown. In 1948, he voted for Truman, and he accepted Truman's invitation to return to Europe as supreme commander of NATO forces. Both parties wanted the affable military leader as their candidate in 1952. But Eisenhower became convinced that Senator Robert A. Taft of Ohio, a leading contender for the Republican nomination, would lead the United States back toward isolationism. Eisenhower entered the contest and won the Republican nomination.

As his running mate, Eisenhower chose Richard Nixon of California, a World War II veteran who had made a name for himself by vigorous anticommunism. He gained national fame by his pursuit of Alger Hiss while a member of the House Un-American Activities Committee. Nixon won election to the U.S. Senate in 1950 in a campaign in which he suggested that the Democratic candidate, Congresswoman Helen Gahagan Douglas, had communist sympathies.

These tactics gave Nixon a lifelong reputation for opportunism and dishonesty. But Nixon was also a shrewd politician, who pioneered efforts to transform the Republican Party's image from defender of business to champion of the "forgotten man"—the hardworking citizen burdened by heavy taxation and unresponsive government bureaucracies. In using populist language to promote free market economics, Nixon helped to lay the foundation for the triumph of conservatism a generation later.

The 1952 Campaign

Almost as soon as he won the vice-presidential nomination, Nixon ran into trouble over press reports that wealthy Californians had created a private fund for his family. Eisenhower considered dropping him from the ticket. But in an emotional nationally televised thirty-minute address in which he drew attention to his ordinary upbringing, war service, and close-knit family, Nixon denied the accusations. The "Checkers speech," named after the family dog—the one gift Nixon acknowledged receiving, but insisted he would not return—rescued his political career. It illustrated how television was beginning to transform politics by allowing candidates to bring a carefully crafted image directly into Americans' living rooms. The 1952 campaign became the first to make extensive use of TV ads. Parties, one observer complained, were "selling the president like toothpaste."

More important to the election's outcome, however, was Eisenhower's popularity (invoked in the Republican campaign slogan "I Like Ike") and the public's weariness with the Korean War. Ike's pledge to "go to Korea" in search of peace signaled his intention to bring the conflict to an end. He won a resounding victory over the Democratic candidate, Adlai Stevenson. Four years later, Eisenhower again defeated Stevenson, by an even wider margin. His popularity, however, did not extend to his party. Republicans won a razor-thin majority in Congress in 1952, but Democrats regained control in 1954 and retained it for the rest of the decade. In 1956, Eisenhower became the first president to be elected without his party controlling either house of Congress.

In his two campaigns for president, the Texas-born Eisenhower made remarkable inroads in the Democratic South, a harbinger of the region's later political realignment. In 1952, he carried seven former slave states and won 48 percent of the votes cast in the states of the Confederacy. He ran strongly among moderate whites living in metropolitan and suburban areas of the upper South and border states. But his personal appeal did not translate into a "coattail" effect. For the time being, Democrats continued to control almost all southern state and local offices.

During the 1950s, voters at home and abroad seemed to find reassurance in selecting familiar, elderly leaders to govern them. At age sixty-two, Eisenhower was one of the oldest men ever elected president. But he seemed positively youthful compared with Winston Churchill, who returned to office as prime minister of Great Britain at age seventy-seven, Charles DeGaulle, who assumed the presidency of France at sixty-eight, and Konrad Adenauer, who served as chancellor of West Germany from age seventy-three until well into his eighties.

Modern Republicanism

With a Republican serving as president for the first time in twenty years, the tone in Washington changed. Wealthy businessmen dominated Eisenhower's cabinet. Defense Secretary Charles Wilson, the former president of General Motors, made the widely publicized statement: "What is good for the country is good for General Motors, and vice versa." A champion of the business community and a fiscal conservative, Ike worked to scale back government spending, including the military budget. But while right-wing Republicans saw his victory as an invitation to roll back the New Deal, Eisenhower realized that such a course would be disastrous. "Should any political party attempt to abolish Social Security, unemployment insurance, and eliminate labor laws and farm programs," he declared, "you would not hear of that party again in our political history."

Eisenhower called his domestic agenda Modern Republicanism. It aimed to sever his party's identification in the minds of many Americans with Herbert Hoover, the Great Depression, and indifference to the economic conditions of ordinary citizens. The core New Deal programs not only remained in place, but expanded. In 1955, millions of agricultural workers became eligible for the first time for Social Security. Nor did Ike reduce the size and scope of government. Despite the use of "free enterprise" as a weapon in the Cold War, the idea of a "mixed economy" in which the government played a major role in planning economic activity was widely accepted throughout the Western world. America's European allies like Britain and France expanded their welfare states and nationalized key industries like steel, shipbuilding, and transportation (that is, the government bought them from private owners and operated and subsidized them).

The United States had a more limited welfare state than western Europe and left the main pillars of the economy in private hands. But it too used government spending to promote productivity and boost employment. Eisenhower presided over the largest public-works enterprise in American history, the interstate highway system, discussed earlier. And when the Soviets launched **Sputnik**, the first artificial earth satellite, in 1957, the administration responded with the **National Defense Education Act**, which for the first time offered direct federal funding to higher education.

All in all, rather than dismantling the New Deal, Eisenhower's Modern Republicanism consolidated and legitimized it. By accepting its basic premises, he ensured that its continuation no longer depended on Democratic control of the presidency.

The Social Contract

The 1950s also witnessed an easing of the labor conflict of the two previous decades. The passage of the Taft-Hartley Act in 1947 (discussed in the previous chapter) had reduced labor militancy. In 1955, the AFL and CIO merged to form a single organization representing 35 percent of all nonagricultural workers. In leading industries, labor and management hammered out what has been called a new **social contract**. Unions signed long-term agreements that left decisions regarding capital investment, plant location, and output in management's hands, and agreed to try to prevent unauthorized "wildcat" strikes. Employers stopped trying to eliminate existing unions and granted wage increases and fringe benefits such as private pension plans, health insurance, and automatic adjustments to pay to reflect rises in the cost of living.

Unionized workers shared fully in 1950s prosperity. Although the social contract did not apply to the majority of workers, who did not belong to unions, it did bring benefits to those who labored in nonunion jobs. For example, trade unions in the 1950s and 1960s were able to use their political power to win a steady increase in the minimum wage, which was earned mostly by non-union workers at the bottom of the employment pyramid. But these "spillover effects" were limited. The majority of workers did not enjoy anything close to the wages, benefits, and job security of unionized workers in such industries as automobiles and steel.

Indeed, nonunion employers continued to fight vehemently against labor organization, and groups like the National Association of Manufacturers still viewed unions as an unacceptable infringement on the power of employers. Some firms continued to shift jobs to the less-unionized suburbs and South. By the end of the 1950s, the social contract was weakening. In 1959, the steel industry sought to tighten work rules and limit wage increases in an attempt to boost profits battered by a recession that hit two years earlier. The plan sparked a strike of 500,000 steelworkers, which successfully beat back the proposed changes.

Massive Retaliation

Soon after he entered office, Eisenhower approved an armistice that ended fighting in Korea. But this failed to ease international tensions. Ike took office at a time when the Cold War had entered an extremely dangerous phase. In 1952, the United States exploded the first hydrogen bomb—a weapon far more powerful than those that had devastated Hiroshima and Nagasaki. The following year, the Soviets matched this achievement. Both sides feverishly developed long-range bombers capable of delivering weapons of mass destruction around the world.

A professional soldier, Ike hated war, which he viewed as a tragic waste. "Every gun that is made," he said in 1953, "every warship launched . . . signifies a theft from those who hunger and are not fed." But his secretary of state, John Foster Dulles, was a grim Cold Warrior. In 1954, Dulles announced an updated version of the doctrine of containment. **Massive retaliation**, as it was called, declared that any Soviet attack on an American ally would be countered by

"H-Bomb Hideaway," a photograph taken in 1955, shows a family in their underground bomb shelter, where—the manufacturer claimed—the occupants could survive for five days after a nuclear war.

a nuclear assault on the Soviet Union itself. In some ways, this reliance on the nuclear threat was a way to enable the budget-conscious Eisenhower to reduce spending on conventional military forces. During his presidency, the size of the armed services fell by nearly half. But the number of American nuclear warheads rose from 1,000 in 1953 to 18,000 in 1960.

Massive retaliation ran the risk that any small conflict, or even a miscalculation, could escalate into a war that would destroy both the United States and the Soviet Union. Critics called the doctrine "brinksmanship," warning of the danger of Dulles's apparent willingness to bring the world to the brink of nuclear war. The reality that all-out war would result in "mutual assured destruction" (or MAD, in military shorthand) did succeed in making both great powers cautious in their direct dealings with one another. But it also inspired widespread fear of impending nuclear war. Government programs encouraging Americans to build bomb shelters in their backyards, and school drills that trained children to hide under their desks in the event of an atomic attack, aimed to convince Americans that nuclear war was survivable. But these measures only increased the atmosphere of fear.

Ike and the Russians

In his inaugural address, Eisenhower repeated the familiar Cold War formula: "Freedom is pitted against slavery; lightness against dark." But the end of the Korean War and the death of Stalin, both of which occurred in 1953, convinced him that rather than being blind zealots, the Soviets were reasonable and could be dealt with in conventional diplomatic terms. In 1955, Ike met in Geneva, Switzerland, with Nikita Khrushchev, the new Soviet leader, at the first "summit" conference since Potsdam a decade earlier. The following year, Khrushchev delivered a speech to the Communist Party Congress in Moscow that detailed Stalin's crimes, including purges of political opponents numbering in the millions. The revelations created a crisis of belief among communists throughout the world. In the United States, three-quarters of the remaining Communist Party members abandoned the organization, realizing that they had been blind to the nature of Stalin's rule.

Khrushchev's call in the same 1956 speech for "peaceful coexistence" with the United States raised the possibility of an easing of the Cold War. The "thaw" was abruptly shaken that fall, however, when Soviet troops put down an anti-communist uprising in Hungary. Many conservative Republicans had urged eastern Europeans to resist communist rule, and Secretary of State Dulles himself had declared "liberation," rather than containment, to be the goal of American policy. But Eisenhower refused to extend aid to the Hungarian rebels, an indication that he believed it impossible to "roll back" Soviet domination of eastern Europe.

In 1958, the two superpowers agreed to a voluntary halt to the testing of nuclear weapons. The pause lasted until 1961. It had been demanded by the National Committee for a Sane Nuclear Policy, which publicized the danger to public health posed by radioactive fallout from nuclear tests. In 1959, Khrushchev toured the United States and had a friendly meeting with Eisenhower at Camp David. But the spirit of cooperation ended abruptly in 1960, when the Soviets shot down an American U-2 spy plane over their territory. Eisenhower first denied that the plane had been involved in espionage and refused to apologize even after the Russians produced the captured pilot. The incident torpedoed another planned summit meeting.

The Emergence of the Third World

Even as Europe, where the Cold War began, settled into what appeared to be a permanent division between a communist East and a capitalist West, an intense rivalry, which sometimes took a military form, persisted in what came to be called the "Third World." The term was invented to describe developing countries aligned with neither of the two Cold War powers and desirous of finding their own model of development between Soviet centralized economic planning and free market capitalism. The **Bandung Conference**, which brought leaders of twenty-nine Asian and African nations together in Indonesia in 1955, seemed to announce the emergence of a new force in global affairs, representing a majority of the world's population. Wary of the leftist principles advanced by many conference attendees, the United States did not send an official representative. But the gathering did attract prominent African Americans, including the novelist Richard Wright and Congressman Adam Clayton Powell Jr., who connected the fight against imperialism abroad with the battle for civil rights at home.

The post–World War II era witnessed the crumbling of European empires. The "winds of change," said British prime minister Harold Macmillan, were sweeping Africa and Asia. Decolonization began when India and Pakistan (the latter carved out of India to give Muslims their own nation) achieved independence in 1947. Ten years later, Britain's Gold Coast colony in West Africa emerged as the independent nation of Ghana. Other new nations—including Indonesia, Malaysia, Nigeria, Kenya, and Tanzania—soon followed. In 1975, Portugal, which five centuries earlier had created the first modern overseas empire, granted independence to its African colonies of Mozambique and Angola.

Decolonization presented the United States with a complex set of choices. It created power vacuums in the former colonies into which, Americans feared, communists would move. The Soviet Union strongly supported the dissolution of Europe's overseas empires, and communists participated in movements for colonial independence. Many noncommunist leaders, like Jawaharlal Nehru of India and Kwame Nkrumah of Ghana, saw socialism of one sort or another as the best route to achieving economic independence and narrowing the social inequalities fostered by imperialism. Most of the newly decolonized nations resisted alignment with either major power bloc, hoping to remain neutral in the Cold War. On the other hand, many nationalists sincerely admired the United States and, indeed, saw the American struggle for independence as a model for their own struggles. Ho Chi Minh, the communist leader of the Vietnamese movement against rule by France, modeled his 1945 proclamation of nationhood on the American Declaration of Independence. He even requested that President Truman establish a protectorate over Vietnam to guarantee its independence.

The Global Cold War

By the end of the 1950s, the division of Europe appeared to be set in stone. Much of the focus of the Cold War shifted to the Third World. The policy of containment easily slid over into opposition to any government, whether communist or not, that seemed to threaten American strategic or economic interests. Jacobo Arbenz Guzmán in Guatemala and Mohammed Mossadegh in Iran were elected, homegrown nationalists, not agents of Moscow. But they were determined to reduce foreign corporations' control over their countries' economies. Arbenz embarked on a sweeping land-reform policy that threatened the domination of Guatemala's economy by the American-owned United Fruit Company. Mossadegh nationalized the Anglo-Iranian Oil Company, whose refinery in Iran was Britain's largest remaining overseas asset. Their foes quickly branded both as communists. In 1953 and 1954, the Central Intelligence Agency organized the ouster of both governments—a clear violation of the UN Charter, which barred a member state from taking military action against another except in self-defense.

In 1956, Israel, France, and Britain—without prior consultation with the United States—invaded Egypt after the country's nationalist leader, Gamal

Abdel Nasser, nationalized the Suez Canal, jointly owned by Britain and France. A furious Eisenhower forced them to abandon the invasion. After the Suez fiasco, the United States moved to replace Britain as the major Western power in the Middle East, and American companies increasingly dominated the region's oil fields. In 1957, Eisenhower extended the principle of containment to the region, issuing the Eisenhower Doctrine, which pledged the United States to defend Middle Eastern governments threatened by communism or Arab nationalism. A year later, Ike dispatched 5,000 American troops to Lebanon to protect a government dominated by pro-Western Christians against Nasser's effort to bring all Arab states into a single regime under his rule.

The military junta installed in Guatemala by the CIA in 1954 enters Guatemala City in a Jeep driven by CIA agent Carlos Castillo Armas. Although hailed by the Eisenhower administration as a triumph for freedom, the new government suppressed democracy in Guatemala and embarked on a murderous campaign to stamp out opposition.

Origins of the Vietnam War

In Vietnam, the expulsion of the Japanese in 1945 led not to independence but to a French military effort to preserve their Asian empire, which dated to the late nineteenth century, against Ho Chi Minh's nationalist forces. Anticommunism led the United States into deeper and deeper involvement. Following a policy initiated by Truman, the Eisenhower administration funneled billions of dollars in aid to bolster French efforts. By the early 1950s, the United States was paying four-fifths of the cost of the war. Wary of becoming bogged down in another land war in Asia immediately after Korea, however, Ike declined to send in American troops when France requested them to avert defeat in 1954. He also rejected the National Security Council's advice to use nuclear weapons, leaving France no alternative but to agree to Vietnamese independence.

Issued from a peace conference in 1954, the **Geneva Accords** divided Vietnam temporarily into northern and southern districts, with elections scheduled for 1956 to unify the country. But the staunchly anticommunist southern leader Ngo Dinh Diem, urged on by the United States, refused to hold elections, which would almost certainly have resulted in a victory for Ho Chi Minh's communists. Diem's close ties to wealthy Catholic families—in predominantly Buddhist South Vietnam—and to landlords in a society dominated by small farmers who had been promised land by Ho alienated an increasing number of his subjects. American aid poured into South Vietnam in order to bolster the Diem regime. By the time Eisenhower left office in 1960, Diem nevertheless faced a full-scale guerrilla revolt by the communist-led National Liberation Front.

Events in Guatemala, Iran, and Vietnam, considered great successes at the time by American policymakers, cast a long shadow over American foreign relations. The United States was becoming accustomed to intervention, both open and secret, in far-flung corners of the world. Despite the Cold War rhetoric of freedom, American leaders seemed more comfortable dealing with reliable military regimes than democratic governments. A series of military governments succeeded Arbenz. The shah of Iran replaced Mossadegh and agreed to give British and American oil companies 40 percent of his nation's oil revenues. He remained in office until 1979 as one of the world's most tyrannical rulers, until his overthrow in a revolution led by the fiercely anti-American radical Islamist Ayatollah Khomeini. In Vietnam, the American decision to prop up Diem's regime laid the groundwork for what would soon become the most disastrous military involvement in American history.

Mass Society and Its Critics

Consensus was the dominant ideal in an era in which McCarthyism had defined criticism of the social and economic order as disloyalty and most Americans located the enjoyment of freedom in private pleasures rather than the public sphere. With the mainstreams of both parties embracing the Cold War, political debate took place within extremely narrow limits. But dissenting voices could be heard. Some intellectuals wondered whether the celebration of affluence and the either-or mentality of the Cold War obscured the extent to which the United States itself fell short of the ideal of freedom. The sociologist C. Wright Mills wrote of a "power elite"—an interlocking directorate of corporate leaders, politicians, and military men whose domination of government and society had made political democracy obsolete. Freedom, Mills insisted, meant more than "the chance to do as one pleases." It rested on the ability "to formulate the available choices," and this most Americans were effectively denied.

Even as the government and media portrayed the United States as a beacon of liberty locked in a titanic struggle with its opposite, one strand of social analysis in the 1950s contended that Americans did not enjoy genuine freedom. Modern mass society, some writers worried, inevitably produced loneliness and anxiety, causing mankind to yearn for stability and authority, not freedom. In *The Lonely Crowd* (1950), the decade's most influential work of social analysis, the sociologist David Riesman described Americans as "other-directed" conformists who lacked the inner resources to lead truly independent lives. Other social critics charged that corporate bureaucracies had transformed employees into "organization men" incapable of independent thought.

Some commentators feared that the Russians had demonstrated a greater ability to sacrifice for common public goals than Americans. What kind of nation, the economist John Kenneth Galbraith asked in *The Affluent Society* (1958), neglected investment in schools, parks, and public services, while producing ever more goods to fulfill desires created by advertising? Was the spectacle of millions of educated middle-class women seeking happiness in suburban dream houses a reason for celebration or a waste of precious "woman power" at a time when the Soviets trumpeted the accomplishments of their female scientists, physicians, and engineers? Books like Galbraith's, along with William Whyte's *The Organization Man* (1956) and Vance Packard's *The Hidden Persuaders* (1957), which criticized the monotony of modern work, the emptiness of suburban life, and the pervasive influence of advertising, created the vocabulary for an assault on the nation's social values that lay just over the horizon.

Rebels without a Cause

The social critics did not offer a political alternative or have any real impact on the parties or government. Nor did other stirrings of dissent. With teenagers a growing part of the population thanks to the baby boom, an emergent popular culture geared to the youth market revealed significant generational tensions beneath the surface of life in the 1950s. J. D. Salinger's 1951 novel *Catcher in the Rye* and the 1955 films *Blackboard Jungle* and *Rebel without a Cause* (the latter starring James Dean as an aimlessly rebellious youth) highlighted the alienation of at least some young people from the world of adult respectability. These works helped to spur a mid-1950s panic about "juvenile delinquency." *Time* magazine devoted a cover story to "Teenagers on the Rampage," and a Senate committee held hearings in 1954 on whether violent comic books caused criminal behavior among young people. (One witness even criticized Superman comics for arousing violent emotions among its readers.) To head off federal regulation, publishers—like movie producers earlier—adopted a code of conduct for their industry that strictly limited the portrayal of crime and violence in comic books.

Cultural life during the 1950s seemed far more daring than politics. Teenagers danced to rock-and-roll music that brought the hard-driving rhythms and sexually provocative movements of Black musicians and dancers to enthusiastic young white audiences. They made Elvis Presley, a rock-and-roll singer with an openly sexual performance style, an immensely popular entertainment celebrity.

Challenges of various kinds also arose to the family-centered image of personal fulfillment. *Playboy* magazine, which began publication in 1953, reached a circulation of more than 1 million copies per month by 1960. It extended the consumer culture into the most intimate realms of life, offering men a fantasy world of sexual gratification outside the family's confines. Although considered deviant by the larger society and subject to constant police harassment, gay men and lesbians created their own subcultures in major cities.

The Beats

In New York City and San Francisco, as well as college towns like Madison, Wisconsin, and Ann Arbor, Michigan, **the Beats**, a small group of poets and writers, railed against mainstream culture. The novelist Jack Kerouac coined the term "beat"—a play on "beaten down" and "beatified" (or saintlike). His *On the Road*, written in the early 1950s but not published until 1957, recounted in a seemingly spontaneous rush of sights, sounds, and images its main character's aimless wanderings across the American landscape. The book became a bible for a generation of young people who rejected the era's middle-class culture but had little to put in its place.

"I saw the best minds of my generation destroyed by madness, starving hysterical naked," wrote the Beat poet Allen Ginsberg in *Howl* (1955), a brilliant

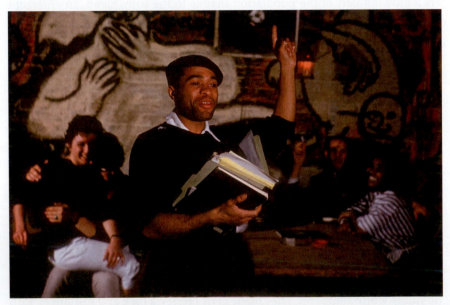

A poetry meeting at a Beat coffeehouse in New York City, photographed in 1959, where poets, artists, and others who rejected 1950s mainstream culture gathered.

protest against materialism and conformism written while the author was under the influence of hallucinogenic drugs. Ginsberg became nationally known when San Francisco police in 1956 confiscated his book and arrested bookstore owners for selling an obscene work. (A judge later overturned the ban on the grounds that *Howl* possessed redeeming social value.) Rejecting the work ethic, the "desperate materialism" of the suburban middle class, and the militarization of American life by the Cold War, the Beats celebrated impulsive action, immediate pleasure (often enhanced by drugs), and sexual experimentation. Despite Cold War slogans, they insisted, personal and political repression, not freedom, were the hallmarks of American society.

THE FREEDOM MOVEMENT

Not until the 1960s would young white rebels find their cause, as the seeds of dissent planted by the social critics and Beats flowered in an outpouring of political activism, new attitudes toward sexuality, and a full-fledged generational rebellion. A more immediate challenge to the status quo of the 1950s arose from the twentieth century's greatest citizens' movement—the Black struggle for equality.

Origins of the Movement

Today, with the birthday of Martin Luther King Jr., a national holiday, and the struggles of Montgomery, Little Rock, Birmingham, and Selma celebrated as heroic episodes in the history of freedom, it is easy to forget that at the time, the civil rights revolution came as a great surprise. Looking back, its causes seem clear: the destabilization of the racial system during World War II; the mass migration out of the segregated South that made Black voters an increasingly important part of the Democratic Party coalition; and the Cold War and rise of independent states in the Third World, both of which made the gap between America's rhetoric and its racial reality an international embarrassment. Yet few predicted the emergence of the southern mass movement for civil rights.

With Blacks' traditional allies on the left decimated by McCarthyism, most union leaders unwilling to challenge racial inequalities within their own ranks, and the NAACP concentrating on court battles, new constituencies and new tactics were sorely needed. The movement found in the southern Black church the organizing power for a militant, nonviolent assault on segregation.

The United States in the 1950s was still a segregated, unequal society. Half of the nation's Black families lived in poverty. Because of labor contracts that linked promotions and firings to seniority, non-white workers, who had joined the industrial labor force later than whites, lost their jobs first in times of economic downturn. In the South, evidence of Jim Crow abounded—in separate public institutions and the signs "white" and "colored" at entrances to buildings, train carriages, drinking fountains, restrooms, and the like. In the North and West, the law did not require segregation, but custom barred Blacks from many colleges, hotels, and restaurants, and from most suburban housing. Las Vegas, Nevada, for example, was as strictly segregated as any southern city. Hotels and casinos did not admit Blacks except in the most menial jobs. Lena Horne, Sammy Davis Jr., Louis Armstrong, and other Black entertainers played the hotel-casinos on the "strip" but could not stay as guests where they performed.

In 1950, seventeen southern and border states and Washington, D.C., had laws requiring the racial segregation of public schools, and several others permitted local districts to impose it. Around 40 percent of the nation's 28 million schoolchildren studied in legally segregated schools, and millions more attended classes in northern communities where housing patterns and school district lines created de facto segregation—separation in fact if not in law. Few white Americans felt any urgency about confronting racial inequality. "Segregation," the white writer John Egerton later recalled, "didn't restrict me in any way, so it was easy to accept things the way they were, to take my freedom for granted and not worry about anyone else's."

The Legal Assault on Segregation

With Truman's civil rights initiative having faded and the Eisenhower administration reluctant to address the issue, it fell to the courts to confront the problem of racial segregation. In the Southwest, the **League of United Latin American Citizens** (LULAC), the counterpart of the NAACP, challenged restrictive housing, employment discrimination, and the segregation of Latino students. It won an important victory in 1946 in the case of *Mendez v. Westminster*, when a federal court ordered the schools of Orange County desegregated. In response, the state legislature repealed all school laws requiring racial segregation. The governor who signed the measure, Earl Warren, had presided over the internment of Japanese Americans during World War II as the state's attorney general. After the war, he became convinced that racial inequality had no place in American life. When Chief Justice Fred Vinson died in 1953, Eisenhower appointed Earl Warren to replace him. Warren would play the key role in deciding ***Brown v. Board of Education***, the momentous case that outlawed school segregation.

For years, the NAACP, under the leadership of attorneys Charles Hamilton Houston and Thurgood Marshall, had pressed legal challenges to the "separate but equal" doctrine laid down by the Court in 1896 in *Plessy v. Ferguson* (see Chapter 17). At first, the NAACP sought to gain admission to white institutions of higher learning for which no Black equivalent existed. In 1938, the Supreme Court ordered the University of Missouri Law School to admit Lloyd Gaines, a Black student, because the state had no such school for Blacks. Missouri responded by setting up a segregated law school, satisfying the courts. But in 1950, the Supreme Court unanimously ordered Heman Sweatt admitted to the University of Texas Law School even though the state had established a "school" for him in a basement containing three classrooms and no library. There was no way, the Court declared, that this hastily constructed law school could be "equal" to the prestigious all-white institution.

The *Brown* Case

Marshall now launched a frontal assault on segregation itself. He brought the NAACP's support to local cases that had arisen when Black parents challenged unfair school policies. To do so required remarkable courage. In Clarendon County, South Carolina, Levi Pearson, a Black farmer who brought a lawsuit on behalf of his children, saw his house burned to the ground. The Clarendon case attacked not segregation itself but the unequal funding of schools. The local school board spent $179 per white child and $43 per Black, and unlike white pupils, Black children attended class in buildings with no running water or indoor toilets and were not provided with buses to transport them to classes. Five such cases from four states and the District of Columbia were combined in a single appeal that reached the Supreme Court late in 1952.

The Court consolidated the cases under the name of a case from the Midwest, not wanting to single out the states of the old Confederacy. Oliver Brown went to court because his daughter, a third grader, was forced to walk across dangerous railroad tracks each morning rather than being allowed to attend a nearby school restricted to whites. The segregation lawsuit became *Brown v. Board of Education of Topeka, Kansas.*

Thurgood Marshall decided that the time had come to attack not the unfair applications of the "separate but equal" principle but the doctrine itself. Even with the same funding and facilities, he insisted, segregation was inherently unequal since it stigmatized one group of citizens as unfit to associate with others. Drawing on studies by New York psychologists Kenneth and Mamie Clark, Marshall argued that segregation did lifelong damage to Black children, undermining their self-esteem. In its legal brief, the Eisenhower administration did not directly support Marshall's position, but it urged the justices to consider "the problem of racial discrimination . . . in the context of the present world struggle between freedom and tyranny." Other peoples, it noted, "cannot understand how such a practice can exist in a country which professes to be a staunch supporter of freedom, justice, and democracy."

Chief Justice Warren managed to create unanimity on a divided Court, some of whose members disliked segregation but feared that a decision to outlaw it would spark widespread violence. On May 17, 1954, Warren himself read aloud the decision, only eleven pages long. Segregation in public education, he concluded, violated the equal protection of the laws guaranteed by the Fourteenth Amendment. "In the field of education, the doctrine of 'separate but equal' has no place. Separate educational facilities are inherently unequal."

The Black press hailed the *Brown* decision as a "second Emancipation Proclamation." And like its predecessor it was in many ways a limited document. The decision did not address segregation in institutions other than public schools or ban all racial classifications in the law, such as statutes prohibiting interracial marriage. It did not address school segregation of the North, which rested on housing patterns and municipal school board practices rather than state law. It did not order immediate implementation but instead called for hearings as to how segregated schooling should be dismantled. But *Brown* marked the emergence of the "Warren Court" as an active agent of social change. And it inspired a wave of optimism that discrimination would soon disappear. "What a wonderful world of possibilities are unfolded for the children," wrote the Black novelist Ralph Ellison.

The Montgomery Bus Boycott

Brown did not cause the modern civil rights movement, which, as noted in the previous two chapters, began during World War II and continued in cities like New York after the war. But the decision did ensure that when the movement resumed after waning in the early 1950s, it would have the backing of the federal courts. Mass action against Jim Crow soon reappeared. On December 1, 1955, Rosa Parks, a Black tailor's assistant who had just completed her day's work in a Montgomery, Alabama, department store, refused to surrender her seat on a city bus to a white rider, as required by local law. Parks's arrest sparked a yearlong **Montgomery bus boycott**, the beginning of the mass phase of the civil rights movement in the South. Within a decade, the civil rights revolution had overturned the structure of legal segregation and regained the right to vote for Black southerners. In 2000, *Time* magazine named Rosa Parks one of the 100 most significant persons of the twentieth century.

Parks is widely remembered today as a "seamstress with tired feet," a symbol of ordinary Blacks' determination to resist the daily injustices and indignities of the Jim Crow South. In fact, her life makes clear that the civil rights revolution built on earlier struggles. Parks was a veteran of Black politics. During the

1930s, she took part in meetings protesting the conviction of the "Scottsboro boys." She served for many years as secretary to E. D. Nixon, the local leader of the NAACP. In 1943, she tried to register to vote, only to be turned away because she supposedly failed a literacy test. After two more attempts, Parks succeeded in becoming one of the few Blacks in Montgomery able to cast a ballot. In 1954, she attended a training session for political activists at the Highlander School in Tennessee, a meeting ground for labor and civil rights radicals.

For years, civil rights activists in Montgomery had been strategizing over how best to confront the city ordinance that required bus segregation. An earlier challenge had been abandoned because the person who refused to move was an unmarried pregnant teenager. The dignified, accomplished

The mug shot of Rosa Parks taken in December 1955 at a Montgomery, Alabama, police station after she was arrested for refusing to give up her seat on a city bus to a white passenger.

Parks was the ideal person to become a symbol of the fight. The date may have been chosen because an all-white jury in Mississippi had just acquitted the murderers of Emmett Till, a Black teenager who had allegedly whistled at a white woman. Till's murder and the judicial outcome shocked the nation. When his body was returned to Chicago, his parents insisted that the casket remain open at the funeral, so people could see his severely bruised and disfigured body—dramatic witness to why the racial status quo desperately needed to change.

Jo Ann Robinson, a professor at the all-Black Alabama State University, had been calling for a boycott of public transportation since 1954. When news of Parks's arrest spread, hundreds of Blacks gathered in a local church and vowed to refuse to ride the buses until accorded equal treatment. For 381 days, despite legal harassment and occasional violence, Black maids, janitors, teachers, and students walked to their destinations or rode an informal network of taxis. Robinson played a leading role in these events, taking part in negotiations with city officials and bus company executives, editing the boycott movement's newsletter, and driving people to and from work. Finally, in November 1956, the Supreme Court ruled segregation in public transportation unconstitutional. The boycott ended in triumph.

THE FREEDOM MOVEMENT ★ 981

The Daybreak of Freedom

The Montgomery bus boycott marked a turning point in postwar American history. It launched the movement for racial justice as a nonviolent crusade based in the Black churches of the South. It gained the support of northern liberals and focused unprecedented and unwelcome international attention on the country's racial policies. And it marked the emergence of twenty-six-year-old Martin Luther King Jr., who had recently arrived in Montgomery to become pastor of a Baptist church, as the movement's national symbol. On the night of the first protest meeting, King's call to action electrified the audience: "We, the disinherited of this land, we who have been oppressed so long, are tired of going through the long night of captivity. And now we are reaching out for the daybreak of freedom and justice and equality."

From the beginning, the language of freedom pervaded the Black movement. It resonated in the speeches of civil rights leaders and in the hand-lettered placards of the struggle's foot soldiers. On the day of Rosa Parks's court appearance in December 1955, even before the bus boycott had officially been announced, a torn piece of cardboard appeared on a bus shelter in Montgomery's Court Square, advising passengers: "Don't ride the buses today. Don't ride it for freedom." During the summer of 1964, when civil rights activists established "freedom schools" for Black children across Mississippi, lessons began with students being asked to define the word. Some gave specific answers ("going to public libraries"), some more abstract ("standing up for your rights"). Some insisted that freedom meant legal equality, others saw it as liberation from years of deference to and fear of whites. "Freedom of the mind," wrote one, was the greatest freedom of all.

For adults as well, freedom had many meanings. It meant enjoying the political rights and economic opportunities taken for granted by whites. It required eradicating historic wrongs such as segregation, disenfranchisement, confinement to low-wage jobs, and the ever-present threat of violence. It meant the right to be served at lunch counters and downtown department stores, central locations in the consumer culture, and to be addressed as "Mr.," "Miss," and "Mrs.," rather than "boy" and "auntie."

The Leadership of King

In King's soaring oratory, the protesters' understandings of freedom fused into a coherent whole. For the title of his first book, relating the boycott's history, King chose the title *Stride Toward Freedom*. His most celebrated oration, the "I Have a Dream" speech of 1963, began by invoking the unfulfilled promise of emancipation ("one hundred years later, the Negro still is not free") and closed with a cry borrowed from a Black spiritual: "Free at last! Free at last! Thank God Almighty, we are free at last!"

A master at appealing to the deep sense of injustice among Blacks and to the conscience of white America, King presented the case for Black rights in a vocabulary that merged the Black experience with that of the nation. Having studied the writings on peaceful civil disobedience of Henry David Thoreau and Mohandas (Mahatma) Gandhi, as well as the nonviolent protests the Congress of Racial Equality had organized in the 1940s, King outlined a philosophy of struggle in which evil must be met with good, hate with Christian love, and violence with peaceful demands for change. "There will be no white persons pulled out of their homes and taken out to some distant road and lynched," he declared in his speech at the launching of the Montgomery bus boycott.

Echoing Christian themes derived from his training in the Black church, King's speeches resonated deeply in both Black communities and the broader culture. He repeatedly invoked the Bible to preach justice and forgiveness. Like Frederick Douglass before him, King appealed to white America by stressing the protesters' love of country and devotion to national values. The "daybreak of freedom," King made clear, meant a new dawn for the whole of American society. And like W. E. B. Du Bois, he linked the American "color line" with the degradation of non-white peoples overseas. "The great struggle of the Twentieth Century," he declared in a 1956 sermon, "has been between the exploited masses questing for freedom and the colonial powers seeking to maintain their domination." If Africa was gaining its freedom, he asked, why must Black America lag behind?

Massive Resistance

Buoyed by success in Montgomery, King in 1956 took the lead in forming the **Southern Christian Leadership Conference**, a coalition of Black ministers and civil rights activists, to press for desegregation. But despite the movement's success in popular mobilization, the fact that Montgomery's city fathers agreed to the boycott's demands only after a Supreme Court ruling indicated that without national backing, local action might not be enough to overturn Jim Crow. The white South's refusal to accept the *Brown* decision reinforced the conviction that Black citizens could not gain their constitutional rights without Washington's intervention. This was not immediately forthcoming. When the Supreme Court finally issued its implementation ruling in 1955, the justices declared that desegregation should proceed "with all deliberate speed." This vague formulation unintentionally encouraged a campaign of "massive resistance" that paralyzed civil rights progress in much of the South.

From REV. WILLIAM H. BORDERS, CONFRONTING SEGREGATION (1957)

The Montgomery Bus Boycott inspired similar demands for change in other southern cities. Not long after the Supreme Court declared segregation in public transportation a violation of the Constitution, a similar protest took place in Atlanta. A group of Black ministers took seats in the front rows of a city bus and refused to move. One of the organizers, Reverend William H. Borders, testified before a Senate subcommittee, explaining the ministers' demands and their strategy of non-violent resistance. Two years later, the Supreme Court ordered Atlanta to integrate its buses.

After the Montgomery Supreme Court decision, we began with the buses. In Atlanta, from many angles a wonderful and marvelous city, some cabs ride only whites. Some ride only Negroes. In spite of our fine schools, magnificent churches, and thriving businesses and industry, Negroes are forced by law to sit in the back of buses.

In 1947 I traveled all over Europe and the Holy Land. In 1955 I traveled after the Baptist World Alliance through Europe, the Holy Land, Egypt, India, China, Japan, Hawaii, and back to Los Angeles. In conversation and in speaking, I told everybody of the United States, one of God's greatest countries, the leader of the free world, the hope of many, many millions. In no place did I see people because of race forced to sit on a particular part of a bus as is the case in most of the States of the South....

If any person is being molested, do not arise to go to his defense but pray for the oppressor and use moral and spiritual force to carry on the struggle for justice....

If cursed, do not curse back. If pushed, do not push back. If struck, do not strike back, but show love and goodwill at all times.

Remember always to pray, especially for those who would persecute anyone....

Whereas riding a bus is a simple matter if rights are violated because of color, it is the urgent business of democracy to rectify this wrong.

I want, Negroes want, democratic and Christian people everywhere want the civil rights bill passed. It will help make the South and our country a more decent place for all its citizenry. Implementing the Constitution, the Supreme Court decision on education and the Montgomery but protest take nothing from whites.

... The only way whites can keep democracy for themselves is to give it to everybody....

The minorities of the United States, especially the Negro, are the social indicators of American democracy. Thank God that bread is being thrown to Hungarians over there. It is a shame that bombs are being thrown at Negro homes and churches over here because they ask to be seated in buses as other people.

... Two-thirds of the world is brown and black. Our international stock drops and our competition for world leadership is wounded if we allow prejudice ... to suck the red blood of healthy hopes.

In the name of decency, in the name of democracy, in the name of world leadership, in the name of God, let us pass strong civil rights legislation.

From THE SOUTHERN MANIFESTO (1956)

Drawn up early in 1956 and signed by ninety-six southern members of the Senate and House of Representatives, the Southern Manifesto repudiated the Supreme Court decision in *Brown v. Board of Education* and offered support to the campaign of resistance in the South.

The unwarranted decision of the Supreme Court in the public school cases is now bearing the fruit always produced when men substitute naked power for established law. . . .

We regard the decisions of the Supreme Court in the school cases as a clear abuse of judicial power. It climaxes a trend in the Federal Judiciary undertaking to legislate, in derogation [violation] of the authority of Congress, and to encroach upon the reserved rights of the States and the people.

The original Constitution does not mention education. Neither does the 14th Amendment nor any other amendment. The debates preceding the submission of the 14th Amendment clearly show that there was no intent that it should affect the system of education maintained by the States.

In the case of *Plessy v. Ferguson* in 1896 the Supreme Court expressly declared that under the 14th Amendment no person was denied any of his rights if the States provided separate but equal facilities. This decision . . . restated time and again, became a part of the life of the people of many of the States and confirmed their habits, traditions, and way of life. It is founded on elemental humanity and commonsense, for parents should not be deprived by Government of the right to direct the lives and education of their own children.

Though there has been no constitutional amendment or act of Congress changing this established legal principle almost a century old, the Supreme Court of the United States, with no legal basis for such action, undertook to exercise their naked judicial power and substituted their personal political and social ideas for the established law of the land.

This unwarranted exercise of power by the Court, contrary to the Constitution, is creating chaos and confusion in the States principally affected. It is destroying the amicable relations between the white and Negro races that have been created through 90 years of patient effort by the good people of both races. It has planted hatred and suspicion where there has been heretofore friendship and understanding.

With the gravest concern for the explosive and dangerous condition created by this decision and inflamed by outside meddlers: . . . we commend the motives of those States which have declared the intention to resist forced integration by any lawful means. . . .

QUESTIONS

1. *Why does Borders refer several times to the international implications of the American system of racial segregation?*

2. *Why does the Southern Manifesto claim that the Supreme Court decision is a threat to constitutional government?*

3. *How do these documents illustrate contrasting understandings of freedom in the wake of the civil rights movement?*

In 1956, 96 of 106 southern congressmen—and every southern senator except Lyndon B. Johnson of Texas and Albert Gore and Estes Kefauver of Tennessee—signed a **Southern Manifesto**, denouncing the *Brown* decision as a "clear abuse of judicial power" and calling for resistance to "forced integration" by "any lawful means." State after state passed laws to block desegregation. Some made it illegal for the NAACP to operate within their borders. Virginia pioneered the strategy of closing any public schools ordered to desegregate and offering funds to enable white pupils, but not Black, to attend private institutions. Prince Edward County, Virginia, shut its schools entirely in 1959; not until 1964 did the Supreme Court order them reopened. Many states adopted "freedom of choice" plans that allowed white students to opt out of integrated schools. As a symbol of defiance, Georgia's legislature incorporated the Confederate battle flag into its state flag in 1956, and Alabama and South Carolina soon began flying the battle flag over their state capitol buildings.

Eisenhower and Civil Rights

The federal government tried to remain aloof from the Black struggle. Thanks to the efforts of Senate majority leader Lyndon B. Johnson, who hoped to win liberal support for a run for president in 1960, Congress in 1957 passed the first national civil rights law since Reconstruction. It targeted the denial of Black voting rights in the South, but with weak enforcement provisions it added few voters to the rolls. President Eisenhower failed to provide moral leadership. He called for Americans to abide by the law, but he made it clear that he found the whole civil rights issue distasteful. He privately told aides that he disagreed with the Supreme Court's reasoning. Ike failed to act in 1956 when a federal court ordered that Autherine Lucy be admitted to the University of Alabama; a mob prevented her from registering and the board of trustees expelled her. The university remained all white into the 1960s.

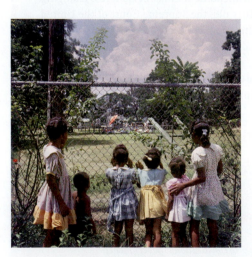

A photograph by Gordon Parks shows black children peering wistfully into a whites-only playground in Mobile, Alabama, in 1956.

In 1957, however, after Governor Orval Faubus of Arkansas used the National Guard to prevent the court-ordered integration of Little Rock's Central High School, Eisenhower dispatched federal troops to the city. In the face of a howling mob, soldiers of the 101st Airborne Division escorted nine Black children into the school. Events in Little Rock showed that in the last instance, the federal government would not allow the flagrant violation of court orders. But because of massive resistance, the pace of the movement slowed in the final years of the 1950s. When Eisenhower left office, fewer than 2 percent of Black students attended desegregated schools in the states of the old Confederacy.

The World Views the United States

Ever since the beginning of the Cold War, American leaders had worried about the impact of segregation on the country's international reputation. President Truman had promoted his civil rights initiative, in part, by reminding Americans that they could not afford to "ignore what the world thinks of our record." The State Department filed a brief in the *Brown* case noting the damage segregation was doing to the country's image overseas.

Foreign nations and colonies paid close attention to the unfolding of the American civil rights movement. The global reaction to the *Brown* decision was overwhelmingly positive. "At Last! Whites and Blacks in the United States on the same school benches!" proclaimed a newspaper in Senegal, West Africa. But the slow pace of change led to criticism that embarrassed American diplomats seeking to win the loyalty of people in the non-white world. In a public forum in India, the American ambassador was peppered with questions about American race relations. Was it true that the Haitian ambassador to the United States had to live in a Black ghetto in Washington? Why did no Black person hold a high public office? Of course, the Soviet Union played up American race relations as part of the global "battle for hearts and minds" that was a key part of the Cold War.

THE ELECTION OF 1960

Kennedy and Nixon

The presidential campaign of 1960 turned out to be one of the closest in American history. Republicans chose Vice President Richard Nixon as their candidate to succeed Eisenhower. Democrats nominated John F. Kennedy, a senator from Massachusetts and a Roman Catholic, whose father, a millionaire Irish American businessman, had served as ambassador to Great Britain during the 1930s. Kennedy's chief rivals for the nomination were Hubert Humphrey, leader of the party's liberal wing, and Lyndon B. Johnson of Texas, the Senate majority leader, who accepted Kennedy's offer to run for vice president.

The atmosphere of tolerance promoted by World War II had weakened traditional anti-Catholicism. But as recently as 1949, Paul Blanshard's *American Freedom and Catholic Power*, which accused the church of being antidemocratic, morally repressive, and essentially un-American, had become a national bestseller. Many Protestants remained reluctant to vote for a Catholic, fearing that Kennedy would be required to support church doctrine on controversial public issues or, in a more extreme version, take orders from the Pope. Kennedy addressed the question directly. "I do not speak for my church on public matters," he insisted, and "the church does not speak for me." His defeat of Humphrey in the Democratic primary in overwhelmingly Protestant West Virginia put the issue of his religion to rest. At age forty-three, Kennedy became the youngest major-party nominee for president in the nation's history.

Both Kennedy and Nixon were ardent Cold Warriors. But Kennedy pointed to Soviet success in putting *Sputnik*, the first earth satellite, into orbit and subsequently testing the first intercontinental ballistic missile (ICBM) as evidence that the United States had lost the sense of national purpose necessary to fight the Cold War. He warned that Republicans had allowed a missile gap to develop in which the Soviets had achieved technological and military superiority over the United States. In fact, as both Kennedy and Nixon well knew, American economic and military capacity far exceeded that of the Soviets. But the charge persuaded many Americans that the time had come for new leadership. The stylishness of Kennedy's wife, Jacqueline, which stood in sharp contrast to the more dowdy public appearance of Mamie Eisenhower and Pat Nixon, reinforced the impression that Kennedy would conduct a more youthful, vigorous presidency.

In the first televised debate between presidential candidates, judging by viewer response, the handsome Kennedy bested Nixon, who was suffering from a cold and appeared tired and nervous. Those who heard the encounter on the radio thought Nixon had won, but, on TV, image counted for more than substance. In November, Kennedy eked out a narrow victory, winning the popular vote by only 120,000 out of 69 million votes cast (and, Republicans charged, benefiting from a fraudulent vote count by the notoriously corrupt Chicago Democratic machine).

The End of the 1950s

In January 1961, shortly before leaving office, Eisenhower delivered a televised Farewell Address, modeled to some extent on George Washington's address of 1796. Knowing that the missile gap was a myth, Ike warned against the drumbeat of calls for a new military buildup. He urged Americans to think about the dangerous power of what he called the **military-industrial complex**— the conjunction of "an immense military establishment" with a "permanent arms industry"—with an influence felt in "every office" in the land. "We must never let the weight of this combination," he advised his countrymen, "endanger our liberties or democratic processes." Few Americans shared Ike's concern—far more saw the alliance of the Defense Department and private industry as a source of jobs and national security rather than a threat to democracy. A few years later, however, with the United States locked in an increasingly unpopular war, Eisenhower's warning would come to seem prophetic.

By then, other underpinnings of 1950s life were generating growing controversy. The tens of millions of

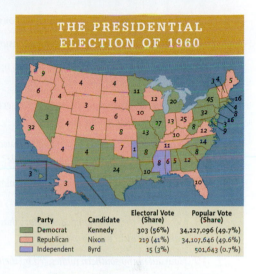

THE PRESIDENTIAL ELECTION OF 1960

Party	Candidate	Electoral Vote (Share)	Popular Vote (Share)
Democrat	Kennedy	303 (56%)	34,227,096 (49.7%)
Republican	Nixon	219 (41%)	34,107,646 (49.6%)
Independent	Byrd	15 (3%)	501,643 (0.7%)

cars that made suburban life possible were spewing toxic lead, an additive to make gasoline more efficient, into the atmosphere. Penned in to the east by mountains that kept automobile emissions from being dispersed by the wind, Los Angeles had become synonymous with smog, a type of air pollution produced by cars. Chlorofluorocarbons, used in air conditioners, deodorants, and aerosol hair sprays, were releasing chemicals into the atmosphere that trapped heat and damaged the ozone layer, producing global warming and an increase in skin cancer. (Both leaded gasoline and chlorofluorocarbons had been invented by General Motors research scientist Thomas Midgley. He "had more impact on the atmosphere," writes one historian, "than any other single organism" in the history of the world.) The chemical insecticides that enabled agricultural conglomerates to produce the country's remarkable abundance of food were poisoning farmworkers, consumers, and the water supply. Housewives were rebelling against a life centered in suburban dream houses. Blacks were increasingly impatient with the slow progress of racial change. The United States, in other words, had entered that most turbulent of decades, the 1960s.

CHAPTER REVIEW

REVIEW QUESTIONS

1. *Explain the meaning of the "American standard of living" during the 1950s.*

2. *Describe how the automobile and new highway construction transformed American life in the 1950s.*

3. *Identify the prescribed roles and aspirations for women during the 1950s.*

4. *What are some ways in which mass consumption was promoted as a patriotic act?*

5. *How did governmental policies, business practices, and individual choices contribute to racially segregated suburbs?*

6. *Explain the ideological rifts between conservatives in the 1950s. Why did many view President Eisenhower as "not one of them"?*

7. *What was the new "social contract" between labor and management, and how did it benefit both sides as well as the nation as a whole?*

8. *How did the United States and Soviet Union shift the focus of the Cold War to the Third World?*

9. *What were the most significant factors that contributed to the growing momentum of the civil rights movement in the 1950s?*

10. *How did many southern whites, led by their elected officials, resist desegregation and civil rights in the name of "freedom"?*

11. *How and why did the federal government's concern with U.S. relations overseas shape its involvement with the* Brown v. Board of Education *case?*

KEY TERMS

Levittown (p. 952)

interstate highway system (p. 956)

baby boom (p. 957)

urban renewal (p. 959)

Indian Urban Relocation Program (p. 960)

"In God We Trust" (p. 962)

Sputnik (p. 968)

National Defense Education Act (p. 968)

social contract (p. 969)

massive retaliation (p. 969)

Bandung Conference (p. 971)

Geneva Accords (p. 973)

the Beats (p. 976)

League of United Latin American Citizens (p. 978)

Brown v. Board of Education (p. 978)

Montgomery bus boycott (p. 980)

Southern Christian Leadership Conference (p. 983)

Southern Manifesto (p. 986)

military-industrial complex (p. 988)

Go to 🐰 INQUIZITIVE

To see what you know—and learn what you've missed—with personalized feedback along the way.

CHAPTER 25

THE SIXTIES

1960–1968

FOCUS QUESTIONS

- What were the major events in the civil rights movement of the early 1960s?

- What were the major crises and policy initiatives of the Kennedy presidency?

- What were the purposes and strategies of Johnson's Great Society programs?

- How did the civil rights movement change in the mid-1960s?

- How did the Vietnam War transform American politics and culture?

- What were the sources and significance of the rights revolution of the late 1960s?

- In what ways was 1968 a climactic year for the Sixties?

O n the afternoon of February 1, 1960, four students from North Carolina Agricultural and Technical State University, a Black college in Greensboro, North Carolina, entered the local Woolworth's department store. After making a few purchases, they sat down at the lunch counter, an area reserved for whites. Told that they could not be served, they remained in their seats until the store closed. They returned the next morning and the next. As the protest continued, other students, including a few local whites, joined in. Demonstrations spread across the country. After resisting for five months, Woolworth's in July agreed to serve Black customers at its lunch counters.

The **sit-in** reflected mounting frustration at the slow pace of racial change. White Greensboro prided itself on being free of prejudice. In 1954, the city had been the first in the South to declare its intention of complying with the *Brown* decision. But by 1960 only a handful of Black students had been admitted to all-white schools, the economic gap between Blacks and whites had not narrowed, and Greensboro was still segregated.

More than any other event, the Greensboro sit-in launched the 1960s: a decade of political activism and social change. Sit-ins had occurred before, but never had they sparked so massive a response. Similar demonstrations soon took place throughout the South, demanding the integration not only of lunch counters but of parks, pools, restaurants, bowling alleys, libraries, and other facilities as well. By the end of 1960, some 70,000 demonstrators had taken part in sit-ins. Angry whites often assaulted them. But having been trained in nonviolent resistance, the protesters did not strike back.

Even more than elevating Blacks to full citizenship, declared the writer James Baldwin, the civil rights movement challenged the United States to rethink "what it really means by freedom"—including whether freedom applied to all Americans or only to part of the population. With their freedom rides, freedom schools, freedom marches, and the insistent cry "Freedom now," Black Americans and their white allies made freedom once again the rallying cry of the dispossessed. Thousands of ordinary men and women—maids and laborers alongside students, teachers, businessmen, and ministers—risked physical and economic retribution to lay claim to freedom. Their courage inspired a host of other challenges to the status quo, including a student movement known as the New Left, the "second wave" of feminism, and activism among other minorities.

By the time the decade ended, these movements had challenged the 1950s' understanding of freedom linked to the Cold War abroad and consumer choice at home. They exposed the limitations of traditional New Deal liberalism. They forced a reconsideration of the nation's foreign policy and extended claims to freedom into the most intimate areas of life. They made American society confront the fact that certain groups, including students, women, members of racial minorities, and gay persons, felt themselves excluded from full enjoyment of American freedom.

Reflecting back years later on the struggles of the 1960s, one Black organizer in Memphis remarked, "All I wanted to do was to live in a free country." Of the movement's accomplishments, he added, "You had to fight for every inch of it. Nobody gave you anything. Nothing."

THE CIVIL RIGHTS REVOLUTION

The Rising Tide of Protest

With the sit-ins, college students for the first time stepped onto the stage of American history as the leading force for social change. In April 1960, Ella Baker, a longtime civil rights organizer, called a meeting of young activists in Raleigh, North Carolina. About 200 Black students and a few whites attended. Out of the gathering came the **Student Nonviolent Coordinating Committee** (SNCC), dedicated to replacing the culture of segregation with a "beloved community" of racial justice and to empowering ordinary Blacks to take control of the decisions that affected their lives. "We can't count on adults," declared SNCC organizer Robert Moses. "Very few . . . are not afraid of the tremendous pressure they will face. This leaves the young people to be the organizers, the agents of social and political change."

Other forms of direct action soon followed the sit-ins. Blacks in Biloxi and Gulfport, Mississippi, engaged in "wade-ins," demanding access to segregated public beaches. Scores were arrested and two Black teenagers were killed. In 1961, the Congress of Racial Equality (CORE) launched the **Freedom Rides**. Integrated groups traveled by bus into the Lower South to test compliance with court orders banning segregation on interstate buses and trains and in terminal facilities. Violent mobs assaulted them. Near Anniston, Alabama, a firebomb was thrown into the vehicle and the passengers beaten as they escaped. In Birmingham, Klansmen attacked riders with bats and chains, while police refused to intervene. Many of the Freedom Riders were arrested. But their actions led the Interstate Commerce Commission to order buses and terminals desegregated.

• CHRONOLOGY •

1960	Greensboro, N.C., sit-in
	Young Americans for Freedom founded
1961	Bay of Pigs
	Freedom Rides
	Berlin Wall constructed
1962	Port Huron Statement
	University of Mississippi desegregated
	Rachel Carson's *Silent Spring*
	Cuban missile crisis
1963	Betty Friedan's *The Feminine Mystique*
	King's "Letter from Birmingham Jail"
	March on Washington
	Kennedy assassinated
1964	Freedom Summer
	Civil Rights Act passed
	Gulf of Tonkin resolution
1965	Voting Rights Act
	Watts uprising
	Hart-Celler Act
1965–1967	Great Society
1966	National Organization for Women organized
1968	Tet offensive
	Martin Luther King Jr. assassinated
	American Indian Movement founded
	Richard Nixon elected
1969	Police raid on Stonewall Inn
	Woodstock festival
1973	*Roe v. Wade*

As protests escalated, so did the resistance of local authorities. Late in 1961, SNCC and other groups launched a campaign of nonviolent protests against racial discrimination in Albany, Georgia. The protests lasted a year, but despite filling the jails with demonstrators—a tactic adopted by the movement to gain national sympathy—they failed to achieve their goals. In September 1962, a court ordered the University of Mississippi to admit James Meredith, a Black student. The state police stood aside as a mob, encouraged by Governor Ross Barnett, rampaged through the streets of Oxford, where the university is located. Two bystanders lost their lives in the riot. President Kennedy was forced to dispatch the army to restore order.

Birmingham

The high point of protest came in the spring of 1963, when demonstrations took place in towns and cities across the South, dramatizing Black discontent over inequality in education, employment, and housing. In one week in June, there were more than 15,000 arrests in 186 cities. The dramatic culmination came in Birmingham, Alabama, a citadel of segregation. Even for the Lower South, Birmingham was a violent city—there had been over fifty bombings of Black homes and institutions since World War II. Local Blacks had been demonstrating, with no result, for greater economic opportunities and an end to segregation by local businesses.

With the movement flagging, some of its leaders invited Martin Luther King Jr. to come to Birmingham. While serving a nine-day prison term in April 1963 for violating a ban on demonstrations, King composed one of his most eloquent pleas for racial justice, the "Letter from Birmingham Jail." Responding to local clergymen who counseled patience, King related the litany of abuses faced by Black southerners, from police brutality to the daily humiliation of having to explain to their children why they could not enter amusement parks or public swimming pools. The "white moderate," King declared, must put aside fear of disorder and commit himself to racial justice.

In May, King made the bold decision to send Black schoolchildren into the streets of Birmingham. Police chief

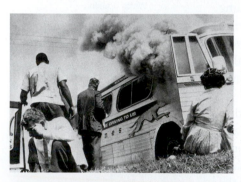

Black and white Freedom Riders rode buses from Washington, D.C., to Alabama in 1961 to press for integration. This Greyhound bus was set aflame by a white mob in Alabama.

Eugene "Bull" Connor unleashed his forces against the thousands of young marchers. The images, broadcast on television, of children being assaulted with nightsticks, high-pressure fire hoses, and attack dogs produced a wave of revulsion throughout the world and turned the Birmingham campaign into a triumph for the civil rights movement. It led President Kennedy, as will be related later, to endorse the movement's goals. Leading businessmen, fearing that the city was becoming an international symbol of brutality, brokered an end to the demonstrations that desegregated downtown stores and restaurants and promised that Black salespeople would be hired.

But more than these modest gains, the events in Birmingham forced white Americans to decide whether they had more in common with fellow citizens demanding their basic rights or with violent segregationists. The question became more insistent in the following weeks. In June 1963, a sniper killed Medgar Evers, field secretary of the NAACP in Mississippi. In September, a bomb exploded at a Black Baptist church in Birmingham, killing four young

During the climactic demonstrations in Birmingham, firemen assaulted young African Americans with high-pressure hoses. Broadcast on television, such pictures posed a serious problem for the United States in its battle for the "hearts and minds" of people around the world and forced the Kennedy administration to confront the contradiction between the rhetoric of freedom and the reality of racism.

THE CIVIL RIGHTS REVOLUTION ★ 995

girls. (Not until 2002 was the last of those who committed this act of domestic terrorism tried and convicted.)

The March on Washington

On August 28, 1963, two weeks before the Birmingham church bombing, 250,000 Black and white Americans converged on the nation's capital for the **March on Washington**, often considered the high point of the nonviolent civil rights movement. Organized by a coalition of civil rights, labor, and church organizations led by A. Philip Randolph, the Black unionist who had threatened a similar march in 1941, it was the largest public demonstration in the nation's history to that time. Calls for the passage of a civil rights bill pending before Congress took center stage. But the march's goals also included a public-works program to reduce unemployment, an increase in the minimum wage, and a law barring discrimination in employment. These demands, and the marchers' slogan, "Jobs and Freedom," revealed how the Black movement had, for the moment, forged an alliance with white liberal groups. On the steps of the Lincoln Memorial, King delivered his most famous speech, including the words, "I have a dream that one day this nation will rise up and live out the true meaning of its creed: 'We hold these truths to be self-evident, that all men are created equal.'"

The March on Washington reflected an unprecedented degree of Black-white cooperation in support of racial and economic justice. But it also revealed some of the movement's limitations, and the tensions within it. Even though female activists like Jo Ann Robinson and Ella Baker had played crucial roles in civil rights organizing, every speaker at the Lincoln Memorial was male. The organizers ordered SNCC leader John Lewis (later a congressman from Georgia) to tone down his speech, the original text of which called on Blacks to "free ourselves of the chains of political and economic slavery" and march "through the heart of Dixie the way Sherman did . . . and burn Jim Crow to the ground." Lewis's rhetoric forecast the more militant turn many in the movement would soon be taking.

"Seek the freedom in 1963 promised in 1863," read one banner at the March on Washington. And civil rights activists resurrected the Civil War–era vision of national authority as the custodian of American freedom. Despite the fact that the federal government had for many decades promoted segregation, Blacks' historical experience suggested that they had more hope for justice from national power than from local governments or civic institutions— home owners' associations, businesses, private clubs—still riddled with racism. It remained unclear whether the federal government would take up this responsibility.

THE KENNEDY YEARS

John F. Kennedy served as president for less than three years and, in domestic affairs, had few tangible accomplishments. But his administration is widely viewed today as a moment of youthful glamour, soaring hopes, and dynamic leadership at home and abroad. Later revelations of the sexual liaisons Kennedy obsessively pursued while in the White House have not significantly damaged his reputation among the general public.

Kennedy's inaugural address of January 1961 announced a watershed in American politics: "The torch has been passed," he declared, "to a new generation of Americans" who would "pay any price, bear any burden," to "assure the survival and success of liberty." The speech seemed to urge Americans to move beyond the self-centered consumer culture of the 1950s: "Ask not what your country can do for you; ask what you can do for your country." But while the sit-ins were by now a year old, the speech said nothing about segregation or race. At the outset of his presidency, Kennedy regarded civil rights as a distraction from his main concern—vigorous conduct of the Cold War.

Kennedy and the World

Kennedy's agenda envisioned new initiatives aimed at countering communist influence in the world. One of his administration's first acts was to establish the Peace Corps, which sent young Americans abroad to aid in the economic and educational progress of developing countries and to improve the image of the United States there. By 1966, more than 15,000 young men and women were serving as Peace Corps volunteers. When the Soviets in April 1961 launched a satellite carrying the first man into orbit around the earth, Kennedy announced that the United States would mobilize its resources to land a man on the moon by the end of the decade. The goal seemed almost impossible when announced, but it was stunningly accomplished in 1969.

Kennedy also formulated a new policy toward Latin America, the Alliance for Progress. A kind of Marshall Plan for the Western Hemisphere, although involving far smaller sums of money, it aimed, Kennedy said, to promote both "political" and "material freedom." Begun in 1961 with much fanfare about alleviating poverty and counteracting the appeal of communism, the Alliance for Progress failed. Unlike the Marshall Plan, military regimes and local elites controlled Alliance for Progress aid. They enriched themselves while the poor saw little benefit.

Like his predecessors, Kennedy viewed the entire world through the lens of the Cold War. This outlook shaped his dealings with Fidel Castro, who led a revolution that in 1959 ousted Cuban dictator Fulgencio Batista. Until Castro took power, Cuba was an economic dependency of the United States. When his government began nationalizing American landholdings and other investments and signed an agreement to sell sugar to the Soviet Union, the Eisenhower administration suspended trade and diplomatic relations with the island. The CIA began training anti-Castro exiles for an invasion of Cuba.

In April 1961, Kennedy allowed the CIA to launch its invasion, at a site known as the Bay of Pigs. Military advisers predicted a popular uprising that would quickly topple the Castro government. But the **Bay of Pigs invasion** proved to be a total failure. Of 1,400 invaders, more than 100 were killed and 1,100 captured. Cuba became ever more closely tied to the Soviet Union. The Kennedy administration tried other methods, including assassination attempts, to get rid of Castro's government.

The Missile Crisis

Meanwhile, relations between the two "superpowers" deteriorated. In August 1961, in order to stem a growing tide of emigrants fleeing from East to West Berlin, the Soviets constructed a wall separating the two parts of the city. Until its demolition in 1989, the Berlin Wall would stand as a tangible symbol of the Cold War and the division of Europe.

The most dangerous crisis of the Kennedy administration, and in many ways of the entire Cold War, came in October 1962, when American spy planes discovered that the Soviet Union was installing missiles in Cuba capable of reaching the United States with nuclear weapons. Rejecting advice from military leaders that he authorize an attack on Cuba, which would almost certainly have triggered a Soviet response in Berlin and perhaps a nuclear war, Kennedy imposed a blockade, or "quarantine," of the island and demanded the missiles' removal. For thirteen days, the world teetered on the brink of all-out nuclear war. After tense behind-the-scenes negotiations, Soviet premier Nikita Khrushchev agreed to withdraw the missiles. Kennedy pledged that the United States would not invade Cuba and secretly agreed to remove American Jupiter missiles from Turkey, from which they could reach the Soviet Union.

The **Cuban missile crisis** seems to have lessened Kennedy's passion for the Cold War. Indeed, he appears to have been shocked by the casual way military leaders spoke of "winning" a nuclear exchange in which tens of millions of Americans and Russians were certain to die. In 1963, Kennedy moved to reduce Cold War tensions. In a speech at American University, he called for greater cooperation with the Soviets. That summer, the two countries agreed to a treaty banning the testing of nuclear weapons in the atmosphere and in space. In announcing the agreement, Kennedy paid tribute to the small movement against nuclear weapons that had been urging such a ban for several years. He even sent word to Castro through a journalist that he desired a more constructive relationship with Cuba.

Kennedy and Civil Rights

In his first two years in office, Kennedy was preoccupied with foreign policy. But in 1963, the crisis over civil rights eclipsed other concerns. Until then, Kennedy had been reluctant to take a forceful stand on Black demands. He seemed to share FBI director J. Edgar Hoover's fear that the movement was inspired by communism. Attorney General Robert F. Kennedy, the president's brother, approved FBI wiretaps on King. Despite promising during the 1960 campaign to ban discrimination in federally assisted housing, Kennedy waited until the end of 1962 to issue the order. He used federal force when obstruction of the law became acute, as at the University of Mississippi. But he failed to protect civil rights workers from violence, insisting that law enforcement was a local matter.

Events in Birmingham in May 1963 forced Kennedy's hand. Kennedy realized that the United States simply could not declare itself the champion of freedom throughout the world while maintaining a system of racial inequality at home. In June, he went on national television to call for the passage of a law banning discrimination in all places of public accommodation, a major goal of the civil rights movement. The nation, he asserted, faced a moral crisis: "We preach freedom around the world, . . . but are we to say to the world, and much more importantly, to each other, that this is a land of the free except for Negroes?"

Kennedy did not live to see his civil rights bill enacted. On November 22, 1963, while riding in a motorcade through Dallas, Texas, he was shot and killed. Most likely, the assassin was Lee Harvey Oswald, a troubled former marine. Partly because Oswald was murdered two days later by a local nightclub owner while in police custody, speculation about a possible conspiracy continues to this day. In any event, Kennedy's death brought an abrupt and utterly unexpected end to his presidency. As with Pearl Harbor or September 11, 2001, an entire generation would always recall the moment when they first heard the news of Kennedy's death. It fell to his successor,

New York City train passengers reading the news of President Kennedy's assassination, November 22, 1963.

Lyndon B. Johnson, to secure passage of the civil rights bill and to launch a program of domestic liberalism far more ambitious than anything Kennedy had envisioned.

LYNDON JOHNSON'S PRESIDENCY

Unlike John F. Kennedy, raised in a wealthy and powerful family, Lyndon Johnson grew up in one of the poorest parts of the United States, the central Texas hill country. Kennedy seemed to view success as his birthright; Johnson had to struggle ferociously to achieve wealth and power. By the 1950s, he had risen to become majority leader of the U.S. Senate. But Johnson never forgot the poor Mexican and white children he had taught in a Texas school in the early 1930s. Far more interested than Kennedy in domestic reform, he continued to hold the New Deal view that government had an obligation to assist less fortunate members of society.

The Civil Rights Act of 1964

When he became president, nobody expected that Johnson would make the passage of civil rights legislation his first order of business or that he would come to identify himself with the Black movement more passionately than any previous president. Just five days after Kennedy's assassination, however, Johnson called on Congress to enact the civil rights bill as the most fitting memorial to his slain predecessor. "We have talked long enough about equal rights in this country," he declared. "It is now time to write the next chapter and write it in the books of law."

In 1964, Congress passed the **Civil Rights Act**, which prohibited racial discrimination in employment, institutions like hospitals and schools, and privately owned public accommodations such as restaurants, hotels, and theaters. Johnson knew that many whites opposed the new law. An aide later claimed that after signing the bill, Johnson remarked, "I think we delivered the South to the Republican Party."

Freedom Summer

The 1964 law did not address a major concern of the civil rights movement—the right to vote in the South. That summer, a coalition of civil rights groups, including SNCC, CORE, and the NAACP, launched a voter registration drive in Mississippi. Hundreds of white college students from the North traveled to the state to take part in Freedom Summer. An outpouring of violence greeted the campaign, including thirty-five bombings and numerous beatings of civil rights workers. In June, three young activists—Michael Schwerner and Andrew Goodman, white students from the North, and James Chaney, a local Black youth—were kidnapped by a group headed by a deputy sheriff and murdered near Philadelphia, Mississippi. Between 1961 and 1965, an estimated twenty-five Black civil rights workers paid with their lives. But the deaths of the two white students focused unprecedented attention on Mississippi and on the apparent inability of the federal government to protect citizens seeking to enjoy their constitutional rights. (In June 2005, forty-one years after Freedom Summer, a Mississippi jury convicted a member of the Ku Klux Klan of manslaughter in the deaths of the three civil rights workers.)

Freedom Summer led directly to one of the most dramatic confrontations of the civil rights era—the campaign by the Mississippi Freedom Democratic Party (MFDP) to take the seats of the state's all-white official party at the 1964 Democratic national convention in Atlantic City, New Jersey. With Blacks unable to participate in the activities of the Democratic Party or register to vote, the civil rights movement in Mississippi had created the MFDP, open to all residents of the state. At televised hearings before the credentials committee, Fannie Lou Hamer of the MFDP held a national audience spellbound with her account of growing up in poverty in the Yazoo-Mississippi Delta and of the savage beatings she had endured at the hands of police. Like many other Black activists, Hamer was a deeply religious person who believed that Christianity rested on the idea of freedom and that the movement had been divinely inspired. "Is this America," she asked, "the land of the free and home of the brave, where . . . we [are] threatened daily because we want to live as decent human beings?" Johnson feared a southern walkout, as had happened at the 1948 party convention, if the MFDP were seated. Party liberals, including Johnson's running mate, Hubert Humphrey, pressed for a compromise in which two Black delegates would be granted seats. But the MFDP rejected the proposal.

The 1964 Election

The events at Atlantic City severely weakened Black activists' faith in the responsiveness of the political system and forecast the impending breakup of the coalition between the civil rights movement and the liberal wing of the Democratic Party. For the moment, however, the movement rallied behind Johnson's campaign for reelection. Johnson's opponent, Senator Barry Goldwater of Arizona, had published *The Conscience of a Conservative* (1960), which sold more than 3 million copies. The book demanded a more aggressive conduct of the Cold War (he even suggested that nuclear war might be "the price of freedom"). But Goldwater directed most of his critique against "internal" dangers to freedom, especially the New Deal welfare state, which he believed stifled individual initiative and independence. He called for the substitution of private charity for public welfare programs and Social Security, and the abolition of the graduated income tax. Goldwater had voted against the Civil Rights Act of 1964. His acceptance speech at the Republican national convention contained the explosive statement, "Extremism in the defense of liberty is no vice."

Stigmatized by the Democrats as an extremist who would repeal Social Security and risk nuclear war, Goldwater went down to a disastrous defeat. Johnson received almost 43 million votes to Goldwater's 27 million. Democrats swept to two-to-one majorities in both houses of Congress. But although few realized it, the 1964 campaign marked a milestone in the resurgence of American conservatism. Goldwater's success in the Lower South, where he carried five states, coupled with the surprisingly strong showing of segregationist governor George Wallace of Alabama in Democratic primaries in Wisconsin, Indiana, and Maryland, suggested that politicians could strike electoral gold by appealing to white opposition to the civil rights movement.

One indication of problems for the Democrats came in California, with the passage by popular referendum of Proposition 14, which repealed a 1963 law banning racial discrimination in the sale of real estate. Backed by the state's realtors and developers, California conservatives made the "freedom" of home owners to control their property the rallying cry of the campaign against the fair housing law. Although Johnson carried California by more than 1 million votes, Proposition 14 received a considerable majority, winning three-fourths of the votes cast by whites.

The Conservative Sixties

The 1960s, today recalled as a decade of radicalism, clearly had a conservative side as well. With the founding in 1960 of Young Americans for Freedom (YAF), conservative students emerged as a force in politics. There were striking parallels between the Sharon Statement, issued by ninety young people who gathered at the estate of conservative intellectual William F. Buckley in Sharon, Connecticut, to establish YAF, and the Port Huron Statement of SDS of 1962 (discussed later in this chapter). Both manifestos portrayed youth as the cutting edge of a new radicalism, and both claimed to offer a route to greater freedom. The Sharon Statement summarized beliefs that had circulated among conservatives during the past decade—the free market underpinned "personal freedom," government must be strictly limited, and "international communism," the gravest threat to liberty, must be destroyed.

YAF aimed initially to take control of the Republican Party from leaders who had made their peace with the New Deal and seemed willing to coexist with communism. YAF members became Barry Goldwater's shock troops in 1964. Despite his landslide defeat in the general election, Goldwater's nomination was a remarkable triumph for a movement widely viewed as composed of fanatics out to "repeal the twentieth century."

Goldwater also brought new constituencies to the conservative cause. His campaign aroused enthusiasm in the rapidly expanding suburbs of southern California and the Southwest. Orange County, California, many of whose residents had recently arrived from the Midwest and worked in defense-related industries, became a nationally known center of grassroots conservative activism. The funds that poured into the Goldwater campaign from the Sunbelt's oilmen and aerospace entrepreneurs established a new financial base for conservatism. And by carrying five states of the Lower South, Goldwater showed that the civil rights revolution had redrawn the nation's political map, opening the door to a "southern strategy" that would eventually lead the entire region into the Republican Party.

Well before the rise of Black Power, a reaction against civil rights gains offered conservatives new opportunities and threatened the stability of the Democratic coalition. During the 1950s, many conservatives had responded favorably to southern whites' condemnation of the *Brown v. Board of Education* desegregation decision as an invasion of states' rights. The *National Review*, an influential conservative magazine, referred to whites as "the advanced race" and defended Black disenfranchisement on the grounds that "the claims of civilization supersede those of universal suffrage." In 1962, YAF bestowed its Freedom Award on Senator Strom Thurmond of South Carolina, one of the country's most prominent segregationists. During the 1960s, most conservatives abandoned talk of racial superiority and inferiority. But conservative appeals to law and order, "freedom of association," and the evils of welfare often had strong racial overtones. Racial divisions would prove to be a political gold mine for conservatives.

The Voting Rights Act

One last legislative triumph, however, lay ahead for the civil rights movement. In January 1965, King launched a voting rights campaign in Selma, Alabama, a city where only 355 of 15,000 Black residents had been allowed to register to vote. In March, defying a ban by Governor Wallace, King attempted to lead a march from Selma to the state capital, Montgomery. When the marchers reached the bridge leading out of the city, state police assaulted them with cattle prods, whips, and tear gas.

Once again, violence against nonviolent demonstrators flashed across television screens throughout the world, compelling the federal government to take action. Calling Selma a milestone in "man's unending search for freedom," Johnson asked Congress to enact a law securing the right to vote. He closed his

A sharecropper's shack alongside Jefferson Davis Highway, the route followed from Selma to Montgomery, Alabama, in 1965, by marchers demanding voting rights. The photograph, by James "Spider" Martin, who chronicled the march, suggests the deep-seated inequalities that persisted a century after the end of the Civil War.

speech by quoting the demonstrators' song, "We Shall Overcome." Never before had the movement received so powerful an endorsement from the federal government. Congress quickly passed the **Voting Rights Act** of 1965, which allowed federal officials to register voters. Black southerners finally regained the suffrage that had been stripped from them at the turn of the twentieth century. In addition, the Twenty-fourth Amendment to the Constitution outlawed the poll tax, which had long prevented poor Blacks (and some whites) from voting in the South.

Immigration Reform

By 1965, the civil rights movement had succeeded in eradicating the legal bases of second-class citizenship. The belief that racism should no longer serve as a foundation of public policy spilled over into other realms. In 1965, the **Hart-Celler Act** abandoned the national-origins quota system of immigration, which had excluded Asians and severely restricted southern and eastern Europeans. The law established new, racially neutral criteria for immigration, notably family reunification and possession of skills in demand in the United States. On the other hand, because of growing hostility in the Southwest to Mexican immigration, the law established the first limit, 120,000, on newcomers from the Western Hemisphere. This created, for the first time, the category of "illegal aliens" from the Americas. Indeed, since the act set a maximum annual immigration quota of 20,000 persons for every country in the world, it guaranteed that a large part of Mexican immigration would be unauthorized, since labor demand for Mexican immigrants in the United States far exceeded that number. As a result, many arrived without documentation, and many Americans came to conflate all Mexicans with "illegal" immigrants. Establishing the same quota for Mexico and, say, Belgium or New Zealand made no sense. However, because of special provisions for refugees from communist countries, immigration soon exceeded these caps.

The immigration law opened the country's borders in significant ways compared to the restrictive quotas in existence since 1924. As Oscar Handlin made plain in the "Who Is an American?" document in Chapter 23, immigrants and their descendants believed that the 1924 quotas suggested that they were not truly welcome in American society. They demanded to be seen as equal members.

The new law had many unexpected results. At the time, immigrants represented only 5 percent of the American population—the lowest proportion since the 1830s. No one anticipated that the new quotas not only would lead to an explosive rise in immigration but also would spark a dramatic shift in which newcomers from Latin America, the Caribbean, and Asia came to outnumber those from Europe. Taken together, the civil rights revolution and immigration reform marked the triumph of a pluralist conception of Americanism. By 1976, 85 percent of respondents to a public-opinion survey agreed with the statement, "The United States was meant to be . . . a country made up of many races, religions, and nationalities."

The Great Society

After his landslide victory of 1964, Johnson outlined the most sweeping proposal for governmental action to promote the general welfare since the New Deal. Johnson's initiatives of 1965–1967, known collectively as the **Great Society**, provided health services to the poor and elderly in the new Medicaid and Medicare programs and poured federal funds into education and urban development. New cabinet offices—the Departments of Transportation and of Housing and Urban Development—and new agencies, such as the Equal Employment Opportunity Commission, the National Endowments for the Humanities and for the Arts, and a national public broadcasting network, were created. These measures greatly expanded the powers of the federal government, and they completed and extended the social agenda (with the exception of national health insurance) that had been stalled in Congress since 1938.

Unlike the New Deal, however, the Great Society was a response to prosperity, not depression. The mid-1960s was a time of rapid economic expansion, fueled by increased government spending and a tax cut on individuals and businesses initially proposed by Kennedy and enacted in 1964. Johnson and Democratic liberals believed that economic growth made it possible to fund ambitious new government programs and to improve the quality of life.

The War on Poverty

The centerpiece of the Great Society, however, was the crusade to eradicate poverty, launched by Johnson early in 1964. After the talk of universal affluence during the 1950s, economic deprivation had been rediscovered by political

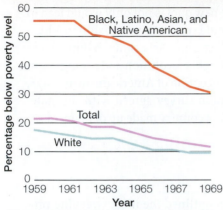

FIGURE 25.1 PERCENTAGE OF POPULATION BELOW POVERTY LEVEL, BY RACE, 1959–1969*

*The poverty threshold for a non-farm family of four was $3,743 in 1969 and $2,973 in 1959.

During the 1960s, an expanding economy and government programs assisting the poor produced a steady decrease in the percentage of Americans living in poverty.

leaders, thanks in part to Michael Harrington's 1962 book *The Other America*. Harrington revealed that 40 to 50 million Americans lived in poverty, often in isolated rural areas or urban slums "invisible" to the middle class. The civil rights movement heightened the urgency of the issue, even though, as Harrington made clear, whites made up a majority of the nation's poor.

During the 1930s, Democrats had attributed poverty to an imbalance of economic power and flawed economic institutions. In the 1960s, the administration attributed it to an absence of skills and a lack of proper attitudes and work habits. Thus, the **War on Poverty** did not consider the most direct ways of eliminating poverty—guaranteeing an annual income for all Americans, creating jobs for the unemployed, promoting the spread of unionization, or making it more difficult for businesses to shift production to the low-wage South or overseas. Nor did it address the economic changes that were reducing the number of well-paid manufacturing jobs and leaving poor families in rural areas like Appalachia and decaying urban neighborhoods with little hope of economic advancement.

One of the Great Society's most popular and successful components, food stamps, offered direct aid to the poor. But, in general, the War on Poverty concentrated on equipping the poor with skills and rebuilding their spirit and motivation. The new Office of Economic Opportunity oversaw a series of initiatives designed to lift the poor into the social and economic mainstream. It provided Head Start (an early childhood education program), job training, legal services, and scholarships for poor college students. It also created VISTA, a domestic version of the Peace Corps for the inner cities. In an echo of SNCC's philosophy of empowering ordinary individuals to take control of their lives, the War on Poverty required that poor people play a leading part in the design and implementation of local policies, a recipe for continuing conflict with local political leaders accustomed to controlling the flow of federal dollars. The grassroots War on Poverty contributed to an upsurge of local radical activism.

Freedom and Equality

Johnson defended the Great Society in a vocabulary of freedom derived from the New Deal, when his own political career began, and reinforced by the civil rights movement. Soon after assuming office in 1963, he resurrected the phrase "freedom from want," all but forgotten during the 1950s. Echoing FDR, Johnson told the 1964 Democratic national convention, "The man who is hungry, who cannot find work or educate his children, who is bowed by want, that man is not fully free." Recognizing that Black poverty was fundamentally different from white, since its roots lay in "past injustice and present prejudice," Johnson sought to redefine the relationship between freedom and equality. Economic liberty, he insisted, meant more than equal opportunity: "You do not wipe away the scars of centuries by saying: Now you are free to go where you want, do as you desire, and choose the leaders you please. . . . We seek . . . not just equality as a right and a theory, but equality as a fact and as a result."

Johnson's Great Society may not have achieved equality "as a fact." But it represented the most expansive effort in the nation's history to mobilize the powers of the national government to address the needs of the least-advantaged Americans, especially those, like Blacks, largely excluded from the original New Deal entitlements such as Social Security.

Coupled with the decade's high rate of economic growth, the War on Poverty succeeded in reducing the incidence of poverty from 22 percent to 13 percent of American families during the 1960s. It has fluctuated around the latter figure ever since. The sum spent, however, was too low to end poverty altogether or to transform conditions of life in poor urban neighborhoods. Today, thanks to the civil rights movement and the Great Society, the historic gap between whites and Blacks in education, income, and access to skilled employment has narrowed considerably. But with deindustrialization and urban decay affecting numerous families, the median wealth of white households remains ten times greater than that of Blacks, and nearly a quarter of all Black children still live in poverty.

THE CHANGING BLACK MOVEMENT

Even at its moment of triumph, the civil rights movement confronted a crisis as it sought to move from access to schools, public accommodations, and the voting booth to the economic divide separating Blacks from other Americans. In the mid-1960s, economic issues rose to the forefront of the civil rights agenda. Violent outbreaks in urban Black communities outside the South drew attention to the national scope of racial injustice and to inequalities in jobs, education, and housing that the dismantling of legal segregation left intact. Much of the animosity that came to characterize race relations arose from the belief of many whites that the legislation of 1964 and 1965 had fulfilled the nation's obligation to assure Blacks equality before the law, while Blacks pushed for more government action, sparking charges of "reverse discrimination."

Urban Rebellions

Between 1964 and 1972, Black insurgencies took place in every major urban center in the country and in many smaller cities. Frequently sparked by an encounter between a Black resident and the predominantly white police (widely seen by many residents as an occupying army), the uprisings often escalated to pitched battles with looting and burning of white-owned businesses. The collective violence revealed the anger of poor, young urban Blacks who grew up in segregated neighborhoods with high unemployment, decaying housing, and police surveillance that disproportionately targeted their communities. The first rebellion erupted in Harlem in 1964. Far larger was the Watts uprising of 1965, which took place in Los Angeles only days after Johnson signed the Voting Rights Act. An estimated 50,000 persons took part in a close to weeklong uprising that was quelled by 15,000 police and National Guardsmen. It left 34 people dead, 23 of whom were killed by the Los Angeles police and National Guard, over 4,000 arrested, and $30 million worth of property destroyed.

By 1967, collective violence had become widespread and frequent. Urban uprisings in large cities that year left 23 dead in Newark and 43 in Detroit, mostly African Americans. In Detroit, entire blocks went up in flames. More than 7,200 arrests were made, and property damage ran into the hundreds of millions of dollars. Seventy other midsize and small cities from Greensboro, North Carolina, to Milwaukee, Wisconsin, witnessed violent outbreaks, a number that would surge in 1968—with 137 separate incidents alone in the month of April following the assassination of Martin Luther King Jr.

The violence led Johnson to appoint a commission headed by Illinois governor Otto Kerner in 1967 to study the causes of the uprisings and propose remedies. The commission's findings blamed the violence on "segregation and poverty" and offered a powerful indictment of "white racism." Its recommendations called for the full integration of Black Americans into the "mainstream of American life" through a massive influx of federal investment into Black communities that would go well beyond the War on Poverty. Without such an investment, the report warned, the nation was in danger of continued incidents of violence, followed by white retaliation, and the forging of a "garrison state." Released in 1968, and published as a paperback, the report sold over 700,000 copies in a few weeks, but few of its recommendations were implemented. Increasingly preoccupied with the war in Vietnam, and finding the report's recommendations politically impractical, Johnson focused instead on curbing the violence through police reform, professionalization, and crime control.

The Northern Black Freedom Struggle

With the violence in the streets of Black urban communities revealing a set of grievances that civil rights legislation left unchanged ("voting rights," one prominent activist declared, "could not be eaten or made into clothing and shelter"), civil rights movement leaders increasingly shifted their focus toward economic goals, looking for ways to "make freedom real" for poor Black Americans. (Black family income was little more than half the white norm.) Already in 1964, King called for a "Bill of Rights for the Disadvantaged" to mobilize the nation's resources to abolish economic deprivation. His proposal was directed against poverty in general, but King also insisted that after "doing something special *against* the Negro for hundreds of years," the United States had an obligation to "do something special *for* him now"—an early call for what would come to be known as "affirmative action."

In 1966, King launched the Chicago Freedom movement, with demands quite different from its predecessors in the South—an end to discrimination by employers and unions, equal access to mortgages, the integration of public housing, and the construction of low-income housing scattered throughout the region. Confronting the entrenched power of Mayor Richard J. Daley's political machine and the ferocious opposition of white home owners, the movement failed. King's tactics—marches, sit-ins, mass arrests—proved ineffective in the face of the North's less pervasive but still powerful system of racial inequality. King's language became more and more radical. He called for nothing less than a "revolution in values" that would create a "better distribution of wealth" for "all God's children."

Malcolm X

The civil rights movement's first phase had produced a clear set of objectives, far-reaching accomplishments, and a series of coherent if sometimes competitive organizations. The second was more diffuse and fragmented, focused less on federal legislative reform and integration than on community control, opening up jobs and representation for African Americans in white-dominated urban politics and establishing Black studies programs on college campuses. Even during the heyday of the integration struggle, the fiery orator Malcolm X had insisted that Blacks must control the political and economic resources of their communities and rely on their own efforts rather than working with whites. His ideas drew upon older Black separatist traditions like Marcus Garvey's Universal Negro Improvement Association (UNIA; discussed in Chapter 19). Malcolm X's parents had been active UNIA organizers. Having committed a string of crimes as a youth, Malcolm Little was converted in jail to the teachings of the Nation of Islam, or Black Muslims, who preached a message of white evil and Black self-discipline. Malcolm dropped his "slave surname" in favor of "X," symbolizing Blacks' separation from their African ancestry. On his release from prison he became a spokesman for the Muslims and a sharp critic of the ideas of integration and nonviolence, and of King's practice of appealing to American values. "I don't see any American dream," he proclaimed. "I see an American nightmare." He called for Black self-defense against violence perpetrated by whites.

On a 1964 trip to Mecca, Saudi Arabia, Islam's spiritual home, Malcolm X witnessed harmony among Muslims of all races. He now began to speak of the possibility of interracial cooperation for radical change in the United States. He broke with the Nation of Islam and formed the Organization for Afro-American Unity. He was assassinated by Nation of Islam members in February 1965. Many white Americans considered Malcolm X an apostle of racial violence, but his appeals to self-defense, community control, and Black nationalism struck a chord among the urban poor and young civil rights activists that resonated well after his death. His *Autobiography*, published in 1966, became a best-seller. Today, streets, parks, and schools are named after him.

The Rise of Black Power

Malcolm X was the intellectual father of **Black Power**, a slogan that came to national attention in 1966 when SNCC leader Stokely Carmichael used it during a civil rights march in Mississippi. Black Power immediately became a rallying cry for those bitter over the federal government's failure to stop violence against civil rights workers, white attempts to determine movement strategy (as at the Democratic convention of 1964), and the civil rights movement's failure to have any impact on the economic problems of the Black urban poor.

Black Power sought to appeal to African Americans to come together as a group to gain access to a wider share of economic and political power. The idea was imprecise enough to encompass distinct visions, ranging from electing more Black officials and supporting Black businesses (hardly radical notions) to the belief that Black Americans were a colonized people whose freedom could be won only through revolutionary struggle for self-determination. In many communities where Black parents felt that the local public education system failed to educate their children adequately, it inspired the establishment of Black-operated local schools that combined traditional learning with an emphasis on pride in African American history and identity. But however employed, the idea reflected the radicalization of young civil rights activists and sparked an explosion of cultural self-assertion. The slogan "Black is Beautiful," a flourishing Black Arts movement, the popularity of African styles of dress, and the "natural," or "Afro," hairdo among both men and women, along with the campaign to establish Black studies programs on campuses, reflected a new sense of group pride.

Inspired by the idea of Black self-determination, SNCC and CORE repudiated their previous interracialism, and new militant groups sprang into existence. Most prominent of the new groups, in terms of publicity, if not numbers, was the Black Panther Party. Founded in Oakland, California, in 1966, it became notorious for advocating armed self-defense in response to police brutality. It demanded the release of Black prisoners because of racism in the criminal justice system. The party's youthful members alarmed whites by wearing military garb, although they also ran health clinics, schools, and children's breakfast programs. But internal disputes and a campaign against the Black Panthers by police and the FBI, which left several leaders dead in shootouts, destroyed the organization. A number of former members successfully made the transition to electoral politics, including Bobby Rush, a long-serving member of Congress from Chicago; Charles Barron, a city councilman in New York and later State Assembly member, and Marion Barry, a four-term mayor of Washington.

By 1967, with the escalation of U.S. military involvement in Vietnam, the War on Poverty ground to a halt. By then, with uprisings punctuating the urban landscape, the antiwar movement assuming massive proportions, and millions of young people ostentatiously rejecting mainstream values, American society faced its greatest crisis since the Depression.

VIETNAM AND THE NEW LEFT

Old and New Lefts

To most Americans, the rise of a protest movement among white youth came as a complete surprise. For most of the century, colleges had been conservative institutions that drew their students from a privileged segment of the population. During the 1950s, young people had been called a "silent generation." If Blacks' grievances appeared self-evident, those of white college students were

Members of Students for a Democratic Society (SDS) in a University of Delaware yearbook photo. Despite their raised fists, they appear eminently respectable compared with radicals who emerged later in the decade. The group is entirely white.

difficult to understand. What persuaded large numbers of children of affluence to reject the values and institutions of their society? In part, the answer lay in a redefinition of the meaning of freedom by what came to be called the **New Left**.

What made the New Left new was its rejection of the intellectual and political categories that had shaped radicalism and liberalism for most of the twentieth century. It challenged not only mainstream America but also what it dismissively called the Old Left. Unlike the Communist Party, it did not take the Soviet Union as a model or see the working class as the main agent of social change. Instead of economic equality and social citizenship, the language of New Deal liberals, the New Left spoke of isolation, and alienation, of powerlessness in the face of bureaucratic institutions and a hunger for authenticity that affluence could not provide. These discontents galvanized a mass movement among what was rapidly becoming a major sector of the American population. By 1968, thanks to the coming of age of the baby-boom generation and the growing number of jobs that required post–high school skills, more than 7 million students attended college, more than the number of farmers or steelworkers.

The New Left was not as new as it claimed. Its call for a democracy of citizen participation harked back to the American Revolution, and its critique of the contrast between American values and American reality, to the abolitionists. Its emphasis on authenticity in the face of conformity recalled the bohemians of the years before World War I, and its critique of consumer culture drew inspiration from 1950s writers on mass society. But the New Left's greatest inspiration was the Black freedom movement. More than any other event, the sit-ins catalyzed white student activism.

Here was the unlikely combination that created the upheaval known as the Sixties—the convergence of society's most excluded members demanding full access to all its benefits, with the children of the middle class rejecting the social mainstream. The Black movement and white New Left shared basic assumptions—that the evils to be corrected were deeply embedded in social institutions and that only direct confrontation could persuade Americans of the urgency of far-reaching change.

The Rise of SDS

The most prominent organization of the student New Left was the **Students for a Democratic Society** (SDS), founded in 1960, as an offshoot of the Socialist League for Industrial Democracy. In 1962, SDS published an influential document, the **Port Huron Statement**, adopted at a meeting of some sixty students in Port Huron, Michigan, that captured the mood and summarized the beliefs of this generation of student protesters. The Port Huron Statement devoted four-fifths of its text to criticism of institutions ranging from political parties to corporations, unions, and the military-industrial complex. But what made the document the guiding spirit of a new radicalism was the remainder, which offered a new vision of social change. "We seek the establishment," it proclaimed, of "a democracy of individual participation, [in which] the individual shares in those social decisions determining the quality and direction of his life." Freedom, for the New Left, meant "participatory democracy." Although rarely defined with precision, this became a standard by which students judged existing social arrangements—workplaces, schools, government—and found them wanting.

By the end of 1962, SDS had grown to 8,000 members. Then, in 1964, events at the University of California at Berkeley revealed the possibility for a far broader mobilization of students in the name of participatory democracy. A Cold War "multiversity," Berkeley was an immense, impersonal institution where enrollments in many classes approached 1,000 students. The spark that set student protests alight was a new rule prohibiting political groups from using a central area of the campus to spread their ideas. Students—including conservatives outraged at being barred from distributing their own literature—responded by creating the Free Speech movement. Freedom of expression, declared Mario Savio, a student leader, "represents the very dignity of what a human being is. . . . That's what marks us off from the stones and the stars. You can speak freely." Likening the university to a factory, Savio called on students to "throw our body against the machines."

Thousands of Berkeley students became involved in the protests in the months that followed. Their program moved from demanding a repeal of the new rule to a critique of the entire structure of the university and of an education geared toward preparing graduates for corporate jobs. When the university gave in on the speech ban early in 1965, one activist exulted that the students had succeeded in reversing "the world-wide drift from freedom."

America and Vietnam

By 1965, the Black movement and the emergence of the New Left had shattered the climate of consensus of the 1950s. But what transformed protest into a full-fledged generational rebellion was the war in Vietnam. The war tragically revealed the danger that Walter Lippmann had warned of at the outset of the Cold War—viewing the entire world and every local situation within it through the either-or lens of an anticommunist crusade. A Vietnam specialist in the State Department who attended a policy meeting in August 1963 later recalled "the abysmal ignorance around the table of the particular facts of Vietnam. . . . They made absolutely no distinctions between countries with completely different historical experiences. . . . They [believed] that we could manipulate other states and build nations; that we knew all the answers."

Few Americans had any knowledge of Vietnam's history and culture. Viewing Asia through the lens of Cold War geopolitics, successive administrations reduced a complex struggle for national independence, led by homegrown communists who enjoyed widespread support throughout their country in addition to Soviet backing, to a test of "containment." As noted in the previous chapter, the Truman and Eisenhower administrations cast their lot with French colonialism in the region. After the French defeat, they financed the creation of a pro-American South Vietnamese government, in violation of the Geneva Accords of 1954 that had promised elections to unify Vietnam. By the 1960s, the United States was committed to the survival of this corrupt regime.

Fear that voters would not forgive them for "losing" Vietnam made it impossible for Presidents Kennedy and Johnson to remove the United States from an increasingly untenable situation. Kennedy's foreign policy advisers saw Vietnam as a test of whether the United States could, through

THE VIETNAM WAR, 1964–1975

A war of aerial bombing and small guerrilla skirmishes rather than fixed land battles, at the time it was fought, Vietnam was among the longest wars in American history and the only one the United States has lost.

"counterinsurgency"—intervention to counter internal uprisings in non-communist countries—halt the spread of Third World revolutions. Despite the dispatch of increased American aid and numerous military advisers, South Vietnamese leader Ngo Dinh Diem lost control of the countryside to the communist-led Viet Cong. Diem resisted American advice to broaden his government's base of support. In October 1963, after large Buddhist demonstrations against his regime, the United States approved a military coup that led to Diem's death. When Kennedy was assassinated the following month, there were 17,000 American military advisers in South Vietnam. Shortly before his death, according to the notes of a White House meeting, Kennedy questioned "the wisdom of involvement in Vietnam." But he took no action to end the American presence.

Lyndon Johnson's War

Lyndon B. Johnson came to the presidency with little experience in foreign relations. Johnson had misgivings about sending American troops to Vietnam. But he was an adept politician and knew that Republicans had used the "loss" of China as a weapon against Truman. "I am not going to be the president," he vowed, "who saw Southeast Asia go the way China went."

In August 1964, North Vietnamese vessels encountered an American ship on a spy mission off its coast. When North Vietnamese patrol boats fired on the American vessel, Johnson proclaimed that the United States was a victim of "aggression." In response, Congress passed the **Gulf of Tonkin resolution**, authorizing the president to take "all necessary measures to repel armed attack" in Vietnam. Only two members—Senators Ernest Gruening of Alaska and Wayne Morse of Oregon—voted against giving Johnson this blank check. The nearest the United States ever came to a formal declaration of war, the resolution passed without any discussion of American goals and strategy in Vietnam.

During the 1964 campaign, Johnson insisted that he had no intention of sending American troops to Vietnam. But immediately after Johnson's reelection, the National Security Council recommended that the United States begin air strikes against North Vietnam and introduce American ground troops in the south. When the Viet Cong in February 1965 attacked an American air base in South Vietnam, Johnson put the plan into effect. At almost the same time, he intervened in the Dominican Republic. Here, military leaders in 1963 had overthrown the left-wing but noncommunist Juan Bosch, the country's first elected president since 1924. In April 1965, another group of military men attempted to restore Bosch to power but were defeated by the ruling junta. Fearing the unrest would lead to "another Cuba," Johnson dispatched 22,000 American troops. The intervention outraged many Latin Americans. But the operation's success seemed to bolster Johnson's determination in Vietnam.

By 1968, the number of American troops in Vietnam exceeded half a million, and the conduct of the war had become more and more brutal. The North Vietnamese mistreated American prisoners of war held in a camp known sardonically by the inmates as the Hanoi Hilton. (One prisoner of war, John McCain, who spent six years there, courageously refused to be exchanged unless his companions were freed with him. McCain later became a senator from Arizona and the Republican candidate for president in 2008.) American planes dropped more tons of bombs on the small countries of North and South Vietnam than both sides used in all of World War II. They spread chemicals that destroyed forests to deprive the Viet Cong of hiding places and dropped incendiary bombs filled with napalm, a gelatinous form of gasoline that clings to the skin of anyone exposed to it as it burns. The army pursued Viet Cong and North Vietnamese forces in "search and destroy" missions that often did not distinguish between combatants and civilians. Weekly reports of enemy losses or "body counts" became a fixation of the administration. But the United States could not break its opponents' ability to fight or make the South Vietnamese government any more able to survive on its own.

The Antiwar Movement

As casualties mounted and American bombs poured down on North and South Vietnam, the Cold War foreign policy consensus began to unravel. By 1968, the war had sidetracked much of the Great Society and had torn families, universities, and the Democratic Party apart. With the entire political leadership, liberal no less than conservative, committed to the war for most of the 1960s, young activists lost all confidence in "the system."

Opposition to the war became the organizing theme that united people with all kinds of doubts and discontents. "We recoil with horror," said a SNCC position paper, "at the inconsistency of a supposedly 'free' society where responsibility to freedom is equated with the responsibility to lend oneself to military aggression." With college students exempted from the draft, the burden of fighting fell on the working class and the poor. In 1967, Martin Luther King Jr. condemned the administration's Vietnam policy as an unconscionable use of violence and for draining resources from needs at home. At this point, King was the most prominent American to speak out against the war.

As for SDS, the war seemed the opposite of participatory democracy, since American involvement had come through secret commitments and decisions made by political elites, with no real public debate. In April 1965, SDS invited opponents of American policy in Vietnam to assemble in Washington, D.C. The turnout of 25,000 amazed the organizers, offering the first hint that the antiwar movement would soon enjoy a mass constituency. At the next antiwar rally, in November 1965, SDS leader Carl Ogelsby openly challenged the foundations of Cold War thinking. He linked Vietnam to a critique of American interventions in Guatemala and Iran, support for South African apartheid, and Johnson's dispatch of troops to the Dominican Republic, all rooted in obsessive anticommunism. Some might feel, Ogelsby concluded, "that I sound mighty anti-American. To these, I say: 'Don't blame *me* for *that*! Blame those who mouthed my liberal values and broke my American heart.'" The speech, observed one reporter, marked a "declaration of independence" for the New Left.

By 1967, young men were burning their draft cards or fleeing to Canada to avoid fighting in what they considered an unjust war. In October of that year, 100,000 antiwar protesters assembled at the Lincoln Memorial in Washington, D.C. Many marched across the Potomac River to the Pentagon, where photographers captured them placing flowers in the rifle barrels of soldiers guarding the nerve center of the American military.

The Counterculture

The New Left's definition of freedom initially centered on participatory democracy, a political concept. But as the 1960s progressed, young Americans' understanding of freedom increasingly expanded to include cultural freedom as well. Although many streams flowed into the generational rebellion known as the **counterculture**, the youth revolt was inconceivable without the war's destruction of young Americans' belief in authority. By the late 1960s, millions of young people openly rejected the values and behavior of their elders. Their ranks included not only college students but also numerous young workers, even though most unions strongly opposed antiwar demonstrations and countercultural displays (a reaction that further separated young radicals from former allies on the traditional left). For the first time in American history, the flamboyant rejection of respectable norms in clothing, language, sexual behavior, and drug use, previously confined to artists and bohemians, became the basis of a mass movement. Its rallying cry was "liberation."

Here was John Winthrop's nightmare of three centuries earlier come to pass—a massive redefinition of freedom as a rejection of all authority. "Your sons and your daughters are beyond your command," Bob Dylan's song "The Times They Are A-Changin'" bluntly informed mainstream America. To be sure, the counterculture in some ways represented not rebellion but the fulfillment of the consumer marketplace. It extended into every realm of life the definition of freedom as the right to individual choice. Given the purchasing power of students and young adults, countercultural emblems—colorful clothing, rock music, images of sexual freedom, even symbols of Black revolution and Native American resistance—were soon being mass-marketed as fashions of the day. Self-indulgence and self-destructive behavior were built into the counterculture. To followers of Timothy Leary, the Harvard scientist turned prophet of mind expansion, the psychedelic drug LSD embodied a new freedom—"the freedom to expand your own consciousness." In 1967, Leary organized a Human Be-In in San Francisco, where he urged a crowd of 20,000 to "turn on, tune in, drop out."

Personal Liberation and the Free Individual

But there was far more to the counterculture than new consumer styles or the famed trio of sex, drugs, and rock and roll. To young dissenters, personal liberation represented a spirit of creative experimentation, a search for a way of life in which friendship and pleasure eclipsed the single-minded pursuit of wealth. It meant a release from bureaucratized education and work, repressive rules of personal behavior, and, above all, a militarized state that, in the name of freedom, rained destruction on a faraway people. It also encouraged new forms of radical action. "Underground" newspapers pioneered a personal and politically committed style of journalism. The Youth International Party, or "yippies," introduced humor and theatricality as elements of protest. From the visitors' gallery of the New York Stock Exchange, yippie founder Abbie Hoffman showered dollar bills onto the floor, bringing trading to a halt as brokers scrambled to retrieve the money.

The counterculture emphasized the ideal of community, establishing quasi-independent neighborhoods in New York City's East Village and San Francisco's Haight-Ashbury district and, in an echo of nineteenth-century utopian communities like New Harmony, some 2,000 communes nationwide. Rock festivals, like Woodstock in upstate New York in 1969, brought together hundreds of thousands of young people to celebrate their alternative lifestyle and independence from adult authority. The opening song at Woodstock, performed by Richie Havens, began with eight repetitions of the single word "freedom."

Religion in the 1960s

Religious conviction, as has been noted, helped to inspire the civil rights movement. A different religious development, the sweeping reforms initiated in Roman Catholic practice (such as the delivery of the Mass in local languages, not Latin) by the Second Vatican Council of 1962–1965, led many priests, nuns, and lay Catholics to become involved in social justice movements. This produced a growing split in the church between liberals and conservatives. Protestant churches also experienced rifts. The National Council of Churches, composed of the more liberal mainline Protestant denominations including United Presbyterian Church and United Church of Christ, came out strongly in support of racial and economic justice. Much like the Social Gospel adherents of the late nineteenth century, they viewed a commitment to social change as a fulfillment of Christian values. Other Protestant churches were divided over civil rights. By the late 1960s, the mainline Protestant churches began a long-term membership decline. Nondenominational evangelical churches surged in growth. In places like California, a "Jesus Movement" blossomed, with evangelical churches welcoming long-haired hippie youth searching for authenticity to worship Christ. Such churches, while theologically conservative, often adopted hip, informal styles, folksy Christian music, large worship services, and a highly personal born-again Christian message. By the late 1970s, they would increasingly mobilize in politics to support conservative social issues. The Sixties also witnessed a burgeoning interest in eastern religions fueled by the counterculture quest for personal authenticity. The Beats of the 1950s had been attracted to Buddhism as a religion that rejected violence and materialism—the antithesis of what they saw as key features of American society. Now, practices derived from Hinduism like yoga and meditation became popular with members of the counterculture (and later entered the suburban mainstream) as a way of promoting spiritual and physical well-being. Some Americans traveled to Tibet and India to seek spiritual guidance from "gurus" (religious teachers) there.

THE NEW MOVEMENTS AND THE RIGHTS REVOLUTION

The civil rights revolution, soon followed by the rise of the New Left, inspired other Americans to voice their grievances and claim their rights. Many borrowed the confrontational tactics of the Black movement and activist students, adopting their language of "power" and "liberation" and their rejection of traditional organizations and approaches. By the late 1960s, new social movements dotted the political landscape.

The counterculture's notion of liberation centered on the free individual. Nowhere was this more evident than in the place occupied by sexual freedom in the generational rebellion. Starting in 1960, the mass marketing of birth-control pills made possible what "free lovers" had long demanded—the separation of sex from procreation. By the late 1960s, sexual freedom had become as much an element of the youth rebellion as long hair, drugs, and rock music. The sexual revolution was central to another mass movement that emerged in the 1960s—the "second wave" of feminism.

The Women's Rights Movement

The achievement of the vote had not seemed to affect women's lack of power and opportunity. When the 1960s began, only a handful of women held political office, newspapers divided job ads into "male" and "female" sections, with the latter limited to low-wage clerical positions, and major universities limited the number of female students they accepted. In many states, husbands still controlled their wives' earnings. As late as 1970, the Ohio Supreme Court held that a wife was "at most a superior servant to her husband," without "legally recognized feelings or rights."

Concerns that the country was wasting its "woman power," a potential weapon in the Cold War, led Kennedy to establish the President's Commission on the Status of Women in 1961. Chaired by Eleanor Roosevelt until her death in 1962, the commission's final report found widespread discrimination in the workplace and called for opening up opportunities. In 1963, Congress passed the Equal Pay Act, barring sex discrimination among holders of the same jobs. Slowly, the law began to address feminist concerns. The Civil Rights Act of 1964 banned discrimination on the grounds of sex as well as race (along with religion and national origin). Civil rights and women's rights activists such as lawyer Pauli Murray had pressed for the inclusion of sex, finding allies among congressional opponents of civil rights who hoped, wrongly, that including the provision would derail the whole bill.

The National Organization for Women

These changes marked the emergence of a new wave of feminist activism. The public reawakening of feminist consciousness was signaled by the publication in 1963 of Betty Friedan's **The Feminine Mystique**. Friedan had written pioneering articles during the 1940s on pay discrimination against women workers and racism in the workplace for the newspaper of the United Electrical Workers' union. But, like other social critics, she now took as her themes the emptiness of consumer culture and the discontents of the middle class. Her opening chapter, "The Problem That Has No Name," painted a devastating picture of talented, educated women trapped in a world that viewed marriage and motherhood as their primary goals. Somehow, after more than a century of agitation for access to the public sphere, women's lives still centered on the home. In Moscow in 1959, Richard Nixon had made the suburban home an emblem of American freedom. For Friedan, invoking the era's most powerful symbol of evil, it was a "comfortable concentration camp."

Friedan's book struck a powerful chord among many college-educated women who had married young, had children during the baby boom, and whose lives now revolved around their families. The book quickly became a best-seller, and Friedan was deluged with letters by readers. "Freedom," wrote an Atlanta woman, "was a word I had always taken for granted. [I now realized that] I had voluntarily enslaved myself." To be sure, a few of Friedan's correspondents insisted that for a woman to create "a comfortable, happy home for her family" was "what God intended." But the immediate result of *The Feminine Mystique* was to focus attention on yet another gap between American rhetoric and American reality.

Feminists had hoped that establishment of the Equal Employment Opportunity Commission under the 1964 Civil Rights Act would provide a powerful lever to break down sex discrimination. But women's rights advocates were disappointed that the commission did not seem to take sex discrimination

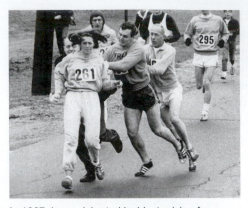

In 1967, in a celebrated incident arising from the new feminism, a race official tried to eject Kathrine Switzer from the Boston Marathon, only to be pushed aside by other runners. Considered too fragile for the marathon (whose course covers more than twenty-six miles), women were prohibited from running. Switzer completed the race, and today hundreds of thousands of women around the world compete in marathons each year.

seriously, refusing to bar employment advertisements segregated by sex, such as ads for female secretaries. Women's rights leaders pressed for bolder action, founding the **National Organization for Women** (NOW) in 1966, with Friedan as president. Modeled on civil rights organizations, it demanded equal opportunity in jobs, education, and political participation and attacked the "false image of women" spread by the mass media.

Women's Liberation

If NOW grew out of a resurgence of feminism that sought to break down barriers to women's full participation in all aspects of American life, a different female revolt was brewing within the civil rights and student movements. As in the days of abolitionism, young women who had embraced an ideology of social equality and personal freedom and learned methods of political organizing encountered inequality and sexual exploitation. Women like Ella Baker and Fannie Lou Hamer had played major roles in grassroots civil rights organizing. But many women in the movement found themselves relegated to typing, cooking, and cleaning for male coworkers. Some were pressured to engage in sexual liaisons. Echoing the words of Abby Kelley a century earlier, a group of female SNCC activists concluded in a 1965 memorandum that "there seem to be many parallels that can be drawn between the treatment of Negroes and the treatment of women in our society as a whole." What bothered them most was the status of women within the movement, where assumptions of male supremacy seemed as deeply rooted as in society at large.

The same complaints arose in SDS. "The Movement is supposed to be for human liberation," wrote one student leader. "How come the condition of women inside it is no better than outside?" The rapidly growing number of women in college provided a ready-made constituency for the new feminism. By 1967, women throughout the country were establishing "consciousness-raising" groups to discuss the sources of their discontent. The time, many concluded, had come to establish a movement of their own, more radical than NOW.

Personal Freedom

The women's liberation movement inspired a major expansion of the idea of freedom by insisting that it should be applied to the most intimate realms of life. Introducing the terms "sexism" and "sexual politics" and the phrase "the personal is political" into public debate, it insisted that sexual relations, conditions of marriage, and standards of beauty were as much "political" questions as the war, civil rights, and the class tensions that had traditionally inspired the left to action. The idea that family life is not off-limits to considerations of power and justice repudiated the family-oriented public culture of the 1950s, and it permanently changed Americans' definition of freedom.

Radical feminists' first public campaign demanded the repeal of state laws that underscored women's lack of self-determination by banning abortions or leaving it up to physicians to decide whether a pregnancy could be terminated. Without the right to control her own reproduction, wrote one activist, "woman's other 'freedoms' are tantalizing mockeries that cannot be exercised." In 1969, a group of feminists disrupted legislative hearings on New York's law banning abortions, where the experts scheduled to testify consisted of fourteen men and a Roman Catholic nun.

The call for legalized abortions merged the nineteenth-century demand that a woman control her own body with the Sixties emphasis on sexual freedom. But the concerns of women's liberation went far beyond sexuality. *Sisterhood Is Powerful*, an influential collection of essays, manifestos, and personal accounts published in 1970, touched on a remarkable array of issues, from violence against women to inequalities in the law, churches, workplaces, and family life. By this time, feminist ideas had entered the mainstream. In 1962, a poll showed that two-thirds of American women did not feel themselves to be victims of discrimination. By 1974, two-thirds did.

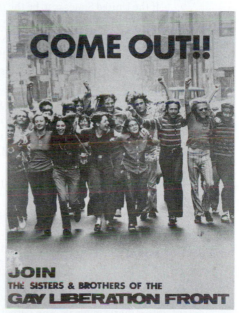

A 1970 poster urging gay men and lesbians to join the Gay Liberation Front, one of the numerous movements that sprang to life in the late 1960s.

Gay Liberation

In a decade full of surprises, perhaps the greatest of all was the emergence of the movement for gay liberation. Efforts of one kind or another for greater rights

From CLYDE WARRIOR, "TO SURVIVE AS A PEOPLE" (1964)

The National Indian Youth council, founded in 1961, brought together a new generation of young Indian activists. Clyde Warrior of the Ponca tribe, one of its most outspoken leaders, outlines their grievances and demands in the following 1964 statement. He embraces the language of "internal colonialism," increasingly deployed by minorities, to press for self-determination and empowerment.

The NIYC is very much in favor of Indian self-government, real, not fictional self-government, and self-determination. . . .

* * *

This system under which Indians live, a horrendous combination of colonialism, segregation, and discrimination has been going on for over 100 years. . . . NIYC feels that there must be some drastic steps in the way of legislation to ameliorate the current American Indian situation. . . .

1. Decision-making power over the lives of people in an Indian community must be legally taken out of the hands of a federal bureau and put where it belongs in the hands of the people, and the community. America cannot afford to continue a system of repressive internal colonialism which parallels the Soviet treatment of its national minorities. . . . Indians must have real self-government.

2. . . . If the United States is to be the moral force in the world which she has aspired to be, morality must begin at home. We only ask the American people to honor their word. Unilateral action by Congress or state governments in regard to Indian treaties is immoral. Indian consent not "consultation" is needed in any restructuring of the relationship, spelled out in treaties and statutes, between the Federal government and Indian tribes.

3. A drastic and revolutionary economic and education program in which Indian communities make the basic decisions with the BIA in an advisory capacity, is needed to amend the century of discrimination which has caused the present conditions of American Indians. The trend must be reversed and Indians must be able to lead a decent life in their own communities.

. . . Colonial rule and deception of Indian communities must not be allowed to continue. . . .

The indignity of a school system which is calculated purposely to turn children against their parents is an aspect of state control as only seen in Nazi Germany, Communist China, and American Indian reservations. This kind of discrimination is an indignity that no other ethnic group has to suffer.

* * *

Disgrace against the Indian in his own home and community is intolerable. It is inconsistent with American Ideals. The perpetual threat that his treaties will be disregarded and his community broken apart is eroding the Indian character and sapping his very life blood. These indignities must be wiped away and the Indian, like any other American, must be able to lead a decent life in a free community.

From STATEMENT OF PURPOSE, NATIONAL ORGANIZATION FOR WOMEN (1966)

Founded in 1966, the National Organization for Women gave voice to the movement for equality for women known as the "second wave" of feminism. Written by Betty Friedan and adopted at the group's organizing meeting in Washington, D.C., the statement of purpose outlined a wide range of areas, public and private, where women continued to be denied full freedom.

The time has come for a new movement toward true equality for all women in America, and toward a fully equal partnership of the sexes, as part of the worldwide revolution of human rights now taking place within and beyond our national borders.

The purpose of NOW is to take action to bring women into full participation in the mainstream of American society now, exercising all the privileges and responsibilities thereof in truly equal partnership with men. . . .

We organize to initiate or support action, nationally, or in any part of this nation, by individuals or organizations, to break through the silken curtain of prejudice and discrimination against women in government, industry, and professions, the churches, the political parties, the judiciary, the labor unions, in education, science, medicine, law, religion and every other field of importance in American society. . . .

The actual position of women in the United States has declined, and is declining, to an alarming degree throughout the 1950's and '60s. . . . Working women are becoming increasingly—not less— concentrated on the bottom of the job ladder. . . . Today, women earn only one in three of the B.A.'s and M.A.'s granted, and one in ten of the Ph.D.'s. In all the professions considered of importance to society, and in the executive ranks of industry and government, women are losing ground. Where they are present it is only a token handful. Women comprise less than 1% of federal judges; less than 4% of all lawyers; 7% of doctors. . . .

We do not accept the traditional assumption that a woman has to choose between marriage and motherhood, on the one hand, and serious participation in industry or the professions on the other. . . . True equality of opportunity and freedom of choice for women requires such practical, and possible innovations as a nationwide network of child-care centers which will make it unnecessary for women to retire completely from society until their children are grown. . . .

We believe that a true partnership between the sexes demands a different concept of marriage and equitable sharing of the responsibilities of home and children and of the economic burdens of their support. We believe that proper recognition should be given to the economic and social value of homemaking and childcare. . . .

QUESTIONS

1. *How does Warrior highlight contradictions between professed ideas about liberty and the situation faced by American Indians?*

2. *What social changes does NOW believe necessary to enable women to enjoy equality and freedom?*

3. *How do the two documents differ in their visions of freedom?*

for racial minorities and women had a long history. Gay Americans, wrote Harry Hay, who in 1951 founded the Mattachine Society, the first gay rights organization, were "the one group of disadvantaged people who didn't even think of themselves as a group." Gay men and lesbians had long been stigmatized as sinful or mentally disordered. Most states made homosexual acts illegal, and police regularly harassed the gay subcultures that existed in major cities like San Francisco and New York. McCarthyism, which viewed homosexuality as a source of national weakness, made the discrimination to which gays were subjected even worse. Although gay persons had achieved considerable success in many fields, especially the arts and fashion, most kept their sexual orientation secret, or "in the closet."

The Mattachine Society worked to persuade the public that apart from their sexual orientation, gays were average Americans who ought not to be persecuted. But as with other groups, the Sixties transformed the gay movement. If one moment marked the advent of "gay liberation," it was a 1969 police raid on the **Stonewall Inn** in New York's Greenwich Village, a gathering place for homosexuals. Rather than bowing to police harassment, as in the past, gays fought back. Five days of rioting followed, and a militant movement was born. Gay men and lesbians stepped out of the "closet" to insist that sexual orientation is a matter of rights, power, and identity. Prejudice against them persisted. But within a few years, "gay pride" marches were being held in numerous cities.

Latino Activism

As in the case of Blacks, a movement for legal rights had long flourished among Mexican Americans. But the mid-1960s saw the flowering of a new militancy

Union activist César Chávez (*right*) breaks bread with Senator Robert F. Kennedy to mark the end of Chávez's twenty-five-day hunger strike in support of striking workers in California's grape fields.

challenging the group's second-class economic status. Like Black Power advocates, the movement emphasized pride in both the Mexican past and the new Chicano culture that had arisen in the United States. Unlike the Black Power movement and SDS, it was closely linked to labor struggles. Beginning in 1965, César Chávez, the son of migrant farm workers and a disciple of King, and Dolores Huerta, a longtime labor activist whose father was a migrant worker and whose mother owned a restaurant and hotel that catered to low-wage farm laborers, led a series of nonviolent protests, including marches, fasts, and a national boycott of California grapes, to pressure growers to agree to labor contracts with the United Farm Workers union (UFW). The UFW was as much a mass movement for civil rights as a campaign for economic betterment. The boycott mobilized Latino communities throughout the Southwest and drew national attention to the pitifully low wages and oppressive working conditions of migrant laborers. In 1970, the major growers agreed to contracts with the UFW.

In New York City, the Young Lords Organization, modeled on the Black Panthers, staged street demonstrations to protest the high unemployment rate among the city's Puerto Ricans and the lack of city services in Latino neighborhoods. (In one protest, they dumped garbage on city streets to draw attention to the city's failure to collect refuse in poor areas.) Like SNCC and SDS, the Latino movement gave rise to feminist dissent. Many Chicano and Puerto Rican men regarded feminist demands as incompatible with the Latino heritage of *machismo* (an exaggerated sense of manliness, including the right to dominate women). Young female activists, however, viewed the sexual double standard and the inequality of women as incompatible with freedom for all members of *la raza* (the race, or people).

Indigenous Activism and Self-Determination

The 1960s also witnessed an upsurge of Indian protest action and militancy. A group of Indian college students rejected the moderate strategies of the National Congress of American Indians (discussed in Chapter 23), founding the National Indian Youth Council in 1961. Using the tactics of the civil rights movement, they brought national visibility to the campaign to restore Native American fishing rights in the Northwest threatened by state governments by conducting "fish-ins." The courts eventually sided with Native Americans in the 1970s.

Like other minorities, Indian activists compared their own status to that of underdeveloped countries overseas. They demanded not simply economic aid but self-determination, like the emerging nations of the Third World. Using language typical of the late 1960s, Clyde Warrior, president of the National Indian Youth Council, declared, "We are not free in the most basic sense of the word. We are not allowed to make those basic human choices about our personal life and the destiny of our communities."

To empower their communities, young urban Native Americans, much like urban Black youth, organized against police discrimination. One group of Minneapolis Native American youth formed neighborhood patrols to monitor police. Soon seeing the need for more militant national action, they founded the **American Indian Movement** (AIM) calling for self-determination and the restoration of economic resources guaranteed in treaties. AIM's establishment

The occupation of Alcatraz Island in San Francisco Bay in 1969 by "Indians of All Tribes" symbolized the emergence of a new militancy among Native Americans.

by young urban Indians showed that urbanization did not abolish Native American identity but instead forged a new generation of pan-Indian activists.

One year later, a group calling itself "Indians of All Tribes" occupied (or from their point of view, reoccupied) Alcatraz Island in San Francisco Bay, claiming that it had been illegally seized from its original inhabitants. The nonviolent protest, which lasted eighteen months, coincided with the rise of the Red Power movement, a period of militant activism seeking greater self-government and redress for the long history of broken treaty rights. Activists took over the Bureau of Indian Affairs in 1972, fortifying windows and doors with overturned desks and filing cabinets. Shortly thereafter activists also occupied Wounded Knee on the Pine Ridge reservation, the site of the massacre of Native Americans by army troops in 1890. A standoff between law enforcement and AIM members ended after seventy-one days. The arrest and imprisonment of key leaders in ongoing confrontations with police destroyed the organization. The outpouring of Indigenous activism in the late 1960s and early 1970s, however, called national attention to the centuries of injustice faced by Native Americans and contributed to significant changes in federal Indian policy in the 1970s.

Silent Spring

Liberation movements among racial minorities, women, and gays challenged long-standing social inequalities. Another movement, environmentalism, called into question different pillars of American life—the equation of progress with endless increases in consumption and the faith that science, technology, and economic growth would advance the social welfare. Concern for preserving the natural environment dated back to the creation of national parks and other conservation efforts during the Progressive era. But in keeping with the spirit of the Sixties, the new environmentalism was more activist and youth oriented, and it spoke the language of empowering citizens to participate in decisions that affected their lives. Its emergence reflected the very affluence celebrated by proponents of the American Way. As the "quality of life"—including physical fitness, health, and opportunities to enjoy leisure activities—occupied a greater role in the lives of middle-class Americans, the environmental consequences of economic growth received increased attention. When the 1960s began, complaints were already being heard about the bulldozing of forests for suburban development and the contamination produced by laundry detergents and chemical lawn fertilizers seeping into drinking supplies.

The publication in 1962 of **Silent Spring** by the marine biologist Rachel Carson brought home to millions of readers the effects of DDT, an insecticide widely used by home owners and farmers against mosquitoes, gypsy moths, and other insects. In chilling detail, Carson related how DDT killed birds and animals and caused sickness among humans. Chemical and pesticide companies launched a campaign to discredit her—some critics called the book part of a communist plot. *Time* magazine even condemned Carson as "hysterical" and "emotional"—words typically used by men to discredit women.

The New Environmentalism

Carson's work launched the modern environmental movement. The Sierra Club, founded in the 1890s to preserve forests, saw its membership more than triple, and other groups sprang into existence to alert the country to the dangers of water contamination, air pollution, lead in paint, and the extinction of animal species. Nearly every state quickly banned the use of DDT. In 1969, television brought home to a national audience the death of birds and fish and the despoiling of beaches caused by a major oil spill off the coast of California, exposing the environmental dangers of oil transportation and ocean drilling for oil.

The postwar economic boom, with its seemingly limitless demand for resources like land, energy, and building materials, placed enormous stress on the natural environment. As highways and suburbs paved over the landscape, more and more Americans became committed to the survival of places of natural beauty.

Despite vigorous opposition from business groups that considered its proposals a violation of property rights, environmentalism attracted the broadest bipartisan support of any of the new social movements. Under Republican president Richard Nixon, Congress during the late 1960s and early 1970s passed a series of measures to protect the environment, including the Clean Air and Clean Water Acts and the Endangered Species Act. On April 22, 1970, the first Earth Day, some 20 million people, most of them under the age of thirty, participated in rallies, concerts, and teach-ins.

Closely related to environmentalism was the consumer movement, spearheaded by the lawyer Ralph Nader. His book *Unsafe at Any Speed* (1965) exposed how auto manufacturers produced highly dangerous vehicles. General Motors, whose Chevrolet Corvair Nader singled out for its tendency to roll over in certain driving situations, hired private investigators to discredit him. When their campaign was exposed, General Motors paid Nader a handsome settlement, which he used to fund investigations of other dangerous products and of misleading advertising.

Nader's campaigns laid the groundwork for the numerous new consumer protection laws and regulations of the 1970s. Unlike 1960s movements that emphasized personal liberation, environmentalism and the consumer movement called for limiting some kinds of freedom—especially the right to use private property in any way the owner desired—in the name of a greater common good.

The Rights Revolution

It is one of the more striking ironies of the 1960s that although the "rights revolution" began in the streets, it achieved constitutional legitimacy through the Supreme Court, historically the most conservative branch of government. Under the guidance of Chief Justice Earl Warren, the Court vastly expanded the rights enjoyed by all Americans and placed them beyond the reach of legislative and local majorities.

As noted in Chapter 21, the Court's emergence as a vigorous guardian of civil liberties had been foreshadowed in 1937, when it abandoned its commitment to freedom of contract while declaring that the right of free expression deserved added protection. The McCarthy era halted progress toward a broader conception of civil liberties. It resumed on June 17, 1957, known as "Red Monday" by conservatives, when the Court moved to rein in the anticommunist crusade. The justices overturned convictions of individuals for advocating the overthrow of the government, failing to answer questions before the House Un-American Activities Committee, and refusing to disclose their political beliefs to state officials. The government, Warren declared, could prosecute illegal actions, but not "unorthodoxy or dissent." By the time Warren retired in 1969, the Court had reaffirmed the right of even the most unpopular viewpoints to First Amendment protection and had dismantled the Cold War loyalty security system.

Civil liberties had gained strength in the 1930s because of association with the rights of labor; in the 1950s and 1960s, they became intertwined with civil rights. Beginning with *NAACP v. Alabama* in 1958, the Court struck down southern laws that sought to destroy civil rights organizations by forcing them to make public their membership lists. In addition, in the landmark ruling in *New York Times v. Sullivan* (1964), it overturned a libel judgment by an Alabama jury against the nation's leading newspaper for carrying an advertisement critical of how local officials treated civil rights demonstrators. The "central meaning of the First Amendment," the justices declared, lay in the right of citizens to criticize their government. For good measure, they declared the Sedition Act of 1798 unconstitutional over a century and a half after it had expired. Before the 1960s, few Supreme Court cases had dealt with newspaper publishing. *Sullivan* created the modern constitutional law of freedom of the press.

Richard and Mildred Loving with their children at their home in 1967. Their desire to live in Virginia as man and wife led to a Supreme Court decision declaring unconstitutional state laws that barred interracial marriages.

The Court in the 1960s continued the push toward racial equality, overturning numerous local Jim Crow laws. In *Loving v. Virginia* (1967), it declared unconstitutional the laws still on the books in sixteen states that prohibited interracial marriage. This aptly named case arose from the interracial marriage of Richard and Mildred Loving. Barred by Virginia law from marrying, they did so in Washington, D.C., and later returned to their home state. Two weeks after their arrival, the local sheriff entered their home in the middle of the night, roused the couple from bed, and arrested them. The Lovings were sentenced to five years in prison, although the judge gave them the option of leaving Virginia instead. They departed for Washington, but five years later, wishing to return, they sued in federal court, claiming that their rights had been violated.

Policing the States

The Court simultaneously pushed forward the process of imposing upon the states the obligation to respect the liberties outlined in the Bill of Rights. It required states to abide by protections against illegal search and seizure, the right of a defendant to a speedy trial, the prohibition against cruel and unusual punishment, and the right of poor persons accused of a crime to receive counsel from publicly supplied attorneys. Among the most important of these decisions was the 5-4 ruling in *Miranda v. Arizona* (1966). This held that an individual in police custody must be informed of the rights to remain silent and to confer with a lawyer before answering questions and must be told that any statements might be used in court. The decision made "Miranda warnings" standard police practice.

The Court also assumed the power to oversee the fairness of democratic procedures at the state and local levels. *Baker v. Carr* (1962) established the principle that districts electing members of state legislatures and Congress must be equal in population. This "one man, one vote" principle overturned apportionment systems in numerous states that had allowed individuals in sparsely inhabited rural areas to enjoy the same representation as residents of populous city districts.

The justices also moved to reinforce the "wall of separation" between church and state. In 1961, they unanimously declared unconstitutional a clause in Maryland's constitution requiring that public officials declare their belief "in the existence of God." In the following year, in *Engel v. Vitale*, they decreed that prayers and Bible readings in public schools also violated the First Amendment. President Kennedy pointed out that Americans remained perfectly free to pray at home or in church, but these rulings proved to be the most unpopular of all the Warren Court's decisions. Polls showed that 80 percent of Americans favored allowing prayer in public schools.

The Right to Privacy

The Warren Court not only expanded existing liberties but also outlined entirely new rights in response to the rapidly changing contours of American society. Most dramatic was its assertion of a constitutional right to privacy in **Griswold v. Connecticut** (1965), which overturned a state law prohibiting the use of contraceptives. Justice William O. Douglas, who wrote the decision, had once declared, "The right to be let alone is the beginning of all freedom." Apart from decisions of the 1920s that affirmed the right to marry and raise children without government interference, however, few legal precedents existed regarding privacy. The Constitution does not mention the word. Nonetheless, Douglas argued that a constitutionally protected "zone of privacy" within marriage could be inferred from the "penumbras" (shadows) of the Bill of Rights.

Griswold linked privacy to the sanctity of marriage. But the Court soon transformed it into a right of individuals. It extended access to birth control to unmarried adults and ultimately to minors—an admission by the Court that law could not reverse the sexual revolution. These decisions led directly to the most controversial decision that built on the rulings of the Warren Court (even though it occurred in 1973, four years after Warren's retirement). This was **Roe v. Wade**, which created a constitutional right to terminate a pregnancy. The Court declared access to abortion a fundamental freedom protected by the Constitution, a fulfillment of radical feminists' earliest demand. *Roe* provoked vigorous opposition, which has continued to this day. Only two states banned contraception when *Griswold* was decided; *Roe* invalidated the laws of no fewer than forty-six.

Griswold and *Roe* unleashed a flood of rulings and laws that seemed to accept the feminist view of the family as a collection of sovereign individuals rather than a unit with a single head. The legal rights of women within the domestic sphere expanded dramatically. Law enforcement authorities for the first time began to prosecute crimes like rape and assault by husbands against their wives. Today, some notion of privacy is central to most Americans' conception of freedom.

The rights revolution completed the transformation of American freedom from a set of entitlements enjoyed mainly by white men into an open-ended claim to equality, recognition, and self-determination. For the rest of the century, the government and legal system would be inundated by demands by aggrieved groups of all kinds, and the Supreme Court would devote much of its time to defining the rights of Americans.

1968

A Year of Turmoil

The Sixties reached their climax in 1968, a year when momentous events succeeded each other so rapidly that the foundations of society seemed to be dissolving. Late January 1968 saw the **Tet offensive**, in which Viet Cong and North Vietnamese troops launched well-organized uprisings in cities throughout South Vietnam, completely surprising American military leaders. The United States drove back the offensive and inflicted heavy losses. But the intensity of the fighting, brought into America's homes on television, shattered public confidence in the Johnson administration, which had repeatedly proclaimed victory to be "just around the corner." Leading members of the press and political establishment joined the chorus criticizing American involvement. Eugene McCarthy, an antiwar senator from Minnesota, announced that he would seek the Democratic nomination for president. Aided by a small army of student volunteers, McCarthy received more than 40 percent of the vote in the New Hampshire primary. With public support dissolving, Johnson rejected the military's request to send 200,000 more troops to Vietnam. Johnson then stunned the nation by announcing that he had decided not to seek reelection. Peace talks soon opened in Paris.

Meanwhile, Martin Luther King Jr. was organizing a Poor People's March, hoping to bring thousands of demonstrators to Washington to demand increased anti-poverty efforts. The campaign included not just poor Blacks but also Puerto Ricans, Mexicans, and a Native American contingent. King did not live long enough to see the march. On April 4, having traveled to Memphis to support a strike of the city's grossly underpaid Black garbage collectors, King was killed by a white assassin. The greatest outbreak of urban violence in the nation's history followed in ghettos across the country. Washington, D.C., had to be occupied by soldiers before order was restored. As a gesture to King's memory, Congress passed its last major civil rights law, the Open Housing Act, which prohibited discrimination in the sale and rental of homes and apartments, although with weak enforcement mechanisms.

At the end of April, students protesting Columbia University's involvement in defense research and its plan to build a gymnasium in a public park occupied seven campus buildings. New York police removed them in an assault that left hundreds of protesters and bystanders injured and led to a strike that closed the campus. In June, a young Palestinian nationalist assassinated Robert F. Kennedy, who was seeking the Democratic nomination as an opponent of the war. In August, tens of thousands of antiwar activists descended on Chicago for protests at the Democratic national convention, where the delegates nominated Vice President Hubert Humphrey as their presidential candidate. The city's police, never known for restraint, assaulted the marchers with nightsticks, producing hundreds of injuries outside the convention hall and pandemonium inside it.

A later investigation called the event a "police riot." Nonetheless, the government indicted eight political radicals for conspiring to incite the violence. They included Tom Hayden of SDS, yippie leader Abbie Hoffman, and Bobby Seale of the Black Panthers. Five were found guilty after a tumultuous trial. But an appeals court overturned the convictions because Judge Julius Hoffman (no relation to Abbie Hoffman) had been flagrantly biased against the defendants.

The Global 1968

Like 1848 and 1919, 1968 was a year of worldwide upheaval. In many countries, young radicals challenged existing power structures, often borrowing language and strategies from the decade's social movements in the United States and adapting them to their own circumstances. Television carried events in one country instantaneously across the globe.

Massive antiwar demonstrations took place in London, Rome, Paris, Munich, and Tokyo, leading to clashes with police and scores of injuries. In Italy, students occupied university buildings, bringing education to a halt. In Paris, a nationwide student uprising began in May 1968 that echoed American demands for educational reform and personal liberation. Unlike in the United States, millions of French workers soon joined the protest, adding their own demands for higher wages and greater democracy in the workplace. The result was a general strike that paralyzed the country and nearly led to the collapse of the government before it ended. In communist Czechoslovakia, leaders bent on reform came to power by promising to institute "socialism with a human face," only to be ousted by a Soviet invasion. Soldiers fired on students demonstrating for greater democracy on the eve of the opening of the Olympic Games in Mexico City, leading to more than 500 deaths. In Northern Ireland, which remained part of Great Britain after the rest of Ireland achieved independence, the police attacked a peaceful march of Catholics demanding an end to religious discrimination who were inspired by the American civil rights movement. This event marked the beginning of The Troubles, a period of both peaceful protest and violent conflict in the region that did not end until the turn of the twenty-first century.

And throughout the world, the second wave of American feminism found echoes among women who resented being relegated to unequal citizenship. As in the United States, personal liberation, including a woman's right to control her own body, became a rallying cry. In Catholic European countries like France and Italy, women's movements won significant legal changes, making it easier to obtain divorces and decriminalizing abortion. *Our Bodies, Ourselves*, a book originally published in 1973 by a group of Boston women, dealt frankly with widely misunderstood aspects of women's health, including pregnancy and childbirth, menopause, birth control, and sexually transmitted diseases. It was quickly translated into twenty languages.

Nixon's Comeback

In the United States, instead of radical change, the year's events opened the door for a conservative reaction. Turmoil in the streets produced a demand for public order. Black militancy produced white "backlash," which played an increasing role in politics. The fact that the unelected Supreme Court was inventing and protecting "rights" fed the argument that faraway bureaucrats rode roughshod over local traditions.

In August, Richard Nixon capped a remarkable political comeback by winning the Republican nomination. He campaigned as the champion of the "silent majority"—ordinary Americans who believed that change had gone too far—and called for a renewed commitment to "law and order." Humphrey could not overcome the deep divide in his party. With 43 percent of the vote, Nixon had only a razor-thin margin over his Democratic rival. But George Wallace, running as an independent and appealing to resentments against Blacks' gains, Great Society programs, and the Warren Court, received an additional 13 percent. Taken together, the Nixon and Wallace totals, which included a considerable number of former Democratic voters, indicated that four years after Johnson's landslide election ushered in the Great Society, liberalism was on the defensive.

The year 1968 did not mark the end of the 1960s. The Great Society would achieve an unlikely culmination during the Nixon administration. The second wave of feminism achieved its largest following during the 1970s. Nixon's election did, however, inaugurate a period of growing conservatism in American politics. The conservative ascendancy would usher in yet another chapter in the story of American freedom.

The Legacy of the Sixties

The 1960s transformed American life in ways unimaginable when the decade began. It produced new rights and new understandings of freedom. It made possible the entrance of numerous members of racial minorities into the mainstream of American life, while leaving unsolved the problem of urban poverty. It set in motion a transformation of the status of women. It changed what Americans expected from government—from clean air and water to medical coverage in old age. At the same time, it undermined public confidence in national leaders. Relations between young and old, men and women, and white and non-white, along with every institution in society, changed as a result.

Just as the Civil War and New Deal established the framework for future political debates, so, it seemed, Americans were condemned to refight the battles of the 1960s long after the decade ended. Race relations, feminism, social policy, the nation's proper role in world affairs—these issues hardly originated in the 1960s. But the events of those years made them more pressing and more divisive. As the country became more conservative, the Sixties would be blamed for every imaginable social ill, from crime and drug abuse to a decline of respect for authority. Yet during the 1960s, the United States became a more open, more tolerant—in a word, a freer—country.

CHAPTER REVIEW

REVIEW QUESTIONS

1. *How did the idea of a "zone of privacy" build on or change earlier notions of rights and freedom?*

2. *In what ways were President Kennedy's foreign policy decisions shaped by Cold War ideology?*

3. *How did immigration policies change in these years, and what were the consequences for the composition of the population in the United States?*

4. Explain why many Blacks, especially in the North, did not believe that the civil rights legislation went far enough in promoting Black freedom.

5. What were the effects of President Johnson's Great Society and War on Poverty programs?

6. In what ways was the New Left not as new as it claimed?

7. How did the goals and actions of the United States in Vietnam cause controversy at home and abroad?

8. Discuss the impact of the civil rights movement on other movements for social change in the 1960s.

9. Identify the origins, goals, and composition of the feminist, or women's liberation, movement.

10. Describe how the social movements of the 1960s in the United States became part of global movements for change by 1968. How did those connections affect the United States' position in the world?

11. How did the counterculture expand the meaning of freedom in these years?

KEY TERMS

sit-in (p. 992)

Student Nonviolent Coordinating Committee (p. 993)

Freedom Rides (p. 993)

March on Washington (p. 996)

Bay of Pigs invasion (p. 998)

Cuban missile crisis (p. 998)

Civil Rights Act (p. 1000)

Voting Rights Act (p. 1004)

Hart-Celler Act (p. 1004)

Great Society (p. 1005)

War on Poverty (p. 1006)

Black Power (p. 1010)

New Left (p. 1012)

Students for a Democratic Society (p. 1013)

Port Huron Statement (p. 1013)

Gulf of Tonkin resolution (p. 1016)

counterculture (p. 1018)

The Feminine Mystique (p. 1021)

National Organization for Women (p. 1022)

Stonewall Inn (p. 1026)

American Indian Movement (p. 1027)

Silent Spring (p. 1029)

Griswold v. Connecticut (p. 1032)

Roe v. Wade (p. 1032)

Tet offensive (p. 1033)

Go to INQUIZITIVE

To see what you know—and learn what you've missed—with personalized feedback along the way.

CHAPTER 26

THE CONSERVATIVE TURN

1969–1988

FOCUS QUESTIONS

- *What were the major policies of the Nixon administration on social and economic issues?*

- *How did the ongoing rights revolutions lead to profound changes in American social life?*

- *How did Vietnam and the Watergate scandal affect popular trust in the government?*

- *In what ways did the opportunities of most Americans diminish in the 1970s?*

- *What were the roots of the rise of conservatism in the 1970s?*

- *How did the Reagan presidency affect American aims at home and abroad?*

On October 27, 1964, Ronald Reagan, a well-known movie star, stood before a Los Angeles audience to campaign for Republican presidential nominee Barry Goldwater. The nation, Reagan warned, faced a crossroads in the struggle for liberty. The choice was to move "up to the ultimate in individual freedom" or down to the welfare state and, eventually, the "totalitarianism of the ant heap." The nationally televised speech launched Reagan's political career, even though, as noted in the previous chapter, voters emphatically rejected Goldwater and his conservative philosophy. That philosophy, however, remained the bedrock of conservatism for years to come: intense anticommunism, a critique of the welfare state for destroying "the dignity of the individual," and a demand for cuts in taxes and government regulations. Less than two decades later, Reagan brought these ideas to the White House.

More than any other previous president, Reagan made freedom his watchword. He repeatedly invoked the idea that America has a divinely appointed mission to be a "beacon of liberty and freedom." Reagan, who became known as "the Great Communicator," reshaped the definition of freedom, and the national agenda, more effectively than any president since Franklin D. Roosevelt. Like Roosevelt, Reagan promised to free government from control by "special interests," but these were racial minorities, unionists, and others hoping to use Washington's power to attack social inequalities, not businessmen seeking political favors, the traditional target of liberals.

The second half of the 1960s and the 1970s witnessed pivotal developments that reshaped American politics—the breakup of the political coalition forged by Franklin D. Roosevelt; an economic crisis that traditional liberal remedies seemed unable to solve; a shift of population and economic resources to conservative strongholds in the Sunbelt of the South and West; the growth of an activist, conservative Christianity increasingly aligned with the Republican Party; and a series of setbacks for the United States overseas. Together, they led to growing popularity for conservatives' ideas, including their understanding of freedom.

PRESIDENT NIXON

Richard Nixon's presidency bridged the eras of liberalism under Kennedy and Johnson and the conservatism of the Reagan era. Nixon was the first president from California, and his

· CHRONOLOGY ·

1968	Oil discovered in Alaska
	My Lai massacre
1970	U.S. invades Cambodia
1971	Pentagon Papers published
	U.S. goes off gold standard
1972	Nixon travels to the People's Republic of China
	Congress passes the Equal Rights Amendment for ratification
	SALT is signed
	Congress approves Title IX
1973	Paris Peace Accords end U.S. involvement in Vietnam War
	CIA-aided Chilean coup
	War Powers Act
1974	Nixon resigns in Watergate scandal
1975	Collapse of South Vietnamese government
1976	Jimmy Carter elected
1978	*Regents of the University of California v. Bakke*
	Camp David Accords signed between Israel and Egypt
1979	Three Mile Island accident
	Sagebrush Rebellion
	Sixty-six Americans taken hostage in Iran
1980	Ronald Reagan elected
1981	Air traffic controllers' strike
1983	Strategic Defense Initiative
1985–1987	Iran-Contra affair
1986	*Bowers v. Hardwick*

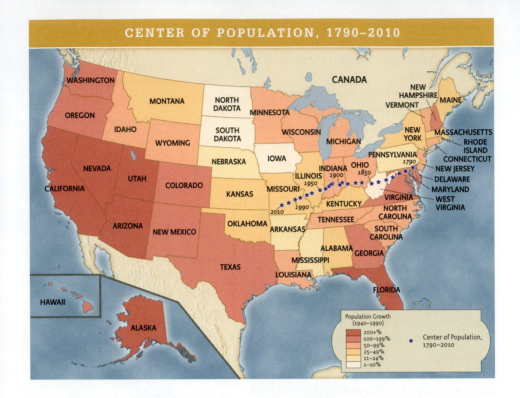

CENTER OF POPULATION, 1790–2010

Population Growth (1940–1990)

- 200+%
- 100–199%
- 50–99%
- 25–49%
- 11–24%
- 1–10%

★ Center of Population, 1790–2010

victory signaled the growing power of the conservative Sunbelt in national politics. From the vantage point of the early twenty-first century, it is difficult to recall how marginal conservatism seemed at the end of World War II. Associated in many minds with conspiracy theories, anti-Semitism, and preference for social hierarchy over democracy and equality, conservatism seemed a relic of a discredited past.

Nonetheless, as noted in the previous two chapters, the 1950s and 1960s witnessed a conservative rebirth. And in 1968, a "backlash" among formerly Democratic voters against both Black assertiveness and antiwar demonstrations helped to propel Richard Nixon into the White House. But conservatives found Nixon no more to their liking than his predecessors. Nixon echoed conservative language, especially in his condemnation of student protesters and his calls for law and order, but in office he expanded the welfare state and moved to improve American relations with the Soviet Union and China. During his presidency, the social changes set in motion by the 1960s—seen by conservatives as forces of moral decay—continued apace.

Nixon's Domestic Policies

Having won the presidency by a very narrow margin, Nixon moved toward the political center on many issues. A shrewd politician, he worked to solidify his support among Republicans while reaching out to disaffected elements of the Democratic coalition. It is difficult to characterize Nixon's domestic agenda according to the traditional categories of liberal and conservative. Mostly interested in foreign policy, he had no desire to battle Congress, still under Democratic control, on domestic issues. Just as Eisenhower had helped to institutionalize the New Deal, Nixon accepted and even expanded many elements of the Great Society.

Conservatives applauded Nixon's New Federalism, which offered federal "block grants" to the states to spend as they saw fit, rather than for specific purposes dictated by Washington. On the other hand, the Nixon administration created a host of new federal agencies. The Environmental Protection Agency oversaw programs to combat water and air pollution, cleaned up hazardous wastes, and required "environmental impact" statements from any project that received federal funding. The Occupational Safety and Health Administration sent inspectors into the nation's workplaces. The National Transportation Safety Board instructed automobile makers on how to make their cars safer.

Nixon spent lavishly on social services and environmental initiatives. He abolished the Office of Economic Opportunity, which had coordinated Johnson's War on Poverty. But he signed congressional measures that expanded the food stamp program and indexed Social Security benefits to inflation—meaning that they would rise automatically as the cost of living increased. The Endangered Species Act prohibited spending federal funds on any project that might extinguish an animal species. The Clean Air Act set air quality standards for carbon monoxide and other chemicals released by cars and factories and led to a dramatic decline in air pollution.

Nixon and Welfare

Perhaps Nixon's most startling initiative was his proposal for a Family Assistance Plan, or "negative income tax," that would replace Aid to Families with Dependent Children (AFDC) by having the federal government guarantee a minimum income for all Americans. Universally known as "welfare," AFDC provided assistance, often quite limited, to poor families who met local eligibility requirements. Originally a New Deal program that mainly served the white poor, welfare had come to be associated with Blacks, who by 1970 accounted for nearly half the recipients. The AFDC rolls expanded rapidly during the 1960s, partly because the federal government relaxed eligibility standards. This arose from an increase in births to unmarried women, which produced a sharp rise in the number of poor female-headed households, and from an aggressive campaign by welfare rights groups to encourage people to apply for benefits. Conservative politicians now attacked recipients of welfare as people who preferred to live at the expense of honest taxpayers rather than by working.

A striking example of Nixon's willingness to break the political mold, his plan to replace welfare with a guaranteed annual income failed to win approval by Congress. It proved too radical for conservatives, who saw it as a reward for laziness, while liberals denounced the proposed level of $1,600 per year for a needy family of four as inadequate.

Nixon and Race

Nixon's racial policies offer a similarly mixed picture. To consolidate support in the white South, he nominated to the Supreme Court two conservative southern jurists with records of support for segregation. Both were rejected by the Senate. On the other hand, because the courts finally lost patience with southern delaying tactics, extensive racial integration at last came to public schools in the South. In Nixon's first three years in office, the proportion of southern Black students attending integrated schools rose from 32 percent to 77 percent. His administration opened the Office of Minority Business Enterprise to fund Black capitalist initiatives, calling on Blacks to embrace self-help strategies to "get a piece of the action." He even courted some Black Power advocates, providing former civil rights leader Floyd McKissick with $14 million to establish Soul City, a town in North Carolina. (The project did not succeed.)

For a time, the Nixon administration also pursued **affirmative action** programs to upgrade minority employment. The Philadelphia Plan required that construction contractors on federal projects hire specific numbers of minority workers. Secretary of Labor George Shultz, who initiated the idea, sincerely hoped to open more jobs for Black workers. Nixon seems to have viewed the plan mainly as a way of fighting inflation by weakening the power of the building trades unions. Their control over the labor market, he believed, pushed wages to unreasonably high levels, raising the cost of construction. And, he calculated, if the plan caused dissension between Blacks and labor unions—two pillars of the Democratic coalition—Republicans could only benefit.

Even as he pursued his southern strategy, President Nixon courted Black support. Here he meets with three African Americans in the White House, including football legend and actor Jim Brown (dressed in white).

Trade unions of skilled workers like plumbers and electricians, which had virtually no Black members, strongly opposed the Philadelphia Plan. After a widely publicized incident in May 1970, when a group of construction workers assaulted antiwar demonstrators in New York City,

Nixon suddenly decided that he might be able to woo blue-collar workers in preparation for his 1972 reelection campaign. He soon abandoned the Philadelphia Plan in favor of an ineffective one that stressed voluntary local efforts toward minority hiring instead of federal requirements.

The Burger Court and Busing

When Earl Warren retired as chief justice in 1969, Nixon appointed Warren Burger, a federal court-of-appeals judge, to succeed him. An outspoken critic of the "judicial activism" of the Warren Court—its willingness to expand old rights and create new ones by overturning acts of Congress and the states—Burger was expected to lead the justices in a conservative direction. But like Nixon, he surprised many of his supporters. While the pace of change slowed, the Burger Court, at least initially, consolidated and expanded many of the judicial innovations of the 1960s.

In 1971, in *Swann v. Charlotte-Mecklenburg Board of Education*, which arose from North Carolina, the justices unanimously approved a lower court's plan that required the extensive transportation of students to achieve school integration. The decision led to hundreds of cases in which judges throughout the country ordered the use of **busing** as a tool to achieve integration. With many white parents determined to keep their children in neighborhood schools and others willing to move to the suburbs or enroll them in private academies to avoid integration, busing became a lightning rod for protests. One of the most bitter fights took place in Boston in the mid-1970s. Residents of the tightly knit Irish American community of South Boston demonstrated vociferously and sometimes violently against a busing plan decreed by a local judge. The protesters adopted the language and strategies associated with the progressive social movements of the 1960s, calling for a restoration of their "rights" and "freedom." The busing issue helped to consolidate white hostility to "too powerful government," a position that would eventually benefit conservatives.

The Supreme Court soon abandoned the idea of overturning local control of schools or moving students great distances to achieve integration. In 1973, it rebuffed a group of Texas Latinos who sued to overturn the use of property taxes to finance public education. Because of the great disparity in wealth between districts, spending on predominantly Mexican American schools stood far below that for white ones. But in *San Antonio Independent School District v. Rodriguez*, a 5-4 Court majority ruled that the Constitution did not require equality of school funding. In the following year, in *Milliken v. Bradley* (1974), the justices overturned a lower court order that required Detroit's predominantly white suburbs to enter into a regional desegregation plan with the city's heavily minority school system. By absolving suburban districts of responsibility for assisting in integrating urban schools, the decision guaranteed that housing segregation would be mirrored in public education. Indeed, by the 1990s, public schools in the North were considerably more segregated than those in the South.

The Court and Affirmative Action

Efforts to promote greater employment opportunities for minorities also spawned opposition. Many whites came to view affirmative action programs as a form of reverse discrimination. Even as such programs quickly spread from Blacks to encompass women, Latinos, Asian Americans, and Native Americans, conservatives demanded that the Supreme Court invalidate them all. The justices refused, but they found it difficult to devise a consistent approach to this politically charged issue.

In *Griggs v. Duke Power Company* (1971), the Court ruled that even racially neutral job requirements such as a written examination were illegal if they operated to exclude a disproportionate number of non-white applicants and were not directly related to job performance. Later in the decade, it upheld a program devised by the Kaiser Aluminum & Chemical Corporation and its union that set quotas for training and hiring non-white workers in skilled jobs.

The justices, however, proved increasingly hostile to governmental affirmative action policies. In *Regents of the University of California v. Bakke* (1978), the Court overturned an admissions program of the University of California at Davis, a public university, which set aside 16 of 100 places in the entering medical school class for minority students. Justice Lewis F. Powell, a Nixon appointee who cast the deciding vote in the 5-4 decision, rejected the idea of fixed affirmative action quotas. He added, however, that race could be used as one factor among many in admissions decisions, so affirmative action continued at most colleges and universities. *Bakke* continues to be the standard by which affirmative action programs are judged today.

GRASSROOTS RIGHTS MOVEMENTS

As noted in the previous chapter, the social activism associated with the 1960s continued in the following decade. Both right and left took part in grassroots movements, ranging from campaigns against nuclear weapons and nuclear power plants and struggles to aid migrant workers to battles to stop the court-ordered busing of public school children and movements against abortion rights. Some movements, such as Native American rights and the disability rights movements, achieved support across the political spectrum. But other movements including women's rights and gay liberation generated intense opposition among religious conservatives.

Indian Tribal Revitalization

The intensified Native American activism of the late 1960s and 1970s contributed to a shift in federal Indian policy. In a 1970 message to Congress, Nixon rejected terminating tribal governance and spoke in favor of self-determination. In the wake of the Wounded Knee occupation in 1973, calls for reform led to the passage of the Indian Self-Determination and Education Assistance Act in 1975. Indians won control over federally funded programs ranging from health and social services to natural resource development, contributing to a revitalization of Indian nations. Many tribes established successful business enterprises and

The renaissance of Native identity and culture that began in the 1970s included new institutions of higher education, including Haskell Indian Nations University in Lawrence, Kansas. Founded by the U.S. government as a residential boarding school, Haskell evolved into a four-year college. Some graduating students chose to wear traditional regalia during this 2015 commencement ceremony.

won back some lost land and resources. Some that had lost federal recognition during the Termination Era (discussed in Chapter 23), including the Menominee of Wisconsin and the Klamath of Washington, saw their status restored. Indian studies programs on college campuses and tribe-controlled community colleges, along with language revitalization efforts, pointed to a renaissance of Native American identity and cultural pride. As a result of a rising sense of self-respect, the number of Americans identifying as Indians quadrupled between 1970 and 2000. A thriving Indian professional class blossomed, and novelists and filmmakers—from Cherokee and Kiowa writer N. Scott Momaday to Cheyenne and Arapaho director Chris Eyres—found wide audiences for their work. These developments, however, did not bring an end to the continued high rates of poverty, infant mortality, and unemployment experienced by many Indians living on reservations and in cities.

Disability Rights

Meanwhile, increased activism demanding equal opportunities and treatment for people with disabilities resulted in passage—unanimously in both houses of Congress—of the Rehabilitation Act of 1973, which prohibited discrimination on the basis of disability in programs conducted by federal agencies or receiving federal financial assistance and in employment practices of federal contractors. The act represented a dramatic repudiation of the "science" of eugenics, discussed in Chapter 19, which encouraged government action to

"improve" the American population and of the practice of involuntary sterilization of the "less fit" practiced by state governments well into the twentieth
century.

Further efforts to enable persons with disabilities to participate fully in society
followed. In 1977, disability activists organized a sit-in at offices of the Department
of Health, Education, and Welfare, forcing the department to issue regulations
to put the law into effect. Over time, public and private buildings ranging from
apartment houses to train stations to sites of business have been redesigned to
improve access for persons with physical disabilities. A major inspiration for these
changes came in the Americans with Disabilities Act, passed in 1990. Modeled on
civil rights legislation of the 1960s, it extended the ban on discrimination against
persons with disabilities to state and local governments and private employers
and required public accommodations such as restaurants to take steps to ensure
that they were fully accessible to those with impaired mobility.

The Continuing Sexual Revolution

But the most profound changes in American life arose from the continuing
sexual revolution. To the alarm of conservatives, during the 1970s the sexual revolution passed from the counterculture into the social mainstream.
The number of Americans who told public-opinion polls that premarital sex
was wrong plummeted. The number of divorces soared, reaching more than
1 million in 1975, double the number ten years earlier. The age at which both
men and women married rose dramatically.
As a result of women's changing aspirations
and the availability of birth control and legal
abortions, the American birthrate declined
dramatically. By 1976, the average woman
was bearing 1.7 children during her lifetime,
less than half the figure of 1957 and below
the level at which a population reproduces
itself. A 1971 survey of the last five graduating
classes at Bryn Mawr, an elite women's college,
reported the birth of more than seventy children. A similar survey covering the classes of
1971 through 1975 found that only three had
been born. (Of course, many of these women
eventually did marry and have children. But
unlike their mothers of the baby-boom generation, they postponed these decisions to
pursue careers.)

TABLE 26.1 Rate of Divorce: Divorces of Existing Marriages per 1,000 New Marriages, 1950–1980

Year	Divorces
1950	385
1955	377
1960	393
1965	479
1970	708
1975	1,036
1980	1,189

During the Nixon years, women made inroads into areas from which they had long been excluded. In 1972, Congress approved **Title IX**, which banned gender discrimination in higher education, and the Equal Credit Opportunity Act, which required that married women be given access to credit in their own name. The giant corporation American Telephone and Telegraph (AT&T) entered into a landmark agreement in which it agreed to pay millions of dollars to workers who had suffered gender discrimination and to upgrade employment opportunities for women. The number of women at work continued its upward climb. In 1960, only 20 percent of women with young children had been in the workforce. The figure reached 40 percent in 1980, and 55 percent in 1990. Working women were motivated by varied aims. Some sought careers in professions and skilled jobs previously open only to men. Others, spurred by the need to bolster family income as the economy faltered, flooded into the traditional, low-wage, "pink-collar" sector, working as cashiers, secretaries, and telephone operators.

In addition, the gay and lesbian movement, born at the end of the 1960s, expanded greatly during the 1970s and became a major concern of the right. In 1969, there had been about fifty local gay rights groups in the United States; ten years later, their numbers reached into the thousands. They began to elect local officials, persuaded many states to decriminalize same-sex relations, and succeeded in convincing cities with large gay populations to pass antidiscrimination laws. They actively encouraged gay men and lesbians to "come out of the closet"—that is, to reveal their sexual orientation. During the 1970s, the American Psychiatric Association removed homosexuality from its list of mental disorders.

FOREIGN POLICY AND WATERGATE

Nixon and Détente

Just as many of the domestic policies and social trends under Nixon disappointed conservatives, they viewed his foreign policy as dangerously "soft" on communism. To be sure, in the Third World, Nixon and Henry Kissinger, his national security adviser and secretary of state, continued their predecessors' policy of attempting to undermine governments deemed dangerous to American strategic or economic interests. Nixon funneled arms to dictatorial pro-American regimes in Iran, the Philippines, and South Africa. After Chile in 1970 elected socialist Salvador Allende as president, the CIA worked with his domestic opponents to destabilize the regime. On September 11, 1973, Allende was overthrown and killed in a military coup, which installed a bloody dictatorship under General Augusto Pinochet. Thousands of Allende backers, including a few Americans then in Chile, were tortured and murdered, and many others fled the country. The Nixon administration knew of the coup plans in advance but failed to warn Allende, and it continued to back Pinochet despite his brutal policies. Democracy did not return to Chile until the end of the 1980s.

In his relations with the major communist powers, however, Nixon fundamentally altered Cold War policies. Nixon had launched his political career as a fierce and, critics charged, unscrupulous anticommunist. But in the language of foreign relations, he and Kissinger were "realists." They had more interest in power than ideology and preferred international stability to relentless conflict. Nixon also hoped that if relations with the Soviet Union improved, the Russians would influence North Vietnam to agree to an end to the Vietnam War on terms acceptable to the United States.

Nixon realized that far from being part of a unified communist bloc, China had its own interests, different from those of the Soviet Union, and was destined to play a major role on the world stage. The policy of refusing to recognize China's communist government had reached a dead end. In 1971, Kissinger flew secretly to China, paving the way for Nixon's own astonishing public visit of February 1972. The trip led to the Beijing government's taking up China's seat at the United Nations, previously occupied by the exiled regime on Taiwan. Full diplomatic relations between the United States and the People's Republic of China were not established until 1979. But Nixon's visit sparked a dramatic increase in trade between the two countries.

Three months after his trip to Beijing, Nixon became the first Cold War American president to visit the Soviet Union, where he engaged in intense negotiations with his Soviet counterpart, Leonid Brezhnev. Out of this "summit" meeting came agreements for increased trade and two landmark arms-control treaties. SALT (named for the **Strategic Arms Limitation Talks** under way since 1969) froze each country's arsenal of intercontinental missiles capable of carrying nuclear warheads. The Anti–Ballistic Missile Treaty banned the development of systems designed to intercept incoming missiles, so that neither side would be tempted to attack the other without fearing devastating retaliation. Nixon and Brezhnev proclaimed a new era of "peaceful coexistence," in which **détente** (cooperation) would replace the hostility of the Cold War.

Nixon and Vietnam

Despite Nixon's foreign policy triumphs, one issue would not go away— Vietnam. Nixon ran for president in 1968 declaring that he had a "secret plan" to end the war. On taking office, he announced a new policy, Vietnamization. Under this plan, American troops would gradually be withdrawn while South

Vietnamese soldiers, backed by continued American bombing, did more and more of the fighting. But Vietnamization neither limited the war nor ended the antiwar movement. Hoping to cut North Vietnamese supply lines, Nixon in 1970 ordered American troops into neutral Cambodia. The invasion did not achieve its military goals, but it destabilized the Cambodian government and set in motion a chain of events that eventually brought to power the Khmer Rouge. Before being ousted by a Vietnamese invasion in 1979, this local communist movement attempted to force virtually all Cambodians into rural communes and committed widespread massacres in that unfortunate country.

As the war escalated, protests again spread on college campuses, partly because the policy of exempting students from the draft had ended. In the wake of the killing of four antiwar protesters at Kent State University by the Ohio National Guard and two by police at Jackson State University in Mississippi, the student movement reached its high-water mark. In the spring of 1970, more than 350 colleges and universities experienced strikes, and troops occupied 21 campuses. The protests at Kent State, a public university with a largely working-class student body, and Jackson State, a Black institution, demonstrated how antiwar sentiment had spread far beyond elite campuses like Berkeley and Columbia.

At the same time, troop morale in Vietnam plummeted. For most of the war, college students had received exemptions. As a result, the army was predominantly composed of working-class whites and members of racial minorities. Of the 2.5 million Americans who served in the military during the war, around 80 percent came from poor and working-class families.

The same social changes sweeping the home front were evident among troops in Vietnam. Soldiers experimented with drugs, openly wore peace and Black Power symbols, refused orders, and even assaulted unpopular

Students peer from a residence hall window—pockmarked by bullet holes—at Jackson State, a historically Black university in Mississippi. Two students were killed when police opened fire on the building, claiming they were returning sniper fire. The event took place eleven days after the tragedy at Kent State University but received much less attention.

officers. In 1971, thousands deserted the army, while at home Vietnam veterans held antiwar demonstrations. The decline of discipline within the army convinced increasing numbers of high-ranking officers that the United States must extricate itself from Vietnam.

Public support for the war was rapidly waning. In 1969, the *New York Times* published details of the **My Lai massacre** of 1968, in which a company of American troops killed some 350 South Vietnamese civilians. After a military investigation, one soldier, Lieutenant William Calley, was found guilty of directing the atrocity. (The courts released him from prison in 1974.) While hardly typical of the behavior of most servicemen, My Lai further undermined public support for the war.

In 1971, the *Times* began publishing the **Pentagon Papers**, a classified report prepared by the Defense Department that traced American involvement in Vietnam back to World War II and revealed how successive presidents had misled the American people about it. In a landmark freedom-of-the-press decision, the Supreme Court rejected Nixon's request for an injunction to halt publication. In 1973, Congress passed the **War Powers Act**. The most vigorous assertion of congressional control over foreign policy in the nation's history, it required the president to seek congressional approval for the commitment of American troops overseas.

The End of the Vietnam War

Early in 1973, Nixon achieved what had eluded his predecessors—a negotiated settlement in Vietnam. The Paris peace agreement, the result of five years of talks, made possible the final withdrawal of American troops. The compromise left in place the government of South Vietnam, but it also left North Vietnamese and Viet Cong soldiers in control of parts of the South. American bombing ceased, and the military draft came to an end. Henceforth, volunteers would make up the armed forces. But the agreement did not solve the basic issue of the war—whether Vietnam would be one country or two. That question was answered in the spring of 1975, when the North Vietnamese launched a final military offensive. The government of South Vietnam collapsed; the United States did not intervene except to evacuate the American embassy, and Vietnam was reunified under communist rule.

Vietnam was a military, political, and social disaster. By the time it ended, 58,000 Americans had been killed, along with 3 million to 4 million Vietnamese. The war cost the United States many hundreds of millions of dollars and diverted funds from needs at home. But the nonmonetary price was far higher. Vietnam undermined Americans' confidence in their own institutions and challenged long-standing beliefs about the country and its purposes. The divisions caused by the war continued in debates over its legacy that persisted for many years. The war's supporters blamed critics at home for undermining a successful and winnable military effort. Others took the lesson that the United States should be extremely reluctant to commit its armed forces overseas—an outlook sometimes called the **Vietnam Syndrome**.

Two decades after the war ended, former secretary of defense Robert McNamara published a memoir in which he admitted that the policy he had helped to shape had been "terribly wrong." Ignorance of the history and culture of Vietnam and a misguided belief that every communist movement in the world was a puppet of Moscow, he wrote, had led the country into a war that he now profoundly regretted. The *New York Times* rejected McNamara's apology. The "ghosts of those unlived lives," the young men sent to their death "for no purpose," it declared, could not so easily be wished away. But the *Times* itself, like the rest of the political establishment, had supported the war for most of its duration. For far too long, the press and political leaders had accepted its basic premise—that the United States had the right to decide the fate of a faraway people about whom it knew almost nothing.

The 1972 Election

To run against Nixon in 1972, Democrats chose Senator George McGovern, a liberal from South Dakota. New rules established in the wake of Hubert Humphrey's nomination in 1968 brought increased diversity to the party's ranks but also opened new rifts. In the primaries, Shirley Chisholm, a member of Congress from Brooklyn, became the first Black woman to seek the presidency. George Wallace rallied the party's southern and blue-collar base with a racial and populist appeal. McGovern, a strong opponent of the Vietnam War, won the nomination to the discomfort of the broad Democratic middle. Many Democratic voters stayed home, or

A campaign poster from the 1972 election does not even name Richard Nixon, referring to him only as "the president." It includes images of some of his accomplishments, including pursuing détente with China (*bottom*) and the Soviet Union (*above and to the left*).

Beat poet Allen Ginsberg and feminist leader Bella Abzug (later elected to Congress from New York City) at the 1972 Democratic national convention in Miami Beach. Their presence illustrated the growing role of the counterculture and new social movements in the party, to the dismay of its traditional leaders.

voted for Nixon, who won in a landslide. McGovern carried only Massachusetts. The loyalty of white southerners and northern white working-class voters to the party of FDR could no longer be taken for granted.

Watergate

Nixon's landslide victory contained the seeds of his downfall. Nixon was obsessed with secrecy and could not accept honest difference of opinion. He viewed every critic as a threat to national security and developed an "enemies list" that included reporters, politicians, and celebrities unfriendly to the administration. When the Pentagon Papers were published, Nixon created a special investigative unit known as the "plumbers" to gather information about Daniel Ellsberg, the former government official who had leaked them to the press. The plumbers raided the office of Ellsberg's psychiatrist in search of incriminating records. In June 1972, five former employees of Nixon's reelection committee took part in a break-in at Democratic Party headquarters in the **Watergate** apartment complex in Washington, D.C. A security guard called police, who arrested the intruders.

No one knows precisely what the Watergate burglars were looking for (perhaps they intended to install listening devices), and the botched robbery played little role in the 1972 presidential campaign. But in 1973, Judge John J. Sirica, before whom the burglars were tried, determined to find out who had sponsored the break-in. A pair of *Washington Post* journalists began publishing investigative stories that made it clear that persons close to the president had ordered the burglary and then tried to cover up White House involvement. Congressional hearings followed that revealed a wider pattern of wiretapping, break-ins, and attempts to sabotage political opposition. When it became known that Nixon had made tape recordings of conversations in his office, Archibald Cox, a special prosecutor appointed to investigate the Watergate affair, demanded copies. Nixon, however, refused to release the tapes and fired Cox, whereupon Attorney General Elliot Richardson resigned in protest. These events, known as the Saturday Night Massacre, further undermined Nixon's standing. The Supreme Court unanimously ordered Nixon to provide the tapes—a decision that reaffirmed the principle that the president is not above the law.

Nixon's Fall

By mid-1974, it had become clear that whether or not Nixon knew in advance of the Watergate break-in, he had become involved immediately afterward in authorizing payments to the burglars to remain silent or commit perjury, and he had ordered the FBI to halt its investigation of the crime. In August 1974, the House Judiciary Committee voted to recommend that Nixon be impeached for conspiracy to obstruct justice. His political support having evaporated, Nixon became the only president in history to resign.

Nixon's presidency remains a classic example of the abuse of political power. In 1973, his vice president, Spiro T. Agnew, resigned after revelations that he had accepted bribes from construction firms while serving as governor of Maryland. Nixon's attorney general, John Mitchell, and White House aides H. R. Haldeman and John Ehrlichman, were convicted of obstruction of justice in the Watergate affair and went to jail. As for the president, he insisted that he had done nothing wrong—or at any rate, that previous presidents had also been guilty of lying and illegality.

Although it hardly excused his behavior, Nixon had a point. His departure from office was followed by Senate hearings headed by Frank Church of Idaho that laid bare a history of abusive actions that involved every administration since the beginning of the Cold War. In violation of the law, the FBI had spied on millions of Americans and had tried to disrupt the civil rights movement. The CIA had conducted secret operations to overthrow foreign governments and had tried to assassinate foreign leaders. It had even recruited a secret army to fight in Laos, a neighbor of Vietnam. Abuses of power, in other words, went far beyond the misdeeds of a single president.

Along with Watergate, the Pentagon Papers, and the Vietnam War itself, the Church Committee revelations seriously undermined Americans' confidence in their own government. They led Congress to enact new restrictions on the power of the FBI and CIA to spy on American citizens or conduct operations abroad without the knowledge of lawmakers. Congress also strengthened the Freedom of Information Act (FOIA), initially enacted in 1966. Since 1974, the FOIA has allowed scholars, journalists, and ordinary citizens to gain access to millions of pages of records of federal agencies.

Liberals, who had despised Nixon throughout his career, celebrated his downfall. They did not realize that the revulsion against Watergate undermined the foundations of liberalism itself, already weakened by the divisions of the 1960s. For liberalism rests, in part, on belief in the ability of government, especially the federal government, to solve social problems and promote both the public good and individual freedom. Nixon's fall and the revelations of years of governmental misconduct helped to convince many Americans that conservatives were correct when they argued that to protect liberty it was necessary to limit Washington's power over Americans' lives. The Watergate crisis also distracted attention from the economic crisis that began in the fall of 1973. Its inability to fashion a response to this crisis, which gripped the United States for much of the 1970s, dealt liberalism yet another blow.

THE END OF THE GOLDEN AGE

The Decline of Manufacturing

During the 1970s, the long period of postwar economic expansion and consumer prosperity came to an end, succeeded by slow growth and high inflation. For the only time in the twentieth century, other than the 1930s, the average American ended the 1970s poorer than when the decade began. There were many reasons for the end of capitalism's "golden age." With American prosperity seemingly unassailable and the military-industrial complex thriving, successive administrations had devoted little attention to the less positive economic consequences of the Cold War. To strengthen its anticommunist allies, the United States promoted the industrial reconstruction of Japan and Germany and the emergence of new centers of manufacturing in places like South Korea and Taiwan. It encouraged American companies to invest in overseas plants and did not complain when allies protected their own industries while seeking unrestricted access to the American market. Imports of foreign steel, for example, led to growing problems for this key industry at home. The strong dollar, linked to gold by the Bretton Woods agreement of 1944, made it harder to sell American goods overseas (discussed in Chapter 22).

In 1971, for the first time in the twentieth century, the United States experienced a merchandise trade deficit—that is, it imported more goods than it exported. By 1980, nearly three-quarters of goods produced in the United States were competing with foreign-made products and the number of manufacturing workers, 38 percent of the American workforce in 1960, had fallen to 28 percent.

In 1971, Nixon announced the most radical change in economic policy since the Great Depression. He took the United States off the gold standard, ending the Bretton Woods agreement that fixed the value of the dollar and other currencies in terms of gold. Henceforth, the world's currencies would "float" in relation to one another, their worth determined not by treaty but by international currency markets. Nixon hoped that lowering the dollar's value in terms of the German mark and Japanese yen would promote exports by making American goods cheaper overseas and reduce imports since foreign products would be more expensive in the United States. But the end of fixed currency rates injected a new element of instability into the world economy. Nixon also ordered wages and prices frozen for ninety days.

Stagflation

These policies temporarily curtailed inflation and reduced imports. But in 1973, a brief war broke out between Israel and its neighbors Egypt and Syria. Middle Eastern Arab states retaliated for Western support of Israel by quadrupling the price of oil and suspending the export of oil to the United States for several months. During the **oil embargo**, long lines of cars appeared at American gas stations, which either ran out of fuel or limited how much a customer could buy. A second "oil shock" occurred in 1979 as a result of the revolution that overthrew the shah of Iran, discussed later.

Because the rapidly growing demand for fuel by cars and factories outstripped domestic supplies, by 1973 the United States imported one-third of its oil. Europe and Japan depended even more heavily on oil imports. To promote energy conservation, Congress lowered the speed limit on interstate highways to fifty-five miles per hour, and many public buildings reduced heat and lighting.

The energy crisis of the 1970s drew increased attention to domestic energy resources like oil, coal, and natural gas. While the rest of the economy stagnated, western energy production grew apace. Oil was discovered in Alaska in 1968, and in 1977 a pipeline opened to facilitate its shipment to the rest of the country. Coal

TABLE 26.2 The Misery Index, 1970–1980

Year	Rate of Inflation (%)	Rate of Unemployment (%)	Misery Index (%)
1970	5.9	4.9	10.8
1971	4.3	5.9	10.2
1972	3.3	5.6	8.9
1973	6.2	4.9	11.1
1974	11.0	5.6	16.6
1975	9.1	8.5	17.6
1976	5.8	7.7	13.5
1977	6.5	7.1	13.6
1978	7.7	6.1	13.8
1979	11.3	5.8	17.1
1980	13.5	7.1	20.6

production in Wyoming boomed. Western energy companies benefited from the high oil prices set by OPEC—the Organization of Petroleum Exporting Countries.

But rising oil prices rippled through the world economy, contributing to the combination of stagnant economic growth and high inflation known as **stagflation**. Between 1973 and 1981, the rate of inflation in developed countries was 10 percent per year, and the rate of economic growth only 2.4 percent, a sharp deterioration from the economic conditions of the 1960s. The so-called misery index—the sum of the unemployment and inflation rates—stood at 10.8 percent when the decade began. By 1980, it had almost doubled. As oil prices rose, many Americans shifted from large domestically produced cars, known for high gasoline consumption, to smaller, more fuel-efficient imports. By the end of the decade, Japan had become the world's leading automobile producer, and imports accounted for nearly 25 percent of car sales in the United States.

The Beleaguered Social Compact

The economic crisis contributed to a breakdown of the postwar social compact. Faced with declining profits and rising overseas competition, corporations stepped up the trend, already under way before 1970, toward eliminating well-paid manufacturing jobs through automation and shifting production to low-wage areas of the United States and overseas. The effects on older industrial cities were devastating. By 1980, Detroit and Chicago had lost more than half the manufacturing jobs that had existed three decades earlier.

Smaller industrial cities suffered even sharper declines. As their tax bases shriveled, many found themselves unable to maintain public services. In Paterson, New Jersey, where great silk factories had arisen in the early twentieth century, **deindustrialization** left a landscape of abandoned manufacturing plants. The poverty rate reached 20 percent, the city sold off public library buildings to raise cash, and the schools became so run down and overcrowded that the state government took control.

In some manufacturing centers, political and economic leaders welcomed the opportunity to remake their cities as finance, information, and entertainment hubs. In New York, the construction of the World Trade Center, completed in 1977, symbolized this shift in the economy. Until destroyed by terrorists twenty-four years later, the 110-story "twin towers" stood as a symbol of New York's grandeur. But to make way for the World Trade Center, the city displaced hundreds of small electronics, printing, and other firms, causing the loss of thousands of manufacturing jobs.

Increasingly, jobs, investment, and population flowed to the nonunion, low-wage states of the **Sunbelt**, a term that came into widespread use to describe the growing economic and political influence of this conservative region. Ninety-six percent of population growth in metropolitan areas during the 1970s occurred in the South and West. Booming Sunbelt cities pursued a different model of development and spatial growth than the older urban centers of the North and Midwest. Businesses and new housing developments sprang up along highways, with cities like Houston, Dallas, and Los Angeles reaching to the horizon. Gated communities became a popular project for developers, promoting a style of life that emphasized security and privacy and that relied on cars, not public transport, to get around.

Labor on the Defensive

Always a junior partner in the Democratic coalition, the labor movement found itself forced onto the defensive. It has remained there ever since. One example of the weakening of unions' power came in 1975 with the New York City fiscal crisis. Deeply in debt and unable to market its bonds, the city faced the prospect of bankruptcy. The solution to the crisis required a reduction of the city's workforce, severe cuts in the budgets of schools, parks, and the subway system, and an end to the century-old policy of free tuition at the City University. Even in this center of unionism, working-class New Yorkers had no choice but to absorb job losses and a drastic decline in public services.

FIGURE 26.1 REAL AVERAGE WEEKLY WAGES, 1955–1990

Because of economic dislocations and deindustrialization, Americans' real wages (wages adjusted to take account of inflation) peaked in the early 1970s and then began a sharp, prolonged decline.

The weakening of unions and the continuation of the economy's long-term shift from manufacturing to service employment had an adverse impact on ordinary Americans. Between 1953 and 1973, median family income had doubled. But in 1973, real wages began to fall. The popular song "The River," by Bruce Springsteen, captured the woes of blue-collar workers: "Is a dream a lie if it don't come true / Or is it something worse?"

The Ford and Carter Administrations

Economic problems dogged the presidencies of Nixon's successors. Gerald Ford, who had been appointed to replace Vice President Agnew, succeeded to the White House when Nixon resigned. Ford named Nelson Rockefeller of

New York as his vice president. Among his first acts as president, Ford pardoned Nixon, shielding him from prosecution for obstruction of justice, a decision that proved to be widely unpopular.

In domestic policy, Ford's brief presidency lacked significant accomplishment. Although inflation fell while he was in office, joblessness continued to rise. During the steep recession of 1974–1975 unemployment exceeded 9 percent, the highest level since the Depression.

In the international arena, 1975 witnessed the major achievement of Ford's presidency. In a continuation of Nixon's policy of détente, the United States and Soviet Union signed an agreement at Helsinki, Finland, that recognized the permanence of Europe's post–World War II boundaries (including the division of Germany). In addition, both superpowers agreed to respect the basic liberties of their citizens. Over time, the **Helsinki Accords** inspired movements for greater freedom within the communist countries of eastern Europe.

In the presidential election of 1976, Jimmy Carter, a former governor of Georgia, narrowly defeated Ford. A graduate of the U.S. Naval Academy who later became a peanut farmer, Carter was virtually unknown outside his state when he launched his campaign for the Democratic nomination. But in the wake of Vietnam and Watergate, he turned his obscurity into an advantage. Carter ran for president as an "outsider," making a virtue of the fact that he had never held federal office. A devout "born-again" Baptist, he spoke openly of his religious convictions. His promise, "I'll never lie to you," resonated with an electorate tired of official dishonesty.

Carter had much in common with Progressives of the early twentieth century. His passions were making government more efficient, protecting the environment, and raising the moral tone of politics. Unlike the Progressives, however, he embraced the aspirations of Black Americans. As president, Carter appointed an unprecedented number of Blacks to important positions, including Andrew Young, a former lieutenant of Martin Luther King Jr., as ambassador to the United Nations.

Carter and the Economic Crisis

The Democratic Party found itself ill-equipped to deal with the economic crisis. The social upheavals of the 1960s had led to the emergence of politicians known as the New Democrats. Representing affluent urban and suburban districts, they prioritized issues like race relations, gender equality, the environment, and improving the political process more than traditional economic matters. Although his party controlled both houses, Carter often found himself at odds with Congress. He viewed inflation, not unemployment, as the country's main economic problem, and to combat it he promoted cuts in spending on domestic programs. In the hope that increased competition would reduce prices, his administration enacted **deregulation** in the airline and trucking industries. Anticipating what would come to be called the supply-side economics of the Reagan administration, Carter in 1978 inaugurated tax cuts for wealthier Americans in the hope that this would stimulate investment and encourage economic growth. In 1980, with Carter's approval, Congress repealed usury laws—laws that limit how much interest lenders can charge—allowing credit card companies to push their interest rates up to 20 percent or even higher. Carter supported the Federal Reserve Bank's decision to raise interest rates to curtail economic activity until both wages and prices fell, traditionally a Republican policy. But oil prices kept rising, thanks to the overthrow of the shah of Iran, discussed later, and inflation did not decline.

Carter also believed that expanded use of nuclear energy could help reduce dependence on imported oil. For years, proponents of nuclear power had hailed it as an inexpensive way of meeting the country's energy needs. By the time Carter took office, more than 200 nuclear plants were operating or on order. But in 1979 the industry suffered a near-fatal blow when an accident at the **Three Mile Island** plant in Pennsylvania released a large amount of radioactive steam into the atmosphere. The rise of the environmental movement had promoted public skepticism about scientific experts who touted the miraculous promise of technological innovations without concern for their social consequences. The Three Mile Island mishap reinforced fears about the environmental hazards associated with nuclear energy and put a halt to the industry's expansion.

Since the New Deal, Democrats had presented themselves as the party of affluence and economic growth. But Carter seemed to be presiding over a period of national decline. It did not help his popularity when, in a speech in 1979, he spoke of a national "crisis of confidence" and seemed to blame it on the American people themselves and their "mistaken idea of freedom" as "self-indulgence and consumption."

The Emergence of Human Rights Politics

Under Carter, a commitment to promoting human rights became a centerpiece of American foreign policy for the first time. He was influenced by the proliferation of information about global denials of human rights that was spread by nongovernmental agencies like Amnesty International, whose American membership grew from 6,000 to 35,000 between 1970 and 1976. Its reports marked a significant break with dominant ideas about international affairs since World War II, which had viewed the basic division in the world as between communist and noncommunist countries. Such reports, along with congressional hearings, fact-finding missions, and academic studies of human rights, exposed misdeeds not only by communist countries but also by American allies, especially the death squads of Latin American dictatorships. Amnesty International pressured the United States to try to do something to promote human rights abroad. In 1977, Amnesty International received the Nobel Peace Prize, an indication of the rapid emergence of human rights as an international issue.

In 1978, Carter cut off aid to the brutal military dictatorship governing Argentina, which in the name of anticommunism had launched a "dirty war" against its own citizens, kidnapping off the streets and secretly murdering an estimated 10,000 to 30,000 persons. Carter's action was a dramatic gesture, as Argentina was one of the most important powers in Latin America and previous American administrations had turned a blind eye to human rights abuses by Cold War allies. By the end of his presidency, the phrase "human rights" had acquired political potency. Its very vagueness was both a weakness and a strength. It was difficult to define exactly what rights should and should not be considered universally applicable, but various groups could and did unite under the umbrella of global human rights.

Carter believed that in the post-Vietnam era, promoting human rights should take priority over what he called "the inordinate fear of communism that once led us to embrace any dictator who joined us in that fear." In one of his first acts as president, he offered an unconditional pardon to Vietnam-era draft resisters.

Carter's emphasis on pursuing peaceful solutions to international problems and his willingness to think outside the Cold War framework yielded important results. In 1978, he brought the leaders of Egypt and Israel to the presidential retreat at Camp David and brokered a historic peace agreement, the **Camp David Accords**, between the two countries. He improved American relations with Latin America by agreeing to a treaty, ratified by the Senate in 1978, that provided for the transfer of the Panama Canal to local control by the year 2000. In 1979 he signed the SALT II agreement with the Soviets, which reduced the number of missiles, bombers, and nuclear warheads. That same year he resisted calls for intervention when a popular revolution led by the left-wing Sandinista movement overthrew Nicaraguan dictator Anastasio Somoza, a longtime ally of the United States. Carter attempted to curb the murderous violence of death squads allied to the right-wing government of El Salvador, and in 1980 he suspended military aid after the murder of four American nuns by members of the country's army. But Carter often found it difficult to translate human rights rhetoric into action. He criticized American arms sales to the rest of the world. But with thousands of jobs and billions of dollars in corporate profits at stake, he did nothing to curtail them. The United States continued its support of allies with serious human rights violations such as the governments of Guatemala, the Philippines, South Korea, and Iran. Indeed, the American connection with the shah of Iran, whose secret police regularly jailed and tortured political opponents, proved to be Carter's undoing.

The Iran Crisis and Afghanistan

Occupying a strategic location on the southern border of the Soviet Union, Iran was a major supplier of oil and an importer of American military equipment. At the end of 1977, Carter traveled there to help celebrate the shah's rule, causing the internal opposition to become more and more anti-American. Early in 1979, a popular revolution inspired by the exiled Muslim cleric Ayatollah Khomeini overthrew the shah and declared Iran an Islamic republic.

The Iranian revolution marked an ideological shift in opposition movements in the Middle East from socialism and Arab nationalism to religious fundamentalism. This would have important long-term consequences for the United States. More immediately, when Carter in November 1979 allowed the deposed shah to seek medical treatment in the United States, Khomeini's followers invaded the American embassy in Tehran and seized sixty-six hostages. Fourteen people (women, African American men, and a white man in ill health) were soon released, leaving fifty-two captives. They did not regain their freedom until January 1981, on the day Carter's term as president ended. Events in Iran made Carter seem helpless and inept and led to a rapid fall in his popularity.

Another crisis that began in 1979 undermined American relations with Moscow. At the end of that year, the Soviet Union sent thousands of troops into Afghanistan to support a friendly government threatened by an Islamic rebellion. In the long run, Afghanistan became the Soviet Vietnam, an unwinnable conflict whose mounting casualties seriously weakened the government at home. Initially, however, it seemed another example of declining American power.

Declaring the invasion the greatest crisis since World War II (a considerable exaggeration), the president announced the Carter Doctrine, declaring that the United States would use military force, if necessary, to protect its interests in the Persian Gulf. He placed an embargo on grain exports

American hostages being paraded by their Iranian captors on the first day of the occupation of the American embassy in Tehran in 1979. Television gave extensive coverage to the plight of the hostages, leading many Americans to view the Carter administration as weak and inept.

to the Soviet Union and organized a Western boycott of the 1980 Olympics, which took place in Moscow. He withdrew the SALT II treaty from consideration by the Senate and dramatically increased American military spending. In a reversion to the Cold War principle that any opponent of the Soviet Union deserved American support, the United States funneled aid to fundamentalist Muslims in Afghanistan who fought a decade-long guerrilla war against the Soviets. The alliance had unforeseen consequences. A faction of Islamic fundamentalists known as the Taliban eventually came to power in Afghanistan. Tragically, they would prove as hostile to the United States as to Moscow.

In an unsuccessful attempt to bring down inflation, Carter had abandoned the Keynesian economic policy of increased government spending to combat recession in favor of high interest rates. He had cut back on social spending and the federal government's economic regulations, while projecting a major increase in the military budget. By 1980, détente had been eclipsed and the Cold War reinvigorated. Thus, many of the conservative policies associated with his successor, Ronald Reagan, were already in place when Carter's presidency ended.

THE RISING TIDE OF CONSERVATISM

The combination of domestic and international dislocations during the 1970s created a widespread sense of anxiety among Americans and offered conservatives new political opportunities. Economic problems heightened the appeal of lower taxes, reduced government regulation, and cuts in social spending to spur business investment. Fears about a decline of American power in the world led to calls for a renewal of the Cold War. The civil rights and sexual revolutions produced resentments that undermined the Democratic coalition. Rising urban crime rates reinforced demands for law and order and attacks on courts considered too lenient toward criminals. These issues brought new converts to the conservative cause.

As the 1970s went on, conservatives abandoned overt opposition to the Black struggle for racial justice. The fiery rhetoric and direct confrontation tactics of Bull Connor, George Wallace, and other proponents of massive resistance were succeeded by appeals to freedom of association, local control, and resistance to the power of the federal government. This language of individual freedom resonated throughout the country, appealing especially to the growing, predominantly white, suburban population that was fleeing the cities and their urban problems. The suburbs would become one of the bastions of modern conservatism.

Like predecessors as diverse as the civil rights and labor movements, conservatives organized at the grassroots. In order to spread conservative doctrines, they ran candidates for office even when they had little chance of winning, and worked to change the policies of local institutions like school boards, town councils, and planning commissions. Conservatives also had allies in Washington. Conservative "think tanks" created during the 1970s, like the Heritage Foundation along with the earlier established American Enterprise Institute, refined and spread conservative ideas.

The Religious Right

The rise of religious fundamentalism during the 1970s expanded conservatism's popular base. Challenged by the secular and material concerns of American society, some denominations tried to bring religion into harmony with these interests; others reasserted more traditional religious values. The latter approach seemed to appeal to growing numbers of Americans. Even as membership in mainstream denominations like Episcopalianism and Presbyterianism declined, evangelical Protestantism flourished. Some observers spoke of a Third Great Awakening (like those of the 1740s and early nineteenth century). The election of Carter, the first "born-again" Christian to become president, highlighted the growing influence of evangelical religion. But unlike Carter, most fundamentalists who entered politics did so as conservatives.

Of course, there was nothing new about the involvement of churches in political life. There is a long tradition in American history of moral stewardship—devout Christians taking on responsibility for social reform and using political means to combat what they perceive as individual or collective sins. During the 1960s, many members of the burgeoning evangelical churches of the suburbs, South, and West had become more and more alienated from a culture that seemed to them to trivialize religion and promote immorality. They demanded the reversal of Supreme Court decisions banning prayer in public schools, protecting pornography as free speech, and legalizing abortion. The Religious Right proved remarkably adept at using modern technology, including mass mailings and televised religious programming, to raise funds for their crusade and spread their message. In 1979, Jerry Falwell, a Virginia minister, created the self-styled **Moral Majority**, devoted to waging a "war against sin" and electing "pro-life, pro-family, pro-America" candidates to office. Falwell identified supporters of abortion rights, easy divorce, and "military unpreparedness" as the forces of Satan.

Christian conservatives were deeply agitated by the ongoing sexual revolution. The growing assertiveness of the new gay movement spurred an especially fierce reaction. In 1977, after a campaign led by the popular singer Anita

Bryant, a familiar fixture in televised orange juice commercials, Dade County, Florida, passed an anti-gay ordinance under the banner "Save Our Children."

The Battle over the Equal Rights Amendment

During the 1970s, "family values" moved to the center of conservative politics, nowhere more so than in the battle over the Equal Rights Amendment (ERA). Originally proposed during the 1920s by Alice Paul and the Woman's Party, the ERA had been revived by second-wave feminists. In the wake of the rights revolution, the amendment's affirmation that "equality of rights under the law" could not be abridged "on account of sex" hardly seemed controversial. In 1972, with broad bipartisan support, Congress approved the ERA and sent it to the states for ratification. Designed to eliminate obstacles to the full participation of women in public life, it aroused unexpected protest from those who claimed it would discredit the role of wife and homemaker.

The ERA debate reflected a division among women as much as a battle of the sexes. To its supporters, the amendment offered a guarantee of women's freedom in the public sphere. To its foes, freedom for women still resided in the divinely appointed roles of wife and mother. Phyllis Schlafly, who helped to organize

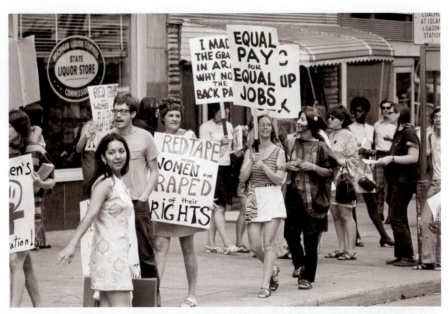

A women's liberation march in Detroit in 1970 highlights the issue of equal pay for equal work. At the time, women earned less than men in virtually every category of employment.

From DECLARATION OF CONTINUING INDEPENDENCE (1974)

The International Indian Treaty Council was established in 1974 to press the case for Native American treaty rights on the international stage. Their founding declaration connected American Indian rights to global decolonization efforts. In 1977, they won consultative status with the United Nations Economic and Social Council and have since continued to press the UN for recognition of Indigenous Rights.

The United States of America has continually violated the independent Native Peoples of this continent by Executive action, Legislative fiat and Judicial decision. By its actions, the U.S. has denied all Native people their International Treaty rights, Treaty lands and basic human rights of freedom and sovereignty....

Might does not make right. Sovereign people of varying cultures have the absolute right to live in harmony with Mother Earth so long as they do not infringe upon this same right of other peoples. The denial of this right to any sovereign people, such as the Native American Indian Nations, must be challenged by truth and action....

* * *

The International Indian Treaty Council recognizes the sovereignty of all Native Nations and will stand in unity to support our Native and international brothers and sisters in their respective and collective struggles concerning international treaties and agreements violated by the United States and other governments.

* * *

We recognize that there is only one color of Mankind in the world who are not represented in the United Nations; that is the indigenous Redman of the Western Hemisphere....

The International Indian Treaty Council established by this conference is directed to make the application to the United Nations for recognition and membership of the sovereign Native Nations. We pledge our support to any similar application by an aboriginal people.

* * *

We, the People of the International Indian Treaty Council, following the guidance of our elders through instructions from the Great Spirit, and out of respect for our sacred Mother Earth, all her children, and those yet unborn, offer our lives for our International Treaty Rights.

QUESTIONS

1. *What does the declaration identify as necessary to achieve American Indian self-determination?*

2. *How does the document connect Native American rights to wider international struggles?*

opposition to the ERA, insisted that the "free enterprise system" was the "real liberator of women," since labor-saving home appliances offered more genuine freedom than "whining about past injustices" or seeking fulfillment outside the home. Opponents claimed that the ERA would let men "off the hook" by denying their responsibility to provide for their wives and children. Polls consistently showed that a majority of Americans, male and female, favored the ERA. But thanks to the mobilization of conservative women, the amendment failed to achieve ratification by the required thirty-eight states.

The Abortion Controversy

An even more acrimonious battle emerged in the 1970s over abortion rights, another example, to conservatives, of how liberals in office promoted sexual immorality at the expense of moral values. The movement to reverse the 1973 *Roe v. Wade* decision began among Roman Catholics, whose church condemned abortion under any circumstances. But it soon enlisted evangelical Protestants and social conservatives more generally. Life, the movement insisted, begins at conception, and abortion is nothing less than murder. Between this position and the feminist insistence that a woman's right to control her body includes the right to a safe, legal abortion, compromise was impossible. Ironically, both sides showed how the rights revolution had reshaped the language of politics. Defenders of abortion exalted "the right to choose" as the essence of freedom. Opponents called themselves the "right to life" movement and claimed to represent the rights of the "unborn child."

The abortion issue drew a bitter, sometimes violent line through American politics. It affected battles over nominees to judicial positions and led to demonstrations at family-planning and abortion clinics. The anti-abortion movement won its first victory in 1976 when Congress, over President Ford's veto, ended federal funding for abortions for poor women through the Medicaid program. By the 1990s, a few fringe anti-abortion activists were placing bombs at medical clinics and murdering doctors who terminated pregnancies. Today, most women continue to have the legal right of access to abortion. But in many areas the procedure became more and more difficult to obtain as hospitals and doctors stopped providing it and states passed laws that limited the number of facilities providing abortions.

Conservatism in the West

The West has always both reflected and contributed to national political trends. In the 1970s and 1980s it offered fertile soil for various strands of conservatism. The population movements of previous decades stimulated this development. Many southerners had left their homes for southern California, bringing with them their distinctive form of evangelical Christianity. Increasingly alienated from a Democratic Party that embraced the rights revolution and with it, evangelicals felt, the decline of traditional values, they gravitated to the California Republican Party, from which emerged national Republican leaders such as Richard Nixon and Ronald Reagan. California conservatives also embraced the new anti-tax mood.

In 1978, conservatives sponsored and California voters approved Proposition 13, a ban on further increases in property taxes. The vote demonstrated that the level of taxation could be a powerful political issue. Economic decline, inflation, and rising property taxes broadened the constituency receptive to demands for lower taxes. To conservatives, tax reductions served the dual purpose of enhancing business profits and reducing the resources available to government, thus making new social programs financially impossible. Proposition 13 proved to be a windfall for businesses and home owners, while reducing funds available for schools, libraries, and other public services. Many voters, however, proved willing to accept this result of lower taxes. As anti-tax mobilization flourished throughout the country, commonly known as the **tax revolt**, many states followed California's lead.

There have always been voices in the West insisting that the region has a colonial relationship with the rest of the country. They point to federal ownership of large swaths of western land, and the dependence of western development on investment from the East. In the late nineteenth century, this view helped give rise to western Populism, when the targets of protest were eastern banks and railroad companies, as well as a national economic policy that favored these corporations. Nearly a century later it became associated with a conservative upsurge known as the Sagebrush Rebellion (the name given to a bill passed by the Nevada legislature in 1979) directed at the federal government. The roots of this "rebellion" lie as far back as the 1920s, when the U.S. Forest Service announced plans to increase grazing fees and mineral rights in national forests and other public lands. Nevada's ranchers went to court to block these fees but were rebuffed by the Supreme Court. In the 1970s, new environmental regulations won fresh recruits to the movement. The Clean Air Act alarmed western coal operators. Westerners who believed the environmental policies of the Carter administration were closing the public domain to exploitation eagerly supported Ronald Reagan's presidential candidacy.

Using the language of freedom from government tyranny, leaders in western states insisted that the states themselves be given decision-making power over issues like grazing rights, mining development, and whether public lands should be closed to fishing and hunting. With the federal government reluctant to give up control over public lands in the West, the Sagebrush Rebellion

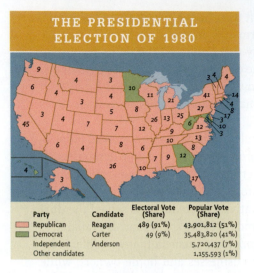

THE PRESIDENTIAL
ELECTION OF 1980

Party	Candidate	Electoral Vote (Share)	Popular Vote (Share)
Republican	Reagan	489 (91%)	43,901,812 (51%)
Democrat	Carter	49 (9%)	35,483,820 (41%)
Independent	Anderson		5,720,437 (7%)
Other candidates			1,155,593 (1%)

had few concrete accomplishments, but it underscored the rising tide of antigovernment sentiment.

The Election of 1980

By 1980, Carter's approval rating had fallen to 21 percent—lower than Nixon's at the time of his resignation. A conservative tide seemed to be rising throughout the Western world. In 1979, Margaret Thatcher became prime minister of Great Britain. She promised to restore economic competitiveness by curtailing the power of unions, reducing taxes, selling state-owned industries to private owners, and cutting back the welfare state. In the United States, Ronald Reagan's 1980 campaign for the presidency brought together the many strands of 1970s conservatism. He pledged to end stagflation and restore the country's dominant role in the world and its confidence in itself. "Let's make America great again," he proclaimed. "The era of self-doubt is over."

Reagan also appealed skillfully to "white backlash." He kicked off his campaign in Philadelphia, Mississippi, where three civil rights workers had been murdered in 1964, with a speech emphasizing his belief in states' rights. Many white southerners understood this doctrine as including opposition to federal intervention on behalf of civil rights. During the campaign, Reagan repeatedly condemned welfare "cheats," school busing, and affirmative action. The Republican platform reversed the party's long-standing support for the Equal Rights Amendment and condemned moral permissiveness. Although not personally religious and the first divorced man to run for president, Reagan won the support of the Religious Right and conservative upholders of "family values."

Riding a wave of dissatisfaction with the country's condition, Reagan swept into the White House. He carried such Democratic strongholds as Illinois, Texas, and New York. Carter received 41 percent of the popular vote, a humiliating defeat for a sitting president.

Jimmy Carter's reputation improved after he left the White House. He went to work for Habitat for Humanity, an organization that constructs homes for poor families. In the 1990s, he negotiated a cease-fire between warring Muslim and Serb forces in Bosnia and arranged a peaceful transfer of power from the military to an elected government in Haiti. In 2002, Carter was awarded the Nobel Peace Prize. His presidency, however, is almost universally considered a failure. And his defeat in 1980 launched the **Reagan Revolution**, which completed the transformation of freedom from the rallying cry of the left to a possession of the right.

THE REAGAN REVOLUTION

Ronald Reagan followed a most unusual path to the presidency. Originally a New Deal Democrat and head of the Screen Actors Guild (the only union leader ever to reach the White House), he emerged in the 1950s as a spokesman for the General Electric Corporation, preaching the virtues of unregulated capitalism. His speech for Barry Goldwater in 1964 (mentioned earlier) brought Reagan to national attention. Two years later, California voters elected Reagan as governor. In 1976, he challenged President Ford for the Republican nomination and came close to winning it. His victory in 1980 brought to power a diverse coalition of old and new conservatives: Sunbelt suburbanites and urban working-class ethnics; antigovernment crusaders and advocates of a more aggressive foreign policy; and libertarians who believed in freeing the individual from restraint and the Christian Right, which sought to restore what they considered traditional moral values to American life.

Reagan and American Freedom

Reagan's opponents often underestimated him. Unlike most modern presidents, he was content to outline broad policy themes and leave their implementation to others. Reagan, however, was hardly a political novice, having governed California during the turbulent 1960s. He was an excellent public speaker, and his optimism and affability appealed to large numbers of Americans. Reagan made conservatism seem progressive, rather than an attempt to turn back the tide of progress. He frequently quoted Thomas Paine: "We have it in our power to begin the world over again."

Overall, Reagan proved remarkably successful at seizing control of the terms of public debate. On issues ranging from taxes to government spending, national security, crime, welfare, and "traditional values," he put Democrats on the defensive. But he also proved to be a pragmatist, recognizing when to compromise so as not to fragment his diverse coalition of supporters.

Reagan's Economic Policies

Like Roosevelt and Johnson before him, Reagan spoke of "economic freedom" and proposed an "economic Bill of Rights." But in contrast to his predecessors, who used these phrases to combat poverty and strengthen economic security, economic freedom for Reagan meant curtailing the power of unions, dismantling regulations, and radically reducing taxes. Taxation, he declared, violated the principle that "the right to earn your own keep and keep what you earn" was "what it means to be free."

In 1981, Reagan persuaded Congress to reduce the top tax rate from 70 percent to 50 percent and to index tax brackets to take inflation into account. Five years later, the Tax Reform Act reduced the rate on the wealthiest Americans to 28 percent. These measures marked a sharp retreat from the principle of progressivity (the idea that the wealthy should pay a higher percentage of their income in taxes than other citizens), one of the ways twentieth-century societies tried to address the unequal distribution of wealth. Reagan also appointed conservative heads of regulatory agencies, who cut back on environmental protection and workplace safety rules about which business had complained for years.

Since the New Deal, liberals had tried to promote economic growth by using the power of the government to bolster ordinary Americans' purchasing power. Reagan's economic program, known as "supply-side economics" by proponents and "trickle-down economics" by critics, relied on high interest rates to curb inflation and lower tax rates, especially for businesses and high-income Americans, to stimulate private investment. The policy assumed that cutting taxes would inspire Americans at all income levels to work harder, since they would keep more of the money they earned. Everyone would benefit from increased business profits, and because of a growing economy, government receipts would rise despite lower tax rates.

Reagan and Labor

Reagan inaugurated an era of hostility between the federal government and organized labor. In August 1981, when 13,000 members of PATCO, the union of air traffic controllers, began a strike in violation of federal law, Reagan fired them all. He used the military to oversee the nation's air traffic system until new controllers could be trained. Reagan's action inspired many private employers to launch anti-union offensives. The hiring of workers to replace permanently those who had gone on strike, a rare occurrence before 1980, became widespread. Manufacturing employment, where union membership was concentrated, meanwhile continued its long-term decline. By the mid-1990s, the steel industry employed only 170,000 persons—down from 600,000 in 1973. When Reagan left office, both the service and retail sectors employed more Americans than manufacturing, and only 11 percent of workers with nongovernment jobs were union members.

Reaganomics, as critics dubbed the administration's policies, initially produced the most severe recession since the 1930s. A long period of economic expansion, however, followed the downturn of 1981–1982. As companies "downsized" their workforces, shifted production overseas, and took advantage of new technologies such as satellite communications, they became more profitable. At the same time, the rate of inflation, 13.5 percent at the beginning of 1981, declined to 3.5 percent in 1988, partly because a period of expanded oil production that drove down prices succeeded the shortages of the 1970s. By the end of Reagan's presidency in 1989, the real gross domestic product had risen by 25 percent and unemployment was down to 5.5 percent. These were significant accomplishments.

The Problem of Inequality

Together, Reagan's policies, rising stock prices, and deindustrialization resulted in a considerable rise in economic inequality. By the mid-1990s, the richest 1 percent of Americans owned 40 percent of the nation's wealth, twice their share twenty years earlier. Most spent their income not on productive investments and charity as supply-side economists had promised, but on luxury goods, real-estate speculation, and corporate buyouts that often led to plant closings as operations were consolidated. The income of middle-class families, especially those with a wife who did not work outside the home, stagnated while that of the poorest one-fifth of the population declined. Because of falling investment in public housing, the release of mental patients from state hospitals, and cuts in welfare, homeless persons became a visible fixture on the streets of cities from New York to Los Angeles.

Deindustrialization and the decline of the labor movement had a particularly devastating impact on minority workers, who had only recently gained a foothold in better-paying manufacturing jobs. Thanks to the opening of colleges and professional schools to minority students as a result of the civil rights movement and affirmative action programs, the Black middle class expanded considerably. But Black workers, traditionally the last hired and first fired, were hard hit by economic changes.

During the 1970s, Jim Crow had finally ended in many workplaces and unions. But just as decades of painful efforts to obtain better jobs bore fruit, hundreds of thousands of Black workers lost their jobs when factories closed their doors. In South Gate, a working-class suburb of Los Angeles, for example, the giant Firestone tire factory shut down in 1980, only a few years after Black and Latino workers made their first breakthroughs in employment. When the national unemployment rate reached 8.9 percent at the end of 1981, the figure for Blacks exceeded 20 percent. Nor did Black workers share fully in the

From BARRY COMMONER, *THE CLOSING CIRCLE* (1971)

Environmentalism, a movement born in the 1960s, expanded rapidly in the following decade. In *The Closing Circle*, Barry Commoner, a biologist later called the Paul Revere of the movement, warned that technological development and the pursuit of economic growth regardless of consequences were creating an environmental crisis. He called on Americans to alter their lifestyles to bring them into harmony with the "ecosphere"—the natural environment within which people live.

The environment has just been rediscovered by the people who live in it. In the United States the event was celebrated in April 1970, during Earth Week. It was a sudden, noisy awakening. School children cleaned up rubbish; college students organized new demonstrations; determined citizens recaptured the streets from the automobile, at least for a day. Everyone seemed to be aroused to the environmental danger and eager to do something about it.

They were offered lots of advice. Almost every writer, almost every speaker, on the college campuses, in the streets and on television and radio broadcasts, was ready to fix the blame and pronounce a cure for the environmental crisis.

Some blamed pollution on the rising population. . . . Some blamed man's innate aggressiveness. . . . Having spent some years in the effort simply to detect and describe the growing list of environmental problems—radioactive fallout, air and water pollution, the deterioration of the soil—and in tracing some of their links to social and political processes, the identification of a single cause and cure seemed a rather bold step. . . .

Any living thing that hopes to live on the earth must fit into the ecosphere or perish. The environmental crisis is a sign that the finely sculpted fit between life and its surroundings has begun to corrode. As the links between one living thing and another, and between all of them and their surroundings, begin to break down, the dynamic interactions that sustain the whole have begun to falter and, in some places, stop. . . .

We have broken out of the circle of life, converting its endless cycles into manmade, linear events; oil is taken from the ground, distilled into fuel, burned in an engine, converted thereby into noxious fumes, which are emitted into the air. At the end of the line is smog. Other man-made breaks in the ecosphere's cycle spew out toxic chemicals, sewage, heaps of rubbish—the testimony to our power to tear the ecological fabric that has, for millions of years, sustained the planet's life.

From RICHARD E. BLAKEMORE, REPORT ON THE SAGEBRUSH REBELLION (1979)

The rapid growth of the environmentalist movement sparked a conservative reaction, especially in the western states. What came to be called the Sagebrush Rebellion denounced federal control of large areas of western land as well as new environmental regulations that, the "rebels" claimed, threatened energy production and long-standing grazing rights. **Richard E. Blakemore**, a member of the Nevada state senate, offered this explanation of the outlook of many westerners.

The "sagebrush rebellion" is a catchy but somewhat misleading term used to describe the western states' demands for a greater role in determining the future of the west. Unlike the dictionary definition, in this rebellion there is no armed or unlawful resistance to government. Neither is western land desolate or worthless as the term "sagebrush" connoted. Moreover, if much of the land in the west ever was considered of little worth, the need for energy has changed that.

Statistics show that much of the west is controlled by the federal government. . . . On average, the federal government controls 52.6 percent of the land in the 12 western states. . . . For many years, the public domain was open to ranching, mining, and outdoor recreation. But a number of federal acts, passed to protect and conserve the environment, have closed great parts of the public domain to traditional uses. . . .

The west today is at the confluence of two major movements—that for protection of the environment and that for production of energy. To a great extent, the success of the attempt for U.S. energy independence depends on resources of the west. In addition, the west is looked to for increased agricultural production and for its reserves of minerals necessary to modern industry. The environmental movement prompted the passage of federal legislation aimed at protecting the environment and maintaining great portions of the country in a natural state. Among the major environmental acts of the past 15 years are the Wilderness Act, the National Environmental Protection Act, the Federal Land Policy Management Act, the Wild and Scenic Rivers Act, and the National Forest Management Act.

The genesis of the sagebrush rebellion can be found in the conflict between the desires to protect and preserve the environment and the demands for food, minerals, and energy from the west. . . .

While the particular issues on which the sagebrush rebellion are based are more common in the west, the principles behind the movement are national in scope. . . .

Because of the federal omnipresence in the west, westerners have reached the crisis first. But reversing the trend towards centralization that threatens the economy, our lands, and our freedoms is of concern to all Americans.

QUESTIONS

1. *How and why does Commoner ask Americans to rethink their definition of freedom?*

2. *What elements of environmental policy does Blakemore see as a threat to "our freedoms"?*

3. *How do the two writers differ in their visions of the future of American society?*

recovery that followed. Few had the education to take advantage of job openings in growing "knowledge-based" industries like technology and information services. Overall, during the 1980s Black males fell farther than any other group in the population in terms of wages and jobs.

The Second Gilded Age

In retrospect, the 1980s, like the 1890s, would be widely remembered as a decade of misplaced values. Buying out companies generated more profits than running them; making deals, not making products, became the way to get rich. The merger of Nabisco and R. J. Reynolds Tobacco Company in 1988 produced close to $1 billion in fees for lawyers, economic advisers, and stockbrokers. "Greed is healthy," declared Wall Street financier Ivan Boesky (who ended up in prison for insider stock trading). Loosened government regulation facilitated irresponsible and risky financial practices.

Taxpayers footed the bill for some of the consequences. The deregulation of savings and loan associations—banks that had generally confined themselves to financing home mortgages—allowed these institutions to invest in unsound real-estate ventures and corporate mergers. Losses piled up, and the Federal Savings and Loan Insurance Corporation, which insured depositors' accounts, faced bankruptcy. After Reagan left office, the federal government bailed out the savings and loan institutions, at a cost to taxpayers estimated at $250 billion.

Supply-side advocates insisted that lowering taxes would enlarge government revenue by stimulating economic activity. But spurred by large increases in funds for the military, federal spending far outstripped income, producing large budget deficits, despite assurances by supply-siders that this would not happen. During Reagan's presidency, the national debt tripled to $2.7 trillion. Nonetheless, Reagan remained immensely popular. He took credit for economic expansion while blaming congressional leaders for the ballooning federal deficit. He won a triumphant reelection in 1984. His opponent, Walter Mondale (best remembered for choosing Congresswoman Geraldine Ferraro of New York as his running mate, the first woman candidate on a major-party presidential ticket), carried only his home state of Minnesota and the District of Columbia.

Reagan and Immigration Reform

Under Reagan, Congress passed the most significant reform of immigration policy since 1965. Large numbers of immigrants had entered the country from Mexico without authorization—the so-called illegals. These newcomers were drawn by strong demand for low-wage labor, which far exceeded the annual legal quotas established under the Hart-Celler Act (discussed in the previous chapter). Calls to stem the flow of undocumented immigrants grew. Reagan viewed immigration as crucial to the country's economic strength. He promised to "continue America's tradition as a land that welcomes people," even as the nation regained control of its borders. The Immigration Reform and Control Act of 1986 provided amnesty and a path to citizenship for nearly 3 million undocumented immigrants who had put down roots in the country but penalized employers who knowingly hired them. But with weak enforcement provisions unauthorized immigration continued.

Conservatives and Reagan

While he implemented their economic policies, Reagan in some ways disappointed ardent conservatives. The administration sharply reduced funding for Great Society antipoverty programs such as food stamps, school lunches, and federal financing of low-income housing. But it left intact core elements of the welfare state, such as Social Security, Medicare, and Medicaid, which many conservatives wished to curtail significantly or repeal. The Reagan era did little to advance the social agenda of the Christian Right. Abortion remained legal, women continued to enter the labor force in unprecedented numbers, and Reagan even appointed the first female member of the Supreme Court, Sandra Day O'Connor. In 1986, in *Bowers v. Hardwick*, in a rare victory for cultural conservatives, the Supreme Court did uphold the constitutionality of state laws outlawing homosexual acts. (In 2003, the justices would reverse the *Bowers* decision, declaring such laws unconstitutional.)

Reagan gave verbal support to a proposed constitutional amendment restoring prayer in public schools but did little to promote its passage. Reagan's Justice Department cut back on civil rights enforcement and worked to curtail affirmative action programs. But to the end of Reagan's presidency, the Supreme Court continued to approve plans by private employers and city and state governments to upgrade minority employment.

The Wars on Crime and Drugs

If Reagan weakened the federal government's power to regulate business, he strengthened its role in crime control. He championed a strand of thought about freedom favored by social conservatives that emphasized law and order to secure "freedom from fear." Reagan built on initiatives begun during the Nixon administration. With reported crime rising sharply and cities gripped by riots, Nixon had called for increased spending on policing and law enforcement, and an expansion of the nation's prisons. Although the number of prisoners

TABLE 26.3 Percentage of Adult Male Population Ever Incarcerated, 1974–2001

	1974	1991	2001
White (%)	1.4	1.9	2.6
Black (%)	8.7	12.0	16.6
Hispanic (%)	2.3	4.9	7.7

As the war on drugs intensified, mandatory minimum sentences and discriminatory policing and enforcement led to stark racial and ethnic differences in incarceration rates.

had remained low and stable for years, Nixon anticipated a large increase as part of a crackdown on the growing use, in cities, suburbs, and on college campuses, of marijuana and heroin. In 1973, Nixon declared an "all-out war on the global drug menace," but with little result.

Reagan expanded on Nixon's "tough on crime" approach. The Comprehensive Crime Control Act of 1984 reinstated the federal death penalty, abolished the federal parole system, and instituted harsh sentencing guidelines for judges to implement. Public fears about the spread of crack in urban areas contributed to support for these punitive policies. Reagan brought national spending on criminal justice to a record high of nearly $3.5 billion. In 1986, the Anti–Drug Abuse Act led to a surge in arrests, and a rapidly expanding prison population. In 1980 there were 50,000 Americans in prison for nonviolent drug violations; by 1997 the number had reached 400,000, most of them Blacks and Hispanics, who were disproportionately targeted by police. But the war on drugs failed to seriously disrupt global supply chains or the domestic demand for drugs.

Reagan and the Cold War

In foreign policy, Reagan breathed new life into the rhetorical division of the world into a free West and unfree East. He resumed vigorous denunciation of the Soviet Union—calling it an "evil empire"—and sponsored the largest military buildup in American history, including new long-range bombers and missiles. In 1983, he proposed an entirely new strategy, the Strategic Defense Initiative, based on developing a space-based system to intercept and destroy enemy missiles. The idea was not remotely feasible technologically, and, if deployed, it would violate the Anti–Ballistic Missile Treaty of 1972. But it appealed to Reagan's desire to reassert America's worldwide power. He persuaded NATO, over much opposition, to introduce short-range nuclear weapons into Europe to counter Soviet forces. But the renewed arms race and Reagan's casual talk of winning a nuclear war caused widespread alarm at home and abroad. In the early 1980s, a movement for a nuclear freeze—a halt to the development of nuclear weapons—attracted millions of supporters in the United States and Europe.

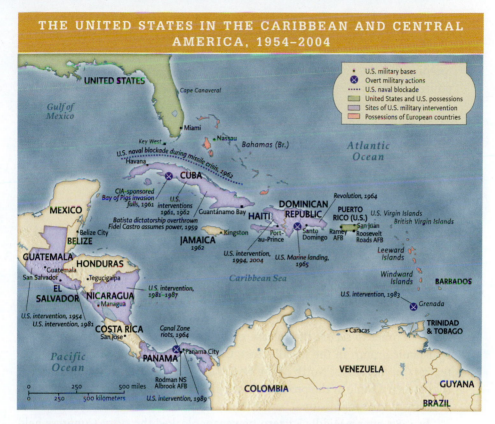

THE UNITED STATES IN THE CARIBBEAN AND CENTRAL AMERICA, 1954–2004

As in the first part of the twentieth century, the United States intervened frequently in Caribbean and Central American countries during and immediately after the Cold War.

Reagan came into office determined to overturn the "Vietnam Syndrome"— as widespread public reluctance to commit American forces overseas was called. He sent American troops to the Caribbean island of Grenada to oust a pro-Cuban government. In 1982, Reagan dispatched marines as a peacekeeping force to Lebanon, where a civil war raged between the Christian government, supported by Israeli forces, and Muslim insurgents. But he quickly withdrew them after a bomb exploded at their barracks, killing 241 Americans. The public, Reagan realized, would support minor operations like Grenada but remained unwilling to sustain heavy casualties abroad.

Reagan generally relied on military aid rather than American troops to pursue his foreign policy objectives. Abandoning the Carter administration's emphasis on human rights, Reagan embraced the idea, advanced in 1979 by neoconservative writer Jeane Kirkpatrick, that the United States should oppose "totalitarian" communists but assist "authoritarian" noncommunist regimes. Kirkpatrick became the American ambassador to the United Nations, and the United States stepped up its alliances with Third World anticommunist dictatorships like the governments of Chile and South Africa. The administration poured in funds to combat insurgencies against the governments of El Salvador and Guatemala, whose armies and associated death squads committed flagrant abuses against their own citizens. When El Salvador's army massacred hundreds of civilians in the town of El Mozote in 1981, the State Department denied that the event, widely reported in the press, had taken place.

The Iran-Contra Affair

American involvement in Central America produced the greatest scandal of Reagan's presidency, the **Iran-Contra affair**. In 1984, Congress banned military aid to the Contras (derived from the Spanish word for "against") fighting the Sandinista government of Nicaragua, which, as noted earlier, had ousted the American-backed dictator Anastasio Somoza in 1979. In 1985, Reagan secretly authorized the sale of arms to Iran—now involved in a war with its neighbor, Iraq—in order to secure the release of a number of American hostages held by Islamic groups in the Middle East. CIA director William Casey and Lieutenant Colonel Oliver North of the National Security Council set up a system that diverted some of the proceeds to buy military supplies for the Contras in defiance of the congressional ban. The scheme continued for nearly two years.

In 1987, after a Middle Eastern newspaper leaked the story, Congress held televised hearings that revealed a pattern of official duplicity and violation of the law reminiscent of the Nixon era. Eleven members of the administration eventually were convicted of perjury or destroying documents or pleaded guilty before being tried. Reagan denied knowledge of the illegal proceedings, but the Iran-Contra affair undermined confidence that he controlled his own administration.

Reagan and Gorbachev

In his second term, to the surprise of both his foes and supporters, Reagan softened his anticommunist rhetoric and established good relations with Soviet premier Mikhail Gorbachev. Gorbachev had come to power in 1985, bent on reforming the Soviet Union's repressive political system and reinvigorating its economy. The country had fallen further and further behind the United States in the production and distribution of consumer goods, and it relied increasingly on agricultural imports to feed itself. Gorbachev inaugurated policies known as *glasnost* (political openness) and *perestroika* (economic reform).

Gorbachev realized that significant change would be impossible without reducing his country's military budget. Reagan was ready to negotiate. A series of talks between 1985 and 1987 yielded more progress on arms control than in the entire postwar period to that point, including an agreement to eliminate intermediate- and short-range nuclear missiles in Europe. In 1988, Gorbachev began pulling Soviet troops out of Afghanistan. Having entered office as an ardent Cold Warrior, Reagan left with hostilities between the superpowers much diminished. He even repudiated his earlier comment that the Soviet Union was an "evil empire," saying that it referred to "another era."

Reagan's Legacy

Reagan's presidency revealed the contradictions at the heart of modern conservatism. In some ways, the Reagan Revolution undermined the very values and institutions conservatives held dear. Intended to discourage reliance on government handouts by rewarding honest work and business initiative, Reagan's policies inspired a speculative frenzy that enriched architects of corporate takeovers and investors in the stock market while leaving in their wake plant closings, job losses, and devastated communities. Nothing proved more threatening to local traditions or family stability than deindustrialization, insecurity about employment, and the relentless downward pressure on wages. Nothing did more to undermine a sense of common national purpose than the widening gap between rich and poor.

Because of the Iran-Contra scandal and the enormous deficits the government had accumulated, Reagan left the presidency with his reputation somewhat tarnished. Nonetheless, few figures have so successfully changed the landscape and language of politics. Reagan's vice president, George H. W. Bush, defeated Michael Dukakis, the governor of Massachusetts, in the 1988 election partly because Dukakis could not respond effectively to the charge that he was a "liberal"—now a term of political abuse. Conservative assumptions about the virtues of the free market and the evils of "big government" dominated the mass media and political debates. Those receiving public assistance had come to be seen not as citizens entitled to help in coping with economic misfortune but as a drain on taxes. During the 1990s, these and other conservative ideas would be embraced almost as fully by President Bill Clinton, a Democrat, as by Reagan and the Republicans.

The Election of 1988

The 1988 election seemed to show politics sinking to new lows. Both parties ran aggressive negative campaigns. Democrats ridiculed the Republican vice-presidential nominee, Senator Dan Quayle of Indiana, for factual and linguistic mistakes. Republicans spread unfounded rumors that Michael Dukakis's wife had burned an American flag during the 1960s. Most controversially, Republicans ran a racially charged campaign ad accusing Dukakis of being "soft on crime." The television ad depicted the threatening image of Willie Horton, a Black felon who attacked a white couple while furloughed from prison during Dukasis's term as governor of Massachusetts. Rarely in the modern era had a major party appealed so blatantly to racial fears.

Although he did not match Reagan's landslide victory of 1984, Bush achieved a substantial majority, winning 54 percent of the popular vote. Democratic success in retaining control of Congress suggested that an electoral base existed for a comeback. But this would occur only if the party fashioned a new appeal to replace traditional liberalism, which had been eclipsed by the triumph of conservatism.

CHAPTER REVIEW

REVIEW QUESTIONS

1. *Describe the legislative efforts to enable persons with disabilities to participate fully in society during this period.*

2. *Why were social issues associated with the sexual revolution so contested by all sides?*

3. *What were continuing challenges to the cohesiveness of the Democratic (New Deal) coalition? What were the consequences of those divisions?*

4. *What were the main features of Nixon's policy of "realism" in dealing with China and the Soviet Union?*

5. *Describe the basic events and the larger significance of the Watergate scandal.*

6. *What were the major causes for the decline of the U.S. economy in the 1970s?*

7. *What were the causes and consequences of the public's disillusionment with the federal government in the 1970s and 1980s?*

8. *Identify the groups and their agendas that combined to create the new conservative base in the 1970s and 1980s.*

9. *How did Reagan view immigration? What was the significance of his reform to immigration policy?*

10. *How did Reagan expand on Nixon's "tough on crime" approach?*

11. *Why was there growth in economic inequality in the 1980s?*

12. *How did various groups see the relationship between women's rights and freedom differently?*

KEY TERMS

affirmative action (p. 1042)

busing (p. 1043)

Title IX (p. 1047)

Strategic Arms Limitation Talks (p. 1048)

détente (p. 1048)

My Lai massacre (p. 1050)

Pentagon Papers (p. 1050)

War Powers Act (p. 1050)

Vietnam Syndrome (p. 1051)

Watergate (p. 1052)

oil embargo (p. 1055)

stagflation (p. 1056)

deindustrialization (p. 1056)

Sunbelt (p. 1056)

Helsinki Accords (p. 1058)

deregulation (p. 1059)

Three Mile Island (p. 1059)

Camp David Accords (p. 1060)

Moral Majority (p. 1063)

tax revolt (p. 1067)

Reagan Revolution (p. 1069)

Reaganomics (p. 1071)

Iran-Contra affair (p. 1078)

Go to 🐰 INQUIZITIVE

To see what you know—and learn what you've missed—with personalized feedback along the way.

CHAPTER 27

A NEW WORLD ORDER

1989–2004

FOCUS QUESTIONS

- *What were the major international initiatives of the Clinton administration in the aftermath of the Cold War?*

- *What forces drove the economic resurgence of the 1990s?*

- *What cultural conflicts emerged in the 1990s?*

- *How did a divisive political partisanship affect the election of 2000?*

- *Why did Al Qaeda attack the United States on September 11, 2001?*

- *What were the major policy elements of the war on terror in the wake of September 11, 2001?*

- *How did the war in Iraq unfold in the wake of 9/11?*

- *How did the war on terror affect the economy and American liberties?*

T he year 1989 was one of the most momentous of the twentieth century. In April, tens of thousands of student demonstrators occupied Tiananmen Square in the heart of Beijing, demanding greater democracy in China. Workers, teachers, and even some government officials joined them, until their numbers swelled to nearly 1 million. The students erected a figure reminiscent of the Statue of Liberty, calling it "The Goddess of Democracy and Freedom." In June, Chinese troops crushed the protest, killing an unknown number of people, possibly thousands.

In the fall of 1989, pro-democracy demonstrations spread across eastern Europe. Soviet leader Mikhail Gorbachev made it clear that unlike in the past, the Soviet Union would not intervene. The climactic event took place on November 9 when crowds breached the Berlin Wall, which since 1961 had stood as the Cold War's most prominent symbol. One by one, the region's communist governments agreed to give up power. In 1990, a reunified German nation absorbed East Germany. The remarkably swift and almost entirely peaceful collapse of communism in eastern Europe became known as the "velvet revolution."

Meanwhile, the Soviet Union itself slipped deeper and deeper into crisis. Gorbachev's attempts at economic reform produced only chaos, and his policy of political openness allowed long-suppressed national and ethnic tensions to rise to the surface. In 1991, Gorbachev resigned from the Communist Party, ending its seventy-four-year rule. One after another, the republics of the Soviet Union declared themselves sovereign states. At the end of 1991, the Soviet Union ceased to exist; in its place were fifteen new independent nations.

The sudden and unexpected collapse of communism marked the end of the Cold War and a stunning triumph for the United States and its allies. For the first time since 1917, there existed a truly worldwide capitalist system. Even China, while remaining under Communist Party rule, had already embarked on market reforms and rushed to attract foreign investment. Other events suggested that the 1990s would be a "decade of democracy." In 1990, South Africa released Nelson Mandela, head of the African National Congress, from prison. Four years

· CHRONOLOGY ·

1989	Communism falls in eastern Europe
1991	Gulf War
	Dissolution of the Soviet Union
1992	Los Angeles riots
	Casey v. Planned Parenthood of Pennsylvania
	Clinton elected president
1993	Israel and Palestine Liberation Organization sign the Oslo Accords
	North American Free Trade Agreement approved
1994	Republicans win Congress; Contract with America
1995	Oklahoma City federal building bombed
1996	Clinton eliminates Aid to Families with Dependent Children
	Defense of Marriage Act
1998– 1999	Clinton impeachment proceedings
1999	Protests in Seattle against the World Trade Organization
	Glass-Steagall Act repealed
2000	*Bush v. Gore*
2001	9/11 attacks
	U.S. enters war in Afghanistan
	USA Patriot Act
2002	Bush identifies "axis of evil"
	Department of Homeland Security established
2003	Iraq War begins

later, as a result of the first democratic elections in the country's history, Mandela became president, ending the system of state-sponsored racial inequality, known as "apartheid," and white minority government.

The sudden shift from a bipolar world to one of unquestioned American predominance promised to redefine the country's global role. President George H. W. Bush spoke of the coming of a **new world order**. But no one knew what its characteristics would be and what new challenges to American power might arise.

THE POST-COLD WAR WORLD

Bush's first major foreign policy action revealed how new threats led to continued U.S. military intervention after the Cold War ended. In 1989, Bush dispatched troops to Panama to overthrow the government of General Manuel Antonio Noriega, a former ally of the United States indicted in two federal courts on drug trafficking charges. Bush, declaring drugs a major international threat, sent troops to Panama, installed a new government, and extradited Noriega to the United States. The Organization of American States protested the violation of international law, but the United States' position as the only remaining superpower emboldened interventionists. Noriega became the first foreign government leader tried and convicted in U.S. courts.

The Gulf War

A far more serious crisis arose in 1990 when Iraq invaded and annexed Kuwait, an oil-rich sheikdom on the Persian Gulf. Fearing that Iraqi dictator Saddam

U.S. soldiers seated under a portrait of Iraqi ruler Saddam Hussein at the border between Iraq and Kuwait during the Gulf War of 1991.

Hussein might next attack Saudi Arabia, a longtime ally that supplied more oil to the United States than any other country, Bush rushed troops to defend Kuwait and warned Iraq to withdraw from the country or face war. The Iraqi invasion so flagrantly violated international law that Bush succeeded in building a forty-nation coalition committed to restoring Kuwait's independence, secured the support of the United Nations, and sent half a million American troops along with a naval armada to the region.

In February 1991, the United States launched Operation Desert Storm, which quickly drove the Iraqi army from Kuwait. Tens of thousands of Iraqis and 184 Americans died in the conflict. The United Nations ordered Iraq to disarm and imposed economic sanctions that produced widespread civilian suffering for the rest of the decade. But Hussein remained in place. So did a large American military establishment in Saudi Arabia, to the outrage of Islamic fundamentalists who deemed its presence an affront to their faith.

The **Gulf War** was the first post–Cold War international crisis. Relying on high-tech weaponry like cruise missiles that reached Iraq from bases and aircraft carriers hundreds of miles away, the United States was able to prevail quickly and avoid the prolonged involvement and high casualties of Vietnam. In the war's immediate aftermath, Bush's public approval rating rose to an unprecedented 89 percent.

The Election of Clinton

Had a presidential election been held in 1991, Bush would undoubtedly have been victorious. But in that year the economy slipped into recession. Despite victory in the Cold War and the Gulf, more and more Americans believed the country was on the wrong track. No one seized more effectively on the widespread sense of unease than Bill Clinton, a former governor of Arkansas. In 1992, Clinton won the Democratic nomination by combining social liberalism (he supported abortion rights, gay rights, and affirmative action for racial minorities) with elements of conservatism (he pledged to reduce government bureaucracy and, borrowing a page from Republicans, promised to "end welfare as we know it"). A charismatic campaigner, Clinton conveyed sincere concern for voters' economic anxieties.

Bush, by contrast, seemed out of touch with the day-to-day lives of ordinary Americans. He was further weakened when conservative leader Pat Buchanan delivered a fiery televised speech at the Republican national convention that declared cultural war against gays, feminists, and supporters of abortion rights. This rallied social conservatives but seemed to confirm the Democratic portrait of Republicans as intolerant and divisive.

A third candidate, the eccentric Texas billionaire Ross Perot, who had never held elected office, also entered the fray. He attacked Bush and Clinton as lacking the economic know-how to deal with the recession and the ever-increasing national debt. That millions of Americans considered Perot a credible candidate testified to widespread dissatisfaction with the major parties. Perot received 19 percent of the popular vote, the best result for a third-party candidate since Theodore Roosevelt in 1912. Clinton won by a substantial margin, a humiliating outcome for Bush, given his earlier popularity.

Clinton in Office

In his first two years in office, Clinton turned away from some of the social and economic policies of the Reagan and Bush years. He appointed several Blacks and women to his cabinet, including Janet Reno, the first female attorney general, and named two supporters of abortion rights, Ruth Bader Ginsburg and Stephen Breyer, to the Supreme Court. He modified the military's strict ban on gay soldiers, instituting a "**Don't ask, don't tell**" policy by which officers would not seek out gays for dismissal from the armed forces. His first budget raised taxes on the wealthy and significantly expanded the Earned Income Tax Credit (EITC)—a cash payment for low-income workers begun during the Ford administration. The most effective antipoverty policy since the Great Society, the EITC raised more than 4 million Americans, half of them children, above the poverty line during Clinton's presidency.

Clinton shared his predecessor's passion for free trade. Despite strong opposition from unions and environmentalists, he obtained congressional approval in 1993 of the **North American Free Trade Agreement** (NAFTA), a treaty negotiated by Bush that created a free-trade zone consisting of Canada, Mexico, and the United States.

The major policy initiative of Clinton's first term was a plan devised by a panel headed by Hillary Rodham Clinton, a successful lawyer and Bill Clinton's wife, to address the rising cost of health care and the increasing number of Americans who lacked health insurance. In Canada and western Europe, governments provided universal medical coverage. The United States had the world's most advanced medical technology and a woefully incomplete system of health insurance. The Great Society had provided coverage for the elderly and poor through the Medicare and Medicaid programs. Many employers offered health insurance to their workers. But tens of millions of Americans lacked any coverage at all, leaving them vulnerable to large debts should they face unexpected serious illness. Too complex to be easily understood by most voters, however, and facing staunch Republican and business opposition, the Clinton plan died in 1994.

The "Freedom Revolution"

With the economy recovering slowly from the recession and Clinton's first two years in office seemingly lacking in significant accomplishments, voters in 1994 turned against the administration. For the first time since the 1950s, Republicans won control of both houses of Congress. They proclaimed their triumph the "Freedom Revolution." Newt Gingrich, a conservative congressman from Georgia who became the new Speaker of the House, masterminded their campaign. Gingrich had devised a platform called the **Contract with America**, which promised to curtail the scope of government, cut back on taxes and economic and environmental regulations, overhaul the welfare system, and end affirmative action.

Viewing their electoral triumph as an endorsement of the contract, Republicans moved swiftly to implement its provisions. Led by Gingrich, they embraced a newly confrontational style of politics favoring conflict over compromise. The House approved deep cuts in social, educational, and environmental programs, including the popular Medicare system. With the president and Congress unable to reach agreement on a budget, the government in December 1995 shut down all nonessential operations, including Washington, D.C., museums and national parks.

Gingrich had assumed that the public shared his intense ideological convictions. He discovered that in 1994 they had voted against Clinton, not for the full implementation of the Contract with America. Most Americans blamed Republicans for the impasse, and Congress soon retreated. But the divisive partisan political style embraced by Gingrich, with harsh rhetoric that demonized opponents and calculated use of news media to sensationalize voter issues, gained growing traction in American politics in the twenty-first century helping to lay the groundwork for Donald Trump's rise.

Clinton's Political Strategy

Like Truman after the Republican sweep of 1946, Clinton rebuilt his popularity by campaigning against a radical Congress. He opposed the most extreme parts of his opponents' program, while adopting others. In his state of the union address of January 1996, he announced that "the era of big government is over," in effect turning his back on the tradition of Democratic Party liberalism and embracing the antigovernment outlook associated with Republicans since the days of Barry Goldwater.

In 1996, ignoring the protests of most Democrats, Clinton signed into law a Republican bill that abolished the program of Aid to Families with Dependent Children (AFDC), commonly known as "welfare." Grants of money to the states, with strict limits on how long recipients could receive payments, replaced it. At the time of its abolition, AFDC assisted 14 million individuals, 9 million of them children. Thanks to stringent new eligibility requirements imposed by the states and the economic boom of the late 1990s, welfare rolls plummeted. But the number of children living in poverty remained essentially unchanged. Nonetheless, Clinton had succeeded in one of his primary goals: by the late 1990s, welfare, a hotly contested issue for twenty years or more, had disappeared from political debate.

Clinton's strategy enabled him to neutralize Republican claims that Democrats were the party of high taxes and lavish spending on persons who preferred dependency to honest labor. Clinton's passion for free trade alienated many working-class Democrats but convinced much of the middle class that the party was not beholden to the unions. Clinton easily defeated Republican Bob Dole in the presidential contest of 1996, becoming the first Democrat elected to two terms since FDR. Clinton accomplished for Reaganism what Eisenhower had done for the New Deal and Nixon for the Great Society—consolidating a basic shift in American politics by accepting many of the premises of his opponents.

Clinton and World Affairs

Like Jimmy Carter before him, Clinton's primary political interests concerned domestic, not international, affairs. But with the United States now indisputably the world's dominant power, Clinton, like Carter, took steps to encourage the settlement of long-standing international conflicts and tried to elevate support for human rights to a central place in international relations. He achieved only mixed success.

Clinton strongly supported a 1993 agreement, negotiated at Oslo, Norway, in which Israel for the first time recognized the legitimacy of the Palestine Liberation Organization. The **Oslo Accords** seemed to outline a road to Mideast peace. But neither side proved willing to implement them fully. Israeli governments continued to build Jewish settlements on Palestinian land in the West Bank—a part of Jordan that Israel had occupied during the 1967 Six-Day War. The new Palestinian Authority, which shared in governing parts of the West Bank as a stepping-stone to full statehood, proved to be corrupt, powerless, and unable to curb the growth of groups bent on violence against Israel. At the end of his presidency, Clinton brought Israeli and Palestinian leaders to Camp David to try to work out a final peace treaty. But the meeting failed, and violence soon resumed.

Like Carter, Clinton found it difficult to balance concern for human rights with strategic and economic interests and to formulate clear guidelines for humanitarian interventions overseas. For example, the United States did nothing in 1994 when tribal massacres racked Rwanda, in central Africa. More than 800,000 people were slaughtered in the **Rwandan genocide**, and 2 million refugees fled the country.

The Balkan Crisis

The most complex foreign policy crisis of the Clinton years arose from the disintegration of Yugoslavia, a multiethnic state in southeastern Europe that had been carved from the old Austro-Hungarian empire after World War I. As in the

EASTERN EUROPE AFTER THE COLD WAR

The end of the Cold War and breakup of the Soviet Union, Czechoslovakia, and Yugoslavia redrew the map of eastern Europe (compare this map with the map of Cold War Europe in Chapter 23). Two additional nations that emerged from the Soviet Union lie to the east and are not indicated here: Kyrgyzstan and Tajikistan.

rest of eastern Europe, the communist government that had ruled Yugoslavia since the 1940s collapsed in 1989. Within a few years, the country's six provinces dissolved into five new states. Conflict plagued several of these new nations. **Ethnic cleansing**—a terrible new term meaning the forcible expulsion of a particular ethnic group—now entered the international vocabulary. By the end of 1993, more than 100,000 Bosnians, nearly all of them civilians, had perished in the **Balkan crisis**.

With the Cold War over, protection of human rights in the Balkans gave NATO a new purpose. After considerable indecision, NATO launched air strikes against Bosnian Serb forces, with American planes contributing. UN troops, including 20,000 Americans, arrived as peacekeepers. In 1998, ethnic cleansing again surfaced, this time by Yugoslavian troops and local Serbs against the Albanian population of Kosovo, a province of Serbia. More than 800,000 Albanians fled the region. To halt the bloodshed, NATO launched a two-month war in 1999 against Yugoslavia that led to the deployment of American and UN forces in Kosovo.

GLOBALIZATION AND ITS DISCONTENTS

In December 1999, delegates from around the world gathered in Seattle for a meeting of the World Trade Organization (WTO), a 135-nation group created five years earlier to reduce barriers to international commerce and settle trade disputes. To the astonishment of residents of the city, more than 30,000 persons gathered to protest the meeting. Their marches and rallies brought together factory workers, who claimed that global free trade encouraged corporations to shift production to low-wage centers overseas, and environmentalists, who complained about the impact of unregulated economic development on the earth's ecology, endangering species whose habitats were disappearing because of widespread destruction of forests by lumber companies and unrestricted ocean fishing.

Protesters also drew attention to the depletion of the ozone in the atmosphere, which shields the earth from harmful solar radiation. The heightened use of aerosol sprays and refrigerants containing damaging chemicals had caused a large hole in the ozone layer.

Globalization in action: workers in a factory at the Foxconn campus in China. With 300,000 employees, this is the world's largest industrial complex, where iPhones are assembled for sale around the world.

Once a center of labor radicalism, the Seattle area in 1999 was best known as the home of Microsoft, developer of the Windows operating system used in most of the world's computers. The company's worldwide reach symbolized **globalization**, the process by which people, investment, goods, information, and culture increasingly flow across national boundaries. During the 1990s, the media resounded with announcements that a new era in human history had opened, with a borderless economy and a "global civilization" that would soon replace traditional cultures.

Globalization, of course, was hardly a new phenomenon. The internationalization of commerce and culture and the reshuffling of the world's peoples have been going on since the explorations of the fifteenth century. But the scale and scope of late-twentieth-century globalization was unprecedented. Thanks to satellites and the Internet, information and popular culture flowed instantaneously to every corner of the world. Manufacturers and financial institutions scoured the world for profitable investment opportunities.

Perhaps most important, the collapse of communism between 1989 and 1991 opened the entire world to the spread of market capitalism and to the idea that government should interfere as little as possible with economic activity. American politicians and social commentators increasingly criticized the regulation of wages and working conditions, assistance to the less fortunate, and environmental protections as burdens on international competitiveness. During the 1990s, presidents Bush, a Republican, and Clinton, a Democrat, both spoke of an American mission to create a single global free market as the path to rising living standards, the spread of democracy, and greater worldwide freedom.

The media called the loose coalition of groups who organized the Seattle protests the "antiglobalization" movement. In fact, they challenged not globalization itself but its social consequences. Globalization, the demonstrators claimed, accelerated the worldwide creation of wealth but widened gaps between rich and poor countries and between haves and have-nots within societies. Decisions affecting the day-to-day lives of millions of people were made by institutions—the World Trade Organization, International Monetary Fund, World Bank, and multinational corporations—that operated without any democratic input. Demonstrators demanded the establishment of international standards for wages, labor conditions, and the environment and greater investment in health and education in poor countries. The Battle of Seattle placed on the national and international agendas a question that reverberated into the twenty-first century—the relationship between globalization, economic justice, and freedom.

The economy's performance in the 1990s at first seemed to justify the claims of globalization's advocates. After recovery from the recession of 1990–1991, economic expansion continued for the rest of the decade. By 2000, unemployment stood below 4 percent, a figure not seen since the 1960s. Because Reagan and Bush had left behind massive budget deficits, Clinton worked hard to balance the federal budget—a goal traditionally associated with fiscal conservatives. Since economic growth produced rising tax revenues, Clinton during his second term not only balanced the budget but actually produced budget surpluses.

The Computer and Internet Revolution

Many commentators spoke of the 1990s as the dawn of a "new economy," in which computers and the Internet would produce vast new efficiencies and

From BILL CLINTON, SPEECH ON SIGNING OF NAFTA (1993)

The North American Free Trade Agreement was signed by President Bill Clinton early in his first term. It created a free-trade zone (an area where goods can travel freely without paying import duties) composed of Canada, the United States, and Mexico. Clinton asked Americans to accept economic globalization as an inevitable form of progress and the path to future prosperity. "There will be no job loss," he promised. Things did not entirely work out that way.

As President, it is my duty to speak frankly to the American people about the world in which we now live. Fifty years ago, at the end of World War II, an unchallenged America was protected by the oceans and by our technological superiority and, very frankly, by the economic devastation of the people who could otherwise have been our competitors. We chose then to try to help rebuild our former enemies and to create a world of free trade supported by institutions which would facilitate it.... As a result, jobs were created, and opportunity thrived all across the world....

For the last 20 years, in all the wealthy countries of the world—because of changes in the global environment, because of the growth of technology, because of increasing competition—the middle class that was created and enlarged by the wise policies of expanding trade at the end of World War II has been under severe stress. Most Americans are working harder for less. They are vulnerable to the fear tactics and the averseness to change that are behind much of the opposition to NAFTA. But I want to say to my fellow Americans: When you live in a time of change, the only way to recover your security and to broaden your horizons is to adapt to the change—to embrace, to move forward.... The only way we can recover the fortunes of the middle class in this country so that people who work harder and smarter can, at least, prosper more, the only way we can pass on the American dream of the last 40 years to our children and their children for the next 40, is to adapt to the changes which are occurring.

In a fundamental sense, this debate about NAFTA is a debate about whether we will embrace these changes and create the jobs of tomorrow or try to resist these changes, hoping we can preserve the economic structures of yesterday.... I believe that NAFTA will create 1 million jobs in the first 5 years of its impact.... NAFTA will generate these jobs by fostering an export boom to Mexico by tearing down tariff walls.... There will be no job loss.

From GLOBAL EXCHANGE, SEATTLE, DECLARATION FOR GLOBAL DEMOCRACY (DECEMBER 1999)

The demonstrations that disrupted the December 1999 meeting of the World Trade Organization in Seattle brought to public attention a widespread dissatisfaction with the effects of economic "globalization." In this declaration, organizers of the protest offered their critique.

As citizens of global society, recognizing that the World Trade Organization is unjustly dominated by corporate interests and run for the enrichment of the few at the expense of all others, we demand:

Representatives from all sectors of society must be included in all levels of trade policy formulations. All global citizens must be democratically represented in the formulation, implementation, and evaluation of all global social and economic policies.

Global trade and investment must not be ends in themselves, but rather the instruments for achieving equitable and sustainable development including protection for workers and the environment.

Global trade agreements must not undermine the ability of each nation-state or local community to meet its citizens' social, environmental, cultural or economic needs.

The World Trade Organization must be replaced by a democratic and transparent body accountable to citizens—not to corporations.

No globalization without representation!

QUESTIONS

1. *Why does Clinton feel that free trade is necessary to American prosperity?*

2. *Why do the Seattle protesters feel that the World Trade Organization is a threat to democracy?*

3. *How do these documents reflect contradictory arguments about the impact of globalization in the United States?*

Two architects of the computer revolution, Steve Jobs (*on the left*), once the head of Apple Computer, and Bill Gates, founder of Microsoft, which makes the operating system used in most of the world's computers.

the production and sale of information would occupy the central place once held by the manufacture of goods. Computers had first been developed during and after World War II to solve scientific problems and do calculations involving enormous amounts of data. The early ones were extremely large, expensive, and, by modern standards, slow. Research for the space program of the 1960s spurred the development of improved computer technology, notably the miniaturization of parts thanks to the development of the microchip on which circuits could be imprinted.

Microchips made possible the development of entirely new consumer products. Videocassette recorders, handheld video games, cellular phones, and digital cameras were mass-produced at affordable prices during the 1990s, mostly in Asia and Latin America rather than the United States. But it was the computer that transformed American life. Beginning in the 1980s, companies like Apple and IBM marketed computers for business and home use. As computers became smaller, faster, and less expensive, they found a place in businesses of every kind. In occupations as diverse as clerical work, banking, architectural design, medical diagnosis, and even factory production, they transformed the American workplace. They also changed private life. By the year 2000, nearly half of all American households owned a personal computer, used for entertainment, shopping, and sending and receiving electronic mail. Centers of computer technology, such as Silicon Valley south of San Francisco, the Seattle and Austin metropolitan areas, and lower Manhattan, boomed during the 1990s.

The Internet, first developed as a high-speed military communications network, was simplified and opened to commercial and individual use through personal computers. The Internet expanded the flow of information and communications more radically than any invention since the printing press. At a time when the ownership of newspapers, television stations, and publishing houses was becoming concentrated in the hands of a few giant media conglomerates, the fact that anyone with a computer could post his or her ideas for worldwide circulation led "netizens" ("citizens" of the Internet) to hail the advent of a new, democratic public sphere in cyberspace. Unfortunately, it also offered cranks, conspiracy theorists, and racists an easy way to spread their views. Emerging social media platforms such as Facebook, which soon attracted billions of users around the globe, became central channels of communication with an unprecedented potential for the rapid dissemination of misinformation. Eyeing their explosive growth, congressional critics began to call for stronger regulation and more effective forms of content moderation.

The Stock Market Boom and Bust

Economic growth and talk of a new economy sparked a frenzied boom in the stock market that was reminiscent of the 1920s. Investors, large and small, poured funds into stocks, spurred by the rise of discount and online firms that advertised aggressively and charged lower fees than traditional brokers.

Investors were especially attracted to the new "dot coms"—companies that conducted business via the Internet and seemed to symbolize the promise of the new economy. Many of these "high-tech" companies never turned a profit. But economic journalists and stockbrokers explained that the new economy had so revolutionized business that traditional methods of assessing a company's value no longer applied. Inevitably, the bubble burst. On April 14, 2000, stocks suffered their largest one-day point drop in history. For the first time since the Depression, stock prices declined for three successive years (2000–2002), wiping out billions of dollars in Americans' net worth and pension funds. By 2001, the American economy had fallen into a recession. Talk of a new economy, it appeared, had been premature.

Only after the market dropped did it become apparent that the stock boom of the 1990s had been fueled in part by fraud. For a time in 2001 and 2002, Americans were treated almost daily to revelations of incredible greed and corruption on the part of respected brokerage firms, accountants, and company executives. Enron, a Houston-based energy company that epitomized the new economy—it bought and sold electricity rather than actually producing it— reported as profits billions of dollars in operating losses.

Fruits of Deregulation

At the height of the 1990s boom, with globalization in full swing, stocks rising, and the economy expanding, the economic model of free trade and deregulation appeared unassailable. But the retreat from government economic regulation, a policy embraced by both the Republican Congress and President Clinton, left no one to represent the public interest.

The sectors of the economy most affected by the scandals—energy, telecommunications, and stock trading—had all been subjects of deregulation. Enron could manipulate energy prices because Congress had granted it an exemption from laws regulating the price of natural gas and electricity. Many stock frauds stemmed from the repeal in 1999 of the Glass-Steagall Act, a New Deal measure that separated commercial banks, which accept deposits and make loans, from investment banks, which invest in stocks and real estate and take larger risks. Banks took their new freedom as an invitation to engage in all sorts of misdeeds, knowing that they had become so big that if anything happened, the federal government would have no choice but to rescue them. Banks poured money into risky mortgages. When the housing bubble collapsed in 2008, the banks suffered losses that threatened to bring down the entire financial system. The Bush and Obama administrations felt they had no choice but to expend hundreds of billions of dollars of taxpayer money to save the banks from their own misconduct.

Rising Inequality

The boom that began in 1995 benefited nearly all Americans. For the first time since the early 1970s, average real wages and family incomes began to grow significantly. Economic expansion at a time of low unemployment brought rapid increases in wages for families at all income levels. It aided low-skilled workers, especially non-whites, who had been left out of previous periods of growth. Yet, despite these gains, in the last two decades of the twentieth century, the poor and the middle class became worse off while the rich became significantly richer. The wealth of the richest Americans exploded during the 1990s. Sales of luxury goods like yachts and mansions boomed. Bill Gates, head of Microsoft and the country's richest person, owned as much wealth as the bottom 40 percent of the American population put together.

Companies continued to shift manufacturing jobs overseas. Thanks to NAFTA, a thriving industrial zone emerged just across the southern border of the United States, where American manufacturers built plants to take advantage of cheap labor and weak environmental and safety regulations. Business, moreover, increasingly relied for profits on financial operations rather than making things. The financial sector of the economy accounted for around 10 percent of total profits in 1950; by 2000 the figure was up to 40 percent. Companies like Ford and General Electric made more money from interest on loans to customers and other financial operations than from selling their products.

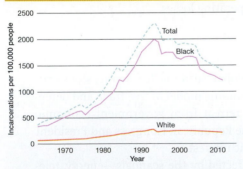

FIGURE 27.1 INCARCERATION RATES, 1970s–2010s

This graph vividly displays the extreme disparity between the incarceration rate for Black and white Americans since the advent of the "wars" on crime and drugs.

Overall, between 1990 and 2008, companies that did business in global markets contributed almost nothing to job growth in the United States. Apple, whose computers, iPads, and iPhones were among the most ubiquitous consumer products of the early twenty-first century, in 2010 employed some 43,000 persons in the United States (the large majority a low-wage sales force in the company's stores). Its contractors, who made these products, had more than 700,000 employees, almost all of them overseas. In 1970, General Motors had been the country's largest corporate employer. In the early twenty-first century, it was replaced by Walmart, a giant discount retail chain that paid most of its 1.6 million workers slightly more than the minimum wage. Walmart aggressively opposed efforts at collective bargaining. Not a single one of its employees belonged to a union.

CULTURE WARS

The end of the Cold War ushered in hopes for a new era of global harmony. Instead, what one observer called a "rebellion of particularisms"—renewed emphasis on group identity and insistent demands for group recognition and power—has racked the international arena. In the nineteenth and twentieth centuries, socialism and nationalism had united people of different backgrounds in pursuit of common goals. Now, in Africa, Asia, the Middle East, and parts of Europe, the waning of movements based on socialism and the declining power of nation-states arising from globalization seemed to unleash long-simmering ethnic and religious antagonisms. Partly in reaction to the global spread of a secular culture based on consumption and mass entertainment, intense religious movements attracted increasing numbers of followers—Hindu nationalism in India, orthodox Judaism in Israel, Islamic fundamentalism in much of the Muslim world, and evangelical Christianity in the United States. Like

Erected on U.S. 5, an interstate highway running from the Mexican to Canadian borders along the Pacific coast, this sign warns motorists to be on the lookout for people (i.e., undocumented immigrant families) crossing the road on foot. The sign's placement north of San Diego, about thirty miles north of Mexico, illustrates how the "border" had become an entire region, not simply a geographical boundary.

other nations, although in a far less extreme way and with little accompanying violence, the United States has experienced divisions arising from the intensification of ethnic and racial identities and religious fundamentalism.

The Newest Immigrants

Because of shifts in immigration, cultural and racial diversity have become increasingly visible in the United States. Until the immigration law of 1965, the vast majority of twentieth-century newcomers hailed from Europe. That measure, as noted in Chapter 25, sparked a wholesale shift in immigrants' origins. Between 1965 and 2015, nearly 58 million immigrants entered the United States. The nation's foreign-born population reached 14 percent, nearing the historic peak of the first immigration wave between 1890 and 1910. About 50 percent came from Latin America and the Caribbean, 35 percent from Asia, and smaller numbers from the Middle East and Africa. Only 10 percent arrived from Europe, mostly from the war-torn Balkans and the former Soviet Union.

In 2020, the number of foreign-born persons living in the United States stood at more than 40 million. The immigrant influx changed the country's religious and racial map. By 2020, close to 4 million Muslims resided in the United States, and the combined population of Buddhists and Hindus exceeded 1 million.

As in the past, many immigrants became urban residents, with New York City, Los Angeles, Chicago, and Miami the most common destinations. New ethnic communities emerged, with homes, shops, restaurants, foreign-language newspapers, radio and television stations, and ethnic professionals like businessmen and lawyers. Unlike in the past, rather than being concentrated in one or two parts of city centers, immigrants quickly moved into outlying neighborhoods and older suburbs. By the turn of the century, more than half of all Latinos lived in suburbs. While most immigrants settled on the East and West coasts, some moved to other parts of the country. They brought cultural and racial diversity to once-homogeneous communities in the American heartland.

Post-1965 immigration formed part of the worldwide uprooting of labor arising from globalization. Those who migrated to the United States came from a wide variety of backgrounds. They included poor, illiterate refugees from places of economic and political crisis—Central Americans escaping the region's civil wars and poverty, Haitians and Cambodians fleeing repressive governments. But many immigrants were well-educated professionals from countries like India and South Korea, where the availability of skilled jobs had not kept pace with the spread of higher education. In the year 2000, more than 40 percent of all immigrants to the United States had a college education.

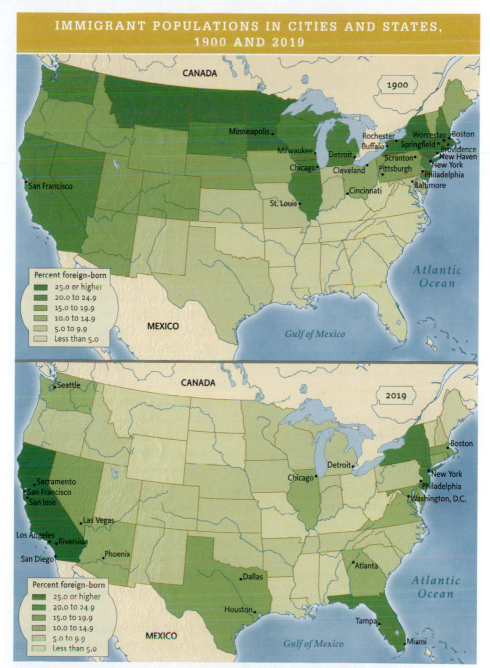

IMMIGRANT POPULATIONS IN CITIES AND STATES, 1900 AND 2019

Maps illustrating states' foreign-born populations and the twenty metropolitan areas with the most immigrants in 1900 and 2019. In 1900 nearly all went to the Northeast and Upper Midwest, the heartland of the industrial economy. In 2019 the largest number headed for cities in the South and West, especially California, although major cities of the Northeast also attracted many newcomers.

FIGURE 27.2 ADULT MEN AND WOMEN IN THE LABOR FORCE, 1950–2019

The percentage of adult men and women in the labor force has declined since the beginning of the Great Recession in 2008. The decline for men is part of a long-term trend sparked by deindustrialization. The decline for women, reversing a process that had gathered strength since 1950, was partly caused by low wages and the difficulty of finding affordable day care.

For the first time in American history, women made up the majority of newcomers, reflecting the decline of manufacturing jobs that had previously absorbed immigrant men, as well as the spread of employment opportunities in traditionally female fields like care of children and the elderly and retail sales. Thanks to cheap global communications and jet travel, modern-day immigrants retain strong ties with their countries of origin, frequently phoning and visiting home.

The New Diversity

Latinos formed the largest single immigrant group. This term was invented in the United States and includes people from quite different origins— Mexicans, Central and South Americans, and migrants from Spanish-speaking Caribbean islands like Cuba, the Dominican Republic, and Puerto Rico (although the last group, of course, are American citizens, not immigrants). With 95 million people, Mexico in 2000 had become the world's largest Spanish-speaking nation. Sharing a border with the United States, it became a source of massive immigration, both legal and undocumented. For many years, most Mexican immigrants settled in the southwestern states that had once been part of Mexico, especially to work in agricultural harvesting and at canneries in Texas and California. But increasingly Mexican immigrants found work in other states, mostly low-wage jobs in domestic labor, packing plants, and other service industries. Today, there is a significant Mexican American community in almost every state, including such places as Kansas, Minnesota, and Georgia, which until recently had very little experience with ethnic diversity.

Numbering just over 62 million in 2020, Latinos made up close to 19 percent of the population in the United States. With a 23 percent increase from 2010 to 2020, Latinos made up over half of the nation's population growth. Latinos were highly visible in entertainment, sports, and politics. The Latino presence transformed American life. Mateo and Santiago were among the ten most popular baby names in Texas in 2020. Smith remained the most common

LOS TIGRES DEL NORTE, "JAULA DE ORO" (1984)

Having sunk roots and established families in the United States but unable to visit Mexico for fear of not being able to return, many undocumented immigrants suffered a crisis of identity. They felt trapped in a "cage of gold" (*jaula de oro*) and alienated from their Americanized children. The Mexican American group Los Tigres del Norte developed these themes in a popular song.

I am established here
In the United States
Many years have passed
Since I crossed as a wetback
With no papers
I'm still an illegal

I have my wife and kids
That I brought so young
And they've already forgotten
My dear Mexico
Which I will never forget
And cannot return to

What use is money
If I'm like a prisoner
In this great nation
When I'm reminded, I cry
Although this cage is made of gold
It's still a prison

Listen son,
Would you like to go back and live in
    Mexico?
"Whatcha talkin' about dad?
I don't want to go back to Mexico,
No way, dad."

My kids don't talk to me
They have learned another language.

And they've forgotten Spanish
They think like Americans
Deny that they're Mexicans
Even though they have my complexion

From my work to my home
I don't know what's wrong with me
Even though I'm man of the house
I barely go outside
Since I'm afraid that they'll catch me
And deport me

What use is money
If I'm like a prisoner
In this great nation
When I'm reminded, I cry
Although this cage is made of gold
It's still a prison

QUESTIONS

1. *What elements of Mexican culture are disappearing in immigrant households, according to the song?*

2. *How do you think the experience of the narrator compares with that of members of previous immigrant groups?*

American surname, but Garcia, Rodriguez, and Martinez were all in the top ten. Although most Latinos voted for the Democratic Party, a significant minority voted Republican. Both parties sought to court the growing Hispanic vote.

A flourishing middle class developed in Los Angeles, Miami, and other cities with large Spanish-speaking populations. But most immigrants from Mexico and Central America competed at the lowest levels in the job market. Latino communities remained far poorer than the general population. In 2020, the Latino poverty rate at 15.7 percent stood at 1.5 times the national figure. Yet this was a historically low rate since first measured in 1972.

Asian Americans also became increasingly visible. There had long been a small population of Asian ancestry in California and New York City, but only after 1965 did immigration from Asia assume large proportions. Between 1990 and 2020, the Asian American population nearly tripled, reaching close to 20 million. Asian Americans made up over 6 percent of the nation's population. Between 2010 and 2020, Asian Americans have been the fastest growing ethnic group overall. Around 45 percent of Americans of Asian origin live in the West, but many others live in the South, Northeast, and Midwest. Like Latinos, Asian Americans were a highly diverse population, including well-educated Korean, Indian, and Japanese origin professionals, as well as poor refugees from Cambodia, Vietnam, and China. Growing up in tight-knit communities that placed great emphasis on education, young Asian Americans poured into American colleges and universities. Once subjected to harsh discrimination, Asian Americans now achieved remarkable success. But more than any other group, Asian Americans clustered at opposite ends of the income spectrum. Large numbers earned either more than $100,000 per year (doctors, engineers, and entrepreneurs) or under $45,000 (unskilled laborers in sweatshops and restaurants).

Multiculturalism

The United States, of course, had long been a multiracial society. But for centuries race relations had been shaped by the Black-white divide and the experience of slavery and segregation. The growing visibility of Latinos and Asians suggested that a two-race system no longer adequately described American life. Multiracial imagery filled television, films, and advertising. Interracial marriage, at one time banned in forty-two states, became more common and acceptable. Among Asian Americans, half of all marriages involved a non-Asian partner. The figure for Latinos was 30 percent. Some commentators spoke of the "end of racism" and the emergence of a truly color-blind society. The census bureau projected that by 2050, less than 50 percent of the American population would be white. The new face of American society went hand in hand with one of the most striking developments of the 1990s—the celebration of group

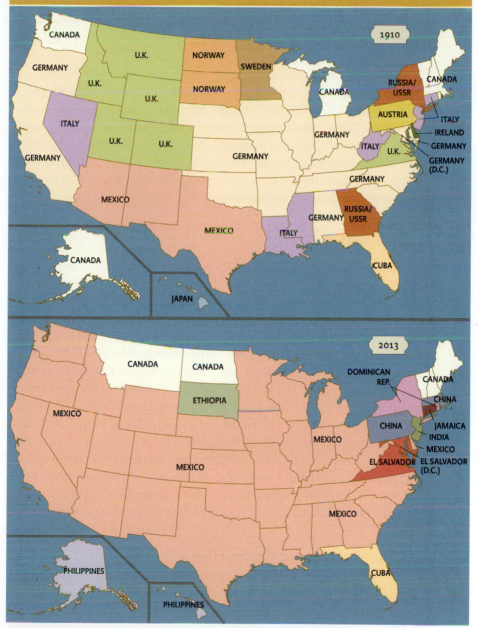

ORIGIN OF LARGEST IMMIGRANT POPULATIONS BY STATE, 1910 AND 2013

Maps depicting the birthplace of each state's largest immigrant population in 1910 and 2013. A century ago, most immigrants hailed from Europe, and the leading country of origin varied among the states. Today, in almost every state outside the Northeast, those born in Mexico constitute the largest number of immigrants.

difference and demands for group recognition. **Multiculturalism** became the term for a new awareness of the diversity of American society, past and present, and for vocal demands that jobs, education, and politics reflect that diversity. As the numbers of minority and female students at the nation's colleges and universities rose, these institutions moved aggressively to diversify their faculties and revise the traditional curriculum.

One sign of multiculturalism could be seen in the spread of academic programs dealing with the experience of specific groups—Black studies, Latino studies, women's studies, and the like. Literature departments added the writings of female and minority authors to those of white men. Conservatives, and some traditional liberals as well, decried "identity politics" for undermining a shared sense of purpose. Numerous scholars now taught and wrote history in ways that stressed the experiences of diverse groups of Americans rather than a common national narrative.

The New Nativism

While many Americans celebrated the growing pluralism of American life, the heightened visibility of immigrants and racial minorities was cause for alarm among other Americans. With the census bureau projecting a majority-minority nation by 2050, conservatives decried what they perceived of as cultural fragmentation and the loss of a common sense of nationhood. Cultural diversity inspired harsh debates over whether immigration should be discouraged. These issues entered politics most dramatically in California in 1994, when a group of conservatives placed a proposition on the ballot to deny undocumented immigrants and their children access to education, health services, and social services. Despite the enormous mobilization among Latinos and others (which would eventually turn the state Democratic), California voters approved the initiative. The state supreme court declared it unconstitutional, but Proposition 187 sparked a series of similar initiatives in other states as well as at the federal level. Such efforts laid the groundwork for the anti-immigrant politics that helped propel Donald Trump to the White House in 2016.

The Changing Face of Black America

Compared with the situation in 1900 or 1950, the most dramatic change in American life at the turn of the century was the absence of legal segregation and the presence of Blacks in areas of American life from which they had once been almost entirely excluded. Thanks to the decline in overt discrimination and the effectiveness of many affirmative action programs, Blacks now worked in unprecedented numbers alongside whites in corporate boardrooms, offices, and factories. The number of Black policemen, for example, rose from 24,000 to 65,000 between 1970 and 2000, and in the latter year, 37 percent of the Black population reported having attended college.

One major change in Black life was the growing visibility of Africans among the nation's immigrants. Between 1970 and 2010, more than twice as many Africans immigrated to the United States as had entered during the entire period of the Atlantic slave trade. For the first time, all the elements of the African diaspora—natives of Africa, Caribbeans, Central and South Americans of African descent, Europeans with African roots—could be found in the United States alongside the descendants of American slaves.

Nigeria, Ghana, and Ethiopia provided the largest number of African immigrants, and they settled overwhelmingly in urban areas, primarily in New York, California, Texas, and the District of Columbia. Some were impoverished refugees fleeing civil wars in Somalia, Sudan, and Ethiopia, but many more were professionals—more than half the African newcomers had college educations, the highest percentage for any immigrant group. While some prospered, others found it difficult to transfer their credentials to the United States and found jobs driving taxis and selling African crafts at street fairs.

The African American middle class continued to expand in the first two decades of the twenty-first century. African Americans increasingly lived in suburbs with close to 40 percent living in suburbs in 2015 compared to 36 percent in cities. But Blacks most often moved to so-called "first-ring" suburbs with cheaper housing but fewer job opportunities. African Americans overall remained in a more precarious situation than whites and many recent immigrants. The Black unemployment rate remained double that of whites and nearly one in three Black children lived in poverty. In every index of social well-being from health to housing quality, Blacks continued to lag. A lower percentage of Blacks than whites owned their homes or held professional or managerial jobs.

Despite the nation's growing racial diversity, school segregation—now resulting from housing patterns and the divide between urban and suburban school districts rather than laws requiring racial separation—was on the rise. Most city public school systems consisted overwhelmingly of minority students, large numbers of whom failed to receive an adequate education. Nearly 80 percent of white students attended schools where they encountered few if any pupils of another race. Since school funding rested on property taxes, poor communities continued to have less to spend on education than wealthy ones. African Americans continued to face discriminatory treatment by police with little accountability, leading to violent community responses. In 1992, an all-white suburban jury found four Los Angeles police officers not guilty in the brutal beating of Black motorist Rodney King, even though the assault had been captured on videotape. The deadliest urban uprising since the New York draft riots of 1863 followed. Some fifty-two people died, and property damage approached $1 billion. Many Latino youths, who shared the resentment of Blacks over mistreatment by the police, joined in the violence. The uprising revealed the limits of the civil rights revolution in addressing the grievances of poor Black Americans and suggested that a renewed racial reckoning was on the horizon.

The Prison-Industrial Complex

In the decades following World War II, the rate of imprisonment had declined from its Prohibition era spike, but in the 1970s, as noted in the prior chapter, politicians of both parties sought to adopt "tough on crime" policies. Multiple inner-city rebellions along with rising crime rates contributed to support for harsh punitive policies. Federal crime legislation under Reagan and, in 1994, a crime bill passed during the Clinton administration fueled prison growth. State governments also adopted increasingly harsh penalties for crimes. (California, for example, required a mandatory life sentence for those convicted of a third felony.) Drug users were imprisoned for possessing even small quantities of drugs, effectively criminalizing addiction. As a result, the number of Americans in prison rose dramatically.

Though crime rates dropped across the country during the 1990s, the number of Americans behind bars continued to rise in the new millennium because of the sentencing laws of the previous decades. The prison population peaked at 2.2 million in 2016, ten times the figure of 1970 and one-fourth of the entire world's inmates. Several million more individuals were on parole, on probation, or under some other kind of criminal supervision. These figures dwarfed those of every other Western society.

As the prison population grew, a "prison-industrial complex" emerged. Struggling communities battered by deindustrialization saw prisons as a source of jobs and income. Between 1990 and 1995, the federal government and the states constructed more than 200 new prisons. In 2008, five states spent more money on their prison systems than on higher education. Convict labor, a practice the labor movement had managed to curtail in the late nineteenth century, revived in the late twentieth. Private companies in Oregon "leased" prisoners for three dollars per day. A call to Trans World Airlines for a flight reservation was likely to be answered by a California inmate. By 2019, the high costs of imprisonment led to a push by members of both parties to reduce prison numbers. The numbers of Americans in prison declined from 2.2 million to 1.8 million, still one of the highest rates of "unfreedom" in the world, in a nation priding itself on liberty.

The Burden of Imprisonment

Members of racial minorities experienced most strongly the growing islands of unfreedom in the United States. In 1950, whites accounted for 70 percent of the nation's prison population and non-whites 30 percent. By 2016, these figures had almost been reversed. Racial disparties in sentencing contributed to this trend. Those convicted of using or selling crack, a particularly potent form of cocaine concentrated among the urban poor, faced severe penalties while the use of powder cocaine, the drug of choice in suburban America, led to far lighter sentences.

The percentage of the Black population in prison stood five times higher than the proportion for white Americans. More than one-quarter of all Black men could expect to serve time in prison at some time during their lives. A criminal record made it very difficult for ex-prisoners to find jobs. Partly because so many young men were in prison, Blacks have a significantly lower rate of marriage than other Americans. And thanks to state laws disenfranchising persons with a felony conviction, as of 2020, around 5 million Americans, mostly Black men, could not vote. In 2018, Florida voters approved a measure to restore this right to nearly all felons after they have served their prison terms but the Republican legislature sharply restricted this right, requiring the payment of all outstanding court fees and fines to be eligible. Critics noted the resemblance of the requirement to post–Civil War poll taxes. The governors of Iowa and Kentucky, however, in 2020 restored the ballot to former felons without requiring such payments as a basic right of citizenship.

Blacks convicted of crimes were also more likely than whites to receive the death penalty. In 1972, the Supreme Court temporarily suspended states' use of this punishment. But the Court soon allowed it to resume, despite evidence of racial disparities in its application. Even as western Europe and other areas of the world abolished the death penalty, the United States executed over 1,400 persons between 1977 and 2015. In the 1830s, Alexis de Tocqueville had described executions as common in Europe but rare in America. By the early-twenty-first century, the United States ranked with China, Iran, and Saudi Arabia as the nations that most often executed their citizens.

The Gay Rights Revolution

Some movements that were descended from the late 1960s achieved great visibility in the 1990s. Prominent among these was the campaign for gay rights, which in the last two decades of the century increasingly turned its attention to combating acquired immunodeficiency syndrome (AIDS), a fatal disease spread by sexual contact, drug use, and transfusions of contaminated blood. AIDS first emerged in the early 1980s. It quickly became epidemic among gay

The AIDS quilt, each square of which represents a person who died of AIDS, on display in Washington, D.C. The quilt was exhibited throughout the country, heightening public awareness of the AIDS epidemic.

men. The gay movement mobilized to promote "safe sex," prevent discrimination against people suffering from AIDS, and press the federal government to devote greater resources to fighting the disease. The Gay Men's Health Crisis organized educational programs and assistance to those affected by the disease and demanded that drug companies put AZT, a drug with some success in treating AIDS, on the market. A more radical group, ACT UP, disrupted a mass at New York's St. Patrick's Cathedral to protest what it called the Catholic Church's prejudices against gays. By 2000, even though more than 400,000 Americans had died of AIDS, its spread among gays had been sharply curtailed. But in other parts of the world, such as Africa, the AIDS epidemic remained out of control.

Gay groups also played an increasing role in politics. In cities with large gay populations, such as New York and San Francisco, politicians vied to attract their votes. Overall, the growth of public tolerance of gay men and lesbians was a striking change in social attitudes. In the second decade of the twenty-first century, this would lead to the remarkably rapid acceptance of the right of gay Americans to form legal marriages.

Native Americans in the New Century

The revitalization of Indian culture, identity, and economic development continued into the new millennium. Those Americans identifying as Indian reached over 5 million in the 2010 census (including people choosing more than one race) and rose to close to 10 million in 2020. This growth reflected a renewed sense of Indian pride that led many Americans for the first time to identify as Native American. Tribes won a number of suits seeking restitution for past injustices. In 2001, a New York court awarded the Cayuga Nation $248 million for illegal land seizures two centuries earlier. In 2014, the Obama administration paid the Navajo nation $554 million to settle claims that the government had over decades mismanaged natural resources and funds. It paid eighty additional nations a total of $2.61 billion to settle cases over the mismanagement of tribal trust funds. The Bureau of Indian Affairs designated Alaskan Native villages as reservations, ending their status of legal limbo. There are now 566 federally recognized tribal governments.

Gains were also made in recognition of Indian rights in the international arena. Efforts by Indigenous tribes in the United States, Canada, Latin America, Australia, and elsewhere led the United Nations to take up Indigenous issues. In 2007, the United Nations established the Declaration on the Rights of Indigenous Peoples with the United States signing on in 2010.

Tribal governments sought to promote economic growth through gaming and natural resource development. Exempt from state legal gambling limits, tribes near large population centers established lucrative casino operations. Gaming led to renewed struggles to define the meaning and extent of Indian self-determination. In 2011, Indian casinos took in over $27 billion, making a few tribes, comprising only a small percentage of Native Americans, spectacularly wealthy. Gaming has enabled some financially stable tribes to reinvest casino profits to improve housing, health care, and education. But most Indian casinos are marginal operations whose low-wage jobs as cashiers, waitresses, and the like have done little to dramatically improve the welfare of tribal members. Critics charge that casino profits have flowed off the reservations to wealthy non-Indian investors and point to gambling's exacerbation of existing

Native activist and photographer Josué Rivas depicts the confrontation between protesters and law enforcement during the 2016 protests at Standing Rock to stop the construction of the Dakota Access pipeline. The photo graphically illustrates the ongoing contests over Native American sovereignty.

social problems. Other forms of Native economic development focused on generating profits from natural resources, but they too proved divisive.

Indians continue to struggle with the highest rates of poverty, infant mortality, and school drop-out rates in the country. Native Americans, like Black Americans, also face disproportional rates of incarceration. In North Dakota, Native people make up 19 percent of the incarcerated population and just 5 percent of the overall population.

In 2016, the struggle to secure Indian self-determination against private efforts to control and use Native land resources came to a head on the Standing Rock Lakota reservation in 2016. The close to 2,000-mile Dakota Access oil pipeline was planned to extend across four states and included land that crossed under the Missouri River and Lake Oahe, the Standing Rock Lakota's primary water supply, on historic tribal lands. A powerful grassroots movement of Indigenous "**water protectors**," known as NoDAPL, sought to block the construction. In a vibrant campaign that gained international attention, Indian tribes and their non-Indian allies established camps of several thousand protesters. A months-long stand-off between police, company security, and protesters led to a large number of arrests and the eventual clearance of the camp. What was perhaps the largest Indigenous protest in close to a century, however, revealed that once again the question of Indian rights and self-determination remains as contested as ever.

Cultural Conservatism

Immigration occupied only one front in what came to be called the **Culture Wars**—battles over moral values that raged throughout the 1990s. The Christian Coalition, founded by evangelical minister Pat Robertson, became a major force in Republican politics. It launched crusades against gay rights, abortion, secularism in public schools, and government aid to the arts. Pat Buchanan's Republican convention speech of 1992 calling for a "religious war for the soul of America," mentioned earlier, alarmed many voters. But cultural conservatives hailed it as their new rallying cry.

It sometimes appeared during the 1990s that the country was refighting old battles between traditional religion and modern secular culture. In an echo of the 1920s, a number of localities required the teaching of creationism, a religious alternative to Darwin's theory of evolution. The battles of the 1960s seemed to be forever unresolved. Many conservatives railed against the erosion of the nuclear family, the changing racial landscape produced by immigration, and what they considered a general decline of traditional values. Cultural conservatives were not satisfied with a few victories over what they considered immorality, such as the **Defense of Marriage Act** of 1996, which barred gay couples from spousal benefits provided by federal law. (The Supreme Court would declare the law unconstitutional in 2013.)

Family Values in Retreat

The censuses of 2000 and 2010 showed **family values** increasingly in disarray. Half of all marriages ended in divorce (70 percent on the West Coast). In 2010, more than 40 percent of births were to unmarried women, not only sexually active teenagers but growing numbers of professional women in their thirties and forties as well. For the first time, fewer than half of all households consisted of married couples, and only one-fifth were "traditional" families—a wife, husband, and their children. More than half of all adults were single or divorced. Two-thirds of married women worked outside the home. The pay gap between men and women, although narrowing, persisted. In 2010, the weekly earnings of women with full-time jobs stood at 82 percent of those of men—up from 63 percent in 1980. In only two occupational categories did women earn more than men—postal service clerks and special education teachers.

Although dominated by conservatives, the Supreme Court, in *Casey v. Planned Parenthood of Pennsylvania* (1992), reaffirmed a woman's right to terminate a pregnancy. The decision overturned a requirement that the husband be notified before the procedure was undertaken. "At the heart of liberty," said the Court, "is the right to . . . make the most intimate and personal choices" without outside interference. In effect, *Casey* repudiated the centuries-old doctrine that a husband has a legal claim to control the body of his wife.

The Antigovernment Extreme

At the radical fringe of conservatism, the belief that the federal government posed a threat to American freedom led to the creation of private militias who armed themselves to fend off oppressive authority. Groups like Aryan Nation, Posse Comitatus, and other self-proclaimed "Christian patriots" spread a mixture of racist, anti-Semitic, and antigovernment ideas. Private armies, like the Militia of Montana, vowed to resist enforcement of federal gun control laws. For millions of Americans, owning a gun became a prime symbol of liberty.

Many militia groups employed the symbolism and language of the American Revolution, sprinkling their appeals with warnings about the dangers of government tyranny drawn from the writings of Thomas Jefferson, Patrick Henry, and Thomas Paine. They warned that leaders of both major parties formed part of a conspiracy to surrender American sovereignty to the United Nations or to some shadowy international conspiracy. Although such organizations had been growing for years, they burst into the national spotlight in 1995 when Timothy McVeigh, a member of the militant antigovernment movement, exploded a bomb at a federal office building in Oklahoma City. The blast killed 168 persons, including numerous children at a day-care center. McVeigh was captured, convicted, and executed. The bombing alerted the nation to the danger of violent antigovernment right-wing groups.

IMPEACHMENT AND THE ELECTION OF 2000

The newly intense partisanship that emerged in the 1990s and continued in the new millennium contributed to Republican efforts to impeach Bill Clinton. Republicans strongly disliked Clinton, despite his move toward the political center. He seemed to symbolize much that conservatives hated about the 1960s. As a college student, the president had smoked marijuana and participated in antiwar demonstrations. He had married a feminist, made a point of leading a multicultural administration, and supported gay rights. Clinton's popularity puzzled and frustrated conservatives, reinforcing their conviction that something was deeply amiss in American life. From the very outset of his administration, Clinton's political opponents and scandal-hungry media stood ready to pounce. Clinton himself provided the ammunition.

The Impeachment of Clinton

Sexual misconduct by public officials had a long history. But in the 1980s and 1990s, scrutiny of politicians' private lives became far more common than in the past. In 1991, Senate hearings on the nomination to the Supreme Court of Clarence Thomas, a Black conservative, became embroiled in dramatic charges of sexual harassment leveled against Thomas by law professor Anita Hill. To the outrage of feminists, the Senate narrowly confirmed him. Nonetheless, because of her testimony, Americans became more aware of the problem of sexual harassment in and out of the workplace, and complaints shot up across the country.

In 1998, it became known that Clinton had carried on an affair with Monica Lewinsky, a White House intern. Kenneth Starr, the special counsel who had been appointed to investigate a previous scandal, shifted his focus to Lewinsky. He issued a lengthy report containing almost pornographic details of Clinton's sexual acts with the young woman and accused the president of lying when he denied the affair under oath. In December 1998, the Republican-controlled House of Representatives voted to impeach Clinton for perjury and obstruction of justice. He became the second president to be tried before the Senate. Early in 1999, the vote took place. Neither charge mustered a simple majority, much less than the two-thirds required to remove Clinton from office.

Clinton's impeachment had to do with what many considered to be a juvenile escapade. Polls suggested that the obsession of Kenneth Starr and members of Congress with Clinton's sexual acts appalled Americans far more than the president's irresponsible behavior. Clinton's continuing popularity throughout the impeachment controversy demonstrated how profoundly traditional attitudes toward sexual morality had changed.

The Disputed Election

Had Clinton been eligible to run for reelection in 2000, he would probably have won. But after the death of FDR, the Constitution had been amended to limit presidents to two terms in office. Democrats nominated Vice President Al Gore to succeed Clinton (pairing him with Senator Joseph Lieberman of Connecticut, the first Jewish vice-presidential nominee). Republicans chose George W. Bush, the governor of Texas and son of Clinton's predecessor, as their candidate, with former secretary of defense Dick Cheney as his running mate.

The election proved to be one of the closest in the nation's history. The outcome remained uncertain until a month after the ballots had been cast. Gore won the popular vote by a tiny margin—540,000 of 100 million cast, or one-half of 1 percent. Victory in the electoral college hinged on which candidate had carried Florida. There, amid widespread confusion at the polls and claims of irregularities in counting the ballots, Bush claimed a margin of a few hundred votes.

As in the disputed election that ended Reconstruction (a contest in which Florida had also played a crucial role), it fell to Supreme Court justices to decide the outcome. On December 12, 2000, by a 5-4 vote, the Court ordered a halt to the recounting of Florida ballots, allowing the state's governor Jeb Bush (George W. Bush's brother) to certify that the Republican candidate had carried the state and had therefore won the presidency.

The decision in **Bush v. Gore** was one of the oddest in Supreme Court history. The majority justified their decision by insisting that the "equal protection" clause of the Fourteenth Amendment required that all ballots within a state be counted in accordance with a single

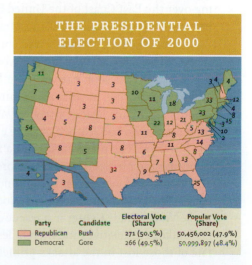

THE PRESIDENTIAL ELECTION OF 2000

Party	Candidate	Electoral Vote (Share)	Popular Vote (Share)
Republican	Bush	271 (50.5%)	50,456,002 (47.9%)
Democrat	Gore	266 (49.5%)	50,999,897 (48.4%)

standard, something impossible given the wide variety of machines and paper ballots used in Florida. Perhaps recognizing that this new constitutional principle threatened to throw into question results throughout the country—since many states had voting systems as complex as Florida's—the Court added that it applied only in this single case.

A Challenged Democracy

Coming at the end of the "decade of democracy," the 2000 election revealed troubling features of the American political system. The electoral college, devised by the founders to enable the country's prominent men rather than ordinary voters to choose the president, gave the White House to a candidate who did not receive the most votes—an odd result in a political democracy. Similarly, in 2016 Republicans won the presidency despite losing the popular vote by 2.8 million votes. Counting both congressional and presidential races, the campaign cost more than $1.5 billion, mostly raised from wealthy individuals and corporate donors. This reinforced the widespread belief that money dominated the political system. The implications for democracy of the ever-closer connection between power in the economic marketplace and power in the marketplace of politics and ideas would be widely debated in the early twenty-first century.

THE ATTACKS OF SEPTEMBER 11

September 11, 2001, a beautiful late-summer morning, began with the sun rising over the East Coast of the United States in a crystal-clear sky. But September 11 soon became one of the most tragic dates in American history.

Around 8 am, hijackers seized control of four jet airliners filled with passengers. They crashed two into the World Trade Center in New York City, igniting infernos that soon caused these buildings, which dominated the lower Manhattan skyline, to collapse. A third plane hit a wing of the Pentagon, the country's military headquarters, in Washington, D.C. On the fourth aircraft, passengers who had learned of these events via their cellphones overpowered the hijackers. The plane crashed in a field near Pittsburgh, killing all aboard. Counting the nineteen hijackers, more than 200 passengers, pilots, and flight attendants, and victims on the ground, around 3,000 people died on September 11. The victims included nearly 400 police and firefighters who had rushed to the World Trade Center in a rescue effort and perished when the "twin towers" collapsed. Relatives and friends desperately seeking information about the fate of those lost in the attacks printed thousands of "missing" posters. These remained in public places in New York and Washington for weeks, grim reminders of the lives extinguished on September 11.

The Bush administration quickly blamed Al Qaeda, a shadowy terrorist organization headed by Osama bin Laden, for the attacks. A wealthy Islamic fundamentalist from Saudi Arabia, bin Laden had joined the fight against the Soviet occupation of Afghanistan in the 1980s. He had developed a relationship with the Central Intelligence Agency and received American funds to help build his mountain bases. But after the Gulf War of 1991, his anger increasingly turned against the United States. Bin Laden was especially outraged by the presence of American military bases in Saudi Arabia and by American support for Israel in its ongoing conflict with the Palestinians. More generally, bin Laden and his followers saw the United States, with its religious pluralism, consumer culture, and open sexual mores, as the antithesis of the rigid values in which they believed.

The twin towers of the World Trade Center after being struck by hijacked airplanes on September 11, 2001. Shortly after this photograph was taken, the towers collapsed.

He feared that American influence was corrupting Saudi Arabia, Islam's spiritual home.

After the Gulf War, Osama bin Laden declared "war" on the United States. Terrorists associated with Al Qaeda exploded a truck-bomb at the World Trade Center in 1993, killing six persons, and set off blasts in 1998 at American embassies in Kenya and Tanzania, in which more than 200 persons, mostly African embassy workers, died. Thus, a rising terrorist threat was visible before September 11. Nonetheless, the attack came as a complete surprise. With the end of the Cold War in 1991, most Americans felt more secure, especially within their own borders, than they had for decades.

The attacks of September 11, 2001, lent new urgency to questions that had recurred many times in American history: Should the United States act in the world as a republic or an empire? What is the proper balance between liberty and security? Who deserves the full enjoyment of American freedom? Suddenly, the Bush administration had to face these questions.

THE ATTACKS OF SEPTEMBER 11 ★ **1115**

THE WAR ON TERRORISM

Islam, America, and the "Clash of Civilizations"

The events of September 11, 2001, placed new pressures on religious liberty. Even before the terrorist attacks, the political scientist Samuel P. Huntington had published a widely noted book, *The Clash of Civilizations and the Remaking of the World Order* (1996), which argued that with the Cold War over, a new global conflict impended between Western and Islamic "civilizations."

Many readers, including politicians, interpreted Huntington, not entirely correctly, as reducing politics and culture to a single characteristic—in this case, religion—forever static, divorced from historical development. ("Islam," in fact, consists of well over a billion people in many different countries ranging from South Asia to the Middle East, Africa, Europe, and the Americas.) Nonetheless, in the aftermath of September 11, the formula that pitted a freedom-loving United States against militant, authoritarian Muslims became widely popular as a way of making sense of the terrorist attacks.

What did this mean for the nearly 5 million Americans who practiced the Muslim religion? President Bush insisted that the war on terrorism was not a war against Islam. But many Americans found it difficult to separate the two, even though most American Muslims were as appalled by the terrorist attacks as their fellow countrymen. Some critics claimed that Islam was fundamentally incompatible with American life—a position reminiscent of prejudice in the nineteenth century against Catholics and Mormons.

"They Hate Freedom"

September 11 transformed the international situation, the domestic political environment, and the Bush presidency. An outpouring of popular patriotism followed the attacks, all the more impressive because it was spontaneous, not orchestrated by the government or private organizations. Throughout the country, people demonstrated their sense of resolve and their sympathy for the victims by displaying the American flag. Public trust in government rose dramatically, and public servants like firemen and policemen became national heroes. After two decades in which the dominant language of American politics centered on deregulation and individualism, the country experienced a renewed feeling of common social purpose.

Bush seized the opportunity to give his administration a new direction and purpose. Like presidents before him, he made freedom the rallying cry for a nation at war. On September 20, 2001, Bush addressed a joint session of Congress and a national television audience. His speech echoed the words of FDR, Truman, and Reagan: "Freedom and fear are at war. The advance of human freedom . . . now depends on us." The country's antagonists, Bush went on, "hate our freedoms, our freedom of religion, our freedom of speech, our freedom to assemble and disagree with each other." In later speeches, he repeated this theme. Why did terrorists attack the United States? the president repeatedly asked. His answer: "Because we love freedom, that's why. And they hate freedom."

The War in Afghanistan

Bush's speech announced a new foreign policy principle, which quickly became known as the **Bush Doctrine**. The United States would launch a **war on terrorism**. Unlike previous wars, this one had a vaguely defined enemy— terrorist groups around the world that might threaten the United States or its allies—and no predictable timetable for victory. The American administration would recognize no middle ground in the new war: "Either you are with us, or you are with the terrorists." Bush demanded that Afghanistan, ruled by a group of Islamic fundamentalists called the Taliban, surrender Osama bin Laden, the architect of the 9/11 attacks, who had established a base in the country. When the Taliban refused, the United States on October 7, 2001, launched air strikes against its strongholds.

Bush gave the **war in Afghanistan** the name "Enduring Freedom." By the end of the year, the combination of American bombing and ground combat by the Northern Alliance (Afghans who had been fighting the Taliban for years) had driven the regime from power. A new government, friendly to and dependent on the United States, took its place. The new government found it difficult to establish full control over the country. U.S. troops fought in Afghanistan for two decades to support the government and weaken the Taliban. By 2021, with polls showing most Americans supported an end to America's longest war, President Joseph Biden withdrew the remaining troops. The American-backed government collapsed with breakneck speed and the Taliban took control of the country.

The "Axis of Evil"

The toppling of the Taliban, Bush repeatedly insisted, marked only the beginning of the war on terrorism. In his State of the Union address of January 2002, the president accused Iraq, Iran, and North Korea of harboring terrorists and developing "weapons of mass destruction"—nuclear, chemical, and biological—that posed a potential threat to the United States. He called the three countries an "axis of evil," even though no evidence connected them with the attacks of September 11 and they had never cooperated with one another (Iraq and Iran, in fact, had fought a long and bloody war in the 1980s).

THE WAR ON TERRORISM ★ **1117**

AN AMERICAN EMPIRE?

The "axis of evil" speech and National Security Strategy sent shock waves around the world. In the immediate aftermath of September 11, a wave of sympathy for the United States had swept across the globe. Most of the world supported the war in Afghanistan as a legitimate response to the terrorist attacks. By late 2002, however, many persons overseas feared that the United States was claiming the right to act as a world policeman in violation of international law.

Charges quickly arose that the United States was bent on establishing itself as a new global empire. Indeed, September 11 and its aftermath highlighted not only the vulnerability of the United States but also its overwhelming strength. In every index of power—military, economic, cultural—the United States far outpaced the rest of the world. The United States was the only country that maintained military bases throughout the world and deployed its navy on every ocean. It was not surprising that in such circumstances many American policymakers felt that the country had a responsibility to impose order in a dangerous world.

Confronting Iraq

These tensions became starkly evident in the Bush administration's next initiative. From the outset of the Bush administration, a group of conservative policymakers including Vice President Dick Cheney, Secretary of Defense Donald Rumsfeld, and Deputy Defense Secretary Paul D. Wolfowitz were determined to oust the Iraqi dictator Saddam Hussein from power. They insisted that the oppressed Iraqi people would welcome an American army as liberators and quickly establish a democratic government, allowing for the early departure of American soldiers. This group seized on the opportunity presented by the attacks of September 11 to press their case, and President Bush adopted their outlook. Secretary of State Colin Powell, who believed the conquest and stabilization of Iraq would require hundreds of thousands of American soldiers and should not be undertaken without the support of America's allies, found himself marginalized in the administration.

Even though no known evidence linked Hussein to the terrorist attacks of September 11, the Bush administration in 2002 announced a goal of "regime change" in Iraq. Hussein, administration spokesmen insisted, must be ousted from power because he had developed an arsenal of chemical and bacterial "weapons of mass destruction" and was seeking to acquire nuclear arms. American newspaper and television journalists repeated these claims with almost no independent investigation. Early in 2003, despite his original misgivings, Secretary of State Powell delivered a speech before the United Nations outlining the administration's case. He claimed that Hussein possessed a mobile chemical weapons laboratory, had hidden weapons of mass destruction in his many palaces, and was seeking to acquire uranium in Africa to build nuclear weapons. (Every one of these assertions later turned out to be false.)

The Iraq War

Foreign policy "realists," including members of previous Republican administrations like Brent Scowcroft, the national security adviser under the first President Bush, warned that the United States could not unilaterally transform the Middle East into a bastion of democracy, as the administration claimed was its long-term aim. The decision to begin the **Iraq War** split the Western alliance and inspired a massive antiwar movement throughout the world. In February 2003, between 10 million and 15 million people across the globe demonstrated against the impending war.

Both traditional foes of the United States like Russia and China and traditional allies like Germany and France refused to support a "preemptive" strike against Iraq. Unable to obtain approval from the United Nations for attacking Iraq, the United States went to war anyway in March 2003, with Great Britain as its sole significant ally. President Bush called the war "Operation Iraqi Freedom." Its purpose, he declared, was to "defend our freedom" and "bring freedom to others." The Hussein regime proved no match for the American armed forces, with their precision bombing, satellite-guided missiles, and well-trained soldiers. Within a month, American troops occupied Baghdad. After hiding out for several months, Hussein was captured by American forces and subsequently put on trial before an Iraqi court. Late in 2006, he was found guilty of ordering the killing of many Iraqis during his reign and was sentenced to death and executed.

Soon after the fall of Baghdad, a triumphant President Bush appeared on the deck of an aircraft carrier beneath a banner reading "Mission Accomplished." But then everything seemed to go wrong. Rather than parades welcoming American liberators, looting and chaos followed the fall of the Iraqi regime. An insurgency quickly developed that targeted American soldiers and Iraqis cooperating with them. Sectarian violence soon swept throughout Iraq, with militias of Shiite and Sunni Muslims fighting each other. (Under Hussein, Sunnis, a minority of Iraq's population, had dominated the government and army; now, the Shiite majority sought to exercise power and exact revenge.)

The war marked a new departure in American foreign policy. While the United States had exerted enormous influence in the Middle East since World War II, never before had it occupied a nation in the center of the world's most volatile region. Rarely in its history had the United States found itself so isolated from world public opinion. Initially, the war in Iraq proved to be popular in the United States. But the realization that in fact Hussein had no weapons of

U.S. PRESENCE IN THE MIDDLE EAST, 1947–2019

SYRIA - Civil war, 2011–
Al-Raqqah

IRAQ - Gulf War, 1990; -Iraq War, 2003–

IRAN - American embassy occupied, 1979–1981

AFGHANISTAN - War against Taliban and Terrorists, 2001–

KUWAIT

JORDAN - Recognition, 1948; -Camp David Accords, 1978; -Wye Memorandum, concerning peace with the Palestinians, 1998

PAKISTAN - Osama bin Laden killed, 2011

EGYPT - Suez crisis, 1956; -Kissinger's shuttle diplomacy, 1974–1975; -Camp David accords, 1978

BAHRAIN

QATAR

UNITED ARAB EMIRATES

OMAN

Oil fields
Air bases
Naval bases
Troops in Syria

1967 Cease-Fire line
1949 Armistice line
1950 Armistice line

Territory under full Palestinian control
Palestinian Authority responsible for social and civil services only
West Bank territory under full Israeli control
Jewish settlements
Israeli military bases

Since World War II, the United States has become more and more deeply involved in the affairs of the Middle East, whose countries are together the world's largest exporter of oil. Note that the positions of U.S. troops in Syria shown here are as of April 2018.

mass destruction discredited the administration's rationale for the war. By early 2007, polls showed that a large majority of Americans considered the invasion of Iraq a mistake and the war a lost cause. Fulfilling a campaign promise to end the war, President Barack Obama withdrew U.S. troops in 2011. Threats by the Islamic State in 2014, however, led to renewed airstrikes and the return of a small number of American forces. In December 2021, President Biden withdrew the remaining 2,500 combat troops.

THE AFTERMATH OF SEPTEMBER 11 AT HOME

Security and Liberty

Like earlier wars, the war on terrorism raised anew the problem of balancing security and liberty. In the immediate aftermath of the attacks, Congress rushed to pass the **USA Patriot Act**, a mammoth bill (it ran to more than 300 pages) that few members of the House or Senate had actually read. It conferred unprecedented powers on law-enforcement agencies charged with preventing the new, vaguely defined crime of "domestic terrorism," including the power to wiretap, spy on citizens, open letters, read email, and obtain personal records from third parties like universities and libraries without the knowledge of a suspect. At least 5,000 foreigners with Middle Eastern connections were rounded up and more than 1,200 arrested. Many with no link to terrorism were held for months, without either a formal charge or a public notice of their fate. The administration also set up a detention camp at the U.S. naval base at **Guantánamo Bay**, Cuba, for persons captured in Afghanistan or otherwise accused of terrorism. More than 700 persons, the nationals of many foreign countries, were detained there.

In November 2001, the Bush administration issued an executive order authorizing the holding of secret military tribunals for noncitizens deemed to have assisted terrorism. In such trials, traditional constitutional protections, such as the right of the accused to choose a lawyer and see all the evidence, would not apply. A few months later, the Justice Department declared that American citizens could be held indefinitely without charge and not allowed to see a lawyer if the government declared them to be "enemy combatants."

The Power of the President

In the new atmosphere of heightened security, numerous court orders and regulations of the 1970s, inspired by abuses of the CIA, FBI, and local police forces, were rescinded, allowing these agencies to resume surveillance of Americans without evidence that a crime had been committed. Soon after September 11, President Bush authorized the National Security Agency (NSA) to eavesdrop on Americans' telephone conversations without a court warrant, a clear violation of a law limiting the NSA to foreign intelligence gathering.

The majority of Americans seemed willing to accept the administration's contention that restraints on time-honored liberties were necessary to fight terrorism. Others recalled previous times when wars produced limitations on civil liberties and public officials equated political dissent with lack of patriotism: the Alien and Sedition Acts during the "quasi war" with France in 1798, the suspension of the writ of habeas corpus during the Civil War, the severe repression of free speech and persecution of German Americans during World War I, Japanese American internment in World War II, and McCarthyism during the Cold War. The debate over liberty and security seemed certain to last as long as the war on terrorism itself.

The Torture Controversy

Officials of the Bush administration also insisted in the aftermath of September 11 that the United States need not be bound by international law in pursuing the war on terrorism. They were especially eager to sidestep the Geneva Conventions and the International Convention against Torture, which regulate the treatment of prisoners of war and prohibit torture and other forms of physical and mental coercion.

Amid strong protests from Secretary of State Powell and senior military officers who feared retaliatory mistreatment of American prisoners of war, in April 2003 the president prohibited the use of torture except where special permission had been granted. Nonetheless, the Defense Department approved methods of interrogation that most observers considered torture. In addition, the CIA set up a series of jails in foreign countries outside the traditional chain of military command and took part in the "rendition" of suspects—that is, kidnapping them and spiriting them to prisons in Egypt, Yemen, Syria, and former communist states of eastern Europe, where torture is practiced.

In this atmosphere and lacking clear rules of behavior, some military personnel—in Afghanistan, at Abu Ghraib prison in Iraq, and at Guantánamo— beat prisoners who were being held for interrogation, subjected them to electric shocks, let them be attacked by dogs, and forced them to strip naked and lie atop other prisoners. Photographs of the maltreatment of prisoners, circulated by email, became public. Their exposure around the world in newspapers, on television, and on the Internet undermined the reputation of the United States as a country that adheres to standards of civilized behavior and the rule of law.

Based on an infamous photograph, circulated around the world, of an Iraqi prisoner abused while in American custody, this 2004 cartoon suggests how such mistreatment damaged the image of the United States.

The full extent of the torture policy did not become known until 2014, when a Senate committee released a scathing report stemming from a long investigation. It revealed a pattern of brutality and deception, while concluding that no useful information had been obtained from tortured prisoners. Torture, it concluded, did not arise from the actions of a few "bad apples" but was systematically employed at secret U.S. prisons around the world.

The Court and the President

The Supreme Court did not prove receptive to President Bush's claim of authority to disregard laws and treaties and to suspend constitutional protections of individual liberties. In a series of decisions, the Court reaffirmed the rule of law both for American citizens and for foreigners held prisoner by the United States.

In *Hamdi v. Rumsfeld*, in 2004, the Court considered the lawsuit of Yasir Hamdi, an American citizen who had moved to Saudi Arabia and been captured in Afghanistan. Hamdi was imprisoned in a military jail in South Carolina without charge or the right to see a lawyer. The Court ruled that he had a right to a judicial hearing. "A state of war," wrote Sandra Day O'Connor for the 8-1 majority, "is not a blank check for the president when it comes to the rights of the nation's citizens."

By the time the next significant case, *Hamdan v. Rumsfeld*, came before the Court in 2006, President Bush had appointed two new justices—Chief Justice John Roberts, to replace William Rehnquist, who died in 2005, and Samuel Alito Jr., who succeeded the retiring Sandra Day O'Connor. The Court was clearly becoming more conservative. But in June 2006, by a 5-3 margin (with Roberts not participating because he had ruled on the case while serving on an appeals court), the justices offered a stinging rebuke to the key presumptions of the Bush administration—that the Geneva Conventions do not apply to prisoners captured in the war on terrorism, that the president can unilaterally set up secret military tribunals in which defendants have very few if any rights. The protections were afforded to prisoners of war by the Geneva Conventions, which, the Court declared, was the law of the land.

In June 2008, the Supreme Court rebuffed the Bush administration's strategy of denying detainees at Guantánamo Bay the normal protections guaranteed by the Constitution. Written by Justice Anthony Kennedy, the 5-4 decision in *Boumediene v. Bush* affirmed the detainees' right to challenge their detention in U.S. courts. "The laws and Constitution are designed," Kennedy wrote, "to survive, and remain in force, in extraordinary times." Security, he added, consists not simply in military might but "in fidelity to freedom's first principles," including freedom from arbitrary arrest and the right of a person to go to court to challenge his or her imprisonment. The decision was a powerful affirmation that constitutional rights remain intact during wartime. But the question of how to find the proper balance between liberty and security was certain to persist in the twenty-first century.

CHAPTER REVIEW

REVIEW QUESTIONS

1. *Why was the year 1989 one of the most momentous in the twentieth century?*

2. *Describe the different visions of the U.S. role in the post–Cold War world as identified by President George H. W. Bush and President Clinton.*

3. *Identify the factors that, in the midst of 1990s prosperity, increased the levels of inequality in the United States.*

4. *What are the similarities and differences between immigration patterns of the 1990s and earlier?*

5. *Explain the main cultural, social, and economic developments in Indian America in the new millennium.*

6. *Assess the role of the Supreme Court in the presidential election of 2000.*

7. *What is globalization, and how did it affect the United States in the 1990s?*

8. *How did the foreign policy initiatives of the George W. Bush administration depart from the policies of other presidents since World War II?*

9. *How did the September 11 attacks transform Americans' understanding of their security? How did the response compare with that after Pearl Harbor?*

10. *What are the similarities and differences between America's involvement in Afghanistan and Iraq since 2001?*

11. *What does the war on terrorism suggest about the tension between freedom and security as priorities of the United States?*

12. *How did Supreme Court decisions since 2001 indicate that the rights revolution was here to stay?*

KEY TERMS

new world order (p. 1084)

Gulf War (p. 1085)

"Don't ask, don't tell" (p. 1086)

North American Free Trade Agreement (p. 1086)

Contract with America (p. 1087)

Oslo Accords (p. 1088)

Rwandan genocide (p. 1088)

ethnic cleansing (p. 1089)

Go to 🐰 INQUIZITIVE

To see what you know—and learn what you've missed—with personalized feedback along the way.

A DIVIDED
NATION

The two decades following the attacks of September 11, 2001, led to one political surprise after another, culminating in one of the most turbulent years in national history: 2020. In 2008, the country experienced the worst economic crisis since the Great Depression. Widespread dissatisfaction with established leadership enabled relative newcomers to national politics to reach the White House in the presidential elections of 2008 and 2016—Barack Obama, a first-term U.S. senator from Illinois and the first African American to win a major party's presidential nomination, and Donald Trump, a New York real estate developer and television personality with no public service experience.

The two men's campaigns had much in common. Both Obama and Trump appealed successfully to a desire for new political leadership and to a sense that the country was headed in the wrong direction. Making effective use of the Internet and new social media to spread their messages, both inspired rapturous enthusiasm from supporters but deep resentment from opponents. In their political philosophies, personal demeanor, and sources of electoral support, however, Obama and Trump could not have been more different. The election and reelection of the first African American president marked an important turning point. Yet the election of Trump to succeed him, with his appeals to white Americans' resentments toward racial minorities and immigrants, suggested that issues as old as the republic—namely, who is an American, who is entitled to full freedom and equality—remained as contested as ever.

Former Democratic Vice President Joseph Biden, a four-time presidential contender—at age seventy-seven, the oldest president to ever assume office—won the presidential election against Donald Trump in 2020. Biden's win suggested that a majority of American voters were tired of the divisiveness and unpredictability of Trump's presidency. But Trump's baseless claims of fraud and his efforts to overturn the results, culminating in a shocking siege of the Capitol on January 6, 2020, raised troubling questions about the health of American democracy. What the long-term future of American politics holds remained to be seen. What these events made clear, however, was that Americans were more deeply divided in their social and political outlooks—indeed in their very understanding of what constituted truth—than at any point since the Civil War.

THE WINDS OF CHANGE

Bush's Second Term

President Bush won a narrow victory in 2004 against Democratic nominee John Kerry, a senator from Massachusetts and the first Catholic to run for president since John F. Kennedy in 1960. With Bush's popularity sliding because of the Iraq War and a widespread sense that Americans were not benefiting from economic growth, Democrats sensed a golden opportunity to retake the White House. But John Kerry, an aloof man who lacked the common touch, proved to be an ineffective candidate. Bush won with a margin of 2 percent of the popular vote and thirty-four electoral votes.

In his second inaugural address, in January 2005, Bush outlined a new American goal—"ending tyranny in the world." Striking a more conciliatory tone than during his first administration, he promised that the United States would not try to impose "our style of government" on others and that it would in the future seek the advice of allies. He said nothing specific about Iraq but tried to shore up falling support for the war by invoking the ideal of freedom. In his first inaugural, in January 2001, Bush had used the words "freedom," "free," or "liberty" seven times. In his second, they appeared forty-nine times. Again and again, Bush insisted that the United States stands for the worldwide triumph of freedom.

But the ongoing chaos in Iraq, coupled with a spate of corruption scandals surrounding Republicans in Congress and the White House, eroded Bush's standing. Vice President Cheney's chief of staff was convicted of perjury in connection with an investigation of the illegal "leak" to the press of the name of a CIA operative whose husband had criticized the manipulation of intelligence before the invasion of Iraq. Bush's popularity continued to decline. At one point in 2006, his approval rating fell to 31 percent.

Hurricane Katrina

A further blow to the Bush administration's standing came in August 2005, when **Hurricane Katrina** slammed ashore near New Orleans. Situated below sea level between the Mississippi River and Lake Pontchartrain, New Orleans has always been vulnerable to flooding. Decades of economic development to boost oil profits had worsened the delicate landscape. Dredged canals and soil erosion brought salt water closer to the city. For years, scientists had predicted a catastrophe if a hurricane hit the city. But the federal government ignored requests to strengthen its levee system. When the storm hit on August 29 the levees broke, and nearly the entire city, with a population of half a million, was inundated. Nearby areas of the Louisiana and Mississippi Gulf Coast were also hard hit.

The disaster response revealed ineptitude from local government to the White House. The mayor of New Orleans had been slow to order an evacuation, fearing this would damage the city's tourist trade. When he finally instructed residents to leave, a day before the storm's arrival, he neglected to provide for the thousands who did not own automobiles and were too poor to find other means of transportation. The Federal Emergency Management Agency (FEMA) had done almost no preparation. When the president finally visited the city, he seemed unaware of the scope of devastation. If the Bush administration had prided itself on anything, it was competence in dealing with disaster. Katrina shattered that image.

The New Orleans Disaster

For days, vast numbers of people, most of them poor African Americans, remained abandoned amid the floodwaters. Bodies floated in the streets and people died in city hospitals and nursing homes. By the time aid began to arrive, damage stood at $80 billion, the death toll was around 1,500, and two-thirds of the city's population had been displaced. The televised images of misery in the streets of New Orleans shocked the world and shamed the country.

Hurricane Katrina shone a bright light on both the heroic and the less praiseworthy sides of American life. Where government failed, individual citizens stepped into the breach. People with boats rescued countless survivors from rooftops and attics, private donations flowed in to aid the

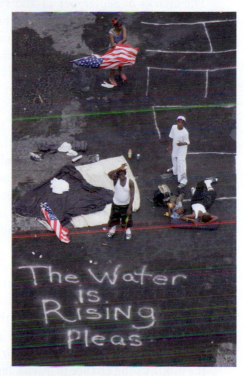

Residents of New Orleans, stranded on a rooftop days after flood waters engulfed the city, frantically attempt to attract the attention of rescue helicopters.

victims, and neighboring states like Texas opened their doors to thousands of refugees. Like the publication of Jacob Riis's *How the Other Half Lives* (1890) and Michael Harrington's *The Other America* (1962), the hurricane's aftermath alerted Americans to the extent of poverty in the world's richest country. The city's rebuilding process also revealed the racial inequalities that structured American life. Although much of the city's public housing survived the flood, the city chose to demolish it in its wake. It proved more difficult for poor Black renters to return. Eligibility requirements for federal financing, moreover, made it harder for Black home owners to rebuild. As a result, while the city's white population returned to pre-flood levels, about 100,000 Black residents displaced by the disaster never returned.

Battle over the Border

The attacks of September 11 and subsequent war on terrorism threw into sharp relief the status of American borders and borderlands, especially in the Southwest. The existence of the borderland embracing parts of the United States and Mexico, with people enjoying well-developed connections with communities in both countries, has always been a source of tension and insecurity in the eyes of many Americans. Fears of terrorists crossing the border merged with older worries about undocumented immigration and the growth of Hispanic culture in the Southwest.

The Bush and Obama administrations greatly accelerated efforts to police the border. By 2013, the number of U.S. Border Patrol officers stood at 20,000, making it the nation's second largest police force after the New York City Police Department, and 400,000 undocumented immigrants were being deported annually, far more than in the past. Latino communities experienced the southwestern borderlands as increasingly militarized, since the "border" stretched far inland and persons accused of having entered the country illegally—almost all of them from Mexico, Guatemala, Honduras, and El Salvador—could be apprehended many miles north of Mexico. Nonetheless, some Americans in the region, claiming that the federal government was not doing enough to enforce the border's status as a dividing line, set up unofficial militias to police the area. Ironically, a major result of tighter controls over border crossing was to reduce back-and-forth migration. Given the diminishing chance of aliens, legal or not, visiting their original homes and then returning, more and more simply stayed put after entering the United States.

In the continuing political debate over immigration, as in other issues of the day, long-standing political divisions continue to simmer. Who has the right to determine the status of millions of undocumented workers—the president, Congress, the states, the courts, or private employers?

In the spring of 2006, the immigration issue suddenly burst again onto the center stage of politics. As we have seen, the Hart-Celler Act of 1965 led to a radical shift in the origins of those entering the United States and especially the rapid growth of the Hispanic population. Many of these newcomers bypassed traditional immigrant destinations and headed for areas in the Midwest, small-town New England, and the Upper South. Racial and ethnic diversity was now a fact of life in the American heartland.

Alongside legal immigrants, undocumented newcomers made their way to the United States, mostly from Mexico. At the end of 2005, it was estimated, there were 11 million "illegal aliens" in the United States, 7 million of them members of the workforce. Economists disagree about their impact. It seems clear that the presence of large numbers of uneducated, low-skilled workers pushes down wages at the bottom of the economic ladder, especially affecting African Americans. On the other hand, immigrants both legal and undocumented receive regular paychecks, spend money, and pay taxes. They fill jobs for which American workers seem to be unavailable because the wages are so low. It is estimated that more than one-fifth of construction workers, domestic workers, and agricultural workers are in the United States illegally.

As governor of Texas, George W. Bush managed to win Hispanic support and downplayed the immigration issue. But in 2006, with many Americans convinced that the United States had lost control of its borders and that immigration was in part responsible for the stagnation of real wages, the House of Representatives approved a bill making it a felony to be in the country illegally and a crime to offer aid to illegal immigrants.

The response was utterly unexpected: a series of massive demonstrations in the spring of 2006 by immigrants—legal and illegal—and their supporters, demanding the right to remain in the country as citizens. In cities from New York to Chicago, Los Angeles, Phoenix, and Dallas, hundreds of thousands of protesters took to the streets. Nashville experienced the largest public demonstration in its history, a march of more than 10,000 mostly Hispanic immigrants. Congress, however, could not agree on a response.

Members of the Texas Minutemen patrolling the U.S.-Mexico border. Claiming that the federal government was failing to prevent undocumented immigrants from entering the United States, vigilantes tried to do so on their own.

The immigration issue was at a stalemate, where it remains today, its ultimate resolution impossible to predict.

The Constitution and Liberty

As in the 1980s and 1990s, conservatives proved far more successful in implementing their views in economic and foreign policy than in the ongoing culture wars. Two significant Supreme Court decisions in June 2003 revealed how the largely conservative justices had come to accept that the social revolution that began during the 1960s could not be undone.

In two cases arising from challenges to the admissions policies of the University of Michigan, the Supreme Court issued its most important rulings on affirmative action since the *Bakke* case twenty-five years earlier. A 5-4 majority upheld the right of colleges and universities to take race into account in admissions decisions. Writing for the majority, Justice Sandra Day O'Connor argued that such institutions have a legitimate interest in creating a "diverse" student body to enhance education. O'Connor was strongly influenced by briefs filed by corporate executives and retired military officers. In today's world, they argued, the United States cannot compete in the global economy or maintain effective armed services without drawing its college-trained business and military leaders from a wide variety of racial and ethnic backgrounds.

In the second decision, in *Lawrence v. Texas*, a 6-3 majority declared unconstitutional a Texas law making sexual acts between persons of the same gender a crime. The *Lawrence* decision paved the way for an even more momentous Supreme Court ruling in 2015, in **Obergefell v. Hodges**, which overturned state laws barring marriages for same-sex couples. Public opinion on this question had evolved with remarkable rapidity, especially among younger Americans. In 2003, two-thirds of Americans opposed legalizing such marriages; by the time of the 2015 ruling, over 60 percent were in favor.

Both decisions relating to gay Americans, written by Justice Anthony Kennedy, repudiated the conservative view that constitutional interpretation must rest either on the "original intent" of the founders and authors of constitutional amendments or on a narrow reading of the text. Instead, Kennedy, generally a conservative, reaffirmed the liberal view of the Constitution as a living document whose protections expand as society changes. "The nature of injustice is such," he wrote in *Obergefell*, "that we may not always see it in our own times. The generations that wrote and ratified the Bill of Rights and the Fourteenth Amendment did not presume to know the extent of freedom in all of its dimensions, and so they entrusted to future generations a charter protecting the right of all persons to enjoy liberty as we learn its meaning."

The Midterm Elections of 2006

With President Bush's popularity having plummeted because of the Iraq War and the Hurricane Katrina disaster, Congress beset by scandal after scandal, and public-opinion polls revealing that a majority of Americans believed the country to be "on the wrong track," Democrats expected to reap major gains in the congressional elections of 2006. They were not disappointed. In a sweeping repudiation of the administration, voters gave Democrats control of both houses of Congress for the first time since 1994. In January 2007, Democrat Nancy Pelosi of California became the first female Speaker of the House in American history.

In January 2009, as Bush's presidency came to an end, only 22 percent of Americans approved of his performance in office—the lowest figure since such polls began in the mid-twentieth century. Because of tax cuts for the wealthy that he pushed through Congress during his first term, as well as the cost of the wars in Iraq and Afghanistan, the large budget surplus he had inherited was transformed into an immense deficit. The percentage of Americans living in poverty and those without health insurance rose substantially during Bush's presidency. And in his final year in office, Bush had to confront the most severe economic crisis since the Great Depression.

THE GREAT RECESSION

The Housing Bubble

At one point in his administration, Bush might have pointed to the economic recovery that began in 2001 as a major success. But late in 2007, the economy entered a recession. And in 2008, the American banking system suddenly found itself on the brink of collapse.

The roots of the crisis of 2008 lay in a combination of public and private policies that favored economic speculation, free-wheeling spending, and get-rich-quick schemes over more traditional avenues to economic growth and personal advancement. For years, the Federal Reserve Bank kept interest rates at unprecedented low levels, first to help the economy recover from the bursting of the technology bubble in 2000 and then to enable more Americans to borrow money to purchase homes. The result was a new bubble, as housing prices rose rapidly. Consumer indebtedness also rose dramatically as people who owned houses took out second mortgages or simply spent to the limits on their credit cards. In mid-2008, when the median family income was around $50,000, the average American family owed an $84,000 home mortgage, $14,000 in auto and student loans, $8,500 to credit card companies, and $10,000 in home equity loans.

All this borrowing fueled increased spending. An immense influx of cheap goods from China accelerated the loss of manufacturing jobs in the United States (which continued their decline despite the overall economic recovery) but also enabled Americans to keep buying, even though for most, household income stagnated during the Bush years. Indeed, China helped to finance the American spending spree by buying up hundreds of billions of dollars' worth of federal bonds—in effect loaning money to the United States so that it could purchase Chinese-made goods. Banks and other lending institutions issued more and more "subprime" mortgages—risky loans to people who lacked the income to meet their monthly payments. The initially low interest rates on these loans were set to rise dramatically after a year or two. Banks assumed that home prices would keep rising, and if they had to foreclose, they could easily resell the property at a profit.

Wall Street bankers developed complex new ways of repackaging and selling these mortgages to investors. Insurance companies, including the world's largest, American International Group (AIG), insured these new financial products against future default. Credit rating agencies gave these securities their highest ratings, even though they were based on loans that clearly would never be repaid. Believing that the market must be left to regulate itself, the Federal Reserve Bank and other regulatory agencies did nothing to slow the speculative frenzy. Banks and investment firms reported billions of dollars in profits and rewarded their executives with unheard-of bonuses.

The Bubble Bursts

In 2006 and 2007, overbuilding had reached the point where home prices began to fall. More and more home owners found themselves owing more money than their homes were worth. As mortgage rates reset, increasing numbers of borrowers defaulted—that is, they could no longer meet their monthly mortgage payments. The value of the new

FIGURE 28.1 PORTRAIT OF A RECESSION

Retail Sales
Change from previous year

Industrial Production
Change from previous year

Unemployment
Percent unemployed
Seasonally adjusted

Consumer Confidence
Conference Board survey

Housing Starts
Annual rate, in millions
Seasonally adjusted

New Home Sales
Annual rate, in millions
Seasonally adjusted

These graphs offer a vivid visual illustration of the steep decline in the American economy in 2008 and the first part of 2009, and the slow recovery to 2012.

mortgage-based securities fell precipitously. Banks suddenly found themselves with billions of dollars of worthless investments on their books. In 2008, the situation became a full-fledged crisis, as banks stopped making loans, business dried up, and the stock market collapsed. Once above 14,000, the Dow Jones Industrial Average plunged to around 8,000—the worst percentage decline since 1931. Lehman Brothers, a venerable investment house, recorded a $2.3 billion loss and went out of existence in history's biggest bankruptcy. Leading banks seemed to be on the verge of failure. With the value of their homes and stock market accounts in free fall, Americans cut back on spending, leading to business failures and a rapid rise in unemployment. By the end of 2008, 2.5 million jobs had been lost—the most in any year since the end of World War II.

In the last three months of 2008, and again in the first three of 2009, the gross domestic product of the United States decreased by 6 percent—a remarkably steep contraction. Even worse than the economic meltdown was the meltdown of confidence as millions of Americans lost their jobs and/or their homes and saw their retirement savings and pensions, if invested in the stock market, disappear. In April 2009, the recession that began in December 2007 became the longest since the Great Depression.

In the **Great Recession**, the mortgage crisis affected minorities the most. Many had been steered by banks into subprime mortgages even when they had the assets and income to qualify for more traditional, lower-cost loans. As a result, foreclosures were highest in minority areas, and the gains Blacks, Asians, and Hispanics had made in home ownership between 1995 and 2004 now eroded. In 2012, Wells Fargo Bank, the nation's largest home mortgage lender, agreed to pay $175 million to settle claims that its brokers had charged higher fees to Blacks and Hispanics who borrowed money to purchase homes during the housing bubble than to whites with comparable incomes and pushed the minorities into risky subprime mortgages.

"A Conspiracy against the Public"

In *The Wealth of Nations* (1776), Adam Smith wrote: "People of the same trade seldom meet together, even for merriment and diversion, but the conversation ends in a conspiracy against the public." This certainly seemed an apt description of the behavior of leading bankers and investment houses whose greed helped to bring down the American economy. Like the scandals of the 1920s and 1990s, those of the Bush era damaged confidence in the ethics of corporate leaders. Indeed, striking parallels existed between these three decades—the get-rich-quick ethos, the close connection between business and government, the passion for deregulation, and widespread corruption.

Damaged by revelations of corporate misdeeds, the reputation of stockbrokers and bankers fell to lows last seen during the Great Depression. One poll showed that of various social groups, bankers ranked third from the bottom in public esteem—just above prostitutes and convicted felons. Resentment was fueled by the fact that Wall Street had long since abandoned the idea that pay should be linked to results. By the end of 2008, the worst year for the stock market since the Depression, Wall Street firms had fired 240,000 employees. But they also paid out $20 billion in bonuses to top executives. Even the executives of Lehman Brothers, which went bankrupt (and, it later turned out, had shortchanged New York City by hundreds of millions of dollars in corporate and other taxes), received $5.7 billion in bonuses in 2007 and 2008. In 2010, Goldman Sachs, the Wall Street banking and investment firm, paid a fine of half a billion dollars to settle charges that it had knowingly marketed to clients mortgage-based securities it knew were bound to fail, and then in effect bet on their failure. (This was like a real-estate agency selling an unsuspecting customer a house with faulty wiring and then taking out insurance so that the agency would be paid when the house burned down.)

Overall, during the next few years, an incredible litany of malfeasance by the world's largest banks became public. Between 2009 and 2016, major banks, American and foreign, were forced by their respective governments to pay fines totaling in excess of $100 billion for such actions as facilitating tax evasion by wealthy clients, fixing foreign currency exchange rates and international interest rates to boost their own profits, often at the expense of their customers, and misleading regulators about their activities. Yet bank profits are so large that the institutions accepted these fines as simply a minor cost of doing business. Even when J. P. Morgan Chase and Citibank pleaded guilty to felony conspiracy charges, no meaningful punishment followed. No individual executive was charged with a crime, and the Securities and Exchange Commission granted waivers from penalties that are supposed to punish criminal behavior, such as being barred from certain kinds of financial transactions.

The Collapse of Market Fundamentalism

The crisis exposed the dark side of market fundamentalism—the ethos of deregulation that had dominated world affairs for the preceding thirty years. Alan Greenspan, the head of the Federal Reserve Bank from 1987 to 2006, had steered the American economy through crises ranging from the stock market collapse of 1987 to the terrorist attacks of 2001. Greenspan had presided over much of the era of deregulation, artificially low interest rates, and excessive borrowing and spending. He and his successors had promoted the housing bubble and saw all sorts of speculative behavior flourish with no governmental intervention. In effect, they allowed securities firms to regulate themselves.

In 2008, Greenspan admitted to Congress that there had been a "flaw" in his long-held conviction that free markets would automatically produce the best results for all and that regulation would damage banks, Wall Street, and the mortgage market. He himself, he said, was in a state of "shocked disbelief," as the crisis turned out to be "much broader than anything I could have imagined." Every president from Ronald Reagan onward had lectured the rest of the world on the need to adopt the American model of unregulated economic competition and berated countries like Japan and Germany for assisting failing businesses. Now, the American model lay in ruins and a new role for government in regulating economic activity seemed inevitable.

Bush and the Financial Crisis

In the fall of 2008, with the presidential election campaign in full swing, the Bush administration seemed unable to come up with a response to the crisis. In keeping with the free market ethos, it allowed Lehman Brothers to fail. But this immediately created a domino effect, with the stock prices of other banks and investment houses collapsing, and the administration quickly reversed course. It persuaded a reluctant Congress to appropriate $700 billion to bail out other floundering firms. Insurance companies like AIG, banks like Citigroup and Bank of America, and giant financial companies like the Federal Home Loan Mortgage Corporation (popularly known as Freddie Mac) and the Federal National Mortgage Association (Fannie Mae), which insured most mortgages in the country, were so interconnected with other institutions that their collapse would drive the economy into a full-fledged depression. Through the federal bailout, taxpayers in effect took temporary ownership of these companies, absorbing the massive losses created by their previous malfeasance. But despite the bailout, the health of the banking system remained fragile.

The crisis also revealed the limits of the American "safety net" compared with other industrialized countries. In western Europe, workers who lose their jobs typically receive many months of unemployment insurance amounting to a significant percentage of their lost wages. In the United States, only one-third of out-of-work persons even qualify for unemployment insurance, and it runs out after a few months. The abolition of "welfare" (the national obligation to assist the neediest Americans) during the Clinton administration left the American safety net a patchwork of a few national programs like food stamps, supplemented by locally administered aid. The poor were dependent on aid from the states, which found their budgets collapsing as revenues from property and sales taxes dried up. Hard-pressed for cash, states used their ability to turn away applicants, greatly enhanced by the welfare reform of the 1990s, to save money. In 2012, only one in five poor children received cash aid, the lowest percentage in half a century.

The Emergence of Barack Obama

A little-known forty-seven-year-old senator from Illinois when the campaign of 2008 began, Barack Obama owed his success both to his own exceptional skills as a speaker and campaigner and to the evolution of American politics and society during his lifetime.

Obama's life story exemplified the enormous changes the United States had undergone since 1960. Without the civil rights movement, his election would have been inconceivable. He was the product of an interracial marriage, which ended in divorce when he was two years old, between a Kenyan immigrant and a white American woman. When Obama was born in 1961, their marriage was still illegal in many states. He attended Harvard Law School and worked in Chicago as a community organizer before going into politics. He also wrote two best-selling books about his upbringing in Indonesia (where his mother worked as an anthropologist) and Hawaii (where his maternal grandparents helped to raise him) and his search for a sense of identity given his complex background. Obama was elected to the U.S. Senate in 2004 and first gained national attention with an eloquent speech at the Democratic national convention that year. His early opposition to the Iraq War won the support of the Democratic Party's large antiwar element, his race galvanized the support of Black voters, and his promise of change appealed to the young.

The 2008 Campaign

In 2008, Obama faced Senator John McCain, the Republican nominee, in the general election. McCain chose Sarah Palin, the little-known governor of Alaska, as his running mate. Palin proved extremely popular with the Republican Party's conservative base. But her performances in speeches and interviews made it clear that she lacked familiarity with many of the domestic and foreign issues a new administration would confront. Her selection raised questions among many Americans about McCain's judgment.

But the main obstacles for the McCain campaign were President Bush's low popularity and the financial crisis that reached bottom in September and October. Obama's promise of change seemed more appealing than ever. On election day, he swept to victory with 53 percent of the popular vote and a large majority in the electoral college. His election redrew the nation's political map. Obama carried not only Democratic strongholds but also states that had been reliably Republican for years. He cracked the solid South, winning Virginia, North Carolina, and Florida. He did extremely well in suburbs throughout the country. He even carried Indiana, where Bush had garnered 60 percent of the vote in 2004, but which now was hard hit by unemployment. Obama put together a "rainbow" coalition, winning nearly the entire Black vote and a large majority of Hispanics (who helped him to carry Colorado, Nevada, and Florida). He did exceptionally well among young voters. Obama carried every age group except persons over sixty-five. Thus, he was elected even though he received only 43 percent of the nation's white vote.

After Jacob Philadelphia, a five-year-old White House visitor, asked if Obama's hair was the same as his, the president bent down so Philadelphia could feel it for himself. Peter Souza's 2009 iconic photo captured the symbolic significance of Obama's ascent to the White House for Black Americans.

Obama's First Inauguration

On January 20, 2009, more than forty-five years after King's "I Have a Dream" speech, Obama was inaugurated as president. More than 1 million people traveled to Washington to view the historic event. In his inaugural address, Obama offered a stark rebuke to eight years of Bush policies and, more broadly, to the premises that had shaped government policy since the election of Reagan. He promised a foreign policy based on diplomacy rather than unilateral force, pledged to protect the environment, spoke of the need to combat income inequality and lack of access to health care, and blamed a culture of "greed and irresponsibility" for helping to bring on the economic crisis. Unlike Bush, Obama said little about freedom in his speech. Instead, he spoke of community and responsibility. His address harked back to the revolutionary-era ideal of putting the common good before individual self-interest.

OBAMA IN OFFICE

In many ways, Obama's first policy initiatives lived up to the promise of change. In his first three months, he announced plans to close the prison at Guantánamo Bay in Cuba, barred the use of torture, launched a diplomatic initiative to repair relations with the Muslim world, reversed the previous administration's executive orders limiting women's reproductive rights, and abandoned Bush's rhetoric about a God-given American mission to spread freedom throughout the world. When Supreme Court justice David Souter announced his retirement, Obama named **Sonia Sotomayor**, the first Hispanic and third woman in the Court's history, to replace him. He also appointed his rival for the nomination, Hillary Clinton, as secretary of state.

Obama's first budget recalled the New Deal and Great Society. Breaking with the Reagan-era motto, "Government is the problem, not the solution," it anticipated active government support for health-care reform, clean energy, and public education, paid for in part by allowing Bush's tax cuts for the wealthy to expire in 2010. He pushed through Congress a "stimulus" package amounting to nearly $800 billion in new government spending—for construction projects, the extension of unemployment benefits, and aid to the states to enable them to balance their budgets. The bill was meant to pump money into the economy in order to save and create jobs and to ignite a resumption of economic activity.

A year into his presidency, in the spring of 2010, Obama had to deal with one of the worst environmental disasters in American history. An oil rig in the Gulf of Mexico owned by British Petroleum (BP) exploded, spewing millions of gallons of oil into the sea. The oil washed up on the beaches of Louisiana, Mississippi, Alabama, and Florida, killing marine life, birds, and other animals and devastating the Gulf tourist industry. It took months to stop the oil from rushing into the Gulf, and much longer to restore the beaches.

The **Gulf oil spill** illustrated some of the downsides of globalization and deregulation. The government agency charged with inspections allowed oil companies to set their own safety standards and looked the other way in the face of BP's long record of cutting corners, safety violations, and accidents. The rig that exploded had been built in South Korea and was operated by a Swiss company under contract to BP. Primary responsibility for safety rested not with the United States but with the Republic of the Marshall Islands, a tiny, impoverished nation in the Pacific Ocean, where the rig was registered. Thus, BP enjoyed freedom from the effective oversight that might have prevented the disaster.

The Health-Care Debate

For most of Obama's first year in office, congressional debate revolved around a plan to restructure the nation's health-care system so as to provide insurance coverage to the millions of Americans who lacked it and to end abusive practices by insurance companies, such as their refusal to cover patients with existing illnesses. After months of increasingly bitter debate, in March 2010, Congress passed the Affordable Care Act, a sweeping health-care measure that required all Americans to purchase health insurance and most businesses to provide it to their employees. It also offered subsidies to persons of modest incomes so they could afford insurance and required insurance companies to accept all applicants. The measure aroused strong partisan opposition. Claiming that it amounted to a "government takeover" of the health-care industry (even though plans for a government-run insurance program had been dropped from the bill), every Republican in Congress voted against the bill.

Throughout Obama's presidency, Republicans remained bitterly opposed to the new law and vowed to repeal it when they could. Indeed, in October 2013, in an effort to get the president to abandon the health-care law, the Republican-dominated Congress shut down the federal government—a tactic that, as during the Clinton administration, backfired. By 2015, what came to be known as Obamacare proved to be a remarkably successful policy. Sixteen million uninsured Americans had obtained medical coverage under its provisions, most of them less affluent Americans who received some sort of government subsidy. The number of uninsured would have been even lower except that twenty-three Republican-controlled states refused to expand Medicaid coverage for their poorest residents, as the new law made possible, even though nearly all the cost would have been covered by the federal government. Despite a conservative majority on the Supreme Court, the justices twice rejected challenges to the constitutionality of Obamacare.

Financial Reform

Another significant measure, enacted in July 2010, was a financial regulatory reform law that sought to place under increased federal oversight many of the transactions that had helped create the economic crisis. Although the details remained to be worked out through specific regulations, the law represented a reversal of the policies of the past fifty years that had given banks a free hand in their operations. But it did not require a breakup of banks deemed "too big to fail" and left open the possibility of future taxpayer bailouts of these institutions. Moreover, officials responsible for issuing new regulations watered them down when banks complained.

Taken together, the measures of Obama's first year and a half in office saw the most dramatic domestic reform legislation since the Great Society of the 1960s. "Change"—the slogan of his election campaign—was significant, but did not go far enough for many of his supporters. The health-care bill failed to include a "public option," in which the government itself would offer medical insurance to those who desired it (much like Medicare for elderly Americans). Obama chose his economic advisers from Wall Street, who underestimated the depth of the crisis and continued the Bush administration policy of pouring

From OPINION OF THE COURT IN *OBERGEFELL V. HODGES* (2015)

In 2015, in a 5-4 decision, the Supreme Court ruled that the Constitution's Fourteenth Amendment establishes a constitutional right to marriage for gay Americans. The ruling reflected a remarkably rapid shift in public opinion regarding gay marriage in the previous few years. Written by Justice Anthony Kennedy, the majority opinion included a powerful exposition of the meaning of freedom in the early twenty-first century.

From their beginning to their most recent page, annals of human history reveal the transcendent importance of marriage. . . . Rising from the most basic human needs, marriage is essential to our most profound hopes and aspirations. . . .

The history of marriage is one of both continuity and change. That institution—even as confined to opposite-sex relations—has evolved over time. For example, marriage was once viewed as an arrangement by the couple's parents based on political, religious, and financial concerns; but by the time of the Nation's founding it was understood to be a voluntary contract between a man and a woman. . . . As the role and status of women changed, the institution further evolved. Under the centuries-old doctrine of coverture, a married man and woman were treated by the State as a single, male-dominated legal entity. As women gained legal, political, and property rights, and as society began to understand that women have their own equal dignity, the law of coverture was abandoned. . . .

New dimensions of freedom become apparent to new generations, often through perspectives that begin in pleas of protests. . . .

This dynamic can be seen in the Nation's experiences with the rights of gays and lesbians. Until the mid-20th century, same-sex intimacy long had been condemned as immoral by the state itself in most Western nations. . . . Only in recent years have psychiatrists and others recognized that sexual orientation is both a normal expression of human sexuality and immutable. . . .

The identification and protection of fundamental rights is an enduring part of the judicial duty to interpret the Constitution. . . . The nature of injustice is such that we may not always see it in our own times. The generations that wrote and ratified the Bill of Rights and the Fourteenth Amendment did not presume to know the extent of freedom in all of its dimensions, and so they entrusted to future generations a charter protecting the right of all persons to enjoy liberty as we learn its meaning. When new insight reveals discord between the Constitution's central protections and a received legal structure, a claim to liberty must be addressed. . . .

The right to marry is a fundamental right inherent in the liberty of the person, and . . . couples of the same sex may not be deprived of that right and that liberty.

From BARACK OBAMA, EULOGY AT EMANUEL AFRICAN METHODIST EPISCOPAL CHURCH (2015)

In the summer of 2015, the nation was shocked by the murder of nine Black parishioners in a Black church in Charleston by a white supremacist gunman. President Obama traveled to the city to deliver a eulogy for one of the victims, Clementa Pinckney, the church's pastor and a member of the South Carolina Senate. His speech reflected on the history of race relations and the condition of Black America fifty years after the height of the civil rights revolution.

The church is and always has been the center of African American life . . . a place to call our own in a too-often hostile world, a sanctuary from so many hardships. . . .

There's no better example of this tradition than Mother Emanuel, . . . a church built by Blacks seeking liberty, burned to the ground because its founders sought to end slavery only to rise up again, a phoenix from these ashes. . . . A sacred place, this church, not just for Blacks, not just for Christians but for every American who cares about the steady expansion . . . of human rights and human dignity in this country, a foundation stone for liberty and justice for all. . . .

We do not know whether the killer of Reverend Pinckney and eight others knew all of this history, but he surely sensed the meaning of his violent act. It was an act that drew on a long history of bombs and arson and shots fired at churches, not random but as a means of control, a way to terrorize and oppress . . . , an act that he presumed would deepen divisions that trace back to our nation's original sin. . . .

For too long, we've been blind to the way past injustices continue to shape the present. Perhaps we see that now. Perhaps this tragedy causes us to ask some tough questions about how we can permit so many of our children to languish in poverty . . . or attend dilapidated schools or grow up without prospects for a job or for a career. Perhaps it causes us to examine what we're doing to cause some of our children to hate. Perhaps it softens hearts towards those lost young men, tens and tens of thousands caught up in the criminal justice system and leads us to make sure that that system's not infected with bias. . . .

None of us can or should expect a transformation in race relations overnight. . . . Whatever solutions we find will necessarily be incomplete. But it would be a betrayal of everything Reverend Pinckney stood for, I believe, if we allow ourselves to slip into a comfortable silence again. . . . That's what we so often do to avoid uncomfortable truths about the prejudice that still infects our society. . . . What is true in the South is true for America. Clem understood that justice grows out of recognition of ourselves in each other; that my liberty depends on you being free, too.

QUESTIONS

1. *How does Justice Kennedy believe we should understand the meaning of freedom?*

2. *Why does President Obama believe that the freedom of some Americans is interconnected with the freedom of others?*

3. *What do these documents suggest about how much has changed in American life in the past half-century and how much has not changed?*

taxpayer money into the banks and assuming responsibility for many of their debts. Little was done to help home owners facing foreclosure. Deindustrialization continued. During 2008 and 2009, the economy lost 8 million jobs. It would take a long time to recover them.

The Problem of Inequality

In 2014, the economic recovery finally gathered momentum. Consumer spending and confidence were on the rise, unemployment was falling, home sales were rising, and the stock market reached record highs. The one exception to these favorable trends, however, was a significant one—Americans' wages remained stagnant. In fact, because of the growing number of low-paid jobs, the continuing decline in the power of unions, and the rising value of stocks, owned primarily by upper-income Americans, virtually the entire benefit of the recovery went to the top 1 percent of earners, while the real incomes of most families declined, deepening the long-term trend toward greater and greater economic inequality. In 2013, the top 10 percent of Americans received nearly half the total income. Meanwhile, the percentage of families in the middle class continued to shrink while those living in poverty continued to grow.

At the bottom of the social scale, Americans employed by some of the country's largest corporations, including McDonald's and Walmart, received pitiably low wages, at or just slightly above the federal minimum wage of $7.25 per hour (a figure lower, in income adjusted for inflation, than fifty years before). Many of these workers were assigned to "flexible" schedules, which means that they did not even know the number of hours they would work each week until a few days prior, making planning for child care and other obligations almost impossible. Nearly three-quarters of people helped by programs designed for the poor, such as food stamps and Medicaid, include a working member, so in effect taxpayers are subsidizing the low-wage policies of highly profitable corporations by enabling their employees to survive.

The Occupy Movement

The problem of inequality burst into public discussion in 2011. On September 17, a few dozen young protesters unrolled sleeping bags in Zuccotti Park, in the heart of New York City's financial district. They vowed to remain—to **Occupy Wall Street,** as they put it—as a protest against growing economic inequality, declining opportunity, and malfeasance by the banks.

Over the next few weeks, hundreds of people camped out in the park and thousands took part in rallies organized by the Occupy movement. Similar encampments sprang up in cities across the country. Using social media and

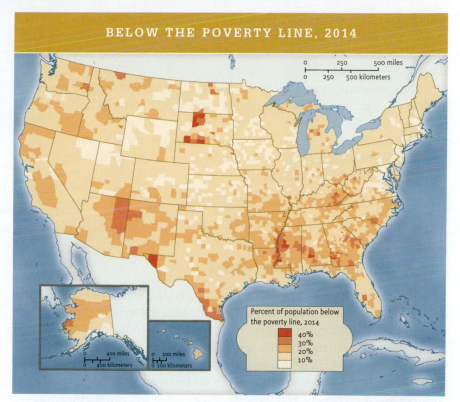

BELOW THE POVERTY LINE, 2014

Percent of population below the poverty line, 2014

- 40%
- 30%
- 20%
- 10%

A map showing the distribution of poverty in the United States. The darker the color, the higher the percentage of families living below the poverty line. Areas with concentrations of African Americans, Latinos, and Native Americans, along with portions of Appalachia inhabited by whites, have the highest poverty rates.

the Internet, the Occupy movement spread its message far and wide. Although the technology was new, the movement bore some resemblance to previous efforts at social change, including the sit-down strikes of the 1930s and the civil disobedience of Henry David Thoreau and Martin Luther King Jr. In the spring of 2012, public authorities began to evict the protesters and the movement seemed to dissipate. But its language, especially the charge that "the 1 percent" (the very richest Americans) dominated political and economic life, had entered the political vocabulary.

The Occupy movement tapped into a widespread feeling of alienation, especially among the young, a sense that society's rules have been fixed in favor of those at the top. And it spurred a movement among low-paid workers, especially in fast-food establishments, demanding a rise in the hourly minimum wage. In 2014, Seattle and Los Angeles raised their minimums to $15 per hour. New York

State followed in 2015 by announcing a $15 minimum for workers in fast-food restaurants. What began as a quixotic movement of the least empowered workers against some of the country's most prominent corporations achieved some remarkable successes.

The problem of income inequality and the shrinking size of the American middle class also energized progressive Democratic political leaders on the national stage. Senator Bernie Sanders of Vermont and Senator Elizabeth Warren of Massachusetts (elected in 2012) called on the party to embrace more ambitious economic reform—from student debt relief to universal health care—to reduce income inequality.

THE OBAMA PRESIDENCY

The Continuing Economic Crisis

The deep recession exacerbated structural trends long under way. Manufacturing employment, which once offered a route into the middle class for those (mostly men) with limited educations, rebounded from its low point of 2009 but remained several million jobs lower than in 2000. Job growth was concentrated at either the high or low end of the pay scale. The financial sector laid off hundreds of thousands of workers, but the incomes of those who kept their jobs remained extremely high. The fastest-growing job categories, however, were those that paid low wages. Indeed, the Bureau of Labor Statistics in 2012 projected that over the next decade, the largest areas of job growth would be in office work, sales, food preparation and service, child care, home health aides, and janitors—every one of which paid less than the median annual wage. The median income of a male full-time worker in 2010 was lower, adjusted for inflation, than in 1973. Rising income inequality afflicted countries across the globe, but among industrialized nations the United States had the highest rate of all.

African Americans suffered most severely from the recession. Unlike other Americans, Blacks tended to own few if any stocks, so did not benefit when the stock market recovered many of its recession losses. A far higher proportion of their family wealth was in their homes, and so the collapse of the housing bubble devastated their economic status. In 2016, the median family wealth of white families was $171,000, that of Black only $17,600, and for Hispanics, $20,700. Black unemployment remained nearly double that of whites, as did the poverty rate. Two-thirds of all Black children lived in low-income families. While the civil rights movement had produced a dramatic increase in the number of well-paid Black professionals (like Obama himself, a lawyer), ordinary African Americans had achieved economic gains by moving into jobs in manufacturing and government (the latter accounting for 20 percent of Black employment), the two sectors hardest hit by the recession.

Postracial America?

Despite this grim reality, Obama's election spurred discussions among political commentators and ordinary Americans that the nation had finally put the legacy of racial inequality behind it. Talk proliferated of a new, "postracial" America, in which racial differences no longer affected public policy or private attitudes. In 2013, the Supreme Court employed this very logic in a 5-4 decision that invalidated the heart of the Voting Rights Act of 1965, a milestone of the civil rights era. Since states identified in the law, most of them in the Old South, no longer discriminated on the basis of race, the majority declared, they should no longer be required to gain permission from the Justice Department before changing their election laws. The decision, in *Shelby County v. Holden*, unleashed a flood of laws in Republican-controlled states, such as limits on early voting and requiring voters to possess state-issued identification. These measures were intended to limit the right to vote for poor people of all races, many of whom do not possess driver's licenses or other official IDs.

A series of events involving the death of unarmed Black men at the hands of police or other authorities also suggested that self-congratulation about the end of racial inequality was premature. In 2012, Trayvon Martin, a Black teenager walking through a Florida neighborhood while visiting his father, was accosted by George Zimmerman, a white member of the "neighborhood

Heavily armed police confront a resident of Ferguson, Missouri, during demonstrations there.

watch." An altercation followed in which Zimmerman shot and killed Martin. Subsequently, a jury acquitted Zimmerman of all charges related to the incident. In 2014, Eric Garner, a forty-four-year-old Black man selling cigarettes on the street in Staten Island, a borough of New York City, died after being wrestled to the ground and choked by police. Although "choke holds" were illegal, a grand jury declined to bring charges. In ensuing months other such incidents followed including the shooting death by a Cleveland police officer of a twelve-year-old Black child who was playing with a toy pistol in a park, the death of a twenty-five-year-old Black man in Baltimore while in a police van after being arrested for carrying a small knife (legal in Maryland), and the fatal shooting in the back of a Black man who ran from police after a traffic stop in North Charleston, South Carolina. In Ferguson, Missouri, a suburb of St. Louis, Michael Brown, an unarmed Black eighteen-year-old, was shot in disputed circumstances by a white police officer, whom a grand jury subsequently cleared of potential charges. In Baltimore and North Charleston, by contrast, local district attorneys moved to indict the police implicated in these cities' deaths.

This cascade of events spurred the emergence of a national movement, **Black Lives Matter**, which demanded that police practices be changed and officers who used excessive force be held accountable. It gave public voice to the countless African Americans who had experienced disrespect, harassment, or violence at the hands of police. The movement used social media to organize protests and disseminate videos of encounters between Black persons and the police. The impact of these images had precedents, notably in the role of television in bringing the war in Vietnam and violent reactions to civil rights demonstrators to national awareness in the 1960s. But the creation of such images was now democratized—most of the videos that spurred outrage were taken by bystanders with cell phones. The Black Lives Matter movement was less an articulation of specific policy demands than a broad claim to Black humanity. In this sense, it had historical precedents in abolitionism, with its slogan "Am I Not a Man and a Brother?" and in "I Am a Man," the defiant claim of Memphis refuse collectors during their 1968 strike, where Martin Luther King Jr. was assassinated.

In Ferguson, Missouri, Brown's death inspired weeks of sometimes violent street demonstrations. These led to the deployment of state police and National Guardsmen dressed in battle gear and armed with assault rifles and armored personnel carriers, as if equipped for a war zone overseas—a sign of how policing had become militarized since the 1960s. The death of Brown and the others, at the very least, suggested that half a century after the urban uprisings of the 1960s, many police departments still relied on excessive force in dealing with Black people and that the criminal justice system remained mired in racism. In Ferguson, investigations after the death of Michael Brown revealed that the almost entirely white police, city government, and local judiciary regularly preyed on Black residents, seeing them not as citizens to be served and protected but as a source of revenue to balance the local budget. Blacks were hauled into court to pay fines for nonexistent driving violations, jaywalking, even walking on the sidewalks too close to the street. Sometimes jail terms ensued for those unable to pay the fine. Over 90 percent of such arrests in Ferguson—which were entirely discretionary—were of Black men and women. Nationally, public reaction to the Black Lives Matter movement revealed a sharp divide between white and Black Americans. In public opinion polls, over 80 percent of Blacks but just 30 percent of whites agreed with the statement that Blacks are victims of discriminatory treatment by the police.

Obama and the World

A significant achievement of Obama's presidency was fulfillment of his campaign promise to end the war in Iraq. At the end of 2011, the last American combat troops came home, although a few hundred advisers remained. In eight years of war, nearly 5,000 American troops and hundreds of thousands of Iraqis, most of them civilians, had died. The war had cost the United States nearly $2 trillion, an almost unimaginable sum. Though the conflict ended Saddam Hussein's dictatorship, it failed to produce a stable, democratic Iraq.

At the same time, Obama continued many of the policies of the Bush administration. Obama dramatically increased the American troop presence in Afghanistan, while pledging to withdraw American forces by the end of 2014 although he failed to meet this deadline. Polls showed that a large majority of Americans felt the war was a mistake and wanted it to end.

Like many of his predecessors, Obama found that criticizing presidential power from outside is one thing, dismantling it another. He reversed his previous promise to abolish the military tribunals Bush had established and to close the military prison at Guantánamo, Cuba. And in 2011 he signed a four-year extension of key provisions of the USA Patriot Act originally passed under Bush. In May 2011, to wide acclaim in the United States, Obama authorized an armed raid into Pakistan that resulted in the death of Osama bin Laden, who had been hiding there for years. And in 2011 Obama sent the air force to participate in a NATO campaign that assisted rebels who overthrew Libyan dictator Muammar Gadhafi. But an endless civil war followed, not the restoration of democracy. Obama did not seek congressional approval of the action, deeming it unnecessary. In fact, throughout Obama's presidency, American troops or planes were involved in combat as part of an expanded war on terrorism not only in Afghanistan but also in Yemen, Pakistan, and

Somalia. American Special Forces were involved in efforts to suppress the drug trade in Honduras and Colombia.

In 2014, Obama abandoned the half-century-old policy of isolating Cuba, and moved to resume diplomatic relations with the island nation. The policy of isolation had long outlived its Cold War origins and had made the United States seem petty and vindictive in the eyes of Latin Americans. In the following year, the administration, in conjunction with the European Union, Russia, and China, worked out an arrangement with Iran to ensure that that nation's nuclear energy program was confined to peaceful purposes and did not lead to the manufacture of nuclear weapons. This was a remarkable achievement in view of the decades of hostility between the United States and Iran dating back to the hostage crisis of 1979–1981. Also in 2015, the United States played a major role in forging the Paris Agreement, which committed every country in the world to reduce emissions (notably from the burning of coal and oil) that contributed to global warming.

Events overseas presented new challenges and opportunities for the Obama administration. Beginning in 2011, to the surprise of almost everyone, popular revolts swept the Middle East. The uprisings brought millions of people into the streets, and toppled long-serving dictators in Tunisia, Egypt, and Libya. Freedom emerged as the rallying cry of those challenging autocratic governments. "I'm in Tahrir Square," one demonstrator yelled into his cellphone while standing at the epicenter of the Egyptian revolution. "In freedom, in freedom, in freedom." Once again, the tension between the ideals of freedom and democracy and American strategic interests posed a difficult challenge for policymakers. After some hesitation, the United States sided with those seeking the ouster of Hosni Mubarak, Egypt's long-serving dictator and a staunch American ally. It then stood on the sidelines throughout 2011 and 2012 as Egypt lurched from popular uprising to military rule, to electoral victory by the Muslim Brotherhood, a previously illegal Islamic group, with the final outcome of the revolution always in doubt. When a military coup in 2014 ousted the elected president and instituted a regime even more repressive than Mubarak's, the Obama administration suspended shipments of military equipment to Egypt, but soon resumed them. In general, like his predecessors during the Cold War, Obama used "human rights" as a political weapon, condemning abuses by adversaries like China while remaining largely silent in the face of serious abuses by allies in the "war on terror" such as Pakistan, Ethiopia, and Saudi Arabia.

The Rise of ISIS

In his second term, Obama faced a new crisis when the self-proclaimed Islamic State took control of parts of Iraq, Syria, and Libya. **ISIS**, as it was called, conducted campaigns of exceptional brutality, beheading prisoners of war and driving religious minorities out of territory it conquered. The videos of these acts posted by ISIS on social media horrified most of the world but also attracted recruits to the organization. ISIS also sponsored terror attacks outside the Middle East. In 2015, over 100 persons were killed in a series of coordinated attacks in Paris. A few weeks later, two followers of ISIS in the United States killed fourteen people in San Bernardino, California. By 2018, in the face of counterattacks by the United States and its allies, ISIS was on the defensive throughout the Middle East, having surrendered the territory it had occupied.

Another area in which Obama continued the policies initiated during the Bush administration's war on terrorism was governmental surveillance, both domestic and overseas. The extent of such activity became known in 2013 when **Edward Snowden**, a former employee of the National Security Agency, released documents online that detailed NSA programs that monitored virtually all telephone, instant messaging, and email traffic in the United States, tracked the location of numerous American cellphones, and spied on the private communications of world leaders, including close allies of the United States such as Chancellor Angela Merkel of Germany and French president François Hollande. The government also secretly worked with major Internet and communications companies like AT&T and Verizon to gain access to the private data of their users. Of course, the overwhelming majority of the people subject to government surveillance had no connection to terrorism or to any crime at all. The Obama administration responded by charging Snowden with violating the Espionage Act of 1917—a law passed during the height of World War I hysteria over security. To avoid prosecution, Snowden took up residence in Russia. But his revelations rekindled the age-old debate over the balance between national security and Americans' civil liberties and offered another example of how, whichever party is in power, the balance always seems to shift in favor of security. In 2015, Congress approved a measure curtailing the government's sweeping surveillance of phone records. But much of the government's prying into Americans' communications continued.

The Republican Resurgence

In nearly all midterm elections in American history, the party in power has lost seats in Congress. But Democrats faced more serious difficulties than usual in the midterm elections of 2010. Grassroots Republicans were energized by hostility to Obama's sweeping legislative enactments. The **Tea Party**, named for the Boston Tea Party of the 1770s and inspired by its opposition to taxation by a faraway government, mobilized grassroots opposition to the administration.

The Tea Party appealed to a long-established American fear of overbearing federal power, as well as to more recent anxieties, especially about immigration. Some supporters advocated repealing the provision of the Fourteenth Amendment granting automatic citizenship to all persons born in the United States. With their opponents energized and their own supporters demoralized by the slow pace of economic recovery, Democrats suffered a severe reversal. Republicans swept to control of the House of Representatives and substantially reduced the Democratic majority in the Senate. The outcome at the national level was political gridlock that lasted for the remainder of Obama's presidency. Obama could no longer get significant legislation through Congress.

Tea Party–inspired conservative gains at the state level in 2010 unleashed a rash of new legislation. Several states moved to curtail abortion rights. In Wisconsin, the legislature and Governor Scott Walker rescinded most of the bargaining rights of unions representing public employees. In Ohio, however, a similar anti-union law was repealed in a popular referendum.

New conservative legislatures also took aim at undocumented immigrants. Alabama, which has no land border with a foreign country and a small population of immigrants compared with other states, enacted the harshest measure, making it a crime for illegal immigrants to apply for a job and for anyone to transport them, even to a church or hospital. During the contest for the Republican presidential nomination in early 2012, candidates vied with each other to demonstrate their determination to drive undocumented immigrants from the country. Oddly, all this took place at a time when undocumented immigration from Mexico, the largest source of undocumented workers, had ceased almost completely because of stricter controls at the border and the drying up of available jobs because of the recession. Despite the fact that the Obama administration had deported far more undocumented immigrants than its predecessor, these measures associated the Republican Party with intense nativism.

The 2012 Campaign

During the campaign for the Republican presidential nomination in 2012 Mitt Romney, the former governor of Massachusetts, emerged as the front-runner. Romney used his personal fortune to outspend his rivals by an enormous amount and became the Republican candidate, the first Mormon to win a major party's nomination—a significant moment in the history of religious toleration in the United States. He chose as his running mate Congressman Paul D. Ryan of Wisconsin, a favorite of the Tea Party and a Roman Catholic. For the first time in its history, the Republican Party's ticket did not contain a traditional Protestant.

President Obama began the 2012 campaign with numerous liabilities. The enthusiasm that greeted his election had long since faded as the worst economic slump since the Great Depression dragged on, and voters became fed up with both the president and Congress because of the intensity of partisanship and legislative gridlock in Washington. The war in Afghanistan was increasingly unpopular, and Obama's signature health-care law was under ferocious assault by Republicans.

Nonetheless, after a heated campaign, Obama emerged victorious, winning 332 electoral votes to Romney's 206, and 51 percent of the popular vote to his opponent's 47 percent. The balance of power in Washington remained essentially unchanged. This set the stage for continued partisan infighting and political gridlock during Obama's second term.

Obama's victory stemmed from many causes, including an extremely efficient "get out the vote" organization on election day, and Romney's weaknesses as a campaigner. More importantly, as in 2008, the result reflected the new diversity of the American population in the twenty-first century. Romney won 60 percent of the white vote, which in previous elections would have guaranteed victory. But Obama carried over 90 percent of the Black vote and over 70 percent of Asians and Hispanics.

Perhaps the most striking feature of the 2012 election was the unprecedented amount of money spent on the campaign. In 2010, in *Citizens United v. Federal Elections Commission*, the conservative majority on the Supreme Court had overturned federal restrictions on political contributions by corporations. At the same time, "political action committees" were allowed to spend as much money as they wished supporting or denigrating candidates for office so long as they did not coordinate their activities with the candidates' campaigns. Meanwhile, the Romney and Obama campaigns themselves raised and spent hundreds of millions of dollars from individual donors. All this resulted in an election that cost, for presidential and congressional races combined, some $6 billion.

PRESIDENT TRUMP

The Candidates in 2016

As the election year 2016 began, all signs pointed to a victory for Hillary Clinton. Most Democrats seemed to feel that she deserved the nomination that Obama had wrested from her eight years earlier. She had long political experience as senator and secretary of state, and many women were galvanized by the prospect of the nation's first female president.

Hillary Clinton at a campaign rally in North Carolina a few days before the 2016 election.

Clinton, however, faced a surprisingly robust challenge for the nomination from Senator Bernie Sanders of Vermont, a self-proclaimed "democratic socialist." By this he meant strengthening and expanding the regulatory policies and social safety net of the New Deal and Great Society through such measures as universal health insurance and limits on corporations' political spending. But beyond specific issues, Sanders spoke to widespread discontent with a society in which those who had plunged the country into economic crisis walked away scot-free while taxpayers were left to pick up the pieces. Adopting themes enunciated by the Occupy Wall Street movement, Sanders accused Clinton of being part of a political establishment whose policies had widened the gap between the 1 percent at the top of the American economy and everyone else. One of the remarkable accomplishments of his campaign was to put the word "socialism"—long banished because of the Cold War—back into the vocabulary of American politics.

With the united support of the Democratic Party establishment, Clinton secured the nomination. Meanwhile, Republicans fractured. Seventeen candidates, including governors, senators, and business leaders, presented themselves. Assuming that Donald Trump, a New York real estate developer and television celebrity, could never be nominated, they tended to ignore him while turning their fire on each other. The result was to weaken each conventional candidate without denting Trump. He shocked the country and the world by winning the Republican nomination.

The Election of Trump

Trump's campaign played on both racial and gender resentments spawned by the growing diversity of American society and the rapid changes in gender roles, as well as the widespread sense, especially in areas suffering from the decline of manufacturing, that millions of ordinary Americans had been left behind by the recovery from the Great Recession.

Trump did not speak much about freedom. He preferred to invoke slogans suggesting military and economic power, such as "Make America Great Again" and "America First." He explicitly rejected the idea that the United States should

From KHIZR KHAN, SPEECH AT DEMOCRATIC NATIONAL CONVENTION (2016)

Donald Trump's incessant attacks on immigrants and association of Muslims with terrorism appealed to many Americans but alienated many others. In a powerful speech at the Democratic convention that nominated Hillary Clinton, with his wife standing at his side, the Pakistani American father of an American soldier killed during the Iraq War responded to Trump's nativist pronouncements. The Khans had moved to the United States in 1980; Khizr Khan graduated from Harvard Law School in 1986, the same year the couple became American citizens.

First, our thoughts and prayers are with our veterans and those who serve today. Tonight, we are honored to stand here as the parents of Capt. Humayun Khan, and as patriotic American Muslims with undivided loyalty to our country.

Like many immigrants, we came to this country empty-handed. We believed in American democracy—that with hard work and the goodness of this country, we could share in and contribute to its blessings. We were blessed to raise our three sons in a nation where they were free to be themselves and follow their dreams. Our son, Humayun, had dreams of being a military lawyer. But he put those dreams aside the day he sacrificed his life to save his fellow soldiers. . . .

If it was up to Donald Trump, he never would have been in America. Donald Trump consistently smears the character of Muslims. He disrespects other minorities—women, judges, even his own party leadership. He vows to build walls and ban us from this country.

Donald Trump . . . let me ask you: Have you even read the U.S. Constitution? I will gladly lend you my copy. In this document, look for the words "liberty" and "equal protection of law." Have you ever been to Arlington Cemetery? Go look at the graves of the brave patriots who died defending America—you will see all faiths, genders, and ethnicities.

We can't solve our problems by building walls and sowing division. We are stronger together.

QUESTIONS

1. *Why does Khan refer to the U.S. Constitution?*

2. *What evidence does he offer of the patriotism of immigrants?*

Donald Trump at a rally in West Virginia during his campaign for the 2016 Republican presidential nomination. He wears a hard hat as part of his appeal for support from the state's coal miners and, more broadly, blue-collar workers suffering from the impact of deindustrialization.

seek to remake other countries in its own image or pay attention to their behavior concerning human rights. He cast doubt on traditional alliances such as NATO. Trump's policies marked a significant change in the national sense of purpose, inspired, in part, by weariness with the seemingly endless wars in Iraq and Afghanistan. No longer would the United States see itself as a global policeman with a mission to uphold freedom across the globe. It would now be one nation—a powerful one to be sure—among many, each pursuing national self-interest.

Trump's political outlook had a strong racial component. In 1989, he had taken out newspaper ads to demand the death penalty for a group of Black and Latino youths accused of the rape of a female jogger. DNA evidence later established that they did not commit the crime, but Trump continued to insist on their guilt. He was a major spokesman for the "birther" movement, which claimed that Obama had been born in Africa and was ineligible to serve as president. (Actually, Obama's birthplace was Hawaii.) When he announced his candidacy, Trump condemned immigrants from Mexico as murderers and rapists and galvanized supporters by promising to build a wall along the long border with Mexico to stop people from entering the country.

Trump ran an unusual campaign. He did not have a conventional campaign organization, spent little on television ads, and did not seek newspaper endorsements. He spread his views via social media and through large rallies where his enthusiastic supporters chanted refrains like "Build That Wall" and "Lock Her Up"—the latter a reference to charges that as secretary of state, Hillary Clinton had illegally used a private server for email. While presidential campaigns have always included scurrilous charges, never before had a major party candidate claimed that his predecessor was not an American citizen or promised to jail his opponent. Trump's polarizing rhetoric and disregard for the truth earned him a great deal of television news coverage. Negative or positive, such attention, driven by profitable ratings, likely helped his campaign.

Despite her long political experience, Clinton failed to address effectively widespread anxiety about the economic and cultural effects of globalization and large-scale immigration. Trump understood that these were the issues of most concern to voters, not his personal foibles and prejudices. He rode this insight to the White House. Trump appealed successfully to nostalgia for a time when people of color and women knew their "place" and American manufacturing dominated the world economy.

Trump was an unusual candidate, but he did not come out of nowhere. The Tea Party had recently shown that hostility to immigrants could pay electoral dividends. Ross Perot in 1992 had run as a businessman whose lack of political experience was a plus and had denounced free-trade agreements for costing millions of Americans their jobs. George Wallace in 1968 and 1972 had appealed to white workers' resentments over racial and economic change, and Richard Nixon's "southern strategy" had won many Wallace voters to the Republican fold.

Trump realized that social media had transformed American politics, allowing him to communicate inexpensively with millions of followers via Facebook and, especially, Twitter. He also understood that on social media, insults, bragging, even expressions of hatred garnered the most attention. Clinton issued long documents outlining her policies on various issues. But at a time when many Americans were dissatisfied with the way the country was headed, political experience such as that possessed by Clinton turned out to be an electoral liability. Like Obama in 2008, Trump promised change to a country unhappy with the status quo. Clinton seemed to represent more of the same.

Throughout 2016, public-opinion polls showed Clinton almost certain to be elected. But Trump triumphed, in possibly the biggest upset in American political history. To be sure, he trailed Clinton by around 3 million popular votes. But by carrying key "swing" states such as Ohio and Florida and by winning Pennsylvania, Michigan, and Wisconsin, where disgruntled white working-class voters who had supported Obama either stayed home or shifted to the Republicans, he gained victory in the electoral college. Overall, the results revealed a sharp divide between rural and small-town America, predominantly white in population and suffering economic decline, which Trump carried with large majorities, and economically thriving, multicultural large metropolitan areas, which went overwhelmingly for Clinton. Trump won 58 percent of white voters but only one-third of Hispanics and 8 percent of Blacks. Clinton carried 54 percent of women voters, but in a humiliating rebuff, a majority of white women voted for Trump.

Trump's victory was part of a global voter revolt against a political establishment many people blamed for job losses, stagnant wages, and large-scale immigration, all elements of globalization. Throughout the world, strongmen who showed a willingness to dispense with democratic norms and stir up hatreds rooted in national or tribal identity consolidated their authority. Whether elected, chosen by a ruling party, or seizing power in a coup d'état, they enjoyed wide popularity—rulers such as Abdel Fattah el-Sisi in Egypt, Vladimir Putin in Russia, Viktor Orbán in Hungary, and Rodrigo Duterte in the Philippines. Trump expressed admiration for all these men. In disorienting times, it seemed, many people wanted strong authority figures at the helm of their nation and a secure sense of belonging and national identity.

Trump in Office

Despite his promise to upend the political system, many of Trump's policies as president, including increased military spending, opposition to women's reproductive rights, deregulation of the economy, and opposition to measures to protect the environment, were standard conservative Republican fare. He and the Republican majority in Congress made strenuous attempts to repeal the Affordable Care Act (Obamacare), but, with nothing to put in its place, their efforts failed. Trump's main legislative achievement during his first two years in office was a massive tax cut. In keeping with the "supply-side" economic outlook embraced by his party since Ronald Reagan's presidency, most of the benefits were directed toward corporations and the wealthiest Americans, on the theory that they would invest the money they saved in economically productive activities and higher wages.

Given a boost by the tax cuts, the economic recovery of the Obama administration continued, with unemployment falling to under 4 percent during 2018. But many corporations used their tax windfall not for productive purposes but to buy back their own stock, enriching investors and corporate executives. Wage increases continued to lag behind inflation so that most Americans saw no economic gain. The typical worker in 2018 earned $44,500 a year, virtually the same as in 1979 when adjusted for inflation. Nearly 80 percent lived paycheck to paycheck, with little economic cushion in case of an emergency. With 560,000 employees, Amazon, the online company that sold every conceivable product, had become, after Walmart, the second largest employer in the United States. Most were low-wage men and women who worked in the company's giant warehouses. Their median pay was $28,000 per year.

Trump did, however, break with Republican free-trade orthodoxy by raising tariffs on goods imported from China, Canada, and the European Union in the hope of promoting American manufacturing. He negotiated a few changes in NAFTA, the free trade agreement with Canada and Mexico that Bill Clinton had worked out in the 1990s. Those with a sense of history noted that he was returning to the Republican Party's protectionist economic outlook of the late nineteenth and early twentieth centuries.

In both foreign and domestic affairs, Trump seemed determined to erase as much of Obama's legacy as possible. He withdrew the United States from the multinational agreement that limited Iran's ability to develop nuclear weapons, preferring to pressure that country with economic sanctions and threats of war. Despite his party's majorities in both houses of Congress, Trump relied on executive orders, not legislation, to erase many of Obama's initiatives, from banking regulations that sought to prevent a repeat of the 2008 financial crisis to rules protecting workers from unsafe conditions and communities from air and water pollution. These and other regulations, Trump declared, were impediments to economic growth.

Early in Trump's presidency, evidence accumulated that the Russian government had interfered in the 2016 election by spreading disinformation on social media and hacking into the email servers of the Democratic National Committee. Russian president Putin seems to have promoted Trump's campaign in the hope that Trump would remove some of the economic sanctions the United States and other countries had instituted after Russia invaded and annexed Crimea, a part of the nation of Ukraine. The Justice Department appointed a special prosecutor, Robert Mueller, to determine whether illegal collusion had occurred between Trump's campaign and Russian officials. As time went on, Mueller expanded his investigation to include other forms of campaign malfeasance, such as secret payments shortly before the election that purchased the silence of two women who claimed to have had affairs with Trump. A number of persons close to the president, including Paul Manafort, his campaign manager; his personal lawyer Michael Cohen; and Michael Flynn, his national security adviser, pleaded guilty to crimes such as tax evasion and lying to the FBI or were convicted of doing so. Mueller's final report, however, found no evidence that Trump had personally conspired with the Russians but did suggest that he had attempted to obstruct the investigation.

Trump and Immigration

As president, Trump kept up his rhetorical attacks on Mexicans, Muslims, and immigrants more generally, but during 2017 and 2018, when his party controlled both houses of Congress, failed to convince lawmakers to authorize the building of his border wall or to legislate at all on immigration. Trump had demanded a complete "shutdown" of Muslim immigration to the United States during the campaign, and one of his first acts as president was to ban travel to the United States from a number of Muslim-majority countries. Federal courts blocked the ban as a form of religious discrimination; eventually, the Supreme Court allowed a watered-down version to go into effect. In the summer of 2018, the administration began removing young children from the custody of parents who had come to the southern border with their families seeking asylum in the United States. The pictures of young children, even toddlers, separated from their parents and held in cage-like structures on abandoned army bases caused an uproar, and a judge ordered the administration to reunite the families.

At the end of 2018, the Trump administration inspired an international uproar when it began separating families seeking to enter the United States from Mexico, holding the children in cage-like structures. The courts ordered that the families be reunited.

Misinformation abounded in the continuing debate over immigration. Trump repeatedly blamed undocumented immigrants for urban crime, even though their crime rate, and that of newcomers legally in the United States, was far lower than that of native-born Americans. About 12 percent of the country's population in 2018 was born abroad, but when asked about the number in polls, Americans gave an average response of 35 percent.

Trump and the Environment

One area in which Trump turned his back not only on Obama's policies but also on the rest of the world was his administration's response to the problem of global warming—a slow rise in the earth's temperature that scientists warn could have disastrous effects on the climate and human life more broadly. Global warming is caused when carbon dioxide released by burning fossil fuels such as oil and coal remains in the upper atmosphere, trapping heat reflected from the earth. Evidence of this development surfaced in the 1980s and 1990s, when scientists studying layers of ice in Greenland concluded that the earth's temperature had risen significantly during the past century.

Today, most scientists consider global warming a serious situation. Climate change threatens to disrupt long-established patterns of agriculture and lead to a

The risks of climate change became increasingly difficult to ignore. Wildfires such as this one in southern California became common as average temperatures rose in increasingly arid lands (*left*). Environmental protest also took on global dimensions. In September 2019, students in Sydney, Australia, participated in the Global Climate Strike to protest government inaction on global warming (*right*).

large expansion of the size of the world's deserts. The melting of glaciers and polar ice caps because of rising temperatures will eventually raise ocean levels, flooding coastal cities. Global warming exacerbates the destructiveness of hurricanes, wildfires, and other natural disasters. But while this was not originally a partisan issue, during the 1990s more and more Republicans came to reject the scientific consensus that human activity causes climate change, and they opposed efforts to promote sources of energy—solar and wind power, for example—that would reduce dependency on oil and coal.

In 2017, Trump withdrew from the **Paris Agreement** on climate change of 2015, making the United States the only country in the world not to commit itself to take steps to reduce emissions that cause climate change. He promised to revive the American coal industry, which was suffering a long decline because of competition from less expensive natural gas as well as from worries about coal's effects on the climate, by weakening restrictions on how much pollution coal-burning power plants spewed into the air. Trump appointed Scott Pruitt of Oklahoma, a close ally of the oil industry who considered global warming a hoax, to head the Environmental Protection Agency. The agency proposed to weaken fuel efficiency standards for automobiles. This would result in cars burning more gasoline and producing more emissions, harming the environment but further enriching oil companies. Late in 2018, government scientists issued a report predicting dire consequences—from widespread flooding to ever more intense storms and wildfires and serious crop failures—if climate change is not addressed. But President Trump declared, "I don't believe it," and the administration continued its efforts to reduce regulations aimed at combating global warming.

A Polarized Nation

Trump's unprecedented conduct as a candidate continued in office. He held virtually no press conferences (and, indeed, denounced the mainstream media as "enemies of the people" who spread "fake news"). Instead, he issued a daily barrage of tweets that promoted his ideas and insulted political opponents, critics, and even political allies such as his attorney general Jeff Sessions. Often, his tweets had a racial component. He declared basketball great LeBron James and Maxine Waters, a Black member of Congress, lacking in intelligence. The tone set by the president helped to produce a coarsening of public discourse, empowering Trump supporters young and old to vent their prejudices on social media, in schools and colleges, and at political rallies.

Trump's presidency exacerbated the intense polarization that had been a feature of politics since Clinton's presidency. His supporters, who represented, according to polls, around 40 percent of Americans, remained steadfastly loyal. Those who disliked Trump's policies or were offended by his behavior were galvanized to express their opposition. Many people were deeply offended by his derogatory remarks about women. On the day after his inauguration, a **Women's March** on Washington brought hundreds of thousands of people to the nation's capital to express their support for women's rights, immigration reform, racial equality, and protection of the environment.

Another expression of women's activism, the **Me Too movement**, brought to light evidence of rampant sexual harassment by entertainment moguls, business leaders, public officials, and other powerful men. Prominent women, including members of Congress and leading actresses, and ordinary ones publicized their experiences in workplaces, universities, and social gatherings and demanded the punishment of offenders. Charges of sexual misconduct led to the firing or resignation of figures as diverse as Minnesota senator Al Franken, TV personality Charlie Rose, and movie producer Harvey Weinstein.

The Elections of 2018

With the economic recovery that had begun under Obama still underway and unemployment at a historic low, a conventional politician would have emphasized economic issues in the midterm elections of 2018. Not Trump. In the last weeks of the campaign he traveled the country, holding rallies where he whipped up fear of immigrants, warning of a coming "invasion" of people bringing crime, disease, and terrorism. These appeals consolidated his political base but alienated more moderate voters. With Democrats, and many independents, galvanized by opposition to Trump's policies and behavior, the elections of 2018 in part reversed the verdict of two years earlier. Democrats replaced Republicans in forty seats in the House of Representatives, regaining control of that body.

Trump's policies and demeaning comments regarding women produced a giant gender gap in voting. Women supported Democratic candidates by 59 to 40 percent. The gap was even wider among young voters; those below age thirty voted Democratic by 35 percentage points. On the other hand, Republicans increased their majority in the Senate.

The 2018 elections revealed other deep divides—between rural areas, strongly Republican, and cities and suburbs dominated by Democrats; and between Republicans' almost entirely white and largely male support and the diversity of Democrats. Republicans won 54 percent of white voters but only 29 percent of Hispanics and 9 percent of Blacks. These patterns were reflected in the new House of Representatives. Over 100 women were elected to the body, the most in American history. Of the forty-two new women members, thirty-eight were Democrats; of twenty-three new people of color elected to Congress, only one was a Republican. The new members of Congress included the first two Native American women (Sharice Davids of Kansas and Deb Haaland of New Mexico, both Democrats) and the first two Muslim women (Ilhan Omar of Minnesota and Rashida Tlaib of Michigan, also Democrats). The year 2018 also saw the election of the first openly gay governor, Democrat Jared Polis of Colorado.

Thus, two visions of America clashed, one based on exclusion and whiteness, the other welcoming and diverse. Both were deeply rooted in the American experience.

The Impeachment of Donald Trump

Soon after the Mueller investigation delivered its inconclusive verdict, Trump faced new charges in 2019 of soliciting foreign interference to benefit his reelection bid. In a recorded telephone conversation revealed by a CIA whistleblower, Trump pressured Ukrainian president Volodymyr Zelenskyy to open investigations into the Biden family to weaken Joseph Biden, his expected challenger in the 2020 election. If Ukraine did not act, Trump threatened to withhold promised U.S. military aid. When Congress opened an investigation into the incident, Trump instructed members of his administration to refuse to cooperate. On December 17, 2019, after testimony from a number of high-placed officials and diplomats, the House of Representatives found Trump guilty of abuse of power and obstruction of justice.

Trump became only the third president to be impeached in U.S. history for "high crimes and misdemeanors." The largely partisan vote for impeachment, however, revealed the deep polarization of the nation and Trump's powerful grip on the Republican Party. The Republican-dominated Senate held only a brief trial and quickly acquitted Trump. Though few members of Congress disputed the facts, they downplayed the seriousness of Trump's actions, arguing that they did not amount to sufficient grounds to remove him from office. Senator Mitt Romney of Utah was the only Republican to vote to convict President Trump.

2020: YEAR OF CRISIS

In many ways comparable to 1968 or 1919, 2020 was a tumultuous year. A series of unprecedented events unfolded with dizzying speed. Within less than thirteen months the nation experienced a global pandemic, a wave of street protests against police violence, two presidential impeachments, and a violent insurrection in the nation's capital. Only during the Civil War had the United States been more deeply divided.

FIGURE 28.2 COVID-19 CASES AND DEATHS IN THE UNITED STATES, 2020

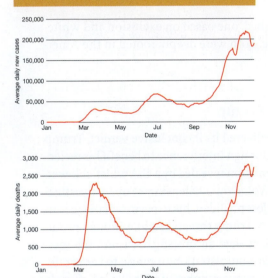

After the initial wave in March and April, the Covid-19 outbreak continued into 2020. In July the United States recorded more than 1.9 million new infections; the death toll surpassed 200,000 by the end of September, over 250,000 by November, and 300,000 by year's end (with more than 1 million deaths reported worldwide).

The Coronavirus Pandemic

In early January 2020, government officials in Wuhan, China, confirmed the outbreak of a dangerous new virus that had infected dozens of patients. By January 11, China reported the first known death, and on January 23, the government cut off air, road, and rail traffic to and from Wuhan to prevent the virus's spread. But by that time, the highly contagious new strain of coronavirus, which scientists named **Covid-19** because it originated in 2019, had spread to other parts of Asia and around the world. The United States confirmed its first case on January 20. By March 11, the World Health Organization elevated Covid-19 to a global pandemic, and the United States soon emerged as one of the countries hardest hit.

To prevent the spread of the virus, governments around the

globe enacted strict measures, banning nonessential travel, closing schools and businesses, and requiring citizens in especially hard-hit areas to shelter in place. The Trump administration suspended travel from China and then barred noncitizens from other countries, declaring a national emergency. By the end of March, the U.S. unemployment rate had risen to close to 15 percent. Spiraling Covid-19 infections taxed the health-care system to the breaking point with overcrowded hospitals and a dearth of essential supplies from masks to ventilators. Succeeding viral waves hit different parts of the country. With only 4 percent of the world's population, the United States had 22 percent of confirmed Covid deaths by September 2020. By the end of December the United States recorded 300,000 deaths (the death rate doubled again in 2021). Only Peru, Brazil, Hungary, Poland, and a few other countries surpassed the United States in reported death rates.

The Pandemic and Politics

In 2018, before Covid-19 emerged, Trump dismantled a global public health task force established in the wake of the 2014 Ebola outbreak to prepare for future pandemics. This left the nation less capable of mounting an early and coordinated response. As the virus spread, Trump downplayed Covid-19's public health dangers, contributing to the spread of misinformation. With escalating hospitalizations and deaths, states scrambled to contain the spread of Covid-19 through testing, tracing the contacts of people who became ill, and issuing mask mandates and stay-at-home orders. With businesses shuttered, Congress passed bills providing $3 trillion in relief. Many Americans received stimulus checks and the government provided small businesses access to special loans and grants.

While many Americans accepted health officials' guidance, others saw public health measures as infringements on individual liberty. Often the heated disagreements over public health policies mirrored partisan divides. Many more Republican than Democrat officials were skeptical of public health guidance. Republican Attorney General William Barr suggested that statewide stay-at-home mandates infringed on constitutional rights. In some states where Democratic governors ordered statewide closures to protect public health, protesters came to their state capitols to signal their opposition. Trump expressed his support for such actions on Twitter, calling on residents to "Liberate" Minnesota and Michigan.

The polarized response to the virus revealed many Americans' deep distrust of government authority. Other countries also experienced protests against public health mandates, but the partisan division over government health measures was greater in the United States than elsewhere. In Germany and in France, for example, trust in government increased in response to government measures to contain the virus. But in the United States faith in government decreased. Misinformation about Covid-19 was spread rapidly through social media. Online platforms such as Facebook were designed to provide their users content they liked, even if the information was false. Platform algorithms contributed to the dissemination of rumors and conspiracy theories about the virus to millions of Americans.

Once a vaccine was authorized by the Food and Drug Administration (FDA) on an emergency basis, opposition and misinformation about vaccines spread rapidly as well. The Trump administration invested billions of dollars of federal funds into public and private partnerships to quickly develop and deliver a vaccine against Covid-19. By December 2020, a vaccine rollout had begun. When Biden took office in January 2021, he declared the goal of vaccinating 70 percent of Americans by July 4. But with vaccine hesitancy gaining strength only around 60 percent of adults in the United States had been vaccinated by the fall of 2021, significantly less than in many other developed countries. The virus continued its spread. Vaccination, however, helped prevent a recurrence of the early surge of hospitalizations and deaths. It remained unclear whether the pandemic would run its course, much like the Spanish flu, or remain a persistent health-care challenge.

The Pandemic and Structural Inequalities

Long-standing structural inequalities contributed to a disproportionate impact of the virus on minority communities. African Americans, Hispanics, and Native Americans became sick and died at higher rates than white Americans due to higher rates of chronic illness, poverty, inconsistent access to health care, and more often living in multigenerational households. African Americans and Latinos frequently worked in low-wage, front-line "essential services" like hospitality, with more exposure to the virus. African Americans had twice the death rate of white Americans. Since 1980, the United States has experienced a widening gap among racial and ethnic groups in life expectancy compared to other industrial, high-income countries such as Denmark, England, France, and Israel. The virus increased the gap. Black Americans' grievances over structural inequalities and police violence led to what many hoped would be a pivotal moment of national racial transformation.

"I Can't Breathe": The Murder of George Floyd

On May 25, 2020, forty-six-year-old George Floyd was arrested by Minneapolis police on suspicion of using a counterfeit twenty dollar bill. Placed in a choke hold for close to nine minutes with an officer's knee pressed into his neck, Floyd pleaded for air until he died. The callous killing, captured by one witness's cell phone camera, reverberated around the nation and the world.

In the wake of Floyd's death, hundreds of thousands across the nation demonstrated for police reform and racial justice. **George Floyd's murder** awakened many Americans to the problem of racially discriminatory policing. Black Americans in 2020 were more than twice as likely as whites to be shot and killed by police. Floyd's killing was only the most highly publicized in a series of police killings of unarmed Black Americans. Since 2015, there have been close to 1,000 lethal shootings by police officers each year, with African Americans disproportionately among the victims.

Incidents of police violence had sparked major rebellions from the Watts riots in Los Angeles in 1965 to Ferguson, Missouri, in 2014. Although the Black Lives Matter movement (discussed above) had mobilized for police reform since 2011, Floyd's murder sparked an unprecedented wave of protest. Demonstrations spread from major cities including Seattle, New York, and Los Angeles to smaller cities and towns with calls for reform, including demands to "defund" the police—that is, transfer money allocated to police departments to social services including mental health treatment. Black Lives Matter witnessed a surge of public support. The House of Representatives approved the George Floyd Justice in Policing Act twice, but it failed to pass the Republican-controlled Senate. Cities such as Seattle banned choke holds, and Maryland limited "no knock" warrants. Floyd's death led to heightened awareness of racial discrimination and intensified appeals for racial justice. Many towns and cities removed Confederate monuments from public spaces. But police reforms amounted to a trickle rather than a flood.

Americans remained deeply divided over policing and the protests. Some localities used violence to repress the demonstrations. At one White House protest against Floyd's killing in June 2020, President Trump called on the National Guard and used tear gas to clear demonstrators for a photo opportunity. Despite the outpouring of protest, the numbers of killings in police custody and the economic grievances faced by poor Blacks have continued largely unchanged.

The 2020 Election

In the midst of the pandemic and the wave of social unrest following Floyd's killing, former Vice President Joe Biden became the Democratic nominee for president after a heated primary campaign. He faced stiff competition from his party's progressive wing. Senator Bernie Sanders of Vermont and Senator Elizabeth Warren of Massachusetts called for raising taxes on the nation's billionaires, providing free college tuition to rein in rising student debt, and establishing universal health care. With the party's backing, however, Biden, who favored more moderate proposals, won the nomination. He claimed that his political experience, experience with bipartisan relationships, and working-class roots made him the candidate most likely to defeat Trump. The support of influential African American officeholders, such as Congressman James Clyburn of South Carolina, helped put Biden's nomination over the top. Biden chose Senator Kamala Harris of California as his running mate, the first female vice-presidential candidate of African American and Asian American heritage. The themes of unity, stability, and economic rebuilding dominated his campaign.

Biden's upbringing in white working-class Scranton, Pennsylvania, along with the disaffection among some of those who voted for Trump in 2016, enabled the former vice president to win back many of the working-class voters the Democrats had lost in 2016. Biden regained the swing states of Michigan, Wisconsin, and Pennsylvania that Trump had won in 2016. Biden triumphed in the electoral college 306 to 232 and carried the popular vote 51 percent to 47 percent. But Democrats saw their majority in the House shrink. They eventually gained a narrow control of the Senate after winning two runoff races in Georgia in January 2021 (discussed on p. 1170), but their slim majorities left Congress gridlocked.

Turnout in 2020 was the highest since 1900, with nearly two-thirds of eligible voters casting a ballot. The seemingly high stakes contributed to record turnout. Trump's followers, who adored his unapologetic "America First" nationalism, were eager to see him secure a second term. His critics feared his strongman style and disregard for past presidential norms; they saw the prospect of four additional years in office as a threat to American democracy.

Public health measures also bolstered the high turnout. To enable voters to safely cast ballots during the pandemic, twenty-nine states instituted early voting or expanded voting by mail. Mail-in and absentee voting had precedents. In Oregon, for example, people had been voting exclusively by mail since 1998. And over the two preceding decades, mail-in voting had increased in many states. In 2020, a majority of those who voted did so in person, either early or on election day, while 43 percent of voters cast their ballots by mail. The increased volume of mail-in balloting required counting millions of ballots that arrived shortly before each state's deadline, usually when the polls closed on election day. The resulting delay set the stage for Trump's unsubstantiated claims that votes had been fraudulently "found."

The Challenge to Democracy

For months ahead of election day, Trump had warned his followers to expect "tremendous fraud" that might cause him to lose. His allegations had precedent.

In 2016, he had falsely blamed "millions and millions" of illegal votes for Hillary Clinton's popular vote majority. In 2020, he spread unfounded claims that mail-in voting would be "substantially fraudulent," establishing the groundwork for challenging the election's legitimacy should he lose.

Trump urged his followers to vote in person. With in-person ballots generally counted first, early returns favored Trump. Late on election night he claimed that he had won even though many states were still counting millions of legally cast ballots. When counting was finished, Biden proved to be the winner. Trump refused to concede. He mounted a series of fruitless legal challenges in close swing states to overturn the results. Two such attempts were turned back by the Supreme Court. But the drumbeat of "flipped" and "stolen votes" amplified over the coming months by Trump and his allies led many Americans to question the legitimacy of the electoral process.

With his legal strategy floundering, Trump pressured Republican officials in swing states to flip electors in his favor. He urged the Georgia Republican secretary of state to "find 11,800 votes," which would erase Biden's slim majority in the state. Trump lobbied Vice President Pence to reject the state-certified results, which would allow the election to be decided by the House of Representatives, where Republicans controlled a majority of the state delegations. Pence refused, citing his oath to defend the Constitution.

The Capitol Attack

On January 6, 2021, Congress assembled to ratify the 2020 election results. This routine process turned into an attack on the seat of American governance. Trump had urged his supporters to gather in Washington to protest a "rigged" election. He held a rally at the National Mall, railing against the "fake news" media and a "stolen" election. At Trump's urging, thousands of those present then marched to the Capitol. Many demonstrated peacefully, but a group of his supporters, including the paramilitary Oath Keepers and the white nationalist Proud Boys, came prepared to instigate violence. Some among the crowd carried chemical sprays and baseball bats and donned battle gear. Rioters smashed barricades, battled police, broke windows, and breached the building. Lawmakers scrambled to safety. The rioters occupied the Senate chambers before the Capitol police, bolstered by the municipal police of Washington, D.C., cleared the building. More than 140 police officers were injured, and one police officer and four Trump loyalists died during the events of that day.

In the immediate aftermath, Democrats and top Republican lawmakers condemned Trump for his role in the **Capitol attack**, laying the blame for the day's violence at his feet. Twitter and Facebook banned Trump from using

Pro-Trump rioters storm the Capitol building on January 6, 2021, to disrupt the 2020 election certification. On January 13, Trump was impeached by the House of Representatives for inciting insurrection.

their platforms. House Democrats charged Trump with "incitement of insurrection" and swiftly proceeded to impeach him on January 13, making him the only president in American history to be impeached twice. The brief Senate trial, however, held after Biden's inauguration, failed to convict. Since Trump was no longer president, Minority Leader Mitch McConnell argued, the Senate had no jurisdiction. In the wake of the trial, McConnell declared Trump's actions "a disgraceful dereliction of duty." But since then, most Republican lawmakers have downplayed what happened. House Republicans ousted Congresswoman Liz Cheney from her leadership position in May 2021 for continuing to condemn Trump for instigating the riot.

Trump's unprecedented effort to overturn the presidential election in 2020 failed, but only future developments will reveal its long-term consequences for American democracy. Many Republican lawmakers backed Trump's unsubstantiated allegations of widespread voter fraud (147 Republican members of Congress voted against the certification of state results), revealing an erosion of the norms of democratic governance. In 2021, Republicans in states they controlled used the concerns generated by claims of voter fraud to pass new laws making it harder to vote. Justified as a means to ensure "ballot integrity," these laws are reminiscent of earlier efforts to suppress voting by Blacks and the poor. Among other restrictive measures, a law passed in Georgia in 2021, for example, makes it illegal for any person to offer water to voters waiting in line to cast their ballots.

A Reinvigoration of Pluralism

Joe Biden was inaugurated on January 20, 2021, ending Trump's tumultuous years in office. The day's events celebrated national traditions of inclusiveness, immigration, and multiculturalism. Two weeks earlier on January 5, Democrats secured control of Congress when Republican senators David Perdue and Kelly

Loeffler lost their reelection bids in a special runoff race. Democrats Raphael Warnock and John Ossoff became the first Black and the first Jewish senators from Georgia. This marked a historic turning point in a state with a deep history of racial discrimination and anti-Semitism. The campaigns owed their success, in no small part, to an energetic and well-organized mobilization among the state's many Black Democratic voters. The events of January 5 and January 6, only a day apart, revealed the ongoing contest between different visions of national identity central to American history—namely, between the United States as an inclusive, plural, interracial democracy and a nation defined by white nationalism.

FREEDOM IN THE TWENTY-FIRST CENTURY

The century that ended in 2000 witnessed vast human progress and unimaginable human tragedy. It saw the decolonization of Asia and Africa, the emergence of women into full citizenship in most parts of the world, and amazing advances in science, medicine, and technology. Thanks to the spread of new products, available at ever-cheaper prices, it brought more improvement in the daily conditions of life to more human beings than any other century in history. Worldwide life expectancy in the twentieth century rose from forty to sixty-seven years, and the literacy rate increased from 25 percent to 80 percent. This was the first century in which the primary economic activity for most of mankind moved beyond the acquisition of basic food, clothing, and shelter. But the twentieth century also witnessed the death of uncounted millions in wars and genocides and the widespread degradation of the natural environment, the underside of progress.

Exceptional America

In the early twenty-first century, people in the United States lived longer and healthier lives compared with previous generations, and they enjoyed a level of material comfort unimagined a century before. In 1900, the typical American had no indoor plumbing, had no telephone or car, and had not graduated from high school. As late as 1940, one-third of American households did not have running water. In 2020 close to 20 million Americans attended college, more than three times the number in 1960. By 2019, health conditions had improved so much that the average life expectancy for men had risen to seventy-seven and for women to eighty-one (from forty-six and forty-eight, respectively, in 1900). In the second decade of the twenty-first century, however, life expectancy trends have tended to stagnate, and during the Covid-19 pandemic, as mentioned earlier, life expectancy averages actually fell.

Overall, however, the rising life expectancy through the years of the twentieth century to the early decades of the twenty-first century suggested that people would enjoy far longer and more productive periods of retirement than in the past. Many of the changes affecting American life, such as the longer life span of the population, better health care, and the transformed role of women, along with the decline of industrial employment, have taken place in all economically advanced societies. In other ways, however, the United States in the twenty-first century has differed sharply from other developed countries. Since 1980, for example, life expectancy in the United States has increased more slowly and poverty, income inequality, and infant mortality in the United States have considerably exceeded that of comparable countries. Fewer than 10 percent of workers in private firms belong to unions, a figure not seen since the nineteenth century. The United States has continued to lag behind Europe in providing social rights to its citizens. In Europe, workers are guaranteed by law a paid vacation each year and a number of paid sick days. American employers are not required to offer either of these benefits to their workers. Only three countries in the world have no national provision for paid leave after a woman gives birth to a child: Papua New Guinea, Suriname, and the United States. In Europe new parents have paid leaves of up to fourteen months. The United States is also an outlier in its low levels of financial support for the care of young children compared to other wealthy countries.

Prevailing ideas of freedom in the United States seemed more attuned to individual advancement than to broad social welfare. In 2003, when asked whether it was more important for the government to guarantee freedom from want or freedom to pursue individual goals, only 35 percent of Americans selected freedom from want, as opposed to 58 percent in Germany, 62 percent in France and Great Britain, and 65 percent in Italy. As a country, the United States is more individualistic than are countries in Europe. A 2019 survey showed that 53 percent of western Europeans and 58 percent of central and eastern Europeans believed that success is determined by forces outside their control. Only 31 percent of Americans agreed. The United States is also far more religious. Close to 50 percent of Americans agreed with the statement "Religion plays a very important part in my life." The comparable figure was 22 percent in western Europe and 19 percent in central and eastern Europe. Close to one in four Americans said they believed in the literal truth of the Bible. A 2006 survey found that nearly one-fifth of Americans believe that God favors the United States in world affairs. Religion and nationalism reinforced one another more powerfully in the United States than in the more secular nations of western Europe.

One of the starkest differences between the United States and other advanced countries is gun ownership and gun violence. Over 40 percent of the world's guns in private hands, from pistols to hunting weapons to assault rifles, are owned in the United States. The United States has over 390 million guns, more than the total American population. As a result, Americans are far more likely to be killed by guns than are residents of other developed countries. In 2017, the United States had close to 38,000 deaths involving guns, including murders, suicides, and accidents, whereas only 58 Americans died from acts classified as terrorism. In 2020, handguns accounted for over 8,000 murders.

In the last years of the twentieth century and first two decades of the twenty-first, the United States was the scene of a horrifying number of mass murders with the attacks becoming increasingly deadly. Eight of the shootings with the highest numbers of mass casualties have happened in the past ten years. Many attacks have been committed at schools.

In 1999, two students killed twelve students and a teacher at Columbine High School in Colorado. In 2007, a student at Virginia Tech University shot and killed thirty-two people. Five years later, a lone gunman killed twenty children aged five and six, and seven adults, at Sandy Hook Elementary School in Newtown, Connecticut. In the 1950s, schools across the country had conducted drills to enable students to survive a nuclear attack. Now they trained pupils in seeking shelter if a gunman entered the building. There were also mass killings at a movie theater in Aurora, Colorado, and at the Washington Navy Yard. In 2015, a gunman influenced by racist Internet sites murdered nine Black participants in a Bible study group, including the minister, at Emanuel African Methodist Episcopal Church in Charleston, South Carolina. Around sixty people were killed by a gunman firing from a hotel window on a crowd gathered for a country and western music festival in Las Vegas in November 2017. Other countries also experienced instances of mass violence, but not with the frequency of the United States.

In March 2018, hundreds of thousands of young people took part in demonstrations across the country for gun control, under the slogan **March for Our**

In 2017, the artist Hank William Thomas and photographer Emily Shur reimagined Norman Rockwell's famous 1943 painting *Freedom from Want* (see Chapter 22) to depict today's more diverse American society. The work also brings to mind the post–Civil War engraving *Uncle Sam's Thanksgiving Dinner* (Chapter 15). Credit: *For Freedoms* (Hank Willis Thomas and Emily Shur in collaboration with Eric Gottesman and Wyatt Gallery of For Freedoms).

Lives. The movement was organized by students at a high school in Parkland, Florida, after a shooting there that left seventeen pupils and teachers dead. But the strong commitment of many Americans to the Second Amendment's guarantee of the right to bear arms, coupled with the remarkable power of the National Rifle Association, one of the country's most influential lobbies, ensured that no new regulations were enacted. At the same time, as noted in the previous chapter, the United States has the world's highest rate of imprisonment and a more punitive approach to crime overall than most of its wealthy peer nations. Most nations have abolished the death penalty, but the United States retains it.

Varieties of Freedom

In the early twenty-first century, Americans were increasingly tolerant of divergent personal lifestyles, cultural backgrounds, and religious persuasions. They enjoyed a degree of freedom of expression unmatched in virtually any country in the world. Thanks to the rights revolution and the political ascendancy of antigovernment conservatives, the dominant definition of freedom stressed the capacity of individuals to realize their desires and fulfill their potential unrestricted by authority. Still other Americans continued to stress alternative visions—freedom as economic security, freedom as active participation in democratic government, freedom as social justice for those long disadvantaged. But many Americans sought freedom within themselves, not through social institutions or public engagement. And, as noted earlier, one of the great ironies of twenty-first-century life is that despite the prominence of ideas about freedom in politics and American identity, the United States has the largest rate of incarceration in the world.

The large number of Americans living in conditions of unfreedom, paradoxically, existed at a time when Americans in the twenty-first century enjoyed much greater personal freedoms than earlier generations—freedom to choose a nonbinary gender identity, for example, or to marry a partner of the same sex. Rising incarceration rates and greater personal freedom were also coupled with the diminishment of what earlier generations called "industrial freedom." Globalization—which treated workers at home and abroad as interchangeable factors of production, capable of being uprooted or dismissed without warning—seemed to render individual and even national sovereignty all but meaningless. Since economic liberty has long been associated with economic security, and rights have historically been linked to democratic participation and membership in a nation-state, these processes had ominous implications for traditional understandings of freedom. A conception of freedom grounded in access to the consumer marketplace and the glorification of individual self-fulfillment unrestrained by government, social citizenship, or a common public culture has left many Americans feeling aggrieved. A concurrent decline in the faith among blue-collar and middle-class white Americans in the possibility of social mobility and the sentiment that their children will be worse off than they were have contributed to the spread of white nationalist, nativist, and exclusionary ideas. Whether or not earlier visions of industrial freedom can be revived and instill a renewed faith in a common culture and social citizenship remains to be seen.

Battles over History

In a politically polarized nation, history itself has become a battleground. Debates proliferate over the fate of public monuments to the Confederacy and its leaders. Some see these statues as harmless expressions of southern civic heritage; to others, they represent the glorification of slavery and racism.

Some statues have recently been taken down, including those of Confederate president Jefferson Davis at the University of Texas, and Chief Justice Roger B. Taney, author of the infamous Dred Scott decision, in Baltimore. New Orleans mayor Mitch Landrieu ordered four removed from public property—statues of Davis, Confederate generals P. G. T. Beauregard and Robert E. Lee, and a monument to the Battle of Liberty Place of 1874, when the White League attempted to violently overthrow Louisiana's biracial Reconstruction government. The inscription on this monument celebrated the league's insurrection as an effort to restore "white supremacy." Landrieu explained his city's decision: "In the second decade of the 21st century, asking African Americans—or anyone else—to drive by property that they own; occupied by reverential statues of men who fought to destroy the country and deny that person's humanity seems perverse and absurd."

The monuments controversy took a deadly turn in August 2017, when a group of white supremacists and neo-Nazis marched in Charlottesville, Virginia, chanting anti-Semitic and racist slogans, to demand that a statue of Robert E. Lee remain in place. They were confronted by opposing demonstrators. Violent clashes ensued, leading to the death of a woman mowed down when a marcher ran his car into the anti-racist crowd. To the dismay of many Americans, including leaders of his own party, President Trump refused to apportion blame, insisting that there were "very fine people" on both sides of the confrontation. He also sent out a tweet lamenting the removal of Confederate statues, claiming such actions tear apart "the history and culture of our great country."

Conflicts over how to represent history have arisen most recently in the nation's schools. In the wake of George Floyd's killing and the heightened public discussions about racial discrimination, some administrators and teachers have sought to more centrally include curriculum on slavery and racial discrimination in the teaching of American history. This effort has been met with backlash by those who believe such teaching amplifies divisions and differences among Americans instead of commonalities. They believe that history teaching should build national pride by providing a celebratory, rather than critical, vision of the American past. Recently, Republican governors in Oklahoma, Tennessee, Iowa, and Texas have signed bills designed to restrict the way history is taught. The ongoing contest over history reflects two distinct visions of America that have deep roots in the nation's past.

Learning from History

"The owl of Minerva takes flight at dusk." Minerva was the Roman goddess of wisdom, and this saying suggests that the meaning of events only becomes clear once they are over. As of 2021, the world seemed far more unstable than anyone could have predicted when the Cold War ended. After a twenty-year war, the United States left Afghanistan in August 2021 in a chaotic evacuation with its enemy, the Taliban, in full control of the country. The future of the entire Middle East remained uncertain. No settlement of the long-standing conflict between Israel and its Arab neighbors seemed in sight. China's rapidly growing economic power and influence challenged American global predominance. No one could predict the long-term outcome of these developments or others yet unimagined.

Despite the U.S. withdrawal from Afghanistan and the rising influence of nationalist and isolationist ideas domestically, it seemed clear that the United States would remain involved in the affairs of the world. The country has nearly

Hundreds of Afghans swarmed Karzai International airport during the rushed U.S. military evacuation on August 16, 2021. Although some rejoiced at the U.S. departure, others were desperate to escape Taliban rule.

800 military bases in around 70 countries. It had 173,000 troops deployed in 150 countries in 2020. A study by American intelligence agencies predicted that by 2025 the United States would remain the world's most powerful nation but that its economic and military predominance would decline significantly. A "multipolar world" with countries like China and India emerging as major powers is succeeding the era of unquestioned American dominance. The consequences of these changes, along with the implications of

the growing numbers of countries with illiberal governments, including India, Hungary, and Brazil, remains unclear. In 2020, the United States witnessed a challenge to the legitimacy of democratic governance not seen since the Civil War and Reconstruction eras. Only time will reveal the long-term implications of such developments.

What *is* clear is that as in the past, freedom remains central to Americans' sense of themselves as individuals and as a nation. Americans continue to debate contemporary issues in a political landscape shaped by ideas of freedom. Indeed, freedom remains, as it has always been, an evolving concept, its definition open to disagreement, its boundaries never fixed or final. Freedom is neither self-enforcing nor self-correcting. It cannot be taken for granted, and its preservation requires eternal vigilance, especially in times of crisis.

More than half a century ago, the African American poet Langston Hughes urged Americans both to celebrate the freedoms they enjoy and to remember that freedom has always been incomplete:

> There are words like *Freedom*
> Sweet and wonderful to say.
> On my heartstrings freedom sings
> All day everyday.
>
> There are words like *Liberty*
> That almost make me cry.
> If you had known what I know
> You would know why.

CHAPTER REVIEW

REVIEW QUESTIONS

1. *What were the political and social effects of Hurricane Katrina? Which were lasting?*

2. *In what ways did the Obama administration diverge from the policies of other recent administrations? In what ways was it similar?*

3. *How did the 2012 election reveal changes in American political and social practices? How did it represent continuities?*

4. *In what ways is the United States different from other economically advanced societies and how is it similar?*

5. *What did Obama's and Trump's presidential campaigns have in common? In what ways did Trump run an unusual presidential campaign?*

6. *How was Trump's victory part of a larger global voter revolt against the political establishment?*

7. *Describe the basic events of the investigation into the Russian government's interference in the 2016 election.*

8. *What are some similarities and differences between the Black Lives Matter movement and the Me Too movement?*

9. *How did responses to the Covid-19 pandemic reflect a divided America?*

10. *Describe the events that led to the two impeachments of Donald Trump.*

11. *How did national debates over Confederate monuments and school curriculum on the teaching of slavery and race illuminate the complexity of representing history? How did they once again raise the question of who is an American?*

KEY TERMS

Hurricane Katrina (p. 1128)

Obergefell v. Hodges (p. 1132)

Great Recession (p. 1135)

Sonia Sotomayor (p. 1140)

Gulf oil spill (p. 1140)

Occupy Wall Street (p. 1144)

Black Lives Matter (p. 1148)

ISIS (p. 1150)

Edward Snowden (p. 1151)

Tea Party (p. 1151)

Paris Agreement (p. 1161)

Women's March (p. 1162)

Me Too movement (p. 1162)

Covid-19 (p. 1164)

George Floyd's murder (p. 1167)

Capitol attack (p. 1169)

March for Our Lives (p. 1173)

Go to 🐰 INQUIZITIVE

To see what you know—and learn what you've missed—with personalized feedback along the way.

SUGGESTED READING

CHAPTER 1

BOOKS

Fernández-Armesto, Felipe. *Pathfinders: A Global History of Exploration* (2006). A history of explorations throughout the centuries, including those of the fifteenth and sixteenth centuries.

Greer, Allen. *Prosperity and Dispossession: Natives, Empires and Land in Early Modern America* (2018). Examines Native and European concepts and use of property across North America from the sixteenth to eighteenth centuries.

Hill, Susan M. *The Clay We Are Made Of: Haudenosaunee Land Tenure on the Grand River* (2017). A path-breaking exploration of Haudenosaunee (Iroquois) history.

Knaut, Andrew L. *The Pueblo Revolt of 1680: Conquest and Resistance in Seventeenth-Century New Mexico* (1997). An account of the conflicts between the Spanish and the people of the Pueblos.

Mancall, Peter C. *Fatal Journey: The Final Expedition of Henry Hudson* (2009). Gripping tale of the seventeenth-century explorer's death and the motivations and limits of colonialism.

Mann, Charles C. *1491: New Revelations of the Americas before Columbus* (2005). A comprehensive portrait of life in the Western Hemisphere before the arrival of Europeans.

Merwick, Donna. *The Shame and the Sorrow: Dutch-Amerindian Encounters in New Netherland* (2006). Explores the high-minded goals and unintended consequences of Dutch colonization.

Pauketat, Timothy R. *Cahokia: Ancient America's Great City on the Mississippi* (2009). A vivid portrait of one of North America's ancient civilizations.

Reséndez, Andrés. *A Land So Strange: The Epic Journey of Cabeza de Vaca* (2007). A lively account of the journey of Cabeza de Vaca, Esteban, and their companions across North America.

Richter, Daniel K. *Before the Revolution: America's Ancient Pasts* (2011). A comparative history of the diverse peoples of North America, Western Europe, and West Africa as their worlds collided.

Rodriguez, Jaime E. *Political Culture in Spanish America, 1500–1830* (2017). Political ideas and practices from colonization through Spanish-American independence.

Romney, Susanah Shaw. *New Netherland Connections: Intimate Networks and Atlantic Ties in Seventeenth-Century America* (2014). Focuses on Dutch, Native, and African women in the making of New Netherland.

Witgen, Michael. *An Infinity of Nations: How the Native New World Shaped Early North America* (2012). A rich account of how Native peoples and Europeans interacted in the Great Lakes region.

WEBSITES

Archive of Early American Images: https://jcb.lunaimaging.com/

Cahokia Mounds: http://cahokiamounds .org

Exploring the Early Americas: www.loc.gov /exhibits/earlyamericas/

France in America (Library of Congress): https://www.loc.gov/collections/france -in-america/

Three North American Beginnings (Smithsonian): https://www.si.edu /exhibitions/jamestown-quebec-santa-fe -three-north-american-beginnings -event-exhib-4531

CHAPTER 2

BOOKS

Anderson, Virginia. *Creatures of Empire: How Domestic Animals Transformed Early America* (2006). Shows how livestock brought by English settlers helped to transform the colonial landscape and provoked conflict with Native Americans.

Brown, Kathleen. *Good Wives, Nasty Wenches, and Anxious Patriarchs: Gender, Race, and Power in Colonial Virginia* (1996). A pioneering study of gender relations and their impact on Virginia society.

Gleach, Frederic W. *Powhatan's World and Colonial Virginia: A Conflict of Cultures* (1997). A study of Powhatan's people and the impact of European colonization upon them.

Horn, James. *1619: Jamestown and the Forging of American Democracy* (2019). Tells the story of this momentous year, in which Jamestown colonists created a representative government, established rules of private property, and began to enslave people of African descent.

Kupperman, Karen Ordahl. *Pocahontas and the English Boys: Caught between Cultures in Early Virginia* (2019). Uses the stories of Pocahontas and three other young people to show relationships between the Powhatans and Jamestown.

Morgan, Jennifer L. *Reckoning with Slavery: Gender, Kinship, and Capitalism in the Early Black Atlantic* (2021). Traces sixteenth- and seventeenth-century African women through capture, the Middle Passage, and enslavement in the Americas.

Noll, Mark. *The Old Religion in a New World: The History of North American Christianity* (2001). Relates how the transplantation of European religions to America changed religious institutions and practices.

Norton, Mary Beth. *Founding Mothers and Fathers: Gendered Power and the Forming of American Society* (2011). An examination of legal cases that illuminate the power relations involving colonial women and men.

Oberg, Michael Leroy. *The Head in Edward Nugent's Hand: Roanoke's Forgotten Indians* (2008). Uses the history of Roanoke to reveal the Native peoples with whom the colonists interacted.

Pestana, Carla G. *The English Atlantic in an Age of Revolution, 1640–1661* (2001). Analyzes how the English Civil War reverberated in the American colonies.

Philbrick, Nathaniel. *Mayflower* (2006). An account of one of the most celebrated voyages of the colonial era and the early history of the Plymouth colony.

Rees, John. *The Leveller Revolution: Radical Political Organization in England, 1640–1650* (2017). The most recent study of history's first democratic popular movement.

Reséndez, Andrés. *The Other Slavery: The Uncovered Story of Indian Enslavement in America* (2016). A careful analysis of the development and extent of Spanish enslavement of Native Americans.

Taylor, Alan. *American Colonies* (2001). A comprehensive survey of the history of North American colonies from their beginnings to 1763.

WEBSITES

The Plymouth Colony Archive Project: www.histarch.illinois.edu/plymouth

Virtual Jamestown: www.virtualjamestown.org

CHAPTER 3

BOOKS

Berlin, Ira. *Many Thousands Gone: The First Two Centuries of Slavery in North America* (1998). The most extensive study of the origins and development of colonial slavery.

Blackhawk, Ned. *Violence Over the Land: Indians and Empires in the Early American West* (2006). A history of how Spanish violence, weapons, and horses brought chaos and change to the Utes, Paiutes, and Shoshones.

Brooks, Lisa. *Our Beloved Kin: A New History of King Philip's War* (2018). Tells King Philip's War from the perspectives of Metacom, Weetamoo, and other Native participants.

Dayton, Cornelia H. *Women before the Bar: Gender, Law, and Society in Connecticut, 1639–1789* (1995). Examines the changing legal status of women in one American colony.

DuVal, Kathleen. *The Native Ground: Indians and Colonists in the Heart of the Continent* (2006). Argues that Native peoples in the Arkansas and Mississippi valleys set the terms of engagement for French, Spanish, and British colonizers and, for a time, the United States.

Harris, Leslie M. *In the Shadow of Slavery: African Americans in New York City, 1626–1863*. A detailed history of free and enslaved Blacks from the founding of New Amsterdam through the transition to English New York, the American Revolution, and the Civil War.

Kidd, Thomas S. *The Great Awakening* (2007). An account of the religious movement that swept the American colonies in the eighteenth century.

Morgan, Edmund S. *American Slavery, American Freedom: The Ordeal of Colonial Virginia* (1975). An influential study of the slow development of slavery in seventeenth-century Virginia.

Norton, Mary Beth. *In the Devil's Snare: The Salem Witchcraft Crisis of 1692* (2002). A study of the witch trials that places them in the context of anxieties over warfare on the Massachusetts frontier.

Pestana, Carla G. *Protestant Empire: Religion and the Making of the British Atlantic World* (2009). Discusses the role of Protestantism in inspiring and justifying British overseas expansion.

WEBSITES

Afro-Louisiana History and Genealogy: www.ibiblio.org/laslave/

Our Beloved Kin: Remapping a New History of King Philip's War: https://ourbelovedkin.com/awikhigan/

CHAPTER 4

BOOKS

Anderson, Fred. *Crucible of War: The Seven Years' War and the Fate of Empire in British North America, 1754–1766* (2000). A general history of the Seven Years' War and its consequences.

Beeman, Richard R. *Varieties of Political Experience in Eighteenth-Century America* (2004). Explores how political life differed from colony to colony, and what characteristics they had in common.

Brown, Vincent. *Tacky's Revolt: The Story of an Atlantic Slave War* (2020). The history of a revolt by enslaved Africans in Jamaica and its repercussions throughout the Atlantic world.

Byrd, Alexander X. *Captives and Voyagers: Black Migrants across the Eighteenth-Century British Atlantic World* (2008). Centers on the stories of enslaved and free Blacks by tracing both forced migrations of the slave trade and free Black immigration to Sierra Leone.

Calloway, Colin G. The *Scratch of a Pen: 1763 and the Transformation of North America* (2006). Examines the impact of the Peace of Paris on North America, especially the Native American population.

Colley, Linda. *Britons: Forging the Nation, 1707–1837* (1992). An influential study of the rise of a sense of national identity in Great Britain, relevant also for the American colonies.

Crouch, Christian. *Nobility Lost: French and Canadian Martial Cultures, Indians, and the End of New France* (2014). A cross-cultural history of the Seven Years' War from the perspectives of those on the French side.

Dowd, Gregory Evans. *War Under Heaven: Pontiac, the Indian Nations, and the British Empire* (2002). An in-depth history of Pontiac's War.

Fuentes, Marisa. *Dispossessed Lives: Enslaved Women, Violence, and the Archive* (2016). A study of enslaved and free women in eighteenth-century Barbados that also reflects on how archives make telling some stories easier than others.

Newman, Simon P. *A New World of Labor: The Development of Plantation Slavery in the British Atlantic* (2013). The most recent account of how slavery emerged and was consolidated in the British empire.

Noll, Mark. *The Rise of Evangelicalism: The Age of Edwards, Whitefield, and the Wesleys* (2004). Explores the Great Awakening on both sides of the Atlantic and its impact on religious life.

Rucker, Walter C. *The River Flows On: Black Resistance, Culture, and Identity Formation in Early America* (2006). Traces the emergence of a new African American identity and how it affected modes of slave resistance.

Smallwood, Stephanie. *Saltwater Slavery: A Middle Passage from Africa to American Diaspora* (2007). An in-depth account of the slave trade from the perspectives of enslaved people, from their capture, through the Middle Passage, to sale in the Americas.

Smith, Barbara Clark. *The Freedoms We Lost: Consent and Resistance in Revolutionary America* (2010). Examines the ways colonial Americans participated in public life and sought to defend their concepts of freedom.

Valerio-Jiménez, Omar S. *River of Hope: Forging Identity and Nation in the Rio Grande Borderlands* (2013). Traces the processes of cultural interaction and the establishment of national power in a major borderlands region.

WEBSITES

Africans in America: https://www.pbs.org/wgbh/aia/home.html

Peoples of the Historical Slave Trade: https://enslaved.org

Slave Voyages: https://www.slavevoyages.org

Web de Anza: https://webdeanza.org/

CHAPTER 5

BOOKS

Armitage, David. *The Declaration of Independence: A Global History* (2007). Traces the international impact of the Declaration of Independence in the years since it was written.

Breen, T. H. *Marketplace of Revolution: How Consumer Politics Shaped American Independence* (2004). An examination of how the colonists' very dependence on British consumer goods led them to resent interference with trade.

Carté, Kate. *Religion and the American Revolution: An Imperial History* (2021). Explores how Christianity shaped the American Revolution and in turn was changed by it.

Countryman, Edward. *The American Revolution* (rev. ed., 2002). A brief summary of the Revolution's causes, conduct, and consequences.

Foner, Eric. *Tom Paine and Revolutionary America* (1976). Examines the ideas of the era's greatest pamphleteer of revolution and how they contributed to the struggle for independence.

Maier, Pauline. *American Scripture: Making the Declaration of Independence* (1997). The most detailed study of the writing of the Declaration and of previous calls for independence within the colonies.

Nash, Gary. *The Urban Crucible: Social Change, Political Consciousness, and the Origins of the American Revolution* (1979). Explores how the social history of American cities contributed to the coming of the Revolution.

Neimeyer, Charles. *America Goes to War: A Social History of the Continental Army* (1995). A history of Washington's army that stresses the role of nonelite Americans in the fighting and the impact of military service on the soldiers.

Polansky, Janet. *Revolutions without Borders: The Call to Liberty in the Atlantic World* (2015). Explores both the revolutions of the late eighteenth century and the kinds of sources historians use to study them.

Raphael, Ray. *A People's History of the American Revolution* (2001). A study of grassroots resistance to Britain before and during the War of Independence.

Saunt, Claudio. *West of the Revolution: An Uncommon History of 1776* (2014). An account of events in North America among Indians, Spanish colonists, and others in the year of the Declaration of Independence.

Taylor, Alan. *American Revolutions: A Continental History, 1750–1804* (2015). A sweeping history of the Revolution as a continental event.

Zabin, Serena. *The Boston Massacre: A Family History* (2020). An in-depth study of both sides of the Boston Massacre.

WEBSITES

The American Revolution and Its Era: Maps and Charts of North America and the West Indies: http://memory.loc.gov /ammem/gmdhtml/armhtml/armhome .html

The Coming of the American Revolution: www.masshist.org/revolution/

CHAPTER 6

BOOKS

Berkin, Carol. *Revolutionary Mothers: Women in the Struggle for American Independence* (2005). Presents profiles of women who took part in the movement for independence.

Calloway, Colin. *The American Revolution in Indian Country* (1995). Examines how the Revolution affected Indians in each region of the United States.

Cameron, Christopher. *To Plead Our Own Cause: African Americans in Massachusetts and the Making of the Antislavery Movement* (2014). Reveals the early origins of the abolition movement among African Americans in Massachusetts.

Davis, David Brion. *The Problem of Slavery in the Age of Revolution* (1975). An influential study of the emergence of slavery as a major public issue in the Atlantic world.

DuVal, Kathleen. *Independence Lost: Lives on the Edge of the American Revolution* (2015). A study of the Revolution as a borderlands conflict on the Gulf Coast, in which European empires and Native Americans fought for their own ideas of power and liberty.

Frey, Sylvia R. *Water from the Rock: Black Resistance in a Revolutionary Age* (1991). A study of the many ways Blacks sought to gain freedom for themselves during the Revolution.

Hatch, Nathan O. *The Democratization of American Christianity* (1989). A comprehensive account of the Revolution's impact on religion and its aftermath.

Jasanoff, Maya. *Liberty's Exiles: American Loyalists in the Revolutionary World* (2011). A study of Americans who remained loyal to Great Britain during the War of Independence.

Kruman, Marc. *Between Authority and Liberty: State Constitution Making in Revolutionary America* (1997). The most detailed account of how state constitutions were changed during the era.

Parkinson, Robert G. *The Common Cause: Creating Race and Nation in the American Revolution* (2016). How hostility to Native Americans and slaves helped to create a sense of shared identity among white patriots fighting for American independence.

Pybus, Cassandra. *Epic Journeys of Freedom: Runaway Slaves of the American Revolution and Their Global Quest for Liberty* (2006). Traces the lives of Harry Washington and others from slavery to freedom.

Taylor, Alan. *The Divided Ground: Indians, Settlers, and the Northern Borderland of the American Revolution* (2006). Examines the Revolution and its consequences in the Haudenosaunee (Iroquois) region of upstate New York.

WEBSITES

Creating the United States: www.loc.gov /exhibits/creating-the-united-states

The Geography of Slavery in Virginia: http://www2.vcdh.virginia.edu/gos/

CHAPTER 7

BOOKS

Cornell, Saul. *The Other Founders: Anti-Federalism and the Dissenting Tradition in America, 1788–1828* (1999). A careful examination of the ideas of those who opposed ratification of the Constitution.

Dowd, Gregory E. *A Spirited Resistance: The North American Indian Struggle for Unity, 1745–1815* (1992). Contains an important discussion of the place of Indians in the new American nation.

Dunbar, Eric Armstrong. *Never Caught: The Washingtons' Relentless Pursuit of Their Runaway Slave Ona Judge* (2017). Uses the fascinating story of one of George and Martha Washington's slaves to illuminate the dilemma of slavery and freedom in the early republic.

Gordon-Reed, Annette. *The Hemingses of Monticello: An American Family* (2008). Reveals the history of Sally Hemings and her ancestors and descendants and how they are related to the family of Thomas Jefferson.

Holton, Woody. *Unruly Americans and the Origins of the Constitution* (2007). Argues that the political activities of ordinary Americans helped to shape the Constitution.

Klarman, Michael. *The Framers' Coup: The Making of the United States Constitution* (2016). Unlike many other books on the Constitutional Convention, emphasizes the deep divides among the delegates rather than eventual consensus.

Maier, Pauline. *Ratification: The People Debate the Constitution, 1787–1788* (2010). The most complete account of the state-by-state debates over ratification of the Constitution.

Milteer, Warren. *Beyond Slavery's Shadow: Free People of Color in the South* (2021). A history of the diverse peoples who made up the category "free people of color."

Nash, Gary. *The Forgotten Fifth: African Americans in the Age of Revolution* (2006). A comprehensive survey of the Revolution's impact on Blacks, slave and free.

Rakove, Jack. *Original Meanings: Politics and Ideas in the Making of the Constitution* (1996). An influential interpretation of the ideas that went into the drafting of the Constitution.

Sleeper-Smith, Susan. *Indigenous Prosperity and American Conquest: Indian Women of the Ohio River Valley, 1690–1792* (2018). In-depth study of the world created by Shawnees, Delawares, Miamis, and other Native peoples as they sought to maintain their independence in a time of increasing European and U.S. power.

Wilentz, Sean. *No Property in Man: Slavery and Antislavery at the Nation's Founding* (2018). Emphasizes the long-term consequences of the framers' refusal to include a direct national acknowledgment of property in man in the Constitution.

WEBSITES

Creating the United States: www.loc.gov /exhibits/creating-the-united-states
Explore the Constitution: http://constitutioncenter.org
The Presidency: http://americanhistory.si .edu/presidency/home.html

CHAPTER 8

BOOKS

Egerton, Douglas R. *Gabriel's Rebellion: The Virginia Slave Conspiracies of 1800 and 1802* (1993). The most comprehensive account of one of the most important slave conspiracies in American history.

Gray, Edward G. *Tom Paine's Iron Bridge: Building a United States* (2016). Reveals how the author of *Common Sense* envisioned infrastructure that would bring disparate states into a united country.

Johnson, Rashauna. *Slavery's Metropolis: Unfree Labor in New Orleans during the Age of Revolutions* (2016). Centers on the rise of slavery in New Orleans from the late years of Spanish and French colonization through its incorporation into the United States as well as the lives of the people enslaved there.

Kerber, Linda K. *Women of the Republic: Intellect and Ideology in Revolutionary America* (1980). A study of prevailing ideas about women's place in the new republic.

Lambert, Frank. *The Barbary Wars: American Independence in the Atlantic World* (2005). An account of the first foreign military conflict conducted by the newly independent United States.

McCoy, Drew. *The Elusive Republic: Political Economy in Jeffersonian America* (1980). An influential study of the economic and political outlooks and policies of Federalists and Jeffersonians.

Perl-Rosenthal, Nathan. *Citizen Sailors: Becoming American in the Age of Revolution* (2015). How sailors, white and Black, asserted their rights as American citizens in the decades after the Revolution.

Ronda, James P. *Lewis and Clark among the Indians* (1984). An account of the most famous exploring party in American history.

Rothman, Adam. *Slave Country: American Expansion and the Origins of the Deep South* (2005). A study of how the United States secured control of what are now the Gulf states, opening the door for the expansion of slavery.

Taylor, Alan. *The Civil War of 1812* (2010). An account of the War of 1812 that stresses how divided Americans were during the conflict.

Waldstreicher, David. *In the Midst of Perpetual Fetes: The Making of American Nationalism, 1776–1820* (1997). Explores how Americans celebrated and thought about their nation's independence in the years of the early republic.

WEBSITE

Rivers, Edens, Empires: Lewis and Clark and the Revealing of America: https://www .loc.gov/exhibits/lewisandclark/

CHAPTER 9

BOOKS

Bergmann, William H. *The American National State and the Early West* (2014). Demonstrates how governmental action was crucial to early western development.

Boydston, Jeanne. *Home and Work: Housework, Wages, and the Ideology of Work in the Early Republic* (1990). Examines how the market revolution affected ideas relating to women's work.

Deyle, Steven. *Carry Me Back: The Domestic Slave Trade in American Life* (2005). The most comprehensive history of the internal slave trade, by which millions of slaves were transported to the Deep South.

Harris, Leslie. *In the Shadow of Slavery: African-Americans in New York City, 1626–1863* (2003). A study that emphasizes the exclusion of African Americans from the economic opportunities offered by the market revolution.

Haselby, Sam. *The Origins of American Religious Nationalism* (2015). Explores how the battle between frontier evangelists and more traditional New England ministers shaped religion and politics in the early republic.

Howe, Daniel W. *What Hath God Wrought: The Transformation of America, 1815–1848* (2007). A comprehensive account of social and political changes in this era, emphasizing the significance of the communications revolution.

Johnson, Paul E. *A Shopkeeper's Millennium: Society and Revivals in Rochester, New York, 1815–1837* (1978). Explores the impact of religious revivals on a key city of upstate New York.

Larson, John L. *The Market Revolution in America: Liberty, Ambition, and the Eclipse of the Common Good* (2010). The most recent account of the market revolution

and its impact on American society and values.

Miles, Tiya. *The Dawn of Detroit: A Chronicle of Slavery and Freedom in the City of the Straits* (2017). Traces the history of unfree labor in Detroit, as it grew from a French trading post to a city on the border of the United States and British Canada.

Rockman, Seth. *Scraping By: Wage Labor, Slavery, and Survival in Early Baltimore* (2009). An in-depth history of poor workers in Baltimore, female and male, enslaved and free.

Ryan, Mary P. *Cradle of the Middle Class: The Family in Oneida County, New York, 1790–1865* (1981). Examines how economic change helped to produce a new kind of middle-class family structure centered on women's dominance of the household.

Zakim, Michael. *Accounting for Capitalism: The World the Clerks Made* (2018). How a new generation of clerks arose in the early nineteenth century and how they personified and helped to shape the market revolution.

WEBSITES

American Transcendentalism: www.vcu.edu /engweb/transcendentalism/

Women in America, 1820–1842: http:// xroads.virginia.edu/~hyper/detoc/fem /home.htm

CHAPTER 10

BOOKS

Balogh, Brian. *A Government Out of Sight: The Mystery of National Authority in Nineteenth-Century America* (2009). Examines the paradox of widespread belief in limited government yet frequent energetic use of federal authority.

Fitz, Caitlin. *Our Sister Republics: The United States in an Age of American Revolutions*

(2016). Traces changes in responses in the United States to the Latin American Wars of Independence, from initial enthusiasm to skepticism as the new nations moved to end slavery.

Forbes, Robert. *The Missouri Compromise and Its Aftermath: Slavery and the Meaning of America* (2007). Places the Missouri controversy in the context of the long national debate over slavery.

Guyatt, Nicholas. *Bind Us Apart: How Enlightened Americans Invented Racial Segregation* (2016). Compares the movements for Indian removal and colonization of African Americans outside the country as precursors to later racial segregation laws.

Keyssar, Alexander. *The Right to Vote: The Contested History of Democracy in the United States* (2000). A history of the right to vote in America from the colonial era to the present.

O'Brien, Jean M. *Firsting and Lasting: Writing Indians out of Existence in New England* (2010). Tells how New England's Native peoples resisted removal and how non-Native New Englanders imagined that they had disappeared.

Ostler, Jeffrey. *Surviving Genocide: Native Nations and the United States from the American Revolution to Bleeding Kansas* (2019). A comprehensive account of how Native nations survived U.S. wars and dispossession.

Saunt, Claudio. *Unworthy Republic: The Dispossession of Native Americans and the Road to Indian Territory* (2020). Details the forced deportations of Native nations and the reasons behind them.

Snyder, Christina. *Great Crossings: Indians, Settlers, and Slaves in the Age of Jackson* (2017). Tells the surprising story of the Choctaw Academy, a school where people of Native, African, and European descent lived and learned from one another.

Watson, Harry. *Liberty and Power: The Politics of Jacksonian America* (1990). A valuable brief account of the politics of the 1820s and 1830s.

Wilentz, Sean. *The Rise of American Democracy: Jefferson to Lincoln* (2005). A comprehensive history of democratic ideas and politics from the American Revolution to the Civil War.

Witgen, Michael John. *Seeing Red: Indigenous Land, American Expansion, and the Political Economy of Plunder in North America* (2021). The history of U.S. expansion into the Great Lakes region, the home of the Anishinaabe (including the Ojibwe, Ottawa, and Potawatomi peoples).

WEBSITES

Democracy in America, Alexis de Tocqueville: https://xroads.virginia.edu/~Hyper /DETOC/toc_indx.html

Legacy: Spain and the United States in the Age of Independence, 1763–1848: https://npg.si.edu/exhibition/legacy -pain-and-united-states-age-independence -1763%E2%80%931848

CHAPTER 11

BOOKS

Baumgartner, Alice. *South to Freedom: Runaway Slaves to Mexico and the Road to the Civil War* (2020).

Beckert, Sven. *The Empire of Cotton* (2014). A history of one of the world's most important commodities, placing the Old South in an international context.

Berlin, Ira. *Slaves without Masters: The Free Negro in the Antebellum South* (1974). A careful study of the status of free Blacks, stressing differences between the Upper and Lower South.

Breen, Patrick H. *The Land Shall Be Deluged in Blood: A New History of the Nat Turner*

Revolt (2016). The most recent account of the most famous slave rebellion in American history.

Camp, Stephanie. *Closer to Freedom: Enslaved Women and Everyday Resistance in the Plantation South* (2004). A pioneering study of how female slaves resisted slavery.

Davis, David Brion. *Inhuman Bondage: The Rise and Fall of Slavery in the New World* (2006). Places the history of slavery in the United States firmly in a hemispheric context.

Foner, Eric. *Gateway to Freedom: The Hidden History of the Underground Railroad* (2015). A study of the operations of the Underground Railroad, focusing on New York City, and of the fugitives it assisted.

Genovese, Eugene D. *Roll, Jordan, Roll: The World the Slaves Made* (1974). A classic study of the paternalist ethos and the culture that developed under slavery.

Gutman, Herbert G. *The Black Family in Slavery and Freedom* (1976). A pioneering examination of how slaves created and sustained families under the harsh conditions of slavery.

Jones-Rogers, Stephanie E. *They Were Her Property: White Women as Slave Owners in the American South* (2019). Combining records left by white women and testimony of former slaves, this account examines the economic relationship of white women to slavery.

Karp, Matthew. *This Vast Southern Empire: Slaveholders at the Helm of American Foreign Policy* (2016). Explores how slave-holders tried to use the power of the federal government to protect slavery in the United States and the rest of the Western Hemisphere.

Kaye, Anthony E. *Joining Places: Slave Neighborhoods in the Old South* (2007). Emphasizes the importance of the local networks established by slaves in Mississippi.

McCurry, Stephanie. *Masters of Small Worlds: Yeoman Households, Gender Relations, and the Political Culture of Antebellum South Carolina* (1995). Studies the lives of men and women in non-slaveholding families to explore their links with the planter class.

Stevenson, Brenda. *Life in Black and White: Family and Community in the Slave South* (1996). Focusing on Virginia, an examination of how slaves adapted to the rise of the interstate slave trade.

WEBSITES

Born in Slavery: Slave Narratives from the Federal Writers' Project: http://lcweb2.loc.gov/ammem/snhtml/snhome.html

Documenting the American South: http://docsouth.unc.edu

Slaves and the Courts, 1740–1860: http://memory.loc.gov/ammem/sthtml/sthome.html

CHAPTER 12

BOOKS

Bestor, Arthur E. *Backwoods Utopias: The Sectarian and Owenite Phases of Communitarian Socialism in America* (1948). An account of some of the numerous communitarian experiments in pre–Civil War America.

Boylan, Anne M. *The Origins of Women's Activism: New York and Boston, 1797–1840* (2002). Considers how middle-class urban women organized numerous associations for social improvement and thereby gained a place in the public sphere.

DuBois, Ellen C. *Suffrage: Women's Long Battle for the Vote* (2020). The most up-to-date history of the movement for woman suffrage from its beginnings to the adoption of the Nineteenth Amendment.

Goodman, Paul. *Of One Blood: Abolitionists and the Origins of Racial Equality*

(1998). Explores the origins of racial egalitarianism in the movement against slavery.

Jeffrey, Julie R. *The Great Silent Army of Abolitionism: Ordinary Women in the Antislavery Movement* (1998). The role of women as the grassroots foot soldiers of the abolitionist movement.

Jones, Martha S. *Vanguard: How Black Women Broke Barriers, Won the Vote, and Insisted on Equality for All* (2020).

Masur, Kate. *Until Justice Be Done: America's First Civil Rights Movement, from the Revolution to Reconstruction* (2021). A history of the struggle, before the Civil War, for recognition of the equal civil rights of Black Americans.

McGreevy, John T. *Catholicism and American Freedom* (2003). Contains an illuminating discussion of how Catholics responded to Protestant-based reform movements.

Sinha, Manisha. *The Slave's Cause: A History of Abolition* (2016). A comprehensive history of the antislavery movement from the colonial era through the Civil War.

Tyrrell, Ian. *Sobering Up: From Temperance to Prohibition in Antebellum America, 1800–1860* (1979). Traces the movement against the sale and use of liquor and how it changed in the first part of the nineteenth century.

Zboray, Ronald J. and Mary. *Voices without Votes: Women and Politics in Antebellum New England* (2010). Shows how women took part in Jacksonian-era politics in ways other than voting.

WEBSITES

Samuel J. May Anti-Slavery Collection: http://dlxs.library.cornell.edu/m/mayantislavery/

Women and Social Movements in the United States, 1600–2000: http://asp6new.alexanderstreet.com/wam2/wam2.index.map.aspx

CHAPTER 13

BOOKS

Cronon, William. *Nature's Metropolis: Chicago and the Great West* (1992). An influential account of the rise of Chicago and the city's relationship to its agricultural hinterland.

DeLay, Brian. *War of a Thousand Deserts: Indian Raids and the U.S.-Mexican War* (2008). A history of the Mexican War that emphasizes its impact on Native Americans.

Foner, Eric. *Free Soil, Free Labor, Free Men: The Ideology of the Republican Party before the Civil War* (1970). A discussion of the basic ideas that united Republicans in the 1850s, especially their "free labor ideology."

Freeman, Joanne B. *The Field of Blood: Violence in Congress and the Road to Civil War* (2018). How fistfights, assaults, and other violence among members of Congress (of which the assault on Charles Sumner was the most prominent example but by no means the only one) reflected and contributed to the growing divide between the sections.

Haas, Lisbeth. *Conquests and Historical Identities in California, 1769–1936* (1995). Contains a detailed description of how California's acquisition by the United States affected the state's diverse population groups.

Lee, Erika. *America for Americans: A History of Xenophobia in the United States* (2019). Traces the history of anti-foreign sentiment, including the Know-Nothing movement of the 1850s.

Maizlish, Stephen E. *A Strife of Tongues: The Compromise of 1850 and the Ideological Foundations of the American Civil War* (2018). A careful account of the long congressional debate over the Compromise of 1850, showing how it revealed the hardening of sectional ideologies.

Montejano, David. *Anglos and Mexicans in the Making of Texas* (1987). A history of cultural relations among the varied populations of Texas.

Potter, David M. *The Impending Crisis, 1848–1861* (1976). Still the standard account of the nation's history in the years before the Civil War.

Ron, Ariel. *Grassroots Leviathan: Agricultural Reform and the Rural North in the Slaveholding Republic* (2020). Emphasizes how a large agricultural reform movement in the northern states increased the differences between the sections.

Sinha, Manisha. *The Counterrevolution of Slavery: Politics and Ideology in Antebellum South Carolina* (2002). A detailed study of how a vigorous defense of slavery developed in South Carolina, which justified the decision for secession.

Stephanson, Anders. *Manifest Destiny: American Expansionism and the Empire of Right* (1995). Considers how the idea of an American mission to spread freedom and democracy has affected American foreign policy throughout the country's history.

WEBSITES

Gold Rush!: www.museumca.org/goldrush/

The Oregon Trail: http://oregontrail101.com

Record of Fugitives: https://exhibitions.cul.columbia.edu/exhibits/show/fugitives/record_fugitives

Uncle Tom's Cabin and American Culture: http://jefferson.village.virginia.edu/utc/

CHAPTER 14

BOOKS

Ayers, Edward L. *In the Presence of Mine Enemies: War in the Heart of America, 1859–1863* (2003), and *The Thin Light of Freedom: The Civil War and Emancipation in the Heart of America* (2017). A two-volume study of the experiences of Americans in two counties—one in Pennsylvania, one in Virginia—in the early years of the Civil War.

Doyle, Don. *The Cause of All Nations: An International History of the Civil War* (2014). Traces how people around the world responded to the American Civil War.

Foner, Eric. *The Fiery Trial: Abraham Lincoln and American Slavery* (2010). A study of the evolution of Lincoln's ideas and policies relating to slavery over the course of his life.

Glatthaar, Joseph T. *Forged in Battle: The Civil War Alliance of Black Soldiers and White Officers* (1990). Relates the complex experience of Black Civil War soldiers and their officers.

Glymph, Thavolia. *The Woman's Fight: The Civil War's Battles for Home, Freedom, and Nation* (2020). A pioneering account of the numerous ways women, both Black and white, engaged with and were affected by the war.

Green, Michael. *Lincoln and Native Americans* (2021). A concise account of how Lincoln and his administration dealt with American Indians and the choices made by Native nations during the conflict.

Lawson, Melinda. *Patriot Fires: Forging a New Nationalism in the Civil War North* (2002). Considers how both public and private groups, in order to mobilize support for the war effort, promoted a new idea of American nationalism.

McCurry, Stephanie. *Confederate Reckoning: Power and Politics in the Civil War South* (2010). A pioneering study of the political mobilization of poorer white women and slaves in the Confederacy.

McPherson, James M. *Battle Cry of Freedom: The Civil War Era* (1988). The standard account of the coming of the war, its conduct, and its consequences.

Neely, Mark E. *The Fate of Liberty: Abraham Lincoln and Civil Liberties* (1991). Explores how the Lincoln administration did and did not meet the challenge of preserving civil liberties while fighting the war.

Oakes, James. *Freedom National: The Destruction of Slavery in the United States* (2012). A careful account of the complex path to emancipation.

Silber, Nina. *Daughters of the Union: Northern Women Fight the Civil War* (2005). Examines the participation of northern women in the war effort and how this did and did not alter their lives.

WEBSITES

Civil War Photographs: http://memory.loc .gov/ammem/cwphtml/cwphome.html

A House Divided: America in the Age of Lincoln: www.digitalhistory.uh.edu /exhibits/ahd/index.html

The Valley of the Shadow: Two Communities in the American Civil War: https://valley .lib.virginia.edu

CHAPTER 15

BOOKS

Bottoms, D. Michael. *An Aristocracy of Color: Race and Reconstruction in California and the West, 1850–1890* (2013). A study of changing race relations, and definitions of race, in the western states.

Downs, Gregory. *Declarations of Dependence: The Long Reconstruction of Popular Politics in the South, 1861–1908* (2011). Traces the changing ways Black and white southerners sought aid and protection from the government during and after the Civil War and Reconstruction.

Downs, James. *Sick from Freedom: The Deadly Consequences of Emancipation* (2012). How disease shaped the experience of freedom and how the Freedmen's Bureau

and other agencies sought to cope with widespread illness among former slaves.

Edwards, Laura. *A Nation of Rights: A Legal History of the Civil War and Reconstruction* (2015). A careful analysis of how this era changed American law and the Constitution.

Fields, Barbara J. *Slavery and Freedom on the Middle Ground: Maryland during the Nineteenth Century* (1985). A study of slavery and emancipation in a key border state.

Foner, Eric. *Reconstruction: America's Unfinished Revolution, 1863–1877* (1988). A comprehensive account of the Reconstruction era.

Foner, Eric. *The Second Founding: How the Civil War and Reconstruction Remade the Constitution* (2019). A study of the Thirteenth, Fourteenth, and Fifteenth Amendments, why they were adopted, how they transformed the Constitution, and how for many decades the courts allowed them to be abrogated in the southern states.

Hahn, Steven. *A Nation under Our Feet: Black Political Struggles in the Rural South from Slavery to the Great Migration* (2003). A detailed study of Black political activism, stressing nationalist consciousness and emigration movements.

Hahn, Steven. *A Nation without Borders: The United States and Its World in an Age of Civil Wars, 1830–1910* (2016). The chapters on Reconstruction emphasize the role of the West during that period.

Karuka, Manu. *Empire's Tracks: Indigenous Nations, Chinese Workers, and the Transcontinental Railroad* (2019). The building of the transcontinental railroad from the perspective of Native peoples and Chinese laborers.

Krauthamer, Barbara. *Black Slaves, Indian Masters: Slavery, Emancipation, and Citizenship in the Native American South* (2013). A study of slavery, emancipation, and race among the Chickasaw and Choctaw nations.

Litwack, Leon F. *Been in the Storm So Long: The Aftermath of Slavery* (1979). A detailed look at the immediate aftermath of the end of slavery and the variety of Black and white responses to emancipation.

Parsons, Elaine F. *Ku-Klux: The Birth of the Klan during Reconstruction* (2016). Emphasizes both the Klan's terrorism and how discourse about it helped to shape politics and culture, North and South.

Reidy, Joseph P. *Illusions of Emancipation: The Pursuit of Freedom and Equality in the Twilight of Slavery* (2020). A detailed study of how the promise of emancipation was partly achieved and partly disappointed in one part of the South.

Rodrigue, John C. *Reconstruction in the Cane Fields: From Slavery to Free Labor in Louisiana's Sugar Parishes, 1862–1880* (2001). A study of how an often-neglected part of the South experienced the aftermath of slavery.

WEBSITES

America's Reconstruction: People and Politics after the Civil War: www.digitalhistory.uh.edu/exhibits/reconstruction/index.html

Freedmen and Southern Society Project: www.history.umd.edu/Freedmen/

Freedmen's Bureau Online: http://www.freedmensbureau.com/

CHAPTER 16

BOOKS

Bensel, Richard F. *The Political Economy of American Industrialization, 1877–1900* (2000). A study of the policies and political divisions that contributed to and resulted from the second industrial revolution.

Deutsch, Sarah. *No Separate Refuge: Culture, Class, and Gender on the Anglo-Hispanic Frontier in the American Southwest, 1880–1940* (1987). A careful analysis of the changing experience of people of Hispanic origin in the Southwest during these years.

Fink, Leon. *Workingmen's Democracy: The Knights of Labor and American Politics* (1983). Examines the rise of the Knights of Labor and their forays into local politics in the mid-1880s.

Foster, Gaines. *Moral Reconstruction: Christian Lobbyists and the Federal Legislation of Morality, 1865–1920* (2002). Traces the rise of efforts to use the federal government to promote Protestant notions of moral behavior.

Freeberg, Ernest. *The Age of Edison: Electric Light and the Invention of Modern America* (2013). Explores the numerous ways electricity altered Americans' lives.

Grinspan, Jon. *The Age of Acrimony: How Americans Fought to Fix Their Democracy, 1865–1915* (2021). A lively account of electoral campaigns during the Gilded Age and efforts to limit democratic participation.

Hamalainen, Pekka. *The Comanche Empire* (2008). The rise and fall of Comanche domination over much of the southwestern United States.

Jeffrey, Julie R. *Frontier Women: "Civilizing" the West? 1840–1880* (rev. ed., 1998). A study, based on letters and diaries, of the experience of women on the western frontier.

Kasson, Joy S. *Buffalo Bill's Wild West: Celebrity, Memory, and Popular History* (2000). An account of the popular theatrical production that helped to fix an image of the Wild West in the American imagination.

Maggor, Noam. *Brahmin Capitalism: Frontiers of Wealth and Populism in America's First Gilded Age* (2017). Explores how Boston capitalists helped to finance the spread of railroads, mining, and other enterprises in the West, and the conflicts over how the fruits of economic development should be distributed.

Ostler, Jeffrey. *The Plains Sioux and U.S. Colonialism from Lewis and Clark to Wounded Knee* (2004). Covering nearly the entire nineteenth century, traces the complex relationship between the federal government and the Sioux Indians.

Postel, Charles. *Equality: An American Dilemma, 1866–1896* (2019). Examines how three large reform movements—the Grange, Woman's Christian Temperance Union, and Knights of Labor— understood and sought to achieve equality.

White, Richard. *The Republic for Which It Stands: The United States during Reconstruction and the Gilded Age* (2017). A comprehensive account of the social, economic, and political history of this transformative era.

WEBSITES

Firsthand Accounts of California 1849–1900: http://memory.loc.gov/ammem/cbhtml /cbhome.html

Indian Peoples of the Northern Great Plains: http://arc.lib.montana.edu/indian-great -plains

CHAPTER 17

BOOKS

Aleinikoff, Alexander. *Semblances of Sovereignty: The Constitution, the State, and American Citizenship* (2002). Includes a careful discussion of the citizenship status of American minorities and residents of overseas possessions.

Blight, David. *Race and Reunion: The Civil War in American Memory* (2001).

Examines how a memory of the Civil War that downplayed the issue of slavery played a part in sectional reconciliation and the rise of segregation.

Blum, Edward. *Reforging the White Republic: Race, Religion, and American Nationalism, 1865–1898* (2005). Explores the development of a shared religious culture that united northern and southern Protestants in support of white supremacy and overseas expansion.

Factor, Robert L. *The Black Response to America: Men, Ideals, and Organization from Frederick Douglass to the NAACP* (1970). Discusses Black social and political thought, including that of Booker T. Washington and his critics.

Goodwyn, Lawrence. *The Populist Moment: A Short History of the Agrarian Revolt in America* (1978). A sympathetic account of the rise and fall of Populism.

Higginbotham, Evelyn. *Righteous Discontent: The Women's Movement in the Black Baptist Church, 1880–1920* (1993). Explains how Black women developed ways of exerting their influence in public life even as Black men were losing the right to vote.

Hoganson, Kristin L. *Consumers' Imperium: The Global Production of American Domesticity, 1865–1920* (2007). Shows how the consumer desires of middle-class women helped to spur the consolidation of an American empire.

Hsu, Madeline. *Dreaming of Gold, Dreaming of Home: Transnationalism and Migration between the United States and South China, 1882–1934* (2000). Examines the enduring connections between Chinese immigrants in the United States and their home communities.

Krause, Paul. *The Battle for Homestead, 1880– 1892: Politics, Culture, and Steel* (1992). An account of the era's most celebrated conflict between capital and labor.

Lake, Marilyn, and Henry Reynolds. *Drawing the Global Color Line* (2008). Traces the global transmission of ideas about white supremacy in the late nineteenth century.

Lew-Williams, Beth. *The Chinese Must Go: Violence, Exclusion, and the Making of the Alien in America* (2018). Discusses the proliferation of anti-Chinese violence in the 1880s and 1890s and how Chinese American communities responded to it.

Linn, Brian M. *The Philippine War, 1899–1902* (2000). A detailed history of America's "forgotten war."

McClain, Charles J. *In Search of Equality: The Chinese Struggle against Discrimination in Nineteenth-Century America* (1994). Explores how Chinese Americans worked to combat the discrimination to which they were subjected and to assert their rights.

McMillen, Neil R. *Dark Journey: Black Mississippians in the Age of Jim Crow* (1989). A powerful account of Black life in the segregation era and the boundaries within which it operated.

Perez, Louis A. *The War of 1898: The United States and Cuba in History and Historiography* (1998). Presents the Cuban side of the Spanish-American War, including a detailed discussion of the Cuban movement for independence and how American intervention affected it.

Postel, Charles. *The Populist Vision* (2007). A history of the Populist movement that stresses how it anticipated many public policies of the twentieth century.

Wilkerson, Isabel. *Caste: The Origins of Our Discontents* (2020). An influential history of racial inequality in the United States, including the segregation era, comparing it to caste systems based on social inequality in India and elsewhere.

Wong, Eddie J. *Racial Reconstruction: Black Inclusion, Chinese Exclusion, and the Fictions of Citizenship* (2015). Juxtaposes policies regarding these two groups in the late nineteenth century.

WEBSITES

1896: The Presidential Campaign: http://projects.vassar.edu/1896/1896home.html

The Rise and Fall of Jim Crow: www.pbs.org/wnet/jimcrow

The World of 1898: The Spanish-American War: www.loc.gov/rr/hispanic/1898

CHAPTER 18

BOOKS

Bodnar, John. *The Transplanted: A History of Immigrants in Urban America* (1985). A comprehensive account of American immigration.

Cott, Nancy F. *The Grounding of Modern Feminism* (1987). A careful study of feminist ideas in the Progressive era.

Dawley, Alan. *Struggles for Justice: Social Responsibility and the Liberal State* (1991). Examines the varieties of Progressive reform and various efforts to use the power of government for social betterment.

Deloria, Phil. *Indians in Unexpected Places* (2004). A rich consideration of Indian people's participation in modern cultural realms in the early twentieth century.

Fields, Kendra. *Growing Up with the Country: Family, Race, and Nation after the Civil War* (2018). A narrative of Black emigration to the West and the intersection between Native American history, Black history, and the struggles over land.

Gerstle, Gary. *Liberty and Coercion: The Paradox of American Government from the Founding to the Present* (2015). A sweeping study of the nature and struggles over the size and scope of government in U.S. history.

Hofstadter, Richard. *The Age of Reform: From Bryan to F.D.R.* (1955). A classic account of the ideas of reformers from Populism to the New Deal.

Johnston, Robert D. *The Radical Middle Class: Populist Democracy and the Question of Capitalism in Progressive Era Portland* (2003). Analyzes how Progressivism operated in one important city.

Jones, Martha. *Vanguard: How Black Women Broke Barriers, Won the Vote, and Insisted on Equality for All* (2020). Illuminates the central role of Black women in the struggle for women's democratic rights before and after the passage of the Nineteenth Amendment.

Lears, Jackson. *Rebirth of a Nation: The Making of Modern America, 1877–1920* (2009). A comprehensive history of the Gilded Age and Progressive era, stressing the extent of social and cultural change.

Molina, Natalia. *Fit to Be Citizens? Public Health and Race in Los Angeles, 1879–1939* (2006). A careful study of the use of public health measures in stigmatizing Chinese, Japanese, and Mexican immigrants in one city.

Rodgers, Daniel T. *Atlantic Crossings: Social Politics in a Progressive Age* (1998). A comprehensive study of the flow of Progressive ideas and policies back and forth across the Atlantic.

Stansell, Christine. *American Moderns: Bohemian New York and the Creation of a New Century* (2000). A colorful account of the Greenwich Village radicals who expanded the idea of personal freedom in the Progressive era.

Stromquist, Shelton. *Re-Inventing "The People": The Progressive Movement, the Class Problem, and the Origins of Modern Liberalism* (2006). Discusses how the desire to re-create social harmony in an age of labor conflict shaped Progressivism.

Tichi, Cecelia. *Civic Passions: Seven Who Launched Progressive America* (2009). An exploration of the careers of some of the most prominent leaders of Progressive reform.

WEBSITES

Evolution of the Conservation Movement, 1860–1920: http://lcweb2.loc.gov /ammem/amrvhtml/conshome.html

Immigration to the United States, 1789–1930: http://ocp.hul.harvard.edu /immigration/

Triangle Shirtwaist Factory Fire: www.ilr .cornell.edu/trianglefire/

Urban Experience in Chicago: Hull House and Its Neighborhoods: http://hullhouse .uic.edu/hull/urbanexp

Votes for Women: http://memory.loc.gov /ammem/naw/nawshome.html

CHAPTER 19

BOOKS

Bristow, Nancy. *American Pandemic: The Lost Worlds of the 1918 Influenza Epidemic* (2012). A social history of the toll of the flu virus in the United States.

Britten, Thomas. *American Indians in World War I: At Home and at War* (1997). A study of Native American soldiers before, during, and after their service in World War I.

Cahill, Kathleen. *Recasting the Vote: How Women of Color Transformed the Suffrage Movement* (2020). Illuminates the role of non-white women in advancing women's political enfranchisement.

Capozzola, Christopher. *Uncle Sam Wants You: World War I and the Making of the Modern American Citizen* (2008). A careful study of public and private efforts to enforce patriotic ideas and actions during World War I.

Dawley, Alan. *Changing the World: American Progressives in War and Revolution* (2003). Presents the war as a fulfillment and betrayal of the Progressive impulse.

Ewing, Adam. *The Age of Garvey: How a Jamaican Activist Created a Mass*

Movement and Changed Global Black Politics (2014). A study of the rise and fall of the Universal Negro Improvement Association and its influence on Black politics internationally.

Greene, Julie. *The Canal Builders: Making American Empire at the Panama Canal* (2009). Tells the story of the construction of the Panama Canal and the tens of thousands of workers who did the work.

Grossman, James R. *Land of Hope: Chicago, Black Southerners, and the Great Migration* (1989). An in-depth study of the migration of Blacks to one American city.

Jensen, Kimberly. *Mobilizing Minerva: American Women in the First World War* (2008). Examines the participation of women in the war effort and its impact on gender relations.

Kazin, Michael. *War Against War: The American Fight for Peace, 1914–1918* (2017). A rich and lively narrative of the broad antiwar movement in the United States.

Kennedy, David M. *Over Here: The First World War and American Society* (1980). A comprehensive account of how the war affected domestic life in the United States.

Ladd-Taylor, Molly. *Fixing the Poor: Eugenic Sterilization and Child Welfare in the Twentieth Century* (2017). A harrowing account of the eugenics movement and the social policies it helped to inspire.

Manela, Erez. *The Wilsonian Moment* (2007). Details how the Wilsonian ideal of self-determination was received around the world, with results Wilson did not anticipate.

Mitchell, David J. *1919: Red Mirage* (1970). A global account of the upheavals of 1919.

Preston, William, Jr. *Aliens and Dissenters: Federal Suppression of Radicals, 1903–1933* (1963). An influential study of the federal government's efforts to suppress dissenting ideas, especially during and immediately after World War I.

Renda, Mary A. *Taking Haiti: Military Occupation and the Culture of U.S. Imperialism, 1915–1940* (2001). Examines the causes and consequences of the American occupation of Haiti.

Sullivan, Patricia. *Lift Every Voice: The NAACP and the Making of the Civil Rights Movement* (2009). A sweeping history of the country's preeminent civil rights organization, from its founding to the 1950s.

Tooze, Adam. *The Deluge: The Great War, America and the Remaking of the Global Order, 1916–1931* (2014). A sweeping account of the legacies of World War I for the United States and the wider world.

Veeser, Cyrus. *A World Safe for Capitalism: Dollar Diplomacy and America's Rise to Global Power* (2002). An in-depth exploration of the entanglement of U.S. business interests and the federal government in the Dominican Republic.

Williams, Chad. *Torchbearers of Democracy: African-American Soldiers in the World War I Era* (2010). Describes the experiences of Black servicemen in Europe and as veterans in the United States.

WEBSITES

The Bisbee Deportation of 1917: https://wayback.archive-it.org/8851/20180304033448/http://www.library.arizona.edu/exhibits/bisbee/index.html

Tulsa Massacre: https://www.tulsahistory.org/exhibit/1921-tulsa-race-massacre/#flexible-content Latin America: www.casahistoria.net/uslatam.htm

CHAPTER 20

BOOKS

Boyle, Kevin. *Arc of Justice: A Saga of Race, Civil Rights, and Murder in the Jazz Age* (2004). A history of the Sweet case, placing it in the context of postwar Detroit and the nation.

Dumenil, Lynn. *The Modern Temper: America in the Twenties* (1995). A brief survey of the main political and cultural trends of the decade.

Garraty, John A. *The Great Depression* (1986). Places the Depression in a global context and compares various governments' responses to it.

Gerstle, Gary. *American Crucible: Race and Nation in the Twentieth Century* (2002). A sweeping survey of how changing ideas of race have affected the concept of American nationality, with a strong account of the debates of the 1920s.

Gordon, Linda. *The Second Coming of the KKK: The Ku Klux Klan of the 1920s and the American Political Tradition* (2017). Illuminates the reasons for the Klan's surprising revival in the 1920s.

Heap, Chad. *Slumming: Sexual and Racial Encounters in American Nightlife, 1885–1940* (2009). An insightful analysis of slumming in urban leisure.

Hernandez, Kelly. *Migra! A History of the U.S. Border Patrol* (2010). A revealing history of the expanding efforts to police the border between Mexico and the United States.

Larson, Edward. *Summer for the Gods: The Scopes Trial and America's Continuing Debate over Science and Religion* (1998). A history of the famous trial and the enduring debate over evolution.

Lewis, David L. *When Harlem Was in Vogue* (1981). A lively account of the Harlem Renaissance of the 1920s.

Marchand, Roland. *Advertising the American Dream: Making Way for Modernity, 1920–1940* (1985). Examines how advertisers responded to and helped to shape changes in American life between the two world wars.

McGirr, Lisa. *The War on Alcohol: Prohibition and the Rise of the American State* (2015). A penetrating analysis of Prohibition's impact on American society and government.

Murphy, Paul L. *World War I and the Origin of Civil Liberties in the United States* (1979). An analysis of how the repression of free speech during World War I paved the way for a heightened awareness of the importance of civil liberties.

Ngai, Mae. *Impossible Subjects: Illegal Aliens and the Making of Modern America* (2004). An influential examination of immigration policy toward Mexicans and Asians and the development of the legal category of "illegal alien."

Ross, William G. *Forging New Freedoms: Nativism, Education, and the Constitution, 1917–1927* (1994). Discusses battles over cultural pluralism in the 1920s and how they laid the groundwork for an expanded definition of personal liberty.

Sanchez, George. *Becoming Mexican American: Ethnicity, Culture, and Identity in Chicano Los Angeles, 1900–1945* (1993). An examination of the formation of the Mexican American community in southern California.

WEBSITES

Chicago and the Great Migration: www.loc.gov/exhibits/african/afam011.html

Emergence of Advertising in America: http://library.duke.edu/digitalcollections/eaa/

Prosperity and Thrift: The Coolidge Era and the Consumer Economy: http://memory.loc.gov/ammem/coolhtml/coolhome.html

Scopes Trial: https://famous-trials.com/scopesmonkey

CHAPTER 21

BOOKS

Badger, Anthony. *FDR: The First Hundred Days* (2008). A brief account of the burst of legislation in the early years of the New Deal.

Blackwelder, Julia Kirk. *Women of the Depression* (1998). Examines how female members of three communities—Anglo, Mexican American, and Black—coped with the Great Depression.

Cohen, Lizabeth. *Making a New Deal: Industrial Workers in Chicago, 1919–1939* (1990). Describes how the assimilation of immigrants and their children paved the way for the creation of the New Deal political coalition.

Denning, Michael. *The Cultural Front: The Laboring of American Culture in the Twentieth Century* (1996). A comprehensive account of the rise of cultural activity associated with the political left and the New Deal.

Egan, Timothy. *The Worst Hard Time* (2006). A social history of the Dust Bowl during the Depression, including the stories of victims and survivors.

Gilmore, Glenda. *Defying Dixie: The Radical Roots of Civil Rights, 1919–1950* (2008). Traces the intersection between the struggle for social justice among Black Americans and the internationalist left during the Depression, 1930s, and post–World War II moment.

Gordon, Linda. *Pitied but Not Entitled: Single Mothers and the History of Welfare, 1890–1935* (1994). Explains the emergence of a gendered welfare state with the establishment of Aid for Families with Dependent Children under the Social Security Act of 1935.

Katznelson, Ira. *Fear Itself: The New Deal and the Origins of Our Time* (2013). Examines the shaping of New Deal policy and especially the compromises Roosevelt had to make to get measures through a Congress dominated by segregationist members from the South.

Kennedy, David. *Freedom from Fear: The American People in Depression and War* (2005). A synthetic narrative account of the New Deal era and World War II.

Kessler-Harris, Alice. *In Pursuit of Equity: Men, Women, and the Quest for Economic Citizenship in 20th-Century America* (2001). Explores how assumptions regarding the proper roles of men and women helped to shape New Deal measures such as Social Security.

Patel, Kiran Klaus. *The New Deal: A Global History* (2016). A comparative account of how different countries, including the United States, Italy, Germany, and the Soviet Union, responded to the Great Depression.

Phillips, Sarah T. *The Land, This Nation: Conservation, Rural America, and the New Deal* (2007). Examines New Deal policies regarding agricultural development, rural conservation, and land use, and its attempt to modernize and uplift rural life.

Smith, Jason B. *Building New Deal Liberalism: The Political Economy of Public Works* (2006). Places the great construction projects of the 1930s at the center of New Deal economic policy.

Williams, Mason B. *City of Ambition: FDR, La Guardia, and the Making of Modern New York* (2014). An illuminating study of the most prominent "little New Deal" and its long-term results.

WEBSITES

America from the Great Depression to World War II: http://memory.loc.gov/ammem/fsowhome.html

Flint Sit-Down Strike: www.historicalvoices.org/flint/

The New Deal: https://livingnewdeal.org

CHAPTER 22

BOOKS

Brinkley, Alan. *The End of Reform: New Deal Liberalism in Recession and War* (1995). Describes how liberals' ideas and policies moved away, during the late New Deal and the war, from combating inequalities of economic power.

Daniels, Roger. *Prisoners without Trial: Japanese Americans in World War II* (1993). A brief history of the internment of Japanese Americans during the war.

Dower, John W. *War without Mercy: Race and Power in the Pacific War* (1986). Explores how racial fears and antagonisms motivated both sides in the Pacific theater.

Escobedo, Elizabeth R. *From Coveralls to Zoot Suits: The Lives of Mexican American Women on the World War II Home Front* (2013). Examines how the rise of racial liberalism during World War II and the opening of new jobs affected Mexican American women.

Klein, Jennifer. *For All These Rights: Business, Labor, and the Shaping of America's Public-Private Welfare State* (2003). Explains how the United States adopted a partially privatized welfare state relying on employers, organized labor, and the government in the wake of the New Deal and World War II.

Rhodes, Richard. *The Making of the Atomic Bomb* (1986). A dramatic account of how the atomic bomb was created.

Rosier, Paul C. *Serving Their Country: American Indian Politics and Patriotism in the Twentieth Century* (2009). An in-depth examination of the history of Native Americans and military service across the twentieth century.

Sparrow, James. *Warfare State: World War II, Americans and the Age of Big Government* (2011). Traces how the war expanded the scope and authority of the federal government.

Von Eschen, Penny. *Race against Empire: Black Americans and Anticolonialism, 1937–1957* (1997). Examines how Black Americans responded to the rise of movements for colonial independence overseas during and after World War II.

Wertheim, Stephen. *Tomorrow the World: The Birth of American Global Supremacy* (2020). Looks at World War II as a critical period that came to embrace the exercise of U.S. global power through military preponderance.

WEBSITES

A More Perfect Union: Japanese Americans and the U.S. Constitution: http://amhistory.si.edu/perfectunion/experience/

A People at War: www.archives.gov/exhibits/a_people_at_war/a_people_at_war.html

Bittersweet Harvest: The Bracero Program 1942–1964: http://americanhistory.si.edu/exhibitions/bittersweet-harvest-bracero-program-1942-1964

Remembering Nagasaki: www.exploratorium.edu/nagasaki/

CHAPTER 23

BOOKS

Biondi, Martha. *To Stand and Fight: The Struggle for Civil Rights in Postwar New York City* (2003). A comprehensive account of the broad coalition that battled for racial justice in New York City, in areas such as jobs, education, and housing.

Canaday, Margot. *The Straight State: Sexuality and Citizenship in Twentieth-Century America* (2009). Details the federal government's efforts to stigmatize and punish homosexuality.

Cobb, Daniel M. *Native Activism in Cold War America: The Struggle for Sovereignty* (2008). Traces the history of Indian mobilization for self-determination and economic reform from 1945 through the 1960s.

Donovan, Robert. *Conflict and Crisis: The Presidency of Harry S. Truman, 1945–1948*

(1977). A careful account of Truman's first administration and his surprising election victory in 1948.

Dudziak, Mary L. *Cold War Civil Rights: Race and the Image of American Democracy* (2000). Analyzes how the Cold War influenced and in some ways encouraged the civil rights movement at home.

Glendon, Mary Ann. *A World Made New: Eleanor Roosevelt and the Universal Declaration of Human Rights* (2001). Relates the drafting of the Universal Declaration of Human Rights and the response of governments around the world, including the United States.

Hajimu, Masuda. *Cold War Crucible: The Korean Conflict and the Postwar World* (2015). A history of the Korean War that combines global and local perspectives and emphasizes how it laid the foundation for a large standing army in the United States and military bases around the world.

Hunt, Michael. *Ideology and U.S. Foreign Policy* (1987). Discusses how ideas, including the idea of freedom, have shaped America's interactions with the rest of the world.

Johnson, David K. *The Lavender Scare: The Cold War Persecution of Gays and Lesbians in the Federal Government* (2004). A study of the persecution of gay men and lesbians during the Cold War, including a view of the gay culture that thrived in Washington.

Saunders, Frances S. *The Cultural Cold War: The CIA and the World of Arts and Letters* (2000). Describes how the CIA and other government agencies secretly funded artists and writers as part of the larger Cold War.

Schrecker, Ellen. *Many Are the Crimes: McCarthyism in America* (1998). A full account of the anticommunist crusade at home and its impact on American intellectual and social life.

Sugrue, Thomas. *Origins of the Urban Crisis: Race and Inequality in Postwar Detroit* (1996). Explores race relations in a key industrial city after World War II and how they set the stage for the upheavals of the 1960s.

Wall, Wendy. *Inventing the "American Way": The Politics of Consensus from the New Deal to the Civil Rights Movement* (2008). Charts how World War II and the Cold War reshaped the idea of American unity, consensus, and capitalism.

Westad, Odd Arne. *The Cold War: A World History* (2017). A comprehensive account of the Cold War emphasizing how the conflict played out in Asia and Africa.

WEBSITES

Cold War International History Project: www.wilsoncenter.org/program/cold-war-international-history-project

The Korean War and Its Origins, 1945–1953: https://www.trumanlibrary.gov/library/online-collections/korean-war-and-its-origins

CHAPTER 24

BOOKS

Freeman, Joshua B. *Working-Class New York: Life and Labor since World War II* (2000). An account of the lives of laborers in the nation's largest city, tracing the rise and decline of the labor movement.

Freund, David. *Colored Property: State Policy and White Racial Politics in Suburban America* (2007). Shows how federal policy contributed to suburban racial inequality in one place.

Inboden, William. *Religion and American Foreign Policy, 1945–1960: The Soul of Containment* (2008). How religious groups influenced American diplomacy at the height of the Cold War.

Jackson, Kenneth T. *Crabgrass Frontier: The Suburbanization of America* (1985). The standard account of the development of American suburbia.

Jacobs, Meg. *Pocketbook Politics: Economic Citizenship in Twentieth-Century America* (2005). Discusses how consumer freedom became central to Americans' national identity after World War II.

Klarman, Michael J. *From Jim Crow to Civil Rights: The Supreme Court and the Struggle for Racial Equality* (2004). A full study of Supreme Court cases dealing with civil rights, and how they both reflected and helped to stimulate social change.

Miller, Douglas K. *Indians on the Move: Native Mobility and Urbanization in the 20th Century* (2019). Examines the effort by the federal government to relocate Native American individuals and families off reservations and into cities to increase their work opportunities.

Needham, Andrew. *Power Lines: Phoenix and the Making of the Modern Southwest* (2014). A rich study of the dependency of suburban metropolitan development upon the rural periphery.

Nicolaides, Becky M. *My Blue Heaven: Life and Politics in the Working-Class Suburbs of Los Angeles, 1920–1965* (2002). Traces the transformation of Southgate, an industrial neighborhood of Los Angeles, into an all-white suburb, and the political results.

Phillips-Fein, Kim. *Invisible Hands: The Making of the Conservative Movement from the New Deal to Reagan* (2009). Relates how a group of economic thinkers and businessmen worked to fashion a conservative movement in an attempt to reverse many of the policies of the New Deal.

Rothstein, Richard. *The Color of Law: A Forgotten History of How Our Government Segregated America* (2017). How actions by federal, state, and local governments, reinforced by banks and real estate developers, promoted housing segregation.

Self, Robert. *American Babylon: Race and the Struggle for Postwar Oakland* (2003). Explains how suburbanization and urban crisis evolved together in the post–World War II era.

WEBSITES

Brown v. Board of Education: www.lib.umich .edu/brown-versus-board-education/

Herblock's History: Political Cartoons from the Crash to the Millennium: www.loc .gov/rr/print/swann/herblock/

CHAPTER 25

BOOKS

Anderson, John A., III. *The Other Side of the Sixties: Young Americans for Freedom and the Rise of Conservative Politics* (1997). Considers conservative students of the 1960s and how they laid the groundwork for the later growth of their movement.

Bradley, Mark. *Vietnam at War* (2009). A concise history of the American war in Vietnam that places it within a longer history of foreign intervention.

Brick, Howard. *Age of Contradiction: American Thought and Culture in the 1960s* (1998). A careful examination of the complex currents of thought that circulated during the decade.

Cobb, Daniel M. *Native Activism in Cold War America: The Struggle for Sovereignty* (2008). An in-depth look at the evolution of Indian activism during the 1960s.

Hinton, Elizabeth. *America on Fire: The Untold History of Police Violence and Black Rebellion since the 1960s* (2021). Examines the scope of Black rebellion in cities both large and small from the late 1960s through the 1990s.

Horwitz, Morton J. *The Warren Court and the Pursuit of Justice* (1998). Analyzes how the Supreme Court redefined the rights of Americans under Chief Justice Earl Warren.

Isserman, Maurice, and Michael Kazin. *America Divided: The Civil War of the 1960s* (2000). A comprehensive account of the social movements and political debates of the 1960s.

Logevall, Frederik. *Embers of War: The Fall of an Empire and the Making of America's Vietnam* (2012). An international account of the origins of American military intervention in Vietnam.

Payne, Charles. *I've Got the Light of Freedom: The Organizing Tradition and the Mississippi Freedom Struggle* (1995, 2007). A rich study of the civil rights struggles at the local grassroots level in one Deep South state.

Rosen, Ruth. *The World Split Open: How the Modern Women's Movement Changed America* (2000). Considers how the "second wave" of feminism transformed the lives of American women and men.

Sugrue, Thomas. *Sweet Land of Liberty: The Forgotten Struggle for Civil Rights in the North* (2015). A broad history of civil rights struggles outside the South, emphasizing regional differences within the movement.

Zelizer, Julian. *The Fierce Urgency of Now: Lyndon Johnson, Congress, and the Battle for the Great Society* (2015). Shows how Johnson's leadership, the mass mobilization of the civil rights movement, and the election of liberal Democrats to Congress in 1964 made possible the enactment of measures that had been stalled since the New Deal.

WEBSITES

A Visual Journey: Photographs by Lisa Law, 1965–1971: https://americanhistory.si.edu/lisalaw/

Free Speech Movement Digital Archive: http://bancroft.berkeley.edu/FSM/

Freedom Now!: http://cds.library.brown.edu/projects/FreedomNow

Women's Liberation Movement Print Culture: https://repository.duke.edu/dc/wlmpc

CHAPTER 26

BOOKS

Borstelman, Thomas. *The 1970s: A New Global History from Civil Rights to Economic Inequality* (2012). Shows how developments in the United States, from economic crisis to greater cultural inclusiveness, played out in other countries as well.

Cowie, Jefferson. *Stayin' Alive: The 1970s and the Last Days of the Working Class* (2016). Traces the decline of manufacturing employment and union power in the 1970s and how these affected the lives of individual workers.

Erickson, Ansley T. *Making the Unequal Metropolis: School Desegregation and Its Limits* (2016). With Nashville as its focus, shows how a combination of federal and local policies, and the actions of real estate developers, thwarted efforts at school desegregation.

Foley, Michael S. *Front Porch Politics: The Forgotten Heyday of American Activism in the 1970s and 1980s* (2013). A lively account of the grassroots movements of both left and right that followed the 1960s.

Jacobs, Meg. *Panic at the Pump: The Energy Crisis and the Transformation of American Politics in the 1970s* (2016). Examines the effects of the energy crisis, including strengthening conservative efforts to reduce the role of government in the economy.

Kruse, Kevin. *White Flight: Atlanta and the Making of Modern Conservatism* (2005). Explores how conservative politics took root in the predominantly white suburbs of Atlanta, with implications for similar communities across the country.

Luker, Kristin. *Abortion and the Politics of Motherhood* (1984). Describes how the abortion issue affected American politics and the ideas about gender relations that lay behind the debate.

McGirr, Lisa. *Suburban Warriors: The Origins of the New American Right* (2001). An influential study of the rise of conservatism in Orange County, California, once one of its more powerful centers.

Minian, Ana Raquel. *Undocumented Lives: The Untold Story of Mexican Migration* (2018). Traces government policies toward migration in Mexico and the United States in the 1960s and 1970s, and the experiences of individual immigrants.

Moreton, Bethany. *To Serve God and Wal-Mart: The Making of Christian Free Enterprise* (2009). Explores how the nation's largest employer drew on evangelical Christianity to justify its often-criticized labor policies.

Nielsen, Kim E. *A Disability History of the United States* (2013). A comprehensive history of the experiences of people with disabilities over the course of American history, including the rise of disability rights activism in the 1970s.

Self, Robert O. *All in the Family: The Realignment of American Democracy Since the 1960s* (2012). A sweeping history of social and political changes since the 1960s, honing in on the political repercussions of the women's rights and gay liberation movements.

Spruill, Marjorie J. *Divided We Stand: The Battle over Women's Rights and Family Values That Polarized American Politics* (2017). How the growth of feminism in the 1970s sparked the emergence of an antifeminist movement led by women committed to traditional definitions of women's role in society.

Stein, Judith. *Pivotal Decade: How the United States Traded Factories for Finance in the Seventies* (2010). A careful analysis of the economic transformations of the 1970s.

Wilentz, Sean. *The Age of Reagan: A History, 1974–2008* (2008). Explores how Ronald Reagan set the terms of public debate during and after his presidency.

Windham, Lane. *Knocking on Labor's Door: Union Organizing in the 1970s and the Roots of a New Economic Divide* (2017). Provides an account of multiple labor organizing efforts in a period of labor decline and employer opposition to unionization.

WEBSITES

National Security Archive: http://nsarchive.gwu.edu

Watergate: http://watergate.info/

CHAPTER 27

BOOKS

Bacevich, Andrew J. *American Empire: The Realities and Consequences of U.S. Diplomacy* (2003). Examines how the idea of an American empire reemerged after September 11, and some of the results.

Cole, David. *Terrorism and the Constitution: Sacrificing Civil Liberties in the Name of National Security* (2006). Explores the constitutional issues raised by the war on terrorism.

Gardner, Lloyd C. *The Long Road to Baghdad: A History of U.S. Foreign Policy from the 1970s to the Present* (2008). A careful study of recent American foreign policy and the origins of the Iraq War.

Hartman, Andrew. *A War for the Soul of America: A History of the Culture Wars*

(2015). An account of the numerous social and cultural cleavages spawned by immigration and the social movements of the 1960s.

Hinton, Elizabeth. *From the War on Poverty to the War on Crime: The Making of Mass Incarceration in America* (2016). Traces the evolution of policies, from Johnson through Reagan, that gave rise to mass incarceration.

Hsu, Madeline Y. *The Good Immigrants: How the Yellow Peril Became the Model Minority* (2015). Examines the history of attitudes toward Asian immigrants and the decline of prejudice against them.

Levitas, Daniel. *The Terrorist Next Door: The Militia Movement and the Radical Right* (2003). A careful study of right-wing extremism of the 1990s.

Lichtenstein, Nelson. *The Retail Revolution: How Wal-Mart Created a Brave New World of Business* (2009). How Wal-Mart became the largest employer in the United States and one of the most profitable.

Phillips, Kevin. *Wealth and Democracy* (2002). A critique of the influence of money on American politics.

Power, Samantha. *A Problem from Hell: America and the Age of Genocide* (2002). Discusses genocides of the 1990s and the problem of the appropriate American response.

Smelser, Neil J., and Jeffrey C. Alexander. *Diversity and Its Discontents: Cultural Conflict and Common Ground in Contemporary American Society* (1999). Describes the new social diversity of the 1990s and the cultural and political tensions arising from it.

Zelizer, Julien. *Burning Down the House: Newt Gingrich, the Fall of a Speaker and the Rise of a New Republican Party* (2020). Focuses on the strategies of House Speaker Newt Gingrich in the mid-1990s and his role in fomenting the greater partisan divide in Congress.

WEBSITES

The AIDS Crisis: http://americanhistory.si.edu/exhibitions/hiv-and-aids-thirty-years-ago

Global Exchange: www.globalexchange.org

Making the Macintosh: Technology and Culture in Silicon Valley: https://web.stanford.edu/dept/SUL/sites/mac/index.html

September 11 Digital Archive: http://911digitalarchive.org

CHAPTER 28

BOOKS

Appiah, Anthony. *The Lies That Bind: Rethinking Identity* (2018). A critique of contemporary ideas of identity based on nation, religion, and race, arguing that they sow divisions within societies and are often based on historical misconceptions.

Cherlin, Andrew J. *Labor's Love Lost: The Rise and Fall of the Working-Class Family in America* (2015). Studies how class differences affect family life and opportunities for social mobility in today's America.

Fraser, Steve. *The Age of Acquiescence* (2015). A comparison of the late nineteenth century with the current era, exploring why protest against inequality was stronger in the former.

Horowitz, Andrew. *Katrina: A History, 1915–2015* (2020). Traces the long history of flooding in New Orleans and the decades of economic development that laid the groundwork for the 2005 disaster.

Hyman, Louis. *Temp: How American Work, American Business, and the American Dream Became Temporary* (2018). Explores the reasons for the rise of temporary jobs as the norm and the impact of prospects for workers moving into the middle class.

Johnson, Walter. *The Broken Heart of America: St. Louis and the Violent History of the United States* (2020). Places the Black uprising in Ferguson, Missouri, in 2014 within a centuries' long history of racial inequality and injustice in St. Louis.

Lakoff, George. *Whose Freedom? The Battle over America's Most Important Idea* (2006). Describes how conservatives and liberals continue to interpret freedom in very different ways.

Lansley, Stewart. *Divided We Stand: Why Inequality Keeps Rising* (2011). A prominent economist explains the reasons for rising economic inequality.

Levitsky, Steve, and Daniel Ziblatt. *How Democracies Die* (2018). A compact and instructive examination of the ways political leaders gradually erode democracy and increase autocratic power.

Mounk, Yascha. *The People vs. Democracy: Why Our Freedom Is in Danger and How to Save It* (2018). Sees the 2016 election as endangering democratic institutions and respect for the rights of minorities in the United States.

Tooze, Adam. *Crashed: How a Decade of Financial Crises Changed the World* (2018). Examines the causes of the financial crisis of 2008, its global implications, and why governments did so little to assist its victims.

Turk, Katherine. *Equality on Trial: Gender and Rights in the Modern American Workplace* (2015). An examination of the persistence of gender inequality in offices, factories, and other sites of work.

Weisser, Michael. *From My Cold Dead Hands: Why Americans Won't Give Up Their Guns* (2018). A judicious examination of the debate over gun control.

Zakaria, Fareed. *The Future of Freedom: Illiberal Democracy at Home and Abroad* (2003). A foreign policy analyst discusses how the United States should respond to threats to freedom in the world.

WEBSITE

The White House: www.whitehouse.gov

THE DECLARATION OF INDEPENDENCE (1776)

When in the course of human events, it becomes necessary for one people to dissolve the political bands which have connected them with another, and to assume among the Powers of the earth, the separate and equal station to which the Laws of Nature and of Nature's God entitle them, a decent respect to the opinions of mankind requires that they should declare the causes which impel them to the separation.

We hold these truths to be self-evident, that all men are created equal, that they are endowed by their Creator with certain unalienable rights, that among these are Life, Liberty, and the pursuit of Happiness. That to secure these rights, Governments are instituted among Men, deriving their just powers from the consent of the governed. That whenever any Form of Government becomes destructive of these ends, it is the Right of the People to alter or to abolish it, and to institute new Government, laying its foundation on such principles and organizing its powers in such form, as to them shall seem most likely to effect their Safety and Happiness. Prudence, indeed, will dictate that Governments long established should not be changed for light and transient causes; and accordingly all experience hath shown, that mankind are more disposed to suffer, while evils are sufferable, than to right themselves by abolishing the forms to which they are accustomed. But when a long train of abuses and usurpations, pursuing invariably the same Object evinces a design to reduce them under absolute Despotism, it is their right, it is their duty, to throw off such Government, and to provide new Guards for their future security.—Such has been the patient sufferance of these Colonies; and such is now the necessity which constrains them to alter their former Systems of Government. The history of the present King of Great Britain is a history of repeated injuries and usurpations, all having in direct object the establishment of an absolute Tyranny over these States. To prove this, let Facts be submitted to a candid world.

He has refused his Assent to Laws, the most wholesome and necessary for the public good.

He has forbidden his Governors to pass Laws of immediate and pressing importance, unless suspended in their operation till his Assent should be obtained; and when so suspended, he has utterly neglected to attend to them.

He has refused to pass other Laws for the accommodation of large districts of people, unless those people would relinquish the right of Representation in the Legislature, a right inestimable to them and formidable to tyrants only.

He has called together legislative bodies at places unusual, uncomfortable, and distant from the depository of their public Records, for the sole purpose of fatiguing them into compliance with his measures.

He has dissolved Representative Houses repeatedly, for opposing with manly firmness his invasions on the rights of the people.

He has refused for a long time, after such dissolutions, to cause others to be elected; whereby the Legislative powers, incapable of Annihilation, have returned to the People at large for their exercise; the State remaining in the mean time exposed to all dangers of invasion from without, and convulsions within.

He has endeavoured to prevent the population of these States; for that purpose obstructing the Laws of Naturalization of Foreigners; refusing to pass others to encourage their migrations hither, and raising the conditions of new Appropriations of Lands.

He has obstructed the Administration of Justice, by refusing his Assent to Laws for establishing Judiciary powers.

He has made Judges dependent on his Will alone, for the tenure of their offices, and the amount and payment of their salaries.

He has erected a multitude of New Offices, and sent hither swarms of Officers to harass our People, and eat out their substance.

He has kept among us, in times of peace, Standing Armies without the Consent of our legislatures.

He has affected to render the Military independent of and superior to the Civil Power.

He has combined with others to subject us to a jurisdiction foreign to our constitution, and unacknowledged by our laws; giving his Assent to their Acts of pretended Legislation:

For quartering large bodies of armed troops among us:

For protecting them, by a mock Trial, from Punishment for any Murders which they should commit on the Inhabitants of these States:

For cutting off our Trade with all parts of the world:

For imposing taxes on us without our Consent:

For depriving us of many cases, of the benefits of Trial by jury:

For transporting us beyond Seas to be tried for pretended offences:

For abolishing the free System of English Laws in a neighbouring Province, establishing therein an Arbitrary government, and enlarging its Boundaries so as to render it at once an example and fit instrument for introducing the same absolute rule into these Colonies:

For taking away our Charters, abolishing our most valuable Laws, and altering fundamentally the Forms of our Governments:

For suspending our own Legislatures, and declaring themselves invested with Power to legislate for us in all cases whatsoever.

He has abdicated Government here, by declaring us out of his Protection and waging War against us.

He has plundered our seas, ravaged our Coasts, burnt our towns, and destroyed the lives of our people.

He is at this time transporting large armies of foreign mercenaries to compleat the works of death, desolation, and tyranny, already begun with circumstances of Cruelty & perfidy scarcely paralleled in the most barbarous ages, and totally unworthy the Head of a civilized nation.

He has constrained our fellow Citizens taken Captive on the high Seas to bear Arms against their Country, to become the executioners of their friends and Brethren, or to fall themselves by their Hands.

He has excited domestic insurrections amongst us, and has endeavoured to bring on the inhabitants of our frontiers, the merciless Indian Savages, whose known rule of warfare, is an undistinguished destruction of all ages, sexes, and conditions.

In every stage of these Oppressions We have Petitioned for Redress in the most humble terms: Our repeated Petitions have been answered only by repeated injury. A Prince, whose character is thus marked by every act which may define a Tyrant, is unfit to be the ruler of a free people.

Nor have We been wanting in attention to our British brethren. We have warned them from time to time of attempts by their legislature to extend an unwarrantable jurisdiction over us. We have reminded them of the circumstances of our emigration and settlement here. We have appealed to their native justice and magnanimity, and we have conjured them by the ties of our common kindred to disavow these usurpations, which, would inevitably interrupt our connections and correspondence. They too must have been deaf to the voice of justice and of consanguinity. We must, therefore, acquiesce in the necessity, which denounces our Separation, and hold them, as we hold the rest of mankind, Enemies in War, in Peace Friends.

WE, THEREFORE, the Representatives of the UNITED STATES OF AMERICA, in General Congress, Assembled, appealing to the Supreme Judge of the world for the rectitude of our intentions, do, in the Name, and by Authority of the good People of these Colonies, solemnly publish and declare, That these United Colonies are, and of Right ought to be FREE AND INDEPENDENT STATES; that they are Absolved from all Allegiance to the British Crown, and that all political connection between them and the State of Great Britain, is and ought to be totally dissolved; and that as Free and Independent States, they have full Power to levy War, conclude Peace, contract Alliances, establish Commerce, and to do all other Acts and Things which Independent States may of right do. And for the support of this Declaration, with a firm reliance on the Protection of Divine Providence, we mutually pledge to each other our Lives, our Fortunes, and our sacred Honor.

The foregoing Declaration was, by order of Congress, engrossed, and signed by the following members:

John Hancock

New Hampshire
Josiah Bartlett
William Whipple
Matthew Thornton

Massachusetts Bay
Samuel Adams
John Adams
Robert Treat Paine
Elbridge Gerry

Rhode Island
Stephen Hopkins
William Ellery

Connecticut
Roger Sherman
Samuel Huntington
William Williams
Oliver Wolcott

New York
William Floyd
Philip Livingston
Francis Lewis
Lewis Morris

New Jersey
Richard Stockton
John Witherspoon
Francis Hopkinson
John Hart
Abraham Clark

Pennsylvania
Robert Morris
Benjamin Rush
Benjamin Franklin
John Morton
George Clymer
James Smith
George Taylor
James Wilson
George Ross

Delaware
Caesar Rodney
George Read
Thomas M'Kean

Maryland
Samuel Chase
William Paca
Thomas Stone
Charles Carroll, of Carrollton

Virginia
George Wythe
Richard Henry Lee
Thomas Jefferson
Benjamin Harrison
Thomas Nelson, Jr.
Francis Lightfoot Lee
Carter Braxton

North Carolina
William Hooper
Joseph Hewes
John Penn

South Carolina
Edward Rutledge
Thomas Heyward, Jr.
Thomas Lynch, Jr.
Arthur Middleton

Georgia
Button Gwinnett
Lyman Hall
George Walton

Resolved, That copies of the Declaration be sent to the several assemblies, conventions, and committees, or councils of safety, and to the several commanding officers of the continental troops; that it be proclaimed in each of the United States, at the head of the army.

THE CONSTITUTION OF THE UNITED STATES (1787)

We the People of the United States, in order to form a more perfect Union, establish Justice, insure domestic Tranquility, provide for the common defence, promote the general Welfare, and secure the Blessings of Liberty to ourselves and our Posterity, do ordain and establish this Constitution for the United States of America.

ARTICLE. I.

Section. 1. All legislative Powers herein granted shall be vested in a Congress of the United States, which shall consist of a Senate and House of Representatives.

Section. 2. The House of Representatives shall be composed of Members chosen every second Year by the People of the several States, and the Electors in each State shall have the Qualifications requisite for Electors of the most numerous Branch of the State Legislature.

No Person shall be a Representative who shall not have attained to the Age of twenty five Years, and been seven Years a Citizen of the United States, and who shall not, when elected, be an Inhabitant of that State in which he shall be chosen.

Representatives and direct Taxes shall be apportioned among the several States which may be included within this Union, according to their respective Numbers, which shall be determined by adding to the whole Number of free Persons, including those bound to Service for a Term of Years, and excluding Indians not taxed, three fifths of all other Persons. The actual Enumeration shall be made within three Years after the first Meeting of the Congress of the United States, and within every subsequent Term of ten Years, in such Manner as they shall by Law direct. The Number of Representatives shall not exceed one for every thirty Thousand, but each State shall have at Least one Representative; and until such enumeration shall be made, the State of New Hampshire shall be entitled to chuse three, Massachusetts eight, Rhode-Island and Providence Plantations one, Connecticut five, New York six, New Jersey four, Pennsylvania eight, Delaware one, Maryland six, Virginia ten, North Carolina five, South Carolina five, and Georgia three.

When vacancies happen in the Representation from any state, the Executive Authority thereof shall issue Writs of Election to fill such Vacancies.

The House of Representatives shall chuse their Speaker and other Officers; and shall have the sole Power of Impeachment.

Section. 3. The Senate of the United States shall be composed of two Senators from each State, chosen by the legislature thereof, for six Years; and each Senator shall have one Vote.

Immediately after they shall be assembled in Consequence of the first Election, they shall be divided as equally as may be into three Classes. The Seats of the Senators of the first Class shall be vacated at the Expiration of the second Year, of the second Class at the Expiration of the fourth Year, and of the third Class at the Expiration of the sixth Year, so that one third may be chosen every second Year; and if Vacancies happen by Resignation, or otherwise, during the Recess of the Legislature of any State, the Executive thereof may make temporary Appointments until the next Meeting of the Legislature, which shall then fill such Vacancies.

No Person shall be a Senator who shall not have attained to the Age of thirty Years, and been nine Years a Citizen of the United States, and who shall not, when elected, be an Inhabitant of that State for which he shall be chosen.

The Vice President of the United States shall be President of the Senate, but shall have no Vote, unless they be equally divided.

The Senate shall chuse their other Officers, and also a President pro tempore, in the Absence of the Vice President, or when he shall exercise the Office of President of the United States.

The Senate shall have the sole Power to try all Impeachments. When sitting for that Purpose, they shall be on Oath or Affirmation. When the President of the United States is tried, the Chief Justice shall preside: And no Person shall be convicted without the Concurrence of two thirds of the Members present.

Judgment in Cases of Impeachment shall not extend further than to removal from Office, and disqualification to hold and enjoy any Office of honor, Trust or Profit under the United States: but the Party convicted shall nevertheless be liable and subject to Indictment, Trial, Judgment and Punishment, according to Law.

Section. 4. The Times, Places and Manner of holding Elections for Senators and Representatives, shall be prescribed in each State by the Legislature thereof; but the Congress may at any time by Law make or alter such Regulations, except as to the Places of chusing Senators.

The Congress shall assemble at least once in every Year, and such Meeting shall be on the first Monday in December, unless they shall by Law appoint a different Day.

Section. 5. Each House shall be the Judge of the Elections, Returns and Qualifications of its own Members, and a Majority of each shall constitute a Quorum to do Business; but a smaller Number may adjourn from day to day, and may be authorized to compel the Attendance of absent Members, in such Manner, and under such Penalties as each House may provide.

Each House may determine the Rules of its Proceedings, punish its Members for disorderly Behaviour, and, with the Concurrence of two thirds, expel a Member.

Each House shall keep a Journal of its Proceedings, and from time to time publish the same, excepting such Parts as may in their Judgment require Secrecy; and the Yeas and Nays of the Members of either House on any question shall, at the Desire of one fifth of those Present, be entered on the Journal.

Neither House, during the Session of Congress, shall, without the Consent of the other, adjourn for more than three days, not to any other Place than that in which the two Houses shall be sitting.

Section. 6. The Senators and Representatives shall receive a Compensation for their Services, to be ascertained by Law, and paid out of the Treasury of the United States. They shall in all Cases, except Treason, Felony and Breach of the Peace, be privileged from Arrest during their Attendance at the Session of their respective Houses, and in going to and returning from the same; and for any Speech or Debate in either House, they shall not be questioned in any other Place.

No Senator or Representative shall, during the Time for which he was elected, be appointed to any civil Office under the Authority of the United States, which shall have been created, or the Emoluments whereof shall have been encreased during such time; and no Person holding any Office under the United States, shall be a Member of either House during his Continuance in Office.

Section. 7. All Bills for raising Revenue shall originate in the House of Representatives; but the Senate may propose or concur with Amendments as on other Bills.

Every Bill which shall have passed the House of Representatives and the Senate shall, before it become a Law, be presented to the President of the United States; If he approve he shall sign it, but if not he shall return it, with his Objections to that House in which it shall have originated, who shall enter the Objections at large on their Journal, and proceed to reconsider it. If after such Reconsideration two thirds of that House shall agree to pass the Bill, it shall be sent, together with the Objections, to the other House, by which it shall likewise be reconsidered, and if approved by two thirds of that House, it shall become a Law. But in all such Cases the Votes of both Houses shall be determined by Yeas and Nays, and the Names of the Persons voting for and against the Bill shall be entered on the Journal of each House respectively. If any Bill shall not be returned by the President within ten Days (Sundays excepted) after it shall have been presented to him, the Same shall be a Law, in like Manner as if he had signed it, unless the Congress by their Adjournment prevent its Return, in which Case it shall not be a Law.

Every Order, Resolution, or Vote to which the Concurrence of the Senate and House of Representatives may be necessary (except on a question of Adjournment) shall be presented to the President of the United States; and before the Same shall take Effect, shall be approved by him, or being disapproved by him, shall be repassed by two thirds of the Senate and House of Representatives, according to the Rules and Limitations prescribed in the Case of a Bill.

Section. 8. The Congress shall have Power To lay and collect Taxes, Duties, Imposts and Excises, to pay the Debts and provide for the common Defence and general Welfare of the United States; but all Duties, Imposts and Excises shall be uniform throughout the United States;

To borrow Money on the credit of the United States;

To regulate Commerce with foreign Nations, and among the several States, and with the Indian Tribes;

To establish an uniform Rule of Naturalization, and uniform Laws on the subject of Bankruptcies throughout the United States;

To coin Money, regulate the Value thereof, and of foreign Coin, and fix the Standard of Weights and Measures;

To provide for the Punishment of counterfeiting the Securities and current Coin of the United States;

To establish Post Offices and Post Roads;

To promote the Progress of Science and useful Arts, by securing for limited Times to Authors and Inventors the exclusive Right to their respective Writings and Discoveries;

To constitute Tribunals inferior to the supreme Court;

To define and punish Piracies and Felonies committed on the high Seas, and Offences against the Law of Nations;

To declare War, grant Letters of Marque and Reprisal, and make Rules concerning Captures on Land and Water;

To raise and support Armies, but no Appropriation of Money to that Use shall be for a longer Term than two Years;

To provide and maintain a Navy;

To make Rules for the Government and Regulation of the land and naval Forces;

To provide for calling forth the Militia to execute the Laws of the Union, suppress Insurrections and repel Invasions;

To provide for organizing, arming, and disciplining, the Militia, and for governing such Part of them as may be employed in the Service of the United States, reserving to the States respectively, the Appointment of the Officers, and the Authority of training the Militia according to the discipline prescribed by Congress;

To exercise exclusive Legislation in all Cases whatsoever, over such District (not exceeding ten Miles square) as may, by Cession of Particular States, and the Acceptance of Congress, become the Seat of the Government of the United States, and to exercise like Authority over all Places purchased by the Consent of the Legislature of the State in which the Same shall be, for the Erection of Forts, Magazines, Arsenals, dock-Yards, and other needful Buildings;—And

To make all Laws which shall be necessary and proper for carrying into Execution the foregoing Powers, and all other Powers vested by this Constitution in the Government of the United States, or in any Department or Officer thereof.

Section. 9. The Migration or Importation of such Persons as any of the States now existing shall think proper to admit, shall not be prohibited by the Congress prior to the Year one thousand eight hundred and eight, but a Tax or duty may be imposed on such Importation, not exceeding ten dollars for each Person.

The Privilege of the Writ of Habeas Corpus shall not be suspended, unless when in Cases of Rebellion or Invasion the public Safety may require it.

No Bill of Attainder or ex post facto Law shall be passed.

No Capitation, or other direct, Tax shall be laid, unless in Proportion to the Census or Enumeration herein before directed to be taken.

No Tax or Duty shall be laid on Articles exported from any State.

No Preference shall be given by any Regulation of Commerce or Revenue to the Ports of one State over those of another: nor shall Vessels bound to, or from, one State, be obliged to enter, clear, or pay Duties in another.

No Money shall be drawn from the Treasury, but in Consequence of Appropriations made by Law; and a regular Statement and Account of the Receipts and Expenditures of all public Money shall be published from time to time.

No Title of Nobility shall be granted by the United States: And no Person holding any Office of Profit or Trust under them, shall, without the Consent of the Congress, accept of any present, Emolument, Office, or Title, of any kind whatever, from any King, Prince, or foreign State.

Section. 10. No State shall enter into any Treaty, Alliance, or Confederation; grant Letters of Marque and Reprisal; coin Money; emit Bills of Credit; make any Thing but gold and silver Coin a Tender in Payment of Debts; pass any Bill of Attainder, ex post facto Law, or Law impairing the Obligation of Contracts, or grant any Title of Nobility.

No State shall, without the Consent of the Congress, lay any Imposts or Duties on Imports or Exports, except what may be absolutely necessary for executing its inspection Laws: and the net Produce of all Duties and Imposts, laid by any State on Imports or Exports, shall be for the Use of the Treasury of the United States; and all such Laws shall be subject to the Revision and Controul of the Congress.

No State shall, without the Consent of Congress, lay any Duty of Tonnage, keep Troops, or Ships of War in time of Peace, enter into any Agreement or Compact with another State, or with a foreign Power, or engage in War, unless actually invaded, or in such imminent Danger as will not admit of delay.

ARTICLE. II.

Section. 1. The executive Power shall be vested in a President of the United States of America. He shall hold his Office during the term of four Years, and, together with the Vice President, chosen for the same Term, be elected, as follows:

Each State shall appoint, in such Manner as the Legislature thereof may direct, a Number of Electors, equal to the whole Number of Senators and Representatives to which the State may be entitled in the Congress: but no Senator or Representative, or Person holding an Office of Trust or Profit under the United States, shall be appointed an Elector.

The Electors shall meet in their respective States, and vote by Ballot for two Persons, of whom one at least shall not be an Inhabitant of the same State with themselves. And they shall make a List of all the Persons voted for, and of the Number of Votes for each; which List they shall sign and certify, and transmit sealed to the Seat of the Government of the United States, directed to the President of the Senate. The President of the Senate shall, in the Presence of the Senate and House of Representatives, open all the Certificates, and the Votes shall then be counted. The Person having the greatest Number of Votes shall be the President, if such Number be a Majority of the whole Number of Electors appointed; and if there be more than one who have such Majority, and have an equal Number of Votes, then the House of Representatives shall immediately chuse by Ballot one of them for President; and if no Person have a Majority, then from the five highest on the List the said House shall in like Manner chuse the President. But in chusing the President, the Votes shall be taken by States, the Representation from each State having one Vote; A quorum for this Purpose shall consist of a Member or Members from two thirds of the States, and a Majority of all the States shall be necessary to a Choice. In every Case, after the Choice of the President, the Person having the greatest Number of Votes of the Electors shall be the Vice President. But if there should remain two or more who have equal Votes, the Senate shall chuse from them by Ballot the Vice President.

The Congress may determine the Time of chusing the Electors, and the Day on which they shall give their Votes; which Day shall be the same throughout the United States.

No Person except a natural born Citizen, or a Citizen of the United States, at the time of the Adoption of this Constitution, shall be eligible to the Office of President; neither shall any Person be eligible to that Office who shall not have attained to the Age of thirty five Years, and been fourteen Years a Resident within the United States.

In Case of the Removal of the President from Office, or of his Death, Resignation, or Inability to discharge the Powers and Duties of the said Office, the Same shall devolve on the Vice President, and the Congress may by Law provide for the Case of Removal, Death, Resignation or Inability, both of the President and Vice President, declaring what Officer shall then act as President, and such Officer shall act accordingly, until the Disability be removed, or a President shall be elected.

The President shall, at stated Times, receive for his Services, a Compensation, which shall neither be encreased or diminished during the Period for which he shall have been elected, and he shall not receive within that Period any other Emolument from the United States, or any of them.

Before he enters on the Execution of his Office, he shall take the following Oath or Affirmation:—"I do solemnly swear (or affirm) that I will faithfully execute the Office of President of the United States, and will to the best of my Ability, preserve, protect and defend the Constitution of the United States."

Section. 2. The President shall be Commander in Chief of the Army and Navy of the United States, and of the Militia of the several States, when called into the actual Service of the United States; he may require the Opinion, in writing, of the principal Officer in each of the executive Departments, upon any Subject relating to the Duties of their respective Offices, and he shall have Power to grant Reprieves and Pardons for Offences against the United States, except in Cases of Impeachment.

He shall have Power, by and with the Advice and Consent of the Senate, to make Treaties, provided two thirds of the Senators present concur; and he shall nominate, and by and with the Advice and Consent of the Senate, shall appoint Ambassadors, other public Ministers and Consuls, Judges of the supreme Court, and all other Officers of the United States, whose Appointments are not herein otherwise provided for, and which shall be established by Law; but the Congress may by Law vest the Appointment of such inferior Officers, as they think proper, in the President alone, in the Courts of Law, or in the Heads of Departments.

The President shall have Power to fill up all Vacancies that may happen during the Recess of the Senate, by granting Commissions which shall expire at the End of their next Session.

Section. 3. He shall from time to time give to the Congress Information of the State of the Union, and recommend to their Consideration such Measures as he shall judge necessary and expedient; he may, on extraordinary Occasions, convene both Houses, or either of them, and in Case of Disagreement between them, with Respect to the Time of Adjournment, he may adjourn them to such Time as he shall think proper; he shall receive Ambassadors and other public Ministers; he shall take Care that the Laws be faithfully executed, and shall Commission all the Officers of the United States.

Section. 4. The President, Vice President and all civil Officers of the United States, shall be removed from Office on Impeachment for, and Conviction of, Treason, Bribery, or other high Crimes and Misdemeanors.

ARTICLE. III.

Section. 1. The judicial Power of the United States, shall be vested in one supreme Court, and in such inferior Courts as the Congress may from time to time ordain and establish. The Judges, both of the supreme and inferior Courts, shall hold their Offices during good Behavior, and shall, at stated Times, receive for their Services, a Compensation, which shall not be diminished during their Continuance in Office.

Section. 2. The judicial Power shall extend to all Cases, in Law and Equity, arising under this Constitution, the Laws of the United States, and Treaties made, or which shall be made, under their Authority;—to all Cases affecting Ambassadors, other public Ministers and Consuls;—to all Cases of admiralty and maritime Jurisdiction;—the Controversies to which the United States shall be a Party;—to Controversies between two or more States;—between a State and Citizens of another State;—between Citizens of different States;—between Citizens of the same State claiming Lands under Grants of different States, and between a State, or the Citizens thereof, and foreign States, Citizens or Subjects.

In all cases affecting Ambassadors, other public Ministers and Consuls, and those in which a State shall be Party, the supreme Court shall have original Jurisdiction. In all the other Cases before mentioned, the supreme Court shall have appellate Jurisdiction, both as to Law and Fact, with such Exceptions, and under such Regulations as the Congress shall make.

The Trial of all Crimes, except in Cases of Impeachment, shall be by Jury; and such Trial shall be held in the State where the said Crimes shall have been committed; but when not committed within any State, the Trial shall be at such Place or Places as the Congress may by Law have directed.

Section. 3. Treason against the United States, shall consist only in levying War against them, or in adhering to their Enemies, giving them Aid and Comfort. No Person shall be convicted of Treason unless on the Testimony of two Witnesses to the same overt Act, or on Confession in open Court.

The Congress shall have Power to declare the Punishment of Treason, but no Attainder of Treason shall work Corruption of Blood, or Forfeiture except during the Life of the Person attainted.

ARTICLE. IV.

Section. 1. Full Faith and Credit shall be given in each State to the public Acts, Records, and judicial Proceedings of every other State. And the Congress may by general Laws prescribe the Manner in which such Acts, Records and Proceedings shall be proved, and the Effect thereof.

Section. 2. The Citizens of each State shall be entitled to all Privileges and Immunities of Citizens in the several States.

A Person charged in any State with Treason, Felony, or other Crime, who shall flee from Justice, and be found in another State, shall on Demand of the executive Authority of the State from which he fled, be delivered up, to be removed to the State having Jurisdiction of the Crime.

No Person held to Service or Labour in one State, under the Laws thereof, escaping into another, shall, in Consequence of any Law or Regulation therein, be discharged from such Service or Labour, but shall be delivered up on Claim of the Party to whom such Service or Labour may be due.

Section. 3. New States may be admitted by the Congress into this Union; but no new State shall be formed or erected within the Jurisdiction of any other State; nor any State be formed by the Junction of two or more States, or Parts of States, without the consent of the Legislatures of the States concerned as well as of the Congress.

The Congress shall have Power to dispose of and make all needful Rules and Regulations respecting the Territory or other Property belonging to the United States; and nothing in this Constitution shall be so construed as to Prejudice any Claims of the United States, or of any particular States.

Section. 4. The United States shall guarantee to every State in this Union a Republican Form of Government, and shall protect each of them against Invasion; and on Application of the Legislature, or of the Executive (when the Legislature cannot be convened) against domestic Violence.

ARTICLE. V.

The Congress, whenever two thirds of both Houses shall deem it necessary, shall propose Amendments to this Constitution, or, on the Application of the Legislatures of two thirds of the several States, shall call a Convention for proposing Amendments, which, in either Case, shall be valid to all Intents and Purposes, as Part of this Constitution, when ratified by the Legislatures of three fourths of the several States, or by Conventions in three fourths thereof, as the one or the other Mode of Ratification may be proposed by the Congress; Provided that no Amendment which may be made prior to the Year One thousand eight hundred and eight shall in any Manner affect the first and fourth Clauses in the Ninth Section of the first Article; and that no State, without its Consent, shall be deprived of its equal Suffrage in the Senate.

ARTICLE. VI.

All Debts contracted and Engagements entered into, before the Adoption of this Constitution, shall be as valid against the United States under this Constitution, as under the Confederation.

This Constitution, and the Laws of the United States which shall be made in Pursuance thereof; and all Treaties made, or which shall be made, under the Authority of the United States, shall be the supreme Law of the Land; and the Judges in every State shall be bound thereby, any Thing in the Constitution or Laws of any State to the Contrary notwithstanding.

The Senators and Representatives before mentioned, and the Members of the several State Legislatures, and all executive and judicial Officers, both of the United States and of the several States, shall be bound by Oath or Affirmation, to support this Constitution; but no religious Test shall ever be required as a Qualification to any Office or public Trust under the United States.

ARTICLE. VII.

The Ratification of the Conventions of nine States, shall be sufficient for the Establishment of this Constitution between the States so ratifying the Same.

Done in Convention by the Unanimous Consent of the States present the Seventeenth Day of September in the Year of our Lord one thousand seven hundred and Eighty seven and of the Independence of the United States of America the Twelfth. In witness thereof We have hereunto subscribed our Names,

G°. WASHINGTON—Presd^t.
and deputy from Virginia

New Hampshire
John Langdon
Nicholas Gilman

Massachusetts
Nathaniel Gorham
Rufus King

Connecticut
Wm Saml Johnson
Roger Sherman

New York
Alexander Hamilton

New Jersey
Wil: Livingston
David A. Brearley
Wm Paterson
Jona: Dayton

Pennsylvania
B Franklin
Thomas Mifflin
Robt Morris
Geo. Clymer
Thos FitzSimons
Jared Ingersoll
James Wilson
Gouv Morris

Delaware
Geo: Read
Gunning Bedford jun
John Dickinson
Richard Bassett
Jaco: Broom

Maryland
James McHenry
Dan of St Thos Jenifer
Danl Carroll

Virginia
John Blair—
James Madison Jr.

North Carolina
Wm Blount
Richd Dobbs Spaight
Hu Williamson

South Carolina
J. Rutledge
Charles Cotesworth Pinckney
Charles Pinckney
Pierce Butler

Georgia
William Few
Abr Baldwin

AMENDMENTS TO THE CONSTITUTION

Articles in addition to, and Amendment of the Constitution of the United States of America, proposed by Congress, and ratified by the Legislatures of the several States, pursuant to the fifth Article of the original Constitution.

AMENDMENT I.*
Congress shall make no law respecting an establishment of religion, or prohibiting the free exercise thereof; or abridging the freedom of speech, or of the press; or the right of the people peaceably to assemble, and to petition the Government for a redress of grievances.

AMENDMENT II.
A well regulated Militia, being necessary to the security of a free State, the right of the people to keep and bear Arms, shall not be infringed.

AMENDMENT III.
No Soldier shall, in time of peace be quartered in any house, without the consent of the Owner, nor in time of war, but in a manner to be prescribed by law.

AMENDMENT IV.
The right of the people to be secure in their persons, houses, papers, and effects, against unreasonable searches and seizures, shall not be violated, and no Warrants shall issue, but upon probable cause, supported by Oath or affirmation, and particularly describing the place to be searched, and the persons or things to be seized.

AMENDMENT V.
No person shall be held to answer for a capital, or otherwise infamous crime, unless on a presentment or indictment of a Grand Jury, except in cases arising in the land or naval forces, or in the Militia, when in actual service in time of War or public danger; nor shall any person be subject for the same offence to be twice put in jeopardy of life or limb; nor shall be compelled in any criminal case to be a witness against himself, nor be deprived of life, liberty, or property, without due process of law; nor shall private property be taken for public use, without just compensation.

*The first ten amendments (the Bill of Rights) were ratified in 1791.

AMENDMENT VI.

In all criminal prosecutions, the accused shall enjoy the right to a speedy and public trial, by an impartial jury of the State and district wherein the crime shall have been committed, which district shall have been previously ascertained by law, and to be informed of the nature and cause of the accusation; to be confronted with the witnesses against him; to have compulsory process for obtaining witnesses in his favor, and to have the Assistance of Counsel for his defence.

AMENDMENT VII.

In Suits at common law, where the value in controversy shall exceed twenty dollars, the right of trial by jury shall be preserved, and no fact tried by a jury, shall be otherwise re-examined in any Court of the United States, than according to the rules of the common law.

AMENDMENT VIII.

Excessive bail shall not be required, nor excessive fines imposed, nor cruel and unusual punishments inflicted.

AMENDMENT IX.

The enumeration in the Constitution, of certain rights, shall not be construed to deny or disparage others retained by the people.

AMENDMENT X.

The powers not delegated to the United States by the Constitution, nor prohibited by it to the States, are reserved to the States respectively, or to the people.

AMENDMENT XI.

The Judicial power of the United States shall not be construed to extend to any suit in law or equity, commenced or prosecuted against one of the United States by Citizens of another State, or by Citizens or Subjects of any Foreign State. [January 8, 1798]

AMENDMENT XII.

The Electors shall meet in their respective states, and vote by ballot for President and Vice-President, one of whom, at least, shall not be an inhabitant of the same state with themselves; they shall name in their ballots the person voted for as President, and in distinct ballots the person voted for as Vice-President, and they shall make distinct lists of all persons voted for as President, and of all persons voted for as Vice President, and of the number of votes for each, which lists they shall sign and certify, and transmit sealed to the seat of the government of the United States, directed to the President of the Senate;— The President of the Senate shall, in the presence of the Senate and House of

Representatives, open all the certificates and the votes shall then be counted;—The person having the greatest number of votes for President, shall be the President, if such number be a majority of the whole number of Electors appointed; and if no person have such majority, then from the persons having the highest numbers not exceeding three on the list of those voted for as President, the House of Representatives shall choose immediately, by ballot, the President. But in choosing the President, the votes shall be taken by states, the representation from each state having one vote; a quorum for this purpose shall consist of a member or members from two-thirds of the states, and a majority of all the states shall be necessary to a choice. And if the House of Representatives shall not choose a President whenever the right of choice shall devolve upon them, before the fourth day of March next following, then the Vice-President shall act as President, as in the case of the death or other constitutional disability of the President.—The person having the greatest number of votes as Vice-President, shall be the Vice-President, if such number be a majority of the whole number of Electors appointed, and if no person have a majority, then from the two highest numbers on the list, the Senate shall choose the Vice-President; a quorum for the purpose shall consist of two-thirds of the whole number of Senators, and a majority of the whole number shall be necessary to a choice. But no person constitutionally ineligible to the office of President shall be eligible to that of Vice-President of the United States. [September 25, 1804]

AMENDMENT XIII.

Section 1. Neither slavery nor involuntary servitude, except as a punishment for crime whereof the party shall have been duly convicted, shall exist within the United States, or any place subject to their jurisdiction.

Section 2. Congress shall have power to enforce this article by appropriate legislation. [December 18, 1865]

AMENDMENT XIV.

Section 1. All persons born or naturalized in the United States, and subject to the jurisdiction thereof, are citizens of the United States and of the State wherein they reside. No State shall make or enforce any law which shall abridge the privileges or immunities of citizens of the United States; nor shall any State deprive any person of life, liberty, or property, without due process of law; nor deny to any person within its jurisdiction the equal protection of the laws.

Section 2. Representatives shall be apportioned among the several States according to their respective numbers, counting the whole number of persons in each State, excluding Indians not taxed. But when the right to vote at any election for the choice of electors for President and Vice President of the United States, Representatives in Congress, the Executive and Judicial officers of a State, or the members of the Legislature thereof, is denied to any of the male inhabitants of such State, being twenty-one years of age, and citizens of the United States, or in any way abridged, except for participation in rebellion, or other crime, the basis of representation therein shall be reduced in the proportion which the number of such male citizens shall bear to the whole number of male citizens twenty-one years of age in such State.

Section 3. No person shall be a Senator or Representative in Congress, or elector of President and Vice President, or hold any office, civil or military, under the United States, or under any State, who, having previously taken an oath, as a member of Congress, or as an officer of the United States, or as a member of any State legislature, or as an executive or judicial officer of any State, to support the Constitution of the United States, shall have engaged in insurrection or rebellion against the same, or given aid or comfort to the enemies thereof. But Congress may by a vote of two-thirds of each House, remove such disability.

Section 4. The validity of the public debt of the United States, authorized by law, including debts incurred for payment of pensions and bounties for services in suppressing insurrection or rebellion, shall not be questioned. But neither the United States nor any State shall assume or pay any debt or obligation incurred in aid of insurrection or rebellion against the United States, or any claim for the loss or emancipation of any slave; but all such debts, obligations and claims shall be held illegal and void.

Section 5. The Congress shall have power to enforce, by appropriate legislation, the provisions of this article. [July 28, 1868]

AMENDMENT XV.
Section 1. The right of citizens of the United States to vote shall not be denied or abridged by the United States or by any State on account of race, color, or previous condition of servitude—

Section 2. The Congress shall have power to enforce this article by appropriate legislation. [March 30, 1870]

AMENDMENT XVI.
The Congress shall have power to lay and collect taxes on incomes, from whatever source derived, without apportionment among the several States, and without regard to any census or enumeration. [February 25, 1913]

AMENDMENT XVII.

The Senate of the United States shall be composed of two senators from each State, elected by the people thereof, for six years; and each Senator shall have one vote. The electors in each State shall have the qualifications requisite for electors of the most numerous branch of the State legislatures.

When vacancies happen in the representation of any State in the Senate, the executive authority of such State shall issue writs of election to fill such vacancies: *Provided,* That the legislature of any State may empower the executive thereof to make temporary appointments until the people fill the vacancies by election as the legislature may direct.

This amendment shall not be so construed as to affect the election or term of any senator chosen before it becomes valid as part of the Constitution. [May 31, 1913]

AMENDMENT XVIII.

After one year from the ratification of this article, the manufacture, sale, or transportation of intoxicating liquors within, the importation thereof into, or the exportation thereof from the United States and all territory subject to the jurisdiction thereof for beverage purposes is hereby prohibited.

The Congress and the several States shall have concurrent power to enforce this article by appropriate legislation.

This article shall be inoperative unless it shall have been ratified as an amendment to the Constitution by the legislatures of the several States, as provided in the Constitution, within seven years from the date of the submission thereof to the States by Congress. [January 29, 1919]

AMENDMENT XIX.

The right of citizens of the United States to vote shall not be denied or abridged by the United States or by any State on account of sex.

The Congress shall have power by appropriate legislation to enforce the provisions of this article. [August 26, 1920]

AMENDMENT XX.

Section 1. The terms of the President and Vice-President shall end at noon on the twentieth day of January, and the terms of Senators and Representatives at noon on the third day of January, of the years in which such terms would have ended if this article had not been ratified; and the terms of their successors shall then begin.

Section 2. The Congress shall assemble at least once in every year, and such meeting shall begin at noon on the third day of January, unless they shall by law appoint a different day.

Section 3. If, at the time fixed for the beginning of the term of the President, the President-elect shall have died, the Vice-President-elect shall become President. If a President shall not have been chosen before the time fixed for the beginning of his term, or if the President-elect shall have failed to qualify, then the Vice-President-elect shall act as President until a President shall have qualified; and the Congress may by law provide for the case wherein neither a President-elect nor a Vice-President-elect shall have qualified, declaring who shall then act as President, or the manner in which one who is to act shall be selected, and such person shall act accordingly until a President or Vice-President shall have qualified.

Section 4. The Congress may by law provide for the case of the death of any of the persons from whom the House of Representatives may choose a President whenever the right of choice shall have devolved upon them, and for the case of the death of any of the persons from whom the Senate may choose a Vice-President whenever the right of choice shall have devolved upon them.

Section 5. Sections 1 and 2 shall take effect on the 15th day of October following the ratification of this article.

Section 6. This article shall be inoperative unless it shall have been ratified as an amendment to the Constitution by the legislatures of three-fourths of the several States within seven years from the date of its submission. [February 6, 1933]

AMENDMENT XXI.

Section 1. The eighteenth article of amendment to the Constitution of the United States is hereby repealed.

Section 2. The transportation or importation into any State, Territory or possession of the United States for delivery or use therein of intoxicating liquors, in violation of the laws thereof, is hereby prohibited.

Section 3. This article shall be inoperative unless it shall have been ratified as an amendment to the Constitution by convention in the several States, as provided in the Constitution, within seven years from the date of the submission thereof to the States by the Congress. [December 5, 1933]

AMENDMENT XXII.

Section 1. No person shall be elected to the office of the President more than twice, and no person who has held the office of President, or acted as President, for more than two years of a term to which some other person was elected President shall be elected to the office of the President more than once. But this

Article shall not apply to any person holding the office of President when this Article was proposed by the Congress, and shall not prevent any person who may be holding the office of President, or acting as President, during the term within which this Article becomes operative from holding the office of President or acting as President during the remainder of such term.

Section 2. This article shall be inoperative unless it shall have been ratified as an amendment to the Constitution by the legislatures of three-fourths of the several States within seven years from the date of its submission to the States by the Congress. [February 27, 1951]

AMENDMENT XXIII.

Section 1. The District constituting the seat of government of the United States shall appoint in such manner as the Congress may direct:

A number of electors of President and Vice-President equal to the whole number of Senators and Representatives in Congress to which the District would be entitled if it were a State, but in no event more than the least populous State; they shall be in addition to those appointed by the States, but they shall be considered, for the purposes of the election of President and Vice-President, to be electors appointed by a State; and they shall meet in the District and perform such duties as provided by the twelfth article of amendment.

Section 2. The Congress shall have the power to enforce this article by appropriate legislation. [March 29, 1961]

AMENDMENT XXIV.

Section 1. The right of citizens of the United States to vote in any primary or other election for President or Vice President, for electors for President or Vice President, or for Senator or Representative in Congress, shall not be denied or abridged by the United States or any State by reason of failure to pay any poll tax or other tax.

Section 2. The Congress shall have power to enforce this article by appropriate legislation. [January 23, 1964]

AMENDMENT XXV.

Section 1. In case of the removal of the President from office or of his death or resignation, the Vice President shall become President.

Section 2. Whenever there is a vacancy in the office of Vice President, the President shall nominate a Vice President who shall take office upon confirmation by a majority vote of both Houses of Congress.

Section 3. Whenever the President transmits to the President pro tempore of the Senate and the Speaker of the House of Representatives his written declaration that he is unable to discharge the powers and duties of his office, and until he transmits to them a written declaration to the contrary, such powers and duties shall be discharged by the Vice President as Acting President.

Section 4. Whenever the Vice President and a majority of either the principal officers of the executive departments or of such other body as Congress may by law provide, transmit to the President pro tempore of the Senate and the Speaker of the House of Representatives their written declaration that the President is unable to discharge the powers and duties of his office, the Vice President shall immediately assume the powers and duties of the office as Acting President.

Thereafter, when the President transmits to the President pro tempore of the Senate and the Speaker of the House of Representatives his written declaration that no inability exists, he shall resume the powers and duties of his office unless the Vice President and a majority of either the principal officers of the executive departments or of such other body as Congress may by law provide, transmit within four days to the President pro tempore of the Senate and the Speaker of the House of Representatives their written declaration that the President is unable to discharge the powers and duties of his office. Thereupon Congress shall decide the issue, assembling within forty-eight hours for that purpose if not in session. If the Congress, within twenty-one days after receipt of the latter written declaration, or, if Congress is not in session, within twenty-one days after Congress is required to assemble, determines by two-thirds vote of both Houses that the President is unable to discharge the powers and duties of his office, the Vice-President shall continue to discharge the same as Acting President; otherwise, the President shall resume the powers and duties of his office. [February 10, 1967]

AMENDMENT XXVI.

Section 1. The right of citizens of the United States, who are eighteen years of age or older, to vote shall not be denied or abridged by the United States or by any State on account of age.

Section 2. The Congress shall have power to enforce this article by appropriate legislation. [June 30, 1971]

AMENDMENT XXVII.

No law, varying the compensation for the services of the Senators and Representatives shall take effect, until an election of Representatives shall have intervened. [May 8, 1992]

GLOSSARY

abolition Social movement of the pre–Civil War era that advocated the immediate emancipation of the slaves and their incorporation into American society as equal citizens.

Act Concerning Religion (or Maryland Toleration Act) 1649 law that granted free exercise of religion to all Christian denominations in colonial Maryland.

Adkins v. Children's Hospital 1923 Supreme Court case that reversed *Muller v. Oregon*, the 1908 case that permitted states to set maximum hours to protect working women; justices ruled in *Adkins* that women no longer deserved special treatment because they could vote.

affirmative action Policy efforts to promote greater employment opportunities for minorities.

Agricultural Adjustment Act New Deal legislation passed in 1933 that established the Agricultural Adjustment Administration (AAA) to improve agricultural prices by limiting market supplies; declared unconstitutional in *United States v. Butler* (1936).

Albany Plan of Union A failed 1754 proposal by the seven northern British colonies in anticipation of the Seven Years' War, urging the unification of the colonies under one crown-appointed president.

Alien and Sedition Acts Four measures passed in 1798 during the undeclared war with France that limited the freedoms of speech and press and restricted the liberty of noncitizens.

America First Committee An influential organization led by prominent businessmen (1940–1941) opposed to American involvement in World War II.

American Anti-Slavery Society Founded in 1833, the organization that sought an immediate end to slavery and the establishment of equality for Black Americans. It split in 1840 after disputes about the role of women within the organization and other issues.

American Civil Liberties Union Organization founded during World War I to protest the suppression of freedom of expression in wartime; played a major role in court cases that achieved judicial recognition of Americans' civil liberties.

American Colonization Society Organized in 1816 to encourage emigration of free Blacks to Africa; West African nation of Liberia founded in 1822 to serve as a homeland for them.

American Federation of Labor A federation of trade unions founded in 1881 composed mostly of skilled, white, native-born workers; its long-term president was Samuel Gompers.

American Indian Movement (AIM) Movement founded in 1963 by Native Americans who were fed up with the poor conditions on Indian reservations and the federal government's unwillingness to help. In 1973, the American Indian Movement led 200 Lakota in the occupation of Wounded Knee. After a ten-week standoff with the federal authorities, the government agreed to re-examine Indian treaty rights and the occupation ended.

"American standard of living" The Progressive-era idea that American workers were entitled to a wage high enough to allow them full participation in the nation's mass consumption economy.

American System Program of internal improvements and protective tariffs promoted by Speaker of the House Henry Clay in his presidential campaign of 1824; his proposals formed the core of Whig ideology in the 1830s and 1840s.

American system of manufactures A system of production that relied on the mass production of interchangeable parts that could be rapidly assembled into standardized finished products; first perfected in Connecticut by clockmaker Eli Terry and by small-arms producer Eli Whitney in the 1840s and 1850s.

Americans with Disabilities Act 1990 law that prohibits the discrimination against persons with disabilities in both hiring and promotion. It also mandates accessible entrances for public buildings.

Amistad Ship that transported slaves from one port in Cuba to another, seized by the slaves in 1839. They made their way northward to the United States, where the status of the slaves became the subject of a celebrated court case; eventually most were able to return to Africa.

Anglican Church The established state church of England, formed by Henry VIII after the pope refused to annul his marriage to Catherine of Aragon.

Anglo-Powhatan War Three wars fought between the Powhatans and the Jamestown colonists in 1610–1614, 1622–1626, and 1644–1646.

annuity system System of yearly payments to Native American nations by which the federal government justified and institutionalized its interference in Indian tribal affairs.

Antietam, Battle of One of the bloodiest battles of the Civil War, fought to a standoff on September 17, 1862, in western Maryland.

Anti-Federalists Opponents of the Constitution who saw it as a limitation on individual and states' rights; their demands led to the addition of a Bill of Rights to the document.

Anti-Imperialist League Coalition of anti-imperialist groups united in 1899 to protest American territorial expansion, especially in the Philippine Islands; its membership included prominent politicians, industrialists, labor leaders, and social reformers.

Appomattox Courthouse, Virginia Site of the surrender of Confederate general Robert E. Lee to Union general Ulysses S. Grant on April 9, 1865, marking the end of the Civil War.

Army-McCarthy hearings Televised U.S. Senate hearings in 1954 on Senator Joseph McCarthy's charges of disloyalty in the army; his tactics contributed to his censure by the Senate.

Articles of Confederation First frame of government for the United States; in effect from 1781 to 1788, it provided for a weak central authority and was soon replaced by the Constitution.

Atlanta Compromise Speech to the Cotton States and International Exposition in 1895 by educator Booker T. Washington, the leading Black spokesman of the day; Black scholar W. E. B. Du Bois gave the speech its derisive name and criticized Washington for encouraging Blacks to accommodate segregation and disenfranchisement.

Atlantic Charter Agreement issued August 12, 1941, following meetings in Newfoundland between President Franklin D. Roosevelt and British Prime Minister Winston Churchill, that signaled the Allies' cooperation and stated their war aims.

Atlantic slave trade The systematic importation of African people from their native continent across the Atlantic Ocean to the Americas, fueled largely by rising demand for sugar, rice, coffee, and tobacco.

Attucks, Crispus One of the protesters against British troops who was killed during the Boston Massacre.

Axis powers In World War II, the nations of Germany, Italy, and Japan.

Aztec The Mesoamerican empire ruled by the Mexica people that was defeated by the Spanish under Hernán Cortés and his Native allies, 1519–1528.

baby boom Markedly higher birthrate in the years following World War II; led to the biggest demographic "bubble" in American history.

backcountry In colonial America, the area stretching from central Pennsylvania southward through the Shenandoah Valley of Virginia and into upland North and South Carolina.

Bacon's Rebellion Unsuccessful 1676 revolt led by planter Nathaniel Bacon against British Governor of Virginia William Berkeley's administration.

Balkan crisis A series of ethnic and political crises that arose following the dissolution of Yugoslavia in the 1990s. Many atrocities were committed during the conflict, and NATO, the United Nations, and the United States intervened several times.

Bandung Conference A 1955 meeting of leaders from twenty-nine Asian and African nations that signaled the new visibility of the "third world," those nations allied with neither of the two Cold War superpowers, who desired to find their own model of economic development.

Bank of the United States Proposed by the first secretary of the treasury, Alexander Hamilton, the bank that opened in 1791 and operated until 1811 to issue a uniform currency, make business loans, and collect tax monies. The Second Bank of the United States was chartered in 1816, but President Andrew Jackson vetoed the recharter bill in 1832.

Bank War Political struggle in the early 1830s between President Jackson and financier Nicholas Biddle over the renewing of the Second Bank's charter.

Barbary Wars The first wars fought by the United States, and the nation's first encounter with the Islamic world. The wars were fought from 1801 to 1805 against plundering pirates off the Mediterranean coast of Africa after President Thomas Jefferson's refusal to pay them tribute to protect American ships.

Bargain of 1877 Deal made by a Republican and Democratic special congressional commission to resolve the disputed presidential election of 1876; Republican Rutherford B. Hayes, who had lost the popular vote, was declared the winner in exchange for the withdrawal of federal troops from involvement in politics in the South, marking the end of Reconstruction.

Bay of Pigs invasion U.S. mission in which the CIA, hoping to inspire a revolt against Fidel Castro, sent 1,500 Cuban exiles to invade their homeland on April 17, 1961; the mission was a spectacular failure.

Beats, the A term coined by Jack Kerouac for a small group of poets and writers who railed against 1950s' mainstream culture.

Bill for Establishing Religious Freedom A Virginia law, drafted by Thomas Jefferson in 1777 and enacted in 1786, that guarantees freedom of, and from, religion.

Bill of Rights First ten amendments to the U.S. Constitution, adopted in 1791 to guarantee individual rights against infringement by the federal government.

birth-control movement An offshoot of the early twentieth-century feminist movement that saw access to birth control and "voluntary motherhood" as essential to women's freedom. The birth-control movement was led by Margaret Sanger.

Black Codes Laws passed from 1865 to 1866 in southern states to restrict the rights of former slaves; to nullify the codes, Congress passed the Civil Rights Act of 1866 and the Fourteenth Amendment.

Black Legend Idea that the Spanish empire was more oppressive toward Indians than other European empires; used as a justification for English imperial expansion.

Black Lives Matter Civil rights movement sparked by a series of incidents of police brutality and lethal force against people of color.

Black Power Post-1966 rallying cry of a more militant civil rights movement.

"Bleeding Kansas" Violence between pro- and antislavery settlers in the Kansas Territory, 1856.

bonanza farms Large farms that covered thousands of acres and employed hundreds of wage laborers in the West in the late nineteenth century.

borderland A place between or near recognized borders where no group of people has complete political control or cultural dominance.

Boston Massacre Clash between British soldiers and a Boston mob, March 5, 1770, in which five colonists were killed.

Boston Tea Party The incident on December 16, 1773, in which the Sons of Liberty dumped hundreds of chests of tea into Boston Harbor to protest the Tea Act of 1773. Under the Tea Act, the British exported to the colonies millions of pounds of cheap—but still taxed—tea, thereby undercutting the price of smuggled tea and forcing payment of the tea duty.

***bracero* program** System agreed to by Mexican and American governments in 1942 under which tens of thousands of Mexicans entered the United States to work temporarily in agricultural jobs in the Southwest; lasted until 1964 and inhibited labor organization among farm workers since *braceros* could be deported at any time.

Brant, Joseph Mohawk military, political, and diplomatic leader who led the Haudenosaunee against the rebelling British colonists in the Revolutionary War; brother of Molly Brant.

Brant, Molly Mohawk leader who coordinated efforts with the British and with Loyalists during the Revolutionary War in Haudenosaunee country; sister of Joseph Brant.

Bretton Woods conference International meeting held in the town of Bretton Woods, New Hampshire, in 1944 in which participants agreed that the American dollar would replace the British pound as the most important international currency. The conference also created the World Bank and International Monetary Fund to promote rebuilding after World War II and to ensure that countries did not devalue their currencies.

Brook Farm Transcendentalist commune in West Roxbury, Massachusetts, populated from 1841 to 1847 principally by writers (Nathaniel Hawthorne, for one) and other intellectuals.

Brown v. Board of Education 1954 U.S. Supreme Court decision that struck down racial segregation in public education and declared "separate but equal" unconstitutional.

Bull Run, first Battle of The first land engagement of the Civil War, which took place on July 21, 1861, at Manassas Junction, Virginia, and at which Union troops quickly retreated.

Bull Run, second Battle of Civil War engagement that took place one year after the first Battle of Bull Run, on August 29–30, during which Confederates captured the federal supply depot at Manassas Junction, Virginia, and forced Union troops back to Washington.

Bunker Hill, Battle of First major battle of the Revolutionary War; it actually took place at nearby Breed's Hill, Massachusetts, on June 17, 1775.

Bush Doctrine President George W. Bush's foreign policy principle wherein the United States would launch a war on terrorism.

Bush v. Gore U.S. Supreme Court case that determined the winner of the disputed 2000 presidential election.

busing The means of transporting students via buses to achieve school integration in the 1970s.

Camp David Accords Peace agreement between the leaders of Israel and Egypt, brokered by President Carter in 1978.

Capitol attack A pro-Trump group of protesters stormed the Capitol on January 6, 2021, to disrupt the certification of the 2020 presidential election results. The violent assault on the nation's capital led to Trump's impeachment by the House of Representatives one week later. After a brief trial, however, the Senate voted against conviction.

captivity narratives Accounts written by colonists after their time in Indian captivity, often stressing the captive's religious convictions.

caravel A fifteenth-century European ship capable of long-distance travel.

carpetbaggers Derisive term for northern emigrants who participated in the Republican governments of the Reconstruction South.

checks and balances A systematic balance to prevent any one branch of the national government from dominating the other two branches.

Chinese Exclusion Act 1882 law that halted Chinese immigration to the United States.

Church of Jesus Christ of Latter-Day Saints Religious sect founded in 1830 by Joseph Smith; it was a product of the intense revivalism of the "burned-over district" of New York. Smith's successor Brigham Young led 15,000 followers to Utah in 1847 to escape persecution.

Civil Rights Act 1964 law that banned discrimination in public accommodations and employment.

Civil Rights Act of 1875 The last piece of Reconstruction legislation, which outlawed racial discrimination in places of public accommodation such as hotels and theaters. Many parts of the act were ruled unconstitutional by the Supreme Court in 1883.

Civil Rights Bill of 1866 Along with the Fourteenth Amendment, legislation that guaranteed the rights of citizenship to former slaves.

Civil Service Act of 1883 Law that established the Civil Service Commission and marked the end of the spoils system.

Civilian Conservation Corps (CCC) 1933 New Deal public work relief program that provided outdoor manual work for unemployed men, rebuilding infrastructure and implementing conservation programs. The program cut the unemployment rate, particularly among young men.

Cold War Term for tensions between the Soviet Union and the United States, the two major world powers after World War II, lasting from 1945 to 1989.

collective bargaining The process of negotiations between an employer and a group of employees to regulate working conditions.

Columbian Exchange The transatlantic flow of goods and people that began with Columbus's voyages in 1492.

Committee of Correspondence Group organized by Samuel Adams in retaliation for the *Gaspée* incident to address American grievances, assert American rights, and form a network of rebellion.

common school Tax-supported state schools of the early nineteenth century open to all children.

Common Sense A pamphlet anonymously written by Thomas Paine in January 1776 that attacked the English principles of hereditary rule and monarchical government.

Commonwealth v. Hunt Landmark 1842 ruling of the Massachusetts Supreme Court establishing the legality of labor unions.

communitarianism Social reform movement of the nineteenth century driven by the belief that by establishing small communities based on common ownership of property, a less competitive and less individualistic society could be developed.

Compromise of 1850 Complex compromise devised by Senator Henry Clay that admitted California as a free state, included a stronger fugitive slave law, and delayed determination of the slave status of the New Mexico and Utah territories.

Congress of Industrial Organizations Umbrella organization of semiskilled industrial unions formed in 1935 as the Committee for Industrial Organization and renamed in 1938.

conquistadores Spanish term for "conquerors," applied to Spanish and Portuguese soldiers who conquered lands held by Indigenous peoples in central and southern America as well as the current states of Florida, Texas, New Mexico, Arizona, and California.

conservation movement A progressive reform movement that focused on the preservation and sustainable management of the nation's natural resources.

Constitutional Convention Meeting in Philadelphia, May 25–September 17, 1787, of representatives from twelve colonies—excepting Rhode Island—to revise the existing Articles of Confederation; the convention soon resolved to produce an entirely new constitution.

containment General U.S. strategy in the Cold War that called for containing Soviet expansion; originally devised by U.S. diplomat George F. Kennan.

Continental army Army authorized by the Continental Congress in 1775 to fight the British; commanded by General George Washington.

Continental Congress First meeting of representatives of the colonies, held in Philadelphia in 1774 to formulate actions against British policies; in the Second Continental Congress (1775–1789), the colonial representatives conducted the war and adopted the Declaration of Independence and the Articles of Confederation.

"the contrabands" Slaves who sought refuge in Union military camps or who lived in areas of the Confederacy under Union control.

Contract with America A list of conservatives' promises in response to the supposed liberalism of the Clinton administration, that was drafted by Speaker of the House Newt Gingrich and other congressional Republicans as the GOP platform for the 1994 midterm elections. It was more a campaign tactic than a practical program; few of its proposed items ever became law.

cotton gin Invented by Eli Whitney in 1793, the machine that separated cotton seed from cotton fiber, speeding cotton processing and making profitable the cultivation of the more hardy, but difficult to clean, short-staple cotton; led directly to the dramatic nineteenth-century expansion of slavery in the South.

"Cotton is king" Phrase from Senator James Henry Hammond's speech extolling the virtues of cotton and, implicitly, the slave system of production that led to its bounty for the South. "King Cotton" became a shorthand phrase for southern political and economic power.

Cotton Kingdom Cotton-producing region, relying predominantly on slave labor, which spanned from North Carolina west to Louisiana and reached as far north as southern Illinois.

counterculture "Hippie" youth culture of the 1960s, which rejected the values of the dominant culture in favor of illicit drugs, communes, free sex, and rock music.

Court packing President Franklin D. Roosevelt's failed 1937 attempt to increase the number of U.S. Supreme Court justices from nine to fifteen in order to save his Second New Deal programs from constitutional challenges.

Covenant Chain Alliance formed in the 1670s between the English colony of New York and the Haudenosaunee League and eventually other colonies and Native nations.

coverture Principle in English and U.S. law that a married woman lost her legal identity, which became "covered" by that of her husband, who therefore controlled her person and the family's economic resources.

Covid-19 A highly contagious virus that emerged in early 2020, leading to a global pandemic. By 2022, the virus had led to the deaths of one million Americans. The United States had a higher recorded death rate than most other countries.

Coxey's Army A march on Washington organized by Jacob Coxey, an Ohio member of the People's Party. Coxey believed in abandoning the gold standard and printing enough legal tender to reinvigorate the economy. The marchers demanded that Congress create jobs and pay workers in paper currency not backed by gold.

creoles Persons born in the Americas of European ancestry.

crop lien Credit extended by merchants to tenants based on their future crops; under this system, high interest rates and the uncertainties of farming often led to inescapable debts.

Cuban missile crisis Tense confrontation caused when the United States discovered Soviet offensive missile sites in Cuba in October 1962; the U.S.-Soviet confrontation was the Cold War's closest brush with nuclear war.

cult of domesticity The nineteenth-century ideology of "virtue" and "modesty" as the qualities that were essential to proper womanhood.

Culture Wars Battles over moral values that occurred throughout the 1990s. The Culture Wars touched many areas of American life—from popular culture to academia. Flashpoints included the future of the nuclear family and the teaching of evolution.

Dartmouth College v. Woodward 1819 U.S. Supreme Court case in which the Court upheld the original charter of the college against New Hampshire's attempt to alter the board of trustees; set the precedent of support of contracts against state interference.

Daughters of Liberty Organization formed by women in 1767 to protest against the British by boycotting British goods, making replacement products such as homespun cloth, and publicizing their efforts to encourage others.

Dawes Act Law passed in 1887 meant to encourage adoption of white norms among Indians; broke up tribal holdings into small farms for Indian families, with the remainder sold to white purchasers.

D-Day June 6, 1944, when an Allied amphibious assault landed on the Normandy coast and established a foothold in Europe, leading to the liberation of France from German occupation.

Declaration of Independence Document adopted on July 4, 1776, that made the break with Britain official; drafted by a committee of the Second Continental Congress, including principal writer Thomas Jefferson.

decolonization The process by which African and Asian colonies of European empires became independent in the years following World War II.

Defense of Marriage Act 1996 law that barred gay couples from receiving federal benefits; ruled unconstitutional in 2013.

deindustrialization Term describing decline of manufacturing in old industrial areas in the late twentieth century as companies shifted production to low-wage centers in the South and West or in other countries.

Deism Enlightenment thought applied to religion; emphasized reason, morality, and natural law.

Democracy in America Two works, published in 1835 and 1840, by the French thinker Alexis de Tocqueville on the subject of American democracy. Tocqueville stressed the cultural nature of American democracy and the importance and prevalence of equality in American life.

Democratic-Republican societies Organizations created in the mid-1790s by opponents of the policies of the Washington administration and supporters of the French Revolution.

Denmark Vesey's conspiracy An 1822 failed slave uprising in Charleston, South Carolina, purported to have been led by Denmark Vesey, a free Black man.

deregulation Legislation during the Reagan-Clinton era that removed regulations on many industries, including finance and air travel.

détente Period of improving relations between the United States and Communist nations, particularly China and the Soviet Union, during the Nixon administration.

disenfranchisement Depriving a person or persons of the right to vote; in the United States, exclusionary policies were used to deny groups, especially African Americans and women, their voting rights.

Dissenters Protestants who belonged to denominations outside of the established Anglican Church.

division of powers The division of political power between the state and federal governments under the U.S. Constitution (also known as federalism).

Dix, Dorothea An important figure in increasing the public's awareness of the plight of the mentally ill. After a two-year investigation of the treatment of the mentally ill in Massachusetts, she presented her findings and won the support of leading reformers. She eventually convinced twenty states to reform their treatment of the mentally ill.

Dixiecrats Lower South delegates who walked out of the 1948 Democratic national convention in protest of the party's support for civil rights legislation and later formed the States' Rights Democratic (Dixiecrat) Party, which nominated Strom Thurmond of South Carolina for president.

Dollar Diplomacy A foreign policy initiative under President William Howard Taft that promoted the spread of American influence through loans and economic investments from American banks.

Dominion of New England Consolidation into a single colony of the New England colonies—and later New York and New Jersey—by royal governor Edmund Andros in 1686; dominion reverted to individual colonial governments three years later.

"Don't ask, don't tell" President Clinton's compromise measure that allowed gay people to serve in the military incognito, as officers could no longer seek them out for dismissal but they could not openly express their identity. "Don't ask, don't tell" was ended under the Obama administration, when gay military service was allowed.

Dorr War A movement in Rhode Island against property qualifications for voting. The movement formed an extralegal constitutional convention for the state and elected Thomas Dorr as a governor but was quashed by federal troops dispatched by President John Tyler.

double-V Led by the *Pittsburgh Courier*, the movement that pressed for victory over fascism abroad and over racism at home. It argued that since African Americans were risking their lives abroad, they should receive full civil rights at home.

dower rights In colonial America, the right of a widowed woman to inherit one-third of her deceased husband's property.

Dred Scott v. Sandford 1857 U.S. Supreme Court decision in which Chief Justice Roger B. Taney ruled that Congress could not prohibit slavery in the territories, on the grounds that such a prohibition would violate the Fifth Amendment rights of slaveholders, and that no Black person could be a citizen of the United States.

Dust Bowl Great Plains counties where millions of tons of topsoil were blown away from parched farmland in the 1930s; massive migration of farm families followed.

Eighteenth Amendment Prohibition amendment passed in 1919 that made illegal the manufacture, sale, or transportation of alcoholic beverages; repealed in 1933.

Ellis Island Reception center in New York Harbor through which most European immigrants to America were processed from 1892 to 1954.

Emancipation Proclamation Declaration issued by President Abraham Lincoln; the preliminary proclamation on September 22, 1862, freed the slaves in areas under Confederate control as of January 1, 1863, the date of the final proclamation, which also authorized the enrollment of Black soldiers into the Union army.

Embargo Act Attempt in 1807 to exert economic pressure by prohibiting all exports from the United States instead of waging war in reaction to continued British impressment of American sailors; smugglers easily circumvented the embargo, and it was repealed two years later.

Emergency Banking Act Passed in 1933, the First New Deal measure that provided for reopening the banks under strict conditions and took the United States off the gold standard.

empire of liberty The idea, expressed by Jefferson, that the United States would expand liberty as it spread west across the continent. White Americans who moved west would eventually be able to apply for admission into the United States as full member states.

enclosure movement A legal process that divided large farm fields in England that were previously collectively owned by groups of peasants into smaller, individually owned plots. The enclosure movement took place over several centuries and resulted in eviction for many peasants.

Enforcement Acts Three laws passed in 1870 and 1871 that tried to eliminate the Ku Klux Klan by outlawing it and other such terrorist societies; the laws allowed the president to deploy the army for that purpose.

English Bill of Rights A series of laws enacted in 1689 that inscribed the rights of English men into law and enumerated parliamentary powers such as taxation.

English liberty The idea that English men were entitled to certain liberties, including trial by jury, habeas corpus, and the right to face one's accuser in court. These rights meant that even the English king was subject to the rule of law.

English Toleration Act A 1690 act of Parliament that allowed all English Protestants to worship freely.

Enlightenment Revolution in thought in the eighteenth century that emphasized reason and science over the authority of traditional religion.

Equal Rights Amendment An amendment to guarantee equal rights for women, introduced in 1923 but not passed by Congress until 1972; it failed to be ratified by the states.

Era of Good Feelings Contemporary characterization of the administration of popular Republican president James Monroe, 1817–1825.

Erie Canal Most important and profitable of the canals of the 1820s and 1830s; stretched from Buffalo to Albany, New York, connecting the Great Lakes to the East Coast and making New York City the nation's largest port.

Espionage Act 1917 law that prohibited spying and interfering with the draft as well as making "false statements" that hurt the war effort.

ethnic cleansing The systematic removal of an ethnic group from a territory through violence or intimidation in order to create a homogeneous society; the term was popularized by the Yugoslav policy brutally targeting Albanian Muslims in Kosovo.

eugenics The study of the alleged mental and physical characteristics of different groups of people aiming to "improve" the quality of the human race through selective breeding.

Ex parte Milligan 1866 Supreme Court case that declared it unconstitutional to bring accused persons before military tribunals where civil courts were operating.

Exposition and Protest Document written in 1828 by Vice President John C. Calhoun of South Carolina to protest the so-called tariff of abominations, which seemed to favor northern industry; introduced the concept of state interposition and became the basis for South Carolina's Nullification Doctrine of 1833.

Fair Deal Domestic reform proposals of the Truman administration; included civil rights legislation, national health insurance, and repeal of the Taft-Hartley Act, but only extensions of some New Deal programs were enacted.

family values Set of beliefs usually associated with conservatism that stressed the superiority of the nuclear family, heterosexual marriage, and traditional gender roles.

family wage Idea that male workers should earn a wage sufficient to enable them to support their entire family without their wives having to work outside the home.

Federal Housing Administration (FHA) A government agency created during the New Deal to guarantee mortgages, allowing lenders to offer long-term (usually thirty-year) loans with low down payments (usually 10 percent of the asking price). The FHA seldom underwrote loans in racially mixed or minority neighborhoods.

Federal Trade Commission (FTC) Independent agency created by the Wilson administration that replaced the Bureau of Corporations as an even more powerful tool to combat unfair trade practices and monopolies.

federalism A system of government in which power is divided between the central government and the states.

Federalist, The Collection of eighty-five essays that appeared in the New York press in 1787–1788 in support of the Constitution; written by Alexander Hamilton, James Madison, and John Jay and published under the pseudonym "Publius."

Federalists and Republicans The two increasingly coherent political parties that appeared in Congress by the mid-1790s. The Federalists, led by George Washington, John Adams, and Alexander Hamilton, favored a strong central government. The Republicans supported a strict interpretation of the Constitution, which they believed would safeguard individual freedoms and states' rights from the threats posed by a strong central government.

Feminine Mystique, The The book widely credited with sparking second-wave feminism in the United States. Author Betty Friedan focused on college-educated women, arguing that they would find fulfillment by engaging in paid employment outside the home.

feminism Term that entered the lexicon in the early twentieth century to describe the movement for full equality for women, in political, social, and personal life.

Fifteenth Amendment Constitutional amendment ratified in 1870, which prohibited states from discriminating in voting privileges on the basis of race.

flappers Young women of the 1920s whose rebellion against prewar standards of femininity included wearing shorter dresses, bobbing their hair, dancing to jazz music, driving cars, smoking cigarettes, and indulging in illegal drinking and gambling.

George Floyd's murder A Minneapolis Black man killed by police on May 25, 2020. A video captured a police officer kneeling on Floyd's neck as he pleaded for air, leading to a wave of protest and calls for police reform.

Force Act 1833 legislation, sparked by the nullification crisis in South Carolina, authorizing the president's use of the army to compel states to comply with federal law.

Fordism Early twentieth-century term describing the economic system pioneered by Ford Motor Company based on high wages and mass consumption.

Fort McHenry Fort in Baltimore Harbor unsuccessfully bombarded by the British in September 1814; Francis Scott Key, a witness to the battle, was moved to write the words to "The Star-Spangled Banner."

Fort Sumter First battle of the Civil War, in which the federal fort in Charleston (South Carolina) Harbor was captured by the Confederates on April 14, 1861, after two days of shelling.

Four Freedoms Freedom of speech, freedom of worship, freedom from want, and freedom from fear, as described by President Franklin D. Roosevelt during his January 6, 1941, State of the Union address.

Fourteen Points President Woodrow Wilson's 1918 plan for peace after World War I; at the Versailles peace conference, however, he failed to incorporate all of the points into the treaty.

Fourteenth Amendment 1868 constitutional amendment that guaranteed rights of citizenship to former slaves, in words similar to those of the Civil Rights Act of 1866.

franchise The right to vote.

free Blacks African American persons not held in slavery; immediately before the Civil War, there were nearly a half million free Blacks in the United States, split almost evenly between North and South.

Free Soil Party Political organization formed in 1848 to oppose slavery in the territory acquired in the Mexican War; nominated Martin Van Buren for president in 1848. By 1854 most of the party's members had joined the Republican Party.

free trade The belief that economic development arises from the exchange of goods between different countries without governmental interference.

Freedmen's Bureau Reconstruction agency established in 1865 to protect the legal rights of former slaves and to assist with their education, jobs, health care, and landowning.

freedom petitions Arguments for liberty presented to courts and legislatures starting in the early 1770s by enslaved African Americans.

Freedom Rides Bus journeys challenging racial segregation in the South in 1961.

French and Indian War The last—and most important—of four colonial wars fought between England and France for control of North America east of the Mississippi River.

Fugitive Slave Act 1850 law that gave the federal government authority in cases involving runaway slaves; aroused considerable opposition in the North.

fugitive slaves Slaves who escaped from their owners.

fundamentalism Anti-modernist Protestant movement started in the early twentieth century that proclaimed the literal truth of the Bible; the name came from *The Fundamentals*, published by conservative leaders.

Gabriel's Rebellion An 1800 uprising planned by Virginian slaves to gain their freedom. The plot led by a blacksmith named Gabriel was discovered and quashed.

Gadsden Purchase Thirty thousand square miles in present-day Arizona and New Mexico bought by Congress from Mexico in 1853 primarily for the Southern Pacific Railroad's transcontinental route.

gag rule Rule adopted by the House of Representatives in 1836 prohibiting consideration of abolitionist petitions; opposition, led by former president John Quincy Adams, succeeded in having it repealed in 1844.

Garvey, Marcus The leading spokesman for Negro Nationalism, which exalted Blackness, Black cultural expression, and Black exclusiveness. He called upon African Americans to liberate themselves from the surrounding white culture and create their own businesses, cultural centers, and newspapers. He was also the founder of the Universal Negro Improvement Association.

Geneva Accords A 1954 document that had promised elections to unify Vietnam and established the Seventeenth Parallel demarcation line that divided North and South Vietnam.

"gentlemen of property and standing" Well-to-do merchants who often had commercial ties to the South and resisted abolitionism, occasionally inciting violence against its adherents.

Gettysburg, Battle of Battle fought in southern Pennsylvania, July 1–3, 1863; the Confederate defeat and the simultaneous loss at Vicksburg marked the military turning point of the Civil War.

Ghost Dance A spiritual and political movement among Native Americans whose followers performed a ceremonial "ghost dance" intended to connect the living with the dead and make the Indians bulletproof in battles intended to restore their homelands.

GI Bill of Rights The 1944 legislation that provided money for education and other benefits to military personnel returning from World War II.

Gibbons v. Ogden 1824 U.S. Supreme Court decision reinforcing the "commerce clause" (the federal government's right to regulate interstate commerce) of the Constitution; Chief Justice John Marshall ruled against the State of New York's granting of steamboat monopolies.

Gilded Age The popular but derogatory name for the period from the end of the Civil War to the turn of the century, after the title of the 1873 novel by Mark Twain and Charles Dudley Warner.

globalization Term that became prominent in the 1990s to describe the rapid acceleration of international flows of commerce, financial resources, labor, and cultural products.

Glorious Revolution A coup in 1688 engineered by a small group of aristocrats that led to William of Orange taking the British throne in place of James II.

gold rush The massive migration of Americans into California territory in the late 1840s and 1850s in pursuit of gold, which was discovered there in 1848.

gold standard Policy at various points in American history by which the value of a dollar was set at a fixed price in terms of gold (in the post–World War II era, for example, $35 per ounce of gold).

gradual emancipation A series of acts passed in state legislatures in the North in the years following the Revolution that freed slaves after they reached a certain age, following lengthy "apprenticeships."

grandfather clause Loophole created by southern disenfranchising legislatures of the 1890s for illiterate white males whose grandfathers had been eligible to vote before the Civil War.

Great Awakening Fervent religious revival movement in the 1720s through the 1740s that was spread in the colonies by ministers like New England Congregationalist Jonathan Edwards and English revivalist George Whitefield.

Great Depression Worst economic depression in American history; it was spurred by the stock market crash of 1929 and lasted until World War II.

Great League of Peace An alliance of the Haudenosaunee (Iroquois) nations, originally formed at least 400 years ago. Each year the Haudenosaunee Great Council, with male representatives chosen by the women of the five (and later six) nations, met to coordinate dealings with outsiders. The League was a major force in the 1600s and 1700s.

Great Migration Large-scale migration of southern Blacks during and after World War I to the North, where jobs had become available during the labor shortage of the war years.

Great Migration (1630s) The migration of approximately 21,000 English Puritans to the Massachusetts Bay Colony.

Great Railroad Strike A series of demonstrations, some violent, held nationwide in support of striking railroad workers in Martinsburg, West Virginia, who refused to work due to wage cuts.

Great Recession A period of major economic stagnation across the United States and western Europe, characterized by rising unemployment and inflation and a 37 percent decline in the stock market between March and December 1974.

Great Society Term coined by President Lyndon B. Johnson in his 1965 State of the Union address, in which he proposed legislation to address problems of voting rights, poverty, diseases, education, immigration, and the environment.

Griswold v. Connecticut Supreme Court decision that, in overturning Connecticut law prohibiting the use of contraceptives, established a constitutional right to privacy.

Guantánamo Bay A detention center at the American naval base at Guantánamo Bay,

Cuba, where beginning in 2002 suspected terrorists and war prisoners were held indefinitely and tried by extrajudicial military tribunals. During his 2008 presidential campaign, Senator Barack Obama pledged to close the prison, but as of 2015 it remained open.

Gulf of Tonkin resolution Legislation passed by Congress in 1964 in reaction to supposedly unprovoked attacks on American warships off the coast of North Vietnam; it gave the president unlimited authority to defend U.S. forces and members of SEATO.

Gulf oil spill Environmental disaster that occurred in 2010 after an explosion on the *Deepwater Horizon* oil rig. Hundreds of millions of gallons of oil were spilled into the Gulf of Mexico, resulting in one of the largest environmental calamities in human history.

Gulf War Military action in 1991 in which an international coalition led by the United States drove Iraq from Kuwait, which it had occupied the previous year.

hacienda Large-scale farm in the Spanish empire worked by Native American laborers.

Haitian Revolution A revolution by enslaved people that led to the establishment of Haiti as an independent country in 1804.

Half-Way Covenant A 1662 religious compromise that allowed baptism and partial church membership to colonial New Englanders whose parents were not among the Puritan elect.

Harlem Renaissance African American literary and artistic movement of the 1920s centered in New York City's Harlem neighborhood; writers Langston Hughes, Jean Toomer, Zora Neale Hurston, and Countee Cullen were among those active in the movement.

Harpers Ferry, Virginia Site of abolitionist John Brown's failed raid on the federal arsenal,

October 16–17, 1859; Brown became a martyr to his cause after his capture and execution.

Hart-Celler Act 1965 law that eliminated the national origins quota system for immigration established by laws in 1921 and 1924; led to radical change in the origins of immigrants to the United States, with Asians and Latin Americans outnumbering Europeans.

Hartford Convention Meeting of New England Federalists on December 15, 1814, to protest the War of 1812; proposed seven constitutional amendments (limiting embargoes and changing requirements for officeholding, declaration of war, and admission of new states), but the war ended before Congress could respond.

Haymarket affair Violence during an anarchist protest at Haymarket Square in Chicago on May 4, 1886; the deaths of eight, including seven policemen, led to the trial of eight anarchist leaders for conspiracy to commit murder.

Haynes, Lemuel A Black member of the Massachusetts militia and celebrated minister who urged that Americans extend their conception of freedom to enslaved Africans during the Revolutionary era.

headright system A land-grant policy that promised fifty acres to any colonist who could afford passage to Virginia, as well as fifty more for any accompanying servants. The headright policy was eventually expanded to include any colonists and was also adopted in other colonies.

Helsinki Accords 1975 agreement between the USSR and the United States that recognized the post–World War II boundaries of Europe and guaranteed the basic liberties of each nation's citizens.

Hessians German soldiers, most from Hesse-Cassel principality (hence, the name),

paid to fight for the British in the Revolutionary War.

Hollywood Ten A group called before the House Un-American Activities Committee who refused to speak about their political leanings or "name names"—that is, identify communists in Hollywood. Some were imprisoned as a result.

Holocaust Systematic racist attempt by the Nazis to exterminate the Jews of Europe, resulting in the murder of over 6 million Jews and more than a million other "undesirables."

Homestead Act 1862 law that authorized Congress to grant 160 acres of public land to a western settler, who had to live on the land for five years to establish title.

horizontal expansion The process by which a corporation acquires or merges with its competitors.

House of Burgesses The first elected assembly in colonial America established in 1619 in Virginia. Only wealthy landowners could vote in its elections.

House Un-American Activities Committee (HUAC) Committee formed in 1938 to investigate subversives in the government and holders of radical ideas more generally; best-known investigations were of Hollywood notables and of former State Department official Alger Hiss, who was accused in 1948 of espionage and Communist Party membership; abolished in 1975.

Hundred Days Extraordinarily productive first three months of President Franklin D. Roosevelt's administration in which a special session of Congress enacted fifteen of his New Deal proposals.

Hurricane Katrina 2005 hurricane that devastated much of the Gulf Coast, especially New

Orleans. The Bush administration's response was widely criticized as inadequate.

illegal alien A new category established by the Immigration Act of 1924 that referred to immigrants crossing U.S. borders in excess of the new immigration quotas.

Immigration Restriction League A political organization founded in 1894 that called for reducing immigration to the United States by requiring a literacy test for immigrants.

impeachment Bringing charges against a public official; for example, the House of Representatives can impeach a president for "treason, bribery, or other high crimes and misdemeanors" by majority vote, and after the trial the Senate can remove the president by a vote of two-thirds. Although three presidents, Andrew Johnson, Bill Clinton, and Donald Trump, were impeached and tried before the Senate, none were convicted.

impressment The British navy's practice of using press-gangs to kidnap men in British and colonial ports who were then forced to serve in the British navy.

"In God We Trust" Phrase placed on all new U.S. currency as of 1954.

indentured servants Settlers who signed on for a temporary period of servitude to a master in exchange for passage to the New World; Virginia and Pennsylvania were largely peopled in the seventeenth and eighteenth centuries by English and German indentured servants.

Indian Citizenship Act 1924 act that conferred American citizenship to all non-citizen Indians born within U.S. territorial boundaries.

Indian New Deal Phrase that refers to the reforms implemented for Native Americans during the New Deal era. John Collier, the commissioner of the Bureau of Indian Affairs (BIA), increased the access Native Americans had to relief programs and employed more Native Americans at the BIA. He worked to pass the Indian Reorganization Act. However, the version of the act passed by Congress was a much diluted version of Collier's original proposal and did not greatly improve the lives of Native Americans.

Indian Removal Act An 1830 law signed by President Andrew Jackson that permitted the negotiation of treaties to obtain Native Americans' lands in exchange for their deportation to what would become Oklahoma.

Indian Urban Relocation Program This federal program during the 1950s and 1960s encouraged Indians to move from reservation lands to cities for better economic opportunity. Although the program was ended after facing criticism for moving Indians from rural poverty to urban poverty, Indian urbanization continued.

individualism Term that entered the language in the 1820s to describe the increasing emphasis on the pursuit of personal advancement and private fulfillment free of outside interference.

Industrial Workers of the World Radical union organized in Chicago in 1905 and nicknamed the Wobblies; its opposition to World War I led to its destruction by the federal government under the Espionage Act.

inflation An economic condition in which prices rise continuously.

initiative A Progressive-era reform that allowed citizens to propose and vote on laws, bypassing state legislatures.

Insular Cases Series of cases between 1901 and 1904 in which the Supreme Court ruled that constitutional protection of individual rights did not fully apply to residents of "insular" territories acquired by the United States in the Spanish-American War, such as Puerto Rico and the Philippines.

Interstate Commerce Commission Organization established by Congress, in reaction to the U.S. Supreme Court's ruling in *Wabash Railroad v. Illinois* (1886), in order to curb abuses in the railroad industry by regulating rates.

interstate highway system National network of interstate superhighways; its construction began in the late 1950s for the purpose of commerce and defense. The interstate highways would enable the rapid movement of military convoys and the evacuation of cities after a nuclear attack.

Intolerable Acts Four parliamentary measures in reaction to the Boston Tea Party that forced payment for the tea, disallowed colonial trials of British soldiers, forced their quartering in private homes, and reduced the number of elected officials in Massachusetts.

Iran-Contra Affair Scandal of the second Reagan administration involving sales of arms to Iran in partial exchange for release of hostages in Lebanon and use of the arms money to aid the Contras in Nicaragua, which had been expressly forbidden by Congress.

Iraq War Military campaign in 2003 in which the United States, unable to gain approval by the United Nations, unilaterally occupied Iraq and removed dictator Saddam Hussein from power.

iron curtain Term coined by Winston Churchill to describe the Cold War divide between western Europe and the Soviet Union's eastern European satellites.

ISIS An insurgency that emerged from the sectarian civil wars that destabilized Syria and post–Saddam Hussein Iraq. Beginning in 2014, ISIS forces attacked towns and cities in Iraq, Syria, and Libya, systematically murdering members of ethnic and religious minorities.

isolationism The desire to avoid foreign entanglements that dominated the U.S. Congress in the 1930s; beginning in 1935, lawmakers passed a series of Neutrality Acts that banned travel on belligerents' ships and the sale of arms to countries at war.

Japanese American internment Policy adopted by the Roosevelt administration in 1942 under which 110,000 persons of Japanese descent, most of them American citizens, were removed from the West Coast and forced to spend most of World War II in internment camps; it was the largest violation of American civil liberties in the twentieth century.

Jay's Treaty Treaty with Britain negotiated in 1794 by Chief Justice John Jay; Britain agreed to vacate forts in the Northwest Territories, and festering disagreements (such as the border with Canada, prewar debts, and shipping claims) would be settled by commission.

Kansas Exodus A migration in 1879 and 1880 by some 40,000–60,000 Blacks to Kansas to escape the oppressive environment of the New South.

Kansas-Nebraska Act 1854 law sponsored by Illinois senator Stephen A. Douglas to allow settlers in newly organized territories north of the Missouri border to decide the slavery issue for themselves; fury over the resulting repeal of the Missouri Compromise of 1820 led to violence in Kansas and to the formation of the Republican Party.

"King Cotton diplomacy" An attempt during the Civil War by the South to encourage British intervention by banning cotton exports.

King Philip's War (Metacom's War) A multiyear conflict that began in 1675 between the English and a Native alliance led by Wampanoags Metacom (King Philip) and Weetamoo. Its end result was broadened freedoms for white New Englanders and the dispossession of the Wampanoags and other Indians.

Knights of Labor Founded in 1869, the first national union; it lasted, under the leadership of Terence V. Powderly, only into the 1890s; supplanted by the American Federation of Labor.

Know-Nothing Party Nativist, anti-Catholic third party organized in 1854 in reaction to large-scale German and Irish immigration; the party's only presidential candidate was Millard Fillmore in 1856.

Korean War Conflict touched off in 1950 when communist North Korea invaded South Korea; fighting, largely by U.S. forces, continued until 1953.

Korematsu v. United States 1944 Supreme Court case that found Executive Order 9066 to be constitutional. Fred Korematsu, an American-born citizen of Japanese descent, defied the military order that banned all persons of Japanese ancestry from designated western coastal areas. The Court upheld Korematsu's arrest and internment.

Ku Klux Klan Group organized in Pulaski, Tennessee, in 1866 to terrorize former slaves who voted and held political offices during Reconstruction; a revived organization in the 1910s and 1920s that stressed white, Anglo-Saxon, fundamentalist Protestant supremacy; revived a third time to fight the civil rights movement of the 1950s and 1960s in the South.

Las Casas, Bartolomé de A Catholic missionary who renounced the Spanish practice of coercively converting Indians and advocated their better treatment. In 1552, he wrote *A Brief Relation of the Destruction of the Indies*, which described the cruel treatment of the Indians by the Spanish.

League of Nations Organization of nations to mediate disputes and avoid war, established after World War I as part of the Treaty of Versailles; President Woodrow Wilson's "Fourteen Points" speech to Congress in 1918 proposed the formation of the league, which the United States never joined.

League of United Latin American Citizens Often called LULAC, an organization that challenged restrictive housing, employment discrimination, and other inequalities faced by Latino Americans.

Lend-Lease Act 1941 law that permitted the United States to lend or lease arms and other supplies to the Allies, signifying the increasing likelihood of American involvement in World War II.

Levittown Low-cost, mass-produced developments of suburban tract housing built by William Levitt after World War II on Long Island in New York and elsewhere.

Lewis and Clark expedition Led by Meriwether Lewis and William Clark, a mission to the Pacific coast commissioned for the purposes of scientific and geographical exploration.

Lexington and Concord, Battles of The first shots fired in the Revolutionary War, on April 19, 1775, near Boston; approximately 100 minutemen and 250 British soldiers were killed.

liberal internationalism Woodrow Wilson's foreign policy theory, which rested on the idea that economic and political freedom went hand in hand, and encouraged American intervention abroad in order to secure these freedoms globally.

liberalism Originally, political philosophy that emphasized the protection of liberty by limiting the power of government to interfere with the natural rights of citizens; in the twentieth century, belief in an activist government promoting greater social and economic equality.

liberty of contract A judicial concept of the late nineteenth and early twentieth centuries whereby the courts overturned laws regulating labor conditions as violations of the economic freedom of both employers and employees.

Liberty Party Abolitionist political party that nominated James G. Birney for president in 1840 and 1844; merged with the Free Soil Party in 1848.

Lincoln-Douglas debates Series of senatorial campaign debates in 1858 focusing on the issue of slavery in the territories; held in Illinois between Republican Abraham Lincoln, who made a national reputation for himself, and incumbent Democratic senator Stephen A. Douglas, who managed to hold on to his seat.

Little Bighorn, Battle of the Most famous battle of the Black Hills War; took place in 1876 in the Montana Territory; Lakota and Cheyenne warriors massacred a vastly outnumbered U.S. Cavalry commanded by Lieutenant Colonel George Armstrong Custer.

Long Telegram A telegram by American diplomat George Kennan in 1946 outlining his views of the Soviet Union that eventually inspired the policy of containment.

Lord Dunmore's proclamation A proclamation issued in 1775 by the earl of Dunmore, the British governor of Virginia, that offered freedom to any men enslaved by rebels who volunteered to fight for the king.

Lords of Trade An English regulatory board established to oversee colonial affairs in 1675.

Lost Cause A romanticized view of slavery, the Old South, and the Confederacy that arose in the decades following the Civil War.

Lost Generation A group of writers and artists who came of age during World War I. Disillusioned with American values and culture, many moved to Europe during the 1920s.

Louisiana Purchase President Thomas Jefferson's 1803 purchase from France of the important port of New Orleans and 828,000 square miles west of the Mississippi River to the Rocky Mountains. In theory, it more than doubled the territory of the United States at a cost of only $15 million; in reality it was still the land of multiple Native nations.

Loyalists Colonists who remained loyal to Great Britain during the War of Independence.

Lusitania British passenger liner sunk by a German U-boat, May 7, 1915, creating a diplomatic crisis and public outrage at the loss of 128 Americans (roughly 10 percent of the total aboard); Germany agreed to pay reparations, and the United States waited two more years to enter World War I.

lynching Practice, particularly widespread in the South between 1890 and 1940, in which persons (usually Blacks) accused of a crime were murdered by mobs before standing trial. Lynchings often took place before large crowds, with law enforcement authorities not intervening.

Manhattan Project Secret American program during World War II to develop an atomic bomb; J. Robert Oppenheimer led the team of physicists at Los Alamos, New Mexico.

manifest destiny Phrase first used in 1845 to urge annexation of Texas; used thereafter to encourage U.S. settlement of European colonial and Native lands in the Great Plains and the West and, more generally, as a justification for American empire.

Marbury v. Madison First U.S. Supreme Court decision to declare a federal law—the Judiciary Act of 1801—unconstitutional.

March for Our Lives Student-led protest on March 24, 2018, against gun violence and for gun control legislation in the United States.

March on Washington Civil rights demonstration on August 28, 1963, where the Reverend Martin Luther King Jr. gave his "I Have a Dream" speech on the steps of the Lincoln Memorial.

Marshall Plan U.S. program for the reconstruction of post–World War II Europe through massive aid to former enemy nations as well as allies; proposed by General George C. Marshall in 1947.

massive retaliation Strategy that used the threat of nuclear warfare as a means of combating the global spread of communism.

maternalist reforms Progressive-era reforms that sought to encourage women's childbearing and childrearing abilities and to promote their economic independence.

Mayflower Compact Document signed in 1620 aboard the *Mayflower* before the Pilgrims landed at Plymouth; the document committed the group to majority-rule government by its male colonists.

McCarran-Walter Act Immigration legislation passed in 1952 that allowed the government to deport immigrants who had been identified as communists, regardless of whether or not they were citizens.

McCarthyism Post–World War II Red Scare focused on the fear of Communists in U.S. government positions; peaked during the Korean War; most closely associated with Joseph McCarthy, a major instigator of the hysteria.

McCulloch v. Maryland 1819 U.S. Supreme Court decision in which Chief Justice John Marshall, holding that Maryland could not tax the Second Bank of the United States, supported the authority of the federal government versus the states.

mercantilism Policy of Great Britain and other imperial powers of regulating the economies of colonies to benefit the mother country.

mestizos Spanish word for persons of mixed Native American and European ancestry.

Metacom Wampanoag leader whom the colonists called King Philip; he led a war against the English colonists, one in which he was killed.

métis Children of marriages between Native American women and French men.

Me Too movement Social movement founded in 2006 by Tarana Burke to help survivors of sexual violence and oppose sexual harassment and assault, particularly in the workplace. In October 2017 it went viral on social media with #MeToo.

Mexican War Controversial war with Mexico for control of California and New Mexico, 1846–1848; the Treaty of Guadalupe Hidalgo fixed the border at the Rio Grande and extended the United States to the Pacific coast, annexing more than a half-million square miles of Mexican territory.

Middle Passage The hellish and often deadly middle leg of the transatlantic "triangular trade" in which European ships carried manufactured goods to Africa, then transported enslaved Africans to the Americas and the Caribbean, and finally conveyed American agricultural products back to Europe; from the late sixteenth to the early nineteenth centuries, some 12 million Africans were transported via the Middle Passage, unknown millions more dying en route.

military-industrial complex The concept of "an immense military establishment" combined with a "permanent arms industry," which President Eisenhower warned against in his 1961 Farewell Address.

mill girls Women who worked at textile mills during the industrial revolution who enjoyed new freedoms and independence not seen before.

Missouri Compromise Deal proposed by Kentucky senator Henry Clay in 1820 to resolve the slave/free imbalance in Congress that would result from Missouri's admission as a slave state; Maine's admission as a free state offset Missouri, and slavery was prohibited in the remainder of the Louisiana Territory north of the southern border of Missouri.

Monroe Doctrine President James Monroe's declaration to Congress on December 2, 1823, that the American continents would be thenceforth closed to European colonization, and that the United States would not interfere in European affairs.

Montgomery bus boycott Sparked by Rosa Parks's arrest on December 1, 1955, for refusing to surrender her seat to a white passenger, a successful yearlong boycott protesting segregation on city buses; led by the Reverend Martin Luther King Jr.

moral imperialism The Wilsonian belief that U.S. foreign policy should be guided by morality and should teach other peoples about democracy. Wilson used this belief to both repudiate Dollar Diplomacy and justify frequent military interventions in Latin America.

Moral Majority An organization of evangelical religious conservatives founded in 1979 to promote conservative social values. Though disbanded in 1989, it helped to establish the Christian Right as an important force within the Republican Party.

moral suasion The abolitionist strategy that sought to end slavery by persuading both slaveowners and complicit northerners that the institution was evil.

muckraking Writing that exposed corruption and abuses in politics, business, meatpacking, child labor, and more, primarily in the first decade of the twentieth century; included popular books and magazine articles that spurred public interest in reform.

Muller v. Oregon 1908 Supreme Court decision that held that state interest in protecting women could override liberty of contract. Louis D. Brandeis, with help from his sister-in-law Josephine Goldmark of the National Consumers League, filed a brief in *Muller* that used statistics about women's health to argue for their protection.

multiculturalism Term that became prominent in the 1990s to describe a growing emphasis on group racial and ethnic identity and demands that jobs, education, and politics reflect the increasingly diverse nature of American society.

Murray, Judith Sargent A writer and early feminist thinker prominent in the years following the American Revolution.

My Lai massacre Massacre of 347 Vietnamese civilians in the village of My Lai by Lieutenant William Calley and troops under his command. U.S. army officers covered up the massacre for a year until an investigation uncovered the events. Eventually twenty-five army officers were charged with complicity in the massacre and its cover-up, but only Calley was convicted. He served little time for his crimes.

Natchez War War begun in 1729 by the Natchez Indians against the French who were building plantations on Natchez land. With help from Native allies, the French won the war and drove the Natchez from their homeland.

Nat Turner's Rebellion An 1831 insurrection in Southampton County, Virginia, led by an enslaved preacher, resulting in the death of about sixty white persons.

National Association for the Advancement of Colored People Founded in 1910, the civil rights organization that brought lawsuits against discriminatory practices and published *The Crisis*, a journal edited by African American scholar W. E. B. Du Bois.

National Defense Education Act 1958 law passed in reaction to America's perceived inferiority in the space race; encouraged education in science and modern languages through student loans, university research grants, and aid to public schools.

National Industrial Recovery Act 1933 law passed on the last of the Hundred Days; it created public-works jobs through the Federal Emergency Relief Administration and established a system of self-regulation for industry through the National Recovery Administration, which was later ruled unconstitutional in 1935.

National Organization for Women Organization founded in 1966 by writer Betty Friedan and other feminists; it pushed for abortion rights, nondiscrimination in the workplace, and other forms of equality for women.

National Recovery Administration (NRA) Controversial federal agency created in 1933 that brought together business and labor leaders to create "codes of fair competition" and "fair labor" policies, including a national minimum wage.

nativism Anti-immigrant and anti-Catholic feeling especially prominent from the 1830s through the 1850s; the largest group of its proponents was New York's Order of the Star-Spangled Banner, which expanded into the American (Know-Nothing) Party in 1854.

Navajo's Long Walk The forced removal of 8,000 Navajos from their lands by Union forces to a reservation in the 1860s.

Navigation Acts Law passed by the English Parliament to control colonial trade and bolster the mercantile system, 1651–1775; enforcement of the act led to growing resentment by colonists.

Neolin A Delaware Indian (Lenape) religious prophet who, by preaching Native American unity and rejection of European technology and commerce, helped inspire Pontiac's War.

Neutrality Acts Series of laws passed between 1935 and 1939 to keep the United States from becoming involved in war by prohibiting American trade and travel to warring nations.

New Deal Franklin D. Roosevelt's campaign promise, in his speech to the Democratic National Convention of 1932, to combat the Great Depression with a "new deal for the American people"; the phrase became a catchword for his ambitious plan of economic programs.

new feminism A new aspect of the women's rights movement that arose in the early part of the twentieth century. New feminism added a focus on individual and sexual freedom to the movement and introduced the word "feminism" into American life.

New Freedom Democrat Woodrow Wilson's political slogan in the presidential campaign of 1912; Wilson wanted to improve the banking system, lower tariffs, and, by breaking up monopolies, give small businesses freedom to compete.

New Harmony Community founded in Indiana by British industrialist Robert Owen in

1825; the short-lived New Harmony Community of Equality was one of the few nineteenth-century communal experiments not based on religious ideology.

new immigrants Wave of newcomers from southern and eastern Europe, including many Jews, who became a majority among immigrants to America after 1890.

New Jersey Plan New Jersey's delegation to the Constitutional Convention's plan for one legislative body with equal representation for each state.

New Left Radical youth protest movement of the 1960s, named by leader Tom Hayden to distinguish it from the Old (Marxist-Leninist) Left of the 1930s.

New Nationalism Platform of the Progressive Party and slogan of former president Theodore Roosevelt in the presidential campaign of 1912; stressed government activism, including regulation of trusts, conservation, and recall of state court decisions that had nullified progressive programs.

New Orleans, Battle of Last battle of the War of 1812, fought on January 8, 1815, weeks after the peace treaty was signed but prior to the news reaching America; General Andrew Jackson led the victorious American troops.

New South *Atlanta Constitution* editor Henry W. Grady's 1886 term for the prosperous post–Civil War South he envisioned: democratic, industrial, urban, and free of nostalgia for the defeated plantation South.

new world order President George H. W. Bush's term for the post–Cold War world.

Ninety-Five Theses The list of moral grievances against the Catholic Church by Martin Luther, a German priest, in 1517.

"No taxation without representation" The rallying cry of opponents to the 1765 Stamp Act. The slogan decried the colonists' lack of representation in Parliament.

North American Free Trade Agreement (NAFTA) Approved in 1993, the agreement with Canada and Mexico that allowed goods to travel across their borders free of tariffs. Critics of the agreement argued that American workers would lose their jobs to cheaper Mexican labor.

North Atlantic Treaty Organization (NATO) Alliance founded in 1949 by ten western European nations, the United States, and Canada to deter Soviet expansion in Europe.

Northwest Ordinance of 1787 Law that created the Northwest Territory (area north of the Ohio River and west of Pennsylvania), established conditions for self-government and statehood, included a Bill of Rights, and permanently prohibited slavery.

Notes on the State of Virginia Thomas Jefferson's 1785 book that claimed, among other things, that Black people were incapable of becoming citizens and living in harmony alongside white people due to the legacy of slavery and what Jefferson believed were the "real distinctions that nature has made" between races.

NSC-68 Top-secret policy paper approved by President Truman in 1950 that outlined a militaristic approach to combating the spread of global communism.

nullification crisis The 1832 attempt by the State of South Carolina to nullify, or invalidate within its borders, the 1832 federal tariff law. President Jackson responded with the Force Act of 1833.

Obergefell v. Hodges 2015 Supreme Court decision that allowed same-sex couples to marry throughout the United States.

...py Wall Street A grassroots movement
... against growing economic inequality,
...ng opportunity, and the depredations of
...et banks.

...o Prohibition on trade in oil
declared by the Organization of Petroleum
Exporting Countries, dominated by Middle
Eastern producers, in October 1973 in response
to U.S. and western European support for Israel
in the 1973 Yom Kippur War. The rise in gas
prices and fuel shortages resulted in a global
economic recession and profoundly affected
the American economy.

Olmstead v. United States 1928 Supreme
Court decision that allowed the federal government's use of wiretapping without a warrant
to prosecute suspected criminals.

Oneida Utopian community founded in 1848;
the Perfectionist religious group practiced
"complex marriage" under leader John Humphrey Noyes.

Open Door Policy Demand in 1899 by Secretary of State John Hay, in hopes of protecting
the Chinese market for U.S. exports, that
Chinese trade be open to all nations.

open immigration American immigration
laws under which nearly all white people
could immigrate to the United States and
become naturalized citizens.

Operation Dixie CIO's largely ineffective
post–World War II campaign to unionize
southern workers.

Ordinance of 1784 A law drafted by Thomas
Jefferson that regulated land ownership and
defined the terms by which western land
would be marketed and settled; it established
stages of self-government for the West. First
Congress would govern a territory; then the
territory would be admitted to the Union as a
full state.

Ordinance of 1785 A law that regulated land
sales in the Old Northwest. The land surveyed
was divided into 640-acre plots and sold at $1
per acre.

Oslo Accords 1993 roadmap for peace
between Israel and the newly created Palestinian Authority, negotiated under the Clinton
administration.

Panama Canal Zone The small strip of land
on either side of the Panama Canal; the Canal
Zone was under U.S. control from 1903 to 1979
as a result of Theodore Roosevelt's assistance
in engineering a coup in Colombia that established Panama's independence.

Panic of 1819 Financial collapse brought on
by sharply falling cotton prices, declining
demand for American exports, and reckless
western land speculation.

Panic of 1837 Beginning of major economic
depression lasting about six years; touched off
by a British financial crisis and made worse
by falling cotton prices, credit and currency
problems, and speculation in land, canals, and
railroads.

Paris Agreement 2016 agreement within the
United Nations Framework Convention on
Climate Change concerned with mitigating
greenhouse gas emissions.

paternalism A moral position developed
during the first half of the nineteenth century,
which claimed that slaves were deprived of
liberty for their own "good." Such a rationalization was adopted by some slaveowners to
justify slavery.

Paya Mataha Chickasaw military and diplo-
matic leader who worked during the era of the
American Revolution to make peace among
Native nations, including the Chickasaw,
Cherokee, and Choctaw, and tried to stay out of
Europeans' infighting.

"peculiar institution" A phrase used by whites in the antebellum South to refer to slavery without using the word "slavery."

Pentagon Papers Informal name for the Defense Department's secret history of the Vietnam conflict; leaked to the press by former official Daniel Ellsberg and published in the *New York Times* in 1971.

Pequot War An armed conflict in 1637 fought between the Pequot Indians and an alliance of Narragansett, Mohegan, and English. The Pequot loss led to most of them being killed, enslaved, or incorporated into other Native nations.

perfectionism The idea that social ills once considered incurable could in fact be eliminated, popularized by the religious revivalism of the nineteenth century.

Perry, Commodore Matthew U.S. naval officer who negotiated the Treaty of Kanagawa in 1854. That treaty was the first step in starting a political and commercial relationship between the United States and Japan.

pet banks Local banks that received deposits while the charter of the Bank of the United States was about to expire in 1836. The choice of these banks was influenced by political and personal connections.

Philippine War American military campaign that suppressed the movement for Philippine independence after the Spanish-American War; America's death toll was over 4,000 and that of the Philippines was far higher.

Pilgrims Puritan separatists who broke completely with the Church of England and sailed to the Americas aboard the *Mayflower*, founding Plymouth Colony on Cape Cod in 1620.

plantation An early word for a colony, a settlement "planted" from abroad among an alien population in Ireland or the Americas; later, a large agricultural enterprise that used unfree labor to produce a crop for the world market.

Platt Amendment 1901 amendment to the Cuban constitution that reserved the right of the United States to intervene in Cuban affairs and that forced newly independent Cuba to host American naval bases on the island.

Plessy v. Ferguson U.S. Supreme Court decision supporting the legality of Jim Crow laws that permitted or required "separate but equal" facilities for Blacks and whites.

Pontiac's War A war inspired by the Delaware prophet Neolin in which allied Native American fighters from the Ohio Valley and Great Lakes successfully attacked British forts and settlements after France ceded to the British its territory east of the Mississippi River as part of the Treaty of Paris in 1763. It helped lead to the Proclamation of 1763.

Popular Front A period during the mid-1930s when the Communist Party sought to ally itself with socialists and New Dealers in movements for social change, urging reform of the capitalist system rather than revolution.

popular sovereignty Program that allowed settlers in a disputed territory to decide the slavery issue for themselves; most closely associated with Senator Stephen A. Douglas of Illinois.

Populists Founded in 1892, a group that advocated a variety of reform issues, including free coinage of silver, income tax, postal savings, regulation of railroads, and direct election of U.S. senators.

Porkopolis Nickname of Cincinnati, coined in the mid-nineteenth century, after its numerous slaughterhouses.

Port Huron Statement A manifesto by Students for a Democratic Society that criticized institutions ranging from political parties to corporations, unions, and the military-industrial complex, while offering a new vision of social change.

Potsdam conference Last meeting of the major Allied powers; the conference that took place outside Berlin from July 17 to August 2, 1945, at which U.S. president Harry Truman, Soviet dictator Joseph Stalin, and British prime minister Clement Attlee finalized plans begun at Yalta.

pragmatism A philosophical movement that emerged in the late nineteenth century, which insisted that institutions and social policies should be judged by their practical effects, not their longevity or whether they reflected traditional religious or political beliefs.

Proclamation of 1763 Royal directive issued after the Seven Years' War and Pontiac's War prohibiting settlement, surveys, and land grants west of the Appalachian Mountains; caused considerable resentment among colonists hoping to move west.

Progressive Party Political party created when former president Theodore Roosevelt broke away from the Republican Party to run for president again in 1912. The party supported progressive reforms similar to those of the Democrats but stopped short of seeking to eliminate trusts; also the name of the party backing Robert La Follette for president in 1924.

Progressivism Broad-based reform movement, 1900–1917, that sought governmental action in solving problems in many areas of American life, including education, public health, the economy, the environment, labor, transportation, and politics.

proslavery argument The series of arguments defending the institution of slavery in the South as a positive good, not a necessary evil. The arguments included the racist belief that Black people were inherently inferior to white people, as well as the belief that slavery, in creating a permanent underclass of laborers, made freedom possible for whites. Other elements of the argument included biblical citations.

Public Works Administration A New Deal agency that contracted with private construction companies to build roads, bridges, schools, hospitals, and other public facilities.

Pueblo Revolt Uprising in 1680 by allied Pueblo led by Popé that temporarily drove Spanish colonists out of New Mexico.

Pure Food and Drug Act Passed in 1906, the first law to regulate manufacturing of food and medicines; prohibited dangerous additives and inaccurate labeling.

Puritans English religious group that sought to purify the Church of England; founded the Massachusetts Bay Colony under John Winthrop in 1630.

Radical Republicans Group within the Republican Party in the 1850s and 1860s that advocated strong resistance to the expansion of slavery, opposition to compromise with the South in the secession crisis of 1860–1861, emancipation and arming of Black soldiers during the Civil War, and equal civil and political rights for Blacks during Reconstruction.

Reagan Revolution The rightward turn of American politics following the 1980 election of Ronald Reagan; the Reagan Revolution made individual "freedom" a rallying cry for the right.

Reaganomics Popular name for President Ronald Reagan's philosophy of "supply-side" economics, which combined tax cuts with an unregulated marketplace.

recall A Progressive-era reform that allowed the removal of public officials by popular vote.

reconquista The "reconquest" of Spain from the Moors completed by King Ferdinand and Queen Isabella in 1492.

Reconstruction Act 1867 law that established temporary military governments in ten Confederate states—except Tennessee—and required that the states ratify the Fourteenth Amendment and permit freedmen to vote.

Reconstruction Finance Corporation Federal program established in 1932 under President Herbert Hoover to loan money to banks and other institutions to help them avert bankruptcy.

Red Scare of 1919–1920 Fear among many Americans after World War I of Communists in particular and noncitizens in general, a reaction to the Russian revolution, mail bombs, strikes, and riots.

Redeemers Post–Civil War Democratic leaders who supposedly saved the South from Yankee domination and preserved the primarily rural economy.

redemptioners Indentured families or persons who received passage to the New World in exchange for a promise to work off their debt in America.

referendum A Progressive-era reform that allowed public policies to be submitted to popular vote.

Regulators Groups of backcountry Carolina settlers who protested colonial policies.

repartimiento system Spanish labor system under which Indians were legally free and able to earn wages but were also required to perform a fixed amount of labor yearly; replaced the *encomienda* system.

repeal The campaign to make the manufacture, transportation, and sale of alcoholic beverages legal again by rescinding the Eighteenth Amendment.

republic Representative political system in which citizens govern themselves by electing representatives, or legislators, to make key decisions on the citizens' behalf.

republican motherhood The ideology that emerged as a result of American independence where women's political role was to train their sons to be future citizens.

republicanism Political theory in eighteenth-century England and America that celebrated active participation in public life by economically independent citizens as central to freedom.

Revolution of 1800 First time that an American political party surrendered power to the opposition party; Jefferson, a Republican, had defeated incumbent Adams, a Federalist, for president.

Roanoke colony Failed English attempt to establish a colony on Roanoke Island in the Outer Banks; the colony disappeared sometime between 1587 and 1590.

robber barons Also known as "captains of industry"; Gilded Age industrial figures who inspired both admiration, for their economic leadership and innovation, and hostility and fear, due to their unscrupulous business methods, repressive labor practices, and unprecedented economic control over entire industries.

Roe v. Wade 1973 U.S. Supreme Court decision requiring states to permit first-trimester abortions.

Roosevelt Corollary 1904 announcement by President Theodore Roosevelt, essentially a corollary to the Monroe Doctrine, stating that the United States could intervene militarily to prevent interference from European powers in the Western Hemisphere.

Rwandan genocide 1994 genocide conducted by the Hutu ethnic group upon the Tutsi minority in Rwanda.

Sacco-Vanzetti case A case held during the 1920s in which two Italian American anarchists were found guilty and executed for a crime in which there was very little evidence linking them to the particular crime.

Salem witch trials A crisis of trials and executions in Salem, Massachusetts, in 1692 that resulted from anxiety over witchcraft.

salutary neglect Informal British policy during the first half of the eighteenth century that allowed the American colonies considerable freedom to pursue their economic and political interests in exchange for colonial obedience.

Sanitary Fairs Fund-raising bazaars led by women on behalf of Civil War soldiers; the fairs offered items such as uniforms and banners, as well as other emblems of war.

Santa Anna, Antonio López de The military leader who, in 1834, seized political power in Mexico and became a dictator. In 1835, Texans rebelled against him, and he led his army to Texas to crush their rebellion. He captured the mission called the Alamo and killed all of its defenders, which inspired Texans to continue their resistance and Americans to volunteer to fight for Texas. The Texans captured Santa Anna during a surprise attack, and he bought his freedom by signing a treaty recognizing Texas's independence.

Saratoga, Battle of Major defeat of British general John Burgoyne and more than 5,000 British troops at Saratoga, New York, on October 17, 1777.

scalawags Southern white Republicans—some former Unionists—who supported Reconstruction governments.

Schenck v. United States 1919 U.S. Supreme Court decision upholding the wartime Espionage and Sedition Acts; in the opinion he wrote for the case, Justice Oliver Wendell Holmes set the now familiar "clear and present danger" standard.

scientific management Management campaign to improve worker efficiency using measurements like "time and motion" studies to achieve greater productivity; introduced by Frederick Winslow Taylor in 1911.

Scopes trial 1925 trial of John Scopes, Tennessee teacher accused of violating state law prohibiting teaching of the theory of evolution; it became a nationally celebrated confrontation between religious fundamentalism and civil liberties.

Scottsboro case Case in which nine Black youths were convicted of raping two white women; in overturning the verdicts of this case, the Court established precedents in *Powell v. Alabama* (1932) that adequate counsel must be appointed in capital cases, and in *Norris v. Alabama* (1935) that African Americans cannot be excluded from juries.

Sea Islands experiment The 1861 pre-Reconstruction social experiment that involved converting slave plantations into places where former slaves could work for wages or own land. Former slaves also received education and access to improved shelter and food.

Second American Revolution The transformation of American government and society brought about by the Civil War.

Second Great Awakening Religious revival movement of the early decades of the nineteenth century, in reaction to the growth of secularism and rationalist religion; began the predominance of the Baptist and Methodist churches.

second Great Migration The movement of Black migrants from the rural South to the cities of the North and West, which occurred from 1941 through World War II, that dwarfed the Great Migration of World War I.

Second Middle Passage The massive trade of slaves from the upper South (Virginia and the Chesapeake) to the lower South (the Gulf states) that took place between 1820 and 1860.

Sedition Act 1918 law that made it a crime to make spoken or printed statements that criticized the U.S. government or encouraged interference with the war effort.

Selective Service Act Law passed in 1917 to quickly increase enlistment in the army for the U.S. entry into World War I; required men to register with the draft.

"separate but equal" Principle underlying legal racial segregation, upheld in *Plessy v. Ferguson* (1896) and struck down in *Brown v. Board of Education* (1954).

separation of powers Feature of the U.S. Constitution, sometimes called "checks and balances," in which power is divided between executive, legislative, and judicial branches of the national government so that no one can dominate the other two and endanger citizens' liberties.

Serra, Father Junípero Missionary who began and directed the California mission system in the 1770s and 1780s. Serra presided over the conversion of many Indians to Christianity sometimes by force.

settlement house Late-nineteenth-century movement to offer a broad array of social services in urban immigrant neighborhoods; Chicago's Hull House was one of hundreds of settlement houses that operated by the early twentieth century.

Seven Years' War The last—and most important—of four colonial wars fought between England and France for control of North America east of the Mississippi River.

Seventeenth Amendment Progressive reform passed in 1913 that required U.S. senators to be elected directly by voters; previously, senators were chosen by state legislatures.

Shakers Religious sect founded by Mother Ann Lee in England; the United Society of Believers in Christ's Second Appearing settled in Watervliet, New York, in 1774, and subsequently established eighteen additional communes in the Northeast, Indiana, and Kentucky.

Share Our Wealth movement Program offered by Huey Long as an alternative to the New Deal. The program proposed to confiscate large personal fortunes, which would be used to guarantee every poor family a cash grant of $5,000 and every worker an annual income of $2,500. It also promised to provide pensions, reduce working hours, and pay veterans' bonuses and ensured a college education to every qualified student.

sharecropping Type of farm tenancy that developed after the Civil War in which landless workers—often former slaves—farmed land in exchange for farm supplies and a share of the crop.

Shays's Rebellion Attempt by Massachusetts farmer Daniel Shays and 1,200 compatriots, seeking debt relief through issuance of paper currency and lower taxes, to prevent courts from seizing property from indebted farmers.

Sherman Antitrust Act Passed in 1890, first law to restrict monopolistic trusts and business combinations; extended by the Clayton Antitrust Act of 1914.

Silent Spring 1962 book by biologist Rachel Carson about the destructive impact of the widely used insecticide DDT that launched the modern environmentalist movement.

single tax Concept of taxing only landowners as a remedy for poverty, promulgated by Henry George in *Progress and Poverty* (1879).

sit-down strike Tactic adopted by labor unions in the mid- and late 1930s, whereby striking workers refused to leave factories, making production impossible; proved highly effective in the organizing drive of the Congress of Industrial Organizations.

sit-in Tactic adopted by young civil rights activists, beginning in 1960, of demanding service at lunch counters or public accommodations and refusing to leave if denied access; marked the beginning of the most militant phase of the civil rights struggle.

Sixteenth Amendment Constitutional amendment passed in 1913 that legalized the federal income tax.

Slave Power The Republican and abolitionist term for proslavery dominance of southern and national governments.

Smith, John An English soldier and explorer who became one of the leaders of the Jamestown colony and helped to establish relations with the Powhatans. His narratives describe the early history of Jamestown as well as his explorations of what became New England.

Smoot-Hawley Tariff 1930 act that raised tariffs to an unprecedented level and worsened the Great Depression by raising prices and discouraging foreign trade.

Snowden, Edward An NSA contractor turned whistleblower, who released classified information relating to U.S. intelligence gathering both at home and abroad.

social contract Agreement hammered out between labor and management in leading industries; called a new "social contract." Unions signed long-term agreements that left decisions regarding capital investment, plant location, and output in management's hands, and they agreed to try to prevent unauthorized "wildcat" strikes.

Social Darwinism Application of Charles Darwin's theory of natural selection to society; used the concept of the "survival of the fittest" to justify class distinctions and to explain poverty.

Social Gospel Ideals preached by liberal Protestant clergymen in the late nineteenth and early twentieth centuries; advocated the application of Christian principles to social problems generated by industrialization.

Social Security Act 1935 law that created the Social Security system with provisions for a retirement pension, unemployment insurance, disability insurance, and public assistance (welfare).

Socialist Party Political party demanding public ownership of major economic enterprises in the United States as well as reforms like recognition of labor unions and woman suffrage; reached peak of influence in 1912 when presidential candidate Eugene V. Debs received over 900,000 votes.

Society of American Indians Organization founded in 1911 that brought together Native American intellectuals of many tribal backgrounds to promote discussion of the plight of Indian peoples.

Society of Friends (Quakers) Religious group in England and America whose members believed all persons possessed the "inner light" or spirit of God; they were early proponents of abolition of slavery and equal rights for women.

soft money and hard money In the 1830s, "soft money" referred to paper currency issued by banks. "Hard money" referred to gold and silver currency—also called specie.

Sons of Liberty Organization formed by Samuel Adams, John Hancock, and other radical men in response to the Stamp Act.

Sotomayor, Sonia First Supreme Court Justice of Hispanic descent. Justice Sotomayor was appointed by President Barack Obama in 2009.

Southern Christian Leadership Conference (SCLC) Civil rights organization founded in 1957 by the Reverend Martin Luther King Jr. and other civil rights leaders.

Southern Manifesto A document written in 1956 that repudiated the Supreme Court decision in *Brown v. Board of Education* and supported the campaign against racial integration in public places.

spoils system The custom of filling federal government jobs with persons loyal to the party of the president; originated in Andrew Jackson's first term.

Sputnik First artificial satellite to orbit the earth; launched October 4, 1957, by the Soviet Union.

stagflation A combination of stagnant economic growth and high inflation present during the 1970s.

Stamp Act Parliament's 1765 requirement that revenue stamps be affixed to all colonial printed matter, documents, and playing cards; the Stamp Act Congress met to formulate a response, and the act was repealed the following year.

staple crops Important cash crops; for example, cotton or tobacco.

steamboats Paddlewheelers that could travel both up- and down-river in deep or shallow waters; they became commercially viable early in the nineteenth century and soon developed into America's first inland freight and passenger service network.

stock market crash Also known as Black Tuesday, a stock market panic in 1929 that resulted in the loss of more than $10 billion in market value (worth approximately ten times more today); one among many causes of the Great Depression.

Stonewall Inn A gathering place for New York's gay community, the site of the 1969 police raids and resulting riots that launched the modern gay rights movement.

Stono Rebellion An uprising by enslaved men in 1739 in South Carolina that led to a severe tightening of the slave code and the temporary imposition of a prohibitive tax on imported slaves.

Strategic Arms Limitation Talks 1972 talks between President Nixon and Secretary Brezhnev that resulted in the Strategic Arms Limitation Treaty (or SALT), which limited the quantity of nuclear warheads each nation could possess, and prohibited the development of missile defense systems.

Student Nonviolent Coordinating Committee (SNCC) Organization founded in 1960 to coordinate civil rights sit-ins and other forms of grassroots protest.

Students for a Democratic Society (SDS) Major organization of the New Left, founded at the University of Michigan in 1960 by Tom Hayden and Al Haber.

suffrage The right to vote.

Sugar Act 1764 decision by Parliament to tax refined sugar and many other colonial products.

Sunbelt The label for an arc that stretched from the Carolinas to California; during the postwar era, much of the urban population growth occurred in this area.

Taft-Hartley Act 1947 law passed over President Harry Truman's veto; the law contained a number of provisions to weaken labor unions, including the banning of closed shops.

tariff of abominations Tariff passed in 1828 by Congress that taxed imported goods at a very high rate; aroused strong opposition in the South.

tariff of 1816 First true protective tariff, intended to protect certain American goods against foreign competition.

tax revolt Local and state anti-tax mobilizations in the late 1970s and early 1980s in the wake of economic decline, inflation, and rising property taxes. Lower tax rates resulted in reducing government funds for public services.

Tea Party A grassroots Republican movement that emerged in 2009 named for the Boston Tea Party of the 1770s. The Tea Party opposed the Obama administration's sweeping legislative enactments and advocated for a more stringent immigration policy.

Teapot Dome Harding administration scandal in which Secretary of the Interior Albert B. Fall profited from secret leasing to private oil companies of government oil reserves at Teapot Dome, Wyoming, and Elk Hills, California.

Tecumseh Shawnee diplomatic and military leader who followed the teachings of his brother Tenskwatawa and tried to unite all Indians into a confederation to resist white encroachment on their lands; his beliefs and leadership made him seem dangerous to the American government. He allied with the British during the War of 1812 and was killed at the Battle of the Thames.

Tejanos Texas settlers of Spanish or Mexican descent.

temperance movement A widespread reform movement, led by militant Christians, focused on reducing the use of alcoholic beverages.

Tennessee Valley Authority Administrative body created in 1933 to control flooding in the Tennessee River valley, provide work for the region's unemployed, and produce inexpensive electric power for the region.

Tenochtitlán The capital city of the Aztec empire; the city was built on marshy islands on the western side of Lake Tetzcoco, which is the site of present-day Mexico City.

Ten-Percent Plan of Reconstruction President Lincoln's proposal for reconstruction, issued in 1863, in which southern states would rejoin the Union if 10 percent of the 1860 electorate signed loyalty pledges, accepted emancipation, and had received presidential pardons.

Tenure of Office Act 1867 law that required the president to obtain Senate approval to remove any official whose appointment had also required Senate approval; President Andrew Johnson's violation of the law by firing Secretary of War Edwin Stanton led to Johnson's impeachment.

Tenskwatawa Shawnee religious prophet who called for complete Native American separation from whites and their goods and influence and resistance to the United States; brother of Tecumseh.

termination era Federal policies in the 1950s and early 1960s that aimed to diminish Native American self-governance and break up reservation lands. Several tribes, including the Menominee and the Klamath, were terminated with devastating economic consequences. (Some tribes later saw their trust status restored.)

Tet offensive Surprise attack by the Viet Cong and North Vietnamese during the Vietnamese New Year of 1968; turned American public opinion strongly against the war in Vietnam.

Texas revolt The 1830s rebellion of residents of the territory of Texas—many of them American emigrants—against Mexican control of the region.

Thirteenth Amendment Constitutional amendment adopted in 1865 that irrevocably abolished slavery throughout the United States.

Three Mile Island Nuclear power plant near Harrisburg, Pennsylvania, site of 1979 accident that released radioactive steam into the air; public reaction ended the nuclear power industry's expansion.

three-fifths clause A provision signed into the Constitution in 1787 that three-fifths of the enslaved population would be counted in determining each state's representation in the House of Representatives and its electoral votes for president.

Title IX Part of the Educational Amendments Act of 1972 that banned gender discrimination in higher education.

totalitarianism The term that describes aggressive, ideologically driven states that seek to subdue all of civil society to their control, thus leaving no room for individual rights or alternative values.

Townshend Acts 1767 parliamentary measures (named for the Chancellor of the Exchequer) that taxed tea and other commodities and established a Board of Customs Commissioners and colonial vice-admiralty courts.

Trail of Tears Cherokee's own term for their forced removal, 1838–1839, from the Southeast to Indian Territory (later Oklahoma). Of 18,000 at the start of the journey, at least 4,500 died.

transcendentalists Philosophy of a small group of mid-nineteenth-century New England writers and thinkers, including Ralph Waldo Emerson, Henry David Thoreau, and Margaret Fuller; they stressed personal and intellectual self-reliance.

transcontinental railroad First line across the continent from Omaha, Nebraska, to Sacramento, California, established in 1869 with the linkage of the Union Pacific and Central Pacific railroads at Promontory, Utah.

Treaty of Greenville A 1795 treaty under which representatives of twelve Native nations ceded most of Ohio and Indiana to the federal government.

Treaty of Paris Signed on September 3, 1783, the treaty that ended the Revolutionary War, recognized American independence from Britain, established the border between Canada and the United States, fixed the western border at the Mississippi River, and ceded Florida to Spain (without setting Florida's border).

Truman Doctrine President Harry S. Truman's program announced in 1947 of aid to European countries—particularly Greece and Turkey—threatened by communism.

trusts Companies combined to limit competition.

Tubman, Harriet Abolitionist who was born a slave, escaped to the North, and then returned to the South nineteen times and guided 300 slaves to freedom.

Tulsa massacre A race riot in 1921—the worst in American history—that occurred in Tulsa, Oklahoma, after a group of Black veterans tried to prevent a lynching. Over 300 African Americans were killed, and 10,000 lost their homes in fires set by white mobs.

Uncle Tom's Cabin Harriet Beecher Stowe's 1852 antislavery novel that popularized the abolitionist position.

Underground Railroad Operating in the decades before the Civil War, a clandestine system of routes and safehouses through which slaves were led to freedom in the North.

United Nations Organization of nations to maintain world peace established in 1945 and headquartered in New York.

urban renewal A series of policies supported by all levels of government that allowed local governments and housing authorities to demolish so-called blighted areas in urban centers to replace them with more valuable real estate usually reserved for white people.

USA Patriot Act A 2001 mammoth bill that conferred unprecedented powers on law enforcement agencies charged with preventing domestic terrorism, including the power to wiretap, read private messages, and spy on citizens.

U.S.S. *Maine* Battleship that exploded in Havana Harbor on February 15, 1898, resulting in 266 deaths; the American public, assuming that the Spanish had mined the ship, clamored for war, and the Spanish-American War was declared two months later.

utopian communities Ideal communities that offered innovative social and economic relationships to those who were interested in achieving salvation.

V-E Day May 8, 1945, the day World War II officially ended in Europe.

Versailles Treaty The treaty signed at the Versailles peace conference after World War I, which established President Woodrow Wilson's vision of an international regulating body, redrew parts of Europe and the Middle East, and assigned economically crippling war reparations to Germany but failed to incorporate all of Wilson's Fourteen Points.

vertical integration Company's avoidance of intermediaries by producing its own supplies and providing for distribution of its product.

Vicksburg, Battle of The fall of Vicksburg, Mississippi, to General Ulysses S. Grant's army on July 4, 1863, after two months of siege; a turning point in the war because it gave the Union control of the Mississippi River.

Vietnam Syndrome Belief that emerged after the end of the Vietnam War that the United States should be extremely cautious in deploying its military forces overseas.

Virginia and Kentucky resolutions Legislation passed in 1798 and 1799 by the Virginia and the Kentucky legislatures; written by James Madison and Thomas Jefferson in response to the Alien and Sedition Acts, the resolutions advanced the state-compact theory of the Constitution. Virginia's resolution called on the federal courts to protect free speech. Jefferson's draft for Kentucky stated that a state could nullify federal law, but this was deleted.

Virginia Company A joint-stock enterprise that King James I chartered in 1606; the company was to spread Christianity in the Americas as well as find ways to make a profit in it.

Virginia Plan Virginia's delegation to the Constitutional Convention's plan for a strong central government and a two-house legislature apportioned by population.

virtual representation The idea that the American colonies, although they had no actual representative in Parliament, were "virtually" represented by all members of Parliament.

Voting Rights Act Law passed in the wake of Martin Luther King Jr.'s Selma-to-Montgomery March in 1965; it authorized federal protection of the right to vote and permitted federal enforcement of minority voting rights in individual counties, mostly in the South.

Wade-Davis Bill Radical Republicans' 1864 plan for reconstruction that required loyalty oaths, abolition of slavery, repudiation of war debts, and denial of political rights to high-ranking Confederate officials; President Lincoln refused to sign the bill.

Wagner Act (National Labor Relations Act of 1935) Law that established the National Labor Relations Board and facilitated unionization by regulating employment and bargaining practices.

Walking Purchase An infamous 1737 purchase of Native American land in which Pennsylvanian colonists tricked the Delaware Indians, who had agreed to cede land equivalent to the distance a man could walk in thirty-six hours, but the colonists marked out an area using a team of runners.

war in Afghanistan War fought against the Taliban and Al Qaeda in Afghanistan following the attacks of September 11, 2001. It remains the longest war in American history.

War Industries Board Board run by financier Bernard Baruch that planned production and allocation of war materiel, supervised purchasing, and fixed prices, 1917–1919.

War of 1812 War fought with Britain, 1812–1814, over issues that included impressment of American sailors, interference with shipping, and collusion with Northwest Territory Indians; settled by the Treaty of Ghent in 1814.

War on Poverty Plan announced by President Lyndon B. Johnson in his 1964 State of the Union address; under the Economic Opportunity Bill signed later that year, Head Start, VISTA, and the Jobs Corps were created, and programs were created for students, farmers, and businesses in efforts to eliminate poverty.

war on terrorism Global crusade to root out anti-American, anti-Western Islamist terrorist cells; launched by President George W. Bush as a response to the 9/11 attacks.

War Powers Act Law passed in 1973, reflecting growing opposition to American involvement in the Vietnam War; required congressional approval before the president sent troops abroad.

Watergate Washington office and apartment complex that lent its name to the 1972–1974 scandal of the Nixon administration; when his knowledge of the break-in at the Watergate and subsequent cover-up were revealed, Nixon resigned the presidency under threat of impeachment.

water protectors A group of Native American activists who organized large-scale protests to block the construction of the Dakota Access pipeline on ancestral Lakota lands that provided the primary water supply to the Standing Rock reservation.

Wealth of Nations, The The 1776 work by economist Adam Smith that argued that the "invisible hand" of the free market directed economic life more effectively and fairly than governmental intervention.

Webster-Hayne debate U.S. Senate debate of January 1830 between Daniel Webster of Massachusetts and Robert Hayne of South Carolina over nullification and states' rights.

welfare state A term that originated in Britain during World War II to refer to a system of income assistance, health coverage, and social services for all citizens.

Whiskey Rebellion Violent protest by western Pennsylvania farmers against the federal excise tax on whiskey in 1794.

Wickersham Commission Established by Herbert Hoover in 1929, the commission was the first large-scale federal study of the problem of crime.

Wilmot Proviso Proposal to prohibit slavery in any land acquired in the Mexican War; defeated by southern senators, led by John C. Calhoun of South Carolina, in 1846 and 1847.

Winthrop, John Puritan leader and governor of the Massachusetts Bay Colony who resolved to use the colony as a refuge for persecuted Puritans and as an instrument of building a "wilderness Zion" in America.

woman suffrage Movement to give women the right to vote through a constitutional amendment, spearheaded by Susan B. Anthony and Elizabeth Cady Stanton's National Woman Suffrage Association.

Women's March International protest on January 21, 2017, for women's rights, LGBT rights, gender equality, and racial equality following the inauguration of President Donald Trump. It was the biggest single-day protest in U.S. history.

Worcester v. Georgia 1832 Supreme Court case that held that the Indian nations were distinct peoples who could not be dealt with by the states—instead, only the federal government could negotiate with them. President Jackson refused to enforce the ruling.

Works Progress Administration (WPA) Part of the Second New Deal; it provided jobs for millions of the unemployed on construction and arts projects.

Wounded Knee massacre Last incident of the Indian Wars; it took place in 1890 in the Dakota Territory, where the U.S. Cavalry killed over 200 Sioux men, women, and children.

writs of assistance One of the colonies' main complaints against Britain; the writs allowed unlimited search warrants without cause to look for evidence of smuggling.

XYZ affair Affair in which French foreign minister Talleyrand's three anonymous agents (designated X, Y, and Z) demanded payments to stop French plundering of American ships in 1797; refusal to pay the bribe was followed by two years of undeclared sea war with France (1798–1800).

Yalta conference Meeting of Franklin D. Roosevelt, Winston Churchill, and Joseph Stalin at a Crimean resort to discuss the postwar world on February 4–11, 1945; Joseph Stalin claimed large areas in eastern Europe for Soviet domination.

Yamasee War War between South Carolina and Yamasee and Muscogee Indians, aggravated by rising debts and slave traders' raids; although the Yamasee lost, the war resulted in the end of South Carolina's Indian slave trade.

yellow press Sensationalism in newspaper publishing that reached a peak in the circulation war between Joseph Pulitzer's *New York World* and William Randolph Hearst's *New York Journal* in the 1890s; the papers' accounts of events in Havana Harbor in 1898 led directly to the Spanish-American War.

yeoman farmers Small landowners (the majority of white families in the Old South) who farmed their own land and usually did not own slaves.

Yorktown, Battle of Last battle of the Revolutionary War; General Lord Charles Cornwallis along with over 7,000 British troops surrendered at Yorktown, Virginia, on October 17, 1781.

Zimmermann Telegram Telegram from the German foreign secretary to the German minister in Mexico, February 1917, instructing the minister to offer to recover Texas, New Mexico, and Arizona for Mexico if it would fight the United States to divert attention from Germany in the event that the United States joined the war.

zoot suit riots 1943 riots in which sailors on leave attacked Mexican American youths.

CREDITS

PHOTOS

Front Matter: Page 25: (Foner): Lynn Garafola; (DuVal): Kristen Chavez, UNC-Chapel Hill College of Arts & Sciences; (McGirr): (c) Tony Rinaldo. Chapter 1: Page 5: Cahokia Mounds State Historic Site, painting by William R. Iseminger; p. 8: Bridgeman Images; p. 17: Granger; p. 21: Science History Images / Alamy Stock Photo; p. 22: Unknown artist, Young Woman With a Harpsichord, 1735–50 Denver Art Museum: Gift of the Collection of Frederick and Jan Mayer, 2014.209. Photo courtesy of Denver Art Museum; p. 25: Bridgeman Images; p. 26: Science History Images / Alamy Stock Photo; p. 38: Granger; p. 39: akg-images. Chapter 2: Page 47: The Picture Art Collection / Alamy Stock Photo; p. 48: Woburn Abbey, Bedfordshire, UK / The Bridgeman Art Library; p. 50: Granger; p. 52: Museum of Art, Rhode Island School of Design. Gift of Robert Winthrop. Photography by Erik Gould; p. 56: National Portrait Gallery, Smithsonian Institution; transfer from the National Gallery of Art; gift of the A.W. Mellon Educational and Charitable Trust, 1942; p. 61: Alamy Stock Photo; p. 66: Courtesy of the John Carter Brown Library at Brown University; p. 68: Worcester Art Museum, Worcester, Massachusetts, Gift of William A. Savage / Bridgeman Images; p. 72: Library of Congress; p. 80: Mrs. Elizabeth Freake and Baby Mary, unknown artist, 1963.134, Worcester Art Museum / Bridgeman Images; p. 84: Scottish National Portrait Gallery / Bridgeman Images. Chapter 3: Page 97: Photograph © 2022 Museum of Fine Arts, Boston. All rights reserved. / Bequest of Maxim Karolik / Bridgeman Images; p. 99: Free Women of Color with Their Children and Servants in a Landscape, 1770-1796 (oil on canvas), Brunias, Agostino (1728-96) / Brooklyn Museum of Art, New York, USA / Gift of Mrs. Carl H. de Silver in memory of her husband, by exchange and gift of George S. Hellman, by exchange / Bridgeman Images; p. 101: 4X5 Coll-Lerner Fine Art II / Superstock; p. 109: The New York Public Library / Art Resource, NY; p. 117: Granger; p. 119: The Library Company of Philadelphia; p. 122:

Collection of the New-York Historical Society / Bridgeman Images; p. 126: Art Resource. Chapter 4: Page 134: Barry Lawrence Ruderman Antique Maps Inc. www.raremaps.com; p. 136: Library of Congress; p. 138: Maidun Collection / Alamy Stock Photo; p. 140: Granger; p. 143: Photo © Christie's Images / Bridgeman Images; p. 144: The Colonial Williamsburg Foundation. Gift of Abby Aldrich Rockefeller; p. 146: Schomburg Center for Research in Black Culture, Photographs and Prints Division, The New York Public Library; p. 149: Eileen Tweedy / REX / Shutterstock; p. 153: The Library Company of Philadelphia; p. 162: Granger; p. 166: Album / Alamy Stock Photo; p. 170: Library of Congress. Chapter 5: Page 182: US 10070.35. Houghton Library, Harvard University; p. 186: Library of Congress; p. 189: Library of Congress; p. 199: Courtesy, American Antiquarian Society; p. 202: Anne S.K. Brown Military Collection, Brown University; p. 203: Collection of the Smithsonian National Museum of African American History and Culture; p. 204: Historic Images / Alamy Stock Photo; p. 205: Image Courtesy of the Museum of the American Revolution; p. 210: Library of Congress. Chapter 6: Page 218: Gianni Dagli Orti / REX / Shutterstock; p. 221: Historical Society of Pennsylvania; p. 224: York County Historical Society, America, USA / The Bridgeman Art Library; p. 227: Library of Congress; p. 235: Corbis / Getty Images; p. 236: Collection of the New-York Historical Society; p. 239: The Colonial Williamsburg Foundation. Museum Purchase, The Friends of Colonial Williamsburg Collections Fund; p. 242: The New York Public Library Digital Collections; p. 243: MPI / Getty Images; p. 245: © The Trustees of the British Museum / Art Resource, NY. Chapter 7: Page 256: Courtesy, American Antiquarian Society; p. 262: Huntington Library and Art Gallery, San Marino, CA, / © The Huntington Library, Art Collections & Botanical Gardens / Bridgeman Images; p. 264: Courtesy of The Library of Virginia; p. 267: Library of Congress; p. 270: Collection of the New-York Historical Society/Bridgeman Images; p. 278: The Picture Art Collection / Alamy Stock

Photo; **p. 283:** Collection of the New-York Historical Society, USA / Bridgeman Images. **Chapter 8: Page 291:** Fenimore Art Museum, Cooperstown, New York, Gift of Stephen C. Clark, N0535.1948. Photograph by Richard Walker; **p. 292:** Division of Home and Community Life, National Museum of American History, Smithsonian Institution; **p. 297:** TopFoto.co.uk; **p. 305:** Photos 12 / Alamy; **p. 312:** Collection of the New-York Historical Society; **p. 315:** Royal Ontario Museum; **p. 318:** © Collection of the New-York Historical Society, USA / Bridgeman Images. **Chapter 9: Page 325:** The New York Public Library Digital Collections; **p. 330:** © Collection of the New-York Historical Society / Bridgeman Images; **p. 343:** Bishop Hill State Historic Site / Illinois Historic Preservation Agency; **p. 350:** The New York Public Library / Art Resource, NY; **p. 355:** Archivart / Alamy Stock Photo; **p. 359:** © Collection of the New-York Historical Society / Bridgeman Images; **p. 360:** Granger. **Chapter 10: Page 367:** Fenimore Art Museum, Cooperstown, New York, Gift of Stephen C. Clark. N0411.1955. Photograph by Richard Walker; **p. 370:** Courtesy of the Pennsylvania Academy of the Fine Arts, Philadelphia, 1879.8.1; **p. 373:** Granger; **p. 393:** Library of Congress; **p. 394:** Library of Congress; **p. 396:** Son of the Forest by William Apes, 1831; **p. 401:** Library of Congress. **Chapter 11: Page 409 (both):** The Historic New Orleans Collection / Bridgeman Images; **p. 411:** Superstock; **p. 414:** Missouri Historical Society; **p. 418:** Granger; **p. 430:** The Historic New Orleans Collection / Bridgeman Images; **p. 432:** Library of Congress; **p. 437:** Pictures Now / Alamy Stock Photo. **Chapter 12: Page 448:** Library of Congress; **p. 452:** Image copyright © The Metropolitan Museum of Art. Image source: Art Resource, NY; **p. 455:** Collection of the Massachusetts Historical Society. Banner, William Lloyd Garrison (1805-1879) "Proclaim Liberty Throughout all the Land unto all the inhabitants thereof." MHS image #332; **p. 457:** Boston Athenaeum; **p. 459:** Granger; **p. 464:** Library of Congress; **p. 467:** Library of Congress; **p. 469:** Gift of Constance Fuller Threinen, great-granddaughter of Margaret Fuller's brother, the Rev. Arthur Buckminster Fuller, who was a Unitarian minister in Boston, a chaplain in the Civil War, and was killed at the Battle of Fredericksburg in 1862. National Portrait Gallery, Smithsonian; **p. 471:** Bettmann / Corbis / Getty Images. **Chapter 13: Page 480:** Library of Congress; **p. 482:** Collection of the New-York Historical Society / Gift of George K. Higgins / Bridgeman Images; **p. 486:** Alfred Sully, Monterey, California Rancho Scene, circa 1849. Watercolor on paper, 15.25 x 18 in. Collection of the Oakland Museum of California. The Oakland Museum of California Kahn Collection; **p. 489:** The Bancroft Library, University of California,

Berkeley; **p. 496:** Fugitive slave law...Hamlet in chains. National anti-slavery standard. Vol. 21 (Oct. 17, 1850), page 82, Rare Book & Manuscript Library, Columbia University in the City of New York; **p. 504:** Collection of the New-York Historical Society / Bridgeman Images; **p. 509:** Collection of the New-York Historical Society / Bridgeman Images; p. 512: Abraham Lincoln Presidential Library and Museum. **Chapter 14: Page 531:** Collection of the New-York Historical Society / Bridgeman Images; **p. 535:** Library of Congress; **p. 536:** Smithsonian Institution, Photographic History Collection, Division of Information Technology; **p. 539:** Courtesy, Daughters of Charity, Province of St. Louise, St. Louis, MO; **p. 542:** Wisconsin Historical Society, WHS-6909; **p. 549 (both):** Louisiana State University Special Collections from the U.S. Civil War Center exhibit Beyond Face Value, courtesy of Jules d'Hemecourt. **Chapter 15: Page 569:** Library of Congress; **p. 573:** Digital Image © Museum Associates / LACMA. Licensed by Art Resource, NY; **p. 579:** Niday Picture Library / Alamy Stock Photo; **p. 582:** Library of Congress; **p. 585:** Library of Congress; **p. 592:** Library of Congress; **p. 594:** Library of Congress. **Chapter 16: Page 610:** Library of Congress; **p. 617:** Bettmann / Getty Images; **p. 621:** bpk, Berlin / Art Resource, NY; **p. 626:** L1987-06_2, 19th and Early 20th Century Labor Prints, Southern Labor Archives. Special Collections and Archives, Georgia State University Library; **p. 629:** Newberry Library, Chicago; **p. 636:** The Michael C. Rockefeller Memorial Collection, Purchase, Nelson A. Rockefeller Gift, 1968, The Metropolitan Museum of Art; **p. 640:** Library of Congress. **Chapter 17: Page 656:** Park, Milton. The Southern Mercury. (Dallas, Tex.), Vol. 10, No. 36, Ed. 1 Thursday, September 3, 1891, newspaper, September 3, 1891; Dallas, Texas. (https://texashistory.unt.edu/ark:/67531 /metapth185428/: accessed June 24, 2019), University of North Texas Libraries, The Portal to Texas History, https://texashistory.unt.edu; **p. 663:** Mary McLeod Bethune with a line of girls from the school. ca 1905. Black & white photonegative. State Archives of Florida, Florida Memory. Accessed 28 Dec. 2018. https:// www.floridamemory.com/items/show/149519; **p. 664:** Library of Congress; **p. 665:** Library of Congress; **p. 669:** Research Division of the Oklahoma Historical Society; **p. 675:** National Archives; **p. 681:** Courtesy of the Hawaii State Archives, Queen Liliuokalani, Photograph Exhibition: Liliuokalani, Withdrawn Photos, PPWD-16-4-019; **p. 689:** North Wind Picture Archives / Alamy. **Chapter 18: Page 696:** Library of Congress; **p. 698:** Library of Congress; **p. 699:** Peter Roberts, The New Immigrants, 1921; **p. 703:** The Art Archive / REX / Shutterstock; **p. 709:** Library of Congress; **p. 715:** Everett Collection Historical / Alamy

Stock Photo; **p. 718:** Library of Congress; **p. 723:** History and Art Collection / Alamy Stock Photo; **p. 724:** Hulton Archive / Getty Images; **p. 731:** Fotosearch / Getty Images. **Chapter 19: Page 743:** Everett Collection Inc / Alamy Stock Photo; **p. 757:** Universal History Archive / UIG / Bridgeman Images; **p. 766:** National Archives; **p. 769:** Everett Collection Inc / Alamy Stock Photo; **p. 771:** © 2022 The Jacob and Gwendolyn Knight Lawrence Foundation, Seattle / Artists Rights Society (ARS), New York. Digital Image © The Museum of Modern Art / Licensed by SCALA / Art Resource, NY; **p. 775:** Courtesy of the author. **Chapter 20: Page 789:** National Archives; **p. 792 (both):** Granger; **p. 801:** Library of Congress; **p. 803:** San Diego Museum of Art / Bridgeman Images; **p. 805:** Smith Archive / Alamy Stock Photo; **p. 806:** Indiana University Campus Art Collection, THB X, Thomas Hart Benton, Indiana Murals: Parks, the Circus, the Klan, the Press. Photograph by Michael Cavanagh and Kevin Montague, Eskenazi Museum of Art at Indiana University; **p. 811:** Schomburg Center / The New York Public Library / Art Resource, NY; **p. 817:** National Archives; **p. 819:** Buyenlarge / Getty Images. **Chapter 21: Page 831:** Geographicus Rare Antique Maps; **p. 839:** Library of Congress; **p. 844:** Bettmann / Getty Images; **p. 852:** Bettmann / Getty Images; **p. 854:** National Archives, Seattle; **p. 857:** Library of Congress. **Chapter 22: Page 870:** "Four Freedoms" illustrations © SEPS licensed by Curtis Licensing Indianapolis, IN. Printed by permission of the Norman Rockwell Family Agency. Copyright ©1943 the Norman Rockwell Family Entities; **p. 883 (left):** Photo © Photo Josse / Bridgeman Images; **(right):** Courtesy Northwestern University Library; **p. 885:** National Archives; **p. 901:** Library of Congress; **p. 909:** Ed Clark / The LIFE Picture Collection / Shutterstock. **Chapter 23: Page 914:** National Archives; **p. 918:** Library of Congress; **p. 920:** AP Photo; **p. 926:** Photofest; **p. 932:** The Jon B. Lovelace Collection of California Photographs in Carol M. Highsmith's America Project, Library of Congress; **p. 934:** Lake County Illinois Discovery Museum, Curt Teich Postcard Archives; **p. 935:** Loomis Dean / The LIFE Picture Collection / Shutterstock; **p. 941:** National Museum of the American Indian, Smithsonian Institution, catalog # 010_pht_306_002. **Chapter 24: Page 950:** Howard Sochurek / The LIFE Picture Collection / Shutterstock; **p. 953:** Ernst Haas / Getty Images; **p. 958:** Yale Joel / The LIFE Picture Collection / Shutterstock; **p. 960:** Bureau of Indian Affairs / Newberry Library; **p. 961:** American Economic Foundation, "Man's Belief in God is Personal," CU Libraries Exhibitions, accessed February 22, 2013, https://exhibitions.cul.columbia.edu/items/show/2829; **p. 963:** Hagley Museum & Library,

Wilmington, Delaware / Bridgeman Images; **p. 970:** Bettmann / Corbis / Getty Images; **p. 973:** AP Photo; **p. 976:** Burt Glinn / Magnum Photos; **p. 981:** AP Photo; **p. 986:** Photograph by Gordon Parks, Courtesy of © The Gordon Parks Foundation. **Chapter 25: Page 994:** Bettmann / Getty Images; **p. 995:** © Bob Adelman; **p. 999:** Carl Mydans / The LIFE Picture Collection / Shutterstock; **p. 1004:** © 1965 Spider Martin; **p. 1012:** Courtesy of the University of Delaware Archives and Records Management; **p. 1022:** Boston Globe via Getty Images; **p. 1023:** © 2022 The Peter Hujar Archive / Artists Rights Society (ARS), New York; Courtesy Pace / MacGill Gallery, New York and Fraenkel Gallery, San Francisco; **p. 1026:** CSU Archives / Everett Collection / Newscom; **p. 1028:** AP Photo; **p. 1031:** The Free Lance-Star via AP. **Chapter 26: Page 1042:** Richard Nixon Presidential Library and Museum, NARA; **p. 1045:** © Shane Keyser / Kansas City Star / TNS / Alamy Live News; **p. 1049:** AP Photo / Jack Thornell; **p. 1051:** Kean Collection / Getty Images; **p. 1052:** Copyright © Diana Mara Henry / www.dianamarahenry.com; **p. 1061:** Bettmann / Corbis / Getty Images; **p. 1064:** Bettmann / Corbis / Getty Images. **Chapter 27: Page 1084:** Peter Turnley / Corbis / VCG via Getty Images; **p. 1090:** Tony Law / Redux; **p. 1094:** © PictureLux / The Hollywood Archive / Alamy; **p. 1097:** AP Photo / Damian Dovarganes; **p. 1108:** Vanessa Vick / Science Source; **p. 1109:** Josue Rivas / Indigena LLC; **p. 1115:** Steve Ludlum / The New York Times / Redux; **p. 1122:** Michael Ramirez / Creators Syndicate. **Chapter 28: Page 1129:** AP Photo; **p. 1131:** AP Photo / Kampha Bouaphanh; **p. 1139:** Official White House Photo by Pete Souza; **p. 1147:** Whitney Curtis, The New York Times, Redux; **p. 1154:** Win McNamee / Getty Images; **p. 1156:** Mark Lyons / Getty Images; **p. 1160:** U.S. Customs and Border Protection via Getty Images; **p. 1161 (left):** f00sion / Getty Images; **(right):** Australian Associated Press; **p. 1170:** Reuters / Alamy Stock Photo; **p. 1173:** For Freedoms (Hank Willis Thomas and Emily Shur in collaboration with Eric Gottesman and Wyatt Gallery of For Freedoms); **p. 1176:** EyePress / Newscom.

TEXT

Chapter 1: Bartolomé de las Casas: "History of the Indies [1528]", excerpt from *History of the Indies*, translated and edited by Andrée Collard (New York: Harper & Row, 1971), pp. 82, 112-115. Copyright © 1971 by Andrée M. Collard, renewed © 1999 by Joyce J. Contrucci. Reprinted by permission of Joyce J. Contrucci. **Marcos de Niza:** "Friar Marco De Niza's Account of His Voyage with Esteban" from *Relación* (1539), translated by John DuVal. Reprinted by permission of John

DuVal. **Chapter 8: Democratic-Republican Society of Pennsylvania**: Excerpt from minutes of The Democratic Society of Pennsylvania, December 18, 1794. The Historical Society of Pennsylvania (HSP), Collection # Am. 315/3150. **Chapter 9: Margaret McCarthy**: "Letter of Margaret McCarthy to Her Family (1850") From "State-Aided Emigration Schemes from Crown Estates in Ireland c. 1850" by Eilish Ellis. *Analecta Hibernica 22* (1960), pp. 390-393. Reprinted by permission of the estate of Eilish Ellis. **Chapter 11: Joseph Taper**: Excerpt from "Letter from Joseph Taper to Joseph Long, November 11, 1840" in the Joseph Long Papers located in the Rare Book, Manuscript, and Special Collections Library, Duke University. **Chapter 21: Woody Guthrie**: 6 lines from "Roll On, Columbia," Words by Woody Guthrie, Music based on "Goodnight, Irene" by Huddie Ledbetter and John Lomax. WGP/TRO @ Copyright 1936, 1957, 1963 (copyrights renewed). Woody Guthrie Publications, Inc. & Ludlow Music, Inc. Reprinted by permission of the publisher, TRO Essex Music Group. International Copyright Secured Made in U.S.A. All Rights Reserved Including Public Performance For Profit. Used by Permission. **John Steinbeck**: Excerpt from *The Harvest Gypsies* by John Steinbeck. Copyright © 1936 by *The San Francisco News*. Reprinted by permission of Heyday Books, Berkeley, California. **Chapter 22: LULAC News**: "Editorial on World War II and Mexican-Americans (1945)" from *LULAC News*, Volume 12, October 1945. Reprinted by permission of LULAC News. **Carlos Bulosan**: Excerpt from *Freedom From Want* essay © SEPS licensed by Curtis Licensing Indianapolis, IN. All rights reserved. **Chapter 23: Oscar Handlin**: "The Immigration Fight Has Only Begun" by Oscar Handlin. Originally published in *Commentary*, July 1952. Reprinted by permission of the Oscar Handlin estate. **Henry Steele Commager**: Excerpts from "Who Is Loyal to America?" Originally published in *Harper's Magazine*, v.195 no. 1168. Subsequently published in *Freedom, Loyalty, Dissent* by Henry Steele Commager (1954), 700w from pp.135-140. By permission of Oxford University Press and the Estate of Henry Steele Commager. **Chapter 25: Clyde Warrior**: "To Survive as a People." From *Say We Are Nations: Documents of Politics and Protest in Indigenous*

American Since 1887 by Daniel M. Cobb. Copyright © 2015 by the University of North Carolina Press. Used by permission of the publisher. www.uncpress.unc .edu. **National Organization for Women**: Excerpts from "The National Organization for Women's 1966 Statement of Purpose," by Betty Friedan. Reprinted with permission of National Organization for Women. This is a historical document and may not reflect the current language or priorities of the organization. **Chapter 26: International Indian Treaty Council**: Excerpts from *Declaration of Continuing Independence by the First International Indian Treaty Council* at Standing Rock Indian Country, June 8-16, 1974. Reprinted by permission of the International Indian Treaty Council. **Barry Commoner**: Excerpts from "Chapter 1: The Environmental Crisis" from *The Closing Circle: Nature, Man, and Technology* by Barry Commoner. Copyright © 1971 by Barry Commoner. Reprinted by permission of Lisa Feiner. **Chapter 27: Global Exchange**: "Declaration for Global Democracy," from Global Exchange, Seattle, December 1999. Reprinted by permission. **Los Tigres del Norte**: *Jaula de Oro*. Fonovisa, 1984. Lyrics by Enrique Franco. Translated by Alana Graffam. Reprinted with permission of TN Ediciones Musicales. **Chapter 28: Khizr Khan:** Excerpt(s) from AN AMERICAN Family: A MEMOIR OF HOPE AND SACRIFICE by Khizr Khan, copyright © 2017 by Khizr Khan. Used by permission of Random House, an imprint and division of Penguin Random House LLC. All rights reserved. Reproduced in the U.K. with permission of Little & Brown Book Group Limited through PLSclear.

LINE ART

M27.2: Map 1 from "Contemporary Immigrant Gateways in Historical Perspective," by Audrey Singer. *Daedalus*, Summer 2013, Vol. 142, No. 3: 76–91. Reprinted by permission of the author. **M27.3**: Map: Where Each State's Largest Immigrant Population Was Born, from "From Germany to Mexico: How America's source of immigrants has changed over a century," by Jens Manuel Krogstad and Michael Keegan. Pew Research Center, October 7, 2015. Courtesy of Pew Research Center.

INDEX

Note: Page numbers in *italics* refer to figures, tables, or illustrations.

Americanization, 797, 805–12, 958
  Catholics and, 809–12
  of immigrants, 762–766, 805–7, 808, 858, 889–90
  see also Americanism; assimilation
Americanization of the World, The; or, the Trend of the Twentieth Century (Stead), 738
American Jewish Committee, 860, 897
American Jewish Congress, 902
American League, 726
American Legion, 939
American Liberty League, 845
American Magazine, The, 170
American Medical Association, 726, 843, 927
American Missionary, 639
American National Exhibition, 948–50, *950*
American National Red Cross, 547
American Party. *see* Know-Nothing Party
American Philosophical Society, 155
American Progress (Gast), *480*
American Protective League (APL), 760
American Psychiatric Association, 1047
American Railway Union, 658
American Revolution, 179–212, 236, 294, 295, 306, 324, 406, 456, 537, 616, 884, 920, 928, 932, 1013
  American advantages in, 201–3
  American mutinies in, 210
  Andrew Jackson in, 364
  Articles of Confederation and, 252–260
  background of, 180–191
  battles of, 204–212, *207, 209*
  Black soldiers in, *202*, 203–4
  as borderlands conflict, 232–34
  British advantages in, 201–3
  casualties in, 202, 523
  creation of national identity and, 274
  debt created by, 289
  democracy and, 216–221
  early battles of, 193–94, 204–206
  economic effect of, 229–30, 258–59
  equality and, 216
  family life and, 243–46, 248
  force strength in, 202–3
  French assistance in, *202*, 206
  indentured servitude and, 202, 215, 227–228, 245
  low point of, 205, 210
  Loyalists in, 230–32, *231*
  map of battles in, *207*
  Native Americans and, 206–8, 216, 233–34, 248
  Paine's view of, 195, 196–98
  religious freedom and, 221–226

slavery and, 216, 234–242, 247, 248, 432, 453
  in South, 208–11
  Spanish help in, 206
  views of elite on, 217–19
  voting rights and, 219–21
  women and, 188, 242–48, *243*
"American Scholar, The" (Emerson), 349–50
Americans with Disabilities Act (1990), 1046
American System, 374–75, 382, 388, 403
American system of manufactures, 339
American Telephone and Telegraph (AT&T), 1047
American Temperance Society, 449
American Tobacco, 73
American Tract Society, 451
American University, 998
American Way, 1029
American Woman Suffrage Association, 592
Ames, Adelbert (1835–1933), 601–600
Ames, Charles G., 688
Am I Not a Man and a Brother?, 462, *464*
Am I Not a Woman and a Sister? (Bourne), *471*
Amistad, 437, *437*
Amity and Commerce, Treaty of (1778), 206
Amnesty International, 1059, 1060
Amsterdam, Netherlands, 35
Anabaptists, 116
anarchism, 621, 626, 757, 764, 783
Anderson, Marian (1897–1993), 856
Anderson, Sherwood (1876–1941), 814
Andersonville, Ga., Confederate prison at, 524, 581
Andes Mountains, 4, 21
Andrews, Sidney (1837–1880), 569, 571
Andros, Edmund (1637–1714), 94, 107–8
Angel Island, 698
Anglican Church, 35, 46, 83, 85, 105, 107, 114, 122, 190
  American Revolution and, 222, 225, 230
  creation of, 46
  Dissenters and, 85, 105, 221–22
  Puritans and, 64
Anglo-Dutch war, 92
Anglo-Iranian Oil Company, 972
Anglo-Powhatan Wars, 56–57
Anglos, 486–87
Angola, 60, 972
Anishinaabe, 128, 167, 398
  see also Ojibwe; Ottawas; Potawatomis
Ann Arbor, Mich., Beats in, 976
Anniston, Ala., 993
annuity system (for Native Americans), 280
Anthony, Susan B. (1820–1906), 474, 591–92, *592*
Anti-Ballistic Missile Treaty (1972), 1048, 1076

anti-Catholicism, 962, 988

Anti-Defamation League of B'nai B'rith, 810

Anti-Drug Abuse Act (1986), 1076

Antietam, Battle of, 528, 532

Anti-Federalists, 267, 269–271, 273

Anti-Imperialist League, 689

Anti-Mask League, 750

Antinomianism, 75

anti-Semitism, 810, 840, 890, 962, 1040, 1111, 1171
  see also Jews

antiwar movement, Vietnam era, 1017–18, 1033–34, 1049, 1049–50

Apaches, 29, 128–29, 162, 163, 281, 281, 479, 637

apartheid, 687, 1017, 1084

Apess, William (1798–1839), 233, 396, 398

Appalachia, 1006, 1145

Appalachian Mountains, 254, 281, 327, 331, 333, 334

Appeal in Favor of That Class of Americans Called Africans, An (Child), 460

Appeal of the Independent Democrats, 497

Appeal to Reason, 708

Appeal to the Coloured Citizens of the World, An (Walker), 455–56, 462

appeasement, 871

Apple Computer, 1094, 1094

appliances, household. see consumerism, and household appliances; specific appliances

Appomattox Courthouse, 560–61, 580

aqueducts, 729

Arabella, 69

Arabs, 778–79, 1055–56
  nationalism and, 972–73, 1061–62

Aragon, 13

Arapahos, 544, 637, 640, 1045

Arbenz Guzmán, Jacobo (1913–1971), 972, 974

Arbuckle, Fatty (1887–1933), 799

Argentina, 631, 643, 1060

Aristotle (384–322 BCE), 14, 217, 367

Arizona, 30–31, 485, 641, 695, 789, 893, 952, 1016

Arizona territory, 629, 630

Arkansas, 281, 281, 331, 354, 799, 1085

Arlington, Vt., 867

Armada Portrait, 48

armed forces, U.S. see military, U.S.

Arminianism, 158

armistice, Korean War, 921, 923

Armory show, 711

Armour, Philip D. (1832–1901), 546

Armstrong, Louis, 978

Armstrong, Samuel (1839–1893), 665

Army, U.S.
  African Americans in, 373, 533–37, 535
  desegregation in, 903
  fear of standing, 290
  Native Americans in, 542, 542–43

Army-McCarthy hearings, 939, 955

Army of Northern Virginia, Confederate, 527

Army of the Potomac, Union, 526–27, 528, 555, 556

Arnold, Benedict (1741–1801), 193, 210, 222

Arthur, Chester A. (1829–1886), 646

Articles of Confederation (1781), 252–60, 263, 266, 289
  weaknesses of, 258–59

artisans, 337, 339, 340–41, 356, 841–42
  see also craftsmen

arts
  African Americans in, 812–13
  during Cold War, 925–26
  Second New Deal and, 841–42

Aryan Nation, 1111

Aryans, 809

Aryans, as "master race," 889, 931

Ashanti people, 136, 144

Asia, 15, 16, 684, 738, 779, 903, 915, 925, 971, 972, 1094, 1097
  decolonization of, 1171
  Native Americans and, 4
  pre–World War II, 870

Asian Americans, Kamala Harris, 1168

Asian immigrants, 283, 674–77, 697–98, 765, 891, 1004–5, 1102–4, 1103
  affirmative action and, 1044
  discrimination against, 589
  naturalization of, 806–7
  New Nationalism and, 734
  World War II and, 893, 896–99, 897

asiento, 134

assemblies, colonial, 154–55, 182

assembly lines, 702–3, 703, 836

assimilation, 809–10, 858, 889–90, 963

associational action, 814, 819

Astor, John Jacob (1763–1848), 355

Astor House, 355

asylum of liberty, U.S. as, 197, 198, 225, 809

asylums, 451, 661

Atkinson, Edward (1827–1905), 616

Atlanta, Ga., Sherman's capture of, 557

"Atlanta Compromise" speech, 665

Atlanta Cotton Exposition, 665

Atlanta University, 768

Atlantic, Battle of the, 876

Atlantic and Pacific Tea Company, 609

Atlantic cable, 610

Atlantic Charter, 909, 927

Barbary Wars, 311–12
Bargain of 1877, 602–3
Barlow, Joel (1754–1812), 284
Barnett, Ross (1898–1987), 994
Barr, William, 1165
Barron, Charles (1950–), 1011
Barrow plantation, maps of, *571*
Barry, Marion (1936–2014), 1011
Bart, Lily, 615
Barton, Bruce (1886–1967), 789
Barton, Clara (1821–1912), 546–47
Baruch, Bernard (1870–1965), 751
baseball, 726, 931
Bataan, 875–76
Bataan (movie), 890
Bataan death march, 875–76
Bateman, Horatio, *585*
Batista, Fulgencio (1901–1973), 869, 997
Baton Rouge, La., 166, 332–33
"Battle Hymn of the Republic" (Howe), 538
Bavaria, 773
Bay of Pigs invasion, 998
Beard, Charles (1874–1948), 789, 820
Beats, *976*, 976–77
Beaufort, South Carolina, *144*
Beauregard, P. G. T. (1818–1893), 522, 1175
Becker, Carl (1873–1945), 753
Beebe, Abner, 232
Beecher, Catharine (1800–1878), 346, 371, 465, 467, 473
Beecher, Henry Ward (1813–1887), 346
Beecher, Lyman (1775–1863), 346
Beekman, Jane, *122*
Beer and Wine Revenue Act, 857–58
Beijing, China, 1048, 1082–83
Belfast, Northern Ireland, 773
Belgium, 746, 872
Bell, John (1797–1869), 512–13
Bellamy, Edward (1850–1898), 622, 623–24, 706, 717
Bellows, George (1882–1925), 696, *803*
Belmont, Alva (1853–1933), 693
Beloved (Morrison), 495
Benedict, Ruth (1887–1948), 809, 890
Benin, 10, 16
Benito Cereno (Melville), 372
Bentham, Jeremy, 248
Benton, Thomas Hart (1782–1858), 392, *806*
Berger, Victor (1860–1929), 706, 776
Bering Strait, 3–4
Berkeley, John (1602–1678), 96
Berkeley, William (1606–1677), 100–101, *101*, 106
Berlin, Germany
    blockade, 919–20, *920*

Berlin Congress of 1884–1885, 678–79
Berlin Wall, 998, 1083
Bernays, Edward (1891–1995), 752, 793
Bethune, Mary McLeod (1875–1955), *663*, 855–56
Better America League, 940
Beveridge, Albert (1862–1927), 689–90
Bible, 17, 23, 64, 69–70, 75, *149*, 158, 161, 431–32, 438, 451, 803, 983, 1032, 1171
    Book of Exodus of, 663
    interpretation of, 804
    Jefferson's version of, 223
    King James, 346
    slavery in, 415, 425
    see also New Testament
Bible Belt, 624
Bible Commonwealth, 70, 71, 78, 108
Biddle, Nicholas (1786–1844), 398–99
Biden, Joseph R. (1942–), 636, 1120, 1127, 1163
    Covid-19 and, 1166
    in election of 2020, 1167–71
    inauguration, 1170–71
Bilbo, Theodore (1877–1947), 857
Bill for Establishing Religious Freedom, Virginia, 224–25
Bill of Rights (American), 271, 274, 584, 587–88, 802, 882, 940, 1031–32, 1132, 1142
Bill of Rights (English), 106, 274
"Bill of Rights for the Disadvantaged," 1009
Biloxi, Miss., 128, 993
bin Laden, Osama (1957–2011), 1115, 1149
Birmingham, Ala., 914, 977
    church bombing in, 995–96
    civil rights campaign in, 994–96, *995*
    Freedom Rides in, *994*, 994–95
    manufacturing in, 662, 929
Birney, James G. (1825–1864), 463, 475, 483
birth control, 714–15, *715*, 754, 792–93, 799, 1020, 1032–33, 1046
birther movement, 1156
Birth of a Nation (movie), 767–68
birthrate, decline in U.S., 357, 673, 817
birthright citizenship, 459–60, 587
Bisbee, Ariz., strikes in, 760
Bishop Hill, Ill., *343*
Bismarck, Otto von (1815–1898), 538
Bisno, Abraham (1866–1929), 701
Black, Hugo (1886–1971), 899
Black Americans. *see* African Americans
Blackbirds (Broadway show), 813
Blackboard Jungle (movie), 975
Black Codes, 581
Black Death, 12, 44
Black Hawk (1767–1838), 6–7, 393
Black Hills, 200, 637

British Empire, 58–60, 198, 679, 738, 773, 779, 908, 915–16, 918, 924
   abolition of slavery in, 417, 529
   American *vs.* British view of, 184–85
   expansion of, 90–98
British Isles, abolitionists in, 458
British liberty. *see* English liberty
British navy, 313, 314
British Petroleum (BP), and Gulf of Mexico oil spill, 1140
Broadway theater, 813
Bronson, Ruth, *941*
Brooke, Edward W. (1919–2015), 594
Brook Farm, 447
Brooklyn, N.Y., 608, 715, *715*, 835
Brooklyn Dodgers, 931
Brooks, Preston (1819–1857), 502–3
Brotherhood of Sleeping Car Porters, 901
Browder, Earl (1891–1973), 859
Brown, Hallie Quinn, 754
Brown, Henry "Box" (b. 1816), 436
Brown, Jim, *1042*
Brown, John (1800–1859), 462, 508–10, *509*
Brown, Joseph E. (1821–1894), 412, 549
Brown, Matt, 578
Brown, Michael, 1148–49
Brown, Oliver (1918–1961), 979
Brown, Olympia, 591
Brown, William Wells, *594*
Brown Fellowship Society, 423
Brownson, Orestes (1803–1876), 361
Brown v. Board of Education, 587, 978–80, 983, 985, 987, 992, 1003
Broz, Josip (Tito; 1892–1980), 907
Bruce, Blanche K. (1841–1898), 594
Bruce, Louis, *941*
Brunias, Agostino (1730?–1796), *99*
Bryan, George (1731–1791), 270
Bryan, William Jennings (1860–1925), 659–60, 689, 729, 743, 747, 804
   "cross of gold" speech of, 660
Bryant, Anita (1940–), 1063–64
Bryce, James, 687
Bryn Mawr, 1046
Buchanan, James (1791–1868), *502*, 503, 516, 635
Buchanan, Pat (1938–), 1085, 1110
Buck, Carrie, 761
Buck, Pearl (1892–1973), 889
Buckley, William F. (1925–2008), 1002
Buck v. Bell, 761
Buddhism
   Buddhists Beats and, 1020
   as immigrants, 1098
   in Vietnam, 973, 1015

Buena Vista, Battle of, 485
buffalo, 6, 26, 635, 636–37, 642, 644
Buffalo, N.Y., 727
Buffalo Bill's Wild West Show, 644
Bulgaria, 915
Bulge, Battle of the, 905
Bulger, Andrew (1789–1858), *315*
Bull Run, First Battle of, 526
Bull Run, Second Battle of, 528
Bulosan, Carlos (1913–1956), 882–83, 895
Bunau-Varilla, Philippe (1859–1940), 741
Bunker Hill, Battle of, 194, 383
Bureau of Indian Affairs, U.S., 640, 716–17, 960, 1028, 1109
Bureau of Intelligence, U.S., 900
Bureau of Labor Statistics, 1146
Burger, Warren (1907–1995), 1043–44
Burger Court, 1043–44
Burgoyne, John (1722–1792), 205, 232
Burke, Edmund (1729–1797), 177, 236, 432
Burlingame, Anson, 588, 590
Burlingame Treaty, 588, 590, 674–75
Burma, 875
Burnside, Ambrose E. (1824–1881), 528, 555
Burr, Aaron (1756–1836), 300, 302–3, *303*
Burr, William Henry, *359*
Busbey, Fred, 926
Bush, George H. W. (1924–2018), 1079–80, 1084, 1091
   in election of 1992, 1085
   Gulf War and, *1084*, 1084–85
   NAFTA and, 1086
Bush, George W. (1946–), 1128–38, 1139, 1141, 1144, 1149
   affirmative action and, 1132
   civil liberties and, 1121–24
   economy under, 1133–37, *1134*
   in election of 2000, *1113*, 1113–14
   foreign policy of, 1116–20, *1120*, 1133
   Hurricane Katrina and, 1128–30, *1129*, 1133
   Iraq War and, 1116–23, *1122*, 1128, 1133
   Latinos and, 1130–32
   Supreme Court and, 1123
   2008 financial crisis and, 1096
Bush, Jeb (1953–), 1113
Bush Doctrine, 1117
Bush v. Gore, 1113–14
business
   government and, 793–798, 886
   horizontal expansion of, 612
   rise of, 611–13
   vertically integrated, 611, 612, *613*
   see also corporations

busing, desegregation of schools and, 1043–44
Butler, Benjamin F. (1818–1893), 530–29, 535
Butte, Mont., 633, 760
Byllesby, Langdon (1803–1890), 360
Byrd, William, III (1728–1777), 124

Cabeza de Vaca, Alvar Núñez (ca. 1490–1557?), 26, 30–31
Cabot, John (ca. 1450–ca. 1499), 18, *19*, 46
Cabral, Pedro (1467–1520), 18, *19*
Cabrillo, Juan Rodriguez (d. 1543), 26
Cacica, 1
Caddoans, 87, 280–81
Caddos, 128–29
Caesar's Column (Donnelly), 622
Cage, John (1912–1992), 926
Cahokia, 5, *5*
Cajuns, 170
Calhoun, Floride (1792–1866), 390–91
Calhoun, John C. (1782–1850), 494
  American System and, 374, 375
  annexation of Texas and, 482
  compact theory of, 391
  concurrent majority theory of, 391
  death of, 497
  Declaration of Independence as viewed by, 418
  Democratic Party and, 402
  Missouri Controversy and, 377
  nationalism and, 390
  nullification crisis and, 390–91
  sectionalism and, 390
  slavery as viewed by, 415, 418
  states' rights and, 390–91
  as vice president, 390–91
  as War Hawk, 314
California, 110, 483, 484–86, *486*, 631, 698, 719–20, 724, 799, 802, 816, 834, 855, 861, 880, *881*, 940, 951–52, 1102, 1104, 1108, 1168
  agriculture in, 695, 788–89, 952
  Asian Americans in, 765, 1102–4, *1103*
  boycott of grapes from, 1027
  Chinese immigrants in, 634
  conservatism in, 1067
  constitution of, 489
  in election of 1934, 839
  in election of 1964, 1002
  enters Union, 494
  gold rush in, *488*, 488–90, 510, 628
  Japanese Americans in, 893, 896–99, *897*
  lumber industry in, 633
  migration to, 478, 788–89
  oil spill off coast of, 1029

population of, 165–66, 479, 488, 489
Proposition 187, 1104
Reagan as governor of, 1069
Russian fur traders in, 165
Spanish settlements in, *164*, 165–66
suburbs in, 953–54
tax law in, 1067
woman suffrage in, 657, 719
California, University of, 954
  at Berkeley, 1013–14, 1049
  at Davis, 1044
California House of Representatives, 675
California Supreme Court, *675*, 676
California Trail, 635
Californios, 166, 479–80, *486*
Call, The, 714–15
Calley, William (1943–), 1050
calumet (peace pipe) ceremony, 87
Calvert, Cecilius, Lord Baltimore (1605–1675), 63, 85
Calvert, Charles, Lord Baltimore (1637–1715), 105, 107
Calvin, John (1509–1564), 64–65
Calvinists, 35, 107
Cambodia, 875, 1049, 1098, 1102
Cambridge, Mass., 69
camera, handheld, 610
Campbell, Helen, 723
Camp David, 971, 1060, 1088
Camp Dodge, Ill., 757
Canada, 6, 166, 177, 184, 185, 318, 383, 643, 807, 824, 1092, *1097*, 1171
  border with United States, 383
  ceded to Great Britain, 170
  D-Day and, 878
  draft dodgers' flight to, 1017–18
  French, 33–35
  Loyalists exiled in, 232–33
  lynching in, 672
  NAFTA and, 1086
  Native Americans in, 90
  as slave refuge, 424, 433, 435, 436, 468, 495
  U.S. invasion of, 318, 398
  War Hawks' plan for annexation of, 314
  see also French Canada
Canadians, Canadian immigrants, 630
canals, 328–30, *329*, 374, 375, 400
Canal Zone, 740–42, *741*
Canary Islands, 16
cancer, skin, 989
Cannery and Agricultural Workers union, 860
Cape Breton Island, 170
Cape Cod, 66, *66*, 398

concentration camps, 871, 878, 890
    see also Japanese immigrants, Japanese Americans
Concord, Battle of, 193, *207*, 228, 295
concurrent majority theory, 391
Conestogas, 176
Confederate Constitution, 545
Confederate monuments, removal of, 1167
Confederate States of America, 517, 548–54, 562–63, 626
    Black soldiers and, 554
    currency of, *549*, 552
    division among, 552
    economic problems of, 548–49, 552–53
    government of, 548–49
    Senate of, 554
    states' rights and, 549
    Union sympathizers in, 553
    women and, 553–54
Conference on Home Building and Home Ownership, 834
conformity, 935
Confronting Segregation (Borders), 984
Congregationalists, 64, 69–70, 114, 160, 222, 465, 680
    American Revolution and, 225
    Half-Way Covenant and, 80
    in Massachusetts, 223–26
Congress, U.S., 392, 645–46, 682, 828, 843, 887, 967, 1043, 1045–46, 1053–54, 1058, 1133
    acquisition of Hawaii and, 681
    African Americans in, 664
    anticommunism and, 941
    apologizes for Japanese American internment, 899
    under Articles of Confederation, 252–60
    authority of, 377, 390
    Bank of the United States and, 398–99
    Civil Rights Act (1964) and, 996
    civil rights and, 986
    coinage and, 288
    under Constitution, 261–64
    currency and, 229, 545–46
    in election of 1946, 930
    in election of 2020, 1168
    Equal Pay Act and, 1021
    FDR and, 848
    federal bailouts and, 1137
    government surveillance and, 1151
    health care bill passed by, 1140–41
    immigration and, 674–77, 806–7, 891, 893
    Independent Treasury policy and, 402
    isolationism and, 871
    League of Nations and, 781

Missouri Compromise and, 377–79, *378*
National Road authorized by, 328, 374
Native American treaty system and, 636–37, 640–41
New Deal and, 828, 831, 850, 887
oaths of allegiance and, 232, 233
petitioned for emancipation, 304
political parties in, 288
presidential veto and, 399, 583, 930, 941
Reagan's defiance of, 1078
Reconstruction policies of, 580, 583–85
Republican control of, 1087
Resolution of Regret, 675
slavery and, 304, 492
"stimulus" package passed by, 1140
Truman Doctrine and, 917
Universal Declaration of Human Rights and, 929
Voting Rights Act passed by, 1003–4
wage and price controls, 229
World War II and, 874
    see also House of Representatives, U.S.; Senate, U.S.
Congressional Medal of Honor, 767
Congress of Industrial Organizations (CIO), 837–38, 841, 851, 858, 859, 861, 863, 902, 929–31, 944, 968
Congress of Racial Equality (CORE), 901–2, 983, 993, 1000–1001, 1011
Connecticut, 253
    slavery in, 241
Connecticut colony, 73–74, 120, 160
    government in, 153
    militia of, 193
    in Pequot War, 72, 72–73
    women in, 126–27
Connor, Eugene "Bull" (1897–1973), 995, 1062
conquistadores, 18, 24, 29, 30–31
Conscience of a Conservative, The (Goldwater), 1001
conservationism, 728–29, 853–54, 1029–30, 1055
conservation movement, 633
conservatism, 888–89, 971, 1001–3, 1030, 1038–1080, 1110–11, 1132
    abortion and, 1063, 1066
    anti-Semitism and, 1040
    Clinton and, 1085–86
    colleges and, 1011–12
    "conspicuous consumption," 615
    libertarians and, 965
    neoconservatism and, 1077
    New Deal and, 886
    Nixon and, 1039–1044
    radical, 1002–3, 1111
    Reagan and, 1075

Mills, C. Wright (1916–1962), 974
Mills, Florence (1895–1927), 813
Milton, John (1608–1674), 83, *239*, *585*
Milwaukee, Wis., 698, 706–7, 1008
Miner, George, *766*
minimum wage, 726, 731, 751, 793, 835, 849, 856, 888, 929, 965, 969, 996, 1097, 1144, 1145–46
mining, *632*, 633–34, 698, 700, 732, 788, 880
    coal, 553, 727–28, 774
    in national parks, 729, 730
    strikes and, 658, 760
    United Mine Workers and, 713
Minneapolis, Minn., 790, 836, 837, 932
Minnesota, 630, 852, 1033, 1074, 1100, 1165
minorities
    home ownership and, 1135
    "subprime" mortgages and, 1135
minstrel shows, 373
Miracle, The (movie), 799
Miranda v. Arizona, 1031–32
misery index, *1055*, 1056
misinformation, spread of, 1094–95, 1166
    in election of 2020, 1169–70
Miss Breme Jones, *239*
missiles, 1076, 1079
    Cold War "missile gap," 988
    cruise, 1085
    Cuba and, 998
    Jupiter, 998
    see also nuclear weapons
missionaries, 29–32, 55, 479, 487, 680, 762
    in Hawaii, 687
    Jesuit, 28, 34
    Spanish, 23–25, 28, 155, *162*, 165–66, *166*
Mission Dolores, 200
Mississippi, 128, 167, 256–57, *257*, 308, 331, 857, *857*, 928, 945, 1010, 1049
    Black voting in, 931
    BP oil spill and, 1140
    "freedom schools" in, 982
    Gulf Coast of, 1129
    population, *334*
    voter registration drive in, 1000–1001
    voting rights in, 754
Mississippi, University of, 994, 999
Mississippians, 5, *5*
Mississippi Delta, segregation in, *857*, *857*
Mississippi Freedom Democratic Party (MFDP), 1001
Mississippi River, 33, 45, 128, 166, 171, *172*, 234, 256–57, *257*, 280, *281*, 308, *309*, 319, 324, 328, *332*, 333, 374, 392, *393*, 1128
Mississippi Valley, 5, *5*, 163, 166, 330, 559

Missouri, 331
    constitution of, 378
    entrance into union of, 377–79, *378*, 453
    population, *334*
    slave trade in, *418*
Missouri, University of, segregation at, 979
Missouri Compromise (1820), 377–79, *378*, 384, 390, 438, 491, 497, *498*, 503, 504, 516
Missouri River, 280, *281*
Missouri Territory, slave population of, 377–79, *378*
Mitchell, John N. (1913–1988), 1053
Mitchell, John P. (1870–1919), 620, 713
Mobile, Ala., 128, 171, 335, *986*
Moby Dick (Melville), 372
Model A, 786
Model T, 702–3, *703*, 786
modernism, 802–3
Modern Republicanism, 967–68
Modern Woman: The Lost Sex, 958
Mohaves, 893
Mohawks, 6, 35, 39, 208
    see also Haudenosaunee (Iroquois)
Mohicans, 317
Molasses Act (1733), 181
Molasses Act (1843), 183
Momaday, N. Scott, 1045
monarchy, U.S. rejection of, 216, 219
Mondale, Walter (1928–), 1074
Monitor, 523
monopolies, 229, 347, 612–13, 626
    Federal Trade Commission and, 735
    "natural," 718
    Theodore Roosevelt and, 727
    see also trusts, business
Monroe, James (1758–1831), 306, 377
    Era of Good Feelings under, 377
    Monrovia named for, 453
Monroe Doctrine, 380–82, *381*, 383, 679, 740, 742
    American foreign policy and, 380–82
    nationalism and, 382, 383
    neutrality and, 381
Monrovia, Liberia, 453–55
Montagnais (Innus), 34
Montagu, Ashley (1905–1999), 890
Montana, 707, 788, 1111
Montana territory, 629
Monterey, Calif., 165
Montesquieu, Baron (1689–1755), 149
Montezuma, Carlos, 716, 807, 809
Montgomery, Ala., 1003, *1004*
    bus boycott in, 977, 980–82, *981*, 983, 984
Montgomery Ward, 609, 880
Moody, Dwight, 680

Reno, Milo, 818

repartimiento system, 25

"Report on Economic Conditions in the South,"
862–63

Report on Manufactures (Hamilton), 289–90

reproductive rights, 1023, 1032–33, 1035, 1140

republicanism, 150–51

Republicanism, Christian, 226

republican motherhood, 245, *245*, 248, 357

Republican Party (Jeffersonian), 293, 294, 295,
300, 302–4, *303*, 317, 374, 377–79, 384

    in election of 1824, 382–83

    in Missouri Compromise, 378–79

    platform of, 294

    press of, 294–95, 301–2

Republican Party (modern), 507, 508, 533, 547–
48, 623, *645*, 645–46, 656, 805, 858, 859,
863, 872–73, 881, 920, 933–34, 939, 940,
966, 967–68, 1000, 1003, 1016, 1041,
1059, 1067–69, *1068*, 1079–80, 1087,
1091, 1095, 1128, 1138–39, 1152–53, 1176

    in 1920s, 793–94

    as antislavery, 501–2, 513, 516

    Black members of, 665–66

    Black voters and, 593

    in campaign of 1960, 987–89, *989*

    Capitol attack, January 6, 2021, 1169–70

    Christianity aligned with, 1039, 1110–11

    Clinton and, 1085–86

    conservatives in, 971

    Contract with America, 1087

    convention of 1964, 1001–2, 1069

    convention of 1992, 1085, 1110

    corruption in, 645

    Dwight Eisenhower and, 966–68

    in election of 1896, *660*, 660–61

    in election of 1916, 747

    in election of 1928, 813–15

    in election of 1936, 848

    in election of 1946, 930

    in election of 1952, 966–67

    in election of 1968, 1035–36

    in election of 1972, 1043

    in election of 1992, 1085

    in election of 2000, *1113*, 1113–14

    in election of 2018, 1162–63

    Equal Rights Amendment and, 1064,
1066

    high tariff supported by, 647

    industrialists and, 620

    Johnson's impeachment and, 586

    Liberal, 599–600, 616–17

    liberal reformers' split from, 616–17

    Lincoln's nomination and, 511–12

    Native Americans and, 640

    North and, 661

    press of, 527, 540

    in Reconstruction, 572, 579–86, 593, 596–603

    rise of, 498–503, 627

    South and, 665–66

    Soviet Union and, 869

    Supreme Court and, 835

    Taft and, 729–30

    Truman Doctrine and, 917

    Trump impeachment, 1163–64

    YAF and, 1002–3

    see also Radical Republicans; specific elec-
tions and campaigns

Republic Steel, 838

Rerum Novarum, 704

reservations, Native American, 640–43, *642*,
716–17, 853–54, 892–93, 1027–28

Resettlement Administration, 833–34

Residence of David Twining, The (Hicks), *126*

Resolution of Regret (2012), 675

Revels, Hiram (1822–1901), 594, *594*

Revenue Act (1767), 183

Revere, Paul (1735–1818), *189*, 193

reverse discrimination, 1008, 1044

"Revolution of 1800," 304

Rhineland, 776, 870

Rhine River, 905

Rhode Island, 260

    Dorr War in, 366

    U.S. Constitution and, 271

    voting rights in, 365–66

Rhode Island colony, 73–74, 84, 106, 114, 203–4,
222, 228

    government in, 152

    religious freedom in, 73–74

    slave trade in, 135, *142*

rice, 134, *426*, 662

    slavery and, 141, 145

    in Southern colonies, 96, 121, 139, 141

Rice, Thomas D., *373*

Richardson, Elliot (1920–1999), 1052

Richmond, Va., *264*, 306, 526, 528, 553, 560, *561*

Richmond Enquirer, 419

Richmond Whig, 414

Rickey, Branch (1881–1965), 931

Ridge, Major (ca. 1771–1839), 315

Riesman, David (1909–2002), 974–75

rifles, in Civil War, 523

"rights of Englishmen," 81

Rights of Man (Paine), 295, 296

right to work laws, 930

Riis, Jacob (1849–1914), 615, *617*, 1130

Rincon Center, *932*

Rindisbacher, Peter (1806–1834), *315*

Rio Grande, 110, 162, 484, 487

riots
Capitol attack, January 6, 2021, 1169–70
food, 552
race, 356, 771–72, 890, 899, 1008–9, 1105–6,
1148–49
Reconstruction, 584–85
zoot suit, 891–92
rise of U.S. government, 728, 1005, 1007
Ritchie, Thomas (1778–1854), 384
Rivas, Josué, *1109*
"River, The," 1057
River Rouge auto plant, 955
Riverside Church, 803
R.J. Reynolds Tobacco Company, 1074
roads, 327–29, *329*, 374–75, 786, 830, 839, 841,
853–54
toll, 328
Road to Serfdom, The (Hayek), 888
Roanoke Island, Va., 44, 47
Roaring Twenties, 785
robber barons, 612–13, 964
Roberts, John (1955–), 1123
Roberts, Lemuel (b. 1751), 193
Robertson, Pat (1930–), 1110
Robeson, Paul (1898–1976), 860, 904, 945
Robin Hood, 940
Robinson, Alfred (1806–1895), 480
Robinson, Bill, 813
Robinson, Earl (1910–1991), 860
Robinson, Jackie (1919–1972), 931
Robinson, Jo Ann (1912–1992), 981, 996
Rochester, N.Y., 328
rock-and-roll, 975, 1018
Rockefeller, John D. (1839–1937), 546, 612–13,
679, 696, 710, 729–30, 803
Rockefeller, Nelson (1908–1979), 869, 1057–58
Rockwell, Norman (1894–1978), 866–68, *870*,
882, 885, 890, 925, *932*, *1173*
Rocky Mountains, 162
Rödel, Peter, 361
Rodgers, Thomas (1792–1856), 355
Roe v. Wade, 1032–33, 1066
Rolfe, John (1585–1622), 56, 57
"Roll on, Columbia" (Guthrie), 823–24
Romania, 915
Rome, ancient, 15
slavery in, 59, *415*, 478
Romney, Mitt (1947–), 1152–53, 1164
Roosevelt, Eleanor (1884–1962), 850–51, 856,
927, 928–29, 1021
Roosevelt, Franklin D. (1882–1945), 662, 693,
775, 840, *844*, 846, 851–52, 857, 859,
874, 879, 899, 904, 907, 915, 932, 940,
1039, 1113, 1116
antilynching law and, 856, 857

Atlantic Charter and, 909
background of, 826–27
Black voters and, 848
"court packing" by, 848–49, 863
death of, 905, *909*
Economic Bill of Rights and, 887–88
First New Deal and, 826–35
Four Freedoms and, 866–68, *870*, 882,
909–10, 963
freedom and, 866–68, *870*, 899, 913
Good Neighbor Policy, 869
Hitler and, 870, 872, 890
on housing, 834
Japanese American internment and, 893,
896–99, *897*
pluralism and, 889
polio and, 827
Second New Deal and, 840–43
South and, 862–63
U.S.-Soviet relations and, 915
West and, 825
World War II strategy of, 876
see also New Deal
Roosevelt, Theodore (1858–1919), 627, 721, 740,
743, 751, 827, 848, 1085
African Americans and, 767
Asian Americans and, 765
as conservationist, 728–29
corporations and, 727–28
New Nationalism of, 732, 734
Panama Canal and, 740–42, *741*
as Progressive candidate, 730–31, 828
as Progressive president, 727–28
as Rough Rider, 683
U.S. government regulatory power and, 728
World War I and, 746
Roosevelt Corollary, 742–43
Rose, Charlie, 1162
Rose, Ernestine (1810–1892), 471
Rose, John (1752/1753–1820), *144*, *239*
rosemary, 15
Rosenberg, Ethel (1915–1953), 938
Rosenberg, Julius (1918–1953), 938
Rosie the Riveter, 884
Ross, Fort, 165
Ross, Frederick (1796–1883), 418–19
Ross, John (1790–1866), 315, 394
Ross, Nellie Taylor, 724
Ross, Thomas J., 576–77
Roubideaux, Ramon, 853
Rough Riders, 683
Rowlandson, Mary (1637?–1711), 72
Royal Africa Company, 92, 104
Royal Air Force, 872
Royal Army, 204

African American loss of, 665–67, 720–21, 768, 851–52, 856, 903, 986, 1000–1001, 1003–4, 1007

for African Americans, 421, 537, 584, 586–87, 754, 903

in American colonies, 152–53, 217–19

citizenship and, 720

in election of 2020, 1168

emancipated slaves and, 566, 570, 584, 586–87

grandfather clause and, 666

for Japanese women, 919

literacy tests and, 666, 721, 754

mail-in ballots, 1168

for Native Americans, 893

poll tax, 98, 666, 754, 932, 1004

property qualifications and, 219, 220–21, 365–66, 368

Puerto Ricans and, 765

registration and Black voters, 666–67, 721

religious freedom and, 222

universal, 592

in U.S., 217–19

Voting Rights Act and, 1003–4

for women, 152, 371, 468, 584, 591–92, *592*, 657, 674, 678, 694, 719, 723–24, *724*, 747, 753–54, 791, 793

Voting Rights Act (1965), 372, 1003–4, 1147

Wabanaki Confederacy, 398

Wabash v. Illinois, 619

Wade, Benjamin F., 586

Wade-Davis Bill, 559

"wade-ins," 993

wages, 227–29, 359, 360, 458–59, 492–93, 774, 858, 1144

African Americans and, 356, 558, 767, 812, 1079, 1131

agricultural work for, 631

consumerism and, 700, 702–3, 723, 787–88

cost of living increases in, 941, 969

cowboys and, 632

decline in real, 400, 547, 1056, 1057, *1057*, 1059, 1067, 1079, 1097

equal pay for equal work and, 467, 1064, *1064*

family, 358

Fordism and, 703

Great Depression and, 816, 838

hourly, 340–41

immigrants and, 700

inflation and increasing, 787

international standards for, 1091

"living wage" and, 732, 753, 843, 851

Mexican immigrants and, 1026–27, 1131

migrant farm workers and, *1026*, 1026–27

minimum, 726, 732, 793, 835, 849, 969, 1097, 1144, 1145–46

New Deal and, 838, 839

overtime and, 849

Prohibition and, 755

right to vote and, 365, 366

rising, 950

slavery compared with working for, 360, 458–59

Social Security tax on, 843, 851–52

stagnation of, 1131

strike for higher, 348, 359–60, 547, 593, 632

tax brackets and, 1070

in U.S. compared with Europe, 614

wage-earning poor, 349

women and, 357–61, 470–71, 677, 767, 885, 1020–21, *1064*, 1111

in World War I, 751

in World War II, 879, 881, 885

Wagner, Fort, 535

Wagner Act (1935), 836, 842, 848–49, 855, 913

Wahhabbism, 159

Wahunsonacock, 55

Waite, Davis (1825–1901), 659

Walden (Thoreau), 351

Waldorf-Astoria Hotel, 615

Walker, David (1796?–1830), 455–56, 462, 509, 904

Walker, Francis Amasa (1840–1897), 673

Walker, Quock, 238

Walker, William (1824–1860), 510

Walking Purchase (1737), 117

Wallace, George (1919–1998), 1002, 1003, 1035, 1051–52, 1062, 1157

Wallace, Henry (1888–1965), 886, 887, 916, 933–28

Walls, Josiah T., *594*

Wall Street, 694, 790, 795, 817, 840, 872, 964, 1074, 1134, 1136, 1141

Occupy Movement and, 1144–46

Wall Street Journal, 793

Walmart, 1097, 1144, 1158

Waltham, Mass., 339

Wampanoags, 67, 71, 90

wampum, *52*, 87

Wanchese, 43–44

War Advertising Council, 884

war bonds, 751, 879, 884, 899

War Department, U.S., 903, 905

Warehouse Act (1916), 732

War Hawks, 314

War Industries Board, 751, 829